State Rankings 2011

Other titles in the State Fact Finder series

City Crime Rankings

Crime State Rankings

Education State Rankings

Health Care State Rankings

State Rankings 2011

A Statistical View of America

Kathleen O'Leary Morgan

and

Scott Morgan

Editors

CQ PRESS

A Division of SAGE

Washington, D.C.

CQ Press
2300 N Street, NW, Suite 800
Washington, DC 20037

Phone: 202-729-1900; toll-free, 1-866-4CQ-PRESS (1-866-427-7737)

Web: www.cqpress.com

Copyright © 2011 by CQ Press, a division of SAGE. CQ Press is a registered
trademark of Congressional Quarterly Inc.

Cover design: Silverander Communications

♾ The paper used in this publication exceeds the requirements of the American
National Standard for Information Sciences—Permanence of Paper for Printed
Library Materials, ANSI Z39.48-1992.

Printed and bound in the United States of America

15 14 13 12 11   1 2 3 4 5

ISBN: 978-1-60871-731-6 (Cloth)
ISBN: 978-1-60871-733-0 (Paper)

Contents

Detailed Table of Contents

VI. EMPLOYMENT AND LABOR

VII. ENERGY AND ENVIRONMENT

XIV. SOCIAL WELFARE

XV. TRANSPORTATION

Introduction and Methodology

Introduction

State Rankings 2011 provides an easily accessible collection of data on a broad range of quality of life factors in the United States. In this latest edition, *State Rankings* compares data from the fifty states and the District of Columbia in 567 tables that fall into fifteen livability categories: agriculture, crime and law enforcement, defense, economy, education, employment and labor, energy and environment, geography, federal government finances, state and local government finances, health, households and housing, population, social welfare, and transportation.

Purpose of This Book

State Rankings 2011 translates complicated and often convoluted statistics into meaningful, easy-to-understand information. Too often there is an abundance of data but far too little information putting that data into context. This book allows researchers, legislators, policy analysts, journalists, and the general public to access information in a manner that provides not only the basic facts about a state's quality of life, but also a meaningful framework by comparing individual states against the rest of the country.

These data and rankings can be used in a variety of ways and by a variety of audiences, including the following:

- Policymakers can use the data to help identify areas that warrant further study.
- Journalists can easily find impartial state information that puts stories into context.
- The general public can see how a particular state is faring compared with other states.
- Librarians can use the data as a quick reference to assist patrons in research and can offer the sources and Web sites included as a starting point for finding related data.

The comparison rankings in *State Rankings 2011* are an annual snapshot of how the states are doing in the fifteen livability categories just listed. Two principal approaches can be taken to using these rankings. The first is to examine how a state is doing compared with all other states via the comparison rankings in this book. The second approach is to compare a state to itself over a given period of time. Both approaches are important to achieving a good understanding of how and whether a state is making progress. It is important to keep in mind that the rankings are not a definitive determination of which state is the "best." Nevertheless, because so many issues are perceived subjectively, tracking them by the numbers can help bring discussions back to a more balanced, unbiased review that, in the end, leads to better decisions.

Data and Limitations

The data featured in *State Rankings 2011* were chosen specifically by the editors from a variety of government and private sector sources. The statistics presented are intended to cover a broad array of quality of life subject areas, giving users of the book a solid collection of state information. Nevertheless, the statistics do not include all the data that might be available.

Previous editions of this book have used the term *most livable* when describing states with the highest livability ranking. However, this term is no longer being used because it is purely descriptive—at no time do the editors attempt to explain *why* a particular state is ranking higher or lower in some livability factors than others or against the national average. This explanation—currently sought by social science researchers—is beyond the scope of this book. Although their selection of factors clearly affects the rankings, the editors believe the rankings constitute a solid measure of how the fifty states and the District of Columbia are faring in quality of life in the United States. Researchers, practitioners, and others can confidently use the data to understand livability issues and guide policy decisions.

Methodology

The editors have determined the comparison rankings for *State Rankings 2011* using the same methodology they have used for the last twenty years. The fifteen livability categories were used to select forty-four quality of life factors from a broad range of economic, educational, health-oriented, public safety, and environmental statistics. The overall comparison rankings were determined by averaging each state's ranking for each category. The scale is one to fifty—the higher the number, the higher the state is in the rankings (that is, fifty is the best score). The data used are for the most recent year for which comparable numbers are available from most states. All factors are given equal weight.

The 567 tables in *State Rankings 2011* are then ranked from highest to lowest without any subjective determination of whether a subject is "positive" or "negative." For the state comparison rankings, the editors do make a subjective determination as to whether something is "positive" or "negative." Twenty-five of the forty-four factors were determined to be negative, and the remaining nineteen were viewed as positive.

The reason for this division between positive and negative is that if a state ranks first in crime rate (that is, it has the highest crime rate), its comparison ranking is reduced. But if a state ranks first in per capita personal income (that is, it has the highest income), its comparison ranking is increased. To account for this fluctuation, the editors subtracted the rankings for the positive factors from fifty-one so that a state with the highest ranking in a positive factor ended up with a fifty for that factor (remember, high numbers are best).

After the editors chose the factors and divided them into positive and negative groupings, they simply averaged the rankings for each state in all forty-four factors. If a state was missing data for a given factor, its standing was based on the average ranking for the remaining factors.

For example, Minnesota ranks thirty-first in the crime rate in 2009 (negative factor), twenty-seventh in the personal bankruptcy rate in 2010 (negative factor), and first in percentage of the eligible population reported voting in 2008 (positive factor). The thirty-first and twenty-seventh rankings go straight into the comparison formula, whereas the number one ranking in percentage of eligible population reported voting is first subtracted from fifty-one, with the resulting fifty going into the ranking. For these three factors for Minnesota, the ratings thirty-one, twenty-seven, and fifty are averaged, for a result of thirty-six. If these three factors were the only ones used, then the resulting average of thirty-six would be the figure used to compare Minnesota with the other forty-nine states. However, for the *State Rankings* comparison rankings, an additional forty-one factors are added into the calculations before the final results are determined.

Designed with the researcher in mind, the numbers shown in *State Rankings* require no additional calculations to convert them from millions, thousands, etc. All states are ranked on a high to low basis, with any ties among the states listed alphabetically for a given ranking. Negative numbers are shown in parentheses. For tables displaying national totals (as opposed to rates, per capita, etc.), a separate column is included that shows what percentage of the national total each state's total represents. This column is headed by "% of USA." This percentage figure is particularly interesting when compared with a state's population in a given year.

To further assist readers, source information and footnotes are shown clearly at the bottom of each page, and the national totals, rates, and percentages are prominently displayed at the top of each table. Every other line is shaded in gray for easier reading. Numerous information-finding tools are also provided: a thorough table of contents, table listings at the beginning of each chapter, and a detailed index. In addition, a roster of sources, with addresses, phone numbers, and Web sites, is found in the back of the book.

The 2011 State Rankings

ALPHA ORDER

RANK	STATE	AVG	10 RANK	CHANGE
47	Alabama	19.52	46	-1
19	Alaska	27.93	18	-1
42	Arizona	20.32	45	3
40	Arkansas	20.59	42	2
33	California	22.20	34	1
18	Colorado	27.95	12	-6
12	Connecticut	29.80	14	2
25	Delaware	25.27	29	4
46	Florida	19.55	44	-2
41	Georgia	20.55	43	2
20	Hawaii	27.48	17	-3
22	Idaho	26.84	23	1
28	Illinois	24.34	30	2
34	Indiana	21.86	33	-1
2	Iowa	33.75	2	0
16	Kansas	29.00	10	-6
48	Kentucky	19.34	48	0
43	Louisiana	20.23	36	-7
9	Maine	30.68	16	7
15	Maryland	29.02	19	4
11	Massachusetts	30.18	11	0
35	Michigan	21.30	35	0
3	Minnesota	33.16	1	-2
50	Mississippi	16.43	49	-1
30	Missouri	23.30	26	-4
21	Montana	27.45	20	-1
5	Nebraska	32.07	3	-2
37	Nevada	21.14	38	1
1	New Hampshire	34.18	4	3
13	New Jersey	29.41	15	2
44	New Mexico	20.07	39	-5
29	New York	24.23	24	-5
31	North Carolina	22.41	41	10
7	North Dakota	31.95	5	-2
38	Ohio	20.95	40	2
36	Oklahoma	21.18	32	-4
24	Oregon	25.70	25	1
26	Pennsylvania	25.16	27	1
27	Rhode Island	24.84	28	1
45	South Carolina	19.66	50	5
8	South Dakota	31.55	7	-1
49	Tennessee	18.91	47	-2
32	Texas	22.25	30	-2
10	Utah	30.45	8	-2
4	Vermont	32.09	9	5
14	Virginia	29.09	13	-1
23	Washington	26.55	22	-1
39	West Virginia	20.66	37	-2
17	Wisconsin	28.57	21	4
5	Wyoming	32.07	6	1

RANK ORDER

RANK	STATE	AVG	10 RANK	CHANGE
1	New Hampshire	34.18	4	3
2	Iowa	33.75	2	0
3	Minnesota	33.16	1	-2
4	Vermont	32.09	9	5
5	Nebraska	32.07	3	-2
5	Wyoming	32.07	6	1
7	North Dakota	31.95	5	-2
8	South Dakota	31.55	7	-1
9	Maine	30.68	16	7
10	Utah	30.45	8	-2
11	Massachusetts	30.18	11	0
12	Connecticut	29.80	14	2
13	New Jersey	29.41	15	2
14	Virginia	29.09	13	-1
15	Maryland	29.02	19	4
16	Kansas	29.00	10	-6
17	Wisconsin	28.57	21	4
18	Colorado	27.95	12	-6
19	Alaska	27.93	18	-1
20	Hawaii	27.48	17	-3
21	Montana	27.45	20	-1
22	Idaho	26.84	23	1
23	Washington	26.55	22	-1
24	Oregon	25.70	25	1
25	Delaware	25.27	29	4
26	Pennsylvania	25.16	27	1
27	Rhode Island	24.84	28	1
28	Illinois	24.34	30	2
29	New York	24.23	24	-5
30	Missouri	23.30	26	-4
31	North Carolina	22.41	41	10
32	Texas	22.25	30	-2
33	California	22.20	34	1
34	Indiana	21.86	33	-1
35	Michigan	21.30	35	0
36	Oklahoma	21.18	32	-4
37	Nevada	21.14	38	1
38	Ohio	20.95	40	2
39	West Virginia	20.66	37	-2
40	Arkansas	20.59	42	2
41	Georgia	20.55	43	2
42	Arizona	20.32	45	3
43	Louisiana	20.23	36	-7
44	New Mexico	20.07	39	-5
45	South Carolina	19.66	50	5
46	Florida	19.55	44	-2
47	Alabama	19.52	46	-1
48	Kentucky	19.34	48	0
49	Tennessee	18.91	47	-2
50	Mississippi	16.43	49	-1

Date Each State Admitted to Statehood*

ALPHA ORDER

RANK	STATE	DATE OF ADMISSION
22	Alabama	December 14, 1819
49	Alaska	January 3, 1959
48	Arizona	February 14, 1912
25	Arkansas	June 15, 1836
31	California	September 9, 1850
38	Colorado	August 1, 1876
5	Connecticut	January 9, 1788
1	Delaware	December 7, 1787
27	Florida	March 3, 1845
4	Georgia	January 2, 1788
50	Hawaii	August 21, 1959
43	Idaho	July 3, 1890
21	Illinois	December 3, 1818
19	Indiana	December 11, 1816
29	Iowa	December 28, 1846
34	Kansas	January 29, 1861
15	Kentucky	June 1, 1792
18	Louisiana	April 30, 1812
23	Maine	March 15, 1820
7	Maryland	April 28, 1788
6	Massachusetts	February 6, 1788
26	Michigan	January 26, 1837
32	Minnesota	May 11, 1858
20	Mississippi	December 10, 1817
24	Missouri	August 10, 1821
41	Montana	November 8, 1889
37	Nebraska	March 1, 1867
36	Nevada	October 31, 1864
9	New Hampshire	June 21, 1788
3	New Jersey	December 18, 1787
47	New Mexico	January 6, 1912
11	New York	July 26, 1788
12	North Carolina	November 21, 1789
39	North Dakota	November 2, 1889
17	Ohio	March 1, 1803
46	Oklahoma	November 16, 1907
33	Oregon	February 14, 1859
2	Pennsylvania	December 12, 1787
13	Rhode Island	May 29, 1790
8	South Carolina	May 23, 1788
39	South Dakota	November 2, 1889
16	Tennessee	June 1, 1796
28	Texas	December 29, 1845
45	Utah	January 4, 1896
14	Vermont	March 4, 1791
10	Virginia	June 26, 1788
42	Washington	November 11, 1889
35	West Virginia	June 20, 1863
30	Wisconsin	May 29, 1848
44	Wyoming	July 10, 1890

RANK ORDER

RANK	STATE	DATE OF ADMISSION
1	Delaware	December 7, 1787
2	Pennsylvania	December 12, 1787
3	New Jersey	December 18, 1787
4	Georgia	January 2, 1788
5	Connecticut	January 9, 1788
6	Massachusetts	February 6, 1788
7	Maryland	April 28, 1788
8	South Carolina	May 23, 1788
9	New Hampshire	June 21, 1788
10	Virginia	June 26, 1788
11	New York	July 26, 1788
12	North Carolina	November 21, 1789
13	Rhode Island	May 29, 1790
14	Vermont	March 4, 1791
15	Kentucky	June 1, 1792
16	Tennessee	June 1, 1796
17	Ohio	March 1, 1803
18	Louisiana	April 30, 1812
19	Indiana	December 11, 1816
20	Mississippi	December 10, 1817
21	Illinois	December 3, 1818
22	Alabama	December 14, 1819
23	Maine	March 15, 1820
24	Missouri	August 10, 1821
25	Arkansas	June 15, 1836
26	Michigan	January 26, 1837
27	Florida	March 3, 1845
28	Texas	December 29, 1845
29	Iowa	December 28, 1846
30	Wisconsin	May 29, 1848
31	California	September 9, 1850
32	Minnesota	May 11, 1858
33	Oregon	February 14, 1859
34	Kansas	January 29, 1861
35	West Virginia	June 20, 1863
36	Nevada	October 31, 1864
37	Nebraska	March 1, 1867
38	Colorado	August 1, 1876
39	North Dakota	November 2, 1889
39	South Dakota	November 2, 1889
41	Montana	November 8, 1889
42	Washington	November 11, 1889
43	Idaho	July 3, 1890
44	Wyoming	July 10, 1890
45	Utah	January 4, 1896
46	Oklahoma	November 16, 1907
47	New Mexico	January 6, 1912
48	Arizona	February 14, 1912
49	Alaska	January 3, 1959
50	Hawaii	August 21, 1959

Source: U.S. Bureau of the Census
   "1980 Census of Population" (vol. 1, part A, PC80-1-A)
*First thirteen states show date of ratification of Constitution.

STATE FAST FACTS

STATE	NICKNAME	CAPITAL	POPULATION*	AREA**
Alabama	Heart of Dixie	Montgomery	4,729,656	52,420
Alaska	The Last Frontier	Juneau	708,862	664,988
Arizona	Grand Canyon State	Phoenix	6,676,627	113,990
Arkansas	The Natural State	Little Rock	2,910,236	53,178
California	Golden State	Sacramento	37,266,600	163,694
Colorado	Centennial State	Denver	5,095,309	104,094
Connecticut	Constitution State	Hartford	3,526,937	5,544
Delaware	First State	Dover	891,464	2,489
Florida	Sunshine State	Tallahassee	18,678,049	65,758
Georgia	Peach State	Atlanta	9,908,357	59,425
Hawaii	Aloha State	Honolulu	1,300,086	10,926
Idaho	Gem State	Boise	1,559,796	83,568
Illinois	Land of Lincoln	Springfield	12,944,410	57,916
Indiana	Hoosier State	Indianapolis	6,445,295	36,417
Iowa	Hawkeye State	Des Moines	3,023,081	56,273
Kansas	Sunflower State	Topeka	2,841,121	82,278
Kentucky	Bluegrass State	Frankfort	4,339,435	40,411
Louisiana	Pelican State	Baton Rouge	4,529,426	51,988
Maine	Pine Tree State	Augusta	1,312,939	35,384
Maryland	Free State	Annapolis	5,737,274	12,406
Massachusetts	Bay State	Boston	6,631,280	10,554
Michigan	Great Lake State	Lansing	9,931,235	96,713
Minnesota	North Star State	St. Paul	5,290,447	86,935
Mississippi	Magnolia State	Jackson	2,960,467	48,432
Missouri	Show Me State	Jefferson City	6,011,741	69,702
Montana	Treasure State	Helena	980,152	147,039
Nebraska	Cornhusker State	Lincoln	1,811,072	77,349
Nevada	Silver State	Carson City	2,654,751	110,572
New Hampshire	Granite State	Concord	1,323,531	9,348
New Jersey	Garden State	Trenton	8,732,811	8,723
New Mexico	Land of Enchantment	Santa Fe	2,033,875	121,590
New York	Empire State	Albany	19,577,730	54,555
North Carolina	Tar Heel State	Raleigh	9,458,888	53,819
North Dakota	Peace Garden State	Bismarck	653,778	70,698
Ohio	Buckeye State	Columbus	11,532,111	44,825
Oklahoma	Sooner State	Oklahoma City	3,724,447	69,899
Oregon	Beaver State	Salem	3,855,536	98,379
Pennsylvania	Keystone State	Harrisburg	12,632,780	46,055
Rhode Island	Ocean State	Providence	1,056,870	1,545
South Carolina	Palmetto State	Columbia	4,596,958	32,021
South Dakota	Mount Rushmore State	Pierre	820,077	77,116
Tennessee	Volunteer State	Nashville	6,338,112	42,144
Texas	Lone Star State	Austin	25,213,445	268,597
Utah	Beehive State	Salt Lake City	2,830,753	84,897
Vermont	Green Mountain State	Montpelier	622,433	9,616
Virginia	Old Dominion	Richmond	7,952,119	42,775
Washington	Evergreen State	Olympia	6,746,199	71,298
West Virginia	Mountain State	Charleston	1,825,513	24,230
Wisconsin	Badger State	Madison	5,668,519	65,496
Wyoming	Equality State	Cheyenne	547,637	97,812

*2010 Census resident population estimates.

**Total of land and water area in square miles.

STATE SONG	STATE FLOWER	STATE TREE	STATE BIRD
Alabama	Camellia	Southern Pine	Yellowhammer
Alaska's Flag	Forget-Me-Not	Sitka Spruce	Willow Ptarmigan
Arizona	Saguaro Cactus Blossom	Palo Verde	Cactus Wren
Arkansas	Apple Blossom	Pine	Mockingbird
I Love You, California	Golden Poppy	California Redwood	California Valley Quail
Where the Columbines Grow	Rocky Mountain Columbine	Colorado Blue Spruce	Lark Bunting
Yankee Doodle Dandy	Mountain Laurel	White Oak	American Robin
Our Delaware	Peach Blossom	American Holly	Blue Hen Chicken
Swanee River	Orange Blossom	Sabal Palmetto Palm	Mockingbird
Georgia On My Mind	Cherokee Rose	Live Oak	Brown Thrasher
Hawaii Ponoi	Yellow Hibiscus	Candlenut	Nene
Here We Have Idaho	Syringa	White Pine	Mountain Bluebird
Illinois	Purple Violet	White Oak	Cardinal
On the Banks of the Wabash, Far Away	Peony	Tulip Poplar	Cardinal
The Song of Iowa	Wild Rose	Oak	Eastern Goldfinch
Home on the Range	Sunflower	Cottonwood	Western Meadowlark
My Old Kentucky Home	Goldenrod	Tulip Tree	Cardinal
Give Me Louisiana	Magnolia	Cypress	Eastern Brown Pelican
State of Maine Song	White Pine Cone and Tassel	Eastern White Pine	Chickadee
Maryland, My Maryland	Black-eyed Susan	White Oak	Baltimore Oriole
All Hail to Massachusetts	Mayflower	American Elm	Chickadee
Michigan, My Michigan	Apple Blossom	White Pine	Robin
Hail! Minnesota	Pink and White Lady's Slipper	Red Pine	Common Loon
Go, Mississippi!	Magnolia	Magnolia	Mockingbird
Missouri Waltz	Hawthorn	Dogwood	Bluebird
Montana	Bitterroot	Ponderosa Pine	Western Meadowlark
Beautiful Nebraska	Goldenrod	Cottonwood	Western Meadowlark
Home Means Nevada	Sagebrush	Single-Leaf Pinon	Mountain Bluebird
Old New Hampshire	Purple Lilac	White Birch	Purple Finch
Ode to New Jersey	Purple Violet	Red Oak	Eastern Goldfinch
O Fair New Mexico	Yucca	Pinon	Roadrunner
I Love New York	Rose	Sugar Maple	Bluebird
The Old North State	Dogwood	Pine	Cardinal
North Dakota Hymn	Wild Prairie Rose	American Elm	Western Meadowlark
Beautiful Ohio	Scarlet Carnation	Buckeye	Cardinal
Oklahoma!	Mistletoe	Redbud	Scissortailed Flycatcher
Oregon, My Oregon	Oregon Grape	Douglas Fir	Western Meadowlark
Hail! Pennsylvania	Mountain Laurel	Hemlock	Ruffed Grouse
Rhode Island	Violet	Red Maple	Rhode Island Red
Carolina	Yellow Jessamine	Palmetto	Carolina Wren
Hail, South Dakota	Pasque Flower	Black Hills Spruce	Ringnecked Pheasant
The Tennessee Waltz	Iris	Tulip Poplar	Mockingbird
Texas, Our Texas	Bluebonnet	Pecan	Mockingbird
Utah, We Love Thee	Sego Lily	Blue Spruce	Seagull
Hail, Vermont	Red Clover	Sugar Maple	Hermit Thrush
Carry Me Back to Old Virginia	Dogwood	Dogwood	Cardinal
Washington, My Home	Western Rhododendron	Western Hemlock	Willow Goldfinch
The West Virginia Hills; This Is My West Virginia; and West Virginia, My Home, Sweet Home	Big Rhododendron	Sugar Maple	Cardinal
On Wisconsin!	Wood Violet	Sugar Maple	Robin
Wyoming	Indian Paintbrush	Cottonwood	Meadowlark

I. Agriculture

Number of Farms in 2009

National Total = 2,200,010 Farms*

ALPHA ORDER

RANK	STATE	FARMS	% of USA
18	Alabama	48,500	2.2%
50	Alaska	680	0.0%
37	Arizona	15,500	0.7%
17	Arkansas	49,100	2.2%
6	California	81,500	3.7%
27	Colorado	36,200	1.6%
45	Connecticut	4,900	0.2%
48	Delaware	2,480	0.1%
20	Florida	47,500	2.2%
19	Georgia	47,600	2.2%
43	Hawaii	7,500	0.3%
33	Idaho	25,500	1.2%
10	Illinois	75,800	3.4%
14	Indiana	61,500	2.8%
3	Iowa	92,600	4.2%
12	Kansas	65,500	3.0%
5	Kentucky	85,500	3.9%
30	Louisiana	30,000	1.4%
41	Maine	8,100	0.4%
38	Maryland	12,800	0.6%
42	Massachusetts	7,700	0.3%
15	Michigan	54,800	2.5%
7	Minnesota	81,000	3.7%
23	Mississippi	42,300	1.9%
2	Missouri	108,000	4.9%
31	Montana	29,800	1.4%
21	Nebraska	47,200	2.1%
47	Nevada	3,080	0.1%
46	New Hampshire	4,150	0.2%
40	New Jersey	10,300	0.5%
35	New Mexico	20,500	0.9%
26	New York	36,600	1.7%
16	North Carolina	52,400	2.4%
28	North Dakota	32,000	1.5%
11	Ohio	74,900	3.4%
4	Oklahoma	86,500	3.9%
25	Oregon	38,600	1.8%
13	Pennsylvania	63,200	2.9%
49	Rhode Island	1,220	0.1%
32	South Carolina	27,000	1.2%
29	South Dakota	31,500	1.4%
8	Tennessee	78,700	3.6%
1	Texas	247,500	11.2%
36	Utah	16,600	0.8%
44	Vermont	7,000	0.3%
22	Virginia	47,000	2.1%
24	Washington	39,500	1.8%
34	West Virginia	23,200	1.1%
9	Wisconsin	78,000	3.5%
39	Wyoming	11,000	0.5%

RANK ORDER

RANK	STATE	FARMS	% of USA
1	Texas	247,500	11.2%
2	Missouri	108,000	4.9%
3	Iowa	92,600	4.2%
4	Oklahoma	86,500	3.9%
5	Kentucky	85,500	3.9%
6	California	81,500	3.7%
7	Minnesota	81,000	3.7%
8	Tennessee	78,700	3.6%
9	Wisconsin	78,000	3.5%
10	Illinois	75,800	3.4%
11	Ohio	74,900	3.4%
12	Kansas	65,500	3.0%
13	Pennsylvania	63,200	2.9%
14	Indiana	61,500	2.8%
15	Michigan	54,800	2.5%
16	North Carolina	52,400	2.4%
17	Arkansas	49,100	2.2%
18	Alabama	48,500	2.2%
19	Georgia	47,600	2.2%
20	Florida	47,500	2.2%
21	Nebraska	47,200	2.1%
22	Virginia	47,000	2.1%
23	Mississippi	42,300	1.9%
24	Washington	39,500	1.8%
25	Oregon	38,600	1.8%
26	New York	36,600	1.7%
27	Colorado	36,200	1.6%
28	North Dakota	32,000	1.5%
29	South Dakota	31,500	1.4%
30	Louisiana	30,000	1.4%
31	Montana	29,800	1.4%
32	South Carolina	27,000	1.2%
33	Idaho	25,500	1.2%
34	West Virginia	23,200	1.1%
35	New Mexico	20,500	0.9%
36	Utah	16,600	0.8%
37	Arizona	15,500	0.7%
38	Maryland	12,800	0.6%
39	Wyoming	11,000	0.5%
40	New Jersey	10,300	0.5%
41	Maine	8,100	0.4%
42	Massachusetts	7,700	0.3%
43	Hawaii	7,500	0.3%
44	Vermont	7,000	0.3%
45	Connecticut	4,900	0.2%
46	New Hampshire	4,150	0.2%
47	Nevada	3,080	0.1%
48	Delaware	2,480	0.1%
49	Rhode Island	1,220	0.1%
50	Alaska	680	0.0%
	District of Columbia	0	0.0%

Source: U.S. Department of Agriculture, National Agricultural Statistics Service
"Farms and Land in Farms" (http://usda.mannlib.cornell.edu/MannUsda/viewDocumentInfo.do?documentID=1259)
*A farm is any establishment from which $1,000 or more of agricultural products were sold or would normally be sold during the year. This includes places with five or more horses, except horses in boarding stables or racetracks.

Land in Farms in 2009

National Total = 919,800,000 Acres*

ALPHA ORDER

RANK	STATE	ACRES	% of USA
31	Alabama	9,000,000	1.0%
44	Alaska	880,000	0.1%
15	Arizona	26,100,000	2.8%
23	Arkansas	13,600,000	1.5%
16	California	25,400,000	2.8%
9	Colorado	31,300,000	3.4%
49	Connecticut	400,000	0.0%
47	Delaware	490,000	0.1%
30	Florida	9,250,000	1.0%
28	Georgia	10,300,000	1.1%
43	Hawaii	1,120,000	0.1%
24	Idaho	11,400,000	1.2%
14	Illinois	26,700,000	2.9%
19	Indiana	14,800,000	1.6%
10	Iowa	30,800,000	3.3%
3	Kansas	46,200,000	5.0%
21	Kentucky	14,000,000	1.5%
33	Louisiana	8,050,000	0.9%
41	Maine	1,350,000	0.1%
40	Maryland	2,050,000	0.2%
46	Massachusetts	520,000	0.1%
29	Michigan	10,000,000	1.1%
13	Minnesota	26,900,000	2.9%
26	Mississippi	11,050,000	1.2%
12	Missouri	29,100,000	3.2%
2	Montana	60,800,000	6.6%
4	Nebraska	45,600,000	5.0%
37	Nevada	5,900,000	0.6%
48	New Hampshire	470,000	0.1%
45	New Jersey	730,000	0.1%
6	New Mexico	43,000,000	4.7%
36	New York	7,100,000	0.8%
32	North Carolina	8,600,000	0.9%
7	North Dakota	39,600,000	4.3%
22	Ohio	13,800,000	1.5%
8	Oklahoma	35,100,000	3.8%
17	Oregon	16,400,000	1.8%
35	Pennsylvania	7,750,000	0.8%
50	Rhode Island	70,000	0.0%
38	South Carolina	4,900,000	0.5%
5	South Dakota	43,700,000	4.8%
27	Tennessee	10,900,000	1.2%
1	Texas	130,400,000	14.2%
25	Utah	11,100,000	1.2%
42	Vermont	1,220,000	0.1%
34	Virginia	8,000,000	0.9%
19	Washington	14,800,000	1.6%
39	West Virginia	3,700,000	0.4%
18	Wisconsin	15,200,000	1.7%
11	Wyoming	30,200,000	3.3%

RANK ORDER

RANK	STATE	ACRES	% of USA
1	Texas	130,400,000	14.2%
2	Montana	60,800,000	6.6%
3	Kansas	46,200,000	5.0%
4	Nebraska	45,600,000	5.0%
5	South Dakota	43,700,000	4.8%
6	New Mexico	43,000,000	4.7%
7	North Dakota	39,600,000	4.3%
8	Oklahoma	35,100,000	3.8%
9	Colorado	31,300,000	3.4%
10	Iowa	30,800,000	3.3%
11	Wyoming	30,200,000	3.3%
12	Missouri	29,100,000	3.2%
13	Minnesota	26,900,000	2.9%
14	Illinois	26,700,000	2.9%
15	Arizona	26,100,000	2.8%
16	California	25,400,000	2.8%
17	Oregon	16,400,000	1.8%
18	Wisconsin	15,200,000	1.7%
19	Indiana	14,800,000	1.6%
19	Washington	14,800,000	1.6%
21	Kentucky	14,000,000	1.5%
22	Ohio	13,800,000	1.5%
23	Arkansas	13,600,000	1.5%
24	Idaho	11,400,000	1.2%
25	Utah	11,100,000	1.2%
26	Mississippi	11,050,000	1.2%
27	Tennessee	10,900,000	1.2%
28	Georgia	10,300,000	1.1%
29	Michigan	10,000,000	1.1%
30	Florida	9,250,000	1.0%
31	Alabama	9,000,000	1.0%
32	North Carolina	8,600,000	0.9%
33	Louisiana	8,050,000	0.9%
34	Virginia	8,000,000	0.9%
35	Pennsylvania	7,750,000	0.8%
36	New York	7,100,000	0.8%
37	Nevada	5,900,000	0.6%
38	South Carolina	4,900,000	0.5%
39	West Virginia	3,700,000	0.4%
40	Maryland	2,050,000	0.2%
41	Maine	1,350,000	0.1%
42	Vermont	1,220,000	0.1%
43	Hawaii	1,120,000	0.1%
44	Alaska	880,000	0.1%
45	New Jersey	730,000	0.1%
46	Massachusetts	520,000	0.1%
47	Delaware	490,000	0.1%
48	New Hampshire	470,000	0.1%
49	Connecticut	400,000	0.0%
50	Rhode Island	70,000	0.0%
	District of Columbia	0	0.0%

Source: U.S. Department of Agriculture, National Agricultural Statistics Service
    "Farms and Land in Farms" (http://usda.mannlib.cornell.edu/MannUsda/viewDocumentInfo.do?documentID=1259)
*A farm is any establishment from which $1,000 or more of agricultural products were sold or would normally be sold during the year. This includes places with five or more horses, except horses in boarding stables or racetracks.

Average Number of Acres per Farm in 2009

National Average = 418 Acres*

ALPHA ORDER

RANK	STATE	ACRES
32	Alabama	186
7	Alaska	1,294
5	Arizona	1,684
22	Arkansas	277
21	California	312
10	Colorado	865
47	Connecticut	82
28	Delaware	198
29	Florida	195
27	Georgia	216
43	Hawaii	149
14	Idaho	447
18	Illinois	352
26	Indiana	241
19	Iowa	333
11	Kansas	705
39	Kentucky	164
24	Louisiana	268
38	Maine	167
41	Maryland	160
49	Massachusetts	68
34	Michigan	182
20	Minnesota	332
25	Mississippi	261
23	Missouri	269
3	Montana	2,040
9	Nebraska	966
4	Nevada	1,916
46	New Hampshire	113
48	New Jersey	71
2	New Mexico	2,098
31	New York	194
39	North Carolina	164
8	North Dakota	1,238
33	Ohio	184
16	Oklahoma	406
15	Oregon	425
45	Pennsylvania	123
50	Rhode Island	57
35	South Carolina	181
6	South Dakota	1,387
44	Tennessee	139
13	Texas	527
12	Utah	669
36	Vermont	174
37	Virginia	170
17	Washington	375
42	West Virginia	159
29	Wisconsin	195
1	Wyoming	2,745

RANK ORDER

RANK	STATE	ACRES
1	Wyoming	2,745
2	New Mexico	2,098
3	Montana	2,040
4	Nevada	1,916
5	Arizona	1,684
6	South Dakota	1,387
7	Alaska	1,294
8	North Dakota	1,238
9	Nebraska	966
10	Colorado	865
11	Kansas	705
12	Utah	669
13	Texas	527
14	Idaho	447
15	Oregon	425
16	Oklahoma	406
17	Washington	375
18	Illinois	352
19	Iowa	333
20	Minnesota	332
21	California	312
22	Arkansas	277
23	Missouri	269
24	Louisiana	268
25	Mississippi	261
26	Indiana	241
27	Georgia	216
28	Delaware	198
29	Florida	195
29	Wisconsin	195
31	New York	194
32	Alabama	186
33	Ohio	184
34	Michigan	182
35	South Carolina	181
36	Vermont	174
37	Virginia	170
38	Maine	167
39	Kentucky	164
39	North Carolina	164
41	Maryland	160
42	West Virginia	159
43	Hawaii	149
44	Tennessee	139
45	Pennsylvania	123
46	New Hampshire	113
47	Connecticut	82
48	New Jersey	71
49	Massachusetts	68
50	Rhode Island	57
	District of Columbia**	NA

Source: U.S. Department of Agriculture, National Agricultural Statistics Service
    "Farms and Land in Farms" (http://usda.mannlib.cornell.edu/MannUsda/viewDocumentInfo.do?documentID=1259)
*A farm is any establishment from which $1,000 or more of agricultural products were sold or would normally be sold during the year. This includes places with five or more horses, except horses in boarding stables or racetracks.
**Not applicable.

Average per-Acre Value of Farmland in 2010

National Average = $2,140 per Acre*

ALPHA ORDER			RANK ORDER		
RANK	STATE	PER-ACRE VALUE	RANK	STATE	PER-ACRE VALUE
30	Alabama	$2,100	1	Rhode Island	$13,600
NA	Alaska**	NA	2	New Jersey	13,100
20	Arizona	3,500	3	Massachusetts	11,600
26	Arkansas	2,500	4	Connecticut	11,500
7	California	6,700	5	Delaware	8,100
41	Colorado	1,080	6	Maryland	7,200
4	Connecticut	11,500	7	California	6,700
5	Delaware	8,100	8	Florida	5,000
8	Florida	5,000	8	Pennsylvania	5,000
15	Georgia	3,900	10	New Hampshire	4,750
NA	Hawaii**	NA	11	Illinois	4,650
30	Idaho	2,100	12	Virginia	4,600
11	Illinois	4,650	13	North Carolina	4,130
14	Indiana	4,100	14	Indiana	4,100
15	Iowa	3,900	15	Georgia	3,900
42	Kansas	1,060	15	Iowa	3,900
24	Kentucky	2,880	15	Ohio	3,900
32	Louisiana	2,050	18	Wisconsin	3,720
35	Maine	2,000	19	Michigan	3,650
6	Maryland	7,200	20	Arizona	3,500
3	Massachusetts	11,600	21	Tennessee	3,450
19	Michigan	3,650	22	Minnesota	2,940
22	Minnesota	2,940	23	South Carolina	2,900
33	Mississippi	2,030	24	Kentucky	2,880
29	Missouri	2,250	25	Vermont	2,750
46	Montana	700	26	Arkansas	2,500
39	Nebraska	1,460	27	New York	2,400
43	Nevada	1,000	27	West Virginia	2,400
10	New Hampshire	4,750	29	Missouri	2,250
2	New Jersey	13,100	30	Alabama	2,100
48	New Mexico	480	30	Idaho	2,100
27	New York	2,400	32	Louisiana	2,050
13	North Carolina	4,130	33	Mississippi	2,030
45	North Dakota	810	33	Washington	2,030
15	Ohio	3,900	35	Maine	2,000
40	Oklahoma	1,180	36	Utah	1,810
37	Oregon	1,780	37	Oregon	1,780
8	Pennsylvania	5,000	38	Texas	1,630
1	Rhode Island	13,600	39	Nebraska	1,460
23	South Carolina	2,900	40	Oklahoma	1,180
44	South Dakota	920	41	Colorado	1,080
21	Tennessee	3,450	42	Kansas	1,060
38	Texas	1,630	43	Nevada	1,000
36	Utah	1,810	44	South Dakota	920
25	Vermont	2,750	45	North Dakota	810
12	Virginia	4,600	46	Montana	700
33	Washington	2,030	47	Wyoming	510
27	West Virginia	2,400	48	New Mexico	480
18	Wisconsin	3,720	NA	Alaska**	NA
47	Wyoming	510	NA	Hawaii**	NA
				District of Columbia**	NA

Source: U.S. Department of Agriculture, National Agricultural Statistics Service
    "Land Values and Cash Rents" (http://usda.mannlib.cornell.edu/MannUsda/viewDocumentInfo.do?documentID=1446)
*As of January 1, 2010. Value of farmland and buildings in nominal dollars.
**Not applicable or available.

Percent Change in Average per-Acre Value of Farmland: 2009 to 2010

National Percent Change = 1.4% Increase*

ALPHA ORDER

RANK	STATE	PERCENT CHANGE
35	Alabama	(2.3)
NA	Alaska**	NA
21	Arizona	0.0
3	Arkansas	4.6
13	California	1.5
31	Colorado	(1.8)
41	Connecticut	(4.2)
47	Delaware	(9.0)
38	Florida	(2.9)
45	Georgia	(4.9)
NA	Hawaii**	NA
43	Idaho	(4.5)
9	Illinois	2.6
12	Indiana	2.0
16	Iowa	1.3
8	Kansas	2.9
17	Kentucky	1.1
5	Louisiana	4.1
44	Maine	(4.8)
40	Maryland	(4.0)
39	Massachusetts	(3.3)
36	Michigan	(2.7)
10	Minnesota	2.4
13	Mississippi	1.5
11	Missouri	2.3
21	Montana	0.0
1	Nebraska	9.0
21	Nevada	0.0
29	New Hampshire	(1.0)
46	New Jersey	(5.1)
21	New Mexico	0.0
21	New York	0.0
37	North Carolina	(2.8)
6	North Dakota	3.8
20	Ohio	0.5
18	Oklahoma	0.9
30	Oregon	(1.1)
34	Pennsylvania	(2.0)
48	Rhode Island	(11.1)
21	South Carolina	0.0
7	South Dakota	3.4
4	Tennessee	4.5
2	Texas	5.2
19	Utah	0.6
31	Vermont	(1.8)
41	Virginia	(4.2)
13	Washington	1.5
21	West Virginia	0.0
28	Wisconsin	(0.8)
33	Wyoming	(1.9)

RANK ORDER

RANK	STATE	PERCENT CHANGE
1	Nebraska	9.0
2	Texas	5.2
3	Arkansas	4.6
4	Tennessee	4.5
5	Louisiana	4.1
6	North Dakota	3.8
7	South Dakota	3.4
8	Kansas	2.9
9	Illinois	2.6
10	Minnesota	2.4
11	Missouri	2.3
12	Indiana	2.0
13	California	1.5
13	Mississippi	1.5
13	Washington	1.5
16	Iowa	1.3
17	Kentucky	1.1
18	Oklahoma	0.9
19	Utah	0.6
20	Ohio	0.5
21	Arizona	0.0
21	Montana	0.0
21	Nevada	0.0
21	New Mexico	0.0
21	New York	0.0
21	South Carolina	0.0
21	West Virginia	0.0
28	Wisconsin	(0.8)
29	New Hampshire	(1.0)
30	Oregon	(1.1)
31	Colorado	(1.8)
31	Vermont	(1.8)
33	Wyoming	(1.9)
34	Pennsylvania	(2.0)
35	Alabama	(2.3)
36	Michigan	(2.7)
37	North Carolina	(2.8)
38	Florida	(2.9)
39	Massachusetts	(3.3)
40	Maryland	(4.0)
41	Connecticut	(4.2)
41	Virginia	(4.2)
43	Idaho	(4.5)
44	Maine	(4.8)
45	Georgia	(4.9)
46	New Jersey	(5.1)
47	Delaware	(9.0)
48	Rhode Island	(11.1)
NA	Alaska**	NA
NA	Hawaii**	NA
	District of Columbia**	NA

Source: U.S. Department of Agriculture, National Agricultural Statistics Service
    "Land Values and Cash Rents" (http://usda.mannlib.cornell.edu/MannUsda/viewDocumentInfo.do?documentID=1446)
*As of January 1, 2010. Value of farmland and buildings in nominal dollars.
**Not applicable or available.

Net Farm Income in 2009

National Total = $62,187,066,485*

ALPHA ORDER

RANK	STATE	FARM INCOME	% of USA
20	Alabama	$1,018,573,553	1.6%
47	Alaska	8,155,388	0.0%
36	Arizona	203,280,889	0.3%
15	Arkansas	1,524,030,186	2.5%
1	California	8,782,066,032	14.1%
25	Colorado	744,917,639	1.2%
41	Connecticut	116,239,535	0.2%
37	Delaware	193,245,774	0.3%
17	Florida	1,280,982,029	2.1%
10	Georgia	2,359,381,109	3.8%
39	Hawaii	132,939,252	0.2%
22	Idaho	926,743,121	1.5%
3	Illinois	3,641,424,489	5.9%
7	Indiana	2,539,974,056	4.1%
2	Iowa	5,012,848,577	8.1%
9	Kansas	2,368,809,057	3.8%
16	Kentucky	1,331,617,780	2.1%
26	Louisiana	689,101,755	1.1%
38	Maine	138,570,535	0.2%
33	Maryland	299,296,738	0.5%
42	Massachusetts	107,792,027	0.2%
19	Michigan	1,070,667,504	1.7%
5	Minnesota	3,020,138,942	4.9%
18	Mississippi	1,220,257,553	2.0%
11	Missouri	2,335,689,549	3.8%
35	Montana	248,098,186	0.4%
4	Nebraska	3,275,706,662	5.3%
43	Nevada	104,698,471	0.2%
45	New Hampshire	19,158,066	0.0%
34	New Jersey	294,894,616	0.5%
31	New Mexico	431,703,463	0.7%
29	New York	552,710,279	0.9%
6	North Carolina	2,739,163,485	4.4%
14	North Dakota	1,935,924,246	3.1%
13	Ohio	2,121,830,262	3.4%
40	Oklahoma	130,238,622	0.2%
28	Oregon	562,777,011	0.9%
23	Pennsylvania	905,066,125	1.5%
46	Rhode Island	13,578,279	0.0%
30	South Carolina	530,831,766	0.9%
8	South Dakota	2,376,051,657	3.8%
27	Tennessee	612,618,369	1.0%
12	Texas	2,123,966,806	3.4%
NA	Utah**	(51,839,438)	-0.1%
44	Vermont	97,099,121	0.2%
32	Virginia	352,075,470	0.6%
21	Washington	962,004,074	1.5%
NA	West Virginia**	(34,897,351)	-0.1%
24	Wisconsin	849,353,556	1.4%
NA	Wyoming**	(32,489,388)	-0.1%

RANK ORDER

RANK	STATE	FARM INCOME	% of USA
1	California	$8,782,066,032	14.1%
2	Iowa	5,012,848,577	8.1%
3	Illinois	3,641,424,489	5.9%
4	Nebraska	3,275,706,662	5.3%
5	Minnesota	3,020,138,942	4.9%
6	North Carolina	2,739,163,485	4.4%
7	Indiana	2,539,974,056	4.1%
8	South Dakota	2,376,051,657	3.8%
9	Kansas	2,368,809,057	3.8%
10	Georgia	2,359,381,109	3.8%
11	Missouri	2,335,689,549	3.8%
12	Texas	2,123,966,806	3.4%
13	Ohio	2,121,830,262	3.4%
14	North Dakota	1,935,924,246	3.1%
15	Arkansas	1,524,030,186	2.5%
16	Kentucky	1,331,617,780	2.1%
17	Florida	1,280,982,029	2.1%
18	Mississippi	1,220,257,553	2.0%
19	Michigan	1,070,667,504	1.7%
20	Alabama	1,018,573,553	1.6%
21	Washington	962,004,074	1.5%
22	Idaho	926,743,121	1.5%
23	Pennsylvania	905,066,125	1.5%
24	Wisconsin	849,353,556	1.4%
25	Colorado	744,917,639	1.2%
26	Louisiana	689,101,755	1.1%
27	Tennessee	612,618,369	1.0%
28	Oregon	562,777,011	0.9%
29	New York	552,710,279	0.9%
30	South Carolina	530,831,766	0.9%
31	New Mexico	431,703,463	0.7%
32	Virginia	352,075,470	0.6%
33	Maryland	299,296,738	0.5%
34	New Jersey	294,894,616	0.5%
35	Montana	248,098,186	0.4%
36	Arizona	203,280,889	0.3%
37	Delaware	193,245,774	0.3%
38	Maine	138,570,535	0.2%
39	Hawaii	132,939,252	0.2%
40	Oklahoma	130,238,622	0.2%
41	Connecticut	116,239,535	0.2%
42	Massachusetts	107,792,027	0.2%
43	Nevada	104,698,471	0.2%
44	Vermont	97,099,121	0.2%
45	New Hampshire	19,158,066	0.0%
46	Rhode Island	13,578,279	0.0%
47	Alaska	8,155,388	0.0%
NA	Wyoming**	(32,489,388)	-0.1%
NA	West Virginia**	(34,897,351)	-0.1%
NA	Utah**	(51,839,438)	-0.1%
	District of Columbia	0	0.0%

Source: U.S. Department of Agriculture, Economic Research Service
"Net Farm Income and Value of Production per Acre for States, 2009
(http://www.ers.usda.gov/data/FarmIncome/FinfidmuXls.htm)
*Net farm income is a measure of the net value of production in a given year. It is determined by subtracting total production expenses from gross farm income.

Net Farm Income per Operation in 2009

National Average = $21,001 per Operation

ALPHA ORDER			RANK ORDER		
RANK	STATE	PER OPERATION	RANK	STATE	PER OPERATION
26	Alabama	$21,002	1	California	$107,755
39	Alaska	11,993	2	Delaware	77,922
38	Arizona	13,115	3	South Dakota	75,430
15	Arkansas	31,039	4	Nebraska	69,401
1	California	107,755	5	North Dakota	60,498
27	Colorado	20,578	6	Iowa	54,134
21	Connecticut	23,722	7	North Carolina	52,274
2	Delaware	77,922	8	Georgia	49,567
19	Florida	26,968	9	Illinois	48,040
8	Georgia	49,567	10	Indiana	41,300
30	Hawaii	17,725	11	Minnesota	37,286
12	Idaho	36,343	12	Idaho	36,343
9	Illinois	48,040	13	Kansas	36,165
10	Indiana	41,300	14	Nevada	33,993
6	Iowa	54,134	15	Arkansas	31,039
13	Kansas	36,165	16	Mississippi	28,848
32	Kentucky	15,574	17	New Jersey	28,631
23	Louisiana	22,970	18	Ohio	28,329
31	Maine	17,107	19	Florida	26,968
22	Maryland	23,383	20	Washington	24,355
36	Massachusetts	13,999	21	Connecticut	23,722
29	Michigan	19,538	22	Maryland	23,383
11	Minnesota	37,286	23	Louisiana	22,970
16	Mississippi	28,848	24	Missouri	21,627
24	Missouri	21,627	25	New Mexico	21,059
43	Montana	8,325	26	Alabama	21,002
4	Nebraska	69,401	27	Colorado	20,578
14	Nevada	33,993	28	South Carolina	19,660
46	New Hampshire	4,616	29	Michigan	19,538
17	New Jersey	28,631	30	Hawaii	17,725
25	New Mexico	21,059	31	Maine	17,107
33	New York	15,101	32	Kentucky	15,574
7	North Carolina	52,274	33	New York	15,101
5	North Dakota	60,498	34	Oregon	14,580
18	Ohio	28,329	35	Pennsylvania	14,321
47	Oklahoma	1,506	36	Massachusetts	13,999
34	Oregon	14,580	37	Vermont	13,871
35	Pennsylvania	14,321	38	Arizona	13,115
40	Rhode Island	11,130	39	Alaska	11,993
28	South Carolina	19,660	40	Rhode Island	11,130
3	South Dakota	75,430	41	Wisconsin	10,889
44	Tennessee	7,784	42	Texas	8,582
42	Texas	8,582	43	Montana	8,325
50	Utah	(3,123)	44	Tennessee	7,784
37	Vermont	13,871	45	Virginia	7,491
45	Virginia	7,491	46	New Hampshire	4,616
20	Washington	24,355	47	Oklahoma	1,506
48	West Virginia	(1,504)	48	West Virginia	(1,504)
41	Wisconsin	10,889	49	Wyoming	(2,954)
49	Wyoming	(2,954)	50	Utah	(3,123)
				District of Columbia*	NA

Source: U.S. Department of Agriculture, Economic Research Service
"Net Farm Income and Value of Production per Acre for States, 2009
(http://www.ers.usda.gov/data/FarmIncome/FinfidmuXls.htm)
*Not applicable.

Net Farm Income per Acre in 2009

National Average = $68 per Acre

ALPHA ORDER

ALPHA ORDER

RANK	STATE	PER ACRE
17	Alabama	$113
44	Alaska	9
45	Arizona	8
18	Arkansas	112
3	California	346
40	Colorado	24
5	Connecticut	291
2	Delaware	394
13	Florida	138
6	Georgia	229
15	Hawaii	119
26	Idaho	81
14	Illinois	136
9	Indiana	172
10	Iowa	163
35	Kansas	51
24	Kentucky	95
25	Louisiana	86
23	Maine	103
12	Maryland	146
7	Massachusetts	207
22	Michigan	107
18	Minnesota	112
20	Mississippi	110
27	Missouri	80
46	Montana	4
30	Nebraska	72
41	Nevada	18
38	New Hampshire	41
1	New Jersey	404
43	New Mexico	10
29	New York	78
4	North Carolina	319
36	North Dakota	49
11	Ohio	154
46	Oklahoma	4
39	Oregon	34
16	Pennsylvania	117
8	Rhode Island	194
21	South Carolina	108
34	South Dakota	54
32	Tennessee	56
42	Texas	16
49	Utah	(5)
27	Vermont	80
37	Virginia	44
31	Washington	65
50	West Virginia	(9)
32	Wisconsin	56
48	Wyoming	(1)

RANK ORDER

RANK	STATE	PER ACRE
1	New Jersey	$404
2	Delaware	394
3	California	346
4	North Carolina	319
5	Connecticut	291
6	Georgia	229
7	Massachusetts	207
8	Rhode Island	194
9	Indiana	172
10	Iowa	163
11	Ohio	154
12	Maryland	146
13	Florida	138
14	Illinois	136
15	Hawaii	119
16	Pennsylvania	117
17	Alabama	113
18	Arkansas	112
18	Minnesota	112
20	Mississippi	110
21	South Carolina	108
22	Michigan	107
23	Maine	103
24	Kentucky	95
25	Louisiana	86
26	Idaho	81
27	Missouri	80
27	Vermont	80
29	New York	78
30	Nebraska	72
31	Washington	65
32	Tennessee	56
32	Wisconsin	56
34	South Dakota	54
35	Kansas	51
36	North Dakota	49
37	Virginia	44
38	New Hampshire	41
39	Oregon	34
40	Colorado	24
41	Nevada	18
42	Texas	16
43	New Mexico	10
44	Alaska	9
45	Arizona	8
46	Montana	4
46	Oklahoma	4
48	Wyoming	(1)
49	Utah	(5)
50	West Virginia	(9)
	District of Columbia*	NA

Source: U.S. Department of Agriculture, Economic Research Service
"Net Farm Income and Value of Production per Acre for States, 2009
(http://www.ers.usda.gov/data/FarmIncome/FinfidmuXls.htm)
*Not applicable.

Farm Income: Cash Receipts from Commodities in 2009

National Total = $283,406,168,000*

ALPHA ORDER

RANK	STATE	FARM INCOME	% of USA
26	Alabama	$4,214,820,000	1.5%
50	Alaska	31,919,000	0.0%
29	Arizona	2,943,464,000	1.0%
12	Arkansas	7,190,056,000	2.5%
1	California	34,840,647,000	12.3%
20	Colorado	5,552,944,000	2.0%
43	Connecticut	535,519,000	0.2%
38	Delaware	1,009,804,000	0.4%
13	Florida	7,099,929,000	2.5%
15	Georgia	6,846,586,000	2.4%
41	Hawaii	581,385,000	0.2%
21	Idaho	5,160,698,000	1.8%
5	Illinois	14,544,878,000	5.1%
9	Indiana	8,757,045,000	3.1%
2	Iowa	21,013,892,000	7.4%
7	Kansas	12,085,411,000	4.3%
25	Kentucky	4,257,623,000	1.5%
34	Louisiana	2,539,158,000	0.9%
42	Maine	577,701,000	0.2%
36	Maryland	1,656,025,000	0.6%
47	Massachusetts	474,824,000	0.2%
19	Michigan	5,579,183,000	2.0%
6	Minnesota	13,325,230,000	4.7%
24	Mississippi	4,327,260,000	1.5%
10	Missouri	7,696,071,000	2.7%
33	Montana	2,565,052,000	0.9%
4	Nebraska	15,309,098,000	5.4%
44	Nevada	533,370,000	0.2%
48	New Hampshire	178,903,000	0.1%
39	New Jersey	1,000,459,000	0.4%
31	New Mexico	2,698,524,000	1.0%
28	New York	3,675,505,000	1.3%
8	North Carolina	9,187,821,000	3.2%
18	North Dakota	6,351,969,000	2.2%
16	Ohio	6,835,590,000	2.4%
23	Oklahoma	4,844,882,000	1.7%
27	Oregon	3,893,448,000	1.4%
22	Pennsylvania	4,979,589,000	1.8%
49	Rhode Island	61,989,000	0.0%
35	South Carolina	2,154,858,000	0.8%
14	South Dakota	6,860,746,000	2.4%
30	Tennessee	2,841,388,000	1.0%
3	Texas	16,573,054,000	5.8%
37	Utah	1,185,844,000	0.4%
45	Vermont	517,256,000	0.2%
32	Virginia	2,641,506,000	0.9%
17	Washington	6,592,649,000	2.3%
46	West Virginia	495,624,000	0.2%
11	Wisconsin	7,609,624,000	2.7%
40	Wyoming	969,649,000	0.3%

RANK ORDER

RANK	STATE	FARM INCOME	% of USA
1	California	$34,840,647,000	12.3%
2	Iowa	21,013,892,000	7.4%
3	Texas	16,573,054,000	5.8%
4	Nebraska	15,309,098,000	5.4%
5	Illinois	14,544,878,000	5.1%
6	Minnesota	13,325,230,000	4.7%
7	Kansas	12,085,411,000	4.3%
8	North Carolina	9,187,821,000	3.2%
9	Indiana	8,757,045,000	3.1%
10	Missouri	7,696,071,000	2.7%
11	Wisconsin	7,609,624,000	2.7%
12	Arkansas	7,190,056,000	2.5%
13	Florida	7,099,929,000	2.5%
14	South Dakota	6,860,746,000	2.4%
15	Georgia	6,846,586,000	2.4%
16	Ohio	6,835,590,000	2.4%
17	Washington	6,592,649,000	2.3%
18	North Dakota	6,351,969,000	2.2%
19	Michigan	5,579,183,000	2.0%
20	Colorado	5,552,944,000	2.0%
21	Idaho	5,160,698,000	1.8%
22	Pennsylvania	4,979,589,000	1.8%
23	Oklahoma	4,844,882,000	1.7%
24	Mississippi	4,327,260,000	1.5%
25	Kentucky	4,257,623,000	1.5%
26	Alabama	4,214,820,000	1.5%
27	Oregon	3,893,448,000	1.4%
28	New York	3,675,505,000	1.3%
29	Arizona	2,943,464,000	1.0%
30	Tennessee	2,841,388,000	1.0%
31	New Mexico	2,698,524,000	1.0%
32	Virginia	2,641,506,000	0.9%
33	Montana	2,565,052,000	0.9%
34	Louisiana	2,539,158,000	0.9%
35	South Carolina	2,154,858,000	0.8%
36	Maryland	1,656,025,000	0.6%
37	Utah	1,185,844,000	0.4%
38	Delaware	1,009,804,000	0.4%
39	New Jersey	1,000,459,000	0.4%
40	Wyoming	969,649,000	0.3%
41	Hawaii	581,385,000	0.2%
42	Maine	577,701,000	0.2%
43	Connecticut	535,519,000	0.2%
44	Nevada	533,370,000	0.2%
45	Vermont	517,256,000	0.2%
46	West Virginia	495,624,000	0.2%
47	Massachusetts	474,824,000	0.2%
48	New Hampshire	178,903,000	0.1%
49	Rhode Island	61,989,000	0.0%
50	Alaska	31,919,000	0.0%
	District of Columbia	0	0.0%

Source: U.S. Department of Agriculture, Economic Research Service
    "Farm Marketings" (http://www.ers.usda.gov/data/FarmIncome/firkdmu.htm)
*Commodities include crops and livestock.

Farm Income: Crops in 2009

National Total = $163,654,539,000

ALPHA ORDER

RANK	STATE	FARM INCOME	% of USA
34	Alabama	$879,677,000	0.5%
50	Alaska	25,709,000	0.0%
25	Arizona	1,765,703,000	1.1%
17	Arkansas	3,225,991,000	2.0%
1	California	27,026,641,000	16.5%
22	Colorado	2,229,599,000	1.4%
40	Connecticut	383,951,000	0.2%
44	Delaware	238,935,000	0.1%
7	Florida	5,997,750,000	3.7%
21	Georgia	2,555,771,000	1.6%
38	Hawaii	509,772,000	0.3%
20	Idaho	2,649,561,000	1.6%
2	Illinois	12,696,303,000	7.8%
6	Indiana	6,388,823,000	3.9%
3	Iowa	12,492,972,000	7.6%
9	Kansas	5,733,270,000	3.5%
24	Kentucky	1,828,561,000	1.1%
26	Louisiana	1,761,590,000	1.1%
42	Maine	319,811,000	0.2%
36	Maryland	750,609,000	0.5%
41	Massachusetts	379,544,000	0.2%
15	Michigan	3,673,750,000	2.2%
4	Minnesota	8,422,873,000	5.1%
29	Mississippi	1,595,401,000	1.0%
14	Missouri	4,382,080,000	2.7%
30	Montana	1,515,648,000	0.9%
5	Nebraska	8,025,772,000	4.9%
43	Nevada	257,002,000	0.2%
47	New Hampshire	103,786,000	0.1%
35	New Jersey	867,646,000	0.5%
37	New Mexico	700,944,000	0.4%
28	New York	1,679,828,000	1.0%
16	North Carolina	3,477,881,000	2.1%
10	North Dakota	5,580,563,000	3.4%
12	Ohio	4,601,244,000	2.8%
31	Oklahoma	1,260,431,000	0.8%
18	Oregon	2,995,176,000	1.8%
23	Pennsylvania	1,932,558,000	1.2%
49	Rhode Island	53,257,000	0.0%
33	South Carolina	907,335,000	0.6%
13	South Dakota	4,499,158,000	2.7%
27	Tennessee	1,704,713,000	1.0%
8	Texas	5,932,189,000	3.6%
39	Utah	421,327,000	0.3%
46	Vermont	118,136,000	0.1%
32	Virginia	1,006,496,000	0.6%
11	Washington	4,952,514,000	3.0%
48	West Virginia	91,407,000	0.1%
19	Wisconsin	2,830,757,000	1.7%
45	Wyoming	224,128,000	0.1%

RANK ORDER

RANK	STATE	FARM INCOME	% of USA
1	California	$27,026,641,000	16.5%
2	Illinois	12,696,303,000	7.8%
3	Iowa	12,492,972,000	7.6%
4	Minnesota	8,422,873,000	5.1%
5	Nebraska	8,025,772,000	4.9%
6	Indiana	6,388,823,000	3.9%
7	Florida	5,997,750,000	3.7%
8	Texas	5,932,189,000	3.6%
9	Kansas	5,733,270,000	3.5%
10	North Dakota	5,580,563,000	3.4%
11	Washington	4,952,514,000	3.0%
12	Ohio	4,601,244,000	2.8%
13	South Dakota	4,499,158,000	2.7%
14	Missouri	4,382,080,000	2.7%
15	Michigan	3,673,750,000	2.2%
16	North Carolina	3,477,881,000	2.1%
17	Arkansas	3,225,991,000	2.0%
18	Oregon	2,995,176,000	1.8%
19	Wisconsin	2,830,757,000	1.7%
20	Idaho	2,649,561,000	1.6%
21	Georgia	2,555,771,000	1.6%
22	Colorado	2,229,599,000	1.4%
23	Pennsylvania	1,932,558,000	1.2%
24	Kentucky	1,828,561,000	1.1%
25	Arizona	1,765,703,000	1.1%
26	Louisiana	1,761,590,000	1.1%
27	Tennessee	1,704,713,000	1.0%
28	New York	1,679,828,000	1.0%
29	Mississippi	1,595,401,000	1.0%
30	Montana	1,515,648,000	0.9%
31	Oklahoma	1,260,431,000	0.8%
32	Virginia	1,006,496,000	0.6%
33	South Carolina	907,335,000	0.6%
34	Alabama	879,677,000	0.5%
35	New Jersey	867,646,000	0.5%
36	Maryland	750,609,000	0.5%
37	New Mexico	700,944,000	0.4%
38	Hawaii	509,772,000	0.3%
39	Utah	421,327,000	0.3%
40	Connecticut	383,951,000	0.2%
41	Massachusetts	379,544,000	0.2%
42	Maine	319,811,000	0.2%
43	Nevada	257,002,000	0.2%
44	Delaware	238,935,000	0.1%
45	Wyoming	224,128,000	0.1%
46	Vermont	118,136,000	0.1%
47	New Hampshire	103,786,000	0.1%
48	West Virginia	91,407,000	0.1%
49	Rhode Island	53,257,000	0.0%
50	Alaska	25,709,000	0.0%
	District of Columbia	0	0.0%

Source: U.S. Department of Agriculture, Economic Research Service
"Farm Marketings" (http://www.ers.usda.gov/data/FarmIncome/firkdmu.htm)

Farm Income: Livestock in 2009

National Total = $119,751,600,000*

ALPHA ORDER

RANK	STATE	FARM INCOME	% of USA
12	Alabama	$3,335,143,000	2.8%
50	Alaska	6,210,000	0.0%
29	Arizona	1,177,761,000	1.0%
10	Arkansas	3,964,065,000	3.3%
3	California	7,814,006,000	6.5%
13	Colorado	3,323,345,000	2.8%
44	Connecticut	151,568,000	0.1%
37	Delaware	770,869,000	0.6%
31	Florida	1,102,179,000	0.9%
9	Georgia	4,290,815,000	3.6%
48	Hawaii	71,613,000	0.1%
17	Idaho	2,511,137,000	2.1%
25	Illinois	1,848,575,000	1.5%
19	Indiana	2,368,222,000	2.0%
2	Iowa	8,520,920,000	7.1%
5	Kansas	6,352,141,000	5.3%
18	Kentucky	2,429,062,000	2.0%
35	Louisiana	777,568,000	0.6%
43	Maine	257,890,000	0.2%
33	Maryland	905,416,000	0.8%
46	Massachusetts	95,280,000	0.1%
24	Michigan	1,905,433,000	1.6%
7	Minnesota	4,902,357,000	4.1%
16	Mississippi	2,731,859,000	2.3%
14	Missouri	3,313,991,000	2.8%
32	Montana	1,049,404,000	0.9%
4	Nebraska	7,283,326,000	6.1%
42	Nevada	276,368,000	0.2%
47	New Hampshire	75,117,000	0.1%
45	New Jersey	132,813,000	0.1%
22	New Mexico	1,997,580,000	1.7%
23	New York	1,995,677,000	1.7%
6	North Carolina	5,709,940,000	4.8%
36	North Dakota	771,406,000	0.6%
21	Ohio	2,234,346,000	1.9%
11	Oklahoma	3,584,451,000	3.0%
34	Oregon	898,272,000	0.8%
15	Pennsylvania	3,047,031,000	2.5%
49	Rhode Island	8,732,000	0.0%
28	South Carolina	1,247,523,000	1.0%
20	South Dakota	2,361,588,000	2.0%
30	Tennessee	1,136,675,000	0.9%
1	Texas	10,640,865,000	8.9%
38	Utah	764,517,000	0.6%
41	Vermont	399,120,000	0.3%
27	Virginia	1,635,010,000	1.4%
26	Washington	1,640,135,000	1.4%
40	West Virginia	404,217,000	0.3%
8	Wisconsin	4,778,867,000	4.0%
39	Wyoming	745,521,000	0.6%

RANK ORDER

RANK	STATE	FARM INCOME	% of USA
1	Texas	$10,640,865,000	8.9%
2	Iowa	8,520,920,000	7.1%
3	California	7,814,006,000	6.5%
4	Nebraska	7,283,326,000	6.1%
5	Kansas	6,352,141,000	5.3%
6	North Carolina	5,709,940,000	4.8%
7	Minnesota	4,902,357,000	4.1%
8	Wisconsin	4,778,867,000	4.0%
9	Georgia	4,290,815,000	3.6%
10	Arkansas	3,964,065,000	3.3%
11	Oklahoma	3,584,451,000	3.0%
12	Alabama	3,335,143,000	2.8%
13	Colorado	3,323,345,000	2.8%
14	Missouri	3,313,991,000	2.8%
15	Pennsylvania	3,047,031,000	2.5%
16	Mississippi	2,731,859,000	2.3%
17	Idaho	2,511,137,000	2.1%
18	Kentucky	2,429,062,000	2.0%
19	Indiana	2,368,222,000	2.0%
20	South Dakota	2,361,588,000	2.0%
21	Ohio	2,234,346,000	1.9%
22	New Mexico	1,997,580,000	1.7%
23	New York	1,995,677,000	1.7%
24	Michigan	1,905,433,000	1.6%
25	Illinois	1,848,575,000	1.5%
26	Washington	1,640,135,000	1.4%
27	Virginia	1,635,010,000	1.4%
28	South Carolina	1,247,523,000	1.0%
29	Arizona	1,177,761,000	1.0%
30	Tennessee	1,136,675,000	0.9%
31	Florida	1,102,179,000	0.9%
32	Montana	1,049,404,000	0.9%
33	Maryland	905,416,000	0.8%
34	Oregon	898,272,000	0.8%
35	Louisiana	777,568,000	0.6%
36	North Dakota	771,406,000	0.6%
37	Delaware	770,869,000	0.6%
38	Utah	764,517,000	0.6%
39	Wyoming	745,521,000	0.6%
40	West Virginia	404,217,000	0.3%
41	Vermont	399,120,000	0.3%
42	Nevada	276,368,000	0.2%
43	Maine	257,890,000	0.2%
44	Connecticut	151,568,000	0.1%
45	New Jersey	132,813,000	0.1%
46	Massachusetts	95,280,000	0.1%
47	New Hampshire	75,117,000	0.1%
48	Hawaii	71,613,000	0.1%
49	Rhode Island	8,732,000	0.0%
50	Alaska	6,210,000	0.0%
	District of Columbia	0	0.0%

Source: U.S. Department of Agriculture, Economic Research Service
"Farm Marketings" (http://www.ers.usda.gov/data/FarmIncome/firkdmu.htm)
*Includes livestock products.

Farm Income: Government Payments in 2009

National Total = $12,262,587,000*

ALPHA ORDER

RANK	STATE	PAYMENTS	% of USA
26	Alabama	$168,824,000	1.4%
50	Alaska	5,820,000	0.0%
32	Arizona	111,572,000	0.9%
7	Arkansas	482,276,000	3.9%
3	California	568,427,000	4.6%
23	Colorado	191,920,000	1.6%
46	Connecticut	12,797,000	0.1%
43	Delaware	15,897,000	0.1%
35	Florida	79,640,000	0.6%
14	Georgia	392,128,000	3.2%
45	Hawaii	13,437,000	0.1%
30	Idaho	140,267,000	1.1%
4	Illinois	566,722,000	4.6%
16	Indiana	305,375,000	2.5%
2	Iowa	767,407,000	6.3%
10	Kansas	475,318,000	3.9%
15	Kentucky	354,875,000	2.9%
21	Louisiana	247,492,000	2.0%
40	Maine	20,446,000	0.2%
36	Maryland	52,787,000	0.4%
44	Massachusetts	15,521,000	0.1%
25	Michigan	179,624,000	1.5%
5	Minnesota	527,900,000	4.3%
8	Mississippi	480,614,000	3.9%
9	Missouri	478,902,000	3.9%
19	Montana	256,456,000	2.1%
12	Nebraska	419,287,000	3.4%
47	Nevada	11,166,000	0.1%
48	New Hampshire	9,107,000	0.1%
42	New Jersey	17,490,000	0.1%
34	New Mexico	81,768,000	0.7%
29	New York	149,065,000	1.2%
6	North Carolina	486,109,000	4.0%
11	North Dakota	441,949,000	3.6%
17	Ohio	288,445,000	2.4%
22	Oklahoma	229,327,000	1.9%
33	Oregon	101,939,000	0.8%
27	Pennsylvania	161,356,000	1.3%
49	Rhode Island	6,383,000	0.1%
28	South Carolina	161,344,000	1.3%
20	South Dakota	256,352,000	2.1%
18	Tennessee	265,398,000	2.2%
1	Texas	1,406,753,000	11.5%
38	Utah	43,963,000	0.4%
37	Vermont	45,044,000	0.4%
31	Virginia	119,813,000	1.0%
24	Washington	189,356,000	1.5%
41	West Virginia	18,362,000	0.1%
13	Wisconsin	406,445,000	3.3%
39	Wyoming	33,924,000	0.3%

RANK ORDER

RANK	STATE	PAYMENTS	% of USA
1	Texas	$1,406,753,000	11.5%
2	Iowa	767,407,000	6.3%
3	California	568,427,000	4.6%
4	Illinois	566,722,000	4.6%
5	Minnesota	527,900,000	4.3%
6	North Carolina	486,109,000	4.0%
7	Arkansas	482,276,000	3.9%
8	Mississippi	480,614,000	3.9%
9	Missouri	478,902,000	3.9%
10	Kansas	475,318,000	3.9%
11	North Dakota	441,949,000	3.6%
12	Nebraska	419,287,000	3.4%
13	Wisconsin	406,445,000	3.3%
14	Georgia	392,128,000	3.2%
15	Kentucky	354,875,000	2.9%
16	Indiana	305,375,000	2.5%
17	Ohio	288,445,000	2.4%
18	Tennessee	265,398,000	2.2%
19	Montana	256,456,000	2.1%
20	South Dakota	256,352,000	2.1%
21	Louisiana	247,492,000	2.0%
22	Oklahoma	229,327,000	1.9%
23	Colorado	191,920,000	1.6%
24	Washington	189,356,000	1.5%
25	Michigan	179,624,000	1.5%
26	Alabama	168,824,000	1.4%
27	Pennsylvania	161,356,000	1.3%
28	South Carolina	161,344,000	1.3%
29	New York	149,065,000	1.2%
30	Idaho	140,267,000	1.1%
31	Virginia	119,813,000	1.0%
32	Arizona	111,572,000	0.9%
33	Oregon	101,939,000	0.8%
34	New Mexico	81,768,000	0.7%
35	Florida	79,640,000	0.6%
36	Maryland	52,787,000	0.4%
37	Vermont	45,044,000	0.4%
38	Utah	43,963,000	0.4%
39	Wyoming	33,924,000	0.3%
40	Maine	20,446,000	0.2%
41	West Virginia	18,362,000	0.1%
42	New Jersey	17,490,000	0.1%
43	Delaware	15,897,000	0.1%
44	Massachusetts	15,521,000	0.1%
45	Hawaii	13,437,000	0.1%
46	Connecticut	12,797,000	0.1%
47	Nevada	11,166,000	0.1%
48	New Hampshire	9,107,000	0.1%
49	Rhode Island	6,383,000	0.1%
50	Alaska	5,820,000	0.0%
	District of Columbia	0	0.0%

Source: U.S. Department of Agriculture, Economic Research Service
  "Farm Income" (http://www.ers.usda.gov/Data/FarmIncome/FinfidmuXls.htm)
*Government payments made directly to farmers in cash.

Acres Planted in 2010

National Total = 316,696,000 Acres*

ALPHA ORDER

RANK	STATE	ACRES	% of USA
31	Alabama	2,115,000	0.7%
NA	Alaska**	NA	NA
38	Arizona	738,000	0.2%
15	Arkansas	7,646,000	2.4%
23	California	4,205,000	1.3%
17	Colorado	6,248,000	2.0%
46	Connecticut	88,000	0.0%
41	Delaware	442,000	0.1%
36	Florida	1,079,000	0.3%
26	Georgia	3,576,000	1.1%
48	Hawaii	17,000	0.0%
21	Idaho	4,371,000	1.4%
3	Illinois	22,716,000	7.2%
10	Indiana	12,190,000	3.8%
1	Iowa	24,595,000	7.8%
2	Kansas	22,729,000	7.2%
18	Kentucky	5,745,000	1.8%
27	Louisiana	3,412,000	1.1%
44	Maine	267,000	0.1%
34	Maryland	1,412,000	0.4%
45	Massachusetts	99,000	0.0%
16	Michigan	6,493,000	2.1%
6	Minnesota	19,823,000	6.3%
22	Mississippi	4,331,000	1.4%
9	Missouri	13,140,000	4.1%
13	Montana	9,285,000	2.9%
7	Nebraska	19,226,000	6.1%
40	Nevada	504,000	0.2%
47	New Hampshire	71,000	0.0%
42	New Jersey	309,000	0.1%
35	New Mexico	1,090,000	0.3%
28	New York	2,943,000	0.9%
20	North Carolina	4,736,000	1.5%
5	North Dakota	21,496,000	6.8%
12	Ohio	10,010,000	3.2%
11	Oklahoma	10,335,000	3.3%
30	Oregon	2,224,000	0.7%
24	Pennsylvania	3,703,000	1.2%
49	Rhode Island	11,000	0.0%
33	South Carolina	1,631,000	0.5%
8	South Dakota	16,133,000	5.1%
19	Tennessee	4,797,000	1.5%
4	Texas	21,972,000	6.9%
37	Utah	1,000,000	0.3%
43	Vermont	287,000	0.1%
29	Virginia	2,774,000	0.9%
25	Washington	3,701,000	1.2%
39	West Virginia	695,000	0.2%
14	Wisconsin	7,864,000	2.5%
32	Wyoming	1,634,000	0.5%

RANK ORDER

RANK	STATE	ACRES	% of USA
1	Iowa	24,595,000	7.8%
2	Kansas	22,729,000	7.2%
3	Illinois	22,716,000	7.2%
4	Texas	21,972,000	6.9%
5	North Dakota	21,496,000	6.8%
6	Minnesota	19,823,000	6.3%
7	Nebraska	19,226,000	6.1%
8	South Dakota	16,133,000	5.1%
9	Missouri	13,140,000	4.1%
10	Indiana	12,190,000	3.8%
11	Oklahoma	10,335,000	3.3%
12	Ohio	10,010,000	3.2%
13	Montana	9,285,000	2.9%
14	Wisconsin	7,864,000	2.5%
15	Arkansas	7,646,000	2.4%
16	Michigan	6,493,000	2.1%
17	Colorado	6,248,000	2.0%
18	Kentucky	5,745,000	1.8%
19	Tennessee	4,797,000	1.5%
20	North Carolina	4,736,000	1.5%
21	Idaho	4,371,000	1.4%
22	Mississippi	4,331,000	1.4%
23	California	4,205,000	1.3%
24	Pennsylvania	3,703,000	1.2%
25	Washington	3,701,000	1.2%
26	Georgia	3,576,000	1.1%
27	Louisiana	3,412,000	1.1%
28	New York	2,943,000	0.9%
29	Virginia	2,774,000	0.9%
30	Oregon	2,224,000	0.7%
31	Alabama	2,115,000	0.7%
32	Wyoming	1,634,000	0.5%
33	South Carolina	1,631,000	0.5%
34	Maryland	1,412,000	0.4%
35	New Mexico	1,090,000	0.3%
36	Florida	1,079,000	0.3%
37	Utah	1,000,000	0.3%
38	Arizona	738,000	0.2%
39	West Virginia	695,000	0.2%
40	Nevada	504,000	0.2%
41	Delaware	442,000	0.1%
42	New Jersey	309,000	0.1%
43	Vermont	287,000	0.1%
44	Maine	267,000	0.1%
45	Massachusetts	99,000	0.0%
46	Connecticut	88,000	0.0%
47	New Hampshire	71,000	0.0%
48	Hawaii	17,000	0.0%
49	Rhode Island	11,000	0.0%
NA	Alaska**	NA	NA
	District of Columbia**	NA	NA

Source: U.S. Department of Agriculture, National Agricultural Statistics Service
    "Crop Production: 2010 Summary" (January 2011)
    (http://usda.mannlib.cornell.edu/MannUsda/viewDocumentInfo.do?documentID=1047)
*Estimated totals.
**No acreage or not available.

Acres Harvested in 2010

National Total = 304,668,000 Acres*

ALPHA ORDER

RANK	STATE	ACRES	% of USA
31	Alabama	2,031,000	0.7%
NA	Alaska**	NA	NA
38	Arizona	730,000	0.2%
15	Arkansas	7,532,000	2.5%
23	California	3,651,000	1.2%
17	Colorado	6,034,000	2.0%
46	Connecticut	84,000	0.0%
41	Delaware	431,000	0.1%
35	Florida	1,053,000	0.3%
27	Georgia	3,309,000	1.1%
48	Hawaii	17,000	0.0%
21	Idaho	4,236,000	1.4%
2	Illinois	22,525,000	7.4%
10	Indiana	12,088,000	4.0%
1	Iowa	24,300,000	8.0%
3	Kansas	22,127,000	7.3%
18	Kentucky	5,555,000	1.8%
26	Louisiana	3,369,000	1.1%
44	Maine	262,000	0.1%
34	Maryland	1,341,000	0.4%
45	Massachusetts	96,000	0.0%
16	Michigan	6,436,000	2.1%
5	Minnesota	19,490,000	6.4%
22	Mississippi	4,207,000	1.4%
9	Missouri	12,862,000	4.2%
12	Montana	8,875,000	2.9%
7	Nebraska	18,792,000	6.2%
40	Nevada	493,000	0.2%
47	New Hampshire	70,000	0.0%
42	New Jersey	301,000	0.1%
37	New Mexico	901,000	0.3%
28	New York	2,903,000	1.0%
20	North Carolina	4,529,000	1.5%
4	North Dakota	21,021,000	6.9%
11	Ohio	9,915,000	3.3%
13	Oklahoma	8,635,000	2.8%
30	Oregon	2,182,000	0.7%
25	Pennsylvania	3,598,000	1.2%
49	Rhode Island	11,000	0.0%
32	South Carolina	1,584,000	0.5%
8	South Dakota	15,747,000	5.2%
19	Tennessee	4,649,000	1.5%
6	Texas	19,107,000	6.3%
36	Utah	931,000	0.3%
43	Vermont	280,000	0.1%
29	Virginia	2,672,000	0.9%
24	Washington	3,631,000	1.2%
39	West Virginia	690,000	0.2%
14	Wisconsin	7,638,000	2.5%
33	Wyoming	1,563,000	0.5%

RANK ORDER

RANK	STATE	ACRES	% of USA
1	Iowa	24,300,000	8.0%
2	Illinois	22,525,000	7.4%
3	Kansas	22,127,000	7.3%
4	North Dakota	21,021,000	6.9%
5	Minnesota	19,490,000	6.4%
6	Texas	19,107,000	6.3%
7	Nebraska	18,792,000	6.2%
8	South Dakota	15,747,000	5.2%
9	Missouri	12,862,000	4.2%
10	Indiana	12,088,000	4.0%
11	Ohio	9,915,000	3.3%
12	Montana	8,875,000	2.9%
13	Oklahoma	8,635,000	2.8%
14	Wisconsin	7,638,000	2.5%
15	Arkansas	7,532,000	2.5%
16	Michigan	6,436,000	2.1%
17	Colorado	6,034,000	2.0%
18	Kentucky	5,555,000	1.8%
19	Tennessee	4,649,000	1.5%
20	North Carolina	4,529,000	1.5%
21	Idaho	4,236,000	1.4%
22	Mississippi	4,207,000	1.4%
23	California	3,651,000	1.2%
24	Washington	3,631,000	1.2%
25	Pennsylvania	3,598,000	1.2%
26	Louisiana	3,369,000	1.1%
27	Georgia	3,309,000	1.1%
28	New York	2,903,000	1.0%
29	Virginia	2,672,000	0.9%
30	Oregon	2,182,000	0.7%
31	Alabama	2,031,000	0.7%
32	South Carolina	1,584,000	0.5%
33	Wyoming	1,563,000	0.5%
34	Maryland	1,341,000	0.4%
35	Florida	1,053,000	0.3%
36	Utah	931,000	0.3%
37	New Mexico	901,000	0.3%
38	Arizona	730,000	0.2%
39	West Virginia	690,000	0.2%
40	Nevada	493,000	0.2%
41	Delaware	431,000	0.1%
42	New Jersey	301,000	0.1%
43	Vermont	280,000	0.1%
44	Maine	262,000	0.1%
45	Massachusetts	96,000	0.0%
46	Connecticut	84,000	0.0%
47	New Hampshire	70,000	0.0%
48	Hawaii	17,000	0.0%
49	Rhode Island	11,000	0.0%
NA	Alaska**	NA	NA
	District of Columbia**	NA	NA

Source: U.S. Department of Agriculture, National Agricultural Statistics Service
"Crop Production: 2010 Summary" (January 2011)
(http://usda.mannlib.cornell.edu/MannUsda/viewDocumentInfo.do?documentID=1047)
*Estimated totals.
**No acreage or not available.

Acres Harvested: Corn in 2010

National Total = 88,192,000 Acres*

ALPHA ORDER

RANK	STATE	ACRES	% of USA
30	Alabama	270,000	0.3%
NA	Alaska**	NA	NA
42	Arizona	45,000	0.1%
25	Arkansas	390,000	0.4%
21	California	610,000	0.7%
16	Colorado	1,330,000	1.5%
44	Connecticut	26,000	0.0%
32	Delaware	180,000	0.2%
40	Florida	60,000	0.1%
29	Georgia	295,000	0.3%
NA	Hawaii**	NA	NA
28	Idaho	320,000	0.4%
2	Illinois	12,600,000	14.3%
5	Indiana	5,900,000	6.7%
1	Iowa	13,400,000	15.2%
6	Kansas	4,850,000	5.5%
15	Kentucky	1,340,000	1.5%
22	Louisiana	510,000	0.6%
43	Maine	28,000	0.0%
23	Maryland	500,000	0.6%
45	Massachusetts	17,000	0.0%
11	Michigan	2,400,000	2.7%
4	Minnesota	7,700,000	8.7%
19	Mississippi	750,000	0.9%
10	Missouri	3,150,000	3.6%
36	Montana	80,000	0.1%
3	Nebraska	9,150,000	10.4%
47	Nevada	4,000	0.0%
46	New Hampshire	15,000	0.0%
36	New Jersey	80,000	0.1%
33	New Mexico	140,000	0.2%
17	New York	1,050,000	1.2%
18	North Carolina	910,000	1.0%
13	North Dakota	2,050,000	2.3%
9	Ohio	3,450,000	3.9%
26	Oklahoma	370,000	0.4%
38	Oregon	70,000	0.1%
14	Pennsylvania	1,350,000	1.5%
48	Rhode Island	2,000	0.0%
27	South Carolina	350,000	0.4%
7	South Dakota	4,550,000	5.2%
20	Tennessee	710,000	0.8%
12	Texas	2,300,000	2.6%
38	Utah	70,000	0.1%
34	Vermont	92,000	0.1%
24	Virginia	490,000	0.6%
31	Washington	200,000	0.2%
41	West Virginia	48,000	0.1%
8	Wisconsin	3,900,000	4.4%
35	Wyoming	90,000	0.1%

RANK ORDER

RANK	STATE	ACRES	% of USA
1	Iowa	13,400,000	15.2%
2	Illinois	12,600,000	14.3%
3	Nebraska	9,150,000	10.4%
4	Minnesota	7,700,000	8.7%
5	Indiana	5,900,000	6.7%
6	Kansas	4,850,000	5.5%
7	South Dakota	4,550,000	5.2%
8	Wisconsin	3,900,000	4.4%
9	Ohio	3,450,000	3.9%
10	Missouri	3,150,000	3.6%
11	Michigan	2,400,000	2.7%
12	Texas	2,300,000	2.6%
13	North Dakota	2,050,000	2.3%
14	Pennsylvania	1,350,000	1.5%
15	Kentucky	1,340,000	1.5%
16	Colorado	1,330,000	1.5%
17	New York	1,050,000	1.2%
18	North Carolina	910,000	1.0%
19	Mississippi	750,000	0.9%
20	Tennessee	710,000	0.8%
21	California	610,000	0.7%
22	Louisiana	510,000	0.6%
23	Maryland	500,000	0.6%
24	Virginia	490,000	0.6%
25	Arkansas	390,000	0.4%
26	Oklahoma	370,000	0.4%
27	South Carolina	350,000	0.4%
28	Idaho	320,000	0.4%
29	Georgia	295,000	0.3%
30	Alabama	270,000	0.3%
31	Washington	200,000	0.2%
32	Delaware	180,000	0.2%
33	New Mexico	140,000	0.2%
34	Vermont	92,000	0.1%
35	Wyoming	90,000	0.1%
36	Montana	80,000	0.1%
36	New Jersey	80,000	0.1%
38	Oregon	70,000	0.1%
38	Utah	70,000	0.1%
40	Florida	60,000	0.1%
41	West Virginia	48,000	0.1%
42	Arizona	45,000	0.1%
43	Maine	28,000	0.0%
44	Connecticut	26,000	0.0%
45	Massachusetts	17,000	0.0%
46	New Hampshire	15,000	0.0%
47	Nevada	4,000	0.0%
48	Rhode Island	2,000	0.0%
NA	Alaska**	NA	NA
NA	Hawaii**	NA	NA
	District of Columbia**	NA	NA

Source: U.S. Department of Agriculture, National Agricultural Statistics Service
   "Crop Production: 2010 Summary" (January 2011)
   (http://usda.mannlib.cornell.edu/MannUsda/viewDocumentInfo.do?documentID=1047)
*Estimated totals. Acres harvested for grain and silage. There were 81,446,000 acres harvested for grain.
**No acreage or not available.

Acres Harvested: Soybeans in 2010

National Total = 76,616,000 Acres*

ALPHA ORDER

RANK	STATE	ACRES	% of USA
24	Alabama	345,000	0.5%
NA	Alaska**	NA	NA
NA	Arizona**	NA	NA
11	Arkansas	3,150,000	4.1%
NA	California**	NA	NA
NA	Colorado**	NA	NA
NA	Connecticut**	NA	NA
28	Delaware	173,000	0.2%
30	Florida	23,000	0.0%
26	Georgia	260,000	0.3%
NA	Hawaii**	NA	NA
NA	Idaho**	NA	NA
2	Illinois	9,050,000	11.8%
4	Indiana	5,330,000	7.0%
1	Iowa	9,730,000	12.7%
8	Kansas	4,250,000	5.5%
17	Kentucky	1,390,000	1.8%
18	Louisiana	1,020,000	1.3%
NA	Maine**	NA	NA
22	Maryland	465,000	0.6%
NA	Massachusetts**	NA	NA
12	Michigan	2,040,000	2.7%
3	Minnesota	7,310,000	9.5%
13	Mississippi	1,980,000	2.6%
6	Missouri	5,070,000	6.6%
NA	Montana**	NA	NA
5	Nebraska	5,100,000	6.7%
NA	Nevada**	NA	NA
NA	New Hampshire**	NA	NA
29	New Jersey	92,000	0.1%
NA	New Mexico**	NA	NA
25	New York	279,000	0.4%
15	North Carolina	1,550,000	2.0%
10	North Dakota	4,070,000	5.3%
7	Ohio	4,590,000	6.0%
21	Oklahoma	475,000	0.6%
NA	Oregon**	NA	NA
20	Pennsylvania	495,000	0.6%
NA	Rhode Island**	NA	NA
23	South Carolina	455,000	0.6%
9	South Dakota	4,140,000	5.4%
16	Tennessee	1,410,000	1.8%
27	Texas	185,000	0.2%
NA	Utah**	NA	NA
NA	Vermont**	NA	NA
19	Virginia	540,000	0.7%
NA	Washington**	NA	NA
31	West Virginia	19,000	0.0%
14	Wisconsin	1,630,000	2.1%
NA	Wyoming**	NA	NA

RANK ORDER

RANK	STATE	ACRES	% of USA
1	Iowa	9,730,000	12.7%
2	Illinois	9,050,000	11.8%
3	Minnesota	7,310,000	9.5%
4	Indiana	5,330,000	7.0%
5	Nebraska	5,100,000	6.7%
6	Missouri	5,070,000	6.6%
7	Ohio	4,590,000	6.0%
8	Kansas	4,250,000	5.5%
9	South Dakota	4,140,000	5.4%
10	North Dakota	4,070,000	5.3%
11	Arkansas	3,150,000	4.1%
12	Michigan	2,040,000	2.7%
13	Mississippi	1,980,000	2.6%
14	Wisconsin	1,630,000	2.1%
15	North Carolina	1,550,000	2.0%
16	Tennessee	1,410,000	1.8%
17	Kentucky	1,390,000	1.8%
18	Louisiana	1,020,000	1.3%
19	Virginia	540,000	0.7%
20	Pennsylvania	495,000	0.6%
21	Oklahoma	475,000	0.6%
22	Maryland	465,000	0.6%
23	South Carolina	455,000	0.6%
24	Alabama	345,000	0.5%
25	New York	279,000	0.4%
26	Georgia	260,000	0.3%
27	Texas	185,000	0.2%
28	Delaware	173,000	0.2%
29	New Jersey	92,000	0.1%
30	Florida	23,000	0.0%
31	West Virginia	19,000	0.0%
NA	Alaska**	NA	NA
NA	Arizona**	NA	NA
NA	California**	NA	NA
NA	Colorado**	NA	NA
NA	Connecticut**	NA	NA
NA	Hawaii**	NA	NA
NA	Idaho**	NA	NA
NA	Maine**	NA	NA
NA	Massachusetts**	NA	NA
NA	Montana**	NA	NA
NA	Nevada**	NA	NA
NA	New Hampshire**	NA	NA
NA	New Mexico**	NA	NA
NA	Oregon**	NA	NA
NA	Rhode Island**	NA	NA
NA	Utah**	NA	NA
NA	Vermont**	NA	NA
NA	Washington**	NA	NA
NA	Wyoming**	NA	NA
	District of Columbia**	NA	NA

Source: U.S. Department of Agriculture, National Agricultural Statistics Service
   "Crop Production: 2010 Summary" (January 2011)
      (http://usda.mannlib.cornell.edu/MannUsda/viewDocumentInfo.do?documentID=1047)
*Estimated totals.
**No acreage or not available.

Acres Harvested: Wheat in 2010

National Total = 47,637,000 Acres*

ALPHA ORDER

RANK	STATE	ACRES	% of USA
32	Alabama	115,000	0.2%
NA	Alaska**	NA	NA
36	Arizona	85,000	0.2%
25	Arkansas	150,000	0.3%
15	California	465,000	1.0%
7	Colorado	2,377,000	5.0%
NA	Connecticut**	NA	NA
37	Delaware	45,000	0.1%
41	Florida	7,000	0.0%
31	Georgia	125,000	0.3%
NA	Hawaii**	NA	NA
11	Idaho	1,345,000	2.8%
17	Illinois	295,000	0.6%
21	Indiana	230,000	0.5%
40	Iowa	10,000	0.0%
2	Kansas	8,000,000	16.8%
20	Kentucky	250,000	0.5%
33	Louisiana	110,000	0.2%
NA	Maine**	NA	NA
28	Maryland	135,000	0.3%
NA	Massachusetts**	NA	NA
14	Michigan	510,000	1.1%
9	Minnesota	1,610,000	3.4%
34	Mississippi	100,000	0.2%
19	Missouri	280,000	0.6%
3	Montana	5,210,000	10.9%
10	Nebraska	1,490,000	3.1%
39	Nevada	12,000	0.0%
NA	New Hampshire**	NA	NA
38	New Jersey	23,000	0.0%
18	New Mexico	290,000	0.6%
34	New York	100,000	0.2%
16	North Carolina	380,000	0.8%
1	North Dakota	8,400,000	17.6%
13	Ohio	750,000	1.6%
4	Oklahoma	3,900,000	8.2%
12	Oregon	947,000	2.0%
25	Pennsylvania	150,000	0.3%
NA	Rhode Island**	NA	NA
30	South Carolina	130,000	0.3%
6	South Dakota	2,725,000	5.7%
23	Tennessee	180,000	0.4%
5	Texas	3,750,000	7.9%
29	Utah	131,000	0.3%
NA	Vermont**	NA	NA
24	Virginia	160,000	0.3%
8	Washington	2,285,000	4.8%
42	West Virginia	5,000	0.0%
21	Wisconsin	230,000	0.5%
27	Wyoming	145,000	0.3%

RANK ORDER

RANK	STATE	ACRES	% of USA
1	North Dakota	8,400,000	17.6%
2	Kansas	8,000,000	16.8%
3	Montana	5,210,000	10.9%
4	Oklahoma	3,900,000	8.2%
5	Texas	3,750,000	7.9%
6	South Dakota	2,725,000	5.7%
7	Colorado	2,377,000	5.0%
8	Washington	2,285,000	4.8%
9	Minnesota	1,610,000	3.4%
10	Nebraska	1,490,000	3.1%
11	Idaho	1,345,000	2.8%
12	Oregon	947,000	2.0%
13	Ohio	750,000	1.6%
14	Michigan	510,000	1.1%
15	California	465,000	1.0%
16	North Carolina	380,000	0.8%
17	Illinois	295,000	0.6%
18	New Mexico	290,000	0.6%
19	Missouri	280,000	0.6%
20	Kentucky	250,000	0.5%
21	Indiana	230,000	0.5%
21	Wisconsin	230,000	0.5%
23	Tennessee	180,000	0.4%
24	Virginia	160,000	0.3%
25	Arkansas	150,000	0.3%
25	Pennsylvania	150,000	0.3%
27	Wyoming	145,000	0.3%
28	Maryland	135,000	0.3%
29	Utah	131,000	0.3%
30	South Carolina	130,000	0.3%
31	Georgia	125,000	0.3%
32	Alabama	115,000	0.2%
33	Louisiana	110,000	0.2%
34	Mississippi	100,000	0.2%
34	New York	100,000	0.2%
36	Arizona	85,000	0.2%
37	Delaware	45,000	0.1%
38	New Jersey	23,000	0.0%
39	Nevada	12,000	0.0%
40	Iowa	10,000	0.0%
41	Florida	7,000	0.0%
42	West Virginia	5,000	0.0%
NA	Alaska**	NA	NA
NA	Connecticut**	NA	NA
NA	Hawaii**	NA	NA
NA	Maine**	NA	NA
NA	Massachusetts**	NA	NA
NA	New Hampshire**	NA	NA
NA	Rhode Island**	NA	NA
NA	Vermont**	NA	NA
	District of Columbia**	NA	NA

Source: U.S. Department of Agriculture, National Agricultural Statistics Service
"Crop Production: 2010 Summary" (January 2011)
(http://usda.mannlib.cornell.edu/MannUsda/viewDocumentInfo.do?documentID=1047)
*Estimated totals.
**No acreage or not available.

Cattle on Farms in 2011

National Total = 92,582,400 Cattle*

ALPHA ORDER

RANK	STATE	CATTLE	% of USA
25	Alabama	1,230,000	1.3%
49	Alaska	13,500	0.0%
32	Arizona	870,000	0.9%
16	Arkansas	1,720,000	1.9%
4	California	5,150,000	5.6%
10	Colorado	2,650,000	2.9%
44	Connecticut	49,000	0.1%
48	Delaware	18,000	0.0%
18	Florida	1,630,000	1.8%
30	Georgia	1,020,000	1.1%
42	Hawaii	141,000	0.2%
13	Idaho	2,200,000	2.4%
27	Illinois	1,100,000	1.2%
33	Indiana	850,000	0.9%
7	Iowa	3,900,000	4.2%
2	Kansas	6,300,000	6.8%
14	Kentucky	2,190,000	2.4%
35	Louisiana	790,000	0.9%
43	Maine	90,000	0.1%
41	Maryland	195,000	0.2%
45	Massachusetts	40,000	0.0%
28	Michigan	1,090,000	1.2%
12	Minnesota	2,380,000	2.6%
31	Mississippi	900,000	1.0%
6	Missouri	3,950,000	4.3%
11	Montana	2,500,000	2.7%
3	Nebraska	6,200,000	6.7%
37	Nevada	460,000	0.5%
46	New Hampshire	34,000	0.0%
47	New Jersey	32,000	0.0%
20	New Mexico	1,540,000	1.7%
22	New York	1,400,000	1.5%
36	North Carolina	780,000	0.8%
17	North Dakota	1,700,000	1.8%
25	Ohio	1,230,000	1.3%
5	Oklahoma	5,100,000	5.5%
23	Oregon	1,330,000	1.4%
19	Pennsylvania	1,610,000	1.7%
50	Rhode Island	4,900	0.0%
38	South Carolina	385,000	0.4%
8	South Dakota	3,700,000	4.0%
15	Tennessee	1,990,000	2.1%
1	Texas	13,300,000	14.4%
34	Utah	800,000	0.9%
40	Vermont	270,000	0.3%
20	Virginia	1,540,000	1.7%
28	Washington	1,090,000	1.2%
39	West Virginia	370,000	0.4%
9	Wisconsin	3,450,000	3.7%
24	Wyoming	1,300,000	1.4%

RANK ORDER

RANK	STATE	CATTLE	% of USA
1	Texas	13,300,000	14.4%
2	Kansas	6,300,000	6.8%
3	Nebraska	6,200,000	6.7%
4	California	5,150,000	5.6%
5	Oklahoma	5,100,000	5.5%
6	Missouri	3,950,000	4.3%
7	Iowa	3,900,000	4.2%
8	South Dakota	3,700,000	4.0%
9	Wisconsin	3,450,000	3.7%
10	Colorado	2,650,000	2.9%
11	Montana	2,500,000	2.7%
12	Minnesota	2,380,000	2.6%
13	Idaho	2,200,000	2.4%
14	Kentucky	2,190,000	2.4%
15	Tennessee	1,990,000	2.1%
16	Arkansas	1,720,000	1.9%
17	North Dakota	1,700,000	1.8%
18	Florida	1,630,000	1.8%
19	Pennsylvania	1,610,000	1.7%
20	New Mexico	1,540,000	1.7%
20	Virginia	1,540,000	1.7%
22	New York	1,400,000	1.5%
23	Oregon	1,330,000	1.4%
24	Wyoming	1,300,000	1.4%
25	Alabama	1,230,000	1.3%
25	Ohio	1,230,000	1.3%
27	Illinois	1,100,000	1.2%
28	Michigan	1,090,000	1.2%
28	Washington	1,090,000	1.2%
30	Georgia	1,020,000	1.1%
31	Mississippi	900,000	1.0%
32	Arizona	870,000	0.9%
33	Indiana	850,000	0.9%
34	Utah	800,000	0.9%
35	Louisiana	790,000	0.9%
36	North Carolina	780,000	0.8%
37	Nevada	460,000	0.5%
38	South Carolina	385,000	0.4%
39	West Virginia	370,000	0.4%
40	Vermont	270,000	0.3%
41	Maryland	195,000	0.2%
42	Hawaii	141,000	0.2%
43	Maine	90,000	0.1%
44	Connecticut	49,000	0.1%
45	Massachusetts	40,000	0.0%
46	New Hampshire	34,000	0.0%
47	New Jersey	32,000	0.0%
48	Delaware	18,000	0.0%
49	Alaska	13,500	0.0%
50	Rhode Island	4,900	0.0%
	District of Columbia	0	0.0%

Source: U.S. Department of Agriculture, National Agricultural Statistics Service
    "Cattle" (http://usda.mannlib.cornell.edu/MannUsda/viewDocumentInfo.do?documentID=1017)
*As of January 1, 2011.

Milk Cows on Farms in 2009

National Total = 9,315,000 Milk Cows*

ALPHA ORDER

RANK	STATE	MILK COWS	% of USA
43	Alabama	12,000	0.1%
50	Alaska	600	0.0%
13	Arizona	186,000	2.0%
40	Arkansas	15,000	0.2%
1	California	1,844,000	19.8%
16	Colorado	128,000	1.4%
37	Connecticut	19,000	0.2%
47	Delaware	6,500	0.1%
17	Florida	120,000	1.3%
26	Georgia	76,000	0.8%
48	Hawaii	1,700	0.0%
4	Idaho	549,000	5.9%
21	Illinois	102,000	1.1%
14	Indiana	167,000	1.8%
12	Iowa	216,000	2.3%
18	Kansas	117,000	1.3%
23	Kentucky	90,000	1.0%
34	Louisiana	26,000	0.3%
32	Maine	33,000	0.4%
30	Maryland	56,000	0.6%
40	Massachusetts	15,000	0.2%
8	Michigan	350,000	3.8%
6	Minnesota	464,000	5.0%
36	Mississippi	20,000	0.2%
20	Missouri	110,000	1.2%
39	Montana	17,000	0.2%
29	Nebraska	58,000	0.6%
33	Nevada	27,000	0.3%
40	New Hampshire	15,000	0.2%
45	New Jersey	10,000	0.1%
9	New Mexico	338,000	3.6%
3	New York	626,000	6.7%
31	North Carolina	47,000	0.5%
34	North Dakota	26,000	0.3%
10	Ohio	280,000	3.0%
27	Oklahoma	64,000	0.7%
19	Oregon	114,000	1.2%
4	Pennsylvania	549,000	5.9%
49	Rhode Island	1,100	0.0%
38	South Carolina	18,000	0.2%
23	South Dakota	90,000	1.0%
28	Tennessee	59,000	0.6%
7	Texas	418,000	4.5%
25	Utah	85,000	0.9%
15	Vermont	140,000	1.5%
22	Virginia	98,000	1.1%
11	Washington	244,000	2.6%
43	West Virginia	12,000	0.1%
2	Wisconsin	1,252,000	13.4%
46	Wyoming	7,000	0.1%

RANK ORDER

RANK	STATE	MILK COWS	% of USA
1	California	1,844,000	19.8%
2	Wisconsin	1,252,000	13.4%
3	New York	626,000	6.7%
4	Idaho	549,000	5.9%
4	Pennsylvania	549,000	5.9%
6	Minnesota	464,000	5.0%
7	Texas	418,000	4.5%
8	Michigan	350,000	3.8%
9	New Mexico	338,000	3.6%
10	Ohio	280,000	3.0%
11	Washington	244,000	2.6%
12	Iowa	216,000	2.3%
13	Arizona	186,000	2.0%
14	Indiana	167,000	1.8%
15	Vermont	140,000	1.5%
16	Colorado	128,000	1.4%
17	Florida	120,000	1.3%
18	Kansas	117,000	1.3%
19	Oregon	114,000	1.2%
20	Missouri	110,000	1.2%
21	Illinois	102,000	1.1%
22	Virginia	98,000	1.1%
23	Kentucky	90,000	1.0%
23	South Dakota	90,000	1.0%
25	Utah	85,000	0.9%
26	Georgia	76,000	0.8%
27	Oklahoma	64,000	0.7%
28	Tennessee	59,000	0.6%
29	Nebraska	58,000	0.6%
30	Maryland	56,000	0.6%
31	North Carolina	47,000	0.5%
32	Maine	33,000	0.4%
33	Nevada	27,000	0.3%
34	Louisiana	26,000	0.3%
34	North Dakota	26,000	0.3%
36	Mississippi	20,000	0.2%
37	Connecticut	19,000	0.2%
38	South Carolina	18,000	0.2%
39	Montana	17,000	0.2%
40	Arkansas	15,000	0.2%
40	Massachusetts	15,000	0.2%
40	New Hampshire	15,000	0.2%
43	Alabama	12,000	0.1%
43	West Virginia	12,000	0.1%
45	New Jersey	10,000	0.1%
46	Wyoming	7,000	0.1%
47	Delaware	6,500	0.1%
48	Hawaii	1,700	0.0%
49	Rhode Island	1,100	0.0%
50	Alaska	600	0.0%
	District of Columbia	0	0.0%

Source: U.S. Department of Agriculture, National Agricultural Statistics Service
   "Milk Production, Disposition and Income: 2009 Summary" (April 2010)
   (http://usda.mannlib.cornell.edu/MannUsda/viewDocumentInfo.do?documentID=1105)
*Average number during year. Excludes heifers not yet fresh.

Milk Production in 2009

National Total = 189,982,000,000 Pounds of Milk*

ALPHA ORDER

RANK	STATE	POUNDS	% of USA
43	Alabama	184,000,000	0.1%
50	Alaska	7,200,000	0.0%
12	Arizona	4,349,000,000	2.3%
42	Arkansas	186,000,000	0.1%
1	California	41,203,000,000	21.7%
15	Colorado	2,935,000,000	1.5%
35	Connecticut	364,000,000	0.2%
47	Delaware	110,000,000	0.1%
19	Florida	2,060,000,000	1.1%
25	Georgia	1,355,000,000	0.7%
49	Hawaii	18,500,000	0.0%
4	Idaho	12,315,000,000	6.5%
20	Illinois	1,894,000,000	1.0%
14	Indiana	3,287,000,000	1.7%
13	Iowa	4,319,000,000	2.3%
17	Kansas	2,415,000,000	1.3%
26	Kentucky	1,210,000,000	0.6%
37	Louisiana	319,000,000	0.2%
32	Maine	603,000,000	0.3%
29	Maryland	1,029,000,000	0.5%
41	Massachusetts	254,000,000	0.1%
9	Michigan	7,763,000,000	4.1%
6	Minnesota	8,782,000,000	4.6%
40	Mississippi	291,000,000	0.2%
24	Missouri	1,615,000,000	0.9%
38	Montana	313,000,000	0.2%
27	Nebraska	1,083,000,000	0.6%
33	Nevada	559,000,000	0.3%
39	New Hampshire	299,000,000	0.2%
45	New Jersey	169,000,000	0.1%
8	New Mexico	7,865,000,000	4.1%
3	New York	12,432,000,000	6.5%
31	North Carolina	892,000,000	0.5%
34	North Dakota	418,000,000	0.2%
11	Ohio	5,130,000,000	2.7%
28	Oklahoma	1,061,000,000	0.6%
18	Oregon	2,254,000,000	1.2%
5	Pennsylvania	10,575,000,000	5.6%
48	Rhode Island	19,900,000	0.0%
36	South Carolina	322,000,000	0.2%
21	South Dakota	1,796,000,000	0.9%
30	Tennessee	948,000,000	0.5%
7	Texas	8,416,000,000	4.4%
22	Utah	1,776,000,000	0.9%
16	Vermont	2,576,000,000	1.4%
23	Virginia	1,726,000,000	0.9%
10	Washington	5,696,000,000	3.0%
44	West Virginia	181,000,000	0.1%
2	Wisconsin	24,472,000,000	12.9%
46	Wyoming	135,700,000	0.1%

RANK ORDER

RANK	STATE	POUNDS	% of USA
1	California	41,203,000,000	21.7%
2	Wisconsin	24,472,000,000	12.9%
3	New York	12,432,000,000	6.5%
4	Idaho	12,315,000,000	6.5%
5	Pennsylvania	10,575,000,000	5.6%
6	Minnesota	8,782,000,000	4.6%
7	Texas	8,416,000,000	4.4%
8	New Mexico	7,865,000,000	4.1%
9	Michigan	7,763,000,000	4.1%
10	Washington	5,696,000,000	3.0%
11	Ohio	5,130,000,000	2.7%
12	Arizona	4,349,000,000	2.3%
13	Iowa	4,319,000,000	2.3%
14	Indiana	3,287,000,000	1.7%
15	Colorado	2,935,000,000	1.5%
16	Vermont	2,576,000,000	1.4%
17	Kansas	2,415,000,000	1.3%
18	Oregon	2,254,000,000	1.2%
19	Florida	2,060,000,000	1.1%
20	Illinois	1,894,000,000	1.0%
21	South Dakota	1,796,000,000	0.9%
22	Utah	1,776,000,000	0.9%
23	Virginia	1,726,000,000	0.9%
24	Missouri	1,615,000,000	0.9%
25	Georgia	1,355,000,000	0.7%
26	Kentucky	1,210,000,000	0.6%
27	Nebraska	1,083,000,000	0.6%
28	Oklahoma	1,061,000,000	0.6%
29	Maryland	1,029,000,000	0.5%
30	Tennessee	948,000,000	0.5%
31	North Carolina	892,000,000	0.5%
32	Maine	603,000,000	0.3%
33	Nevada	559,000,000	0.3%
34	North Dakota	418,000,000	0.2%
35	Connecticut	364,000,000	0.2%
36	South Carolina	322,000,000	0.2%
37	Louisiana	319,000,000	0.2%
38	Montana	313,000,000	0.2%
39	New Hampshire	299,000,000	0.2%
40	Mississippi	291,000,000	0.2%
41	Massachusetts	254,000,000	0.1%
42	Arkansas	186,000,000	0.1%
43	Alabama	184,000,000	0.1%
44	West Virginia	181,000,000	0.1%
45	New Jersey	169,000,000	0.1%
46	Wyoming	135,700,000	0.1%
47	Delaware	110,000,000	0.1%
48	Rhode Island	19,900,000	0.0%
49	Hawaii	18,500,000	0.0%
50	Alaska	7,200,000	0.0%
	District of Columbia	0	0.0%

Source: U.S. Department of Agriculture, National Agricultural Statistics Service
    "Milk Production, Disposition and Income: 2009 Summary" (April 2010)
    (http://usda.mannlib.cornell.edu/MannUsda/viewDocumentInfo.do?documentID=1105)
*Excludes milk suckled by calves.

Milk Production per Milk Cow in 2009

National Average = 20,395 Pounds of Milk per Cow*

ALPHA ORDER

RANK	STATE	POUNDS
42	Alabama	15,333
49	Alaska	12,000
1	Arizona	23,382
47	Arkansas	12,400
6	California	22,344
4	Colorado	22,930
21	Connecticut	19,158
37	Delaware	16,923
35	Florida	17,167
33	Georgia	17,829
50	Hawaii	10,882
5	Idaho	22,432
25	Illinois	18,569
17	Indiana	19,683
12	Iowa	19,995
10	Kansas	20,641
46	Kentucky	13,444
48	Louisiana	12,269
30	Maine	18,273
28	Maryland	18,375
36	Massachusetts	16,933
7	Michigan	22,180
23	Minnesota	18,927
45	Mississippi	14,550
44	Missouri	14,682
26	Montana	18,412
24	Nebraska	18,672
9	Nevada	20,704
14	New Hampshire	19,933
38	New Jersey	16,900
3	New Mexico	23,269
15	New York	19,859
22	North Carolina	18,979
40	North Dakota	16,077
29	Ohio	18,321
39	Oklahoma	16,578
16	Oregon	19,772
20	Pennsylvania	19,262
31	Rhode Island	18,091
32	South Carolina	17,889
13	South Dakota	19,956
41	Tennessee	16,068
11	Texas	20,134
8	Utah	20,894
27	Vermont	18,400
34	Virginia	17,612
2	Washington	23,344
43	West Virginia	15,083
18	Wisconsin	19,546
19	Wyoming	19,386

RANK ORDER

RANK	STATE	POUNDS
1	Arizona	23,382
2	Washington	23,344
3	New Mexico	23,269
4	Colorado	22,930
5	Idaho	22,432
6	California	22,344
7	Michigan	22,180
8	Utah	20,894
9	Nevada	20,704
10	Kansas	20,641
11	Texas	20,134
12	Iowa	19,995
13	South Dakota	19,956
14	New Hampshire	19,933
15	New York	19,859
16	Oregon	19,772
17	Indiana	19,683
18	Wisconsin	19,546
19	Wyoming	19,386
20	Pennsylvania	19,262
21	Connecticut	19,158
22	North Carolina	18,979
23	Minnesota	18,927
24	Nebraska	18,672
25	Illinois	18,569
26	Montana	18,412
27	Vermont	18,400
28	Maryland	18,375
29	Ohio	18,321
30	Maine	18,273
31	Rhode Island	18,091
32	South Carolina	17,889
33	Georgia	17,829
34	Virginia	17,612
35	Florida	17,167
36	Massachusetts	16,933
37	Delaware	16,923
38	New Jersey	16,900
39	Oklahoma	16,578
40	North Dakota	16,077
41	Tennessee	16,068
42	Alabama	15,333
43	West Virginia	15,083
44	Missouri	14,682
45	Mississippi	14,550
46	Kentucky	13,444
47	Arkansas	12,400
48	Louisiana	12,269
49	Alaska	12,000
50	Hawaii	10,882

District of Columbia**   NA

Source: U.S. Department of Agriculture, National Agricultural Statistics Service
    "Milk Production, Disposition and Income: 2009 Summary" (April 2010)
        (http://usda.mannlib.cornell.edu/MannUsda/viewDocumentInfo.do?documentID=1105)
*Excludes milk suckled by calves.
**Not applicable.

Hogs and Pigs on Farms in 2010

National Total = 64,325,000 Hogs and Pigs*

ALPHA ORDER

RANK	STATE	HOGS AND PIGS	% of USA
28	Alabama	130,000	0.2%
48	Alaska	1,200	0.0%
24	Arizona	165,000	0.3%
25	Arkansas	160,000	0.2%
30	California	105,000	0.2%
15	Colorado	720,000	1.1%
42	Connecticut	3,400	0.0%
39	Delaware	5,500	0.0%
34	Florida	15,000	0.0%
25	Georgia	160,000	0.2%
35	Hawaii	12,500	0.0%
NA	Idaho**	NA	NA
4	Illinois	4,300,000	6.7%
5	Indiana	3,650,000	5.7%
1	Iowa	18,900,000	29.4%
10	Kansas	1,810,000	2.8%
20	Kentucky	325,000	0.5%
37	Louisiana	10,000	0.0%
41	Maine	4,700	0.0%
32	Maryland	26,000	0.0%
36	Massachusetts	11,000	0.0%
13	Michigan	1,040,000	1.6%
3	Minnesota	7,700,000	12.0%
17	Mississippi	385,000	0.6%
7	Missouri	2,900,000	4.5%
22	Montana	180,000	0.3%
6	Nebraska	3,100,000	4.8%
47	Nevada	1,400	0.0%
43	New Hampshire	3,300	0.0%
38	New Jersey	8,000	0.0%
46	New Mexico	1,500	0.0%
29	New York	108,000	0.2%
2	North Carolina	8,800,000	13.7%
27	North Dakota	143,000	0.2%
9	Ohio	2,030,000	3.2%
8	Oklahoma	2,330,000	3.6%
33	Oregon	16,000	0.0%
12	Pennsylvania	1,110,000	1.7%
45	Rhode Island	1,800	0.0%
21	South Carolina	230,000	0.4%
11	South Dakota	1,290,000	2.0%
23	Tennessee	170,000	0.3%
16	Texas	660,000	1.0%
14	Utah	740,000	1.2%
44	Vermont	2,700	0.0%
18	Virginia	355,000	0.6%
NA	Washington**	NA	NA
40	West Virginia	5,000	0.0%
19	Wisconsin	340,000	0.5%
31	Wyoming	99,000	0.2%

RANK ORDER

RANK	STATE	HOGS AND PIGS	% of USA
1	Iowa	18,900,000	29.4%
2	North Carolina	8,800,000	13.7%
3	Minnesota	7,700,000	12.0%
4	Illinois	4,300,000	6.7%
5	Indiana	3,650,000	5.7%
6	Nebraska	3,100,000	4.8%
7	Missouri	2,900,000	4.5%
8	Oklahoma	2,330,000	3.6%
9	Ohio	2,030,000	3.2%
10	Kansas	1,810,000	2.8%
11	South Dakota	1,290,000	2.0%
12	Pennsylvania	1,110,000	1.7%
13	Michigan	1,040,000	1.6%
14	Utah	740,000	1.2%
15	Colorado	720,000	1.1%
16	Texas	660,000	1.0%
17	Mississippi	385,000	0.6%
18	Virginia	355,000	0.6%
19	Wisconsin	340,000	0.5%
20	Kentucky	325,000	0.5%
21	South Carolina	230,000	0.4%
22	Montana	180,000	0.3%
23	Tennessee	170,000	0.3%
24	Arizona	165,000	0.3%
25	Arkansas	160,000	0.2%
25	Georgia	160,000	0.2%
27	North Dakota	143,000	0.2%
28	Alabama	130,000	0.2%
29	New York	108,000	0.2%
30	California	105,000	0.2%
31	Wyoming	99,000	0.2%
32	Maryland	26,000	0.0%
33	Oregon	16,000	0.0%
34	Florida	15,000	0.0%
35	Hawaii	12,500	0.0%
36	Massachusetts	11,000	0.0%
37	Louisiana	10,000	0.0%
38	New Jersey	8,000	0.0%
39	Delaware	5,500	0.0%
40	West Virginia	5,000	0.0%
41	Maine	4,700	0.0%
42	Connecticut	3,400	0.0%
43	New Hampshire	3,300	0.0%
44	Vermont	2,700	0.0%
45	Rhode Island	1,800	0.0%
46	New Mexico	1,500	0.0%
47	Nevada	1,400	0.0%
48	Alaska	1,200	0.0%
NA	Idaho**	NA	NA
NA	Washington**	NA	NA
	District of Columbia	0	0.0%

Source: U.S. Department of Agriculture, National Agricultural Statistics Service
   "Quarterly Hogs and Pigs" (http://usda.mannlib.cornell.edu/MannUsda/viewDocumentInfo.do?documentID=1086)
*As of December 1, 2010.
**Not available. Figures for Idaho and Washington withheld to avoid disclosing data for individual operations.

Chickens in 2009 (Leading States Only)

National Total = 8,550,500,000 Chickens*

ALPHA ORDER					RANK ORDER			

RANK	STATE	CHICKENS	% of USA		RANK	STATE	CHICKENS	% of USA
3	Alabama	1,002,300,000	11.7%		1	Georgia	1,322,000,000	15.5%
NA	Alaska***	NA	NA		2	Arkansas	1,050,900,000	12.3%
NA	Arizona***	NA	NA		3	Alabama	1,002,300,000	11.7%
2	Arkansas	1,050,900,000	12.3%		4	Mississippi	793,400,000	9.3%
NA	California**	NA	NA		5	North Carolina	759,600,000	8.9%
NA	Colorado***	NA	NA		6	Texas	668,700,000	7.8%
NA	Connecticut**	NA	NA		7	Kentucky	307,000,000	3.6%
11	Delaware	231,500,000	2.7%		8	Maryland	291,900,000	3.4%
19	Florida	42,000,000	0.5%		9	Virginia	240,800,000	2.8%
1	Georgia	1,322,000,000	15.5%		10	South Carolina	237,800,000	2.8%
NA	Hawaii***	NA	NA		11	Delaware	231,500,000	2.7%
NA	Idaho***	NA	NA		12	Oklahoma	226,000,000	2.6%
NA	Illinois***	NA	NA		13	Tennessee	189,700,000	2.2%
NA	Indiana**	NA	NA		14	Pennsylvania	153,500,000	1.8%
NA	Iowa**	NA	NA		15	West Virginia	82,700,000	1.0%
NA	Kansas***	NA	NA		16	Ohio	56,400,000	0.7%
7	Kentucky	307,000,000	3.6%		17	Wisconsin	45,800,000	0.5%
NA	Louisiana**	NA	NA		18	Minnesota	44,800,000	0.5%
NA	Maine***	NA	NA		19	Florida	42,000,000	0.5%
8	Maryland	291,900,000	3.4%		NA	Alaska***	NA	NA
NA	Massachusetts***	NA	NA		NA	Arizona***	NA	NA
NA	Michigan**	NA	NA		NA	California**	NA	NA
18	Minnesota	44,800,000	0.5%		NA	Colorado***	NA	NA
4	Mississippi	793,400,000	9.3%		NA	Connecticut**	NA	NA
NA	Missouri**	NA	NA		NA	Hawaii***	NA	NA
NA	Montana***	NA	NA		NA	Idaho***	NA	NA
NA	Nebraska**	NA	NA		NA	Illinois***	NA	NA
NA	Nevada***	NA	NA		NA	Indiana**	NA	NA
NA	New Hampshire***	NA	NA		NA	Iowa**	NA	NA
NA	New Jersey***	NA	NA		NA	Kansas***	NA	NA
NA	New Mexico***	NA	NA		NA	Louisiana**	NA	NA
NA	New York**	NA	NA		NA	Maine***	NA	NA
5	North Carolina	759,600,000	8.9%		NA	Massachusetts***	NA	NA
NA	North Dakota***	NA	NA		NA	Michigan**	NA	NA
16	Ohio	56,400,000	0.7%		NA	Missouri**	NA	NA
12	Oklahoma	226,000,000	2.6%		NA	Montana***	NA	NA
NA	Oregon**	NA	NA		NA	Nebraska**	NA	NA
14	Pennsylvania	153,500,000	1.8%		NA	Nevada***	NA	NA
NA	Rhode Island***	NA	NA		NA	New Hampshire***	NA	NA
10	South Carolina	237,800,000	2.8%		NA	New Jersey***	NA	NA
NA	South Dakota***	NA	NA		NA	New Mexico***	NA	NA
13	Tennessee	189,700,000	2.2%		NA	New York**	NA	NA
6	Texas	668,700,000	7.8%		NA	North Dakota***	NA	NA
NA	Utah***	NA	NA		NA	Oregon**	NA	NA
NA	Vermont***	NA	NA		NA	Rhode Island***	NA	NA
9	Virginia	240,800,000	2.8%		NA	South Dakota***	NA	NA
NA	Washington**	NA	NA		NA	Utah***	NA	NA
15	West Virginia	82,700,000	1.0%		NA	Vermont***	NA	NA
17	Wisconsin	45,800,000	0.5%		NA	Washington**	NA	NA
NA	Wyoming***	NA	NA		NA	Wyoming***	NA	NA
						District of Columbia***	NA	NA

Source: U.S. Department of Agriculture, National Agricultural Statistics Service
  "Poultry - Production and Value: 2009 Summary" (April 2010)
   (http://usda.mannlib.cornell.edu/MannUsda/viewDocumentInfo.do?documentID=1130)
*Broilers. Total includes numbers for states not shown separately but excludes states producing less than 500,000 birds. **These states produced a combined total of 803,700,000 chickens. They are combined to avoid disclosing individual operations. National total does not include chickens used for egg production. ***Produces fewer than 500,000 chickens or are not available.

Eggs Produced in 2009

National Total = 90,359,000,000 Eggs

ALPHA ORDER

RANK	STATE	EGGS	% of USA
14	Alabama	2,106,000,000	2.3%
NA	Alaska*	NA	NA
NA	Arizona*	NA	NA
9	Arkansas	2,935,000,000	3.2%
5	California	5,304,000,000	5.9%
23	Colorado	1,110,000,000	1.2%
27	Connecticut	767,000,000	0.8%
NA	Delaware*	NA	NA
13	Florida	2,670,000,000	3.0%
7	Georgia	4,467,000,000	4.9%
36	Hawaii	69,500,000	0.1%
NA	Idaho*	NA	NA
19	Illinois	1,253,000,000	1.4%
4	Indiana	6,460,000,000	7.1%
1	Iowa	14,475,000,000	16.0%
NA	Kansas*	NA	NA
21	Kentucky	1,130,000,000	1.3%
32	Louisiana	455,000,000	0.5%
25	Maine	916,000,000	1.0%
31	Maryland	554,000,000	0.6%
38	Massachusetts	36,000,000	0.0%
10	Michigan	2,784,000,000	3.1%
11	Minnesota	2,777,000,000	3.1%
17	Mississippi	1,440,000,000	1.6%
15	Missouri	1,973,000,000	2.2%
35	Montana	107,000,000	0.1%
12	Nebraska	2,749,000,000	3.0%
NA	Nevada*	NA	NA
NA	New Hampshire*	NA	NA
NA	New Jersey*	NA	NA
NA	New Mexico*	NA	NA
20	New York	1,192,000,000	1.3%
8	North Carolina	3,148,000,000	3.5%
NA	North Dakota*	NA	NA
2	Ohio	7,392,000,000	8.2%
26	Oklahoma	769,000,000	0.9%
29	Oregon	732,000,000	0.8%
3	Pennsylvania	6,509,000,000	7.2%
NA	Rhode Island*	NA	NA
22	South Carolina	1,128,000,000	1.2%
30	South Dakota	696,000,000	0.8%
33	Tennessee	323,000,000	0.4%
6	Texas	4,985,000,000	5.5%
24	Utah	918,000,000	1.0%
37	Vermont	57,000,000	0.1%
28	Virginia	741,000,000	0.8%
16	Washington	1,705,000,000	1.9%
34	West Virginia	212,000,000	0.2%
18	Wisconsin	1,350,000,000	1.5%
39	Wyoming	2,400,000	0.0%

RANK ORDER

RANK	STATE	EGGS	% of USA
1	Iowa	14,475,000,000	16.0%
2	Ohio	7,392,000,000	8.2%
3	Pennsylvania	6,509,000,000	7.2%
4	Indiana	6,460,000,000	7.1%
5	California	5,304,000,000	5.9%
6	Texas	4,985,000,000	5.5%
7	Georgia	4,467,000,000	4.9%
8	North Carolina	3,148,000,000	3.5%
9	Arkansas	2,935,000,000	3.2%
10	Michigan	2,784,000,000	3.1%
11	Minnesota	2,777,000,000	3.1%
12	Nebraska	2,749,000,000	3.0%
13	Florida	2,670,000,000	3.0%
14	Alabama	2,106,000,000	2.3%
15	Missouri	1,973,000,000	2.2%
16	Washington	1,705,000,000	1.9%
17	Mississippi	1,440,000,000	1.6%
18	Wisconsin	1,350,000,000	1.5%
19	Illinois	1,253,000,000	1.4%
20	New York	1,192,000,000	1.3%
21	Kentucky	1,130,000,000	1.3%
22	South Carolina	1,128,000,000	1.2%
23	Colorado	1,110,000,000	1.2%
24	Utah	918,000,000	1.0%
25	Maine	916,000,000	1.0%
26	Oklahoma	769,000,000	0.9%
27	Connecticut	767,000,000	0.8%
28	Virginia	741,000,000	0.8%
29	Oregon	732,000,000	0.8%
30	South Dakota	696,000,000	0.8%
31	Maryland	554,000,000	0.6%
32	Louisiana	455,000,000	0.5%
33	Tennessee	323,000,000	0.4%
34	West Virginia	212,000,000	0.2%
35	Montana	107,000,000	0.1%
36	Hawaii	69,500,000	0.1%
37	Vermont	57,000,000	0.1%
38	Massachusetts	36,000,000	0.0%
39	Wyoming	2,400,000	0.0%
NA	Alaska*	NA	NA
NA	Arizona*	NA	NA
NA	Delaware*	NA	NA
NA	Idaho*	NA	NA
NA	Kansas*	NA	NA
NA	Nevada*	NA	NA
NA	New Hampshire*	NA	NA
NA	New Jersey*	NA	NA
NA	New Mexico*	NA	NA
NA	North Dakota*	NA	NA
NA	Rhode Island*	NA	NA
	District of Columbia	0	0.0%

Source: U.S. Department of Agriculture, National Agricultural Statistics Service
   "Poultry - Production and Value: 2009 Summary" (April 2010)
   (http://usda.mannlib.cornell.edu/MannUsda/viewDocumentInfo.do?documentID=1130)
*These states produced a combined 1,963,000,000 eggs. They are combined to avoid disclosing individual operations.

II. Crime and Law Enforcement

Crimes in 2009

National Total = 10,639,369 Crimes*

ALPHA ORDER

RANK	STATE	CRIMES	% of USA
20	Alabama	198,808	1.9%
46	Alaska	24,998	0.2%
13	Arizona	261,511	2.5%
27	Arkansas	123,997	1.2%
1	California	1,184,073	11.1%
25	Colorado	150,944	1.4%
34	Connecticut	92,689	0.9%
40	Delaware	35,283	0.3%
3	Florida	825,551	7.8%
7	Georgia	402,280	3.8%
39	Hawaii	50,978	0.5%
41	Idaho	34,271	0.3%
5	Illinois	417,532	3.9%
15	Indiana	221,564	2.1%
36	Iowa	77,838	0.7%
30	Kansas	101,698	1.0%
29	Kentucky	119,560	1.1%
21	Louisiana	198,305	1.9%
42	Maine	33,264	0.3%
16	Maryland	216,045	2.0%
22	Massachusetts	182,050	1.7%
9	Michigan	332,465	3.1%
24	Minnesota	151,925	1.4%
33	Mississippi	95,485	0.9%
14	Missouri	232,142	2.2%
45	Montana	26,497	0.2%
37	Nebraska	54,673	0.5%
31	Nevada	99,322	0.9%
43	New Hampshire	30,738	0.3%
18	New Jersey	208,218	2.0%
35	New Mexico	87,518	0.8%
4	New York	453,491	4.3%
8	North Carolina	382,027	3.6%
50	North Dakota	13,800	0.1%
6	Ohio	415,885	3.9%
26	Oklahoma	150,243	1.4%
28	Oregon	123,255	1.2%
10	Pennsylvania	325,477	3.1%
44	Rhode Island	30,157	0.3%
19	South Carolina	207,965	2.0%
49	South Dakota	15,476	0.1%
11	Tennessee	278,406	2.6%
2	Texas	1,116,813	10.5%
32	Utah	97,129	0.9%
47	Vermont	15,748	0.1%
17	Virginia	209,332	2.0%
12	Washington	266,424	2.5%
38	West Virginia	51,377	0.5%
23	Wisconsin	162,019	1.5%
48	Wyoming	15,596	0.1%

RANK ORDER

RANK	STATE	CRIMES	% of USA
1	California	1,184,073	11.1%
2	Texas	1,116,813	10.5%
3	Florida	825,551	7.8%
4	New York	453,491	4.3%
5	Illinois	417,532	3.9%
6	Ohio	415,885	3.9%
7	Georgia	402,280	3.8%
8	North Carolina	382,027	3.6%
9	Michigan	332,465	3.1%
10	Pennsylvania	325,477	3.1%
11	Tennessee	278,406	2.6%
12	Washington	266,424	2.5%
13	Arizona	261,511	2.5%
14	Missouri	232,142	2.2%
15	Indiana	221,564	2.1%
16	Maryland	216,045	2.0%
17	Virginia	209,332	2.0%
18	New Jersey	208,218	2.0%
19	South Carolina	207,965	2.0%
20	Alabama	198,808	1.9%
21	Louisiana	198,305	1.9%
22	Massachusetts	182,050	1.7%
23	Wisconsin	162,019	1.5%
24	Minnesota	151,925	1.4%
25	Colorado	150,944	1.4%
26	Oklahoma	150,243	1.4%
27	Arkansas	123,997	1.2%
28	Oregon	123,255	1.2%
29	Kentucky	119,560	1.1%
30	Kansas	101,698	1.0%
31	Nevada	99,322	0.9%
32	Utah	97,129	0.9%
33	Mississippi	95,485	0.9%
34	Connecticut	92,689	0.9%
35	New Mexico	87,518	0.8%
36	Iowa	77,838	0.7%
37	Nebraska	54,673	0.5%
38	West Virginia	51,377	0.5%
39	Hawaii	50,978	0.5%
40	Delaware	35,283	0.3%
41	Idaho	34,271	0.3%
42	Maine	33,264	0.3%
43	New Hampshire	30,738	0.3%
44	Rhode Island	30,157	0.3%
45	Montana	26,497	0.2%
46	Alaska	24,998	0.2%
47	Vermont	15,748	0.1%
48	Wyoming	15,596	0.1%
49	South Dakota	15,476	0.1%
50	North Dakota	13,800	0.1%
	District of Columbia	36,527	0.3%

Source: CQ Press using reported data from the Federal Bureau of Investigation
    "Crime in the United States 2009" (Uniform Crime Reports, September 13, 2010, http://www.fbi.gov/ucr/ucr.htm)
*Includes murder, rape, robbery, aggravated assault, burglary, larceny-theft, and motor vehicle theft.

Percent Change in Number of Crimes: 2008 to 2009

National Percent Change = 4.7% Decrease*

ALPHA ORDER				RANK ORDER		
RANK	STATE	PERCENT CHANGE		RANK	STATE	PERCENT CHANGE
32	Alabama	(6.0)		1	Oklahoma	3.5
5	Alaska	1.7		2	Hawaii	3.1
50	Arizona	(11.9)		3	Texas	2.1
8	Arkansas	(0.2)		4	New Hampshire	1.8
36	California	(6.5)		5	Alaska	1.7
23	Colorado	(4.6)		6	Mississippi	0.1
28	Connecticut	(5.4)		7	West Virginia	0.0
34	Delaware	(6.1)		8	Arkansas	(0.2)
38	Florida	(6.7)		9	Louisiana	(1.2)
41	Georgia	(7.4)		9	Washington	(1.2)
2	Hawaii	3.1		11	Utah	(1.3)
23	Idaho	(4.6)		12	New Mexico	(1.4)
40	Illinois	(7.0)		12	Wyoming	(1.4)
29	Indiana	(5.5)		14	Massachusetts	(2.1)
26	Iowa	(5.0)		15	Maine	(2.2)
25	Kansas	(4.8)		16	North Dakota	(2.5)
31	Kentucky	(5.9)		17	New York	(2.7)
9	Louisiana	(1.2)		18	South Dakota	(2.9)
15	Maine	(2.2)		19	Virginia	(3.4)
44	Maryland	(7.5)		20	Michigan	(3.9)
14	Massachusetts	(2.1)		20	Nebraska	(3.9)
20	Michigan	(3.9)		22	Ohio	(4.0)
39	Minnesota	(6.8)		23	Colorado	(4.6)
6	Mississippi	0.1		23	Idaho	(4.6)
30	Missouri	(5.7)		25	Kansas	(4.8)
49	Montana	(9.4)		26	Iowa	(5.0)
20	Nebraska	(3.9)		27	Wisconsin	(5.2)
48	Nevada	(8.7)		28	Connecticut	(5.4)
4	New Hampshire	1.8		29	Indiana	(5.5)
46	New Jersey	(8.5)		30	Missouri	(5.7)
12	New Mexico	(1.4)		31	Kentucky	(5.9)
17	New York	(2.7)		32	Alabama	(6.0)
45	North Carolina	(8.1)		32	Vermont	(6.0)
16	North Dakota	(2.5)		34	Delaware	(6.1)
22	Ohio	(4.0)		34	Tennessee	(6.1)
1	Oklahoma	3.5		36	California	(6.5)
47	Oregon	(8.6)		37	South Carolina	(6.6)
41	Pennsylvania	(7.4)		38	Florida	(6.7)
41	Rhode Island	(7.4)		39	Minnesota	(6.8)
37	South Carolina	(6.6)		40	Illinois	(7.0)
18	South Dakota	(2.9)		41	Georgia	(7.4)
34	Tennessee	(6.1)		41	Pennsylvania	(7.4)
3	Texas	2.1		41	Rhode Island	(7.4)
11	Utah	(1.3)		44	Maryland	(7.5)
32	Vermont	(6.0)		45	North Carolina	(8.1)
19	Virginia	(3.4)		46	New Jersey	(8.5)
9	Washington	(1.2)		47	Oregon	(8.6)
7	West Virginia	0.0		48	Nevada	(8.7)
27	Wisconsin	(5.2)		49	Montana	(9.4)
12	Wyoming	(1.4)		50	Arizona	(11.9)

	District of Columbia	(5.7)

Source: CQ Press using reported data from the Federal Bureau of Investigation

"Crime in the United States 2009" (Uniform Crime Reports, September 13, 2010, http://www.fbi.gov/ucr/ucr.htm)

*Includes murder, rape, robbery, aggravated assault, burglary, larceny-theft, and motor vehicle theft.

Crime Rate in 2009

National Rate = 3,465.5 Crimes per 100,000 Population*

ALPHA ORDER

RANK	STATE	RATE
8	Alabama	4,222.2
21	Alaska	3,579.0
14	Arizona	3,964.8
7	Arkansas	4,291.4
28	California	3,203.5
30	Colorado	3,004.0
40	Connecticut	2,634.5
13	Delaware	3,986.2
3	Florida	4,453.3
9	Georgia	4,092.7
15	Hawaii	3,936.0
48	Idaho	2,217.1
26	Illinois	3,234.1
23	Indiana	3,449.4
41	Iowa	2,587.9
19	Kansas	3,607.9
36	Kentucky	2,771.4
5	Louisiana	4,414.6
44	Maine	2,523.3
17	Maryland	3,790.6
37	Massachusetts	2,761.1
24	Michigan	3,334.8
31	Minnesota	2,884.9
25	Mississippi	3,234.6
16	Missouri	3,877.1
38	Montana	2,717.6
29	Nebraska	3,043.1
18	Nevada	3,757.8
47	New Hampshire	2,320.6
45	New Jersey	2,391.2
6	New Mexico	4,354.8
46	New York	2,320.7
11	North Carolina	4,072.4
49	North Dakota	2,133.5
20	Ohio	3,603.0
10	Oklahoma	4,074.9
27	Oregon	3,221.8
42	Pennsylvania	2,582.1
34	Rhode Island	2,863.4
1	South Carolina	4,559.4
50	South Dakota	1,905.0
4	Tennessee	4,421.8
2	Texas	4,506.4
22	Utah	3,488.1
43	Vermont	2,532.8
39	Virginia	2,655.6
12	Washington	3,997.9
35	West Virginia	2,823.2
33	Wisconsin	2,865.2
32	Wyoming	2,865.5

RANK ORDER

RANK	STATE	RATE
1	South Carolina	4,559.4
2	Texas	4,506.4
3	Florida	4,453.3
4	Tennessee	4,421.8
5	Louisiana	4,414.6
6	New Mexico	4,354.8
7	Arkansas	4,291.4
8	Alabama	4,222.2
9	Georgia	4,092.7
10	Oklahoma	4,074.9
11	North Carolina	4,072.4
12	Washington	3,997.9
13	Delaware	3,986.2
14	Arizona	3,964.8
15	Hawaii	3,936.0
16	Missouri	3,877.1
17	Maryland	3,790.6
18	Nevada	3,757.8
19	Kansas	3,607.9
20	Ohio	3,603.0
21	Alaska	3,579.0
22	Utah	3,488.1
23	Indiana	3,449.4
24	Michigan	3,334.8
25	Mississippi	3,234.6
26	Illinois	3,234.1
27	Oregon	3,221.8
28	California	3,203.5
29	Nebraska	3,043.1
30	Colorado	3,004.0
31	Minnesota	2,884.9
32	Wyoming	2,865.5
33	Wisconsin	2,865.2
34	Rhode Island	2,863.4
35	West Virginia	2,823.2
36	Kentucky	2,771.4
37	Massachusetts	2,761.1
38	Montana	2,717.6
39	Virginia	2,655.6
40	Connecticut	2,634.5
41	Iowa	2,587.9
42	Pennsylvania	2,582.1
43	Vermont	2,532.8
44	Maine	2,523.3
45	New Jersey	2,391.2
46	New York	2,320.7
47	New Hampshire	2,320.6
48	Idaho	2,217.1
49	North Dakota	2,133.5
50	South Dakota	1,905.0

District of Columbia 6,091.3

Source: CQ Press using reported data from the Federal Bureau of Investigation
  "Crime in the United States 2009" (Uniform Crime Reports, September 13, 2010, http://www.fbi.gov/ucr/ucr.htm)
*Includes murder, rape, robbery, aggravated assault, burglary, larceny-theft, and motor vehicle theft.

Percent Change in Crime Rate: 2008 to 2009

National Percent Change = 5.5% Decrease*

ALPHA ORDER			RANK ORDER		
RANK	STATE	PERCENT CHANGE	RANK	STATE	PERCENT CHANGE
33	Alabama	(6.6)	1	Hawaii	2.5
4	Alaska	0.2	2	Oklahoma	2.3
50	Arizona	(13.2)	3	New Hampshire	1.6
8	Arkansas	(0.9)	4	Alaska	0.2
38	California	(7.4)	4	Texas	0.2
31	Colorado	(6.3)	6	Mississippi	(0.3)
27	Connecticut	(5.8)	6	West Virginia	(0.3)
34	Delaware	(7.0)	8	Arkansas	(0.9)
36	Florida	(7.3)	9	Louisiana	(2.1)
44	Georgia	(8.7)	9	Maine	(2.1)
1	Hawaii	2.5	11	New Mexico	(2.5)
26	Idaho	(5.7)	12	Washington	(2.6)
40	Illinois	(7.5)	13	Massachusetts	(2.9)
28	Indiana	(6.0)	14	New York	(3.1)
23	Iowa	(5.4)	15	North Dakota	(3.3)
24	Kansas	(5.5)	16	Utah	(3.4)
32	Kentucky	(6.5)	17	Wyoming	(3.5)
9	Louisiana	(2.1)	18	Michigan	(3.6)
9	Maine	(2.1)	19	South Dakota	(3.9)
43	Maryland	(8.1)	20	Ohio	(4.1)
13	Massachusetts	(2.9)	21	Virginia	(4.5)
18	Michigan	(3.6)	22	Nebraska	(4.6)
38	Minnesota	(7.4)	23	Iowa	(5.4)
6	Mississippi	(0.3)	24	Kansas	(5.5)
30	Missouri	(6.2)	25	Wisconsin	(5.6)
49	Montana	(10.0)	26	Idaho	(5.7)
22	Nebraska	(4.6)	27	Connecticut	(5.8)
47	Nevada	(9.6)	28	Indiana	(6.0)
3	New Hampshire	1.6	29	Vermont	(6.1)
45	New Jersey	(8.9)	30	Missouri	(6.2)
11	New Mexico	(2.5)	31	Colorado	(6.3)
14	New York	(3.1)	32	Kentucky	(6.5)
46	North Carolina	(9.4)	33	Alabama	(6.6)
15	North Dakota	(3.3)	34	Delaware	(7.0)
20	Ohio	(4.1)	34	Tennessee	(7.0)
2	Oklahoma	2.3	36	Florida	(7.3)
47	Oregon	(9.6)	36	Rhode Island	(7.3)
41	Pennsylvania	(7.6)	38	California	(7.4)
36	Rhode Island	(7.3)	38	Minnesota	(7.4)
42	South Carolina	(7.8)	40	Illinois	(7.5)
19	South Dakota	(3.9)	41	Pennsylvania	(7.6)
34	Tennessee	(7.0)	42	South Carolina	(7.8)
4	Texas	0.2	43	Maryland	(8.1)
16	Utah	(3.4)	44	Georgia	(8.7)
29	Vermont	(6.1)	45	New Jersey	(8.9)
21	Virginia	(4.5)	46	North Carolina	(9.4)
12	Washington	(2.6)	47	Nevada	(9.6)
6	West Virginia	(0.3)	47	Oregon	(9.6)
25	Wisconsin	(5.6)	49	Montana	(10.0)
17	Wyoming	(3.5)	50	Arizona	(13.2)

	District of Columbia	(7.2)

Source: CQ Press using reported data from the Federal Bureau of Investigation
   "Crime in the United States 2009" (Uniform Crime Reports, September 13, 2010, http://www.fbi.gov/ucr/ucr.htm)
*Includes murder, rape, robbery, aggravated assault, burglary, larceny-theft, and motor vehicle theft.

Violent Crimes in 2009

National Total = 1,318,398 Violent Crimes*

ALPHA ORDER

RANK	STATE	CRIMES	% of USA
21	Alabama	21,179	1.6%
40	Alaska	4,421	0.3%
18	Arizona	26,929	2.0%
26	Arkansas	14,959	1.1%
1	California	174,459	13.2%
25	Colorado	16,976	1.3%
32	Connecticut	10,508	0.8%
37	Delaware	5,635	0.4%
3	Florida	113,541	8.6%
9	Georgia	41,880	3.2%
41	Hawaii	3,559	0.3%
42	Idaho	3,530	0.3%
5	Illinois	64,185	4.9%
20	Indiana	21,404	1.6%
34	Iowa	8,397	0.6%
30	Kansas	11,278	0.9%
31	Kentucky	11,159	0.8%
16	Louisiana	27,849	2.1%
46	Maine	1,579	0.1%
12	Maryland	33,623	2.6%
14	Massachusetts	30,136	2.3%
6	Michigan	49,547	3.8%
28	Minnesota	12,842	1.0%
35	Mississippi	8,304	0.6%
15	Missouri	29,444	2.2%
44	Montana	2,473	0.2%
39	Nebraska	5,059	0.4%
22	Nevada	18,559	1.4%
45	New Hampshire	2,114	0.2%
17	New Jersey	27,121	2.1%
29	New Mexico	12,440	0.9%
4	New York	75,176	5.7%
11	North Carolina	37,929	2.9%
48	North Dakota	1,298	0.1%
10	Ohio	38,332	2.9%
23	Oklahoma	18,474	1.4%
33	Oregon	9,744	0.7%
7	Pennsylvania	47,965	3.6%
43	Rhode Island	2,660	0.2%
13	South Carolina	30,596	2.3%
47	South Dakota	1,508	0.1%
8	Tennessee	42,041	3.2%
2	Texas	121,668	9.2%
36	Utah	5,924	0.4%
50	Vermont	817	0.1%
24	Virginia	17,879	1.4%
19	Washington	22,056	1.7%
38	West Virginia	5,396	0.4%
27	Wisconsin	14,533	1.1%
49	Wyoming	1,242	0.1%

RANK ORDER

RANK	STATE	CRIMES	% of USA
1	California	174,459	13.2%
2	Texas	121,668	9.2%
3	Florida	113,541	8.6%
4	New York	75,176	5.7%
5	Illinois	64,185	4.9%
6	Michigan	49,547	3.8%
7	Pennsylvania	47,965	3.6%
8	Tennessee	42,041	3.2%
9	Georgia	41,880	3.2%
10	Ohio	38,332	2.9%
11	North Carolina	37,929	2.9%
12	Maryland	33,623	2.6%
13	South Carolina	30,596	2.3%
14	Massachusetts	30,136	2.3%
15	Missouri	29,444	2.2%
16	Louisiana	27,849	2.1%
17	New Jersey	27,121	2.1%
18	Arizona	26,929	2.0%
19	Washington	22,056	1.7%
20	Indiana	21,404	1.6%
21	Alabama	21,179	1.6%
22	Nevada	18,559	1.4%
23	Oklahoma	18,474	1.4%
24	Virginia	17,879	1.4%
25	Colorado	16,976	1.3%
26	Arkansas	14,959	1.1%
27	Wisconsin	14,533	1.1%
28	Minnesota	12,842	1.0%
29	New Mexico	12,440	0.9%
30	Kansas	11,278	0.9%
31	Kentucky	11,159	0.8%
32	Connecticut	10,508	0.8%
33	Oregon	9,744	0.7%
34	Iowa	8,397	0.6%
35	Mississippi	8,304	0.6%
36	Utah	5,924	0.4%
37	Delaware	5,635	0.4%
38	West Virginia	5,396	0.4%
39	Nebraska	5,059	0.4%
40	Alaska	4,421	0.3%
41	Hawaii	3,559	0.3%
42	Idaho	3,530	0.3%
43	Rhode Island	2,660	0.2%
44	Montana	2,473	0.2%
45	New Hampshire	2,114	0.2%
46	Maine	1,579	0.1%
47	South Dakota	1,508	0.1%
48	North Dakota	1,298	0.1%
49	Wyoming	1,242	0.1%
50	Vermont	817	0.1%
	District of Columbia	8,071	0.6%

Source: Reported data from the Federal Bureau of Investigation
"Crime in the United States 2009" (Uniform Crime Reports, September 13, 2010, http://www.fbi.gov/ucr/ucr.htm)
*Violent crimes are offenses of murder, forcible rape, robbery, and aggravated assault.

Percent Change in Number of Violent Crimes: 2008 to 2009

National Percent Change = 5.3% Decrease*

ALPHA ORDER

RANK	STATE	PERCENT CHANGE
8	Alabama	0.3
15	Alaska	(1.3)
48	Arizona	(13.9)
3	Arkansas	3.4
33	California	(5.8)
12	Colorado	(0.9)
18	Connecticut	(2.1)
42	Delaware	(8.9)
43	Florida	(10.1)
45	Georgia	(11.8)
5	Hawaii	1.4
24	Idaho	(4.0)
32	Illinois	(5.4)
10	Indiana	(0.5)
20	Iowa	(2.9)
19	Kansas	(2.7)
47	Kentucky	(12.9)
33	Louisiana	(5.8)
7	Maine	0.4
29	Maryland	(5.0)
6	Massachusetts	0.8
23	Michigan	(3.6)
39	Minnesota	(6.7)
40	Mississippi	(7.2)
12	Missouri	(0.9)
49	Montana	(15.3)
41	Nebraska	(8.6)
17	Nevada	(1.9)
11	New Hampshire	(0.6)
26	New Jersey	(4.3)
28	New Mexico	(4.4)
21	New York	(3.1)
46	North Carolina	(12.0)
2	North Dakota	6.7
29	Ohio	(5.0)
24	Oklahoma	(4.0)
14	Oregon	(1.0)
35	Pennsylvania	(6.0)
9	Rhode Island	0.2
38	South Carolina	(6.6)
50	South Dakota	(32.1)
37	Tennessee	(6.5)
16	Texas	(1.6)
22	Utah	(3.4)
26	Vermont	(4.3)
44	Virginia	(10.8)
4	Washington	1.5
1	West Virginia	7.3
36	Wisconsin	(6.2)
31	Wyoming	(5.3)

RANK ORDER

RANK	STATE	PERCENT CHANGE
1	West Virginia	7.3
2	North Dakota	6.7
3	Arkansas	3.4
4	Washington	1.5
5	Hawaii	1.4
6	Massachusetts	0.8
7	Maine	0.4
8	Alabama	0.3
9	Rhode Island	0.2
10	Indiana	(0.5)
11	New Hampshire	(0.6)
12	Colorado	(0.9)
12	Missouri	(0.9)
14	Oregon	(1.0)
15	Alaska	(1.3)
16	Texas	(1.6)
17	Nevada	(1.9)
18	Connecticut	(2.1)
19	Kansas	(2.7)
20	Iowa	(2.9)
21	New York	(3.1)
22	Utah	(3.4)
23	Michigan	(3.6)
24	Idaho	(4.0)
24	Oklahoma	(4.0)
26	New Jersey	(4.3)
26	Vermont	(4.3)
28	New Mexico	(4.4)
29	Maryland	(5.0)
29	Ohio	(5.0)
31	Wyoming	(5.3)
32	Illinois	(5.4)
33	California	(5.8)
33	Louisiana	(5.8)
35	Pennsylvania	(6.0)
36	Wisconsin	(6.2)
37	Tennessee	(6.5)
38	South Carolina	(6.6)
39	Minnesota	(6.7)
40	Mississippi	(7.2)
41	Nebraska	(8.6)
42	Delaware	(8.9)
43	Florida	(10.1)
44	Virginia	(10.8)
45	Georgia	(11.8)
46	North Carolina	(12.0)
47	Kentucky	(12.9)
48	Arizona	(13.9)
49	Montana	(15.3)
50	South Dakota	(32.1)

District of Columbia (5.1)

Source: Reported data from the Federal Bureau of Investigation
"Crime in the United States 2009" (Uniform Crime Reports, September 13, 2010, http://www.fbi.gov/ucr/ucr.htm)
*Violent crimes are offenses of murder, forcible rape, robbery, and aggravated assault.

Violent Crime Rate in 2009

National Rate = 429.4 Violent Crimes per 100,000 Population*

ALPHA ORDER

RANK	STATE	RATE
18	Alabama	449.8
5	Alaska	633.0
20	Arizona	408.3
10	Arkansas	517.7
16	California	472.0
25	Colorado	337.8
30	Connecticut	298.7
4	Delaware	636.6
8	Florida	612.5
19	Georgia	426.1
35	Hawaii	274.8
42	Idaho	228.4
12	Illinois	497.2
26	Indiana	333.2
34	Iowa	279.2
22	Kansas	400.1
36	Kentucky	258.7
6	Louisiana	620.0
50	Maine	119.8
9	Maryland	589.9
17	Massachusetts	457.1
13	Michigan	497.0
41	Minnesota	243.9
33	Mississippi	281.3
14	Missouri	491.8
39	Montana	253.6
32	Nebraska	281.6
1	Nevada	702.2
48	New Hampshire	159.6
29	New Jersey	311.5
7	New Mexico	619.0
23	New York	384.7
21	North Carolina	404.3
46	North Dakota	200.7
27	Ohio	332.1
11	Oklahoma	501.1
38	Oregon	254.7
24	Pennsylvania	380.5
40	Rhode Island	252.6
2	South Carolina	670.8
47	South Dakota	185.6
3	Tennessee	667.7
15	Texas	490.9
45	Utah	212.7
49	Vermont	131.4
44	Virginia	226.8
28	Washington	331.0
31	West Virginia	296.5
37	Wisconsin	257.0
43	Wyoming	228.2

RANK ORDER

RANK	STATE	RATE
1	Nevada	702.2
2	South Carolina	670.8
3	Tennessee	667.7
4	Delaware	636.6
5	Alaska	633.0
6	Louisiana	620.0
7	New Mexico	619.0
8	Florida	612.5
9	Maryland	589.9
10	Arkansas	517.7
11	Oklahoma	501.1
12	Illinois	497.2
13	Michigan	497.0
14	Missouri	491.8
15	Texas	490.9
16	California	472.0
17	Massachusetts	457.1
18	Alabama	449.8
19	Georgia	426.1
20	Arizona	408.3
21	North Carolina	404.3
22	Kansas	400.1
23	New York	384.7
24	Pennsylvania	380.5
25	Colorado	337.8
26	Indiana	333.2
27	Ohio	332.1
28	Washington	331.0
29	New Jersey	311.5
30	Connecticut	298.7
31	West Virginia	296.5
32	Nebraska	281.6
33	Mississippi	281.3
34	Iowa	279.2
35	Hawaii	274.8
36	Kentucky	258.7
37	Wisconsin	257.0
38	Oregon	254.7
39	Montana	253.6
40	Rhode Island	252.6
41	Minnesota	243.9
42	Idaho	228.4
43	Wyoming	228.2
44	Virginia	226.8
45	Utah	212.7
46	North Dakota	200.7
47	South Dakota	185.6
48	New Hampshire	159.6
49	Vermont	131.4
50	Maine	119.8
	District of Columbia	1,345.9

Source: Reported data from the Federal Bureau of Investigation
"Crime in the United States 2009" (Uniform Crime Reports, September 13, 2010, http://www.fbi.gov/ucr/ucr.htm)
*Violent crimes are offenses of murder, forcible rape, robbery, and aggravated assault.

Percent Change in Violent Crime Rate: 2008 to 2009

National Percent Change = 6.1% Decrease*

ALPHA ORDER				RANK ORDER		
RANK	**STATE**	**PERCENT CHANGE**		**RANK**	**STATE**	**PERCENT CHANGE**
9	Alabama	(0.3)		1	West Virginia	7.1
16	Alaska	(2.8)		2	North Dakota	5.8
48	Arizona	(15.2)		3	Arkansas	2.6
3	Arkansas	2.6		4	Hawaii	0.8
35	California	(6.8)		5	Maine	0.6
15	Colorado	(2.7)		6	Rhode Island	0.2
14	Connecticut	(2.6)		7	Massachusetts	0.1
42	Delaware	(9.8)		8	Washington	0.0
43	Florida	(10.6)		9	Alabama	(0.3)
45	Georgia	(12.9)		10	New Hampshire	(0.8)
4	Hawaii	0.8		11	Indiana	(1.1)
27	Idaho	(5.2)		12	Missouri	(1.4)
31	Illinois	(5.9)		13	Oregon	(2.1)
11	Indiana	(1.1)		14	Connecticut	(2.6)
19	Iowa	(3.4)		15	Colorado	(2.7)
19	Kansas	(3.4)		16	Alaska	(2.8)
47	Kentucky	(13.5)		17	Nevada	(2.9)
33	Louisiana	(6.7)		18	Michigan	(3.3)
5	Maine	0.6		19	Iowa	(3.4)
30	Maryland	(5.7)		19	Kansas	(3.4)
7	Massachusetts	0.1		19	New York	(3.4)
18	Michigan	(3.3)		22	Texas	(3.5)
38	Minnesota	(7.4)		23	Vermont	(4.4)
39	Mississippi	(7.6)		24	New Jersey	(4.8)
12	Missouri	(1.4)		25	Ohio	(5.1)
49	Montana	(15.9)		25	Oklahoma	(5.1)
41	Nebraska	(9.4)		27	Idaho	(5.2)
17	Nevada	(2.9)		28	Utah	(5.3)
10	New Hampshire	(0.8)		29	New Mexico	(5.5)
24	New Jersey	(4.8)		30	Maryland	(5.7)
29	New Mexico	(5.5)		31	Illinois	(5.9)
19	New York	(3.4)		32	Pennsylvania	(6.3)
46	North Carolina	(13.3)		33	Louisiana	(6.7)
2	North Dakota	5.8		33	Wisconsin	(6.7)
25	Ohio	(5.1)		35	California	(6.8)
25	Oklahoma	(5.1)		36	Tennessee	(7.3)
13	Oregon	(2.1)		36	Wyoming	(7.3)
32	Pennsylvania	(6.3)		38	Minnesota	(7.4)
6	Rhode Island	0.2		39	Mississippi	(7.6)
40	South Carolina	(7.8)		40	South Carolina	(7.8)
50	South Dakota	(32.8)		41	Nebraska	(9.4)
36	Tennessee	(7.3)		42	Delaware	(9.8)
22	Texas	(3.5)		43	Florida	(10.6)
28	Utah	(5.3)		44	Virginia	(11.8)
23	Vermont	(4.4)		45	Georgia	(12.9)
44	Virginia	(11.8)		46	North Carolina	(13.3)
8	Washington	0.0		47	Kentucky	(13.5)
1	West Virginia	7.1		48	Arizona	(15.2)
33	Wisconsin	(6.7)		49	Montana	(15.9)
36	Wyoming	(7.3)		50	South Dakota	(32.8)

	District of Columbia	(6.7)

Source: Reported data from the Federal Bureau of Investigation
  "Crime in the United States 2009" (Uniform Crime Reports, September 13, 2010, http://www.fbi.gov/ucr/ucr.htm)
*Violent crimes are offenses of murder, forcible rape, robbery, and aggravated assault.

Murders in 2009

National Total = 15,241 Murders*

RANK	STATE	MURDERS	% of USA
17	Alabama	323	2.1%
43	Alaska	22	0.1%
15	Arizona	354	2.3%
23	Arkansas	179	1.2%
1	California	1,972	12.9%
26	Colorado	175	1.1%
32	Connecticut	107	0.7%
36	Delaware	41	0.3%
3	Florida	1,017	6.7%
8	Georgia	566	3.7%
43	Hawaii	22	0.1%
43	Idaho	22	0.1%
5	Illinois	773	5.1%
19	Indiana	310	2.0%
39	Iowa	34	0.2%
31	Kansas	119	0.8%
25	Kentucky	178	1.2%
9	Louisiana	530	3.5%
42	Maine	26	0.2%
13	Maryland	438	2.9%
28	Massachusetts	172	1.1%
7	Michigan	627	4.1%
35	Minnesota	74	0.5%
22	Mississippi	190	1.2%
14	Missouri	383	2.5%
41	Montana	28	0.2%
37	Nebraska	40	0.3%
29	Nevada	157	1.0%
48	New Hampshire	10	0.1%
18	New Jersey	319	2.1%
26	New Mexico	175	1.1%
4	New York	778	5.1%
11	North Carolina	494	3.2%
48	North Dakota	10	0.1%
10	Ohio	519	3.4%
21	Oklahoma	228	1.5%
33	Oregon	85	0.6%
6	Pennsylvania	661	4.3%
40	Rhode Island	31	0.2%
20	South Carolina	287	1.9%
46	South Dakota	21	0.1%
12	Tennessee	461	3.0%
2	Texas	1,328	8.7%
38	Utah	37	0.2%
50	Vermont	7	0.0%
16	Virginia	347	2.3%
23	Washington	179	1.2%
34	West Virginia	84	0.6%
30	Wisconsin	144	0.9%
47	Wyoming	13	0.1%

RANK	STATE	MURDERS	% of USA
1	California	1,972	12.9%
2	Texas	1,328	8.7%
3	Florida	1,017	6.7%
4	New York	778	5.1%
5	Illinois	773	5.1%
6	Pennsylvania	661	4.3%
7	Michigan	627	4.1%
8	Georgia	566	3.7%
9	Louisiana	530	3.5%
10	Ohio	519	3.4%
11	North Carolina	494	3.2%
12	Tennessee	461	3.0%
13	Maryland	438	2.9%
14	Missouri	383	2.5%
15	Arizona	354	2.3%
16	Virginia	347	2.3%
17	Alabama	323	2.1%
18	New Jersey	319	2.1%
19	Indiana	310	2.0%
20	South Carolina	287	1.9%
21	Oklahoma	228	1.5%
22	Mississippi	190	1.2%
23	Arkansas	179	1.2%
23	Washington	179	1.2%
25	Kentucky	178	1.2%
26	Colorado	175	1.1%
26	New Mexico	175	1.1%
28	Massachusetts	172	1.1%
29	Nevada	157	1.0%
30	Wisconsin	144	0.9%
31	Kansas	119	0.8%
32	Connecticut	107	0.7%
33	Oregon	85	0.6%
34	West Virginia	84	0.6%
35	Minnesota	74	0.5%
36	Delaware	41	0.3%
37	Nebraska	40	0.3%
38	Utah	37	0.2%
39	Iowa	34	0.2%
40	Rhode Island	31	0.2%
41	Montana	28	0.2%
42	Maine	26	0.2%
43	Alaska	22	0.1%
43	Hawaii	22	0.1%
43	Idaho	22	0.1%
46	South Dakota	21	0.1%
47	Wyoming	13	0.1%
48	New Hampshire	10	0.1%
48	North Dakota	10	0.1%
50	Vermont	7	0.0%
	District of Columbia	144	0.9%

Source: Reported data from the Federal Bureau of Investigation
"Crime in the United States 2009" (Uniform Crime Reports, September 13, 2010, http://www.fbi.gov/ucr/ucr.htm)
*Includes nonnegligent manslaughter.

Murder Rate in 2009

National Rate = 5.0 Murders per 100,000 Population*

ALPHA ORDER

RANK	STATE	RATE
5	Alabama	6.9
31	Alaska	3.1
16	Arizona	5.4
10	Arkansas	6.2
18	California	5.3
30	Colorado	3.5
32	Connecticut	3.0
22	Delaware	4.6
15	Florida	5.5
14	Georgia	5.8
43	Hawaii	1.7
45	Idaho	1.4
12	Illinois	6.0
21	Indiana	4.8
48	Iowa	1.1
26	Kansas	4.2
27	Kentucky	4.1
1	Louisiana	11.8
42	Maine	2.0
3	Maryland	7.7
36	Massachusetts	2.6
8	Michigan	6.3
45	Minnesota	1.4
6	Mississippi	6.4
6	Missouri	6.4
33	Montana	2.9
40	Nebraska	2.2
13	Nevada	5.9
50	New Hampshire	0.8
29	New Jersey	3.7
2	New Mexico	8.7
28	New York	4.0
18	North Carolina	5.3
44	North Dakota	1.5
24	Ohio	4.5
10	Oklahoma	6.2
40	Oregon	2.2
20	Pennsylvania	5.2
33	Rhode Island	2.9
8	South Carolina	6.3
36	South Dakota	2.6
4	Tennessee	7.3
16	Texas	5.4
47	Utah	1.3
48	Vermont	1.1
25	Virginia	4.4
35	Washington	2.7
22	West Virginia	4.6
38	Wisconsin	2.5
39	Wyoming	2.4

RANK ORDER

RANK	STATE	RATE
1	Louisiana	11.8
2	New Mexico	8.7
3	Maryland	7.7
4	Tennessee	7.3
5	Alabama	6.9
6	Mississippi	6.4
6	Missouri	6.4
8	Michigan	6.3
8	South Carolina	6.3
10	Arkansas	6.2
10	Oklahoma	6.2
12	Illinois	6.0
13	Nevada	5.9
14	Georgia	5.8
15	Florida	5.5
16	Arizona	5.4
16	Texas	5.4
18	California	5.3
18	North Carolina	5.3
20	Pennsylvania	5.2
21	Indiana	4.8
22	Delaware	4.6
22	West Virginia	4.6
24	Ohio	4.5
25	Virginia	4.4
26	Kansas	4.2
27	Kentucky	4.1
28	New York	4.0
29	New Jersey	3.7
30	Colorado	3.5
31	Alaska	3.1
32	Connecticut	3.0
33	Montana	2.9
33	Rhode Island	2.9
35	Washington	2.7
36	Massachusetts	2.6
36	South Dakota	2.6
38	Wisconsin	2.5
39	Wyoming	2.4
40	Nebraska	2.2
40	Oregon	2.2
42	Maine	2.0
43	Hawaii	1.7
44	North Dakota	1.5
45	Idaho	1.4
45	Minnesota	1.4
47	Utah	1.3
48	Iowa	1.1
48	Vermont	1.1
50	New Hampshire	0.8
	District of Columbia	24.0

Source: Reported data from the Federal Bureau of Investigation
"Crime in the United States 2009" (Uniform Crime Reports, September 13, 2010, http://www.fbi.gov/ucr/ucr.htm)
*Includes nonnegligent manslaughter.

Percent of Murders Involving Firearms in 2009

National Percent = 67.1% of Murders*

ALPHA ORDER

RANK	STATE	PERCENT
6	Alabama	72.0
31	Alaska	59.1
29	Arizona	60.1
26	Arkansas	62.6
15	California	69.0
35	Colorado	56.3
23	Connecticut	65.4
3	Delaware	75.6
NA	Florida**	NA
12	Georgia	69.6
44	Hawaii	38.1
48	Idaho	22.7
2	Illinois*	80.6
8	Indiana	71.3
47	Iowa	32.4
6	Kansas	72.0
22	Kentucky	65.9
1	Louisiana	82.7
42	Maine	42.3
12	Maryland	69.6
37	Massachusetts	55.0
10	Michigan	69.9
39	Minnesota	52.8
14	Mississippi	69.5
5	Missouri	72.4
18	Montana	67.9
34	Nebraska	57.5
32	Nevada	58.3
43	New Hampshire	40.0
15	New Jersey	69.0
38	New Mexico	54.2
28	New York	61.7
11	North Carolina	69.8
46	North Dakota	33.3
27	Ohio	62.0
36	Oklahoma	55.6
41	Oregon	49.4
9	Pennsylvania	71.1
33	Rhode Island	58.1
17	South Carolina	68.9
45	South Dakota	36.4
25	Tennessee	64.0
24	Texas	65.1
19	Utah	67.6
49	Vermont	0.0
20	Virginia	66.0
30	Washington	59.8
40	West Virginia	50.0
20	Wisconsin	66.0
4	Wyoming	72.7

RANK ORDER

RANK	STATE	PERCENT
1	Louisiana	82.7
2	Illinois*	80.6
3	Delaware	75.6
4	Wyoming	72.7
5	Missouri	72.4
6	Alabama	72.0
6	Kansas	72.0
8	Indiana	71.3
9	Pennsylvania	71.1
10	Michigan	69.9
11	North Carolina	69.8
12	Georgia	69.6
12	Maryland	69.6
14	Mississippi	69.5
15	California	69.0
15	New Jersey	69.0
17	South Carolina	68.9
18	Montana	67.9
19	Utah	67.6
20	Virginia	66.0
20	Wisconsin	66.0
22	Kentucky	65.9
23	Connecticut	65.4
24	Texas	65.1
25	Tennessee	64.0
26	Arkansas	62.6
27	Ohio	62.0
28	New York	61.7
29	Arizona	60.1
30	Washington	59.8
31	Alaska	59.1
32	Nevada	58.3
33	Rhode Island	58.1
34	Nebraska	57.5
35	Colorado	56.3
36	Oklahoma	55.6
37	Massachusetts	55.0
38	New Mexico	54.2
39	Minnesota	52.8
40	West Virginia	50.0
41	Oregon	49.4
42	Maine	42.3
43	New Hampshire	40.0
44	Hawaii	38.1
45	South Dakota	36.4
46	North Dakota	33.3
47	Iowa	32.4
48	Idaho	22.7
49	Vermont	0.0
NA	Florida**	NA

District of Columbia   78.5

Source: CQ Press using reported data from the Federal Bureau of Investigation

"Crime in the United States 2009" (Uniform Crime Reports, September 13, 2010, http://www.fbi.gov/ucr/ucr.htm)

*Of the 13,636 murders in 2009 for which supplemental data were received by the F.B.I. There were an additional 1,605 murders for which the type of murder weapon was not reported to the F.B.I. Includes nonnegligent manslaughter. National and state percents based on reporting jurisdictions only. Illinois's percent is for Chicago and Rockford only.

**Not available.

Rapes in 2009

National Total = 88,097 Rapes*

ALPHA ORDER

RANK	STATE	RAPES	% of USA
23	Alabama	1,504	1.7%
39	Alaska	512	0.6%
13	Arizona	2,110	2.4%
24	Arkansas	1,368	1.6%
1	California	8,713	9.9%
12	Colorado	2,242	2.5%
36	Connecticut	651	0.7%
45	Delaware	338	0.4%
3	Florida	5,501	6.2%
11	Georgia	2,301	2.6%
43	Hawaii	392	0.4%
38	Idaho	552	0.6%
6	Illinois	3,901	4.4%
17	Indiana	1,640	1.9%
35	Iowa	853	1.0%
29	Kansas	1,096	1.2%
22	Kentucky	1,509	1.7%
25	Louisiana	1,359	1.5%
44	Maine	376	0.4%
27	Maryland	1,156	1.3%
16	Massachusetts	1,701	1.9%
4	Michigan	4,514	5.1%
15	Minnesota	1,789	2.0%
33	Mississippi	939	1.1%
19	Missouri	1,607	1.8%
46	Montana	294	0.3%
37	Nebraska	595	0.7%
32	Nevada	1,021	1.2%
42	New Hampshire	400	0.5%
31	New Jersey	1,041	1.2%
30	New Mexico	1,057	1.2%
8	New York	2,586	2.9%
10	North Carolina	2,306	2.6%
48	North Dakota	225	0.3%
5	Ohio	4,022	4.6%
20	Oklahoma	1,529	1.7%
26	Oregon	1,168	1.3%
7	Pennsylvania	3,651	4.1%
47	Rhode Island	287	0.3%
18	South Carolina	1,612	1.8%
40	South Dakota	445	0.5%
14	Tennessee	1,993	2.3%
2	Texas	8,287	9.4%
34	Utah	905	1.0%
50	Vermont	124	0.1%
21	Virginia	1,511	1.7%
9	Washington	2,539	2.9%
41	West Virginia	433	0.5%
28	Wisconsin	1,108	1.3%
49	Wyoming	184	0.2%

RANK ORDER

RANK	STATE	RAPES	% of USA
1	California	8,713	9.9%
2	Texas	8,287	9.4%
3	Florida	5,501	6.2%
4	Michigan	4,514	5.1%
5	Ohio	4,022	4.6%
6	Illinois	3,901	4.4%
7	Pennsylvania	3,651	4.1%
8	New York	2,586	2.9%
9	Washington	2,539	2.9%
10	North Carolina	2,306	2.6%
11	Georgia	2,301	2.6%
12	Colorado	2,242	2.5%
13	Arizona	2,110	2.4%
14	Tennessee	1,993	2.3%
15	Minnesota	1,789	2.0%
16	Massachusetts	1,701	1.9%
17	Indiana	1,640	1.9%
18	South Carolina	1,612	1.8%
19	Missouri	1,607	1.8%
20	Oklahoma	1,529	1.7%
21	Virginia	1,511	1.7%
22	Kentucky	1,509	1.7%
23	Alabama	1,504	1.7%
24	Arkansas	1,368	1.6%
25	Louisiana	1,359	1.5%
26	Oregon	1,168	1.3%
27	Maryland	1,156 ·	1.3%
28	Wisconsin	1,108	1.3%
29	Kansas	1,096	1.2%
30	New Mexico	1,057	1.2%
31	New Jersey	1,041	1.2%
32	Nevada	1,021	1.2%
33	Mississippi	939	1.1%
34	Utah	905	1.0%
35	Iowa	853	1.0%
36	Connecticut	651	0.7%
37	Nebraska	595	0.7%
38	Idaho	552	0.6%
39	Alaska	512	0.6%
40	South Dakota	445	0.5%
41	West Virginia	433	0.5%
42	New Hampshire	400	0.5%
43	Hawaii	392	0.4%
44	Maine	376	0.4%
45	Delaware	338	0.4%
46	Montana	294	0.3%
47	Rhode Island	287	0.3%
48	North Dakota	225	0.3%
49	Wyoming	184	0.2%
50	Vermont	124	0.1%
	District of Columbia	150	0.2%

Source: Reported data from the Federal Bureau of Investigation
     "Crime in the United States 2009" (Uniform Crime Reports, September 13, 2010, http://www.fbi.gov/ucr/ucr.htm)
*Forcible rape is the carnal knowledge of a female forcibly and against her will. Assaults or attempts to commit rape by force or threat of force are included. However, statutory rape without force and other sex offenses are excluded.

Rape Rate in 2009

National Rate = 28.7 Rapes per 100,000 Population*

ALPHA ORDER

RANK	STATE	RATE
23	Alabama	31.9
1	Alaska	73.3
22	Arizona	32.0
4	Arkansas	47.3
42	California	23.6
6	Colorado	44.6
48	Connecticut	18.5
10	Delaware	38.2
32	Florida	29.7
43	Georgia	23.4
27	Hawaii	30.3
12	Idaho	35.7
29	Illinois	30.2
39	Indiana	25.5
35	Iowa	28.4
8	Kansas	38.9
14	Kentucky	35.0
27	Louisiana	30.3
34	Maine	28.5
44	Maryland	20.3
38	Massachusetts	25.8
5	Michigan	45.3
17	Minnesota	34.0
24	Mississippi	31.8
37	Missouri	26.8
29	Montana	30.2
20	Nebraska	33.1
9	Nevada	38.6
29	New Hampshire	30.2
50	New Jersey	12.0
3	New Mexico	52.6
49	New York	13.2
40	North Carolina	24.6
15	North Dakota	34.8
15	Ohio	34.8
7	Oklahoma	41.5
26	Oregon	30.5
33	Pennsylvania	29.0
36	Rhode Island	27.3
13	South Carolina	35.3
2	South Dakota	54.8
25	Tennessee	31.7
19	Texas	33.4
21	Utah	32.5
45	Vermont	19.9
47	Virginia	19.2
11	Washington	38.1
41	West Virginia	23.8
46	Wisconsin	19.6
18	Wyoming	33.8

RANK ORDER

RANK	STATE	RATE
1	Alaska	73.3
2	South Dakota	54.8
3	New Mexico	52.6
4	Arkansas	47.3
5	Michigan	45.3
6	Colorado	44.6
7	Oklahoma	41.5
8	Kansas	38.9
9	Nevada	38.6
10	Delaware	38.2
11	Washington	38.1
12	Idaho	35.7
13	South Carolina	35.3
14	Kentucky	35.0
15	North Dakota	34.8
15	Ohio	34.8
17	Minnesota	34.0
18	Wyoming	33.8
19	Texas	33.4
20	Nebraska	33.1
21	Utah	32.5
22	Arizona	32.0
23	Alabama	31.9
24	Mississippi	31.8
25	Tennessee	31.7
26	Oregon	30.5
27	Hawaii	30.3
27	Louisiana	30.3
29	Illinois	30.2
29	Montana	30.2
29	New Hampshire	30.2
32	Florida	29.7
33	Pennsylvania	29.0
34	Maine	28.5
35	Iowa	28.4
36	Rhode Island	27.3
37	Missouri	26.8
38	Massachusetts	25.8
39	Indiana	25.5
40	North Carolina	24.6
41	West Virginia	23.8
42	California	23.6
43	Georgia	23.4
44	Maryland	20.3
45	Vermont	19.9
46	Wisconsin	19.6
47	Virginia	19.2
48	Connecticut	18.5
49	New York	13.2
50	New Jersey	12.0

District of Columbia   25.0

Source: Reported data from the Federal Bureau of Investigation
    "Crime in the United States 2009" (Uniform Crime Reports, September 13, 2010, http://www.fbi.gov/ucr/ucr.htm)
*Forcible rape is the carnal knowledge of a female forcibly and against her will. Assaults or attempts to commit rape by force or threat of force are included. However, statutory rape without force and other sex offenses are excluded.

Robberies in 2009

National Total = 408,217 Robberies*

ALPHA ORDER

RANK	STATE	ROBBERIES	% of USA
19	Alabama	6,259	1.5%
42	Alaska	655	0.2%
14	Arizona	8,099	2.0%
31	Arkansas	2,582	0.6%
1	California	64,093	15.7%
28	Colorado	3,387	0.8%
25	Connecticut	3,990	1.0%
35	Delaware	1,671	0.4%
3	Florida	30,911	7.6%
8	Georgia	14,603	3.6%
39	Hawaii	1,034	0.3%
45	Idaho	245	0.1%
5	Illinois	22,923	5.6%
17	Indiana	7,352	1.8%
38	Iowa	1,195	0.3%
34	Kansas	1,786	0.4%
26	Kentucky	3,629	0.9%
21	Louisiana	6,105	1.5%
44	Maine	399	0.1%
10	Maryland	12,007	2.9%
16	Massachusetts	7,427	1.8%
9	Michigan	12,330	3.0%
27	Minnesota	3,619	0.9%
30	Mississippi	2,965	0.7%
15	Missouri	7,452	1.8%
46	Montana	216	0.1%
37	Nebraska	1,219	0.3%
22	Nevada	6,021	1.5%
43	New Hampshire	455	0.1%
12	New Jersey	11,639	2.9%
33	New Mexico	1,870	0.5%
4	New York	28,136	6.9%
11	North Carolina	11,825	2.9%
49	North Dakota	105	0.0%
6	Ohio	17,782	4.4%
29	Oklahoma	3,343	0.8%
32	Oregon	2,461	0.6%
7	Pennsylvania	17,514	4.3%
41	Rhode Island	786	0.2%
23	South Carolina	5,735	1.4%
47	South Dakota	111	0.0%
13	Tennessee	9,647	2.4%
2	Texas	38,035	9.3%
36	Utah	1,299	0.3%
47	Vermont	111	0.0%
20	Virginia	6,257	1.5%
18	Washington	6,699	1.6%
40	West Virginia	917	0.2%
24	Wisconsin	4,850	1.2%
50	Wyoming	77	0.0%

RANK ORDER

RANK	STATE	ROBBERIES	% of USA
1	California	64,093	15.7%
2	Texas	38,035	9.3%
3	Florida	30,911	7.6%
4	New York	28,136	6.9%
5	Illinois	22,923	5.6%
6	Ohio	17,782	4.4%
7	Pennsylvania	17,514	4.3%
8	Georgia	14,603	3.6%
9	Michigan	12,330	3.0%
10	Maryland	12,007	2.9%
11	North Carolina	11,825	2.9%
12	New Jersey	11,639	2.9%
13	Tennessee	9,647	2.4%
14	Arizona	8,099	2.0%
15	Missouri	7,452	1.8%
16	Massachusetts	7,427	1.8%
17	Indiana	7,352	1.8%
18	Washington	6,699	1.6%
19	Alabama	6,259	1.5%
20	Virginia	6,257	1.5%
21	Louisiana	6,105	1.5%
22	Nevada	6,021	1.5%
23	South Carolina	5,735	1.4%
24	Wisconsin	4,850	1.2%
25	Connecticut	3,990	1.0%
26	Kentucky	3,629	0.9%
27	Minnesota	3,619	0.9%
28	Colorado	3,387	0.8%
29	Oklahoma	3,343	0.8%
30	Mississippi	2,965	0.7%
31	Arkansas	2,582	0.6%
32	Oregon	2,461	0.6%
33	New Mexico	1,870	0.5%
34	Kansas	1,786	0.4%
35	Delaware	1,671	0.4%
36	Utah	1,299	0.3%
37	Nebraska	1,219	0.3%
38	Iowa	1,195	0.3%
39	Hawaii	1,034	0.3%
40	West Virginia	917	0.2%
41	Rhode Island	786	0.2%
42	Alaska	655	0.2%
43	New Hampshire	455	0.1%
44	Maine	399	0.1%
45	Idaho	245	0.1%
46	Montana	216	0.1%
47	South Dakota	111	0.0%
47	Vermont	111	0.0%
49	North Dakota	105	0.0%
50	Wyoming	77	0.0%
	District of Columbia	4,389	1.1%

Source: Reported data from the Federal Bureau of Investigation
    "Crime in the United States 2009" (Uniform Crime Reports, September 13, 2010, http://www.fbi.gov/ucr/ucr.htm)
*Robbery is the taking or attempting to take anything of value by force or threat of force.

Robbery Rate in 2009

National Rate = 133.0 Robberies per 100,000 Population*

ALPHA ORDER

RANK	STATE	RATE
15	Alabama	132.9
26	Alaska	93.8
20	Arizona	122.8
29	Arkansas	89.4
5	California	173.4
37	Colorado	67.4
22	Connecticut	113.4
3	Delaware	188.8
6	Florida	166.7
10	Georgia	148.6
32	Hawaii	79.8
48	Idaho	15.8
4	Illinois	177.6
21	Indiana	114.5
42	Iowa	39.7
39	Kansas	63.4
31	Kentucky	84.1
13	Louisiana	135.9
44	Maine	30.3
2	Maryland	210.7
23	Massachusetts	112.6
19	Michigan	123.7
35	Minnesota	68.7
25	Mississippi	100.4
18	Missouri	124.5
45	Montana	22.2
36	Nebraska	67.8
1	Nevada	227.8
43	New Hampshire	34.4
14	New Jersey	133.7
27	New Mexico	93.1
11	New York	144.0
16	North Carolina	126.1
47	North Dakota	16.2
7	Ohio	154.1
28	Oklahoma	90.7
38	Oregon	64.3
12	Pennsylvania	138.9
34	Rhode Island	74.6
17	South Carolina	125.7
50	South Dakota	13.7
9	Tennessee	153.2
8	Texas	153.5
41	Utah	46.6
46	Vermont	17.9
33	Virginia	79.4
24	Washington	100.5
40	West Virginia	50.4
30	Wisconsin	85.8
49	Wyoming	14.1

RANK ORDER

RANK	STATE	RATE
1	Nevada	227.8
2	Maryland	210.7
3	Delaware	188.8
4	Illinois	177.6
5	California	173.4
6	Florida	166.7
7	Ohio	154.1
8	Texas	153.5
9	Tennessee	153.2
10	Georgia	148.6
11	New York	144.0
12	Pennsylvania	138.9
13	Louisiana	135.9
14	New Jersey	133.7
15	Alabama	132.9
16	North Carolina	126.1
17	South Carolina	125.7
18	Missouri	124.5
19	Michigan	123.7
20	Arizona	122.8
21	Indiana	114.5
22	Connecticut	113.4
23	Massachusetts	112.6
24	Washington	100.5
25	Mississippi	100.4
26	Alaska	93.8
27	New Mexico	93.1
28	Oklahoma	90.7
29	Arkansas	89.4
30	Wisconsin	85.8
31	Kentucky	84.1
32	Hawaii	79.8
33	Virginia	79.4
34	Rhode Island	74.6
35	Minnesota	68.7
36	Nebraska	67.8
37	Colorado	67.4
38	Oregon	64.3
39	Kansas	63.4
40	West Virginia	50.4
41	Utah	46.6
42	Iowa	39.7
43	New Hampshire	34.4
44	Maine	30.3
45	Montana	22.2
46	Vermont	17.9
47	North Dakota	16.2
48	Idaho	15.8
49	Wyoming	14.1
50	South Dakota	13.7
	District of Columbia	731.9

Source: Reported data from the Federal Bureau of Investigation
"Crime in the United States 2009" (Uniform Crime Reports, September 13, 2010, http://www.fbi.gov/ucr/ucr.htm)
*Robbery is the taking or attempting to take anything of value by force or threat of force.

Aggravated Assaults in 2009

National Total = 806,843 Aggravated Assaults*

ALPHA ORDER

RANK	STATE	ASSAULTS	% of USA
20	Alabama	13,093	1.6%
39	Alaska	3,232	0.4%
16	Arizona	16,366	2.0%
25	Arkansas	10,830	1.3%
1	California	99,681	12.4%
24	Colorado	11,172	1.4%
34	Connecticut	5,760	0.7%
38	Delaware	3,585	0.4%
2	Florida	76,112	9.4%
9	Georgia	24,410	3.0%
42	Hawaii	2,111	0.3%
41	Idaho	2,711	0.3%
5	Illinois	36,588	4.5%
22	Indiana	12,102	1.5%
31	Iowa	6,315	0.8%
29	Kansas	8,277	1.0%
33	Kentucky	5,843	0.7%
15	Louisiana	19,855	2.5%
49	Maine	778	0.1%
13	Maryland	20,022	2.5%
12	Massachusetts	20,836	2.6%
6	Michigan	32,076	4.0%
30	Minnesota	7,360	0.9%
35	Mississippi	4,210	0.5%
14	Missouri	20,002	2.5%
43	Montana	1,935	0.2%
40	Nebraska	3,205	0.4%
23	Nevada	11,360	1.4%
45	New Hampshire	1,249	0.2%
18	New Jersey	14,122	1.8%
27	New Mexico	9,338	1.2%
4	New York	43,676	5.4%
10	North Carolina	23,304	2.9%
47	North Dakota	958	0.1%
17	Ohio	16,009	2.0%
19	Oklahoma	13,374	1.7%
32	Oregon	6,030	0.7%
8	Pennsylvania	26,139	3.2%
44	Rhode Island	1,556	0.2%
11	South Carolina	22,962	2.8%
48	South Dakota	931	0.1%
7	Tennessee	29,940	3.7%
3	Texas	74,018	9.2%
37	Utah	3,683	0.5%
50	Vermont	575	0.1%
26	Virginia	9,764	1.2%
21	Washington	12,639	1.6%
36	West Virginia	3,962	0.5%
28	Wisconsin	8,431	1.0%
46	Wyoming	968	0.1%

RANK ORDER

RANK	STATE	ASSAULTS	% of USA
1	California	99,681	12.4%
2	Florida	76,112	9.4%
3	Texas	74,018	9.2%
4	New York	43,676	5.4%
5	Illinois	36,588	4.5%
6	Michigan	32,076	4.0%
7	Tennessee	29,940	3.7%
8	Pennsylvania	26,139	3.2%
9	Georgia	24,410	3.0%
10	North Carolina	23,304	2.9%
11	South Carolina	22,962	2.8%
12	Massachusetts	20,836	2.6%
13	Maryland	20,022	2.5%
14	Missouri	20,002	2.5%
15	Louisiana	19,855	2.5%
16	Arizona	16,366	2.0%
17	Ohio	16,009	2.0%
18	New Jersey	14,122	1.8%
19	Oklahoma	13,374	1.7%
20	Alabama	13,093	1.6%
21	Washington	12,639	1.6%
22	Indiana	12,102	1.5%
23	Nevada	11,360	1.4%
24	Colorado	11,172	1.4%
25	Arkansas	10,830	1.3%
26	Virginia	9,764	1.2%
27	New Mexico	9,338	1.2%
28	Wisconsin	8,431	1.0%
29	Kansas	8,277	1.0%
30	Minnesota	7,360	0.9%
31	Iowa	6,315	0.8%
32	Oregon	6,030	0.7%
33	Kentucky	5,843	0.7%
34	Connecticut	5,760	0.7%
35	Mississippi	4,210	0.5%
36	West Virginia	3,962	0.5%
37	Utah	3,683	0.5%
38	Delaware	3,585	0.4%
39	Alaska	3,232	0.4%
40	Nebraska	3,205	0.4%
41	Idaho	2,711	0.3%
42	Hawaii	2,111	0.3%
43	Montana	1,935	0.2%
44	Rhode Island	1,556	0.2%
45	New Hampshire	1,249	0.2%
46	Wyoming	968	0.1%
47	North Dakota	958	0.1%
48	South Dakota	931	0.1%
49	Maine	778	0.1%
50	Vermont	575	0.1%
	District of Columbia	3,388	0.4%

Source: Reported data from the Federal Bureau of Investigation
   "Crime in the United States 2009" (Uniform Crime Reports, September 13, 2010, http://www.fbi.gov/ucr/ucr.htm)
*Aggravated assault is an attack for the purpose of inflicting severe bodily injury.

Aggravated Assault Rate in 2009

National Rate = 262.8 Aggravated Assaults per 100,000 Population*

ALPHA ORDER

RANK	STATE	RATE
18	Alabama	278.1
4	Alaska	462.7
22	Arizona	248.1
9	Arkansas	374.8
19	California	269.7
24	Colorado	222.3
34	Connecticut	163.7
8	Delaware	405.0
7	Florida	410.6
21	Georgia	248.3
35	Hawaii	163.0
33	Idaho	175.4
17	Illinois	283.4
30	Indiana	188.4
26	Iowa	210.0
16	Kansas	293.6
44	Kentucky	135.4
5	Louisiana	442.0
50	Maine	59.0
11	Maryland	351.3
14	Massachusetts	316.0
13	Michigan	321.7
42	Minnesota	139.8
41	Mississippi	142.6
12	Missouri	334.1
28	Montana	198.5
31	Nebraska	178.4
6	Nevada	429.8
48	New Hampshire	94.3
36	New Jersey	162.2
3	New Mexico	464.7
23	New York	223.5
20	North Carolina	248.4
39	North Dakota	148.1
43	Ohio	138.7
10	Oklahoma	362.7
37	Oregon	157.6
27	Pennsylvania	207.4
40	Rhode Island	147.7
1	South Carolina	503.4
47	South Dakota	114.6
2	Tennessee	475.5
15	Texas	298.7
45	Utah	132.3
49	Vermont	92.5
46	Virginia	123.9
29	Washington	189.7
25	West Virginia	217.7
38	Wisconsin	149.1
32	Wyoming	177.9

RANK ORDER

RANK	STATE	RATE
1	South Carolina	503.4
2	Tennessee	475.5
3	New Mexico	464.7
4	Alaska	462.7
5	Louisiana	442.0
6	Nevada	429.8
7	Florida	410.6
8	Delaware	405.0
9	Arkansas	374.8
10	Oklahoma	362.7
11	Maryland	351.3
12	Missouri	334.1
13	Michigan	321.7
14	Massachusetts	316.0
15	Texas	298.7
16	Kansas	293.6
17	Illinois	283.4
18	Alabama	278.1
19	California	269.7
20	North Carolina	248.4
21	Georgia	248.3
22	Arizona	248.1
23	New York	223.5
24	Colorado	222.3
25	West Virginia	217.7
26	Iowa	210.0
27	Pennsylvania	207.4
28	Montana	198.5
29	Washington	189.7
30	Indiana	188.4
31	Nebraska	178.4
32	Wyoming	177.9
33	Idaho	175.4
34	Connecticut	163.7
35	Hawaii	163.0
36	New Jersey	162.2
37	Oregon	157.6
38	Wisconsin	149.1
39	North Dakota	148.1
40	Rhode Island	147.7
41	Mississippi	142.6
42	Minnesota	139.8
43	Ohio	138.7
44	Kentucky	135.4
45	Utah	132.3
46	Virginia	123.9
47	South Dakota	114.6
48	New Hampshire	94.3
49	Vermont	92.5
50	Maine	59.0
	District of Columbia	565.0

Source: Reported data from the Federal Bureau of Investigation
"Crime in the United States 2009" (Uniform Crime Reports, September 13, 2010, http://www.fbi.gov/ucr/ucr.htm)
*Aggravated assault is an attack for the purpose of inflicting severe bodily injury.

Property Crimes in 2009

National Total = 9,320,971 Property Crimes*

ALPHA ORDER

RANK	STATE	CRIMES	% of USA
19	Alabama	177,629	1.9%
46	Alaska	20,577	0.2%
13	Arizona	234,582	2.5%
28	Arkansas	109,038	1.2%
1	California	1,009,614	10.8%
25	Colorado	133,968	1.4%
33	Connecticut	82,181	0.9%
42	Delaware	29,648	0.3%
3	Florida	712,010	7.6%
6	Georgia	360,400	3.9%
38	Hawaii	47,419	0.5%
41	Idaho	30,741	0.3%
7	Illinois	353,347	3.8%
15	Indiana	200,160	2.1%
36	Iowa	69,441	0.7%
31	Kansas	90,420	1.0%
29	Kentucky	108,401	1.2%
21	Louisiana	170,456	1.8%
40	Maine	31,685	0.3%
17	Maryland	182,422	2.0%
22	Massachusetts	151,914	1.6%
9	Michigan	282,918	3.0%
24	Minnesota	139,083	1.5%
32	Mississippi	87,181	0.9%
14	Missouri	202,698	2.2%
45	Montana	24,024	0.3%
37	Nebraska	49,614	0.5%
34	Nevada	80,763	0.9%
43	New Hampshire	28,624	0.3%
18	New Jersey	181,097	1.9%
35	New Mexico	75,078	0.8%
4	New York	378,315	4.1%
8	North Carolina	344,098	3.7%
50	North Dakota	12,502	0.1%
5	Ohio	377,553	4.1%
26	Oklahoma	131,769	1.4%
27	Oregon	113,511	1.2%
10	Pennsylvania	277,512	3.0%
44	Rhode Island	27,497	0.3%
20	South Carolina	177,369	1.9%
49	South Dakota	13,968	0.1%
12	Tennessee	236,365	2.5%
2	Texas	995,145	10.7%
30	Utah	91,205	1.0%
47	Vermont	14,931	0.2%
16	Virginia	191,453	2.1%
11	Washington	244,368	2.6%
39	West Virginia	45,981	0.5%
23	Wisconsin	147,486	1.6%
48	Wyoming	14,354	0.2%

RANK ORDER

RANK	STATE	CRIMES	% of USA
1	California	1,009,614	10.8%
2	Texas	995,145	10.7%
3	Florida	712,010	7.6%
4	New York	378,315	4.1%
5	Ohio	377,553	4.1%
6	Georgia	360,400	3.9%
7	Illinois	353,347	3.8%
8	North Carolina	344,098	3.7%
9	Michigan	282,918	3.0%
10	Pennsylvania	277,512	3.0%
11	Washington	244,368	2.6%
12	Tennessee	236,365	2.5%
13	Arizona	234,582	2.5%
14	Missouri	202,698	2.2%
15	Indiana	200,160	2.1%
16	Virginia	191,453	2.1%
17	Maryland	182,422	2.0%
18	New Jersey	181,097	1.9%
19	Alabama	177,629	1.9%
20	South Carolina	177,369	1.9%
21	Louisiana	170,456	1.8%
22	Massachusetts	151,914	1.6%
23	Wisconsin	147,486	1.6%
24	Minnesota	139,083	1.5%
25	Colorado	133,968	1.4%
26	Oklahoma	131,769	1.4%
27	Oregon	113,511	1.2%
28	Arkansas	109,038	1.2%
29	Kentucky	108,401	1.2%
30	Utah	91,205	1.0%
31	Kansas	90,420	1.0%
32	Mississippi	87,181	0.9%
33	Connecticut	82,181	0.9%
34	Nevada	80,763	0.9%
35	New Mexico	75,078	0.8%
36	Iowa	69,441	0.7%
37	Nebraska	49,614	0.5%
38	Hawaii	47,419	0.5%
39	West Virginia	45,981	0.5%
40	Maine	31,685	0.3%
41	Idaho	30,741	0.3%
42	Delaware	29,648	0.3%
43	New Hampshire	28,624	0.3%
44	Rhode Island	27,497	0.3%
45	Montana	24,024	0.3%
46	Alaska	20,577	0.2%
47	Vermont	14,931	0.2%
48	Wyoming	14,354	0.2%
49	South Dakota	13,968	0.1%
50	North Dakota	12,502	0.1%
	District of Columbia	28,456	0.3%

Source: Reported data from the Federal Bureau of Investigation
"Crime in the United States 2009" (Uniform Crime Reports, September 13, 2010, http://www.fbi.gov/ucr/ucr.htm)
*Property crimes are offenses of burglary, larceny-theft, and motor vehicle theft.

Percent Change in Number of Property Crimes: 2008 to 2009

National Percent Change = 4.6% Decrease*

ALPHA ORDER			RANK ORDER		
RANK	STATE	PERCENT CHANGE	RANK	STATE	PERCENT CHANGE
38	Alabama	(6.7)	1	Oklahoma	4.7
4	Alaska	2.4	2	Hawaii	3.2
50	Arizona	(11.7)	3	Texas	2.6
9	Arkansas	(0.7)	4	Alaska	2.4
36	California	(6.6)	5	New Hampshire	2.0
25	Colorado	(5.1)	6	South Dakota	1.8
30	Connecticut	(5.8)	7	Mississippi	0.9
29	Delaware	(5.5)	8	Louisiana	(0.4)
34	Florida	(6.2)	9	Arkansas	(0.7)
40	Georgia	(6.9)	10	West Virginia	(0.8)
2	Hawaii	3.2	11	New Mexico	(0.9)
23	Idaho	(4.7)	12	Wyoming	(1.1)
41	Illinois	(7.3)	13	Utah	(1.2)
31	Indiana	(6.0)	14	Washington	(1.4)
27	Iowa	(5.2)	15	Maine	(2.3)
24	Kansas	(5.0)	16	New York	(2.6)
27	Kentucky	(5.2)	17	Massachusetts	(2.7)
8	Louisiana	(0.4)	17	Virginia	(2.7)
15	Maine	(2.3)	19	Nebraska	(3.3)
44	Maryland	(7.9)	19	North Dakota	(3.3)
17	Massachusetts	(2.7)	21	Ohio	(3.9)
22	Michigan	(4.0)	22	Michigan	(4.0)
39	Minnesota	(6.8)	23	Idaho	(4.7)
7	Mississippi	0.9	24	Kansas	(5.0)
35	Missouri	(6.4)	25	Colorado	(5.1)
46	Montana	(8.7)	25	Wisconsin	(5.1)
19	Nebraska	(3.3)	27	Iowa	(5.2)
49	Nevada	(10.1)	27	Kentucky	(5.2)
5	New Hampshire	2.0	29	Delaware	(5.5)
47	New Jersey	(9.1)	30	Connecticut	(5.8)
11	New Mexico	(0.9)	31	Indiana	(6.0)
16	New York	(2.6)	32	Tennessee	(6.1)
43	North Carolina	(7.7)	32	Vermont	(6.1)
19	North Dakota	(3.3)	34	Florida	(6.2)
21	Ohio	(3.9)	35	Missouri	(6.4)
1	Oklahoma	4.7	36	California	(6.6)
48	Oregon	(9.2)	36	South Carolina	(6.6)
42	Pennsylvania	(7.6)	38	Alabama	(6.7)
45	Rhode Island	(8.0)	39	Minnesota	(6.8)
36	South Carolina	(6.6)	40	Georgia	(6.9)
6	South Dakota	1.8	41	Illinois	(7.3)
32	Tennessee	(6.1)	42	Pennsylvania	(7.6)
3	Texas	2.6	43	North Carolina	(7.7)
13	Utah	(1.2)	44	Maryland	(7.9)
32	Vermont	(6.1)	45	Rhode Island	(8.0)
17	Virginia	(2.7)	46	Montana	(8.7)
14	Washington	(1.4)	47	New Jersey	(9.1)
10	West Virginia	(0.8)	48	Oregon	(9.2)
25	Wisconsin	(5.1)	49	Nevada	(10.1)
12	Wyoming	(1.1)	50	Arizona	(11.7)
				District of Columbia	(5.8)

Source: Reported data from the Federal Bureau of Investigation
   "Crime in the United States 2009" (Uniform Crime Reports, September 13, 2010, http://www.fbi.gov/ucr/ucr.htm)
*Property crimes are offenses of burglary, larceny-theft, and motor vehicle theft.

Property Crime Rate in 2009

National Rate = 3,036.1 Property Crimes per 100,000 Population*

ALPHA ORDER

RANK	STATE	RATE
6	Alabama	3,772.4
25	Alaska	2,946.0
14	Arizona	3,556.5
5	Arkansas	3,773.7
29	California	2,731.5
30	Colorado	2,666.2
41	Connecticut	2,335.8
16	Delaware	3,349.6
3	Florida	3,840.8
11	Georgia	3,666.6
12	Hawaii	3,661.2
47	Idaho	1,988.7
28	Illinois	2,736.9
21	Indiana	3,116.2
42	Iowa	2,308.7
19	Kansas	3,207.8
36	Kentucky	2,512.7
4	Louisiana	3,794.6
39	Maine	2,403.5
20	Maryland	3,200.7
43	Massachusetts	2,304.0
26	Michigan	2,837.8
31	Minnesota	2,641.0
24	Mississippi	2,953.3
15	Missouri	3,385.3
37	Montana	2,464.0
27	Nebraska	2,761.5
22	Nevada	3,055.6
45	New Hampshire	2,161.0
46	New Jersey	2,079.7
8	New Mexico	3,735.8
48	New York	1,936.0
9	North Carolina	3,668.1
49	North Dakota	1,932.8
18	Ohio	3,270.9
13	Oklahoma	3,573.8
23	Oregon	2,967.1
44	Pennsylvania	2,201.6
33	Rhode Island	2,610.8
2	South Carolina	3,888.6
50	South Dakota	1,719.4
7	Tennessee	3,754.1
1	Texas	4,015.5
17	Utah	3,275.4
40	Vermont	2,401.4
38	Virginia	2,428.8
10	Washington	3,666.9
35	West Virginia	2,526.7
34	Wisconsin	2,608.2
32	Wyoming	2,637.3

RANK ORDER

RANK	STATE	RATE
1	Texas	4,015.5
2	South Carolina	3,888.6
3	Florida	3,840.8
4	Louisiana	3,794.6
5	Arkansas	3,773.7
6	Alabama	3,772.4
7	Tennessee	3,754.1
8	New Mexico	3,735.8
9	North Carolina	3,668.1
10	Washington	3,666.9
11	Georgia	3,666.6
12	Hawaii	3,661.2
13	Oklahoma	3,573.8
14	Arizona	3,556.5
15	Missouri	3,385.3
16	Delaware	3,349.6
17	Utah	3,275.4
18	Ohio	3,270.9
19	Kansas	3,207.8
20	Maryland	3,200.7
21	Indiana	3,116.2
22	Nevada	3,055.6
23	Oregon	2,967.1
24	Mississippi	2,953.3
25	Alaska	2,946.0
26	Michigan	2,837.8
27	Nebraska	2,761.5
28	Illinois	2,736.9
29	California	2,731.5
30	Colorado	2,666.2
31	Minnesota	2,641.0
32	Wyoming	2,637.3
33	Rhode Island	2,610.8
34	Wisconsin	2,608.2
35	West Virginia	2,526.7
36	Kentucky	2,512.7
37	Montana	2,464.0
38	Virginia	2,428.8
39	Maine	2,403.5
40	Vermont	2,401.4
41	Connecticut	2,335.8
42	Iowa	2,308.7
43	Massachusetts	2,304.0
44	Pennsylvania	2,201.6
45	New Hampshire	2,161.0
46	New Jersey	2,079.7
47	Idaho	1,988.7
48	New York	1,936.0
49	North Dakota	1,932.8
50	South Dakota	1,719.4

District of Columbia   4,745.4

Source: Reported data from the Federal Bureau of Investigation
"Crime in the United States 2009" (Uniform Crime Reports, September 13, 2010, http://www.fbi.gov/ucr/ucr.htm)
*Property crimes are offenses of burglary, larceny-theft, and motor vehicle theft.

Percent Change in Property Crime Rate: 2008 to 2009

National Percent Change = 5.5% Decrease*

ALPHA ORDER

RANK ORDER

RANK	STATE	PERCENT CHANGE		RANK	STATE	PERCENT CHANGE
36	Alabama	(7.3)		1	Oklahoma	3.4
4	Alaska	0.9		2	Hawaii	2.6
50	Arizona	(13.0)		3	New Hampshire	1.8
10	Arkansas	(1.4)		4	Alaska	0.9
38	California	(7.5)		5	South Dakota	0.8
32	Colorado	(6.8)		6	Texas	0.6
28	Connecticut	(6.2)		7	Mississippi	0.4
30	Delaware	(6.5)		8	West Virginia	(1.1)
32	Florida	(6.8)		9	Louisiana	(1.3)
43	Georgia	(8.1)		10	Arkansas	(1.4)
2	Hawaii	2.6		11	New Mexico	(2.0)
27	Idaho	(5.8)		12	Maine	(2.2)
39	Illinois	(7.8)		13	Washington	(2.9)
30	Indiana	(6.5)		14	New York	(3.0)
24	Iowa	(5.7)		15	Wyoming	(3.1)
24	Kansas	(5.7)		16	Utah	(3.2)
24	Kentucky	(5.7)		17	Massachusetts	(3.4)
9	Louisiana	(1.3)		18	Michigan	(3.7)
12	Maine	(2.2)		18	Virginia	(3.7)
44	Maryland	(8.6)		20	Ohio	(4.0)
17	Massachusetts	(3.4)		21	Nebraska	(4.1)
18	Michigan	(3.7)		22	North Dakota	(4.2)
37	Minnesota	(7.4)		23	Wisconsin	(5.5)
7	Mississippi	0.4		24	Iowa	(5.7)
34	Missouri	(6.9)		24	Kansas	(5.7)
46	Montana	(9.4)		24	Kentucky	(5.7)
21	Nebraska	(4.1)		27	Idaho	(5.8)
49	Nevada	(11.1)		28	Connecticut	(6.2)
3	New Hampshire	1.8		28	Vermont	(6.2)
47	New Jersey	(9.5)		30	Delaware	(6.5)
11	New Mexico	(2.0)		30	Indiana	(6.5)
14	New York	(3.0)		32	Colorado	(6.8)
45	North Carolina	(9.0)		32	Florida	(6.8)
22	North Dakota	(4.2)		34	Missouri	(6.9)
20	Ohio	(4.0)		34	Tennessee	(6.9)
1	Oklahoma	3.4		36	Alabama	(7.3)
48	Oregon	(10.2)		37	Minnesota	(7.4)
41	Pennsylvania	(7.9)		38	California	(7.5)
42	Rhode Island	(8.0)		39	Illinois	(7.8)
39	South Carolina	(7.8)		39	South Carolina	(7.8)
5	South Dakota	0.8		41	Pennsylvania	(7.9)
34	Tennessee	(6.9)		42	Rhode Island	(8.0)
6	Texas	0.6		43	Georgia	(8.1)
16	Utah	(3.2)		44	Maryland	(8.6)
28	Vermont	(6.2)		45	North Carolina	(9.0)
18	Virginia	(3.7)		46	Montana	(9.4)
13	Washington	(2.9)		47	New Jersey	(9.5)
8	West Virginia	(1.1)		48	Oregon	(10.2)
23	Wisconsin	(5.5)		49	Nevada	(11.1)
15	Wyoming	(3.1)		50	Arizona	(13.0)

District of Columbia   (7.3)

Source: Reported data from the Federal Bureau of Investigation
   "Crime in the United States 2009" (Uniform Crime Reports, September 13, 2010, http://www.fbi.gov/ucr/ucr.htm)
*Property crimes are offenses of burglary, larceny-theft, and motor vehicle theft.

Burglaries in 2009

National Total = 2,199,125 Burglaries*

ALPHA ORDER

RANK	STATE	BURGLARIES	% of USA
15	Alabama	48,837	2.2%
45	Alaska	3,597	0.2%
12	Arizona	53,412	2.4%
22	Arkansas	34,764	1.6%
2	California	230,137	10.5%
28	Colorado	26,649	1.2%
36	Connecticut	15,073	0.7%
40	Delaware	6,932	0.3%
3	Florida	181,884	8.3%
6	Georgia	98,362	4.5%
38	Hawaii	9,178	0.4%
42	Idaho	6,558	0.3%
7	Illinois	77,850	3.5%
14	Indiana	48,910	2.2%
34	Iowa	16,224	0.7%
32	Kansas	19,469	0.9%
25	Kentucky	29,701	1.4%
16	Louisiana	46,246	2.1%
41	Maine	6,728	0.3%
21	Maryland	37,032	1.7%
23	Massachusetts	34,665	1.6%
8	Michigan	75,815	3.4%
29	Minnesota	25,488	1.2%
26	Mississippi	29,162	1.3%
18	Missouri	43,787	2.0%
47	Montana	3,386	0.2%
39	Nebraska	8,701	0.4%
31	Nevada	21,994	1.0%
44	New Hampshire	4,928	0.2%
20	New Jersey	37,262	1.7%
30	New Mexico	22,022	1.0%
10	New York	62,842	2.9%
4	North Carolina	107,830	4.9%
49	North Dakota	2,354	0.1%
5	Ohio	104,213	4.7%
19	Oklahoma	37,975	1.7%
33	Oregon	19,377	0.9%
11	Pennsylvania	54,797	2.5%
43	Rhode Island	5,749	0.3%
17	South Carolina	45,282	2.1%
48	South Dakota	2,479	0.1%
9	Tennessee	63,646	2.9%
1	Texas	240,233	10.9%
35	Utah	15,159	0.7%
46	Vermont	3,452	0.2%
24	Virginia	31,576	1.4%
13	Washington	52,791	2.4%
37	West Virginia	11,951	0.5%
27	Wisconsin	26,740	1.2%
50	Wyoming	2,230	0.1%

RANK ORDER

RANK	STATE	BURGLARIES	% of USA
1	Texas	240,233	10.9%
2	California	230,137	10.5%
3	Florida	181,884	8.3%
4	North Carolina	107,830	4.9%
5	Ohio	104,213	4.7%
6	Georgia	98,362	4.5%
7	Illinois	77,850	3.5%
8	Michigan	75,815	3.4%
9	Tennessee	63,646	2.9%
10	New York	62,842	2.9%
11	Pennsylvania	54,797	2.5%
12	Arizona	53,412	2.4%
13	Washington	52,791	2.4%
14	Indiana	48,910	2.2%
15	Alabama	48,837	2.2%
16	Louisiana	46,246	2.1%
17	South Carolina	45,282	2.1%
18	Missouri	43,787	2.0%
19	Oklahoma	37,975	1.7%
20	New Jersey	37,262	1.7%
21	Maryland	37,032	1.7%
22	Arkansas	34,764	1.6%
23	Massachusetts	34,665	1.6%
24	Virginia	31,576	1.4%
25	Kentucky	29,701	1.4%
26	Mississippi	29,162	1.3%
27	Wisconsin	26,740	1.2%
28	Colorado	26,649	1.2%
29	Minnesota	25,488	1.2%
30	New Mexico	22,022	1.0%
31	Nevada	21,994	1.0%
32	Kansas	19,469	0.9%
33	Oregon	19,377	0.9%
34	Iowa	16,224	0.7%
35	Utah	15,159	0.7%
36	Connecticut	15,073	0.7%
37	West Virginia	11,951	0.5%
38	Hawaii	9,178	0.4%
39	Nebraska	8,701	0.4%
40	Delaware	6,932	0.3%
41	Maine	6,728	0.3%
42	Idaho	6,558	0.3%
43	Rhode Island	5,749	0.3%
44	New Hampshire	4,928	0.2%
45	Alaska	3,597	0.2%
46	Vermont	3,452	0.2%
47	Montana	3,386	0.2%
48	South Dakota	2,479	0.1%
49	North Dakota	2,354	0.1%
50	Wyoming	2,230	0.1%
	District of Columbia	3,696	0.2%

Source: Reported data from the Federal Bureau of Investigation
"Crime in the United States 2009" (Uniform Crime Reports, September 13, 2010, http://www.fbi.gov/ucr/ucr.htm)
*Burglary is the unlawful entry of a structure to commit a felony or theft. Attempts are included.

Burglary Rate in 2009

National Rate = 716.3 Burglaries per 100,000 Population*

ALPHA ORDER

RANK	STATE	RATE
4	Alabama	1,037.2
34	Alaska	515.0
15	Arizona	809.8
1	Arkansas	1,203.1
26	California	622.6
32	Colorado	530.4
41	Connecticut	428.4
17	Delaware	783.2
11	Florida	981.1
8	Georgia	1,000.7
21	Hawaii	708.6
43	Idaho	424.2
27	Illinois	603.0
18	Indiana	761.5
31	Iowa	539.4
22	Kansas	690.7
23	Kentucky	688.5
6	Louisiana	1,029.5
35	Maine	510.4
25	Maryland	649.7
33	Massachusetts	525.7
19	Michigan	760.5
38	Minnesota	484.0
10	Mississippi	987.9
20	Missouri	731.3
48	Montana	347.3
37	Nebraska	484.3
14	Nevada	832.1
46	New Hampshire	372.0
42	New Jersey	427.9
3	New Mexico	1,095.8
49	New York	321.6
2	North Carolina	1,149.5
47	North Dakota	363.9
13	Ohio	902.9
5	Oklahoma	1,030.0
36	Oregon	506.5
40	Pennsylvania	434.7
29	Rhode Island	545.9
9	South Carolina	992.8
50	South Dakota	305.2
7	Tennessee	1,010.9
12	Texas	969.4
30	Utah	544.4
28	Vermont	555.2
45	Virginia	400.6
16	Washington	792.2
24	West Virginia	656.7
39	Wisconsin	472.9
44	Wyoming	409.7

RANK ORDER

RANK	STATE	RATE
1	Arkansas	1,203.1
2	North Carolina	1,149.5
3	New Mexico	1,095.8
4	Alabama	1,037.2
5	Oklahoma	1,030.0
6	Louisiana	1,029.5
7	Tennessee	1,010.9
8	Georgia	1,000.7
9	South Carolina	992.8
10	Mississippi	987.9
11	Florida	981.1
12	Texas	969.4
13	Ohio	902.9
14	Nevada	832.1
15	Arizona	809.8
16	Washington	792.2
17	Delaware	783.2
18	Indiana	761.5
19	Michigan	760.5
20	Missouri	731.3
21	Hawaii	708.6
22	Kansas	690.7
23	Kentucky	688.5
24	West Virginia	656.7
25	Maryland	649.7
26	California	622.6
27	Illinois	603.0
28	Vermont	555.2
29	Rhode Island	545.9
30	Utah	544.4
31	Iowa	539.4
32	Colorado	530.4
33	Massachusetts	525.7
34	Alaska	515.0
35	Maine	510.4
36	Oregon	506.5
37	Nebraska	484.3
38	Minnesota	484.0
39	Wisconsin	472.9
40	Pennsylvania	434.7
41	Connecticut	428.4
42	New Jersey	427.9
43	Idaho	424.2
44	Wyoming	409.7
45	Virginia	400.6
46	New Hampshire	372.0
47	North Dakota	363.9
48	Montana	347.3
49	New York	321.6
50	South Dakota	305.2

| | District of Columbia | 616.4 |

Source: Reported data from the Federal Bureau of Investigation
"Crime in the United States 2009" (Uniform Crime Reports, September 13, 2010, http://www.fbi.gov/ucr/ucr.htm)
*Burglary is the unlawful entry of a structure to commit a felony or theft. Attempts are included.

Larceny-Thefts in 2009

National Total = 6,327,230 Larceny-Thefts*

ALPHA ORDER

RANK	STATE	THEFTS	% of USA
20	Alabama	117,711	1.9%
46	Alaska	15,291	0.2%
13	Arizona	155,184	2.5%
30	Arkansas	68,171	1.1%
2	California	615,456	9.7%
25	Colorado	94,861	1.5%
32	Connecticut	59,632	0.9%
43	Delaware	20,809	0.3%
3	Florida	479,867	7.6%
7	Georgia	228,893	3.6%
38	Hawaii	33,422	0.5%
41	Idaho	22,741	0.4%
6	Illinois	248,821	3.9%
16	Indiana	137,371	2.2%
34	Iowa	49,329	0.8%
31	Kansas	64,997	1.0%
28	Kentucky	72,620	1.1%
21	Louisiana	112,493	1.8%
40	Maine	23,936	0.4%
18	Maryland	125,771	2.0%
23	Massachusetts	105,514	1.7%
10	Michigan	177,720	2.8%
24	Minnesota	105,076	1.7%
33	Mississippi	52,618	0.8%
15	Missouri	141,432	2.2%
45	Montana	19,182	0.3%
37	Nebraska	37,432	0.6%
36	Nevada	46,390	0.7%
42	New Hampshire	22,572	0.4%
17	New Jersey	128,327	2.0%
35	New Mexico	46,580	0.7%
4	New York	293,603	4.6%
8	North Carolina	216,244	3.4%
50	North Dakota	9,296	0.1%
5	Ohio	250,450	4.0%
27	Oklahoma	83,390	1.3%
26	Oregon	84,265	1.3%
9	Pennsylvania	204,894	3.2%
44	Rhode Island	19,355	0.3%
19	South Carolina	118,521	1.9%
49	South Dakota	10,676	0.2%
12	Tennessee	157,746	2.5%
1	Texas	678,353	10.7%
29	Utah	69,142	1.1%
48	Vermont	11,031	0.2%
14	Virginia	148,458	2.3%
11	Washington	167,897	2.7%
39	West Virginia	31,289	0.5%
22	Wisconsin	111,820	1.8%
47	Wyoming	11,353	0.2%

RANK ORDER

RANK	STATE	THEFTS	% of USA
1	Texas	678,353	10.7%
2	California	615,456	9.7%
3	Florida	479,867	7.6%
4	New York	293,603	4.6%
5	Ohio	250,450	4.0%
6	Illinois	248,821	3.9%
7	Georgia	228,893	3.6%
8	North Carolina	216,244	3.4%
9	Pennsylvania	204,894	3.2%
10	Michigan	177,720	2.8%
11	Washington	167,897	2.7%
12	Tennessee	157,746	2.5%
13	Arizona	155,184	2.5%
14	Virginia	148,458	2.3%
15	Missouri	141,432	2.2%
16	Indiana	137,371	2.2%
17	New Jersey	128,327	2.0%
18	Maryland	125,771	2.0%
19	South Carolina	118,521	1.9%
20	Alabama	117,711	1.9%
21	Louisiana	112,493	1.8%
22	Wisconsin	111,820	1.8%
23	Massachusetts	105,514	1.7%
24	Minnesota	105,076	1.7%
25	Colorado	94,861	1.5%
26	Oregon	84,265	1.3%
27	Oklahoma	83,390	1.3%
28	Kentucky	72,620	1.1%
29	Utah	69,142	1.1%
30	Arkansas	68,171	1.1%
31	Kansas	64,997	1.0%
32	Connecticut	59,632	0.9%
33	Mississippi	52,618	0.8%
34	Iowa	49,329	0.8%
35	New Mexico	46,580	0.7%
36	Nevada	46,390	0.7%
37	Nebraska	37,432	0.6%
38	Hawaii	33,422	0.5%
39	West Virginia	31,289	0.5%
40	Maine	23,936	0.4%
41	Idaho	22,741	0.4%
42	New Hampshire	22,572	0.4%
43	Delaware	20,809	0.3%
44	Rhode Island	19,355	0.3%
45	Montana	19,182	0.3%
46	Alaska	15,291	0.2%
47	Wyoming	11,353	0.2%
48	Vermont	11,031	0.2%
49	South Dakota	10,676	0.2%
50	North Dakota	9,296	0.1%
	District of Columbia	19,228	0.3%

Source: Reported data from the Federal Bureau of Investigation
"Crime in the United States 2009" (Uniform Crime Reports, September 13, 2010, http://www.fbi.gov/ucr/ucr.htm)
*Larceny-theft is the unlawful taking of property without use of force, violence, or fraud. Attempts are included. Motor vehicle thefts are excluded.

Larceny-Theft Rate in 2009

National Rate = 2,060.9 Larceny-Thefts per 100,000 Population*

ALPHA ORDER

RANK	STATE	RATE
8	Alabama	2,499.9
21	Alaska	2,189.2
12	Arizona	2,352.8
11	Arkansas	2,359.3
42	California	1,665.1
30	Colorado	1,887.9
40	Connecticut	1,694.9
13	Delaware	2,351.0
3	Florida	2,588.6
14	Georgia	2,328.7
4	Hawaii	2,580.5
48	Idaho	1,471.1
29	Illinois	1,927.3
23	Indiana	2,138.7
43	Iowa	1,640.0
16	Kansas	2,305.9
41	Kentucky	1,683.3
7	Louisiana	2,504.3
33	Maine	1,815.7
19	Maryland	2,206.7
45	Massachusetts	1,600.3
34	Michigan	1,782.6
26	Minnesota	1,995.3
35	Mississippi	1,782.5
10	Missouri	2,362.1
28	Montana	1,967.4
25	Nebraska	2,083.5
37	Nevada	1,755.1
39	New Hampshire	1,704.1
47	New Jersey	1,473.7
15	New Mexico	2,317.8
46	New York	1,502.5
17	North Carolina	2,305.2
49	North Dakota	1,437.1
22	Ohio	2,169.8
18	Oklahoma	2,261.7
20	Oregon	2,202.6
44	Pennsylvania	1,625.5
32	Rhode Island	1,837.7
2	South Carolina	2,598.4
50	South Dakota	1,314.2
6	Tennessee	2,505.4
1	Texas	2,737.2
9	Utah	2,483.0
36	Vermont	1,774.2
31	Virginia	1,883.4
5	Washington	2,519.4
38	West Virginia	1,719.4
27	Wisconsin	1,977.4
24	Wyoming	2,085.9

RANK ORDER

RANK	STATE	RATE
1	Texas	2,737.2
2	South Carolina	2,598.4
3	Florida	2,588.6
4	Hawaii	2,580.5
5	Washington	2,519.4
6	Tennessee	2,505.4
7	Louisiana	2,504.3
8	Alabama	2,499.9
9	Utah	2,483.0
10	Missouri	2,362.1
11	Arkansas	2,359.3
12	Arizona	2,352.8
13	Delaware	2,351.0
14	Georgia	2,328.7
15	New Mexico	2,317.8
16	Kansas	2,305.9
17	North Carolina	2,305.2
18	Oklahoma	2,261.7
19	Maryland	2,206.7
20	Oregon	2,202.6
21	Alaska	2,189.2
22	Ohio	2,169.8
23	Indiana	2,138.7
24	Wyoming	2,085.9
25	Nebraska	2,083.5
26	Minnesota	1,995.3
27	Wisconsin	1,977.4
28	Montana	1,967.4
29	Illinois	1,927.3
30	Colorado	1,887.9
31	Virginia	1,883.4
32	Rhode Island	1,837.7
33	Maine	1,815.7
34	Michigan	1,782.6
35	Mississippi	1,782.5
36	Vermont	1,774.2
37	Nevada	1,755.1
38	West Virginia	1,719.4
39	New Hampshire	1,704.1
40	Connecticut	1,694.9
41	Kentucky	1,683.3
42	California	1,665.1
43	Iowa	1,640.0
44	Pennsylvania	1,625.5
45	Massachusetts	1,600.3
46	New York	1,502.5
47	New Jersey	1,473.7
48	Idaho	1,471.1
49	North Dakota	1,437.1
50	South Dakota	1,314.2

| | District of Columbia | 3,206.5 |

Source: Reported data from the Federal Bureau of Investigation
    "Crime in the United States 2009" (Uniform Crime Reports, September 13, 2010, http://www.fbi.gov/ucr/ucr.htm)
*Larceny-theft is the unlawful taking of property without use of force, violence, or fraud. Attempts are included. Motor vehicle thefts are excluded.

Motor Vehicle Thefts in 2009

National Total = 794,616 Motor Vehicle Thefts*

ALPHA ORDER

RANK	STATE	THEFTS	% of USA
24	Alabama	11,081	1.4%
42	Alaska	1,689	0.2%
7	Arizona	25,986	3.3%
32	Arkansas	6,103	0.8%
1	California	164,021	20.6%
19	Colorado	12,458	1.6%
29	Connecticut	7,476	0.9%
41	Delaware	1,907	0.2%
3	Florida	50,259	6.3%
4	Georgia	33,145	4.2%
36	Hawaii	4,819	0.6%
44	Idaho	1,442	0.2%
6	Illinois	26,676	3.4%
17	Indiana	13,879	1.7%
37	Iowa	3,888	0.5%
34	Kansas	5,954	0.7%
33	Kentucky	6,080	0.8%
22	Louisiana	11,717	1.5%
46	Maine	1,021	0.1%
12	Maryland	19,619	2.5%
21	Massachusetts	11,735	1.5%
5	Michigan	29,383	3.7%
28	Minnesota	8,519	1.1%
35	Mississippi	5,401	0.7%
14	Missouri	17,479	2.2%
43	Montana	1,456	0.2%
38	Nebraska	3,481	0.4%
20	Nevada	12,379	1.6%
45	New Hampshire	1,124	0.1%
15	New Jersey	15,508	2.0%
31	New Mexico	6,476	0.8%
10	New York	21,870	2.8%
11	North Carolina	20,024	2.5%
47	North Dakota	852	0.1%
9	Ohio	22,890	2.9%
25	Oklahoma	10,404	1.3%
26	Oregon	9,869	1.2%
13	Pennsylvania	17,821	2.2%
40	Rhode Island	2,393	0.3%
18	South Carolina	13,566	1.7%
48	South Dakota	813	0.1%
16	Tennessee	14,973	1.9%
2	Texas	76,559	9.6%
30	Utah	6,904	0.9%
50	Vermont	448	0.1%
23	Virginia	11,419	1.4%
8	Washington	23,680	3.0%
39	West Virginia	2,741	0.3%
27	Wisconsin	8,926	1.1%
49	Wyoming	771	0.1%

RANK ORDER

RANK	STATE	THEFTS	% of USA
1	California	164,021	20.6%
2	Texas	76,559	9.6%
3	Florida	50,259	6.3%
4	Georgia	33,145	4.2%
5	Michigan	29,383	3.7%
6	Illinois	26,676	3.4%
7	Arizona	25,986	3.3%
8	Washington	23,680	3.0%
9	Ohio	22,890	2.9%
10	New York	21,870	2.8%
11	North Carolina	20,024	2.5%
12	Maryland	19,619	2.5%
13	Pennsylvania	17,821	2.2%
14	Missouri	17,479	2.2%
15	New Jersey	15,508	2.0%
16	Tennessee	14,973	1.9%
17	Indiana	13,879	1.7%
18	South Carolina	13,566	1.7%
19	Colorado	12,458	1.6%
20	Nevada	12,379	1.6%
21	Massachusetts	11,735	1.5%
22	Louisiana	11,717	1.5%
23	Virginia	11,419	1.4%
24	Alabama	11,081	1.4%
25	Oklahoma	10,404	1.3%
26	Oregon	9,869	1.2%
27	Wisconsin	8,926	1.1%
28	Minnesota	8,519	1.1%
29	Connecticut	7,476	0.9%
30	Utah	6,904	0.9%
31	New Mexico	6,476	0.8%
32	Arkansas	6,103	0.8%
33	Kentucky	6,080	0.8%
34	Kansas	5,954	0.7%
35	Mississippi	5,401	0.7%
36	Hawaii	4,819	0.6%
37	Iowa	3,888	0.5%
38	Nebraska	3,481	0.4%
39	West Virginia	2,741	0.3%
40	Rhode Island	2,393	0.3%
41	Delaware	1,907	0.2%
42	Alaska	1,689	0.2%
43	Montana	1,456	0.2%
44	Idaho	1,442	0.2%
45	New Hampshire	1,124	0.1%
46	Maine	1,021	0.1%
47	North Dakota	852	0.1%
48	South Dakota	813	0.1%
49	Wyoming	771	0.1%
50	Vermont	448	0.1%
	District of Columbia	5,532	0.7%

Source: Reported data from the Federal Bureau of Investigation
"Crime in the United States 2009" (Uniform Crime Reports, September 13, 2010, http://www.fbi.gov/ucr/ucr.htm)
*Includes the theft or attempted theft of a self-propelled vehicle. Excludes motorboats, construction equipment, airplanes, and farming equipment.

Motor Vehicle Theft Rate in 2009

National Rate = 258.8 Motor Vehicle Thefts per 100,000 Population*

ALPHA ORDER

RANK	STATE	RATE
21	Alabama	235.3
19	Alaska	241.8
3	Arizona	394.0
27	Arkansas	211.2
2	California	443.8
17	Colorado	247.9
26	Connecticut	212.5
24	Delaware	215.5
14	Florida	271.1
7	Georgia	337.2
4	Hawaii	372.1
47	Idaho	93.3
29	Illinois	206.6
23	Indiana	216.1
44	Iowa	129.3
27	Kansas	211.2
42	Kentucky	140.9
15	Louisiana	260.8
49	Maine	77.4
6	Maryland	344.2
34	Massachusetts	178.0
11	Michigan	294.7
35	Minnesota	161.8
32	Mississippi	183.0
12	Missouri	291.9
38	Montana	149.3
31	Nebraska	193.8
1	Nevada	468.4
48	New Hampshire	84.9
33	New Jersey	178.1
8	New Mexico	322.2
45	New York	111.9
25	North Carolina	213.5
43	North Dakota	131.7
30	Ohio	198.3
13	Oklahoma	282.2
16	Oregon	258.0
41	Pennsylvania	141.4
22	Rhode Island	227.2
10	South Carolina	297.4
46	South Dakota	100.1
20	Tennessee	237.8
9	Texas	308.9
17	Utah	247.9
50	Vermont	72.1
39	Virginia	144.9
5	Washington	355.3
37	West Virginia	150.6
36	Wisconsin	157.8
40	Wyoming	141.7

RANK ORDER

RANK	STATE	RATE
1	Nevada	468.4
2	California	443.8
3	Arizona	394.0
4	Hawaii	372.1
5	Washington	355.3
6	Maryland	344.2
7	Georgia	337.2
8	New Mexico	322.2
9	Texas	308.9
10	South Carolina	297.4
11	Michigan	294.7
12	Missouri	291.9
13	Oklahoma	282.2
14	Florida	271.1
15	Louisiana	260.8
16	Oregon	258.0
17	Colorado	247.9
17	Utah	247.9
19	Alaska	241.8
20	Tennessee	237.8
21	Alabama	235.3
22	Rhode Island	227.2
23	Indiana	216.1
24	Delaware	215.5
25	North Carolina	213.5
26	Connecticut	212.5
27	Arkansas	211.2
27	Kansas	211.2
29	Illinois	206.6
30	Ohio	198.3
31	Nebraska	193.8
32	Mississippi	183.0
33	New Jersey	178.1
34	Massachusetts	178.0
35	Minnesota	161.8
36	Wisconsin	157.8
37	West Virginia	150.6
38	Montana	149.3
39	Virginia	144.9
40	Wyoming	141.7
41	Pennsylvania	141.4
42	Kentucky	140.9
43	North Dakota	131.7
44	Iowa	129.3
45	New York	111.9
46	South Dakota	100.1
47	Idaho	93.3
48	New Hampshire	84.9
49	Maine	77.4
50	Vermont	72.1
	District of Columbia	922.5

Source: Reported data from the Federal Bureau of Investigation
   "Crime in the United States 2009" (Uniform Crime Reports, September 13, 2010, http://www.fbi.gov/ucr/ucr.htm)
*Includes the theft or attempted theft of a self-propelled vehicle. Excludes motorboats, construction equipment, airplanes, and farming equipment.

Rate of Consumer Fraud Complaints in 2009

National Rate = 342.8 Complaints per 100,000 Population*

ALPHA ORDER

RANK	STATE	RATE
20	Alabama	296.1
6	Alaska	377.7
11	Arizona	352.7
47	Arkansas	222.5
14	California	332.3
2	Colorado	412.4
29	Connecticut	284.6
8	Delaware	369.3
10	Florida	361.9
15	Georgia	321.6
12	Hawaii	352.0
17	Idaho	307.1
31	Illinois	279.9
27	Indiana	287.3
44	Iowa	237.8
32	Kansas	278.2
46	Kentucky	226.7
38	Louisiana	267.1
37	Maine	269.7
4	Maryland	393.6
24	Massachusetts	291.0
39	Michigan	264.6
33	Minnesota	276.5
50	Mississippi	188.0
13	Missouri	347.1
16	Montana	316.4
36	Nebraska	271.5
1	Nevada	412.9
3	New Hampshire	397.2
18	New Jersey	306.4
34	New Mexico	276.2
40	New York	263.3
28	North Carolina	287.2
48	North Dakota	199.0
25	Ohio	289.5
43	Oklahoma	254.2
5	Oregon	391.7
19	Pennsylvania	300.5
42	Rhode Island	257.4
35	South Carolina	271.9
49	South Dakota	195.5
21	Tennessee	295.3
30	Texas	280.6
23	Utah	293.3
26	Vermont	287.4
9	Virginia	366.8
7	Washington	376.1
45	West Virginia	230.1
41	Wisconsin	260.9
21	Wyoming	295.3

RANK ORDER

RANK	STATE	RATE
1	Nevada	412.9
2	Colorado	412.4
3	New Hampshire	397.2
4	Maryland	393.6
5	Oregon	391.7
6	Alaska	377.7
7	Washington	376.1
8	Delaware	369.3
9	Virginia	366.8
10	Florida	361.9
11	Arizona	352.7
12	Hawaii	352.0
13	Missouri	347.1
14	California	332.3
15	Georgia	321.6
16	Montana	316.4
17	Idaho	307.1
18	New Jersey	306.4
19	Pennsylvania	300.5
20	Alabama	296.1
21	Tennessee	295.3
21	Wyoming	295.3
23	Utah	293.3
24	Massachusetts	291.0
25	Ohio	289.5
26	Vermont	287.4
27	Indiana	287.3
28	North Carolina	287.2
29	Connecticut	284.6
30	Texas	280.6
31	Illinois	279.9
32	Kansas	278.2
33	Minnesota	276.5
34	New Mexico	276.2
35	South Carolina	271.9
36	Nebraska	271.5
37	Maine	269.7
38	Louisiana	267.1
39	Michigan	264.6
40	New York	263.3
41	Wisconsin	260.9
42	Rhode Island	257.4
43	Oklahoma	254.2
44	Iowa	237.8
45	West Virginia	230.1
46	Kentucky	226.7
47	Arkansas	222.5
48	North Dakota	199.0
49	South Dakota	195.5
50	Mississippi	188.0
	District of Columbia	528.8

Source: Federal Trade Commission, Consumer Sentinel
"Consumer Fraud and Identity Theft Complaint Data, January - December 2009" (February 2010, http://www.ftc.gov/sentinel/)
*National rate includes complaints not shown by state. Rates do not include identity theft or "Do Not Call" registry complaints.

Rate of Identity Theft Complaints in 2009

National Rate = 90.6 Complaints per 100,000 Population*

ALPHA ORDER

RANK	STATE	RATE
16	Alabama	76.2
43	Alaska	44.8
2	Arizona	119.4
31	Arkansas	64.4
4	California	114.2
9	Colorado	95.0
16	Connecticut	76.2
13	Delaware	81.9
1	Florida	122.3
7	Georgia	97.2
42	Hawaii	45.1
39	Idaho	48.8
10	Illinois	93.8
30	Indiana	64.8
47	Iowa	39.2
26	Kansas	67.6
40	Kentucky	48.4
22	Louisiana	72.4
48	Maine	38.8
11	Maryland	91.8
25	Massachusetts	69.0
18	Michigan	75.5
35	Minnesota	54.6
19	Mississippi	73.2
32	Missouri	64.3
46	Montana	41.8
36	Nebraska	52.2
5	Nevada	106.0
45	New Hampshire	44.1
12	New Jersey	84.5
6	New Mexico	98.0
8	New York	96.7
21	North Carolina	72.5
49	North Dakota	29.7
29	Ohio	65.2
23	Oklahoma	71.4
27	Oregon	67.5
14	Pennsylvania	78.4
33	Rhode Island	63.8
28	South Carolina	67.3
50	South Dakota	29.1
24	Tennessee	69.4
3	Texas	116.4
34	Utah	62.4
44	Vermont	44.6
20	Virginia	72.8
15	Washington	77.2
41	West Virginia	46.2
38	Wisconsin	49.1
37	Wyoming	49.2

RANK ORDER

RANK	STATE	RATE
1	Florida	122.3
2	Arizona	119.4
3	Texas	116.4
4	California	114.2
5	Nevada	106.0
6	New Mexico	98.0
7	Georgia	97.2
8	New York	96.7
9	Colorado	95.0
10	Illinois	93.8
11	Maryland	91.8
12	New Jersey	84.5
13	Delaware	81.9
14	Pennsylvania	78.4
15	Washington	77.2
16	Alabama	76.2
16	Connecticut	76.2
18	Michigan	75.5
19	Mississippi	73.2
20	Virginia	72.8
21	North Carolina	72.5
22	Louisiana	72.4
23	Oklahoma	71.4
24	Tennessee	69.4
25	Massachusetts	69.0
26	Kansas	67.6
27	Oregon	67.5
28	South Carolina	67.3
29	Ohio	65.2
30	Indiana	64.8
31	Arkansas	64.4
32	Missouri	64.3
33	Rhode Island	63.8
34	Utah	62.4
35	Minnesota	54.6
36	Nebraska	52.2
37	Wyoming	49.2
38	Wisconsin	49.1
39	Idaho	48.8
40	Kentucky	48.4
41	West Virginia	46.2
42	Hawaii	45.1
43	Alaska	44.8
44	Vermont	44.6
45	New Hampshire	44.1
46	Montana	41.8
47	Iowa	39.2
48	Maine	38.8
49	North Dakota	29.7
50	South Dakota	29.1

	District of Columbia	150.4

Source: Federal Trade Commission, Consumer Sentinel
"Consumer Fraud and Identity Theft Complaint Data, January - December 2009" (February 2010, http://www.ftc.gov/sentinel/)
*National rate includes complaints not shown by state. Rates do not include consumer fraud or "Do Not Call" registry complaints.

Reported Arrest Rate in 2009

National Rate = 4,563.9 Reported Arrests per 100,000 Population*

ALPHA ORDER

RANK	STATE	RATE
14	Alabama	5,257.5
7	Alaska	5,912.0
15	Arizona	5,175.3
17	Arkansas	5,099.2
38	California	4,008.4
24	Colorado	4,711.4
39	Connecticut	3,942.3
22	Delaware	4,790.7
11	Florida	5,670.3
23	Georgia	4,737.4
28	Hawaii	4,519.2
21	Idaho	4,821.8
NA	Illinois**	NA
25	Indiana	4,651.6
37	Iowa	4,010.0
35	Kansas	4,137.8
9	Kentucky	5,817.4
10	Louisiana	5,796.0
32	Maine	4,295.2
18	Maryland	4,994.5
49	Massachusetts	2,418.5
47	Michigan	3,093.1
41	Minnesota	3,758.5
1	Mississippi	7,578.5
8	Missouri	5,850.2
43	Montana	3,448.3
13	Nebraska	5,285.3
4	Nevada	6,774.9
33	New Hampshire	4,252.9
26	New Jersey	4,548.0
5	New Mexico	6,265.8
46	New York	3,241.2
12	North Carolina	5,616.1
30	North Dakota	4,447.8
45	Ohio	3,276.6
27	Oklahoma	4,522.7
42	Oregon	3,655.0
40	Pennsylvania	3,779.5
44	Rhode Island	3,363.1
29	South Carolina	4,515.4
34	South Dakota	4,180.2
6	Tennessee	6,243.3
20	Texas	4,838.6
19	Utah	4,945.1
48	Vermont	2,581.2
31	Virginia	4,360.2
36	Washington	4,103.9
16	West Virginia	5,136.7
3	Wisconsin	6,864.8
2	Wyoming	7,180.2

RANK ORDER

RANK	STATE	RATE
1	Mississippi	7,578.5
2	Wyoming	7,180.2
3	Wisconsin	6,864.8
4	Nevada	6,774.9
5	New Mexico	6,265.8
6	Tennessee	6,243.3
7	Alaska	5,912.0
8	Missouri	5,850.2
9	Kentucky	5,817.4
10	Louisiana	5,796.0
11	Florida	5,670.3
12	North Carolina	5,616.1
13	Nebraska	5,285.3
14	Alabama	5,257.5
15	Arizona	5,175.3
16	West Virginia	5,136.7
17	Arkansas	5,099.2
18	Maryland	4,994.5
19	Utah	4,945.1
20	Texas	4,838.6
21	Idaho	4,821.8
22	Delaware	4,790.7
23	Georgia	4,737.4
24	Colorado	4,711.4
25	Indiana	4,651.6
26	New Jersey	4,548.0
27	Oklahoma	4,522.7
28	Hawaii	4,519.2
29	South Carolina	4,515.4
30	North Dakota	4,447.8
31	Virginia	4,360.2
32	Maine	4,295.2
33	New Hampshire	4,252.9
34	South Dakota	4,180.2
35	Kansas	4,137.8
36	Washington	4,103.9
37	Iowa	4,010.0
38	California	4,008.4
39	Connecticut	3,942.3
40	Pennsylvania	3,779.5
41	Minnesota	3,758.5
42	Oregon	3,655.0
43	Montana	3,448.3
44	Rhode Island	3,363.1
45	Ohio	3,276.6
46	New York	3,241.2
47	Michigan	3,093.1
48	Vermont	2,581.2
49	Massachusetts	2,418.5
NA	Illinois**	NA
	District of Columbia**	NA

Source: CQ Press using reported data from the Federal Bureau of Investigation

"Crime in the United States 2009" (Uniform Crime Reports, September 13, 2010, http://www.fbi.gov/ucr/ucr.htm)

*By law enforcement agencies submitting complete reports to the F.B.I. for 12 months in 2009. These rates based on population estimates for areas under the jurisdiction of those agencies reporting. Arrest rate based on the F.B.I. estimate of total arrests is 4,458.3 reported and unreported arrests per 100,000 population. See important note at beginning of this chapter.

**Not available.

Reported Juvenile Arrest Rate in 2009

National Rate = 5,920.6 Reported Arrests per 100,000 Juvenile Population*

<table>
<tr><td colspan="3">ALPHA ORDER</td><td colspan="3">RANK ORDER</td></tr>
<tr><td>RANK</td><td>STATE</td><td>RATE</td><td>RANK</td><td>STATE</td><td>RATE</td></tr>
<tr><td>46</td><td>Alabama</td><td>2,800.9</td><td>1</td><td>Wisconsin</td><td>15,012.5</td></tr>
<tr><td>38</td><td>Alaska</td><td>4,858.3</td><td>2</td><td>Wyoming</td><td>10,925.2</td></tr>
<tr><td>16</td><td>Arizona</td><td>7,181.0</td><td>3</td><td>Hawaii</td><td>10,490.5</td></tr>
<tr><td>41</td><td>Arkansas</td><td>4,443.7</td><td>4</td><td>North Dakota</td><td>10,291.9</td></tr>
<tr><td>35</td><td>California</td><td>4,981.8</td><td>5</td><td>Nevada</td><td>8,721.0</td></tr>
<tr><td>8</td><td>Colorado</td><td>8,210.4</td><td>6</td><td>Nebraska</td><td>8,569.2</td></tr>
<tr><td>36</td><td>Connecticut</td><td>4,958.1</td><td>7</td><td>South Dakota</td><td>8,516.0</td></tr>
<tr><td>13</td><td>Delaware</td><td>7,369.0</td><td>8</td><td>Colorado</td><td>8,210.4</td></tr>
<tr><td>26</td><td>Florida</td><td>5,952.9</td><td>9</td><td>Minnesota</td><td>7,912.1</td></tr>
<tr><td>28</td><td>Georgia</td><td>5,617.2</td><td>10</td><td>Idaho</td><td>7,860.0</td></tr>
<tr><td>3</td><td>Hawaii</td><td>10,490.5</td><td>11</td><td>Utah</td><td>7,776.6</td></tr>
<tr><td>10</td><td>Idaho</td><td>7,860.0</td><td>12</td><td>Montana</td><td>7,594.0</td></tr>
<tr><td>NA</td><td>Illinois**</td><td>NA</td><td>13</td><td>Delaware</td><td>7,369.0</td></tr>
<tr><td>19</td><td>Indiana</td><td>6,874.8</td><td>14</td><td>Pennsylvania</td><td>7,281.8</td></tr>
<tr><td>23</td><td>Iowa</td><td>6,335.9</td><td>15</td><td>Missouri</td><td>7,250.8</td></tr>
<tr><td>37</td><td>Kansas</td><td>4,894.1</td><td>16</td><td>Arizona</td><td>7,181.0</td></tr>
<tr><td>45</td><td>Kentucky</td><td>3,328.3</td><td>17</td><td>Louisiana</td><td>7,043.4</td></tr>
<tr><td>17</td><td>Louisiana</td><td>7,043.4</td><td>18</td><td>Maryland</td><td>6,948.5</td></tr>
<tr><td>29</td><td>Maine</td><td>5,400.5</td><td>19</td><td>Indiana</td><td>6,874.8</td></tr>
<tr><td>18</td><td>Maryland</td><td>6,948.5</td><td>20</td><td>Tennessee</td><td>6,842.2</td></tr>
<tr><td>47</td><td>Massachusetts</td><td>2,649.3</td><td>21</td><td>Oregon</td><td>6,690.6</td></tr>
<tr><td>44</td><td>Michigan</td><td>3,398.1</td><td>22</td><td>Mississippi</td><td>6,357.3</td></tr>
<tr><td>9</td><td>Minnesota</td><td>7,912.1</td><td>23</td><td>Iowa</td><td>6,335.9</td></tr>
<tr><td>22</td><td>Mississippi</td><td>6,357.3</td><td>24</td><td>New Hampshire</td><td>6,145.9</td></tr>
<tr><td>15</td><td>Missouri</td><td>7,250.8</td><td>25</td><td>Texas</td><td>6,095.2</td></tr>
<tr><td>12</td><td>Montana</td><td>7,594.0</td><td>26</td><td>Florida</td><td>5,952.9</td></tr>
<tr><td>6</td><td>Nebraska</td><td>8,569.2</td><td>27</td><td>New Mexico</td><td>5,898.3</td></tr>
<tr><td>5</td><td>Nevada</td><td>8,721.0</td><td>28</td><td>Georgia</td><td>5,617.2</td></tr>
<tr><td>24</td><td>New Hampshire</td><td>6,145.9</td><td>29</td><td>Maine</td><td>5,400.5</td></tr>
<tr><td>31</td><td>New Jersey</td><td>5,358.5</td><td>30</td><td>Oklahoma</td><td>5,374.0</td></tr>
<tr><td>27</td><td>New Mexico</td><td>5,898.3</td><td>31</td><td>New Jersey</td><td>5,358.5</td></tr>
<tr><td>43</td><td>New York</td><td>3,811.2</td><td>32</td><td>Washington</td><td>5,138.2</td></tr>
<tr><td>33</td><td>North Carolina</td><td>5,107.9</td><td>33</td><td>North Carolina</td><td>5,107.9</td></tr>
<tr><td>4</td><td>North Dakota</td><td>10,291.9</td><td>34</td><td>Rhode Island</td><td>5,090.8</td></tr>
<tr><td>40</td><td>Ohio</td><td>4,616.1</td><td>35</td><td>California</td><td>4,981.8</td></tr>
<tr><td>30</td><td>Oklahoma</td><td>5,374.0</td><td>36</td><td>Connecticut</td><td>4,958.1</td></tr>
<tr><td>21</td><td>Oregon</td><td>6,690.6</td><td>37</td><td>Kansas</td><td>4,894.1</td></tr>
<tr><td>14</td><td>Pennsylvania</td><td>7,281.8</td><td>38</td><td>Alaska</td><td>4,858.3</td></tr>
<tr><td>34</td><td>Rhode Island</td><td>5,090.8</td><td>39</td><td>South Carolina</td><td>4,665.1</td></tr>
<tr><td>39</td><td>South Carolina</td><td>4,665.1</td><td>40</td><td>Ohio</td><td>4,616.1</td></tr>
<tr><td>7</td><td>South Dakota</td><td>8,516.0</td><td>41</td><td>Arkansas</td><td>4,443.7</td></tr>
<tr><td>20</td><td>Tennessee</td><td>6,842.2</td><td>42</td><td>Virginia</td><td>4,427.9</td></tr>
<tr><td>25</td><td>Texas</td><td>6,095.2</td><td>43</td><td>New York</td><td>3,811.2</td></tr>
<tr><td>11</td><td>Utah</td><td>7,776.6</td><td>44</td><td>Michigan</td><td>3,398.1</td></tr>
<tr><td>48</td><td>Vermont</td><td>2,606.5</td><td>45</td><td>Kentucky</td><td>3,328.3</td></tr>
<tr><td>42</td><td>Virginia</td><td>4,427.9</td><td>46</td><td>Alabama</td><td>2,800.9</td></tr>
<tr><td>32</td><td>Washington</td><td>5,138.2</td><td>47</td><td>Massachusetts</td><td>2,649.3</td></tr>
<tr><td>49</td><td>West Virginia</td><td>2,526.3</td><td>48</td><td>Vermont</td><td>2,606.5</td></tr>
<tr><td>1</td><td>Wisconsin</td><td>15,012.5</td><td>49</td><td>West Virginia</td><td>2,526.3</td></tr>
<tr><td>2</td><td>Wyoming</td><td>10,925.2</td><td>NA</td><td>Illinois**</td><td>NA</td></tr>
<tr><td></td><td></td><td></td><td></td><td>District of Columbia**</td><td>NA</td></tr>
</table>

Source: CQ Press using reported data from the Federal Bureau of Investigation

"Crime in the United States 2009" (Uniform Crime Reports, September 13, 2010, http://www.fbi.gov/ucr/ucr.htm)

*By law enforcement agencies submitting complete reports to the F.B.I. for 12 months in 2009. Arrests of youths 17 years and younger divided into population of 10 to 17 year olds. See important note at beginning of this chapter.

**Not available.

Prisoners in State Correctional Institutions: Year End 2009

National Total = 1,405,622 State Prisoners*

ALPHA ORDER

RANK	STATE	PRISONERS	% of USA
14	Alabama	31,874	2.3%
41	Alaska	5,285	0.4%
10	Arizona	40,627	2.9%
28	Arkansas	15,208	1.1%
1	California	171,275	12.2%
22	Colorado	22,795	1.6%
26	Connecticut	19,716	1.4%
36	Delaware	6,794	0.5%
3	Florida	103,915	7.4%
5	Georgia	53,371	3.8%
40	Hawaii	5,891	0.4%
35	Idaho	7,400	0.5%
9	Illinois	45,161	3.2%
16	Indiana	28,808	2.0%
33	Iowa	8,813	0.6%
34	Kansas	8,641	0.6%
24	Kentucky	21,638	1.5%
12	Louisiana	39,780	2.8%
48	Maine	2,206	0.2%
23	Maryland	22,255	1.6%
31	Massachusetts	11,316	0.8%
8	Michigan	45,478	3.2%
32	Minnesota	9,986	0.7%
25	Mississippi	21,482	1.5%
15	Missouri	30,563	2.2%
44	Montana	3,605	0.3%
42	Nebraska	4,474	0.3%
30	Nevada	12,482	0.9%
46	New Hampshire	2,731	0.2%
19	New Jersey	25,382	1.8%
38	New Mexico	6,519	0.5%
4	New York	58,687	4.2%
11	North Carolina	39,860	2.8%
50	North Dakota	1,486	0.1%
6	Ohio	51,606	3.7%
18	Oklahoma	26,397	1.9%
29	Oregon	14,403	1.0%
7	Pennsylvania	51,429	3.7%
43	Rhode Island	3,674	0.3%
20	South Carolina	24,288	1.7%
45	South Dakota	3,434	0.2%
17	Tennessee	26,965	1.9%
2	Texas	171,249	12.2%
37	Utah	6,533	0.5%
47	Vermont	2,220	0.2%
13	Virginia	38,092	2.7%
27	Washington	18,233	1.3%
39	West Virginia	6,367	0.5%
21	Wisconsin	23,153	1.6%
49	Wyoming	2,075	0.1%

RANK ORDER

RANK	STATE	PRISONERS	% of USA
1	California	171,275	12.2%
2	Texas	171,249	12.2%
3	Florida	103,915	7.4%
4	New York	58,687	4.2%
5	Georgia	53,371	3.8%
6	Ohio	51,606	3.7%
7	Pennsylvania	51,429	3.7%
8	Michigan	45,478	3.2%
9	Illinois	45,161	3.2%
10	Arizona	40,627	2.9%
11	North Carolina	39,860	2.8%
12	Louisiana	39,780	2.8%
13	Virginia	38,092	2.7%
14	Alabama	31,874	2.3%
15	Missouri	30,563	2.2%
16	Indiana	28,808	2.0%
17	Tennessee	26,965	1.9%
18	Oklahoma	26,397	1.9%
19	New Jersey	25,382	1.8%
20	South Carolina	24,288	1.7%
21	Wisconsin	23,153	1.6%
22	Colorado	22,795	1.6%
23	Maryland	22,255	1.6%
24	Kentucky	21,638	1.5%
25	Mississippi	21,482	1.5%
26	Connecticut	19,716	1.4%
27	Washington	18,233	1.3%
28	Arkansas	15,208	1.1%
29	Oregon	14,403	1.0%
30	Nevada	12,482	0.9%
31	Massachusetts	11,316	0.8%
32	Minnesota	9,986	0.7%
33	Iowa	8,813	0.6%
34	Kansas	8,641	0.6%
35	Idaho	7,400	0.5%
36	Delaware	6,794	0.5%
37	Utah	6,533	0.5%
38	New Mexico	6,519	0.5%
39	West Virginia	6,367	0.5%
40	Hawaii	5,891	0.4%
41	Alaska	5,285	0.4%
42	Nebraska	4,474	0.3%
43	Rhode Island	3,674	0.3%
44	Montana	3,605	0.3%
45	South Dakota	3,434	0.2%
46	New Hampshire	2,731	0.2%
47	Vermont	2,220	0.2%
48	Maine	2,206	0.2%
49	Wyoming	2,075	0.1%
50	North Dakota	1,486	0.1%
	District of Columbia**	NA	NA

Source: U.S. Department of Justice, Bureau of Justice Statistics
    "Prisoners in 2009" (December 2010, NCJ 231675, http://bjs.ojp.usdoj.gov/)
*Advance figures as of December 31, 2009. Totals reflect all prisoners, including those sentenced to a year or less and those unsentenced. National total does not include 208,118 prisoners under federal jurisdiction. State and federal prisoners combined total 1,613,740.
**Responsibility for sentenced felons in D.C. was transferred to the Federal Bureau of Prisons in 2001.

State Prisoner Imprisonment Rate in 2009

National Rate = 442 State Prisoners per 100,000 Population*

ALPHA ORDER

RANK	STATE	RATE
4	Alabama	650
32	Alaska	357
6	Arizona	580
9	Arkansas	522
16	California	458
18	Colorado	450
25	Connecticut	382
19	Delaware	447
7	Florida	559
8	Georgia	526
35	Hawaii	317
14	Idaho	476
33	Illinois	349
19	Indiana	447
39	Iowa	292
37	Kansas	305
13	Kentucky	478
1	Louisiana	881
50	Maine	150
25	Maryland	382
46	Massachusetts	213
17	Michigan	457
49	Minnesota	189
2	Mississippi	702
11	Missouri	509
31	Montana	368
43	Nebraska	243
15	Nevada	470
48	New Hampshire	206
40	New Jersey	291
36	New Mexico	316
38	New York	298
29	North Carolina	369
45	North Dakota	228
21	Ohio	446
3	Oklahoma	657
28	Oregon	373
24	Pennsylvania	406
47	Rhode Island	211
10	South Carolina	512
23	South Dakota	420
22	Tennessee	426
5	Texas	648
44	Utah	232
41	Vermont	277
12	Virginia	480
42	Washington	271
34	West Virginia	346
29	Wisconsin	369
27	Wyoming	377

RANK ORDER

RANK	STATE	RATE
1	Louisiana	881
2	Mississippi	702
3	Oklahoma	657
4	Alabama	650
5	Texas	648
6	Arizona	580
7	Florida	559
8	Georgia	526
9	Arkansas	522
10	South Carolina	512
11	Missouri	509
12	Virginia	480
13	Kentucky	478
14	Idaho	476
15	Nevada	470
16	California	458
17	Michigan	457
18	Colorado	450
19	Delaware	447
19	Indiana	447
21	Ohio	446
22	Tennessee	426
23	South Dakota	420
24	Pennsylvania	406
25	Connecticut	382
25	Maryland	382
27	Wyoming	377
28	Oregon	373
29	North Carolina	369
29	Wisconsin	369
31	Montana	368
32	Alaska	357
33	Illinois	349
34	West Virginia	346
35	Hawaii	317
36	New Mexico	316
37	Kansas	305
38	New York	298
39	Iowa	292
40	New Jersey	291
41	Vermont	277
42	Washington	271
43	Nebraska	243
44	Utah	232
45	North Dakota	228
46	Massachusetts	213
47	Rhode Island	211
48	New Hampshire	206
49	Minnesota	189
50	Maine	150
	District of Columbia**	NA

Source: U.S. Department of Justice, Bureau of Justice Statistics
   "Prisoners in 2009" (December 2010, NCJ 231675, http://bjs.ojp.usdoj.gov/)
*As of December 31, 2009. Includes only inmates sentenced to more than one year. Does not include federal imprisonment rate
of 61 prisoners per 100,000 population. State and federal combined imprisonment rate is 502 prisoners per 100,000 population.
**Responsibility for sentenced felons in D.C. was transferred to the Federal Bureau of Prisons in 2001.

Percent Change in Number of State Prisoners: 2008 to 2009

National Percent Change = 0.2% Decrease*

ALPHA ORDER

RANK	STATE	PERCENT CHANGE
4	Alabama	4.5
1	Alaska	5.4
9	Arizona	2.6
7	Arkansas	3.3
40	California	(1.4)
42	Colorado	(2.1)
46	Connecticut	(4.6)
45	Delaware	(4.0)
17	Florida	1.5
19	Georgia	1.2
39	Hawaii	(1.1)
17	Idaho	1.5
33	Illinois	(0.7)
13	Indiana	1.7
25	Iowa	0.5
19	Kansas	1.2
29	Kentucky	(0.3)
6	Louisiana	3.6
25	Maine	0.5
46	Maryland	(4.6)
35	Massachusetts	(0.8)
49	Michigan	(6.7)
24	Minnesota	0.8
48	Mississippi	(5.6)
19	Missouri	1.2
13	Montana	1.7
36	Nebraska	(1.0)
41	Nevada	(2.0)
22	New Hampshire	1.1
43	New Jersey	(2.2)
12	New Mexico	1.8
44	New York	(2.8)
23	North Carolina	1.0
10	North Dakota	2.3
27	Ohio	(0.2)
11	Oklahoma	2.1
13	Oregon	1.7
4	Pennsylvania	4.5
50	Rhode Island	(9.2)
27	South Carolina	(0.2)
8	South Dakota	2.8
36	Tennessee	(1.0)
33	Texas	(0.7)
29	Utah	(0.3)
3	Vermont	4.9
32	Virginia	(0.5)
13	Washington	1.7
2	West Virginia	5.1
36	Wisconsin	(1.0)
31	Wyoming	(0.4)

RANK ORDER

RANK	STATE	PERCENT CHANGE
1	Alaska	5.4
2	West Virginia	5.1
3	Vermont	4.9
4	Alabama	4.5
4	Pennsylvania	4.5
6	Louisiana	3.6
7	Arkansas	3.3
8	South Dakota	2.8
9	Arizona	2.6
10	North Dakota	2.3
11	Oklahoma	2.1
12	New Mexico	1.8
13	Indiana	1.7
13	Montana	1.7
13	Oregon	1.7
13	Washington	1.7
17	Florida	1.5
17	Idaho	1.5
19	Georgia	1.2
19	Kansas	1.2
19	Missouri	1.2
22	New Hampshire	1.1
23	North Carolina	1.0
24	Minnesota	0.8
25	Iowa	0.5
25	Maine	0.5
27	Ohio	(0.2)
27	South Carolina	(0.2)
29	Kentucky	(0.3)
29	Utah	(0.3)
31	Wyoming	(0.4)
32	Virginia	(0.5)
33	Illinois	(0.7)
33	Texas	(0.7)
35	Massachusetts	(0.8)
36	Nebraska	(1.0)
36	Tennessee	(1.0)
36	Wisconsin	(1.0)
39	Hawaii	(1.1)
40	California	(1.4)
41	Nevada	(2.0)
42	Colorado	(2.1)
43	New Jersey	(2.2)
44	New York	(2.8)
45	Delaware	(4.0)
46	Connecticut	(4.6)
46	Maryland	(4.6)
48	Mississippi	(5.6)
49	Michigan	(6.7)
50	Rhode Island	(9.2)
	District of Columbia**	NA

Source: U.S. Department of Justice, Bureau of Justice Statistics
    "Prisoners in 2009" (December 2010, NCJ 231675, http://bjs.ojp.usdoj.gov/)
*From December 31, 2008 to December 31, 2009. Includes inmates sentenced to more than one year and those sentenced to a year or less or with no sentence. The percent change in number of prisoners under federal jurisdiction during the same period was an 3.4% increase. The combined state and federal increase was 0.2%.
**Responsibility for sentenced felons in D.C. was transferred to the Federal Bureau of Prisons in 2001.

Prisoners under Sentence of Death in 2009

National Total = 3,118 State Prisoners*

ALPHA ORDER

RANK	STATE	PRISONERS	% of USA
5	Alabama	200	6.4%
NA	Alaska**	NA	NA
8	Arizona	131	4.2%
17	Arkansas	40	1.3%
1	California	684	21.9%
31	Colorado	2	0.1%
26	Connecticut	10	0.3%
20	Delaware	17	0.5%
2	Florida	389	12.5%
9	Georgia	101	3.2%
NA	Hawaii**	NA	NA
22	Idaho	14	0.4%
21	Illinois	16	0.5%
22	Indiana	14	0.4%
NA	Iowa**	NA	NA
28	Kansas	9	0.3%
18	Kentucky	35	1.1%
11	Louisiana	83	2.7%
NA	Maine**	NA	NA
30	Maryland	5	0.2%
NA	Massachusetts**	NA	NA
NA	Michigan**	NA	NA
NA	Minnesota**	NA	NA
14	Mississippi	60	1.9%
16	Missouri	51	1.6%
31	Montana	2	0.1%
25	Nebraska	11	0.4%
12	Nevada	80	2.6%
35	New Hampshire	1	0.0%
NA	New Jersey**	NA	NA
31	New Mexico	2	0.1%
37	New York	0	0.0%
7	North Carolina	159	5.1%
NA	North Dakota**	NA	NA
6	Ohio	165	5.3%
13	Oklahoma	79	2.5%
19	Oregon	31	1.0%
4	Pennsylvania	218	7.0%
NA	Rhode Island**	NA	NA
15	South Carolina	55	1.8%
31	South Dakota	2	0.1%
10	Tennessee	89	2.9%
3	Texas	331	10.6%
26	Utah	10	0.3%
NA	Vermont**	NA	NA
24	Virginia	13	0.4%
29	Washington	8	0.3%
NA	West Virginia**	NA	NA
NA	Wisconsin**	NA	NA
35	Wyoming	1	0.0%

RANK ORDER

RANK	STATE	PRISONERS	% of USA
1	California	684	21.9%
2	Florida	389	12.5%
3	Texas	331	10.6%
4	Pennsylvania	218	7.0%
5	Alabama	200	6.4%
6	Ohio	165	5.3%
7	North Carolina	159	5.1%
8	Arizona	131	4.2%
9	Georgia	101	3.2%
10	Tennessee	89	2.9%
11	Louisiana	83	2.7%
12	Nevada	80	2.6%
13	Oklahoma	79	2.5%
14	Mississippi	60	1.9%
15	South Carolina	55	1.8%
16	Missouri	51	1.6%
17	Arkansas	40	1.3%
18	Kentucky	35	1.1%
19	Oregon	31	1.0%
20	Delaware	17	0.5%
21	Illinois	16	0.5%
22	Idaho	14	0.4%
22	Indiana	14	0.4%
24	Virginia	13	0.4%
25	Nebraska	11	0.4%
26	Connecticut	10	0.3%
26	Utah	10	0.3%
28	Kansas	9	0.3%
29	Washington	8	0.3%
30	Maryland	5	0.2%
31	Colorado	2	0.1%
31	Montana	2	0.1%
31	New Mexico	2	0.1%
31	South Dakota	2	0.1%
35	New Hampshire	1	0.0%
35	Wyoming	1	0.0%
37	New York	0	0.0%
NA	Alaska**	NA	NA
NA	Hawaii**	NA	NA
NA	Iowa**	NA	NA
NA	Maine**	NA	NA
NA	Massachusetts**	NA	NA
NA	Michigan**	NA	NA
NA	Minnesota**	NA	NA
NA	New Jersey**	NA	NA
NA	North Dakota**	NA	NA
NA	Rhode Island**	NA	NA
NA	Vermont**	NA	NA
NA	West Virginia**	NA	NA
NA	Wisconsin**	NA	NA
	District of Columbia**	NA	NA

Source: U.S. Department of Justice, Bureau of Justice Statistics
   "Capital Punishment 2009" (Bulletin, December 2010, NCJ 231676, http://bjs.ojp.usdoj.gov/)
*As of December 31, 2009. Does not include 55 federal prisoners under sentence of death. There were 52 executions in 2009.
**No death penalty as of December 31, 2009.

Rate of State and Local Police Officers in 2009

National Rate = 23.4 Officers per 10,000 Population*

ALPHA ORDER

RANK	STATE	RATE
17	Alabama	22.9
45	Alaska	17.0
37	Arizona	19.7
25	Arkansas	21.9
32	California	20.9
15	Colorado	23.1
16	Connecticut	23.0
19	Delaware	22.8
11	Florida	23.8
27	Georgia	21.7
13	Hawaii	23.7
35	Idaho	20.4
5	Illinois	28.7
34	Indiana	20.7
39	Iowa	18.6
11	Kansas	23.8
41	Kentucky	18.4
4	Louisiana	29.2
44	Maine	17.4
10	Maryland	24.0
3	Massachusetts	30.2
42	Michigan	18.3
43	Minnesota	17.6
8	Mississippi	25.8
17	Missouri	22.9
40	Montana	18.5
28	Nebraska	21.5
36	Nevada	20.0
20	New Hampshire	22.7
2	New Jersey	31.2
23	New Mexico	22.5
1	New York	38.5
13	North Carolina	23.7
38	North Dakota	18.7
30	Ohio	21.2
31	Oklahoma	21.1
48	Oregon	16.6
24	Pennsylvania	22.2
6	Rhode Island	28.5
9	South Carolina	25.0
29	South Dakota	21.4
20	Tennessee	22.7
32	Texas	20.9
50	Utah	16.1
48	Vermont	16.6
25	Virginia	21.9
45	Washington	17.0
45	West Virginia	17.0
22	Wisconsin	22.6
7	Wyoming	28.1

RANK ORDER

RANK	STATE	RATE
1	New York	38.5
2	New Jersey	31.2
3	Massachusetts	30.2
4	Louisiana	29.2
5	Illinois	28.7
6	Rhode Island	28.5
7	Wyoming	28.1
8	Mississippi	25.8
9	South Carolina	25.0
10	Maryland	24.0
11	Florida	23.8
11	Kansas	23.8
13	Hawaii	23.7
13	North Carolina	23.7
15	Colorado	23.1
16	Connecticut	23.0
17	Alabama	22.9
17	Missouri	22.9
19	Delaware	22.8
20	New Hampshire	22.7
20	Tennessee	22.7
22	Wisconsin	22.6
23	New Mexico	22.5
24	Pennsylvania	22.2
25	Arkansas	21.9
25	Virginia	21.9
27	Georgia	21.7
28	Nebraska	21.5
29	South Dakota	21.4
30	Ohio	21.2
31	Oklahoma	21.1
32	California	20.9
32	Texas	20.9
34	Indiana	20.7
35	Idaho	20.4
36	Nevada	20.0
37	Arizona	19.7
38	North Dakota	18.7
39	Iowa	18.6
40	Montana	18.5
41	Kentucky	18.4
42	Michigan	18.3
43	Minnesota	17.6
44	Maine	17.4
45	Alaska	17.0
45	Washington	17.0
45	West Virginia	17.0
48	Oregon	16.6
48	Vermont	16.6
50	Utah	16.1
	District of Columbia	67.8

Source: CQ Press using data from U.S. Bureau of the Census, Governments Division
   "Government Employment and Payroll" (http://www.census.gov/govs/apes/index.html)
*Full-time equivalent as of March 2009. Does not include employees of police departments who are not officers.

Per Capita State and Local Government
Expenditures for Police Protection in 2008
National Per Capita = $295*

ALPHA ORDER			RANK ORDER		
RANK	STATE	PER CAPITA	RANK	STATE	PER CAPITA
37	Alabama	$223	1	New York	$419
4	Alaska	381	2	Nevada	412
7	Arizona	332	3	California	407
49	Arkansas	172	4	Alaska	381
3	California	407	5	Florida	366
16	Colorado	294	6	New Jersey	356
18	Connecticut	284	7	Arizona	332
8	Delaware	330	8	Delaware	330
5	Florida	366	8	Illinois	330
30	Georgia	236	10	Maryland	325
24	Hawaii	260	11	Wyoming	319
40	Idaho	210	12	New Mexico	303
8	Illinois	330	13	Rhode Island	301
44	Indiana	191	14	Louisiana	298
42	Iowa	205	15	Nebraska	296
26	Kansas	245	16	Colorado	294
50	Kentucky	164	17	Minnesota	292
14	Louisiana	298	18	Connecticut	284
46	Maine	177	19	Massachusetts	282
10	Maryland	325	20	Wisconsin	276
19	Massachusetts	282	21	Missouri	274
27	Michigan	242	21	Ohio	274
17	Minnesota	292	23	Oregon	267
43	Mississippi	204	24	Hawaii	260
21	Missouri	274	25	Virginia	258
33	Montana	233	26	Kansas	245
15	Nebraska	296	27	Michigan	242
2	Nevada	412	28	New Hampshire	240
28	New Hampshire	240	28	North Carolina	240
6	New Jersey	356	30	Georgia	236
12	New Mexico	303	30	Tennessee	236
1	New York	419	32	Utah	235
28	North Carolina	240	33	Montana	233
45	North Dakota	186	34	Texas	231
21	Ohio	274	35	Vermont	227
41	Oklahoma	209	36	Pennsylvania	226
23	Oregon	267	37	Alabama	223
36	Pennsylvania	226	38	Washington	220
13	Rhode Island	301	39	South Carolina	218
39	South Carolina	218	40	Idaho	210
47	South Dakota	175	41	Oklahoma	209
30	Tennessee	236	42	Iowa	205
34	Texas	231	43	Mississippi	204
32	Utah	235	44	Indiana	191
35	Vermont	227	45	North Dakota	186
25	Virginia	258	46	Maine	177
38	Washington	220	47	South Dakota	175
48	West Virginia	173	48	West Virginia	173
20	Wisconsin	276	49	Arkansas	172
11	Wyoming	319	50	Kentucky	164
				District of Columbia	1,001

Source: CQ Press using data from U.S. Bureau of the Census, Governments Division
   "2008 State and Local Government Finances" (http://www.census.gov/govs/estimate/index.html)
*Direct general expenditures.

Per Capita State and Local Government Expenditures for Corrections in 2008

National Per Capita = $240*

ALPHA ORDER

RANK	STATE	PER CAPITA
45	Alabama	$150
3	Alaska	362
15	Arizona	253
34	Arkansas	174
2	California	375
20	Colorado	232
24	Connecticut	204
4	Delaware	320
13	Florida	258
19	Georgia	237
37	Hawaii	170
25	Idaho	203
43	Illinois	154
38	Indiana	166
47	Iowa	147
38	Kansas	166
35	Kentucky	171
8	Louisiana	279
41	Maine	161
5	Maryland	298
22	Massachusetts	215
16	Michigan	246
33	Minnesota	175
38	Mississippi	166
47	Missouri	147
25	Montana	203
32	Nebraska	181
7	Nevada	294
50	New Hampshire	127
18	New Jersey	238
8	New Mexico	279
5	New York	298
28	North Carolina	192
49	North Dakota	131
35	Ohio	171
27	Oklahoma	193
10	Oregon	269
17	Pennsylvania	243
21	Rhode Island	216
41	South Carolina	161
30	South Dakota	190
44	Tennessee	153
23	Texas	214
31	Utah	186
28	Vermont	192
11	Virginia	267
12	Washington	264
45	West Virginia	150
14	Wisconsin	257
1	Wyoming	451

RANK ORDER

RANK	STATE	PER CAPITA
1	Wyoming	$451
2	California	375
3	Alaska	362
4	Delaware	320
5	Maryland	298
5	New York	298
7	Nevada	294
8	Louisiana	279
8	New Mexico	279
10	Oregon	269
11	Virginia	267
12	Washington	264
13	Florida	258
14	Wisconsin	257
15	Arizona	253
16	Michigan	246
17	Pennsylvania	243
18	New Jersey	238
19	Georgia	237
20	Colorado	232
21	Rhode Island	216
22	Massachusetts	215
23	Texas	214
24	Connecticut	204
25	Idaho	203
25	Montana	203
27	Oklahoma	193
28	North Carolina	192
28	Vermont	192
30	South Dakota	190
31	Utah	186
32	Nebraska	181
33	Minnesota	175
34	Arkansas	174
35	Kentucky	171
35	Ohio	171
37	Hawaii	170
38	Indiana	166
38	Kansas	166
38	Mississippi	166
41	Maine	161
41	South Carolina	161
43	Illinois	154
44	Tennessee	153
45	Alabama	150
45	West Virginia	150
47	Iowa	147
47	Missouri	147
49	North Dakota	131
50	New Hampshire	127

District of Columbia	453

Source: CQ Press using data from U.S. Bureau of the Census, Governments Division
"2008 State and Local Government Finances" (http://www.census.gov/govs/estimate/index.html)
*Direct general expenditures.

Per Capita State and Local Government Expenditures for Judicial and Legal Services in 2008
National Per Capita = $136*

ALPHA ORDER

RANK	STATE	PER CAPITA
41	Alabama	$88
1	Alaska	309
11	Arizona	155
48	Arkansas	73
2	California	254
30	Colorado	104
5	Connecticut	189
7	Delaware	177
18	Florida	125
28	Georgia	105
3	Hawaii	251
24	Idaho	111
31	Illinois	102
46	Indiana	81
24	Iowa	111
36	Kansas	98
31	Kentucky	102
14	Louisiana	139
42	Maine	84
15	Maryland	137
12	Massachusetts	148
27	Michigan	109
17	Minnesota	126
47	Mississippi	75
45	Missouri	82
16	Montana	133
39	Nebraska	92
8	Nevada	168
35	New Hampshire	99
9	New Jersey	167
10	New Mexico	157
4	New York	196
48	North Carolina	73
38	North Dakota	94
13	Ohio	146
42	Oklahoma	84
26	Oregon	110
19	Pennsylvania	123
23	Rhode Island	113
50	South Carolina	71
44	South Dakota	83
37	Tennessee	95
40	Texas	90
21	Utah	118
22	Vermont	114
31	Virginia	102
20	Washington	122
34	West Virginia	101
28	Wisconsin	105
6	Wyoming	186

RANK ORDER

RANK	STATE	PER CAPITA
1	Alaska	$309
2	California	254
3	Hawaii	251
4	New York	196
5	Connecticut	189
6	Wyoming	186
7	Delaware	177
8	Nevada	168
9	New Jersey	167
10	New Mexico	157
11	Arizona	155
12	Massachusetts	148
13	Ohio	146
14	Louisiana	139
15	Maryland	137
16	Montana	133
17	Minnesota	126
18	Florida	125
19	Pennsylvania	123
20	Washington	122
21	Utah	118
22	Vermont	114
23	Rhode Island	113
24	Idaho	111
24	Iowa	111
26	Oregon	110
27	Michigan	109
28	Georgia	105
28	Wisconsin	105
30	Colorado	104
31	Illinois	102
31	Kentucky	102
31	Virginia	102
34	West Virginia	101
35	New Hampshire	99
36	Kansas	98
37	Tennessee	95
38	North Dakota	94
39	Nebraska	92
40	Texas	90
41	Alabama	88
42	Maine	84
42	Oklahoma	84
44	South Dakota	83
45	Missouri	82
46	Indiana	81
47	Mississippi	75
48	Arkansas	73
48	North Carolina	73
50	South Carolina	71

| District of Columbia | 183 |

Source: CQ Press using data from U.S. Bureau of the Census, Governments Division
"2008 State and Local Government Finances" (http://www.census.gov/govs/estimate/index.html)
*Direct general expenditures. Includes courts, prosecution and legal services, and public defense.

III. Defense

Homeland Security Grants in 2010

National Total = $1,726,359,956*

ALPHA ORDER

RANK	STATE	GRANTS	% of USA
30	Alabama	$11,293,846	0.7%
36	Alaska	7,358,300	0.4%
14	Arizona	30,086,524	1.7%
39	Arkansas	7,093,544	0.4%
2	California	268,685,401	15.6%
22	Colorado	19,209,759	1.1%
25	Connecticut	14,954,871	0.9%
46	Delaware	6,727,997	0.4%
5	Florida	71,139,501	4.1%
11	Georgia	33,716,473	2.0%
29	Hawaii	11,810,295	0.7%
43	Idaho	6,743,796	0.4%
4	Illinois	87,934,150	5.1%
21	Indiana	19,314,399	1.1%
37	Iowa	7,097,117	0.4%
35	Kansas	7,409,670	0.4%
31	Kentucky	11,045,187	0.6%
17	Louisiana	23,694,494	1.4%
44	Maine	6,738,762	0.4%
16	Maryland	27,342,383	1.6%
9	Massachusetts	35,713,314	2.1%
10	Michigan	34,075,707	2.0%
19	Minnesota	19,907,805	1.2%
38	Mississippi	7,095,565	0.4%
15	Missouri	28,169,120	1.6%
45	Montana	6,730,288	0.4%
34	Nebraska	8,398,024	0.5%
23	Nevada	16,492,596	1.0%
41	New Hampshire	7,056,165	0.4%
6	New Jersey	62,035,995	3.6%
40	New Mexico	7,072,396	0.4%
1	New York	277,150,581	16.1%
18	North Carolina	21,273,139	1.2%
48	North Dakota	6,722,374	0.4%
8	Ohio	40,437,889	2.3%
27	Oklahoma	13,999,310	0.8%
24	Oregon	15,401,772	0.9%
7	Pennsylvania	57,855,730	3.4%
28	Rhode Island	11,814,031	0.7%
33	South Carolina	8,412,080	0.5%
47	South Dakota	6,726,325	0.4%
20	Tennessee	19,564,050	1.1%
3	Texas	143,036,730	8.3%
32	Utah	9,990,734	0.6%
49	Vermont	6,721,884	0.4%
12	Virginia	30,915,010	1.8%
13	Washington	30,615,761	1.8%
42	West Virginia	6,750,853	0.4%
26	Wisconsin	14,609,829	0.8%
50	Wyoming	6,719,732	0.4%

RANK ORDER

RANK	STATE	GRANTS	% of USA
1	New York	$277,150,581	16.1%
2	California	268,685,401	15.6%
3	Texas	143,036,730	8.3%
4	Illinois	87,934,150	5.1%
5	Florida	71,139,501	4.1%
6	New Jersey	62,035,995	3.6%
7	Pennsylvania	57,855,730	3.4%
8	Ohio	40,437,889	2.3%
9	Massachusetts	35,713,314	2.1%
10	Michigan	34,075,707	2.0%
11	Georgia	33,716,473	2.0%
12	Virginia	30,915,010	1.8%
13	Washington	30,615,761	1.8%
14	Arizona	30,086,524	1.7%
15	Missouri	28,169,120	1.6%
16	Maryland	27,342,383	1.6%
17	Louisiana	23,694,494	1.4%
18	North Carolina	21,273,139	1.2%
19	Minnesota	19,907,805	1.2%
20	Tennessee	19,564,050	1.1%
21	Indiana	19,314,399	1.1%
22	Colorado	19,209,759	1.1%
23	Nevada	16,492,596	1.0%
24	Oregon	15,401,772	0.9%
25	Connecticut	14,954,871	0.9%
26	Wisconsin	14,609,829	0.8%
27	Oklahoma	13,999,310	0.8%
28	Rhode Island	11,814,031	0.7%
29	Hawaii	11,810,295	0.7%
30	Alabama	11,293,846	0.7%
31	Kentucky	11,045,187	0.6%
32	Utah	9,990,734	0.6%
33	South Carolina	8,412,080	0.5%
34	Nebraska	8,398,024	0.5%
35	Kansas	7,409,670	0.4%
36	Alaska	7,358,300	0.4%
37	Iowa	7,097,117	0.4%
38	Mississippi	7,095,565	0.4%
39	Arkansas	7,093,544	0.4%
40	New Mexico	7,072,396	0.4%
41	New Hampshire	7,056,165	0.4%
42	West Virginia	6,750,853	0.4%
43	Idaho	6,743,796	0.4%
44	Maine	6,738,762	0.4%
45	Montana	6,730,288	0.4%
46	Delaware	6,727,997	0.4%
47	South Dakota	6,726,325	0.4%
48	North Dakota	6,722,374	0.4%
49	Vermont	6,721,884	0.4%
50	Wyoming	6,719,732	0.4%
	District of Columbia	69,574,433	4.0%

Source: CQ Press using data from U.S. Department of Homeland Security
   "FY 2010 Preparedness Grant Programs Overview" (http://www.dhs.gov/xgovt/grants/)
*For fiscal year ending September 30. National total includes $15,924,265 in grants to U.S. territories. The Homeland Security Grant Program includes several sub-grant programs such as State Homeland Security, Urban Area Security Initiative, Law Enforcement Terrorism Prevention Program, and Emergency Management Performance.

Per Capita Homeland Security Grants in 2010

National Per Capita = $5.57*

RANK	STATE	PER CAPITA
46	Alabama	$2.40
5	Alaska	10.53
25	Arizona	4.56
45	Arkansas	2.45
10	California	7.27
31	Colorado	3.82
27	Connecticut	4.25
9	Delaware	7.60
30	Florida	3.84
38	Georgia	3.43
7	Hawaii	9.12
26	Idaho	4.36
13	Illinois	6.81
41	Indiana	3.01
48	Iowa	2.36
42	Kansas	2.63
44	Kentucky	2.56
18	Louisiana	5.27
19	Maine	5.11
20	Maryland	4.80
16	Massachusetts	5.42
39	Michigan	3.42
33	Minnesota	3.78
46	Mississippi	2.40
21	Missouri	4.70
12	Montana	6.90
22	Nebraska	4.67
14	Nevada	6.24
17	New Hampshire	5.33
11	New Jersey	7.12
36	New Mexico	3.52
1	New York	14.18
49	North Carolina	2.27
6	North Dakota	10.39
37	Ohio	3.50
32	Oklahoma	3.80
28	Oregon	4.03
23	Pennsylvania	4.59
3	Rhode Island	11.22
50	South Carolina	1.84
8	South Dakota	8.28
40	Tennessee	3.11
15	Texas	5.77
35	Utah	3.59
4	Vermont	10.81
29	Virginia	3.92
23	Washington	4.59
34	West Virginia	3.71
43	Wisconsin	2.58
2	Wyoming	12.35

RANK	STATE	PER CAPITA
1	New York	$14.18
2	Wyoming	12.35
3	Rhode Island	11.22
4	Vermont	10.81
5	Alaska	10.53
6	North Dakota	10.39
7	Hawaii	9.12
8	South Dakota	8.28
9	Delaware	7.60
10	California	7.27
11	New Jersey	7.12
12	Montana	6.90
13	Illinois	6.81
14	Nevada	6.24
15	Texas	5.77
16	Massachusetts	5.42
17	New Hampshire	5.33
18	Louisiana	5.27
19	Maine	5.11
20	Maryland	4.80
21	Missouri	4.70
22	Nebraska	4.67
23	Pennsylvania	4.59
23	Washington	4.59
25	Arizona	4.56
26	Idaho	4.36
27	Connecticut	4.25
28	Oregon	4.03
29	Virginia	3.92
30	Florida	3.84
31	Colorado	3.82
32	Oklahoma	3.80
33	Minnesota	3.78
34	West Virginia	3.71
35	Utah	3.59
36	New Mexico	3.52
37	Ohio	3.50
38	Georgia	3.43
39	Michigan	3.42
40	Tennessee	3.11
41	Indiana	3.01
42	Kansas	2.63
43	Wisconsin	2.58
44	Kentucky	2.56
45	Arkansas	2.45
46	Alabama	2.40
46	Mississippi	2.40
48	Iowa	2.36
49	North Carolina	2.27
50	South Carolina	1.84

District of Columbia	116.02

Source: CQ Press using data from U.S. Department of Homeland Security
   "FY 2010 Preparedness Grant Programs Overview" (http://www.dhs.gov/xgovt/grants/)
*For fiscal year ending September 30. National per capita does not include grants to U.S. territories. The Homeland Security Grant Program includes several sub-grant programs such as State Homeland Security, Urban Area Security Initiative, Law Enforcement Terrorism Prevention Program, and Emergency Management Performance.

U.S. Department of Defense Domestic Expenditures in 2009

National Total = $527,824,146,000*

ALPHA ORDER

ALPHA ORDER

RANK ORDER

RANK	STATE	EXPENDITURES	% of USA
11	Alabama	$14,291,629,000	2.7%
31	Alaska	4,888,348,000	0.9%
8	Arizona	15,308,486,000	2.9%
37	Arkansas	2,673,622,000	0.5%
2	California	56,742,620,000	10.8%
18	Colorado	10,725,693,000	2.0%
15	Connecticut	12,638,248,000	2.4%
47	Delaware	876,158,000	0.2%
4	Florida	22,802,179,000	4.3%
6	Georgia	18,607,996,000	3.5%
25	Hawaii	8,800,669,000	1.7%
46	Idaho	934,634,000	0.2%
20	Illinois	9,237,211,000	1.8%
21	Indiana	9,188,013,000	1.7%
40	Iowa	2,089,452,000	0.4%
28	Kansas	6,867,835,000	1.3%
16	Kentucky	12,285,425,000	2.3%
22	Louisiana	9,149,589,000	1.7%
38	Maine	2,382,017,000	0.5%
5	Maryland	19,926,029,000	3.8%
9	Massachusetts	15,081,759,000	2.9%
26	Michigan	7,288,503,000	1.4%
35	Minnesota	2,806,926,000	0.5%
29	Mississippi	5,689,655,000	1.1%
12	Missouri	14,281,251,000	2.7%
48	Montana	853,639,000	0.2%
39	Nebraska	2,142,336,000	0.4%
34	Nevada	3,268,456,000	0.6%
41	New Hampshire	2,014,350,000	0.4%
17	New Jersey	11,019,807,000	2.1%
33	New Mexico	3,270,536,000	0.6%
13	New York	13,562,174,000	2.6%
10	North Carolina	14,677,953,000	2.8%
43	North Dakota	1,100,340,000	0.2%
19	Ohio	10,256,353,000	1.9%
27	Oklahoma	7,103,675,000	1.3%
36	Oregon	2,695,604,000	0.5%
7	Pennsylvania	16,789,144,000	3.2%
42	Rhode Island	1,431,162,000	0.3%
23	South Carolina	9,020,997,000	1.7%
45	South Dakota	1,026,194,000	0.2%
30	Tennessee	5,362,492,000	1.0%
3	Texas	42,082,905,000	8.0%
32	Utah	4,361,476,000	0.8%
49	Vermont	828,433,000	0.2%
1	Virginia	56,933,799,000	10.8%
14	Washington	13,524,233,000	2.6%
44	West Virginia	1,063,251,000	0.2%
24	Wisconsin	8,898,053,000	1.7%
50	Wyoming	566,662,000	0.1%

RANK	STATE	EXPENDITURES	% of USA
1	Virginia	$56,933,799,000	10.8%
2	California	56,742,620,000	10.8%
3	Texas	42,082,905,000	8.0%
4	Florida	22,802,179,000	4.3%
5	Maryland	19,926,029,000	3.8%
6	Georgia	18,607,996,000	3.5%
7	Pennsylvania	16,789,144,000	3.2%
8	Arizona	15,308,486,000	2.9%
9	Massachusetts	15,081,759,000	2.9%
10	North Carolina	14,677,953,000	2.8%
11	Alabama	14,291,629,000	2.7%
12	Missouri	14,281,251,000	2.7%
13	New York	13,562,174,000	2.6%
14	Washington	13,524,233,000	2.6%
15	Connecticut	12,638,248,000	2.4%
16	Kentucky	12,285,425,000	2.3%
17	New Jersey	11,019,807,000	2.1%
18	Colorado	10,725,693,000	2.0%
19	Ohio	10,256,353,000	1.9%
20	Illinois	9,237,211,000	1.8%
21	Indiana	9,188,013,000	1.7%
22	Louisiana	9,149,589,000	1.7%
23	South Carolina	9,020,997,000	1.7%
24	Wisconsin	8,898,053,000	1.7%
25	Hawaii	8,800,669,000	1.7%
26	Michigan	7,288,503,000	1.4%
27	Oklahoma	7,103,675,000	1.3%
28	Kansas	6,867,835,000	1.3%
29	Mississippi	5,689,655,000	1.1%
30	Tennessee	5,362,492,000	1.0%
31	Alaska	4,888,348,000	0.9%
32	Utah	4,361,476,000	0.8%
33	New Mexico	3,270,536,000	0.6%
34	Nevada	3,268,456,000	0.6%
35	Minnesota	2,806,926,000	0.5%
36	Oregon	2,695,604,000	0.5%
37	Arkansas	2,673,622,000	0.5%
38	Maine	2,382,017,000	0.5%
39	Nebraska	2,142,336,000	0.4%
40	Iowa	2,089,452,000	0.4%
41	New Hampshire	2,014,350,000	0.4%
42	Rhode Island	1,431,162,000	0.3%
43	North Dakota	1,100,340,000	0.2%
44	West Virginia	1,063,251,000	0.2%
45	South Dakota	1,026,194,000	0.2%
46	Idaho	934,634,000	0.2%
47	Delaware	876,158,000	0.2%
48	Montana	853,639,000	0.2%
49	Vermont	828,433,000	0.2%
50	Wyoming	566,662,000	0.1%
	District of Columbia	8,406,175,000	1.6%

Source: U.S. Department of Defense

"Atlas/Data Abstract for the United States" (http://siadapp.dmdc.osd.mil/personnel/L03/fy09/09top.htm)

*Expenditures for payroll, grants, and prime contracts ($25,000 or more) for civil and military functions. Does not include payroll, contracts, or grants to U.S. territories and other countries.

Per Capita U.S. Department of Defense Domestic Expenditures in 2009

National Per Capita = $1,719*

ALPHA ORDER

RANK	STATE	PER CAPITA
6	Alabama	$3,035
2	Alaska	6,999
10	Arizona	2,321
39	Arkansas	925
26	California	1,535
12	Colorado	2,135
4	Connecticut	3,592
38	Delaware	990
35	Florida	1,230
18	Georgia	1,893
3	Hawaii	6,795
48	Idaho	605
44	Illinois	715
28	Indiana	1,430
46	Iowa	695
8	Kansas	2,436
7	Kentucky	2,848
13	Louisiana	2,037
19	Maine	1,807
5	Maryland	3,496
11	Massachusetts	2,287
43	Michigan	731
50	Minnesota	533
16	Mississippi	1,927
9	Missouri	2,385
41	Montana	876
36	Nebraska	1,192
34	Nevada	1,237
27	New Hampshire	1,521
32	New Jersey	1,266
22	New Mexico	1,627
47	New York	694
25	North Carolina	1,565
20	North Dakota	1,701
40	Ohio	889
16	Oklahoma	1,927
45	Oregon	705
30	Pennsylvania	1,332
29	Rhode Island	1,359
15	South Carolina	1,978
33	South Dakota	1,263
42	Tennessee	852
21	Texas	1,698
24	Utah	1,566
30	Vermont	1,332
1	Virginia	7,223
14	Washington	2,029
49	West Virginia	584
23	Wisconsin	1,574
37	Wyoming	1,041

RANK ORDER

RANK	STATE	PER CAPITA
1	Virginia	$7,223
2	Alaska	6,999
3	Hawaii	6,795
4	Connecticut	3,592
5	Maryland	3,496
6	Alabama	3,035
7	Kentucky	2,848
8	Kansas	2,436
9	Missouri	2,385
10	Arizona	2,321
11	Massachusetts	2,287
12	Colorado	2,135
13	Louisiana	2,037
14	Washington	2,029
15	South Carolina	1,978
16	Mississippi	1,927
16	Oklahoma	1,927
18	Georgia	1,893
19	Maine	1,807
20	North Dakota	1,701
21	Texas	1,698
22	New Mexico	1,627
23	Wisconsin	1,574
24	Utah	1,566
25	North Carolina	1,565
26	California	1,535
27	New Hampshire	1,521
28	Indiana	1,430
29	Rhode Island	1,359
30	Pennsylvania	1,332
30	Vermont	1,332
32	New Jersey	1,266
33	South Dakota	1,263
34	Nevada	1,237
35	Florida	1,230
36	Nebraska	1,192
37	Wyoming	1,041
38	Delaware	990
39	Arkansas	925
40	Ohio	889
41	Montana	876
42	Tennessee	852
43	Michigan	731
44	Illinois	715
45	Oregon	705
46	Iowa	695
47	New York	694
48	Idaho	605
49	West Virginia	584
50	Minnesota	533

District of Columbia   14,018

Source: CQ Press using data from U.S. Department of Defense
"Atlas/Data Abstract for the United States" (http://siadapp.dmdc.osd.mil/personnel/L03/fy09/09top.htm)
*Expenditures for payroll, grants, and prime contracts ($25,000 or more) for civil and military functions. Does not include payroll, contracts, or grants to U.S. territories and other countries.

U.S. Department of Defense Total Contracts in 2009

National Total = $327,461,911,000*

ALPHA ORDER

RANK	STATE	CONTRACTS	% of USA
11	Alabama	$9,501,617,000	2.9%
32	Alaska	2,180,004,000	0.7%
8	Arizona	12,064,904,000	3.7%
40	Arkansas	985,545,000	0.3%
1	California	41,697,621,000	12.7%
21	Colorado	5,544,160,000	1.7%
9	Connecticut	11,817,700,000	3.6%
47	Delaware	315,358,000	0.1%
5	Florida	13,188,889,000	4.0%
15	Georgia	7,039,405,000	2.1%
30	Hawaii	2,377,271,000	0.7%
49	Idaho	166,118,000	0.1%
20	Illinois	5,936,547,000	1.8%
16	Indiana	6,795,168,000	2.1%
39	Iowa	1,285,344,000	0.4%
27	Kansas	3,158,303,000	1.0%
17	Kentucky	6,534,291,000	2.0%
18	Louisiana	6,407,579,000	2.0%
38	Maine	1,407,038,000	0.4%
6	Maryland	12,911,613,000	3.9%
4	Massachusetts	13,347,134,000	4.1%
22	Michigan	5,331,864,000	1.6%
37	Minnesota	1,529,964,000	0.5%
26	Mississippi	3,447,072,000	1.1%
10	Missouri	10,453,949,000	3.2%
48	Montana	288,759,000	0.1%
41	Nebraska	931,306,000	0.3%
33	Nevada	1,818,505,000	0.6%
35	New Hampshire	1,567,821,000	0.5%
13	New Jersey	8,226,697,000	2.5%
34	New Mexico	1,604,488,000	0.5%
12	New York	8,544,864,000	2.6%
25	North Carolina	3,994,861,000	1.2%
45	North Dakota	437,227,000	0.1%
19	Ohio	6,249,462,000	1.9%
29	Oklahoma	2,880,203,000	0.9%
36	Oregon	1,545,991,000	0.5%
7	Pennsylvania	12,362,728,000	3.8%
42	Rhode Island	661,794,000	0.2%
23	South Carolina	5,298,645,000	1.6%
44	South Dakota	444,618,000	0.1%
28	Tennessee	3,083,056,000	0.9%
3	Texas	22,483,566,000	6.9%
31	Utah	2,206,025,000	0.7%
43	Vermont	549,931,000	0.2%
2	Virginia	38,731,568,000	11.8%
24	Washington	5,173,959,000	1.6%
46	West Virginia	396,440,000	0.1%
14	Wisconsin	7,673,970,000	2.3%
50	Wyoming	140,406,000	0.0%

RANK ORDER

RANK	STATE	CONTRACTS	% of USA
1	California	$41,697,621,000	12.7%
2	Virginia	38,731,568,000	11.8%
3	Texas	22,483,566,000	6.9%
4	Massachusetts	13,347,134,000	4.1%
5	Florida	13,188,889,000	4.0%
6	Maryland	12,911,613,000	3.9%
7	Pennsylvania	12,362,728,000	3.8%
8	Arizona	12,064,904,000	3.7%
9	Connecticut	11,817,700,000	3.6%
10	Missouri	10,453,949,000	3.2%
11	Alabama	9,501,617,000	2.9%
12	New York	8,544,864,000	2.6%
13	New Jersey	8,226,697,000	2.5%
14	Wisconsin	7,673,970,000	2.3%
15	Georgia	7,039,405,000	2.1%
16	Indiana	6,795,168,000	2.1%
17	Kentucky	6,534,291,000	2.0%
18	Louisiana	6,407,579,000	2.0%
19	Ohio	6,249,462,000	1.9%
20	Illinois	5,936,547,000	1.8%
21	Colorado	5,544,160,000	1.7%
22	Michigan	5,331,864,000	1.6%
23	South Carolina	5,298,645,000	1.6%
24	Washington	5,173,959,000	1.6%
25	North Carolina	3,994,861,000	1.2%
26	Mississippi	3,447,072,000	1.1%
27	Kansas	3,158,303,000	1.0%
28	Tennessee	3,083,056,000	0.9%
29	Oklahoma	2,880,203,000	0.9%
30	Hawaii	2,377,271,000	0.7%
31	Utah	2,206,025,000	0.7%
32	Alaska	2,180,004,000	0.7%
33	Nevada	1,818,505,000	0.6%
34	New Mexico	1,604,488,000	0.5%
35	New Hampshire	1,567,821,000	0.5%
36	Oregon	1,545,991,000	0.5%
37	Minnesota	1,529,964,000	0.5%
38	Maine	1,407,038,000	0.4%
39	Iowa	1,285,344,000	0.4%
40	Arkansas	985,545,000	0.3%
41	Nebraska	931,306,000	0.3%
42	Rhode Island	661,794,000	0.2%
43	Vermont	549,931,000	0.2%
44	South Dakota	444,618,000	0.1%
45	North Dakota	437,227,000	0.1%
46	West Virginia	396,440,000	0.1%
47	Delaware	315,358,000	0.1%
48	Montana	288,759,000	0.1%
49	Idaho	166,118,000	0.1%
50	Wyoming	140,406,000	0.0%
	District of Columbia	4,740,563,000	1.4%

Source: U.S. Department of Defense
   "Atlas/Data Abstract for the United States" (http://siadapp.dmdc.osd.mil/personnel/L03/fy09/09top.htm)
*Includes prime contracts ($25,000 or more) for civil and military functions. Does not include contracts to U.S. territories and other countries.

Per Capita U.S. Department of Defense Total Contracts in 2009

National Per Capita = $1,067*

ALPHA ORDER			RANK ORDER		
RANK	STATE	PER CAPITA	RANK	STATE	PER CAPITA
6	Alabama	$2,018	1	Virginia	$4,914
3	Alaska	3,121	2	Connecticut	3,359
8	Arizona	1,829	3	Alaska	3,121
45	Arkansas	341	4	Maryland	2,265
16	California	1,128	5	Massachusetts	2,024
18	Colorado	1,103	6	Alabama	2,018
2	Connecticut	3,359	7	Hawaii	1,835
44	Delaware	356	8	Arizona	1,829
30	Florida	711	9	Missouri	1,746
29	Georgia	716	10	Kentucky	1,515
7	Hawaii	1,835	11	Louisiana	1,426
50	Idaho	107	12	Wisconsin	1,357
39	Illinois	460	13	New Hampshire	1,184
20	Indiana	1,058	14	Mississippi	1,168
41	Iowa	427	15	South Carolina	1,162
17	Kansas	1,120	16	California	1,128
10	Kentucky	1,515	17	Kansas	1,120
11	Louisiana	1,426	18	Colorado	1,103
19	Maine	1,067	19	Maine	1,067
4	Maryland	2,265	20	Indiana	1,058
5	Massachusetts	2,024	21	Pennsylvania	981
36	Michigan	535	22	New Jersey	945
47	Minnesota	291	23	Texas	907
14	Mississippi	1,168	24	Vermont	884
9	Missouri	1,746	25	New Mexico	798
46	Montana	296	26	Utah	792
37	Nebraska	518	27	Oklahoma	781
31	Nevada	688	28	Washington	776
13	New Hampshire	1,184	29	Georgia	716
22	New Jersey	945	30	Florida	711
25	New Mexico	798	31	Nevada	688
40	New York	437	32	North Dakota	676
42	North Carolina	426	33	Rhode Island	628
32	North Dakota	676	34	South Dakota	547
35	Ohio	541	35	Ohio	541
27	Oklahoma	781	36	Michigan	535
43	Oregon	404	37	Nebraska	518
21	Pennsylvania	981	38	Tennessee	490
33	Rhode Island	628	39	Illinois	460
15	South Carolina	1,162	40	New York	437
34	South Dakota	547	41	Iowa	427
38	Tennessee	490	42	North Carolina	426
23	Texas	907	43	Oregon	404
26	Utah	792	44	Delaware	356
24	Vermont	884	45	Arkansas	341
1	Virginia	4,914	46	Montana	296
28	Washington	776	47	Minnesota	291
49	West Virginia	218	48	Wyoming	258
12	Wisconsin	1,357	49	West Virginia	218
48	Wyoming	258	50	Idaho	107
				District of Columbia	7,905

Source: CQ Press using data from U.S. Department of Defense
"Atlas/Data Abstract for the United States" (http://siadapp.dmdc.osd.mil/personnel/L03/fy09/09top.htm)
*Includes prime contracts ($25,000 or more) for civil and military functions. Does not include contracts to U.S. territories and other countries.

U.S. Department of Defense Grants in 2009

National Total = $5,192,057,000*

ALPHA ORDER

RANK	STATE	GRANTS	% of USA
27	Alabama	$66,056,000	1.3%
35	Alaska	48,783,000	0.9%
17	Arizona	105,948,000	2.0%
26	Arkansas	66,370,000	1.3%
2	California	476,541,000	9.2%
31	Colorado	56,411,000	1.1%
18	Connecticut	100,249,000	1.9%
47	Delaware	24,042,000	0.5%
7	Florida	195,371,000	3.8%
21	Georgia	73,944,000	1.4%
20	Hawaii	78,931,000	1.5%
28	Idaho	59,296,000	1.1%
9	Illinois	172,126,000	3.3%
32	Indiana	54,724,000	1.1%
30	Iowa	56,852,000	1.1%
37	Kansas	41,857,000	0.8%
23	Kentucky	70,382,000	1.4%
33	Louisiana	53,861,000	1.0%
12	Maine	128,298,000	2.5%
1	Maryland	476,575,000	9.2%
4	Massachusetts	243,995,000	4.7%
11	Michigan	129,652,000	2.5%
24	Minnesota	68,900,000	1.3%
49	Mississippi	18,237,000	0.4%
38	Missouri	40,466,000	0.8%
46	Montana	24,236,000	0.5%
29	Nebraska	59,049,000	1.1%
43	Nevada	35,345,000	0.7%
42	New Hampshire	35,647,000	0.7%
16	New Jersey	121,890,000	2.3%
39	New Mexico	39,587,000	0.8%
6	New York	198,631,000	3.8%
14	North Carolina	124,942,000	2.4%
44	North Dakota	32,174,000	0.6%
8	Ohio	172,421,000	3.3%
15	Oklahoma	123,839,000	2.4%
19	Oregon	98,566,000	1.9%
5	Pennsylvania	216,030,000	4.2%
45	Rhode Island	26,333,000	0.5%
41	South Carolina	39,365,000	0.8%
25	South Dakota	67,933,000	1.3%
36	Tennessee	44,134,000	0.9%
3	Texas	300,450,000	5.8%
40	Utah	39,483,000	0.8%
50	Vermont	16,997,000	0.3%
10	Virginia	130,816,000	2.5%
13	Washington	126,539,000	2.4%
34	West Virginia	49,988,000	1.0%
22	Wisconsin	72,192,000	1.4%
48	Wyoming	21,236,000	0.4%

RANK ORDER

RANK	STATE	GRANTS	% of USA
1	Maryland	$476,575,000	9.2%
2	California	476,541,000	9.2%
3	Texas	300,450,000	5.8%
4	Massachusetts	243,995,000	4.7%
5	Pennsylvania	216,030,000	4.2%
6	New York	198,631,000	3.8%
7	Florida	195,371,000	3.8%
8	Ohio	172,421,000	3.3%
9	Illinois	172,126,000	3.3%
10	Virginia	130,816,000	2.5%
11	Michigan	129,652,000	2.5%
12	Maine	128,298,000	2.5%
13	Washington	126,539,000	2.4%
14	North Carolina	124,942,000	2.4%
15	Oklahoma	123,839,000	2.4%
16	New Jersey	121,890,000	2.3%
17	Arizona	105,948,000	2.0%
18	Connecticut	100,249,000	1.9%
19	Oregon	98,566,000	1.9%
20	Hawaii	78,931,000	1.5%
21	Georgia	73,944,000	1.4%
22	Wisconsin	72,192,000	1.4%
23	Kentucky	70,382,000	1.4%
24	Minnesota	68,900,000	1.3%
25	South Dakota	67,933,000	1.3%
26	Arkansas	66,370,000	1.3%
27	Alabama	66,056,000	1.3%
28	Idaho	59,296,000	1.1%
29	Nebraska	59,049,000	1.1%
30	Iowa	56,852,000	1.1%
31	Colorado	56,411,000	1.1%
32	Indiana	54,724,000	1.1%
33	Louisiana	53,861,000	1.0%
34	West Virginia	49,988,000	1.0%
35	Alaska	48,783,000	0.9%
36	Tennessee	44,134,000	0.9%
37	Kansas	41,857,000	0.8%
38	Missouri	40,466,000	0.8%
39	New Mexico	39,587,000	0.8%
40	Utah	39,483,000	0.8%
41	South Carolina	39,365,000	0.8%
42	New Hampshire	35,647,000	0.7%
43	Nevada	35,345,000	0.7%
44	North Dakota	32,174,000	0.6%
45	Rhode Island	26,333,000	0.5%
46	Montana	24,236,000	0.5%
47	Delaware	24,042,000	0.5%
48	Wyoming	21,236,000	0.4%
49	Mississippi	18,237,000	0.4%
50	Vermont	16,997,000	0.3%
	District of Columbia	66,367,000	1.3%

Source: U.S. Department of Defense
   "Atlas/Data Abstract for the United States" (http://siadapp.dmdc.osd.mil/personnel/L03/fy09/09top.htm)
*Includes grants for civil and military functions. Does not include contracts to U.S. territories and other countries.

Per Capita U.S. Department of Defense Grants in 2009

National Per Capita = $16.91*

ALPHA ORDER

RANK	STATE	PER CAPITA
31	Alabama	$14.03
4	Alaska	69.84
27	Arizona	16.06
20	Arkansas	22.97
38	California	12.89
42	Colorado	11.23
12	Connecticut	28.49
15	Delaware	27.16
43	Florida	10.54
47	Georgia	7.52
5	Hawaii	60.94
8	Idaho	38.36
34	Illinois	13.33
46	Indiana	8.52
23	Iowa	18.90
29	Kansas	14.85
26	Kentucky	16.31
41	Louisiana	11.99
1	Maine	97.32
2	Maryland	83.62
9	Massachusetts	37.00
37	Michigan	13.00
36	Minnesota	13.08
50	Mississippi	6.18
49	Missouri	6.76
19	Montana	24.86
11	Nebraska	32.87
33	Nevada	13.37
16	New Hampshire	26.91
32	New Jersey	14.00
21	New Mexico	19.70
44	New York	10.16
35	North Carolina	13.32
6	North Dakota	49.74
28	Ohio	14.94
10	Oklahoma	33.59
17	Oregon	25.76
24	Pennsylvania	17.14
18	Rhode Island	25.00
45	South Carolina	8.63
2	South Dakota	83.62
48	Tennessee	7.01
40	Texas	12.12
30	Utah	14.18
14	Vermont	27.34
25	Virginia	16.60
22	Washington	18.99
13	West Virginia	27.47
39	Wisconsin	12.77
7	Wyoming	39.02

RANK ORDER

RANK	STATE	PER CAPITA
1	Maine	$97.32
2	Maryland	83.62
2	South Dakota	83.62
4	Alaska	69.84
5	Hawaii	60.94
6	North Dakota	49.74
7	Wyoming	39.02
8	Idaho	38.36
9	Massachusetts	37.00
10	Oklahoma	33.59
11	Nebraska	32.87
12	Connecticut	28.49
13	West Virginia	27.47
14	Vermont	27.34
15	Delaware	27.16
16	New Hampshire	26.91
17	Oregon	25.76
18	Rhode Island	25.00
19	Montana	24.86
20	Arkansas	22.97
21	New Mexico	19.70
22	Washington	18.99
23	Iowa	18.90
24	Pennsylvania	17.14
25	Virginia	16.60
26	Kentucky	16.31
27	Arizona	16.06
28	Ohio	14.94
29	Kansas	14.85
30	Utah	14.18
31	Alabama	14.03
32	New Jersey	14.00
33	Nevada	13.37
34	Illinois	13.33
35	North Carolina	13.32
36	Minnesota	13.08
37	Michigan	13.00
38	California	12.89
39	Wisconsin	12.77
40	Texas	12.12
41	Louisiana	11.99
42	Colorado	11.23
43	Florida	10.54
44	New York	10.16
45	South Carolina	8.63
46	Indiana	8.52
47	Georgia	7.52
48	Tennessee	7.01
49	Missouri	6.76
50	Mississippi	6.18
	District of Columbia	110.67

Source: CQ Press using data from U.S. Department of Defense
"Atlas/Data Abstract for the United States" (http://siadapp.dmdc.osd.mil/personnel/L03/fy09/09top.htm)
*Includes grants for civil and military functions. Does not include contracts to U.S. territories and other countries.

U.S. Department of Defense Domestic Personnel in 2009

National Total = 2,617,048 Personnel*

ALPHA ORDER

RANK	STATE	PERSONNEL	% of USA
17	Alabama	58,789	2.2%
26	Alaska	33,281	1.3%
21	Arizona	44,662	1.7%
31	Arkansas	23,936	0.9%
1	California	236,963	9.1%
15	Colorado	59,480	2.3%
43	Connecticut	10,908	0.4%
44	Delaware	10,373	0.4%
6	Florida	105,724	4.0%
5	Georgia	140,358	5.4%
10	Hawaii	68,550	2.6%
41	Idaho	12,575	0.5%
19	Illinois	50,965	1.9%
25	Indiana	35,113	1.3%
38	Iowa	15,419	0.6%
20	Kansas	44,761	1.7%
11	Kentucky	65,226	2.5%
22	Louisiana	42,056	1.6%
42	Maine	11,829	0.5%
8	Maryland	80,126	3.1%
30	Massachusetts	25,458	1.0%
29	Michigan	29,448	1.1%
32	Minnesota	23,905	0.9%
24	Mississippi	36,351	1.4%
18	Missouri	51,676	2.0%
47	Montana	9,967	0.4%
36	Nebraska	18,128	0.7%
35	Nevada	18,440	0.7%
49	New Hampshire	5,973	0.2%
23	New Jersey	39,202	1.5%
33	New Mexico	23,266	0.9%
9	New York	72,233	2.8%
4	North Carolina	159,041	6.1%
39	North Dakota	13,788	0.5%
14	Ohio	61,785	2.4%
16	Oklahoma	59,428	2.3%
37	Oregon	15,646	0.6%
12	Pennsylvania	64,619	2.5%
45	Rhode Island	10,300	0.4%
13	South Carolina	62,026	2.4%
46	South Dakota	10,280	0.4%
28	Tennessee	32,084	1.2%
2	Texas	235,972	9.0%
27	Utah	33,054	1.3%
50	Vermont	5,246	0.2%
3	Virginia	177,982	6.8%
7	Washington	93,611	3.6%
40	West Virginia	12,648	0.5%
34	Wisconsin	20,689	0.8%
48	Wyoming	7,818	0.3%

RANK ORDER

RANK	STATE	PERSONNEL	% of USA
1	California	236,963	9.1%
2	Texas	235,972	9.0%
3	Virginia	177,982	6.8%
4	North Carolina	159,041	6.1%
5	Georgia	140,358	5.4%
6	Florida	105,724	4.0%
7	Washington	93,611	3.6%
8	Maryland	80,126	3.1%
9	New York	72,233	2.8%
10	Hawaii	68,550	2.6%
11	Kentucky	65,226	2.5%
12	Pennsylvania	64,619	2.5%
13	South Carolina	62,026	2.4%
14	Ohio	61,785	2.4%
15	Colorado	59,480	2.3%
16	Oklahoma	59,428	2.3%
17	Alabama	58,789	2.2%
18	Missouri	51,676	2.0%
19	Illinois	50,965	1.9%
20	Kansas	44,761	1.7%
21	Arizona	44,662	1.7%
22	Louisiana	42,056	1.6%
23	New Jersey	39,202	1.5%
24	Mississippi	36,351	1.4%
25	Indiana	35,113	1.3%
26	Alaska	33,281	1.3%
27	Utah	33,054	1.3%
28	Tennessee	32,084	1.2%
29	Michigan	29,448	1.1%
30	Massachusetts	25,458	1.0%
31	Arkansas	23,936	0.9%
32	Minnesota	23,905	0.9%
33	New Mexico	23,266	0.9%
34	Wisconsin	20,689	0.8%
35	Nevada	18,440	0.7%
36	Nebraska	18,128	0.7%
37	Oregon	15,646	0.6%
38	Iowa	15,419	0.6%
39	North Dakota	13,788	0.5%
40	West Virginia	12,648	0.5%
41	Idaho	12,575	0.5%
42	Maine	11,829	0.5%
43	Connecticut	10,908	0.4%
44	Delaware	10,373	0.4%
45	Rhode Island	10,300	0.4%
46	South Dakota	10,280	0.4%
47	Montana	9,967	0.4%
48	Wyoming	7,818	0.3%
49	New Hampshire	5,973	0.2%
50	Vermont	5,246	0.2%
	District of Columbia	35,890	1.4%

Source: U.S. Department of Defense
"Atlas/Data Abstract for the United States" (http://siadapp.dmdc.osd.mil/personnel/L03/fy09/09top.htm)
*Includes Active Duty Military, Civilian, Reserve, and National Guard personnel. Does not include personnel in U.S. territories or in other countries.

U.S. Department of Defense Active Duty Military Personnel in 2009

National Total = 1,088,465 Personnel*

ALPHA ORDER

RANK	STATE	PERSONNEL	% of USA
20	Alabama	11,896	1.1%
15	Alaska	23,178	2.1%
17	Arizona	21,343	2.0%
28	Arkansas	6,717	0.6%
2	California	117,806	10.8%
10	Colorado	35,404	3.3%
42	Connecticut	1,914	0.2%
34	Delaware	3,870	0.4%
8	Florida	42,642	3.9%
4	Georgia	73,988	6.8%
9	Hawaii	40,874	3.8%
32	Idaho	4,967	0.5%
22	Illinois	10,111	0.9%
39	Indiana	3,108	0.3%
46	Iowa	1,296	0.1%
14	Kansas	25,482	2.3%
7	Kentucky	43,138	4.0%
19	Louisiana	17,398	1.6%
48	Maine	730	0.1%
13	Maryland	29,160	2.7%
38	Massachusetts	3,205	0.3%
40	Michigan	2,858	0.3%
43	Minnesota	1,897	0.2%
24	Mississippi	9,895	0.9%
18	Missouri	17,925	1.6%
35	Montana	3,623	0.3%
27	Nebraska	6,845	0.6%
23	Nevada	10,034	0.9%
49	New Hampshire	675	0.1%
29	New Jersey	6,673	0.6%
21	New Mexico	11,038	1.0%
12	New York	29,553	2.7%
3	North Carolina	116,073	10.7%
26	North Dakota	7,209	0.7%
25	Ohio	8,261	0.8%
16	Oklahoma	21,673	2.0%
44	Oregon	1,615	0.1%
31	Pennsylvania	5,215	0.5%
45	Rhode Island	1,490	0.1%
11	South Carolina	32,518	3.0%
33	South Dakota	3,910	0.4%
36	Tennessee	3,511	0.3%
1	Texas	131,548	12.1%
30	Utah	6,237	0.6%
50	Vermont	565	0.1%
5	Virginia	63,160	5.8%
6	Washington	46,161	4.2%
47	West Virginia	1,199	0.1%
41	Wisconsin	2,046	0.2%
37	Wyoming	3,407	0.3%

RANK ORDER

RANK	STATE	PERSONNEL	% of USA
1	Texas	131,548	12.1%
2	California	117,806	10.8%
3	North Carolina	116,073	10.7%
4	Georgia	73,988	6.8%
5	Virginia	63,160	5.8%
6	Washington	46,161	4.2%
7	Kentucky	43,138	4.0%
8	Florida	42,642	3.9%
9	Hawaii	40,874	3.8%
10	Colorado	35,404	3.3%
11	South Carolina	32,518	3.0%
12	New York	29,553	2.7%
13	Maryland	29,160	2.7%
14	Kansas	25,482	2.3%
15	Alaska	23,178	2.1%
16	Oklahoma	21,673	2.0%
17	Arizona	21,343	2.0%
18	Missouri	17,925	1.6%
19	Louisiana	17,398	1.6%
20	Alabama	11,896	1.1%
21	New Mexico	11,038	1.0%
22	Illinois	10,111	0.9%
23	Nevada	10,034	0.9%
24	Mississippi	9,895	0.9%
25	Ohio	8,261	0.8%
26	North Dakota	7,209	0.7%
27	Nebraska	6,845	0.6%
28	Arkansas	6,717	0.6%
29	New Jersey	6,673	0.6%
30	Utah	6,237	0.6%
31	Pennsylvania	5,215	0.5%
32	Idaho	4,967	0.5%
33	South Dakota	3,910	0.4%
34	Delaware	3,870	0.4%
35	Montana	3,623	0.3%
36	Tennessee	3,511	0.3%
37	Wyoming	3,407	0.3%
38	Massachusetts	3,205	0.3%
39	Indiana	3,108	0.3%
40	Michigan	2,858	0.3%
41	Wisconsin	2,046	0.2%
42	Connecticut	1,914	0.2%
43	Minnesota	1,897	0.2%
44	Oregon	1,615	0.1%
45	Rhode Island	1,490	0.1%
46	Iowa	1,296	0.1%
47	West Virginia	1,199	0.1%
48	Maine	730	0.1%
49	New Hampshire	675	0.1%
50	Vermont	565	0.1%
	District of Columbia	13,424	1.2%

Source: U.S. Department of Defense
"Atlas/Data Abstract for the United States" (http://siadapp.dmdc.osd.mil/personnel/L03/fy09/09top.htm)
*Does not include active duty personnel in U.S. territories, in other countries or others undistributed.

U.S. Department of Defense Domestic Civilian Personnel in 2009

National Total = 709,265 Personnel*

ALPHA ORDER

RANK	STATE	PERSONNEL	% of USA
10	Alabama	24,794	3.5%
32	Alaska	5,356	0.8%
22	Arizona	9,591	1.4%
34	Arkansas	4,168	0.6%
2	California	61,365	8.7%
18	Colorado	11,585	1.6%
39	Connecticut	2,625	0.4%
45	Delaware	1,622	0.2%
6	Florida	28,429	4.0%
4	Georgia	37,012	5.2%
13	Hawaii	18,400	2.6%
44	Idaho	1,716	0.2%
14	Illinois	15,770	2.2%
19	Indiana	10,932	1.5%
43	Iowa	1,733	0.2%
27	Kansas	7,800	1.1%
25	Kentucky	8,962	1.3%
31	Louisiana	6,647	0.9%
29	Maine	6,946	1.0%
5	Maryland	34,966	4.9%
30	Massachusetts	6,918	1.0%
24	Michigan	8,972	1.3%
38	Minnesota	2,752	0.4%
23	Mississippi	9,124	1.3%
21	Missouri	9,982	1.4%
46	Montana	1,596	0.2%
35	Nebraska	3,785	0.5%
40	Nevada	2,319	0.3%
49	New Hampshire	1,047	0.1%
15	New Jersey	15,217	2.1%
28	New Mexico	7,029	1.0%
17	New York	12,318	1.7%
12	North Carolina	20,426	2.9%
42	North Dakota	1,910	0.3%
9	Ohio	25,001	3.5%
11	Oklahoma	22,115	3.1%
36	Oregon	3,561	0.5%
8	Pennsylvania	27,107	3.8%
33	Rhode Island	4,372	0.6%
20	South Carolina	10,406	1.5%
47	South Dakota	1,388	0.2%
26	Tennessee	7,967	1.1%
3	Texas	48,057	6.8%
16	Utah	14,818	2.1%
50	Vermont	729	0.1%
1	Virginia	89,713	12.6%
7	Washington	27,980	3.9%
41	West Virginia	2,146	0.3%
37	Wisconsin	2,810	0.4%
48	Wyoming	1,193	0.2%

RANK ORDER

RANK	STATE	PERSONNEL	% of USA
1	Virginia	89,713	12.6%
2	California	61,365	8.7%
3	Texas	48,057	6.8%
4	Georgia	37,012	5.2%
5	Maryland	34,966	4.9%
6	Florida	28,429	4.0%
7	Washington	27,980	3.9%
8	Pennsylvania	27,107	3.8%
9	Ohio	25,001	3.5%
10	Alabama	24,794	3.5%
11	Oklahoma	22,115	3.1%
12	North Carolina	20,426	2.9%
13	Hawaii	18,400	2.6%
14	Illinois	15,770	2.2%
15	New Jersey	15,217	2.1%
16	Utah	14,818	2.1%
17	New York	12,318	1.7%
18	Colorado	11,585	1.6%
19	Indiana	10,932	1.5%
20	South Carolina	10,406	1.5%
21	Missouri	9,982	1.4%
22	Arizona	9,591	1.4%
23	Mississippi	9,124	1.3%
24	Michigan	8,972	1.3%
25	Kentucky	8,962	1.3%
26	Tennessee	7,967	1.1%
27	Kansas	7,800	1.1%
28	New Mexico	7,029	1.0%
29	Maine	6,946	1.0%
30	Massachusetts	6,918	1.0%
31	Louisiana	6,647	0.9%
32	Alaska	5,356	0.8%
33	Rhode Island	4,372	0.6%
34	Arkansas	4,168	0.6%
35	Nebraska	3,785	0.5%
36	Oregon	3,561	0.5%
37	Wisconsin	2,810	0.4%
38	Minnesota	2,752	0.4%
39	Connecticut	2,625	0.4%
40	Nevada	2,319	0.3%
41	West Virginia	2,146	0.3%
42	North Dakota	1,910	0.3%
43	Iowa	1,733	0.2%
44	Idaho	1,716	0.2%
45	Delaware	1,622	0.2%
46	Montana	1,596	0.2%
47	South Dakota	1,388	0.2%
48	Wyoming	1,193	0.2%
49	New Hampshire	1,047	0.1%
50	Vermont	729	0.1%
	District of Columbia	16,088	2.3%

Source: U.S. Department of Defense

"Atlas/Data Abstract for the United States" (http://siadapp.dmdc.osd.mil/personnel/L03/fy09/09top.htm)

*Does not include civilian personnel in U.S. territories or civilian personnel in other countries. Includes military and civil functions.

U.S. Department of Defense Reserve and National Guard Personnel in 2009

National Total = 819,318 Personnel*

ALPHA ORDER

RANK	STATE	PERSONNEL	% of USA
12	Alabama	22,099	2.7%
44	Alaska	4,747	0.6%
26	Arizona	13,728	1.7%
28	Arkansas	13,051	1.6%
1	California	57,792	7.1%
29	Colorado	12,491	1.5%
37	Connecticut	6,369	0.8%
42	Delaware	4,881	0.6%
3	Florida	34,653	4.2%
6	Georgia	29,358	3.6%
35	Hawaii	9,276	1.1%
39	Idaho	5,892	0.7%
9	Illinois	25,084	3.1%
13	Indiana	21,073	2.6%
30	Iowa	12,390	1.5%
32	Kansas	11,479	1.4%
27	Kentucky	13,126	1.6%
18	Louisiana	18,011	2.2%
48	Maine	4,153	0.5%
22	Maryland	16,000	2.0%
25	Massachusetts	15,335	1.9%
19	Michigan	17,618	2.2%
16	Minnesota	19,256	2.4%
20	Mississippi	17,332	2.1%
10	Missouri	23,769	2.9%
43	Montana	4,748	0.6%
36	Nebraska	7,498	0.9%
38	Nevada	6,087	0.7%
47	New Hampshire	4,251	0.5%
21	New Jersey	17,312	2.1%
40	New Mexico	5,199	0.6%
5	New York	30,362	3.7%
11	North Carolina	22,542	2.8%
45	North Dakota	4,669	0.6%
7	Ohio	28,523	3.5%
24	Oklahoma	15,640	1.9%
33	Oregon	10,470	1.3%
4	Pennsylvania	32,297	3.9%
46	Rhode Island	4,438	0.5%
17	South Carolina	19,102	2.3%
41	South Dakota	4,982	0.6%
14	Tennessee	20,606	2.5%
2	Texas	56,367	6.9%
31	Utah	11,999	1.5%
49	Vermont	3,952	0.5%
8	Virginia	25,109	3.1%
15	Washington	19,470	2.4%
34	West Virginia	9,303	1.1%
23	Wisconsin	15,833	1.9%
50	Wyoming	3,218	0.4%

RANK ORDER

RANK	STATE	PERSONNEL	% of USA
1	California	57,792	7.1%
2	Texas	56,367	6.9%
3	Florida	34,653	4.2%
4	Pennsylvania	32,297	3.9%
5	New York	30,362	3.7%
6	Georgia	29,358	3.6%
7	Ohio	28,523	3.5%
8	Virginia	25,109	3.1%
9	Illinois	25,084	3.1%
10	Missouri	23,769	2.9%
11	North Carolina	22,542	2.8%
12	Alabama	22,099	2.7%
13	Indiana	21,073	2.6%
14	Tennessee	20,606	2.5%
15	Washington	19,470	2.4%
16	Minnesota	19,256	2.4%
17	South Carolina	19,102	2.3%
18	Louisiana	18,011	2.2%
19	Michigan	17,618	2.2%
20	Mississippi	17,332	2.1%
21	New Jersey	17,312	2.1%
22	Maryland	16,000	2.0%
23	Wisconsin	15,833	1.9%
24	Oklahoma	15,640	1.9%
25	Massachusetts	15,335	1.9%
26	Arizona	13,728	1.7%
27	Kentucky	13,126	1.6%
28	Arkansas	13,051	1.6%
29	Colorado	12,491	1.5%
30	Iowa	12,390	1.5%
31	Utah	11,999	1.5%
32	Kansas	11,479	1.4%
33	Oregon	10,470	1.3%
34	West Virginia	9,303	1.1%
35	Hawaii	9,276	1.1%
36	Nebraska	7,498	0.9%
37	Connecticut	6,369	0.8%
38	Nevada	6,087	0.7%
39	Idaho	5,892	0.7%
40	New Mexico	5,199	0.6%
41	South Dakota	4,982	0.6%
42	Delaware	4,881	0.6%
43	Montana	4,748	0.6%
44	Alaska	4,747	0.6%
45	North Dakota	4,669	0.6%
46	Rhode Island	4,438	0.5%
47	New Hampshire	4,251	0.5%
48	Maine	4,153	0.5%
49	Vermont	3,952	0.5%
50	Wyoming	3,218	0.4%
	District of Columbia	6,378	0.8%

Source: U.S. Department of Defense

"Atlas/Data Abstract for the United States" (http://siadapp.dmdc.osd.mil/personnel/L03/fy09/09top.htm)

*Does not include reserve and national guard personnel in U.S. territories.

U.S. Department of Defense Total Compensation in 2009

National Total = $195,170,178,000*

ALPHA ORDER

RANK	STATE	COMPENSATION	% of USA
13	Alabama	$4,723,956,000	2.4%
24	Alaska	2,659,561,000	1.4%
20	Arizona	3,137,634,000	1.6%
31	Arkansas	1,621,707,000	0.8%
3	California	14,568,458,000	7.5%
11	Colorado	5,125,122,000	2.6%
41	Connecticut	720,299,000	0.4%
46	Delaware	536,758,000	0.3%
6	Florida	9,417,919,000	4.8%
4	Georgia	11,494,647,000	5.9%
9	Hawaii	6,344,467,000	3.3%
42	Idaho	709,220,000	0.4%
21	Illinois	3,128,538,000	1.6%
25	Indiana	2,338,121,000	1.2%
39	Iowa	747,256,000	0.4%
19	Kansas	3,667,675,000	1.9%
10	Kentucky	5,680,752,000	2.9%
22	Louisiana	2,688,149,000	1.4%
38	Maine	846,681,000	0.4%
8	Maryland	6,537,841,000	3.3%
32	Massachusetts	1,490,630,000	0.8%
29	Michigan	1,826,987,000	0.9%
34	Minnesota	1,208,062,000	0.6%
27	Mississippi	2,224,346,000	1.1%
17	Missouri	3,786,836,000	1.9%
45	Montana	540,644,000	0.3%
35	Nebraska	1,151,981,000	0.6%
33	Nevada	1,414,606,000	0.7%
48	New Hampshire	410,882,000	0.2%
23	New Jersey	2,671,220,000	1.4%
30	New Mexico	1,626,461,000	0.8%
12	New York	4,818,679,000	2.5%
5	North Carolina	10,558,150,000	5.4%
43	North Dakota	630,939,000	0.3%
16	Ohio	3,834,470,000	2.0%
15	Oklahoma	4,099,633,000	2.1%
37	Oregon	1,051,047,000	0.5%
14	Pennsylvania	4,210,386,000	2.2%
40	Rhode Island	743,035,000	0.4%
18	South Carolina	3,682,987,000	1.9%
47	South Dakota	513,643,000	0.3%
26	Tennessee	2,235,302,000	1.1%
1	Texas	19,298,889,000	9.9%
28	Utah	2,115,968,000	1.1%
50	Vermont	261,505,000	0.1%
2	Virginia	18,071,415,000	9.3%
7	Washington	8,223,735,000	4.2%
44	West Virginia	616,823,000	0.3%
36	Wisconsin	1,151,891,000	0.6%
49	Wyoming	405,020,000	0.2%

RANK ORDER

RANK	STATE	COMPENSATION	% of USA
1	Texas	$19,298,889,000	9.9%
2	Virginia	18,071,415,000	9.3%
3	California	14,568,458,000	7.5%
4	Georgia	11,494,647,000	5.9%
5	North Carolina	10,558,150,000	5.4%
6	Florida	9,417,919,000	4.8%
7	Washington	8,223,735,000	4.2%
8	Maryland	6,537,841,000	3.3%
9	Hawaii	6,344,467,000	3.3%
10	Kentucky	5,680,752,000	2.9%
11	Colorado	5,125,122,000	2.6%
12	New York	4,818,679,000	2.5%
13	Alabama	4,723,956,000	2.4%
14	Pennsylvania	4,210,386,000	2.2%
15	Oklahoma	4,099,633,000	2.1%
16	Ohio	3,834,470,000	2.0%
17	Missouri	3,786,836,000	1.9%
18	South Carolina	3,682,987,000	1.9%
19	Kansas	3,667,675,000	1.9%
20	Arizona	3,137,634,000	1.6%
21	Illinois	3,128,538,000	1.6%
22	Louisiana	2,688,149,000	1.4%
23	New Jersey	2,671,220,000	1.4%
24	Alaska	2,659,561,000	1.4%
25	Indiana	2,338,121,000	1.2%
26	Tennessee	2,235,302,000	1.1%
27	Mississippi	2,224,346,000	1.1%
28	Utah	2,115,968,000	1.1%
29	Michigan	1,826,987,000	0.9%
30	New Mexico	1,626,461,000	0.8%
31	Arkansas	1,621,707,000	0.8%
32	Massachusetts	1,490,630,000	0.8%
33	Nevada	1,414,606,000	0.7%
34	Minnesota	1,208,062,000	0.6%
35	Nebraska	1,151,981,000	0.6%
36	Wisconsin	1,151,891,000	0.6%
37	Oregon	1,051,047,000	0.5%
38	Maine	846,681,000	0.4%
39	Iowa	747,256,000	0.4%
40	Rhode Island	743,035,000	0.4%
41	Connecticut	720,299,000	0.4%
42	Idaho	709,220,000	0.4%
43	North Dakota	630,939,000	0.3%
44	West Virginia	616,823,000	0.3%
45	Montana	540,644,000	0.3%
46	Delaware	536,758,000	0.3%
47	South Dakota	513,643,000	0.3%
48	New Hampshire	410,882,000	0.2%
49	Wyoming	405,020,000	0.2%
50	Vermont	261,505,000	0.1%
	District of Columbia	3,599,245,000	1.8%

Source: U.S. Department of Defense
   "Atlas/Data Abstract for the United States" (http://siadapp.dmdc.osd.mil/personnel/L03/fy09/09top.htm)
*Includes Civilian Pay, Military Active Duty Pay, Reserve, National Guard Pay, and Retired Military Pay. Based on location
of recipient. Does not include recipients in U.S. territories and other countries.

U.S. Department of Defense Military Active Duty Pay in 2009

National Total = $84,459,939,000*

ALPHA ORDER

RANK	STATE	PAYROLL	% of USA
20	Alabama	$1,254,790,000	1.5%
13	Alaska	2,077,719,000	2.5%
19	Arizona	1,262,572,000	1.5%
28	Arkansas	435,036,000	0.5%
5	California	5,182,809,000	6.1%
9	Colorado	2,965,503,000	3.5%
41	Connecticut	198,163,000	0.2%
38	Delaware	216,219,000	0.3%
10	Florida	2,816,465,000	3.3%
3	Georgia	6,668,434,000	7.9%
6	Hawaii	4,529,364,000	5.4%
36	Idaho	261,607,000	0.3%
21	Illinois	738,269,000	0.9%
31	Indiana	350,647,000	0.4%
45	Iowa	140,071,000	0.2%
12	Kansas	2,465,253,000	2.9%
8	Kentucky	4,339,243,000	5.1%
17	Louisiana	1,417,143,000	1.7%
47	Maine	113,348,000	0.1%
14	Maryland	2,012,820,000	2.4%
33	Massachusetts	319,863,000	0.4%
35	Michigan	263,638,000	0.3%
39	Minnesota	206,036,000	0.2%
23	Mississippi	629,352,000	0.7%
18	Missouri	1,310,799,000	1.6%
42	Montana	187,506,000	0.2%
29	Nebraska	434,949,000	0.5%
24	Nevada	600,019,000	0.7%
49	New Hampshire	73,429,000	0.1%
27	New Jersey	543,053,000	0.6%
26	New Mexico	571,288,000	0.7%
11	New York	2,701,191,000	3.2%
2	North Carolina	7,012,462,000	8.3%
32	North Dakota	335,954,000	0.4%
22	Ohio	640,496,000	0.8%
15	Oklahoma	1,678,570,000	2.0%
44	Oregon	140,868,000	0.2%
25	Pennsylvania	574,034,000	0.7%
46	Rhode Island	120,400,000	0.1%
16	South Carolina	1,530,304,000	1.8%
40	South Dakota	198,438,000	0.2%
34	Tennessee	282,250,000	0.3%
1	Texas	11,128,462,000	13.2%
30	Utah	431,738,000	0.5%
50	Vermont	64,177,000	0.1%
4	Virginia	6,214,491,000	7.4%
7	Washington	4,407,343,000	5.2%
48	West Virginia	106,870,000	0.1%
37	Wisconsin	222,262,000	0.3%
43	Wyoming	177,223,000	0.2%

RANK ORDER

RANK	STATE	PAYROLL	% of USA
1	Texas	$11,128,462,000	13.2%
2	North Carolina	7,012,462,000	8.3%
3	Georgia	6,668,434,000	7.9%
4	Virginia	6,214,491,000	7.4%
5	California	5,182,809,000	6.1%
6	Hawaii	4,529,364,000	5.4%
7	Washington	4,407,343,000	5.2%
8	Kentucky	4,339,243,000	5.1%
9	Colorado	2,965,503,000	3.5%
10	Florida	2,816,465,000	3.3%
11	New York	2,701,191,000	3.2%
12	Kansas	2,465,253,000	2.9%
13	Alaska	2,077,719,000	2.5%
14	Maryland	2,012,820,000	2.4%
15	Oklahoma	1,678,570,000	2.0%
16	South Carolina	1,530,304,000	1.8%
17	Louisiana	1,417,143,000	1.7%
18	Missouri	1,310,799,000	1.6%
19	Arizona	1,262,572,000	1.5%
20	Alabama	1,254,790,000	1.5%
21	Illinois	738,269,000	0.9%
22	Ohio	640,496,000	0.8%
23	Mississippi	629,352,000	0.7%
24	Nevada	600,019,000	0.7%
25	Pennsylvania	574,034,000	0.7%
26	New Mexico	571,288,000	0.7%
27	New Jersey	543,053,000	0.6%
28	Arkansas	435,036,000	0.5%
29	Nebraska	434,949,000	0.5%
30	Utah	431,738,000	0.5%
31	Indiana	350,647,000	0.4%
32	North Dakota	335,954,000	0.4%
33	Massachusetts	319,863,000	0.4%
34	Tennessee	282,250,000	0.3%
35	Michigan	263,638,000	0.3%
36	Idaho	261,607,000	0.3%
37	Wisconsin	222,262,000	0.3%
38	Delaware	216,219,000	0.3%
39	Minnesota	206,036,000	0.2%
40	South Dakota	198,438,000	0.2%
41	Connecticut	198,163,000	0.2%
42	Montana	187,506,000	0.2%
43	Wyoming	177,223,000	0.2%
44	Oregon	140,868,000	0.2%
45	Iowa	140,071,000	0.2%
46	Rhode Island	120,400,000	0.1%
47	Maine	113,348,000	0.1%
48	West Virginia	106,870,000	0.1%
49	New Hampshire	73,429,000	0.1%
50	Vermont	64,177,000	0.1%
	District of Columbia	1,906,999,000	2.3%

Source: U.S. Department of Defense
"Atlas/Data Abstract for the United States" (http://siadapp.dmdc.osd.mil/personnel/L03/fy09/09top.htm)
*Based on location of recipient. Does not include recipients in U.S. territories and other countries.

U.S. Department of Defense Civilian Pay in 2009

National Total = $49,735,662,000*

ALPHA ORDER

RANK	STATE	PAYROLL	% of USA
9	Alabama	$1,808,239,000	3.6%
33	Alaska	321,206,000	0.6%
22	Arizona	626,966,000	1.3%
35	Arkansas	235,881,000	0.5%
2	California	4,570,024,000	9.2%
17	Colorado	786,177,000	1.6%
37	Connecticut	184,190,000	0.4%
45	Delaware	98,410,000	0.2%
6	Florida	1,942,655,000	3.9%
5	Georgia	2,288,362,000	4.6%
14	Hawaii	1,163,627,000	2.3%
44	Idaho	100,861,000	0.2%
15	Illinois	1,069,790,000	2.2%
20	Indiana	705,646,000	1.4%
43	Iowa	102,185,000	0.2%
29	Kansas	471,455,000	0.9%
26	Kentucky	508,305,000	1.0%
31	Louisiana	414,120,000	0.8%
30	Maine	440,345,000	0.9%
3	Maryland	2,995,038,000	6.0%
25	Massachusetts	539,474,000	1.1%
19	Michigan	705,769,000	1.4%
38	Minnesota	177,452,000	0.4%
24	Mississippi	585,976,000	1.2%
23	Missouri	586,610,000	1.2%
46	Montana	91,395,000	0.2%
34	Nebraska	250,642,000	0.5%
40	Nevada	143,070,000	0.3%
48	New Hampshire	74,277,000	0.1%
12	New Jersey	1,290,072,000	2.6%
27	New Mexico	483,878,000	1.0%
18	New York	784,658,000	1.6%
13	North Carolina	1,210,521,000	2.4%
42	North Dakota	108,116,000	0.2%
8	Ohio	1,824,865,000	3.7%
11	Oklahoma	1,339,260,000	2.7%
36	Oregon	231,630,000	0.5%
10	Pennsylvania	1,788,532,000	3.6%
32	Rhode Island	391,187,000	0.8%
21	South Carolina	638,047,000	1.3%
47	South Dakota	76,881,000	0.2%
28	Tennessee	476,959,000	1.0%
4	Texas	2,917,913,000	5.9%
16	Utah	954,215,000	1.9%
50	Vermont	44,921,000	0.1%
1	Virginia	7,447,686,000	15.0%
7	Washington	1,873,338,000	3.8%
41	West Virginia	126,119,000	0.3%
39	Wisconsin	160,743,000	0.3%
49	Wyoming	69,027,000	0.1%

RANK ORDER

RANK	STATE	PAYROLL	% of USA
1	Virginia	$7,447,686,000	15.0%
2	California	4,570,024,000	9.2%
3	Maryland	2,995,038,000	6.0%
4	Texas	2,917,913,000	5.9%
5	Georgia	2,288,362,000	4.6%
6	Florida	1,942,655,000	3.9%
7	Washington	1,873,338,000	3.8%
8	Ohio	1,824,865,000	3.7%
9	Alabama	1,808,239,000	3.6%
10	Pennsylvania	1,788,532,000	3.6%
11	Oklahoma	1,339,260,000	2.7%
12	New Jersey	1,290,072,000	2.6%
13	North Carolina	1,210,521,000	2.4%
14	Hawaii	1,163,627,000	2.3%
15	Illinois	1,069,790,000	2.2%
16	Utah	954,215,000	1.9%
17	Colorado	786,177,000	1.6%
18	New York	784,658,000	1.6%
19	Michigan	705,769,000	1.4%
20	Indiana	705,646,000	1.4%
21	South Carolina	638,047,000	1.3%
22	Arizona	626,966,000	1.3%
23	Missouri	586,610,000	1.2%
24	Mississippi	585,976,000	1.2%
25	Massachusetts	539,474,000	1.1%
26	Kentucky	508,305,000	1.0%
27	New Mexico	483,878,000	1.0%
28	Tennessee	476,959,000	1.0%
29	Kansas	471,455,000	0.9%
30	Maine	440,345,000	0.9%
31	Louisiana	414,120,000	0.8%
32	Rhode Island	391,187,000	0.8%
33	Alaska	321,206,000	0.6%
34	Nebraska	250,642,000	0.5%
35	Arkansas	235,881,000	0.5%
36	Oregon	231,630,000	0.5%
37	Connecticut	184,190,000	0.4%
38	Minnesota	177,452,000	0.4%
39	Wisconsin	160,743,000	0.3%
40	Nevada	143,070,000	0.3%
41	West Virginia	126,119,000	0.3%
42	North Dakota	108,116,000	0.2%
43	Iowa	102,185,000	0.2%
44	Idaho	100,861,000	0.2%
45	Delaware	98,410,000	0.2%
46	Montana	91,395,000	0.2%
47	South Dakota	76,881,000	0.2%
48	New Hampshire	74,277,000	0.1%
49	Wyoming	69,027,000	0.1%
50	Vermont	44,921,000	0.1%
	District of Columbia	1,508,947,000	3.0%

Source: U.S. Department of Defense
"Atlas/Data Abstract for the United States" (http://siadapp.dmdc.osd.mil/personnel/L03/fy09/09top.htm)
*Based on location of recipient. Does not include recipients in U.S. territories and other countries.

U.S. Department of Defense Reserve and National Guard Pay in 2009

National Total = $22,758,996,000*

ALPHA ORDER

RANK	STATE	PAYROLL	% of USA
11	Alabama	$617,055,000	2.7%
46	Alaska	90,592,000	0.4%
36	Arizona	180,724,000	0.8%
18	Arkansas	518,376,000	2.3%
2	California	1,391,094,000	6.1%
33	Colorado	285,229,000	1.3%
38	Connecticut	149,873,000	0.7%
49	Delaware	74,623,000	0.3%
7	Florida	826,134,000	3.6%
6	Georgia	868,244,000	3.8%
30	Hawaii	315,642,000	1.4%
41	Idaho	116,236,000	0.5%
10	Illinois	680,329,000	3.0%
5	Indiana	905,556,000	4.0%
29	Iowa	321,928,000	1.4%
28	Kansas	334,444,000	1.5%
27	Kentucky	391,231,000	1.7%
26	Louisiana	410,608,000	1.8%
47	Maine	87,175,000	0.4%
25	Maryland	421,636,000	1.9%
31	Massachusetts	312,302,000	1.4%
24	Michigan	437,538,000	1.9%
17	Minnesota	557,666,000	2.5%
16	Mississippi	558,821,000	2.5%
3	Missouri	1,268,807,000	5.6%
43	Montana	110,398,000	0.5%
35	Nebraska	198,307,000	0.9%
37	Nevada	151,343,000	0.7%
48	New Hampshire	78,753,000	0.3%
19	New Jersey	507,311,000	2.2%
39	New Mexico	148,491,000	0.7%
8	New York	782,279,000	3.4%
9	North Carolina	729,587,000	3.2%
44	North Dakota	110,138,000	0.5%
12	Ohio	609,867,000	2.7%
20	Oklahoma	496,151,000	2.2%
32	Oregon	300,719,000	1.3%
4	Pennsylvania	1,011,822,000	4.4%
40	Rhode Island	117,397,000	0.5%
21	South Carolina	485,464,000	2.1%
42	South Dakota	115,571,000	0.5%
14	Tennessee	572,830,000	2.5%
1	Texas	1,520,699,000	6.7%
23	Utah	448,935,000	2.0%
45	Vermont	92,561,000	0.4%
13	Virginia	603,453,000	2.7%
15	Washington	563,322,000	2.5%
34	West Virginia	216,627,000	1.0%
22	Wisconsin	470,144,000	2.1%
50	Wyoming	70,775,000	0.3%

RANK ORDER

RANK	STATE	PAYROLL	% of USA
1	Texas	$1,520,699,000	6.7%
2	California	1,391,094,000	6.1%
3	Missouri	1,268,807,000	5.6%
4	Pennsylvania	1,011,822,000	4.4%
5	Indiana	905,556,000	4.0%
6	Georgia	868,244,000	3.8%
7	Florida	826,134,000	3.6%
8	New York	782,279,000	3.4%
9	North Carolina	729,587,000	3.2%
10	Illinois	680,329,000	3.0%
11	Alabama	617,055,000	2.7%
12	Ohio	609,867,000	2.7%
13	Virginia	603,453,000	2.7%
14	Tennessee	572,830,000	2.5%
15	Washington	563,322,000	2.5%
16	Mississippi	558,821,000	2.5%
17	Minnesota	557,666,000	2.5%
18	Arkansas	518,376,000	2.3%
19	New Jersey	507,311,000	2.2%
20	Oklahoma	496,151,000	2.2%
21	South Carolina	485,464,000	2.1%
22	Wisconsin	470,144,000	2.1%
23	Utah	448,935,000	2.0%
24	Michigan	437,538,000	1.9%
25	Maryland	421,636,000	1.9%
26	Louisiana	410,608,000	1.8%
27	Kentucky	391,231,000	1.7%
28	Kansas	334,444,000	1.5%
29	Iowa	321,928,000	1.4%
30	Hawaii	315,642,000	1.4%
31	Massachusetts	312,302,000	1.4%
32	Oregon	300,719,000	1.3%
33	Colorado	285,229,000	1.3%
34	West Virginia	216,627,000	1.0%
35	Nebraska	198,307,000	0.9%
36	Arizona	180,724,000	0.8%
37	Nevada	151,343,000	0.7%
38	Connecticut	149,873,000	0.7%
39	New Mexico	148,491,000	0.7%
40	Rhode Island	117,397,000	0.5%
41	Idaho	116,236,000	0.5%
42	South Dakota	115,571,000	0.5%
43	Montana	110,398,000	0.5%
44	North Dakota	110,138,000	0.5%
45	Vermont	92,561,000	0.4%
46	Alaska	90,592,000	0.4%
47	Maine	87,175,000	0.4%
48	New Hampshire	78,753,000	0.3%
49	Delaware	74,623,000	0.3%
50	Wyoming	70,775,000	0.3%
	District of Columbia	124,189,000	0.5%

Source: U.S. Department of Defense
  "Atlas/Data Abstract for the United States" (http://siadapp.dmdc.osd.mil/personnel/L03/fy09/09top.htm)
*Based on location of recipient. Does not include recipients in U.S. territories and other countries.

U.S. Department of Defense Retired Military Pay in 2009

National Total = $38,215,581,000*

ALPHA ORDER

RANK	STATE	PAYROLL	% of USA
11	Alabama	$1,043,872,000	2.7%
42	Alaska	170,044,000	0.4%
10	Arizona	1,067,372,000	2.8%
24	Arkansas	432,414,000	1.1%
4	California	3,424,531,000	9.0%
9	Colorado	1,088,213,000	2.8%
39	Connecticut	188,073,000	0.5%
45	Delaware	147,506,000	0.4%
1	Florida	3,832,665,000	10.0%
5	Georgia	1,669,607,000	4.4%
30	Hawaii	335,834,000	0.9%
37	Idaho	230,516,000	0.6%
16	Illinois	640,150,000	1.7%
29	Indiana	376,272,000	1.0%
41	Iowa	183,072,000	0.5%
27	Kansas	396,523,000	1.0%
23	Kentucky	441,973,000	1.2%
22	Louisiana	446,278,000	1.2%
38	Maine	205,813,000	0.5%
8	Maryland	1,108,347,000	2.9%
32	Massachusetts	318,991,000	0.8%
26	Michigan	420,042,000	1.1%
36	Minnesota	266,908,000	0.7%
21	Mississippi	450,197,000	1.2%
17	Missouri	620,620,000	1.6%
44	Montana	151,345,000	0.4%
35	Nebraska	268,083,000	0.7%
20	Nevada	520,174,000	1.4%
40	New Hampshire	184,423,000	0.5%
31	New Jersey	330,784,000	0.9%
25	New Mexico	422,804,000	1.1%
19	New York	550,551,000	1.4%
6	North Carolina	1,605,580,000	4.2%
49	North Dakota	76,731,000	0.2%
15	Ohio	759,242,000	2.0%
18	Oklahoma	585,652,000	1.5%
28	Oregon	377,830,000	1.0%
14	Pennsylvania	835,998,000	2.2%
47	Rhode Island	114,051,000	0.3%
12	South Carolina	1,029,172,000	2.7%
46	South Dakota	122,753,000	0.3%
13	Tennessee	903,263,000	2.4%
3	Texas	3,731,815,000	9.8%
34	Utah	281,080,000	0.7%
50	Vermont	59,846,000	0.2%
2	Virginia	3,805,785,000	10.0%
7	Washington	1,379,732,000	3.6%
43	West Virginia	167,207,000	0.4%
33	Wisconsin	298,742,000	0.8%
48	Wyoming	87,995,000	0.2%

RANK ORDER

RANK	STATE	PAYROLL	% of USA
1	Florida	$3,832,665,000	10.0%
2	Virginia	3,805,785,000	10.0%
3	Texas	3,731,815,000	9.8%
4	California	3,424,531,000	9.0%
5	Georgia	1,669,607,000	4.4%
6	North Carolina	1,605,580,000	4.2%
7	Washington	1,379,732,000	3.6%
8	Maryland	1,108,347,000	2.9%
9	Colorado	1,088,213,000	2.8%
10	Arizona	1,067,372,000	2.8%
11	Alabama	1,043,872,000	2.7%
12	South Carolina	1,029,172,000	2.7%
13	Tennessee	903,263,000	2.4%
14	Pennsylvania	835,998,000	2.2%
15	Ohio	759,242,000	2.0%
16	Illinois	640,150,000	1.7%
17	Missouri	620,620,000	1.6%
18	Oklahoma	585,652,000	1.5%
19	New York	550,551,000	1.4%
20	Nevada	520,174,000	1.4%
21	Mississippi	450,197,000	1.2%
22	Louisiana	446,278,000	1.2%
23	Kentucky	441,973,000	1.2%
24	Arkansas	432,414,000	1.1%
25	New Mexico	422,804,000	1.1%
26	Michigan	420,042,000	1.1%
27	Kansas	396,523,000	1.0%
28	Oregon	377,830,000	1.0%
29	Indiana	376,272,000	1.0%
30	Hawaii	335,834,000	0.9%
31	New Jersey	330,784,000	0.9%
32	Massachusetts	318,991,000	0.8%
33	Wisconsin	298,742,000	0.8%
34	Utah	281,080,000	0.7%
35	Nebraska	268,083,000	0.7%
36	Minnesota	266,908,000	0.7%
37	Idaho	230,516,000	0.6%
38	Maine	205,813,000	0.5%
39	Connecticut	188,073,000	0.5%
40	New Hampshire	184,423,000	0.5%
41	Iowa	183,072,000	0.5%
42	Alaska	170,044,000	0.4%
43	West Virginia	167,207,000	0.4%
44	Montana	151,345,000	0.4%
45	Delaware	147,506,000	0.4%
46	South Dakota	122,753,000	0.3%
47	Rhode Island	114,051,000	0.3%
48	Wyoming	87,995,000	0.2%
49	North Dakota	76,731,000	0.2%
50	Vermont	59,846,000	0.2%
	District of Columbia	59,110,000	0.2%

Source: U.S. Department of Defense
"Atlas/Data Abstract for the United States" (http://siadapp.dmdc.osd.mil/personnel/L03/fy09/09top.htm)
*Based on location of recipient. Does not include recipients in U.S. territories and other countries.

Veterans in 2010

National Total = 22,658,145 Veterans*

ALPHA ORDER

RANK	STATE	VETERANS	% of USA
22	Alabama	405,624	1.8%
45	Alaska	77,025	0.3%
13	Arizona	556,729	2.5%
29	Arkansas	254,664	1.1%
1	California	1,971,959	8.7%
19	Colorado	421,342	1.9%
32	Connecticut	229,734	1.0%
44	Delaware	78,247	0.3%
3	Florida	1,650,876	7.3%
9	Georgia	773,858	3.4%
42	Hawaii	116,166	0.5%
40	Idaho	136,625	0.6%
8	Illinois	782,747	3.5%
16	Indiana	491,605	2.2%
31	Iowa	234,552	1.0%
33	Kansas	225,091	1.0%
25	Kentucky	335,670	1.5%
28	Louisiana	304,889	1.3%
39	Maine	138,551	0.6%
17	Maryland	471,238	2.1%
23	Massachusetts	393,722	1.7%
11	Michigan	703,970	3.1%
24	Minnesota	381,309	1.7%
34	Mississippi	205,644	0.9%
14	Missouri	505,916	2.2%
43	Montana	102,015	0.5%
38	Nebraska	145,237	0.6%
30	Nevada	243,867	1.1%
41	New Hampshire	127,964	0.6%
18	New Jersey	443,161	2.0%
35	New Mexico	174,687	0.8%
5	New York	950,417	4.2%
10	North Carolina	765,942	3.4%
48	North Dakota	56,310	0.2%
6	Ohio	890,340	3.9%
27	Oklahoma	324,714	1.4%
26	Oregon	333,752	1.5%
4	Pennsylvania	964,132	4.3%
47	Rhode Island	71,216	0.3%
21	South Carolina	406,729	1.8%
46	South Dakota	71,762	0.3%
15	Tennessee	495,766	2.2%
2	Texas	1,693,791	7.5%
37	Utah	153,623	0.7%
50	Vermont	52,082	0.2%
7	Virginia	822,312	3.6%
12	Washington	632,210	2.8%
36	West Virginia	167,182	0.7%
20	Wisconsin	417,654	1.8%
49	Wyoming	55,850	0.2%

RANK ORDER

RANK	STATE	VETERANS	% of USA
1	California	1,971,959	8.7%
2	Texas	1,693,791	7.5%
3	Florida	1,650,876	7.3%
4	Pennsylvania	964,132	4.3%
5	New York	950,417	4.2%
6	Ohio	890,340	3.9%
7	Virginia	822,312	3.6%
8	Illinois	782,747	3.5%
9	Georgia	773,858	3.4%
10	North Carolina	765,942	3.4%
11	Michigan	703,970	3.1%
12	Washington	632,210	2.8%
13	Arizona	556,729	2.5%
14	Missouri	505,916	2.2%
15	Tennessee	495,766	2.2%
16	Indiana	491,605	2.2%
17	Maryland	471,238	2.1%
18	New Jersey	443,161	2.0%
19	Colorado	421,342	1.9%
20	Wisconsin	417,654	1.8%
21	South Carolina	406,729	1.8%
22	Alabama	405,624	1.8%
23	Massachusetts	393,722	1.7%
24	Minnesota	381,309	1.7%
25	Kentucky	335,670	1.5%
26	Oregon	333,752	1.5%
27	Oklahoma	324,714	1.4%
28	Louisiana	304,889	1.3%
29	Arkansas	254,664	1.1%
30	Nevada	243,867	1.1%
31	Iowa	234,552	1.0%
32	Connecticut	229,734	1.0%
33	Kansas	225,091	1.0%
34	Mississippi	205,644	0.9%
35	New Mexico	174,687	0.8%
36	West Virginia	167,182	0.7%
37	Utah	153,623	0.7%
38	Nebraska	145,237	0.6%
39	Maine	138,551	0.6%
40	Idaho	136,625	0.6%
41	New Hampshire	127,964	0.6%
42	Hawaii	116,166	0.5%
43	Montana	102,015	0.5%
44	Delaware	78,247	0.3%
45	Alaska	77,025	0.3%
46	South Dakota	71,762	0.3%
47	Rhode Island	71,216	0.3%
48	North Dakota	56,310	0.2%
49	Wyoming	55,850	0.2%
50	Vermont	52,082	0.2%
	District of Columbia	37,268	0.2%

Source: U.S. Department of Veteran Affairs
   "Veteran Data and Information" (http://www.va.gov/vetdata/Veteran_Population.asp)
*Estimates based on 2006 data. Includes 210,410 veterans in U.S. territories or other countries.

Percent of Adult Population Who Are Veterans: 2010

National Percent = 9.7%*

ALPHA ORDER

RANK	STATE	PERCENT
20	Alabama	11.3
1	Alaska	15.0
18	Arizona	11.4
10	Arkansas	11.7
48	California	7.2
23	Colorado	11.1
44	Connecticut	8.5
17	Delaware	11.5
18	Florida	11.4
28	Georgia	10.7
16	Hawaii	11.6
9	Idaho	12.1
45	Illinois	8.0
32	Indiana	10.2
32	Iowa	10.2
29	Kansas	10.6
32	Kentucky	10.2
42	Louisiana	9.1
5	Maine	13.2
25	Maryland	10.8
47	Massachusetts	7.6
41	Michigan	9.2
38	Minnesota	9.5
40	Mississippi	9.4
23	Missouri	11.1
3	Montana	13.5
25	Nebraska	10.8
6	Nevada	12.4
6	New Hampshire	12.4
49	New Jersey	6.7
10	New Mexico	11.7
50	New York	6.3
25	North Carolina	10.8
22	North Dakota	11.2
35	Ohio	10.1
10	Oklahoma	11.7
20	Oregon	11.3
36	Pennsylvania	9.8
43	Rhode Island	8.6
10	South Carolina	11.7
10	South Dakota	11.7
31	Tennessee	10.3
38	Texas	9.5
45	Utah	8.0
30	Vermont	10.5
2	Virginia	13.6
6	Washington	12.4
10	West Virginia	11.7
37	Wisconsin	9.6
3	Wyoming	13.5

RANK ORDER

RANK	STATE	PERCENT
1	Alaska	15.0
2	Virginia	13.6
3	Montana	13.5
3	Wyoming	13.5
5	Maine	13.2
6	Nevada	12.4
6	New Hampshire	12.4
6	Washington	12.4
9	Idaho	12.1
10	Arkansas	11.7
10	New Mexico	11.7
10	Oklahoma	11.7
10	South Carolina	11.7
10	South Dakota	11.7
10	West Virginia	11.7
16	Hawaii	11.6
17	Delaware	11.5
18	Arizona	11.4
18	Florida	11.4
20	Alabama	11.3
20	Oregon	11.3
22	North Dakota	11.2
23	Colorado	11.1
23	Missouri	11.1
25	Maryland	10.8
25	Nebraska	10.8
25	North Carolina	10.8
28	Georgia	10.7
29	Kansas	10.6
30	Vermont	10.5
31	Tennessee	10.3
32	Indiana	10.2
32	Iowa	10.2
32	Kentucky	10.2
35	Ohio	10.1
36	Pennsylvania	9.8
37	Wisconsin	9.6
38	Minnesota	9.5
38	Texas	9.5
40	Mississippi	9.4
41	Michigan	9.2
42	Louisiana	9.1
43	Rhode Island	8.6
44	Connecticut	8.5
45	Illinois	8.0
45	Utah	8.0
47	Massachusetts	7.6
48	California	7.2
49	New Jersey	6.7
50	New York	6.3

District of Columbia — 7.7

Source: CQ Press using data from U.S. Department of Veteran Affairs
"Veteran Data and Information" (http://www.va.gov/vetdata/Veteran_Population.asp)
*Estimates based on 2006 data. National figures does not include veterans in U.S. territories or other countries. Percent calculated with population 18 years old and older in 2009.

U.S. Military Fatalities in Iraq and Afghanistan as of January 24, 2011

National Total = 5,881 Fatalities*

ALPHA ORDER

RANK	STATE	FATALITIES	% of USA
23	Alabama	96	1.6%
45	Alaska	22	0.4%
12	Arizona	132	2.2%
28	Arkansas	78	1.3%
1	California	610	10.4%
27	Colorado	83	1.4%
38	Connecticut	38	0.6%
49	Delaware	17	0.3%
3	Florida	281	4.8%
9	Georgia	189	3.2%
43	Hawaii	31	0.5%
39	Idaho	37	0.6%
7	Illinois	231	3.9%
12	Indiana	132	2.2%
32	Iowa	60	1.0%
31	Kansas	61	1.0%
22	Kentucky	99	1.7%
19	Louisiana	109	1.9%
36	Maine	45	0.8%
21	Maryland	102	1.7%
17	Massachusetts	110	1.9%
8	Michigan	196	3.3%
26	Minnesota	85	1.4%
30	Mississippi	70	1.2%
14	Missouri	128	2.2%
39	Montana	37	0.6%
33	Nebraska	54	0.9%
34	Nevada	52	0.9%
39	New Hampshire	37	0.6%
20	New Jersey	103	1.8%
35	New Mexico	51	0.9%
5	New York	257	4.4%
11	North Carolina	151	2.6%
47	North Dakota	19	0.3%
6	Ohio	233	4.0%
23	Oklahoma	96	1.6%
25	Oregon	94	1.6%
4	Pennsylvania	261	4.4%
50	Rhode Island	13	0.2%
28	South Carolina	78	1.3%
45	South Dakota	22	0.4%
15	Tennessee	127	2.2%
2	Texas	523	8.9%
37	Utah	39	0.7%
44	Vermont	25	0.4%
10	Virginia	170	2.9%
16	Washington	125	2.1%
42	West Virginia	36	0.6%
17	Wisconsin	110	1.9%
47	Wyoming	19	0.3%

RANK ORDER

RANK	STATE	FATALITIES	% of USA
1	California	610	10.4%
2	Texas	523	8.9%
3	Florida	281	4.8%
4	Pennsylvania	261	4.4%
5	New York	257	4.4%
6	Ohio	233	4.0%
7	Illinois	231	3.9%
8	Michigan	196	3.3%
9	Georgia	189	3.2%
10	Virginia	170	2.9%
11	North Carolina	151	2.6%
12	Arizona	132	2.2%
12	Indiana	132	2.2%
14	Missouri	128	2.2%
15	Tennessee	127	2.2%
16	Washington	125	2.1%
17	Massachusetts	110	1.9%
17	Wisconsin	110	1.9%
19	Louisiana	109	1.9%
20	New Jersey	103	1.8%
21	Maryland	102	1.7%
22	Kentucky	99	1.7%
23	Alabama	96	1.6%
23	Oklahoma	96	1.6%
25	Oregon	94	1.6%
26	Minnesota	85	1.4%
27	Colorado	83	1.4%
28	Arkansas	78	1.3%
28	South Carolina	78	1.3%
30	Mississippi	70	1.2%
31	Kansas	61	1.0%
32	Iowa	60	1.0%
33	Nebraska	54	0.9%
34	Nevada	52	0.9%
35	New Mexico	51	0.9%
36	Maine	45	0.8%
37	Utah	39	0.7%
38	Connecticut	38	0.6%
39	Idaho	37	0.6%
39	Montana	37	0.6%
39	New Hampshire	37	0.6%
42	West Virginia	36	0.6%
43	Hawaii	31	0.5%
44	Vermont	25	0.4%
45	Alaska	22	0.4%
45	South Dakota	22	0.4%
47	North Dakota	19	0.3%
47	Wyoming	19	0.3%
49	Delaware	17	0.3%
50	Rhode Island	13	0.2%
	District of Columbia	8	0.1%

Source: U.S. Department of Defense, Statistical Information Analysis Department
"Military Casualty Information (http://siadapp.dmdc.osd.mil/personnel/CASUALTY/castop.htm)
*Total includes 99 deaths of soldiers from U.S. territories. Total does not include deaths of United Kingdom soldiers or other coalition nations. Includes 4,623 combat and 1,258 noncombat deaths. Includes 4,408 deaths in Iraq and 1,473 deaths in Afghanistan.

Rate of U.S. Military Fatalities in Iraq and Afghanistan as of January 24, 2011

National Rate = 1.9 Fatalities per 100,000 Population*

ALPHA ORDER

RANK	STATE	RATE
25	Alabama	2.0
5	Alaska	3.1
25	Arizona	2.0
9	Arkansas	2.7
39	California	1.7
39	Colorado	1.7
50	Connecticut	1.1
33	Delaware	1.9
45	Florida	1.5
33	Georgia	1.9
14	Hawaii	2.4
14	Idaho	2.4
37	Illinois	1.8
21	Indiana	2.1
25	Iowa	2.0
19	Kansas	2.2
18	Kentucky	2.3
14	Louisiana	2.4
4	Maine	3.4
37	Maryland	1.8
39	Massachusetts	1.7
25	Michigan	2.0
43	Minnesota	1.6
14	Mississippi	2.4
21	Missouri	2.1
2	Montana	3.8
6	Nebraska	3.0
25	Nevada	2.0
8	New Hampshire	2.8
48	New Jersey	1.2
12	New Mexico	2.5
47	New York	1.3
43	North Carolina	1.6
7	North Dakota	2.9
25	Ohio	2.0
11	Oklahoma	2.6
12	Oregon	2.5
21	Pennsylvania	2.1
48	Rhode Island	1.2
39	South Carolina	1.7
9	South Dakota	2.7
25	Tennessee	2.0
21	Texas	2.1
46	Utah	1.4
1	Vermont	4.0
19	Virginia	2.2
33	Washington	1.9
25	West Virginia	2.0
33	Wisconsin	1.9
3	Wyoming	3.5

RANK ORDER

RANK	STATE	RATE
1	Vermont	4.0
2	Montana	3.8
3	Wyoming	3.5
4	Maine	3.4
5	Alaska	3.1
6	Nebraska	3.0
7	North Dakota	2.9
8	New Hampshire	2.8
9	Arkansas	2.7
9	South Dakota	2.7
11	Oklahoma	2.6
12	New Mexico	2.5
12	Oregon	2.5
14	Hawaii	2.4
14	Idaho	2.4
14	Louisiana	2.4
14	Mississippi	2.4
18	Kentucky	2.3
19	Kansas	2.2
19	Virginia	2.2
21	Indiana	2.1
21	Missouri	2.1
21	Pennsylvania	2.1
21	Texas	2.1
25	Alabama	2.0
25	Arizona	2.0
25	Iowa	2.0
25	Michigan	2.0
25	Nevada	2.0
25	Ohio	2.0
25	Tennessee	2.0
25	West Virginia	2.0
33	Delaware	1.9
33	Georgia	1.9
33	Washington	1.9
33	Wisconsin	1.9
37	Illinois	1.8
37	Maryland	1.8
39	California	1.7
39	Colorado	1.7
39	Massachusetts	1.7
39	South Carolina	1.7
43	Minnesota	1.6
43	North Carolina	1.6
45	Florida	1.5
46	Utah	1.4
47	New York	1.3
48	New Jersey	1.2
48	Rhode Island	1.2
50	Connecticut	1.1
	District of Columbia	1.3

Source: CQ Press using data from U.S. Department of Defense, Statistical Information Analysis Department
"Military Casualty Information (http://siadapp.dmdc.osd.mil/personnel/CASUALTY/castop.htm)
*National rate does not include deaths of soldiers from U.S. territories. Includes combat and noncombat deaths. Calculated with 2009 population estimates.

IV. Economy

Gross Domestic Product in 2009

National Total = $14,150,826,000,000*

ALPHA ORDER

RANK	STATE	G.D.P.	% of USA
25	Alabama	$169,856,000,000	1.2%
45	Alaska	45,709,000,000	0.3%
18	Arizona	256,364,000,000	1.8%
34	Arkansas	101,818,000,000	0.7%
1	California	1,891,363,000,000	13.4%
19	Colorado	252,657,000,000	1.8%
23	Connecticut	227,405,000,000	1.6%
40	Delaware	60,588,000,000	0.4%
4	Florida	737,038,000,000	5.2%
11	Georgia	395,194,000,000	2.8%
38	Hawaii	66,431,000,000	0.5%
42	Idaho	54,005,000,000	0.4%
5	Illinois	630,398,000,000	4.5%
16	Indiana	262,647,000,000	1.9%
30	Iowa	142,282,000,000	1.0%
32	Kansas	124,921,000,000	0.9%
28	Kentucky	156,553,000,000	1.1%
24	Louisiana	208,377,000,000	1.5%
43	Maine	51,293,000,000	0.4%
15	Maryland	286,797,000,000	2.0%
13	Massachusetts	365,182,000,000	2.6%
12	Michigan	368,401,000,000	2.6%
17	Minnesota	260,692,000,000	1.8%
35	Mississippi	95,905,000,000	0.7%
22	Missouri	239,752,000,000	1.7%
48	Montana	35,954,000,000	0.3%
36	Nebraska	86,439,000,000	0.6%
31	Nevada	126,503,000,000	0.9%
41	New Hampshire	59,400,000,000	0.4%
7	New Jersey	482,967,000,000	3.4%
37	New Mexico	74,801,000,000	0.5%
3	New York	1,093,219,000,000	7.7%
10	North Carolina	398,042,000,000	2.8%
49	North Dakota	31,872,000,000	0.2%
8	Ohio	471,264,000,000	3.3%
29	Oklahoma	153,778,000,000	1.1%
26	Oregon	165,648,000,000	1.2%
6	Pennsylvania	554,774,000,000	3.9%
44	Rhode Island	47,837,000,000	0.3%
27	South Carolina	159,647,000,000	1.1%
46	South Dakota	38,308,000,000	0.3%
20	Tennessee	244,508,000,000	1.7%
2	Texas	1,144,695,000,000	8.1%
33	Utah	112,941,000,000	0.8%
50	Vermont	25,438,000,000	0.2%
9	Virginia	408,443,000,000	2.9%
14	Washington	338,334,000,000	2.4%
39	West Virginia	63,344,000,000	0.4%
21	Wisconsin	244,370,000,000	1.7%
47	Wyoming	37,544,000,000	0.3%

RANK ORDER

RANK	STATE	G.D.P.	% of USA
1	California	$1,891,363,000,000	13.4%
2	Texas	1,144,695,000,000	8.1%
3	New York	1,093,219,000,000	7.7%
4	Florida	737,038,000,000	5.2%
5	Illinois	630,398,000,000	4.5%
6	Pennsylvania	554,774,000,000	3.9%
7	New Jersey	482,967,000,000	3.4%
8	Ohio	471,264,000,000	3.3%
9	Virginia	408,443,000,000	2.9%
10	North Carolina	398,042,000,000	2.8%
11	Georgia	395,194,000,000	2.8%
12	Michigan	368,401,000,000	2.6%
13	Massachusetts	365,182,000,000	2.6%
14	Washington	338,334,000,000	2.4%
15	Maryland	286,797,000,000	2.0%
16	Indiana	262,647,000,000	1.9%
17	Minnesota	260,692,000,000	1.8%
18	Arizona	256,364,000,000	1.8%
19	Colorado	252,657,000,000	1.8%
20	Tennessee	244,508,000,000	1.7%
21	Wisconsin	244,370,000,000	1.7%
22	Missouri	239,752,000,000	1.7%
23	Connecticut	227,405,000,000	1.6%
24	Louisiana	208,377,000,000	1.5%
25	Alabama	169,856,000,000	1.2%
26	Oregon	165,648,000,000	1.2%
27	South Carolina	159,647,000,000	1.1%
28	Kentucky	156,553,000,000	1.1%
29	Oklahoma	153,778,000,000	1.1%
30	Iowa	142,282,000,000	1.0%
31	Nevada	126,503,000,000	0.9%
32	Kansas	124,921,000,000	0.9%
33	Utah	112,941,000,000	0.8%
34	Arkansas	101,818,000,000	0.7%
35	Mississippi	95,905,000,000	0.7%
36	Nebraska	86,439,000,000	0.6%
37	New Mexico	74,801,000,000	0.5%
38	Hawaii	66,431,000,000	0.5%
39	West Virginia	63,344,000,000	0.4%
40	Delaware	60,588,000,000	0.4%
41	New Hampshire	59,400,000,000	0.4%
42	Idaho	54,005,000,000	0.4%
43	Maine	51,293,000,000	0.4%
44	Rhode Island	47,837,000,000	0.3%
45	Alaska	45,709,000,000	0.3%
46	South Dakota	38,308,000,000	0.3%
47	Wyoming	37,544,000,000	0.3%
48	Montana	35,954,000,000	0.3%
49	North Dakota	31,872,000,000	0.2%
50	Vermont	25,438,000,000	0.2%
	District of Columbia	99,129,000,000	0.7%

Source: U.S. Department of Commerce, Bureau of Economic Analysis
   "Gross Domestic Product Data" (http://www.bea.gov/regional/gsp/)
*G.D.P. is the market value of goods and services produced by the labor and property located in a state. It is the state counterpart to the nation's Gross Domestic Product. This was formerly known as Gross State Product (G.S.P.).

Percent Change in Gross Domestic Product: 2005 to 2009
(Adjusted to Constant 2005 Dollars)
National Percent Change = 2.8% Increase*

ALPHA ORDER

RANK	STATE	PERCENT CHANGE
30	Alabama	2.1
8	Alaska	10.1
19	Arizona	4.5
17	Arkansas	5.4
26	California	2.8
14	Colorado	6.7
21	Connecticut	4.4
40	Delaware	0.4
45	Florida	(1.7)
44	Georgia	(0.7)
18	Hawaii	4.7
24	Idaho	3.4
41	Illinois	0.3
39	Indiana	0.5
9	Iowa	9.2
10	Kansas	9.0
33	Kentucky	1.7
49	Louisiana	(4.7)
32	Maine	1.8
19	Maryland	4.5
25	Massachusetts	3.1
50	Michigan	(9.3)
41	Minnesota	0.3
13	Mississippi	7.3
38	Missouri	0.7
14	Montana	6.7
10	Nebraska	9.0
46	Nevada	(2.0)
36	New Hampshire	1.5
33	New Jersey	1.7
37	New Mexico	1.0
31	New York	2.0
27	North Carolina	2.7
2	North Dakota	19.0
48	Ohio	(3.4)
3	Oklahoma	18.1
6	Oregon	12.0
22	Pennsylvania	3.7
47	Rhode Island	(2.2)
35	South Carolina	1.6
5	South Dakota	12.4
43	Tennessee	0.0
12	Texas	8.5
4	Utah	12.6
28	Vermont	2.6
22	Virginia	3.7
7	Washington	10.6
16	West Virginia	5.9
29	Wisconsin	2.3
1	Wyoming	25.6

RANK ORDER

RANK	STATE	PERCENT CHANGE
1	Wyoming	25.6
2	North Dakota	19.0
3	Oklahoma	18.1
4	Utah	12.6
5	South Dakota	12.4
6	Oregon	12.0
7	Washington	10.6
8	Alaska	10.1
9	Iowa	9.2
10	Kansas	9.0
10	Nebraska	9.0
12	Texas	8.5
13	Mississippi	7.3
14	Colorado	6.7
14	Montana	6.7
16	West Virginia	5.9
17	Arkansas	5.4
18	Hawaii	4.7
19	Arizona	4.5
19	Maryland	4.5
21	Connecticut	4.4
22	Pennsylvania	3.7
22	Virginia	3.7
24	Idaho	3.4
25	Massachusetts	3.1
26	California	2.8
27	North Carolina	2.7
28	Vermont	2.6
29	Wisconsin	2.3
30	Alabama	2.1
31	New York	2.0
32	Maine	1.8
33	Kentucky	1.7
33	New Jersey	1.7
35	South Carolina	1.6
36	New Hampshire	1.5
37	New Mexico	1.0
38	Missouri	0.7
39	Indiana	0.5
40	Delaware	0.4
41	Illinois	0.3
41	Minnesota	0.3
43	Tennessee	0.0
44	Georgia	(0.7)
45	Florida	(1.7)
46	Nevada	(2.0)
47	Rhode Island	(2.2)
48	Ohio	(3.4)
49	Louisiana	(4.7)
50	Michigan	(9.3)

District of Columbia	6.0

Source: CQ Press using data from U.S. Department of Commerce, Bureau of Economic Analysis
   "Gross Domestic Product Data" (http://www.bea.gov/regional/gsp/)
*G.D.P. is the market value of goods and services produced by the labor and property located in a state. It is the state counterpart to the nation's Gross Domestic Product. This was formerly known as Gross State Product (G.S.P.). Adjusted for inflation using chained 2005 dollars.

Average Annual Change in Gross Domestic Product: 2005 to 2009
(Adjusted to Constant 2005 Dollars)
National Annual Percent Change = 0.6% Increase*

ALPHA ORDER

RANK ORDER

RANK	STATE	PERCENT CHANGE	RANK	STATE	PERCENT CHANGE
30	Alabama	0.4	1	Wyoming	4.7
8	Alaska	1.9	2	North Dakota	3.5
18	Arizona	0.9	3	Oklahoma	3.4
17	Arkansas	1.1	4	South Dakota	2.4
25	California	0.6	4	Utah	2.4
14	Colorado	1.3	6	Oregon	2.3
18	Connecticut	0.9	7	Washington	2.0
38	Delaware	0.1	8	Alaska	1.9
45	Florida	(0.3)	9	Iowa	1.8
44	Georgia	(0.1)	10	Kansas	1.7
18	Hawaii	0.9	10	Nebraska	1.7
22	Idaho	0.7	10	Texas	1.7
38	Illinois	0.1	13	Mississippi	1.4
38	Indiana	0.1	14	Colorado	1.3
9	Iowa	1.8	14	Montana	1.3
10	Kansas	1.7	16	West Virginia	1.2
33	Kentucky	0.3	17	Arkansas	1.1
49	Louisiana	(1.0)	18	Arizona	0.9
30	Maine	0.4	18	Connecticut	0.9
18	Maryland	0.9	18	Hawaii	0.9
25	Massachusetts	0.6	18	Maryland	0.9
50	Michigan	(1.9)	22	Idaho	0.7
38	Minnesota	0.1	22	Pennsylvania	0.7
13	Mississippi	1.4	22	Virginia	0.7
38	Missouri	0.1	25	California	0.6
14	Montana	1.3	25	Massachusetts	0.6
10	Nebraska	1.7	27	North Carolina	0.5
46	Nevada	(0.4)	27	Vermont	0.5
33	New Hampshire	0.3	27	Wisconsin	0.5
33	New Jersey	0.3	30	Alabama	0.4
37	New Mexico	0.2	30	Maine	0.4
30	New York	0.4	30	New York	0.4
27	North Carolina	0.5	33	Kentucky	0.3
2	North Dakota	3.5	33	New Hampshire	0.3
48	Ohio	(0.7)	33	New Jersey	0.3
3	Oklahoma	3.4	33	South Carolina	0.3
6	Oregon	2.3	37	New Mexico	0.2
22	Pennsylvania	0.7	38	Delaware	0.1
47	Rhode Island	(0.5)	38	Illinois	0.1
33	South Carolina	0.3	38	Indiana	0.1
4	South Dakota	2.4	38	Minnesota	0.1
43	Tennessee	0.0	38	Missouri	0.1
10	Texas	1.7	43	Tennessee	0.0
4	Utah	2.4	44	Georgia	(0.1)
27	Vermont	0.5	45	Florida	(0.3)
22	Virginia	0.7	46	Nevada	(0.4)
7	Washington	2.0	47	Rhode Island	(0.5)
16	West Virginia	1.2	48	Ohio	(0.7)
27	Wisconsin	0.5	49	Louisiana	(1.0)
1	Wyoming	4.7	50	Michigan	(1.9)

District of Columbia   1.2

Source: CQ Press using data from U.S. Department of Commerce, Bureau of Economic Analysis
   "Gross Domestic Product Data" (http://www.bea.gov/regional/gsp/)
*G.D.P. is the market value of goods and services produced by the labor and property located in a state. It is the state
counterpart to the nation's Gross Domestic Product. This was formerly known as Gross State Product (G.S.P.). Adjusted for
inflation using chained 2005 dollars.

Per Capita Gross Domestic Product in 2009

National Per Capita = $46,093*

ALPHA ORDER			RANK ORDER		
RANK	STATE	PER CAPITA	RANK	STATE	PER CAPITA
45	Alabama	$36,073	1	Wyoming	$68,980
3	Alaska	65,441	2	Delaware	68,452
39	Arizona	38,868	3	Alaska	65,441
46	Arkansas	35,238	4	Connecticut	64,635
10	California	51,171	5	New York	55,944
13	Colorado	50,283	6	New Jersey	55,464
4	Connecticut	64,635	7	Massachusetts	55,384
2	Delaware	68,452	8	Virginia	51,816
37	Florida	39,758	9	Hawaii	51,291
35	Georgia	40,206	10	California	51,171
9	Hawaii	51,291	11	Washington	50,769
48	Idaho	34,937	12	Maryland	50,320
16	Illinois	48,829	13	Colorado	50,283
32	Indiana	40,891	14	Minnesota	49,503
19	Iowa	47,303	15	North Dakota	49,273
25	Kansas	44,318	16	Illinois	48,829
44	Kentucky	36,289	17	Nebraska	48,112
21	Louisiana	46,388	18	Nevada	47,862
38	Maine	38,908	19	Iowa	47,303
12	Maryland	50,320	20	South Dakota	47,155
7	Massachusetts	55,384	21	Louisiana	46,388
42	Michigan	36,952	22	Texas	46,190
14	Minnesota	49,503	23	Rhode Island	45,420
50	Mississippi	32,488	24	New Hampshire	44,845
36	Missouri	40,042	25	Kansas	44,318
43	Montana	36,876	26	Pennsylvania	44,013
17	Nebraska	48,112	27	Oregon	43,299
18	Nevada	47,862	28	Wisconsin	43,215
24	New Hampshire	44,845	29	North Carolina	42,431
6	New Jersey	55,464	30	Oklahoma	41,708
41	New Mexico	37,221	31	Vermont	40,913
5	New York	55,944	32	Indiana	40,891
29	North Carolina	42,431	33	Ohio	40,828
15	North Dakota	49,273	34	Utah	40,560
33	Ohio	40,828	35	Georgia	40,206
30	Oklahoma	41,708	36	Missouri	40,042
27	Oregon	43,299	37	Florida	39,758
26	Pennsylvania	44,013	38	Maine	38,908
23	Rhode Island	45,420	39	Arizona	38,868
47	South Carolina	35,001	40	Tennessee	38,834
20	South Dakota	47,155	41	New Mexico	37,221
40	Tennessee	38,834	42	Michigan	36,952
22	Texas	46,190	43	Montana	36,876
34	Utah	40,560	44	Kentucky	36,289
31	Vermont	40,913	45	Alabama	36,073
8	Virginia	51,816	46	Arkansas	35,238
11	Washington	50,769	47	South Carolina	35,001
49	West Virginia	34,809	48	Idaho	34,937
28	Wisconsin	43,215	49	West Virginia	34,809
1	Wyoming	68,980	50	Mississippi	32,488
				District of Columbia	165,310

Source: CQ Press using data from U.S. Department of Commerce, Bureau of Economic Analysis
"Gross Domestic Product Data" (http://www.bea.gov/regional/gsp/)
*G.D.P. is the market value of goods and services produced by the labor and property located in a state. It is the state counterpart to the nation's Gross Domestic Product. This was formerly known as Gross State Product (G.S.P.).

Percent Change in Per Capita Gross Domestic Product: 2005 to 2009
(Adjusted to Constant 2005 Dollars)
National Percent Change = 1.0% Decrease*

ALPHA ORDER

RANK	STATE	PERCENT CHANGE
33	Alabama	(1.5)
9	Alaska	5.6
46	Arizona	(5.4)
19	Arkansas	1.3
28	California	(0.4)
30	Colorado	(1.1)
13	Connecticut	3.2
42	Delaware	(4.8)
47	Florida	(5.7)
48	Georgia	(8.1)
14	Hawaii	2.4
40	Idaho	(4.6)
33	Illinois	(1.5)
35	Indiana	(2.1)
5	Iowa	7.0
7	Kansas	6.0
32	Kentucky	(1.4)
40	Louisiana	(4.6)
19	Maine	1.3
14	Maryland	2.4
22	Massachusetts	0.9
49	Michigan	(8.2)
37	Minnesota	(2.8)
10	Mississippi	5.5
36	Missouri	(2.4)
16	Montana	2.3
6	Nebraska	6.3
50	Nevada	(10.7)
27	New Hampshire	(0.3)
24	New Jersey	0.7
38	New Mexico	(3.7)
22	New York	0.9
44	North Carolina	(5.1)
1	North Dakota	16.9
39	Ohio	(3.9)
3	Oklahoma	13.1
8	Oregon	5.9
17	Pennsylvania	2.1
31	Rhode Island	(1.2)
45	South Carolina	(5.2)
4	South Dakota	7.9
42	Tennessee	(4.8)
26	Texas	(0.1)
21	Utah	1.1
17	Vermont	2.1
29	Virginia	(0.5)
12	Washington	3.9
11	West Virginia	5.0
25	Wisconsin	0.3
2	Wyoming	16.8

RANK ORDER

RANK	STATE	PERCENT CHANGE
1	North Dakota	16.9
2	Wyoming	16.8
3	Oklahoma	13.1
4	South Dakota	7.9
5	Iowa	7.0
6	Nebraska	6.3
7	Kansas	6.0
8	Oregon	5.9
9	Alaska	5.6
10	Mississippi	5.5
11	West Virginia	5.0
12	Washington	3.9
13	Connecticut	3.2
14	Hawaii	2.4
14	Maryland	2.4
16	Montana	2.3
17	Pennsylvania	2.1
17	Vermont	2.1
19	Arkansas	1.3
19	Maine	1.3
21	Utah	1.1
22	Massachusetts	0.9
22	New York	0.9
24	New Jersey	0.7
25	Wisconsin	0.3
26	Texas	(0.1)
27	New Hampshire	(0.3)
28	California	(0.4)
29	Virginia	(0.5)
30	Colorado	(1.1)
31	Rhode Island	(1.2)
32	Kentucky	(1.4)
33	Alabama	(1.5)
33	Illinois	(1.5)
35	Indiana	(2.1)
36	Missouri	(2.4)
37	Minnesota	(2.8)
38	New Mexico	(3.7)
39	Ohio	(3.9)
40	Idaho	(4.6)
40	Louisiana	(4.6)
42	Delaware	(4.8)
42	Tennessee	(4.8)
44	North Carolina	(5.1)
45	South Carolina	(5.2)
46	Arizona	(5.4)
47	Florida	(5.7)
48	Georgia	(8.1)
49	Michigan	(8.2)
50	Nevada	(10.7)

District of Columbia   2.8

Source: CQ Press using data from U.S. Department of Commerce, Bureau of Economic Analysis
    "Gross Domestic Product Data" (http://www.bea.gov/regional/gsp/)

*G.D.P. is the market value of goods and services produced by the labor and property located in a state. It is the state counterpart to the nation's Gross Domestic Product. This was formerly known as Gross State Product (G.S.P.). Adjusted for inflation using chained 2005 dollars.

Personal Income in 2009

National Total = $12,165,474,000,000*

ALPHA ORDER

RANK	STATE	INCOME	% of USA
25	Alabama	$157,084,638,000	1.3%
47	Alaska	30,180,493,000	0.2%
17	Arizona	219,269,042,000	1.8%
33	Arkansas	93,685,218,000	0.8%
1	California	1,572,650,187,000	12.9%
22	Colorado	210,228,137,000	1.7%
23	Connecticut	193,726,193,000	1.6%
44	Delaware	35,359,927,000	0.3%
4	Florida	720,949,106,000	5.9%
11	Georgia	333,996,035,000	2.7%
40	Hawaii	54,495,000,000	0.4%
41	Idaho	48,943,709,000	0.4%
5	Illinois	540,994,727,000	4.4%
18	Indiana	217,818,929,000	1.8%
30	Iowa	113,166,035,000	0.9%
31	Kansas	110,673,440,000	0.9%
27	Kentucky	139,370,151,000	1.1%
24	Louisiana	168,544,450,000	1.4%
42	Maine	48,089,690,000	0.4%
15	Maryland	275,143,448,000	2.3%
12	Massachusetts	327,323,542,000	2.7%
10	Michigan	342,302,212,000	2.8%
16	Minnesota	220,437,583,000	1.8%
34	Mississippi	89,818,194,000	0.7%
20	Missouri	215,180,697,000	1.8%
45	Montana	33,923,301,000	0.3%
36	Nebraska	70,564,913,000	0.6%
32	Nevada	99,620,809,000	0.8%
39	New Hampshire	56,407,553,000	0.5%
7	New Jersey	435,465,803,000	3.6%
37	New Mexico	66,744,715,000	0.5%
3	New York	907,885,800,000	7.5%
13	North Carolina	325,695,372,000	2.7%
48	North Dakota	26,343,904,000	0.2%
8	Ohio	410,799,065,000	3.4%
29	Oklahoma	132,143,775,000	1.1%
28	Oregon	138,203,200,000	1.1%
6	Pennsylvania	506,215,135,000	4.2%
43	Rhode Island	43,522,321,000	0.4%
26	South Carolina	147,501,612,000	1.2%
46	South Dakota	31,039,584,000	0.3%
19	Tennessee	215,612,104,000	1.8%
2	Texas	955,264,348,000	7.9%
35	Utah	88,025,491,000	0.7%
50	Vermont	24,261,430,000	0.2%
9	Virginia	347,849,874,000	2.9%
14	Washington	286,113,771,000	2.4%
38	West Virginia	58,355,071,000	0.5%
21	Wisconsin	211,477,916,000	1.7%
49	Wyoming	26,221,601,000	0.2%

RANK ORDER

RANK	STATE	INCOME	% of USA
1	California	$1,572,650,187,000	12.9%
2	Texas	955,264,348,000	7.9%
3	New York	907,885,800,000	7.5%
4	Florida	720,949,106,000	5.9%
5	Illinois	540,994,727,000	4.4%
6	Pennsylvania	506,215,135,000	4.2%
7	New Jersey	435,465,803,000	3.6%
8	Ohio	410,799,065,000	3.4%
9	Virginia	347,849,874,000	2.9%
10	Michigan	342,302,212,000	2.8%
11	Georgia	333,996,035,000	2.7%
12	Massachusetts	327,323,542,000	2.7%
13	North Carolina	325,695,372,000	2.7%
14	Washington	286,113,771,000	2.4%
15	Maryland	275,143,448,000	2.3%
16	Minnesota	220,437,583,000	1.8%
17	Arizona	219,269,042,000	1.8%
18	Indiana	217,818,929,000	1.8%
19	Tennessee	215,612,104,000	1.8%
20	Missouri	215,180,697,000	1.8%
21	Wisconsin	211,477,916,000	1.7%
22	Colorado	210,228,137,000	1.7%
23	Connecticut	193,726,193,000	1.6%
24	Louisiana	168,544,450,000	1.4%
25	Alabama	157,084,638,000	1.3%
26	South Carolina	147,501,612,000	1.2%
27	Kentucky	139,370,151,000	1.1%
28	Oregon	138,203,200,000	1.1%
29	Oklahoma	132,143,775,000	1.1%
30	Iowa	113,166,035,000	0.9%
31	Kansas	110,673,440,000	0.9%
32	Nevada	99,620,809,000	0.8%
33	Arkansas	93,685,218,000	0.8%
34	Mississippi	89,818,194,000	0.7%
35	Utah	88,025,491,000	0.7%
36	Nebraska	70,564,913,000	0.6%
37	New Mexico	66,744,715,000	0.5%
38	West Virginia	58,355,071,000	0.5%
39	New Hampshire	56,407,553,000	0.5%
40	Hawaii	54,495,000,000	0.4%
41	Idaho	48,943,709,000	0.4%
42	Maine	48,089,690,000	0.4%
43	Rhode Island	43,522,321,000	0.4%
44	Delaware	35,359,927,000	0.3%
45	Montana	33,923,301,000	0.3%
46	South Dakota	31,039,584,000	0.3%
47	Alaska	30,180,493,000	0.2%
48	North Dakota	26,343,904,000	0.2%
49	Wyoming	26,221,601,000	0.2%
50	Vermont	24,261,430,000	0.2%
	District of Columbia	40,784,749,000	0.3%

Source: U.S. Department of Commerce, Bureau of Economic Analysis
"Annual State Personal Income" (http://www.bea.gov/regional/spi/)
*The national total shown here is the sum of the state estimates. It differs from the national income and product accounts
(NIPA) estimate of personal income because it omits the earnings of federal civilian and military personnel stationed abroad and
of U.S. residents employed abroad temporarily by private U.S. firms.

Change in Personal Income: 2008 to 2009

National Percent Change = 1.7% Decrease*

ALPHA ORDER

RANK	STATE	PERCENT CHANGE
17	Alabama	(0.9)
25	Alaska	(1.2)
37	Arizona	(2.2)
5	Arkansas	(0.1)
40	California	(2.4)
35	Colorado	(2.1)
49	Connecticut	(3.4)
23	Delaware	(1.1)
39	Florida	(2.3)
37	Georgia	(2.2)
6	Hawaii	(0.2)
46	Idaho	(2.8)
40	Illinois	(2.4)
40	Indiana	(2.4)
23	Iowa	(1.1)
29	Kansas	(1.4)
2	Kentucky	0.4
13	Louisiana	(0.6)
6	Maine	(0.2)
2	Maryland	0.4
34	Massachusetts	(2.0)
47	Michigan	(3.1)
43	Minnesota	(2.5)
13	Mississippi	(0.6)
31	Missouri	(1.7)
12	Montana	(0.5)
26	Nebraska	(1.3)
50	Nevada	(5.0)
35	New Hampshire	(2.1)
44	New Jersey	(2.6)
4	New Mexico	0.0
47	New York	(3.1)
17	North Carolina	(0.9)
20	North Dakota	(1.0)
26	Ohio	(1.3)
33	Oklahoma	(1.8)
16	Oregon	(0.7)
8	Pennsylvania	(0.3)
20	Rhode Island	(1.0)
13	South Carolina	(0.6)
31	South Dakota	(1.7)
30	Tennessee	(1.6)
26	Texas	(1.3)
20	Utah	(1.0)
10	Vermont	(0.4)
8	Virginia	(0.3)
10	Washington	(0.4)
1	West Virginia	2.0
17	Wisconsin	(0.9)
45	Wyoming	(2.7)

RANK ORDER

RANK	STATE	PERCENT CHANGE
1	West Virginia	2.0
2	Kentucky	0.4
2	Maryland	0.4
4	New Mexico	0.0
5	Arkansas	(0.1)
6	Hawaii	(0.2)
6	Maine	(0.2)
8	Pennsylvania	(0.3)
8	Virginia	(0.3)
10	Vermont	(0.4)
10	Washington	(0.4)
12	Montana	(0.5)
13	Louisiana	(0.6)
13	Mississippi	(0.6)
13	South Carolina	(0.6)
16	Oregon	(0.7)
17	Alabama	(0.9)
17	North Carolina	(0.9)
17	Wisconsin	(0.9)
20	North Dakota	(1.0)
20	Rhode Island	(1.0)
20	Utah	(1.0)
23	Delaware	(1.1)
23	Iowa	(1.1)
25	Alaska	(1.2)
26	Nebraska	(1.3)
26	Ohio	(1.3)
26	Texas	(1.3)
29	Kansas	(1.4)
30	Tennessee	(1.6)
31	Missouri	(1.7)
31	South Dakota	(1.7)
33	Oklahoma	(1.8)
34	Massachusetts	(2.0)
35	Colorado	(2.1)
35	New Hampshire	(2.1)
37	Arizona	(2.2)
37	Georgia	(2.2)
39	Florida	(2.3)
40	California	(2.4)
40	Illinois	(2.4)
40	Indiana	(2.4)
43	Minnesota	(2.5)
44	New Jersey	(2.6)
45	Wyoming	(2.7)
46	Idaho	(2.8)
47	Michigan	(3.1)
47	New York	(3.1)
49	Connecticut	(3.4)
50	Nevada	(5.0)

District of Columbia   1.1

Source: CQ Press using data from U.S. Department of Commerce, Bureau of Economic Analysis
    "Annual State Personal Income" (http://www.bea.gov/regional/spi/)
*Based on revised 2008 figures.

Per Capita Personal Income in 2009

National Per Capita = $39,626*

ALPHA ORDER

RANK	STATE	PER CAPITA
41	Alabama	$33,360
8	Alaska	43,209
42	Arizona	33,244
44	Arkansas	32,423
11	California	42,548
15	Colorado	41,839
1	Connecticut	55,063
19	Delaware	39,949
23	Florida	38,890
39	Georgia	33,980
12	Hawaii	42,075
48	Idaho	31,662
13	Illinois	41,904
40	Indiana	33,912
27	Iowa	37,623
21	Kansas	39,263
46	Kentucky	32,306
28	Louisiana	37,520
30	Maine	36,479
4	Maryland	48,275
3	Massachusetts	49,643
37	Michigan	34,334
14	Minnesota	41,859
50	Mississippi	30,426
32	Missouri	35,938
35	Montana	34,794
20	Nebraska	39,277
26	Nevada	37,691
10	New Hampshire	42,585
2	New Jersey	50,009
43	New Mexico	33,212
6	New York	46,459
36	North Carolina	34,719
17	North Dakota	40,727
34	Ohio	35,590
33	Oklahoma	35,840
31	Oregon	36,125
18	Pennsylvania	40,161
16	Rhode Island	41,324
45	South Carolina	32,338
25	South Dakota	38,208
38	Tennessee	34,245
24	Texas	38,546
49	Utah	31,612
22	Vermont	39,021
7	Virginia	44,129
9	Washington	42,933
47	West Virginia	32,067
29	Wisconsin	37,398
5	Wyoming	48,178

RANK ORDER

RANK	STATE	PER CAPITA
1	Connecticut	$55,063
2	New Jersey	50,009
3	Massachusetts	49,643
4	Maryland	48,275
5	Wyoming	48,178
6	New York	46,459
7	Virginia	44,129
8	Alaska	43,209
9	Washington	42,933
10	New Hampshire	42,585
11	California	42,548
12	Hawaii	42,075
13	Illinois	41,904
14	Minnesota	41,859
15	Colorado	41,839
16	Rhode Island	41,324
17	North Dakota	40,727
18	Pennsylvania	40,161
19	Delaware	39,949
20	Nebraska	39,277
21	Kansas	39,263
22	Vermont	39,021
23	Florida	38,890
24	Texas	38,546
25	South Dakota	38,208
26	Nevada	37,691
27	Iowa	37,623
28	Louisiana	37,520
29	Wisconsin	37,398
30	Maine	36,479
31	Oregon	36,125
32	Missouri	35,938
33	Oklahoma	35,840
34	Ohio	35,590
35	Montana	34,794
36	North Carolina	34,719
37	Michigan	34,334
38	Tennessee	34,245
39	Georgia	33,980
40	Indiana	33,912
41	Alabama	33,360
42	Arizona	33,244
43	New Mexico	33,212
44	Arkansas	32,423
45	South Carolina	32,338
46	Kentucky	32,306
47	West Virginia	32,067
48	Idaho	31,662
49	Utah	31,612
50	Mississippi	30,426
	District of Columbia	68,013

Source: U.S. Department of Commerce, Bureau of Economic Analysis
    "Annual State Personal Income" (http://www.bea.gov/regional/spi/)
*The national figure is based on the sum of the state estimates. It differs from the national income and product accounts (NIPA) estimate of personal income because it omits the earnings of federal civilian and military personnel stationed abroad and of U.S. residents employed abroad temporarily by private U.S. firms.

Change in Per Capita Personal Income: 2008 to 2009

National Percent Change = 2.6% Decrease*

ALPHA ORDER			RANK ORDER		
RANK	STATE	PERCENT CHANGE	RANK	STATE	PERCENT CHANGE
17	Alabama	(1.6)	1	West Virginia	1.8
31	Alaska	(2.7)	2	Maine	(0.1)
45	Arizona	(3.6)	3	Kentucky	(0.2)
7	Arkansas	(0.8)	4	Maryland	(0.3)
42	California	(3.4)	5	Vermont	(0.5)
46	Colorado	(3.8)	6	Pennsylvania	(0.6)
46	Connecticut	(3.8)	7	Arkansas	(0.8)
23	Delaware	(2.1)	7	Hawaii	(0.8)
34	Florida	(2.9)	9	Mississippi	(1.0)
44	Georgia	(3.5)	9	Rhode Island	(1.0)
7	Hawaii	(0.8)	11	New Mexico	(1.1)
48	Idaho	(4.0)	12	Montana	(1.3)
34	Illinois	(2.9)	13	Ohio	(1.4)
34	Indiana	(2.9)	13	Virginia	(1.4)
17	Iowa	(1.6)	13	Wisconsin	(1.4)
25	Kansas	(2.2)	16	Louisiana	(1.5)
3	Kentucky	(0.2)	17	Alabama	(1.6)
16	Louisiana	(1.5)	17	Iowa	(1.6)
2	Maine	(0.1)	19	North Dakota	(1.8)
4	Maryland	(0.3)	19	Oregon	(1.8)
31	Massachusetts	(2.7)	19	South Carolina	(1.8)
33	Michigan	(2.8)	19	Washington	(1.8)
40	Minnesota	(3.2)	23	Delaware	(2.1)
9	Mississippi	(1.0)	23	Nebraska	(2.1)
26	Missouri	(2.3)	25	Kansas	(2.2)
12	Montana	(1.3)	26	Missouri	(2.3)
23	Nebraska	(2.1)	26	New Hampshire	(2.3)
50	Nevada	(6.0)	26	North Carolina	(2.3)
26	New Hampshire	(2.3)	29	Tennessee	(2.4)
39	New Jersey	(3.1)	30	South Dakota	(2.6)
11	New Mexico	(1.1)	31	Alaska	(2.7)
42	New York	(3.4)	31	Massachusetts	(2.7)
26	North Carolina	(2.3)	33	Michigan	(2.8)
19	North Dakota	(1.8)	34	Florida	(2.9)
13	Ohio	(1.4)	34	Illinois	(2.9)
34	Oklahoma	(2.9)	34	Indiana	(2.9)
19	Oregon	(1.8)	34	Oklahoma	(2.9)
6	Pennsylvania	(0.6)	38	Utah	(3.0)
9	Rhode Island	(1.0)	39	New Jersey	(3.1)
19	South Carolina	(1.8)	40	Minnesota	(3.2)
30	South Dakota	(2.6)	40	Texas	(3.2)
29	Tennessee	(2.4)	42	California	(3.4)
40	Texas	(3.2)	42	New York	(3.4)
38	Utah	(3.0)	44	Georgia	(3.5)
5	Vermont	(0.5)	45	Arizona	(3.6)
13	Virginia	(1.4)	46	Colorado	(3.8)
19	Washington	(1.8)	46	Connecticut	(3.8)
1	West Virginia	1.8	48	Idaho	(4.0)
13	Wisconsin	(1.4)	49	Wyoming	(4.8)
49	Wyoming	(4.8)	50	Nevada	(6.0)
				District of Columbia	(0.5)

Source: CQ Press using data from U.S. Department of Commerce, Bureau of Economic Analysis
    "Annual State Personal Income" (http://www.bea.gov/regional/spi/)
*Based on revised 2008 figures.

Per Capita Disposable Personal Income in 2009

National Per Capita = $35,916*

ALPHA ORDER

RANK	STATE	PER CAPITA
42	Alabama	$30,758
8	Alaska	39,620
41	Arizona	30,807
45	Arkansas	29,861
12	California	38,300
14	Colorado	37,899
1	Connecticut	47,797
19	Delaware	36,130
20	Florida	36,031
39	Georgia	31,096
11	Hawaii	38,556
48	Idaho	29,171
13	Illinois	37,913
40	Indiana	30,983
27	Iowa	34,385
22	Kansas	35,714
46	Kentucky	29,526
28	Louisiana	34,249
30	Maine	33,359
5	Maryland	42,902
4	Massachusetts	43,884
38	Michigan	31,475
16	Minnesota	37,583
50	Mississippi	28,387
32	Missouri	32,781
36	Montana	31,853
21	Nebraska	35,939
26	Nevada	34,914
10	New Hampshire	39,124
2	New Jersey	44,416
43	New Mexico	30,721
6	New York	40,348
37	North Carolina	31,635
17	North Dakota	37,286
34	Ohio	32,445
31	Oklahoma	32,831
33	Oregon	32,717
18	Pennsylvania	36,255
15	Rhode Island	37,636
44	South Carolina	29,900
24	South Dakota	35,662
35	Tennessee	32,135
25	Texas	35,472
49	Utah	28,856
23	Vermont	35,703
9	Virginia	39,606
7	Washington	39,699
47	West Virginia	29,416
29	Wisconsin	33,857
3	Wyoming	43,929

RANK ORDER

RANK	STATE	PER CAPITA
1	Connecticut	$47,797
2	New Jersey	44,416
3	Wyoming	43,929
4	Massachusetts	43,884
5	Maryland	42,902
6	New York	40,348
7	Washington	39,699
8	Alaska	39,620
9	Virginia	39,606
10	New Hampshire	39,124
11	Hawaii	38,556
12	California	38,300
13	Illinois	37,913
14	Colorado	37,899
15	Rhode Island	37,636
16	Minnesota	37,583
17	North Dakota	37,286
18	Pennsylvania	36,255
19	Delaware	36,130
20	Florida	36,031
21	Nebraska	35,939
22	Kansas	35,714
23	Vermont	35,703
24	South Dakota	35,662
25	Texas	35,472
26	Nevada	34,914
27	Iowa	34,385
28	Louisiana	34,249
29	Wisconsin	33,857
30	Maine	33,359
31	Oklahoma	32,831
32	Missouri	32,781
33	Oregon	32,717
34	Ohio	32,445
35	Tennessee	32,135
36	Montana	31,853
37	North Carolina	31,635
38	Michigan	31,475
39	Georgia	31,096
40	Indiana	30,983
41	Arizona	30,807
42	Alabama	30,758
43	New Mexico	30,721
44	South Carolina	29,900
45	Arkansas	29,861
46	Kentucky	29,526
47	West Virginia	29,416
48	Idaho	29,171
49	Utah	28,856
50	Mississippi	28,387

District of Columbia   60,751

Source: U.S. Department of Commerce, Bureau of Economic Analysis
"Annual State Personal Income" (http://www.bea.gov/regional/spi/)
*Disposable personal income is personal income less personal tax and nontax payments. It is the income available to persons for spending or saving.

Median Household Income in 2009

National Median = $50,618*

ALPHA ORDER

RANK	STATE	INCOME
44	Alabama	$42,652
5	Alaska	63,505
35	Arizona	47,106
49	Arkansas	39,392
13	California	56,862
9	Colorado	59,964
2	Connecticut	65,213
17	Delaware	53,032
38	Florida	45,897
37	Georgia	46,570
7	Hawaii	61,055
29	Idaho	48,299
16	Illinois	53,413
36	Indiana	46,579
22	Iowa	50,422
32	Kansas	47,527
46	Kentucky	41,489
45	Louisiana	42,528
30	Maine	48,032
3	Maryland	65,183
8	Massachusetts	59,981
27	Michigan	48,888
12	Minnesota	56,956
50	Mississippi	36,650
33	Missouri	47,408
43	Montana	42,778
24	Nebraska	50,333
14	Nevada	53,964
1	New Hampshire	66,654
4	New Jersey	64,143
40	New Mexico	43,790
23	New York	50,372
41	North Carolina	43,229
26	North Dakota	49,450
31	Ohio	47,809
39	Oklahoma	45,507
20	Oregon	50,866
25	Pennsylvania	49,829
15	Rhode Island	53,584
42	South Carolina	42,945
28	South Dakota	48,416
47	Tennessee	40,895
34	Texas	47,143
11	Utah	58,722
21	Vermont	50,619
6	Virginia	61,151
10	Washington	58,964
48	West Virginia	40,627
19	Wisconsin	51,763
18	Wyoming	52,010

RANK ORDER

RANK	STATE	INCOME
1	New Hampshire	$66,654
2	Connecticut	65,213
3	Maryland	65,183
4	New Jersey	64,143
5	Alaska	63,505
6	Virginia	61,151
7	Hawaii	61,055
8	Massachusetts	59,981
9	Colorado	59,964
10	Washington	58,964
11	Utah	58,722
12	Minnesota	56,956
13	California	56,862
14	Nevada	53,964
15	Rhode Island	53,584
16	Illinois	53,413
17	Delaware	53,032
18	Wyoming	52,010
19	Wisconsin	51,763
20	Oregon	50,866
21	Vermont	50,619
22	Iowa	50,422
23	New York	50,372
24	Nebraska	50,333
25	Pennsylvania	49,829
26	North Dakota	49,450
27	Michigan	48,888
28	South Dakota	48,416
29	Idaho	48,299
30	Maine	48,032
31	Ohio	47,809
32	Kansas	47,527
33	Missouri	47,408
34	Texas	47,143
35	Arizona	47,106
36	Indiana	46,579
37	Georgia	46,570
38	Florida	45,897
39	Oklahoma	45,507
40	New Mexico	43,790
41	North Carolina	43,229
42	South Carolina	42,945
43	Montana	42,778
44	Alabama	42,652
45	Louisiana	42,528
46	Kentucky	41,489
47	Tennessee	40,895
48	West Virginia	40,627
49	Arkansas	39,392
50	Mississippi	36,650
	District of Columbia	53,685

Source: U.S. Bureau of the Census
   "Median Household Income by State" (http://www.census.gov/hhes/www/income/data/historical/household/index.html)
*This is a 3-year-average of inflation-adjusted single-year medians for the years 2007 through 2009.

Bankruptcy Filings in 2010

National Total = 1,596,355 Bankruptcies*

ALPHA ORDER

RANK	STATE	BANKRUPTCIES	% of USA
15	Alabama	34,689	2.2%
50	Alaska	1,132	0.1%
11	Arizona	42,216	2.6%
29	Arkansas	16,818	1.1%
1	California	255,115	16.0%
18	Colorado	32,636	2.0%
32	Connecticut	11,554	0.7%
42	Delaware	4,459	0.3%
2	Florida	111,550	7.0%
4	Georgia	78,793	4.9%
44	Hawaii	3,862	0.2%
36	Idaho	8,392	0.5%
3	Illinois	82,511	5.2%
10	Indiana	48,443	3.0%
34	Iowa	10,154	0.6%
33	Kansas	11,379	0.7%
23	Kentucky	25,652	1.6%
27	Louisiana	19,236	1.2%
43	Maine	4,149	0.3%
21	Maryland	29,938	1.9%
24	Massachusetts	23,485	1.5%
6	Michigan	69,970	4.4%
25	Minnesota	22,628	1.4%
31	Mississippi	14,572	0.9%
17	Missouri	33,487	2.1%
45	Montana	3,167	0.2%
37	Nebraska	7,924	0.5%
19	Nevada	30,637	1.9%
40	New Hampshire	5,671	0.4%
12	New Jersey	40,775	2.6%
38	New Mexico	6,659	0.4%
8	New York	57,941	3.6%
22	North Carolina	27,358	1.7%
48	North Dakota	1,651	0.1%
5	Ohio	72,507	4.5%
30	Oklahoma	15,228	1.0%
26	Oregon	20,460	1.3%
13	Pennsylvania	39,471	2.5%
41	Rhode Island	5,365	0.3%
35	South Carolina	9,559	0.6%
46	South Dakota	2,018	0.1%
9	Tennessee	51,597	3.2%
7	Texas	58,118	3.6%
28	Utah	17,888	1.1%
47	Vermont	1,676	0.1%
14	Virginia	37,684	2.4%
16	Washington	34,142	2.1%
39	West Virginia	6,489	0.4%
20	Wisconsin	30,228	1.9%
49	Wyoming	1,560	0.1%

RANK ORDER

RANK	STATE	BANKRUPTCIES	% of USA
1	California	255,115	16.0%
2	Florida	111,550	7.0%
3	Illinois	82,511	5.2%
4	Georgia	78,793	4.9%
5	Ohio	72,507	4.5%
6	Michigan	69,970	4.4%
7	Texas	58,118	3.6%
8	New York	57,941	3.6%
9	Tennessee	51,597	3.2%
10	Indiana	48,443	3.0%
11	Arizona	42,216	2.6%
12	New Jersey	40,775	2.6%
13	Pennsylvania	39,471	2.5%
14	Virginia	37,684	2.4%
15	Alabama	34,689	2.2%
16	Washington	34,142	2.1%
17	Missouri	33,487	2.1%
18	Colorado	32,636	2.0%
19	Nevada	30,637	1.9%
20	Wisconsin	30,228	1.9%
21	Maryland	29,938	1.9%
22	North Carolina	27,358	1.7%
23	Kentucky	25,652	1.6%
24	Massachusetts	23,485	1.5%
25	Minnesota	22,628	1.4%
26	Oregon	20,460	1.3%
27	Louisiana	19,236	1.2%
28	Utah	17,888	1.1%
29	Arkansas	16,818	1.1%
30	Oklahoma	15,228	1.0%
31	Mississippi	14,572	0.9%
32	Connecticut	11,554	0.7%
33	Kansas	11,379	0.7%
34	Iowa	10,154	0.6%
35	South Carolina	9,559	0.6%
36	Idaho	8,392	0.5%
37	Nebraska	7,924	0.5%
38	New Mexico	6,659	0.4%
39	West Virginia	6,489	0.4%
40	New Hampshire	5,671	0.4%
41	Rhode Island	5,365	0.3%
42	Delaware	4,459	0.3%
43	Maine	4,149	0.3%
44	Hawaii	3,862	0.2%
45	Montana	3,167	0.2%
46	South Dakota	2,018	0.1%
47	Vermont	1,676	0.1%
48	North Dakota	1,651	0.1%
49	Wyoming	1,560	0.1%
50	Alaska	1,132	0.1%
	District of Columbia	1,286	0.1%

Source: CQ Press using data from Administrative Office of the U.S. Courts
"Table F-2, U.S. Bankruptcy Courts" (http://www.uscourts.gov/Statistics/BankruptcyStatistics.aspx)
*For 12 months through September 2010. Includes business (58,322) and non-business (1,538,033) filings. Includes all chapters of bankruptcy. National total includes 12,476 bankruptcies in U.S. territories.

Personal Bankruptcy Rate in 2010

National Rate = 497 Personal Bankruptcies per 100,000 Population*

ALPHA ORDER			RANK ORDER		
RANK	STATE	RATE	RANK	STATE	RATE
5	Alabama	720	1	Nevada	1,121
50	Alaska	150	2	Tennessee	801
11	Arizona	614	3	Georgia	774
15	Arkansas	563	4	Indiana	739
7	California	665	5	Alabama	720
9	Colorado	620	6	Michigan	682
37	Connecticut	315	7	California	665
32	Delaware	373	8	Illinois	621
14	Florida	575	9	Colorado	620
3	Georgia	774	10	Utah	617
41	Hawaii	287	11	Arizona	614
19	Idaho	517	12	Ohio	612
8	Illinois	621	13	Kentucky	582
4	Indiana	739	14	Florida	575
35	Iowa	326	15	Arkansas	563
30	Kansas	391	16	Missouri	546
13	Kentucky	582	17	Oregon	520
28	Louisiana	411	18	Wisconsin	518
40	Maine	298	19	Idaho	517
20	Maryland	510	20	Maryland	510
33	Massachusetts	348	21	Washington	495
6	Michigan	682	22	Rhode Island	493
27	Minnesota	414	23	Mississippi	476
23	Mississippi	476	24	Virginia	463
16	Missouri	546	25	New Jersey	451
38	Montana	307	26	Nebraska	424
26	Nebraska	424	27	Minnesota	414
1	Nevada	1,121	28	Louisiana	411
31	New Hampshire	383	29	Oklahoma	398
25	New Jersey	451	30	Kansas	391
36	New Mexico	317	31	New Hampshire	383
42	New York	283	32	Delaware	373
43	North Carolina	276	33	Massachusetts	348
46	North Dakota	245	34	West Virginia	345
12	Ohio	612	35	Iowa	326
29	Oklahoma	398	36	New Mexico	317
17	Oregon	520	37	Connecticut	315
39	Pennsylvania	301	38	Montana	307
22	Rhode Island	493	39	Pennsylvania	301
49	South Carolina	201	40	Maine	298
47	South Dakota	235	41	Hawaii	287
2	Tennessee	801	42	New York	283
48	Texas	217	43	North Carolina	276
10	Utah	617	44	Wyoming	272
45	Vermont	259	45	Vermont	259
24	Virginia	463	46	North Dakota	245
21	Washington	495	47	South Dakota	235
34	West Virginia	345	48	Texas	217
18	Wisconsin	518	49	South Carolina	201
44	Wyoming	272	50	Alaska	150
				District of Columbia	196

Source: CQ Press using data from Administrative Office of the U.S. Courts
   "Table F-2, U.S. Bankruptcy Courts" (http://www.uscourts.gov/Statistics/BankruptcyStatistics.aspx)
*For 12 months through September 2010. National rate does not include bankruptcies or population in U.S. territories. Includes
all nonbusiness bankruptcies.

Percent Change in Personal Bankruptcy Rate: 2009 to 2010

National Percent Change = 14.5% Increase*

ALPHA ORDER				RANK ORDER		
RANK	STATE	PERCENT CHANGE		RANK	STATE	PERCENT CHANGE
48	Alabama	(0.3)		1	Arizona	37.4
6	Alaska	25.0		2	California	34.9
1	Arizona	37.4		3	Hawaii	31.7
40	Arkansas	4.5		4	Utah	31.6
2	California	34.9		5	Wyoming	27.1
9	Colorado	23.3		6	Alaska	25.0
14	Connecticut	19.8		7	Maryland	24.7
11	Delaware	20.7		8	Florida	23.7
8	Florida	23.7		9	Colorado	23.3
31	Georgia	7.8		10	Montana	21.3
3	Hawaii	31.7		11	Delaware	20.7
19	Idaho	15.9		12	New Jersey	20.6
16	Illinois	19.0		13	Massachusetts	20.0
43	Indiana	3.2		14	Connecticut	19.8
43	Iowa	3.2		14	Oregon	19.8
32	Kansas	7.7		16	Illinois	19.0
42	Kentucky	4.1		17	Washington	16.2
36	Louisiana	5.9		18	New Mexico	16.1
25	Maine	11.6		19	Idaho	15.9
7	Maryland	24.7		20	South Dakota	14.1
13	Massachusetts	20.0		21	New Hampshire	14.0
38	Michigan	4.6		22	Wisconsin	13.8
26	Minnesota	11.3		23	Oklahoma	12.7
47	Mississippi	0.2		24	Missouri	11.9
24	Missouri	11.9		25	Maine	11.6
10	Montana	21.3		26	Minnesota	11.3
30	Nebraska	8.2		27	Nevada	11.1
27	Nevada	11.1		28	Texas	10.7
21	New Hampshire	14.0		29	Vermont	9.7
12	New Jersey	20.6		30	Nebraska	8.2
18	New Mexico	16.1		31	Georgia	7.8
35	New York	6.4		32	Kansas	7.7
46	North Carolina	1.1		33	Pennsylvania	7.5
41	North Dakota	4.3		34	Virginia	6.7
38	Ohio	4.6		35	New York	6.4
23	Oklahoma	12.7		36	Louisiana	5.9
14	Oregon	19.8		37	Rhode Island	5.3
33	Pennsylvania	7.5		38	Michigan	4.6
37	Rhode Island	5.3		38	Ohio	4.6
49	South Carolina	(1.5)		40	Arkansas	4.5
20	South Dakota	14.1		41	North Dakota	4.3
50	Tennessee	(5.0)		42	Kentucky	4.1
28	Texas	10.7		43	Indiana	3.2
4	Utah	31.6		43	Iowa	3.2
29	Vermont	9.7		45	West Virginia	2.1
34	Virginia	6.7		46	North Carolina	1.1
17	Washington	16.2		47	Mississippi	0.2
45	West Virginia	2.1		48	Alabama	(0.3)
22	Wisconsin	13.8		49	South Carolina	(1.5)
5	Wyoming	27.1		50	Tennessee	(5.0)
				District of Columbia		16.0

Source: CQ Press using data from Administrative Office of the U.S. Courts
"Table F-2, U.S. Bankruptcy Courts" (http://www.uscourts.gov/Statistics/BankruptcyStatistics.aspx)
*Twelve months ending in September 2009 to 12 months ending in September 2010. National rate does not include bankruptcies or population in U.S. territories. Includes all nonbusiness bankruptcies.

Business Bankruptcy Rate in 2009

National Rate = 1.0% of Existing Firms*

ALPHA ORDER

RANK	STATE	RATE
11	Alabama	0.9
27	Alaska	0.6
4	Arizona	1.3
11	Arkansas	0.9
19	California	0.7
11	Colorado	0.9
36	Connecticut	0.5
1	Delaware	6.4
6	Florida	1.1
3	Georgia	1.4
45	Hawaii	0.4
17	Idaho	0.8
11	Illinois	0.9
36	Indiana	0.5
36	Iowa	0.5
36	Kansas	0.5
19	Kentucky	0.7
17	Louisiana	0.8
27	Maine	0.6
19	Maryland	0.7
45	Massachusetts	0.4
8	Michigan	1.0
27	Minnesota	0.6
11	Mississippi	0.9
27	Missouri	0.6
45	Montana	0.4
19	Nebraska	0.7
2	Nevada	1.7
4	New Hampshire	1.3
19	New Jersey	0.7
19	New Mexico	0.7
19	New York	0.7
19	North Carolina	0.7
49	North Dakota	0.3
11	Ohio	0.9
27	Oklahoma	0.6
36	Oregon	0.5
36	Pennsylvania	0.5
36	Rhode Island	0.5
36	South Carolina	0.5
36	South Dakota	0.5
6	Tennessee	1.1
8	Texas	1.0
8	Utah	1.0
49	Vermont	0.3
27	Virginia	0.6
27	Washington	0.6
27	West Virginia	0.6
27	Wisconsin	0.6
45	Wyoming	0.4

RANK ORDER

RANK	STATE	RATE
1	Delaware	6.4
2	Nevada	1.7
3	Georgia	1.4
4	Arizona	1.3
4	New Hampshire	1.3
6	Florida	1.1
6	Tennessee	1.1
8	Michigan	1.0
8	Texas	1.0
8	Utah	1.0
11	Alabama	0.9
11	Arkansas	0.9
11	Colorado	0.9
11	Illinois	0.9
11	Mississippi	0.9
11	Ohio	0.9
17	Idaho	0.8
17	Louisiana	0.8
19	California	0.7
19	Kentucky	0.7
19	Maryland	0.7
19	Nebraska	0.7
19	New Jersey	0.7
19	New Mexico	0.7
19	New York	0.7
19	North Carolina	0.7
27	Alaska	0.6
27	Maine	0.6
27	Minnesota	0.6
27	Missouri	0.6
27	Oklahoma	0.6
27	Virginia	0.6
27	Washington	0.6
27	West Virginia	0.6
27	Wisconsin	0.6
36	Connecticut	0.5
36	Indiana	0.5
36	Iowa	0.5
36	Kansas	0.5
36	Oregon	0.5
36	Pennsylvania	0.5
36	Rhode Island	0.5
36	South Carolina	0.5
36	South Dakota	0.5
45	Hawaii	0.4
45	Massachusetts	0.4
45	Montana	0.4
45	Wyoming	0.4
49	North Dakota	0.3
49	Vermont	0.3
	District of Columbia	0.4

Source: CQ Press using data from U.S. Small Business Administration
"The Small Business Economy 2010" (http://www.sba.gov/advo/research/)
*Firms can be in more than one state. Firms filing for bankruptcy in 2009 as a percent of employer firms existing in 2009.

2011 State Business Tax Climate Index

National Average Score = 5.00*

ALPHA ORDER

RANK	STATE	SCORE
28	Alabama	4.99
2	Alaska	7.39
34	Arizona	4.81
39	Arkansas	4.55
49	California	3.78
15	Colorado	5.57
47	Connecticut	4.01
8	Delaware	6.03
5	Florida	6.53
25	Georgia	5.02
22	Hawaii	5.06
18	Idaho	5.27
23	Illinois	5.05
10	Indiana	5.79
45	Iowa	4.20
35	Kansas	4.76
19	Kentucky	5.22
36	Louisiana	4.71
29	Maine	4.98
44	Maryland	4.25
32	Massachusetts	4.89
17	Michigan	5.40
43	Minnesota	4.40
21	Mississippi	5.09
16	Missouri	5.48
6	Montana	6.39
29	Nebraska	4.98
4	Nevada	6.74
7	New Hampshire	6.18
48	New Jersey	3.96
32	New Mexico	4.89
50	New York	3.73
41	North Carolina	4.47
20	North Dakota	5.14
46	Ohio	4.16
29	Oklahoma	4.98
14	Oregon	5.61
26	Pennsylvania	5.01
42	Rhode Island	4.46
24	South Carolina	5.04
1	South Dakota	7.43
27	Tennessee	5.00
13	Texas	5.63
9	Utah	5.80
38	Vermont	4.66
12	Virginia	5.67
11	Washington	5.78
37	West Virginia	4.67
39	Wisconsin	4.55
3	Wyoming	7.30

RANK ORDER

RANK	STATE	SCORE
1	South Dakota	7.43
2	Alaska	7.39
3	Wyoming	7.30
4	Nevada	6.74
5	Florida	6.53
6	Montana	6.39
7	New Hampshire	6.18
8	Delaware	6.03
9	Utah	5.80
10	Indiana	5.79
11	Washington	5.78
12	Virginia	5.67
13	Texas	5.63
14	Oregon	5.61
15	Colorado	5.57
16	Missouri	5.48
17	Michigan	5.40
18	Idaho	5.27
19	Kentucky	5.22
20	North Dakota	5.14
21	Mississippi	5.09
22	Hawaii	5.06
23	Illinois	5.05
24	South Carolina	5.04
25	Georgia	5.02
26	Pennsylvania	5.01
27	Tennessee	5.00
28	Alabama	4.99
29	Maine	4.98
29	Nebraska	4.98
29	Oklahoma	4.98
32	Massachusetts	4.89
32	New Mexico	4.89
34	Arizona	4.81
35	Kansas	4.76
36	Louisiana	4.71
37	West Virginia	4.67
38	Vermont	4.66
39	Arkansas	4.55
39	Wisconsin	4.55
41	North Carolina	4.47
42	Rhode Island	4.46
43	Minnesota	4.40
44	Maryland	4.25
45	Iowa	4.20
46	Ohio	4.16
47	Connecticut	4.01
48	New Jersey	3.96
49	California	3.78
50	New York	3.73
	District of Columbia	4.57

Source: The Tax Foundation

"State Business Tax Climate Index" (October 2010, http://www.taxfoundation.org/publications/show/22658.html)

*This index looks at levels of taxation and complexity of compliance to compare the states on how "business friendly" each state is compared to the others. The scale for each factor considered is one to ten, with ten being the "best."

Fortune 500 Companies in 2010

National Total = 500 Companies*

RANK	STATE	COMPANIES	% of USA
35	Alabama	1	0.2%
40	Alaska	0	0.0%
23	Arizona	5	1.0%
26	Arkansas	4	0.8%
1	California	57	11.4%
18	Colorado	8	1.6%
15	Connecticut	11	2.2%
35	Delaware	1	0.2%
11	Florida	16	3.2%
12	Georgia	14	2.8%
40	Hawaii	0	0.0%
35	Idaho	1	0.2%
4	Illinois	31	6.2%
23	Indiana	5	1.0%
28	Iowa	3	0.6%
32	Kansas	2	0.4%
21	Kentucky	6	1.2%
28	Louisiana	3	0.6%
40	Maine	0	0.0%
21	Maryland	6	1.2%
14	Massachusetts	13	2.6%
9	Michigan	18	3.6%
7	Minnesota	21	4.2%
40	Mississippi	0	0.0%
15	Missouri	11	2.2%
40	Montana	0	0.0%
23	Nebraska	5	1.0%
28	Nevada	3	0.6%
40	New Hampshire	0	0.0%
9	New Jersey	18	3.6%
40	New Mexico	0	0.0%
3	New York	56	11.2%
12	North Carolina	14	2.8%
35	North Dakota	1	0.2%
6	Ohio	23	4.6%
26	Oklahoma	4	0.8%
32	Oregon	2	0.4%
5	Pennsylvania	25	5.0%
32	Rhode Island	2	0.4%
28	South Carolina	3	0.6%
40	South Dakota	0	0.0%
18	Tennessee	8	1.6%
1	Texas	57	11.4%
35	Utah	1	0.2%
40	Vermont	0	0.0%
8	Virginia	20	4.0%
20	Washington	7	1.4%
40	West Virginia	0	0.0%
17	Wisconsin	10	2.0%
40	Wyoming	0	0.0%

RANK	STATE	COMPANIES	% of USA
1	California	57	11.4%
1	Texas	57	11.4%
3	New York	56	11.2%
4	Illinois	31	6.2%
5	Pennsylvania	25	5.0%
6	Ohio	23	4.6%
7	Minnesota	21	4.2%
8	Virginia	20	4.0%
9	Michigan	18	3.6%
9	New Jersey	18	3.6%
11	Florida	16	3.2%
12	Georgia	14	2.8%
12	North Carolina	14	2.8%
14	Massachusetts	13	2.6%
15	Connecticut	11	2.2%
15	Missouri	11	2.2%
17	Wisconsin	10	2.0%
18	Colorado	8	1.6%
18	Tennessee	8	1.6%
20	Washington	7	1.4%
21	Kentucky	6	1.2%
21	Maryland	6	1.2%
23	Arizona	5	1.0%
23	Indiana	5	1.0%
23	Nebraska	5	1.0%
26	Arkansas	4	0.8%
26	Oklahoma	4	0.8%
28	Iowa	3	0.6%
28	Louisiana	3	0.6%
28	Nevada	3	0.6%
28	South Carolina	3	0.6%
32	Kansas	2	0.4%
32	Oregon	2	0.4%
32	Rhode Island	2	0.4%
35	Alabama	1	0.2%
35	Delaware	1	0.2%
35	Idaho	1	0.2%
35	North Dakota	1	0.2%
35	Utah	1	0.2%
40	Alaska	0	0.0%
40	Hawaii	0	0.0%
40	Maine	0	0.0%
40	Mississippi	0	0.0%
40	Montana	0	0.0%
40	New Hampshire	0	0.0%
40	New Mexico	0	0.0%
40	South Dakota	0	0.0%
40	Vermont	0	0.0%
40	West Virginia	0	0.0%
40	Wyoming	0	0.0%
	District of Columbia	4	0.8%

Source: Fortune magazine
   "Fortune 500" (http://money.cnn.com/magazines/fortune/fortune500/2010/index.html)
*By state where each company's headquarters is located.

Employer Firms in 2009

National Total = 5,815,800 Firms*

ALPHA ORDER

RANK	STATE	FIRMS	% of USA
27	Alabama	87,531	1.5%
50	Alaska	17,306	0.3%
21	Arizona	128,046	2.2%
33	Arkansas	68,679	1.2%
1	California	1,219,760	21.0%
15	Colorado	153,981	2.6%
26	Connecticut	97,837	1.7%
45	Delaware	25,980	0.4%
3	Florida	464,190	8.0%
9	Georgia	211,334	3.6%
44	Hawaii	31,242	0.5%
36	Idaho	49,232	0.8%
5	Illinois	302,293	5.2%
20	Indiana	130,250	2.2%
30	Iowa	72,352	1.2%
31	Kansas	71,462	1.2%
28	Kentucky	84,726	1.5%
24	Louisiana	103,256	1.8%
39	Maine	41,152	0.7%
16	Maryland	138,766	2.4%
13	Massachusetts	189,900	3.3%
10	Michigan	206,883	3.6%
18	Minnesota	133,298	2.3%
35	Mississippi	55,784	1.0%
17	Missouri	137,262	2.4%
41	Montana	36,988	0.6%
37	Nebraska	48,281	0.8%
34	Nevada	58,146	1.0%
40	New Hampshire	40,826	0.7%
7	New Jersey	235,184	4.0%
38	New Mexico	45,177	0.8%
2	New York	494,607	8.5%
12	North Carolina	198,849	3.4%
49	North Dakota	20,560	0.4%
8	Ohio	227,429	3.9%
29	Oklahoma	82,632	1.4%
23	Oregon	110,380	1.9%
6	Pennsylvania	285,010	4.9%
43	Rhode Island	33,024	0.6%
25	South Carolina	99,063	1.7%
46	South Dakota	25,515	0.4%
22	Tennessee	113,176	1.9%
4	Texas	449,677	7.7%
32	Utah	69,668	1.2%
47	Vermont	21,863	0.4%
14	Virginia	189,292	3.3%
11	Washington	206,482	3.6%
42	West Virginia	35,895	0.6%
19	Wisconsin	130,925	2.3%
48	Wyoming	21,861	0.4%

RANK ORDER

RANK	STATE	FIRMS	% of USA
1	California	1,219,760	21.0%
2	New York	494,607	8.5%
3	Florida	464,190	8.0%
4	Texas	449,677	7.7%
5	Illinois	302,293	5.2%
6	Pennsylvania	285,010	4.9%
7	New Jersey	235,184	4.0%
8	Ohio	227,429	3.9%
9	Georgia	211,334	3.6%
10	Michigan	206,883	3.6%
11	Washington	206,482	3.6%
12	North Carolina	198,849	3.4%
13	Massachusetts	189,900	3.3%
14	Virginia	189,292	3.3%
15	Colorado	153,981	2.6%
16	Maryland	138,766	2.4%
17	Missouri	137,262	2.4%
18	Minnesota	133,298	2.3%
19	Wisconsin	130,925	2.3%
20	Indiana	130,250	2.2%
21	Arizona	128,046	2.2%
22	Tennessee	113,176	1.9%
23	Oregon	110,380	1.9%
24	Louisiana	103,256	1.8%
25	South Carolina	99,063	1.7%
26	Connecticut	97,837	1.7%
27	Alabama	87,531	1.5%
28	Kentucky	84,726	1.5%
29	Oklahoma	82,632	1.4%
30	Iowa	72,352	1.2%
31	Kansas	71,462	1.2%
32	Utah	69,668	1.2%
33	Arkansas	68,679	1.2%
34	Nevada	58,146	1.0%
35	Mississippi	55,784	1.0%
36	Idaho	49,232	0.8%
37	Nebraska	48,281	0.8%
38	New Mexico	45,177	0.8%
39	Maine	41,152	0.7%
40	New Hampshire	40,826	0.7%
41	Montana	36,988	0.6%
42	West Virginia	35,895	0.6%
43	Rhode Island	33,024	0.6%
44	Hawaii	31,242	0.5%
45	Delaware	25,980	0.4%
46	South Dakota	25,515	0.4%
47	Vermont	21,863	0.4%
48	Wyoming	21,861	0.4%
49	North Dakota	20,560	0.4%
50	Alaska	17,306	0.3%
	District of Columbia	28,633	0.5%

Source: U.S. Small Business Administration
    "The Small Business Economy 2010" (http://www.sba.gov/advo/research/)
*State totals do not add to the U.S. figure as firms can be in more than one state.

New Employer Firms in 2008

National Total = 874,816 New Firms*

ALPHA ORDER

RANK	STATE	FIRMS	% of USA
28	Alabama	9,194	1.1%
49	Alaska	1,922	0.2%
18	Arizona	15,847	1.8%
32	Arkansas	8,499	1.0%
1	California	103,572	11.8%
13	Colorado	21,921	2.5%
29	Connecticut	9,164	1.0%
45	Delaware	2,980	0.3%
2	Florida	72,203	8.3%
8	Georgia	28,980	3.3%
42	Hawaii	3,475	0.4%
34	Idaho	6,854	0.8%
7	Illinois	31,493	3.6%
20	Indiana	13,959	1.6%
36	Iowa	5,893	0.7%
33	Kansas	8,156	0.9%
31	Kentucky	8,821	1.0%
27	Louisiana	9,527	1.1%
40	Maine	4,202	0.5%
16	Maryland	18,392	2.1%
15	Massachusetts	18,581	2.1%
12	Michigan	22,090	2.5%
23	Minnesota	11,811	1.4%
37	Mississippi	5,776	0.7%
19	Missouri	15,061	1.7%
41	Montana	4,181	0.5%
38	Nebraska	4,602	0.5%
26	Nevada	10,202	1.2%
39	New Hampshire	4,587	0.5%
9	New Jersey	26,774	3.1%
35	New Mexico	5,971	0.7%
3	New York	65,624	7.5%
11	North Carolina	24,153	2.8%
50	North Dakota	1,842	0.2%
14	Ohio	20,361	2.3%
30	Oklahoma	8,943	1.0%
21	Oregon	13,952	1.6%
5	Pennsylvania	35,587	4.1%
44	Rhode Island	3,310	0.4%
24	South Carolina	11,634	1.3%
48	South Dakota	2,127	0.2%
17	Tennessee	17,167	2.0%
4	Texas	55,214	6.3%
25	Utah	11,238	1.3%
47	Vermont	2,146	0.2%
10	Virginia	25,517	2.9%
6	Washington	33,701	3.9%
43	West Virginia	3,363	0.4%
22	Wisconsin	12,905	1.5%
46	Wyoming	2,593	0.3%

RANK ORDER

RANK	STATE	FIRMS	% of USA
1	California	103,572	11.8%
2	Florida	72,203	8.3%
3	New York	65,624	7.5%
4	Texas	55,214	6.3%
5	Pennsylvania	35,587	4.1%
6	Washington	33,701	3.9%
7	Illinois	31,493	3.6%
8	Georgia	28,980	3.3%
9	New Jersey	26,774	3.1%
10	Virginia	25,517	2.9%
11	North Carolina	24,153	2.8%
12	Michigan	22,090	2.5%
13	Colorado	21,921	2.5%
14	Ohio	20,361	2.3%
15	Massachusetts	18,581	2.1%
16	Maryland	18,392	2.1%
17	Tennessee	17,167	2.0%
18	Arizona	15,847	1.8%
19	Missouri	15,061	1.7%
20	Indiana	13,959	1.6%
21	Oregon	13,952	1.6%
22	Wisconsin	12,905	1.5%
23	Minnesota	11,811	1.4%
24	South Carolina	11,634	1.3%
25	Utah	11,238	1.3%
26	Nevada	10,202	1.2%
27	Louisiana	9,527	1.1%
28	Alabama	9,194	1.1%
29	Connecticut	9,164	1.0%
30	Oklahoma	8,943	1.0%
31	Kentucky	8,821	1.0%
32	Arkansas	8,499	1.0%
33	Kansas	8,156	0.9%
34	Idaho	6,854	0.8%
35	New Mexico	5,971	0.7%
36	Iowa	5,893	0.7%
37	Mississippi	5,776	0.7%
38	Nebraska	4,602	0.5%
39	New Hampshire	4,587	0.5%
40	Maine	4,202	0.5%
41	Montana	4,181	0.5%
42	Hawaii	3,475	0.4%
43	West Virginia	3,363	0.4%
44	Rhode Island	3,310	0.4%
45	Delaware	2,980	0.3%
46	Wyoming	2,593	0.3%
47	Vermont	2,146	0.2%
48	South Dakota	2,127	0.2%
49	Alaska	1,922	0.2%
50	North Dakota	1,842	0.2%
	District of Columbia	3,939	0.5%

Source: U.S. Small Business Administration
  "The Small Business Economy 2009" (http://www.sba.gov/advo/research/)
*National total includes Puerto Rico and Virgin Islands.

Rate of New Employer Firms in 2008

National Rate = 14.3% of Existing Firms*

ALPHA ORDER

RANK	STATE	RATE
33	Alabama	10.2
22	Alaska	11.1
19	Arizona	11.8
13	Arkansas	12.6
47	California	8.8
6	Colorado	13.7
43	Connecticut	9.2
22	Delaware	11.1
5	Florida	14.3
8	Georgia	13.4
22	Hawaii	11.1
8	Idaho	13.4
31	Illinois	10.5
30	Indiana	10.7
50	Iowa	8.2
21	Kansas	11.5
33	Kentucky	10.2
42	Louisiana	9.3
36	Maine	9.9
12	Maryland	12.9
35	Massachusetts	10.0
36	Michigan	9.9
48	Minnesota	8.7
32	Mississippi	10.3
29	Missouri	10.8
22	Montana	11.1
41	Nebraska	9.6
1	Nevada	17.0
22	New Hampshire	11.1
27	New Jersey	11.0
10	New Mexico	13.1
10	New York	13.1
17	North Carolina	12.1
45	North Dakota	9.1
46	Ohio	9.0
27	Oklahoma	11.0
14	Oregon	12.4
16	Pennsylvania	12.3
39	Rhode Island	9.8
19	South Carolina	11.8
49	South Dakota	8.5
4	Tennessee	14.9
14	Texas	12.4
3	Utah	15.9
40	Vermont	9.7
7	Virginia	13.6
2	Washington	16.6
43	West Virginia	9.2
36	Wisconsin	9.9
17	Wyoming	12.1

RANK ORDER

RANK	STATE	RATE
1	Nevada	17.0
2	Washington	16.6
3	Utah	15.9
4	Tennessee	14.9
5	Florida	14.3
6	Colorado	13.7
7	Virginia	13.6
8	Georgia	13.4
8	Idaho	13.4
10	New Mexico	13.1
10	New York	13.1
12	Maryland	12.9
13	Arkansas	12.6
14	Oregon	12.4
14	Texas	12.4
16	Pennsylvania	12.3
17	North Carolina	12.1
17	Wyoming	12.1
19	Arizona	11.8
19	South Carolina	11.8
21	Kansas	11.5
22	Alaska	11.1
22	Delaware	11.1
22	Hawaii	11.1
22	Montana	11.1
22	New Hampshire	11.1
27	New Jersey	11.0
27	Oklahoma	11.0
29	Missouri	10.8
30	Indiana	10.7
31	Illinois	10.5
32	Mississippi	10.3
33	Alabama	10.2
33	Kentucky	10.2
35	Massachusetts	10.0
36	Maine	9.9
36	Michigan	9.9
36	Wisconsin	9.9
39	Rhode Island	9.8
40	Vermont	9.7
41	Nebraska	9.6
42	Louisiana	9.3
43	Connecticut	9.2
43	West Virginia	9.2
45	North Dakota	9.1
46	Ohio	9.0
47	California	8.8
48	Minnesota	8.7
49	South Dakota	8.5
50	Iowa	8.2

District of Columbia	14.2

Source: CQ Press using data from U.S. Small Business Administration
    "The Small Business Economy 2009" and unpublished data (http://www.sba.gov/advo/research/)
*Firms can be in more than one state. Rate figure represents the number of employer firms started in 2008 as a percent of existing firms at the beginning of 2008.

Employer Firm Terminations in 2008

National Total = 966,647 Terminations*

ALPHA ORDER

RANK	STATE	FIRMS	% of USA
26	Alabama	11,468	1.2%
46	Alaska	2,879	0.3%
16	Arizona	21,219	2.2%
34	Arkansas	7,511	0.8%
1	California	150,314	15.6%
11	Colorado	27,591	2.9%
25	Connecticut	11,488	1.2%
45	Delaware	3,698	0.4%
2	Florida	72,003	7.4%
10	Georgia	29,945	3.1%
44	Hawaii	3,973	0.4%
35	Idaho	7,273	0.8%
7	Illinois	35,689	3.7%
20	Indiana	14,380	1.5%
31	Iowa	7,679	0.8%
33	Kansas	7,648	0.8%
28	Kentucky	8,790	0.9%
32	Louisiana	7,656	0.8%
40	Maine	5,095	0.5%
15	Maryland	21,251	2.2%
18	Massachusetts	20,223	2.1%
8	Michigan	34,272	3.5%
23	Minnesota	12,597	1.3%
36	Mississippi	6,800	0.7%
14	Missouri	21,290	2.2%
41	Montana	4,771	0.5%
39	Nebraska	5,200	0.5%
27	Nevada	10,771	1.1%
38	New Hampshire	5,515	0.6%
9	New Jersey	31,167	3.2%
37	New Mexico	5,972	0.6%
3	New York	69,267	7.2%
13	North Carolina	23,734	2.5%
49	North Dakota	2,344	0.2%
17	Ohio	21,038	2.2%
30	Oklahoma	7,787	0.8%
21	Oregon	14,182	1.5%
4	Pennsylvania	42,318	4.4%
43	Rhode Island	4,459	0.5%
24	South Carolina	11,657	1.2%
50	South Dakota	2,311	0.2%
19	Tennessee	18,614	1.9%
6	Texas	36,108	3.7%
29	Utah	8,105	0.8%
48	Vermont	2,555	0.3%
12	Virginia	23,971	2.5%
5	Washington	37,955	3.9%
42	West Virginia	4,644	0.5%
22	Wisconsin	12,711	1.3%
47	Wyoming	2,703	0.3%

RANK ORDER

RANK	STATE	FIRMS	% of USA
1	California	150,314	15.6%
2	Florida	72,003	7.4%
3	New York	69,267	7.2%
4	Pennsylvania	42,318	4.4%
5	Washington	37,955	3.9%
6	Texas	36,108	3.7%
7	Illinois	35,689	3.7%
8	Michigan	34,272	3.5%
9	New Jersey	31,167	3.2%
10	Georgia	29,945	3.1%
11	Colorado	27,591	2.9%
12	Virginia	23,971	2.5%
13	North Carolina	23,734	2.5%
14	Missouri	21,290	2.2%
15	Maryland	21,251	2.2%
16	Arizona	21,219	2.2%
17	Ohio	21,038	2.2%
18	Massachusetts	20,223	2.1%
19	Tennessee	18,614	1.9%
20	Indiana	14,380	1.5%
21	Oregon	14,182	1.5%
22	Wisconsin	12,711	1.3%
23	Minnesota	12,597	1.3%
24	South Carolina	11,657	1.2%
25	Connecticut	11,488	1.2%
26	Alabama	11,468	1.2%
27	Nevada	10,771	1.1%
28	Kentucky	8,790	0.9%
29	Utah	8,105	0.8%
30	Oklahoma	7,787	0.8%
31	Iowa	7,679	0.8%
32	Louisiana	7,656	0.8%
33	Kansas	7,648	0.8%
34	Arkansas	7,511	0.8%
35	Idaho	7,273	0.8%
36	Mississippi	6,800	0.7%
37	New Mexico	5,972	0.6%
38	New Hampshire	5,515	0.6%
39	Nebraska	5,200	0.5%
40	Maine	5,095	0.5%
41	Montana	4,771	0.5%
42	West Virginia	4,644	0.5%
43	Rhode Island	4,459	0.5%
44	Hawaii	3,973	0.4%
45	Delaware	3,698	0.4%
46	Alaska	2,879	0.3%
47	Wyoming	2,703	0.3%
48	Vermont	2,555	0.3%
49	North Dakota	2,344	0.2%
50	South Dakota	2,311	0.2%
	District of Columbia	2,765	0.3%

Source: U.S. Small Business Administration
   "The Small Business Economy 2009" (http://www.sba.gov/advo/research/)
*National total includes Puerto Rico and Virgin Islands.

Rate of Employer Firm Terminations in 2008

National Rate = 15.8% of Existing Firms*

ALPHA ORDER

RANK	STATE	RATE
21	Alabama	12.7
4	Alaska	16.7
6	Arizona	15.9
37	Arkansas	11.1
21	California	12.7
3	Colorado	17.2
33	Connecticut	11.6
14	Delaware	13.8
11	Florida	14.3
14	Georgia	13.8
21	Hawaii	12.7
12	Idaho	14.2
29	Illinois	11.9
38	Indiana	11.0
41	Iowa	10.7
41	Kansas	10.7
43	Kentucky	10.2
50	Louisiana	7.5
29	Maine	11.9
9	Maryland	14.9
39	Massachusetts	10.9
7	Michigan	15.3
46	Minnesota	9.3
28	Mississippi	12.1
8	Missouri	15.2
21	Montana	12.7
40	Nebraska	10.8
2	Nevada	17.9
16	New Hampshire	13.4
19	New Jersey	12.8
18	New Mexico	13.1
13	New York	13.9
31	North Carolina	11.8
33	North Dakota	11.6
46	Ohio	9.3
45	Oklahoma	9.6
26	Oregon	12.6
10	Pennsylvania	14.6
17	Rhode Island	13.2
31	South Carolina	11.8
48	South Dakota	9.2
5	Tennessee	16.1
49	Texas	8.1
36	Utah	11.5
33	Vermont	11.6
19	Virginia	12.8
1	Washington	18.7
21	West Virginia	12.7
44	Wisconsin	9.7
26	Wyoming	12.6

RANK ORDER

RANK	STATE	RATE
1	Washington	18.7
2	Nevada	17.9
3	Colorado	17.2
4	Alaska	16.7
5	Tennessee	16.1
6	Arizona	15.9
7	Michigan	15.3
8	Missouri	15.2
9	Maryland	14.9
10	Pennsylvania	14.6
11	Florida	14.3
12	Idaho	14.2
13	New York	13.9
14	Delaware	13.8
14	Georgia	13.8
16	New Hampshire	13.4
17	Rhode Island	13.2
18	New Mexico	13.1
19	New Jersey	12.8
19	Virginia	12.8
21	Alabama	12.7
21	California	12.7
21	Hawaii	12.7
21	Montana	12.7
21	West Virginia	12.7
26	Oregon	12.6
26	Wyoming	12.6
28	Mississippi	12.1
29	Illinois	11.9
29	Maine	11.9
31	North Carolina	11.8
31	South Carolina	11.8
33	Connecticut	11.6
33	North Dakota	11.6
33	Vermont	11.6
36	Utah	11.5
37	Arkansas	11.1
38	Indiana	11.0
39	Massachusetts	10.9
40	Nebraska	10.8
41	Iowa	10.7
41	Kansas	10.7
43	Kentucky	10.2
44	Wisconsin	9.7
45	Oklahoma	9.6
46	Minnesota	9.3
46	Ohio	9.3
48	South Dakota	9.2
49	Texas	8.1
50	Louisiana	7.5
	District of Columbia	9.9

Source: CQ Press using data from U.S. Small Business Administration
    "The Small Business Economy 2009" and unpublished data (http://www.sba.gov/advo/research/)
*Firms can be in more than one state. Firms with paid employees ceasing operations in 2008 as a percent of employer firms existing in 2008. Some state terminations result in successor firms which are not listed as new firms, thus making terminations higher than formations for most states.

V. Education

Estimated Percent of School-Age Population in Public Schools in 2009

National Percent = 92.1%*

ALPHA ORDER

RANK	STATE	PERCENT
32	Alabama	91.3
1	Alaska	101.2
41	Arizona	89.5
7	Arkansas	94.8
17	California	93.4
9	Colorado	94.7
12	Connecticut	94.0
50	Delaware	84.2
33	Florida	91.0
36	Georgia	90.4
43	Hawaii	89.1
18	Idaho	93.3
20	Illinois	92.8
31	Indiana	91.5
7	Iowa	94.8
10	Kansas	94.3
24	Kentucky	92.3
49	Louisiana	85.2
16	Maine	93.5
46	Maryland	86.9
30	Massachusetts	91.6
12	Michigan	94.0
23	Minnesota	92.4
39	Mississippi	90.2
42	Missouri	89.3
39	Montana	90.2
24	Nebraska	92.3
35	Nevada	90.8
24	New Hampshire	92.3
22	New Jersey	92.6
29	New Mexico	91.7
48	New York	85.6
36	North Carolina	90.4
11	North Dakota	94.2
28	Ohio	91.9
3	Oklahoma	99.7
44	Oregon	89.0
45	Pennsylvania	87.3
47	Rhode Island	86.1
18	South Carolina	93.3
38	South Dakota	90.3
33	Tennessee	91.0
4	Texas	98.5
12	Utah	94.0
5	Vermont	96.1
12	Virginia	94.0
21	Washington	92.7
2	West Virginia	100.8
24	Wisconsin	92.3
6	Wyoming	95.1

RANK ORDER

RANK	STATE	PERCENT
1	Alaska	101.2
2	West Virginia	100.8
3	Oklahoma	99.7
4	Texas	98.5
5	Vermont	96.1
6	Wyoming	95.1
7	Arkansas	94.8
7	Iowa	94.8
9	Colorado	94.7
10	Kansas	94.3
11	North Dakota	94.2
12	Connecticut	94.0
12	Michigan	94.0
12	Utah	94.0
12	Virginia	94.0
16	Maine	93.5
17	California	93.4
18	Idaho	93.3
18	South Carolina	93.3
20	Illinois	92.8
21	Washington	92.7
22	New Jersey	92.6
23	Minnesota	92.4
24	Kentucky	92.3
24	Nebraska	92.3
24	New Hampshire	92.3
24	Wisconsin	92.3
28	Ohio	91.9
29	New Mexico	91.7
30	Massachusetts	91.6
31	Indiana	91.5
32	Alabama	91.3
33	Florida	91.0
33	Tennessee	91.0
35	Nevada	90.8
36	Georgia	90.4
36	North Carolina	90.4
38	South Dakota	90.3
39	Mississippi	90.2
39	Montana	90.2
41	Arizona	89.5
42	Missouri	89.3
43	Hawaii	89.1
44	Oregon	89.0
45	Pennsylvania	87.3
46	Maryland	86.9
47	Rhode Island	86.1
48	New York	85.6
49	Louisiana	85.2
50	Delaware	84.2

District of Columbia — 89.3

Source: CQ Press using data from U.S. Department of Education, National Center for Education Statistics
"Numbers and Types of Public Elementary and Secondary Schools" (http://nces.ed.gov/pubs2010/2010345.pdf)
*Estimate based on 2009 Census population estimates for 5- to 17-year-olds compared to estimated 2008-2009 school year public school student membership. Student membership figures include counts for pre-kindergarten programs. Figures higher than 100 percent reflect using different sources for population-age for student membership.

Regular Public Elementary and Secondary School Districts in 2009

National Total = 13,809 Districts*

ALPHA ORDER

RANK	STATE	DISTRICTS	% of USA
35	Alabama	133	1.0%
43	Alaska	53	0.4%
23	Arizona	225	1.6%
22	Arkansas	245	1.8%
2	California	960	7.0%
27	Colorado	178	1.3%
30	Connecticut	166	1.2%
48	Delaware	19	0.1%
41	Florida	67	0.5%
26	Georgia	180	1.3%
50	Hawaii	1	0.0%
37	Idaho	115	0.8%
3	Illinois	869	6.3%
18	Indiana	294	2.1%
13	Iowa	362	2.6%
16	Kansas	318	2.3%
29	Kentucky	174	1.3%
40	Louisiana	69	0.5%
20	Maine	283	2.0%
47	Maryland	24	0.2%
14	Massachusetts	352	2.5%
7	Michigan	552	4.0%
15	Minnesota	340	2.5%
32	Mississippi	152	1.1%
9	Missouri	523	3.8%
12	Montana	420	3.0%
21	Nebraska	256	1.9%
49	Nevada	17	0.1%
27	New Hampshire	178	1.3%
5	New Jersey	616	4.5%
38	New Mexico	89	0.6%
4	New York	696	5.0%
36	North Carolina	116	0.8%
25	North Dakota	187	1.4%
6	Ohio	614	4.4%
8	Oklahoma	534	3.9%
24	Oregon	194	1.4%
10	Pennsylvania	501	3.6%
46	Rhode Island	32	0.2%
39	South Carolina	85	0.6%
31	South Dakota	161	1.2%
33	Tennessee	136	1.0%
1	Texas	1,032	7.5%
45	Utah	40	0.3%
19	Vermont	292	2.1%
34	Virginia	134	1.0%
17	Washington	295	2.1%
42	West Virginia	55	0.4%
11	Wisconsin	426	3.1%
44	Wyoming	48	0.3%

RANK ORDER

RANK	STATE	DISTRICTS	% of USA
1	Texas	1,032	7.5%
2	California	960	7.0%
3	Illinois	869	6.3%
4	New York	696	5.0%
5	New Jersey	616	4.5%
6	Ohio	614	4.4%
7	Michigan	552	4.0%
8	Oklahoma	534	3.9%
9	Missouri	523	3.8%
10	Pennsylvania	501	3.6%
11	Wisconsin	426	3.1%
12	Montana	420	3.0%
13	Iowa	362	2.6%
14	Massachusetts	352	2.5%
15	Minnesota	340	2.5%
16	Kansas	318	2.3%
17	Washington	295	2.1%
18	Indiana	294	2.1%
19	Vermont	292	2.1%
20	Maine	283	2.0%
21	Nebraska	256	1.9%
22	Arkansas	245	1.8%
23	Arizona	225	1.6%
24	Oregon	194	1.4%
25	North Dakota	187	1.4%
26	Georgia	180	1.3%
27	Colorado	178	1.3%
27	New Hampshire	178	1.3%
29	Kentucky	174	1.3%
30	Connecticut	166	1.2%
31	South Dakota	161	1.2%
32	Mississippi	152	1.1%
33	Tennessee	136	1.0%
34	Virginia	134	1.0%
35	Alabama	133	1.0%
36	North Carolina	116	0.8%
37	Idaho	115	0.8%
38	New Mexico	89	0.6%
39	South Carolina	85	0.6%
40	Louisiana	69	0.5%
41	Florida	67	0.5%
42	West Virginia	55	0.4%
43	Alaska	53	0.4%
44	Wyoming	48	0.3%
45	Utah	40	0.3%
46	Rhode Island	32	0.2%
47	Maryland	24	0.2%
48	Delaware	19	0.1%
49	Nevada	17	0.1%
50	Hawaii	1	0.0%
	District of Columbia	1	0.0%

Source: U.S. Department of Education, National Center for Education Statistics
    "Numbers and Types of Public Elementary and Secondary Education Agencies" (http://nces.ed.gov/pubs2010/2010346.pdf)
*For school year 2008-2009. Regular school districts are agencies responsible for providing free public education for school-age children residing within their jurisdiction. Included in these figures are districts that reported having no students. This can occur when a small district has no pupils or contracts with another district to seducate the students under its jurisdiction.

Public Elementary and Secondary Schools in 2009

National Total = 98,706 Schools*

ALPHA ORDER

RANK	STATE	SCHOOLS	% of USA
24	Alabama	1,605	1.6%
44	Alaska	507	0.5%
16	Arizona	2,186	2.2%
32	Arkansas	1,129	1.1%
1	California	10,029	10.2%
21	Colorado	1,779	1.8%
31	Connecticut	1,150	1.2%
50	Delaware	240	0.2%
6	Florida	3,985	4.0%
11	Georgia	2,472	2.5%
49	Hawaii	290	0.3%
39	Idaho	735	0.7%
4	Illinois	4,402	4.5%
18	Indiana	1,973	2.0%
26	Iowa	1,490	1.5%
28	Kansas	1,428	1.4%
25	Kentucky	1,531	1.6%
23	Louisiana	1,643	1.7%
41	Maine	663	0.7%
27	Maryland	1,457	1.5%
19	Massachusetts	1,855	1.9%
5	Michigan	4,078	4.1%
15	Minnesota	2,263	2.3%
34	Mississippi	1,077	1.1%
12	Missouri	2,423	2.5%
37	Montana	830	0.8%
33	Nebraska	1,122	1.1%
42	Nevada	617	0.6%
45	New Hampshire	492	0.5%
9	New Jersey	2,588	2.6%
36	New Mexico	853	0.9%
3	New York	4,690	4.8%
10	North Carolina	2,548	2.6%
43	North Dakota	525	0.5%
7	Ohio	3,852	3.9%
20	Oklahoma	1,796	1.8%
29	Oregon	1,304	1.3%
8	Pennsylvania	3,248	3.3%
48	Rhode Island	327	0.3%
30	South Carolina	1,211	1.2%
40	South Dakota	721	0.7%
22	Tennessee	1,755	1.8%
2	Texas	8,530	8.6%
35	Utah	1,029	1.0%
47	Vermont	328	0.3%
17	Virginia	2,009	2.0%
13	Washington	2,321	2.4%
38	West Virginia	762	0.8%
14	Wisconsin	2,268	2.3%
46	Wyoming	360	0.4%

RANK ORDER

RANK	STATE	SCHOOLS	% of USA
1	California	10,029	10.2%
2	Texas	8,530	8.6%
3	New York	4,690	4.8%
4	Illinois	4,402	4.5%
5	Michigan	4,078	4.1%
6	Florida	3,985	4.0%
7	Ohio	3,852	3.9%
8	Pennsylvania	3,248	3.3%
9	New Jersey	2,588	2.6%
10	North Carolina	2,548	2.6%
11	Georgia	2,472	2.5%
12	Missouri	2,423	2.5%
13	Washington	2,321	2.4%
14	Wisconsin	2,268	2.3%
15	Minnesota	2,263	2.3%
16	Arizona	2,186	2.2%
17	Virginia	2,009	2.0%
18	Indiana	1,973	2.0%
19	Massachusetts	1,855	1.9%
20	Oklahoma	1,796	1.8%
21	Colorado	1,779	1.8%
22	Tennessee	1,755	1.8%
23	Louisiana	1,643	1.7%
24	Alabama	1,605	1.6%
25	Kentucky	1,531	1.6%
26	Iowa	1,490	1.5%
27	Maryland	1,457	1.5%
28	Kansas	1,428	1.4%
29	Oregon	1,304	1.3%
30	South Carolina	1,211	1.2%
31	Connecticut	1,150	1.2%
32	Arkansas	1,129	1.1%
33	Nebraska	1,122	1.1%
34	Mississippi	1,077	1.1%
35	Utah	1,029	1.0%
36	New Mexico	853	0.9%
37	Montana	830	0.8%
38	West Virginia	762	0.8%
39	Idaho	735	0.7%
40	South Dakota	721	0.7%
41	Maine	663	0.7%
42	Nevada	617	0.6%
43	North Dakota	525	0.5%
44	Alaska	507	0.5%
45	New Hampshire	492	0.5%
46	Wyoming	360	0.4%
47	Vermont	328	0.3%
48	Rhode Island	327	0.3%
49	Hawaii	290	0.3%
50	Delaware	240	0.2%
	District of Columbia	230	0.2%

Source: U.S. Department of Education, National Center for Education Statistics
"Numbers and Types of Public Elementary and Secondary Schools" (http://nces.ed.gov/pubs2010/2010345.pdf)
*For school year 2008-2009.

Private Elementary and Secondary Schools in 2008

National Total = 33,740 Schools*

ALPHA ORDER

RANK	STATE	SCHOOLS	% of USA
22	Alabama	423	1.3%
48	Alaska	63	0.2%
28	Arizona	361	1.1%
30	Arkansas**	305	0.9%
1	California	4,013	11.9%
24	Colorado	415	1.2%
22	Connecticut	423	1.3%
37	Delaware**	214	0.6%
4	Florida	1,938	5.7%
11	Georgia	910	2.7%
46	Hawaii	136	0.4%
40	Idaho**	190	0.6%
5	Illinois	1,924	5.7%
15	Indiana	807	2.4%
33	Iowa	242	0.7%
32	Kansas	246	0.7%
26	Kentucky	404	1.2%
27	Louisiana	393	1.2%
39	Maine	200	0.6%
14	Maryland	823	2.4%
10	Massachusetts	947	2.8%
12	Michigan	908	2.7%
19	Minnesota	585	1.7%
36	Mississippi	219	0.6%
17	Missouri	690	2.0%
44	Montana**	141	0.4%
35	Nebraska	223	0.7%
41	Nevada	161	0.5%
29	New Hampshire	312	0.9%
7	New Jersey	1,441	4.3%
38	New Mexico	212	0.6%
3	New York	2,130	6.3%
18	North Carolina	656	1.9%
49	North Dakota	50	0.1%
8	Ohio	1,189	3.5%
31	Oklahoma**	300	0.9%
20	Oregon	564	1.7%
2	Pennsylvania	2,503	7.4%
34	Rhode Island	226	0.7%
25	South Carolina	409	1.2%
47	South Dakota	80	0.2%
21	Tennessee	557	1.7%
6	Texas	1,651	4.9%
43	Utah	146	0.4%
42	Vermont	150	0.4%
13	Virginia	872	2.6%
16	Washington	730	2.2%
45	West Virginia	139	0.4%
9	Wisconsin	990	2.9%
50	Wyoming	38	0.1%

RANK ORDER

RANK	STATE	SCHOOLS	% of USA
1	California	4,013	11.9%
2	Pennsylvania	2,503	7.4%
3	New York	2,130	6.3%
4	Florida	1,938	5.7%
5	Illinois	1,924	5.7%
6	Texas	1,651	4.9%
7	New Jersey	1,441	4.3%
8	Ohio	1,189	3.5%
9	Wisconsin	990	2.9%
10	Massachusetts	947	2.8%
11	Georgia	910	2.7%
12	Michigan	908	2.7%
13	Virginia	872	2.6%
14	Maryland	823	2.4%
15	Indiana	807	2.4%
16	Washington	730	2.2%
17	Missouri	690	2.0%
18	North Carolina	656	1.9%
19	Minnesota	585	1.7%
20	Oregon	564	1.7%
21	Tennessee	557	1.7%
22	Alabama	423	1.3%
22	Connecticut	423	1.3%
24	Colorado	415	1.2%
25	South Carolina	409	1.2%
26	Kentucky	404	1.2%
27	Louisiana	393	1.2%
28	Arizona	361	1.1%
29	New Hampshire	312	0.9%
30	Arkansas**	305	0.9%
31	Oklahoma**	300	0.9%
32	Kansas	246	0.7%
33	Iowa	242	0.7%
34	Rhode Island	226	0.7%
35	Nebraska	223	0.7%
36	Mississippi	219	0.6%
37	Delaware**	214	0.6%
38	New Mexico	212	0.6%
39	Maine	200	0.6%
40	Idaho**	190	0.6%
41	Nevada	161	0.5%
42	Vermont	150	0.4%
43	Utah	146	0.4%
44	Montana**	141	0.4%
45	West Virginia	139	0.4%
46	Hawaii	136	0.4%
47	South Dakota	80	0.2%
48	Alaska	63	0.2%
49	North Dakota	50	0.1%
50	Wyoming	38	0.1%
	District of Columbia	92	0.3%

Source: U.S. Department of Education, National Center for Education Statistics
    "Characteristics of Private Schools in the United States" (http://nces.ed.gov/pubs2009/2009313.pdf)
*For school year 2007-2008.
**Interpret data for these states with caution.

Private Elementary and Secondary School Enrollment in 2008

National Total = 5,072,451 Students*

ALPHA ORDER

RANK	STATE	STUDENTS	% of USA
23	Alabama	72,037	1.4%
49	Alaska	4,173	0.1%
27	Arizona	51,590	1.0%
33	Arkansas**	34,850	0.7%
1	California	607,141	12.0%
28	Colorado	48,945	1.0%
22	Connecticut	76,520	1.5%
36	Delaware	26,403	0.5%
3	Florida	329,646	6.5%
11	Georgia	136,987	2.7%
35	Hawaii	33,441	0.7%
41	Idaho**	20,878	0.4%
5	Illinois	264,012	5.2%
19	Indiana	104,062	2.1%
31	Iowa	41,796	0.8%
30	Kansas	43,413	0.9%
24	Kentucky	67,376	1.3%
13	Louisiana	123,476	2.4%
42	Maine	19,553	0.4%
9	Maryland	143,661	2.8%
12	Massachusetts	127,967	2.5%
10	Michigan	139,314	2.7%
20	Minnesota	90,973	1.8%
29	Mississippi	47,955	0.9%
16	Missouri	112,368	2.2%
44	Montana**	13,778	0.3%
32	Nebraska	35,872	0.7%
40	Nevada	22,310	0.4%
39	New Hampshire	23,200	0.5%
8	New Jersey	204,486	4.0%
38	New Mexico	23,582	0.5%
2	New York	458,231	9.0%
17	North Carolina	108,810	2.1%
48	North Dakota	6,345	0.1%
7	Ohio	215,592	4.3%
34	Oklahoma	34,354	0.7%
26	Oregon	53,243	1.0%
4	Pennsylvania	281,958	5.6%
37	Rhode Island	23,951	0.5%
25	South Carolina	56,492	1.1%
47	South Dakota	10,692	0.2%
18	Tennessee	106,097	2.1%
6	Texas	235,241	4.6%
43	Utah	17,551	0.3%
46	Vermont	11,713	0.2%
15	Virginia	116,934	2.3%
21	Washington	86,811	1.7%
45	West Virginia	13,400	0.3%
14	Wisconsin	123,174	2.4%
50	Wyoming	2,113	0.0%

RANK ORDER

RANK	STATE	STUDENTS	% of USA
1	California	607,141	12.0%
2	New York	458,231	9.0%
3	Florida	329,646	6.5%
4	Pennsylvania	281,958	5.6%
5	Illinois	264,012	5.2%
6	Texas	235,241	4.6%
7	Ohio	215,592	4.3%
8	New Jersey	204,486	4.0%
9	Maryland	143,661	2.8%
10	Michigan	139,314	2.7%
11	Georgia	136,987	2.7%
12	Massachusetts	127,967	2.5%
13	Louisiana	123,476	2.4%
14	Wisconsin	123,174	2.4%
15	Virginia	116,934	2.3%
16	Missouri	112,368	2.2%
17	North Carolina	108,810	2.1%
18	Tennessee	106,097	2.1%
19	Indiana	104,062	2.1%
20	Minnesota	90,973	1.8%
21	Washington	86,811	1.7%
22	Connecticut	76,520	1.5%
23	Alabama	72,037	1.4%
24	Kentucky	67,376	1.3%
25	South Carolina	56,492	1.1%
26	Oregon	53,243	1.0%
27	Arizona	51,590	1.0%
28	Colorado	48,945	1.0%
29	Mississippi	47,955	0.9%
30	Kansas	43,413	0.9%
31	Iowa	41,796	0.8%
32	Nebraska	35,872	0.7%
33	Arkansas**	34,850	0.7%
34	Oklahoma	34,354	0.7%
35	Hawaii	33,441	0.7%
36	Delaware	26,403	0.5%
37	Rhode Island	23,951	0.5%
38	New Mexico	23,582	0.5%
39	New Hampshire	23,200	0.5%
40	Nevada	22,310	0.4%
41	Idaho**	20,878	0.4%
42	Maine	19,553	0.4%
43	Utah	17,551	0.3%
44	Montana**	13,778	0.3%
45	West Virginia	13,400	0.3%
46	Vermont	11,713	0.2%
47	South Dakota	10,692	0.2%
48	North Dakota	6,345	0.1%
49	Alaska	4,173	0.1%
50	Wyoming	2,113	0.0%
	District of Columbia	17,985	0.4%

Source: U.S. Department of Education, National Center for Education Statistics
   "Characteristics of Private Schools in the United States" (http://nces.ed.gov/pubs2009/2009313.pdf)
*For school year 2007-2008.
**Interpret data for these states with caution.

Public Elementary and Secondary Schools Enrollment in 2009

National Total = 49,265,044 Students*

ALPHA ORDER

RANK	STATE	STUDENTS	% of USA
23	Alabama	745,668	1.5%
45	Alaska	130,662	0.3%
13	Arizona	1,087,817	2.2%
33	Arkansas	478,965	1.0%
1	California	6,322,528	12.8%
22	Colorado	818,443	1.7%
29	Connecticut	567,198	1.2%
47	Delaware	125,430	0.3%
4	Florida	2,631,020	5.3%
9	Georgia	1,655,792	3.4%
42	Hawaii	179,478	0.4%
39	Idaho	275,154	0.6%
5	Illinois	2,119,707	4.3%
14	Indiana	1,046,147	2.1%
32	Iowa	487,559	1.0%
34	Kansas	471,060	1.0%
26	Kentucky	670,030	1.4%
25	Louisiana	684,873	1.4%
41	Maine	192,935	0.4%
20	Maryland	843,861	1.7%
17	Massachusetts	958,910	1.9%
8	Michigan	1,659,921	3.4%
21	Minnesota	836,048	1.7%
31	Mississippi	491,962	1.0%
18	Missouri	917,871	1.9%
44	Montana	141,899	0.3%
37	Nebraska	292,590	0.6%
35	Nevada	433,371	0.9%
40	New Hampshire	197,934	0.4%
11	New Jersey	1,381,420	2.8%
36	New Mexico	330,245	0.7%
3	New York	2,740,805	5.6%
10	North Carolina	1,488,645	3.0%
48	North Dakota	94,728	0.2%
6	Ohio	1,817,163	3.7%
27	Oklahoma	645,108	1.3%
28	Oregon	575,393	1.2%
7	Pennsylvania	1,775,029	3.6%
43	Rhode Island	145,342	0.3%
24	South Carolina	718,113	1.5%
46	South Dakota	126,764	0.3%
16	Tennessee	971,950	2.0%
2	Texas	4,752,148	9.6%
30	Utah	559,778	1.1%
49	Vermont	92,446	0.2%
12	Virginia	1,235,795	2.5%
15	Washington	1,037,018	2.1%
38	West Virginia	282,729	0.6%
19	Wisconsin	873,750	1.8%
50	Wyoming	87,161	0.2%

RANK ORDER

RANK	STATE	STUDENTS	% of USA
1	California	6,322,528	12.8%
2	Texas	4,752,148	9.6%
3	New York	2,740,805	5.6%
4	Florida	2,631,020	5.3%
5	Illinois	2,119,707	4.3%
6	Ohio	1,817,163	3.7%
7	Pennsylvania	1,775,029	3.6%
8	Michigan	1,659,921	3.4%
9	Georgia	1,655,792	3.4%
10	North Carolina	1,488,645	3.0%
11	New Jersey	1,381,420	2.8%
12	Virginia	1,235,795	2.5%
13	Arizona	1,087,817	2.2%
14	Indiana	1,046,147	2.1%
15	Washington	1,037,018	2.1%
16	Tennessee	971,950	2.0%
17	Massachusetts	958,910	1.9%
18	Missouri	917,871	1.9%
19	Wisconsin	873,750	1.8%
20	Maryland	843,861	1.7%
21	Minnesota	836,048	1.7%
22	Colorado	818,443	1.7%
23	Alabama	745,668	1.5%
24	South Carolina	718,113	1.5%
25	Louisiana	684,873	1.4%
26	Kentucky	670,030	1.4%
27	Oklahoma	645,108	1.3%
28	Oregon	575,393	1.2%
29	Connecticut	567,198	1.2%
30	Utah	559,778	1.1%
31	Mississippi	491,962	1.0%
32	Iowa	487,559	1.0%
33	Arkansas	478,965	1.0%
34	Kansas	471,060	1.0%
35	Nevada	433,371	0.9%
36	New Mexico	330,245	0.7%
37	Nebraska	292,590	0.6%
38	West Virginia	282,729	0.6%
39	Idaho	275,154	0.6%
40	New Hampshire	197,934	0.4%
41	Maine	192,935	0.4%
42	Hawaii	179,478	0.4%
43	Rhode Island	145,342	0.3%
44	Montana	141,899	0.3%
45	Alaska	130,662	0.3%
46	South Dakota	126,764	0.3%
47	Delaware	125,430	0.3%
48	North Dakota	94,728	0.2%
49	Vermont	92,446	0.2%
50	Wyoming	87,161	0.2%
	District of Columbia	68,681	0.1%

Source: U.S. Department of Education, National Center for Education Statistics
"Public Elementary and Secondary School Student Enrollment and Staff"
(http://nces.ed.gov/pubsearch/pubsinfo.asp?pubid=2010347)
*School year 2008-2009.

Public Elementary and Secondary School Teachers in 2009

National Total = 3,221,917 Teachers*

ALPHA ORDER

RANK	STATE	TEACHERS	% of USA
26	Alabama	47,819	1.5%
49	Alaska	7,927	0.2%
19	Arizona	54,696	1.7%
29	Arkansas	37,162	1.2%
2	California	303,647	9.4%
24	Colorado	48,692	1.5%
25	Connecticut	48,463	1.5%
47	Delaware	8,322	0.3%
4	Florida	186,361	5.8%
7	Georgia	118,839	3.7%
43	Hawaii	11,295	0.4%
41	Idaho	15,148	0.5%
5	Illinois	135,704	4.2%
16	Indiana	62,668	1.9%
30	Iowa	35,961	1.1%
31	Kansas	35,883	1.1%
28	Kentucky	43,451	1.3%
23	Louisiana	49,377	1.5%
39	Maine	15,912	0.5%
18	Maryland	58,940	1.8%
13	Massachusetts	70,398	2.2%
11	Michigan	94,754	2.9%
21	Minnesota	53,083	1.6%
32	Mississippi	33,358	1.0%
14	Missouri	67,737	2.1%
44	Montana	10,467	0.3%
36	Nebraska	22,057	0.7%
37	Nevada	21,993	0.7%
40	New Hampshire	15,661	0.5%
8	New Jersey	114,713	3.6%
35	New Mexico	22,825	0.7%
3	New York	217,944	6.8%
10	North Carolina	109,634	3.4%
48	North Dakota	8,181	0.3%
9	Ohio	112,845	3.5%
27	Oklahoma	46,571	1.4%
33	Oregon	30,152	0.9%
6	Pennsylvania	129,708	4.0%
42	Rhode Island	11,356	0.4%
22	South Carolina	49,941	1.6%
45	South Dakota	9,244	0.3%
15	Tennessee	64,926	2.0%
1	Texas	327,905	10.2%
34	Utah	23,657	0.7%
46	Vermont	8,766	0.3%
12	Virginia	71,415	2.2%
20	Washington	54,428	1.7%
38	West Virginia	20,209	0.6%
17	Wisconsin	59,401	1.8%
50	Wyoming	7,000	0.2%

RANK ORDER

RANK	STATE	TEACHERS	% of USA
1	Texas	327,905	10.2%
2	California	303,647	9.4%
3	New York	217,944	6.8%
4	Florida	186,361	5.8%
5	Illinois	135,704	4.2%
6	Pennsylvania	129,708	4.0%
7	Georgia	118,839	3.7%
8	New Jersey	114,713	3.6%
9	Ohio	112,845	3.5%
10	North Carolina	109,634	3.4%
11	Michigan	94,754	2.9%
12	Virginia	71,415	2.2%
13	Massachusetts	70,398	2.2%
14	Missouri	67,737	2.1%
15	Tennessee	64,926	2.0%
16	Indiana	62,668	1.9%
17	Wisconsin	59,401	1.8%
18	Maryland	58,940	1.8%
19	Arizona	54,696	1.7%
20	Washington	54,428	1.7%
21	Minnesota	53,083	1.6%
22	South Carolina	49,941	1.6%
23	Louisiana	49,377	1.5%
24	Colorado	48,692	1.5%
25	Connecticut	48,463	1.5%
26	Alabama	47,819	1.5%
27	Oklahoma	46,571	1.4%
28	Kentucky	43,451	1.3%
29	Arkansas	37,162	1.2%
30	Iowa	35,961	1.1%
31	Kansas	35,883	1.1%
32	Mississippi	33,358	1.0%
33	Oregon	30,152	0.9%
34	Utah	23,657	0.7%
35	New Mexico	22,825	0.7%
36	Nebraska	22,057	0.7%
37	Nevada	21,993	0.7%
38	West Virginia	20,209	0.6%
39	Maine	15,912	0.5%
40	New Hampshire	15,661	0.5%
41	Idaho	15,148	0.5%
42	Rhode Island	11,356	0.4%
43	Hawaii	11,295	0.4%
44	Montana	10,467	0.3%
45	South Dakota	9,244	0.3%
46	Vermont	8,766	0.3%
47	Delaware	8,322	0.3%
48	North Dakota	8,181	0.3%
49	Alaska	7,927	0.2%
50	Wyoming	7,000	0.2%
	District of Columbia	5,321	0.2%

Source: U.S. Department of Education, National Center for Education Statistics
    "Common Core of Data (CCD) Database" (http://nces.ed.gov/ccd/)
*School year 2008-2009. Counts are full-time equivalent figures.

Pupil-Teacher Ratio in Public Elementary and Secondary Schools in 2009

National Ratio = 15.3 Pupils per Teacher*

ALPHA ORDER

RANK ORDER

RANK	STATE	RATIO	RANK	STATE	RATIO
16	Alabama	15.6	1	Utah	23.7
12	Alaska	16.5	2	California	20.8
3	Arizona	19.9	3	Arizona	19.9
41	Arkansas	12.9	4	Nevada	19.7
2	California	20.8	5	Oregon	19.1
10	Colorado	16.8	5	Washington	19.1
48	Connecticut	11.7	7	Idaho	18.2
19	Delaware	15.1	8	Michigan	17.5
27	Florida	14.1	9	Virginia	17.3
29	Georgia	13.9	10	Colorado	16.8
14	Hawaii	15.9	11	Indiana	16.7
7	Idaho	18.2	12	Alaska	16.5
16	Illinois	15.6	13	Ohio	16.1
11	Indiana	16.7	14	Hawaii	15.9
34	Iowa	13.6	15	Minnesota	15.7
40	Kansas	13.1	16	Alabama	15.6
18	Kentucky	15.4	16	Illinois	15.6
29	Louisiana	13.9	18	Kentucky	15.4
46	Maine	12.1	19	Delaware	15.1
26	Maryland	14.3	20	Tennessee	15.0
34	Massachusetts	13.6	21	Mississippi	14.7
8	Michigan	17.5	21	Wisconsin	14.7
15	Minnesota	15.7	23	New Mexico	14.5
21	Mississippi	14.7	23	Texas	14.5
34	Missouri	13.6	25	South Carolina	14.4
34	Montana	13.6	26	Maryland	14.3
39	Nebraska	13.3	27	Florida	14.1
4	Nevada	19.7	28	West Virginia	14.0
43	New Hampshire	12.6	29	Georgia	13.9
47	New Jersey	12.0	29	Louisiana	13.9
23	New Mexico	14.5	29	Oklahoma	13.9
43	New York	12.6	32	Pennsylvania	13.7
34	North Carolina	13.6	32	South Dakota	13.7
49	North Dakota	11.6	34	Iowa	13.6
13	Ohio	16.1	34	Massachusetts	13.6
29	Oklahoma	13.9	34	Missouri	13.6
5	Oregon	19.1	34	Montana	13.6
32	Pennsylvania	13.7	34	North Carolina	13.6
42	Rhode Island	12.8	39	Nebraska	13.3
25	South Carolina	14.4	40	Kansas	13.1
32	South Dakota	13.7	41	Arkansas	12.9
20	Tennessee	15.0	42	Rhode Island	12.8
23	Texas	14.5	43	New Hampshire	12.6
1	Utah	23.7	43	New York	12.6
50	Vermont	10.5	45	Wyoming	12.5
9	Virginia	17.3	46	Maine	12.1
5	Washington	19.1	47	New Jersey	12.0
28	West Virginia	14.0	48	Connecticut	11.7
21	Wisconsin	14.7	49	North Dakota	11.6
45	Wyoming	12.5	50	Vermont	10.5
				District of Columbia	12.9

Source: U.S. Department of Education, National Center for Education Statistics
"Public Elementary and Secondary School Student Enrollment and Staff"
(http://nces.ed.gov/pubsearch/pubsinfo.asp?pubid=2010347)
*For school year 2008-2009. Based on full-time equivalency counts of teachers.

Estimated Average Salary of Public School Teachers in 2011
(National Education Association)
National Average = $56,069*

ALPHA ORDER

RANK	STATE	SALARY
32	Alabama	$48,282
8	Alaska	61,093
35	Arizona	47,553
34	Arkansas	47,700
3	California	69,434
28	Colorado	49,938
5	Connecticut	65,571
12	Delaware	57,934
46	Florida	46,702
17	Georgia	53,906
16	Hawaii	55,063
37	Idaho	47,416
7	Illinois	63,005
25	Indiana	50,407
24	Iowa	50,634
41	Kansas	47,080
27	Kentucky	50,038
29	Louisiana	49,634
39	Maine	47,182
6	Maryland	65,113
2	Massachusetts	71,017
11	Michigan	58,595
19	Minnesota	53,215
45	Mississippi	46,818
48	Missouri	46,411
40	Montana	47,132
36	Nebraska	47,521
20	Nevada	53,023
21	New Hampshire	52,792
4	New Jersey	66,985
43	New Mexico	46,950
1	New York	72,708
44	North Carolina	46,850
49	North Dakota	44,266
13	Ohio	57,291
31	Oklahoma	49,039
15	Oregon	56,387
10	Pennsylvania	60,536
9	Rhode Island	60,923
30	South Carolina	49,434
50	South Dakota	35,201
42	Tennessee	47,043
33	Texas	48,261
47	Utah	46,571
26	Vermont	50,141
23	Virginia	51,559
18	Washington	53,796
38	West Virginia	47,253
22	Wisconsin	52,031
14	Wyoming	56,978

RANK ORDER

RANK	STATE	SALARY
1	New York	$72,708
2	Massachusetts	71,017
3	California	69,434
4	New Jersey	66,985
5	Connecticut	65,571
6	Maryland	65,113
7	Illinois	63,005
8	Alaska	61,093
9	Rhode Island	60,923
10	Pennsylvania	60,536
11	Michigan	58,595
12	Delaware	57,934
13	Ohio	57,291
14	Wyoming	56,978
15	Oregon	56,387
16	Hawaii	55,063
17	Georgia	53,906
18	Washington	53,796
19	Minnesota	53,215
20	Nevada	53,023
21	New Hampshire	52,792
22	Wisconsin	52,031
23	Virginia	51,559
24	Iowa	50,634
25	Indiana	50,407
26	Vermont	50,141
27	Kentucky	50,038
28	Colorado	49,938
29	Louisiana	49,634
30	South Carolina	49,434
31	Oklahoma	49,039
32	Alabama	48,282
33	Texas	48,261
34	Arkansas	47,700
35	Arizona	47,553
36	Nebraska	47,521
37	Idaho	47,416
38	West Virginia	47,253
39	Maine	47,182
40	Montana	47,132
41	Kansas	47,080
42	Tennessee	47,043
43	New Mexico	46,950
44	North Carolina	46,850
45	Mississippi	46,818
46	Florida	46,702
47	Utah	46,571
48	Missouri	46,411
49	North Dakota	44,266
50	South Dakota	35,201
	District of Columbia	66,601

Source: National Education Association, Washington, D.C.

"Rankings and Estimates" (Copyright © 2010, NEA, used with permission, http://www.nea.org/home/30896.htm)

*Estimates for school year 2010-2011 for classroom teachers.

Average Teacher's Salary as a Percent of Average Annual Pay in 2009

National Average = 120.2% of Average Annual Pay*

ALPHA ORDER

RANK	STATE	PERCENT
31	Alabama	119.8
20	Alaska	125.3
47	Arizona	108.9
12	Arkansas	131.9
9	California	132.2
49	Colorado	104.2
46	Connecticut	110.4
34	Delaware	119.1
39	Florida	114.3
24	Georgia	123.5
5	Hawaii	134.0
5	Idaho	134.0
18	Illinois	127.6
14	Indiana	130.1
9	Iowa	132.2
27	Kansas	122.0
17	Kentucky	128.2
30	Louisiana	120.2
23	Maine	124.0
19	Maryland	125.4
29	Massachusetts	120.8
11	Michigan	132.1
38	Minnesota	115.1
8	Mississippi	133.2
43	Missouri	111.9
7	Montana	133.6
22	Nebraska	124.4
35	Nevada	118.8
42	New Hampshire	112.7
37	New Jersey	116.2
33	New Mexico	119.4
28	New York	121.9
31	North Carolina	119.8
36	North Dakota	117.6
3	Ohio	135.2
25	Oklahoma	122.9
4	Oregon	134.1
15	Pennsylvania	129.8
1	Rhode Island	135.9
16	South Carolina	129.1
45	South Dakota	110.8
41	Tennessee	114.1
48	Texas	104.4
40	Utah	114.2
21	Vermont	125.0
50	Virginia	102.0
44	Washington	111.2
25	West Virginia	122.9
13	Wisconsin	130.8
2	Wyoming	135.7

RANK ORDER

RANK	STATE	PERCENT
1	Rhode Island	135.9
2	Wyoming	135.7
3	Ohio	135.2
4	Oregon	134.1
5	Hawaii	134.0
5	Idaho	134.0
7	Montana	133.6
8	Mississippi	133.2
9	California	132.2
9	Iowa	132.2
11	Michigan	132.1
12	Arkansas	131.9
13	Wisconsin	130.8
14	Indiana	130.1
15	Pennsylvania	129.8
16	South Carolina	129.1
17	Kentucky	128.2
18	Illinois	127.6
19	Maryland	125.4
20	Alaska	125.3
21	Vermont	125.0
22	Nebraska	124.4
23	Maine	124.0
24	Georgia	123.5
25	Oklahoma	122.9
25	West Virginia	122.9
27	Kansas	122.0
28	New York	121.9
29	Massachusetts	120.8
30	Louisiana	120.2
31	Alabama	119.8
31	North Carolina	119.8
33	New Mexico	119.4
34	Delaware	119.1
35	Nevada	118.8
36	North Dakota	117.6
37	New Jersey	116.2
38	Minnesota	115.1
39	Florida	114.3
40	Utah	114.2
41	Tennessee	114.1
42	New Hampshire	112.7
43	Missouri	111.9
44	Washington	111.2
45	South Dakota	110.8
46	Connecticut	110.4
47	Arizona	108.9
48	Texas	104.4
49	Colorado	104.2
50	Virginia	102.0

District of Columbia 82.0

Source: CQ Press using data from National Education Association, Washington, D.C.
"Rankings and Estimates" (Copyright © 2010, NEA, used with permission, http://www.nea.org/home/30896.htm)
"Quarterly Census of Employment and Wages" (http://www.bls.gov/cew/home.htm)
*Average of public elementary and secondary teacher salary for school years 2008-2009 and 2009-2010 compared to each state's 2009 average annual pay for all workers covered by federal unemployment.

Percent of Public School Fourth Graders
Proficient or Better in Reading in 2009
National Percent = 32%*

ALPHA ORDER

RANK	STATE	PERCENT
37	Alabama	28
42	Alaska	27
45	Arizona	25
35	Arkansas	29
46	California	24
5	Colorado	40
2	Connecticut	42
17	Delaware	35
11	Florida	36
35	Georgia	29
43	Hawaii	26
29	Idaho	32
29	Illinois	32
23	Indiana	34
23	Iowa	34
17	Kansas	35
11	Kentucky	36
50	Louisiana	18
17	Maine	35
8	Maryland	37
1	Massachusetts	47
34	Michigan	30
8	Minnesota	37
48	Mississippi	22
11	Missouri	36
17	Montana	35
17	Nebraska	35
46	Nevada	24
3	New Hampshire	41
5	New Jersey	40
49	New Mexico	20
11	New York	36
29	North Carolina	32
17	North Dakota	35
11	Ohio	36
37	Oklahoma	28
32	Oregon	31
8	Pennsylvania	37
11	Rhode Island	36
37	South Carolina	28
25	South Dakota	33
37	Tennessee	28
37	Texas	28
32	Utah	31
3	Vermont	41
7	Virginia	38
25	Washington	33
43	West Virginia	26
25	Wisconsin	33
25	Wyoming	33

RANK ORDER

RANK	STATE	PERCENT
1	Massachusetts	47
2	Connecticut	42
3	New Hampshire	41
3	Vermont	41
5	Colorado	40
5	New Jersey	40
7	Virginia	38
8	Maryland	37
8	Minnesota	37
8	Pennsylvania	37
11	Florida	36
11	Kentucky	36
11	Missouri	36
11	New York	36
11	Ohio	36
11	Rhode Island	36
17	Delaware	35
17	Kansas	35
17	Maine	35
17	Montana	35
17	Nebraska	35
17	North Dakota	35
23	Indiana	34
23	Iowa	34
25	South Dakota	33
25	Washington	33
25	Wisconsin	33
25	Wyoming	33
29	Idaho	32
29	Illinois	32
29	North Carolina	32
32	Oregon	31
32	Utah	31
34	Michigan	30
35	Arkansas	29
35	Georgia	29
37	Alabama	28
37	Oklahoma	28
37	South Carolina	28
37	Tennessee	28
37	Texas	28
42	Alaska	27
43	Hawaii	26
43	West Virginia	26
45	Arizona	25
46	California	24
46	Nevada	24
48	Mississippi	22
49	New Mexico	20
50	Louisiana	18
	District of Columbia	17

Source: U.S. Department of Education, National Center for Education Statistics
"The Nation's Report Card: Reading 2009" (http://nces.ed.gov/nationsreportcard/)
*There are four achievement levels: Below Basic, Basic, Proficient, and Advanced. Proficient represents solid academic mastery for 4th graders. Students reaching this level have demonstrated competency over challenging subject matter, including subject matter knowledge, application of such knowledge to real-world situations, and analytical skills appropriate to the subject matter.

Percent of Public School Eighth Graders Proficient or Better in Reading in 2009
National Percent = 30%*

	ALPHA ORDER				RANK ORDER	
RANK	STATE	PERCENT		RANK	STATE	PERCENT
42	Alabama	24		1	Connecticut	43
36	Alaska	27		1	Massachusetts	43
36	Arizona	27		3	New Jersey	42
36	Arkansas	27		4	Vermont	41
44	California	22		5	Pennsylvania	40
26	Colorado	32		6	New Hampshire	39
1	Connecticut	43		7	Minnesota	38
31	Delaware	31		7	Montana	38
26	Florida	32		9	Ohio	37
36	Georgia	27		9	South Dakota	37
44	Hawaii	22		11	Maryland	36
19	Idaho	33		11	Washington	36
19	Illinois	33		13	Maine	35
26	Indiana	32		13	Nebraska	35
26	Iowa	32		15	Missouri	34
19	Kansas	33		15	North Dakota	34
19	Kentucky	33		15	Wisconsin	34
49	Louisiana	20		15	Wyoming	34
13	Maine	35		19	Idaho	33
11	Maryland	36		19	Illinois	33
1	Massachusetts	43		19	Kansas	33
31	Michigan	31		19	Kentucky	33
7	Minnesota	38		19	New York	33
50	Mississippi	19		19	Oregon	33
15	Missouri	34		19	Utah	33
7	Montana	38		26	Colorado	32
13	Nebraska	35		26	Florida	32
44	Nevada	22		26	Indiana	32
6	New Hampshire	39		26	Iowa	32
3	New Jersey	42		26	Virginia	32
44	New Mexico	22		31	Delaware	31
19	New York	33		31	Michigan	31
33	North Carolina	29		33	North Carolina	29
15	North Dakota	34		34	Rhode Island	28
9	Ohio	37		34	Tennessee	28
41	Oklahoma	26		36	Alaska	27
19	Oregon	33		36	Arizona	27
5	Pennsylvania	40		36	Arkansas	27
34	Rhode Island	28		36	Georgia	27
42	South Carolina	24		36	Texas	27
9	South Dakota	37		41	Oklahoma	26
34	Tennessee	28		42	Alabama	24
36	Texas	27		42	South Carolina	24
19	Utah	33		44	California	22
4	Vermont	41		44	Hawaii	22
26	Virginia	32		44	Nevada	22
11	Washington	36		44	New Mexico	22
44	West Virginia	22		44	West Virginia	22
15	Wisconsin	34		49	Louisiana	20
15	Wyoming	34		50	Mississippi	19

District of Columbia   14

Source: U.S. Department of Education, National Center for Education Statistics
    "The Nation's Report Card: Reading 2009" (http://nces.ed.gov/nationsreportcard/)
*There are four achievement levels: Below Basic, Basic, Proficient, and Advanced. Proficient represents solid academic mastery for 8th graders. Students reaching this level have demonstrated competency over challenging subject matter, including subject matter knowledge, application of such knowledge to real-world situations, and analytical skills appropriate to the subject matter.

Percent of Public School Fourth Graders Proficient or Better in Mathematics in 2009
National Percent = 38%*

ALPHA ORDER

RANK	STATE	PERCENT
48	Alabama	24
29	Alaska	38
44	Arizona	28
36	Arkansas	36
43	California	30
9	Colorado	45
6	Connecticut	46
36	Delaware	36
25	Florida	40
39	Georgia	34
33	Hawaii	37
21	Idaho	41
29	Illinois	38
19	Indiana	42
21	Iowa	41
6	Kansas	46
33	Kentucky	37
49	Louisiana	23
9	Maine	45
15	Maryland	44
1	Massachusetts	57
38	Michigan	35
3	Minnesota	54
50	Mississippi	22
21	Missouri	41
9	Montana	45
29	Nebraska	38
42	Nevada	32
2	New Hampshire	56
5	New Jersey	49
47	New Mexico	26
25	New York	40
16	North Carolina	43
9	North Dakota	45
9	Ohio	45
41	Oklahoma	33
33	Oregon	37
6	Pennsylvania	46
28	Rhode Island	39
39	South Carolina	34
19	South Dakota	42
44	Tennessee	28
29	Texas	38
21	Utah	41
4	Vermont	51
16	Virginia	43
16	Washington	43
44	West Virginia	28
9	Wisconsin	45
25	Wyoming	40

RANK ORDER

RANK	STATE	PERCENT
1	Massachusetts	57
2	New Hampshire	56
3	Minnesota	54
4	Vermont	51
5	New Jersey	49
6	Connecticut	46
6	Kansas	46
6	Pennsylvania	46
9	Colorado	45
9	Maine	45
9	Montana	45
9	North Dakota	45
9	Ohio	45
9	Wisconsin	45
15	Maryland	44
16	North Carolina	43
16	Virginia	43
16	Washington	43
19	Indiana	42
19	South Dakota	42
21	Idaho	41
21	Iowa	41
21	Missouri	41
21	Utah	41
25	Florida	40
25	New York	40
25	Wyoming	40
28	Rhode Island	39
29	Alaska	38
29	Illinois	38
29	Nebraska	38
29	Texas	38
33	Hawaii	37
33	Kentucky	37
33	Oregon	37
36	Arkansas	36
36	Delaware	36
38	Michigan	35
39	Georgia	34
39	South Carolina	34
41	Oklahoma	33
42	Nevada	32
43	California	30
44	Arizona	28
44	Tennessee	28
44	West Virginia	28
47	New Mexico	26
48	Alabama	24
49	Louisiana	23
50	Mississippi	22
	District of Columbia	17

Source: U.S. Department of Education, National Center for Education Statistics
    "NAEP 2009: The Nation's Report Card, Mathematics 2009" (NCES 2010-451, http://nces.ed.gov/nationsreportcard/)
*There are four achievement levels: Below Basic, Basic, Proficient, and Advanced. Proficient represents solid academic mastery for 4th graders. Students reaching this level have demonstrated competency over challenging subject matter, including subject matter knowledge, application of such knowledge to real-world situations, and analytical skills appropriate to the subject matter.

Percent of Public School Eighth Graders Proficient or Better in Mathematics in 2009
National Percent = 33%*

ALPHA ORDER

RANK	STATE	PERCENT
46	Alabama	20
30	Alaska	33
35	Arizona	29
38	Arkansas	27
45	California	23
9	Colorado	40
9	Connecticut	40
32	Delaware	32
35	Florida	29
38	Georgia	27
41	Hawaii	25
16	Idaho	38
30	Illinois	33
18	Indiana	36
28	Iowa	34
13	Kansas	39
38	Kentucky	27
46	Louisiana	20
23	Maine	35
9	Maryland	40
1	Massachusetts	52
33	Michigan	31
2	Minnesota	47
50	Mississippi	15
23	Missouri	35
3	Montana	44
23	Nebraska	35
41	Nevada	25
5	New Hampshire	43
3	New Jersey	44
46	New Mexico	20
28	New York	34
18	North Carolina	36
5	North Dakota	43
18	Ohio	36
44	Oklahoma	24
17	Oregon	37
9	Pennsylvania	40
37	Rhode Island	28
34	South Carolina	30
8	South Dakota	42
41	Tennessee	25
18	Texas	36
23	Utah	35
5	Vermont	43
18	Virginia	36
13	Washington	39
49	West Virginia	19
13	Wisconsin	39
23	Wyoming	35

RANK ORDER

RANK	STATE	PERCENT
1	Massachusetts	52
2	Minnesota	47
3	Montana	44
3	New Jersey	44
5	New Hampshire	43
5	North Dakota	43
5	Vermont	43
8	South Dakota	42
9	Colorado	40
9	Connecticut	40
9	Maryland	40
9	Pennsylvania	40
13	Kansas	39
13	Washington	39
13	Wisconsin	39
16	Idaho	38
17	Oregon	37
18	Indiana	36
18	North Carolina	36
18	Ohio	36
18	Texas	36
18	Virginia	36
23	Maine	35
23	Missouri	35
23	Nebraska	35
23	Utah	35
23	Wyoming	35
28	Iowa	34
28	New York	34
30	Alaska	33
30	Illinois	33
32	Delaware	32
33	Michigan	31
34	South Carolina	30
35	Arizona	29
35	Florida	29
37	Rhode Island	28
38	Arkansas	27
38	Georgia	27
38	Kentucky	27
41	Hawaii	25
41	Nevada	25
41	Tennessee	25
44	Oklahoma	24
45	California	23
46	Alabama	20
46	Louisiana	20
46	New Mexico	20
49	West Virginia	19
50	Mississippi	15

District of Columbia   11

Source: U.S. Department of Education, National Center for Education Statistics
   "NAEP 2009: The Nation's Report Card, Mathematics 2009" (NCES 2010-451, http://nces.ed.gov/nationsreportcard/)
*There are four achievement levels: Below Basic, Basic, Proficient, and Advanced. Proficient represents solid academic mastery for 8th graders. Students reaching this level have demonstrated competency over challenging subject matter, including subject matter knowledge, application of such knowledge to real-world situations, and analytical skills appropriate to the subject matter.

Percent of Population Graduated from High School in 2009

National Percent = 85.3%*

<u>ALPHA ORDER</u>

RANK	STATE	PERCENT
46	Alabama	82.1
3	Alaska	91.4
37	Arizona	84.2
44	Arkansas	82.4
48	California	80.6
17	Colorado	89.3
20	Connecticut	88.6
26	Delaware	87.4
33	Florida	85.3
38	Georgia	83.9
8	Hawaii	90.4
21	Idaho	88.4
31	Illinois	86.4
29	Indiana	86.6
7	Iowa	90.5
15	Kansas	89.7
47	Kentucky	81.7
45	Louisiana	82.2
10	Maine	90.2
22	Maryland	88.2
19	Massachusetts	89.0
23	Michigan	87.9
2	Minnesota	91.5
49	Mississippi	80.4
28	Missouri	86.8
6	Montana	90.8
13	Nebraska	89.8
38	Nevada	83.9
4	New Hampshire	91.3
26	New Jersey	87.4
42	New Mexico	82.8
34	New York	84.7
36	North Carolina	84.3
11	North Dakota	90.1
25	Ohio	87.6
32	Oklahoma	85.6
18	Oregon	89.1
23	Pennsylvania	87.9
34	Rhode Island	84.7
40	South Carolina	83.6
12	South Dakota	89.9
41	Tennessee	83.1
50	Texas	79.9
8	Utah	90.4
5	Vermont	91.0
29	Virginia	86.6
15	Washington	89.7
42	West Virginia	82.8
13	Wisconsin	89.8
1	Wyoming	91.8

<u>RANK ORDER</u>

RANK	STATE	PERCENT
1	Wyoming	91.8
2	Minnesota	91.5
3	Alaska	91.4
4	New Hampshire	91.3
5	Vermont	91.0
6	Montana	90.8
7	Iowa	90.5
8	Hawaii	90.4
8	Utah	90.4
10	Maine	90.2
11	North Dakota	90.1
12	South Dakota	89.9
13	Nebraska	89.8
13	Wisconsin	89.8
15	Kansas	89.7
15	Washington	89.7
17	Colorado	89.3
18	Oregon	89.1
19	Massachusetts	89.0
20	Connecticut	88.6
21	Idaho	88.4
22	Maryland	88.2
23	Michigan	87.9
23	Pennsylvania	87.9
25	Ohio	87.6
26	Delaware	87.4
26	New Jersey	87.4
28	Missouri	86.8
29	Indiana	86.6
29	Virginia	86.6
31	Illinois	86.4
32	Oklahoma	85.6
33	Florida	85.3
34	New York	84.7
34	Rhode Island	84.7
36	North Carolina	84.3
37	Arizona	84.2
38	Georgia	83.9
38	Nevada	83.9
40	South Carolina	83.6
41	Tennessee	83.1
42	New Mexico	82.8
42	West Virginia	82.8
44	Arkansas	82.4
45	Louisiana	82.2
46	Alabama	82.1
47	Kentucky	81.7
48	California	80.6
49	Mississippi	80.4
50	Texas	79.9

District of Columbia	87.1

Source: U.S. Bureau of the Census, American Community Survey
   "2009 American Community Survey" (http://www.census.gov/acs/www/index.html)
*Persons age 25 and older. Includes equivalency status.

Public High School Graduates in 2008

National Total = 2,965,286 Graduates*

ALPHA ORDER

RANK	STATE	GRADUATES	% of USA
23	Alabama	41,346	1.4%
45	Alaska	7,855	0.3%
17	Arizona	61,667	2.1%
31	Arkansas	28,725	1.0%
1	California	374,561	12.6%
22	Colorado	46,082	1.6%
25	Connecticut	38,419	1.3%
47	Delaware	7,388	0.2%
4	Florida	149,046	5.0%
10	Georgia	83,505	2.8%
41	Hawaii	11,613	0.4%
38	Idaho	16,567	0.6%
5	Illinois	135,143	4.6%
15	Indiana	61,901	2.1%
28	Iowa	34,573	1.2%
30	Kansas	30,737	1.0%
24	Kentucky	39,339	1.3%
29	Louisiana	34,401	1.2%
40	Maine	14,350	0.5%
20	Maryland	59,171	2.0%
13	Massachusetts	65,197	2.2%
8	Michigan	115,183	3.9%
19	Minnesota	60,409	2.0%
33	Mississippi	24,795	0.8%
16	Missouri	61,717	2.1%
42	Montana	10,396	0.4%
34	Nebraska	20,035	0.7%
37	Nevada	17,149	0.6%
39	New Hampshire	14,982	0.5%
9	New Jersey	94,994	3.2%
35	New Mexico	18,264	0.6%
3	New York	176,310	5.9%
11	North Carolina	83,307	2.8%
48	North Dakota	6,999	0.2%
7	Ohio	120,758	4.1%
26	Oklahoma	37,630	1.3%
27	Oregon	34,949	1.2%
6	Pennsylvania	130,298	4.4%
43	Rhode Island	10,347	0.3%
NA	South Carolina**	NA	NA
44	South Dakota	8,582	0.3%
21	Tennessee	57,486	1.9%
2	Texas	252,121	8.5%
32	Utah	28,167	0.9%
46	Vermont	7,392	0.2%
12	Virginia	77,369	2.6%
18	Washington	61,625	2.1%
36	West Virginia	17,489	0.6%
14	Wisconsin	65,183	2.2%
49	Wyoming	5,494	0.2%

RANK ORDER

RANK	STATE	GRADUATES	% of USA
1	California	374,561	12.6%
2	Texas	252,121	8.5%
3	New York	176,310	5.9%
4	Florida	149,046	5.0%
5	Illinois	135,143	4.6%
6	Pennsylvania	130,298	4.4%
7	Ohio	120,758	4.1%
8	Michigan	115,183	3.9%
9	New Jersey	94,994	3.2%
10	Georgia	83,505	2.8%
11	North Carolina	83,307	2.8%
12	Virginia	77,369	2.6%
13	Massachusetts	65,197	2.2%
14	Wisconsin	65,183	2.2%
15	Indiana	61,901	2.1%
16	Missouri	61,717	2.1%
17	Arizona	61,667	2.1%
18	Washington	61,625	2.1%
19	Minnesota	60,409	2.0%
20	Maryland	59,171	2.0%
21	Tennessee	57,486	1.9%
22	Colorado	46,082	1.6%
23	Alabama	41,346	1.4%
24	Kentucky	39,339	1.3%
25	Connecticut	38,419	1.3%
26	Oklahoma	37,630	1.3%
27	Oregon	34,949	1.2%
28	Iowa	34,573	1.2%
29	Louisiana	34,401	1.2%
30	Kansas	30,737	1.0%
31	Arkansas	28,725	1.0%
32	Utah	28,167	0.9%
33	Mississippi	24,795	0.8%
34	Nebraska	20,035	0.7%
35	New Mexico	18,264	0.6%
36	West Virginia	17,489	0.6%
37	Nevada	17,149	0.6%
38	Idaho	16,567	0.6%
39	New Hampshire	14,982	0.5%
40	Maine	14,350	0.5%
41	Hawaii	11,613	0.4%
42	Montana	10,396	0.4%
43	Rhode Island	10,347	0.3%
44	South Dakota	8,582	0.3%
45	Alaska	7,855	0.3%
46	Vermont	7,392	0.2%
47	Delaware	7,388	0.2%
48	North Dakota	6,999	0.2%
49	Wyoming	5,494	0.2%
NA	South Carolina**	NA	NA
	District of Columbia	3,352	0.1%

Source: U.S. Department of Education, National Center for Education Statistics
"Public School Graduates and Dropouts from the Common Core of Data: School Year 2007-08" (NCES 2010341)
(http://nces.ed.gov/pubsearch/pubsinfo.asp?pubid=2010341)

*National total is for reporting states only. Data for school year 2007-2008. Excludes persons receiving high school equivalency certificates and graduates of federal schools for American Indians.
**Not available.

Averaged Freshman Graduation Rate for Public High Schools in 2008

National Average = 74.9%*

ALPHA ORDER

RANK	STATE	PERCENT
43	Alabama	69.0
42	Alaska	69.1
41	Arizona	70.7
25	Arkansas	76.4
39	California	71.2
30	Colorado	75.4
12	Connecticut	82.2
37	Delaware	72.1
44	Florida	66.9
46	Georgia	65.4
28	Hawaii	76.0
17	Idaho	80.1
15	Illinois	80.4
34	Indiana	74.1
3	Iowa	86.4
18	Kansas	79.1
32	Kentucky	74.4
48	Louisiana	63.5
18	Maine	79.1
15	Maryland	80.4
14	Massachusetts	81.5
27	Michigan	76.3
3	Minnesota	86.4
47	Mississippi	63.9
11	Missouri	82.4
13	Montana	82.0
7	Nebraska	83.8
49	Nevada	51.3
9	New Hampshire	83.4
5	New Jersey	84.6
40	New Mexico	70.8
45	New York	66.8
36	North Carolina	72.8
7	North Dakota	83.8
20	Ohio	79.0
21	Oklahoma	78.0
24	Oregon	76.7
10	Pennsylvania	82.7
25	Rhode Island	76.4
NA	South Carolina**	NA
6	South Dakota	84.4
31	Tennessee	74.9
35	Texas	73.1
33	Utah	74.3
2	Vermont	89.3
23	Virginia	77.0
38	Washington	71.9
22	West Virginia	77.3
1	Wisconsin	89.6
28	Wyoming	76.0

RANK ORDER

RANK	STATE	PERCENT
1	Wisconsin	89.6
2	Vermont	89.3
3	Iowa	86.4
3	Minnesota	86.4
5	New Jersey	84.6
6	South Dakota	84.4
7	Nebraska	83.8
7	North Dakota	83.8
9	New Hampshire	83.4
10	Pennsylvania	82.7
11	Missouri	82.4
12	Connecticut	82.2
13	Montana	82.0
14	Massachusetts	81.5
15	Illinois	80.4
15	Maryland	80.4
17	Idaho	80.1
18	Kansas	79.1
18	Maine	79.1
20	Ohio	79.0
21	Oklahoma	78.0
22	West Virginia	77.3
23	Virginia	77.0
24	Oregon	76.7
25	Arkansas	76.4
25	Rhode Island	76.4
27	Michigan	76.3
28	Hawaii	76.0
28	Wyoming	76.0
30	Colorado	75.4
31	Tennessee	74.9
32	Kentucky	74.4
33	Utah	74.3
34	Indiana	74.1
35	Texas	73.1
36	North Carolina	72.8
37	Delaware	72.1
38	Washington	71.9
39	California	71.2
40	New Mexico	70.8
41	Arizona	70.7
42	Alaska	69.1
43	Alabama	69.0
44	Florida	66.9
45	New York	66.8
46	Georgia	65.4
47	Mississippi	63.9
48	Louisiana	63.5
49	Nevada	51.3
NA	South Carolina**	NA

District of Columbia	56.0

Source: U.S. Department of Education, National Center for Education Statistics
    "Public School Graduates and Dropouts from the Common Core of Data: School Year 2007-08" (NCES 2010341)
    (http://nces.ed.gov/pubsearch/pubsinfo.asp?pubid=2010341)
*This rate is calculated by comparing the incoming freshman class enrollment of school year 2004-2005 with the number of
graduates with regular diplomas four years later (2007-2008). The incoming class enrollment figure is an average of the 8th grade
from five years earlier, the 9th grade four years earlier, and the 10th grade from three years earlier. **Not available.

Public High School Dropout Rate in 2008

National Rate = 4.1%*

ALPHA ORDER

RANK	STATE	RATE
45	Alabama	2.2
2	Alaska	7.3
3	Arizona	6.7
18	Arkansas	4.7
15	California	5.0
4	Colorado	6.4
35	Connecticut	2.8
6	Delaware	6.0
31	Florida	3.3
22	Georgia	4.3
8	Hawaii	5.4
46	Idaho	2.0
10	Illinois	5.2
47	Indiana	1.7
34	Iowa	2.9
40	Kansas	2.5
35	Kentucky	2.8
1	Louisiana	7.5
20	Maine	4.4
NA	Maryland**	NA
30	Massachusetts	3.4
5	Michigan	6.2
35	Minnesota	2.8
19	Mississippi	4.6
17	Missouri	4.9
10	Montana	5.2
40	Nebraska	2.5
14	Nevada	5.1
33	New Hampshire	3.0
47	New Jersey	1.7
26	New Mexico	3.9
10	New York	5.2
10	North Carolina	5.2
42	North Dakota	2.4
22	Ohio	4.3
32	Oklahoma	3.1
29	Oregon	3.8
39	Pennsylvania	2.6
9	Rhode Island	5.3
26	South Carolina	3.9
43	South Dakota	2.3
26	Tennessee	3.9
25	Texas	4.0
24	Utah	4.2
NA	Vermont**	NA
38	Virginia	2.7
7	Washington	5.7
20	West Virginia	4.4
43	Wisconsin	2.3
15	Wyoming	5.0

RANK ORDER

RANK	STATE	RATE
1	Louisiana	7.5
2	Alaska	7.3
3	Arizona	6.7
4	Colorado	6.4
5	Michigan	6.2
6	Delaware	6.0
7	Washington	5.7
8	Hawaii	5.4
9	Rhode Island	5.3
10	Illinois	5.2
10	Montana	5.2
10	New York	5.2
10	North Carolina	5.2
14	Nevada	5.1
15	California	5.0
15	Wyoming	5.0
17	Missouri	4.9
18	Arkansas	4.7
19	Mississippi	4.6
20	Maine	4.4
20	West Virginia	4.4
22	Georgia	4.3
22	Ohio	4.3
24	Utah	4.2
25	Texas	4.0
26	New Mexico	3.9
26	South Carolina	3.9
26	Tennessee	3.9
29	Oregon	3.8
30	Massachusetts	3.4
31	Florida	3.3
32	Oklahoma	3.1
33	New Hampshire	3.0
34	Iowa	2.9
35	Connecticut	2.8
35	Kentucky	2.8
35	Minnesota	2.8
38	Virginia	2.7
39	Pennsylvania	2.6
40	Kansas	2.5
40	Nebraska	2.5
42	North Dakota	2.4
43	South Dakota	2.3
43	Wisconsin	2.3
45	Alabama	2.2
46	Idaho	2.0
47	Indiana	1.7
47	New Jersey	1.7
NA	Maryland**	NA
NA	Vermont**	NA

District of Columbia   5.5

Source: U.S. Department of Education, National Center for Education Statistics
    "Public School Graduates and Dropouts from the Common Core of Data: School Year 2007-08" (NCES 2010341)
    (http://nces.ed.gov/pubsearch/pubsinfo.asp?pubid=2010341)
*"Event" dropout rates showing the number of 9th-12th grade dropouts divided by the number of students enrolled at the beginning of the school year in those grades. National rate is for reporting states.
**Not available.

ACT Average Composite Score in 2010

National Average = 21.0*

ALPHA ORDER			RANK ORDER		
RANK	STATE	AVERAGE SCORE	RANK	STATE	AVERAGE SCORE
39	Alabama	20.3	1	Massachusetts	24.0
32	Alaska	21.1	2	Connecticut	23.7
43	Arizona	20.0	2	New Hampshire	23.7
39	Arkansas	20.3	4	New York	23.3
15	California	22.2	5	Maine	23.2
38	Colorado	20.6	5	New Jersey	23.2
2	Connecticut	23.7	5	Vermont	23.2
8	Delaware	23.0	8	Delaware	23.0
48	Florida	19.5	8	Washington	23.0
34	Georgia	20.7	10	Minnesota	22.9
27	Hawaii	21.6	11	Rhode Island	22.8
23	Idaho	21.8	12	Indiana	22.3
34	Illinois	20.7	12	Maryland	22.3
12	Indiana	22.3	12	Virginia	22.3
15	Iowa	22.2	15	California	22.2
19	Kansas	22.0	15	Iowa	22.2
49	Kentucky	19.4	17	Nebraska	22.1
41	Louisiana	20.1	17	Wisconsin	22.1
5	Maine	23.2	19	Kansas	22.0
12	Maryland	22.3	19	Montana	22.0
1	Massachusetts	24.0	21	North Carolina	21.9
46	Michigan	19.7	21	Pennsylvania	21.9
10	Minnesota	22.9	23	Idaho	21.8
50	Mississippi	18.8	23	Ohio	21.8
27	Missouri	21.6	23	South Dakota	21.8
19	Montana	22.0	23	Utah	21.8
17	Nebraska	22.1	27	Hawaii	21.6
29	Nevada	21.5	27	Missouri	21.6
2	New Hampshire	23.7	29	Nevada	21.5
5	New Jersey	23.2	29	North Dakota	21.5
41	New Mexico	20.1	29	Oregon	21.5
4	New York	23.3	32	Alaska	21.1
21	North Carolina	21.9	33	Texas	20.8
29	North Dakota	21.5	34	Georgia	20.7
23	Ohio	21.8	34	Illinois	20.7
34	Oklahoma	20.7	34	Oklahoma	20.7
29	Oregon	21.5	34	West Virginia	20.7
21	Pennsylvania	21.9	38	Colorado	20.6
11	Rhode Island	22.8	39	Alabama	20.3
43	South Carolina	20.0	39	Arkansas	20.3
23	South Dakota	21.8	41	Louisiana	20.1
47	Tennessee	19.6	41	New Mexico	20.1
33	Texas	20.8	43	Arizona	20.0
23	Utah	21.8	43	South Carolina	20.0
5	Vermont	23.2	43	Wyoming	20.0
12	Virginia	22.3	46	Michigan	19.7
8	Washington	23.0	47	Tennessee	19.6
34	West Virginia	20.7	48	Florida	19.5
17	Wisconsin	22.1	49	Kentucky	19.4
43	Wyoming	20.0	50	Mississippi	18.8
				District of Columbia	19.8

Source: The American College Testing Program (Copyright © 2010)
    "Average ACT Scores by State" (http://www.act.org/news/data/10/states.html)
*The ACT score range is 1 to 36. Approximately 1.6 million 2010 U.S. high school students took the test. Caution should be used in using ACT scores to compare states. The percentage of high school students taking the test varies greatly from one state to another. For example, all 11th grade students in Colorado, Illinois, Kentucky, Michigan, Tennessee, and Wyoming are required to take the test but, in Maine, only 10 percent of 11th grade students took the test.

Education Expenditures by State and Local Governments in 2008

National Total = $826,063,178,000*

ALPHA ORDER

RANK	STATE	EXPENDITURES	% of USA
21	Alabama	$13,021,210,000	1.6%
43	Alaska	3,010,437,000	0.4%
19	Arizona	14,040,853,000	1.7%
34	Arkansas	6,986,178,000	0.8%
1	California	103,871,032,000	12.6%
22	Colorado	12,602,587,000	1.5%
26	Connecticut	11,126,438,000	1.3%
45	Delaware	2,878,324,000	0.3%
4	Florida	41,309,887,000	5.0%
10	Georgia	25,650,665,000	3.1%
40	Hawaii	3,393,565,000	0.4%
42	Idaho	3,168,770,000	0.4%
6	Illinois	32,736,157,000	4.0%
17	Indiana	15,418,944,000	1.9%
30	Iowa	8,689,821,000	1.1%
31	Kansas	7,506,496,000	0.9%
27	Kentucky	10,632,513,000	1.3%
25	Louisiana	11,810,100,000	1.4%
41	Maine	3,188,930,000	0.4%
15	Maryland	17,201,575,000	2.1%
14	Massachusetts	17,305,941,000	2.1%
9	Michigan	28,310,913,000	3.4%
18	Minnesota	14,802,409,000	1.8%
33	Mississippi	7,154,566,000	0.9%
20	Missouri	13,938,656,000	1.7%
46	Montana	2,522,784,000	0.3%
37	Nebraska	5,090,389,000	0.6%
35	Nevada	6,226,566,000	0.8%
39	New Hampshire	3,419,245,000	0.4%
8	New Jersey	30,503,321,000	3.7%
36	New Mexico	5,911,778,000	0.7%
3	New York	64,743,134,000	7.8%
11	North Carolina	22,785,386,000	2.8%
49	North Dakota	1,844,941,000	0.2%
7	Ohio	30,882,319,000	3.7%
29	Oklahoma	9,144,590,000	1.1%
28	Oregon	9,674,161,000	1.2%
5	Pennsylvania	33,107,240,000	4.0%
44	Rhode Island	2,936,240,000	0.4%
24	South Carolina	12,252,525,000	1.5%
50	South Dakota	1,753,268,000	0.2%
23	Tennessee	12,375,698,000	1.5%
2	Texas	65,970,133,000	8.0%
32	Utah	7,470,556,000	0.9%
48	Vermont	2,214,713,000	0.3%
12	Virginia	22,692,652,000	2.7%
13	Washington	18,041,972,000	2.2%
38	West Virginia	4,683,675,000	0.6%
16	Wisconsin	15,592,365,000	1.9%
47	Wyoming	2,239,914,000	0.3%

RANK ORDER

RANK	STATE	EXPENDITURES	% of USA
1	California	$103,871,032,000	12.6%
2	Texas	65,970,133,000	8.0%
3	New York	64,743,134,000	7.8%
4	Florida	41,309,887,000	5.0%
5	Pennsylvania	33,107,240,000	4.0%
6	Illinois	32,736,157,000	4.0%
7	Ohio	30,882,319,000	3.7%
8	New Jersey	30,503,321,000	3.7%
9	Michigan	28,310,913,000	3.4%
10	Georgia	25,650,665,000	3.1%
11	North Carolina	22,785,386,000	2.8%
12	Virginia	22,692,652,000	2.7%
13	Washington	18,041,972,000	2.2%
14	Massachusetts	17,305,941,000	2.1%
15	Maryland	17,201,575,000	2.1%
16	Wisconsin	15,592,365,000	1.9%
17	Indiana	15,418,944,000	1.9%
18	Minnesota	14,802,409,000	1.8%
19	Arizona	14,040,853,000	1.7%
20	Missouri	13,938,656,000	1.7%
21	Alabama	13,021,210,000	1.6%
22	Colorado	12,602,587,000	1.5%
23	Tennessee	12,375,698,000	1.5%
24	South Carolina	12,252,525,000	1.5%
25	Louisiana	11,810,100,000	1.4%
26	Connecticut	11,126,438,000	1.3%
27	Kentucky	10,632,513,000	1.3%
28	Oregon	9,674,161,000	1.2%
29	Oklahoma	9,144,590,000	1.1%
30	Iowa	8,689,821,000	1.1%
31	Kansas	7,506,496,000	0.9%
32	Utah	7,470,556,000	0.9%
33	Mississippi	7,154,566,000	0.9%
34	Arkansas	6,986,178,000	0.8%
35	Nevada	6,226,566,000	0.8%
36	New Mexico	5,911,778,000	0.7%
37	Nebraska	5,090,389,000	0.6%
38	West Virginia	4,683,675,000	0.6%
39	New Hampshire	3,419,245,000	0.4%
40	Hawaii	3,393,565,000	0.4%
41	Maine	3,188,930,000	0.4%
42	Idaho	3,168,770,000	0.4%
43	Alaska	3,010,437,000	0.4%
44	Rhode Island	2,936,240,000	0.4%
45	Delaware	2,878,324,000	0.3%
46	Montana	2,522,784,000	0.3%
47	Wyoming	2,239,914,000	0.3%
48	Vermont	2,214,713,000	0.3%
49	North Dakota	1,844,941,000	0.2%
50	South Dakota	1,753,268,000	0.2%
	District of Columbia	2,226,646,000	0.3%

Source: U.S. Bureau of the Census, Governments Division
"2008 State and Local Government Finances" (http://www.census.gov/govs/estimate/index.html)
*Direct general expenditures for higher, secondary, elementary, and, "other" education. Includes capital outlays.

Per Capita State and Local Government Expenditures for Education in 2008

National Per Capita = $2,714*

ALPHA ORDER				RANK ORDER		
RANK	STATE	PER CAPITA		RANK	STATE	PER CAPITA
18	Alabama	$2,784		1	Alaska	$4,375
1	Alaska	4,375		2	Wyoming	4,203
48	Arizona	2,160		3	Vermont	3,566
40	Arkansas	2,436		4	New Jersey	3,521
14	California	2,840		5	New York	3,326
35	Colorado	2,554		6	Delaware	3,285
7	Connecticut	3,176		7	Connecticut	3,176
6	Delaware	3,285		8	Maryland	3,040
46	Florida	2,242		9	New Mexico	2,976
27	Georgia	2,645		10	Virginia	2,911
29	Hawaii	2,636		11	Iowa	2,902
49	Idaho	2,074		12	North Dakota	2,876
36	Illinois	2,549		13	Nebraska	2,857
43	Indiana	2,414		14	California	2,840
11	Iowa	2,902		15	Michigan	2,830
24	Kansas	2,683		15	Minnesota	2,830
38	Kentucky	2,480		17	Rhode Island	2,787
26	Louisiana	2,653		18	Alabama	2,784
42	Maine	2,416		19	Wisconsin	2,771
8	Maryland	3,040		20	Washington	2,748
27	Massachusetts	2,645		21	Utah	2,739
15	Michigan	2,830		22	South Carolina	2,721
15	Minnesota	2,830		23	Texas	2,714
41	Mississippi	2,433		24	Kansas	2,683
45	Missouri	2,340		25	Ohio	2,679
31	Montana	2,606		26	Louisiana	2,653
13	Nebraska	2,857		27	Georgia	2,645
44	Nevada	2,380		27	Massachusetts	2,645
32	New Hampshire	2,587		29	Hawaii	2,636
4	New Jersey	3,521		30	Pennsylvania	2,635
9	New Mexico	2,976		31	Montana	2,606
5	New York	3,326		32	New Hampshire	2,587
39	North Carolina	2,464		33	West Virginia	2,581
12	North Dakota	2,876		34	Oregon	2,557
25	Ohio	2,679		35	Colorado	2,554
37	Oklahoma	2,509		36	Illinois	2,549
34	Oregon	2,557		37	Oklahoma	2,509
30	Pennsylvania	2,635		38	Kentucky	2,480
17	Rhode Island	2,787		39	North Carolina	2,464
22	South Carolina	2,721		40	Arkansas	2,436
47	South Dakota	2,179		41	Mississippi	2,433
50	Tennessee	1,983		42	Maine	2,416
23	Texas	2,714		43	Indiana	2,414
21	Utah	2,739		44	Nevada	2,380
3	Vermont	3,566		45	Missouri	2,340
10	Virginia	2,911		46	Florida	2,242
20	Washington	2,748		47	South Dakota	2,179
33	West Virginia	2,581		48	Arizona	2,160
19	Wisconsin	2,771		49	Idaho	2,074
2	Wyoming	4,203		50	Tennessee	1,983
					District of Columbia	3,774

Source: CQ Press using data from U.S. Bureau of the Census, Governments Division
   "2008 State and Local Government Finances" (http://www.census.gov/govs/estimate/index.html)
*Direct general expenditures for higher, secondary, elementary, and, "other" education. Includes capital outlays.

Expenditures for Education as a Percent of All State and Local Government Expenditures in 2008
National Percent = 34.4%*

ALPHA ORDER

RANK	STATE	PERCENT
3	Alabama	39.9
50	Alaska	26.1
41	Arizona	32.5
8	Arkansas	39.1
43	California	31.0
26	Colorado	35.4
17	Connecticut	36.6
24	Delaware	35.6
47	Florida	29.8
6	Georgia	39.3
48	Hawaii	29.0
39	Idaho	32.7
33	Illinois	34.0
29	Indiana	34.7
12	Iowa	37.7
22	Kansas	35.9
19	Kentucky	36.1
49	Louisiana	28.6
44	Maine	30.9
14	Maryland	37.6
45	Massachusetts	30.6
7	Michigan	39.2
35	Minnesota	33.6
42	Mississippi	31.9
25	Missouri	35.5
28	Montana	34.8
15	Nebraska	37.1
31	Nevada	34.2
10	New Hampshire	38.3
9	New Jersey	38.7
31	New Mexico	34.2
46	New York	30.5
20	North Carolina	36.0
20	North Dakota	36.0
23	Ohio	35.7
11	Oklahoma	38.1
30	Oregon	34.4
27	Pennsylvania	35.0
38	Rhode Island	32.8
18	South Carolina	36.4
35	South Dakota	33.6
39	Tennessee	32.7
2	Texas	40.5
3	Utah	39.9
1	Vermont	40.7
5	Virginia	39.7
34	Washington	33.7
12	West Virginia	37.7
16	Wisconsin	36.7
37	Wyoming	32.9

RANK ORDER

RANK	STATE	PERCENT
1	Vermont	40.7
2	Texas	40.5
3	Alabama	39.9
3	Utah	39.9
5	Virginia	39.7
6	Georgia	39.3
7	Michigan	39.2
8	Arkansas	39.1
9	New Jersey	38.7
10	New Hampshire	38.3
11	Oklahoma	38.1
12	Iowa	37.7
12	West Virginia	37.7
14	Maryland	37.6
15	Nebraska	37.1
16	Wisconsin	36.7
17	Connecticut	36.6
18	South Carolina	36.4
19	Kentucky	36.1
20	North Carolina	36.0
20	North Dakota	36.0
22	Kansas	35.9
23	Ohio	35.7
24	Delaware	35.6
25	Missouri	35.5
26	Colorado	35.4
27	Pennsylvania	35.0
28	Montana	34.8
29	Indiana	34.7
30	Oregon	34.4
31	Nevada	34.2
31	New Mexico	34.2
33	Illinois	34.0
34	Washington	33.7
35	Minnesota	33.6
35	South Dakota	33.6
37	Wyoming	32.9
38	Rhode Island	32.8
39	Idaho	32.7
39	Tennessee	32.7
41	Arizona	32.5
42	Mississippi	31.9
43	California	31.0
44	Maine	30.9
45	Massachusetts	30.6
46	New York	30.5
47	Florida	29.8
48	Hawaii	29.0
49	Louisiana	28.6
50	Alaska	26.1

District of Columbia 20.9

Source: CQ Press using data from U.S. Bureau of the Census, Governments Division
"2008 State and Local Government Finances" (http://www.census.gov/govs/estimate/index.html)
*Direct general expenditures for higher, secondary, elementary, and "other" education as a percent of all direct general expenditures. Includes capital outlays.

State and Local Government Expenditures for Elementary and Secondary Education in 2008
National Total = $565,631,236,000*

ALPHA ORDER

RANK	STATE	EXPENDITURES	% of USA
25	Alabama	$7,736,839,000	1.4%
42	Alaska	2,236,207,000	0.4%
20	Arizona	9,183,710,000	1.6%
33	Arkansas	4,456,722,000	0.8%
1	California	70,687,156,000	12.5%
21	Colorado	8,444,895,000	1.5%
23	Connecticut	8,178,903,000	1.4%
45	Delaware	1,718,975,000	0.3%
4	Florida	30,484,206,000	5.4%
9	Georgia	18,615,660,000	3.3%
41	Hawaii	2,248,990,000	0.4%
44	Idaho	1,927,885,000	0.3%
7	Illinois	22,985,805,000	4.1%
18	Indiana	9,684,117,000	1.7%
30	Iowa	5,191,110,000	0.9%
31	Kansas	4,758,174,000	0.8%
27	Kentucky	6,330,937,000	1.1%
26	Louisiana	7,510,264,000	1.3%
40	Maine	2,277,615,000	0.4%
14	Maryland	11,675,002,000	2.1%
13	Massachusetts	12,489,925,000	2.2%
10	Michigan	17,985,160,000	3.2%
17	Minnesota	9,714,168,000	1.7%
34	Mississippi	4,292,984,000	0.8%
19	Missouri	9,536,565,000	1.7%
46	Montana	1,535,395,000	0.3%
37	Nebraska	3,208,957,000	0.6%
32	Nevada	4,633,015,000	0.8%
39	New Hampshire	2,493,623,000	0.4%
5	New Jersey	24,039,648,000	4.3%
36	New Mexico	3,557,284,000	0.6%
2	New York	51,185,161,000	9.0%
12	North Carolina	13,468,428,000	2.4%
50	North Dakota	1,021,318,000	0.2%
8	Ohio	21,135,711,000	3.7%
29	Oklahoma	5,583,723,000	1.0%
28	Oregon	6,112,891,000	1.1%
6	Pennsylvania	23,697,574,000	4.2%
43	Rhode Island	2,165,460,000	0.4%
24	South Carolina	7,920,103,000	1.4%
49	South Dakota	1,129,781,000	0.2%
22	Tennessee	8,355,853,000	1.5%
3	Texas	45,440,154,000	8.0%
35	Utah	4,236,242,000	0.7%
48	Vermont	1,383,151,000	0.2%
11	Virginia	15,228,627,000	2.7%
15	Washington	11,237,122,000	2.0%
38	West Virginia	2,813,769,000	0.5%
16	Wisconsin	10,091,255,000	1.8%
47	Wyoming	1,507,073,000	0.3%

RANK ORDER

RANK	STATE	EXPENDITURES	% of USA
1	California	$70,687,156,000	12.5%
2	New York	51,185,161,000	9.0%
3	Texas	45,440,154,000	8.0%
4	Florida	30,484,206,000	5.4%
5	New Jersey	24,039,648,000	4.3%
6	Pennsylvania	23,697,574,000	4.2%
7	Illinois	22,985,805,000	4.1%
8	Ohio	21,135,711,000	3.7%
9	Georgia	18,615,660,000	3.3%
10	Michigan	17,985,160,000	3.2%
11	Virginia	15,228,627,000	2.7%
12	North Carolina	13,468,428,000	2.4%
13	Massachusetts	12,489,925,000	2.2%
14	Maryland	11,675,002,000	2.1%
15	Washington	11,237,122,000	2.0%
16	Wisconsin	10,091,255,000	1.8%
17	Minnesota	9,714,168,000	1.7%
18	Indiana	9,684,117,000	1.7%
19	Missouri	9,536,565,000	1.7%
20	Arizona	9,183,710,000	1.6%
21	Colorado	8,444,895,000	1.5%
22	Tennessee	8,355,853,000	1.5%
23	Connecticut	8,178,903,000	1.4%
24	South Carolina	7,920,103,000	1.4%
25	Alabama	7,736,839,000	1.4%
26	Louisiana	7,510,264,000	1.3%
27	Kentucky	6,330,937,000	1.1%
28	Oregon	6,112,891,000	1.1%
29	Oklahoma	5,583,723,000	1.0%
30	Iowa	5,191,110,000	0.9%
31	Kansas	4,758,174,000	0.8%
32	Nevada	4,633,015,000	0.8%
33	Arkansas	4,456,722,000	0.8%
34	Mississippi	4,292,984,000	0.8%
35	Utah	4,236,242,000	0.7%
36	New Mexico	3,557,284,000	0.6%
37	Nebraska	3,208,957,000	0.6%
38	West Virginia	2,813,769,000	0.5%
39	New Hampshire	2,493,623,000	0.4%
40	Maine	2,277,615,000	0.4%
41	Hawaii	2,248,990,000	0.4%
42	Alaska	2,236,207,000	0.4%
43	Rhode Island	2,165,460,000	0.4%
44	Idaho	1,927,885,000	0.3%
45	Delaware	1,718,975,000	0.3%
46	Montana	1,535,395,000	0.3%
47	Wyoming	1,507,073,000	0.3%
48	Vermont	1,383,151,000	0.2%
49	South Dakota	1,129,781,000	0.2%
50	North Dakota	1,021,318,000	0.2%
	District of Columbia	2,097,944,000	0.4%

Source: U.S. Bureau of the Census, Governments Division
"2008 State and Local Government Finances" (http://www.census.gov/govs/estimate/index.html)
*Direct general expenditures. Includes capital outlays.

Per Capita State and Local Government Expenditures for Elementary and Secondary Education in 2008
National Per Capita = $1,858*

<table>
<tr><td colspan="3">ALPHA ORDER</td><td colspan="3">RANK ORDER</td></tr>
<tr><td>RANK</td><td>STATE</td><td>PER CAPITA</td><td>RANK</td><td>STATE</td><td>PER CAPITA</td></tr>
<tr><td>34</td><td>Alabama</td><td>$1,654</td><td>1</td><td>Alaska</td><td>$3,250</td></tr>
<tr><td>1</td><td>Alaska</td><td>3,250</td><td>2</td><td>Wyoming</td><td>2,828</td></tr>
<tr><td>47</td><td>Arizona</td><td>1,413</td><td>3</td><td>New Jersey</td><td>2,775</td></tr>
<tr><td>39</td><td>Arkansas</td><td>1,554</td><td>4</td><td>New York</td><td>2,629</td></tr>
<tr><td>11</td><td>California</td><td>1,932</td><td>5</td><td>Connecticut</td><td>2,335</td></tr>
<tr><td>29</td><td>Colorado</td><td>1,711</td><td>6</td><td>Vermont</td><td>2,227</td></tr>
<tr><td>5</td><td>Connecticut</td><td>2,335</td><td>7</td><td>Maryland</td><td>2,063</td></tr>
<tr><td>9</td><td>Delaware</td><td>1,962</td><td>8</td><td>Rhode Island</td><td>2,055</td></tr>
<tr><td>33</td><td>Florida</td><td>1,655</td><td>9</td><td>Delaware</td><td>1,962</td></tr>
<tr><td>12</td><td>Georgia</td><td>1,920</td><td>10</td><td>Virginia</td><td>1,954</td></tr>
<tr><td>26</td><td>Hawaii</td><td>1,747</td><td>11</td><td>California</td><td>1,932</td></tr>
<tr><td>50</td><td>Idaho</td><td>1,262</td><td>12</td><td>Georgia</td><td>1,920</td></tr>
<tr><td>22</td><td>Illinois</td><td>1,790</td><td>13</td><td>Massachusetts</td><td>1,909</td></tr>
<tr><td>43</td><td>Indiana</td><td>1,516</td><td>14</td><td>New Hampshire</td><td>1,886</td></tr>
<tr><td>27</td><td>Iowa</td><td>1,734</td><td>14</td><td>Pennsylvania</td><td>1,886</td></tr>
<tr><td>31</td><td>Kansas</td><td>1,701</td><td>16</td><td>Texas</td><td>1,870</td></tr>
<tr><td>44</td><td>Kentucky</td><td>1,476</td><td>17</td><td>Minnesota</td><td>1,857</td></tr>
<tr><td>32</td><td>Louisiana</td><td>1,687</td><td>18</td><td>Ohio</td><td>1,833</td></tr>
<tr><td>28</td><td>Maine</td><td>1,726</td><td>19</td><td>Nebraska</td><td>1,801</td></tr>
<tr><td>7</td><td>Maryland</td><td>2,063</td><td>20</td><td>Michigan</td><td>1,798</td></tr>
<tr><td>13</td><td>Massachusetts</td><td>1,909</td><td>21</td><td>Wisconsin</td><td>1,793</td></tr>
<tr><td>20</td><td>Michigan</td><td>1,798</td><td>22</td><td>Illinois</td><td>1,790</td></tr>
<tr><td>17</td><td>Minnesota</td><td>1,857</td><td>22</td><td>New Mexico</td><td>1,790</td></tr>
<tr><td>45</td><td>Mississippi</td><td>1,460</td><td>24</td><td>Nevada</td><td>1,771</td></tr>
<tr><td>36</td><td>Missouri</td><td>1,601</td><td>25</td><td>South Carolina</td><td>1,759</td></tr>
<tr><td>38</td><td>Montana</td><td>1,586</td><td>26</td><td>Hawaii</td><td>1,747</td></tr>
<tr><td>19</td><td>Nebraska</td><td>1,801</td><td>27</td><td>Iowa</td><td>1,734</td></tr>
<tr><td>24</td><td>Nevada</td><td>1,771</td><td>28</td><td>Maine</td><td>1,726</td></tr>
<tr><td>14</td><td>New Hampshire</td><td>1,886</td><td>29</td><td>Colorado</td><td>1,711</td></tr>
<tr><td>3</td><td>New Jersey</td><td>2,775</td><td>29</td><td>Washington</td><td>1,711</td></tr>
<tr><td>22</td><td>New Mexico</td><td>1,790</td><td>31</td><td>Kansas</td><td>1,701</td></tr>
<tr><td>4</td><td>New York</td><td>2,629</td><td>32</td><td>Louisiana</td><td>1,687</td></tr>
<tr><td>46</td><td>North Carolina</td><td>1,456</td><td>33</td><td>Florida</td><td>1,655</td></tr>
<tr><td>37</td><td>North Dakota</td><td>1,592</td><td>34</td><td>Alabama</td><td>1,654</td></tr>
<tr><td>18</td><td>Ohio</td><td>1,833</td><td>35</td><td>Oregon</td><td>1,616</td></tr>
<tr><td>42</td><td>Oklahoma</td><td>1,532</td><td>36</td><td>Missouri</td><td>1,601</td></tr>
<tr><td>35</td><td>Oregon</td><td>1,616</td><td>37</td><td>North Dakota</td><td>1,592</td></tr>
<tr><td>14</td><td>Pennsylvania</td><td>1,886</td><td>38</td><td>Montana</td><td>1,586</td></tr>
<tr><td>8</td><td>Rhode Island</td><td>2,055</td><td>39</td><td>Arkansas</td><td>1,554</td></tr>
<tr><td>25</td><td>South Carolina</td><td>1,759</td><td>40</td><td>Utah</td><td>1,553</td></tr>
<tr><td>48</td><td>South Dakota</td><td>1,404</td><td>41</td><td>West Virginia</td><td>1,550</td></tr>
<tr><td>49</td><td>Tennessee</td><td>1,339</td><td>42</td><td>Oklahoma</td><td>1,532</td></tr>
<tr><td>16</td><td>Texas</td><td>1,870</td><td>43</td><td>Indiana</td><td>1,516</td></tr>
<tr><td>40</td><td>Utah</td><td>1,553</td><td>44</td><td>Kentucky</td><td>1,476</td></tr>
<tr><td>6</td><td>Vermont</td><td>2,227</td><td>45</td><td>Mississippi</td><td>1,460</td></tr>
<tr><td>10</td><td>Virginia</td><td>1,954</td><td>46</td><td>North Carolina</td><td>1,456</td></tr>
<tr><td>29</td><td>Washington</td><td>1,711</td><td>47</td><td>Arizona</td><td>1,413</td></tr>
<tr><td>41</td><td>West Virginia</td><td>1,550</td><td>48</td><td>South Dakota</td><td>1,404</td></tr>
<tr><td>21</td><td>Wisconsin</td><td>1,793</td><td>49</td><td>Tennessee</td><td>1,339</td></tr>
<tr><td>2</td><td>Wyoming</td><td>2,828</td><td>50</td><td>Idaho</td><td>1,262</td></tr>
<tr><td></td><td></td><td></td><td></td><td>District of Columbia</td><td>3,555</td></tr>
</table>

Source: CQ Press using data from U.S. Bureau of the Census, Governments Division
   "2008 State and Local Government Finances" (http://www.census.gov/govs/estimate/index.html)
*Direct general expenditures. Includes capital outlays.

Expenditures for Elementary and Secondary Education as a Percent of All State and Local Government Expenditures in 2008
National Percent = 23.6%*

ALPHA ORDER

RANK	STATE	PERCENT
19	Alabama	23.7
47	Alaska	19.4
40	Arizona	21.2
11	Arkansas	24.9
42	California	21.1
19	Colorado	23.7
5	Connecticut	26.9
38	Delaware	21.3
32	Florida	22.0
2	Georgia	28.5
48	Hawaii	19.2
46	Idaho	19.9
17	Illinois	23.9
34	Indiana	21.8
27	Iowa	22.5
24	Kansas	22.8
37	Kentucky	21.5
50	Louisiana	18.2
29	Maine	22.1
7	Maryland	25.5
29	Massachusetts	22.1
11	Michigan	24.9
32	Minnesota	22.0
49	Mississippi	19.1
14	Missouri	24.3
40	Montana	21.2
22	Nebraska	23.4
8	Nevada	25.4
3	New Hampshire	27.9
1	New Jersey	30.5
44	New Mexico	20.6
16	New York	24.1
38	North Carolina	21.3
45	North Dakota	20.0
13	Ohio	24.5
23	Oklahoma	23.3
35	Oregon	21.7
10	Pennsylvania	25.0
15	Rhode Island	24.2
21	South Carolina	23.5
36	South Dakota	21.6
29	Tennessee	22.1
3	Texas	27.9
26	Utah	22.6
8	Vermont	25.4
6	Virginia	26.7
43	Washington	21.0
25	West Virginia	22.7
18	Wisconsin	23.8
28	Wyoming	22.2

RANK ORDER

RANK	STATE	PERCENT
1	New Jersey	30.5
2	Georgia	28.5
3	New Hampshire	27.9
3	Texas	27.9
5	Connecticut	26.9
6	Virginia	26.7
7	Maryland	25.5
8	Nevada	25.4
8	Vermont	25.4
10	Pennsylvania	25.0
11	Arkansas	24.9
11	Michigan	24.9
13	Ohio	24.5
14	Missouri	24.3
15	Rhode Island	24.2
16	New York	24.1
17	Illinois	23.9
18	Wisconsin	23.8
19	Alabama	23.7
19	Colorado	23.7
21	South Carolina	23.5
22	Nebraska	23.4
23	Oklahoma	23.3
24	Kansas	22.8
25	West Virginia	22.7
26	Utah	22.6
27	Iowa	22.5
28	Wyoming	22.2
29	Maine	22.1
29	Massachusetts	22.1
29	Tennessee	22.1
32	Florida	22.0
32	Minnesota	22.0
34	Indiana	21.8
35	Oregon	21.7
36	South Dakota	21.6
37	Kentucky	21.5
38	Delaware	21.3
38	North Carolina	21.3
40	Arizona	21.2
40	Montana	21.2
42	California	21.1
43	Washington	21.0
44	New Mexico	20.6
45	North Dakota	20.0
46	Idaho	19.9
47	Alaska	19.4
48	Hawaii	19.2
49	Mississippi	19.1
50	Louisiana	18.2

District of Columbia   19.6

Source: CQ Press using data from U.S. Bureau of the Census, Governments Division
"2008 State and Local Government Finances" (http://www.census.gov/govs/estimate/index.html)
*Direct general expenditures as a percent of all direct general expenditures. Includes capital outlays.

Estimated Per Pupil Public Elementary and Secondary School Expenditures in 2011
National Per Pupil = $10,826*

ALPHA ORDER

RANK	STATE	PER PUPIL
35	Alabama	$9,483
22	Alaska	11,147
50	Arizona	6,448
14	Arkansas	11,999
42	California	8,689
33	Colorado	9,588
8	Connecticut	14,989
10	Delaware	13,960
40	Florida	9,124
23	Georgia	10,971
17	Hawaii	11,819
46	Idaho	8,101
16	Illinois	11,896
27	Indiana	10,390
30	Iowa	9,856
38	Kansas	9,254
32	Kentucky	9,612
25	Louisiana	10,578
7	Maine	15,032
6	Maryland	15,268
9	Massachusetts	14,828
13	Michigan	12,015
15	Minnesota	11,905
48	Mississippi	8,003
36	Missouri	9,422
29	Montana	9,973
26	Nebraska	10,452
47	Nevada	8,089
11	New Hampshire	13,797
2	New Jersey	17,717
21	New Mexico	11,346
1	New York	17,750
45	North Carolina	8,303
41	North Dakota	8,880
34	Ohio	9,512
44	Oklahoma	8,311
24	Oregon	10,959
12	Pennsylvania	13,334
5	Rhode Island	15,803
31	South Carolina	9,616
37	South Dakota	9,310
43	Tennessee	8,393
39	Texas	9,128
49	Utah	7,056
3	Vermont	17,447
19	Virginia	11,753
28	Washington	10,367
20	West Virginia	11,369
18	Wisconsin	11,791
4	Wyoming	16,066

RANK ORDER

RANK	STATE	PER PUPIL
1	New York	$17,750
2	New Jersey	17,717
3	Vermont	17,447
4	Wyoming	16,066
5	Rhode Island	15,803
6	Maryland	15,268
7	Maine	15,032
8	Connecticut	14,989
9	Massachusetts	14,828
10	Delaware	13,960
11	New Hampshire	13,797
12	Pennsylvania	13,334
13	Michigan	12,015
14	Arkansas	11,999
15	Minnesota	11,905
16	Illinois	11,896
17	Hawaii	11,819
18	Wisconsin	11,791
19	Virginia	11,753
20	West Virginia	11,369
21	New Mexico	11,346
22	Alaska	11,147
23	Georgia	10,971
24	Oregon	10,959
25	Louisiana	10,578
26	Nebraska	10,452
27	Indiana	10,390
28	Washington	10,367
29	Montana	9,973
30	Iowa	9,856
31	South Carolina	9,616
32	Kentucky	9,612
33	Colorado	9,588
34	Ohio	9,512
35	Alabama	9,483
36	Missouri	9,422
37	South Dakota	9,310
38	Kansas	9,254
39	Texas	9,128
40	Florida	9,124
41	North Dakota	8,880
42	California	8,689
43	Tennessee	8,393
44	Oklahoma	8,311
45	North Carolina	8,303
46	Idaho	8,101
47	Nevada	8,089
48	Mississippi	8,003
49	Utah	7,056
50	Arizona	6,448

| | District of Columbia | 13,803 |

Source: National Education Association, Washington, D.C.
    "Rankings and Estimates" (Copyright © 2010, NEA, used with permission, http://www.nea.org/home/30896.htm)
*Estimates for school year 2010-2011. Based on fall enrollment.

Higher Education Expenditures by State and Local Governments in 2008

National Total = $223,293,543,000*

ALPHA ORDER

RANK	STATE	EXPENDITURES	% of USA
17	Alabama	$4,633,538,000	2.1%
47	Alaska	689,043,000	0.3%
18	Arizona	4,249,844,000	1.9%
34	Arkansas	2,163,658,000	1.0%
1	California	29,521,423,000	13.2%
20	Colorado	3,810,196,000	1.7%
33	Connecticut	2,295,141,000	1.0%
41	Delaware	965,046,000	0.4%
6	Florida	8,428,750,000	3.8%
12	Georgia	5,502,908,000	2.5%
40	Hawaii	1,088,738,000	0.5%
39	Idaho	1,090,867,000	0.5%
7	Illinois	8,285,709,000	3.7%
15	Indiana	4,889,472,000	2.2%
29	Iowa	3,090,466,000	1.4%
32	Kansas	2,524,847,000	1.1%
23	Kentucky	3,428,364,000	1.5%
24	Louisiana	3,393,688,000	1.5%
45	Maine	761,420,000	0.3%
16	Maryland	4,820,946,000	2.2%
22	Massachusetts	3,775,661,000	1.7%
4	Michigan	9,453,150,000	4.2%
19	Minnesota	4,146,530,000	1.9%
31	Mississippi	2,535,787,000	1.1%
21	Missouri	3,780,498,000	1.7%
42	Montana	835,991,000	0.4%
36	Nebraska	1,661,241,000	0.7%
37	Nevada	1,423,939,000	0.6%
43	New Hampshire	816,592,000	0.4%
13	New Jersey	5,264,672,000	2.4%
35	New Mexico	1,996,106,000	0.9%
3	New York	11,560,476,000	5.2%
5	North Carolina	8,585,568,000	3.8%
44	North Dakota	763,460,000	0.3%
8	Ohio	7,811,295,000	3.5%
28	Oklahoma	3,117,467,000	1.4%
26	Oregon	3,269,146,000	1.5%
9	Pennsylvania	7,561,411,000	3.4%
49	Rhode Island	584,364,000	0.3%
25	South Carolina	3,299,145,000	1.5%
50	South Dakota	519,368,000	0.2%
27	Tennessee	3,147,970,000	1.4%
2	Texas	18,763,935,000	8.4%
30	Utah	2,952,595,000	1.3%
46	Vermont	695,113,000	0.3%
10	Virginia	6,640,745,000	3.0%
11	Washington	5,566,909,000	2.5%
38	West Virginia	1,398,144,000	0.6%
14	Wisconsin	4,966,931,000	2.2%
48	Wyoming	636,568,000	0.3%

RANK ORDER

RANK	STATE	EXPENDITURES	% of USA
1	California	$29,521,423,000	13.2%
2	Texas	18,763,935,000	8.4%
3	New York	11,560,476,000	5.2%
4	Michigan	9,453,150,000	4.2%
5	North Carolina	8,585,568,000	3.8%
6	Florida	8,428,750,000	3.8%
7	Illinois	8,285,709,000	3.7%
8	Ohio	7,811,295,000	3.5%
9	Pennsylvania	7,561,411,000	3.4%
10	Virginia	6,640,745,000	3.0%
11	Washington	5,566,909,000	2.5%
12	Georgia	5,502,908,000	2.5%
13	New Jersey	5,264,672,000	2.4%
14	Wisconsin	4,966,931,000	2.2%
15	Indiana	4,889,472,000	2.2%
16	Maryland	4,820,946,000	2.2%
17	Alabama	4,633,538,000	2.1%
18	Arizona	4,249,844,000	1.9%
19	Minnesota	4,146,530,000	1.9%
20	Colorado	3,810,196,000	1.7%
21	Missouri	3,780,498,000	1.7%
22	Massachusetts	3,775,661,000	1.7%
23	Kentucky	3,428,364,000	1.5%
24	Louisiana	3,393,688,000	1.5%
25	South Carolina	3,299,145,000	1.5%
26	Oregon	3,269,146,000	1.5%
27	Tennessee	3,147,970,000	1.4%
28	Oklahoma	3,117,467,000	1.4%
29	Iowa	3,090,466,000	1.4%
30	Utah	2,952,595,000	1.3%
31	Mississippi	2,535,787,000	1.1%
32	Kansas	2,524,847,000	1.1%
33	Connecticut	2,295,141,000	1.0%
34	Arkansas	2,163,658,000	1.0%
35	New Mexico	1,996,106,000	0.9%
36	Nebraska	1,661,241,000	0.7%
37	Nevada	1,423,939,000	0.6%
38	West Virginia	1,398,144,000	0.6%
39	Idaho	1,090,867,000	0.5%
40	Hawaii	1,088,738,000	0.5%
41	Delaware	965,046,000	0.4%
42	Montana	835,991,000	0.4%
43	New Hampshire	816,592,000	0.4%
44	North Dakota	763,460,000	0.3%
45	Maine	761,420,000	0.3%
46	Vermont	695,113,000	0.3%
47	Alaska	689,043,000	0.3%
48	Wyoming	636,568,000	0.3%
49	Rhode Island	584,364,000	0.3%
50	South Dakota	519,368,000	0.2%
	District of Columbia	128,702,000	0.1%

Source: U.S. Bureau of the Census, Governments Division
    "2008 State and Local Government Finances" (http://www.census.gov/govs/estimate/index.html)
*Direct general expenditures. Includes capital outlays.

Per Capita State and Local Government Expenditures for Higher Education in 2008
National Per Capita = $734*

ALPHA ORDER

RANK	STATE	PER CAPITA
9	Alabama	$991
8	Alaska	1,001
36	Arizona	654
31	Arkansas	754
23	California	807
26	Colorado	772
35	Connecticut	655
4	Delaware	1,101
50	Florida	457
46	Georgia	567
22	Hawaii	846
33	Idaho	714
38	Illinois	645
29	Indiana	765
6	Iowa	1,032
13	Kansas	903
24	Kentucky	800
30	Louisiana	762
44	Maine	577
19	Maryland	852
44	Massachusetts	577
10	Michigan	945
25	Minnesota	793
17	Mississippi	862
39	Missouri	635
15	Montana	864
11	Nebraska	932
48	Nevada	544
40	New Hampshire	618
41	New Jersey	608
7	New Mexico	1,005
43	New York	594
12	North Carolina	928
2	North Dakota	1,190
34	Ohio	678
18	Oklahoma	856
15	Oregon	864
42	Pennsylvania	602
47	Rhode Island	555
32	South Carolina	733
37	South Dakota	646
49	Tennessee	504
26	Texas	772
5	Utah	1,083
3	Vermont	1,119
19	Virginia	852
21	Washington	848
28	West Virginia	770
14	Wisconsin	883
1	Wyoming	1,194

RANK ORDER

RANK	STATE	PER CAPITA
1	Wyoming	$1,194
2	North Dakota	1,190
3	Vermont	1,119
4	Delaware	1,101
5	Utah	1,083
6	Iowa	1,032
7	New Mexico	1,005
8	Alaska	1,001
9	Alabama	991
10	Michigan	945
11	Nebraska	932
12	North Carolina	928
13	Kansas	903
14	Wisconsin	883
15	Montana	864
15	Oregon	864
17	Mississippi	862
18	Oklahoma	856
19	Maryland	852
19	Virginia	852
21	Washington	848
22	Hawaii	846
23	California	807
24	Kentucky	800
25	Minnesota	793
26	Colorado	772
26	Texas	772
28	West Virginia	770
29	Indiana	765
30	Louisiana	762
31	Arkansas	754
32	South Carolina	733
33	Idaho	714
34	Ohio	678
35	Connecticut	655
36	Arizona	654
37	South Dakota	646
38	Illinois	645
39	Missouri	635
40	New Hampshire	618
41	New Jersey	608
42	Pennsylvania	602
43	New York	594
44	Maine	577
44	Massachusetts	577
46	Georgia	567
47	Rhode Island	555
48	Nevada	544
49	Tennessee	504
50	Florida	457

District of Columbia	218

Source: CQ Press using data from U.S. Bureau of the Census, Governments Division
   "2008 State and Local Government Finances" (http://www.census.gov/govs/estimate/index.html)
*Direct general expenditures. Includes capital outlays.

Expenditures for Higher Education as a Percent
of All State and Local Government Expenditures in 2008
National Percent = 9.3%*

ALPHA ORDER

RANK	STATE	PERCENT
3	Alabama	14.2
49	Alaska	6.0
28	Arizona	9.8
9	Arkansas	12.1
36	California	8.8
24	Colorado	10.7
43	Connecticut	7.5
12	Delaware	12.0
48	Florida	6.1
38	Georgia	8.4
33	Hawaii	9.3
22	Idaho	11.2
37	Illinois	8.6
23	Indiana	11.0
5	Iowa	13.4
9	Kansas	12.1
14	Kentucky	11.6
40	Louisiana	8.2
44	Maine	7.4
25	Maryland	10.5
45	Massachusetts	6.7
6	Michigan	13.1
31	Minnesota	9.4
20	Mississippi	11.3
30	Missouri	9.6
18	Montana	11.5
9	Nebraska	12.1
42	Nevada	7.8
34	New Hampshire	9.1
45	New Jersey	6.7
14	New Mexico	11.6
50	New York	5.4
4	North Carolina	13.5
2	North Dakota	14.9
35	Ohio	9.0
7	Oklahoma	13.0
14	Oregon	11.6
41	Pennsylvania	8.0
47	Rhode Island	6.5
28	South Carolina	9.8
27	South Dakota	9.9
39	Tennessee	8.3
18	Texas	11.5
1	Utah	15.8
8	Vermont	12.8
14	Virginia	11.6
26	Washington	10.4
20	West Virginia	11.3
13	Wisconsin	11.7
31	Wyoming	9.4

RANK ORDER

RANK	STATE	PERCENT
1	Utah	15.8
2	North Dakota	14.9
3	Alabama	14.2
4	North Carolina	13.5
5	Iowa	13.4
6	Michigan	13.1
7	Oklahoma	13.0
8	Vermont	12.8
9	Arkansas	12.1
9	Kansas	12.1
9	Nebraska	12.1
12	Delaware	12.0
13	Wisconsin	11.7
14	Kentucky	11.6
14	New Mexico	11.6
14	Oregon	11.6
14	Virginia	11.6
18	Montana	11.5
18	Texas	11.5
20	Mississippi	11.3
20	West Virginia	11.3
22	Idaho	11.2
23	Indiana	11.0
24	Colorado	10.7
25	Maryland	10.5
26	Washington	10.4
27	South Dakota	9.9
28	Arizona	9.8
28	South Carolina	9.8
30	Missouri	9.6
31	Minnesota	9.4
31	Wyoming	9.4
33	Hawaii	9.3
34	New Hampshire	9.1
35	Ohio	9.0
36	California	8.8
37	Illinois	8.6
38	Georgia	8.4
39	Tennessee	8.3
40	Louisiana	8.2
41	Pennsylvania	8.0
42	Nevada	7.8
43	Connecticut	7.5
44	Maine	7.4
45	Massachusetts	6.7
45	New Jersey	6.7
47	Rhode Island	6.5
48	Florida	6.1
49	Alaska	6.0
50	New York	5.4

| | District of Columbia | 1.2 |

Source: CQ Press using data from U.S. Bureau of the Census, Governments Division
  "2008 State and Local Government Finances" (http://www.census.gov/govs/estimate/index.html)
*Direct general expenditures for higher education as a percent of all direct general expenditures. Includes capital outlays.

Average Faculty Salary at Institutions of Higher Education in 2009

National Average = $73,570*

ALPHA ORDER

RANK	STATE	AVERAGE SALARY
38	Alabama	$63,086
26	Alaska	68,104
13	Arizona	75,466
49	Arkansas	54,600
4	California	87,736
24	Colorado	68,753
2	Connecticut	90,314
5	Delaware	85,476
27	Florida	68,068
32	Georgia	67,190
10	Hawaii	78,957
44	Idaho	57,786
14	Illinois	75,346
21	Indiana	69,408
29	Iowa	67,526
39	Kansas	62,666
42	Kentucky	60,003
37	Louisiana	63,098
18	Maine	70,138
15	Maryland	73,023
1	Massachusetts	91,612
12	Michigan	77,147
19	Minnesota	70,044
48	Mississippi	55,302
33	Missouri	66,082
46	Montana	56,689
35	Nebraska	64,340
9	Nevada	79,794
8	New Hampshire	80,335
3	New Jersey	89,013
40	New Mexico	61,853
6	New York	82,642
30	North Carolina	67,498
50	North Dakota	54,551
22	Ohio	69,235
41	Oklahoma	61,106
34	Oregon	64,928
11	Pennsylvania	77,822
7	Rhode Island	82,332
43	South Carolina	59,920
47	South Dakota	55,667
36	Tennessee	63,167
23	Texas	69,131
17	Utah	71,309
20	Vermont	69,851
16	Virginia	71,924
31	Washington	67,287
45	West Virginia	57,440
25	Wisconsin	68,531
28	Wyoming	68,020

RANK ORDER

RANK	STATE	AVERAGE SALARY
1	Massachusetts	$91,612
2	Connecticut	90,314
3	New Jersey	89,013
4	California	87,736
5	Delaware	85,476
6	New York	82,642
7	Rhode Island	82,332
8	New Hampshire	80,335
9	Nevada	79,794
10	Hawaii	78,957
11	Pennsylvania	77,822
12	Michigan	77,147
13	Arizona	75,466
14	Illinois	75,346
15	Maryland	73,023
16	Virginia	71,924
17	Utah	71,309
18	Maine	70,138
19	Minnesota	70,044
20	Vermont	69,851
21	Indiana	69,408
22	Ohio	69,235
23	Texas	69,131
24	Colorado	68,753
25	Wisconsin	68,531
26	Alaska	68,104
27	Florida	68,068
28	Wyoming	68,020
29	Iowa	67,526
30	North Carolina	67,498
31	Washington	67,287
32	Georgia	67,190
33	Missouri	66,082
34	Oregon	64,928
35	Nebraska	64,340
36	Tennessee	63,167
37	Louisiana	63,098
38	Alabama	63,086
39	Kansas	62,666
40	New Mexico	61,853
41	Oklahoma	61,106
42	Kentucky	60,003
43	South Carolina	59,920
44	Idaho	57,786
45	West Virginia	57,440
46	Montana	56,689
47	South Dakota	55,667
48	Mississippi	55,302
49	Arkansas	54,600
50	North Dakota	54,551
	District of Columbia	88,635

Source: U.S. Department of Education, National Center for Education Statistics
    "Digest of Education Statistics 2009" (NCES 2010-013, April 2010, http://nces.ed.gov/programs/digest/d09/)
*For 2008-2009 school year. For full-time instructional faculty on 9-month contracts at four-year and two-year public and private degree-granting institutions.

Average Student Costs at Public Institutions of Higher Education in 2009

National Average = $14,256*

ALPHA ORDER

RANK	STATE	AVERAGE COSTS
34	Alabama	$12,166
29	Alaska	12,970
24	Arizona	13,995
39	Arkansas	11,669
15	California	15,683
21	Colorado	14,240
6	Connecticut	17,364
8	Delaware	17,185
41	Florida	11,506
40	Georgia	11,540
26	Hawaii	13,434
48	Idaho	10,408
4	Illinois	18,213
18	Indiana	14,973
25	Iowa	13,831
37	Kansas	12,012
28	Kentucky	13,190
49	Louisiana	10,384
13	Maine	16,112
14	Maryland	16,111
9	Massachusetts	17,112
10	Michigan	17,039
17	Minnesota	15,105
46	Mississippi	11,047
23	Missouri	14,009
38	Montana	11,970
31	Nebraska	12,641
30	Nevada	12,869
3	New Hampshire	19,242
1	New Jersey	20,735
45	New Mexico	11,266
20	New York	14,865
44	North Carolina	11,333
42	North Dakota	11,418
11	Ohio	16,582
33	Oklahoma	12,333
16	Oregon	15,179
5	Pennsylvania	18,124
7	Rhode Island	17,266
12	South Carolina	16,136
43	South Dakota	11,373
36	Tennessee	12,026
27	Texas	13,222
50	Utah	10,352
2	Vermont	19,661
19	Virginia	14,868
22	Washington	14,165
35	West Virginia	12,131
32	Wisconsin	12,406
47	Wyoming	10,556

RANK ORDER

RANK	STATE	AVERAGE COSTS
1	New Jersey	$20,735
2	Vermont	19,661
3	New Hampshire	19,242
4	Illinois	18,213
5	Pennsylvania	18,124
6	Connecticut	17,364
7	Rhode Island	17,266
8	Delaware	17,185
9	Massachusetts	17,112
10	Michigan	17,039
11	Ohio	16,582
12	South Carolina	16,136
13	Maine	16,112
14	Maryland	16,111
15	California	15,683
16	Oregon	15,179
17	Minnesota	15,105
18	Indiana	14,973
19	Virginia	14,868
20	New York	14,865
21	Colorado	14,240
22	Washington	14,165
23	Missouri	14,009
24	Arizona	13,995
25	Iowa	13,831
26	Hawaii	13,434
27	Texas	13,222
28	Kentucky	13,190
29	Alaska	12,970
30	Nevada	12,869
31	Nebraska	12,641
32	Wisconsin	12,406
33	Oklahoma	12,333
34	Alabama	12,166
35	West Virginia	12,131
36	Tennessee	12,026
37	Kansas	12,012
38	Montana	11,970
39	Arkansas	11,669
40	Georgia	11,540
41	Florida	11,506
42	North Dakota	11,418
43	South Dakota	11,373
44	North Carolina	11,333
45	New Mexico	11,266
46	Mississippi	11,047
47	Wyoming	10,556
48	Idaho	10,408
49	Louisiana	10,384
50	Utah	10,352
	District of Columbia**	NA

Source: U.S. Department of Education, National Center for Education Statistics
   "Digest of Education Statistics 2009" (NCES 2010-013, April 2010, http://nces.ed.gov/programs/digest/d09/)
*Data for 2008-2009 school year. Based on average in-state tuition, room and board, and fees for full-time students in public
four-year institutions for an entire academic year.
**Not available.

Average Student Costs at Private Institutions of Higher Education in 2009

National Average = $31,704*

ALPHA ORDER

RANK	STATE	AVERAGE COSTS
40	Alabama	$22,444
24	Alaska	28,837
41	Arizona	21,813
44	Arkansas	21,053
8	California	37,017
22	Colorado	29,331
2	Connecticut	42,268
43	Delaware	21,454
25	Florida	28,185
20	Georgia	30,594
37	Hawaii	22,957
49	Idaho	11,724
14	Illinois	32,359
18	Indiana	31,310
32	Iowa	25,280
34	Kansas	23,842
36	Kentucky	23,691
15	Louisiana	32,013
11	Maine	34,784
5	Maryland	38,453
1	Massachusetts	43,522
39	Michigan	22,862
16	Minnesota	31,706
46	Mississippi	19,358
28	Missouri	26,509
38	Montana	22,884
35	Nebraska	23,722
29	Nevada	25,897
9	New Hampshire	36,786
7	New Jersey	37,156
30	New Mexico	25,458
4	New York	38,488
19	North Carolina	30,963
47	North Dakota	15,614
17	Ohio	31,611
33	Oklahoma	24,762
12	Oregon	33,763
6	Pennsylvania	37,964
3	Rhode Island	39,072
31	South Carolina	25,336
42	South Dakota	21,697
26	Tennessee	27,364
23	Texas	29,228
48	Utah	13,482
10	Vermont	36,101
27	Virginia	27,280
13	Washington	33,455
45	West Virginia	19,859
21	Wisconsin	30,001
NA	Wyoming**	NA

RANK ORDER

RANK	STATE	AVERAGE COSTS
1	Massachusetts	$43,522
2	Connecticut	42,268
3	Rhode Island	39,072
4	New York	38,488
5	Maryland	38,453
6	Pennsylvania	37,964
7	New Jersey	37,156
8	California	37,017
9	New Hampshire	36,786
10	Vermont	36,101
11	Maine	34,784
12	Oregon	33,763
13	Washington	33,455
14	Illinois	32,359
15	Louisiana	32,013
16	Minnesota	31,706
17	Ohio	31,611
18	Indiana	31,310
19	North Carolina	30,963
20	Georgia	30,594
21	Wisconsin	30,001
22	Colorado	29,331
23	Texas	29,228
24	Alaska	28,837
25	Florida	28,185
26	Tennessee	27,364
27	Virginia	27,280
28	Missouri	26,509
29	Nevada	25,897
30	New Mexico	25,458
31	South Carolina	25,336
32	Iowa	25,280
33	Oklahoma	24,762
34	Kansas	23,842
35	Nebraska	23,722
36	Kentucky	23,691
37	Hawaii	22,957
38	Montana	22,884
39	Michigan	22,862
40	Alabama	22,444
41	Arizona	21,813
42	South Dakota	21,697
43	Delaware	21,454
44	Arkansas	21,053
45	West Virginia	19,859
46	Mississippi	19,358
47	North Dakota	15,614
48	Utah	13,482
49	Idaho	11,724
NA	Wyoming**	NA
	District of Columbia	37,554

Source: U.S. Department of Education, National Center for Education Statistics
    "Digest of Education Statistics 2009" (NCES 2010-013, April 2010, http://nces.ed.gov/programs/digest/d09/)
*Data for 2008-2009 school year. Based on average in-state tuition, room and board, and fees for full-time students in private four-year institutions for an entire academic year.
**Not available.

Institutions of Higher Education in 2009

National Total = 4,409 Institutions*

ALPHA ORDER

RANK	STATE	INSTITUTIONS	% of USA
23	Alabama	72	1.6%
50	Alaska	7	0.2%
20	Arizona	75	1.7%
31	Arkansas	50	1.1%
1	California	426	9.7%
18	Colorado	80	1.8%
32	Connecticut	46	1.0%
49	Delaware	10	0.2%
6	Florida	188	4.3%
8	Georgia	135	3.1%
44	Hawaii	21	0.5%
46	Idaho	14	0.3%
7	Illinois	180	4.1%
14	Indiana	107	2.4%
25	Iowa	66	1.5%
25	Kansas	66	1.5%
22	Kentucky	73	1.7%
17	Louisiana	85	1.9%
38	Maine	30	0.7%
30	Maryland	57	1.3%
11	Massachusetts	124	2.8%
15	Michigan	106	2.4%
12	Minnesota	114	2.6%
36	Mississippi	40	0.9%
10	Missouri	131	3.0%
42	Montana	23	0.5%
34	Nebraska	42	1.0%
44	Nevada	21	0.5%
39	New Hampshire	28	0.6%
27	New Jersey	63	1.4%
34	New Mexico	42	1.0%
2	New York	307	7.0%
9	North Carolina	133	3.0%
43	North Dakota	22	0.5%
5	Ohio	209	4.7%
29	Oklahoma	59	1.3%
28	Oregon	60	1.4%
3	Pennsylvania	262	5.9%
47	Rhode Island	13	0.3%
24	South Carolina	69	1.6%
41	South Dakota	24	0.5%
16	Tennessee	105	2.4%
4	Texas	218	4.9%
37	Utah	38	0.9%
40	Vermont	25	0.6%
12	Virginia	114	2.6%
19	Washington	78	1.8%
33	West Virginia	44	1.0%
20	Wisconsin	75	1.7%
48	Wyoming	11	0.2%

RANK ORDER

RANK	STATE	INSTITUTIONS	% of USA
1	California	426	9.7%
2	New York	307	7.0%
3	Pennsylvania	262	5.9%
4	Texas	218	4.9%
5	Ohio	209	4.7%
6	Florida	188	4.3%
7	Illinois	180	4.1%
8	Georgia	135	3.1%
9	North Carolina	133	3.0%
10	Missouri	131	3.0%
11	Massachusetts	124	2.8%
12	Minnesota	114	2.6%
12	Virginia	114	2.6%
14	Indiana	107	2.4%
15	Michigan	106	2.4%
16	Tennessee	105	2.4%
17	Louisiana	85	1.9%
18	Colorado	80	1.8%
19	Washington	78	1.8%
20	Arizona	75	1.7%
20	Wisconsin	75	1.7%
22	Kentucky	73	1.7%
23	Alabama	72	1.6%
24	South Carolina	69	1.6%
25	Iowa	66	1.5%
25	Kansas	66	1.5%
27	New Jersey	63	1.4%
28	Oregon	60	1.4%
29	Oklahoma	59	1.3%
30	Maryland	57	1.3%
31	Arkansas	50	1.1%
32	Connecticut	46	1.0%
33	West Virginia	44	1.0%
34	Nebraska	42	1.0%
34	New Mexico	42	1.0%
36	Mississippi	40	0.9%
37	Utah	38	0.9%
38	Maine	30	0.7%
39	New Hampshire	28	0.6%
40	Vermont	25	0.6%
41	South Dakota	24	0.5%
42	Montana	23	0.5%
43	North Dakota	22	0.5%
44	Hawaii	21	0.5%
44	Nevada	21	0.5%
46	Idaho	14	0.3%
47	Rhode Island	13	0.3%
48	Wyoming	11	0.2%
49	Delaware	10	0.2%
50	Alaska	7	0.2%
	District of Columbia	16	0.4%

Source: U.S. Department of Education, National Center for Education Statistics
    "Digest of Education Statistics 2009" (NCES 2010-013, April 2010, http://nces.ed.gov/programs/digest/d09/)
*For 2008-2009 school year. Consists of 2,719 four-year and 1,690 two-year public and private degree-granting institutions.
Includes five U.S. Service Schools not shown by state.

Enrollment in Institutions of Higher Education in 2007

National Total = 18,248,128 Students*

ALPHA ORDER

RANK	STATE	ENROLLMENT	% of USA
23	Alabama	268,183	1.5%
50	Alaska	30,616	0.2%
9	Arizona	624,147	3.4%
34	Arkansas	152,168	0.8%
1	California	2,529,522	13.9%
21	Colorado	310,637	1.7%
32	Connecticut	179,005	1.0%
44	Delaware	52,343	0.3%
4	Florida	913,793	5.0%
13	Georgia	453,711	2.5%
43	Hawaii	66,601	0.4%
40	Idaho	78,846	0.4%
5	Illinois	837,018	4.6%
17	Indiana	380,477	2.1%
25	Iowa	256,259	1.4%
31	Kansas	194,102	1.1%
24	Kentucky	258,213	1.4%
26	Louisiana	224,754	1.2%
42	Maine	67,173	0.4%
20	Maryland	327,597	1.8%
12	Massachusetts	463,366	2.5%
7	Michigan	643,279	3.5%
15	Minnesota	392,393	2.2%
33	Mississippi	155,232	0.9%
16	Missouri	384,366	2.1%
47	Montana	47,371	0.3%
36	Nebraska	127,378	0.7%
38	Nevada	116,276	0.6%
41	New Hampshire	70,724	0.4%
14	New Jersey	398,136	2.2%
35	New Mexico	134,375	0.7%
3	New York	1,172,811	6.4%
10	North Carolina	502,330	2.8%
45	North Dakota	49,945	0.3%
8	Ohio	630,497	3.5%
28	Oklahoma	206,382	1.1%
30	Oregon	202,928	1.1%
6	Pennsylvania	725,397	4.0%
39	Rhode Island	82,900	0.5%
27	South Carolina	217,755	1.2%
46	South Dakota	49,747	0.3%
22	Tennessee	297,785	1.6%
2	Texas	1,269,098	7.0%
29	Utah	203,679	1.1%
48	Vermont	42,191	0.2%
11	Virginia	478,268	2.6%
18	Washington	352,075	1.9%
37	West Virginia	116,848	0.6%
19	Wisconsin	343,747	1.9%
49	Wyoming	35,246	0.2%

RANK ORDER

RANK	STATE	ENROLLMENT	% of USA
1	California	2,529,522	13.9%
2	Texas	1,269,098	7.0%
3	New York	1,172,811	6.4%
4	Florida	913,793	5.0%
5	Illinois	837,018	4.6%
6	Pennsylvania	725,397	4.0%
7	Michigan	643,279	3.5%
8	Ohio	630,497	3.5%
9	Arizona	624,147	3.4%
10	North Carolina	502,330	2.8%
11	Virginia	478,268	2.6%
12	Massachusetts	463,366	2.5%
13	Georgia	453,711	2.5%
14	New Jersey	398,136	2.2%
15	Minnesota	392,393	2.2%
16	Missouri	384,366	2.1%
17	Indiana	380,477	2.1%
18	Washington	352,075	1.9%
19	Wisconsin	343,747	1.9%
20	Maryland	327,597	1.8%
21	Colorado	310,637	1.7%
22	Tennessee	297,785	1.6%
23	Alabama	268,183	1.5%
24	Kentucky	258,213	1.4%
25	Iowa	256,259	1.4%
26	Louisiana	224,754	1.2%
27	South Carolina	217,755	1.2%
28	Oklahoma	206,382	1.1%
29	Utah	203,679	1.1%
30	Oregon	202,928	1.1%
31	Kansas	194,102	1.1%
32	Connecticut	179,005	1.0%
33	Mississippi	155,232	0.9%
34	Arkansas	152,168	0.8%
35	New Mexico	134,375	0.7%
36	Nebraska	127,378	0.7%
37	West Virginia	116,848	0.6%
38	Nevada	116,276	0.6%
39	Rhode Island	82,900	0.5%
40	Idaho	78,846	0.4%
41	New Hampshire	70,724	0.4%
42	Maine	67,173	0.4%
43	Hawaii	66,601	0.4%
44	Delaware	52,343	0.3%
45	North Dakota	49,945	0.3%
46	South Dakota	49,747	0.3%
47	Montana	47,371	0.3%
48	Vermont	42,191	0.2%
49	Wyoming	35,246	0.2%
50	Alaska	30,616	0.2%
	District of Columbia	115,153	0.6%

Source: U.S. Department of Education, National Center for Education Statistics
"Digest of Education Statistics 2009" (NCES 2010-013, April 2010, http://nces.ed.gov/programs/digest/d09/)
*Fall 2007 enrollment. Includes full-time and part-time students at Title IV eligible, degree-granting four-year and two-year institutions. National total includes 15,285 students at U.S. Service Schools not shown by state.

Enrollment Rate in Institutions of Higher Education in 2007

National Rate = 619 Students per 1,000 Population 18 to 24 Years Old*

ALPHA ORDER

RANK	STATE	RATE
27	Alabama	600
50	Alaska	418
1	Arizona	1,056
35	Arkansas	577
15	California	660
10	Colorado	675
37	Connecticut	555
22	Delaware	617
36	Florida	573
48	Georgia	502
40	Hawaii	540
42	Idaho	536
17	Illinois	648
18	Indiana	629
2	Iowa	839
12	Kansas	669
11	Kentucky	673
49	Louisiana	482
29	Maine	598
23	Maryland	607
6	Massachusetts	723
14	Michigan	661
3	Minnesota	773
45	Mississippi	513
8	Missouri	688
47	Montana	503
9	Nebraska	682
39	Nevada	553
30	New Hampshire	594
44	New Jersey	520
16	New Mexico	656
30	New York	594
33	North Carolina	587
28	North Dakota	599
34	Ohio	586
37	Oklahoma	555
26	Oregon	604
24	Pennsylvania	606
5	Rhode Island	724
46	South Carolina	505
25	South Dakota	605
40	Tennessee	540
43	Texas	522
21	Utah	622
7	Vermont	689
19	Virginia	628
32	Washington	589
4	West Virginia	734
20	Wisconsin	625
13	Wyoming	666

RANK ORDER

RANK	STATE	RATE
1	Arizona	1,056
2	Iowa	839
3	Minnesota	773
4	West Virginia	734
5	Rhode Island	724
6	Massachusetts	723
7	Vermont	689
8	Missouri	688
9	Nebraska	682
10	Colorado	675
11	Kentucky	673
12	Kansas	669
13	Wyoming	666
14	Michigan	661
15	California	660
16	New Mexico	656
17	Illinois	648
18	Indiana	629
19	Virginia	628
20	Wisconsin	625
21	Utah	622
22	Delaware	617
23	Maryland	607
24	Pennsylvania	606
25	South Dakota	605
26	Oregon	604
27	Alabama	600
28	North Dakota	599
29	Maine	598
30	New Hampshire	594
30	New York	594
32	Washington	589
33	North Carolina	587
34	Ohio	586
35	Arkansas	577
36	Florida	573
37	Connecticut	555
37	Oklahoma	555
39	Nevada	553
40	Hawaii	540
40	Tennessee	540
42	Idaho	536
43	Texas	522
44	New Jersey	520
45	Mississippi	513
46	South Carolina	505
47	Montana	503
48	Georgia	502
49	Louisiana	482
50	Alaska	418

District of Columbia   1,562

Source: CQ Press using data from U.S. Department of Education, National Center for Education Statistics
   "Digest of Education Statistics 2009" (NCES 2010-013, April 2010, http://nces.ed.gov/programs/digest/d09/)
*Based on fall 2007 enrollment and population. National rate includes U.S. Service Schools. Includes students at four-year and two-year public and private degree-granting institutions. Enrollment based on location of institution. Population based on residence.

Enrollment in Public Institutions of Higher Education in 2007

National Total = 13,490,780 Students*

ALPHA ORDER

RANK	STATE	ENROLLMENT	% of USA
19	Alabama	237,632	1.8%
49	Alaska	29,381	0.2%
12	Arizona	332,154	2.5%
33	Arkansas	135,525	1.0%
1	California	2,136,087	15.8%
20	Colorado	227,984	1.7%
35	Connecticut	114,072	0.8%
46	Delaware	39,092	0.3%
3	Florida	683,328	5.1%
11	Georgia	359,883	2.7%
40	Hawaii	50,454	0.4%
39	Idaho	60,526	0.4%
5	Illinois	550,940	4.1%
15	Indiana	278,951	2.1%
30	Iowa	154,644	1.1%
28	Kansas	170,054	1.3%
22	Kentucky	211,234	1.6%
25	Louisiana	193,316	1.4%
41	Maine	48,357	0.4%
17	Maryland	269,719	2.0%
24	Massachusetts	198,700	1.5%
6	Michigan	519,449	3.9%
18	Minnesota	250,397	1.9%
32	Mississippi	139,931	1.0%
21	Missouri	223,155	1.7%
43	Montana	42,857	0.3%
37	Nebraska	96,680	0.7%
36	Nevada	104,797	0.8%
44	New Hampshire	41,982	0.3%
13	New Jersey	318,296	2.4%
34	New Mexico	124,773	0.9%
4	New York	652,428	4.8%
8	North Carolina	410,746	3.0%
42	North Dakota	43,016	0.3%
7	Ohio	460,240	3.4%
27	Oklahoma	177,643	1.3%
29	Oregon	165,260	1.2%
9	Pennsylvania	396,774	2.9%
45	Rhode Island	41,503	0.3%
26	South Carolina	180,479	1.3%
47	South Dakota	38,917	0.3%
23	Tennessee	208,524	1.5%
2	Texas	1,109,666	8.2%
31	Utah	147,982	1.1%
50	Vermont	24,829	0.2%
10	Virginia	370,486	2.7%
14	Washington	301,793	2.2%
38	West Virginia	87,838	0.7%
16	Wisconsin	273,708	2.0%
48	Wyoming	33,705	0.2%

RANK ORDER

RANK	STATE	ENROLLMENT	% of USA
1	California	2,136,087	15.8%
2	Texas	1,109,666	8.2%
3	Florida	683,328	5.1%
4	New York	652,428	4.8%
5	Illinois	550,940	4.1%
6	Michigan	519,449	3.9%
7	Ohio	460,240	3.4%
8	North Carolina	410,746	3.0%
9	Pennsylvania	396,774	2.9%
10	Virginia	370,486	2.7%
11	Georgia	359,883	2.7%
12	Arizona	332,154	2.5%
13	New Jersey	318,296	2.4%
14	Washington	301,793	2.2%
15	Indiana	278,951	2.1%
16	Wisconsin	273,708	2.0%
17	Maryland	269,719	2.0%
18	Minnesota	250,397	1.9%
19	Alabama	237,632	1.8%
20	Colorado	227,984	1.7%
21	Missouri	223,155	1.7%
22	Kentucky	211,234	1.6%
23	Tennessee	208,524	1.5%
24	Massachusetts	198,700	1.5%
25	Louisiana	193,316	1.4%
26	South Carolina	180,479	1.3%
27	Oklahoma	177,643	1.3%
28	Kansas	170,054	1.3%
29	Oregon	165,260	1.2%
30	Iowa	154,644	1.1%
31	Utah	147,982	1.1%
32	Mississippi	139,931	1.0%
33	Arkansas	135,525	1.0%
34	New Mexico	124,773	0.9%
35	Connecticut	114,072	0.8%
36	Nevada	104,797	0.8%
37	Nebraska	96,680	0.7%
38	West Virginia	87,838	0.7%
39	Idaho	60,526	0.4%
40	Hawaii	50,454	0.4%
41	Maine	48,357	0.4%
42	North Dakota	43,016	0.3%
43	Montana	42,857	0.3%
44	New Hampshire	41,982	0.3%
45	Rhode Island	41,503	0.3%
46	Delaware	39,092	0.3%
47	South Dakota	38,917	0.3%
48	Wyoming	33,705	0.2%
49	Alaska	29,381	0.2%
50	Vermont	24,829	0.2%
	District of Columbia	5,608	0.0%

Source: U.S. Department of Education, National Center for Education Statistics
    "Digest of Education Statistics 2009" (NCES 2010-013, April 2010, http://nces.ed.gov/programs/digest/d09/)
*Fall 2007 enrollment. Includes full-time and part-time students at Title IV eligible, degree-granting four-year and two-year institutions. National total includes 15,285 students at U.S. Service Schools not shown by state.

Enrollment in Private Institutions of Higher Education in 2007

National Total = 4,757,348 Students*

ALPHA ORDER

RANK	STATE	ENROLLMENT	% of USA
32	Alabama	30,551	0.6%
50	Alaska	1,235	0.0%
4	Arizona	291,993	6.1%
40	Arkansas	16,643	0.3%
2	California	393,435	8.3%
19	Colorado	82,653	1.7%
22	Connecticut	64,933	1.4%
43	Delaware	13,251	0.3%
7	Florida	230,465	4.8%
16	Georgia	93,828	2.0%
41	Hawaii	16,147	0.3%
38	Idaho	18,320	0.4%
5	Illinois	286,078	6.0%
15	Indiana	101,526	2.1%
14	Iowa	101,615	2.1%
36	Kansas	24,048	0.5%
26	Kentucky	46,979	1.0%
30	Louisiana	31,438	0.7%
37	Maine	18,816	0.4%
23	Maryland	57,878	1.2%
6	Massachusetts	264,666	5.6%
12	Michigan	123,830	2.6%
11	Minnesota	141,996	3.0%
42	Mississippi	15,301	0.3%
9	Missouri	161,211	3.4%
48	Montana	4,514	0.1%
31	Nebraska	30,698	0.6%
44	Nevada	11,479	0.2%
34	New Hampshire	28,742	0.6%
20	New Jersey	79,840	1.7%
46	New Mexico	9,602	0.2%
1	New York	520,383	10.9%
17	North Carolina	91,584	1.9%
47	North Dakota	6,929	0.1%
8	Ohio	170,257	3.6%
35	Oklahoma	28,739	0.6%
28	Oregon	37,668	0.8%
3	Pennsylvania	328,623	6.9%
27	Rhode Island	41,397	0.9%
29	South Carolina	37,276	0.8%
45	South Dakota	10,830	0.2%
18	Tennessee	89,261	1.9%
10	Texas	159,432	3.4%
24	Utah	55,697	1.2%
39	Vermont	17,362	0.4%
13	Virginia	107,782	2.3%
25	Washington	50,282	1.1%
33	West Virginia	29,010	0.6%
21	Wisconsin	70,039	1.5%
49	Wyoming	1,541	0.0%

RANK ORDER

RANK	STATE	ENROLLMENT	% of USA
1	New York	520,383	10.9%
2	California	393,435	8.3%
3	Pennsylvania	328,623	6.9%
4	Arizona	291,993	6.1%
5	Illinois	286,078	6.0%
6	Massachusetts	264,666	5.6%
7	Florida	230,465	4.8%
8	Ohio	170,257	3.6%
9	Missouri	161,211	3.4%
10	Texas	159,432	3.4%
11	Minnesota	141,996	3.0%
12	Michigan	123,830	2.6%
13	Virginia	107,782	2.3%
14	Iowa	101,615	2.1%
15	Indiana	101,526	2.1%
16	Georgia	93,828	2.0%
17	North Carolina	91,584	1.9%
18	Tennessee	89,261	1.9%
19	Colorado	82,653	1.7%
20	New Jersey	79,840	1.7%
21	Wisconsin	70,039	1.5%
22	Connecticut	64,933	1.4%
23	Maryland	57,878	1.2%
24	Utah	55,697	1.2%
25	Washington	50,282	1.1%
26	Kentucky	46,979	1.0%
27	Rhode Island	41,397	0.9%
28	Oregon	37,668	0.8%
29	South Carolina	37,276	0.8%
30	Louisiana	31,438	0.7%
31	Nebraska	30,698	0.6%
32	Alabama	30,551	0.6%
33	West Virginia	29,010	0.6%
34	New Hampshire	28,742	0.6%
35	Oklahoma	28,739	0.6%
36	Kansas	24,048	0.5%
37	Maine	18,816	0.4%
38	Idaho	18,320	0.4%
39	Vermont	17,362	0.4%
40	Arkansas	16,643	0.3%
41	Hawaii	16,147	0.3%
42	Mississippi	15,301	0.3%
43	Delaware	13,251	0.3%
44	Nevada	11,479	0.2%
45	South Dakota	10,830	0.2%
46	New Mexico	9,602	0.2%
47	North Dakota	6,929	0.1%
48	Montana	4,514	0.1%
49	Wyoming	1,541	0.0%
50	Alaska	1,235	0.0%
	District of Columbia	109,545	2.3%

Source: U.S. Department of Education, National Center for Education Statistics
    "Digest of Education Statistics 2009" (NCES 2010-013, April 2010, http://nces.ed.gov/programs/digest/d09/)
*Fall 2007 enrollment. Includes full-time and part-time students at Title IV eligible, degree-granting four-year and two-year institutions.

Percent of Population with a Bachelor's Degree or More in 2009

National Percent = 27.9%*

ALPHA ORDER

ALPHA ORDER

RANK	STATE	PERCENT
44	Alabama	22.0
24	Alaska	26.6
29	Arizona	25.6
49	Arkansas	18.9
14	California	29.9
2	Colorado	35.9
4	Connecticut	35.6
18	Delaware	28.7
31	Florida	25.3
20	Georgia	27.5
15	Hawaii	29.6
39	Idaho	23.9
12	Illinois	30.6
43	Indiana	22.5
34	Iowa	25.1
16	Kansas	29.5
47	Kentucky	21.0
46	Louisiana	21.4
23	Maine	26.9
3	Maryland	35.7
1	Massachusetts	38.2
36	Michigan	24.6
10	Minnesota	31.5
48	Mississippi	19.6
33	Missouri	25.2
21	Montana	27.4
21	Nebraska	27.4
45	Nevada	21.8
9	New Hampshire	32.0
5	New Jersey	34.5
31	New Mexico	25.3
8	New York	32.4
25	North Carolina	26.5
27	North Dakota	25.8
38	Ohio	24.1
42	Oklahoma	22.7
17	Oregon	29.2
26	Pennsylvania	26.4
13	Rhode Island	30.5
37	South Carolina	24.3
34	South Dakota	25.1
41	Tennessee	23.0
30	Texas	25.5
19	Utah	28.5
7	Vermont	33.1
6	Virginia	34.0
11	Washington	31.0
50	West Virginia	17.3
28	Wisconsin	25.7
40	Wyoming	23.8

RANK ORDER

RANK	STATE	PERCENT
1	Massachusetts	38.2
2	Colorado	35.9
3	Maryland	35.7
4	Connecticut	35.6
5	New Jersey	34.5
6	Virginia	34.0
7	Vermont	33.1
8	New York	32.4
9	New Hampshire	32.0
10	Minnesota	31.5
11	Washington	31.0
12	Illinois	30.6
13	Rhode Island	30.5
14	California	29.9
15	Hawaii	29.6
16	Kansas	29.5
17	Oregon	29.2
18	Delaware	28.7
19	Utah	28.5
20	Georgia	27.5
21	Montana	27.4
21	Nebraska	27.4
23	Maine	26.9
24	Alaska	26.6
25	North Carolina	26.5
26	Pennsylvania	26.4
27	North Dakota	25.8
28	Wisconsin	25.7
29	Arizona	25.6
30	Texas	25.5
31	Florida	25.3
31	New Mexico	25.3
33	Missouri	25.2
34	Iowa	25.1
34	South Dakota	25.1
36	Michigan	24.6
37	South Carolina	24.3
38	Ohio	24.1
39	Idaho	23.9
40	Wyoming	23.8
41	Tennessee	23.0
42	Oklahoma	22.7
43	Indiana	22.5
44	Alabama	22.0
45	Nevada	21.8
46	Louisiana	21.4
47	Kentucky	21.0
48	Mississippi	19.6
49	Arkansas	18.9
50	West Virginia	17.3

District of Columbia 48.5

Source: U.S. Bureau of the Census, American Community Survey
"2009 American Community Survey" (http://www.census.gov/acs/www/index.html)
*Persons age 25 and older.

Percent of Population Who Have Completed an Advanced Degree: 2009

National Percent = 10.3%*

ALPHA ORDER

ALPHA ORDER

RANK ORDER

RANK	STATE	PERCENT		RANK	STATE	PERCENT
40	Alabama	7.7		1	Massachusetts	16.4
27	Alaska	9.0		2	Maryland	16.0
25	Arizona	9.3		3	Connecticut	15.5
50	Arkansas	6.1		4	Virginia	14.1
14	California	10.7		5	New York	14.0
8	Colorado	12.7		6	Vermont	13.3
3	Connecticut	15.5		7	New Jersey	12.9
11	Delaware	11.4		8	Colorado	12.7
27	Florida	9.0		9	Illinois	11.7
20	Georgia	9.9		9	Rhode Island	11.7
20	Hawaii	9.9		11	Delaware	11.4
42	Idaho	7.5		12	New Hampshire	11.2
9	Illinois	11.7		13	Washington	11.1
37	Indiana	8.1		14	California	10.7
43	Iowa	7.4		15	New Mexico	10.4
18	Kansas	10.2		15	Oregon	10.4
32	Kentucky	8.5		17	Minnesota	10.3
47	Louisiana	6.9		18	Kansas	10.2
22	Maine	9.6		18	Pennsylvania	10.2
2	Maryland	16.0		20	Georgia	9.9
1	Massachusetts	16.4		20	Hawaii	9.9
24	Michigan	9.4		22	Maine	9.6
17	Minnesota	10.3		23	Missouri	9.5
46	Mississippi	7.1		24	Michigan	9.4
23	Missouri	9.5		25	Arizona	9.3
36	Montana	8.3		26	Utah	9.1
29	Nebraska	8.8		27	Alaska	9.0
41	Nevada	7.6		27	Florida	9.0
12	New Hampshire	11.2		29	Nebraska	8.8
7	New Jersey	12.9		29	North Carolina	8.8
15	New Mexico	10.4		29	Ohio	8.8
5	New York	14.0		32	Kentucky	8.5
29	North Carolina	8.8		32	Texas	8.5
48	North Dakota	6.7		34	South Carolina	8.4
29	Ohio	8.8		34	Wisconsin	8.4
43	Oklahoma	7.4		36	Montana	8.3
15	Oregon	10.4		37	Indiana	8.1
18	Pennsylvania	10.2		38	Tennessee	7.9
9	Rhode Island	11.7		38	Wyoming	7.9
34	South Carolina	8.4		40	Alabama	7.7
45	South Dakota	7.3		41	Nevada	7.6
38	Tennessee	7.9		42	Idaho	7.5
32	Texas	8.5		43	Iowa	7.4
26	Utah	9.1		43	Oklahoma	7.4
6	Vermont	13.3		45	South Dakota	7.3
4	Virginia	14.1		46	Mississippi	7.1
13	Washington	11.1		47	Louisiana	6.9
48	West Virginia	6.7		48	North Dakota	6.7
34	Wisconsin	8.4		48	West Virginia	6.7
38	Wyoming	7.9		50	Arkansas	6.1
					District of Columbia	28.0

Source: U.S. Bureau of the Census, American Community Survey
   "2009 American Community Survey" (http://www.census.gov/acs/www/index.html)
*Persons age 25 and older who have earned a master's degree or higher.

Public Libraries and Branches in 2008

National Total = 16,671 Libraries and Branches*

ALPHA ORDER

RANK	STATE	LIBRARIES	% of USA
23	Alabama	288	1.7%
44	Alaska	102	0.6%
32	Arizona	207	1.2%
30	Arkansas	216	1.3%
1	California	1,117	6.7%
26	Colorado	250	1.5%
27	Connecticut	242	1.5%
50	Delaware	33	0.2%
9	Florida	518	3.1%
15	Georgia	387	2.3%
49	Hawaii	51	0.3%
40	Idaho	140	0.8%
4	Illinois	791	4.7%
13	Indiana	434	2.6%
8	Iowa	559	3.4%
16	Kansas	376	2.3%
34	Kentucky	196	1.2%
21	Louisiana	332	2.0%
25	Maine	278	1.7%
36	Maryland	183	1.1%
10	Massachusetts	474	2.8%
6	Michigan	657	3.9%
17	Minnesota	360	2.2%
28	Mississippi	237	1.4%
18	Missouri	359	2.2%
43	Montana	110	0.7%
24	Nebraska	287	1.7%
46	Nevada	85	0.5%
29	New Hampshire	236	1.4%
12	New Jersey	454	2.7%
41	New Mexico	118	0.7%
2	New York	1,069	6.4%
14	North Carolina	389	2.3%
45	North Dakota	90	0.5%
5	Ohio	725	4.3%
33	Oklahoma	206	1.2%
31	Oregon	212	1.3%
	Pennsylvania	629	3.8%
48	Rhode Island	72	0.4%
35	South Carolina	189	1.1%
39	South Dakota	150	0.9%
22	Tennessee	289	1.7%
3	Texas	864	5.2%
42	Utah	116	0.7%
36	Vermont	183	1.1%
19	Virginia	343	2.1%
20	Washington	334	2.0%
38	West Virginia	173	1.0%
11	Wisconsin	458	2.7%
47	Wyoming	76	0.5%

RANK ORDER

RANK	STATE	LIBRARIES	% of USA
1	California	1,117	6.7%
2	New York	1,069	6.4%
3	Texas	864	5.2%
4	Illinois	791	4.7%
5	Ohio	725	4.3%
6	Michigan	657	3.9%
7	Pennsylvania	629	3.8%
8	Iowa	559	3.4%
9	Florida	518	3.1%
10	Massachusetts	474	2.8%
11	Wisconsin	458	2.7%
12	New Jersey	454	2.7%
13	Indiana	434	2.6%
14	North Carolina	389	2.3%
15	Georgia	387	2.3%
16	Kansas	376	2.3%
17	Minnesota	360	2.2%
18	Missouri	359	2.2%
19	Virginia	343	2.1%
20	Washington	334	2.0%
21	Louisiana	332	2.0%
22	Tennessee	289	1.7%
23	Alabama	288	1.7%
24	Nebraska	287	1.7%
25	Maine	278	1.7%
26	Colorado	250	1.5%
27	Connecticut	242	1.5%
28	Mississippi	237	1.4%
29	New Hampshire	236	1.4%
30	Arkansas	216	1.3%
31	Oregon	212	1.3%
32	Arizona	207	1.2%
33	Oklahoma	206	1.2%
34	Kentucky	196	1.2%
35	South Carolina	189	1.1%
36	Maryland	183	1.1%
36	Vermont	183	1.1%
38	West Virginia	173	1.0%
39	South Dakota	150	0.9%
40	Idaho	140	0.8%
41	New Mexico	118	0.7%
42	Utah	116	0.7%
43	Montana	110	0.7%
44	Alaska	102	0.6%
45	North Dakota	90	0.5%
46	Nevada	85	0.5%
47	Wyoming	76	0.5%
48	Rhode Island	72	0.4%
49	Hawaii	51	0.3%
50	Delaware	33	0.2%
	District of Columbia	27	0.2%

Source: Institute of Museum and Library Services

"Public Library Survey Fiscal Year 2008" (June 2010, http://harvester.census.gov/imls/index.asp)

*For fiscal year 2008. Total of central and branch outlets. Does not include bookmobiles. There are 9,221 public libraries.

Rate of Public Libraries and Branches in 2008

National Average = 18,258 Population per Library*

ALPHA ORDER			RANK ORDER		
RANK	STATE	RATE	RANK	STATE	RATE
25	Alabama	16,241	1	Florida	35,567
44	Alaska	6,746	2	California	32,749
3	Arizona	31,398	3	Arizona	31,398
35	Arkansas	13,277	4	Maryland	30,922
2	California	32,749	5	Nevada	30,774
17	Colorado	19,741	6	Texas	28,130
32	Connecticut	14,475	7	Delaware	26,552
7	Delaware	26,552	8	Hawaii	25,245
1	Florida	35,567	9	Georgia	25,059
9	Georgia	25,059	10	South Carolina	23,827
8	Hawaii	25,245	11	North Carolina	23,772
38	Idaho	10,911	12	Utah	23,512
26	Illinois	16,236	13	Virginia	22,727
29	Indiana	14,720	14	Kentucky	21,877
48	Iowa	5,356	15	Tennessee	21,593
41	Kansas	7,440	16	Pennsylvania	19,978
14	Kentucky	21,877	17	Colorado	19,741
34	Louisiana	13,408	18	Washington	19,659
49	Maine	4,747	19	New Jersey	19,082
4	Maryland	30,922	20	New York	18,211
33	Massachusetts	13,805	21	Oregon	17,844
28	Michigan	15,224	22	Oklahoma	17,689
31	Minnesota	14,529	23	New Mexico	16,837
36	Mississippi	12,406	24	Missouri	16,591
24	Missouri	16,591	25	Alabama	16,241
40	Montana	8,800	26	Illinois	16,236
45	Nebraska	6,209	27	Ohio	15,901
5	Nevada	30,774	28	Michigan	15,224
46	New Hampshire	5,601	29	Indiana	14,720
19	New Jersey	19,082	30	Rhode Island	14,632
23	New Mexico	16,837	31	Minnesota	14,529
20	New York	18,211	32	Connecticut	14,475
11	North Carolina	23,772	33	Massachusetts	13,805
42	North Dakota	7,127	34	Louisiana	13,408
27	Ohio	15,901	35	Arkansas	13,277
22	Oklahoma	17,689	36	Mississippi	12,406
21	Oregon	17,844	37	Wisconsin	12,287
16	Pennsylvania	19,978	38	Idaho	10,911
30	Rhode Island	14,632	39	West Virginia	10,491
10	South Carolina	23,827	40	Montana	8,800
47	South Dakota	5,364	41	Kansas	7,440
15	Tennessee	21,593	42	North Dakota	7,127
6	Texas	28,130	43	Wyoming	7,013
12	Utah	23,512	44	Alaska	6,746
50	Vermont	3,394	45	Nebraska	6,209
13	Virginia	22,727	46	New Hampshire	5,601
18	Washington	19,659	47	South Dakota	5,364
39	West Virginia	10,491	48	Iowa	5,356
37	Wisconsin	12,287	49	Maine	4,747
43	Wyoming	7,013	50	Vermont	3,394

District of Columbia 21,855

Source: CQ Press using data from Institute of Museum and Library Services
"Public Library Survey Fiscal Year 2008" (June 2010, http://harvester.census.gov/imls/index.asp)
*For fiscal year 2008. Based on total of central and branch outlets. Does not include bookmobiles.

Rate of Books in Public Libraries in 2008

National Rate = 2,681 Books per 1,000 Population*

ALPHA ORDER

RANK	STATE	RATE
40	Alabama	2,056
16	Alaska	3,620
50	Arizona	1,326
37	Arkansas	2,249
41	California	2,028
32	Colorado	2,439
6	Connecticut	4,456
36	Delaware	2,272
47	Florida	1,777
49	Georgia	1,659
26	Hawaii	2,640
25	Idaho	2,744
18	Illinois	3,524
10	Indiana	4,050
8	Iowa	4,087
15	Kansas	3,711
42	Kentucky	2,023
27	Louisiana	2,615
2	Maine	4,929
28	Maryland	2,541
1	Massachusetts	4,999
20	Michigan	3,455
22	Minnesota	2,822
44	Mississippi	1,881
21	Missouri	3,028
22	Montana	2,822
14	Nebraska	3,728
39	Nevada	2,066
3	New Hampshire	4,698
19	New Jersey	3,502
35	New Mexico	2,304
12	New York	3,834
46	North Carolina	1,820
13	North Dakota	3,824
9	Ohio	4,068
43	Oklahoma	1,989
30	Oregon	2,487
34	Pennsylvania	2,374
7	Rhode Island	4,196
38	South Carolina	2,092
11	South Dakota	3,895
45	Tennessee	1,858
48	Texas	1,720
33	Utah	2,404
4	Vermont	4,670
31	Virginia	2,461
29	Washington	2,503
24	West Virginia	2,821
17	Wisconsin	3,526
5	Wyoming	4,591

RANK ORDER

RANK	STATE	RATE
1	Massachusetts	4,999
2	Maine	4,929
3	New Hampshire	4,698
4	Vermont	4,670
5	Wyoming	4,591
6	Connecticut	4,456
7	Rhode Island	4,196
8	Iowa	4,087
9	Ohio	4,068
10	Indiana	4,050
11	South Dakota	3,895
12	New York	3,834
13	North Dakota	3,824
14	Nebraska	3,728
15	Kansas	3,711
16	Alaska	3,620
17	Wisconsin	3,526
18	Illinois	3,524
19	New Jersey	3,502
20	Michigan	3,455
21	Missouri	3,028
22	Minnesota	2,822
22	Montana	2,822
24	West Virginia	2,821
25	Idaho	2,744
26	Hawaii	2,640
27	Louisiana	2,615
28	Maryland	2,541
29	Washington	2,503
30	Oregon	2,487
31	Virginia	2,461
32	Colorado	2,439
33	Utah	2,404
34	Pennsylvania	2,374
35	New Mexico	2,304
36	Delaware	2,272
37	Arkansas	2,249
38	South Carolina	2,092
39	Nevada	2,066
40	Alabama	2,056
41	California	2,028
42	Kentucky	2,023
43	Oklahoma	1,989
44	Mississippi	1,881
45	Tennessee	1,858
46	North Carolina	1,820
47	Florida	1,777
48	Texas	1,720
49	Georgia	1,659
50	Arizona	1,326
	District of Columbia	3,496

Source: CQ Press using data from Institute of Museum and Library Services
"Public Library Survey Fiscal Year 2008" (June 2010, http://harvester.census.gov/imls/index.asp)
*For fiscal year 2008.

Rate of Electronic Books in Public Libraries in 2008

National Rate = 46 Electronic Books per 1,000 Population*

ALPHA ORDER

RANK	STATE	RATE
7	Alabama	91
22	Alaska	21
13	Arizona	40
32	Arkansas	11
32	California	11
18	Colorado	30
25	Connecticut	16
NA	Delaware**	NA
12	Florida	46
38	Georgia	7
38	Hawaii	7
42	Idaho	4
14	Illinois	39
27	Indiana	14
26	Iowa	15
4	Kansas	252
17	Kentucky	31
30	Louisiana	13
46	Maine	2
41	Maryland	6
22	Massachusetts	21
24	Michigan	19
2	Minnesota	395
42	Mississippi	4
15	Missouri	38
3	Montana	268
5	Nebraska	209
21	Nevada	24
16	New Hampshire	37
30	New Jersey	13
44	New Mexico	3
18	New York	30
20	North Carolina	28
9	North Dakota	65
11	Ohio	55
46	Oklahoma	2
38	Oregon	7
10	Pennsylvania	57
36	Rhode Island	9
27	South Carolina	14
8	South Dakota	76
34	Tennessee	10
36	Texas	9
27	Utah	14
NA	Vermont**	NA
6	Virginia	107
34	Washington	10
44	West Virginia	3
1	Wisconsin	535
48	Wyoming	1

RANK ORDER

RANK	STATE	RATE
1	Wisconsin	535
2	Minnesota	395
3	Montana	268
4	Kansas	252
5	Nebraska	209
6	Virginia	107
7	Alabama	91
8	South Dakota	76
9	North Dakota	65
10	Pennsylvania	57
11	Ohio	55
12	Florida	46
13	Arizona	40
14	Illinois	39
15	Missouri	38
16	New Hampshire	37
17	Kentucky	31
18	Colorado	30
18	New York	30
20	North Carolina	28
21	Nevada	24
22	Alaska	21
22	Massachusetts	21
24	Michigan	19
25	Connecticut	16
26	Iowa	15
27	Indiana	14
27	South Carolina	14
27	Utah	14
30	Louisiana	13
30	New Jersey	13
32	Arkansas	11
32	California	11
34	Tennessee	10
34	Washington	10
36	Rhode Island	9
36	Texas	9
38	Georgia	7
38	Hawaii	7
38	Oregon	7
41	Maryland	6
42	Idaho	4
42	Mississippi	4
44	New Mexico	3
44	West Virginia	3
46	Maine	2
46	Oklahoma	2
48	Wyoming	1
NA	Delaware**	NA
NA	Vermont**	NA
	District of Columbia	3

Source: CQ Press using data from Institute of Museum and Library Services
"Public Library Survey Fiscal Year 2008" (June 2010, http://harvester.census.gov/imls/index.asp)
*For fiscal year 2008.
**Not available.

Internet Terminals in Public Libraries in 2008

National Total = 219,736 Terminals*

ALPHA ORDER

RANK	STATE	TERMINALS	% of USA
19	Alabama	4,445	2.0%
47	Alaska	558	0.3%
24	Arizona	3,686	1.7%
34	Arkansas	1,855	0.8%
1	California	17,505	8.0%
21	Colorado	3,971	1.8%
26	Connecticut	3,434	1.6%
50	Delaware	459	0.2%
4	Florida	13,200	6.0%
11	Georgia	6,328	2.9%
48	Hawaii	530	0.2%
38	Idaho	1,245	0.6%
6	Illinois	10,509	4.8%
9	Indiana	6,944	3.2%
25	Iowa	3,580	1.6%
29	Kansas	3,015	1.4%
27	Kentucky	3,278	1.5%
20	Louisiana	4,365	2.0%
36	Maine	1,437	0.7%
23	Maryland	3,790	1.7%
14	Massachusetts	5,030	2.3%
7	Michigan	9,725	4.4%
17	Minnesota	4,467	2.0%
32	Mississippi	2,047	0.9%
15	Missouri	4,592	2.1%
45	Montana	855	0.4%
33	Nebraska	1,906	0.9%
41	Nevada	1,076	0.5%
40	New Hampshire	1,152	0.5%
10	New Jersey	6,539	3.0%
37	New Mexico	1,405	0.6%
3	New York	14,604	6.6%
12	North Carolina	6,119	2.8%
49	North Dakota	501	0.2%
5	Ohio	11,480	5.2%
31	Oklahoma	2,179	1.0%
30	Oregon	2,240	1.0%
8	Pennsylvania	7,166	3.3%
42	Rhode Island	1,024	0.5%
28	South Carolina	3,020	1.4%
43	South Dakota	920	0.4%
22	Tennessee	3,918	1.8%
2	Texas	14,831	6.7%
35	Utah	1,529	0.7%
43	Vermont	920	0.4%
13	Virginia	5,129	2.3%
18	Washington	4,465	2.0%
39	West Virginia	1,207	0.5%
16	Wisconsin	4,519	2.1%
46	Wyoming	712	0.3%

RANK ORDER

RANK	STATE	TERMINALS	% of USA
1	California	17,505	8.0%
2	Texas	14,831	6.7%
3	New York	14,604	6.6%
4	Florida	13,200	6.0%
5	Ohio	11,480	5.2%
6	Illinois	10,509	4.8%
7	Michigan	9,725	4.4%
8	Pennsylvania	7,166	3.3%
9	Indiana	6,944	3.2%
10	New Jersey	6,539	3.0%
11	Georgia	6,328	2.9%
12	North Carolina	6,119	2.8%
13	Virginia	5,129	2.3%
14	Massachusetts	5,030	2.3%
15	Missouri	4,592	2.1%
16	Wisconsin	4,519	2.1%
17	Minnesota	4,467	2.0%
18	Washington	4,465	2.0%
19	Alabama	4,445	2.0%
20	Louisiana	4,365	2.0%
21	Colorado	3,971	1.8%
22	Tennessee	3,918	1.8%
23	Maryland	3,790	1.7%
24	Arizona	3,686	1.7%
25	Iowa	3,580	1.6%
26	Connecticut	3,434	1.6%
27	Kentucky	3,278	1.5%
28	South Carolina	3,020	1.4%
29	Kansas	3,015	1.4%
30	Oregon	2,240	1.0%
31	Oklahoma	2,179	1.0%
32	Mississippi	2,047	0.9%
33	Nebraska	1,906	0.9%
34	Arkansas	1,855	0.8%
35	Utah	1,529	0.7%
36	Maine	1,437	0.7%
37	New Mexico	1,405	0.6%
38	Idaho	1,245	0.6%
39	West Virginia	1,207	0.5%
40	New Hampshire	1,152	0.5%
41	Nevada	1,076	0.5%
42	Rhode Island	1,024	0.5%
43	South Dakota	920	0.4%
43	Vermont	920	0.4%
45	Montana	855	0.4%
46	Wyoming	712	0.3%
47	Alaska	558	0.3%
48	Hawaii	530	0.2%
49	North Dakota	501	0.2%
50	Delaware	459	0.2%
	District of Columbia	325	0.1%

Source: Institute of Museum and Library Services
"Public Library Survey Fiscal Year 2008" (June 2010, http://harvester.census.gov/imls/index.asp)
*For fiscal year 2008. Total of public-use Internet terminals in central and branch outlets.

Rate of Internet Terminals in Public Libraries in 2008

National Rate = 13.2 Terminals per Library*

ALPHA ORDER

RANK	STATE	RATE
13	Alabama	15.4
47	Alaska	5.5
3	Arizona	17.8
38	Arkansas	8.6
11	California	15.7
9	Colorado	15.9
17	Connecticut	14.2
19	Delaware	13.9
1	Florida	25.5
6	Georgia	16.4
34	Hawaii	10.4
37	Idaho	8.9
23	Illinois	13.3
7	Indiana	16.0
44	Iowa	6.4
40	Kansas	8.0
5	Kentucky	16.7
25	Louisiana	13.1
48	Maine	5.2
2	Maryland	20.7
31	Massachusetts	10.6
15	Michigan	14.8
28	Minnesota	12.4
38	Mississippi	8.6
26	Missouri	12.8
41	Montana	7.8
43	Nebraska	6.6
27	Nevada	12.7
50	New Hampshire	4.9
16	New Jersey	14.4
29	New Mexico	11.9
20	New York	13.7
11	North Carolina	15.7
46	North Dakota	5.6
10	Ohio	15.8
31	Oklahoma	10.6
31	Oregon	10.6
30	Pennsylvania	11.4
17	Rhode Island	14.2
7	South Carolina	16.0
45	South Dakota	6.1
21	Tennessee	13.6
4	Texas	17.2
24	Utah	13.2
49	Vermont	5.0
14	Virginia	15.0
22	Washington	13.4
42	West Virginia	7.0
35	Wisconsin	9.9
36	Wyoming	9.4

RANK ORDER

RANK	STATE	RATE
1	Florida	25.5
2	Maryland	20.7
3	Arizona	17.8
4	Texas	17.2
5	Kentucky	16.7
6	Georgia	16.4
7	Indiana	16.0
7	South Carolina	16.0
9	Colorado	15.9
10	Ohio	15.8
11	California	15.7
11	North Carolina	15.7
13	Alabama	15.4
14	Virginia	15.0
15	Michigan	14.8
16	New Jersey	14.4
17	Connecticut	14.2
17	Rhode Island	14.2
19	Delaware	13.9
20	New York	13.7
21	Tennessee	13.6
22	Washington	13.4
23	Illinois	13.3
24	Utah	13.2
25	Louisiana	13.1
26	Missouri	12.8
27	Nevada	12.7
28	Minnesota	12.4
29	New Mexico	11.9
30	Pennsylvania	11.4
31	Massachusetts	10.6
31	Oklahoma	10.6
31	Oregon	10.6
34	Hawaii	10.4
35	Wisconsin	9.9
36	Wyoming	9.4
37	Idaho	8.9
38	Arkansas	8.6
38	Mississippi	8.6
40	Kansas	8.0
41	Montana	7.8
42	West Virginia	7.0
43	Nebraska	6.6
44	Iowa	6.4
45	South Dakota	6.1
46	North Dakota	5.6
47	Alaska	5.5
48	Maine	5.2
49	Vermont	5.0
50	New Hampshire	4.9

| | District of Columbia | 12.0 |

Source: CQ Press using data from Institute of Museum and Library Services
   "Public Library Survey Fiscal Year 2008" (June 2010, http://harvester.census.gov/imls/index.asp)
*For fiscal year 2008. Total of public-use Internet terminals in central and branch outlets divided by the number of outlets.

Per Capita State Art Agencies' Legislative Appropriations in 2010

National Per Capita = $0.91*

ALPHA ORDER

RANK	STATE	PER CAPITA
20	Alabama	$0.98
20	Alaska	0.98
48	Arizona	0.14
31	Arkansas	0.56
50	California	0.11
44	Colorado	0.23
11	Connecticut	1.78
7	Delaware	1.97
41	Florida	0.28
43	Georgia	0.24
3	Hawaii	4.76
2	Idaho	5.54
45	Illinois	0.22
47	Indiana	0.16
39	Iowa	0.38
17	Kansas	1.13
46	Kentucky	0.17
16	Louisiana	1.24
34	Maine	0.52
5	Maryland	2.34
12	Massachusetts	1.47
48	Michigan	0.14
1	Minnesota	5.75
29	Mississippi	0.58
9	Missouri	1.91
35	Montana	0.47
25	Nebraska	0.82
37	Nevada	0.40
38	New Hampshire	0.39
8	New Jersey	1.96
22	New Mexico	0.97
4	New York	2.66
24	North Carolina	0.93
18	North Dakota	1.06
30	Ohio	0.57
15	Oklahoma	1.29
33	Oregon	0.55
23	Pennsylvania	0.95
10	Rhode Island	1.82
27	South Carolina	0.67
28	South Dakota	0.64
14	Tennessee	1.33
40	Texas	0.31
19	Utah	1.05
25	Vermont	0.82
31	Virginia	0.56
41	Washington	0.28
13	West Virginia	1.37
36	Wisconsin	0.43
6	Wyoming	2.10

RANK ORDER

RANK	STATE	PER CAPITA
1	Minnesota	$5.75
2	Idaho	5.54
3	Hawaii	4.76
4	New York	2.66
5	Maryland	2.34
6	Wyoming	2.10
7	Delaware	1.97
8	New Jersey	1.96
9	Missouri	1.91
10	Rhode Island	1.82
11	Connecticut	1.78
12	Massachusetts	1.47
13	West Virginia	1.37
14	Tennessee	1.33
15	Oklahoma	1.29
16	Louisiana	1.24
17	Kansas	1.13
18	North Dakota	1.06
19	Utah	1.05
20	Alabama	0.98
20	Alaska	0.98
22	New Mexico	0.97
23	Pennsylvania	0.95
24	North Carolina	0.93
25	Nebraska	0.82
25	Vermont	0.82
27	South Carolina	0.67
28	South Dakota	0.64
29	Mississippi	0.58
30	Ohio	0.57
31	Arkansas	0.56
31	Virginia	0.56
33	Oregon	0.55
34	Maine	0.52
35	Montana	0.47
36	Wisconsin	0.43
37	Nevada	0.40
38	New Hampshire	0.39
39	Iowa	0.38
40	Texas	0.31
41	Florida	0.28
41	Washington	0.28
43	Georgia	0.24
44	Colorado	0.23
45	Illinois	0.22
46	Kentucky	0.17
47	Indiana	0.16
48	Arizona	0.14
48	Michigan	0.14
50	California	0.11

District of Columbia   10.90

Source: CQ Press using data from National Assembly of State Arts Agencies
"Current State Arts Agency Budgets" (http://www.nasaa-arts.org/Research/Funding/)
*Enacted figures for fiscal year 2010. Includes line item appropriations. Line items are legislative appropriations that are not controlled by the state art agencies but are passed through their budgets directly to another entity. Calculated using 2009 census population estimates. National per capita does not include appropriations or population in U.S. territories.

Federal Allocations for Head Start Program in 2008

National Total = $6,643,860,725*

ALPHA ORDER

RANK	STATE	ALLOCATIONS	% of USA
18	Alabama	$106,910,747	1.6%
49	Alaska	12,505,529	0.2%
19	Arizona	103,773,998	1.6%
29	Arkansas	64,696,986	1.0%
1	California	833,853,590	12.6%
28	Colorado	68,519,283	1.0%
32	Connecticut	52,035,272	0.8%
48	Delaware	13,270,758	0.2%
5	Florida	263,828,726	4.0%
9	Georgia	168,952,317	2.5%
40	Hawaii	22,946,443	0.3%
41	Idaho	22,873,982	0.3%
4	Illinois	271,476,845	4.1%
22	Indiana	96,453,542	1.5%
33	Iowa	51,685,391	0.8%
34	Kansas	51,060,945	0.8%
17	Kentucky	108,129,820	1.6%
11	Louisiana	146,286,727	2.2%
38	Maine	27,683,563	0.4%
26	Maryland	78,239,829	1.2%
16	Massachusetts	108,635,529	1.6%
7	Michigan	235,167,867	3.5%
27	Minnesota	72,193,111	1.1%
10	Mississippi	162,115,749	2.4%
15	Missouri	119,305,226	1.8%
43	Montana	21,004,313	0.3%
37	Nebraska	36,153,536	0.5%
39	Nevada	24,343,835	0.4%
47	New Hampshire	13,421,239	0.2%
13	New Jersey	129,353,152	1.9%
31	New Mexico	52,437,413	0.8%
3	New York	434,333,488	6.5%
12	North Carolina	141,647,045	2.1%
45	North Dakota	17,220,056	0.3%
6	Ohio	247,546,666	3.7%
25	Oklahoma	81,263,182	1.2%
30	Oregon	59,625,878	0.9%
8	Pennsylvania	228,773,267	3.4%
42	Rhode Island	22,073,130	0.3%
24	South Carolina	82,719,421	1.2%
44	South Dakota	18,874,909	0.3%
14	Tennessee	119,654,435	1.8%
2	Texas	479,971,393	7.2%
36	Utah	37,863,769	0.6%
46	Vermont	13,595,041	0.2%
21	Virginia	99,358,903	1.5%
20	Washington	100,626,555	1.5%
35	West Virginia	50,776,400	0.8%
23	Wisconsin	91,117,239	1.4%
50	Wyoming	12,403,894	0.2%

RANK ORDER

RANK	STATE	ALLOCATIONS	% of USA
1	California	$833,853,590	12.6%
2	Texas	479,971,393	7.2%
3	New York	434,333,488	6.5%
4	Illinois	271,476,845	4.1%
5	Florida	263,828,726	4.0%
6	Ohio	247,546,666	3.7%
7	Michigan	235,167,867	3.5%
8	Pennsylvania	228,773,267	3.4%
9	Georgia	168,952,317	2.5%
10	Mississippi	162,115,749	2.4%
11	Louisiana	146,286,727	2.2%
12	North Carolina	141,647,045	2.1%
13	New Jersey	129,353,152	1.9%
14	Tennessee	119,654,435	1.8%
15	Missouri	119,305,226	1.8%
16	Massachusetts	108,635,529	1.6%
17	Kentucky	108,129,820	1.6%
18	Alabama	106,910,747	1.6%
19	Arizona	103,773,998	1.6%
20	Washington	100,626,555	1.5%
21	Virginia	99,358,903	1.5%
22	Indiana	96,453,542	1.5%
23	Wisconsin	91,117,239	1.4%
24	South Carolina	82,719,421	1.2%
25	Oklahoma	81,263,182	1.2%
26	Maryland	78,239,829	1.2%
27	Minnesota	72,193,111	1.1%
28	Colorado	68,519,283	1.0%
29	Arkansas	64,696,986	1.0%
30	Oregon	59,625,878	0.9%
31	New Mexico	52,437,413	0.8%
32	Connecticut	52,035,272	0.8%
33	Iowa	51,685,391	0.8%
34	Kansas	51,060,945	0.8%
35	West Virginia	50,776,400	0.8%
36	Utah	37,863,769	0.6%
37	Nebraska	36,153,536	0.5%
38	Maine	27,683,563	0.4%
39	Nevada	24,343,835	0.4%
40	Hawaii	22,946,443	0.3%
41	Idaho	22,873,982	0.3%
42	Rhode Island	22,073,130	0.3%
43	Montana	21,004,313	0.3%
44	South Dakota	18,874,909	0.3%
45	North Dakota	17,220,056	0.3%
46	Vermont	13,595,041	0.2%
47	New Hampshire	13,421,239	0.2%
48	Delaware	13,270,758	0.2%
49	Alaska	12,505,529	0.2%
50	Wyoming	12,403,894	0.2%
	District of Columbia	25,173,901	0.4%

Source: U.S. Department of Health and Human Services, Administration for Children and Families
    "Head Start Fact Sheet" (http://www.acf.hhs.gov/programs/ohs/about/fy2009.html)
*For fiscal year 2008. National total includes $475,604,336 to Migrant and Native American programs and $265,322,554 to U.S.
territories. Does not include $233,270,538 in "support activities" expenditures.

Head Start Program Enrollment in 2008

National Total = 906,992 Children*

ALPHA ORDER

RANK	STATE	ENROLLMENT	% of USA
15	Alabama	16,284	1.8%
49	Alaska	1,631	0.2%
22	Arizona	12,946	1.4%
26	Arkansas	10,661	1.2%
1	California	97,942	10.8%
30	Colorado	9,820	1.1%
35	Connecticut	7,036	0.8%
46	Delaware	2,059	0.2%
7	Florida	35,402	3.9%
10	Georgia	23,359	2.6%
40	Hawaii	3,049	0.3%
42	Idaho	2,903	0.3%
4	Illinois	39,534	4.4%
18	Indiana	14,190	1.6%
32	Iowa	7,677	0.8%
31	Kansas	8,324	0.9%
16	Kentucky	16,030	1.8%
11	Louisiana	21,663	2.4%
38	Maine	3,820	0.4%
27	Maryland	10,347	1.1%
23	Massachusetts	12,742	1.4%
8	Michigan	34,949	3.9%
28	Minnesota	10,306	1.1%
9	Mississippi	26,633	2.9%
13	Missouri	17,433	1.9%
41	Montana	2,919	0.3%
37	Nebraska	5,059	0.6%
44	Nevada	2,754	0.3%
48	New Hampshire	1,632	0.2%
17	New Jersey	14,850	1.6%
34	New Mexico	7,249	0.8%
3	New York	48,084	5.3%
12	North Carolina	18,903	2.1%
45	North Dakota	2,353	0.3%
5	Ohio	36,975	4.1%
21	Oklahoma	13,474	1.5%
29	Oregon	10,175	1.1%
6	Pennsylvania	35,456	3.9%
39	Rhode Island	3,083	0.3%
24	South Carolina	12,248	1.4%
43	South Dakota	2,827	0.3%
14	Tennessee	16,339	1.8%
2	Texas	67,680	7.5%
36	Utah	5,518	0.6%
50	Vermont	1,552	0.2%
19	Virginia	13,578	1.5%
25	Washington	11,277	1.2%
33	West Virginia	7,610	0.8%
20	Wisconsin	13,476	1.5%
47	Wyoming	1,792	0.2%

RANK ORDER

RANK	STATE	ENROLLMENT	% of USA
1	California	97,942	10.8%
2	Texas	67,680	7.5%
3	New York	48,084	5.3%
4	Illinois	39,534	4.4%
5	Ohio	36,975	4.1%
6	Pennsylvania	35,456	3.9%
7	Florida	35,402	3.9%
8	Michigan	34,949	3.9%
9	Mississippi	26,633	2.9%
10	Georgia	23,359	2.6%
11	Louisiana	21,663	2.4%
12	North Carolina	18,903	2.1%
13	Missouri	17,433	1.9%
14	Tennessee	16,339	1.8%
15	Alabama	16,284	1.8%
16	Kentucky	16,030	1.8%
17	New Jersey	14,850	1.6%
18	Indiana	14,190	1.6%
19	Virginia	13,578	1.5%
20	Wisconsin	13,476	1.5%
21	Oklahoma	13,474	1.5%
22	Arizona	12,946	1.4%
23	Massachusetts	12,742	1.4%
24	South Carolina	12,248	1.4%
25	Washington	11,277	1.2%
26	Arkansas	10,661	1.2%
27	Maryland	10,347	1.1%
28	Minnesota	10,306	1.1%
29	Oregon	10,175	1.1%
30	Colorado	9,820	1.1%
31	Kansas	8,324	0.9%
32	Iowa	7,677	0.8%
33	West Virginia	7,610	0.8%
34	New Mexico	7,249	0.8%
35	Connecticut	7,036	0.8%
36	Utah	5,518	0.6%
37	Nebraska	5,059	0.6%
38	Maine	3,820	0.4%
39	Rhode Island	3,083	0.3%
40	Hawaii	3,049	0.3%
41	Montana	2,919	0.3%
42	Idaho	2,903	0.3%
43	South Dakota	2,827	0.3%
44	Nevada	2,754	0.3%
45	North Dakota	2,353	0.3%
46	Delaware	2,059	0.2%
47	Wyoming	1,792	0.2%
48	New Hampshire	1,632	0.2%
49	Alaska	1,631	0.2%
50	Vermont	1,552	0.2%
	District of Columbia	3,403	0.4%

Source: U.S. Department of Health and Human Services, Administration for Children and Families
"Head Start Fact Sheet" (http://www.acf.hhs.gov/programs/ohs/about/fy2009.html)
*For fiscal year 2008. National total includes 59,199 enrollees in Migrant and Native American programs and 40,787 enrollees in U.S. territories.

VI. Employment and Labor

Average Annual Pay in 2009

National Average = $45,559*

ALPHA ORDER

RANK	STATE	ANNUAL PAY
31	Alabama	$39,422
11	Alaska	47,103
20	Arizona	42,832
46	Arkansas	35,692
5	California	51,566
12	Colorado	46,861
1	Connecticut	57,771
9	Delaware	47,770
23	Florida	40,970
19	Georgia	42,902
22	Hawaii	41,328
47	Idaho	34,124
7	Illinois	48,358
36	Indiana	38,270
40	Iowa	37,158
37	Kansas	38,154
38	Kentucky	37,996
27	Louisiana	40,579
44	Maine	36,617
6	Maryland	50,579
3	Massachusetts	56,267
17	Michigan	43,645
14	Minnesota	45,319
48	Mississippi	33,847
29	Missouri	40,022
49	Montana	33,762
43	Nebraska	36,644
21	Nevada	42,743
15	New Hampshire	44,932
4	New Jersey	55,168
35	New Mexico	38,529
2	New York	57,739
30	North Carolina	39,844
45	North Dakota	35,970
24	Ohio	40,900
39	Oklahoma	37,238
25	Oregon	40,757
16	Pennsylvania	44,829
18	Rhode Island	43,439
42	South Carolina	36,759
50	South Dakota	33,352
28	Tennessee	40,242
13	Texas	45,692
34	Utah	38,614
33	Vermont	38,778
8	Virginia	48,239
10	Washington	47,470
41	West Virginia	36,897
32	Wisconsin	39,131
26	Wyoming	40,709

RANK ORDER

RANK	STATE	ANNUAL PAY
1	Connecticut	$57,771
2	New York	57,739
3	Massachusetts	56,267
4	New Jersey	55,168
5	California	51,566
6	Maryland	50,579
7	Illinois	48,358
8	Virginia	48,239
9	Delaware	47,770
10	Washington	47,470
11	Alaska	47,103
12	Colorado	46,861
13	Texas	45,692
14	Minnesota	45,319
15	New Hampshire	44,932
16	Pennsylvania	44,829
17	Michigan	43,645
18	Rhode Island	43,439
19	Georgia	42,902
20	Arizona	42,832
21	Nevada	42,743
22	Hawaii	41,328
23	Florida	40,970
24	Ohio	40,900
25	Oregon	40,757
26	Wyoming	40,709
27	Louisiana	40,579
28	Tennessee	40,242
29	Missouri	40,022
30	North Carolina	39,844
31	Alabama	39,422
32	Wisconsin	39,131
33	Vermont	38,778
34	Utah	38,614
35	New Mexico	38,529
36	Indiana	38,270
37	Kansas	38,154
38	Kentucky	37,996
39	Oklahoma	37,238
40	Iowa	37,158
41	West Virginia	36,897
42	South Carolina	36,759
43	Nebraska	36,644
44	Maine	36,617
45	North Dakota	35,970
46	Arkansas	35,692
47	Idaho	34,124
48	Mississippi	33,847
49	Montana	33,762
50	South Dakota	33,352
	District of Columbia	77,483

Source: U.S. Department of Labor, Bureau of Labor Statistics
   "Quarterly Census of Employment and Wages" (http://www.bls.gov/cew/home.htm)
*Computed by dividing total annual wages of employees covered by unemployment insurance programs by the average monthly
number of these employees. Includes bonuses, cash value of meals and lodging, tips and, in many states, employer
contributions to certain deferred compensation plans such as 401(k) plans.

Percent Change in Average Annual Pay: 2008 to 2009

National Percent Change = 0.0% Change*

ALPHA ORDER			RANK ORDER		
RANK	STATE	PERCENT CHANGE	RANK	STATE	PERCENT CHANGE
8	Alabama	1.8	1	Alaska	2.8
1	Alaska	2.8	2	North Dakota	2.6
23	Arizona	0.7	3	West Virginia	2.5
4	Arkansas	2.2	4	Arkansas	2.2
34	California	0.2	5	Maryland	2.1
28	Colorado	0.5	5	Virginia	2.1
45	Connecticut	(1.1)	7	Washington	1.9
31	Delaware	0.4	8	Alabama	1.8
18	Florida	1.0	9	Utah	1.7
23	Georgia	0.7	10	Hawaii	1.6
10	Hawaii	1.6	10	New Mexico	1.6
23	Idaho	0.7	12	Kentucky	1.5
42	Illinois	(0.7)	13	Montana	1.4
39	Indiana	(0.3)	13	New Hampshire	1.4
28	Iowa	0.5	13	South Carolina	1.4
36	Kansas	(0.1)	16	Vermont	1.2
12	Kentucky	1.5	17	Nebraska	1.1
28	Louisiana	0.5	18	Florida	1.0
22	Maine	0.8	18	Mississippi	1.0
5	Maryland	2.1	18	Pennsylvania	1.0
43	Massachusetts	(0.8)	18	Rhode Island	1.0
47	Michigan	(1.4)	22	Maine	0.8
45	Minnesota	(1.1)	23	Arizona	0.7
18	Mississippi	1.0	23	Georgia	0.7
43	Missouri	(0.8)	23	Idaho	0.7
13	Montana	1.4	26	Oregon	0.6
17	Nebraska	1.1	26	Tennessee	0.6
41	Nevada	(0.6)	28	Colorado	0.5
13	New Hampshire	1.4	28	Iowa	0.5
38	New Jersey	(0.2)	28	Louisiana	0.5
10	New Mexico	1.6	31	Delaware	0.4
49	New York	(4.2)	32	North Carolina	0.3
32	North Carolina	0.3	32	Ohio	0.3
2	North Dakota	2.6	34	California	0.2
32	Ohio	0.3	35	Wisconsin	0.0
36	Oklahoma	(0.1)	36	Kansas	(0.1)
26	Oregon	0.6	36	Oklahoma	(0.1)
18	Pennsylvania	1.0	38	New Jersey	(0.2)
18	Rhode Island	1.0	39	Indiana	(0.3)
13	South Carolina	1.4	40	Texas	(0.5)
50	South Dakota	(9.4)	41	Nevada	(0.6)
26	Tennessee	0.6	42	Illinois	(0.7)
40	Texas	(0.5)	43	Massachusetts	(0.8)
9	Utah	1.7	43	Missouri	(0.8)
16	Vermont	1.2	45	Connecticut	(1.1)
5	Virginia	2.1	45	Minnesota	(1.1)
7	Washington	1.9	47	Michigan	(1.4)
3	West Virginia	2.5	48	Wyoming	(1.9)
35	Wisconsin	0.0	49	New York	(4.2)
48	Wyoming	(1.9)	50	South Dakota	(9.4)
				District of Columbia	1.3

Source: CQ Press using data from U.S. Department of Labor, Bureau of Labor Statistics
"Quarterly Census of Employment and Wages" (http://www.bls.gov/cew/home.htm)
*Includes bonuses, cash value of meals and lodging, tips and, in many states, employer contributions to certain deferred compensation plans such as 401(k) plans.

Median Earnings of Male Full-Time Workers in 2009

National Median = $45,485

ALPHA ORDER

RANK	STATE	EARNINGS
34	Alabama	$41,331
6	Alaska	51,019
32	Arizona	41,916
50	Arkansas	36,465
13	California	48,389
16	Colorado	47,983
1	Connecticut	59,387
15	Delaware	48,038
47	Florida	39,122
28	Georgia	42,667
19	Hawaii	45,911
38	Idaho	40,440
10	Illinois	49,336
26	Indiana	43,631
29	Iowa	42,634
30	Kansas	42,494
35	Kentucky	40,748
25	Louisiana	44,174
31	Maine	42,156
4	Maryland	55,116
3	Massachusetts	56,902
14	Michigan	48,066
12	Minnesota	48,492
48	Mississippi	37,528
33	Missouri	41,660
41	Montana	39,830
44	Nebraska	39,516
27	Nevada	43,425
7	New Hampshire	50,837
2	New Jersey	57,738
43	New Mexico	39,562
11	New York	49,174
39	North Carolina	40,359
36	North Dakota	40,693
24	Ohio	44,563
46	Oklahoma	39,174
23	Oregon	44,572
18	Pennsylvania	46,747
9	Rhode Island	49,439
42	South Carolina	39,648
49	South Dakota	36,977
45	Tennessee	39,509
37	Texas	40,621
20	Utah	45,800
21	Vermont	45,234
8	Virginia	50,236
5	Washington	51,305
40	West Virginia	40,231
22	Wisconsin	44,812
17	Wyoming	47,828

RANK ORDER

RANK	STATE	EARNINGS
1	Connecticut	$59,387
2	New Jersey	57,738
3	Massachusetts	56,902
4	Maryland	55,116
5	Washington	51,305
6	Alaska	51,019
7	New Hampshire	50,837
8	Virginia	50,236
9	Rhode Island	49,439
10	Illinois	49,336
11	New York	49,174
12	Minnesota	48,492
13	California	48,389
14	Michigan	48,066
15	Delaware	48,038
16	Colorado	47,983
17	Wyoming	47,828
18	Pennsylvania	46,747
19	Hawaii	45,911
20	Utah	45,800
21	Vermont	45,234
22	Wisconsin	44,812
23	Oregon	44,572
24	Ohio	44,563
25	Louisiana	44,174
26	Indiana	43,631
27	Nevada	43,425
28	Georgia	42,667
29	Iowa	42,634
30	Kansas	42,494
31	Maine	42,156
32	Arizona	41,916
33	Missouri	41,660
34	Alabama	41,331
35	Kentucky	40,748
36	North Dakota	40,693
37	Texas	40,621
38	Idaho	40,440
39	North Carolina	40,359
40	West Virginia	40,231
41	Montana	39,830
42	South Carolina	39,648
43	New Mexico	39,562
44	Nebraska	39,516
45	Tennessee	39,509
46	Oklahoma	39,174
47	Florida	39,122
48	Mississippi	37,528
49	South Dakota	36,977
50	Arkansas	36,465
	District of Columbia	61,993

Source: U.S. Bureau of the Census
 "2009 American Community Survey" (http://www.census.gov/acs/www/index.html)

Median Earnings of Female Full-Time Workers in 2009

National Median = $35,549

ALPHA ORDER

RANK	STATE	EARNINGS
38	Alabama	$30,658
9	Alaska	39,017
20	Arizona	34,651
46	Arkansas	28,640
6	California	40,019
11	Colorado	38,058
4	Connecticut	43,900
14	Delaware	37,645
30	Florida	32,109
23	Georgia	33,665
16	Hawaii	35,977
45	Idaho	29,122
13	Illinois	37,841
32	Indiana	31,762
33	Iowa	31,431
28	Kansas	32,341
41	Kentucky	30,481
44	Louisiana	29,350
29	Maine	32,314
2	Maryland	44,937
1	Massachusetts	45,062
21	Michigan	34,542
12	Minnesota	38,025
48	Mississippi	28,506
31	Missouri	31,993
49	Montana	28,461
40	Nebraska	30,562
17	Nevada	35,691
15	New Hampshire	37,527
3	New Jersey	44,166
39	New Mexico	30,578
5	New York	40,584
27	North Carolina	32,576
42	North Dakota	29,742
24	Ohio	33,616
43	Oklahoma	29,413
22	Oregon	34,121
18	Pennsylvania	35,301
8	Rhode Island	39,248
37	South Carolina	31,010
47	South Dakota	28,515
35	Tennessee	31,222
26	Texas	32,578
36	Utah	31,186
19	Vermont	35,276
7	Virginia	39,354
10	Washington	38,521
50	West Virginia	27,855
25	Wisconsin	33,611
34	Wyoming	31,308

RANK ORDER

RANK	STATE	EARNINGS
1	Massachusetts	$45,062
2	Maryland	44,937
3	New Jersey	44,166
4	Connecticut	43,900
5	New York	40,584
6	California	40,019
7	Virginia	39,354
8	Rhode Island	39,248
9	Alaska	39,017
10	Washington	38,521
11	Colorado	38,058
12	Minnesota	38,025
13	Illinois	37,841
14	Delaware	37,645
15	New Hampshire	37,527
16	Hawaii	35,977
17	Nevada	35,691
18	Pennsylvania	35,301
19	Vermont	35,276
20	Arizona	34,651
21	Michigan	34,542
22	Oregon	34,121
23	Georgia	33,665
24	Ohio	33,616
25	Wisconsin	33,611
26	Texas	32,578
27	North Carolina	32,576
28	Kansas	32,341
29	Maine	32,314
30	Florida	32,109
31	Missouri	31,993
32	Indiana	31,762
33	Iowa	31,431
34	Wyoming	31,308
35	Tennessee	31,222
36	Utah	31,186
37	South Carolina	31,010
38	Alabama	30,658
39	New Mexico	30,578
40	Nebraska	30,562
41	Kentucky	30,481
42	North Dakota	29,742
43	Oklahoma	29,413
44	Louisiana	29,350
45	Idaho	29,122
46	Arkansas	28,640
47	South Dakota	28,515
48	Mississippi	28,506
49	Montana	28,461
50	West Virginia	27,855

| | District of Columbia | 54,698 |

Source: U.S. Bureau of the Census
"2009 American Community Survey" (http://www.census.gov/acs/www/index.html)

State Minimum Wage Rates in 2011

National Rate = $7.25 per Hour*

ALPHA ORDER				RANK ORDER		
RANK	STATE	MINIMUM WAGE		RANK	STATE	MINIMUM WAGE
NA	Alabama**	NA		1	Washington	$8.67
9	Alaska	7.75		2	Oregon	8.50
16	Arizona	7.35		3	Connecticut	8.25
42	Arkansas	6.25		3	Illinois	8.25
7	California	8.00		3	Nevada	8.25
15	Colorado	7.36		6	Vermont	8.15
3	Connecticut	8.25		7	California	8.00
18	Delaware	7.25		7	Massachusetts	8.00
18	Florida	7.25		9	Alaska	7.75
44	Georgia	5.15		10	Maine	7.50
18	Hawaii	7.25		10	New Mexico	7.50
18	Idaho	7.25		12	Michigan	7.40
3	Illinois	8.25		12	Ohio	7.40
18	Indiana	7.25		12	Rhode Island	7.40
18	Iowa	7.25		15	Colorado	7.36
18	Kansas	7.25		16	Arizona	7.35
18	Kentucky	7.25		16	Montana	7.35
NA	Louisiana**	NA		18	Delaware	7.25
10	Maine	7.50		18	Florida	7.25
18	Maryland	7.25		18	Hawaii	7.25
7	Massachusetts	8.00		18	Idaho	7.25
12	Michigan	7.40		18	Indiana	7.25
43	Minnesota	6.15		18	Iowa	7.25
NA	Mississippi**	NA		18	Kansas	7.25
18	Missouri	7.25		18	Kentucky	7.25
16	Montana	7.35		18	Maryland	7.25
18	Nebraska	7.25		18	Missouri	7.25
3	Nevada	8.25		18	Nebraska	7.25
18	New Hampshire	7.25		18	New Hampshire	7.25
18	New Jersey	7.25		18	New Jersey	7.25
10	New Mexico	7.50		18	New York	7.25
18	New York	7.25		18	North Carolina	7.25
18	North Carolina	7.25		18	North Dakota	7.25
18	North Dakota	7.25		18	Oklahoma	7.25
12	Ohio	7.40		18	Pennsylvania	7.25
18	Oklahoma	7.25		18	South Dakota	7.25
2	Oregon	8.50		18	Texas	7.25
18	Pennsylvania	7.25		18	Utah	7.25
12	Rhode Island	7.40		18	Virginia	7.25
NA	South Carolina**	NA		18	West Virginia	7.25
18	South Dakota	7.25		18	Wisconsin	7.25
NA	Tennessee**	NA		42	Arkansas	6.25
18	Texas	7.25		43	Minnesota	6.15
18	Utah	7.25		44	Georgia	5.15
6	Vermont	8.15		44	Wyoming	5.15
18	Virginia	7.25		NA	Alabama**	NA
1	Washington	8.67		NA	Louisiana**	NA
18	West Virginia	7.25		NA	Mississippi**	NA
18	Wisconsin	7.25		NA	South Carolina**	NA
44	Wyoming	5.15		NA	Tennessee**	NA
					District of Columbia	8.25

Source: U.S. Department of Labor, Employment Standards Administration

"Minimum Wage Laws in the States" (http://www.dol.gov/esa/minwage/america.htm)

*As of January 1, 2011. State minimum wage rates are for those employers and jobs not covered by the federal program.

**No separate state program.

Average Hourly Earnings of Production Workers on Manufacturing Payrolls in 2010
National Average = $18.73*

	ALPHA ORDER				RANK ORDER	
RANK	STATE	HOURLY EARNINGS		RANK	STATE	HOURLY EARNINGS
41	Alabama	$15.90		1	Alaska	$24.63
1	Alaska	24.63		2	Connecticut	24.60
32	Arizona	16.86		3	Washington	23.65
50	Arkansas	14.10		4	Colorado	22.43
14	California	19.22		5	Michigan	21.88
4	Colorado	22.43		6	Idaho	21.31
2	Connecticut	24.60		7	Wyoming	20.90
36	Delaware	16.61		8	Louisiana	20.78
16	Florida	18.97		9	Maryland	20.40
35	Georgia	16.73		10	Maine	20.16
21	Hawaii	18.47		11	Massachusetts	20.02
6	Idaho	21.31		12	Kentucky	19.56
29	Illinois	17.22		13	Kansas	19.41
19	Indiana	18.65		14	California	19.22
31	Iowa	16.92		15	Minnesota	19.16
13	Kansas	19.41		16	Florida	18.97
12	Kentucky	19.56		17	New Jersey	18.93
8	Louisiana	20.78		18	Ohio	18.86
10	Maine	20.16		19	Indiana	18.65
9	Maryland	20.40		20	New York	18.60
11	Massachusetts	20.02		21	Hawaii	18.47
5	Michigan	21.88		22	Missouri	18.42
15	Minnesota	19.16		23	Utah	18.41
48	Mississippi	14.84		24	Wisconsin	18.26
22	Missouri	18.42		25	West Virginia	18.23
30	Montana	17.08		26	Virginia	18.22
39	Nebraska	16.19		27	New Hampshire	18.12
45	Nevada	15.56		28	Oregon	17.33
27	New Hampshire	18.12		29	Illinois	17.22
17	New Jersey	18.93		30	Montana	17.08
40	New Mexico	16.04		31	Iowa	16.92
20	New York	18.60		32	Arizona	16.86
43	North Carolina	15.87		33	Pennsylvania	16.85
44	North Dakota	15.71		34	South Carolina	16.79
18	Ohio	18.86		35	Georgia	16.73
49	Oklahoma	14.49		36	Delaware	16.61
28	Oregon	17.33		37	Vermont	16.51
33	Pennsylvania	16.85		38	Texas	16.43
47	Rhode Island	14.85		39	Nebraska	16.19
34	South Carolina	16.79		40	New Mexico	16.04
46	South Dakota	15.38		41	Alabama	15.90
41	Tennessee	15.90		41	Tennessee	15.90
38	Texas	16.43		43	North Carolina	15.87
23	Utah	18.41		44	North Dakota	15.71
37	Vermont	16.51		45	Nevada	15.56
26	Virginia	18.22		46	South Dakota	15.38
3	Washington	23.65		47	Rhode Island	14.85
25	West Virginia	18.23		48	Mississippi	14.84
24	Wisconsin	18.26		49	Oklahoma	14.49
7	Wyoming	20.90		50	Arkansas	14.10
					District of Columbia**	NA

Source: U.S. Department of Labor, Bureau of Labor Statistics
   "State and Metro Area Employment, Hours and Earnings" (http://www.bls.gov/sae/home.htm)
*Preliminary data for December 2010. Not seasonally adjusted.
**Not available.

Average Weekly Earnings of Production Workers
on Manufacturing Payrolls in 2010
National Average = $781.04*

ALPHA ORDER

RANK	STATE	WEEKLY EARNINGS
40	Alabama	$645.54
5	Alaska	889.14
31	Arizona	687.89
49	Arkansas	573.87
15	California	788.02
6	Colorado	877.01
1	Connecticut	1,020.90
33	Delaware	676.03
19	Florida	760.70
36	Georgia	662.51
41	Hawaii	644.60
9	Idaho	833.22
32	Illinois	683.63
14	Indiana	800.09
28	Iowa	705.56
12	Kansas	803.57
10	Kentucky	827.39
4	Louisiana	895.62
11	Maine	826.56
8	Maryland	844.56
13	Massachusetts	800.80
3	Michigan	964.91
16	Minnesota	779.81
47	Mississippi	587.66
25	Missouri	718.38
30	Montana	693.45
38	Nebraska	653.93
50	Nevada	558.60
21	New Hampshire	759.23
17	New Jersey	762.88
43	New Mexico	631.98
18	New York	762.60
37	North Carolina	657.02
46	North Dakota	596.98
20	Ohio	760.06
45	Oklahoma	601.34
34	Oregon	675.87
35	Pennsylvania	674.00
48	Rhode Island	582.12
27	South Carolina	711.90
44	South Dakota	621.35
42	Tennessee	634.41
29	Texas	696.63
26	Utah	716.15
39	Vermont	650.49
24	Virginia	721.51
2	Washington	976.75
23	West Virginia	734.67
22	Wisconsin	752.31
7	Wyoming	854.81

RANK ORDER

RANK	STATE	WEEKLY EARNINGS
1	Connecticut	$1,020.90
2	Washington	976.75
3	Michigan	964.91
4	Louisiana	895.62
5	Alaska	889.14
6	Colorado	877.01
7	Wyoming	854.81
8	Maryland	844.56
9	Idaho	833.22
10	Kentucky	827.39
11	Maine	826.56
12	Kansas	803.57
13	Massachusetts	800.80
14	Indiana	800.09
15	California	788.02
16	Minnesota	779.81
17	New Jersey	762.88
18	New York	762.60
19	Florida	760.70
20	Ohio	760.06
21	New Hampshire	759.23
22	Wisconsin	752.31
23	West Virginia	734.67
24	Virginia	721.51
25	Missouri	718.38
26	Utah	716.15
27	South Carolina	711.90
28	Iowa	705.56
29	Texas	696.63
30	Montana	693.45
31	Arizona	687.89
32	Illinois	683.63
33	Delaware	676.03
34	Oregon	675.87
35	Pennsylvania	674.00
36	Georgia	662.51
37	North Carolina	657.02
38	Nebraska	653.93
39	Vermont	650.49
40	Alabama	645.54
41	Hawaii	644.60
42	Tennessee	634.41
43	New Mexico	631.98
44	South Dakota	621.35
45	Oklahoma	601.34
46	North Dakota	596.98
47	Mississippi	587.66
48	Rhode Island	582.12
49	Arkansas	573.87
50	Nevada	558.60
	District of Columbia**	NA

Source: U.S. Department of Labor, Bureau of Labor Statistics
   "State and Metro Area Employment, Hours and Earnings" (http://www.bls.gov/sae/home.htm)
*Preliminary data for December 2010. Not seasonally adjusted.
**Not available.

Average Work Week of Production Workers
on Manufacturing Payrolls in 2010
National Average = 41.7 Hours per Week*

ALPHA ORDER

RANK	STATE	WEEKLY HOURS
25	Alabama	40.6
48	Alaska	36.1
20	Arizona	40.8
21	Arkansas	40.7
16	California	41.0
42	Colorado	39.1
9	Connecticut	41.5
21	Delaware	40.7
31	Florida	40.1
36	Georgia	39.6
50	Hawaii	34.9
42	Idaho	39.1
35	Illinois	39.7
3	Indiana	42.9
8	Iowa	41.7
11	Kansas	41.4
6	Kentucky	42.3
2	Louisiana	43.1
16	Maine	41.0
11	Maryland	41.4
32	Massachusetts	40.0
1	Michigan	44.1
21	Minnesota	40.7
36	Mississippi	39.6
44	Missouri	39.0
25	Montana	40.6
21	Nebraska	40.7
49	Nevada	35.9
7	New Hampshire	41.9
28	New Jersey	40.3
39	New Mexico	39.4
16	New York	41.0
11	North Carolina	41.4
47	North Dakota	38.0
28	Ohio	40.3
9	Oklahoma	41.5
44	Oregon	39.0
32	Pennsylvania	40.0
41	Rhode Island	39.2
4	South Carolina	42.4
27	South Dakota	40.4
34	Tennessee	39.9
4	Texas	42.4
46	Utah	38.9
39	Vermont	39.4
36	Virginia	39.6
14	Washington	41.3
28	West Virginia	40.3
15	Wisconsin	41.2
19	Wyoming	40.9

RANK ORDER

RANK	STATE	WEEKLY HOURS
1	Michigan	44.1
2	Louisiana	43.1
3	Indiana	42.9
4	South Carolina	42.4
4	Texas	42.4
6	Kentucky	42.3
7	New Hampshire	41.9
8	Iowa	41.7
9	Connecticut	41.5
9	Oklahoma	41.5
11	Kansas	41.4
11	Maryland	41.4
11	North Carolina	41.4
14	Washington	41.3
15	Wisconsin	41.2
16	California	41.0
16	Maine	41.0
16	New York	41.0
19	Wyoming	40.9
20	Arizona	40.8
21	Arkansas	40.7
21	Delaware	40.7
21	Minnesota	40.7
21	Nebraska	40.7
25	Alabama	40.6
25	Montana	40.6
27	South Dakota	40.4
28	New Jersey	40.3
28	Ohio	40.3
28	West Virginia	40.3
31	Florida	40.1
32	Massachusetts	40.0
32	Pennsylvania	40.0
34	Tennessee	39.9
35	Illinois	39.7
36	Georgia	39.6
36	Mississippi	39.6
36	Virginia	39.6
39	New Mexico	39.4
39	Vermont	39.4
41	Rhode Island	39.2
42	Colorado	39.1
42	Idaho	39.1
44	Missouri	39.0
44	Oregon	39.0
46	Utah	38.9
47	North Dakota	38.0
48	Alaska	36.1
49	Nevada	35.9
50	Hawaii	34.9

District of Columbia**   NA

Source: U.S. Department of Labor, Bureau of Labor Statistics
   "State and Metro Area Employment, Hours and Earnings" (http://www.bls.gov/sae/home.htm)
*Preliminary data for December 2010. Not seasonally adjusted.
**Not available.

Average Weekly Unemployment Benefit in 2010

National Average = $300.77 a Week

ALPHA ORDER

RANK	STATE	BENEFIT
49	Alabama	$205.50
43	Alaska	238.49
47	Arizona	213.85
30	Arkansas	277.53
22	California	301.10
8	Colorado	345.69
11	Connecticut	326.52
41	Delaware	246.57
45	Florida	230.81
34	Georgia	272.86
1	Hawaii	416.16
38	Idaho	253.16
17	Illinois	315.48
26	Indiana	293.38
13	Iowa	319.78
12	Kansas	324.77
29	Kentucky	288.19
48	Louisiana	207.50
32	Maine	273.84
15	Maryland	315.87
3	Massachusetts	390.74
24	Michigan	295.34
7	Minnesota	354.76
50	Mississippi	189.78
42	Missouri	243.31
36	Montana	269.81
39	Nebraska	251.52
14	Nevada	316.84
35	New Hampshire	271.68
2	New Jersey	397.39
18	New Mexico	315.14
20	New York	306.38
23	North Carolina	297.74
21	North Dakota	306.05
6	Ohio	366.01
31	Oklahoma	276.00
27	Oregon	289.86
9	Pennsylvania	337.40
5	Rhode Island	379.40
44	South Carolina	236.12
40	South Dakota	247.97
46	Tennessee	224.07
16	Texas	315.76
19	Utah	314.78
25	Vermont	294.38
28	Virginia	288.25
4	Washington	381.04
37	West Virginia	257.58
33	Wisconsin	272.88
10	Wyoming	335.56

RANK ORDER

RANK	STATE	BENEFIT
1	Hawaii	$416.16
2	New Jersey	397.39
3	Massachusetts	390.74
4	Washington	381.04
5	Rhode Island	379.40
6	Ohio	366.01
7	Minnesota	354.76
8	Colorado	345.69
9	Pennsylvania	337.40
10	Wyoming	335.56
11	Connecticut	326.52
12	Kansas	324.77
13	Iowa	319.78
14	Nevada	316.84
15	Maryland	315.87
16	Texas	315.76
17	Illinois	315.48
18	New Mexico	315.14
19	Utah	314.78
20	New York	306.38
21	North Dakota	306.05
22	California	301.10
23	North Carolina	297.74
24	Michigan	295.34
25	Vermont	294.38
26	Indiana	293.38
27	Oregon	289.86
28	Virginia	288.25
29	Kentucky	288.19
30	Arkansas	277.53
31	Oklahoma	276.00
32	Maine	273.84
33	Wisconsin	272.88
34	Georgia	272.86
35	New Hampshire	271.68
36	Montana	269.81
37	West Virginia	257.58
38	Idaho	253.16
39	Nebraska	251.52
40	South Dakota	247.97
41	Delaware	246.57
42	Missouri	243.31
43	Alaska	238.49
44	South Carolina	236.12
45	Florida	230.81
46	Tennessee	224.07
47	Arizona	213.85
48	Louisiana	207.50
49	Alabama	205.50
50	Mississippi	189.78
	District of Columbia	298.96

Source: CQ Press using data from U.S. Department of Labor, Bureau of Labor Statistics
"Unemployment Insurance Data Summary" (http://workforcesecurity.doleta.gov/unemploy/content/data.asp)

Workers' Compensation Benefit Payments in 2008

National Total = $57,632,944,000*

ALPHA ORDER

RANK	STATE	PAYMENTS	% of USA
27	Alabama	$648,094,000	1.1%
45	Alaska	205,363,000	0.4%
26	Arizona	648,664,000	1.1%
43	Arkansas	215,404,000	0.4%
1	California	9,426,019,000	16.4%
19	Colorado	875,440,000	1.5%
23	Connecticut	781,480,000	1.4%
44	Delaware	208,562,000	0.4%
5	Florida	2,787,022,000	4.8%
9	Georgia	1,601,644,000	2.8%
41	Hawaii	245,763,000	0.4%
37	Idaho	280,276,000	0.5%
3	Illinois	2,994,420,000	5.2%
28	Indiana	623,737,000	1.1%
31	Iowa	575,072,000	1.0%
32	Kansas	417,517,000	0.7%
25	Kentucky	696,185,000	1.2%
24	Louisiana	733,650,000	1.3%
39	Maine	261,736,000	0.5%
17	Maryland	935,948,000	1.6%
20	Massachusetts	842,705,000	1.5%
12	Michigan	1,404,976,000	2.4%
15	Minnesota	1,007,193,000	1.7%
34	Mississippi	361,015,000	0.6%
16	Missouri	937,299,000	1.6%
40	Montana	252,648,000	0.4%
35	Nebraska	345,108,000	0.6%
33	Nevada	392,663,000	0.7%
42	New Hampshire	239,290,000	0.4%
8	New Jersey	1,916,466,000	3.3%
38	New Mexico	271,573,000	0.5%
2	New York	3,536,944,000	6.1%
10	North Carolina	1,526,320,000	2.6%
50	North Dakota	105,837,000	0.2%
6	Ohio	2,490,080,000	4.3%
22	Oklahoma	782,091,000	1.4%
30	Oregon	601,849,000	1.0%
4	Pennsylvania	2,902,243,000	5.0%
46	Rhode Island	158,006,000	0.3%
18	South Carolina	915,014,000	1.6%
49	South Dakota	113,555,000	0.2%
21	Tennessee	827,757,000	1.4%
11	Texas	1,514,130,000	2.6%
36	Utah	301,116,000	0.5%
48	Vermont	127,204,000	0.2%
13	Virginia	1,148,354,000	2.0%
7	Washington	2,192,885,000	3.8%
29	West Virginia	603,073,000	1.0%
14	Wisconsin	1,011,334,000	1.8%
47	Wyoming	137,133,000	0.2%

RANK ORDER

RANK	STATE	PAYMENTS	% of USA
1	California	$9,426,019,000	16.4%
2	New York	3,536,944,000	6.1%
3	Illinois	2,994,420,000	5.2%
4	Pennsylvania	2,902,243,000	5.0%
5	Florida	2,787,022,000	4.8%
6	Ohio	2,490,080,000	4.3%
7	Washington	2,192,885,000	3.8%
8	New Jersey	1,916,466,000	3.3%
9	Georgia	1,601,644,000	2.8%
10	North Carolina	1,526,320,000	2.6%
11	Texas	1,514,130,000	2.6%
12	Michigan	1,404,976,000	2.4%
13	Virginia	1,148,354,000	2.0%
14	Wisconsin	1,011,334,000	1.8%
15	Minnesota	1,007,193,000	1.7%
16	Missouri	937,299,000	1.6%
17	Maryland	935,948,000	1.6%
18	South Carolina	915,014,000	1.6%
19	Colorado	875,440,000	1.5%
20	Massachusetts	842,705,000	1.5%
21	Tennessee	827,757,000	1.4%
22	Oklahoma	782,091,000	1.4%
23	Connecticut	781,480,000	1.4%
24	Louisiana	733,650,000	1.3%
25	Kentucky	696,185,000	1.2%
26	Arizona	648,664,000	1.1%
27	Alabama	648,094,000	1.1%
28	Indiana	623,737,000	1.1%
29	West Virginia	603,073,000	1.0%
30	Oregon	601,849,000	1.0%
31	Iowa	575,072,000	1.0%
32	Kansas	417,517,000	0.7%
33	Nevada	392,663,000	0.7%
34	Mississippi	361,015,000	0.6%
35	Nebraska	345,108,000	0.6%
36	Utah	301,116,000	0.5%
37	Idaho	280,276,000	0.5%
38	New Mexico	271,573,000	0.5%
39	Maine	261,736,000	0.5%
40	Montana	252,648,000	0.4%
41	Hawaii	245,763,000	0.4%
42	New Hampshire	239,290,000	0.4%
43	Arkansas	215,404,000	0.4%
44	Delaware	208,562,000	0.4%
45	Alaska	205,363,000	0.4%
46	Rhode Island	158,006,000	0.3%
47	Wyoming	137,133,000	0.2%
48	Vermont	127,204,000	0.2%
49	South Dakota	113,555,000	0.2%
50	North Dakota	105,837,000	0.2%
	District of Columbia	81,263,000	0.1%

Source: National Academy of Social Insurance (Washington, DC)
      "Workers' Compensation: Benefits, Coverage, and Costs, 2008" (http://www.nasi.org)
*Estimated payments from private insurance, state and federal funds, and self insurance. National total includes payments for federal civilian employee program, Black Lung Program, and other federal programs.

Workers' Compensation Benefit Payment per Covered Worker in 2008

National Average = $441*

ALPHA ORDER

RANK	STATE	AVERAGE
34	Alabama	$358
3	Alaska	689
46	Arizona	256
50	Arkansas	193
4	California	618
25	Colorado	390
14	Connecticut	469
10	Delaware	501
27	Florida	388
19	Georgia	418
18	Hawaii	419
16	Idaho	438
7	Illinois	522
48	Indiana	221
24	Iowa	394
43	Kansas	311
21	Kentucky	398
22	Louisiana	396
15	Maine	447
26	Maryland	389
45	Massachusetts	264
33	Michigan	360
30	Minnesota	383
38	Mississippi	343
32	Missouri	369
5	Montana	596
29	Nebraska	384
41	Nevada	318
28	New Hampshire	385
11	New Jersey	495
36	New Mexico	355
19	New York	418
23	North Carolina	395
42	North Dakota	313
13	Ohio	483
7	Oklahoma	522
35	Oregon	357
6	Pennsylvania	524
37	Rhode Island	344
9	South Carolina	514
44	South Dakota	296
40	Tennessee	321
49	Texas	198
47	Utah	255
17	Vermont	433
39	Virginia	336
2	Washington	778
1	West Virginia	901
31	Wisconsin	379
12	Wyoming	492

RANK ORDER

RANK	STATE	AVERAGE
1	West Virginia	$901
2	Washington	778
3	Alaska	689
4	California	618
5	Montana	596
6	Pennsylvania	524
7	Illinois	522
7	Oklahoma	522
9	South Carolina	514
10	Delaware	501
11	New Jersey	495
12	Wyoming	492
13	Ohio	483
14	Connecticut	469
15	Maine	447
16	Idaho	438
17	Vermont	433
18	Hawaii	419
19	Georgia	418
19	New York	418
21	Kentucky	398
22	Louisiana	396
23	North Carolina	395
24	Iowa	394
25	Colorado	390
26	Maryland	389
27	Florida	388
28	New Hampshire	385
29	Nebraska	384
30	Minnesota	383
31	Wisconsin	379
32	Missouri	369
33	Michigan	360
34	Alabama	358
35	Oregon	357
36	New Mexico	355
37	Rhode Island	344
38	Mississippi	343
39	Virginia	336
40	Tennessee	321
41	Nevada	318
42	North Dakota	313
43	Kansas	311
44	South Dakota	296
45	Massachusetts	264
46	Arizona	256
47	Utah	255
48	Indiana	221
49	Texas	198
50	Arkansas	193
	District of Columbia	166

Source: CQ Press using data from National Academy of Social Insurance (Washington, DC)
"Workers' Compensation: Benefits, Coverage, and Costs, 2008" (http://www.nasi.org)
*Estimated payments from private insurance, state and federal funds, and self insurance. National rate includes payments for federal civilian employee program, Black Lung Program, and other federal programs. Total divided by number of workers covered by workers' compensation.

Percent Change in Workers' Compensation Benefit Payments: 2007 to 2008

National Percent Change = 4.4% Increase*

ALPHA ORDER

RANK	STATE	PERCENT CHANGE
11	Alabama	10.8
15	Alaska	9.1
42	Arizona	0.2
31	Arkansas	4.6
44	California	(0.9)
30	Colorado	4.7
19	Connecticut	7.7
25	Delaware	6.1
39	Florida	2.6
17	Georgia	8.1
43	Hawaii	(0.6)
28	Idaho	5.1
14	Illinois	9.4
32	Indiana	4.4
4	Iowa	15.9
26	Kansas	6.0
16	Kentucky	9.0
1	Louisiana	19.5
45	Maine	(4.1)
9	Maryland	10.9
46	Massachusetts	(4.9)
49	Michigan	(6.8)
27	Minnesota	5.8
13	Mississippi	9.7
28	Missouri	5.1
33	Montana	4.0
2	Nebraska	18.7
34	Nevada	3.8
3	New Hampshire	17.1
34	New Jersey	3.8
7	New Mexico	12.0
6	New York	12.7
5	North Carolina	13.2
9	North Dakota	10.9
41	Ohio	0.5
8	Oklahoma	11.4
39	Oregon	2.6
37	Pennsylvania	3.5
34	Rhode Island	3.8
38	South Carolina	3.4
46	South Dakota	(4.9)
22	Tennessee	6.8
21	Texas	7.0
24	Utah	6.6
22	Vermont	6.8
20	Virginia	7.4
12	Washington	9.9
46	West Virginia	(4.9)
50	Wisconsin	(7.6)
18	Wyoming	8.0

RANK ORDER

RANK	STATE	PERCENT CHANGE
1	Louisiana	19.5
2	Nebraska	18.7
3	New Hampshire	17.1
4	Iowa	15.9
5	North Carolina	13.2
6	New York	12.7
7	New Mexico	12.0
8	Oklahoma	11.4
9	Maryland	10.9
9	North Dakota	10.9
11	Alabama	10.8
12	Washington	9.9
13	Mississippi	9.7
14	Illinois	9.4
15	Alaska	9.1
16	Kentucky	9.0
17	Georgia	8.1
18	Wyoming	8.0
19	Connecticut	7.7
20	Virginia	7.4
21	Texas	7.0
22	Tennessee	6.8
22	Vermont	6.8
24	Utah	6.6
25	Delaware	6.1
26	Kansas	6.0
27	Minnesota	5.8
28	Idaho	5.1
28	Missouri	5.1
30	Colorado	4.7
31	Arkansas	4.6
32	Indiana	4.4
33	Montana	4.0
34	Nevada	3.8
34	New Jersey	3.8
34	Rhode Island	3.8
37	Pennsylvania	3.5
38	South Carolina	3.4
39	Florida	2.6
39	Oregon	2.6
41	Ohio	0.5
42	Arizona	0.2
43	Hawaii	(0.6)
44	California	(0.9)
45	Maine	(4.1)
46	Massachusetts	(4.9)
46	South Dakota	(4.9)
46	West Virginia	(4.9)
49	Michigan	(6.8)
50	Wisconsin	(7.6)
	District of Columbia	(3.3)

Source: National Academy of Social Insurance (Washington, DC)
    "Workers' Compensation: Benefits, Coverage, and Costs, 2008" (http://www.nasi.org)
*Estimated payments from private insurance, state and federal funds, and self insurance. National rate includes payments for federal civilian employee program, Black Lung Program, and other federal programs.

Civilian Labor Force in 2010

National Total = 153,690,000 Workers*

RANK	STATE	EMPLOYEES	% of USA
24	Alabama	2,132,100	1.4%
48	Alaska	363,300	0.2%
15	Arizona	3,172,000	2.1%
32	Arkansas	1,358,200	0.9%
1	California	18,214,800	11.9%
22	Colorado	2,665,200	1.7%
28	Connecticut	1,897,600	1.2%
46	Delaware	422,600	0.3%
4	Florida	9,245,400	6.0%
9	Georgia	4,672,500	3.0%
42	Hawaii	633,600	0.4%
39	Idaho	756,000	0.5%
5	Illinois	6,687,500	4.4%
16	Indiana	3,127,600	2.0%
30	Iowa	1,675,800	1.1%
31	Kansas	1,502,400	1.0%
26	Kentucky	2,091,200	1.4%
25	Louisiana	2,104,600	1.4%
41	Maine	697,900	0.5%
20	Maryland	2,977,900	1.9%
14	Massachusetts	3,498,000	2.3%
8	Michigan	4,763,100	3.1%
21	Minnesota	2,953,800	1.9%
35	Mississippi	1,321,500	0.9%
19	Missouri	3,003,800	2.0%
44	Montana	494,700	0.3%
36	Nebraska	973,900	0.6%
34	Nevada	1,331,700	0.9%
40	New Hampshire	747,800	0.5%
10	New Jersey	4,487,000	2.9%
37	New Mexico	957,600	0.6%
3	New York	9,630,400	6.3%
11	North Carolina	4,470,700	2.9%
47	North Dakota	369,000	0.2%
7	Ohio	5,906,500	3.8%
29	Oklahoma	1,755,200	1.1%
27	Oregon	1,993,500	1.3%
6	Pennsylvania	6,357,700	4.1%
43	Rhode Island	573,200	0.4%
23	South Carolina	2,161,800	1.4%
45	South Dakota	443,700	0.3%
17	Tennessee	3,067,300	2.0%
2	Texas	12,210,500	7.9%
33	Utah	1,356,400	0.9%
49	Vermont	358,600	0.2%
12	Virginia	4,182,000	2.7%
13	Washington	3,540,600	2.3%
38	West Virginia	779,100	0.5%
18	Wisconsin	3,050,100	2.0%
50	Wyoming	293,100	0.2%

RANK	STATE	EMPLOYEES	% of USA
1	California	18,214,800	11.9%
2	Texas	12,210,500	7.9%
3	New York	9,630,400	6.3%
4	Florida	9,245,400	6.0%
5	Illinois	6,687,500	4.4%
6	Pennsylvania	6,357,700	4.1%
7	Ohio	5,906,500	3.8%
8	Michigan	4,763,100	3.1%
9	Georgia	4,672,500	3.0%
10	New Jersey	4,487,000	2.9%
11	North Carolina	4,470,700	2.9%
12	Virginia	4,182,000	2.7%
13	Washington	3,540,600	2.3%
14	Massachusetts	3,498,000	2.3%
15	Arizona	3,172,000	2.1%
16	Indiana	3,127,600	2.0%
17	Tennessee	3,067,300	2.0%
18	Wisconsin	3,050,100	2.0%
19	Missouri	3,003,800	2.0%
20	Maryland	2,977,900	1.9%
21	Minnesota	2,953,800	1.9%
22	Colorado	2,665,200	1.7%
23	South Carolina	2,161,800	1.4%
24	Alabama	2,132,100	1.4%
25	Louisiana	2,104,600	1.4%
26	Kentucky	2,091,200	1.4%
27	Oregon	1,993,500	1.3%
28	Connecticut	1,897,600	1.2%
29	Oklahoma	1,755,200	1.1%
30	Iowa	1,675,800	1.1%
31	Kansas	1,502,400	1.0%
32	Arkansas	1,358,200	0.9%
33	Utah	1,356,400	0.9%
34	Nevada	1,331,700	0.9%
35	Mississippi	1,321,500	0.9%
36	Nebraska	973,900	0.6%
37	New Mexico	957,600	0.6%
38	West Virginia	779,100	0.5%
39	Idaho	756,000	0.5%
40	New Hampshire	747,800	0.5%
41	Maine	697,900	0.5%
42	Hawaii	633,600	0.4%
43	Rhode Island	573,200	0.4%
44	Montana	494,700	0.3%
45	South Dakota	443,700	0.3%
46	Delaware	422,600	0.3%
47	North Dakota	369,000	0.2%
48	Alaska	363,300	0.2%
49	Vermont	358,600	0.2%
50	Wyoming	293,100	0.2%
	District of Columbia	332,300	0.2%

Source: U.S. Department of Labor, Bureau of Labor Statistics
"Regional and State Employment and Unemployment" (press release, January 25, 2011, www.bls.gov/bls/newsrels.htm)
*Seasonally adjusted preliminary data as of December 2010. National total calculated through a different formula.

Employed Civilian Labor Force in 2010

National Total = 139,206,000 Employed Workers*

ALPHA ORDER

RANK	STATE	EMPLOYED	% of USA
23	Alabama	1,937,400	1.4%
49	Alaska	334,000	0.2%
15	Arizona	2,875,200	2.1%
33	Arkansas	1,250,400	0.9%
1	California	15,945,500	11.5%
22	Colorado	2,431,900	1.7%
28	Connecticut	1,727,700	1.2%
46	Delaware	386,700	0.3%
4	Florida	8,137,100	5.8%
9	Georgia	4,193,700	3.0%
42	Hawaii	593,300	0.4%
40	Idaho	684,100	0.5%
5	Illinois	6,066,900	4.4%
16	Indiana	2,830,900	2.0%
30	Iowa	1,569,800	1.1%
31	Kansas	1,399,800	1.0%
26	Kentucky	1,876,700	1.3%
24	Louisiana	1,936,600	1.4%
41	Maine	646,700	0.5%
19	Maryland	2,758,900	2.0%
14	Massachusetts	3,209,700	2.3%
8	Michigan	4,207,800	3.0%
20	Minnesota	2,748,000	2.0%
34	Mississippi	1,187,600	0.9%
21	Missouri	2,718,700	2.0%
44	Montana	459,000	0.3%
36	Nebraska	930,700	0.7%
35	Nevada	1,139,200	0.8%
38	New Hampshire	707,000	0.5%
10	New Jersey	4,079,200	2.9%
37	New Mexico	876,000	0.6%
3	New York	8,837,600	6.3%
11	North Carolina	4,031,500	2.9%
47	North Dakota	355,000	0.3%
7	Ohio	5,339,900	3.8%
29	Oklahoma	1,635,300	1.2%
27	Oregon	1,782,900	1.3%
6	Pennsylvania	5,819,400	4.2%
43	Rhode Island	507,200	0.4%
25	South Carolina	1,929,800	1.4%
45	South Dakota	423,300	0.3%
18	Tennessee	2,777,700	2.0%
2	Texas	11,202,400	8.0%
32	Utah	1,254,700	0.9%
48	Vermont	337,900	0.2%
12	Virginia	3,903,400	2.8%
13	Washington	3,212,000	2.3%
39	West Virginia	704,400	0.5%
17	Wisconsin	2,822,400	2.0%
50	Wyoming	274,300	0.2%

RANK ORDER

RANK	STATE	EMPLOYED	% of USA
1	California	15,945,500	11.5%
2	Texas	11,202,400	8.0%
3	New York	8,837,600	6.3%
4	Florida	8,137,100	5.8%
5	Illinois	6,066,900	4.4%
6	Pennsylvania	5,819,400	4.2%
7	Ohio	5,339,900	3.8%
8	Michigan	4,207,800	3.0%
9	Georgia	4,193,700	3.0%
10	New Jersey	4,079,200	2.9%
11	North Carolina	4,031,500	2.9%
12	Virginia	3,903,400	2.8%
13	Washington	3,212,000	2.3%
14	Massachusetts	3,209,700	2.3%
15	Arizona	2,875,200	2.1%
16	Indiana	2,830,900	2.0%
17	Wisconsin	2,822,400	2.0%
18	Tennessee	2,777,700	2.0%
19	Maryland	2,758,900	2.0%
20	Minnesota	2,748,000	2.0%
21	Missouri	2,718,700	2.0%
22	Colorado	2,431,900	1.7%
23	Alabama	1,937,400	1.4%
24	Louisiana	1,936,600	1.4%
25	South Carolina	1,929,800	1.4%
26	Kentucky	1,876,700	1.3%
27	Oregon	1,782,900	1.3%
28	Connecticut	1,727,700	1.2%
29	Oklahoma	1,635,300	1.2%
30	Iowa	1,569,800	1.1%
31	Kansas	1,399,800	1.0%
32	Utah	1,254,700	0.9%
33	Arkansas	1,250,400	0.9%
34	Mississippi	1,187,600	0.9%
35	Nevada	1,139,200	0.8%
36	Nebraska	930,700	0.7%
37	New Mexico	876,000	0.6%
38	New Hampshire	707,000	0.5%
39	West Virginia	704,400	0.5%
40	Idaho	684,100	0.5%
41	Maine	646,700	0.5%
42	Hawaii	593,300	0.4%
43	Rhode Island	507,200	0.4%
44	Montana	459,000	0.3%
45	South Dakota	423,300	0.3%
46	Delaware	386,700	0.3%
47	North Dakota	355,000	0.3%
48	Vermont	337,900	0.2%
49	Alaska	334,000	0.2%
50	Wyoming	274,300	0.2%
	District of Columbia	300,100	0.2%

Source: CQ Press using data from U.S. Department of Labor, Bureau of Labor Statistics
"Regional and State Employment and Unemployment" (press release, January 25, 2011, www.bls.gov/bls/newsrels.htm)
*Seasonally adjusted preliminary data as of December 2010. National total calculated through a different formula.

Employment to Population Ratio in 2010

National Percent = 57.8% of Population 16 Years and Older Employed*

ALPHA ORDER				RANK ORDER		
RANK	STATE	PERCENT		RANK	STATE	PERCENT
49	Alabama	52.2		1	North Dakota	68.3
13	Alaska	62.3		2	Nebraska	66.7
31	Arizona	57.0		3	South Dakota	66.6
41	Arkansas	55.3		4	Minnesota	66.2
38	California	55.7		5	Iowa	66.0
14	Colorado	61.9		5	Vermont	66.0
15	Connecticut	61.5		7	New Hampshire	65.9
42	Delaware	55.1		8	Wyoming	64.2
45	Florida	54.4		9	Kansas	63.9
38	Georgia	55.7		10	Utah	62.7
29	Hawaii	57.2		10	Wisconsin	62.7
25	Idaho	58.4		12	Virginia	62.5
20	Illinois	60.1		13	Alaska	62.3
34	Indiana	56.4		14	Colorado	61.9
5	Iowa	66.0		15	Connecticut	61.5
9	Kansas	63.9		16	Maryland	61.2
43	Kentucky	54.9		17	Washington	60.9
40	Louisiana	55.4		18	Massachusetts	60.2
21	Maine	59.7		18	Texas	60.2
16	Maryland	61.2		20	Illinois	60.1
18	Massachusetts	60.2		21	Maine	59.7
47	Michigan	53.2		22	Rhode Island	59.3
4	Minnesota	66.2		23	New Jersey	59.1
48	Mississippi	52.3		24	Montana	58.7
28	Missouri	57.5		25	Idaho	58.4
24	Montana	58.7		25	Oregon	58.4
2	Nebraska	66.7		27	Ohio	58.3
36	Nevada	56.0		28	Missouri	57.5
7	New Hampshire	65.9		29	Hawaii	57.2
23	New Jersey	59.1		29	Pennsylvania	57.2
35	New Mexico	56.3		31	Arizona	57.0
33	New York	56.5		31	Oklahoma	57.0
44	North Carolina	54.8		33	New York	56.5
1	North Dakota	68.3		34	Indiana	56.4
27	Ohio	58.3		35	New Mexico	56.3
31	Oklahoma	57.0		36	Nevada	56.0
25	Oregon	58.4		37	Tennessee	55.9
29	Pennsylvania	57.2		38	California	55.7
22	Rhode Island	59.3		38	Georgia	55.7
46	South Carolina	53.5		40	Louisiana	55.4
3	South Dakota	66.6		41	Arkansas	55.3
37	Tennessee	55.9		42	Delaware	55.1
18	Texas	60.2		43	Kentucky	54.9
10	Utah	62.7		44	North Carolina	54.8
5	Vermont	66.0		45	Florida	54.4
12	Virginia	62.5		46	South Carolina	53.5
17	Washington	60.9		47	Michigan	53.2
50	West Virginia	47.6		48	Mississippi	52.3
10	Wisconsin	62.7		49	Alabama	52.2
8	Wyoming	64.2		50	West Virginia	47.6
					District of Columbia	60.2

Source: CQ Press using data from U.S. Department of Labor, Bureau of Labor Statistics
"Regional and State Employment and Unemployment" (press release, January 25, 2011, www.bls.gov/bls/newsrels.htm)
*Seasonally adjusted preliminary data as of December 2010. Calculated with 2009 population data.

Unemployed Civilian Labor Force in 2010

National Total = 14,485,000 Unemployed Workers*

ALPHA ORDER

RANK	STATE	UNEMPLOYED	% of USA
26	Alabama	194,700	1.3%
46	Alaska	29,300	0.2%
13	Arizona	296,800	2.0%
32	Arkansas	107,800	0.7%
1	California	2,269,300	15.7%
19	Colorado	233,300	1.6%
28	Connecticut	169,900	1.2%
44	Delaware	35,900	0.2%
2	Florida	1,108,300	7.7%
9	Georgia	478,800	3.3%
43	Hawaii	40,300	0.3%
38	Idaho	71,900	0.5%
5	Illinois	620,600	4.3%
14	Indiana	296,700	2.0%
33	Iowa	106,000	0.7%
34	Kansas	102,600	0.7%
23	Kentucky	214,500	1.5%
29	Louisiana	168,000	1.2%
40	Maine	51,200	0.4%
22	Maryland	219,000	1.5%
16	Massachusetts	288,300	2.0%
7	Michigan	555,300	3.8%
25	Minnesota	205,800	1.4%
30	Mississippi	133,900	0.9%
17	Missouri	285,100	2.0%
45	Montana	35,700	0.2%
41	Nebraska	43,200	0.3%
27	Nevada	192,500	1.3%
42	New Hampshire	40,800	0.3%
11	New Jersey	407,800	2.8%
36	New Mexico	81,600	0.6%
4	New York	792,800	5.5%
10	North Carolina	439,200	3.0%
50	North Dakota	14,000	0.1%
6	Ohio	566,600	3.9%
31	Oklahoma	119,900	0.8%
24	Oregon	210,600	1.5%
8	Pennsylvania	538,300	3.7%
39	Rhode Island	66,000	0.5%
20	South Carolina	232,000	1.6%
48	South Dakota	20,400	0.1%
15	Tennessee	289,600	2.0%
3	Texas	1,008,100	7.0%
35	Utah	101,700	0.7%
47	Vermont	20,700	0.1%
18	Virginia	278,600	1.9%
12	Washington	328,600	2.3%
37	West Virginia	74,700	0.5%
21	Wisconsin	227,700	1.6%
49	Wyoming	18,800	0.1%

RANK ORDER

RANK	STATE	UNEMPLOYED	% of USA
1	California	2,269,300	15.7%
2	Florida	1,108,300	7.7%
3	Texas	1,008,100	7.0%
4	New York	792,800	5.5%
5	Illinois	620,600	4.3%
6	Ohio	566,600	3.9%
7	Michigan	555,300	3.8%
8	Pennsylvania	538,300	3.7%
9	Georgia	478,800	3.3%
10	North Carolina	439,200	3.0%
11	New Jersey	407,800	2.8%
12	Washington	328,600	2.3%
13	Arizona	296,800	2.0%
14	Indiana	296,700	2.0%
15	Tennessee	289,600	2.0%
16	Massachusetts	288,300	2.0%
17	Missouri	285,100	2.0%
18	Virginia	278,600	1.9%
19	Colorado	233,300	1.6%
20	South Carolina	232,000	1.6%
21	Wisconsin	227,700	1.6%
22	Maryland	219,000	1.5%
23	Kentucky	214,500	1.5%
24	Oregon	210,600	1.5%
25	Minnesota	205,800	1.4%
26	Alabama	194,700	1.3%
27	Nevada	192,500	1.3%
28	Connecticut	169,900	1.2%
29	Louisiana	168,000	1.2%
30	Mississippi	133,900	0.9%
31	Oklahoma	119,900	0.8%
32	Arkansas	107,800	0.7%
33	Iowa	106,000	0.7%
34	Kansas	102,600	0.7%
35	Utah	101,700	0.7%
36	New Mexico	81,600	0.6%
37	West Virginia	74,700	0.5%
38	Idaho	71,900	0.5%
39	Rhode Island	66,000	0.5%
40	Maine	51,200	0.4%
41	Nebraska	43,200	0.3%
42	New Hampshire	40,800	0.3%
43	Hawaii	40,300	0.3%
44	Delaware	35,900	0.2%
45	Montana	35,700	0.2%
46	Alaska	29,300	0.2%
47	Vermont	20,700	0.1%
48	South Dakota	20,400	0.1%
49	Wyoming	18,800	0.1%
50	North Dakota	14,000	0.1%
	District of Columbia	32,200	0.2%

Source: U.S. Department of Labor, Bureau of Labor Statistics
   "Regional and State Employment and Unemployment" (press release, January 25, 2011, www.bls.gov/bls/newsrels.htm)
*Seasonally adjusted preliminary data as of December 2010. National total calculated through a different formula.

Unemployment Rate in 2010

National Rate = 9.4% of Labor Force Unemployed*

ALPHA ORDER

RANK	STATE	PERCENT
21	Alabama	9.1
31	Alaska	8.1
17	Arizona	9.4
33	Arkansas	7.9
2	California	12.5
24	Colorado	8.8
23	Connecticut	9.0
25	Delaware	8.5
3	Florida	12.0
9	Georgia	10.2
43	Hawaii	6.4
14	Idaho	9.5
19	Illinois	9.3
14	Indiana	9.5
45	Iowa	6.3
40	Kansas	6.8
8	Kentucky	10.3
32	Louisiana	8.0
37	Maine	7.3
36	Maryland	7.4
29	Massachusetts	8.2
4	Michigan	11.7
39	Minnesota	7.0
10	Mississippi	10.1
14	Missouri	9.5
38	Montana	7.2
49	Nebraska	4.4
1	Nevada	14.5
47	New Hampshire	5.5
21	New Jersey	9.1
25	New Mexico	8.5
29	New York	8.2
11	North Carolina	9.8
50	North Dakota	3.8
12	Ohio	9.6
40	Oklahoma	6.8
7	Oregon	10.6
25	Pennsylvania	8.5
5	Rhode Island	11.5
6	South Carolina	10.7
48	South Dakota	4.6
17	Tennessee	9.4
28	Texas	8.3
34	Utah	7.5
46	Vermont	5.8
42	Virginia	6.7
19	Washington	9.3
12	West Virginia	9.6
34	Wisconsin	7.5
43	Wyoming	6.4

RANK ORDER

RANK	STATE	PERCENT
1	Nevada	14.5
2	California	12.5
3	Florida	12.0
4	Michigan	11.7
5	Rhode Island	11.5
6	South Carolina	10.7
7	Oregon	10.6
8	Kentucky	10.3
9	Georgia	10.2
10	Mississippi	10.1
11	North Carolina	9.8
12	Ohio	9.6
12	West Virginia	9.6
14	Idaho	9.5
14	Indiana	9.5
14	Missouri	9.5
17	Arizona	9.4
17	Tennessee	9.4
19	Illinois	9.3
19	Washington	9.3
21	Alabama	9.1
21	New Jersey	9.1
23	Connecticut	9.0
24	Colorado	8.8
25	Delaware	8.5
25	New Mexico	8.5
25	Pennsylvania	8.5
28	Texas	8.3
29	Massachusetts	8.2
29	New York	8.2
31	Alaska	8.1
32	Louisiana	8.0
33	Arkansas	7.9
34	Utah	7.5
34	Wisconsin	7.5
36	Maryland	7.4
37	Maine	7.3
38	Montana	7.2
39	Minnesota	7.0
40	Kansas	6.8
40	Oklahoma	6.8
42	Virginia	6.7
43	Hawaii	6.4
43	Wyoming	6.4
45	Iowa	6.3
46	Vermont	5.8
47	New Hampshire	5.5
48	South Dakota	4.6
49	Nebraska	4.4
50	North Dakota	3.8

	District of Columbia	9.7

Source: U.S. Department of Labor, Bureau of Labor Statistics
   "Regional and State Employment and Unemployment" (press release, January 25, 2011, www.bls.gov/bls/newsrels.htm)
*Seasonally adjusted preliminary data as of December 2010. National rate calculated through a different formula.

Women in Civilian Labor Force in 2009

National Total = 71,954,000 Women*

ALPHA ORDER

RANK	STATE	WOMEN	% of USA
24	Alabama	1,014,000	1.4%
49	Alaska	167,000	0.2%
20	Arizona	1,414,000	2.0%
32	Arkansas	642,000	0.9%
1	California	8,218,000	11.4%
22	Colorado	1,225,000	1.7%
28	Connecticut	914,000	1.3%
46	Delaware	213,000	0.3%
4	Florida	4,303,000	6.0%
9	Georgia	2,219,000	3.1%
42	Hawaii	297,000	0.4%
40	Idaho	335,000	0.5%
5	Illinois	3,083,000	4.3%
15	Indiana	1,511,000	2.1%
30	Iowa	810,000	1.1%
31	Kansas	718,000	1.0%
26	Kentucky	967,000	1.3%
25	Louisiana	983,000	1.4%
40	Maine	335,000	0.5%
17	Maryland	1,489,000	2.1%
13	Massachusetts	1,690,000	2.3%
8	Michigan	2,306,000	3.2%
21	Minnesota	1,395,000	1.9%
33	Mississippi	609,000	0.8%
18	Missouri	1,481,000	2.1%
44	Montana	235,000	0.3%
36	Nebraska	469,000	0.7%
34	Nevada	598,000	0.8%
39	New Hampshire	353,000	0.5%
11	New Jersey	2,134,000	3.0%
37	New Mexico	443,000	0.6%
3	New York	4,607,000	6.4%
10	North Carolina	2,162,000	3.0%
48	North Dakota	171,000	0.2%
7	Ohio	2,851,000	4.0%
29	Oklahoma	832,000	1.2%
27	Oregon	919,000	1.3%
6	Pennsylvania	3,036,000	4.2%
43	Rhode Island	274,000	0.4%
23	South Carolina	1,042,000	1.4%
45	South Dakota	214,000	0.3%
19	Tennessee	1,428,000	2.0%
2	Texas	5,271,000	7.3%
35	Utah	595,000	0.8%
47	Vermont	178,000	0.2%
12	Virginia	1,989,000	2.8%
14	Washington	1,650,000	2.3%
38	West Virginia	369,000	0.5%
16	Wisconsin	1,494,000	2.1%
50	Wyoming	133,000	0.2%

RANK ORDER

RANK	STATE	WOMEN	% of USA
1	California	8,218,000	11.4%
2	Texas	5,271,000	7.3%
3	New York	4,607,000	6.4%
4	Florida	4,303,000	6.0%
5	Illinois	3,083,000	4.3%
6	Pennsylvania	3,036,000	4.2%
7	Ohio	2,851,000	4.0%
8	Michigan	2,306,000	3.2%
9	Georgia	2,219,000	3.1%
10	North Carolina	2,162,000	3.0%
11	New Jersey	2,134,000	3.0%
12	Virginia	1,989,000	2.8%
13	Massachusetts	1,690,000	2.3%
14	Washington	1,650,000	2.3%
15	Indiana	1,511,000	2.1%
16	Wisconsin	1,494,000	2.1%
17	Maryland	1,489,000	2.1%
18	Missouri	1,481,000	2.1%
19	Tennessee	1,428,000	2.0%
20	Arizona	1,414,000	2.0%
21	Minnesota	1,395,000	1.9%
22	Colorado	1,225,000	1.7%
23	South Carolina	1,042,000	1.4%
24	Alabama	1,014,000	1.4%
25	Louisiana	983,000	1.4%
26	Kentucky	967,000	1.3%
27	Oregon	919,000	1.3%
28	Connecticut	914,000	1.3%
29	Oklahoma	832,000	1.2%
30	Iowa	810,000	1.1%
31	Kansas	718,000	1.0%
32	Arkansas	642,000	0.9%
33	Mississippi	609,000	0.8%
34	Nevada	598,000	0.8%
35	Utah	595,000	0.8%
36	Nebraska	469,000	0.7%
37	New Mexico	443,000	0.6%
38	West Virginia	369,000	0.5%
39	New Hampshire	353,000	0.5%
40	Idaho	335,000	0.5%
40	Maine	335,000	0.5%
42	Hawaii	297,000	0.4%
43	Rhode Island	274,000	0.4%
44	Montana	235,000	0.3%
45	South Dakota	214,000	0.3%
46	Delaware	213,000	0.3%
47	Vermont	178,000	0.2%
48	North Dakota	171,000	0.2%
49	Alaska	167,000	0.2%
50	Wyoming	133,000	0.2%
	District of Columbia	169,000	0.2%

Source: U.S. Department of Labor, Bureau of Labor Statistics
"Geographic Profiles of Employment and Unemployment, 2009" (http://www.bls.gov/gps/)
*Annual averages.

Percent of Women in the Civilian Labor Force in 2009

National Percent = 59.2% of Women*

ALPHA ORDER

RANK	STATE	PERCENT
48	Alabama	53.1
9	Alaska	65.6
42	Arizona	56.2
45	Arkansas	55.9
36	California	57.7
14	Colorado	63.5
13	Connecticut	63.9
29	Delaware	59.0
40	Florida	56.8
32	Georgia	58.2
31	Hawaii	58.3
33	Idaho	57.9
23	Illinois	60.6
28	Indiana	59.8
3	Iowa	68.0
8	Kansas	65.9
46	Kentucky	55.8
47	Louisiana	54.7
23	Maine	60.6
12	Maryland	64.0
18	Massachusetts	61.9
37	Michigan	57.4
6	Minnesota	67.4
49	Mississippi	52.1
19	Missouri	61.7
21	Montana	60.9
5	Nebraska	67.6
25	Nevada	60.4
10	New Hampshire	65.5
22	New Jersey	60.8
42	New Mexico	56.2
38	New York	57.3
33	North Carolina	57.9
4	North Dakota	67.7
20	Ohio	61.1
35	Oklahoma	57.8
27	Oregon	59.9
30	Pennsylvania	58.6
17	Rhode Island	62.6
41	South Carolina	56.5
2	South Dakota	68.3
42	Tennessee	56.2
39	Texas	57.0
25	Utah	60.4
1	Vermont	68.8
15	Virginia	63.3
16	Washington	62.9
50	West Virginia	49.2
7	Wisconsin	66.5
11	Wyoming	64.2

RANK ORDER

RANK	STATE	PERCENT
1	Vermont	68.8
2	South Dakota	68.3
3	Iowa	68.0
4	North Dakota	67.7
5	Nebraska	67.6
6	Minnesota	67.4
7	Wisconsin	66.5
8	Kansas	65.9
9	Alaska	65.6
10	New Hampshire	65.5
11	Wyoming	64.2
12	Maryland	64.0
13	Connecticut	63.9
14	Colorado	63.5
15	Virginia	63.3
16	Washington	62.9
17	Rhode Island	62.6
18	Massachusetts	61.9
19	Missouri	61.7
20	Ohio	61.1
21	Montana	60.9
22	New Jersey	60.8
23	Illinois	60.6
23	Maine	60.6
25	Nevada	60.4
25	Utah	60.4
27	Oregon	59.9
28	Indiana	59.8
29	Delaware	59.0
30	Pennsylvania	58.6
31	Hawaii	58.3
32	Georgia	58.2
33	Idaho	57.9
33	North Carolina	57.9
35	Oklahoma	57.8
36	California	57.7
37	Michigan	57.4
38	New York	57.3
39	Texas	57.0
40	Florida	56.8
41	South Carolina	56.5
42	Arizona	56.2
42	New Mexico	56.2
42	Tennessee	56.2
45	Arkansas	55.9
46	Kentucky	55.8
47	Louisiana	54.7
48	Alabama	53.1
49	Mississippi	52.1
50	West Virginia	49.2
	District of Columbia	64.4

Source: U.S. Department of Labor, Bureau of Labor Statistics
   "Geographic Profiles of Employment and Unemployment, 2009" (http://www.bls.gov/gps/)
*Annual averages.

Percent of Civilian Labor Force Comprised of Women in 2009

National Percent = 46.7% of Civilian Labor Force*

ALPHA ORDER

RANK	STATE	PERCENT
27	Alabama	47.1
41	Alaska	46.1
44	Arizona	44.9
35	Arkansas	46.8
43	California	45.0
44	Colorado	44.9
7	Connecticut	48.4
4	Delaware	48.6
22	Florida	47.3
40	Georgia	46.2
29	Hawaii	47.0
46	Idaho	44.7
37	Illinois	46.7
25	Indiana	47.2
14	Iowa	48.0
29	Kansas	47.0
33	Kentucky	46.9
20	Louisiana	47.4
9	Maine	48.2
2	Maryland	49.0
6	Massachusetts	48.5
29	Michigan	47.0
17	Minnesota	47.6
13	Mississippi	48.1
8	Missouri	48.3
22	Montana	47.3
16	Nebraska	47.8
49	Nevada	44.2
18	New Hampshire	47.5
33	New Jersey	46.9
25	New Mexico	47.2
20	New York	47.4
22	North Carolina	47.3
29	North Dakota	47.0
9	Ohio	48.2
35	Oklahoma	46.8
37	Oregon	46.7
18	Pennsylvania	47.5
4	Rhode Island	48.6
3	South Carolina	48.9
15	South Dakota	47.9
27	Tennessee	47.1
48	Texas	44.3
50	Utah	43.1
1	Vermont	49.6
9	Virginia	48.2
37	Washington	46.7
42	West Virginia	45.1
9	Wisconsin	48.2
47	Wyoming	44.5

RANK ORDER

RANK	STATE	PERCENT
1	Vermont	49.6
2	Maryland	49.0
3	South Carolina	48.9
4	Delaware	48.6
4	Rhode Island	48.6
6	Massachusetts	48.5
7	Connecticut	48.4
8	Missouri	48.3
9	Maine	48.2
9	Ohio	48.2
9	Virginia	48.2
9	Wisconsin	48.2
13	Mississippi	48.1
14	Iowa	48.0
15	South Dakota	47.9
16	Nebraska	47.8
17	Minnesota	47.6
18	New Hampshire	47.5
18	Pennsylvania	47.5
20	Louisiana	47.4
20	New York	47.4
22	Florida	47.3
22	Montana	47.3
22	North Carolina	47.3
25	Indiana	47.2
25	New Mexico	47.2
27	Alabama	47.1
27	Tennessee	47.1
29	Hawaii	47.0
29	Kansas	47.0
29	Michigan	47.0
29	North Dakota	47.0
33	Kentucky	46.9
33	New Jersey	46.9
35	Arkansas	46.8
35	Oklahoma	46.8
37	Illinois	46.7
37	Oregon	46.7
37	Washington	46.7
40	Georgia	46.2
41	Alaska	46.1
42	West Virginia	45.1
43	California	45.0
44	Arizona	44.9
44	Colorado	44.9
46	Idaho	44.7
47	Wyoming	44.5
48	Texas	44.3
49	Nevada	44.2
50	Utah	43.1

District of Columbia	50.1

Source: CQ Press using data from U.S. Department of Labor, Bureau of Labor Statistics
    "Geographic Profiles of Employment and Unemployment, 2009" (http://www.bls.gov/gps/)
*Annual averages.

Percent of Children under 6 Years Old with All Parents Working: 2009

National Percent = 64.4%

ALPHA ORDER

RANK	STATE	PERCENT
30	Alabama	65.4
47	Alaska	57.8
46	Arizona	59.3
22	Arkansas	66.8
43	California	60.9
39	Colorado	62.0
9	Connecticut	70.4
13	Delaware	69.0
21	Florida	67.5
33	Georgia	64.8
12	Hawaii	69.4
48	Idaho	57.2
28	Illinois	65.9
31	Indiana	64.9
2	Iowa	75.4
14	Kansas	68.5
37	Kentucky	63.5
24	Louisiana	66.4
17	Maine	68.4
10	Maryland	70.3
14	Massachusetts	68.5
26	Michigan	66.1
6	Minnesota	72.2
18	Mississippi	68.1
14	Missouri	68.5
35	Montana	64.4
3	Nebraska	73.5
38	Nevada	62.5
11	New Hampshire	69.6
33	New Jersey	64.8
41	New Mexico	61.7
40	New York	61.9
29	North Carolina	65.8
1	North Dakota	76.1
19	Ohio	68.0
41	Oklahoma	61.7
36	Oregon	63.7
23	Pennsylvania	66.7
8	Rhode Island	70.7
19	South Carolina	68.0
5	South Dakota	72.7
27	Tennessee	66.0
45	Texas	59.5
50	Utah	49.6
7	Vermont	71.7
31	Virginia	64.9
44	Washington	60.0
49	West Virginia	57.1
4	Wisconsin	72.9
24	Wyoming	66.4

RANK ORDER

RANK	STATE	PERCENT
1	North Dakota	76.1
2	Iowa	75.4
3	Nebraska	73.5
4	Wisconsin	72.9
5	South Dakota	72.7
6	Minnesota	72.2
7	Vermont	71.7
8	Rhode Island	70.7
9	Connecticut	70.4
10	Maryland	70.3
11	New Hampshire	69.6
12	Hawaii	69.4
13	Delaware	69.0
14	Kansas	68.5
14	Massachusetts	68.5
14	Missouri	68.5
17	Maine	68.4
18	Mississippi	68.1
19	Ohio	68.0
19	South Carolina	68.0
21	Florida	67.5
22	Arkansas	66.8
23	Pennsylvania	66.7
24	Louisiana	66.4
24	Wyoming	66.4
26	Michigan	66.1
27	Tennessee	66.0
28	Illinois	65.9
29	North Carolina	65.8
30	Alabama	65.4
31	Indiana	64.9
31	Virginia	64.9
33	Georgia	64.8
33	New Jersey	64.8
35	Montana	64.4
36	Oregon	63.7
37	Kentucky	63.5
38	Nevada	62.5
39	Colorado	62.0
40	New York	61.9
41	New Mexico	61.7
41	Oklahoma	61.7
43	California	60.9
44	Washington	60.0
45	Texas	59.5
46	Arizona	59.3
47	Alaska	57.8
48	Idaho	57.2
49	West Virginia	57.1
50	Utah	49.6
	District of Columbia	71.2

Source: U.S. Bureau of the Census
"2009 American Community Survey" (http://www.census.gov/acs/www/index.html)

Job Growth: 2009 to 2010

National Percent Change = 0.2% Decrease*

ALPHA ORDER

RANK	STATE	PERCENT CHANGE
43	Alabama	(1.6)
7	Alaska	0.7
16	Arizona	0.3
27	Arkansas	(0.5)
45	California	(1.8)
40	Colorado	(1.1)
23	Connecticut	(0.1)
19	Delaware	0.2
47	Florida	(2.0)
33	Georgia	(0.9)
10	Hawaii	0.6
31	Idaho	(0.8)
23	Illinois	(0.1)
26	Indiana	(0.4)
14	Iowa	0.4
21	Kansas	0.0
6	Kentucky	0.8
19	Louisiana	0.2
13	Maine	0.5
23	Maryland	(0.1)
10	Massachusetts	0.6
21	Michigan	0.0
16	Minnesota	0.3
33	Mississippi	(0.9)
49	Missouri	(2.2)
42	Montana	(1.2)
7	Nebraska	0.7
50	Nevada	(4.1)
1	New Hampshire	1.4
48	New Jersey	(2.1)
46	New Mexico	(1.9)
29	New York	(0.6)
30	North Carolina	(0.7)
1	North Dakota	1.4
44	Ohio	(1.7)
40	Oklahoma	(1.1)
33	Oregon	(0.9)
14	Pennsylvania	0.4
33	Rhode Island	(0.9)
38	South Carolina	(1.0)
3	South Dakota	1.1
38	Tennessee	(1.0)
5	Texas	0.9
31	Utah	(0.8)
3	Vermont	1.1
27	Virginia	(0.5)
33	Washington	(0.9)
16	West Virginia	0.3
7	Wisconsin	0.7
10	Wyoming	0.6

RANK ORDER

RANK	STATE	PERCENT CHANGE
1	New Hampshire	1.4
1	North Dakota	1.4
3	South Dakota	1.1
3	Vermont	1.1
5	Texas	0.9
6	Kentucky	0.8
7	Alaska	0.7
7	Nebraska	0.7
7	Wisconsin	0.7
10	Hawaii	0.6
10	Massachusetts	0.6
10	Wyoming	0.6
13	Maine	0.5
14	Iowa	0.4
14	Pennsylvania	0.4
16	Arizona	0.3
16	Minnesota	0.3
16	West Virginia	0.3
19	Delaware	0.2
19	Louisiana	0.2
21	Kansas	0.0
21	Michigan	0.0
23	Connecticut	(0.1)
23	Illinois	(0.1)
23	Maryland	(0.1)
26	Indiana	(0.4)
27	Arkansas	(0.5)
27	Virginia	(0.5)
29	New York	(0.6)
30	North Carolina	(0.7)
31	Idaho	(0.8)
31	Utah	(0.8)
33	Georgia	(0.9)
33	Mississippi	(0.9)
33	Oregon	(0.9)
33	Rhode Island	(0.9)
33	Washington	(0.9)
38	South Carolina	(1.0)
38	Tennessee	(1.0)
40	Colorado	(1.1)
40	Oklahoma	(1.1)
42	Montana	(1.2)
43	Alabama	(1.6)
44	Ohio	(1.7)
45	California	(1.8)
46	New Mexico	(1.9)
47	Florida	(2.0)
48	New Jersey	(2.1)
49	Missouri	(2.2)
50	Nevada	(4.1)

District of Columbia   1.8

Source: CQ Press using data from U.S. Department of Labor, Bureau of Labor Statistics
   "Regional and State Employment and Unemployment" (press release, January 25, 2011, www.bls.gov/bls/newsrels.htm)
*Nonfarm jobs. December 2000 to December 2010, seasonally adjusted. National figure based on nonfarm employment from a different survey.

Employees on Nonfarm Payrolls in 2010

National Total = 130,712,000 Employees*

ALPHA ORDER

RANK	STATE	EMPLOYEES	% of USA
24	Alabama	1,857,600	1.4%
48	Alaska	323,000	0.2%
21	Arizona	2,419,600	1.9%
33	Arkansas	1,166,400	0.9%
1	California	13,897,100	10.6%
22	Colorado	2,209,400	1.7%
27	Connecticut	1,613,400	1.2%
45	Delaware	410,700	0.3%
4	Florida	7,193,900	5.5%
11	Georgia	3,805,200	2.9%
42	Hawaii	589,800	0.5%
40	Idaho	606,900	0.5%
6	Illinois	5,604,500	4.3%
15	Indiana	2,783,900	2.1%
30	Iowa	1,474,200	1.1%
31	Kansas	1,330,200	1.0%
26	Kentucky	1,778,000	1.4%
23	Louisiana	1,906,300	1.5%
41	Maine	591,600	0.5%
20	Maryland	2,520,600	1.9%
13	Massachusetts	3,183,200	2.4%
9	Michigan	3,831,500	2.9%
17	Minnesota	2,649,700	2.0%
35	Mississippi	1,091,200	0.8%
18	Missouri	2,647,400	2.0%
44	Montana	426,000	0.3%
36	Nebraska	945,300	0.7%
34	Nevada	1,106,800	0.8%
39	New Hampshire	638,200	0.5%
10	New Jersey	3,828,000	2.9%
37	New Mexico	801,700	0.6%
3	New York	8,497,900	6.5%
8	North Carolina	3,896,700	3.0%
47	North Dakota	373,000	0.3%
7	Ohio	5,002,900	3.8%
29	Oklahoma	1,541,000	1.2%
28	Oregon	1,602,400	1.2%
5	Pennsylvania	5,619,800	4.3%
43	Rhode Island	449,500	0.3%
25	South Carolina	1,828,400	1.4%
46	South Dakota	405,000	0.3%
19	Tennessee	2,611,300	2.0%
2	Texas	10,449,700	8.0%
32	Utah	1,190,500	0.9%
49	Vermont	295,300	0.2%
12	Virginia	3,637,200	2.8%
14	Washington	2,809,100	2.1%
38	West Virginia	740,900	0.6%
16	Wisconsin	2,731,000	2.1%
50	Wyoming	284,000	0.2%

RANK ORDER

RANK	STATE	EMPLOYEES	% of USA
1	California	13,897,100	10.6%
2	Texas	10,449,700	8.0%
3	New York	8,497,900	6.5%
4	Florida	7,193,900	5.5%
5	Pennsylvania	5,619,800	4.3%
6	Illinois	5,604,500	4.3%
7	Ohio	5,002,900	3.8%
8	North Carolina	3,896,700	3.0%
9	Michigan	3,831,500	2.9%
10	New Jersey	3,828,000	2.9%
11	Georgia	3,805,200	2.9%
12	Virginia	3,637,200	2.8%
13	Massachusetts	3,183,200	2.4%
14	Washington	2,809,100	2.1%
15	Indiana	2,783,900	2.1%
16	Wisconsin	2,731,000	2.1%
17	Minnesota	2,649,700	2.0%
18	Missouri	2,647,400	2.0%
19	Tennessee	2,611,300	2.0%
20	Maryland	2,520,600	1.9%
21	Arizona	2,419,600	1.9%
22	Colorado	2,209,400	1.7%
23	Louisiana	1,906,300	1.5%
24	Alabama	1,857,600	1.4%
25	South Carolina	1,828,400	1.4%
26	Kentucky	1,778,000	1.4%
27	Connecticut	1,613,400	1.2%
28	Oregon	1,602,400	1.2%
29	Oklahoma	1,541,000	1.2%
30	Iowa	1,474,200	1.1%
31	Kansas	1,330,200	1.0%
32	Utah	1,190,500	0.9%
33	Arkansas	1,166,400	0.9%
34	Nevada	1,106,800	0.8%
35	Mississippi	1,091,200	0.8%
36	Nebraska	945,300	0.7%
37	New Mexico	801,700	0.6%
38	West Virginia	740,900	0.6%
39	New Hampshire	638,200	0.5%
40	Idaho	606,900	0.5%
41	Maine	591,600	0.5%
42	Hawaii	589,800	0.5%
43	Rhode Island	449,500	0.3%
44	Montana	426,000	0.3%
45	Delaware	410,700	0.3%
46	South Dakota	405,000	0.3%
47	North Dakota	373,000	0.3%
48	Alaska	323,000	0.2%
49	Vermont	295,300	0.2%
50	Wyoming	284,000	0.2%
	District of Columbia	723,600	0.6%

Source: U.S. Department of Labor, Bureau of Labor Statistics
   "Regional and State Employment and Unemployment" (press release, January 25, 2011, www.bls.gov/bls/newsrels.htm)
*Seasonally adjusted preliminary data as of December 2010. National total calculated through a different formula.

Employees in Construction in 2010

National Total = 5,603,000 Employees*

ALPHA ORDER

RANK	STATE	EMPLOYEES	% of USA
23	Alabama	82,700	1.5%
49	Alaska	14,700	0.3%
16	Arizona	113,000	2.0%
33	Arkansas	52,600	0.9%
2	California	535,600	9.6%
17	Colorado	111,600	2.0%
34	Connecticut	49,400	0.9%
47	Delaware**	19,100	0.3%
3	Florida	338,400	6.0%
11	Georgia	145,100	2.6%
39	Hawaii**	30,100	0.5%
40	Idaho	28,000	0.5%
6	Illinois	201,200	3.6%
18	Indiana	109,200	1.9%
30	Iowa	61,400	1.1%
31	Kansas	59,100	1.1%
29	Kentucky	62,300	1.1%
13	Louisiana	127,400	2.3%
41	Maine	24,100	0.4%
10	Maryland**	148,400	2.6%
19	Massachusetts	106,900	1.9%
15	Michigan	117,000	2.1%
23	Minnesota	82,700	1.5%
35	Mississippi	46,100	0.8%
21	Missouri	101,300	1.8%
44	Montana	20,500	0.4%
36	Nebraska**	45,100	0.8%
32	Nevada	57,300	1.0%
42	New Hampshire	22,800	0.4%
14	New Jersey	125,200	2.2%
37	New Mexico	44,400	0.8%
4	New York	305,800	5.5%
8	North Carolina	166,400	3.0%
46	North Dakota	19,600	0.3%
9	Ohio	163,900	2.9%
26	Oklahoma	72,300	1.3%
28	Oregon	65,200	1.2%
5	Pennsylvania	216,200	3.9%
48	Rhode Island	15,700	0.3%
25	South Carolina	80,100	1.4%
45	South Dakota**	20,400	0.4%
20	Tennessee**	102,600	1.8%
1	Texas	586,300	10.5%
27	Utah	67,200	1.2%
50	Vermont	11,800	0.2%
7	Virginia	176,600	3.2%
12	Washington	138,900	2.5%
38	West Virginia	30,500	0.5%
22	Wisconsin	90,300	1.6%
43	Wyoming	22,200	0.4%

RANK ORDER

RANK	STATE	EMPLOYEES	% of USA
1	Texas	586,300	10.5%
2	California	535,600	9.6%
3	Florida	338,400	6.0%
4	New York	305,800	5.5%
5	Pennsylvania	216,200	3.9%
6	Illinois	201,200	3.6%
7	Virginia	176,600	3.2%
8	North Carolina	166,400	3.0%
9	Ohio	163,900	2.9%
10	Maryland**	148,400	2.6%
11	Georgia	145,100	2.6%
12	Washington	138,900	2.5%
13	Louisiana	127,400	2.3%
14	New Jersey	125,200	2.2%
15	Michigan	117,000	2.1%
16	Arizona	113,000	2.0%
17	Colorado	111,600	2.0%
18	Indiana	109,200	1.9%
19	Massachusetts	106,900	1.9%
20	Tennessee**	102,600	1.8%
21	Missouri	101,300	1.8%
22	Wisconsin	90,300	1.6%
23	Alabama	82,700	1.5%
23	Minnesota	82,700	1.5%
25	South Carolina	80,100	1.4%
26	Oklahoma	72,300	1.3%
27	Utah	67,200	1.2%
28	Oregon	65,200	1.2%
29	Kentucky	62,300	1.1%
30	Iowa	61,400	1.1%
31	Kansas	59,100	1.1%
32	Nevada	57,300	1.0%
33	Arkansas	52,600	0.9%
34	Connecticut	49,400	0.9%
35	Mississippi	46,100	0.8%
36	Nebraska**	45,100	0.8%
37	New Mexico	44,400	0.8%
38	West Virginia	30,500	0.5%
39	Hawaii**	30,100	0.5%
40	Idaho	28,000	0.5%
41	Maine	24,100	0.4%
42	New Hampshire	22,800	0.4%
43	Wyoming	22,200	0.4%
44	Montana	20,500	0.4%
45	South Dakota**	20,400	0.4%
46	North Dakota	19,600	0.3%
47	Delaware**	19,100	0.3%
48	Rhode Island	15,700	0.3%
49	Alaska	14,700	0.3%
50	Vermont	11,800	0.2%
	District of Columbia**	11,100	0.2%

Source: U.S. Department of Labor, Bureau of Labor Statistics

"Regional and State Employment and Unemployment" (press release, January 25, 2011, www.bls.gov/bls/newsrels.htm)

*Seasonally adjusted preliminary data as of December 2010. National total calculated through a different formula.

**Figures for states include employees in mining and logging.

Percent of Nonfarm Employees in Construction in 2010

National Percent = 4.3% of Employees*

ALPHA ORDER

RANK	STATE	PERCENT
22	Alabama	4.5
20	Alaska	4.6
16	Arizona	4.7
22	Arkansas	4.5
33	California	3.9
9	Colorado	5.1
48	Connecticut	3.1
16	Delaware**	4.7
16	Florida	4.7
36	Georgia	3.8
9	Hawaii**	5.1
20	Idaho	4.6
39	Illinois	3.6
33	Indiana	3.9
27	Iowa	4.2
24	Kansas	4.4
42	Kentucky	3.5
2	Louisiana	6.7
29	Maine	4.1
3	Maryland**	5.9
44	Massachusetts	3.4
48	Michigan	3.1
48	Minnesota	3.1
27	Mississippi	4.2
36	Missouri	3.8
14	Montana	4.8
14	Nebraska**	4.8
8	Nevada	5.2
39	New Hampshire	3.6
45	New Jersey	3.3
6	New Mexico	5.5
39	New York	3.6
26	North Carolina	4.3
7	North Dakota	5.3
45	Ohio	3.3
16	Oklahoma	4.7
29	Oregon	4.1
36	Pennsylvania	3.8
42	Rhode Island	3.5
24	South Carolina	4.4
11	South Dakota**	5.0
33	Tennessee**	3.9
4	Texas	5.6
4	Utah	5.6
32	Vermont	4.0
12	Virginia	4.9
12	Washington	4.9
29	West Virginia	4.1
45	Wisconsin	3.3
1	Wyoming	7.8

RANK ORDER

RANK	STATE	PERCENT
1	Wyoming	7.8
2	Louisiana	6.7
3	Maryland**	5.9
4	Texas	5.6
4	Utah	5.6
6	New Mexico	5.5
7	North Dakota	5.3
8	Nevada	5.2
9	Colorado	5.1
9	Hawaii**	5.1
11	South Dakota**	5.0
12	Virginia	4.9
12	Washington	4.9
14	Montana	4.8
14	Nebraska**	4.8
16	Arizona	4.7
16	Delaware**	4.7
16	Florida	4.7
16	Oklahoma	4.7
20	Alaska	4.6
20	Idaho	4.6
22	Alabama	4.5
22	Arkansas	4.5
24	Kansas	4.4
24	South Carolina	4.4
26	North Carolina	4.3
27	Iowa	4.2
27	Mississippi	4.2
29	Maine	4.1
29	Oregon	4.1
29	West Virginia	4.1
32	Vermont	4.0
33	California	3.9
33	Indiana	3.9
33	Tennessee**	3.9
36	Georgia	3.8
36	Missouri	3.8
36	Pennsylvania	3.8
39	Illinois	3.6
39	New Hampshire	3.6
39	New York	3.6
42	Kentucky	3.5
42	Rhode Island	3.5
44	Massachusetts	3.4
45	New Jersey	3.3
45	Ohio	3.3
45	Wisconsin	3.3
48	Connecticut	3.1
48	Michigan	3.1
48	Minnesota	3.1

District of Columbia**   1.5

Source: CQ Press using data from U.S. Department of Labor, Bureau of Labor Statistics
    "Regional and State Employment and Unemployment" (press release, January 25, 2011, www.bls.gov/bls/newsrels.htm)
*Seasonally adjusted preliminary data as of December 2010. National figure calculated through a different formula.
**Figures for states include employees in mining and logging.

Employees in Education and Health Services in 2010

National Total = 19,772,000 Employees*

ALPHA ORDER

RANK ORDER

RANK	STATE	EMPLOYEES	% of USA	RANK	STATE	EMPLOYEES	% of USA
28	Alabama	213,000	1.1%	1	California	1,777,900	9.0%
49	Alaska	41,900	0.2%	2	New York	1,711,900	8.7%
21	Arizona	348,500	1.8%	3	Texas	1,407,200	7.1%
32	Arkansas	171,900	0.9%	4	Pennsylvania	1,146,400	5.8%
1	California	1,777,900	9.0%	5	Florida	1,104,500	5.6%
24	Colorado	269,200	1.4%	6	Ohio	839,200	4.2%
22	Connecticut	310,300	1.6%	7	Illinois	834,600	4.2%
44	Delaware	66,300	0.3%	8	Massachusetts	666,900	3.4%
5	Florida	1,104,500	5.6%	9	Michigan	624,900	3.2%
12	Georgia	490,500	2.5%	10	New Jersey	601,600	3.0%
43	Hawaii	76,800	0.4%	11	North Carolina	551,200	2.8%
42	Idaho	87,400	0.4%	12	Georgia	490,500	2.5%
7	Illinois	834,600	4.2%	13	Virginia	465,100	2.4%
16	Indiana	421,200	2.1%	14	Minnesota	464,900	2.4%
27	Iowa	214,300	1.1%	15	Wisconsin	426,000	2.2%
31	Kansas	181,200	0.9%	16	Indiana	421,200	2.1%
25	Kentucky	251,100	1.3%	17	Missouri	408,600	2.1%
23	Louisiana	279,200	1.4%	18	Maryland	404,200	2.0%
38	Maine	120,000	0.6%	19	Washington	386,200	2.0%
18	Maryland	404,200	2.0%	20	Tennessee	376,500	1.9%
8	Massachusetts	666,900	3.4%	21	Arizona	348,500	1.8%
9	Michigan	624,900	3.2%	22	Connecticut	310,300	1.6%
14	Minnesota	464,900	2.4%	23	Louisiana	279,200	1.4%
35	Mississippi	136,400	0.7%	24	Colorado	269,200	1.4%
17	Missouri	408,600	2.1%	25	Kentucky	251,100	1.3%
46	Montana	62,800	0.3%	26	Oregon	226,600	1.1%
34	Nebraska	139,300	0.7%	27	Iowa	214,300	1.1%
41	Nevada	100,500	0.5%	28	Alabama	213,000	1.1%
39	New Hampshire	109,700	0.6%	29	South Carolina	212,800	1.1%
10	New Jersey	601,600	3.0%	30	Oklahoma	211,200	1.1%
36	New Mexico	128,000	0.6%	31	Kansas	181,200	0.9%
2	New York	1,711,900	8.7%	32	Arkansas	171,900	0.9%
11	North Carolina	551,200	2.8%	33	Utah	158,200	0.8%
48	North Dakota	54,700	0.3%	34	Nebraska	139,300	0.7%
6	Ohio	839,200	4.2%	35	Mississippi	136,400	0.7%
30	Oklahoma	211,200	1.1%	36	New Mexico	128,000	0.6%
26	Oregon	226,600	1.1%	37	West Virginia	120,800	0.6%
4	Pennsylvania	1,146,400	5.8%	38	Maine	120,000	0.6%
40	Rhode Island	101,200	0.5%	39	New Hampshire	109,700	0.6%
29	South Carolina	212,800	1.1%	40	Rhode Island	101,200	0.5%
45	South Dakota	64,200	0.3%	41	Nevada	100,500	0.5%
20	Tennessee	376,500	1.9%	42	Idaho	87,400	0.4%
3	Texas	1,407,200	7.1%	43	Hawaii	76,800	0.4%
33	Utah	158,200	0.8%	44	Delaware	66,300	0.3%
47	Vermont	61,200	0.3%	45	South Dakota	64,200	0.3%
13	Virginia	465,100	2.4%	46	Montana	62,800	0.3%
19	Washington	386,200	2.0%	47	Vermont	61,200	0.3%
37	West Virginia	120,800	0.6%	48	North Dakota	54,700	0.3%
15	Wisconsin	426,000	2.2%	49	Alaska	41,900	0.2%
NA	Wyoming**	NA	NA	NA	Wyoming**	NA	NA
				District of Columbia		108,600	0.5%

Source: U.S. Department of Labor, Bureau of Labor Statistics
"Regional and State Employment and Unemployment" (press release, January 25, 2011, www.bls.gov/bls/newsrels.htm)
*Seasonally adjusted preliminary data as of December 2010. National total calculated through a different formula.
**The Bureau of Labor Statistics does not publish seasonally adjusted figures in this category for Wyoming.

Percent of Nonfarm Employees in Education and Health Services in 2010

National Percent = 15.1% of Employees*

ALPHA ORDER

RANK	STATE	PERCENT
48	Alabama	11.5
40	Alaska	13.0
29	Arizona	14.4
23	Arkansas	14.7
43	California	12.8
46	Colorado	12.2
7	Connecticut	19.2
13	Delaware	16.1
19	Florida	15.4
42	Georgia	12.9
40	Hawaii	13.0
29	Idaho	14.4
22	Illinois	14.9
21	Indiana	15.1
28	Iowa	14.5
37	Kansas	13.6
32	Kentucky	14.1
27	Louisiana	14.6
5	Maine	20.3
14	Maryland	16.0
2	Massachusetts	21.0
11	Michigan	16.3
8	Minnesota	17.5
45	Mississippi	12.5
19	Missouri	15.4
23	Montana	14.7
23	Nebraska	14.7
49	Nevada	9.1
9	New Hampshire	17.2
17	New Jersey	15.7
14	New Mexico	16.0
6	New York	20.1
32	North Carolina	14.1
23	North Dakota	14.7
10	Ohio	16.8
35	Oklahoma	13.7
32	Oregon	14.1
4	Pennsylvania	20.4
1	Rhode Island	22.5
47	South Carolina	11.6
16	South Dakota	15.9
29	Tennessee	14.4
38	Texas	13.5
39	Utah	13.3
3	Vermont	20.7
43	Virginia	12.8
35	Washington	13.7
11	West Virginia	16.3
18	Wisconsin	15.6
NA	Wyoming**	NA

RANK ORDER

RANK	STATE	PERCENT
1	Rhode Island	22.5
2	Massachusetts	21.0
3	Vermont	20.7
4	Pennsylvania	20.4
5	Maine	20.3
6	New York	20.1
7	Connecticut	19.2
8	Minnesota	17.5
9	New Hampshire	17.2
10	Ohio	16.8
11	Michigan	16.3
11	West Virginia	16.3
13	Delaware	16.1
14	Maryland	16.0
14	New Mexico	16.0
16	South Dakota	15.9
17	New Jersey	15.7
18	Wisconsin	15.6
19	Florida	15.4
19	Missouri	15.4
21	Indiana	15.1
22	Illinois	14.9
23	Arkansas	14.7
23	Montana	14.7
23	Nebraska	14.7
23	North Dakota	14.7
27	Louisiana	14.6
28	Iowa	14.5
29	Arizona	14.4
29	Idaho	14.4
29	Tennessee	14.4
32	Kentucky	14.1
32	North Carolina	14.1
32	Oregon	14.1
35	Oklahoma	13.7
35	Washington	13.7
37	Kansas	13.6
38	Texas	13.5
39	Utah	13.3
40	Alaska	13.0
40	Hawaii	13.0
42	Georgia	12.9
43	California	12.8
43	Virginia	12.8
45	Mississippi	12.5
46	Colorado	12.2
47	South Carolina	11.6
48	Alabama	11.5
49	Nevada	9.1
NA	Wyoming**	NA

District of Columbia 15.0

Source: CQ Press using data from U.S. Department of Labor, Bureau of Labor Statistics
   "Regional and State Employment and Unemployment" (press release, January 25, 2011, www.bls.gov/bls/newsrels.htm)
*Seasonally adjusted preliminary data as of December 2010. National figure calculated through a different formula.
**The Bureau of Labor Statistics does not publish seasonally adjusted figures in this category for Wyoming.

Employees in Financial Activities in 2010

National Total = 7,585,000 Employees*

ALPHA ORDER

RANK	STATE	EMPLOYEES	% of USA
27	Alabama	91,200	1.2%
47	Alaska	14,900	0.2%
15	Arizona	162,200	2.1%
35	Arkansas	50,800	0.7%
1	California	785,500	10.4%
18	Colorado	141,400	1.9%
22	Connecticut	134,400	1.8%
36	Delaware	42,700	0.6%
4	Florida	463,800	6.1%
11	Georgia	193,800	2.6%
43	Hawaii	27,200	0.4%
40	Idaho	30,600	0.4%
5	Illinois	359,400	4.7%
23	Indiana	131,500	1.7%
25	Iowa	100,600	1.3%
32	Kansas	67,300	0.9%
29	Kentucky	84,700	1.1%
28	Louisiana	88,300	1.2%
39	Maine	30,700	0.4%
19	Maryland	137,700	1.8%
9	Massachusetts	210,900	2.8%
12	Michigan	183,200	2.4%
14	Minnesota	167,900	2.2%
NA	Mississippi**	NA	NA
16	Missouri	157,300	2.1%
45	Montana	20,500	0.3%
33	Nebraska	67,200	0.9%
34	Nevada	51,800	0.7%
37	New Hampshire	35,200	0.5%
8	New Jersey	252,700	3.3%
38	New Mexico	32,300	0.4%
2	New York	667,500	8.8%
10	North Carolina	200,000	2.6%
46	North Dakota	20,300	0.3%
7	Ohio	261,800	3.5%
30	Oklahoma	84,300	1.1%
26	Oregon	93,500	1.2%
6	Pennsylvania	309,900	4.1%
41	Rhode Island	30,300	0.4%
24	South Carolina	103,900	1.4%
42	South Dakota	28,300	0.4%
20	Tennessee	136,300	1.8%
3	Texas	631,100	8.3%
31	Utah	70,700	0.9%
48	Vermont	12,800	0.2%
13	Virginia	175,700	2.3%
20	Washington	136,300	1.8%
44	West Virginia	27,000	0.4%
17	Wisconsin	153,400	2.0%
49	Wyoming	11,000	0.1%

RANK ORDER

RANK	STATE	EMPLOYEES	% of USA
1	California	785,500	10.4%
2	New York	667,500	8.8%
3	Texas	631,100	8.3%
4	Florida	463,800	6.1%
5	Illinois	359,400	4.7%
6	Pennsylvania	309,900	4.1%
7	Ohio	261,800	3.5%
8	New Jersey	252,700	3.3%
9	Massachusetts	210,900	2.8%
10	North Carolina	200,000	2.6%
11	Georgia	193,800	2.6%
12	Michigan	183,200	2.4%
13	Virginia	175,700	2.3%
14	Minnesota	167,900	2.2%
15	Arizona	162,200	2.1%
16	Missouri	157,300	2.1%
17	Wisconsin	153,400	2.0%
18	Colorado	141,400	1.9%
19	Maryland	137,700	1.8%
20	Tennessee	136,300	1.8%
20	Washington	136,300	1.8%
22	Connecticut	134,400	1.8%
23	Indiana	131,500	1.7%
24	South Carolina	103,900	1.4%
25	Iowa	100,600	1.3%
26	Oregon	93,500	1.2%
27	Alabama	91,200	1.2%
28	Louisiana	88,300	1.2%
29	Kentucky	84,700	1.1%
30	Oklahoma	84,300	1.1%
31	Utah	70,700	0.9%
32	Kansas	67,300	0.9%
33	Nebraska	67,200	0.9%
34	Nevada	51,800	0.7%
35	Arkansas	50,800	0.7%
36	Delaware	42,700	0.6%
37	New Hampshire	35,200	0.5%
38	New Mexico	32,300	0.4%
39	Maine	30,700	0.4%
40	Idaho	30,600	0.4%
41	Rhode Island	30,300	0.4%
42	South Dakota	28,300	0.4%
43	Hawaii	27,200	0.4%
44	West Virginia	27,000	0.4%
45	Montana	20,500	0.3%
46	North Dakota	20,300	0.3%
47	Alaska	14,900	0.2%
48	Vermont	12,800	0.2%
49	Wyoming	11,000	0.1%
NA	Mississippi**	NA	NA
	District of Columbia	26,200	0.3%

Source: U.S. Department of Labor, Bureau of Labor Statistics

"Regional and State Employment and Unemployment" (press release, January 25, 2011, www.bls.gov/bls/newsrels.htm)
*Seasonally adjusted preliminary data as of December 2010. National total calculated through a different formula. Financial activities include insurance and real estate.
**The Bureau of Labor Statistics does not publish seasonally adjusted figures in this category for these states.

Percent of Nonfarm Employees in Financial Activities in 2010

National Percent = 5.8% of Employees*

ALPHA ORDER

RANK	STATE	PERCENT
34	Alabama	4.9
42	Alaska	4.6
7	Arizona	6.7
45	Arkansas	4.4
19	California	5.7
11	Colorado	6.4
2	Connecticut	8.3
1	Delaware	10.4
11	Florida	6.4
30	Georgia	5.1
42	Hawaii	4.6
33	Idaho	5.0
11	Illinois	6.4
40	Indiana	4.7
6	Iowa	6.8
30	Kansas	5.1
36	Kentucky	4.8
42	Louisiana	4.6
27	Maine	5.2
22	Maryland	5.5
9	Massachusetts	6.6
36	Michigan	4.8
14	Minnesota	6.3
NA	Mississippi**	NA
16	Missouri	5.9
36	Montana	4.8
4	Nebraska	7.1
40	Nevada	4.7
22	New Hampshire	5.5
9	New Jersey	6.6
47	New Mexico	4.0
3	New York	7.9
30	North Carolina	5.1
26	North Dakota	5.4
27	Ohio	5.2
22	Oklahoma	5.5
18	Oregon	5.8
22	Pennsylvania	5.5
7	Rhode Island	6.7
19	South Carolina	5.7
5	South Dakota	7.0
27	Tennessee	5.2
15	Texas	6.0
16	Utah	5.9
46	Vermont	4.3
36	Virginia	4.8
34	Washington	4.9
49	West Virginia	3.6
21	Wisconsin	5.6
48	Wyoming	3.9

RANK ORDER

RANK	STATE	PERCENT
1	Delaware	10.4
2	Connecticut	8.3
3	New York	7.9
4	Nebraska	7.1
5	South Dakota	7.0
6	Iowa	6.8
7	Arizona	6.7
7	Rhode Island	6.7
9	Massachusetts	6.6
9	New Jersey	6.6
11	Colorado	6.4
11	Florida	6.4
11	Illinois	6.4
14	Minnesota	6.3
15	Texas	6.0
16	Missouri	5.9
16	Utah	5.9
18	Oregon	5.8
19	California	5.7
19	South Carolina	5.7
21	Wisconsin	5.6
22	Maryland	5.5
22	New Hampshire	5.5
22	Oklahoma	5.5
22	Pennsylvania	5.5
26	North Dakota	5.4
27	Maine	5.2
27	Ohio	5.2
27	Tennessee	5.2
30	Georgia	5.1
30	Kansas	5.1
30	North Carolina	5.1
33	Idaho	5.0
34	Alabama	4.9
34	Washington	4.9
36	Kentucky	4.8
36	Michigan	4.8
36	Montana	4.8
36	Virginia	4.8
40	Indiana	4.7
40	Nevada	4.7
42	Alaska	4.6
42	Hawaii	4.6
42	Louisiana	4.6
45	Arkansas	4.4
46	Vermont	4.3
47	New Mexico	4.0
48	Wyoming	3.9
49	West Virginia	3.6
NA	Mississippi**	NA
	District of Columbia	3.6

Source: CQ Press using data from U.S. Department of Labor, Bureau of Labor Statistics
   "Regional and State Employment and Unemployment" (press release, January 25, 2011, www.bls.gov/bls/newsrels.htm)
*Seasonally adjusted preliminary data as of December 2010. National figure calculated through a different formula. Financial activities include insurance and real estate.
**The Bureau of Labor Statistics does not publish seasonally adjusted figures in this category for these states.

Employees in Government in 2010

National Total = 22,259,000 Employees*

ALPHA ORDER

RANK	STATE	EMPLOYEES	% of USA
23	Alabama	385,000	1.7%
44	Alaska	85,000	0.4%
21	Arizona	408,700	1.8%
34	Arkansas	212,600	1.0%
1	California	2,449,100	11.0%
22	Colorado	390,500	1.8%
32	Connecticut	243,200	1.1%
48	Delaware	62,200	0.3%
4	Florida	1,108,200	5.0%
10	Georgia	680,600	3.1%
39	Hawaii	125,000	0.6%
40	Idaho	118,200	0.5%
5	Illinois	856,300	3.8%
17	Indiana	428,900	1.9%
30	Iowa	252,600	1.1%
29	Kansas	259,800	1.2%
27	Kentucky	324,000	1.5%
24	Louisiana	364,900	1.6%
41	Maine	101,000	0.5%
14	Maryland	499,500	2.2%
16	Massachusetts	438,600	2.0%
11	Michigan	623,400	2.8%
20	Minnesota	410,300	1.8%
31	Mississippi	246,400	1.1%
15	Missouri	458,500	2.1%
43	Montana	86,900	0.4%
36	Nebraska	169,000	0.8%
37	Nevada	151,000	0.7%
42	New Hampshire	99,200	0.4%
12	New Jersey	622,200	2.8%
35	New Mexico	198,400	0.9%
3	New York	1,466,700	6.6%
8	North Carolina	727,900	3.3%
45	North Dakota	78,700	0.4%
6	Ohio	776,900	3.5%
26	Oklahoma	329,100	1.5%
28	Oregon	297,100	1.3%
7	Pennsylvania	757,200	3.4%
49	Rhode Island	61,200	0.3%
25	South Carolina	352,100	1.6%
46	South Dakota	78,000	0.4%
17	Tennessee	428,900	1.9%
2	Texas	1,844,900	8.3%
33	Utah	215,800	1.0%
50	Vermont	54,100	0.2%
9	Virginia	700,300	3.1%
13	Washington	543,400	2.4%
38	West Virginia	150,400	0.7%
19	Wisconsin	427,300	1.9%
47	Wyoming	72,700	0.3%

RANK ORDER

RANK	STATE	EMPLOYEES	% of USA
1	California	2,449,100	11.0%
2	Texas	1,844,900	8.3%
3	New York	1,466,700	6.6%
4	Florida	1,108,200	5.0%
5	Illinois	856,300	3.8%
6	Ohio	776,900	3.5%
7	Pennsylvania	757,200	3.4%
8	North Carolina	727,900	3.3%
9	Virginia	700,300	3.1%
10	Georgia	680,600	3.1%
11	Michigan	623,400	2.8%
12	New Jersey	622,200	2.8%
13	Washington	543,400	2.4%
14	Maryland	499,500	2.2%
15	Missouri	458,500	2.1%
16	Massachusetts	438,600	2.0%
17	Indiana	428,900	1.9%
17	Tennessee	428,900	1.9%
19	Wisconsin	427,300	1.9%
20	Minnesota	410,300	1.8%
21	Arizona	408,700	1.8%
22	Colorado	390,500	1.8%
23	Alabama	385,000	1.7%
24	Louisiana	364,900	1.6%
25	South Carolina	352,100	1.6%
26	Oklahoma	329,100	1.5%
27	Kentucky	324,000	1.5%
28	Oregon	297,100	1.3%
29	Kansas	259,800	1.2%
30	Iowa	252,600	1.1%
31	Mississippi	246,400	1.1%
32	Connecticut	243,200	1.1%
33	Utah	215,800	1.0%
34	Arkansas	212,600	1.0%
35	New Mexico	198,400	0.9%
36	Nebraska	169,000	0.8%
37	Nevada	151,000	0.7%
38	West Virginia	150,400	0.7%
39	Hawaii	125,000	0.6%
40	Idaho	118,200	0.5%
41	Maine	101,000	0.5%
42	New Hampshire	99,200	0.4%
43	Montana	86,900	0.4%
44	Alaska	85,000	0.4%
45	North Dakota	78,700	0.4%
46	South Dakota	78,000	0.4%
47	Wyoming	72,700	0.3%
48	Delaware	62,200	0.3%
49	Rhode Island	61,200	0.3%
50	Vermont	54,100	0.2%
	District of Columbia	252,000	1.1%

Source: U.S. Department of Labor, Bureau of Labor Statistics
    "Regional and State Employment and Unemployment" (press release, January 25, 2011, www.bls.gov/bls/newsrels.htm)
*Seasonally adjusted preliminary data as of December 2010. National total calculated through a different formula.

Percent of Nonfarm Employees in Government in 2010

National Percent = 17.0% of Employees*

ALPHA ORDER

RANK	STATE	PERCENT
8	Alabama	20.7
1	Alaska	26.3
34	Arizona	16.9
22	Arkansas	18.2
29	California	17.6
27	Colorado	17.7
45	Connecticut	15.1
45	Delaware	15.1
42	Florida	15.4
25	Georgia	17.9
6	Hawaii	21.2
12	Idaho	19.5
44	Illinois	15.3
42	Indiana	15.4
32	Iowa	17.1
12	Kansas	19.5
22	Kentucky	18.2
18	Louisiana	19.1
32	Maine	17.1
11	Maryland	19.8
47	Massachusetts	13.8
36	Michigan	16.3
39	Minnesota	15.5
4	Mississippi	22.6
30	Missouri	17.3
9	Montana	20.4
25	Nebraska	17.9
48	Nevada	13.6
39	New Hampshire	15.5
36	New Jersey	16.3
3	New Mexico	24.7
30	New York	17.3
19	North Carolina	18.7
7	North Dakota	21.1
39	Ohio	15.5
5	Oklahoma	21.4
20	Oregon	18.5
50	Pennsylvania	13.5
48	Rhode Island	13.6
14	South Carolina	19.3
14	South Dakota	19.3
35	Tennessee	16.4
27	Texas	17.7
24	Utah	18.1
21	Vermont	18.3
14	Virginia	19.3
14	Washington	19.3
10	West Virginia	20.3
38	Wisconsin	15.6
2	Wyoming	25.6

RANK ORDER

RANK	STATE	PERCENT
1	Alaska	26.3
2	Wyoming	25.6
3	New Mexico	24.7
4	Mississippi	22.6
5	Oklahoma	21.4
6	Hawaii	21.2
7	North Dakota	21.1
8	Alabama	20.7
9	Montana	20.4
10	West Virginia	20.3
11	Maryland	19.8
12	Idaho	19.5
12	Kansas	19.5
14	South Carolina	19.3
14	South Dakota	19.3
14	Virginia	19.3
14	Washington	19.3
18	Louisiana	19.1
19	North Carolina	18.7
20	Oregon	18.5
21	Vermont	18.3
22	Arkansas	18.2
22	Kentucky	18.2
24	Utah	18.1
25	Georgia	17.9
25	Nebraska	17.9
27	Colorado	17.7
27	Texas	17.7
29	California	17.6
30	Missouri	17.3
30	New York	17.3
32	Iowa	17.1
32	Maine	17.1
34	Arizona	16.9
35	Tennessee	16.4
36	Michigan	16.3
36	New Jersey	16.3
38	Wisconsin	15.6
39	Minnesota	15.5
39	New Hampshire	15.5
39	Ohio	15.5
42	Florida	15.4
42	Indiana	15.4
44	Illinois	15.3
45	Connecticut	15.1
45	Delaware	15.1
47	Massachusetts	13.8
48	Nevada	13.6
48	Rhode Island	13.6
50	Pennsylvania	13.5
	District of Columbia	34.8

Source: CQ Press using data from U.S. Department of Labor, Bureau of Labor Statistics

"Regional and State Employment and Unemployment" (press release, January 25, 2011, www.bls.gov/bls/newsrels.htm)

*Seasonally adjusted preliminary data as of December 2010. National figure calculated through a different formula.

Employees in Leisure and Hospitality in 2010

National Total = 13,231,000 Employees*

ALPHA ORDER

RANK	STATE	EMPLOYEES	% of USA
26	Alabama	172,900	1.3%
48	Alaska	32,900	0.2%
20	Arizona	257,200	1.9%
36	Arkansas	99,400	0.8%
1	California	1,502,900	11.4%
17	Colorado	264,800	2.0%
30	Connecticut	137,700	1.0%
46	Delaware	42,100	0.3%
3	Florida	928,700	7.0%
9	Georgia	381,100	2.9%
35	Hawaii	104,300	0.8%
42	Idaho	59,500	0.4%
5	Illinois	506,200	3.8%
16	Indiana	270,900	2.0%
31	Iowa	132,500	1.0%
33	Kansas	110,500	0.8%
27	Kentucky	170,800	1.3%
25	Louisiana	198,300	1.5%
41	Maine	59,900	0.5%
23	Maryland	236,900	1.8%
14	Massachusetts	298,200	2.3%
10	Michigan	374,000	2.8%
22	Minnesota	244,400	1.8%
32	Mississippi	120,500	0.9%
15	Missouri	276,000	2.1%
43	Montana	56,800	0.4%
38	Nebraska	81,000	0.6%
13	Nevada	301,400	2.3%
40	New Hampshire	66,200	0.5%
12	New Jersey	332,400	2.5%
37	New Mexico	85,600	0.6%
4	New York	724,100	5.5%
8	North Carolina	384,400	2.9%
47	North Dakota	34,800	0.3%
7	Ohio	481,100	3.6%
29	Oklahoma	144,100	1.1%
28	Oregon	164,200	1.2%
6	Pennsylvania	501,900	3.8%
44	Rhode Island	46,600	0.4%
24	South Carolina	205,700	1.6%
45	South Dakota	43,700	0.3%
19	Tennessee	260,600	2.0%
2	Texas	1,026,600	7.8%
34	Utah	108,400	0.8%
49	Vermont	31,900	0.2%
11	Virginia	337,900	2.6%
18	Washington	264,100	2.0%
39	West Virginia	72,900	0.6%
21	Wisconsin	249,600	1.9%
50	Wyoming	31,500	0.2%

RANK ORDER

RANK	STATE	EMPLOYEES	% of USA
1	California	1,502,900	11.4%
2	Texas	1,026,600	7.8%
3	Florida	928,700	7.0%
4	New York	724,100	5.5%
5	Illinois	506,200	3.8%
6	Pennsylvania	501,900	3.8%
7	Ohio	481,100	3.6%
8	North Carolina	384,400	2.9%
9	Georgia	381,100	2.9%
10	Michigan	374,000	2.8%
11	Virginia	337,900	2.6%
12	New Jersey	332,400	2.5%
13	Nevada	301,400	2.3%
14	Massachusetts	298,200	2.3%
15	Missouri	276,000	2.1%
16	Indiana	270,900	2.0%
17	Colorado	264,800	2.0%
18	Washington	264,100	2.0%
19	Tennessee	260,600	2.0%
20	Arizona	257,200	1.9%
21	Wisconsin	249,600	1.9%
22	Minnesota	244,400	1.8%
23	Maryland	236,900	1.8%
24	South Carolina	205,700	1.6%
25	Louisiana	198,300	1.5%
26	Alabama	172,900	1.3%
27	Kentucky	170,800	1.3%
28	Oregon	164,200	1.2%
29	Oklahoma	144,100	1.1%
30	Connecticut	137,700	1.0%
31	Iowa	132,500	1.0%
32	Mississippi	120,500	0.9%
33	Kansas	110,500	0.8%
34	Utah	108,400	0.8%
35	Hawaii	104,300	0.8%
36	Arkansas	99,400	0.8%
37	New Mexico	85,600	0.6%
38	Nebraska	81,000	0.6%
39	West Virginia	72,900	0.6%
40	New Hampshire	66,200	0.5%
41	Maine	59,900	0.5%
42	Idaho	59,500	0.4%
43	Montana	56,800	0.4%
44	Rhode Island	46,600	0.4%
45	South Dakota	43,700	0.3%
46	Delaware	42,100	0.3%
47	North Dakota	34,800	0.3%
48	Alaska	32,900	0.2%
49	Vermont	31,900	0.2%
50	Wyoming	31,500	0.2%
	District of Columbia	59,200	0.4%

Source: U.S. Department of Labor, Bureau of Labor Statistics
"Regional and State Employment and Unemployment" (press release, January 25, 2011, www.bls.gov/bls/newsrels.htm)
*Seasonally adjusted preliminary data as of December 2010. National total calculated through a different formula.

Percent of Nonfarm Employees in Leisure and Hospitality in 2010

National Percent = 10.1% of Employees*

ALPHA ORDER

RANK	STATE	PERCENT
36	Alabama	9.3
19	Alaska	10.2
13	Arizona	10.6
47	Arkansas	8.5
9	California	10.8
5	Colorado	12.0
47	Connecticut	8.5
18	Delaware	10.3
4	Florida	12.9
22	Georgia	10.0
2	Hawaii	17.7
25	Idaho	9.8
42	Illinois	9.0
29	Indiana	9.7
42	Iowa	9.0
50	Kansas	8.3
30	Kentucky	9.6
14	Louisiana	10.4
21	Maine	10.1
32	Maryland	9.4
32	Massachusetts	9.4
25	Michigan	9.8
39	Minnesota	9.2
8	Mississippi	11.0
14	Missouri	10.4
3	Montana	13.3
46	Nebraska	8.6
1	Nevada	27.2
14	New Hampshire	10.4
45	New Jersey	8.7
12	New Mexico	10.7
47	New York	8.5
24	North Carolina	9.9
36	North Dakota	9.3
30	Ohio	9.6
32	Oklahoma	9.4
19	Oregon	10.2
44	Pennsylvania	8.9
14	Rhode Island	10.4
6	South Carolina	11.3
9	South Dakota	10.8
22	Tennessee	10.0
25	Texas	9.8
40	Utah	9.1
9	Vermont	10.8
36	Virginia	9.3
32	Washington	9.4
25	West Virginia	9.8
40	Wisconsin	9.1
7	Wyoming	11.1

RANK ORDER

RANK	STATE	PERCENT
1	Nevada	27.2
2	Hawaii	17.7
3	Montana	13.3
4	Florida	12.9
5	Colorado	12.0
6	South Carolina	11.3
7	Wyoming	11.1
8	Mississippi	11.0
9	California	10.8
9	South Dakota	10.8
9	Vermont	10.8
12	New Mexico	10.7
13	Arizona	10.6
14	Louisiana	10.4
14	Missouri	10.4
14	New Hampshire	10.4
14	Rhode Island	10.4
18	Delaware	10.3
19	Alaska	10.2
19	Oregon	10.2
21	Maine	10.1
22	Georgia	10.0
22	Tennessee	10.0
24	North Carolina	9.9
25	Idaho	9.8
25	Michigan	9.8
25	Texas	9.8
25	West Virginia	9.8
29	Indiana	9.7
30	Kentucky	9.6
30	Ohio	9.6
32	Maryland	9.4
32	Massachusetts	9.4
32	Oklahoma	9.4
32	Washington	9.4
36	Alabama	9.3
36	North Dakota	9.3
36	Virginia	9.3
39	Minnesota	9.2
40	Utah	9.1
40	Wisconsin	9.1
42	Illinois	9.0
42	Iowa	9.0
44	Pennsylvania	8.9
45	New Jersey	8.7
46	Nebraska	8.6
47	Arkansas	8.5
47	Connecticut	8.5
47	New York	8.5
50	Kansas	8.3

District of Columbia — 8.2

Source: CQ Press using data from U.S. Department of Labor, Bureau of Labor Statistics
"Regional and State Employment and Unemployment" (press release, January 25, 2011, www.bls.gov/bls/newsrels.htm)
*Seasonally adjusted preliminary data as of December 2010. National figure calculated through a different formula.

Employees in Manufacturing in 2010

National Total = 11,670,000 Employees*

ALPHA ORDER

RANK	STATE	EMPLOYEES	% of USA
NA	Alabama**	NA	NA
46	Alaska	12,900	0.1%
27	Arizona	149,400	1.3%
24	Arkansas	164,000	1.4%
1	California	1,244,100	10.6%
31	Colorado	122,600	1.0%
23	Connecticut	166,900	1.4%
NA	Delaware**	NA	NA
13	Florida	300,100	2.6%
11	Georgia	333,700	2.8%
NA	Hawaii**	NA	NA
36	Idaho	54,900	0.5%
4	Illinois	563,200	4.8%
8	Indiana	439,000	3.7%
22	Iowa	205,800	1.8%
25	Kansas	161,600	1.4%
20	Kentucky	214,600	1.8%
28	Louisiana	138,700	1.2%
37	Maine	53,200	0.5%
33	Maryland	109,900	0.9%
17	Massachusetts	253,900	2.2%
6	Michigan	460,400	3.9%
14	Minnesota	299,600	2.5%
29	Mississippi	134,500	1.1%
18	Missouri	246,400	2.1%
45	Montana	17,900	0.2%
34	Nebraska	92,100	0.8%
41	Nevada	37,600	0.3%
35	New Hampshire	66,800	0.6%
15	New Jersey	257,300	2.2%
43	New Mexico	30,700	0.3%
7	New York	459,200	3.9%
9	North Carolina	434,400	3.7%
44	North Dakota	23,700	0.2%
3	Ohio	620,200	5.3%
30	Oklahoma	125,600	1.1%
26	Oregon	159,700	1.4%
5	Pennsylvania	561,900	4.8%
39	Rhode Island	39,600	0.3%
21	South Carolina	211,800	1.8%
40	South Dakota	38,200	0.3%
12	Tennessee	301,700	2.6%
2	Texas	840,500	7.1%
32	Utah	110,700	0.9%
42	Vermont	31,700	0.3%
19	Virginia	228,700	1.9%
15	Washington	257,300	2.2%
38	West Virginia	50,300	0.4%
10	Wisconsin	431,900	3.7%
47	Wyoming	9,200	0.1%

RANK ORDER

RANK	STATE	EMPLOYEES	% of USA
1	California	1,244,100	10.6%
2	Texas	840,500	7.1%
3	Ohio	620,200	5.3%
4	Illinois	563,200	4.8%
5	Pennsylvania	561,900	4.8%
6	Michigan	460,400	3.9%
7	New York	459,200	3.9%
8	Indiana	439,000	3.7%
9	North Carolina	434,400	3.7%
10	Wisconsin	431,900	3.7%
11	Georgia	333,700	2.8%
12	Tennessee	301,700	2.6%
13	Florida	300,100	2.6%
14	Minnesota	299,600	2.5%
15	New Jersey	257,300	2.2%
15	Washington	257,300	2.2%
17	Massachusetts	253,900	2.2%
18	Missouri	246,400	2.1%
19	Virginia	228,700	1.9%
20	Kentucky	214,600	1.8%
21	South Carolina	211,800	1.8%
22	Iowa	205,800	1.8%
23	Connecticut	166,900	1.4%
24	Arkansas	164,000	1.4%
25	Kansas	161,600	1.4%
26	Oregon	159,700	1.4%
27	Arizona	149,400	1.3%
28	Louisiana	138,700	1.2%
29	Mississippi	134,500	1.1%
30	Oklahoma	125,600	1.1%
31	Colorado	122,600	1.0%
32	Utah	110,700	0.9%
33	Maryland	109,900	0.9%
34	Nebraska	92,100	0.8%
35	New Hampshire	66,800	0.6%
36	Idaho	54,900	0.5%
37	Maine	53,200	0.5%
38	West Virginia	50,300	0.4%
39	Rhode Island	39,600	0.3%
40	South Dakota	38,200	0.3%
41	Nevada	37,600	0.3%
42	Vermont	31,700	0.3%
43	New Mexico	30,700	0.3%
44	North Dakota	23,700	0.2%
45	Montana	17,900	0.2%
46	Alaska	12,900	0.1%
47	Wyoming	9,200	0.1%
NA	Alabama**	NA	NA
NA	Delaware**	NA	NA
NA	Hawaii**	NA	NA
	District of Columbia**	NA	NA

Source: U.S. Department of Labor, Bureau of Labor Statistics
"Regional and State Employment and Unemployment" (press release, January 25, 2011, www.bls.gov/bls/newsrels.htm)
*Seasonally adjusted preliminary data as of December 2010. National total calculated through a different formula.
**The Bureau of Labor Statistics does not publish seasonally adjusted figures in this category for these states.

Percent of Nonfarm Employees in Manufacturing in 2010

National Percent = 9.0% of Employees*

ALPHA ORDER

RANK	STATE	PERCENT
NA	Alabama**	NA
44	Alaska	4.0
38	Arizona	6.2
3	Arkansas	14.1
25	California	9.0
39	Colorado	5.5
16	Connecticut	10.3
NA	Delaware**	NA
42	Florida	4.2
28	Georgia	8.8
NA	Hawaii**	NA
25	Idaho	9.0
17	Illinois	10.0
1	Indiana	15.8
4	Iowa	14.0
7	Kansas	12.1
7	Kentucky	12.1
33	Louisiana	7.3
25	Maine	9.0
41	Maryland	4.4
31	Massachusetts	8.0
9	Michigan	12.0
12	Minnesota	11.3
6	Mississippi	12.3
22	Missouri	9.3
42	Montana	4.2
20	Nebraska	9.7
46	Nevada	3.4
15	New Hampshire	10.5
35	New Jersey	6.7
45	New Mexico	3.8
40	New York	5.4
13	North Carolina	11.1
36	North Dakota	6.4
5	Ohio	12.4
30	Oklahoma	8.2
17	Oregon	10.0
17	Pennsylvania	10.0
28	Rhode Island	8.8
10	South Carolina	11.6
21	South Dakota	9.4
10	Tennessee	11.6
31	Texas	8.0
22	Utah	9.3
14	Vermont	10.7
37	Virginia	6.3
24	Washington	9.2
34	West Virginia	6.8
1	Wisconsin	15.8
47	Wyoming	3.2

RANK ORDER

RANK	STATE	PERCENT
1	Indiana	15.8
1	Wisconsin	15.8
3	Arkansas	14.1
4	Iowa	14.0
5	Ohio	12.4
6	Mississippi	12.3
7	Kansas	12.1
7	Kentucky	12.1
9	Michigan	12.0
10	South Carolina	11.6
10	Tennessee	11.6
12	Minnesota	11.3
13	North Carolina	11.1
14	Vermont	10.7
15	New Hampshire	10.5
16	Connecticut	10.3
17	Illinois	10.0
17	Oregon	10.0
17	Pennsylvania	10.0
20	Nebraska	9.7
21	South Dakota	9.4
22	Missouri	9.3
22	Utah	9.3
24	Washington	9.2
25	California	9.0
25	Idaho	9.0
25	Maine	9.0
28	Georgia	8.8
28	Rhode Island	8.8
30	Oklahoma	8.2
31	Massachusetts	8.0
31	Texas	8.0
33	Louisiana	7.3
34	West Virginia	6.8
35	New Jersey	6.7
36	North Dakota	6.4
37	Virginia	6.3
38	Arizona	6.2
39	Colorado	5.5
40	New York	5.4
41	Maryland	4.4
42	Florida	4.2
42	Montana	4.2
44	Alaska	4.0
45	New Mexico	3.8
46	Nevada	3.4
47	Wyoming	3.2
NA	Alabama**	NA
NA	Delaware**	NA
NA	Hawaii**	NA
	District of Columbia**	NA

Source: CQ Press using data from U.S. Department of Labor, Bureau of Labor Statistics

"Regional and State Employment and Unemployment" (press release, January 25, 2011, www.bls.gov/bls/newsrels.htm)

*Seasonally adjusted preliminary data as of December 2010. National figure calculated through a different formula.

**The Bureau of Labor Statistics does not publish seasonally adjusted figures in this category for these states.

Employees in Mining and Logging in 2010

National Total = 770,000 Employees*

ALPHA ORDER

RANK	STATE	EMPLOYEES	% of USA
14	Alabama	11,800	1.5%
11	Alaska	14,100	1.8%
13	Arizona	11,900	1.5%
19	Arkansas	9,900	1.3%
7	California	24,000	3.1%
9	Colorado	23,200	3.0%
43	Connecticut	700	0.1%
NA	Delaware**	NA	NA
29	Florida	5,500	0.7%
23	Georgia	8,900	1.2%
NA	Hawaii**	NA	NA
35	Idaho	3,000	0.4%
17	Illinois	10,200	1.3%
27	Indiana	7,100	0.9%
38	Iowa	2,300	0.3%
21	Kansas	9,400	1.2%
8	Kentucky	23,400	3.0%
2	Louisiana	49,700	6.5%
36	Maine	2,900	0.4%
NA	Maryland**	NA	NA
40	Massachusetts	1,400	0.2%
24	Michigan	7,500	1.0%
31	Minnesota	5,000	0.6%
22	Mississippi	9,100	1.2%
34	Missouri	3,800	0.5%
24	Montana	7,500	1.0%
NA	Nebraska**	NA	NA
12	Nevada	12,200	1.6%
41	New Hampshire	800	0.1%
39	New Jersey	1,700	0.2%
10	New Mexico	17,700	2.3%
30	New York	5,400	0.7%
28	North Carolina	6,100	0.8%
20	North Dakota	9,500	1.2%
14	Ohio	11,800	1.5%
3	Oklahoma	47,300	6.1%
26	Oregon	7,300	0.9%
6	Pennsylvania	26,000	3.4%
44	Rhode Island	200	0.0%
33	South Carolina	4,400	0.6%
NA	South Dakota**	NA	NA
NA	Tennessee**	NA	NA
1	Texas	231,600	30.1%
16	Utah	10,400	1.4%
41	Vermont	800	0.1%
18	Virginia	10,000	1.3%
32	Washington	4,900	0.6%
4	West Virginia	30,600	4.0%
36	Wisconsin	2,900	0.4%
5	Wyoming	27,600	3.6%

RANK ORDER

RANK	STATE	EMPLOYEES	% of USA
1	Texas	231,600	30.1%
2	Louisiana	49,700	6.5%
3	Oklahoma	47,300	6.1%
4	West Virginia	30,600	4.0%
5	Wyoming	27,600	3.6%
6	Pennsylvania	26,000	3.4%
7	California	24,000	3.1%
8	Kentucky	23,400	3.0%
9	Colorado	23,200	3.0%
10	New Mexico	17,700	2.3%
11	Alaska	14,100	1.8%
12	Nevada	12,200	1.6%
13	Arizona	11,900	1.5%
14	Alabama	11,800	1.5%
14	Ohio	11,800	1.5%
16	Utah	10,400	1.4%
17	Illinois	10,200	1.3%
18	Virginia	10,000	1.3%
19	Arkansas	9,900	1.3%
20	North Dakota	9,500	1.2%
21	Kansas	9,400	1.2%
22	Mississippi	9,100	1.2%
23	Georgia	8,900	1.2%
24	Michigan	7,500	1.0%
24	Montana	7,500	1.0%
26	Oregon	7,300	0.9%
27	Indiana	7,100	0.9%
28	North Carolina	6,100	0.8%
29	Florida	5,500	0.7%
30	New York	5,400	0.7%
31	Minnesota	5,000	0.6%
32	Washington	4,900	0.6%
33	South Carolina	4,400	0.6%
34	Missouri	3,800	0.5%
35	Idaho	3,000	0.4%
36	Maine	2,900	0.4%
36	Wisconsin	2,900	0.4%
38	Iowa	2,300	0.3%
39	New Jersey	1,700	0.2%
40	Massachusetts	1,400	0.2%
41	New Hampshire	800	0.1%
41	Vermont	800	0.1%
43	Connecticut	700	0.1%
44	Rhode Island	200	0.0%
NA	Delaware**	NA	NA
NA	Hawaii**	NA	NA
NA	Maryland**	NA	NA
NA	Nebraska**	NA	NA
NA	South Dakota**	NA	NA
NA	Tennessee**	NA	NA
	District of Columbia**	NA	NA

Source: U.S. Department of Labor, Bureau of Labor Statistics
   "Regional and State Employment and Unemployment" (press release, January 25, 2011, www.bls.gov/bls/newsrels.htm)
*Not seasonally adjusted preliminary data as of December 2010. National total calculated through a different formula.
**Mining and logging is combined with construction for these states.

Percent of Nonfarm Employees in Mining and Logging in 2010

National Percent = 0.6% of Employees*

<table>
<tr><td colspan="3">ALPHA ORDER</td><td colspan="3">RANK ORDER</td></tr>
<tr><td>RANK</td><td>STATE</td><td>PERCENT</td><td>RANK</td><td>STATE</td><td>PERCENT</td></tr>
<tr><td>17</td><td>Alabama</td><td>0.6</td><td>1</td><td>Wyoming</td><td>9.7</td></tr>
<tr><td>2</td><td>Alaska</td><td>4.4</td><td>2</td><td>Alaska</td><td>4.4</td></tr>
<tr><td>18</td><td>Arizona</td><td>0.5</td><td>3</td><td>West Virginia</td><td>4.1</td></tr>
<tr><td>14</td><td>Arkansas</td><td>0.8</td><td>4</td><td>Oklahoma</td><td>3.1</td></tr>
<tr><td>26</td><td>California</td><td>0.2</td><td>5</td><td>Louisiana</td><td>2.6</td></tr>
<tr><td>11</td><td>Colorado</td><td>1.1</td><td>6</td><td>North Dakota</td><td>2.5</td></tr>
<tr><td>41</td><td>Connecticut</td><td>0.0</td><td>7</td><td>New Mexico</td><td>2.2</td></tr>
<tr><td>NA</td><td>Delaware**</td><td>NA</td><td>7</td><td>Texas</td><td>2.2</td></tr>
<tr><td>36</td><td>Florida</td><td>0.1</td><td>9</td><td>Montana</td><td>1.8</td></tr>
<tr><td>26</td><td>Georgia</td><td>0.2</td><td>10</td><td>Kentucky</td><td>1.3</td></tr>
<tr><td>NA</td><td>Hawaii**</td><td>NA</td><td>11</td><td>Colorado</td><td>1.1</td></tr>
<tr><td>18</td><td>Idaho</td><td>0.5</td><td>11</td><td>Nevada</td><td>1.1</td></tr>
<tr><td>26</td><td>Illinois</td><td>0.2</td><td>13</td><td>Utah</td><td>0.9</td></tr>
<tr><td>23</td><td>Indiana</td><td>0.3</td><td>14</td><td>Arkansas</td><td>0.8</td></tr>
<tr><td>26</td><td>Iowa</td><td>0.2</td><td>14</td><td>Mississippi</td><td>0.8</td></tr>
<tr><td>16</td><td>Kansas</td><td>0.7</td><td>16</td><td>Kansas</td><td>0.7</td></tr>
<tr><td>10</td><td>Kentucky</td><td>1.3</td><td>17</td><td>Alabama</td><td>0.6</td></tr>
<tr><td>5</td><td>Louisiana</td><td>2.6</td><td>18</td><td>Arizona</td><td>0.5</td></tr>
<tr><td>18</td><td>Maine</td><td>0.5</td><td>18</td><td>Idaho</td><td>0.5</td></tr>
<tr><td>NA</td><td>Maryland**</td><td>NA</td><td>18</td><td>Maine</td><td>0.5</td></tr>
<tr><td>41</td><td>Massachusetts</td><td>0.0</td><td>18</td><td>Oregon</td><td>0.5</td></tr>
<tr><td>26</td><td>Michigan</td><td>0.2</td><td>18</td><td>Pennsylvania</td><td>0.5</td></tr>
<tr><td>26</td><td>Minnesota</td><td>0.2</td><td>23</td><td>Indiana</td><td>0.3</td></tr>
<tr><td>14</td><td>Mississippi</td><td>0.8</td><td>23</td><td>Vermont</td><td>0.3</td></tr>
<tr><td>36</td><td>Missouri</td><td>0.1</td><td>23</td><td>Virginia</td><td>0.3</td></tr>
<tr><td>9</td><td>Montana</td><td>1.8</td><td>26</td><td>California</td><td>0.2</td></tr>
<tr><td>NA</td><td>Nebraska**</td><td>NA</td><td>26</td><td>Georgia</td><td>0.2</td></tr>
<tr><td>11</td><td>Nevada</td><td>1.1</td><td>26</td><td>Illinois</td><td>0.2</td></tr>
<tr><td>36</td><td>New Hampshire</td><td>0.1</td><td>26</td><td>Iowa</td><td>0.2</td></tr>
<tr><td>41</td><td>New Jersey</td><td>0.0</td><td>26</td><td>Michigan</td><td>0.2</td></tr>
<tr><td>7</td><td>New Mexico</td><td>2.2</td><td>26</td><td>Minnesota</td><td>0.2</td></tr>
<tr><td>36</td><td>New York</td><td>0.1</td><td>26</td><td>North Carolina</td><td>0.2</td></tr>
<tr><td>26</td><td>North Carolina</td><td>0.2</td><td>26</td><td>Ohio</td><td>0.2</td></tr>
<tr><td>6</td><td>North Dakota</td><td>2.5</td><td>26</td><td>South Carolina</td><td>0.2</td></tr>
<tr><td>26</td><td>Ohio</td><td>0.2</td><td>26</td><td>Washington</td><td>0.2</td></tr>
<tr><td>4</td><td>Oklahoma</td><td>3.1</td><td>36</td><td>Florida</td><td>0.1</td></tr>
<tr><td>18</td><td>Oregon</td><td>0.5</td><td>36</td><td>Missouri</td><td>0.1</td></tr>
<tr><td>18</td><td>Pennsylvania</td><td>0.5</td><td>36</td><td>New Hampshire</td><td>0.1</td></tr>
<tr><td>41</td><td>Rhode Island</td><td>0.0</td><td>36</td><td>New York</td><td>0.1</td></tr>
<tr><td>26</td><td>South Carolina</td><td>0.2</td><td>36</td><td>Wisconsin</td><td>0.1</td></tr>
<tr><td>NA</td><td>South Dakota**</td><td>NA</td><td>41</td><td>Connecticut</td><td>0.0</td></tr>
<tr><td>NA</td><td>Tennessee**</td><td>NA</td><td>41</td><td>Massachusetts</td><td>0.0</td></tr>
<tr><td>7</td><td>Texas</td><td>2.2</td><td>41</td><td>New Jersey</td><td>0.0</td></tr>
<tr><td>13</td><td>Utah</td><td>0.9</td><td>41</td><td>Rhode Island</td><td>0.0</td></tr>
<tr><td>23</td><td>Vermont</td><td>0.3</td><td>NA</td><td>Delaware**</td><td>NA</td></tr>
<tr><td>23</td><td>Virginia</td><td>0.3</td><td>NA</td><td>Hawaii**</td><td>NA</td></tr>
<tr><td>26</td><td>Washington</td><td>0.2</td><td>NA</td><td>Maryland**</td><td>NA</td></tr>
<tr><td>3</td><td>West Virginia</td><td>4.1</td><td>NA</td><td>Nebraska**</td><td>NA</td></tr>
<tr><td>36</td><td>Wisconsin</td><td>0.1</td><td>NA</td><td>South Dakota**</td><td>NA</td></tr>
<tr><td>1</td><td>Wyoming</td><td>9.7</td><td>NA</td><td>Tennessee**</td><td>NA</td></tr>
<tr><td></td><td></td><td></td><td></td><td>District of Columbia**</td><td>NA</td></tr>
</table>

Source: CQ Press using data from U.S. Department of Labor, Bureau of Labor Statistics
   "Regional and State Employment and Unemployment" (press release, January 25, 2011, www.bls.gov/bls/newsrels.htm)
*Not seasonally adjusted preliminary data as of December 2010. National figure calculated through a different formula.
**Mining and logging is combined with construction for these states.

Employees in Professional and Business Services in 2010

National Total = 16,854,000 Employees*

ALPHA ORDER

RANK	STATE	EMPLOYEES	% of USA
24	Alabama	200,000	1.2%
48	Alaska	26,200	0.2%
15	Arizona	355,500	2.1%
34	Arkansas	114,600	0.7%
1	California	2,085,700	12.4%
17	Colorado	327,500	1.9%
26	Connecticut	188,400	1.1%
43	Delaware	53,400	0.3%
4	Florida	1,038,400	6.2%
11	Georgia	512,300	3.0%
39	Hawaii	69,500	0.4%
38	Idaho	74,200	0.4%
5	Illinois	781,500	4.6%
21	Indiana	284,800	1.7%
33	Iowa	124,900	0.7%
32	Kansas	137,400	0.8%
27	Kentucky	184,200	1.1%
25	Louisiana	194,000	1.2%
42	Maine	55,900	0.3%
14	Maryland	392,900	2.3%
13	Massachusetts	466,500	2.8%
10	Michigan	519,800	3.1%
18	Minnesota	316,000	1.9%
37	Mississippi	90,300	0.5%
19	Missouri	308,400	1.8%
45	Montana	38,500	0.2%
35	Nebraska	102,400	0.6%
31	Nevada	140,300	0.8%
40	New Hampshire	66,400	0.4%
9	New Jersey	585,700	3.5%
36	New Mexico	92,200	0.5%
3	New York	1,098,200	6.5%
12	North Carolina	485,200	2.9%
46	North Dakota	29,700	0.2%
8	Ohio	621,600	3.7%
29	Oklahoma	167,500	1.0%
28	Oregon	180,700	1.1%
6	Pennsylvania	676,900	4.0%
44	Rhode Island	50,700	0.3%
23	South Carolina	212,900	1.3%
47	South Dakota	27,100	0.2%
20	Tennessee	304,600	1.8%
2	Texas	1,287,300	7.6%
30	Utah	153,400	0.9%
49	Vermont	22,300	0.1%
7	Virginia	657,600	3.9%
16	Washington	335,900	2.0%
41	West Virginia	59,600	0.4%
22	Wisconsin	257,300	1.5%
50	Wyoming	16,900	0.1%

RANK ORDER

RANK	STATE	EMPLOYEES	% of USA
1	California	2,085,700	12.4%
2	Texas	1,287,300	7.6%
3	New York	1,098,200	6.5%
4	Florida	1,038,400	6.2%
5	Illinois	781,500	4.6%
6	Pennsylvania	676,900	4.0%
7	Virginia	657,600	3.9%
8	Ohio	621,600	3.7%
9	New Jersey	585,700	3.5%
10	Michigan	519,800	3.1%
11	Georgia	512,300	3.0%
12	North Carolina	485,200	2.9%
13	Massachusetts	466,500	2.8%
14	Maryland	392,900	2.3%
15	Arizona	355,500	2.1%
16	Washington	335,900	2.0%
17	Colorado	327,500	1.9%
18	Minnesota	316,000	1.9%
19	Missouri	308,400	1.8%
20	Tennessee	304,600	1.8%
21	Indiana	284,800	1.7%
22	Wisconsin	257,300	1.5%
23	South Carolina	212,900	1.3%
24	Alabama	200,000	1.2%
25	Louisiana	194,000	1.2%
26	Connecticut	188,400	1.1%
27	Kentucky	184,200	1.1%
28	Oregon	180,700	1.1%
29	Oklahoma	167,500	1.0%
30	Utah	153,400	0.9%
31	Nevada	140,300	0.8%
32	Kansas	137,400	0.8%
33	Iowa	124,900	0.7%
34	Arkansas	114,600	0.7%
35	Nebraska	102,400	0.6%
36	New Mexico	92,200	0.5%
37	Mississippi	90,300	0.5%
38	Idaho	74,200	0.4%
39	Hawaii	69,500	0.4%
40	New Hampshire	66,400	0.4%
41	West Virginia	59,600	0.4%
42	Maine	55,900	0.3%
43	Delaware	53,400	0.3%
44	Rhode Island	50,700	0.3%
45	Montana	38,500	0.2%
46	North Dakota	29,700	0.2%
47	South Dakota	27,100	0.2%
48	Alaska	26,200	0.2%
49	Vermont	22,300	0.1%
50	Wyoming	16,900	0.1%
	District of Columbia	157,300	0.9%

Source: U.S. Department of Labor, Bureau of Labor Statistics
"Regional and State Employment and Unemployment" (press release, January 25, 2011, www.bls.gov/bls/newsrels.htm)
*Seasonally adjusted preliminary data as of December 2010. National total calculated through a different formula.

Percent of Nonfarm Employees in Professional and Business Services in 2010

National Percent = 12.9% of Employees*

ALPHA ORDER

RANK	STATE	PERCENT
32	Alabama	10.8
45	Alaska	8.1
6	Arizona	14.7
39	Arkansas	9.8
4	California	15.0
5	Colorado	14.8
24	Connecticut	11.7
12	Delaware	13.0
8	Florida	14.4
11	Georgia	13.5
23	Hawaii	11.8
19	Idaho	12.2
9	Illinois	13.9
37	Indiana	10.2
43	Iowa	8.5
36	Kansas	10.3
34	Kentucky	10.4
37	Louisiana	10.2
40	Maine	9.4
2	Maryland	15.6
6	Massachusetts	14.7
10	Michigan	13.6
22	Minnesota	11.9
44	Mississippi	8.3
26	Missouri	11.6
42	Montana	9.0
32	Nebraska	10.8
15	Nevada	12.7
34	New Hampshire	10.4
3	New Jersey	15.3
28	New Mexico	11.5
13	New York	12.9
16	North Carolina	12.5
46	North Dakota	8.0
17	Ohio	12.4
31	Oklahoma	10.9
29	Oregon	11.3
20	Pennsylvania	12.0
29	Rhode Island	11.3
26	South Carolina	11.6
49	South Dakota	6.7
24	Tennessee	11.7
18	Texas	12.3
13	Utah	12.9
48	Vermont	7.6
1	Virginia	18.1
20	Washington	12.0
46	West Virginia	8.0
40	Wisconsin	9.4
50	Wyoming	6.0

RANK ORDER

RANK	STATE	PERCENT
1	Virginia	18.1
2	Maryland	15.6
3	New Jersey	15.3
4	California	15.0
5	Colorado	14.8
6	Arizona	14.7
6	Massachusetts	14.7
8	Florida	14.4
9	Illinois	13.9
10	Michigan	13.6
11	Georgia	13.5
12	Delaware	13.0
13	New York	12.9
13	Utah	12.9
15	Nevada	12.7
16	North Carolina	12.5
17	Ohio	12.4
18	Texas	12.3
19	Idaho	12.2
20	Pennsylvania	12.0
20	Washington	12.0
22	Minnesota	11.9
23	Hawaii	11.8
24	Connecticut	11.7
24	Tennessee	11.7
26	Missouri	11.6
26	South Carolina	11.6
28	New Mexico	11.5
29	Oregon	11.3
29	Rhode Island	11.3
31	Oklahoma	10.9
32	Alabama	10.8
32	Nebraska	10.8
34	Kentucky	10.4
34	New Hampshire	10.4
36	Kansas	10.3
37	Indiana	10.2
37	Louisiana	10.2
39	Arkansas	9.8
40	Maine	9.4
40	Wisconsin	9.4
42	Montana	9.0
43	Iowa	8.5
44	Mississippi	8.3
45	Alaska	8.1
46	North Dakota	8.0
46	West Virginia	8.0
48	Vermont	7.6
49	South Dakota	6.7
50	Wyoming	6.0

	District of Columbia	21.7

Source: CQ Press using data from U.S. Department of Labor, Bureau of Labor Statistics
   "Regional and State Employment and Unemployment" (press release, January 25, 2011, www.bls.gov/bls/newsrels.htm)
*Seasonally adjusted preliminary data as of December 2010. National figure calculated through a different formula.

Employees in Trade, Transportation, and Public Utilities in 2010

National Total = 24,880,000 Employees*

ALPHA ORDER

RANK	STATE	EMPLOYEES	% of USA
25	Alabama	365,300	1.5%
48	Alaska	62,900	0.3%
20	Arizona	489,800	2.0%
33	Arkansas	228,800	0.9%
1	California	2,568,900	10.3%
22	Colorado	395,200	1.6%
29	Connecticut	287,000	1.2%
46	Delaware	72,800	0.3%
3	Florida	1,456,800	5.9%
9	Georgia	799,300	3.2%
42	Hawaii	108,300	0.4%
40	Idaho	120,300	0.5%
5	Illinois	1,128,300	4.5%
14	Indiana	550,100	2.2%
28	Iowa	291,300	1.2%
31	Kansas	256,100	1.0%
24	Kentucky	366,300	1.5%
23	Louisiana	372,700	1.5%
41	Maine	115,500	0.5%
21	Maryland	436,500	1.8%
15	Massachusetts	536,900	2.2%
11	Michigan	705,600	2.8%
19	Minnesota	491,700	2.0%
34	Mississippi	214,300	0.9%
17	Missouri	506,300	2.0%
43	Montana	89,700	0.4%
36	Nebraska	196,800	0.8%
35	Nevada	207,300	0.8%
37	New Hampshire	135,400	0.5%
8	New Jersey	807,800	3.2%
39	New Mexico	128,100	0.5%
4	New York	1,435,300	5.8%
10	North Carolina	710,500	2.9%
45	North Dakota	78,600	0.3%
7	Ohio	942,500	3.8%
30	Oklahoma	277,500	1.1%
27	Oregon	314,000	1.3%
6	Pennsylvania	1,077,500	4.3%
47	Rhode Island	71,300	0.3%
26	South Carolina	346,100	1.4%
44	South Dakota	82,200	0.3%
13	Tennessee	554,300	2.2%
2	Texas	2,040,600	8.2%
32	Utah	231,700	0.9%
49	Vermont	54,600	0.2%
12	Virginia	623,900	2.5%
16	Washington	534,900	2.1%
38	West Virginia	132,600	0.5%
18	Wisconsin	505,300	2.0%
50	Wyoming	52,200	0.2%

RANK ORDER

RANK	STATE	EMPLOYEES	% of USA
1	California	2,568,900	10.3%
2	Texas	2,040,600	8.2%
3	Florida	1,456,800	5.9%
4	New York	1,435,300	5.8%
5	Illinois	1,128,300	4.5%
6	Pennsylvania	1,077,500	4.3%
7	Ohio	942,500	3.8%
8	New Jersey	807,800	3.2%
9	Georgia	799,300	3.2%
10	North Carolina	710,500	2.9%
11	Michigan	705,600	2.8%
12	Virginia	623,900	2.5%
13	Tennessee	554,300	2.2%
14	Indiana	550,100	2.2%
15	Massachusetts	536,900	2.2%
16	Washington	534,900	2.1%
17	Missouri	506,300	2.0%
18	Wisconsin	505,300	2.0%
19	Minnesota	491,700	2.0%
20	Arizona	489,800	2.0%
21	Maryland	436,500	1.8%
22	Colorado	395,200	1.6%
23	Louisiana	372,700	1.5%
24	Kentucky	366,300	1.5%
25	Alabama	365,300	1.5%
26	South Carolina	346,100	1.4%
27	Oregon	314,000	1.3%
28	Iowa	291,300	1.2%
29	Connecticut	287,000	1.2%
30	Oklahoma	277,500	1.1%
31	Kansas	256,100	1.0%
32	Utah	231,700	0.9%
33	Arkansas	228,800	0.9%
34	Mississippi	214,300	0.9%
35	Nevada	207,300	0.8%
36	Nebraska	196,800	0.8%
37	New Hampshire	135,400	0.5%
38	West Virginia	132,600	0.5%
39	New Mexico	128,100	0.5%
40	Idaho	120,300	0.5%
41	Maine	115,500	0.5%
42	Hawaii	108,300	0.4%
43	Montana	89,700	0.4%
44	South Dakota	82,200	0.3%
45	North Dakota	78,600	0.3%
46	Delaware	72,800	0.3%
47	Rhode Island	71,300	0.3%
48	Alaska	62,900	0.3%
49	Vermont	54,600	0.2%
50	Wyoming	52,200	0.2%
	District of Columbia	26,100	0.1%

Source: U.S. Department of Labor, Bureau of Labor Statistics
"Regional and State Employment and Unemployment" (press release, January 25, 2011, www.bls.gov/bls/newsrels.htm)
*Seasonally adjusted preliminary data as of December 2010. National total calculated through a different formula.

Percent of Nonfarm Employees in
Trade, Transportation, and Public Utilities in 2010
National Percent = 19.0% of Employees*

ALPHA ORDER

RANK	STATE	PERCENT
16	Alabama	19.7
21	Alaska	19.5
11	Arizona	20.2
17	Arkansas	19.6
33	California	18.5
41	Colorado	17.9
43	Connecticut	17.8
44	Delaware	17.7
9	Florida	20.3
6	Georgia	21.0
36	Hawaii	18.4
13	Idaho	19.8
12	Illinois	20.1
13	Indiana	19.8
13	Iowa	19.8
25	Kansas	19.3
8	Kentucky	20.6
17	Louisiana	19.6
21	Maine	19.5
45	Maryland	17.3
47	Massachusetts	16.9
36	Michigan	18.4
32	Minnesota	18.6
17	Mississippi	19.6
27	Missouri	19.1
3	Montana	21.1
7	Nebraska	20.8
31	Nevada	18.7
1	New Hampshire	21.2
3	New Jersey	21.1
49	New Mexico	16.0
47	New York	16.9
39	North Carolina	18.2
3	North Dakota	21.1
30	Ohio	18.8
40	Oklahoma	18.0
17	Oregon	19.6
26	Pennsylvania	19.2
50	Rhode Island	15.9
29	South Carolina	18.9
9	South Dakota	20.3
1	Tennessee	21.2
21	Texas	19.5
21	Utah	19.5
33	Vermont	18.5
46	Virginia	17.2
28	Washington	19.0
41	West Virginia	17.9
33	Wisconsin	18.5
36	Wyoming	18.4

RANK ORDER

RANK	STATE	PERCENT
1	New Hampshire	21.2
1	Tennessee	21.2
3	Montana	21.1
3	New Jersey	21.1
3	North Dakota	21.1
6	Georgia	21.0
7	Nebraska	20.8
8	Kentucky	20.6
9	Florida	20.3
9	South Dakota	20.3
11	Arizona	20.2
12	Illinois	20.1
13	Idaho	19.8
13	Indiana	19.8
13	Iowa	19.8
16	Alabama	19.7
17	Arkansas	19.6
17	Louisiana	19.6
17	Mississippi	19.6
17	Oregon	19.6
21	Alaska	19.5
21	Maine	19.5
21	Texas	19.5
21	Utah	19.5
25	Kansas	19.3
26	Pennsylvania	19.2
27	Missouri	19.1
28	Washington	19.0
29	South Carolina	18.9
30	Ohio	18.8
31	Nevada	18.7
32	Minnesota	18.6
33	California	18.5
33	Vermont	18.5
33	Wisconsin	18.5
36	Hawaii	18.4
36	Michigan	18.4
36	Wyoming	18.4
39	North Carolina	18.2
40	Oklahoma	18.0
41	Colorado	17.9
41	West Virginia	17.9
43	Connecticut	17.8
44	Delaware	17.7
45	Maryland	17.3
46	Virginia	17.2
47	Massachusetts	16.9
47	New York	16.9
49	New Mexico	16.0
50	Rhode Island	15.9

District of Columbia 3.6

Source: CQ Press using data from U.S. Department of Labor, Bureau of Labor Statistics
"Regional and State Employment and Unemployment" (press release, January 25, 2011, www.bls.gov/bls/newsrels.htm)
*Seasonally adjusted preliminary data as of December 2010. National figure calculated through a different formula.

VII. Energy and Environment

Energy Consumption in 2008

National Total = 99,382,100,000,000,000 BTUs*

ALPHA ORDER

RANK	STATE	BTUs	% of USA
16	Alabama	2,065,000,000,000,000	2.1%
39	Alaska	650,800,000,000,000	0.7%
24	Arizona	1,552,800,000,000,000	1.6%
31	Arkansas	1,124,700,000,000,000	1.1%
2	California	8,381,500,000,000,000	8.4%
25	Colorado	1,498,100,000,000,000	1.5%
34	Connecticut	809,900,000,000,000	0.8%
47	Delaware	295,300,000,000,000	0.3%
3	Florida	4,447,400,000,000,000	4.5%
9	Georgia	3,015,400,000,000,000	3.0%
48	Hawaii	283,800,000,000,000	0.3%
41	Idaho	529,300,000,000,000	0.5%
4	Illinois	4,088,700,000,000,000	4.1%
11	Indiana	2,857,400,000,000,000	2.9%
28	Iowa	1,414,400,000,000,000	1.4%
30	Kansas	1,135,600,000,000,000	1.1%
18	Kentucky	1,982,800,000,000,000	2.0%
8	Louisiana	3,487,500,000,000,000	3.5%
42	Maine	469,300,000,000,000	0.5%
27	Maryland	1,446,900,000,000,000	1.5%
26	Massachusetts	1,475,000,000,000,000	1.5%
10	Michigan	2,918,300,000,000,000	2.9%
19	Minnesota	1,979,100,000,000,000	2.0%
29	Mississippi	1,185,600,000,000,000	1.2%
20	Missouri	1,937,000,000,000,000	1.9%
44	Montana	434,300,000,000,000	0.4%
36	Nebraska	781,900,000,000,000	0.8%
37	Nevada	750,100,000,000,000	0.8%
46	New Hampshire	311,300,000,000,000	0.3%
13	New Jersey	2,637,100,000,000,000	2.7%
38	New Mexico	693,300,000,000,000	0.7%
5	New York	3,988,100,000,000,000	4.0%
12	North Carolina	2,702,200,000,000,000	2.7%
43	North Dakota	440,900,000,000,000	0.4%
6	Ohio	3,987,000,000,000,000	4.0%
23	Oklahoma	1,603,400,000,000,000	1.6%
32	Oregon	1,104,700,000,000,000	1.1%
7	Pennsylvania	3,899,700,000,000,000	3.9%
49	Rhode Island	220,100,000,000,000	0.2%
22	South Carolina	1,659,500,000,000,000	1.7%
45	South Dakota	350,200,000,000,000	0.4%
15	Tennessee	2,261,100,000,000,000	2.3%
1	Texas	11,552,200,000,000,000	11.6%
35	Utah	799,400,000,000,000	0.8%
50	Vermont	154,400,000,000,000	0.2%
14	Virginia	2,513,700,000,000,000	2.5%
17	Washington	2,050,200,000,000,000	2.1%
33	West Virginia	830,800,000,000,000	0.8%
21	Wisconsin	1,862,400,000,000,000	1.9%
40	Wyoming	541,600,000,000,000	0.5%

RANK ORDER

RANK	STATE	BTUs	% of USA
1	Texas	11,552,200,000,000,000	11.6%
2	California	8,381,500,000,000,000	8.4%
3	Florida	4,447,400,000,000,000	4.5%
4	Illinois	4,088,700,000,000,000	4.1%
5	New York	3,988,100,000,000,000	4.0%
6	Ohio	3,987,000,000,000,000	4.0%
7	Pennsylvania	3,899,700,000,000,000	3.9%
8	Louisiana	3,487,500,000,000,000	3.5%
9	Georgia	3,015,400,000,000,000	3.0%
10	Michigan	2,918,300,000,000,000	2.9%
11	Indiana	2,857,400,000,000,000	2.9%
12	North Carolina	2,702,200,000,000,000	2.7%
13	New Jersey	2,637,100,000,000,000	2.7%
14	Virginia	2,513,700,000,000,000	2.5%
15	Tennessee	2,261,100,000,000,000	2.3%
16	Alabama	2,065,000,000,000,000	2.1%
17	Washington	2,050,200,000,000,000	2.1%
18	Kentucky	1,982,800,000,000,000	2.0%
19	Minnesota	1,979,100,000,000,000	2.0%
20	Missouri	1,937,000,000,000,000	1.9%
21	Wisconsin	1,862,400,000,000,000	1.9%
22	South Carolina	1,659,500,000,000,000	1.7%
23	Oklahoma	1,603,400,000,000,000	1.6%
24	Arizona	1,552,800,000,000,000	1.6%
25	Colorado	1,498,100,000,000,000	1.5%
26	Massachusetts	1,475,000,000,000,000	1.5%
27	Maryland	1,446,900,000,000,000	1.5%
28	Iowa	1,414,400,000,000,000	1.4%
29	Mississippi	1,185,600,000,000,000	1.2%
30	Kansas	1,135,600,000,000,000	1.1%
31	Arkansas	1,124,700,000,000,000	1.1%
32	Oregon	1,104,700,000,000,000	1.1%
33	West Virginia	830,800,000,000,000	0.8%
34	Connecticut	809,900,000,000,000	0.8%
35	Utah	799,400,000,000,000	0.8%
36	Nebraska	781,900,000,000,000	0.8%
37	Nevada	750,100,000,000,000	0.8%
38	New Mexico	693,300,000,000,000	0.7%
39	Alaska	650,800,000,000,000	0.7%
40	Wyoming	541,600,000,000,000	0.5%
41	Idaho	529,300,000,000,000	0.5%
42	Maine	469,300,000,000,000	0.5%
43	North Dakota	440,900,000,000,000	0.4%
44	Montana	434,300,000,000,000	0.4%
45	South Dakota	350,200,000,000,000	0.4%
46	New Hampshire	311,300,000,000,000	0.3%
47	Delaware	295,300,000,000,000	0.3%
48	Hawaii	283,800,000,000,000	0.3%
49	Rhode Island	220,100,000,000,000	0.2%
50	Vermont	154,400,000,000,000	0.2%
	District of Columbia	180,400,000,000,000	0.2%

Source: U.S. Department of Energy, Energy Information Administration
  "State Energy Data 2008: Consumption" (http://www.eia.doe.gov/emeu/states/_seds.html)
*British Thermal Units: The amount of heat required to raise the temperature of one pound of water one degree. National total includes 40.8 trillion Btu of net imports of coal coke that are not allocated to the states.

Per Capita Energy Consumption in 2008

National Per Capita = 326,512,198 BTUs*

ALPHA ORDER				RANK ORDER		
RANK	STATE	BTUs		RANK	STATE	BTUs
11	Alabama	441,478,545		1	Wyoming	1,016,171,308
2	Alaska	945,758,401		2	Alaska	945,758,401
43	Arizona	238,915,207		3	Louisiana	783,441,495
17	Arkansas	392,187,084		4	North Dakota	687,380,051
46	California	229,125,615		5	Texas	475,315,263
34	Colorado	303,553,261		6	Iowa	472,413,541
45	Connecticut	231,206,315		7	Kentucky	462,414,157
25	Delaware	337,019,280		8	West Virginia	457,773,078
42	Florida	241,393,262		9	Montana	448,640,803
31	Georgia	310,935,283		10	Indiana	447,285,815
48	Hawaii	220,430,437		11	Alabama	441,478,545
23	Idaho	346,512,551		12	Oklahoma	440,007,958
29	Illinois	318,361,336		13	Nebraska	438,789,213
10	Indiana	447,285,815		14	South Dakota	435,284,115
6	Iowa	472,413,541		15	Kansas	405,952,009
15	Kansas	405,952,009		16	Mississippi	403,236,229
7	Kentucky	462,414,157		17	Arkansas	392,187,084
3	Louisiana	783,441,495		18	Minnesota	378,371,981
21	Maine	355,613,549		19	South Carolina	368,509,176
40	Maryland	255,696,804		20	Tennessee	362,329,291
47	Massachusetts	225,411,261		21	Maine	355,613,549
38	Michigan	291,757,469		22	New Mexico	348,959,589
18	Minnesota	378,371,981		23	Idaho	346,512,551
16	Mississippi	403,236,229		24	Ohio	345,851,414
27	Missouri	325,199,976		25	Delaware	337,019,280
9	Montana	448,640,803		26	Wisconsin	330,939,777
13	Nebraska	438,789,213		27	Missouri	325,199,976
39	Nevada	286,760,467		28	Virginia	322,458,406
44	New Hampshire	235,499,352		29	Illinois	318,361,336
33	New Jersey	304,395,573		30	Washington	312,241,426
22	New Mexico	348,959,589		31	Georgia	310,935,283
50	New York	204,856,340		32	Pennsylvania	310,328,330
36	North Carolina	292,220,271		33	New Jersey	304,395,573
4	North Dakota	687,380,051		34	Colorado	303,553,261
24	Ohio	345,851,414		35	Utah	293,105,781
12	Oklahoma	440,007,958		36	North Carolina	292,220,271
37	Oregon	292,017,613		37	Oregon	292,017,613
32	Pennsylvania	310,328,330		38	Michigan	291,757,469
49	Rhode Island	208,922,242		39	Nevada	286,760,467
19	South Carolina	368,509,176		40	Maryland	255,696,804
14	South Dakota	435,284,115		41	Vermont	248,611,623
20	Tennessee	362,329,291		42	Florida	241,393,262
5	Texas	475,315,263		43	Arizona	238,915,207
35	Utah	293,105,781		44	New Hampshire	235,499,352
41	Vermont	248,611,623		45	Connecticut	231,206,315
28	Virginia	322,458,406		46	California	229,125,615
30	Washington	312,241,426		47	Massachusetts	225,411,261
8	West Virginia	457,773,078		48	Hawaii	220,430,437
26	Wisconsin	330,939,777		49	Rhode Island	208,922,242
1	Wyoming	1,016,171,308		50	New York	204,856,340
					District of Columbia	305,724,367

Source: CQ Press using data from U.S. Department of Energy, Energy Information Administration
"State Energy Data 2008: Consumption" (http://www.eia.doe.gov/emeu/states/_seds.html)
*British Thermal Units: The amount of heat required to raise the temperature of one pound of water one degree. National figure includes 40.8 trillion Btu of net imports of coal coke that are not allocated to the states.

Energy Prices in 2008

National Rate = $21.44 per Million BTUs*

ALPHA ORDER

RANK	STATE	RATE
40	Alabama	$19.21
11	Alaska	23.78
12	Arizona	23.77
34	Arkansas	20.01
15	California	23.03
36	Colorado	19.77
2	Connecticut	28.83
10	Delaware	24.23
9	Florida	25.02
22	Georgia	20.95
1	Hawaii	36.21
45	Idaho	18.12
35	Illinois	19.91
49	Indiana	17.15
46	Iowa	17.99
33	Kansas	20.10
41	Kentucky	19.05
48	Louisiana	17.92
24	Maine	20.57
8	Maryland	25.12
3	Massachusetts	27.51
38	Michigan	19.61
39	Minnesota	19.58
20	Mississippi	21.23
29	Missouri	20.32
32	Montana	20.14
42	Nebraska	18.69
14	Nevada	23.48
5	New Hampshire	26.64
13	New Jersey	23.71
16	New Mexico	22.54
7	New York	25.21
17	North Carolina	22.04
50	North Dakota	15.77
30	Ohio	20.30
25	Oklahoma	20.56
23	Oregon	20.83
19	Pennsylvania	21.32
6	Rhode Island	26.24
26	South Carolina	20.54
37	South Dakota	19.65
26	Tennessee	20.54
18	Texas	21.50
43	Utah	18.68
4	Vermont	27.26
21	Virginia	21.14
28	Washington	20.53
44	West Virginia	18.16
31	Wisconsin	20.18
47	Wyoming	17.97

RANK ORDER

RANK	STATE	RATE
1	Hawaii	$36.21
2	Connecticut	28.83
3	Massachusetts	27.51
4	Vermont	27.26
5	New Hampshire	26.64
6	Rhode Island	26.24
7	New York	25.21
8	Maryland	25.12
9	Florida	25.02
10	Delaware	24.23
11	Alaska	23.78
12	Arizona	23.77
13	New Jersey	23.71
14	Nevada	23.48
15	California	23.03
16	New Mexico	22.54
17	North Carolina	22.04
18	Texas	21.50
19	Pennsylvania	21.32
20	Mississippi	21.23
21	Virginia	21.14
22	Georgia	20.95
23	Oregon	20.83
24	Maine	20.57
25	Oklahoma	20.56
26	South Carolina	20.54
26	Tennessee	20.54
28	Washington	20.53
29	Missouri	20.32
30	Ohio	20.30
31	Wisconsin	20.18
32	Montana	20.14
33	Kansas	20.10
34	Arkansas	20.01
35	Illinois	19.91
36	Colorado	19.77
37	South Dakota	19.65
38	Michigan	19.61
39	Minnesota	19.58
40	Alabama	19.21
41	Kentucky	19.05
42	Nebraska	18.69
43	Utah	18.68
44	West Virginia	18.16
45	Idaho	18.12
46	Iowa	17.99
47	Wyoming	17.97
48	Louisiana	17.92
49	Indiana	17.15
50	North Dakota	15.77
	District of Columbia	27.37

Source: U.S. Department of Energy, Energy Information Administration
"State Energy Data 2008: Prices and Expenditures" (http://www.eia.doe.gov/emeu/states/_seds.html)
*British Thermal Units: The amount of heat required to raise the temperature of one pound of water one degree.

Energy Expenditures in 2008

National Total = $1,411,921,600,000*

ALPHA ORDER

RANK	STATE	EXPENDITURES	% of USA
21	Alabama	$24,889,300,000	1.8%
40	Alaska	7,509,200,000	0.5%
24	Arizona	22,610,300,000	1.6%
32	Arkansas	14,715,400,000	1.0%
2	California	136,508,100,000	9.7%
27	Colorado	19,750,800,000	1.4%
29	Connecticut	16,460,000,000	1.2%
47	Delaware	4,390,200,000	0.3%
4	Florida	67,907,300,000	4.8%
9	Georgia	41,568,100,000	2.9%
41	Hawaii	6,849,800,000	0.5%
42	Idaho	6,122,300,000	0.4%
5	Illinois	55,890,700,000	4.0%
14	Indiana	33,150,700,000	2.3%
28	Iowa	16,913,600,000	1.2%
33	Kansas	14,569,400,000	1.0%
23	Kentucky	23,264,100,000	1.6%
11	Louisiana	38,905,900,000	2.8%
39	Maine	7,517,400,000	0.5%
22	Maryland	24,349,400,000	1.7%
16	Massachusetts	28,997,000,000	2.1%
10	Michigan	39,849,300,000	2.8%
18	Minnesota	26,301,300,000	1.9%
30	Mississippi	15,502,500,000	1.1%
19	Missouri	26,055,000,000	1.8%
44	Montana	5,684,300,000	0.4%
37	Nebraska	9,077,500,000	0.6%
34	Nevada	11,192,400,000	0.8%
43	New Hampshire	6,085,000,000	0.4%
8	New Jersey	46,132,700,000	3.3%
38	New Mexico	8,893,200,000	0.6%
3	New York	72,462,100,000	5.1%
12	North Carolina	37,853,800,000	2.7%
46	North Dakota	4,945,900,000	0.4%
7	Ohio	54,144,300,000	3.8%
26	Oklahoma	20,743,400,000	1.5%
31	Oregon	14,881,900,000	1.1%
6	Pennsylvania	55,531,300,000	3.9%
49	Rhode Island	4,223,500,000	0.3%
25	South Carolina	21,438,100,000	1.5%
48	South Dakota	4,232,600,000	0.3%
15	Tennessee	29,365,300,000	2.1%
1	Texas	165,334,300,000	11.7%
35	Utah	9,901,000,000	0.7%
50	Vermont	3,012,000,000	0.2%
13	Virginia	34,886,200,000	2.5%
17	Washington	26,668,800,000	1.9%
36	West Virginia	9,634,400,000	0.7%
20	Wisconsin	25,443,600,000	1.8%
45	Wyoming	5,611,800,000	0.4%

RANK ORDER

RANK	STATE	EXPENDITURES	% of USA
1	Texas	$165,334,300,000	11.7%
2	California	136,508,100,000	9.7%
3	New York	72,462,100,000	5.1%
4	Florida	67,907,300,000	4.8%
5	Illinois	55,890,700,000	4.0%
6	Pennsylvania	55,531,300,000	3.9%
7	Ohio	54,144,300,000	3.8%
8	New Jersey	46,132,700,000	3.3%
9	Georgia	41,568,100,000	2.9%
10	Michigan	39,849,300,000	2.8%
11	Louisiana	38,905,900,000	2.8%
12	North Carolina	37,853,800,000	2.7%
13	Virginia	34,886,200,000	2.5%
14	Indiana	33,150,700,000	2.3%
15	Tennessee	29,365,300,000	2.1%
16	Massachusetts	28,997,000,000	2.1%
17	Washington	26,668,800,000	1.9%
18	Minnesota	26,301,300,000	1.9%
19	Missouri	26,055,000,000	1.8%
20	Wisconsin	25,443,600,000	1.8%
21	Alabama	24,889,300,000	1.8%
22	Maryland	24,349,400,000	1.7%
23	Kentucky	23,264,100,000	1.6%
24	Arizona	22,610,300,000	1.6%
25	South Carolina	21,438,100,000	1.5%
26	Oklahoma	20,743,400,000	1.5%
27	Colorado	19,750,800,000	1.4%
28	Iowa	16,913,600,000	1.2%
29	Connecticut	16,460,000,000	1.2%
30	Mississippi	15,502,500,000	1.1%
31	Oregon	14,881,900,000	1.1%
32	Arkansas	14,715,400,000	1.0%
33	Kansas	14,569,400,000	1.0%
34	Nevada	11,192,400,000	0.8%
35	Utah	9,901,000,000	0.7%
36	West Virginia	9,634,400,000	0.7%
37	Nebraska	9,077,500,000	0.6%
38	New Mexico	8,893,200,000	0.6%
39	Maine	7,517,400,000	0.5%
40	Alaska	7,509,200,000	0.5%
41	Hawaii	6,849,800,000	0.5%
42	Idaho	6,122,300,000	0.4%
43	New Hampshire	6,085,000,000	0.4%
44	Montana	5,684,300,000	0.4%
45	Wyoming	5,611,800,000	0.4%
46	North Dakota	4,945,900,000	0.4%
47	Delaware	4,390,200,000	0.3%
48	South Dakota	4,232,600,000	0.3%
49	Rhode Island	4,223,500,000	0.3%
50	Vermont	3,012,000,000	0.2%
	District of Columbia	2,529,500,000	0.2%

Source: U.S. Department of Energy, Energy Information Administration
  "State Energy Data 2008: Prices and Expenditures" (http://www.eia.doe.gov/emeu/states/_seds.html)
*The national total includes $1,465.5 million for coal coke net imports, which are not allocated to the states.

Per Capita Energy Expenditures in 2008

National Per Capita = $4,639

<table>
<tr><th colspan="3">ALPHA ORDER</th><th colspan="3">RANK ORDER</th></tr>
<tr><th>RANK</th><th>STATE</th><th>PER CAPITA</th><th>RANK</th><th>STATE</th><th>PER CAPITA</th></tr>
<tr><td>12</td><td>Alabama</td><td>$5,321</td><td>1</td><td>Alaska</td><td>$10,913</td></tr>
<tr><td>1</td><td>Alaska</td><td>10,913</td><td>2</td><td>Wyoming</td><td>10,529</td></tr>
<tr><td>50</td><td>Arizona</td><td>3,479</td><td>3</td><td>Louisiana</td><td>8,740</td></tr>
<tr><td>19</td><td>Arkansas</td><td>5,131</td><td>4</td><td>North Dakota</td><td>7,711</td></tr>
<tr><td>46</td><td>California</td><td>3,732</td><td>5</td><td>Texas</td><td>6,803</td></tr>
<tr><td>43</td><td>Colorado</td><td>4,002</td><td>6</td><td>Montana</td><td>5,872</td></tr>
<tr><td>26</td><td>Connecticut</td><td>4,699</td><td>7</td><td>Maine</td><td>5,696</td></tr>
<tr><td>22</td><td>Delaware</td><td>5,010</td><td>8</td><td>Oklahoma</td><td>5,692</td></tr>
<tr><td>48</td><td>Florida</td><td>3,686</td><td>9</td><td>Iowa</td><td>5,649</td></tr>
<tr><td>37</td><td>Georgia</td><td>4,286</td><td>10</td><td>Kentucky</td><td>5,425</td></tr>
<tr><td>13</td><td>Hawaii</td><td>5,320</td><td>11</td><td>New Jersey</td><td>5,325</td></tr>
<tr><td>42</td><td>Idaho</td><td>4,008</td><td>12</td><td>Alabama</td><td>5,321</td></tr>
<tr><td>35</td><td>Illinois</td><td>4,352</td><td>13</td><td>Hawaii</td><td>5,320</td></tr>
<tr><td>18</td><td>Indiana</td><td>5,189</td><td>14</td><td>West Virginia</td><td>5,309</td></tr>
<tr><td>9</td><td>Iowa</td><td>5,649</td><td>15</td><td>Mississippi</td><td>5,273</td></tr>
<tr><td>17</td><td>Kansas</td><td>5,208</td><td>16</td><td>South Dakota</td><td>5,261</td></tr>
<tr><td>10</td><td>Kentucky</td><td>5,425</td><td>17</td><td>Kansas</td><td>5,208</td></tr>
<tr><td>3</td><td>Louisiana</td><td>8,740</td><td>18</td><td>Indiana</td><td>5,189</td></tr>
<tr><td>7</td><td>Maine</td><td>5,696</td><td>19</td><td>Arkansas</td><td>5,131</td></tr>
<tr><td>36</td><td>Maryland</td><td>4,303</td><td>20</td><td>Nebraska</td><td>5,094</td></tr>
<tr><td>32</td><td>Massachusetts</td><td>4,431</td><td>21</td><td>Minnesota</td><td>5,028</td></tr>
<tr><td>44</td><td>Michigan</td><td>3,984</td><td>22</td><td>Delaware</td><td>5,010</td></tr>
<tr><td>21</td><td>Minnesota</td><td>5,028</td><td>23</td><td>Vermont</td><td>4,850</td></tr>
<tr><td>15</td><td>Mississippi</td><td>5,273</td><td>24</td><td>South Carolina</td><td>4,761</td></tr>
<tr><td>34</td><td>Missouri</td><td>4,374</td><td>25</td><td>Tennessee</td><td>4,706</td></tr>
<tr><td>6</td><td>Montana</td><td>5,872</td><td>26</td><td>Connecticut</td><td>4,699</td></tr>
<tr><td>20</td><td>Nebraska</td><td>5,094</td><td>27</td><td>Ohio</td><td>4,697</td></tr>
<tr><td>38</td><td>Nevada</td><td>4,279</td><td>28</td><td>New Hampshire</td><td>4,603</td></tr>
<tr><td>28</td><td>New Hampshire</td><td>4,603</td><td>29</td><td>Wisconsin</td><td>4,521</td></tr>
<tr><td>11</td><td>New Jersey</td><td>5,325</td><td>30</td><td>New Mexico</td><td>4,476</td></tr>
<tr><td>30</td><td>New Mexico</td><td>4,476</td><td>31</td><td>Virginia</td><td>4,475</td></tr>
<tr><td>47</td><td>New York</td><td>3,722</td><td>32</td><td>Massachusetts</td><td>4,431</td></tr>
<tr><td>39</td><td>North Carolina</td><td>4,094</td><td>33</td><td>Pennsylvania</td><td>4,419</td></tr>
<tr><td>4</td><td>North Dakota</td><td>7,711</td><td>34</td><td>Missouri</td><td>4,374</td></tr>
<tr><td>27</td><td>Ohio</td><td>4,697</td><td>35</td><td>Illinois</td><td>4,352</td></tr>
<tr><td>8</td><td>Oklahoma</td><td>5,692</td><td>36</td><td>Maryland</td><td>4,303</td></tr>
<tr><td>45</td><td>Oregon</td><td>3,934</td><td>37</td><td>Georgia</td><td>4,286</td></tr>
<tr><td>33</td><td>Pennsylvania</td><td>4,419</td><td>38</td><td>Nevada</td><td>4,279</td></tr>
<tr><td>41</td><td>Rhode Island</td><td>4,009</td><td>39</td><td>North Carolina</td><td>4,094</td></tr>
<tr><td>24</td><td>South Carolina</td><td>4,761</td><td>40</td><td>Washington</td><td>4,062</td></tr>
<tr><td>16</td><td>South Dakota</td><td>5,261</td><td>41</td><td>Rhode Island</td><td>4,009</td></tr>
<tr><td>25</td><td>Tennessee</td><td>4,706</td><td>42</td><td>Idaho</td><td>4,008</td></tr>
<tr><td>5</td><td>Texas</td><td>6,803</td><td>43</td><td>Colorado</td><td>4,002</td></tr>
<tr><td>49</td><td>Utah</td><td>3,630</td><td>44</td><td>Michigan</td><td>3,984</td></tr>
<tr><td>23</td><td>Vermont</td><td>4,850</td><td>45</td><td>Oregon</td><td>3,934</td></tr>
<tr><td>31</td><td>Virginia</td><td>4,475</td><td>46</td><td>California</td><td>3,732</td></tr>
<tr><td>40</td><td>Washington</td><td>4,062</td><td>47</td><td>New York</td><td>3,722</td></tr>
<tr><td>14</td><td>West Virginia</td><td>5,309</td><td>48</td><td>Florida</td><td>3,686</td></tr>
<tr><td>29</td><td>Wisconsin</td><td>4,521</td><td>49</td><td>Utah</td><td>3,630</td></tr>
<tr><td>2</td><td>Wyoming</td><td>10,529</td><td>50</td><td>Arizona</td><td>3,479</td></tr>
<tr><td></td><td></td><td></td><td></td><td>District of Columbia</td><td>4,287</td></tr>
</table>

Source: CQ Press using data from U.S. Department of Energy, Energy Information Administration
"State Energy Data 2008: Prices and Expenditures" (http://www.eia.doe.gov/emeu/states/_seds.html)

Average Monthly Electric Bill for Industrial Customers in 2009

National Average = $6,761 per Month

ALPHA ORDER

RANK	STATE	MONTHLY BILL
11	Alabama	$15,807
21	Alaska	10,511
25	Arizona	8,622
48	Arkansas	2,224
33	California	5,265
36	Colorado	4,843
24	Connecticut	9,404
10	Delaware	17,165
29	Florida	6,423
22	Georgia	9,662
1	Hawaii	80,927
49	Idaho	1,329
6	Illinois	25,400
18	Indiana	11,409
15	Iowa	12,113
47	Kansas	2,243
7	Kentucky	25,300
32	Louisiana	6,050
26	Maine	8,278
35	Maryland	4,979
14	Massachusetts	12,158
13	Michigan	12,205
20	Minnesota	10,867
17	Mississippi	11,514
27	Missouri	7,569
39	Montana	4,149
50	Nebraska	1,102
8	Nevada	24,488
28	New Hampshire	6,619
31	New Jersey	6,127
37	New Mexico	4,467
16	New York	11,728
19	North Carolina	11,015
30	North Dakota	6,400
12	Ohio	13,118
44	Oklahoma	3,221
46	Oregon	2,376
23	Pennsylvania	9,541
34	Rhode Island	5,018
5	South Carolina	27,251
43	South Dakota	3,488
2	Tennessee	73,543
40	Texas	3,997
42	Utah	3,636
3	Vermont	47,194
9	Virginia	18,179
45	Washington	3,011
41	West Virginia	3,932
4	Wisconsin	27,880
38	Wyoming	4,308

RANK ORDER

RANK	STATE	MONTHLY BILL
1	Hawaii	$80,927
2	Tennessee	73,543
3	Vermont	47,194
4	Wisconsin	27,880
5	South Carolina	27,251
6	Illinois	25,400
7	Kentucky	25,300
8	Nevada	24,488
9	Virginia	18,179
10	Delaware	17,165
11	Alabama	15,807
12	Ohio	13,118
13	Michigan	12,205
14	Massachusetts	12,158
15	Iowa	12,113
16	New York	11,728
17	Mississippi	11,514
18	Indiana	11,409
19	North Carolina	11,015
20	Minnesota	10,867
21	Alaska	10,511
22	Georgia	9,662
23	Pennsylvania	9,541
24	Connecticut	9,404
25	Arizona	8,622
26	Maine	8,278
27	Missouri	7,569
28	New Hampshire	6,619
29	Florida	6,423
30	North Dakota	6,400
31	New Jersey	6,127
32	Louisiana	6,050
33	California	5,265
34	Rhode Island	5,018
35	Maryland	4,979
36	Colorado	4,843
37	New Mexico	4,467
38	Wyoming	4,308
39	Montana	4,149
40	Texas	3,997
41	West Virginia	3,932
42	Utah	3,636
43	South Dakota	3,488
44	Oklahoma	3,221
45	Washington	3,011
46	Oregon	2,376
47	Kansas	2,243
48	Arkansas	2,224
49	Idaho	1,329
50	Nebraska	1,102
	District of Columbia	534,538

Source: U.S. Department of Energy, Energy Information Administration
"Electric Sales, Revenue and Average Price 2009" (http://www.eia.doe.gov/cneaf/electricity/esr/esr_sum.html)

Average Monthly Electric Bill for Commercial Customers in 2009

National Average = $636 per Month

ALPHA ORDER

RANK	STATE	MONTHLY BILL
24	Alabama	$519
13	Alaska	723
9	Arizona	765
41	Arkansas	407
10	California	752
44	Colorado	389
1	Connecticut	1,257
6	Delaware	852
12	Florida	736
15	Georgia	629
3	Hawaii	1,014
49	Idaho	324
7	Illinois	824
30	Indiana	481
47	Iowa	341
35	Kansas	450
42	Kentucky	405
20	Louisiana	555
29	Maine	484
2	Maryland	1,225
16	Massachusetts	606
19	Michigan	560
22	Minnesota	538
33	Mississippi	462
31	Missouri	478
48	Montana	331
46	Nebraska	369
25	Nevada	517
18	New Hampshire	581
4	New Jersey	953
35	New Mexico	450
5	New York	941
32	North Carolina	473
35	North Dakota	450
17	Ohio	595
43	Oklahoma	395
40	Oregon	422
21	Pennsylvania	543
11	Rhode Island	745
34	South Carolina	454
45	South Dakota	382
28	Tennessee	492
14	Texas	665
26	Utah	503
39	Vermont	429
8	Virginia	772
27	Washington	497
50	West Virginia	318
23	Wisconsin	532
38	Wyoming	438

RANK ORDER

RANK	STATE	MONTHLY BILL
1	Connecticut	$1,257
2	Maryland	1,225
3	Hawaii	1,014
4	New Jersey	953
5	New York	941
6	Delaware	852
7	Illinois	824
8	Virginia	772
9	Arizona	765
10	California	752
11	Rhode Island	745
12	Florida	736
13	Alaska	723
14	Texas	665
15	Georgia	629
16	Massachusetts	606
17	Ohio	595
18	New Hampshire	581
19	Michigan	560
20	Louisiana	555
21	Pennsylvania	543
22	Minnesota	538
23	Wisconsin	532
24	Alabama	519
25	Nevada	517
26	Utah	503
27	Washington	497
28	Tennessee	492
29	Maine	484
30	Indiana	481
31	Missouri	478
32	North Carolina	473
33	Mississippi	462
34	South Carolina	454
35	Kansas	450
35	New Mexico	450
35	North Dakota	450
38	Wyoming	438
39	Vermont	429
40	Oregon	422
41	Arkansas	407
42	Kentucky	405
43	Oklahoma	395
44	Colorado	389
45	South Dakota	382
46	Nebraska	369
47	Iowa	341
48	Montana	331
49	Idaho	324
50	West Virginia	318
	District of Columbia	3,426

Source: U.S. Department of Energy, Energy Information Administration
"Electric Sales, Revenue and Average Price 2009" (http://www.eia.doe.gov/cneaf/electricity/esr/esr_sum.html)

Average Monthly Electric Bill for Residential Customers in 2009

National Average = $105 per Month

ALPHA ORDER

RANK	STATE	MONTHLY BILL
6	Alabama	$131
15	Alaska	112
13	Arizona	115
22	Arkansas	98
37	California	85
48	Colorado	69
3	Connecticut	147
7	Delaware	129
5	Florida	140
13	Georgia	115
2	Hawaii	149
39	Idaho	84
41	Illinois	82
25	Indiana	94
34	Iowa	86
34	Kansas	86
24	Kentucky	96
18	Louisiana	103
41	Maine	82
1	Maryland	154
18	Massachusetts	103
47	Michigan	75
44	Minnesota	80
8	Mississippi	124
28	Missouri	91
45	Montana	76
37	Nebraska	85
11	Nevada	121
21	New Hampshire	101
17	New Jersey	110
50	New Mexico	64
20	New York	102
15	North Carolina	112
32	North Dakota	87
25	Ohio	94
27	Oklahoma	93
29	Oregon	88
22	Pennsylvania	98
29	Rhode Island	88
10	South Carolina	123
32	South Dakota	87
12	Tennessee	116
4	Texas	141
49	Utah	66
34	Vermont	86
8	Virginia	124
39	Washington	84
29	West Virginia	88
41	Wisconsin	82
45	Wyoming	76

RANK ORDER

RANK	STATE	MONTHLY BILL
1	Maryland	$154
2	Hawaii	149
3	Connecticut	147
4	Texas	141
5	Florida	140
6	Alabama	131
7	Delaware	129
8	Mississippi	124
8	Virginia	124
10	South Carolina	123
11	Nevada	121
12	Tennessee	116
13	Arizona	115
13	Georgia	115
15	Alaska	112
15	North Carolina	112
17	New Jersey	110
18	Louisiana	103
18	Massachusetts	103
20	New York	102
21	New Hampshire	101
22	Arkansas	98
22	Pennsylvania	98
24	Kentucky	96
25	Indiana	94
25	Ohio	94
27	Oklahoma	93
28	Missouri	91
29	Oregon	88
29	Rhode Island	88
29	West Virginia	88
32	North Dakota	87
32	South Dakota	87
34	Iowa	86
34	Kansas	86
34	Vermont	86
37	California	85
37	Nebraska	85
39	Idaho	84
39	Washington	84
41	Illinois	82
41	Maine	82
41	Wisconsin	82
44	Minnesota	80
45	Montana	76
45	Wyoming	76
47	Michigan	75
48	Colorado	69
49	Utah	66
50	New Mexico	64
	District of Columbia	98

Source: U.S. Department of Energy, Energy Information Administration
"Electric Sales, Revenue and Average Price 2009" (http://www.eia.doe.gov/cneaf/electricity/esr/esr_sum.html)

Electricity Generated through Renewable Sources in 2008

National Total = 381,043,759,000 Kilowatthours*

ALPHA ORDER

RANK	STATE	KWH	% of USA
8	Alabama	9,493,461,000	2.5%
42	Alaska	1,176,551,000	0.3%
10	Arizona	7,399,560,000	1.9%
14	Arkansas	6,173,130,000	1.6%
2	California	48,911,746,000	12.8%
16	Colorado	5,323,778,000	1.4%
41	Connecticut	1,289,691,000	0.3%
50	Delaware	163,375,000	0.0%
20	Florida	4,509,026,000	1.2%
19	Georgia	4,926,588,000	1.3%
47	Hawaii	861,140,000	0.2%
7	Idaho	10,110,913,000	2.7%
26	Illinois	3,173,526,000	0.8%
45	Indiana	948,173,000	0.2%
17	Iowa	5,070,146,000	1.3%
38	Kansas	1,769,986,000	0.5%
33	Kentucky	2,377,089,000	0.6%
22	Louisiana	3,774,048,000	1.0%
9	Maine	8,515,390,000	2.2%
31	Maryland	2,586,563,000	0.7%
32	Massachusetts	2,411,189,000	0.6%
21	Michigan	3,955,519,000	1.0%
12	Minnesota	6,577,943,000	1.7%
40	Mississippi	1,391,326,000	0.4%
34	Missouri	2,292,799,000	0.6%
6	Montana	10,815,024,000	2.8%
48	Nebraska	621,569,000	0.2%
25	Nevada	3,289,453,000	0.9%
30	New Hampshire	2,808,208,000	0.7%
46	New Jersey	931,063,000	0.2%
35	New Mexico	1,973,960,000	0.5%
4	New York	30,041,788,000	7.9%
18	North Carolina	4,955,855,000	1.3%
28	North Dakota	2,959,175,000	0.8%
43	Ohio	1,009,811,000	0.3%
13	Oklahoma	6,361,977,000	1.7%
3	Oregon	37,228,123,000	9.8%
15	Pennsylvania	5,352,634,000	1.4%
49	Rhode Island	163,384,000	0.0%
29	South Carolina	2,938,940,000	0.8%
27	South Dakota	3,139,908,000	0.8%
11	Tennessee	6,611,383,000	1.7%
5	Texas	18,678,562,000	4.9%
44	Utah	969,946,000	0.3%
36	Vermont	1,918,242,000	0.5%
23	Virginia	3,709,452,000	1.0%
1	Washington	82,575,196,000	21.7%
39	West Virginia	1,639,557,000	0.4%
24	Wisconsin	3,370,077,000	0.9%
37	Wyoming	1,797,817,000	0.5%

RANK ORDER

RANK	STATE	KWH	% of USA
1	Washington	82,575,196,000	21.7%
2	California	48,911,746,000	12.8%
3	Oregon	37,228,123,000	9.8%
4	New York	30,041,788,000	7.9%
5	Texas	18,678,562,000	4.9%
6	Montana	10,815,024,000	2.8%
7	Idaho	10,110,913,000	2.7%
8	Alabama	9,493,461,000	2.5%
9	Maine	8,515,390,000	2.2%
10	Arizona	7,399,560,000	1.9%
11	Tennessee	6,611,383,000	1.7%
12	Minnesota	6,577,943,000	1.7%
13	Oklahoma	6,361,977,000	1.7%
14	Arkansas	6,173,130,000	1.6%
15	Pennsylvania	5,352,634,000	1.4%
16	Colorado	5,323,778,000	1.4%
17	Iowa	5,070,146,000	1.3%
18	North Carolina	4,955,855,000	1.3%
19	Georgia	4,926,588,000	1.3%
20	Florida	4,509,026,000	1.2%
21	Michigan	3,955,519,000	1.0%
22	Louisiana	3,774,048,000	1.0%
23	Virginia	3,709,452,000	1.0%
24	Wisconsin	3,370,077,000	0.9%
25	Nevada	3,289,453,000	0.9%
26	Illinois	3,173,526,000	0.8%
27	South Dakota	3,139,908,000	0.8%
28	North Dakota	2,959,175,000	0.8%
29	South Carolina	2,938,940,000	0.8%
30	New Hampshire	2,808,208,000	0.7%
31	Maryland	2,586,563,000	0.7%
32	Massachusetts	2,411,189,000	0.6%
33	Kentucky	2,377,089,000	0.6%
34	Missouri	2,292,799,000	0.6%
35	New Mexico	1,973,960,000	0.5%
36	Vermont	1,918,242,000	0.5%
37	Wyoming	1,797,817,000	0.5%
38	Kansas	1,769,986,000	0.5%
39	West Virginia	1,639,557,000	0.4%
40	Mississippi	1,391,326,000	0.4%
41	Connecticut	1,289,691,000	0.3%
42	Alaska	1,176,551,000	0.3%
43	Ohio	1,009,811,000	0.3%
44	Utah	969,946,000	0.3%
45	Indiana	948,173,000	0.2%
46	New Jersey	931,063,000	0.2%
47	Hawaii	861,140,000	0.2%
48	Nebraska	621,569,000	0.2%
49	Rhode Island	163,384,000	0.0%
50	Delaware	163,375,000	0.0%
	District of Columbia**	NA	NA

Source: U.S. Department of Energy, Energy Information Administration
"Renewable Energy Trends, 2008" (http://www.eia.doe.gov/cneaf/solar.renewables/page/trends/rentrends.html)
*Includes hydroelectric, geothermal, solar, wind, MSW/landfill gas, wood/wood waste and other biomass.
**Not reported.

Percent of Electricity Generated through Renewable Sources in 2008

National Percent = 9.3%*

ALPHA ORDER

RANK	STATE	PERCENT
21	Alabama	6.5
10	Alaska	17.4
22	Arizona	6.2
13	Arkansas	11.2
8	California	23.5
14	Colorado	10.0
29	Connecticut	4.2
41	Delaware	2.2
43	Florida	2.1
34	Georgia	3.6
19	Hawaii	7.6
1	Idaho	84.5
47	Illinois	1.6
49	Indiana	0.7
15	Iowa	9.6
33	Kansas	3.8
39	Kentucky	2.4
30	Louisiana	4.1
4	Maine	49.8
24	Maryland	5.5
23	Massachusetts	5.7
35	Michigan	3.4
12	Minnesota	12.0
36	Mississippi	2.9
38	Missouri	2.5
6	Montana	36.5
45	Nebraska	1.9
16	Nevada	9.4
11	New Hampshire	12.3
48	New Jersey	1.5
25	New Mexico	5.3
9	New York	21.4
31	North Carolina	4.0
17	North Dakota	9.0
49	Ohio	0.7
18	Oklahoma	8.3
3	Oregon	63.4
39	Pennsylvania	2.4
41	Rhode Island	2.2
36	South Carolina	2.9
5	South Dakota	44.3
20	Tennessee	7.3
28	Texas	4.6
43	Utah	2.1
7	Vermont	28.1
27	Virginia	5.1
2	Washington	74.5
46	West Virginia	1.8
25	Wisconsin	5.3
32	Wyoming	3.9

RANK ORDER

RANK	STATE	PERCENT
1	Idaho	84.5
2	Washington	74.5
3	Oregon	63.4
4	Maine	49.8
5	South Dakota	44.3
6	Montana	36.5
7	Vermont	28.1
8	California	23.5
9	New York	21.4
10	Alaska	17.4
11	New Hampshire	12.3
12	Minnesota	12.0
13	Arkansas	11.2
14	Colorado	10.0
15	Iowa	9.6
16	Nevada	9.4
17	North Dakota	9.0
18	Oklahoma	8.3
19	Hawaii	7.6
20	Tennessee	7.3
21	Alabama	6.5
22	Arizona	6.2
23	Massachusetts	5.7
24	Maryland	5.5
25	New Mexico	5.3
25	Wisconsin	5.3
27	Virginia	5.1
28	Texas	4.6
29	Connecticut	4.2
30	Louisiana	4.1
31	North Carolina	4.0
32	Wyoming	3.9
33	Kansas	3.8
34	Georgia	3.6
35	Michigan	3.4
36	Mississippi	2.9
36	South Carolina	2.9
38	Missouri	2.5
39	Kentucky	2.4
39	Pennsylvania	2.4
41	Delaware	2.2
41	Rhode Island	2.2
43	Florida	2.1
43	Utah	2.1
45	Nebraska	1.9
46	West Virginia	1.8
47	Illinois	1.6
48	New Jersey	1.5
49	Indiana	0.7
49	Ohio	0.7
	District of Columbia**	NA

Source: U.S. Department of Energy, Energy Information Administration
"Renewable Energy Trends, 2008" (http://www.eia.doe.gov/cneaf/solar.renewables/page/trends/rentrends.html)
*Includes hydroelectric, geothermal, solar, wind, MSW/landfill gas, wood/wood waste and other biomass.
**Not reported.

Average Price of Natural Gas Delivered to Industrial Customers in 2009

National Average = $5.33 per Thousand Cubic Feet

ALPHA ORDER

RANK	STATE	RATE
34	Alabama	$6.48
50	Alaska	4.02
24	Arizona	8.19
22	Arkansas	8.47
31	California	6.57
31	Colorado	6.57
23	Connecticut	8.44
2	Delaware	13.99
15	Florida	9.41
36	Georgia	6.21
1	Hawaii	19.05
21	Idaho	8.53
27	Illinois	7.31
30	Indiana	6.91
35	Iowa	6.23
47	Kansas	4.59
39	Kentucky	6.05
48	Louisiana	4.31
16	Maine	9.12
9	Maryland	10.70
6	Massachusetts	12.07
11	Michigan	9.63
42	Minnesota	5.66
33	Mississippi	6.53
12	Missouri	9.55
17	Montana	9.06
40	Nebraska	6.02
8	Nevada	11.22
3	New Hampshire	12.86
18	New Jersey	8.96
45	New Mexico	5.41
13	New York	9.52
20	North Carolina	8.66
46	North Dakota	5.21
19	Ohio	8.93
5	Oklahoma	12.55
10	Oregon	9.70
14	Pennsylvania	9.42
4	Rhode Island	12.58
38	South Carolina	6.06
37	South Dakota	6.07
29	Tennessee	7.08
49	Texas	4.05
43	Utah	5.62
25	Vermont	7.93
28	Virginia	7.14
7	Washington	11.68
44	West Virginia	5.55
26	Wisconsin	7.82
41	Wyoming	5.79

RANK ORDER

RANK	STATE	RATE
1	Hawaii	$19.05
2	Delaware	13.99
3	New Hampshire	12.86
4	Rhode Island	12.58
5	Oklahoma	12.55
6	Massachusetts	12.07
7	Washington	11.68
8	Nevada	11.22
9	Maryland	10.70
10	Oregon	9.70
11	Michigan	9.63
12	Missouri	9.55
13	New York	9.52
14	Pennsylvania	9.42
15	Florida	9.41
16	Maine	9.12
17	Montana	9.06
18	New Jersey	8.96
19	Ohio	8.93
20	North Carolina	8.66
21	Idaho	8.53
22	Arkansas	8.47
23	Connecticut	8.44
24	Arizona	8.19
25	Vermont	7.93
26	Wisconsin	7.82
27	Illinois	7.31
28	Virginia	7.14
29	Tennessee	7.08
30	Indiana	6.91
31	California	6.57
31	Colorado	6.57
33	Mississippi	6.53
34	Alabama	6.48
35	Iowa	6.23
36	Georgia	6.21
37	South Dakota	6.07
38	South Carolina	6.06
39	Kentucky	6.05
40	Nebraska	6.02
41	Wyoming	5.79
42	Minnesota	5.66
43	Utah	5.62
44	West Virginia	5.55
45	New Mexico	5.41
46	North Dakota	5.21
47	Kansas	4.59
48	Louisiana	4.31
49	Texas	4.05
50	Alaska	4.02
	District of Columbia*	NA

Source: U.S. Department of Energy, Energy Information Administration
    "Natural Gas Monthly January 2011" (http://www.eia.doe.gov/oil_gas/natural_gas/info_glance/natural_gas.html)
*Not available.

Average Price of Natural Gas Delivered to Commercial Customers in 2009

National Average = $10.06 per Thousand Cubic Feet

ALPHA ORDER

RANK	STATE	RATE
4	Alabama	$14.93
33	Alaska	9.51
11	Arizona	12.15
23	Arkansas	10.71
44	California	7.75
46	Colorado	7.56
31	Connecticut	9.92
2	Delaware	15.87
17	Florida	11.09
14	Georgia	11.70
1	Hawaii	30.00
32	Idaho	9.77
39	Illinois	8.65
37	Indiana	9.18
43	Iowa	7.88
30	Kansas	10.01
19	Kentucky	10.89
26	Louisiana	10.46
7	Maine	13.94
20	Maryland	10.87
9	Massachusetts	12.85
36	Michigan	9.38
42	Minnesota	7.96
34	Mississippi	9.48
21	Missouri	10.80
35	Montana	9.41
48	Nebraska	7.44
18	Nevada	10.92
5	New Hampshire	14.37
29	New Jersey	10.20
47	New Mexico	7.52
22	New York	10.72
15	North Carolina	11.63
50	North Dakota	7.41
27	Ohio	10.41
25	Oklahoma	10.60
12	Oregon	11.86
13	Pennsylvania	11.83
3	Rhode Island	15.14
16	South Carolina	11.16
49	South Dakota	7.42
24	Tennessee	10.67
40	Texas	8.16
45	Utah	7.57
8	Vermont	12.96
28	Virginia	10.31
10	Washington	12.26
6	West Virginia	14.24
38	Wisconsin	8.95
41	Wyoming	8.01

RANK ORDER

RANK	STATE	RATE
1	Hawaii	$30.00
2	Delaware	15.87
3	Rhode Island	15.14
4	Alabama	14.93
5	New Hampshire	14.37
6	West Virginia	14.24
7	Maine	13.94
8	Vermont	12.96
9	Massachusetts	12.85
10	Washington	12.26
11	Arizona	12.15
12	Oregon	11.86
13	Pennsylvania	11.83
14	Georgia	11.70
15	North Carolina	11.63
16	South Carolina	11.16
17	Florida	11.09
18	Nevada	10.92
19	Kentucky	10.89
20	Maryland	10.87
21	Missouri	10.80
22	New York	10.72
23	Arkansas	10.71
24	Tennessee	10.67
25	Oklahoma	10.60
26	Louisiana	10.46
27	Ohio	10.41
28	Virginia	10.31
29	New Jersey	10.20
30	Kansas	10.01
31	Connecticut	9.92
32	Idaho	9.77
33	Alaska	9.51
34	Mississippi	9.48
35	Montana	9.41
36	Michigan	9.38
37	Indiana	9.18
38	Wisconsin	8.95
39	Illinois	8.65
40	Texas	8.16
41	Wyoming	8.01
42	Minnesota	7.96
43	Iowa	7.88
44	California	7.75
45	Utah	7.57
46	Colorado	7.56
47	New Mexico	7.52
48	Nebraska	7.44
49	South Dakota	7.42
50	North Dakota	7.41

| | District of Columbia | 12.99 |

Source: U.S. Department of Energy, Energy Information Administration
"Natural Gas Monthly January 2011" (http://www.eia.doe.gov/oil_gas/natural_gas/info_glance/natural_gas.html)

Average Price of Natural Gas Delivered to Residential Customers in 2009

National Average = $12.14 per Thousand Cubic Feet

ALPHA ORDER

RANK	STATE	RATE
3	Alabama	$18.12
38	Alaska	10.23
5	Arizona	17.65
23	Arkansas	13.39
42	California	9.43
49	Colorado	8.80
14	Connecticut	14.81
4	Delaware	17.79
2	Florida	20.18
9	Georgia	16.30
1	Hawaii	36.37
37	Idaho	10.54
47	Illinois	8.98
35	Indiana	10.81
39	Iowa	9.83
34	Kansas	11.10
29	Kentucky	11.96
25	Louisiana	13.15
8	Maine	16.43
22	Maryland	13.73
13	Massachusetts	14.85
31	Michigan	11.27
46	Minnesota	8.99
32	Mississippi	11.22
27	Missouri	12.61
41	Montana	9.50
44	Nebraska	9.34
24	Nevada	13.18
10	New Hampshire	15.33
17	New Jersey	14.54
40	New Mexico	9.53
11	New York	15.05
19	North Carolina	14.25
50	North Dakota	8.46
26	Ohio	12.68
30	Oklahoma	11.39
18	Oregon	14.52
16	Pennsylvania	14.74
7	Rhode Island	17.06
12	South Carolina	14.91
45	South Dakota	9.14
28	Tennessee	12.16
33	Texas	11.19
48	Utah	8.95
6	Vermont	17.29
21	Virginia	13.83
20	Washington	13.95
15	West Virginia	14.75
36	Wisconsin	10.76
43	Wyoming	9.39

RANK ORDER

RANK	STATE	RATE
1	Hawaii	$36.37
2	Florida	20.18
3	Alabama	18.12
4	Delaware	17.79
5	Arizona	17.65
6	Vermont	17.29
7	Rhode Island	17.06
8	Maine	16.43
9	Georgia	16.30
10	New Hampshire	15.33
11	New York	15.05
12	South Carolina	14.91
13	Massachusetts	14.85
14	Connecticut	14.81
15	West Virginia	14.75
16	Pennsylvania	14.74
17	New Jersey	14.54
18	Oregon	14.52
19	North Carolina	14.25
20	Washington	13.95
21	Virginia	13.83
22	Maryland	13.73
23	Arkansas	13.39
24	Nevada	13.18
25	Louisiana	13.15
26	Ohio	12.68
27	Missouri	12.61
28	Tennessee	12.16
29	Kentucky	11.96
30	Oklahoma	11.39
31	Michigan	11.27
32	Mississippi	11.22
33	Texas	11.19
34	Kansas	11.10
35	Indiana	10.81
36	Wisconsin	10.76
37	Idaho	10.54
38	Alaska	10.23
39	Iowa	9.83
40	New Mexico	9.53
41	Montana	9.50
42	California	9.43
43	Wyoming	9.39
44	Nebraska	9.34
45	South Dakota	9.14
46	Minnesota	8.99
47	Illinois	8.98
48	Utah	8.95
49	Colorado	8.80
50	North Dakota	8.46
	District of Columbia	13.92

Source: U.S. Department of Energy, Energy Information Administration
"Natural Gas Monthly January 2011" (http://www.eia.doe.gov/oil_gas/natural_gas/info_glance/natural_gas.html)

Natural Gas Consumption in 2009

National Total = 22,839,158,000,000 Cubic Feet*

ALPHA ORDER

RANK	STATE	CUBIC FEET	% of USA
15	Alabama	454,268,000,000	2.0%
21	Alaska	342,268,000,000	1.5%
19	Arizona	368,927,000,000	1.6%
30	Arkansas	244,189,000,000	1.1%
2	California	2,328,506,000,000	10.2%
12	Colorado	520,206,000,000	2.3%
37	Connecticut	184,304,000,000	0.8%
48	Delaware	50,152,000,000	0.2%
5	Florida	1,055,369,000,000	4.6%
14	Georgia	462,919,000,000	2.0%
50	Hawaii	2,607,000,000	0.0%
42	Idaho	84,918,000,000	0.4%
6	Illinois	946,019,000,000	4.1%
13	Indiana	506,623,000,000	2.2%
23	Iowa	315,186,000,000	1.4%
25	Kansas	284,014,000,000	1.2%
34	Kentucky	206,534,000,000	0.9%
3	Louisiana	1,187,283,000,000	5.2%
44	Maine	69,824,000,000	0.3%
35	Maryland	197,313,000,000	0.9%
16	Massachusetts	395,920,000,000	1.7%
9	Michigan	731,474,000,000	3.2%
17	Minnesota	394,140,000,000	1.7%
20	Mississippi	364,382,000,000	1.6%
27	Missouri	264,631,000,000	1.2%
43	Montana	75,588,000,000	0.3%
38	Nebraska	162,989,000,000	0.7%
26	Nevada	275,197,000,000	1.2%
46	New Hampshire	59,934,000,000	0.3%
11	New Jersey	620,853,000,000	2.7%
31	New Mexico	240,388,000,000	1.1%
4	New York	1,142,156,000,000	5.0%
29	North Carolina	244,962,000,000	1.1%
47	North Dakota	54,562,000,000	0.2%
8	Ohio	738,596,000,000	3.2%
10	Oklahoma	656,657,000,000	2.9%
28	Oregon	248,779,000,000	1.1%
7	Pennsylvania	804,077,000,000	3.5%
41	Rhode Island	92,765,000,000	0.4%
36	South Carolina	190,542,000,000	0.8%
45	South Dakota	66,185,000,000	0.3%
32	Tennessee	216,506,000,000	0.9%
1	Texas	3,364,425,000,000	14.7%
33	Utah	214,163,000,000	0.9%
49	Vermont	8,637,000,000	0.0%
22	Virginia	319,065,000,000	1.4%
24	Washington	310,112,000,000	1.4%
40	West Virginia	105,275,000,000	0.5%
18	Wisconsin	387,063,000,000	1.7%
39	Wyoming	141,335,000,000	0.6%

RANK ORDER

RANK	STATE	CUBIC FEET	% of USA
1	Texas	3,364,425,000,000	14.7%
2	California	2,328,506,000,000	10.2%
3	Louisiana	1,187,283,000,000	5.2%
4	New York	1,142,156,000,000	5.0%
5	Florida	1,055,369,000,000	4.6%
6	Illinois	946,019,000,000	4.1%
7	Pennsylvania	804,077,000,000	3.5%
8	Ohio	738,596,000,000	3.2%
9	Michigan	731,474,000,000	3.2%
10	Oklahoma	656,657,000,000	2.9%
11	New Jersey	620,853,000,000	2.7%
12	Colorado	520,206,000,000	2.3%
13	Indiana	506,623,000,000	2.2%
14	Georgia	462,919,000,000	2.0%
15	Alabama	454,268,000,000	2.0%
16	Massachusetts	395,920,000,000	1.7%
17	Minnesota	394,140,000,000	1.7%
18	Wisconsin	387,063,000,000	1.7%
19	Arizona	368,927,000,000	1.6%
20	Mississippi	364,382,000,000	1.6%
21	Alaska	342,268,000,000	1.5%
22	Virginia	319,065,000,000	1.4%
23	Iowa	315,186,000,000	1.4%
24	Washington	310,112,000,000	1.4%
25	Kansas	284,014,000,000	1.2%
26	Nevada	275,197,000,000	1.2%
27	Missouri	264,631,000,000	1.2%
28	Oregon	248,779,000,000	1.1%
29	North Carolina	244,962,000,000	1.1%
30	Arkansas	244,189,000,000	1.1%
31	New Mexico	240,388,000,000	1.1%
32	Tennessee	216,506,000,000	0.9%
33	Utah	214,163,000,000	0.9%
34	Kentucky	206,534,000,000	0.9%
35	Maryland	197,313,000,000	0.9%
36	South Carolina	190,542,000,000	0.8%
37	Connecticut	184,304,000,000	0.8%
38	Nebraska	162,989,000,000	0.7%
39	Wyoming	141,335,000,000	0.6%
40	West Virginia	105,275,000,000	0.5%
41	Rhode Island	92,765,000,000	0.4%
42	Idaho	84,918,000,000	0.4%
43	Montana	75,588,000,000	0.3%
44	Maine	69,824,000,000	0.3%
45	South Dakota	66,185,000,000	0.3%
46	New Hampshire	59,934,000,000	0.3%
47	North Dakota	54,562,000,000	0.2%
48	Delaware	50,152,000,000	0.2%
49	Vermont	8,637,000,000	0.0%
50	Hawaii	2,607,000,000	0.0%
	District of Columbia	32,397,000,000	0.1%

Source: U.S. Department of Energy, Energy Information Administration
   "Natural Gas Annual 2009" (http://www.eia.doe.gov/oil_gas/natural_gas/info_glance/natural_gas.html)
*National total includes 103,976,000,000 cubic feet of consumption in the Gulf of Mexico not shown by state.

Coal Mines in 2009

National Total = 1,406 Mines*

ALPHA ORDER

RANK	STATE	MINES	% of USA
5	Alabama	57	4.1%
22	Alaska	1	0.1%
22	Arizona	1	0.1%
19	Arkansas	2	0.1%
NA	California**	NA	NA
13	Colorado	11	0.8%
NA	Connecticut**	NA	NA
NA	Delaware**	NA	NA
NA	Florida**	NA	NA
NA	Georgia**	NA	NA
NA	Hawaii**	NA	NA
NA	Idaho**	NA	NA
9	Illinois	22	1.6%
7	Indiana	33	2.3%
NA	Iowa**	NA	NA
22	Kansas	1	0.1%
1	Kentucky	449	31.9%
19	Louisiana	2	0.1%
NA	Maine**	NA	NA
9	Maryland	22	1.6%
NA	Massachusetts**	NA	NA
NA	Michigan**	NA	NA
NA	Minnesota**	NA	NA
22	Mississippi	1	0.1%
19	Missouri	2	0.1%
16	Montana	6	0.4%
NA	Nebraska**	NA	NA
NA	Nevada**	NA	NA
NA	New Hampshire**	NA	NA
NA	New Jersey**	NA	NA
17	New Mexico	5	0.4%
NA	New York**	NA	NA
NA	North Carolina**	NA	NA
18	North Dakota	4	0.3%
6	Ohio	46	3.3%
14	Oklahoma	10	0.7%
NA	Oregon**	NA	NA
3	Pennsylvania	244	17.4%
NA	Rhode Island**	NA	NA
NA	South Carolina**	NA	NA
NA	South Dakota**	NA	NA
8	Tennessee	25	1.8%
12	Texas	12	0.9%
15	Utah	8	0.6%
NA	Vermont**	NA	NA
4	Virginia	109	7.8%
NA	Washington**	NA	NA
2	West Virginia	282	20.1%
NA	Wisconsin**	NA	NA
11	Wyoming	20	1.4%

RANK ORDER

RANK	STATE	MINES	% of USA
1	Kentucky	449	31.9%
2	West Virginia	282	20.1%
3	Pennsylvania	244	17.4%
4	Virginia	109	7.8%
5	Alabama	57	4.1%
6	Ohio	46	3.3%
7	Indiana	33	2.3%
8	Tennessee	25	1.8%
9	Illinois	22	1.6%
9	Maryland	22	1.6%
11	Wyoming	20	1.4%
12	Texas	12	0.9%
13	Colorado	11	0.8%
14	Oklahoma	10	0.7%
15	Utah	8	0.6%
16	Montana	6	0.4%
17	New Mexico	5	0.4%
18	North Dakota	4	0.3%
19	Arkansas	2	0.1%
19	Louisiana	2	0.1%
19	Missouri	2	0.1%
22	Alaska	1	0.1%
22	Arizona	1	0.1%
22	Kansas	1	0.1%
22	Mississippi	1	0.1%
NA	California**	NA	NA
NA	Connecticut**	NA	NA
NA	Delaware**	NA	NA
NA	Florida**	NA	NA
NA	Georgia**	NA	NA
NA	Hawaii**	NA	NA
NA	Idaho**	NA	NA
NA	Iowa**	NA	NA
NA	Maine**	NA	NA
NA	Massachusetts**	NA	NA
NA	Michigan**	NA	NA
NA	Minnesota**	NA	NA
NA	Nebraska**	NA	NA
NA	Nevada**	NA	NA
NA	New Hampshire**	NA	NA
NA	New Jersey**	NA	NA
NA	New York**	NA	NA
NA	North Carolina**	NA	NA
NA	Oregon**	NA	NA
NA	Rhode Island**	NA	NA
NA	South Carolina**	NA	NA
NA	South Dakota**	NA	NA
NA	Vermont**	NA	NA
NA	Washington**	NA	NA
NA	Wisconsin**	NA	NA
	District of Columbia**	NA	NA

Source: U.S. Department of Energy, Energy Information Administration
   "Annual Coal Report" (http://www.eia.doe.gov/cneaf/coal/page/acr/acr_sum.html)
*National total includes 31 coal mines in refuse recovery not shown by state.
**Not available or no mines.

Coal Production in 2009

National Total = 1,074,923,000 Short Tons*

ALPHA ORDER

RANK	STATE	SHORT TONS	% of USA
15	Alabama	18,796,000	1.7%
21	Alaska	1,860,000	0.2%
16	Arizona	7,474,000	0.7%
25	Arkansas	5,000	0.0%
NA	California**	NA	NA
10	Colorado	28,267,000	2.6%
NA	Connecticut**	NA	NA
NA	Delaware**	NA	NA
NA	Florida**	NA	NA
NA	Georgia**	NA	NA
NA	Hawaii**	NA	NA
NA	Idaho**	NA	NA
8	Illinois	33,748,000	3.1%
6	Indiana	35,655,000	3.3%
NA	Iowa**	NA	NA
24	Kansas	185,000	0.0%
3	Kentucky	107,338,000	10.0%
17	Louisiana	3,657,000	0.3%
NA	Maine**	NA	NA
19	Maryland	2,305,000	0.2%
NA	Massachusetts**	NA	NA
NA	Michigan**	NA	NA
NA	Minnesota**	NA	NA
18	Mississippi	3,440,000	0.3%
23	Missouri	452,000	0.0%
5	Montana	39,486,000	3.7%
NA	Nebraska**	NA	NA
NA	Nevada**	NA	NA
NA	New Hampshire**	NA	NA
NA	New Jersey**	NA	NA
12	New Mexico	25,124,000	2.3%
NA	New York**	NA	NA
NA	North Carolina**	NA	NA
9	North Dakota	29,945,000	2.8%
11	Ohio	27,501,000	2.6%
22	Oklahoma	956,000	0.1%
NA	Oregon**	NA	NA
4	Pennsylvania	57,979,000	5.4%
NA	Rhode Island**	NA	NA
NA	South Carolina**	NA	NA
NA	South Dakota**	NA	NA
20	Tennessee	1,996,000	0.2%
7	Texas	35,093,000	3.3%
13	Utah	21,718,000	2.0%
NA	Vermont**	NA	NA
14	Virginia	21,175,000	2.0%
NA	Washington**	NA	NA
2	West Virginia	136,971,000	12.7%
NA	Wisconsin**	NA	NA
1	Wyoming	431,107,000	40.1%

RANK ORDER

RANK	STATE	SHORT TONS	% of USA
1	Wyoming	431,107,000	40.1%
2	West Virginia	136,971,000	12.7%
3	Kentucky	107,338,000	10.0%
4	Pennsylvania	57,979,000	5.4%
5	Montana	39,486,000	3.7%
6	Indiana	35,655,000	3.3%
7	Texas	35,093,000	3.3%
8	Illinois	33,748,000	3.1%
9	North Dakota	29,945,000	2.8%
10	Colorado	28,267,000	2.6%
11	Ohio	27,501,000	2.6%
12	New Mexico	25,124,000	2.3%
13	Utah	21,718,000	2.0%
14	Virginia	21,175,000	2.0%
15	Alabama	18,796,000	1.7%
16	Arizona	7,474,000	0.7%
17	Louisiana	3,657,000	0.3%
18	Mississippi	3,440,000	0.3%
19	Maryland	2,305,000	0.2%
20	Tennessee	1,996,000	0.2%
21	Alaska	1,860,000	0.2%
22	Oklahoma	956,000	0.1%
23	Missouri	452,000	0.0%
24	Kansas	185,000	0.0%
25	Arkansas	5,000	0.0%
NA	California**	NA	NA
NA	Connecticut**	NA	NA
NA	Delaware**	NA	NA
NA	Florida**	NA	NA
NA	Georgia**	NA	NA
NA	Hawaii**	NA	NA
NA	Idaho**	NA	NA
NA	Iowa**	NA	NA
NA	Maine**	NA	NA
NA	Massachusetts**	NA	NA
NA	Michigan**	NA	NA
NA	Minnesota**	NA	NA
NA	Nebraska**	NA	NA
NA	Nevada**	NA	NA
NA	New Hampshire**	NA	NA
NA	New Jersey**	NA	NA
NA	New York**	NA	NA
NA	North Carolina**	NA	NA
NA	Oregon**	NA	NA
NA	Rhode Island**	NA	NA
NA	South Carolina**	NA	NA
NA	South Dakota**	NA	NA
NA	Vermont**	NA	NA
NA	Washington**	NA	NA
NA	Wisconsin**	NA	NA
	District of Columbia**	NA	NA

Source: U.S. Department of Energy, Energy Information Administration
   "Annual Coal Report" (http://www.eia.doe.gov/cneaf/coal/page/acr/acr_sum.html)
*National total includes 2,688,000 short tons from refuse recovery not shown by state.
**Not available or no production.

Gasoline Used in 2009

National Total = 136,877,949,000 Gallons*

RANK	STATE	GALLONS	% of USA
21	Alabama	2,606,494,000	1.9%
50	Alaska	291,998,000	0.2%
20	Arizona	2,641,520,000	1.9%
32	Arkansas	1,462,818,000	1.1%
1	California	14,831,535,000	10.8%
26	Colorado	2,098,699,000	1.5%
31	Connecticut	1,512,081,000	1.1%
45	Delaware	448,038,000	0.3%
3	Florida	8,324,683,000	6.1%
8	Georgia	4,885,861,000	3.6%
43	Hawaii	451,748,000	0.3%
41	Idaho	663,652,000	0.5%
7	Illinois	4,897,738,000	3.6%
15	Indiana	3,083,882,000	2.3%
28	Iowa	1,649,741,000	1.2%
33	Kansas	1,327,603,000	1.0%
25	Kentucky	2,215,613,000	1.6%
24	Louisiana	2,291,745,000	1.7%
40	Maine	667,266,000	0.5%
16	Maryland	3,034,582,000	2.2%
17	Massachusetts	2,765,743,000	2.0%
9	Michigan	4,559,708,000	3.3%
22	Minnesota	2,551,975,000	1.9%
29	Mississippi	1,576,657,000	1.2%
13	Missouri	3,199,622,000	2.3%
42	Montana	496,496,000	0.4%
38	Nebraska	829,122,000	0.6%
34	Nevada	1,106,660,000	0.8%
39	New Hampshire	717,118,000	0.5%
11	New Jersey	4,193,947,000	3.1%
36	New Mexico	963,947,000	0.7%
4	New York	5,644,564,000	4.1%
10	North Carolina	4,433,153,000	3.2%
47	North Dakota	373,325,000	0.3%
6	Ohio	5,018,943,000	3.7%
27	Oklahoma	1,842,403,000	1.3%
30	Oregon	1,540,800,000	1.1%
5	Pennsylvania	5,075,465,000	3.7%
46	Rhode Island	395,776,000	0.3%
18	South Carolina	2,721,888,000	2.0%
44	South Dakota	448,495,000	0.3%
14	Tennessee	3,163,364,000	2.3%
2	Texas	12,008,645,000	8.8%
35	Utah	1,060,216,000	0.8%
49	Vermont	334,571,000	0.2%
12	Virginia	3,927,895,000	2.9%
19	Washington	2,708,318,000	2.0%
37	West Virginia	834,175,000	0.6%
23	Wisconsin	2,517,353,000	1.8%
48	Wyoming	368,671,000	0.3%

RANK	STATE	GALLONS	% of USA
1	California	14,831,535,000	10.8%
2	Texas	12,008,645,000	8.8%
3	Florida	8,324,683,000	6.1%
4	New York	5,644,564,000	4.1%
5	Pennsylvania	5,075,465,000	3.7%
6	Ohio	5,018,943,000	3.7%
7	Illinois	4,897,738,000	3.6%
8	Georgia	4,885,861,000	3.6%
9	Michigan	4,559,708,000	3.3%
10	North Carolina	4,433,153,000	3.2%
11	New Jersey	4,193,947,000	3.1%
12	Virginia	3,927,895,000	2.9%
13	Missouri	3,199,622,000	2.3%
14	Tennessee	3,163,364,000	2.3%
15	Indiana	3,083,882,000	2.3%
16	Maryland	3,034,582,000	2.2%
17	Massachusetts	2,765,743,000	2.0%
18	South Carolina	2,721,888,000	2.0%
19	Washington	2,708,318,000	2.0%
20	Arizona	2,641,520,000	1.9%
21	Alabama	2,606,494,000	1.9%
22	Minnesota	2,551,975,000	1.9%
23	Wisconsin	2,517,353,000	1.8%
24	Louisiana	2,291,745,000	1.7%
25	Kentucky	2,215,613,000	1.6%
26	Colorado	2,098,699,000	1.5%
27	Oklahoma	1,842,403,000	1.3%
28	Iowa	1,649,741,000	1.2%
29	Mississippi	1,576,657,000	1.2%
30	Oregon	1,540,800,000	1.1%
31	Connecticut	1,512,081,000	1.1%
32	Arkansas	1,462,818,000	1.1%
33	Kansas	1,327,603,000	1.0%
34	Nevada	1,106,660,000	0.8%
35	Utah	1,060,216,000	0.8%
36	New Mexico	963,947,000	0.7%
37	West Virginia	834,175,000	0.6%
38	Nebraska	829,122,000	0.6%
39	New Hampshire	717,118,000	0.5%
40	Maine	667,266,000	0.5%
41	Idaho	663,652,000	0.5%
42	Montana	496,496,000	0.4%
43	Hawaii	451,748,000	0.3%
44	South Dakota	448,495,000	0.3%
45	Delaware	448,038,000	0.3%
46	Rhode Island	395,776,000	0.3%
47	North Dakota	373,325,000	0.3%
48	Wyoming	368,671,000	0.3%
49	Vermont	334,571,000	0.2%
50	Alaska	291,998,000	0.2%
	District of Columbia	111,637,000	0.1%

Source: U.S. Department of Transportation, Federal Highway Administration
"Highway Statistics 2009" (Table MF-21) (http://www.fhwa.dot.gov/policyinformation/statistics/2009/)
*Includes gasoline for highway and nonhighway uses. "Gasoline" includes gasohol but excludes "special fuels" such as diesel.

Per Capita Gasoline Used in 2009

National Per Capita = 446 Gallons*

ALPHA ORDER

RANK	STATE	GALLONS
4	Alabama	554
39	Alaska	418
45	Arizona	400
15	Arkansas	506
44	California	401
39	Colorado	418
35	Connecticut	430
15	Delaware	506
32	Florida	449
21	Georgia	497
49	Hawaii	349
36	Idaho	429
47	Illinois	379
25	Indiana	480
6	Iowa	548
28	Kansas	471
12	Kentucky	514
13	Louisiana	510
15	Maine	506
11	Maryland	532
37	Massachusetts	419
31	Michigan	457
22	Minnesota	485
9	Mississippi	534
9	Missouri	534
14	Montana	509
29	Nebraska	461
37	Nevada	419
7	New Hampshire	541
24	New Jersey	482
25	New Mexico	480
50	New York	289
27	North Carolina	473
3	North Dakota	577
34	Ohio	435
19	Oklahoma	500
42	Oregon	403
42	Pennsylvania	403
48	Rhode Island	376
2	South Carolina	597
5	South Dakota	552
18	Tennessee	502
22	Texas	485
46	Utah	381
8	Vermont	538
20	Virginia	498
41	Washington	406
30	West Virginia	458
33	Wisconsin	445
1	Wyoming	677

RANK ORDER

RANK	STATE	GALLONS
1	Wyoming	677
2	South Carolina	597
3	North Dakota	577
4	Alabama	554
5	South Dakota	552
6	Iowa	548
7	New Hampshire	541
8	Vermont	538
9	Mississippi	534
9	Missouri	534
11	Maryland	532
12	Kentucky	514
13	Louisiana	510
14	Montana	509
15	Arkansas	506
15	Delaware	506
15	Maine	506
18	Tennessee	502
19	Oklahoma	500
20	Virginia	498
21	Georgia	497
22	Minnesota	485
22	Texas	485
24	New Jersey	482
25	Indiana	480
25	New Mexico	480
27	North Carolina	473
28	Kansas	471
29	Nebraska	461
30	West Virginia	458
31	Michigan	457
32	Florida	449
33	Wisconsin	445
34	Ohio	435
35	Connecticut	430
36	Idaho	429
37	Massachusetts	419
37	Nevada	419
39	Alaska	418
39	Colorado	418
41	Washington	406
42	Oregon	403
42	Pennsylvania	403
44	California	401
45	Arizona	400
46	Utah	381
47	Illinois	379
48	Rhode Island	376
49	Hawaii	349
50	New York	289

District of Columbia	186

Source: CQ Press using data from U.S. Department of Transportation, Federal Highway Administration
"Highway Statistics 2009" (Table MF-21) (http://www.fhwa.dot.gov/policyinformation/statistics/2009/)
*Includes gasoline for highway and nonhighway uses. "Gasoline" includes gasohol but excludes "special fuels" such as diesel.

Daily Production of Crude Oil in 2009

National Total = 5,360,537 Barrels a Day*

ALPHA ORDER

RANK	STATE	BARRELS	% of USA
15	Alabama	19,696	0.4%
2	Alaska	645,205	12.0%
30	Arizona	126	0.0%
18	Arkansas	15,838	0.3%
3	California	567,381	10.6%
10	Colorado	77,600	1.4%
NA	Connecticut**	NA	NA
NA	Delaware**	NA	NA
25	Florida	1,907	0.0%
NA	Georgia**	NA	NA
NA	Hawaii**	NA	NA
NA	Idaho**	NA	NA
14	Illinois	24,929	0.5%
23	Indiana	4,942	0.1%
NA	Iowa**	NA	NA
9	Kansas	108,121	2.0%
20	Kentucky	7,148	0.1%
5	Louisiana	189,047	3.5%
NA	Maine**	NA	NA
NA	Maryland**	NA	NA
NA	Massachusetts**	NA	NA
16	Michigan	16,164	0.3%
NA	Minnesota**	NA	NA
12	Mississippi	63,649	1.2%
29	Missouri	258	0.0%
11	Montana	75,868	1.4%
21	Nebraska	6,134	0.1%
26	Nevada	1,247	0.0%
NA	New Hampshire**	NA	NA
NA	New Jersey**	NA	NA
7	New Mexico	167,523	3.1%
27	New York	929	0.0%
NA	North Carolina**	NA	NA
4	North Dakota	218,455	4.1%
17	Ohio	15,984	0.3%
6	Oklahoma	183,611	3.4%
NA	Oregon**	NA	NA
19	Pennsylvania	9,701	0.2%
NA	Rhode Island**	NA	NA
NA	South Carolina**	NA	NA
24	South Dakota	4,542	0.1%
28	Tennessee	734	0.0%
1	Texas	1,106,293	20.6%
13	Utah	62,814	1.2%
NA	Vermont**	NA	NA
31	Virginia	38	0.0%
NA	Washington**	NA	NA
22	West Virginia	5,107	0.1%
NA	Wisconsin**	NA	NA
8	Wyoming	140,638	2.6%

RANK ORDER

RANK	STATE	BARRELS	% of USA
1	Texas	1,106,293	20.6%
2	Alaska	645,205	12.0%
3	California	567,381	10.6%
4	North Dakota	218,455	4.1%
5	Louisiana	189,047	3.5%
6	Oklahoma	183,611	3.4%
7	New Mexico	167,523	3.1%
8	Wyoming	140,638	2.6%
9	Kansas	108,121	2.0%
10	Colorado	77,600	1.4%
11	Montana	75,868	1.4%
12	Mississippi	63,649	1.2%
13	Utah	62,814	1.2%
14	Illinois	24,929	0.5%
15	Alabama	19,696	0.4%
16	Michigan	16,164	0.3%
17	Ohio	15,984	0.3%
18	Arkansas	15,838	0.3%
19	Pennsylvania	9,701	0.2%
20	Kentucky	7,148	0.1%
21	Nebraska	6,134	0.1%
22	West Virginia	5,107	0.1%
23	Indiana	4,942	0.1%
24	South Dakota	4,542	0.1%
25	Florida	1,907	0.0%
26	Nevada	1,247	0.0%
27	New York	929	0.0%
28	Tennessee	734	0.0%
29	Missouri	258	0.0%
30	Arizona	126	0.0%
31	Virginia	38	0.0%
NA	Connecticut**	NA	NA
NA	Delaware**	NA	NA
NA	Georgia**	NA	NA
NA	Hawaii**	NA	NA
NA	Idaho**	NA	NA
NA	Iowa**	NA	NA
NA	Maine**	NA	NA
NA	Maryland**	NA	NA
NA	Massachusetts**	NA	NA
NA	Minnesota**	NA	NA
NA	New Hampshire**	NA	NA
NA	New Jersey**	NA	NA
NA	North Carolina**	NA	NA
NA	Oregon**	NA	NA
NA	Rhode Island**	NA	NA
NA	South Carolina**	NA	NA
NA	Vermont**	NA	NA
NA	Washington**	NA	NA
NA	Wisconsin**	NA	NA
	District of Columbia**	NA	NA

Source: CQ Press using data from U.S. Department of Energy, Energy Information Administration
    "Petroleum Supply Annual 2009, Volume 1" (http://tonto.eia.doe.gov/dnav/pet/pet_crd_crpdn_adc_mbbl_m.htm)
*National total includes 1,618,910 barrels a day in federal offshore production. Figures for Alaska, California, Louisiana, and Texas include state offshore production.
**No reported production.

Fossil Fuel Emissions in 2008

National Total = 5,735,500,000 Metric Tons of Carbon Dioxide (CO2)*

ALPHA ORDER

RANK	STATE	TONS OF CO2	% of USA
14	Alabama	139,100,000	2.4%
40	Alaska	39,400,000	0.7%
23	Arizona	103,000,000	1.8%
33	Arkansas	64,800,000	1.1%
2	California	392,300,000	6.8%
24	Colorado	97,500,000	1.7%
41	Connecticut	38,100,000	0.7%
46	Delaware	16,400,000	0.3%
6	Florida	240,400,000	4.2%
11	Georgia	174,400,000	3.0%
43	Hawaii	19,700,000	0.3%
47	Idaho	15,600,000	0.3%
5	Illinois	241,700,000	4.2%
7	Indiana	232,000,000	4.0%
25	Iowa	88,100,000	1.5%
28	Kansas	77,300,000	1.3%
12	Kentucky	154,900,000	2.7%
10	Louisiana	174,800,000	3.0%
45	Maine	18,800,000	0.3%
30	Maryland	74,400,000	1.3%
29	Massachusetts	75,500,000	1.3%
9	Michigan	176,200,000	3.0%
22	Minnesota	103,800,000	1.8%
34	Mississippi	63,700,000	1.1%
15	Missouri	137,800,000	2.4%
42	Montana	36,000,000	0.6%
37	Nebraska	46,200,000	0.8%
39	Nevada	41,000,000	0.7%
44	New Hampshire	18,900,000	0.3%
16	New Jersey	127,800,000	2.2%
35	New Mexico	57,600,000	1.0%
8	New York	190,900,000	3.3%
13	North Carolina	150,100,000	2.6%
36	North Dakota	53,000,000	0.9%
4	Ohio	262,300,000	4.5%
20	Oklahoma	112,100,000	1.9%
38	Oregon	43,000,000	0.7%
3	Pennsylvania	265,100,000	4.6%
49	Rhode Island	10,700,000	0.2%
26	South Carolina	86,000,000	1.5%
48	South Dakota	14,900,000	0.3%
17	Tennessee	120,100,000	2.1%
1	Texas	622,700,000	10.8%
31	Utah	69,900,000	1.2%
50	Vermont	6,100,000	0.1%
18	Virginia	118,400,000	2.0%
27	Washington	79,400,000	1.4%
19	West Virginia	112,900,000	2.0%
21	Wisconsin	105,900,000	1.8%
32	Wyoming	66,900,000	1.2%

RANK ORDER

RANK	STATE	TONS OF CO2	% of USA
1	Texas	622,700,000	10.8%
2	California	392,300,000	6.8%
3	Pennsylvania	265,100,000	4.6%
4	Ohio	262,300,000	4.5%
5	Illinois	241,700,000	4.2%
6	Florida	240,400,000	4.2%
7	Indiana	232,000,000	4.0%
8	New York	190,900,000	3.3%
9	Michigan	176,200,000	3.0%
10	Louisiana	174,800,000	3.0%
11	Georgia	174,400,000	3.0%
12	Kentucky	154,900,000	2.7%
13	North Carolina	150,100,000	2.6%
14	Alabama	139,100,000	2.4%
15	Missouri	137,800,000	2.4%
16	New Jersey	127,800,000	2.2%
17	Tennessee	120,100,000	2.1%
18	Virginia	118,400,000	2.0%
19	West Virginia	112,900,000	2.0%
20	Oklahoma	112,100,000	1.9%
21	Wisconsin	105,900,000	1.8%
22	Minnesota	103,800,000	1.8%
23	Arizona	103,000,000	1.8%
24	Colorado	97,500,000	1.7%
25	Iowa	88,100,000	1.5%
26	South Carolina	86,000,000	1.5%
27	Washington	79,400,000	1.4%
28	Kansas	77,300,000	1.3%
29	Massachusetts	75,500,000	1.3%
30	Maryland	74,400,000	1.3%
31	Utah	69,900,000	1.2%
32	Wyoming	66,900,000	1.2%
33	Arkansas	64,800,000	1.1%
34	Mississippi	63,700,000	1.1%
35	New Mexico	57,600,000	1.0%
36	North Dakota	53,000,000	0.9%
37	Nebraska	46,200,000	0.8%
38	Oregon	43,000,000	0.7%
39	Nevada	41,000,000	0.7%
40	Alaska	39,400,000	0.7%
41	Connecticut	38,100,000	0.7%
42	Montana	36,000,000	0.6%
43	Hawaii	19,700,000	0.3%
44	New Hampshire	18,900,000	0.3%
45	Maine	18,800,000	0.3%
46	Delaware	16,400,000	0.3%
47	Idaho	15,600,000	0.3%
48	South Dakota	14,900,000	0.3%
49	Rhode Island	10,700,000	0.2%
50	Vermont	6,100,000	0.1%
	District of Columbia	2,300,000	0.0%

Source: U.S. Environmental Protection Agency
   "Energy CO2 Emissions by State" (http://www.eia.doe.gov/oiaf/1605/state/state_emissions.html)
*National total determined using a different methodology. Carbon dioxide (CO2) emissions from fossil fuel combustion
represented the largest source (98%) of total CO2 emissions from all emission sources. The EPA estimates that an
additional 103,800,000 metric tons of CO2 were emitted from other sources.

Per Capita Fossil Fuel Emissions in 2008

National Per Capita = 19.0 Metric Tons of Carbon Dioxide (CO_2)*

ALPHA ORDER

RANK	STATE	PER CAPITA
10	Alabama	29.7
4	Alaska	57.3
33	Arizona	15.8
19	Arkansas	22.6
46	California	10.7
22	Colorado	19.8
45	Connecticut	10.9
28	Delaware	18.7
41	Florida	13.0
30	Georgia	18.0
35	Hawaii	15.3
47	Idaho	10.2
26	Illinois	18.8
7	Indiana	36.3
11	Iowa	29.4
13	Kansas	27.6
8	Kentucky	36.1
5	Louisiana	39.3
39	Maine	14.2
40	Maryland	13.1
43	Massachusetts	11.5
31	Michigan	17.6
22	Minnesota	19.8
20	Mississippi	21.7
17	Missouri	23.1
6	Montana	37.2
14	Nebraska	25.9
34	Nevada	15.7
38	New Hampshire	14.3
37	New Jersey	14.8
12	New Mexico	29.0
49	New York	9.8
32	North Carolina	16.2
2	North Dakota	82.6
18	Ohio	22.8
9	Oklahoma	30.8
44	Oregon	11.4
21	Pennsylvania	21.1
47	Rhode Island	10.2
25	South Carolina	19.1
29	South Dakota	18.5
24	Tennessee	19.2
15	Texas	25.6
15	Utah	25.6
49	Vermont	9.8
36	Virginia	15.2
42	Washington	12.1
3	West Virginia	62.2
26	Wisconsin	18.8
1	Wyoming	125.5

RANK ORDER

RANK	STATE	PER CAPITA
1	Wyoming	125.5
2	North Dakota	82.6
3	West Virginia	62.2
4	Alaska	57.3
5	Louisiana	39.3
6	Montana	37.2
7	Indiana	36.3
8	Kentucky	36.1
9	Oklahoma	30.8
10	Alabama	29.7
11	Iowa	29.4
12	New Mexico	29.0
13	Kansas	27.6
14	Nebraska	25.9
15	Texas	25.6
15	Utah	25.6
17	Missouri	23.1
18	Ohio	22.8
19	Arkansas	22.6
20	Mississippi	21.7
21	Pennsylvania	21.1
22	Colorado	19.8
22	Minnesota	19.8
24	Tennessee	19.2
25	South Carolina	19.1
26	Illinois	18.8
26	Wisconsin	18.8
28	Delaware	18.7
29	South Dakota	18.5
30	Georgia	18.0
31	Michigan	17.6
32	North Carolina	16.2
33	Arizona	15.8
34	Nevada	15.7
35	Hawaii	15.3
36	Virginia	15.2
37	New Jersey	14.8
38	New Hampshire	14.3
39	Maine	14.2
40	Maryland	13.1
41	Florida	13.0
42	Washington	12.1
43	Massachusetts	11.5
44	Oregon	11.4
45	Connecticut	10.9
46	California	10.7
47	Idaho	10.2
47	Rhode Island	10.2
49	New York	9.8
49	Vermont	9.8
	District of Columbia	3.9

Source: CQ Press using data from U.S. Environmental Protection Agency
"Energy CO_2 Emissions by State" (http://www.eia.doe.gov/oiaf/1605/state/state_emissions.html)
*National figure determined using a different methodology. Carbon dioxide (CO_2) emissions from fossil fuel combustion represented the largest source (98%) of total CO_2 emissions from all emission sources. The EPA estimates that an additional 103,800,000 metric tons of CO_2 were emitted from other sources.

Percent Change in Fossil Fuel Emissions: 2004 to 2008

National Percent Change = 2.2% Decrease*

ALPHA ORDER

RANK	STATE	PERCENT CHANGE
26	Alabama	(0.9)
49	Alaska	(15.8)
7	Arizona	6.5
14	Arkansas	2.0
21	California	(0.1)
11	Colorado	4.6
48	Connecticut	(14.6)
31	Delaware	(2.4)
37	Florida	(6.9)
24	Georgia	(0.4)
44	Hawaii	(12.8)
17	Idaho	1.3
15	Illinois	1.7
33	Indiana	(3.0)
2	Iowa	10.8
16	Kansas	1.4
18	Kentucky	1.2
37	Louisiana	(6.9)
50	Maine	(19.0)
41	Maryland	(9.0)
42	Massachusetts	(9.1)
37	Michigan	(6.9)
12	Minnesota	3.2
27	Mississippi	(1.5)
28	Missouri	(1.7)
10	Montana	4.7
4	Nebraska	7.4
47	Nevada	(13.9)
46	New Hampshire	(13.7)
22	New Jersey	(0.2)
30	New Mexico	(1.9)
43	New York	(11.3)
22	North Carolina	(0.2)
5	North Dakota	6.9
25	Ohio	(0.7)
1	Oklahoma	12.1
8	Oregon	5.9
36	Pennsylvania	(4.7)
19	Rhode Island	0.9
32	South Carolina	(2.7)
3	South Dakota	9.6
34	Tennessee	(3.5)
35	Texas	(4.6)
5	Utah	6.9
45	Vermont	(12.9)
40	Virginia	(7.8)
13	Washington	3.1
20	West Virginia	0.0
29	Wisconsin	(1.8)
9	Wyoming	5.2

RANK ORDER

RANK	STATE	PERCENT CHANGE
1	Oklahoma	12.1
2	Iowa	10.8
3	South Dakota	9.6
4	Nebraska	7.4
5	North Dakota	6.9
5	Utah	6.9
7	Arizona	6.5
8	Oregon	5.9
9	Wyoming	5.2
10	Montana	4.7
11	Colorado	4.6
12	Minnesota	3.2
13	Washington	3.1
14	Arkansas	2.0
15	Illinois	1.7
16	Kansas	1.4
17	Idaho	1.3
18	Kentucky	1.2
19	Rhode Island	0.9
20	West Virginia	0.0
21	California	(0.1)
22	New Jersey	(0.2)
22	North Carolina	(0.2)
24	Georgia	(0.4)
25	Ohio	(0.7)
26	Alabama	(0.9)
27	Mississippi	(1.5)
28	Missouri	(1.7)
29	Wisconsin	(1.8)
30	New Mexico	(1.9)
31	Delaware	(2.4)
32	South Carolina	(2.7)
33	Indiana	(3.0)
34	Tennessee	(3.5)
35	Texas	(4.6)
36	Pennsylvania	(4.7)
37	Florida	(6.9)
37	Louisiana	(6.9)
37	Michigan	(6.9)
40	Virginia	(7.8)
41	Maryland	(9.0)
42	Massachusetts	(9.1)
43	New York	(11.3)
44	Hawaii	(12.8)
45	Vermont	(12.9)
46	New Hampshire	(13.7)
47	Nevada	(13.9)
48	Connecticut	(14.6)
49	Alaska	(15.8)
50	Maine	(19.0)
	District of Columbia	(25.8)

Source: CQ Press using data from U.S. Environmental Protection Agency
   "Energy CO2 Emissions by State" (http://www.eia.doe.gov/oiaf/1605/state/state_emissions.html)
*Based on metric tons of carbon dioxide (CO2).

Toxic Releases: Total Pollution Released in 2009

National Total = 3,367,548,904 Pounds of Toxins*

ALPHA ORDER

RANK	STATE	POUNDS	% of USA
11	Alabama	91,075,650	2.7%
1	Alaska	695,927,854	20.7%
18	Arizona	60,899,299	1.8%
28	Arkansas	34,009,523	1.0%
26	California	36,718,326	1.1%
37	Colorado	20,169,013	0.6%
46	Connecticut	3,314,913	0.1%
43	Delaware	8,085,313	0.2%
13	Florida	84,941,381	2.5%
14	Georgia	79,824,749	2.4%
47	Hawaii	2,947,264	0.1%
22	Idaho	47,871,236	1.4%
10	Illinois	95,068,572	2.8%
7	Indiana	132,074,361	3.9%
23	Iowa	46,477,055	1.4%
36	Kansas	21,123,404	0.6%
6	Kentucky	142,607,547	4.2%
9	Louisiana	119,527,406	3.5%
42	Maine	8,463,681	0.3%
27	Maryland	35,759,311	1.1%
44	Massachusetts	5,375,009	0.2%
16	Michigan	70,746,325	2.1%
34	Minnesota	22,229,740	0.7%
20	Mississippi	54,116,796	1.6%
15	Missouri	75,727,384	2.2%
25	Montana	41,169,093	1.2%
30	Nebraska	29,562,754	0.9%
3	Nevada	183,371,163	5.4%
48	New Hampshire	2,899,274	0.1%
41	New Jersey	12,944,597	0.4%
40	New Mexico	15,297,901	0.5%
33	New York	23,279,524	0.7%
17	North Carolina	63,582,646	1.9%
35	North Dakota	21,204,560	0.6%
4	Ohio	158,508,558	4.7%
31	Oklahoma	29,553,945	0.9%
38	Oregon	17,263,571	0.5%
8	Pennsylvania	120,400,308	3.6%
49	Rhode Island	395,231	0.0%
21	South Carolina	49,401,851	1.5%
45	South Dakota	4,589,642	0.1%
12	Tennessee	89,101,753	2.6%
2	Texas	189,779,393	5.6%
5	Utah	147,373,378	4.4%
50	Vermont	262,030	0.0%
19	Virginia	56,035,192	1.7%
39	Washington	15,629,587	0.5%
24	West Virginia	42,942,705	1.3%
29	Wisconsin	32,934,598	1.0%
32	Wyoming	24,960,729	0.7%

RANK ORDER

RANK	STATE	POUNDS	% of USA
1	Alaska	695,927,854	20.7%
2	Texas	189,779,393	5.6%
3	Nevada	183,371,163	5.4%
4	Ohio	158,508,558	4.7%
5	Utah	147,373,378	4.4%
6	Kentucky	142,607,547	4.2%
7	Indiana	132,074,361	3.9%
8	Pennsylvania	120,400,308	3.6%
9	Louisiana	119,527,406	3.5%
10	Illinois	95,068,572	2.8%
11	Alabama	91,075,650	2.7%
12	Tennessee	89,101,753	2.6%
13	Florida	84,941,381	2.5%
14	Georgia	79,824,749	2.4%
15	Missouri	75,727,384	2.2%
16	Michigan	70,746,325	2.1%
17	North Carolina	63,582,646	1.9%
18	Arizona	60,899,299	1.8%
19	Virginia	56,035,192	1.7%
20	Mississippi	54,116,796	1.6%
21	South Carolina	49,401,851	1.5%
22	Idaho	47,871,236	1.4%
23	Iowa	46,477,055	1.4%
24	West Virginia	42,942,705	1.3%
25	Montana	41,169,093	1.2%
26	California	36,718,326	1.1%
27	Maryland	35,759,311	1.1%
28	Arkansas	34,009,523	1.0%
29	Wisconsin	32,934,598	1.0%
30	Nebraska	29,562,754	0.9%
31	Oklahoma	29,553,945	0.9%
32	Wyoming	24,960,729	0.7%
33	New York	23,279,524	0.7%
34	Minnesota	22,229,740	0.7%
35	North Dakota	21,204,560	0.6%
36	Kansas	21,123,404	0.6%
37	Colorado	20,169,013	0.6%
38	Oregon	17,263,571	0.5%
39	Washington	15,629,587	0.5%
40	New Mexico	15,297,901	0.5%
41	New Jersey	12,944,597	0.4%
42	Maine	8,463,681	0.3%
43	Delaware	8,085,313	0.2%
44	Massachusetts	5,375,009	0.2%
45	South Dakota	4,589,642	0.1%
46	Connecticut	3,314,913	0.1%
47	Hawaii	2,947,264	0.1%
48	New Hampshire	2,899,274	0.1%
49	Rhode Island	395,231	0.0%
50	Vermont	262,030	0.0%
	District of Columbia	23,809	0.0%

Source: U.S. Environmental Protection Agency, Office of Pollution Prevention and Toxics Information Management
   "2009 Toxics Release Inventory" (http://www.epa.gov/triexplorer/)
*National total does not include 7,354,400 pounds of toxins in U.S. territories. Includes discharges to air, surface water, underground injection, and surface land. Includes both original (or manufacturing) industries and those added by EPA since it began tracking releases.

Toxic Releases: Total Air Emissions in 2009

National Total = 908,216,183 Pounds*

ALPHA ORDER

RANK	STATE	POUNDS	% of USA
10	Alabama	34,644,696	3.8%
48	Alaska	523,423	0.1%
38	Arizona	2,676,813	0.3%
23	Arkansas	14,424,785	1.6%
24	California	9,470,079	1.0%
41	Colorado	2,230,182	0.2%
44	Connecticut	1,895,394	0.2%
36	Delaware	3,172,033	0.3%
4	Florida	52,608,616	5.8%
5	Georgia	50,026,656	5.5%
42	Hawaii	2,228,566	0.2%
37	Idaho	3,164,624	0.3%
15	Illinois	29,269,611	3.2%
8	Indiana	45,177,118	5.0%
18	Iowa	18,121,768	2.0%
27	Kansas	8,011,645	0.9%
7	Kentucky	45,556,053	5.0%
6	Louisiana	45,678,225	5.0%
33	Maine	3,850,480	0.4%
14	Maryland	30,057,084	3.3%
35	Massachusetts	3,247,046	0.4%
11	Michigan	32,625,341	3.6%
26	Minnesota	8,466,169	0.9%
19	Mississippi	16,200,094	1.8%
20	Missouri	15,101,172	1.7%
40	Montana	2,298,035	0.3%
31	Nebraska	5,489,038	0.6%
45	Nevada	1,632,904	0.2%
39	New Hampshire	2,668,581	0.3%
32	New Jersey	4,326,346	0.5%
47	New Mexico	1,090,664	0.1%
25	New York	8,866,265	1.0%
9	North Carolina	35,138,777	3.9%
34	North Dakota	3,594,546	0.4%
1	Ohio	75,123,706	8.3%
21	Oklahoma	14,764,742	1.6%
30	Oregon	6,048,391	0.7%
3	Pennsylvania	54,012,237	5.9%
49	Rhode Island	173,218	0.0%
12	South Carolina	32,579,702	3.6%
46	South Dakota	1,403,506	0.2%
13	Tennessee	31,946,016	3.5%
2	Texas	62,696,316	6.9%
29	Utah	6,871,172	0.8%
50	Vermont	25,433	0.0%
16	Virginia	28,415,306	3.1%
28	Washington	6,948,213	0.8%
17	West Virginia	27,008,533	3.0%
22	Wisconsin	14,593,359	1.6%
43	Wyoming	2,072,352	0.2%

RANK ORDER

RANK	STATE	POUNDS	% of USA
1	Ohio	75,123,706	8.3%
2	Texas	62,696,316	6.9%
3	Pennsylvania	54,012,237	5.9%
4	Florida	52,608,616	5.8%
5	Georgia	50,026,656	5.5%
6	Louisiana	45,678,225	5.0%
7	Kentucky	45,556,053	5.0%
8	Indiana	45,177,118	5.0%
9	North Carolina	35,138,777	3.9%
10	Alabama	34,644,696	3.8%
11	Michigan	32,625,341	3.6%
12	South Carolina	32,579,702	3.6%
13	Tennessee	31,946,016	3.5%
14	Maryland	30,057,084	3.3%
15	Illinois	29,269,611	3.2%
16	Virginia	28,415,306	3.1%
17	West Virginia	27,008,533	3.0%
18	Iowa	18,121,768	2.0%
19	Mississippi	16,200,094	1.8%
20	Missouri	15,101,172	1.7%
21	Oklahoma	14,764,742	1.6%
22	Wisconsin	14,593,359	1.6%
23	Arkansas	14,424,785	1.6%
24	California	9,470,079	1.0%
25	New York	8,866,265	1.0%
26	Minnesota	8,466,169	0.9%
27	Kansas	8,011,645	0.9%
28	Washington	6,948,213	0.8%
29	Utah	6,871,172	0.8%
30	Oregon	6,048,391	0.7%
31	Nebraska	5,489,038	0.6%
32	New Jersey	4,326,346	0.5%
33	Maine	3,850,480	0.4%
34	North Dakota	3,594,546	0.4%
35	Massachusetts	3,247,046	0.4%
36	Delaware	3,172,033	0.3%
37	Idaho	3,164,624	0.3%
38	Arizona	2,676,813	0.3%
39	New Hampshire	2,668,581	0.3%
40	Montana	2,298,035	0.3%
41	Colorado	2,230,182	0.2%
42	Hawaii	2,228,566	0.2%
43	Wyoming	2,072,352	0.2%
44	Connecticut	1,895,394	0.2%
45	Nevada	1,632,904	0.2%
46	South Dakota	1,403,506	0.2%
47	New Mexico	1,090,664	0.1%
48	Alaska	523,423	0.1%
49	Rhode Island	173,218	0.0%
50	Vermont	25,433	0.0%
	District of Columbia	1,152	0.0%

Source: U.S. Environmental Protection Agency, Office of Pollution Prevention and Toxics Information Management
  "2009 Toxics Release Inventory" (http://www.epa.gov/triexplorer/)
*National total does not include 5,689,026 pounds of emissions in U.S. territories. Includes both original (or manufacturing)
industries and those added by EPA since it began tracking releases.

Toxic Releases: Total Surface Water Discharges in 2009

National Total = 204,478,624 Pounds*

ALPHA ORDER

RANK	STATE	POUNDS	% of USA
9	Alabama	9,068,652	4.4%
40	Alaska	155,625	0.1%
48	Arizona	1,343	0.0%
17	Arkansas	4,803,137	2.3%
27	California	1,703,704	0.8%
30	Colorado	1,568,743	0.8%
36	Connecticut	306,541	0.1%
28	Delaware	1,590,477	0.8%
31	Florida	1,542,877	0.8%
5	Georgia	11,989,648	5.9%
39	Hawaii	222,963	0.1%
23	Idaho	2,466,293	1.2%
8	Illinois	10,223,373	5.0%
3	Indiana	15,033,514	7.4%
15	Iowa	5,178,235	2.5%
35	Kansas	620,384	0.3%
16	Kentucky	4,940,511	2.4%
6	Louisiana	11,803,721	5.8%
21	Maine	2,872,118	1.4%
34	Maryland	1,106,395	0.5%
46	Massachusetts	6,194	0.0%
24	Michigan	2,204,842	1.1%
33	Minnesota	1,204,104	0.6%
12	Mississippi	7,481,611	3.7%
25	Missouri	1,939,698	0.9%
37	Montana	259,491	0.1%
2	Nebraska	15,174,936	7.4%
50	Nevada	118	0.0%
47	New Hampshire	1,719	0.0%
14	New Jersey	5,829,664	2.9%
44	New Mexico	38,361	0.0%
11	New York	7,818,447	3.8%
7	North Carolina	11,510,539	5.6%
38	North Dakota	238,518	0.1%
13	Ohio	6,138,487	3.0%
19	Oklahoma	3,022,328	1.5%
26	Oregon	1,900,205	0.9%
10	Pennsylvania	8,859,207	4.3%
49	Rhode Island	693	0.0%
18	South Carolina	3,285,646	1.6%
43	South Dakota	90,320	0.0%
20	Tennessee	3,008,403	1.5%
4	Texas	12,562,451	6.1%
42	Utah	100,856	0.0%
41	Vermont	118,276	0.1%
1	Virginia	18,572,616	9.1%
29	Washington	1,573,902	0.8%
32	West Virginia	1,500,598	0.7%
22	Wisconsin	2,825,699	1.4%
45	Wyoming	10,577	0.0%

RANK ORDER

RANK	STATE	POUNDS	% of USA
1	Virginia	18,572,616	9.1%
2	Nebraska	15,174,936	7.4%
3	Indiana	15,033,514	7.4%
4	Texas	12,562,451	6.1%
5	Georgia	11,989,648	5.9%
6	Louisiana	11,803,721	5.8%
7	North Carolina	11,510,539	5.6%
8	Illinois	10,223,373	5.0%
9	Alabama	9,068,652	4.4%
10	Pennsylvania	8,859,207	4.3%
11	New York	7,818,447	3.8%
12	Mississippi	7,481,611	3.7%
13	Ohio	6,138,487	3.0%
14	New Jersey	5,829,664	2.9%
15	Iowa	5,178,235	2.5%
16	Kentucky	4,940,511	2.4%
17	Arkansas	4,803,137	2.3%
18	South Carolina	3,285,646	1.6%
19	Oklahoma	3,022,328	1.5%
20	Tennessee	3,008,403	1.5%
21	Maine	2,872,118	1.4%
22	Wisconsin	2,825,699	1.4%
23	Idaho	2,466,293	1.2%
24	Michigan	2,204,842	1.1%
25	Missouri	1,939,698	0.9%
26	Oregon	1,900,205	0.9%
27	California	1,703,704	0.8%
28	Delaware	1,590,477	0.8%
29	Washington	1,573,902	0.8%
30	Colorado	1,568,743	0.8%
31	Florida	1,542,877	0.8%
32	West Virginia	1,500,598	0.7%
33	Minnesota	1,204,104	0.6%
34	Maryland	1,106,395	0.5%
35	Kansas	620,384	0.3%
36	Connecticut	306,541	0.1%
37	Montana	259,491	0.1%
38	North Dakota	238,518	0.1%
39	Hawaii	222,963	0.1%
40	Alaska	155,625	0.1%
41	Vermont	118,276	0.1%
42	Utah	100,856	0.0%
43	South Dakota	90,320	0.0%
44	New Mexico	38,361	0.0%
45	Wyoming	10,577	0.0%
46	Massachusetts	6,194	0.0%
47	New Hampshire	1,719	0.0%
48	Arizona	1,343	0.0%
49	Rhode Island	693	0.0%
50	Nevada	118	0.0%
	District of Columbia	1,864	0.0%

Source: U.S. Environmental Protection Agency, Office of Pollution Prevention and Toxics Information Management
   "2009 Toxics Release Inventory" (http://www.epa.gov/triexplorer/)
*National total does not include 286,667 pounds of discharges in U.S. territories. Includes both original (or manufacturing)
industries and those added by EPA since it began tracking releases.

Hazardous Waste Sites on the National Priority List in 2010

National Total = 1,342 Sites*

ALPHA ORDER

RANK	STATE	SITES	% of USA
25	Alabama	15	1.1%
44	Alaska	6	0.4%
39	Arizona	9	0.7%
43	Arkansas	8	0.6%
3	California	95	7.1%
20	Colorado	20	1.5%
25	Connecticut	15	1.1%
25	Delaware	15	1.1%
6	Florida	55	4.1%
24	Georgia	16	1.2%
46	Hawaii	3	0.2%
39	Idaho	9	0.7%
8	Illinois	49	3.7%
13	Indiana	32	2.4%
33	Iowa	12	0.9%
33	Kansas	12	0.9%
29	Kentucky	14	1.0%
37	Louisiana	11	0.8%
33	Maine	12	0.9%
20	Maryland	20	1.5%
13	Massachusetts	32	2.4%
5	Michigan	69	5.1%
18	Minnesota	25	1.9%
44	Mississippi	6	0.4%
13	Missouri	32	2.4%
23	Montana	17	1.3%
31	Nebraska	13	1.0%
49	Nevada	1	0.1%
19	New Hampshire	21	1.6%
1	New Jersey	113	8.4%
29	New Mexico	14	1.0%
4	New York	88	6.6%
12	North Carolina	37	2.8%
50	North Dakota	0	0.0%
10	Ohio	42	3.1%
39	Oklahoma	9	0.7%
31	Oregon	13	1.0%
2	Pennsylvania	97	7.2%
33	Rhode Island	12	0.9%
17	South Carolina	26	1.9%
47	South Dakota	2	0.1%
25	Tennessee	15	1.1%
7	Texas	51	3.8%
22	Utah	19	1.4%
37	Vermont	11	0.8%
16	Virginia	31	2.3%
9	Washington	48	3.6%
39	West Virginia	9	0.7%
11	Wisconsin	39	2.9%
47	Wyoming	2	0.1%

RANK ORDER

RANK	STATE	SITES	% of USA
1	New Jersey	113	8.4%
2	Pennsylvania	97	7.2%
3	California	95	7.1%
4	New York	88	6.6%
5	Michigan	69	5.1%
6	Florida	55	4.1%
7	Texas	51	3.8%
8	Illinois	49	3.7%
9	Washington	48	3.6%
10	Ohio	42	3.1%
11	Wisconsin	39	2.9%
12	North Carolina	37	2.8%
13	Indiana	32	2.4%
13	Massachusetts	32	2.4%
13	Missouri	32	2.4%
16	Virginia	31	2.3%
17	South Carolina	26	1.9%
18	Minnesota	25	1.9%
19	New Hampshire	21	1.6%
20	Colorado	20	1.5%
20	Maryland	20	1.5%
22	Utah	19	1.4%
23	Montana	17	1.3%
24	Georgia	16	1.2%
25	Alabama	15	1.1%
25	Connecticut	15	1.1%
25	Delaware	15	1.1%
25	Tennessee	15	1.1%
29	Kentucky	14	1.0%
29	New Mexico	14	1.0%
31	Nebraska	13	1.0%
31	Oregon	13	1.0%
33	Iowa	12	0.9%
33	Kansas	12	0.9%
33	Maine	12	0.9%
33	Rhode Island	12	0.9%
37	Louisiana	11	0.8%
37	Vermont	11	0.8%
39	Arizona	9	0.7%
39	Idaho	9	0.7%
39	Oklahoma	9	0.7%
39	West Virginia	9	0.7%
43	Arkansas	8	0.6%
44	Alaska	6	0.4%
44	Mississippi	6	0.4%
46	Hawaii	3	0.2%
47	South Dakota	2	0.1%
47	Wyoming	2	0.1%
49	Nevada	1	0.1%
50	North Dakota	0	0.0%
	District of Columbia	1	0.1%

Source: U.S. Environmental Protection Agency
    "National Priorities List (NPL) Sites in the United States" (http://www.epa.gov/superfund/sites/npl/)
*As of November 29, 2010. Includes final and proposed General Superfund and Federal Facilities Sites. National total includes 16
sites in Puerto Rico, two in Guam, and one in the U.S. Virgin Islands.

Hazardous Waste Sites on the National Priority List
per 10,000 Square Miles in 2010
National Rate = 3.5 Sites per 10,000 Square Miles*

ALPHA ORDER

RANK ORDER

RANK	STATE	RATE		RANK	STATE	RATE
27	Alabama	2.9		1	New Jersey	129.5
48	Alaska	0.1		2	Rhode Island	77.7
45	Arizona	0.8		3	Delaware	60.3
37	Arkansas	1.5		4	Massachusetts	30.3
21	California	5.8		5	Connecticut	27.1
34	Colorado	1.9		6	New Hampshire	22.5
5	Connecticut	27.1		7	Pennsylvania	21.1
3	Delaware	60.3		8	Maryland	16.1
14	Florida	8.4		8	New York	16.1
29	Georgia	2.7		10	Vermont	11.4
29	Hawaii	2.7		11	Ohio	9.4
44	Idaho	1.1		12	Indiana	8.8
13	Illinois	8.5		13	Illinois	8.5
12	Indiana	8.8		14	Florida	8.4
32	Iowa	2.1		15	South Carolina	8.1
37	Kansas	1.5		16	Virginia	7.2
25	Kentucky	3.5		17	Michigan	7.1
32	Louisiana	2.1		18	North Carolina	6.9
26	Maine	3.4		19	Washington	6.7
8	Maryland	16.1		20	Wisconsin	6.0
4	Massachusetts	30.3		21	California	5.8
17	Michigan	7.1		22	Missouri	4.6
27	Minnesota	2.9		23	West Virginia	3.7
41	Mississippi	1.2		24	Tennessee	3.6
22	Missouri	4.6		25	Kentucky	3.5
41	Montana	1.2		26	Maine	3.4
36	Nebraska	1.7		27	Alabama	2.9
48	Nevada	0.1		27	Minnesota	2.9
6	New Hampshire	22.5		29	Georgia	2.7
1	New Jersey	129.5		29	Hawaii	2.7
41	New Mexico	1.2		31	Utah	2.2
8	New York	16.1		32	Iowa	2.1
18	North Carolina	6.9		32	Louisiana	2.1
50	North Dakota	0.0		34	Colorado	1.9
11	Ohio	9.4		34	Texas	1.9
39	Oklahoma	1.3		36	Nebraska	1.7
39	Oregon	1.3		37	Arkansas	1.5
7	Pennsylvania	21.1		37	Kansas	1.5
2	Rhode Island	77.7		39	Oklahoma	1.3
15	South Carolina	8.1		39	Oregon	1.3
46	South Dakota	0.3		41	Mississippi	1.2
24	Tennessee	3.6		41	Montana	1.2
34	Texas	1.9		41	New Mexico	1.2
31	Utah	2.2		44	Idaho	1.1
10	Vermont	11.4		45	Arizona	0.8
16	Virginia	7.2		46	South Dakota	0.3
19	Washington	6.7		47	Wyoming	0.2
23	West Virginia	3.7		48	Alaska	0.1
20	Wisconsin	6.0		48	Nevada	0.1
47	Wyoming	0.2		50	North Dakota	0.0

District of Columbia**   NA

Source: CQ Press using data from U.S. Environmental Protection Agency
    "National Priorities List (NPL) Sites in the United States" (http://www.epa.gov/superfund/sites/npl/)
*As of November 29, 2010. Includes final and proposed General Superfund and Federal Facilities Sites. National rate excludes
sites and square miles in Puerto Rico, Guam and the Virgin Islands. Based on land and water area of states.
**The District of Columbia has one site in its 68 square miles.

Hazardous Waste Sites Deleted from the National Priorities List as of 2010

National Total = 347 Sites*

ALPHA ORDER

RANK	STATE	SITES	% of USA
42	Alabama	1	0.3%
30	Alaska	3	0.9%
30	Arizona	3	0.9%
13	Arkansas	7	2.0%
8	California	12	3.5%
30	Colorado	3	0.9%
30	Connecticut	3	0.9%
15	Delaware	6	1.7%
4	Florida	23	6.6%
19	Georgia	5	1.4%
42	Hawaii	1	0.3%
30	Idaho	3	0.9%
30	Illinois	3	0.9%
12	Indiana	9	2.6%
10	Iowa	10	2.9%
19	Kansas	5	1.4%
15	Kentucky	6	1.7%
8	Louisiana	12	3.5%
37	Maine	2	0.6%
23	Maryland	4	1.2%
23	Massachusetts	4	1.2%
6	Michigan	17	4.9%
5	Minnesota	21	6.1%
30	Mississippi	3	0.9%
19	Missouri	5	1.4%
48	Montana	0	0.0%
42	Nebraska	1	0.3%
48	Nevada	0	0.0%
48	New Hampshire	0	0.0%
1	New Jersey	30	8.6%
23	New Mexico	4	1.2%
3	New York	26	7.5%
42	North Carolina	1	0.3%
37	North Dakota	2	0.6%
13	Ohio	7	2.0%
19	Oklahoma	5	1.4%
23	Oregon	4	1.2%
2	Pennsylvania	28	8.1%
42	Rhode Island	1	0.3%
23	South Carolina	4	1.2%
37	South Dakota	2	0.6%
15	Tennessee	6	1.7%
10	Texas	10	2.9%
23	Utah	4	1.2%
37	Vermont	2	0.6%
23	Virginia	4	1.2%
6	Washington	17	4.9%
37	West Virginia	2	0.6%
15	Wisconsin	6	1.7%
42	Wyoming	1	0.3%

RANK ORDER

RANK	STATE	SITES	% of USA
1	New Jersey	30	8.6%
2	Pennsylvania	28	8.1%
3	New York	26	7.5%
4	Florida	23	6.6%
5	Minnesota	21	6.1%
6	Michigan	17	4.9%
6	Washington	17	4.9%
8	California	12	3.5%
8	Louisiana	12	3.5%
10	Iowa	10	2.9%
10	Texas	10	2.9%
12	Indiana	9	2.6%
13	Arkansas	7	2.0%
13	Ohio	7	2.0%
15	Delaware	6	1.7%
15	Kentucky	6	1.7%
15	Tennessee	6	1.7%
15	Wisconsin	6	1.7%
19	Georgia	5	1.4%
19	Kansas	5	1.4%
19	Missouri	5	1.4%
19	Oklahoma	5	1.4%
23	Maryland	4	1.2%
23	Massachusetts	4	1.2%
23	New Mexico	4	1.2%
23	Oregon	4	1.2%
23	South Carolina	4	1.2%
23	Utah	4	1.2%
23	Virginia	4	1.2%
30	Alaska	3	0.9%
30	Arizona	3	0.9%
30	Colorado	3	0.9%
30	Connecticut	3	0.9%
30	Idaho	3	0.9%
30	Illinois	3	0.9%
30	Mississippi	3	0.9%
37	Maine	2	0.6%
37	North Dakota	2	0.6%
37	South Dakota	2	0.6%
37	Vermont	2	0.6%
37	West Virginia	2	0.6%
42	Alabama	1	0.3%
42	Hawaii	1	0.3%
42	Nebraska	1	0.3%
42	North Carolina	1	0.3%
42	Rhode Island	1	0.3%
42	Wyoming	1	0.3%
48	Montana	0	0.0%
48	Nevada	0	0.0%
48	New Hampshire	0	0.0%
	District of Columbia	0	0.0%

Source: U.S. Environmental Protection Agency
"National Priorities List (NPL) Sites in the United States" (http://www.epa.gov/superfund/sites/npl/)
*Cumulative total as of November 29, 2010. National total includes five sites in Puerto Rico and four in other U.S. territories.

VIII. Geography

Total Area of States in Square Miles in 2009

National Total = 3,795,951 Square Miles*

ALPHA ORDER

RANK	STATE	MILES	% of USA
30	Alabama	52,420	1.4%
1	Alaska	664,988	17.5%
6	Arizona	113,990	3.0%
29	Arkansas	53,178	1.4%
3	California	163,694	4.3%
8	Colorado	104,094	2.7%
48	Connecticut	5,544	0.1%
49	Delaware	2,489	0.1%
22	Florida	65,758	1.7%
24	Georgia	59,425	1.6%
43	Hawaii	10,926	0.3%
14	Idaho	83,568	2.2%
25	Illinois	57,916	1.5%
38	Indiana	36,417	1.0%
26	Iowa	56,273	1.5%
15	Kansas	82,278	2.2%
37	Kentucky	40,411	1.1%
31	Louisiana	51,988	1.4%
39	Maine	35,384	0.9%
42	Maryland	12,406	0.3%
44	Massachusetts	10,554	0.3%
11	Michigan	96,713	2.5%
12	Minnesota	86,935	2.3%
32	Mississippi	48,432	1.3%
21	Missouri	69,702	1.8%
4	Montana	147,039	3.9%
16	Nebraska	77,349	2.0%
7	Nevada	110,572	2.9%
46	New Hampshire	9,348	0.2%
47	New Jersey	8,723	0.2%
5	New Mexico	121,590	3.2%
27	New York	54,555	1.4%
28	North Carolina	53,819	1.4%
19	North Dakota	70,698	1.9%
34	Ohio	44,825	1.2%
20	Oklahoma	69,899	1.8%
9	Oregon	98,379	2.6%
33	Pennsylvania	46,055	1.2%
50	Rhode Island	1,545	0.0%
40	South Carolina	32,021	0.8%
17	South Dakota	77,116	2.0%
36	Tennessee	42,144	1.1%
2	Texas	268,597	7.1%
13	Utah	84,897	2.2%
45	Vermont	9,616	0.3%
35	Virginia	42,775	1.1%
18	Washington	71,298	1.9%
41	West Virginia	24,230	0.6%
23	Wisconsin	65,496	1.7%
10	Wyoming	97,812	2.6%

RANK ORDER

RANK	STATE	MILES	% of USA
1	Alaska	664,988	17.5%
2	Texas	268,597	7.1%
3	California	163,694	4.3%
4	Montana	147,039	3.9%
5	New Mexico	121,590	3.2%
6	Arizona	113,990	3.0%
7	Nevada	110,572	2.9%
8	Colorado	104,094	2.7%
9	Oregon	98,379	2.6%
10	Wyoming	97,812	2.6%
11	Michigan	96,713	2.5%
12	Minnesota	86,935	2.3%
13	Utah	84,897	2.2%
14	Idaho	83,568	2.2%
15	Kansas	82,278	2.2%
16	Nebraska	77,349	2.0%
17	South Dakota	77,116	2.0%
18	Washington	71,298	1.9%
19	North Dakota	70,698	1.9%
20	Oklahoma	69,899	1.8%
21	Missouri	69,702	1.8%
22	Florida	65,758	1.7%
23	Wisconsin	65,496	1.7%
24	Georgia	59,425	1.6%
25	Illinois	57,916	1.5%
26	Iowa	56,273	1.5%
27	New York	54,555	1.4%
28	North Carolina	53,819	1.4%
29	Arkansas	53,178	1.4%
30	Alabama	52,420	1.4%
31	Louisiana	51,988	1.4%
32	Mississippi	48,432	1.3%
33	Pennsylvania	46,055	1.2%
34	Ohio	44,825	1.2%
35	Virginia	42,775	1.1%
36	Tennessee	42,144	1.1%
37	Kentucky	40,411	1.1%
38	Indiana	36,417	1.0%
39	Maine	35,384	0.9%
40	South Carolina	32,021	0.8%
41	West Virginia	24,230	0.6%
42	Maryland	12,406	0.3%
43	Hawaii	10,926	0.3%
44	Massachusetts	10,554	0.3%
45	Vermont	9,616	0.3%
46	New Hampshire	9,348	0.2%
47	New Jersey	8,723	0.2%
48	Connecticut	5,544	0.1%
49	Delaware	2,489	0.1%
50	Rhode Island	1,545	0.0%
	District of Columbia	68	0.0%

Source: U.S. Bureau of the Census
"Statistical Abstract 2010" (http://www.census.gov/compendia/statab/)
*Total of land and water area. Revised figures.

Land Area of States in Square Miles in 2009

National Total = 3,531,822 Square Miles of Land Area*

ALPHA ORDER

RANK	STATE	MILES	% of USA
28	Alabama	50,644	1.4%
1	Alaska	570,665	16.2%
6	Arizona	113,595	3.2%
27	Arkansas	52,030	1.5%
3	California	155,766	4.4%
8	Colorado	103,641	2.9%
48	Connecticut	4,840	0.1%
49	Delaware	1,949	0.1%
26	Florida	53,603	1.5%
21	Georgia	57,501	1.6%
47	Hawaii	6,428	0.2%
11	Idaho	82,643	2.3%
24	Illinois	55,518	1.6%
38	Indiana	35,823	1.0%
23	Iowa	55,858	1.6%
13	Kansas	81,762	2.3%
37	Kentucky	39,492	1.1%
33	Louisiana	43,199	1.2%
39	Maine	30,841	0.9%
42	Maryland	9,705	0.3%
45	Massachusetts	7,801	0.2%
22	Michigan	56,528	1.6%
14	Minnesota	79,607	2.3%
31	Mississippi	46,920	1.3%
18	Missouri	68,716	1.9%
4	Montana	145,541	4.1%
15	Nebraska	76,825	2.2%
7	Nevada	109,780	3.1%
44	New Hampshire	8,952	0.3%
46	New Jersey	7,354	0.2%
5	New Mexico	121,297	3.4%
30	New York	47,126	1.3%
29	North Carolina	48,619	1.4%
17	North Dakota	69,001	2.0%
35	Ohio	40,858	1.2%
19	Oklahoma	68,603	1.9%
10	Oregon	95,985	2.7%
32	Pennsylvania	44,739	1.3%
50	Rhode Island	1,034	0.0%
40	South Carolina	30,070	0.9%
16	South Dakota	75,811	2.1%
34	Tennessee	41,235	1.2%
2	Texas	261,226	7.4%
12	Utah	82,191	2.3%
43	Vermont	9,217	0.3%
36	Virginia	39,493	1.1%
20	Washington	66,449	1.9%
41	West Virginia	24,038	0.7%
25	Wisconsin	54,154	1.5%
9	Wyoming	97,088	2.7%

RANK ORDER

RANK	STATE	MILES	% of USA
1	Alaska	570,665	16.2%
2	Texas	261,226	7.4%
3	California	155,766	4.4%
4	Montana	145,541	4.1%
5	New Mexico	121,297	3.4%
6	Arizona	113,595	3.2%
7	Nevada	109,780	3.1%
8	Colorado	103,641	2.9%
9	Wyoming	97,088	2.7%
10	Oregon	95,985	2.7%
11	Idaho	82,643	2.3%
12	Utah	82,191	2.3%
13	Kansas	81,762	2.3%
14	Minnesota	79,607	2.3%
15	Nebraska	76,825	2.2%
16	South Dakota	75,811	2.1%
17	North Dakota	69,001	2.0%
18	Missouri	68,716	1.9%
19	Oklahoma	68,603	1.9%
20	Washington	66,449	1.9%
21	Georgia	57,501	1.6%
22	Michigan	56,528	1.6%
23	Iowa	55,858	1.6%
24	Illinois	55,518	1.6%
25	Wisconsin	54,154	1.5%
26	Florida	53,603	1.5%
27	Arkansas	52,030	1.5%
28	Alabama	50,644	1.4%
29	North Carolina	48,619	1.4%
30	New York	47,126	1.3%
31	Mississippi	46,920	1.3%
32	Pennsylvania	44,739	1.3%
33	Louisiana	43,199	1.2%
34	Tennessee	41,235	1.2%
35	Ohio	40,858	1.2%
36	Virginia	39,493	1.1%
37	Kentucky	39,492	1.1%
38	Indiana	35,823	1.0%
39	Maine	30,841	0.9%
40	South Carolina	30,070	0.9%
41	West Virginia	24,038	0.7%
42	Maryland	9,705	0.3%
43	Vermont	9,217	0.3%
44	New Hampshire	8,952	0.3%
45	Massachusetts	7,801	0.2%
46	New Jersey	7,354	0.2%
47	Hawaii	6,428	0.2%
48	Connecticut	4,840	0.1%
49	Delaware	1,949	0.1%
50	Rhode Island	1,034	0.0%
	District of Columbia	61	0.0%

Source: U.S. Bureau of the Census
"Statistical Abstract 2010" (http://www.census.gov/compendia/statab/)
*Includes dry land temporarily or partially covered by water, such as marshland, swamps, etc.; streams and canals under
one-eighth mile wide; and lakes, reservoirs, and ponds under 40 acres. Revised figures.

Water Area of States in Square Miles in 2009

National Total = 264,129 Square Miles of Water*

ALPHA ORDER

RANK	STATE	MILES	% of USA
23	Alabama	1,776	0.7%
1	Alaska	94,323	35.7%
47	Arizona	396	0.1%
31	Arkansas	1,149	0.4%
6	California	7,928	3.0%
44	Colorado	454	0.2%
38	Connecticut	703	0.3%
40	Delaware	539	0.2%
3	Florida	12,154	4.6%
22	Georgia	1,924	0.7%
13	Hawaii	4,499	1.7%
33	Idaho	926	0.4%
19	Illinois	2,398	0.9%
39	Indiana	594	0.2%
45	Iowa	415	0.2%
42	Kansas	516	0.2%
34	Kentucky	919	0.3%
5	Louisiana	8,789	3.3%
12	Maine	4,543	1.7%
18	Maryland	2,700	1.0%
16	Massachusetts	2,754	1.0%
2	Michigan	40,185	15.2%
9	Minnesota	7,328	2.8%
25	Mississippi	1,512	0.6%
32	Missouri	987	0.4%
26	Montana	1,498	0.6%
41	Nebraska	524	0.2%
36	Nevada	792	0.3%
47	New Hampshire	396	0.1%
27	New Jersey	1,369	0.5%
49	New Mexico	293	0.1%
7	New York	7,429	2.8%
10	North Carolina	5,200	2.0%
24	North Dakota	1,697	0.6%
14	Ohio	3,967	1.5%
30	Oklahoma	1,296	0.5%
20	Oregon	2,394	0.9%
28	Pennsylvania	1,316	0.5%
43	Rhode Island	511	0.2%
21	South Carolina	1,951	0.7%
29	South Dakota	1,305	0.5%
35	Tennessee	910	0.3%
8	Texas	7,371	2.8%
17	Utah	2,706	1.0%
46	Vermont	400	0.2%
15	Virginia	3,282	1.2%
11	Washington	4,849	1.8%
50	West Virginia	192	0.1%
4	Wisconsin	11,342	4.3%
37	Wyoming	724	0.3%

RANK ORDER

RANK	STATE	MILES	% of USA
1	Alaska	94,323	35.7%
2	Michigan	40,185	15.2%
3	Florida	12,154	4.6%
4	Wisconsin	11,342	4.3%
5	Louisiana	8,789	3.3%
6	California	7,928	3.0%
7	New York	7,429	2.8%
8	Texas	7,371	2.8%
9	Minnesota	7,328	2.8%
10	North Carolina	5,200	2.0%
11	Washington	4,849	1.8%
12	Maine	4,543	1.7%
13	Hawaii	4,499	1.7%
14	Ohio	3,967	1.5%
15	Virginia	3,282	1.2%
16	Massachusetts	2,754	1.0%
17	Utah	2,706	1.0%
18	Maryland	2,700	1.0%
19	Illinois	2,398	0.9%
20	Oregon	2,394	0.9%
21	South Carolina	1,951	0.7%
22	Georgia	1,924	0.7%
23	Alabama	1,776	0.7%
24	North Dakota	1,697	0.6%
25	Mississippi	1,512	0.6%
26	Montana	1,498	0.6%
27	New Jersey	1,369	0.5%
28	Pennsylvania	1,316	0.5%
29	South Dakota	1,305	0.5%
30	Oklahoma	1,296	0.5%
31	Arkansas	1,149	0.4%
32	Missouri	987	0.4%
33	Idaho	926	0.4%
34	Kentucky	919	0.3%
35	Tennessee	910	0.3%
36	Nevada	792	0.3%
37	Wyoming	724	0.3%
38	Connecticut	703	0.3%
39	Indiana	594	0.2%
40	Delaware	539	0.2%
41	Nebraska	524	0.2%
42	Kansas	516	0.2%
43	Rhode Island	511	0.2%
44	Colorado	454	0.2%
45	Iowa	415	0.2%
46	Vermont	400	0.2%
47	Arizona	396	0.1%
47	New Hampshire	396	0.1%
49	New Mexico	293	0.1%
50	West Virginia	192	0.1%
	District of Columbia	7	0.0%

Source: U.S. Bureau of the Census
"Statistical Abstract 2010" (http://www.census.gov/compendia/statab/)
*Includes permanent inland water surface, such as lakes, reservoirs, and ponds having an area of 40 acres or more, canals one-eighth mile or more in width; coastal waters behind or sheltered by headlands or islands separated by less than 1 nautical mile of water, and islands under 40 acres in area. Excludes areas of oceans, bays, etc., lying within U.S. jurisdiction but not defined as inland water. Revised figures.

Highest Point of Elevation in Feet

National High Point = 20,320 Feet Above Sea Level (Mt. McKinley, Alaska)

ALPHA ORDER

RANK	STATE	HIGHEST POINT
35	Alabama	2,407
1	Alaska	20,320
12	Arizona	12,633
34	Arkansas	2,753
2	California	14,494
3	Colorado	14,433
36	Connecticut	2,380
49	Delaware	448
50	Florida	345
25	Georgia	4,784
6	Hawaii	13,796
11	Idaho	12,662
45	Illinois	1,235
44	Indiana	1,257
42	Iowa	1,670
28	Kansas	4,039
27	Kentucky	4,145
48	Louisiana	535
22	Maine	5,268
32	Maryland	3,360
31	Massachusetts	3,491
38	Michigan	1,979
37	Minnesota	2,301
47	Mississippi	806
41	Missouri	1,772
10	Montana	12,799
20	Nebraska	5,424
9	Nevada	13,140
18	New Hampshire	6,288
40	New Jersey	1,803
8	New Mexico	13,161
21	New York	5,344
16	North Carolina	6,684
30	North Dakota	3,506
43	Ohio	1,550
23	Oklahoma	4,973
13	Oregon	11,239
33	Pennsylvania	3,213
46	Rhode Island	812
29	South Carolina	3,560
15	South Dakota	7,242
17	Tennessee	6,643
14	Texas	8,749
7	Utah	13,528
26	Vermont	4,393
19	Virginia	5,729
4	Washington	14,411
24	West Virginia	4,863
39	Wisconsin	1,951
5	Wyoming	13,804

RANK ORDER

RANK	STATE	HIGHEST POINT
1	Alaska	20,320
2	California	14,494
3	Colorado	14,433
4	Washington	14,411
5	Wyoming	13,804
6	Hawaii	13,796
7	Utah	13,528
8	New Mexico	13,161
9	Nevada	13,140
10	Montana	12,799
11	Idaho	12,662
12	Arizona	12,633
13	Oregon	11,239
14	Texas	8,749
15	South Dakota	7,242
16	North Carolina	6,684
17	Tennessee	6,643
18	New Hampshire	6,288
19	Virginia	5,729
20	Nebraska	5,424
21	New York	5,344
22	Maine	5,268
23	Oklahoma	4,973
24	West Virginia	4,863
25	Georgia	4,784
26	Vermont	4,393
27	Kentucky	4,145
28	Kansas	4,039
29	South Carolina	3,560
30	North Dakota	3,506
31	Massachusetts	3,491
32	Maryland	3,360
33	Pennsylvania	3,213
34	Arkansas	2,753
35	Alabama	2,407
36	Connecticut	2,380
37	Minnesota	2,301
38	Michigan	1,979
39	Wisconsin	1,951
40	New Jersey	1,803
41	Missouri	1,772
42	Iowa	1,670
43	Ohio	1,550
44	Indiana	1,257
45	Illinois	1,235
46	Rhode Island	812
47	Mississippi	806
48	Louisiana	535
49	Delaware	448
50	Florida	345
	District of Columbia	410

Source: U.S. Department of Interior, U.S. Geological Survey
"Elevations and Distances in the United States" (http://erg.usgs.gov/isb/pubs/booklets/elvadist/elvadist.html)

Lowest Point of Elevation in Feet

National Low Point = 282 Feet Below Sea Level (Death Valley, California)*

ALPHA ORDER

RANK	STATE	LOWEST POINT
3	Alabama	0
3	Alaska	0
26	Arizona	70
25	Arkansas	55
1	California	(282)
50	Colorado	3,315
3	Connecticut	0
3	Delaware	0
3	Florida	0
3	Georgia	0
3	Hawaii	0
42	Idaho	710
32	Illinois	279
34	Indiana	320
37	Iowa	480
41	Kansas	679
31	Kentucky	257
2	Louisiana	(8)
3	Maine	0
3	Maryland	0
3	Massachusetts	0
38	Michigan	571
40	Minnesota	601
3	Mississippi	0
29	Missouri	230
46	Montana	1,800
44	Nebraska	840
36	Nevada	479
3	New Hampshire	0
3	New Jersey	0
48	New Mexico	2,842
3	New York	0
3	North Carolina	0
43	North Dakota	750
35	Ohio	455
33	Oklahoma	289
3	Oregon	0
3	Pennsylvania	0
3	Rhode Island	0
3	South Carolina	0
45	South Dakota	966
28	Tennessee	178
3	Texas	0
47	Utah	2,000
27	Vermont	95
3	Virginia	0
3	Washington	0
30	West Virginia	240
39	Wisconsin	579
49	Wyoming	3,099

RANK ORDER

RANK	STATE	LOWEST POINT
1	California	(282)
2	Louisiana	(8)
3	Alabama*	0
3	Alaska	0
3	Connecticut	0
3	Delaware	0
3	Florida	0
3	Georgia	0
3	Hawaii	0
3	Maine	0
3	Maryland	0
3	Massachusetts	0
3	Mississippi	0
3	New Hampshire	0
3	New Jersey	0
3	New York	0
3	North Carolina	0
3	Oregon	0
3	Pennsylvania	0
3	Rhode Island	0
3	South Carolina	0
3	Texas	0
3	Virginia	0
3	Washington	0
25	Arkansas	55
26	Arizona	70
27	Vermont	95
28	Tennessee	178
29	Missouri	230
30	West Virginia	240
31	Kentucky	257
32	Illinois	279
33	Oklahoma	289
34	Indiana	320
35	Ohio	455
36	Nevada	479
37	Iowa	480
38	Michigan	571
39	Wisconsin	579
40	Minnesota	601
41	Kansas	679
42	Idaho	710
43	North Dakota	750
44	Nebraska	840
45	South Dakota	966
46	Montana	1,800
47	Utah	2,000
48	New Mexico	2,842
49	Wyoming	3,099
50	Colorado	3,315

District of Columbia	1

Source: U.S. Department of Interior, U.S. Geological Survey

"Elevations and Distances in the United States" (http://erg.usgs.gov/isb/pubs/booklets/elvadist/elvadist.html)

*States with "0" have sea level as lowest point.

Approximate Mean Elevation in Feet

Approximate National Mean Elevation = 2,500 Feet Above Sea Level

ALPHA ORDER

RANK	STATE	MEAN ELEVATION
40	Alabama	500
15	Alaska	1,900
7	Arizona	4,100
36	Arkansas	650
11	California	2,900
1	Colorado	6,800
40	Connecticut	500
50	Delaware	60
48	Florida	100
37	Georgia	600
10	Hawaii	3,030
6	Idaho	5,000
37	Illinois	600
34	Indiana	700
22	Iowa	1,100
14	Kansas	2,000
33	Kentucky	750
48	Louisiana	100
37	Maine	600
43	Maryland	350
40	Massachusetts	500
29	Michigan	900
21	Minnesota	1,200
45	Mississippi	300
32	Missouri	800
8	Montana	3,400
12	Nebraska	2,600
5	Nevada	5,500
25	New Hampshire	1,000
46	New Jersey	250
4	New Mexico	5,700
25	New York	1,000
34	North Carolina	700
15	North Dakota	1,900
31	Ohio	850
20	Oklahoma	1,300
9	Oregon	3,300
22	Pennsylvania	1,100
47	Rhode Island	200
43	South Carolina	350
13	South Dakota	2,200
29	Tennessee	900
17	Texas	1,700
3	Utah	6,100
25	Vermont	1,000
28	Virginia	950
17	Washington	1,700
19	West Virginia	1,500
24	Wisconsin	1,050
2	Wyoming	6,700

RANK ORDER

RANK	STATE	MEAN ELEVATION
1	Colorado	6,800
2	Wyoming	6,700
3	Utah	6,100
4	New Mexico	5,700
5	Nevada	5,500
6	Idaho	5,000
7	Arizona	4,100
8	Montana	3,400
9	Oregon	3,300
10	Hawaii	3,030
11	California	2,900
12	Nebraska	2,600
13	South Dakota	2,200
14	Kansas	2,000
15	Alaska	1,900
15	North Dakota	1,900
17	Texas	1,700
17	Washington	1,700
19	West Virginia	1,500
20	Oklahoma	1,300
21	Minnesota	1,200
22	Iowa	1,100
22	Pennsylvania	1,100
24	Wisconsin	1,050
25	New Hampshire	1,000
25	New York	1,000
25	Vermont	1,000
28	Virginia	950
29	Michigan	900
29	Tennessee	900
31	Ohio	850
32	Missouri	800
33	Kentucky	750
34	Indiana	700
34	North Carolina	700
36	Arkansas	650
37	Georgia	600
37	Illinois	600
37	Maine	600
40	Alabama	500
40	Connecticut	500
40	Massachusetts	500
43	Maryland	350
43	South Carolina	350
45	Mississippi	300
46	New Jersey	250
47	Rhode Island	200
48	Florida	100
48	Louisiana	100
50	Delaware	60

District of Columbia	150

Source: U.S. Department of Interior, U.S. Geological Survey
"Elevations and Distances in the United States" (http://erg.usgs.gov/isb/pubs/booklets/elvadist/elvadist.html)

Normal Daily Mean Temperature*

ALPHA ORDER				RANK ORDER		
RANK	STATE	MEAN TEMPERATURE		RANK	STATE	MEAN TEMPERATURE
5	Alabama	66.8		1	Hawaii	77.5
50	Alaska	41.5		2	Arizona	74.2
2	Arizona	74.2		3	Florida**	72.4
9	Arkansas	62.1		4	Louisiana	68.8
11	California**	61.5		5	Alabama	66.8
35	Colorado	50.1		6	Texas**	66.3
34	Connecticut	50.2		7	Mississippi	64.1
22	Delaware	54.4		8	South Carolina	63.6
3	Florida**	72.4		9	Arkansas	62.1
9	Georgia	62.1		9	Georgia	62.1
1	Hawaii	77.5		11	California**	61.5
29	Idaho	51.9		12	Tennessee**	60.6
36	Illinois**	50.0		13	North Carolina**	60.5
26	Indiana	52.5		14	Oklahoma	60.1
36	Iowa	50.0		15	Virginia**	58.6
18	Kansas	56.4		16	Kentucky	56.9
16	Kentucky	56.9		17	New Mexico	56.8
4	Louisiana	68.8		18	Kansas	56.4
42	Maine	45.7		19	Missouri**	55.3
20	Maryland	54.6		20	Maryland	54.6
30	Massachusetts	51.6		21	West Virginia	54.5
46	Michigan**	44.9		22	Delaware	54.4
48	Minnesota**	42.3		23	New Jersey	53.5
7	Mississippi	64.1		23	Oregon	53.5
19	Missouri**	55.3		25	Pennsylvania**	53.2
47	Montana	43.7		26	Indiana	52.5
33	Nebraska	50.7		27	Ohio**	52.2
31	Nevada	51.3		28	Utah	52.0
41	New Hampshire	45.9		29	Idaho	51.9
23	New Jersey	53.5		30	Massachusetts	51.6
17	New Mexico	56.8		31	Nevada	51.3
36	New York**	50.0		32	Rhode Island	51.1
13	North Carolina**	60.5		33	Nebraska	50.7
48	North Dakota	42.3		34	Connecticut	50.2
27	Ohio**	52.2		35	Colorado	50.1
14	Oklahoma	60.1		36	Illinois**	50.0
23	Oregon	53.5		36	Iowa	50.0
25	Pennsylvania**	53.2		36	New York**	50.0
32	Rhode Island	51.1		39	Washington**	49.8
8	South Carolina	63.6		40	Wisconsin	47.5
44	South Dakota	45.1		41	New Hampshire	45.9
12	Tennessee**	60.6		42	Maine	45.7
6	Texas**	66.3		43	Vermont	45.2
28	Utah	52.0		44	South Dakota	45.1
43	Vermont	45.2		45	Wyoming	45.0
15	Virginia**	58.6		46	Michigan**	44.9
39	Washington**	49.8		47	Montana	43.7
21	West Virginia	54.5		48	Minnesota**	42.3
40	Wisconsin	47.5		48	North Dakota	42.3
45	Wyoming	45.0		50	Alaska	41.5
					District of Columbia	57.5

Source: U.S. Department of Commerce, National Oceanic and Atmospheric Administration
    "Climatography of the United States" (No. 81) (www.ncdc.noaa.gov/oa/climate/online/ccd/nrmavg.txt)
*Based on standard 30 year period, 1971-2000.
**Temperatures from multiple reporting cities within one state were averaged to determine a state's mean temperature.

Percent of Days That Are Sunny*

RANK	STATE	PERCENT OF DAYS SUNNY
26	Alabama	58
50	Alaska	38
1	Arizona	85
8	Arkansas	66
4	California	72
4	Colorado	72
35	Connecticut**	56
37	Delaware**	55
7	Florida	67
16	Georgia	63
11	Hawaii	65
14	Idaho	64
31	Illinois	57
26	Indiana	58
22	Iowa	60
8	Kansas	66
31	Kentucky	57
14	Louisiana	64
31	Maine**	57
31	Maryland	57
37	Massachusetts	55
44	Michigan	49
37	Minnesota	55
16	Mississippi	63
26	Missouri	58
24	Montana	59
16	Nebraska	63
2	Nevada	76
48	New Hampshire	44
35	New Jersey**	56
3	New Mexico	75
42	New York	51
22	North Carolina	60
24	North Dakota	59
42	Ohio	51
11	Oklahoma	65
46	Oregon**	48
41	Pennsylvania	53
26	Rhode Island**	58
20	South Carolina	62
16	South Dakota	63
26	Tennessee	58
11	Texas	65
6	Utah	68
44	Vermont**	49
21	Virginia	61
47	Washington	45
49	West Virginia**	40
40	Wisconsin	54
8	Wyoming	66

RANK	STATE	PERCENT OF DAYS SUNNY
1	Arizona	85
2	Nevada	76
3	New Mexico	75
4	California	72
4	Colorado	72
6	Utah	68
7	Florida	67
8	Arkansas	66
8	Kansas	66
8	Wyoming	66
11	Hawaii	65
11	Oklahoma	65
11	Texas	65
14	Idaho	64
14	Louisiana	64
16	Georgia	63
16	Mississippi	63
16	Nebraska	63
16	South Dakota	63
20	South Carolina	62
21	Virginia	61
22	Iowa	60
22	North Carolina	60
24	Montana	59
24	North Dakota	59
26	Alabama	58
26	Indiana	58
26	Missouri	58
26	Rhode Island**	58
26	Tennessee	58
31	Illinois	57
31	Kentucky	57
31	Maine**	57
31	Maryland	57
35	Connecticut**	56
35	New Jersey**	56
37	Delaware**	55
37	Massachusetts	55
37	Minnesota	55
40	Wisconsin	54
41	Pennsylvania	53
42	New York	51
42	Ohio	51
44	Michigan	49
44	Vermont**	49
46	Oregon**	48
47	Washington	45
48	New Hampshire	44
49	West Virginia**	40
50	Alaska	38

District of Columbia** 56

Source: CQ Press using data from U.S. Department of Commerce, National Oceanic and Atmospheric Administration
    "Comparative Climatic Data" (annual) (http://www.ncdc.noaa.gov/oa/climate/online/ccd/pctpos.txt)
*Averages over various years.
**Percentages from these states are from a single location. All other states are from two or more reporting cities within each state, which were averaged to determine each state's average percentage of sunny days.

Average Wind Speed (MPH)*

ALPHA ORDER

RANK	STATE	MILES PER HOUR
29	Alabama	8.8
39	Alaska	8.2
49	Arizona	6.2
43	Arkansas	7.7
39	California**	8.2
31	Colorado	8.7
36	Connecticut	8.4
24	Delaware	9.0
35	Florida**	8.5
22	Georgia	9.1
7	Hawaii	11.2
31	Idaho	8.7
14	Illinois**	10.1
18	Indiana	9.6
10	Iowa	10.7
4	Kansas	12.2
38	Kentucky	8.3
39	Louisiana	8.2
31	Maine	8.7
31	Maryland	8.7
3	Massachusetts	12.3
17	Michigan**	9.7
9	Minnesota**	10.8
45	Mississippi	6.9
14	Missouri**	10.1
2	Montana	12.5
11	Nebraska	10.5
48	Nevada	6.6
47	New Hampshire	6.7
16	New Jersey	9.8
27	New Mexico	8.9
19	New York**	9.3
44	North Carolina**	7.5
13	North Dakota	10.2
19	Ohio**	9.3
4	Oklahoma	12.2
42	Oregon	7.9
19	Pennsylvania**	9.3
12	Rhode Island	10.4
46	South Carolina	6.8
8	South Dakota	11.0
36	Tennessee**	8.4
24	Texas**	9.0
29	Utah	8.8
24	Vermont	9.0
22	Virginia**	9.1
27	Washington**	8.9
50	West Virginia	5.8
6	Wisconsin	11.5
1	Wyoming	12.9

RANK ORDER

RANK	STATE	MILES PER HOUR
1	Wyoming	12.9
2	Montana	12.5
3	Massachusetts	12.3
4	Kansas	12.2
4	Oklahoma	12.2
6	Wisconsin	11.5
7	Hawaii	11.2
8	South Dakota	11.0
9	Minnesota**	10.8
10	Iowa	10.7
11	Nebraska	10.5
12	Rhode Island	10.4
13	North Dakota	10.2
14	Illinois**	10.1
14	Missouri**	10.1
16	New Jersey	9.8
17	Michigan**	9.7
18	Indiana	9.6
19	New York**	9.3
19	Ohio**	9.3
19	Pennsylvania**	9.3
22	Georgia	9.1
22	Virginia**	9.1
24	Delaware	9.0
24	Texas**	9.0
24	Vermont	9.0
27	New Mexico	8.9
27	Washington**	8.9
29	Alabama	8.8
29	Utah	8.8
31	Colorado	8.7
31	Idaho	8.7
31	Maine	8.7
31	Maryland	8.7
35	Florida**	8.5
36	Connecticut	8.4
36	Tennessee**	8.4
38	Kentucky	8.3
39	Alaska	8.2
39	California**	8.2
39	Louisiana	8.2
42	Oregon	7.9
43	Arkansas	7.7
44	North Carolina**	7.5
45	Mississippi	6.9
46	South Carolina	6.8
47	New Hampshire	6.7
48	Nevada	6.6
49	Arizona	6.2
50	West Virginia	5.8

| | District of Columbia | 9.4 |

Source: U.S. Department of Commerce, National Oceanic and Atmospheric Administration
"Comparative Climatic Data" (annual) (http://www.ncdc.noaa.gov/oa/climate/online/ccd/wndspd.txt)
*Averages over various years.
**Wind speeds from multiple reporting cities within one state were averaged to determine a state's average wind speed.

Tornadoes in 2010

National Total = 1,543 Tornadoes*

ALPHA ORDER

RANK	STATE	TORNADOES	% of USA
14	Alabama	43	2.8%
45	Alaska	0	0.0%
27	Arizona	17	1.1%
15	Arkansas	39	2.5%
30	California	11	0.7%
9	Colorado	66	4.3%
34	Connecticut	6	0.4%
45	Delaware	0	0.0%
25	Florida	22	1.4%
30	Georgia	11	0.7%
45	Hawaii	0	0.0%
38	Idaho	3	0.2%
10	Illinois	65	4.2%
22	Indiana	29	1.9%
11	Iowa	52	3.4%
4	Kansas	94	6.1%
23	Kentucky	27	1.7%
18	Louisiana	34	2.2%
34	Maine	6	0.4%
36	Maryland	5	0.3%
45	Massachusetts	0	0.0%
21	Michigan	30	1.9%
1	Minnesota	145	9.4%
3	Mississippi	100	6.5%
5	Missouri	80	5.2%
19	Montana	33	2.1%
12	Nebraska	46	3.0%
45	Nevada	0	0.0%
41	New Hampshire	1	0.1%
41	New Jersey	1	0.1%
30	New Mexico	11	0.7%
28	New York	16	1.0%
20	North Carolina	32	2.1%
7	North Dakota	68	4.4%
13	Ohio	45	2.9%
6	Oklahoma	74	4.8%
41	Oregon	1	0.1%
29	Pennsylvania	15	1.0%
45	Rhode Island	0	0.0%
25	South Carolina	22	1.4%
16	South Dakota	37	2.4%
17	Tennessee	36	2.3%
2	Texas	105	6.8%
40	Utah	2	0.1%
41	Vermont	1	0.1%
33	Virginia	10	0.6%
38	Washington	3	0.2%
36	West Virginia	5	0.3%
7	Wisconsin	68	4.4%
24	Wyoming	26	1.7%

RANK ORDER

RANK	STATE	TORNADOES	% of USA
1	Minnesota	145	9.4%
2	Texas	105	6.8%
3	Mississippi	100	6.5%
4	Kansas	94	6.1%
5	Missouri	80	5.2%
6	Oklahoma	74	4.8%
7	North Dakota	68	4.4%
7	Wisconsin	68	4.4%
9	Colorado	66	4.3%
10	Illinois	65	4.2%
11	Iowa	52	3.4%
12	Nebraska	46	3.0%
13	Ohio	45	2.9%
14	Alabama	43	2.8%
15	Arkansas	39	2.5%
16	South Dakota	37	2.4%
17	Tennessee	36	2.3%
18	Louisiana	34	2.2%
19	Montana	33	2.1%
20	North Carolina	32	2.1%
21	Michigan	30	1.9%
22	Indiana	29	1.9%
23	Kentucky	27	1.7%
24	Wyoming	26	1.7%
25	Florida	22	1.4%
25	South Carolina	22	1.4%
27	Arizona	17	1.1%
28	New York	16	1.0%
29	Pennsylvania	15	1.0%
30	California	11	0.7%
30	Georgia	11	0.7%
30	New Mexico	11	0.7%
33	Virginia	10	0.6%
34	Connecticut	6	0.4%
34	Maine	6	0.4%
36	Maryland	5	0.3%
36	West Virginia	5	0.3%
38	Idaho	3	0.2%
38	Washington	3	0.2%
40	Utah	2	0.1%
41	New Hampshire	1	0.1%
41	New Jersey	1	0.1%
41	Oregon	1	0.1%
41	Vermont	1	0.1%
45	Alaska	0	0.0%
45	Delaware	0	0.0%
45	Hawaii	0	0.0%
45	Massachusetts	0	0.0%
45	Nevada	0	0.0%
45	Rhode Island	0	0.0%
	District of Columbia	0	0.0%

Source: National Weather Service, Storm Prediction Center
    "Annual Severe Weather Report Summary - 2010" (www.spc.ncep.noaa.gov/climo/online/monthly/2010_annual_summary.html)
*Preliminary figures. Tornadoes striking more than one state are counted in each state.

Hazardous Weather Fatalities in 2009

National Total = 324 Fatalities*

ALPHA ORDER

RANK	STATE	FATALITIES	% of USA
17	Alabama	6	1.9%
34	Alaska	2	0.6%
34	Arizona	2	0.6%
7	Arkansas	13	4.0%
4	California	17	5.2%
30	Colorado	3	0.9%
30	Connecticut	3	0.9%
45	Delaware	0	0.0%
1	Florida	35	10.8%
8	Georgia	12	3.7%
25	Hawaii	4	1.2%
30	Idaho	3	0.9%
2	Illinois	29	9.0%
38	Indiana	1	0.3%
38	Iowa	1	0.3%
14	Kansas	7	2.2%
13	Kentucky	8	2.5%
14	Louisiana	7	2.2%
38	Maine	1	0.3%
38	Maryland	1	0.3%
38	Massachusetts	1	0.3%
25	Michigan	4	1.2%
12	Minnesota	10	3.1%
19	Mississippi	5	1.5%
9	Missouri	11	3.4%
19	Montana	5	1.5%
38	Nebraska	1	0.3%
17	Nevada	6	1.9%
38	New Hampshire	1	0.3%
19	New Jersey	5	1.5%
19	New Mexico	5	1.5%
9	New York	11	3.4%
5	North Carolina	15	4.6%
45	North Dakota	0	0.0%
25	Ohio	4	1.2%
9	Oklahoma	11	3.4%
19	Oregon	5	1.5%
30	Pennsylvania	3	0.9%
45	Rhode Island	0	0.0%
19	South Carolina	5	1.5%
45	South Dakota	0	0.0%
5	Tennessee	15	4.6%
3	Texas	27	8.3%
45	Utah	0	0.0%
45	Vermont	0	0.0%
34	Virginia	2	0.6%
25	Washington	4	1.2%
34	West Virginia	2	0.6%
14	Wisconsin	7	2.2%
25	Wyoming	4	1.2%

RANK ORDER

RANK	STATE	FATALITIES	% of USA
1	Florida	35	10.8%
2	Illinois	29	9.0%
3	Texas	27	8.3%
4	California	17	5.2%
5	North Carolina	15	4.6%
5	Tennessee	15	4.6%
7	Arkansas	13	4.0%
8	Georgia	12	3.7%
9	Missouri	11	3.4%
9	New York	11	3.4%
9	Oklahoma	11	3.4%
12	Minnesota	10	3.1%
13	Kentucky	8	2.5%
14	Kansas	7	2.2%
14	Louisiana	7	2.2%
14	Wisconsin	7	2.2%
17	Alabama	6	1.9%
17	Nevada	6	1.9%
19	Mississippi	5	1.5%
19	Montana	5	1.5%
19	New Jersey	5	1.5%
19	New Mexico	5	1.5%
19	Oregon	5	1.5%
19	South Carolina	5	1.5%
25	Hawaii	4	1.2%
25	Michigan	4	1.2%
25	Ohio	4	1.2%
25	Washington	4	1.2%
25	Wyoming	4	1.2%
30	Colorado	3	0.9%
30	Connecticut	3	0.9%
30	Idaho	3	0.9%
30	Pennsylvania	3	0.9%
34	Alaska	2	0.6%
34	Arizona	2	0.6%
34	Virginia	2	0.6%
34	West Virginia	2	0.6%
38	Indiana	1	0.3%
38	Iowa	1	0.3%
38	Maine	1	0.3%
38	Maryland	1	0.3%
38	Massachusetts	1	0.3%
38	Nebraska	1	0.3%
38	New Hampshire	1	0.3%
45	Delaware	0	0.0%
45	North Dakota	0	0.0%
45	Rhode Island	0	0.0%
45	South Dakota	0	0.0%
45	Utah	0	0.0%
45	Vermont	0	0.0%
	District of Columbia	0	0.0%

Source: National Weather Service, Water and Weather Services
   "2009 Summary of Hazardous Weather Fatalities" (http://www.nws.noaa.gov/om/hazstats/state09.pdf)
*Includes lightning, tornado, thunderstorm, extreme temperature, flood, coastal storm, rip current, hurricane, winter storm, fog, avalanche, and other weather events. National total does not include 42 fatalities in U.S. waters or territories.

Cost of Damage from Hazardous Weather in 2009

National Total = $7,205,890,000*

ALPHA ORDER

RANK	STATE	DAMAGE	% of USA
31	Alabama	$47,440,000	0.7%
33	Alaska	30,820,000	0.4%
34	Arizona	15,410,000	0.2%
1	Arkansas	1,146,460,000	15.9%
24	California	54,400,000	0.8%
4	Colorado	647,300,000	9.0%
43	Connecticut	2,680,000	0.0%
30	Delaware	47,530,000	0.7%
12	Florida	156,010,000	2.2%
6	Georgia	400,850,000	5.6%
50	Hawaii	10,000	0.0%
42	Idaho	2,980,000	0.0%
7	Illinois	390,920,000	5.4%
26	Indiana	52,660,000	0.7%
5	Iowa	420,570,000	5.8%
13	Kansas	140,270,000	1.9%
8	Kentucky	365,790,000	5.1%
2	Louisiana	783,170,000	10.9%
38	Maine	5,390,000	0.1%
41	Maryland	3,110,000	0.0%
40	Massachusetts	3,140,000	0.0%
23	Michigan	55,220,000	0.8%
37	Minnesota	7,980,000	0.1%
25	Mississippi	53,670,000	0.7%
9	Missouri	348,610,000	4.8%
39	Montana	4,890,000	0.1%
29	Nebraska	48,850,000	0.7%
48	Nevada	660,000	0.0%
46	New Hampshire	1,130,000	0.0%
11	New Jersey	195,610,000	2.7%
36	New Mexico	9,300,000	0.1%
10	New York	224,910,000	3.1%
32	North Carolina	30,840,000	0.4%
20	North Dakota	56,550,000	0.8%
28	Ohio	49,020,000	0.7%
17	Oklahoma	74,420,000	1.0%
45	Oregon	1,910,000	0.0%
19	Pennsylvania	57,600,000	0.8%
49	Rhode Island	90,000	0.0%
21	South Carolina	56,320,000	0.8%
16	South Dakota	76,290,000	1.1%
14	Tennessee	131,280,000	1.8%
3	Texas	691,470,000	9.6%
47	Utah	940,000	0.0%
44	Vermont	2,220,000	0.0%
22	Virginia	55,440,000	0.8%
15	Washington	123,940,000	1.7%
27	West Virginia	51,210,000	0.7%
18	Wisconsin	69,180,000	1.0%
35	Wyoming	9,430,000	0.1%

RANK ORDER

RANK	STATE	DAMAGE	% of USA
1	Arkansas	$1,146,460,000	15.9%
2	Louisiana	783,170,000	10.9%
3	Texas	691,470,000	9.6%
4	Colorado	647,300,000	9.0%
5	Iowa	420,570,000	5.8%
6	Georgia	400,850,000	5.6%
7	Illinois	390,920,000	5.4%
8	Kentucky	365,790,000	5.1%
9	Missouri	348,610,000	4.8%
10	New York	224,910,000	3.1%
11	New Jersey	195,610,000	2.7%
12	Florida	156,010,000	2.2%
13	Kansas	140,270,000	1.9%
14	Tennessee	131,280,000	1.8%
15	Washington	123,940,000	1.7%
16	South Dakota	76,290,000	1.1%
17	Oklahoma	74,420,000	1.0%
18	Wisconsin	69,180,000	1.0%
19	Pennsylvania	57,600,000	0.8%
20	North Dakota	56,550,000	0.8%
21	South Carolina	56,320,000	0.8%
22	Virginia	55,440,000	0.8%
23	Michigan	55,220,000	0.8%
24	California	54,400,000	0.8%
25	Mississippi	53,670,000	0.7%
26	Indiana	52,660,000	0.7%
27	West Virginia	51,210,000	0.7%
28	Ohio	49,020,000	0.7%
29	Nebraska	48,850,000	0.7%
30	Delaware	47,530,000	0.7%
31	Alabama	47,440,000	0.7%
32	North Carolina	30,840,000	0.4%
33	Alaska	30,820,000	0.4%
34	Arizona	15,410,000	0.2%
35	Wyoming	9,430,000	0.1%
36	New Mexico	9,300,000	0.1%
37	Minnesota	7,980,000	0.1%
38	Maine	5,390,000	0.1%
39	Montana	4,890,000	0.1%
40	Massachusetts	3,140,000	0.0%
41	Maryland	3,110,000	0.0%
42	Idaho	2,980,000	0.0%
43	Connecticut	2,680,000	0.0%
44	Vermont	2,220,000	0.0%
45	Oregon	1,910,000	0.0%
46	New Hampshire	1,130,000	0.0%
47	Utah	940,000	0.0%
48	Nevada	660,000	0.0%
49	Rhode Island	90,000	0.0%
50	Hawaii	10,000	0.0%
	District of Columbia	0	0.0%

Source: National Weather Service, Water and Weather Services
    "2009 Summary of Hazardous Weather Fatalities" (http://www.nws.noaa.gov/om/hazstats/state09.pdf)
*Includes lightning, tornado, thunderstorm, extreme temperature, flood, coastal storm, rip current, hurricane, winter storm, fog, avalanche, and other weather events. National total does not include damage costs in U.S. territories.

Percent of Land Owned by the Federal Government in 2004

National Percent = 28.8%*

ALPHA ORDER

RANK	STATE	PERCENT
43	Alabama	1.6
2	Alaska	69.1
6	Arizona	48.1
22	Arkansas	7.2
7	California	45.3
10	Colorado	36.6
49	Connecticut	0.4
37	Delaware	2.0
18	Florida	8.2
29	Georgia	3.8
13	Hawaii	19.4
5	Idaho	50.2
41	Illinois	1.8
37	Indiana	2.0
47	Iowa	0.8
45	Kansas	1.2
26	Kentucky	5.4
27	Louisiana	5.1
46	Maine	1.1
34	Maryland	2.8
39	Massachusetts	1.9
16	Michigan	10.0
24	Minnesota	5.6
21	Mississippi	7.3
28	Missouri	5.0
12	Montana	29.9
44	Nebraska	1.4
1	Nevada	84.5
14	New Hampshire	13.5
32	New Jersey	3.1
9	New Mexico	41.8
47	New York	0.8
15	North Carolina	11.8
35	North Dakota	2.7
42	Ohio	1.7
30	Oklahoma	3.6
4	Oregon	53.1
36	Pennsylvania	2.5
49	Rhode Island	0.4
33	South Carolina	2.9
23	South Dakota	6.2
31	Tennessee	3.2
39	Texas	1.9
3	Utah	57.5
19	Vermont	7.5
17	Virginia	9.9
11	Washington	30.3
20	West Virginia	7.4
24	Wisconsin	5.6
8	Wyoming	42.3

RANK ORDER

RANK	STATE	PERCENT
1	Nevada	84.5
2	Alaska	69.1
3	Utah	57.5
4	Oregon	53.1
5	Idaho	50.2
6	Arizona	48.1
7	California	45.3
8	Wyoming	42.3
9	New Mexico	41.8
10	Colorado	36.6
11	Washington	30.3
12	Montana	29.9
13	Hawaii	19.4
14	New Hampshire	13.5
15	North Carolina	11.8
16	Michigan	10.0
17	Virginia	9.9
18	Florida	8.2
19	Vermont	7.5
20	West Virginia	7.4
21	Mississippi	7.3
22	Arkansas	7.2
23	South Dakota	6.2
24	Minnesota	5.6
24	Wisconsin	5.6
26	Kentucky	5.4
27	Louisiana	5.1
28	Missouri	5.0
29	Georgia	3.8
30	Oklahoma	3.6
31	Tennessee	3.2
32	New Jersey	3.1
33	South Carolina	2.9
34	Maryland	2.8
35	North Dakota	2.7
36	Pennsylvania	2.5
37	Delaware	2.0
37	Indiana	2.0
39	Massachusetts	1.9
39	Texas	1.9
41	Illinois	1.8
42	Ohio	1.7
43	Alabama	1.6
44	Nebraska	1.4
45	Kansas	1.2
46	Maine	1.1
47	Iowa	0.8
47	New York	0.8
49	Connecticut	0.4
49	Rhode Island	0.4

| | District of Columbia | 24.7 |

Source: Government Services Administration, Office of Governmentwide Real Property Policy
   "Federal Real Property Profile" (http://www.gsa.gov/realpropertyprofile)
*As of September 30, 2004. Does not include land owned by the federal government in U.S. territories or in foreign countries.

National Park Service Land in 2010

National Total = 84,383,361 Acres*

ALPHA ORDER

RANK	STATE	ACRES	% of USA
41	Alabama	22,737	0.0%
1	Alaska	54,654,000	64.4%
3	Arizona	2,962,853	3.5%
25	Arkansas	104,977	0.1%
2	California	8,111,386	9.6%
12	Colorado	673,589	0.8%
46	Connecticut	7,782	0.0%
50	Delaware	0	0.0%
4	Florida	2,638,389	3.1%
34	Georgia	63,420	0.1%
17	Hawaii	369,124	0.4%
13	Idaho	518,033	0.6%
48	Illinois	115	0.0%
43	Indiana	15,378	0.0%
47	Iowa	2,713	0.0%
44	Kansas	11,636	0.0%
27	Kentucky	95,416	0.1%
39	Louisiana	24,107	0.0%
29	Maine	90,285	0.1%
31	Maryland	73,388	0.1%
35	Massachusetts	57,962	0.1%
11	Michigan	718,228	0.8%
19	Minnesota	301,343	0.4%
24	Mississippi	118,733	0.1%
30	Missouri	83,475	0.1%
8	Montana	1,274,374	1.5%
36	Nebraska	45,735	0.1%
10	Nevada	778,512	0.9%
42	New Hampshire	21,889	0.0%
26	New Jersey	99,206	0.1%
15	New Mexico	391,364	0.5%
32	New York	72,898	0.1%
14	North Carolina	406,268	0.5%
33	North Dakota	72,579	0.1%
37	Ohio	34,150	0.0%
45	Oklahoma	10,241	0.0%
21	Oregon	199,095	0.2%
22	Pennsylvania	137,663	0.2%
49	Rhode Island	5	0.0%
38	South Carolina	32,184	0.0%
20	South Dakota	297,413	0.4%
16	Tennessee	385,805	0.5%
9	Texas	1,245,085	1.5%
6	Utah	2,117,043	2.5%
40	Vermont	23,193	0.0%
18	Virginia	363,664	0.4%
7	Washington	1,967,436	2.3%
28	West Virginia	92,670	0.1%
23	Wisconsin	133,754	0.2%
5	Wyoming	2,396,390	2.8%

RANK ORDER

RANK	STATE	ACRES	% of USA
1	Alaska	54,654,000	64.4%
2	California	8,111,386	9.6%
3	Arizona	2,962,853	3.5%
4	Florida	2,638,389	3.1%
5	Wyoming	2,396,390	2.8%
6	Utah	2,117,043	2.5%
7	Washington	1,967,436	2.3%
8	Montana	1,274,374	1.5%
9	Texas	1,245,085	1.5%
10	Nevada	778,512	0.9%
11	Michigan	718,228	0.8%
12	Colorado	673,589	0.8%
13	Idaho	518,033	0.6%
14	North Carolina	406,268	0.5%
15	New Mexico	391,364	0.5%
16	Tennessee	385,805	0.5%
17	Hawaii	369,124	0.4%
18	Virginia	363,664	0.4%
19	Minnesota	301,343	0.4%
20	South Dakota	297,413	0.4%
21	Oregon	199,095	0.2%
22	Pennsylvania	137,663	0.2%
23	Wisconsin	133,754	0.2%
24	Mississippi	118,733	0.1%
25	Arkansas	104,977	0.1%
26	New Jersey	99,206	0.1%
27	Kentucky	95,416	0.1%
28	West Virginia	92,670	0.1%
29	Maine	90,285	0.1%
30	Missouri	83,475	0.1%
31	Maryland	73,388	0.1%
32	New York	72,898	0.1%
33	North Dakota	72,579	0.1%
34	Georgia	63,420	0.1%
35	Massachusetts	57,962	0.1%
36	Nebraska	45,735	0.1%
37	Ohio	34,150	0.0%
38	South Carolina	32,184	0.0%
39	Louisiana	24,107	0.0%
40	Vermont	23,193	0.0%
41	Alabama	22,737	0.0%
42	New Hampshire	21,889	0.0%
43	Indiana	15,378	0.0%
44	Kansas	11,636	0.0%
45	Oklahoma	10,241	0.0%
46	Connecticut	7,782	0.0%
47	Iowa	2,713	0.0%
48	Illinois	115	0.0%
49	Rhode Island	5	0.0%
50	Delaware	0	0.0%
	District of Columbia	7,090	0.0%

Source: National Park Service
   "Listing of Acreage by State" (unpublished data)
*As of December 31, 2010. Includes federal and nonfederal land in national parks, monuments, historic sites, recreation areas, preserves, battlefields, grasslands, seashores, parkways, trails, and rivers. Does not include land in national forest or wildlife areas. Includes 55,585 acres in U.S. territories.

Recreation Visits to National Park Service Areas in 2009

National Total = 285,579,941 Visits*

ALPHA ORDER

RANK	STATE	VISITS	% of USA
36	Alabama	790,752	0.3%
26	Alaska	2,278,488	0.8%
5	Arizona	10,713,122	3.8%
24	Arkansas	3,031,842	1.1%
1	California	35,318,711	12.4%
18	Colorado	5,443,039	1.9%
49	Connecticut	19,386	0.0%
50	Delaware	0	0.0%
7	Florida	9,495,437	3.3%
14	Georgia	6,475,874	2.3%
19	Hawaii	4,312,818	1.5%
39	Idaho	494,196	0.2%
40	Illinois	464,074	0.2%
27	Indiana	2,230,024	0.8%
44	Iowa	241,063	0.1%
45	Kansas	101,906	0.0%
29	Kentucky	1,828,340	0.6%
42	Louisiana	443,314	0.2%
28	Maine	2,227,698	0.8%
23	Maryland	3,445,530	1.2%
6	Massachusetts	9,772,738	3.4%
32	Michigan	1,628,704	0.6%
37	Minnesota	650,156	0.2%
13	Mississippi	6,582,890	2.3%
22	Missouri	3,933,043	1.4%
20	Montana	4,195,484	1.5%
43	Nebraska	273,444	0.1%
16	Nevada	5,836,491	2.0%
47	New Hampshire	34,558	0.0%
17	New Jersey	5,828,477	2.0%
31	New Mexico	1,659,574	0.6%
4	New York	17,327,234	6.1%
3	North Carolina	18,198,530	6.4%
38	North Dakota	631,459	0.2%
25	Ohio	2,882,593	1.0%
34	Oklahoma	1,249,011	0.4%
35	Oregon	891,783	0.3%
8	Pennsylvania	8,885,894	3.1%
46	Rhode Island	50,397	0.0%
33	South Carolina	1,504,680	0.5%
21	South Dakota	4,134,663	1.4%
10	Tennessee	8,061,848	2.8%
12	Texas	6,938,238	2.4%
9	Utah	8,755,401	3.1%
48	Vermont	31,129	0.0%
2	Virginia	22,953,894	8.0%
11	Washington	7,559,552	2.6%
30	West Virginia	1,803,552	0.6%
41	Wisconsin	452,365	0.2%
15	Wyoming	5,895,719	2.1%

RANK ORDER

RANK	STATE	VISITS	% of USA
1	California	35,318,711	12.4%
2	Virginia	22,953,894	8.0%
3	North Carolina	18,198,530	6.4%
4	New York	17,327,234	6.1%
5	Arizona	10,713,122	3.8%
6	Massachusetts	9,772,738	3.4%
7	Florida	9,495,437	3.3%
8	Pennsylvania	8,885,894	3.1%
9	Utah	8,755,401	3.1%
10	Tennessee	8,061,848	2.8%
11	Washington	7,559,552	2.6%
12	Texas	6,938,238	2.4%
13	Mississippi	6,582,890	2.3%
14	Georgia	6,475,874	2.3%
15	Wyoming	5,895,719	2.1%
16	Nevada	5,836,491	2.0%
17	New Jersey	5,828,477	2.0%
18	Colorado	5,443,039	1.9%
19	Hawaii	4,312,818	1.5%
20	Montana	4,195,484	1.5%
21	South Dakota	4,134,663	1.4%
22	Missouri	3,933,043	1.4%
23	Maryland	3,445,530	1.2%
24	Arkansas	3,031,842	1.1%
25	Ohio	2,882,593	1.0%
26	Alaska	2,278,488	0.8%
27	Indiana	2,230,024	0.8%
28	Maine	2,227,698	0.8%
29	Kentucky	1,828,340	0.6%
30	West Virginia	1,803,552	0.6%
31	New Mexico	1,659,574	0.6%
32	Michigan	1,628,704	0.6%
33	South Carolina	1,504,680	0.5%
34	Oklahoma	1,249,011	0.4%
35	Oregon	891,783	0.3%
36	Alabama	790,752	0.3%
37	Minnesota	650,156	0.2%
38	North Dakota	631,459	0.2%
39	Idaho	494,196	0.2%
40	Illinois	464,074	0.2%
41	Wisconsin	452,365	0.2%
42	Louisiana	443,314	0.2%
43	Nebraska	273,444	0.1%
44	Iowa	241,063	0.1%
45	Kansas	101,906	0.0%
46	Rhode Island	50,397	0.0%
47	New Hampshire	34,558	0.0%
48	Vermont	31,129	0.0%
49	Connecticut	19,386	0.0%
50	Delaware	0	0.0%
	District of Columbia	35,695,833	12.5%

Source: National Park Service, Public Use Statistics Office
    "National Park Service Statistical Abstract 2009" (http://www.nature.nps.gov/stats/abstracts/abst2009.pdf)
*National total includes 1,924,944 visits in U.S. territories.

Percent Change in National Park Service Recreation Visits: 2008 to 2009

National Percent Change = 3.9% Increase*

ALPHA ORDER			RANK ORDER		
RANK	STATE	PERCENT CHANGE	RANK	STATE	PERCENT CHANGE
40	Alabama	0.2	1	Illinois	38.3
46	Alaska	(5.2)	2	Florida	19.6
37	Arizona	0.3	3	Texas	19.5
22	Arkansas	5.5	4	Kansas	18.1
29	California	2.7	4	South Dakota	18.1
34	Colorado	1.1	6	New Hampshire	15.9
23	Connecticut	4.7	7	Michigan	14.6
NA	Delaware**	NA	8	Missouri	14.5
2	Florida	19.6	9	North Dakota	14.2
36	Georgia	0.8	10	Iowa	14.1
44	Hawaii	(4.9)	11	Mississippi	11.6
48	Idaho	(9.1)	12	Montana	9.8
1	Illinois	38.3	13	Rhode Island	9.2
18	Indiana	6.5	14	Maine	7.3
10	Iowa	14.1	15	Oregon	7.2
4	Kansas	18.1	16	Kentucky	7.0
16	Kentucky	7.0	17	New Mexico	6.6
28	Louisiana	2.8	18	Indiana	6.5
14	Maine	7.3	18	Wisconsin	6.5
42	Maryland	(2.8)	20	Washington	5.9
44	Massachusetts	(4.9)	21	Wyoming	5.8
7	Michigan	14.6	22	Arkansas	5.5
32	Minnesota	1.5	23	Connecticut	4.7
11	Mississippi	11.6	24	South Carolina	4.4
8	Missouri	14.5	25	Tennessee	4.2
12	Montana	9.8	26	Utah	3.6
27	Nebraska	2.9	27	Nebraska	2.9
34	Nevada	1.1	28	Louisiana	2.8
6	New Hampshire	15.9	29	California	2.7
37	New Jersey	0.3	30	New York	2.4
17	New Mexico	6.6	31	Virginia	1.8
30	New York	2.4	32	Minnesota	1.5
33	North Carolina	1.2	33	North Carolina	1.2
9	North Dakota	14.2	34	Colorado	1.1
47	Ohio	(7.6)	34	Nevada	1.1
37	Oklahoma	0.3	36	Georgia	0.8
15	Oregon	7.2	37	Arizona	0.3
43	Pennsylvania	(3.3)	37	New Jersey	0.3
13	Rhode Island	9.2	37	Oklahoma	0.3
24	South Carolina	4.4	40	Alabama	0.2
4	South Dakota	18.1	41	West Virginia	(0.5)
25	Tennessee	4.2	42	Maryland	(2.8)
3	Texas	19.5	43	Pennsylvania	(3.3)
26	Utah	3.6	44	Hawaii	(4.9)
49	Vermont	(16.1)	44	Massachusetts	(4.9)
31	Virginia	1.8	46	Alaska	(5.2)
20	Washington	5.9	47	Ohio	(7.6)
41	West Virginia	(0.5)	48	Idaho	(9.1)
18	Wisconsin	6.5	49	Vermont	(16.1)
21	Wyoming	5.8	NA	Delaware**	NA
				District of Columbia	7.6

Source: National Park Service, Public Use Statistics Office
    "National Park Service Statistical Abstract 2009" (http://www.nature.nps.gov/stats/abstracts/abst2009.pdf)
*National percent change includes visits in U.S. territories.
**Not applicable.

State Parks, Recreation Areas, and Natural Areas in 2008

National Total = 6,547 Areas*

ALPHA ORDER

RANK	STATE	AREAS	% of USA
50	Alabama	22	0.3%
12	Alaska	139	2.1%
45	Arizona	32	0.5%
35	Arkansas	52	0.8%
5	California	279	4.3%
10	Colorado	164	2.5%
13	Connecticut	137	2.1%
43	Delaware	34	0.5%
11	Florida	161	2.5%
26	Georgia	73	1.1%
27	Hawaii	70	1.1%
43	Idaho	34	0.5%
4	Illinois	316	4.8%
40	Indiana	37	0.6%
9	Iowa	179	2.7%
47	Kansas	25	0.4%
33	Kentucky	53	0.8%
31	Louisiana	58	0.9%
14	Maine	136	2.1%
30	Maryland	65	1.0%
3	Massachusetts	339	5.2%
19	Michigan	97	1.5%
8	Minnesota	212	3.2%
47	Mississippi	25	0.4%
22	Missouri	85	1.3%
2	Montana	392	6.0%
22	Nebraska	85	1.3%
47	Nevada	25	0.4%
21	New Hampshire	90	1.4%
17	New Jersey	118	1.8%
41	New Mexico	36	0.5%
1	New York	1,417	21.6%
29	North Carolina	66	1.0%
46	North Dakota	30	0.5%
24	Ohio	74	1.1%
36	Oklahoma	51	0.8%
6	Oregon	253	3.9%
16	Pennsylvania	120	1.8%
24	Rhode Island	74	1.1%
32	South Carolina	56	0.9%
15	South Dakota	131	2.0%
33	Tennessee	53	0.8%
20	Texas	93	1.4%
37	Utah	50	0.8%
18	Vermont	103	1.6%
39	Virginia	41	0.6%
7	Washington	214	3.3%
38	West Virginia	47	0.7%
28	Wisconsin	68	1.0%
41	Wyoming	36	0.5%

RANK ORDER

RANK	STATE	AREAS	% of USA
1	New York	1,417	21.6%
2	Montana	392	6.0%
3	Massachusetts	339	5.2%
4	Illinois	316	4.8%
5	California	279	4.3%
6	Oregon	253	3.9%
7	Washington	214	3.3%
8	Minnesota	212	3.2%
9	Iowa	179	2.7%
10	Colorado	164	2.5%
11	Florida	161	2.5%
12	Alaska	139	2.1%
13	Connecticut	137	2.1%
14	Maine	136	2.1%
15	South Dakota	131	2.0%
16	Pennsylvania	120	1.8%
17	New Jersey	118	1.8%
18	Vermont	103	1.6%
19	Michigan	97	1.5%
20	Texas	93	1.4%
21	New Hampshire	90	1.4%
22	Missouri	85	1.3%
22	Nebraska	85	1.3%
24	Ohio	74	1.1%
24	Rhode Island	74	1.1%
26	Georgia	73	1.1%
27	Hawaii	70	1.1%
28	Wisconsin	68	1.0%
29	North Carolina	66	1.0%
30	Maryland	65	1.0%
31	Louisiana	58	0.9%
32	South Carolina	56	0.9%
33	Kentucky	53	0.8%
33	Tennessee	53	0.8%
35	Arkansas	52	0.8%
36	Oklahoma	51	0.8%
37	Utah	50	0.8%
38	West Virginia	47	0.7%
39	Virginia	41	0.6%
40	Indiana	37	0.6%
41	New Mexico	36	0.5%
41	Wyoming	36	0.5%
43	Delaware	34	0.5%
43	Idaho	34	0.5%
45	Arizona	32	0.5%
46	North Dakota	30	0.5%
47	Kansas	25	0.4%
47	Mississippi	25	0.4%
47	Nevada	25	0.4%
50	Alabama	22	0.3%

District of Columbia**		NA	NA

Source: The National Association of State Parks Directors
    "Annual Information Exchange" (http://www.naspd.org/)
*For the period July 1, 2007 through June 30, 2008. Includes operating and nonoperating state parks, recreation areas, natural areas, and other areas.
**Not applicable.

Visitors to State Parks and Recreation Areas in 2008

National Total = 744,943,195 Visitors*

ALPHA ORDER

RANK	STATE	VISITORS	% of USA
36	Alabama	5,141,690	0.7%
38	Alaska	4,976,546	0.7%
44	Arizona	2,348,313	0.3%
24	Arkansas	8,399,016	1.1%
1	California	76,833,187	10.3%
19	Colorado	11,833,500	1.6%
26	Connecticut	7,504,358	1.0%
37	Delaware	5,021,946	0.7%
10	Florida	20,737,052	2.8%
21	Georgia	10,351,102	1.4%
23	Hawaii	10,181,733	1.4%
41	Idaho	4,031,348	0.5%
4	Illinois	45,158,558	6.1%
13	Indiana	18,043,306	2.4%
17	Iowa	13,381,541	1.8%
33	Kansas	6,875,114	0.9%
30	Kentucky	7,081,930	1.0%
46	Louisiana	1,679,173	0.2%
45	Maine	2,124,134	0.3%
20	Maryland	11,329,786	1.5%
9	Massachusetts	31,635,247	4.2%
11	Michigan	19,309,161	2.6%
25	Minnesota	8,379,570	1.1%
48	Mississippi	1,212,391	0.2%
14	Missouri	15,142,186	2.0%
35	Montana	5,332,502	0.7%
22	Nebraska	10,236,147	1.4%
42	Nevada	3,131,766	0.4%
47	New Hampshire	1,625,683	0.2%
12	New Jersey	18,543,109	2.5%
39	New Mexico	4,603,901	0.6%
2	New York	61,771,320	8.3%
18	North Carolina	12,868,493	1.7%
49	North Dakota	878,550	0.1%
3	Ohio	49,658,857	6.7%
16	Oklahoma	13,485,280	1.8%
5	Oregon	42,604,811	5.7%
7	Pennsylvania	33,209,574	4.5%
34	Rhode Island	6,216,588	0.8%
31	South Carolina	7,050,146	0.9%
27	South Dakota	7,374,723	1.0%
8	Tennessee	32,264,499	4.3%
29	Texas	7,142,382	1.0%
40	Utah	4,553,590	0.6%
50	Vermont	697,989	0.1%
32	Virginia	7,039,993	0.9%
6	Washington	41,590,112	5.6%
28	West Virginia	7,324,322	1.0%
15	Wisconsin	14,516,272	1.9%
43	Wyoming	2,510,698	0.3%

RANK ORDER

RANK	STATE	VISITORS	% of USA
1	California	76,833,187	10.3%
2	New York	61,771,320	8.3%
3	Ohio	49,658,857	6.7%
4	Illinois	45,158,558	6.1%
5	Oregon	42,604,811	5.7%
6	Washington	41,590,112	5.6%
7	Pennsylvania	33,209,574	4.5%
8	Tennessee	32,264,499	4.3%
9	Massachusetts	31,635,247	4.2%
10	Florida	20,737,052	2.8%
11	Michigan	19,309,161	2.6%
12	New Jersey	18,543,109	2.5%
13	Indiana	18,043,306	2.4%
14	Missouri	15,142,186	2.0%
15	Wisconsin	14,516,272	1.9%
16	Oklahoma	13,485,280	1.8%
17	Iowa	13,381,541	1.8%
18	North Carolina	12,868,493	1.7%
19	Colorado	11,833,500	1.6%
20	Maryland	11,329,786	1.5%
21	Georgia	10,351,102	1.4%
22	Nebraska	10,236,147	1.4%
23	Hawaii	10,181,733	1.4%
24	Arkansas	8,399,016	1.1%
25	Minnesota	8,379,570	1.1%
26	Connecticut	7,504,358	1.0%
27	South Dakota	7,374,723	1.0%
28	West Virginia	7,324,322	1.0%
29	Texas	7,142,382	1.0%
30	Kentucky	7,081,930	1.0%
31	South Carolina	7,050,146	0.9%
32	Virginia	7,039,993	0.9%
33	Kansas	6,875,114	0.9%
34	Rhode Island	6,216,588	0.8%
35	Montana	5,332,502	0.7%
36	Alabama	5,141,690	0.7%
37	Delaware	5,021,946	0.7%
38	Alaska	4,976,546	0.7%
39	New Mexico	4,603,901	0.6%
40	Utah	4,553,590	0.6%
41	Idaho	4,031,348	0.5%
42	Nevada	3,131,766	0.4%
43	Wyoming	2,510,698	0.3%
44	Arizona	2,348,313	0.3%
45	Maine	2,124,134	0.3%
46	Louisiana	1,679,173	0.2%
47	New Hampshire	1,625,683	0.2%
48	Mississippi	1,212,391	0.2%
49	North Dakota	878,550	0.1%
50	Vermont	697,989	0.1%
	District of Columbia**	NA	NA

Source: The National Association of State Parks Directors
  "Annual Information Exchange" (http://www.naspd.org/)
*For the period July 1, 2007 through June 30, 2008. Includes operating and nonoperating state parks, recreation areas, natural areas, and other areas. Includes day and overnight visitors.
**Not applicable.

IX. Government Finances: Federal

Internal Revenue Service Gross Collections in 2009

National Total = $2,345,337,177,000*

ALPHA ORDER

RANK	STATE	COLLECTIONS	% of USA
30	Alabama	$20,093,422,000	0.9%
46	Alaska	4,670,157,000	0.2%
24	Arizona	32,372,226,000	1.4%
25	Arkansas	25,727,268,000	1.1%
1	California	264,868,391,000	11.3%
22	Colorado	38,484,608,000	1.6%
16	Connecticut	44,684,141,000	1.9%
36	Delaware	13,683,353,000	0.6%
5	Florida	110,156,809,000	4.7%
12	Georgia	59,486,251,000	2.5%
42	Hawaii	6,747,592,000	0.3%
41	Idaho	6,859,632,000	0.3%
4	Illinois	116,130,852,000	5.0%
20	Indiana	42,108,854,000	1.8%
32	Iowa	17,614,407,000	0.8%
29	Kansas	20,374,354,000	0.9%
27	Kentucky	23,313,696,000	1.0%
23	Louisiana	34,882,848,000	1.5%
44	Maine	6,105,799,000	0.3%
17	Maryland	44,484,984,000	1.9%
9	Massachusetts	70,108,079,000	3.0%
14	Michigan	56,050,689,000	2.4%
10	Minnesota	67,646,589,000	2.9%
38	Mississippi	9,603,121,000	0.4%
18	Missouri	44,310,000,000	1.9%
47	Montana	4,136,011,000	0.2%
33	Nebraska	16,200,400,000	0.7%
35	Nevada	13,770,576,000	0.6%
39	New Hampshire	8,739,838,000	0.4%
8	New Jersey	103,548,696,000	4.4%
40	New Mexico	8,188,815,000	0.3%
3	New York	193,446,916,000	8.2%
11	North Carolina	63,348,252,000	2.7%
48	North Dakota	4,115,943,000	0.2%
7	Ohio	103,638,344,000	4.4%
26	Oklahoma	24,297,410,000	1.0%
28	Oregon	21,736,643,000	0.9%
6	Pennsylvania	106,613,979,000	4.5%
37	Rhode Island	10,909,205,000	0.5%
31	South Carolina	17,806,603,000	0.8%
45	South Dakota	4,888,826,000	0.2%
19	Tennessee	44,047,939,000	1.9%
2	Texas	200,521,512,000	8.5%
34	Utah	14,270,839,000	0.6%
50	Vermont	3,366,627,000	0.1%
13	Virginia	58,598,281,000	2.5%
15	Washington	48,587,720,000	2.1%
43	West Virginia	6,332,264,000	0.3%
21	Wisconsin	38,642,363,000	1.6%
49	Wyoming	3,833,691,000	0.2%

RANK ORDER

RANK	STATE	COLLECTIONS	% of USA
1	California	$264,868,391,000	11.3%
2	Texas	200,521,512,000	8.5%
3	New York	193,446,916,000	8.2%
4	Illinois	116,130,852,000	5.0%
5	Florida	110,156,809,000	4.7%
6	Pennsylvania	106,613,979,000	4.5%
7	Ohio	103,638,344,000	4.4%
8	New Jersey	103,548,696,000	4.4%
9	Massachusetts	70,108,079,000	3.0%
10	Minnesota	67,646,589,000	2.9%
11	North Carolina	63,348,252,000	2.7%
12	Georgia	59,486,251,000	2.5%
13	Virginia	58,598,281,000	2.5%
14	Michigan	56,050,689,000	2.4%
15	Washington	48,587,720,000	2.1%
16	Connecticut	44,684,141,000	1.9%
17	Maryland	44,484,984,000	1.9%
18	Missouri	44,310,000,000	1.9%
19	Tennessee	44,047,939,000	1.9%
20	Indiana	42,108,854,000	1.8%
21	Wisconsin	38,642,363,000	1.6%
22	Colorado	38,484,608,000	1.6%
23	Louisiana	34,882,848,000	1.5%
24	Arizona	32,372,226,000	1.4%
25	Arkansas	25,727,268,000	1.1%
26	Oklahoma	24,297,410,000	1.0%
27	Kentucky	23,313,696,000	1.0%
28	Oregon	21,736,643,000	0.9%
29	Kansas	20,374,354,000	0.9%
30	Alabama	20,093,422,000	0.9%
31	South Carolina	17,806,603,000	0.8%
32	Iowa	17,614,407,000	0.8%
33	Nebraska	16,200,400,000	0.7%
34	Utah	14,270,839,000	0.6%
35	Nevada	13,770,576,000	0.6%
36	Delaware	13,683,353,000	0.6%
37	Rhode Island	10,909,205,000	0.5%
38	Mississippi	9,603,121,000	0.4%
39	New Hampshire	8,739,838,000	0.4%
40	New Mexico	8,188,815,000	0.3%
41	Idaho	6,859,632,000	0.3%
42	Hawaii	6,747,592,000	0.3%
43	West Virginia	6,332,264,000	0.3%
44	Maine	6,105,799,000	0.3%
45	South Dakota	4,888,826,000	0.2%
46	Alaska	4,670,157,000	0.2%
47	Montana	4,136,011,000	0.2%
48	North Dakota	4,115,943,000	0.2%
49	Wyoming	3,833,691,000	0.2%
50	Vermont	3,366,627,000	0.1%
	District of Columbia	19,487,689,000	0.8%

Source: U.S. Department of the Treasury, Internal Revenue Service
   "Fiscal Year 2009 IRS Data Book" (http://www.irs.gov/taxstats/index.html)
*Total includes $24,538,954,000 from U.S. citizens abroad and other miscellaneous returns not shown separately.

Per Capita Internal Revenue Service Gross Collections in 2009

National Per Capita = $7,569*

ALPHA ORDER

RANK	STATE	PER CAPITA
45	Alabama	$4,267
26	Alaska	6,686
42	Arizona	4,908
11	Arkansas	8,904
21	California	7,166
16	Colorado	7,659
3	Connecticut	12,701
1	Delaware	15,459
33	Florida	5,942
31	Georgia	6,052
39	Hawaii	5,210
44	Idaho	4,438
9	Illinois	8,995
29	Indiana	6,556
34	Iowa	5,856
20	Kansas	7,228
38	Kentucky	5,404
15	Louisiana	7,765
43	Maine	4,632
14	Maryland	7,805
5	Massachusetts	10,633
36	Michigan	5,622
2	Minnesota	12,845
50	Mississippi	3,253
18	Missouri	7,400
46	Montana	4,242
8	Nebraska	9,017
39	Nevada	5,210
27	New Hampshire	6,598
4	New Jersey	11,892
47	New Mexico	4,075
7	New York	9,899
25	North Carolina	6,753
30	North Dakota	6,363
10	Ohio	8,979
28	Oklahoma	6,590
35	Oregon	5,682
12	Pennsylvania	8,458
6	Rhode Island	10,358
48	South Carolina	3,904
32	South Dakota	6,018
23	Tennessee	6,996
13	Texas	8,091
41	Utah	5,125
37	Vermont	5,415
17	Virginia	7,434
19	Washington	7,291
49	West Virginia	3,480
24	Wisconsin	6,834
22	Wyoming	7,044

RANK ORDER

RANK	STATE	PER CAPITA
1	Delaware	$15,459
2	Minnesota	12,845
3	Connecticut	12,701
4	New Jersey	11,892
5	Massachusetts	10,633
6	Rhode Island	10,358
7	New York	9,899
8	Nebraska	9,017
9	Illinois	8,995
10	Ohio	8,979
11	Arkansas	8,904
12	Pennsylvania	8,458
13	Texas	8,091
14	Maryland	7,805
15	Louisiana	7,765
16	Colorado	7,659
17	Virginia	7,434
18	Missouri	7,400
19	Washington	7,291
20	Kansas	7,228
21	California	7,166
22	Wyoming	7,044
23	Tennessee	6,996
24	Wisconsin	6,834
25	North Carolina	6,753
26	Alaska	6,686
27	New Hampshire	6,598
28	Oklahoma	6,590
29	Indiana	6,556
30	North Dakota	6,363
31	Georgia	6,052
32	South Dakota	6,018
33	Florida	5,942
34	Iowa	5,856
35	Oregon	5,682
36	Michigan	5,622
37	Vermont	5,415
38	Kentucky	5,404
39	Hawaii	5,210
39	Nevada	5,210
41	Utah	5,125
42	Arizona	4,908
43	Maine	4,632
44	Idaho	4,438
45	Alabama	4,267
46	Montana	4,242
47	New Mexico	4,075
48	South Carolina	3,904
49	West Virginia	3,480
50	Mississippi	3,253

District of Columbia	32,498

Source: CQ Press using data from U.S. Department of the Treasury, Internal Revenue Service
"Fiscal Year 2009 IRS Data Book" (http://www.irs.gov/taxstats/index.html)
*National per capita does not include collections from U.S. citizens abroad and other miscellaneous returns not shown separately.

Federal Individual Income Tax Collections in 2009

National Total = $2,048,546,621,000*

ALPHA ORDER

RANK	STATE	COLLECTIONS	% of USA
28	Alabama	$19,053,914,000	0.9%
46	Alaska	4,387,073,000	0.2%
24	Arizona	28,564,174,000	1.4%
27	Arkansas	19,431,278,000	0.9%
1	California	230,209,894,000	11.2%
22	Colorado	34,005,912,000	1.7%
18	Connecticut	39,059,563,000	1.9%
36	Delaware	10,832,715,000	0.5%
4	Florida	102,968,650,000	5.0%
13	Georgia	51,636,705,000	2.5%
42	Hawaii	6,134,814,000	0.3%
41	Idaho	6,249,425,000	0.3%
5	Illinois	100,734,255,000	4.9%
20	Indiana	38,686,817,000	1.9%
32	Iowa	15,963,661,000	0.8%
30	Kansas	17,803,520,000	0.9%
25	Kentucky	21,512,933,000	1.1%
23	Louisiana	32,971,179,000	1.6%
44	Maine	5,692,584,000	0.3%
16	Maryland	41,674,214,000	2.0%
9	Massachusetts	63,808,820,000	3.1%
12	Michigan	52,053,616,000	2.5%
10	Minnesota	57,135,872,000	2.8%
37	Mississippi	8,738,012,000	0.4%
19	Missouri	39,048,966,000	1.9%
47	Montana	3,864,272,000	0.2%
35	Nebraska	12,121,294,000	0.6%
34	Nevada	12,802,614,000	0.6%
38	New Hampshire	8,118,357,000	0.4%
8	New Jersey	87,095,421,000	4.3%
40	New Mexico	7,713,273,000	0.4%
2	New York	171,565,629,000	8.4%
11	North Carolina	53,783,272,000	2.6%
48	North Dakota	3,816,679,000	0.2%
7	Ohio	91,350,121,000	4.5%
29	Oklahoma	17,936,398,000	0.9%
26	Oregon	20,196,879,000	1.0%
6	Pennsylvania	92,949,541,000	4.5%
39	Rhode Island	8,063,988,000	0.4%
31	South Carolina	16,524,564,000	0.8%
45	South Dakota	4,664,408,000	0.2%
17	Tennessee	39,436,002,000	1.9%
3	Texas	158,798,111,000	7.8%
33	Utah	12,906,483,000	0.6%
50	Vermont	3,066,551,000	0.1%
14	Virginia	50,669,866,000	2.5%
15	Washington	42,552,023,000	2.1%
43	West Virginia	5,852,802,000	0.3%
21	Wisconsin	34,662,866,000	1.7%
49	Wyoming	3,407,742,914	0.2%

RANK ORDER

RANK	STATE	COLLECTIONS	% of USA
1	California	$230,209,894,000	11.2%
2	New York	171,565,629,000	8.4%
3	Texas	158,798,111,000	7.8%
4	Florida	102,968,650,000	5.0%
5	Illinois	100,734,255,000	4.9%
6	Pennsylvania	92,949,541,000	4.5%
7	Ohio	91,350,121,000	4.5%
8	New Jersey	87,095,421,000	4.3%
9	Massachusetts	63,808,820,000	3.1%
10	Minnesota	57,135,872,000	2.8%
11	North Carolina	53,783,272,000	2.6%
12	Michigan	52,053,616,000	2.5%
13	Georgia	51,636,705,000	2.5%
14	Virginia	50,669,866,000	2.5%
15	Washington	42,552,023,000	2.1%
16	Maryland	41,674,214,000	2.0%
17	Tennessee	39,436,002,000	1.9%
18	Connecticut	39,059,563,000	1.9%
19	Missouri	39,048,966,000	1.9%
20	Indiana	38,686,817,000	1.9%
21	Wisconsin	34,662,866,000	1.7%
22	Colorado	34,005,912,000	1.7%
23	Louisiana	32,971,179,000	1.6%
24	Arizona	28,564,174,000	1.4%
25	Kentucky	21,512,933,000	1.1%
26	Oregon	20,196,879,000	1.0%
27	Arkansas	19,431,278,000	0.9%
28	Alabama	19,053,914,000	0.9%
29	Oklahoma	17,936,398,000	0.9%
30	Kansas	17,803,520,000	0.9%
31	South Carolina	16,524,564,000	0.8%
32	Iowa	15,963,661,000	0.8%
33	Utah	12,906,483,000	0.6%
34	Nevada	12,802,614,000	0.6%
35	Nebraska	12,121,294,000	0.6%
36	Delaware	10,832,715,000	0.5%
37	Mississippi	8,738,012,000	0.4%
38	New Hampshire	8,118,357,000	0.4%
39	Rhode Island	8,063,988,000	0.4%
40	New Mexico	7,713,273,000	0.4%
41	Idaho	6,249,425,000	0.3%
42	Hawaii	6,134,814,000	0.3%
43	West Virginia	5,852,802,000	0.3%
44	Maine	5,692,584,000	0.3%
45	South Dakota	4,664,408,000	0.2%
46	Alaska	4,387,073,000	0.2%
47	Montana	3,864,272,000	0.2%
48	North Dakota	3,816,679,000	0.2%
49	Wyoming	3,407,742,914	0.2%
50	Vermont	3,066,551,000	0.1%
	District of Columbia	17,896,573,000	0.9%

Source: U.S. Department of the Treasury, Internal Revenue Service
"Fiscal Year 2009 IRS Data Book" (http://www.irs.gov/taxstats/index.html)
*Total includes $18,372,324,000 from U.S. citizens abroad and other miscellaneous returns not shown separately.

Average Revenue Collection per Federal Individual Income Tax Return in 2009

National Average = $14,216 per Return*

ALPHA ORDER

RANK	STATE	PER RETURN
44	Alabama	$9,134
27	Alaska	12,220
39	Arizona	10,497
10	Arkansas	15,847
18	California	13,936
15	Colorado	14,497
2	Connecticut	22,303
1	Delaware	25,355
32	Florida	11,548
28	Georgia	12,083
43	Hawaii	9,292
42	Idaho	9,351
8	Illinois	16,422
24	Indiana	12,782
36	Iowa	11,232
21	Kansas	13,378
34	Kentucky	11,457
7	Louisiana	16,722
45	Maine	8,903
13	Maryland	14,961
5	Massachusetts	19,759
37	Michigan	11,212
3	Minnesota	22,193
50	Mississippi	6,948
16	Missouri	14,235
47	Montana	8,069
17	Nebraska	14,103
40	Nevada	10,043
29	New Hampshire	12,054
4	New Jersey	20,158
46	New Mexico	8,334
6	New York	18,505
23	North Carolina	12,799
31	North Dakota	11,786
9	Ohio	16,372
38	Oklahoma	11,109
33	Oregon	11,482
12	Pennsylvania	15,110
11	Rhode Island	15,687
48	South Carolina	8,047
30	South Dakota	11,952
19	Tennessee	13,831
14	Texas	14,774
35	Utah	11,235
41	Vermont	9,526
20	Virginia	13,530
22	Washington	13,314
49	West Virginia	7,409
25	Wisconsin	12,503
26	Wyoming	12,424

RANK ORDER

RANK	STATE	PER RETURN
1	Delaware	$25,355
2	Connecticut	22,303
3	Minnesota	22,193
4	New Jersey	20,158
5	Massachusetts	19,759
6	New York	18,505
7	Louisiana	16,722
8	Illinois	16,422
9	Ohio	16,372
10	Arkansas	15,847
11	Rhode Island	15,687
12	Pennsylvania	15,110
13	Maryland	14,961
14	Texas	14,774
15	Colorado	14,497
16	Missouri	14,235
17	Nebraska	14,103
18	California	13,936
19	Tennessee	13,831
20	Virginia	13,530
21	Kansas	13,378
22	Washington	13,314
23	North Carolina	12,799
24	Indiana	12,782
25	Wisconsin	12,503
26	Wyoming	12,424
27	Alaska	12,220
28	Georgia	12,083
29	New Hampshire	12,054
30	South Dakota	11,952
31	North Dakota	11,786
32	Florida	11,548
33	Oregon	11,482
34	Kentucky	11,457
35	Utah	11,235
36	Iowa	11,232
37	Michigan	11,212
38	Oklahoma	11,109
39	Arizona	10,497
40	Nevada	10,043
41	Vermont	9,526
42	Idaho	9,351
43	Hawaii	9,292
44	Alabama	9,134
45	Maine	8,903
46	New Mexico	8,334
47	Montana	8,069
48	South Carolina	8,047
49	West Virginia	7,409
50	Mississippi	6,948
	District of Columbia	58,699

Source: CQ Press using data from U.S. Department of the Treasury, Internal Revenue Service
"Fiscal Year 2009 IRS Data Book" (http://www.irs.gov/taxstats/index.html)
*National Rate includes collections and returns from U.S. citizens abroad and other miscellaneous returns not shown separately.

Adjusted Gross Income in 2008

National Total = $8,178,369,208,000*

ALPHA ORDER

RANK	STATE	A.G.I.	% of USA
25	Alabama	$99,243,507,000	1.2%
46	Alaska	20,827,932,000	0.3%
21	Arizona	141,787,560,000	1.7%
34	Arkansas	54,402,707,000	0.7%
1	California	1,029,474,051,000	12.6%
20	Colorado	143,080,084,000	1.7%
19	Connecticut	143,946,830,000	1.8%
44	Delaware	24,263,346,000	0.3%
4	Florida	472,429,878,000	5.8%
12	Georgia	215,392,407,000	2.6%
40	Hawaii	33,877,950,000	0.4%
41	Idaho	30,717,579,000	0.4%
5	Illinois	374,548,593,000	4.6%
18	Indiana	144,377,323,000	1.8%
30	Iowa	71,528,220,000	0.9%
32	Kansas	70,890,584,000	0.9%
28	Kentucky	85,903,879,000	1.1%
24	Louisiana	106,362,237,000	1.3%
42	Maine	29,682,577,000	0.4%
15	Maryland	185,108,742,000	2.3%
11	Massachusetts	226,476,203,000	2.8%
10	Michigan	231,683,311,000	2.8%
16	Minnesota	151,773,983,000	1.9%
35	Mississippi	52,321,579,000	0.6%
22	Missouri	139,187,724,000	1.7%
45	Montana	21,406,639,000	0.3%
36	Nebraska	43,894,512,000	0.5%
31	Nevada	71,050,701,000	0.9%
38	New Hampshire	40,335,754,000	0.5%
7	New Jersey	315,972,205,000	3.9%
37	New Mexico	41,547,512,000	0.5%
3	New York	630,575,468,000	7.7%
13	North Carolina	209,057,409,000	2.6%
49	North Dakota	16,858,774,000	0.2%
8	Ohio	270,208,208,000	3.3%
29	Oklahoma	82,099,684,000	1.0%
27	Oregon	88,955,156,000	1.1%
6	Pennsylvania	334,701,855,000	4.1%
43	Rhode Island	28,211,010,000	0.3%
26	South Carolina	93,513,472,000	1.1%
47	South Dakota	19,073,893,000	0.2%
23	Tennessee	134,950,699,000	1.7%
2	Texas	639,971,478,000	7.8%
33	Utah	60,032,402,000	0.7%
50	Vermont	15,950,073,000	0.2%
9	Virginia	238,153,992,000	2.9%
14	Washington	194,217,775,000	2.4%
39	West Virginia	34,937,804,000	0.4%
17	Wisconsin	145,009,304,000	1.8%
48	Wyoming	17,864,578,000	0.2%

RANK ORDER

RANK	STATE	A.G.I.	% of USA
1	California	$1,029,474,051,000	12.6%
2	Texas	639,971,478,000	7.8%
3	New York	630,575,468,000	7.7%
4	Florida	472,429,878,000	5.8%
5	Illinois	374,548,593,000	4.6%
6	Pennsylvania	334,701,855,000	4.1%
7	New Jersey	315,972,205,000	3.9%
8	Ohio	270,208,208,000	3.3%
9	Virginia	238,153,992,000	2.9%
10	Michigan	231,683,311,000	2.8%
11	Massachusetts	226,476,203,000	2.8%
12	Georgia	215,392,407,000	2.6%
13	North Carolina	209,057,409,000	2.6%
14	Washington	194,217,775,000	2.4%
15	Maryland	185,108,742,000	2.3%
16	Minnesota	151,773,983,000	1.9%
17	Wisconsin	145,009,304,000	1.8%
18	Indiana	144,377,323,000	1.8%
19	Connecticut	143,946,830,000	1.8%
20	Colorado	143,080,084,000	1.7%
21	Arizona	141,787,560,000	1.7%
22	Missouri	139,187,724,000	1.7%
23	Tennessee	134,950,699,000	1.7%
24	Louisiana	106,362,237,000	1.3%
25	Alabama	99,243,507,000	1.2%
26	South Carolina	93,513,472,000	1.1%
27	Oregon	88,955,156,000	1.1%
28	Kentucky	85,903,879,000	1.1%
29	Oklahoma	82,099,684,000	1.0%
30	Iowa	71,528,220,000	0.9%
31	Nevada	71,050,701,000	0.9%
32	Kansas	70,890,584,000	0.9%
33	Utah	60,032,402,000	0.7%
34	Arkansas	54,402,707,000	0.7%
35	Mississippi	52,321,579,000	0.6%
36	Nebraska	43,894,512,000	0.5%
37	New Mexico	41,547,512,000	0.5%
38	New Hampshire	40,335,754,000	0.5%
39	West Virginia	34,937,804,000	0.4%
40	Hawaii	33,877,950,000	0.4%
41	Idaho	30,717,579,000	0.4%
42	Maine	29,682,577,000	0.4%
43	Rhode Island	28,211,010,000	0.3%
44	Delaware	24,263,346,000	0.3%
45	Montana	21,406,639,000	0.3%
46	Alaska	20,827,932,000	0.3%
47	South Dakota	19,073,893,000	0.2%
48	Wyoming	17,864,578,000	0.2%
49	North Dakota	16,858,774,000	0.2%
50	Vermont	15,950,073,000	0.2%
	District of Columbia	22,495,366,000	0.3%

Source: U.S. Department of the Treasury, Internal Revenue Service
    "Individual Tax Statistics, State Income" (http://www.irs.gov/)
*Total includes $88,034,698,000 from U.S. citizens abroad and other miscellaneous returns not shown separately.

Per Capita Adjusted Gross Income in 2008

National Per Capita = $26,580*

ALPHA ORDER

ALPHA ORDER

RANK	STATE	PER CAPITA
43	Alabama	$21,217
9	Alaska	30,268
41	Arizona	21,816
49	Arkansas	18,970
14	California	28,143
13	Colorado	28,992
1	Connecticut	41,093
15	Delaware	27,691
24	Florida	25,642
38	Georgia	22,210
20	Hawaii	26,313
46	Idaho	20,110
11	Illinois	29,164
35	Indiana	22,600
28	Iowa	23,891
25	Kansas	25,342
47	Kentucky	20,034
27	Louisiana	23,894
37	Maine	22,492
5	Maryland	32,712
3	Massachusetts	34,610
33	Michigan	23,163
12	Minnesota	29,017
50	Mississippi	17,795
32	Missouri	23,368
39	Montana	22,113
26	Nebraska	24,633
16	Nevada	27,162
8	New Hampshire	30,514
2	New Jersey	36,472
44	New Mexico	20,912
6	New York	32,391
34	North Carolina	22,608
21	North Dakota	26,283
31	Ohio	23,439
36	Oklahoma	22,530
30	Oregon	23,515
18	Pennsylvania	26,635
17	Rhode Island	26,778
45	South Carolina	20,766
29	South Dakota	23,708
42	Tennessee	21,625
19	Texas	26,332
40	Utah	22,011
23	Vermont	25,682
7	Virginia	30,550
10	Washington	29,579
48	West Virginia	19,251
22	Wisconsin	25,767
4	Wyoming	33,518

RANK ORDER

RANK	STATE	PER CAPITA
1	Connecticut	$41,093
2	New Jersey	36,472
3	Massachusetts	34,610
4	Wyoming	33,518
5	Maryland	32,712
6	New York	32,391
7	Virginia	30,550
8	New Hampshire	30,514
9	Alaska	30,268
10	Washington	29,579
11	Illinois	29,164
12	Minnesota	29,017
13	Colorado	28,992
14	California	28,143
15	Delaware	27,691
16	Nevada	27,162
17	Rhode Island	26,778
18	Pennsylvania	26,635
19	Texas	26,332
20	Hawaii	26,313
21	North Dakota	26,283
22	Wisconsin	25,767
23	Vermont	25,682
24	Florida	25,642
25	Kansas	25,342
26	Nebraska	24,633
27	Louisiana	23,894
28	Iowa	23,891
29	South Dakota	23,708
30	Oregon	23,515
31	Ohio	23,439
32	Missouri	23,368
33	Michigan	23,163
34	North Carolina	22,608
35	Indiana	22,600
36	Oklahoma	22,530
37	Maine	22,492
38	Georgia	22,210
39	Montana	22,113
40	Utah	22,011
41	Arizona	21,816
42	Tennessee	21,625
43	Alabama	21,217
44	New Mexico	20,912
45	South Carolina	20,766
46	Idaho	20,110
47	Kentucky	20,034
48	West Virginia	19,251
49	Arkansas	18,970
50	Mississippi	17,795
	District of Columbia	38,123

Source: CQ Press using data from U.S. Department of the Treasury, Internal Revenue Service
"Individual Tax Statistics, State Income" (http://www.irs.gov/)
*National per capita does not include income from U.S. citizens abroad and other miscellaneous returns not shown separately.

Federal Business Income Tax Collections in 2009

National Total = $225,481,588,000*

ALPHA ORDER

RANK	STATE	COLLECTIONS	% of USA
36	Alabama	$690,741,000	0.3%
45	Alaska	222,515,000	0.1%
26	Arizona	2,471,398,000	1.1%
12	Arkansas	5,524,663,000	2.5%
1	California	27,095,063,000	12.0%
23	Colorado	2,856,472,000	1.3%
15	Connecticut	4,800,755,000	2.1%
25	Delaware	2,725,766,000	1.2%
16	Florida	4,426,304,000	2.0%
11	Georgia	5,671,371,000	2.5%
41	Hawaii	423,772,000	0.2%
39	Idaho	501,992,000	0.2%
5	Illinois	12,991,659,000	5.8%
22	Indiana	2,883,236,000	1.3%
30	Iowa	1,427,436,000	0.6%
32	Kansas	1,267,195,000	0.6%
29	Kentucky	1,446,147,000	0.6%
31	Louisiana	1,326,230,000	0.6%
48	Maine	177,487,000	0.1%
28	Maryland	2,186,965,000	1.0%
14	Massachusetts	5,014,595,000	2.2%
20	Michigan	3,429,151,000	1.5%
8	Minnesota	8,850,168,000	3.9%
38	Mississippi	554,850,000	0.2%
18	Missouri	3,861,265,000	1.7%
49	Montana	177,339,000	0.1%
17	Nebraska	3,941,704,000	1.7%
35	Nevada	728,916,000	0.3%
40	New Hampshire	467,026,000	0.2%
4	New Jersey	14,950,946,000	6.6%
43	New Mexico	284,268,000	0.1%
3	New York	18,213,230,000	8.1%
7	North Carolina	9,039,509,000	4.0%
44	North Dakota	261,179,000	0.1%
9	Ohio	8,826,533,000	3.9%
27	Oklahoma	2,387,976,000	1.1%
33	Oregon	1,147,789,000	0.5%
6	Pennsylvania	10,612,832,000	4.7%
24	Rhode Island	2,745,130,000	1.2%
34	South Carolina	937,804,000	0.4%
50	South Dakota	171,290,000	0.1%
19	Tennessee	3,651,310,000	1.6%
2	Texas	24,235,172,000	10.7%
37	Utah	686,104,000	0.3%
47	Vermont	209,377,000	0.1%
10	Virginia	7,229,899,000	3.2%
13	Washington	5,161,652,000	2.3%
42	West Virginia	370,444,000	0.2%
21	Wisconsin	3,288,051,000	1.5%
46	Wyoming	214,410,000	0.1%

RANK ORDER

RANK	STATE	COLLECTIONS	% of USA
1	California	$27,095,063,000	12.0%
2	Texas	24,235,172,000	10.7%
3	New York	18,213,230,000	8.1%
4	New Jersey	14,950,946,000	6.6%
5	Illinois	12,991,659,000	5.8%
6	Pennsylvania	10,612,832,000	4.7%
7	North Carolina	9,039,509,000	4.0%
8	Minnesota	8,850,168,000	3.9%
9	Ohio	8,826,533,000	3.9%
10	Virginia	7,229,899,000	3.2%
11	Georgia	5,671,371,000	2.5%
12	Arkansas	5,524,663,000	2.5%
13	Washington	5,161,652,000	2.3%
14	Massachusetts	5,014,595,000	2.2%
15	Connecticut	4,800,755,000	2.1%
16	Florida	4,426,304,000	2.0%
17	Nebraska	3,941,704,000	1.7%
18	Missouri	3,861,265,000	1.7%
19	Tennessee	3,651,310,000	1.6%
20	Michigan	3,429,151,000	1.5%
21	Wisconsin	3,288,051,000	1.5%
22	Indiana	2,883,236,000	1.3%
23	Colorado	2,856,472,000	1.3%
24	Rhode Island	2,745,130,000	1.2%
25	Delaware	2,725,766,000	1.2%
26	Arizona	2,471,398,000	1.1%
27	Oklahoma	2,387,976,000	1.1%
28	Maryland	2,186,965,000	1.0%
29	Kentucky	1,446,147,000	0.6%
30	Iowa	1,427,436,000	0.6%
31	Louisiana	1,326,230,000	0.6%
32	Kansas	1,267,195,000	0.6%
33	Oregon	1,147,789,000	0.5%
34	South Carolina	937,804,000	0.4%
35	Nevada	728,916,000	0.3%
36	Alabama	690,741,000	0.3%
37	Utah	686,104,000	0.3%
38	Mississippi	554,850,000	0.2%
39	Idaho	501,992,000	0.2%
40	New Hampshire	467,026,000	0.2%
41	Hawaii	423,772,000	0.2%
42	West Virginia	370,444,000	0.2%
43	New Mexico	284,268,000	0.1%
44	North Dakota	261,179,000	0.1%
45	Alaska	222,515,000	0.1%
46	Wyoming	214,410,000	0.1%
47	Vermont	209,377,000	0.1%
48	Maine	177,487,000	0.1%
49	Montana	177,339,000	0.1%
50	South Dakota	171,290,000	0.1%
	District of Columbia	1,466,547,000	0.7%

Source: U.S. Department of the Treasury, Internal Revenue Service
"Fiscal Year 2009 IRS Data Book" (http://www.irs.gov/taxstats/index.html)
*Total includes collections and returns from international sources and others not distributed by state. Includes taxes on corporation income, farmers' cooperatives, and "unrelated business income" from tax-exempt organizations.

Average Revenue Collection per Federal Business Income Tax Return in 2009

National Average = $32,343 per Return*

ALPHA ORDER

RANK	STATE	PER RETURN
43	Alabama	$9,381
31	Alaska	18,133
27	Arizona	20,023
3	Arkansas	98,381
17	California	36,310
30	Colorado	18,164
5	Connecticut	84,283
1	Delaware	107,751
49	Florida	5,473
22	Georgia	24,369
36	Hawaii	14,622
38	Idaho	13,532
14	Illinois	38,310
23	Indiana	24,150
25	Iowa	22,892
24	Kansas	23,581
26	Kentucky	20,611
35	Louisiana	14,814
48	Maine	5,528
32	Maryland	17,390
19	Massachusetts	33,626
34	Michigan	16,732
7	Minnesota	66,821
39	Mississippi	12,857
16	Missouri	36,312
50	Montana	5,167
4	Nebraska	89,860
46	Nevada	9,118
28	New Hampshire	19,302
6	New Jersey	68,764
47	New Mexico	9,037
21	New York	28,320
12	North Carolina	44,966
29	North Dakota	18,257
11	Ohio	45,821
20	Oklahoma	32,644
37	Oregon	14,187
10	Pennsylvania	47,440
2	Rhode Island	106,442
42	South Carolina	10,270
45	South Dakota	9,142
9	Tennessee	51,502
8	Texas	57,171
44	Utah	9,277
41	Vermont	12,194
13	Virginia	43,073
15	Washington	36,646
33	West Virginia	17,055
18	Wisconsin	33,692
40	Wyoming	12,234

RANK ORDER

RANK	STATE	PER RETURN
1	Delaware	$107,751
2	Rhode Island	106,442
3	Arkansas	98,381
4	Nebraska	89,860
5	Connecticut	84,283
6	New Jersey	68,764
7	Minnesota	66,821
8	Texas	57,171
9	Tennessee	51,502
10	Pennsylvania	47,440
11	Ohio	45,821
12	North Carolina	44,966
13	Virginia	43,073
14	Illinois	38,310
15	Washington	36,646
16	Missouri	36,312
17	California	36,310
18	Wisconsin	33,692
19	Massachusetts	33,626
20	Oklahoma	32,644
21	New York	28,320
22	Georgia	24,369
23	Indiana	24,150
24	Kansas	23,581
25	Iowa	22,892
26	Kentucky	20,611
27	Arizona	20,023
28	New Hampshire	19,302
29	North Dakota	18,257
30	Colorado	18,164
31	Alaska	18,133
32	Maryland	17,390
33	West Virginia	17,055
34	Michigan	16,732
35	Louisiana	14,814
36	Hawaii	14,622
37	Oregon	14,187
38	Idaho	13,532
39	Mississippi	12,857
40	Wyoming	12,234
41	Vermont	12,194
42	South Carolina	10,270
43	Alabama	9,381
44	Utah	9,277
45	South Dakota	9,142
46	Nevada	9,118
47	New Mexico	9,037
48	Maine	5,528
49	Florida	5,473
50	Montana	5,167

District of Columbia   87,875

Source: CQ Press using data from U.S. Department of the Treasury, Internal Revenue Service
"Fiscal Year 2009 IRS Data Book" (http://www.irs.gov/taxstats/index.html)
*National per capita does not include income from U.S. citizens abroad and other miscellaneous returns not shown separately.
Includes taxes on corporation income, farmers' cooperatives, and "unrelated business income" from tax-exempt organizations.

Federal Tax Returns Filed in 2009

National Total = 236,503,362 Returns*

ALPHA ORDER

RANK	STATE	RETURNS	% of USA
23	Alabama	3,236,095	1.4%
47	Alaska	599,905	0.3%
18	Arizona	4,502,431	1.9%
33	Arkansas	2,000,505	0.8%
1	California	28,260,324	11.9%
22	Colorado	4,295,109	1.8%
27	Connecticut	3,043,281	1.3%
45	Delaware	756,353	0.3%
3	Florida	15,961,643	6.7%
9	Georgia	6,849,726	2.9%
40	Hawaii	1,120,099	0.5%
39	Idaho	1,180,254	0.5%
5	Illinois	10,164,459	4.3%
15	Indiana	4,716,842	2.0%
30	Iowa	2,433,424	1.0%
31	Kansas	2,270,579	1.0%
28	Kentucky	2,925,694	1.2%
24	Louisiana	3,233,892	1.4%
42	Maine	1,086,128	0.5%
19	Maryland	4,479,310	1.9%
14	Massachusetts	5,398,461	2.3%
8	Michigan	7,356,862	3.1%
20	Minnesota	4,397,408	1.9%
35	Mississippi	1,926,246	0.8%
17	Missouri	4,513,764	1.9%
43	Montana	929,547	0.4%
37	Nebraska	1,482,383	0.6%
32	Nevada	2,099,474	0.9%
41	New Hampshire	1,094,476	0.5%
11	New Jersey	6,569,654	2.8%
36	New Mexico	1,484,974	0.6%
4	New York	14,753,061	6.2%
10	North Carolina	6,764,007	2.9%
48	North Dakota	596,641	0.3%
6	Ohio	8,724,712	3.7%
29	Oklahoma	2,736,079	1.2%
26	Oregon	3,130,465	1.3%
7	Pennsylvania	8,630,524	3.6%
44	Rhode Island	881,686	0.4%
25	South Carolina	3,230,416	1.4%
46	South Dakota	716,575	0.3%
21	Tennessee	4,363,775	1.8%
2	Texas	17,559,699	7.4%
34	Utah	1,999,045	0.8%
49	Vermont	566,859	0.2%
12	Virginia	6,148,801	2.6%
13	Washington	5,516,349	2.3%
38	West Virginia	1,215,461	0.5%
16	Wisconsin	4,520,831	1.9%
50	Wyoming	527,345	0.2%

RANK ORDER

RANK	STATE	RETURNS	% of USA
1	California	28,260,324	11.9%
2	Texas	17,559,699	7.4%
3	Florida	15,961,643	6.7%
4	New York	14,753,061	6.2%
5	Illinois	10,164,459	4.3%
6	Ohio	8,724,712	3.7%
7	Pennsylvania	8,630,524	3.6%
8	Michigan	7,356,862	3.1%
9	Georgia	6,849,726	2.9%
10	North Carolina	6,764,007	2.9%
11	New Jersey	6,569,654	2.8%
12	Virginia	6,148,801	2.6%
13	Washington	5,516,349	2.3%
14	Massachusetts	5,398,461	2.3%
15	Indiana	4,716,842	2.0%
16	Wisconsin	4,520,831	1.9%
17	Missouri	4,513,764	1.9%
18	Arizona	4,502,431	1.9%
19	Maryland	4,479,310	1.9%
20	Minnesota	4,397,408	1.9%
21	Tennessee	4,363,775	1.8%
22	Colorado	4,295,109	1.8%
23	Alabama	3,236,095	1.4%
24	Louisiana	3,233,892	1.4%
25	South Carolina	3,230,416	1.4%
26	Oregon	3,130,465	1.3%
27	Connecticut	3,043,281	1.3%
28	Kentucky	2,925,694	1.2%
29	Oklahoma	2,736,079	1.2%
30	Iowa	2,433,424	1.0%
31	Kansas	2,270,579	1.0%
32	Nevada	2,099,474	0.9%
33	Arkansas	2,000,505	0.8%
34	Utah	1,999,045	0.8%
35	Mississippi	1,926,246	0.8%
36	New Mexico	1,484,974	0.6%
37	Nebraska	1,482,383	0.6%
38	West Virginia	1,215,461	0.5%
39	Idaho	1,180,254	0.5%
40	Hawaii	1,120,099	0.5%
41	New Hampshire	1,094,476	0.5%
42	Maine	1,086,128	0.5%
43	Montana	929,547	0.4%
44	Rhode Island	881,686	0.4%
45	Delaware	756,353	0.3%
46	South Dakota	716,575	0.3%
47	Alaska	599,905	0.3%
48	North Dakota	596,641	0.3%
49	Vermont	566,859	0.2%
50	Wyoming	527,345	0.2%
	District of Columbia	528,808	0.2%

Source: U.S. Department of the Treasury, Internal Revenue Service
"Fiscal Year 2009 IRS Data Book" (http://www.irs.gov/taxstats/index.html)
*Total includes returns from international sources and other miscellaneous returns not shown separately.

Federal Individual Income Tax Returns Filed in 2009

National Total = 144,103,375 Returns*

ALPHA ORDER

RANK	STATE	RETURNS	% of USA
23	Alabama	2,085,986	1.4%
47	Alaska	359,017	0.2%
20	Arizona	2,721,160	1.9%
34	Arkansas	1,226,213	0.9%
1	California	16,519,265	11.5%
22	Colorado	2,345,659	1.6%
28	Connecticut	1,751,325	1.2%
45	Delaware	427,241	0.3%
4	Florida	8,916,953	6.2%
10	Georgia	4,273,666	3.0%
41	Hawaii	660,232	0.5%
40	Idaho	668,331	0.5%
6	Illinois	6,134,205	4.3%
15	Indiana	3,026,559	2.1%
30	Iowa	1,421,256	1.0%
31	Kansas	1,330,840	0.9%
26	Kentucky	1,877,646	1.3%
25	Louisiana	1,971,715	1.4%
42	Maine	639,377	0.4%
17	Maryland	2,785,531	1.9%
13	Massachusetts	3,229,387	2.2%
8	Michigan	4,642,834	3.2%
21	Minnesota	2,574,508	1.8%
33	Mississippi	1,257,683	0.9%
19	Missouri	2,743,210	1.9%
44	Montana	478,918	0.3%
37	Nebraska	859,500	0.6%
32	Nevada	1,274,794	0.9%
39	New Hampshire	673,510	0.5%
9	New Jersey	4,320,565	3.0%
36	New Mexico	925,510	0.6%
3	New York	9,271,451	6.4%
11	North Carolina	4,202,065	2.9%
48	North Dakota	323,832	0.2%
7	Ohio	5,579,715	3.9%
29	Oklahoma	1,614,595	1.1%
27	Oregon	1,759,057	1.2%
5	Pennsylvania	6,151,409	4.3%
43	Rhode Island	514,047	0.4%
24	South Carolina	2,053,587	1.4%
46	South Dakota	390,265	0.3%
16	Tennessee	2,851,378	2.0%
2	Texas	10,748,636	7.5%
35	Utah	1,148,817	0.8%
49	Vermont	321,923	0.2%
12	Virginia	3,745,024	2.6%
14	Washington	3,196,039	2.2%
38	West Virginia	789,947	0.5%
18	Wisconsin	2,772,429	1.9%
50	Wyoming	274,279	0.2%

RANK ORDER

RANK	STATE	RETURNS	% of USA
1	California	16,519,265	11.5%
2	Texas	10,748,636	7.5%
3	New York	9,271,451	6.4%
4	Florida	8,916,953	6.2%
5	Pennsylvania	6,151,409	4.3%
6	Illinois	6,134,205	4.3%
7	Ohio	5,579,715	3.9%
8	Michigan	4,642,834	3.2%
9	New Jersey	4,320,565	3.0%
10	Georgia	4,273,666	3.0%
11	North Carolina	4,202,065	2.9%
12	Virginia	3,745,024	2.6%
13	Massachusetts	3,229,387	2.2%
14	Washington	3,196,039	2.2%
15	Indiana	3,026,559	2.1%
16	Tennessee	2,851,378	2.0%
17	Maryland	2,785,531	1.9%
18	Wisconsin	2,772,429	1.9%
19	Missouri	2,743,210	1.9%
20	Arizona	2,721,160	1.9%
21	Minnesota	2,574,508	1.8%
22	Colorado	2,345,659	1.6%
23	Alabama	2,085,986	1.4%
24	South Carolina	2,053,587	1.4%
25	Louisiana	1,971,715	1.4%
26	Kentucky	1,877,646	1.3%
27	Oregon	1,759,057	1.2%
28	Connecticut	1,751,325	1.2%
29	Oklahoma	1,614,595	1.1%
30	Iowa	1,421,256	1.0%
31	Kansas	1,330,840	0.9%
32	Nevada	1,274,794	0.9%
33	Mississippi	1,257,683	0.9%
34	Arkansas	1,226,213	0.9%
35	Utah	1,148,817	0.8%
36	New Mexico	925,510	0.6%
37	Nebraska	859,500	0.6%
38	West Virginia	789,947	0.5%
39	New Hampshire	673,510	0.5%
40	Idaho	668,331	0.5%
41	Hawaii	660,232	0.5%
42	Maine	639,377	0.4%
43	Rhode Island	514,047	0.4%
44	Montana	478,918	0.3%
45	Delaware	427,241	0.3%
46	South Dakota	390,265	0.3%
47	Alaska	359,017	0.2%
48	North Dakota	323,832	0.2%
49	Vermont	321,923	0.2%
50	Wyoming	274,279	0.2%
	District of Columbia	304,889	0.2%

Source: U.S. Department of the Treasury, Internal Revenue Service
"Fiscal Year 2009 IRS Data Book" (http://www.irs.gov/taxstats/index.html)
*Total includes returns from international sources and other miscellaneous returns not shown separately.

Federal Corporate Income Tax Returns Filed in 2009

National Total = 6,971,470 Returns*

ALPHA ORDER

RANK	STATE	RETURNS	% of USA
27	Alabama	73,629	1.1%
50	Alaska	12,271	0.2%
18	Arizona	123,426	1.8%
33	Arkansas	56,156	0.8%
2	California	746,222	10.7%
13	Colorado	157,261	2.3%
32	Connecticut	56,960	0.8%
43	Delaware	25,297	0.4%
1	Florida	808,700	11.6%
6	Georgia	232,729	3.3%
41	Hawaii	28,982	0.4%
37	Idaho	37,096	0.5%
5	Illinois	339,123	4.9%
19	Indiana	119,389	1.7%
31	Iowa	62,355	0.9%
34	Kansas	53,739	0.8%
30	Kentucky	70,163	1.0%
23	Louisiana	89,523	1.3%
39	Maine	32,106	0.5%
17	Maryland	125,758	1.8%
14	Massachusetts	149,129	2.1%
9	Michigan	204,948	2.9%
16	Minnesota	132,446	1.9%
36	Mississippi	43,155	0.6%
20	Missouri	106,337	1.5%
38	Montana	34,320	0.5%
35	Nebraska	43,865	0.6%
25	Nevada	79,940	1.1%
44	New Hampshire	24,196	0.3%
8	New Jersey	217,425	3.1%
40	New Mexico	31,456	0.5%
3	New York	643,113	9.2%
10	North Carolina	201,030	2.9%
49	North Dakota	14,306	0.2%
11	Ohio	192,629	2.8%
28	Oklahoma	73,153	1.0%
24	Oregon	80,906	1.2%
7	Pennsylvania	223,709	3.2%
42	Rhode Island	25,790	0.4%
22	South Carolina	91,312	1.3%
46	South Dakota	18,737	0.3%
29	Tennessee	70,896	1.0%
4	Texas	423,907	6.1%
26	Utah	73,957	1.1%
48	Vermont	17,170	0.2%
12	Virginia	167,851	2.4%
15	Washington	140,853	2.0%
45	West Virginia	21,720	0.3%
21	Wisconsin	97,592	1.4%
47	Wyoming	17,526	0.3%

RANK ORDER

RANK	STATE	RETURNS	% of USA
1	Florida	808,700	11.6%
2	California	746,222	10.7%
3	New York	643,113	9.2%
4	Texas	423,907	6.1%
5	Illinois	339,123	4.9%
6	Georgia	232,729	3.3%
7	Pennsylvania	223,709	3.2%
8	New Jersey	217,425	3.1%
9	Michigan	204,948	2.9%
10	North Carolina	201,030	2.9%
11	Ohio	192,629	2.8%
12	Virginia	167,851	2.4%
13	Colorado	157,261	2.3%
14	Massachusetts	149,129	2.1%
15	Washington	140,853	2.0%
16	Minnesota	132,446	1.9%
17	Maryland	125,758	1.8%
18	Arizona	123,426	1.8%
19	Indiana	119,389	1.7%
20	Missouri	106,337	1.5%
21	Wisconsin	97,592	1.4%
22	South Carolina	91,312	1.3%
23	Louisiana	89,523	1.3%
24	Oregon	80,906	1.2%
25	Nevada	79,940	1.1%
26	Utah	73,957	1.1%
27	Alabama	73,629	1.1%
28	Oklahoma	73,153	1.0%
29	Tennessee	70,896	1.0%
30	Kentucky	70,163	1.0%
31	Iowa	62,355	0.9%
32	Connecticut	56,960	0.8%
33	Arkansas	56,156	0.8%
34	Kansas	53,739	0.8%
35	Nebraska	43,865	0.6%
36	Mississippi	43,155	0.6%
37	Idaho	37,096	0.5%
38	Montana	34,320	0.5%
39	Maine	32,106	0.5%
40	New Mexico	31,456	0.5%
41	Hawaii	28,982	0.4%
42	Rhode Island	25,790	0.4%
43	Delaware	25,297	0.4%
44	New Hampshire	24,196	0.3%
45	West Virginia	21,720	0.3%
46	South Dakota	18,737	0.3%
47	Wyoming	17,526	0.3%
48	Vermont	17,170	0.2%
49	North Dakota	14,306	0.2%
50	Alaska	12,271	0.2%
	District of Columbia	16,689	0.2%

Source: U.S. Department of the Treasury, Internal Revenue Service
  "Fiscal Year 2009 IRS Data Book" (http://www.irs.gov/taxstats/index.html)
*Total includes returns from international sources and other miscellaneous returns not shown separately.

Federal Tax Refunds in 2009

National Total = 126,937,150 Refunds*

ALPHA ORDER

RANK	STATE	REFUNDS	% of USA
23	Alabama	1,871,289	1.5%
48	Alaska	277,069	0.2%
20	Arizona	2,391,161	1.9%
34	Arkansas	1,092,004	0.9%
1	California	14,302,483	11.3%
22	Colorado	2,023,808	1.6%
27	Connecticut	1,514,719	1.2%
45	Delaware	386,238	0.3%
4	Florida	8,087,177	6.4%
9	Georgia	3,848,604	3.0%
41	Hawaii	576,105	0.5%
40	Idaho	587,008	0.5%
5	Illinois	5,462,754	4.3%
15	Indiana	2,712,863	2.1%
30	Iowa	1,214,777	1.0%
32	Kansas	1,135,797	0.9%
26	Kentucky	1,682,571	1.3%
25	Louisiana	1,773,460	1.4%
42	Maine	564,635	0.4%
17	Maryland	2,448,450	1.9%
14	Massachusetts	2,800,235	2.2%
8	Michigan	4,072,829	3.2%
21	Minnesota	2,183,186	1.7%
33	Mississippi	1,124,657	0.9%
18	Missouri	2,412,633	1.9%
44	Montana	405,910	0.3%
37	Nebraska	738,394	0.6%
31	Nevada	1,153,046	0.9%
39	New Hampshire	596,465	0.5%
10	New Jersey	3,739,852	2.9%
36	New Mexico	811,783	0.6%
3	New York	8,104,582	6.4%
11	North Carolina	3,710,439	2.9%
49	North Dakota	266,444	0.2%
7	Ohio	4,972,857	3.9%
29	Oklahoma	1,419,836	1.1%
28	Oregon	1,508,567	1.2%
6	Pennsylvania	5,432,646	4.3%
43	Rhode Island	471,016	0.4%
24	South Carolina	1,807,122	1.4%
46	South Dakota	333,441	0.3%
16	Tennessee	2,574,322	2.0%
2	Texas	9,848,172	7.8%
35	Utah	1,034,321	0.8%
47	Vermont	278,417	0.2%
12	Virginia	3,313,300	2.6%
13	Washington	2,857,929	2.3%
38	West Virginia	717,661	0.6%
19	Wisconsin	2,395,672	1.9%
50	Wyoming	244,555	0.2%

RANK ORDER

RANK	STATE	REFUNDS	% of USA
1	California	14,302,483	11.3%
2	Texas	9,848,172	7.8%
3	New York	8,104,582	6.4%
4	Florida	8,087,177	6.4%
5	Illinois	5,462,754	4.3%
6	Pennsylvania	5,432,646	4.3%
7	Ohio	4,972,857	3.9%
8	Michigan	4,072,829	3.2%
9	Georgia	3,848,604	3.0%
10	New Jersey	3,739,852	2.9%
11	North Carolina	3,710,439	2.9%
12	Virginia	3,313,300	2.6%
13	Washington	2,857,929	2.3%
14	Massachusetts	2,800,235	2.2%
15	Indiana	2,712,863	2.1%
16	Tennessee	2,574,322	2.0%
17	Maryland	2,448,450	1.9%
18	Missouri	2,412,633	1.9%
19	Wisconsin	2,395,672	1.9%
20	Arizona	2,391,161	1.9%
21	Minnesota	2,183,186	1.7%
22	Colorado	2,023,808	1.6%
23	Alabama	1,871,289	1.5%
24	South Carolina	1,807,122	1.4%
25	Louisiana	1,773,460	1.4%
26	Kentucky	1,682,571	1.3%
27	Connecticut	1,514,719	1.2%
28	Oregon	1,508,567	1.2%
29	Oklahoma	1,419,836	1.1%
30	Iowa	1,214,777	1.0%
31	Nevada	1,153,046	0.9%
32	Kansas	1,135,797	0.9%
33	Mississippi	1,124,657	0.9%
34	Arkansas	1,092,004	0.9%
35	Utah	1,034,321	0.8%
36	New Mexico	811,783	0.6%
37	Nebraska	738,394	0.6%
38	West Virginia	717,661	0.6%
39	New Hampshire	596,465	0.5%
40	Idaho	587,008	0.5%
41	Hawaii	576,105	0.5%
42	Maine	564,635	0.4%
43	Rhode Island	471,016	0.4%
44	Montana	405,910	0.3%
45	Delaware	386,238	0.3%
46	South Dakota	333,441	0.3%
47	Vermont	278,417	0.2%
48	Alaska	277,069	0.2%
49	North Dakota	266,444	0.2%
50	Wyoming	244,555	0.2%
	District of Columbia	269,071	0.2%

Source: U.S. Department of the Treasury, Internal Revenue Service
"Fiscal Year 2009 IRS Data Book" (http://www.irs.gov/taxstats/index.html)
*Total includes refunds to international sources and other miscellaneous refunds not shown separately.

Value of Federal Tax Refunds in 2009

National Total = $437,685,634,000*

ALPHA ORDER

RANK	STATE	REFUNDS	% of USA
24	Alabama	$6,098,291,000	1.4%
49	Alaska	664,943,000	0.2%
21	Arizona	7,542,986,000	1.7%
35	Arkansas	2,976,225,000	0.7%
1	California	51,095,106,000	11.7%
23	Colorado	6,544,713,000	1.5%
12	Connecticut	11,396,126,000	2.6%
36	Delaware	2,264,967,000	0.5%
4	Florida	25,376,172,000	5.8%
10	Georgia	12,769,290,000	2.9%
44	Hawaii	1,440,194,000	0.3%
39	Idaho	1,748,906,000	0.4%
5	Illinois	21,219,482,000	4.8%
19	Indiana	7,722,319,000	1.8%
31	Iowa	3,914,658,000	0.9%
32	Kansas	3,226,317,000	0.7%
29	Kentucky	4,287,140,000	1.0%
25	Louisiana	5,225,979,000	1.2%
41	Maine	1,611,141,000	0.4%
17	Maryland	8,226,217,000	1.9%
15	Massachusetts	9,474,090,000	2.2%
11	Michigan	12,232,118,000	2.8%
18	Minnesota	8,129,971,000	1.9%
33	Mississippi	3,200,666,000	0.7%
20	Missouri	7,603,775,000	1.7%
46	Montana	872,382,000	0.2%
38	Nebraska	1,901,856,000	0.4%
27	Nevada	4,385,906,000	1.0%
42	New Hampshire	1,606,544,000	0.4%
6	New Jersey	18,138,194,000	4.1%
37	New Mexico	1,973,250,000	0.5%
3	New York	35,050,285,000	8.0%
9	North Carolina	14,472,956,000	3.3%
50	North Dakota	645,682,000	0.1%
7	Ohio	16,267,342,000	3.7%
28	Oklahoma	4,368,872,000	1.0%
30	Oregon	3,916,882,000	0.9%
8	Pennsylvania	16,072,952,000	3.7%
43	Rhode Island	1,490,875,000	0.3%
26	South Carolina	4,971,348,000	1.1%
45	South Dakota	904,307,000	0.2%
14	Tennessee	9,614,649,000	2.2%
2	Texas	37,022,653,000	8.5%
34	Utah	3,016,625,000	0.7%
48	Vermont	703,197,000	0.2%
13	Virginia	10,557,647,000	2.4%
16	Washington	8,686,164,000	2.0%
40	West Virginia	1,688,140,000	0.4%
22	Wisconsin	6,660,933,000	1.5%
47	Wyoming	793,390,000	0.2%

RANK ORDER

RANK	STATE	REFUNDS	% of USA
1	California	$51,095,106,000	11.7%
2	Texas	37,022,653,000	8.5%
3	New York	35,050,285,000	8.0%
4	Florida	25,376,172,000	5.8%
5	Illinois	21,219,482,000	4.8%
6	New Jersey	18,138,194,000	4.1%
7	Ohio	16,267,342,000	3.7%
8	Pennsylvania	16,072,952,000	3.7%
9	North Carolina	14,472,956,000	3.3%
10	Georgia	12,769,290,000	2.9%
11	Michigan	12,232,118,000	2.8%
12	Connecticut	11,396,126,000	2.6%
13	Virginia	10,557,647,000	2.4%
14	Tennessee	9,614,649,000	2.2%
15	Massachusetts	9,474,090,000	2.2%
16	Washington	8,686,164,000	2.0%
17	Maryland	8,226,217,000	1.9%
18	Minnesota	8,129,971,000	1.9%
19	Indiana	7,722,319,000	1.8%
20	Missouri	7,603,775,000	1.7%
21	Arizona	7,542,986,000	1.7%
22	Wisconsin	6,660,933,000	1.5%
23	Colorado	6,544,713,000	1.5%
24	Alabama	6,098,291,000	1.4%
25	Louisiana	5,225,979,000	1.2%
26	South Carolina	4,971,348,000	1.1%
27	Nevada	4,385,906,000	1.0%
28	Oklahoma	4,368,872,000	1.0%
29	Kentucky	4,287,140,000	1.0%
30	Oregon	3,916,882,000	0.9%
31	Iowa	3,914,658,000	0.9%
32	Kansas	3,226,317,000	0.7%
33	Mississippi	3,200,666,000	0.7%
34	Utah	3,016,625,000	0.7%
35	Arkansas	2,976,225,000	0.7%
36	Delaware	2,264,967,000	0.5%
37	New Mexico	1,973,250,000	0.5%
38	Nebraska	1,901,856,000	0.4%
39	Idaho	1,748,906,000	0.4%
40	West Virginia	1,688,140,000	0.4%
41	Maine	1,611,141,000	0.4%
42	New Hampshire	1,606,544,000	0.4%
43	Rhode Island	1,490,875,000	0.3%
44	Hawaii	1,440,194,000	0.3%
45	South Dakota	904,307,000	0.2%
46	Montana	872,382,000	0.2%
47	Wyoming	793,390,000	0.2%
48	Vermont	703,197,000	0.2%
49	Alaska	664,943,000	0.2%
50	North Dakota	645,682,000	0.1%
	District of Columbia	990,283,000	0.2%

Source: U.S. Department of the Treasury, Internal Revenue Service
"Fiscal Year 2009 IRS Data Book" (http://www.irs.gov/taxstats/index.html)
*Total includes refunds to international sources and other miscellaneous refunds not shown separately.

Average Value of Federal Tax Refunds in 2009

National Average = $3,448*

ALPHA ORDER				RANK ORDER		
RANK	STATE	AVERAGE REFUND		RANK	STATE	AVERAGE REFUND
16	Alabama	$3,259		1	Connecticut	$7,524
48	Alaska	2,400		2	Delaware	5,864
22	Arizona	3,155		3	New Jersey	4,850
38	Arkansas	2,725		4	New York	4,325
11	California	3,572		5	North Carolina	3,901
18	Colorado	3,234		6	Illinois	3,884
1	Connecticut	7,524		7	Nevada	3,804
2	Delaware	5,864		8	Texas	3,759
24	Florida	3,138		9	Tennessee	3,735
14	Georgia	3,318		10	Minnesota	3,724
45	Hawaii	2,500		11	California	3,572
28	Idaho	2,979		12	Massachusetts	3,383
6	Illinois	3,884		13	Maryland	3,360
33	Indiana	2,847		14	Georgia	3,318
19	Iowa	3,223		15	Ohio	3,271
35	Kansas	2,841		16	Alabama	3,259
43	Kentucky	2,548		17	Wyoming	3,244
30	Louisiana	2,947		18	Colorado	3,234
32	Maine	2,853		19	Iowa	3,223
13	Maryland	3,360		20	Virginia	3,186
12	Massachusetts	3,383		21	Rhode Island	3,165
27	Michigan	3,003		22	Arizona	3,155
10	Minnesota	3,724		23	Missouri	3,152
34	Mississippi	2,846		24	Florida	3,138
23	Missouri	3,152		25	Oklahoma	3,077
50	Montana	2,149		26	Washington	3,039
42	Nebraska	2,576		27	Michigan	3,003
7	Nevada	3,804		28	Idaho	2,979
40	New Hampshire	2,693		29	Pennsylvania	2,959
3	New Jersey	4,850		30	Louisiana	2,947
46	New Mexico	2,431		31	Utah	2,917
4	New York	4,325		32	Maine	2,853
5	North Carolina	3,901		33	Indiana	2,847
47	North Dakota	2,423		34	Mississippi	2,846
15	Ohio	3,271		35	Kansas	2,841
25	Oklahoma	3,077		36	Wisconsin	2,780
41	Oregon	2,596		37	South Carolina	2,751
29	Pennsylvania	2,959		38	Arkansas	2,725
21	Rhode Island	3,165		39	South Dakota	2,712
37	South Carolina	2,751		40	New Hampshire	2,693
39	South Dakota	2,712		41	Oregon	2,596
9	Tennessee	3,735		42	Nebraska	2,576
8	Texas	3,759		43	Kentucky	2,548
31	Utah	2,917		44	Vermont	2,526
44	Vermont	2,526		45	Hawaii	2,500
20	Virginia	3,186		46	New Mexico	2,431
26	Washington	3,039		47	North Dakota	2,423
49	West Virginia	2,352		48	Alaska	2,400
36	Wisconsin	2,780		49	West Virginia	2,352
17	Wyoming	3,244		50	Montana	2,149
					District of Columbia	3,680

Source: CQ Press using data from U.S. Department of the Treasury, Internal Revenue Service
   "Fiscal Year 2009 IRS Data Book" (http://www.irs.gov/taxstats/index.html)
*National average includes refunds to international sources and other miscellaneous refunds not shown separately.

Value of Federal Individual Income Tax Refunds in 2009

National Total = $321,327,766,000*

ALPHA ORDER					RANK ORDER			
RANK	STATE	REFUNDS	% of USA		RANK	STATE	REFUNDS	% of USA
23	Alabama	$4,624,164,000	1.4%		1	California	$38,473,304,000	12.0%
48	Alaska	584,812,000	0.2%		2	Texas	26,133,286,000	8.1%
18	Arizona	6,201,515,000	1.9%		3	Florida	22,235,484,000	6.9%
35	Arkansas	2,490,834,000	0.8%		4	New York	21,563,626,000	6.7%
1	California	38,473,304,000	12.0%		5	Illinois	14,500,342,000	4.5%
22	Colorado	4,951,470,000	1.5%		6	Pennsylvania	12,542,632,000	3.9%
25	Connecticut	4,310,093,000	1.3%		7	Ohio	10,920,352,000	3.4%
44	Delaware	898,953,000	0.3%		8	New Jersey	10,495,063,000	3.3%
3	Florida	22,235,484,000	6.9%		9	Georgia	9,898,113,000	3.1%
9	Georgia	9,898,113,000	3.1%		10	Michigan	9,522,460,000	3.0%
41	Hawaii	1,243,331,000	0.4%		11	North Carolina	8,724,855,000	2.7%
39	Idaho	1,447,434,000	0.5%		12	Virginia	8,487,666,000	2.6%
5	Illinois	14,500,342,000	4.5%		13	Massachusetts	7,369,445,000	2.3%
16	Indiana	6,367,606,000	2.0%		14	Washington	6,999,046,000	2.2%
32	Iowa	2,720,568,000	0.8%		15	Maryland	6,462,008,000	2.0%
33	Kansas	2,547,749,000	0.8%		16	Indiana	6,367,606,000	2.0%
27	Kentucky	3,850,677,000	1.2%		17	Tennessee	6,212,298,000	1.9%
24	Louisiana	4,530,197,000	1.4%		18	Arizona	6,201,515,000	1.9%
42	Maine	1,147,528,000	0.4%		19	Missouri	5,486,056,000	1.7%
15	Maryland	6,462,008,000	2.0%		20	Wisconsin	5,229,475,000	1.6%
13	Massachusetts	7,369,445,000	2.3%		21	Minnesota	5,092,983,000	1.6%
10	Michigan	9,522,460,000	3.0%		22	Colorado	4,951,470,000	1.5%
21	Minnesota	5,092,983,000	1.6%		23	Alabama	4,624,164,000	1.4%
31	Mississippi	2,847,630,000	0.9%		24	Louisiana	4,530,197,000	1.4%
19	Missouri	5,486,056,000	1.7%		25	Connecticut	4,310,093,000	1.3%
45	Montana	799,367,000	0.2%		26	South Carolina	4,129,058,000	1.3%
37	Nebraska	1,599,410,000	0.5%		27	Kentucky	3,850,677,000	1.2%
28	Nevada	3,375,392,000	1.1%		28	Nevada	3,375,392,000	1.1%
40	New Hampshire	1,429,392,000	0.4%		29	Oregon	3,316,536,000	1.0%
8	New Jersey	10,495,063,000	3.3%		30	Oklahoma	3,228,128,000	1.0%
36	New Mexico	1,795,030,000	0.6%		31	Mississippi	2,847,630,000	0.9%
4	New York	21,563,626,000	6.7%		32	Iowa	2,720,568,000	0.8%
11	North Carolina	8,724,855,000	2.7%		33	Kansas	2,547,749,000	0.8%
50	North Dakota	566,657,000	0.2%		34	Utah	2,500,731,000	0.8%
7	Ohio	10,920,352,000	3.4%		35	Arkansas	2,490,834,000	0.8%
30	Oklahoma	3,228,128,000	1.0%		36	New Mexico	1,795,030,000	0.6%
29	Oregon	3,316,536,000	1.0%		37	Nebraska	1,599,410,000	0.5%
6	Pennsylvania	12,542,632,000	3.9%		38	West Virginia	1,521,758,000	0.5%
43	Rhode Island	1,097,757,000	0.3%		39	Idaho	1,447,434,000	0.5%
26	South Carolina	4,129,058,000	1.3%		40	New Hampshire	1,429,392,000	0.4%
46	South Dakota	719,021,000	0.2%		41	Hawaii	1,243,331,000	0.4%
17	Tennessee	6,212,298,000	1.9%		42	Maine	1,147,528,000	0.4%
2	Texas	26,133,286,000	8.1%		43	Rhode Island	1,097,757,000	0.3%
34	Utah	2,500,731,000	0.8%		44	Delaware	898,953,000	0.3%
49	Vermont	576,389,000	0.2%		45	Montana	799,367,000	0.2%
12	Virginia	8,487,666,000	2.6%		46	South Dakota	719,021,000	0.2%
14	Washington	6,999,046,000	2.2%		47	Wyoming	697,798,000	0.2%
38	West Virginia	1,521,758,000	0.5%		48	Alaska	584,812,000	0.2%
20	Wisconsin	5,229,475,000	1.6%		49	Vermont	576,389,000	0.2%
47	Wyoming	697,798,000	0.2%		50	North Dakota	566,657,000	0.2%
						District of Columbia	726,373,000	0.2%

Source: U.S. Department of the Treasury, Internal Revenue Service
  "Fiscal Year 2009 IRS Data Book" (http://www.irs.gov/taxstats/index.html)
*Total includes refunds to international sources and other miscellaneous refunds not shown separately.

Average Value of Federal Individual Income Tax Refunds in 2009

National Average = $3,302*

ALPHA ORDER				RANK ORDER		
RANK	**STATE**	**AVERAGE REFUND**		**RANK**	**STATE**	**AVERAGE REFUND**
18	Alabama	$3,269		1	Wyoming	$3,842
29	Alaska	3,008		2	Nevada	3,835
10	Arizona	3,458		3	Florida	3,658
26	Arkansas	3,050		4	Connecticut	3,618
6	California	3,573		5	New Jersey	3,597
19	Colorado	3,243		6	California	3,573
4	Connecticut	3,618		7	Texas	3,556
25	Delaware	3,054		8	Louisiana	3,494
3	Florida	3,658		9	New York	3,472
13	Georgia	3,406		10	Arizona	3,458
40	Hawaii	2,894		11	Mississippi	3,425
17	Idaho	3,292		12	Maryland	3,414
14	Illinois	3,401		13	Georgia	3,406
35	Indiana	2,967		14	Illinois	3,401
41	Iowa	2,850		15	Massachusetts	3,375
37	Kansas	2,941		16	Virginia	3,313
33	Kentucky	2,971		17	Idaho	3,292
8	Louisiana	3,494		18	Alabama	3,269
50	Maine	2,585		19	Colorado	3,243
12	Maryland	3,414		20	Utah	3,235
15	Massachusetts	3,375		21	Washington	3,221
32	Michigan	2,975		22	Tennessee	3,137
34	Minnesota	2,968		23	Oklahoma	3,084
11	Mississippi	3,425		24	North Carolina	3,074
36	Missouri	2,955		25	Delaware	3,054
48	Montana	2,646		26	Arkansas	3,050
43	Nebraska	2,803		27	New Hampshire	3,027
2	Nevada	3,835		28	Rhode Island	3,021
27	New Hampshire	3,027		29	Alaska	3,008
5	New Jersey	3,597		30	South Carolina	2,997
31	New Mexico	2,992		31	New Mexico	2,992
9	New York	3,472		32	Michigan	2,975
24	North Carolina	3,074		33	Kentucky	2,971
45	North Dakota	2,786		34	Minnesota	2,968
44	Ohio	2,798		35	Indiana	2,967
23	Oklahoma	3,084		36	Missouri	2,955
39	Oregon	2,900		37	Kansas	2,941
38	Pennsylvania	2,920		38	Pennsylvania	2,920
28	Rhode Island	3,021		39	Oregon	2,900
30	South Carolina	2,997		40	Hawaii	2,894
42	South Dakota	2,831		41	Iowa	2,850
22	Tennessee	3,137		42	South Dakota	2,831
7	Texas	3,556		43	Nebraska	2,803
20	Utah	3,235		44	Ohio	2,798
49	Vermont	2,643		45	North Dakota	2,786
16	Virginia	3,313		46	West Virginia	2,747
21	Washington	3,221		47	Wisconsin	2,744
46	West Virginia	2,747		48	Montana	2,646
47	Wisconsin	2,744		49	Vermont	2,643
1	Wyoming	3,842		50	Maine	2,585
					District of Columbia	3,657

Source: CQ Press using data from U.S. Department of the Treasury, Internal Revenue Service
   "Fiscal Year 2009 IRS Data Book" (http://www.irs.gov/taxstats/index.html)
*National average includes refunds to international sources and other miscellaneous refunds not shown separately. Does not include stimulus payments.

Value of Federal Business Income Tax Refunds in 2009

National Total = $95,200,297,000*

ALPHA ORDER

RANK	STATE	REFUNDS	% of USA
21	Alabama	$1,212,959,000	1.3%
49	Alaska	27,048,000	0.0%
26	Arizona	973,271,000	1.0%
35	Arkansas	329,410,000	0.3%
2	California	10,177,851,000	10.7%
19	Colorado	1,239,541,000	1.3%
5	Connecticut	6,767,133,000	7.1%
22	Delaware	1,176,662,000	1.2%
14	Florida	1,809,714,000	1.9%
12	Georgia	2,212,619,000	2.3%
41	Hawaii	109,857,000	0.1%
37	Idaho	223,942,000	0.2%
6	Illinois	5,762,047,000	6.1%
25	Indiana	991,087,000	1.0%
24	Iowa	1,062,453,000	1.1%
30	Kansas	519,432,000	0.5%
40	Kentucky	193,848,000	0.2%
33	Louisiana	388,060,000	0.4%
32	Maine	390,440,000	0.4%
18	Maryland	1,414,307,000	1.5%
17	Massachusetts	1,519,240,000	1.6%
13	Michigan	2,201,708,000	2.3%
11	Minnesota	2,659,074,000	2.8%
38	Mississippi	215,933,000	0.2%
15	Missouri	1,693,573,000	1.8%
50	Montana	22,654,000	0.0%
39	Nebraska	210,717,000	0.2%
28	Nevada	814,125,000	0.9%
43	New Hampshire	101,827,000	0.1%
4	New Jersey	6,965,673,000	7.3%
45	New Mexico	57,920,000	0.1%
1	New York	11,758,050,000	12.4%
7	North Carolina	5,184,145,000	5.4%
48	North Dakota	48,821,000	0.1%
8	Ohio	4,721,463,000	5.0%
27	Oklahoma	816,642,000	0.9%
31	Oregon	392,582,000	0.4%
10	Pennsylvania	2,660,145,000	2.8%
36	Rhode Island	293,909,000	0.3%
29	South Carolina	622,023,000	0.7%
42	South Dakota	105,107,000	0.1%
9	Tennessee	3,065,319,000	3.2%
3	Texas	9,178,598,000	9.6%
34	Utah	329,815,000	0.3%
44	Vermont	90,139,000	0.1%
16	Virginia	1,567,308,000	1.6%
20	Washington	1,232,252,000	1.3%
47	West Virginia	53,471,000	0.1%
23	Wisconsin	1,158,896,000	1.2%
46	Wyoming	55,542,000	0.1%

RANK ORDER

RANK	STATE	REFUNDS	% of USA
1	New York	$11,758,050,000	12.4%
2	California	10,177,851,000	10.7%
3	Texas	9,178,598,000	9.6%
4	New Jersey	6,965,673,000	7.3%
5	Connecticut	6,767,133,000	7.1%
6	Illinois	5,762,047,000	6.1%
7	North Carolina	5,184,145,000	5.4%
8	Ohio	4,721,463,000	5.0%
9	Tennessee	3,065,319,000	3.2%
10	Pennsylvania	2,660,145,000	2.8%
11	Minnesota	2,659,074,000	2.8%
12	Georgia	2,212,619,000	2.3%
13	Michigan	2,201,708,000	2.3%
14	Florida	1,809,714,000	1.9%
15	Missouri	1,693,573,000	1.8%
16	Virginia	1,567,308,000	1.6%
17	Massachusetts	1,519,240,000	1.6%
18	Maryland	1,414,307,000	1.5%
19	Colorado	1,239,541,000	1.3%
20	Washington	1,232,252,000	1.3%
21	Alabama	1,212,959,000	1.3%
22	Delaware	1,176,662,000	1.2%
23	Wisconsin	1,158,896,000	1.2%
24	Iowa	1,062,453,000	1.1%
25	Indiana	991,087,000	1.0%
26	Arizona	973,271,000	1.0%
27	Oklahoma	816,642,000	0.9%
28	Nevada	814,125,000	0.9%
29	South Carolina	622,023,000	0.7%
30	Kansas	519,432,000	0.5%
31	Oregon	392,582,000	0.4%
32	Maine	390,440,000	0.4%
33	Louisiana	388,060,000	0.4%
34	Utah	329,815,000	0.3%
35	Arkansas	329,410,000	0.3%
36	Rhode Island	293,909,000	0.3%
37	Idaho	223,942,000	0.2%
38	Mississippi	215,933,000	0.2%
39	Nebraska	210,717,000	0.2%
40	Kentucky	193,848,000	0.2%
41	Hawaii	109,857,000	0.1%
42	South Dakota	105,107,000	0.1%
43	New Hampshire	101,827,000	0.1%
44	Vermont	90,139,000	0.1%
45	New Mexico	57,920,000	0.1%
46	Wyoming	55,542,000	0.1%
47	West Virginia	53,471,000	0.1%
48	North Dakota	48,821,000	0.1%
49	Alaska	27,048,000	0.0%
50	Montana	22,654,000	0.0%
	District of Columbia	184,868,000	0.2%

Source: U.S. Department of the Treasury, Internal Revenue Service
   "Fiscal Year 2009 IRS Data Book" (http://www.irs.gov/taxstats/index.html)
*Total includes refunds to international sources and other miscellaneous refunds not shown separately.   Includes taxes on corporation income, farmers' cooperatives, and "unrelated business income" from tax-exempt organizations.

Average Value of Federal Business Income Tax Refunds in 2009

National Average = $174,041*

ALPHA ORDER

RANK	STATE	AVERAGE REFUND
11	Alabama	$205,308
48	Alaska	24,500
27	Arizona	109,455
31	Arkansas	78,189
17	California	143,096
21	Colorado	130,327
1	Connecticut	1,139,248
2	Delaware	535,333
37	Florida	49,764
15	Georgia	147,488
44	Hawaii	31,033
34	Idaho	68,171
8	Illinois	252,877
24	Indiana	121,785
22	Iowa	127,976
33	Kansas	76,522
42	Kentucky	39,272
36	Louisiana	50,118
20	Maine	137,576
18	Maryland	140,448
16	Massachusetts	143,365
26	Michigan	114,256
9	Minnesota	238,546
38	Mississippi	49,143
14	Missouri	153,793
50	Montana	5,988
41	Nebraska	43,402
23	Nevada	127,546
43	New Hampshire	35,234
3	New Jersey	463,051
49	New Mexico	19,541
4	New York	355,357
5	North Carolina	352,136
47	North Dakota	24,757
7	Ohio	262,187
19	Oklahoma	138,203
39	Oregon	46,680
13	Pennsylvania	164,156
12	Rhode Island	173,091
28	South Carolina	100,521
40	South Dakota	44,499
6	Tennessee	345,934
10	Texas	219,889
32	Utah	77,512
35	Vermont	52,744
25	Virginia	114,830
29	Washington	95,052
46	West Virginia	26,379
30	Wisconsin	94,875
45	Wyoming	29,004

RANK ORDER

RANK	STATE	AVERAGE REFUND
1	Connecticut	$1,139,248
2	Delaware	535,333
3	New Jersey	463,051
4	New York	355,357
5	North Carolina	352,136
6	Tennessee	345,934
7	Ohio	262,187
8	Illinois	252,877
9	Minnesota	238,546
10	Texas	219,889
11	Alabama	205,308
12	Rhode Island	173,091
13	Pennsylvania	164,156
14	Missouri	153,793
15	Georgia	147,488
16	Massachusetts	143,365
17	California	143,096
18	Maryland	140,448
19	Oklahoma	138,203
20	Maine	137,576
21	Colorado	130,327
22	Iowa	127,976
23	Nevada	127,546
24	Indiana	121,785
25	Virginia	114,830
26	Michigan	114,256
27	Arizona	109,455
28	South Carolina	100,521
29	Washington	95,052
30	Wisconsin	94,875
31	Arkansas	78,189
32	Utah	77,512
33	Kansas	76,522
34	Idaho	68,171
35	Vermont	52,744
36	Louisiana	50,118
37	Florida	49,764
38	Mississippi	49,143
39	Oregon	46,680
40	South Dakota	44,499
41	Nebraska	43,402
42	Kentucky	39,272
43	New Hampshire	35,234
44	Hawaii	31,033
45	Wyoming	29,004
46	West Virginia	26,379
47	North Dakota	24,757
48	Alaska	24,500
49	New Mexico	19,541
50	Montana	5,988
	District of Columbia	136,838

Source: CQ Press using data from U.S. Department of the Treasury, Internal Revenue Service
"Fiscal Year 2009 IRS Data Book" (http://www.irs.gov/taxstats/index.html)
*National average includes refunds to international sources and other miscellaneous refunds not shown separately.

Federal Tax Burden per Household in 2007

National Average = $23,524*

ALPHA ORDER

ALPHA ORDER

RANK ORDER

RANK	STATE	TAXES	RANK	STATE	TAXES
43	Alabama	$17,201	1	Connecticut	$38,331
11	Alaska	25,955	2	New Jersey	34,400
24	Arizona	20,193	3	Massachusetts	32,157
48	Arkansas	15,422	4	New York	29,919
5	California	29,729	5	California	29,729
18	Colorado	24,030	6	Maryland	29,483
1	Connecticut	38,331	7	Nevada	27,367
9	Delaware	26,049	8	Virginia	26,058
19	Florida	23,956	9	Delaware	26,049
25	Georgia	20,104	10	New Hampshire	26,030
14	Hawaii	24,716	11	Alaska	25,955
42	Idaho	17,366	12	Wyoming	25,851
13	Illinois	25,808	13	Illinois	25,808
33	Indiana	18,841	14	Hawaii	24,716
37	Iowa	17,913	15	Rhode Island	24,643
29	Kansas	19,501	16	Washington	24,613
47	Kentucky	16,205	17	Minnesota	24,368
44	Louisiana	17,094	18	Colorado	24,030
40	Maine	17,391	19	Florida	23,956
6	Maryland	29,483	20	Texas	22,539
3	Massachusetts	32,157	21	Pennsylvania	22,214
23	Michigan	20,263	22	Wisconsin	20,276
17	Minnesota	24,368	23	Michigan	20,263
50	Mississippi	14,126	24	Arizona	20,193
36	Missouri	18,489	25	Georgia	20,104
38	Montana	17,523	26	Vermont	19,855
30	Nebraska	19,356	27	Oregon	19,757
7	Nevada	27,367	28	Utah	19,752
10	New Hampshire	26,030	29	Kansas	19,501
2	New Jersey	34,400	30	Nebraska	19,356
45	New Mexico	16,997	31	South Dakota	19,340
4	New York	29,919	32	Ohio	18,913
34	North Carolina	18,602	33	Indiana	18,841
41	North Dakota	17,371	34	North Carolina	18,602
32	Ohio	18,913	35	Tennessee	18,529
39	Oklahoma	17,508	36	Missouri	18,489
27	Oregon	19,757	37	Iowa	17,913
21	Pennsylvania	22,214	38	Montana	17,523
15	Rhode Island	24,643	39	Oklahoma	17,508
46	South Carolina	16,734	40	Maine	17,391
31	South Dakota	19,340	41	North Dakota	17,371
35	Tennessee	18,529	42	Idaho	17,366
20	Texas	22,539	43	Alabama	17,201
28	Utah	19,752	44	Louisiana	17,094
26	Vermont	19,855	45	New Mexico	16,997
8	Virginia	26,058	46	South Carolina	16,734
16	Washington	24,613	47	Kentucky	16,205
49	West Virginia	14,408	48	Arkansas	15,422
22	Wisconsin	20,276	49	West Virginia	14,408
12	Wyoming	25,851	50	Mississippi	14,126
				District of Columbia	34,777

Source: The Tax Foundation
   "2008 Facts and Figures" (http://www.taxfoundation.org/files/2008 facts and figures.pdf)
*A household is a separate living quarters occupied by one or more people.

Per Capita Federal Economic Stimulus Funds in 2010

National Per Capita = $807*

ALPHA ORDER				RANK ORDER		
RANK	STATE	PER CAPITA		RANK	STATE	PER CAPITA
34	Alabama	$748		1	Alaska	$3,049
1	Alaska	3,049		2	North Dakota	1,667
37	Arizona	741		3	South Dakota	1,614
26	Arkansas	795		4	Vermont	1,573
38	California	734		5	Montana	1,542
18	Colorado	968		6	New Mexico	1,344
46	Connecticut	682		7	Hawaii	1,211
12	Delaware	1,079		8	Wyoming	1,196
50	Florida	589		9	Washington	1,133
47	Georgia	675		10	Rhode Island	1,104
7	Hawaii	1,211		11	Idaho	1,093
11	Idaho	1,093		12	Delaware	1,079
28	Illinois	792		13	Maryland	1,053
45	Indiana	701		14	Maine	1,022
43	Iowa	717		15	Massachusetts	1,018
22	Kansas	833		16	South Carolina	1,005
25	Kentucky	801		17	West Virginia	984
42	Louisiana	718		18	Colorado	968
14	Maine	1,022		19	Mississippi	929
13	Maryland	1,053		20	Tennessee	926
15	Massachusetts	1,018		21	Oklahoma	844
23	Michigan	829		22	Kansas	833
33	Minnesota	750		23	Michigan	829
19	Mississippi	929		24	Oregon	819
27	Missouri	794		25	Kentucky	801
5	Montana	1,542		26	Arkansas	795
35	Nebraska	747		27	Missouri	794
44	Nevada	708		28	Illinois	792
39	New Hampshire	733		29	New York	791
49	New Jersey	616		30	Utah	781
6	New Mexico	1,344		31	North Carolina	778
29	New York	791		32	Virginia	767
31	North Carolina	778		33	Minnesota	750
2	North Dakota	1,667		34	Alabama	748
36	Ohio	745		35	Nebraska	747
21	Oklahoma	844		36	Ohio	745
24	Oregon	819		37	Arizona	741
40	Pennsylvania	729		38	California	734
10	Rhode Island	1,104		39	New Hampshire	733
16	South Carolina	1,005		40	Pennsylvania	729
3	South Dakota	1,614		41	Wisconsin	722
20	Tennessee	926		42	Louisiana	718
48	Texas	660		43	Iowa	717
30	Utah	781		44	Nevada	708
4	Vermont	1,573		45	Indiana	701
32	Virginia	767		46	Connecticut	682
9	Washington	1,133		47	Georgia	675
17	West Virginia	984		48	Texas	660
41	Wisconsin	722		49	New Jersey	616
8	Wyoming	1,196		50	Florida	589
					District of Columbia	8,131

Source: Recovery Accountability and Transparency Board
   "State and Territory Totals by Agency" (http://www.recovery.gov/Pages/home.aspx)
*Funds awarded from February 17, 2009 to September 30, 2010. Calculated using 2009 Census population estimates.

Federal Government Expenditures in 2009

National Total = $3,238,360,000,000*

ALPHA ORDER

RANK	STATE	EXPENDITURES	% of USA
21	Alabama	$54,674,000,000	1.7%
42	Alaska	14,215,000,000	0.4%
18	Arizona	63,029,000,000	1.9%
34	Arkansas	27,302,000,000	0.8%
1	California	345,970,000,000	10.7%
24	Colorado	47,806,000,000	1.5%
27	Connecticut	42,589,000,000	1.3%
48	Delaware	8,137,000,000	0.3%
4	Florida	175,684,000,000	5.4%
12	Georgia	83,917,000,000	2.6%
35	Hawaii	24,610,000,000	0.8%
40	Idaho	14,898,000,000	0.5%
7	Illinois	116,070,000,000	3.6%
20	Indiana	61,149,000,000	1.9%
32	Iowa	29,369,000,000	0.9%
29	Kansas	34,705,000,000	1.1%
22	Kentucky	50,012,000,000	1.5%
23	Louisiana	48,357,000,000	1.5%
41	Maine	14,242,000,000	0.4%
9	Maryland	92,155,000,000	2.8%
13	Massachusetts	83,890,000,000	2.6%
10	Michigan	92,003,000,000	2.8%
26	Minnesota	45,691,000,000	1.4%
31	Mississippi	32,848,000,000	1.0%
16	Missouri	67,942,000,000	2.1%
45	Montana	10,925,000,000	0.3%
39	Nebraska	16,526,000,000	0.5%
38	Nevada	18,894,000,000	0.6%
43	New Hampshire	11,844,000,000	0.4%
14	New Jersey	80,647,000,000	2.5%
33	New Mexico	27,472,000,000	0.8%
3	New York	194,975,000,000	6.0%
11	North Carolina	84,830,000,000	2.6%
47	North Dakota	8,618,000,000	0.3%
8	Ohio	107,975,000,000	3.3%
28	Oklahoma	37,516,000,000	1.2%
30	Oregon	33,594,000,000	1.0%
6	Pennsylvania	135,687,000,000	4.2%
44	Rhode Island	11,517,000,000	0.4%
25	South Carolina	46,904,000,000	1.4%
46	South Dakota	9,499,000,000	0.3%
15	Tennessee	68,546,000,000	2.1%
2	Texas	227,108,000,000	7.0%
36	Utah	20,702,000,000	0.6%
49	Vermont	7,092,000,000	0.2%
5	Virginia	155,554,000,000	4.8%
17	Washington	66,560,000,000	2.1%
37	West Virginia	19,808,000,000	0.6%
19	Wisconsin	61,280,000,000	1.9%
50	Wyoming	6,278,000,000	0.2%

RANK ORDER

RANK	STATE	EXPENDITURES	% of USA
1	California	$345,970,000,000	10.7%
2	Texas	227,108,000,000	7.0%
3	New York	194,975,000,000	6.0%
4	Florida	175,684,000,000	5.4%
5	Virginia	155,554,000,000	4.8%
6	Pennsylvania	135,687,000,000	4.2%
7	Illinois	116,070,000,000	3.6%
8	Ohio	107,975,000,000	3.3%
9	Maryland	92,155,000,000	2.8%
10	Michigan	92,003,000,000	2.8%
11	North Carolina	84,830,000,000	2.6%
12	Georgia	83,917,000,000	2.6%
13	Massachusetts	83,890,000,000	2.6%
14	New Jersey	80,647,000,000	2.5%
15	Tennessee	68,546,000,000	2.1%
16	Missouri	67,942,000,000	2.1%
17	Washington	66,560,000,000	2.1%
18	Arizona	63,029,000,000	1.9%
19	Wisconsin	61,280,000,000	1.9%
20	Indiana	61,149,000,000	1.9%
21	Alabama	54,674,000,000	1.7%
22	Kentucky	50,012,000,000	1.5%
23	Louisiana	48,357,000,000	1.5%
24	Colorado	47,806,000,000	1.5%
25	South Carolina	46,904,000,000	1.4%
26	Minnesota	45,691,000,000	1.4%
27	Connecticut	42,589,000,000	1.3%
28	Oklahoma	37,516,000,000	1.2%
29	Kansas	34,705,000,000	1.1%
30	Oregon	33,594,000,000	1.0%
31	Mississippi	32,848,000,000	1.0%
32	Iowa	29,369,000,000	0.9%
33	New Mexico	27,472,000,000	0.8%
34	Arkansas	27,302,000,000	0.8%
35	Hawaii	24,610,000,000	0.8%
36	Utah	20,702,000,000	0.6%
37	West Virginia	19,808,000,000	0.6%
38	Nevada	18,894,000,000	0.6%
39	Nebraska	16,526,000,000	0.5%
40	Idaho	14,898,000,000	0.5%
41	Maine	14,242,000,000	0.4%
42	Alaska	14,215,000,000	0.4%
43	New Hampshire	11,844,000,000	0.4%
44	Rhode Island	11,517,000,000	0.4%
45	Montana	10,925,000,000	0.3%
46	South Dakota	9,499,000,000	0.3%
47	North Dakota	8,618,000,000	0.3%
48	Delaware	8,137,000,000	0.3%
49	Vermont	7,092,000,000	0.2%
50	Wyoming	6,278,000,000	0.2%
	District of Columbia	49,889,000,000	1.5%

Source: U.S. Bureau of the Census
   "Consolidated Federal Funds Report: 2009" (CFFR/09, August 2010, http://www.census.gov/govs/cffr/)
*Total includes $24,723,000,000 in U.S. territories ($21,406,000,000 in Puerto Rico) and $22,130,000,000 in expenditures not distributed by state.

Per Capita Federal Government Expenditures in 2009

National Per Capita = $10,396*

ALPHA ORDER

RANK	STATE	PER CAPITA
11	Alabama	$11,611
1	Alaska	20,352
31	Arizona	9,556
35	Arkansas	9,449
36	California	9,360
33	Colorado	9,514
9	Connecticut	12,105
41	Delaware	9,193
34	Florida	9,477
48	Georgia	8,538
3	Hawaii	19,001
30	Idaho	9,638
44	Illinois	8,990
32	Indiana	9,520
29	Iowa	9,764
8	Kansas	12,312
12	Kentucky	11,593
23	Louisiana	10,765
22	Maine	10,803
4	Maryland	16,169
7	Massachusetts	12,723
39	Michigan	9,228
47	Minnesota	8,676
17	Mississippi	11,127
15	Missouri	11,347
16	Montana	11,205
40	Nebraska	9,198
50	Nevada	7,148
45	New Hampshire	8,942
38	New Jersey	9,262
5	New Mexico	13,670
28	New York	9,978
43	North Carolina	9,043
6	North Dakota	13,323
37	Ohio	9,354
26	Oklahoma	10,175
46	Oregon	8,781
23	Pennsylvania	10,765
18	Rhode Island	10,935
25	South Carolina	10,283
10	South Dakota	11,693
19	Tennessee	10,887
42	Texas	9,164
49	Utah	7,435
14	Vermont	11,406
2	Virginia	19,734
27	Washington	9,988
20	West Virginia	10,885
21	Wisconsin	10,837
13	Wyoming	11,535

RANK ORDER

RANK	STATE	PER CAPITA
1	Alaska	$20,352
2	Virginia	19,734
3	Hawaii	19,001
4	Maryland	16,169
5	New Mexico	13,670
6	North Dakota	13,323
7	Massachusetts	12,723
8	Kansas	12,312
9	Connecticut	12,105
10	South Dakota	11,693
11	Alabama	11,611
12	Kentucky	11,593
13	Wyoming	11,535
14	Vermont	11,406
15	Missouri	11,347
16	Montana	11,205
17	Mississippi	11,127
18	Rhode Island	10,935
19	Tennessee	10,887
20	West Virginia	10,885
21	Wisconsin	10,837
22	Maine	10,803
23	Louisiana	10,765
23	Pennsylvania	10,765
25	South Carolina	10,283
26	Oklahoma	10,175
27	Washington	9,988
28	New York	9,978
29	Iowa	9,764
30	Idaho	9,638
31	Arizona	9,556
32	Indiana	9,520
33	Colorado	9,514
34	Florida	9,477
35	Arkansas	9,449
36	California	9,360
37	Ohio	9,354
38	New Jersey	9,262
39	Michigan	9,228
40	Nebraska	9,198
41	Delaware	9,193
42	Texas	9,164
43	North Carolina	9,043
44	Illinois	8,990
45	New Hampshire	8,942
46	Oregon	8,781
47	Minnesota	8,676
48	Georgia	8,538
49	Utah	7,435
50	Nevada	7,148
	District of Columbia	83,196

Source: CQ Press using data from U.S. Bureau of the Census
 "Consolidated Federal Funds Report: 2009" (CFFR/09, August 2010, http://www.census.gov/govs/cffr/)
*National per capita excludes expenditures and population for territories and undistributed amounts.

Federal Government Grants in 2009

National Total = $744,115,000,000*

ALPHA ORDER

RANK	STATE	GRANTS	% of USA
24	Alabama	$10,008,000,000	1.3%
39	Alaska	3,706,000,000	0.5%
17	Arizona	14,479,000,000	1.9%
33	Arkansas	6,937,000,000	0.9%
1	California	90,919,000,000	12.2%
26	Colorado	8,854,000,000	1.2%
27	Connecticut	8,829,000,000	1.2%
50	Delaware	2,125,000,000	0.3%
4	Florida	31,979,000,000	4.3%
12	Georgia	19,185,000,000	2.6%
42	Hawaii	3,258,000,000	0.4%
43	Idaho	3,099,000,000	0.4%
5	Illinois	31,485,000,000	4.2%
19	Indiana	13,346,000,000	1.8%
31	Iowa	7,578,000,000	1.0%
34	Kansas	5,386,000,000	0.7%
23	Kentucky	11,366,000,000	1.5%
16	Louisiana	15,249,000,000	2.0%
37	Maine	4,084,000,000	0.5%
21	Maryland	11,805,000,000	1.6%
8	Massachusetts	22,382,000,000	3.0%
9	Michigan	21,120,000,000	2.8%
22	Minnesota	11,744,000,000	1.6%
30	Mississippi	8,305,000,000	1.1%
18	Missouri	13,568,000,000	1.8%
44	Montana	2,940,000,000	0.4%
40	Nebraska	3,656,000,000	0.5%
38	Nevada	3,757,000,000	0.5%
45	New Hampshire	2,612,000,000	0.4%
14	New Jersey	16,785,000,000	2.3%
32	New Mexico	6,953,000,000	0.9%
2	New York	62,419,000,000	8.4%
10	North Carolina	20,942,000,000	2.8%
48	North Dakota	2,254,000,000	0.3%
7	Ohio	25,414,000,000	3.4%
29	Oklahoma	8,554,000,000	1.1%
28	Oregon	8,705,000,000	1.2%
6	Pennsylvania	27,363,000,000	3.7%
41	Rhode Island	3,609,000,000	0.5%
25	South Carolina	9,249,000,000	1.2%
47	South Dakota	2,467,000,000	0.3%
13	Tennessee	17,064,000,000	2.3%
3	Texas	55,671,000,000	7.5%
35	Utah	4,945,000,000	0.7%
49	Vermont	2,162,000,000	0.3%
20	Virginia	12,670,000,000	1.7%
15	Washington	15,261,000,000	2.1%
36	West Virginia	4,922,000,000	0.7%
11	Wisconsin	19,219,000,000	2.6%
46	Wyoming	2,604,000,000	0.3%

RANK ORDER

RANK	STATE	GRANTS	% of USA
1	California	$90,919,000,000	12.2%
2	New York	62,419,000,000	8.4%
3	Texas	55,671,000,000	7.5%
4	Florida	31,979,000,000	4.3%
5	Illinois	31,485,000,000	4.2%
6	Pennsylvania	27,363,000,000	3.7%
7	Ohio	25,414,000,000	3.4%
8	Massachusetts	22,382,000,000	3.0%
9	Michigan	21,120,000,000	2.8%
10	North Carolina	20,942,000,000	2.8%
11	Wisconsin	19,219,000,000	2.6%
12	Georgia	19,185,000,000	2.6%
13	Tennessee	17,064,000,000	2.3%
14	New Jersey	16,785,000,000	2.3%
15	Washington	15,261,000,000	2.1%
16	Louisiana	15,249,000,000	2.0%
17	Arizona	14,479,000,000	1.9%
18	Missouri	13,568,000,000	1.8%
19	Indiana	13,346,000,000	1.8%
20	Virginia	12,670,000,000	1.7%
21	Maryland	11,805,000,000	1.6%
22	Minnesota	11,744,000,000	1.6%
23	Kentucky	11,366,000,000	1.5%
24	Alabama	10,008,000,000	1.3%
25	South Carolina	9,249,000,000	1.2%
26	Colorado	8,854,000,000	1.2%
27	Connecticut	8,829,000,000	1.2%
28	Oregon	8,705,000,000	1.2%
29	Oklahoma	8,554,000,000	1.1%
30	Mississippi	8,305,000,000	1.1%
31	Iowa	7,578,000,000	1.0%
32	New Mexico	6,953,000,000	0.9%
33	Arkansas	6,937,000,000	0.9%
34	Kansas	5,386,000,000	0.7%
35	Utah	4,945,000,000	0.7%
36	West Virginia	4,922,000,000	0.7%
37	Maine	4,084,000,000	0.5%
38	Nevada	3,757,000,000	0.5%
39	Alaska	3,706,000,000	0.5%
40	Nebraska	3,656,000,000	0.5%
41	Rhode Island	3,609,000,000	0.5%
42	Hawaii	3,258,000,000	0.4%
43	Idaho	3,099,000,000	0.4%
44	Montana	2,940,000,000	0.4%
45	New Hampshire	2,612,000,000	0.4%
46	Wyoming	2,604,000,000	0.3%
47	South Dakota	2,467,000,000	0.3%
48	North Dakota	2,254,000,000	0.3%
49	Vermont	2,162,000,000	0.3%
50	Delaware	2,125,000,000	0.3%
	District of Columbia	12,022,000,000	1.6%

Source: U.S. Bureau of the Census

"Consolidated Federal Funds Report: 2009" (CFFR/09, August 2010, http://www.census.gov/govs/cffr/)

*Total includes $9,081,000,000 in U.S. territories ($7,526,000,000 in Puerto Rico) and $20,000,000 in expenditures not distributed by state.

Per Capita Expenditures for Federal Government Grants in 2009

National Per Capita = $2,394*

ALPHA ORDER

RANK	STATE	PER CAPITA
35	Alabama	$2,125
1	Alaska	5,306
33	Arizona	2,195
23	Arkansas	2,401
21	California	2,460
47	Colorado	1,762
20	Connecticut	2,509
23	Delaware	2,401
48	Florida	1,725
43	Georgia	1,952
19	Hawaii	2,515
41	Idaho	2,005
22	Illinois	2,439
37	Indiana	2,078
18	Iowa	2,519
45	Kansas	1,911
17	Kentucky	2,635
8	Louisiana	3,395
11	Maine	3,098
38	Maryland	2,071
8	Massachusetts	3,395
36	Michigan	2,118
31	Minnesota	2,230
14	Mississippi	2,813
28	Missouri	2,266
13	Montana	3,015
39	Nebraska	2,035
50	Nevada	1,421
42	New Hampshire	1,972
44	New Jersey	1,928
5	New Mexico	3,460
10	New York	3,194
30	North Carolina	2,232
3	North Dakota	3,485
32	Ohio	2,202
25	Oklahoma	2,320
27	Oregon	2,275
34	Pennsylvania	2,171
6	Rhode Island	3,427
40	South Carolina	2,028
12	South Dakota	3,037
15	Tennessee	2,710
29	Texas	2,246
46	Utah	1,776
4	Vermont	3,477
49	Virginia	1,607
26	Washington	2,290
16	West Virginia	2,705
7	Wisconsin	3,399
2	Wyoming	4,784

RANK ORDER

RANK	STATE	PER CAPITA
1	Alaska	$5,306
2	Wyoming	4,784
3	North Dakota	3,485
4	Vermont	3,477
5	New Mexico	3,460
6	Rhode Island	3,427
7	Wisconsin	3,399
8	Louisiana	3,395
8	Massachusetts	3,395
10	New York	3,194
11	Maine	3,098
12	South Dakota	3,037
13	Montana	3,015
14	Mississippi	2,813
15	Tennessee	2,710
16	West Virginia	2,705
17	Kentucky	2,635
18	Iowa	2,519
19	Hawaii	2,515
20	Connecticut	2,509
21	California	2,460
22	Illinois	2,439
23	Arkansas	2,401
23	Delaware	2,401
25	Oklahoma	2,320
26	Washington	2,290
27	Oregon	2,275
28	Missouri	2,266
29	Texas	2,246
30	North Carolina	2,232
31	Minnesota	2,230
32	Ohio	2,202
33	Arizona	2,195
34	Pennsylvania	2,171
35	Alabama	2,125
36	Michigan	2,118
37	Indiana	2,078
38	Maryland	2,071
39	Nebraska	2,035
40	South Carolina	2,028
41	Idaho	2,005
42	New Hampshire	1,972
43	Georgia	1,952
44	New Jersey	1,928
45	Kansas	1,911
46	Utah	1,776
47	Colorado	1,762
48	Florida	1,725
49	Virginia	1,607
50	Nevada	1,421
	District of Columbia	20,048

Source: CQ Press using data from U.S. Bureau of the Census
    "Consolidated Federal Funds Report: 2009" (CFFR/09, August 2010, http://www.census.gov/govs/cffr/)
*National per capita excludes expenditures and population for territories and undistributed amounts.

Federal Government Procurement Contract Awards in 2009

National Total = $550,803,000,000*

ALPHA ORDER

RANK	STATE	EXPENDITURES	% of USA
16	Alabama	$10,396,000,000	1.9%
28	Alaska	4,968,000,000	0.9%
9	Arizona	13,932,000,000	2.5%
43	Arkansas	993,000,000	0.2%
2	California	68,979,000,000	12.5%
14	Colorado	11,123,000,000	2.0%
11	Connecticut	13,005,000,000	2.4%
46	Delaware	621,000,000	0.1%
6	Florida	18,531,000,000	3.4%
24	Georgia	7,705,000,000	1.4%
39	Hawaii	1,819,000,000	0.3%
32	Idaho	3,427,000,000	0.6%
13	Illinois	11,510,000,000	2.1%
22	Indiana	7,936,000,000	1.4%
36	Iowa	2,323,000,000	0.4%
34	Kansas	3,004,000,000	0.5%
25	Kentucky	6,972,000,000	1.3%
30	Louisiana	4,036,000,000	0.7%
40	Maine	1,431,000,000	0.3%
4	Maryland	34,339,000,000	6.2%
5	Massachusetts	18,892,000,000	3.4%
18	Michigan	9,316,000,000	1.7%
29	Minnesota	4,776,000,000	0.9%
27	Mississippi	4,988,000,000	0.9%
10	Missouri	13,508,000,000	2.5%
48	Montana	508,000,000	0.1%
41	Nebraska	1,164,000,000	0.2%
37	Nevada	2,065,000,000	0.4%
38	New Hampshire	1,921,000,000	0.3%
12	New Jersey	12,051,000,000	2.2%
23	New Mexico	7,736,000,000	1.4%
8	New York	14,507,000,000	2.6%
26	North Carolina	5,203,000,000	0.9%
49	North Dakota	474,000,000	0.1%
20	Ohio	9,103,000,000	1.7%
33	Oklahoma	3,149,000,000	0.6%
35	Oregon	2,469,000,000	0.4%
7	Pennsylvania	18,098,000,000	3.3%
45	Rhode Island	689,000,000	0.1%
21	South Carolina	8,211,000,000	1.5%
47	South Dakota	569,000,000	0.1%
15	Tennessee	10,425,000,000	1.9%
3	Texas	39,311,000,000	7.1%
31	Utah	3,636,000,000	0.7%
42	Vermont	1,075,000,000	0.2%
1	Virginia	81,797,000,000	14.9%
19	Washington	9,214,000,000	1.7%
44	West Virginia	822,000,000	0.1%
17	Wisconsin	9,514,000,000	1.7%
50	Wyoming	260,000,000	0.0%

RANK ORDER

RANK	STATE	EXPENDITURES	% of USA
1	Virginia	$81,797,000,000	14.9%
2	California	68,979,000,000	12.5%
3	Texas	39,311,000,000	7.1%
4	Maryland	34,339,000,000	6.2%
5	Massachusetts	18,892,000,000	3.4%
6	Florida	18,531,000,000	3.4%
7	Pennsylvania	18,098,000,000	3.3%
8	New York	14,507,000,000	2.6%
9	Arizona	13,932,000,000	2.5%
10	Missouri	13,508,000,000	2.5%
11	Connecticut	13,005,000,000	2.4%
12	New Jersey	12,051,000,000	2.2%
13	Illinois	11,510,000,000	2.1%
14	Colorado	11,123,000,000	2.0%
15	Tennessee	10,425,000,000	1.9%
16	Alabama	10,396,000,000	1.9%
17	Wisconsin	9,514,000,000	1.7%
18	Michigan	9,316,000,000	1.7%
19	Washington	9,214,000,000	1.7%
20	Ohio	9,103,000,000	1.7%
21	South Carolina	8,211,000,000	1.5%
22	Indiana	7,936,000,000	1.4%
23	New Mexico	7,736,000,000	1.4%
24	Georgia	7,705,000,000	1.4%
25	Kentucky	6,972,000,000	1.3%
26	North Carolina	5,203,000,000	0.9%
27	Mississippi	4,988,000,000	0.9%
28	Alaska	4,968,000,000	0.9%
29	Minnesota	4,776,000,000	0.9%
30	Louisiana	4,036,000,000	0.7%
31	Utah	3,636,000,000	0.7%
32	Idaho	3,427,000,000	0.6%
33	Oklahoma	3,149,000,000	0.6%
34	Kansas	3,004,000,000	0.5%
35	Oregon	2,469,000,000	0.4%
36	Iowa	2,323,000,000	0.4%
37	Nevada	2,065,000,000	0.4%
38	New Hampshire	1,921,000,000	0.3%
39	Hawaii	1,819,000,000	0.3%
40	Maine	1,431,000,000	0.3%
41	Nebraska	1,164,000,000	0.2%
42	Vermont	1,075,000,000	0.2%
43	Arkansas	993,000,000	0.2%
44	West Virginia	822,000,000	0.1%
45	Rhode Island	689,000,000	0.1%
46	Delaware	621,000,000	0.1%
47	South Dakota	569,000,000	0.1%
48	Montana	508,000,000	0.1%
49	North Dakota	474,000,000	0.1%
50	Wyoming	260,000,000	0.0%
	District of Columbia	7,750,000,000	1.4%

Source: U.S. Bureau of the Census

"Consolidated Federal Funds Report: 2009" (CFFR/09, August 2010, http://www.census.gov/govs/cffr/)

*Total includes $956,000,000 in U.S. territories ($572,000,000 in Puerto Rico) and $19,597,000,000 in expenditures not distributed by state.

Per Capita Expenditures for Federal Government
Procurement Contract Awards in 2009
National Per Capita = $1,727*

ALPHA ORDER

RANK	STATE	PER CAPITA
10	Alabama	$2,208
2	Alaska	7,113
11	Arizona	2,112
50	Arkansas	344
12	California	1,866
9	Colorado	2,214
5	Connecticut	3,696
41	Delaware	702
29	Florida	1,000
36	Georgia	784
22	Hawaii	1,404
8	Idaho	2,217
33	Illinois	892
26	Indiana	1,236
38	Iowa	772
28	Kansas	1,066
18	Kentucky	1,616
32	Louisiana	898
27	Maine	1,085
3	Maryland	6,025
6	Massachusetts	2,865
30	Michigan	934
31	Minnesota	907
15	Mississippi	1,690
7	Missouri	2,256
47	Montana	521
44	Nebraska	648
37	Nevada	781
20	New Hampshire	1,450
23	New Jersey	1,384
4	New Mexico	3,849
39	New York	742
46	North Carolina	555
40	North Dakota	733
35	Ohio	789
34	Oklahoma	854
45	Oregon	645
21	Pennsylvania	1,436
43	Rhode Island	654
13	South Carolina	1,800
42	South Dakota	700
17	Tennessee	1,656
19	Texas	1,586
25	Utah	1,306
14	Vermont	1,729
1	Virginia	10,377
24	Washington	1,383
49	West Virginia	452
16	Wisconsin	1,682
48	Wyoming	478

RANK ORDER

RANK	STATE	PER CAPITA
1	Virginia	$10,377
2	Alaska	7,113
3	Maryland	6,025
4	New Mexico	3,849
5	Connecticut	3,696
6	Massachusetts	2,865
7	Missouri	2,256
8	Idaho	2,217
9	Colorado	2,214
10	Alabama	2,208
11	Arizona	2,112
12	California	1,866
13	South Carolina	1,800
14	Vermont	1,729
15	Mississippi	1,690
16	Wisconsin	1,682
17	Tennessee	1,656
18	Kentucky	1,616
19	Texas	1,586
20	New Hampshire	1,450
21	Pennsylvania	1,436
22	Hawaii	1,404
23	New Jersey	1,384
24	Washington	1,383
25	Utah	1,306
26	Indiana	1,236
27	Maine	1,085
28	Kansas	1,066
29	Florida	1,000
30	Michigan	934
31	Minnesota	907
32	Louisiana	898
33	Illinois	892
34	Oklahoma	854
35	Ohio	789
36	Georgia	784
37	Nevada	781
38	Iowa	772
39	New York	742
40	North Dakota	733
41	Delaware	702
42	South Dakota	700
43	Rhode Island	654
44	Nebraska	648
45	Oregon	645
46	North Carolina	555
47	Montana	521
48	Wyoming	478
49	West Virginia	452
50	Arkansas	344

	District of Columbia	12,924

Source: CQ Press using data from U.S. Bureau of the Census
"Consolidated Federal Funds Report: 2009" (CFFR/09, August 2010, http://www.census.gov/govs/cffr/)
*National per capita excludes expenditures and population for territories and undistributed amounts.

Federal Government Direct Payments for Retirement and Disability in 2009
National Total = $881,105,000,000*

ALPHA ORDER

RANK	STATE	PAYMENTS	% of USA
20	Alabama	$17,448,000,000	2.0%
50	Alaska	1,537,000,000	0.2%
18	Arizona	17,862,000,000	2.0%
29	Arkansas	10,066,000,000	1.1%
1	California	81,796,000,000	9.3%
26	Colorado	12,341,000,000	1.4%
30	Connecticut	9,763,000,000	1.1%
45	Delaware	2,941,000,000	0.3%
2	Florida	62,292,000,000	7.1%
11	Georgia	25,199,000,000	2.9%
41	Hawaii	4,222,000,000	0.5%
40	Idaho	4,373,000,000	0.5%
7	Illinois	32,570,000,000	3.7%
15	Indiana	18,805,000,000	2.1%
32	Iowa	8,905,000,000	1.0%
33	Kansas	8,202,000,000	0.9%
23	Kentucky	14,327,000,000	1.6%
25	Louisiana	12,614,000,000	1.4%
39	Maine	4,772,000,000	0.5%
17	Maryland	18,449,000,000	2.1%
19	Massachusetts	17,781,000,000	2.0%
8	Michigan	30,851,000,000	3.5%
24	Minnesota	13,654,000,000	1.5%
31	Mississippi	9,468,000,000	1.1%
16	Missouri	18,475,000,000	2.1%
43	Montana	3,244,000,000	0.4%
38	Nebraska	5,192,000,000	0.6%
35	Nevada	6,967,000,000	0.8%
42	New Hampshire	4,150,000,000	0.5%
12	New Jersey	23,873,000,000	2.7%
36	New Mexico	6,455,000,000	0.7%
4	New York	51,663,000,000	5.9%
9	North Carolina	28,595,000,000	3.2%
48	North Dakota	1,865,000,000	0.2%
6	Ohio	33,686,000,000	3.8%
27	Oklahoma	12,234,000,000	1.4%
28	Oregon	11,629,000,000	1.3%
5	Pennsylvania	41,892,000,000	4.8%
44	Rhode Island	3,229,000,000	0.4%
22	South Carolina	15,401,000,000	1.7%
46	South Dakota	2,444,000,000	0.3%
13	Tennessee	20,389,000,000	2.3%
3	Texas	58,300,000,000	6.6%
37	Utah	5,796,000,000	0.7%
47	Vermont	1,931,000,000	0.2%
10	Virginia	27,318,000,000	3.1%
14	Washington	19,748,000,000	2.2%
34	West Virginia	7,518,000,000	0.9%
21	Wisconsin	16,114,000,000	1.8%
49	Wyoming	1,580,000,000	0.2%

RANK ORDER

RANK	STATE	PAYMENTS	% of USA
1	California	$81,796,000,000	9.3%
2	Florida	62,292,000,000	7.1%
3	Texas	58,300,000,000	6.6%
4	New York	51,663,000,000	5.9%
5	Pennsylvania	41,892,000,000	4.8%
6	Ohio	33,686,000,000	3.8%
7	Illinois	32,570,000,000	3.7%
8	Michigan	30,851,000,000	3.5%
9	North Carolina	28,595,000,000	3.2%
10	Virginia	27,318,000,000	3.1%
11	Georgia	25,199,000,000	2.9%
12	New Jersey	23,873,000,000	2.7%
13	Tennessee	20,389,000,000	2.3%
14	Washington	19,748,000,000	2.2%
15	Indiana	18,805,000,000	2.1%
16	Missouri	18,475,000,000	2.1%
17	Maryland	18,449,000,000	2.1%
18	Arizona	17,862,000,000	2.0%
19	Massachusetts	17,781,000,000	2.0%
20	Alabama	17,448,000,000	2.0%
21	Wisconsin	16,114,000,000	1.8%
22	South Carolina	15,401,000,000	1.7%
23	Kentucky	14,327,000,000	1.6%
24	Minnesota	13,654,000,000	1.5%
25	Louisiana	12,614,000,000	1.4%
26	Colorado	12,341,000,000	1.4%
27	Oklahoma	12,234,000,000	1.4%
28	Oregon	11,629,000,000	1.3%
29	Arkansas	10,066,000,000	1.1%
30	Connecticut	9,763,000,000	1.1%
31	Mississippi	9,468,000,000	1.1%
32	Iowa	8,905,000,000	1.0%
33	Kansas	8,202,000,000	0.9%
34	West Virginia	7,518,000,000	0.9%
35	Nevada	6,967,000,000	0.8%
36	New Mexico	6,455,000,000	0.7%
37	Utah	5,796,000,000	0.7%
38	Nebraska	5,192,000,000	0.6%
39	Maine	4,772,000,000	0.5%
40	Idaho	4,373,000,000	0.5%
41	Hawaii	4,222,000,000	0.5%
42	New Hampshire	4,150,000,000	0.5%
43	Montana	3,244,000,000	0.4%
44	Rhode Island	3,229,000,000	0.4%
45	Delaware	2,941,000,000	0.3%
46	South Dakota	2,444,000,000	0.3%
47	Vermont	1,931,000,000	0.2%
48	North Dakota	1,865,000,000	0.2%
49	Wyoming	1,580,000,000	0.2%
50	Alaska	1,537,000,000	0.2%
	District of Columbia	2,847,000,000	0.3%

Source: U.S. Bureau of the Census

"Consolidated Federal Funds Report: 2009" (CFFR/09, August 2010, http://www.census.gov/govs/cffr/)

*Total includes $8,312,000,000 in U.S. territories ($7,708,000,000 in Puerto Rico) and $20,000,000 in expenditures not distributed by state. "Direct Payments for Retirement and Disability" include Social Security, federal retirement and disability payments, and veterans benefits.

Per Capita Federal Government Direct Payments for Retirement and Disability in 2009
National Per Capita = $2,843*

ALPHA ORDER

RANK	STATE	PER CAPITA
2	Alabama	$3,705
49	Alaska	2,201
39	Arizona	2,708
4	Arkansas	3,484
48	California	2,213
46	Colorado	2,456
37	Connecticut	2,775
10	Delaware	3,323
7	Florida	3,360
44	Georgia	2,564
13	Hawaii	3,260
35	Idaho	2,829
45	Illinois	2,523
28	Indiana	2,928
27	Iowa	2,961
30	Kansas	2,910
11	Kentucky	3,321
36	Louisiana	2,808
3	Maine	3,620
15	Maryland	3,237
40	Massachusetts	2,697
20	Michigan	3,094
43	Minnesota	2,593
17	Mississippi	3,207
21	Missouri	3,086
8	Montana	3,327
32	Nebraska	2,890
42	Nevada	2,636
18	New Hampshire	3,133
38	New Jersey	2,742
16	New Mexico	3,212
41	New York	2,644
23	North Carolina	3,048
33	North Dakota	2,883
29	Ohio	2,918
12	Oklahoma	3,318
24	Oregon	3,040
9	Pennsylvania	3,324
22	Rhode Island	3,066
6	South Carolina	3,376
25	South Dakota	3,008
14	Tennessee	3,238
47	Texas	2,352
50	Utah	2,081
19	Vermont	3,106
5	Virginia	3,466
26	Washington	2,963
1	West Virginia	4,131
34	Wisconsin	2,850
31	Wyoming	2,903

RANK ORDER

RANK	STATE	PER CAPITA
1	West Virginia	$4,131
2	Alabama	3,705
3	Maine	3,620
4	Arkansas	3,484
5	Virginia	3,466
6	South Carolina	3,376
7	Florida	3,360
8	Montana	3,327
9	Pennsylvania	3,324
10	Delaware	3,323
11	Kentucky	3,321
12	Oklahoma	3,318
13	Hawaii	3,260
14	Tennessee	3,238
15	Maryland	3,237
16	New Mexico	3,212
17	Mississippi	3,207
18	New Hampshire	3,133
19	Vermont	3,106
20	Michigan	3,094
21	Missouri	3,086
22	Rhode Island	3,066
23	North Carolina	3,048
24	Oregon	3,040
25	South Dakota	3,008
26	Washington	2,963
27	Iowa	2,961
28	Indiana	2,928
29	Ohio	2,918
30	Kansas	2,910
31	Wyoming	2,903
32	Nebraska	2,890
33	North Dakota	2,883
34	Wisconsin	2,850
35	Idaho	2,829
36	Louisiana	2,808
37	Connecticut	2,775
38	New Jersey	2,742
39	Arizona	2,708
40	Massachusetts	2,697
41	New York	2,644
42	Nevada	2,636
43	Minnesota	2,593
44	Georgia	2,564
45	Illinois	2,523
46	Colorado	2,456
47	Texas	2,352
48	California	2,213
49	Alaska	2,201
50	Utah	2,081

District of Columbia   4,748

Source: CQ Press using data from U.S. Bureau of the Census

"Consolidated Federal Funds Report: 2009" (CFFR/09, August 2010, http://www.census.gov/govs/cffr/)

*National per capita excludes expenditures and population for territories and undistributed amounts. "Direct Payments for Retirement and Disability" include Social Security, federal retirement and disability payments, and veterans benefits.

Federal Government "Other" Direct Payments in 2009

National Total = $762,924,000,000*

ALPHA ORDER

RANK	STATE	PAYMENTS	% of USA
24	Alabama	$12,119,000,000	1.6%
50	Alaska	875,000,000	0.1%
23	Arizona	12,138,000,000	1.6%
34	Arkansas	7,065,000,000	0.9%
1	California	80,814,000,000	10.6%
31	Colorado	8,644,000,000	1.1%
27	Connecticut	9,226,000,000	1.2%
47	Delaware	1,795,000,000	0.2%
3	Florida	50,666,000,000	6.6%
12	Georgia	18,197,000,000	2.4%
28	Hawaii	9,155,000,000	1.2%
45	Idaho	2,848,000,000	0.4%
7	Illinois	32,976,000,000	4.3%
13	Indiana	17,353,000,000	2.3%
29	Iowa	8,899,000,000	1.2%
18	Kansas	13,775,000,000	1.8%
25	Kentucky	10,655,000,000	1.4%
21	Louisiana	12,616,000,000	1.7%
44	Maine	2,883,000,000	0.4%
17	Maryland	14,331,000,000	1.9%
10	Massachusetts	20,570,000,000	2.7%
8	Michigan	26,237,000,000	3.4%
22	Minnesota	12,443,000,000	1.6%
33	Mississippi	7,456,000,000	1.0%
15	Missouri	16,212,000,000	2.1%
40	Montana	3,135,000,000	0.4%
35	Nebraska	4,917,000,000	0.6%
37	Nevada	4,293,000,000	0.6%
46	New Hampshire	2,315,000,000	0.3%
9	New Jersey	22,745,000,000	3.0%
38	New Mexico	3,806,000,000	0.5%
2	New York	53,965,000,000	7.1%
11	North Carolina	18,450,000,000	2.4%
42	North Dakota	3,065,000,000	0.4%
6	Ohio	33,135,000,000	4.3%
30	Oklahoma	8,869,000,000	1.2%
32	Oregon	8,382,000,000	1.1%
5	Pennsylvania	40,010,000,000	5.2%
41	Rhode Island	3,079,000,000	0.4%
26	South Carolina	10,177,000,000	1.3%
43	South Dakota	3,051,000,000	0.4%
14	Tennessee	17,106,000,000	2.2%
4	Texas	49,452,000,000	6.5%
39	Utah	3,478,000,000	0.5%
48	Vermont	1,346,000,000	0.2%
16	Virginia	15,515,000,000	2.0%
20	Washington	13,108,000,000	1.7%
36	West Virginia	4,676,000,000	0.6%
19	Wisconsin	13,772,000,000	1.8%
49	Wyoming	1,165,000,000	0.2%

RANK ORDER

RANK	STATE	PAYMENTS	% of USA
1	California	$80,814,000,000	10.6%
2	New York	53,965,000,000	7.1%
3	Florida	50,666,000,000	6.6%
4	Texas	49,452,000,000	6.5%
5	Pennsylvania	40,010,000,000	5.2%
6	Ohio	33,135,000,000	4.3%
7	Illinois	32,976,000,000	4.3%
8	Michigan	26,237,000,000	3.4%
9	New Jersey	22,745,000,000	3.0%
10	Massachusetts	20,570,000,000	2.7%
11	North Carolina	18,450,000,000	2.4%
12	Georgia	18,197,000,000	2.4%
13	Indiana	17,353,000,000	2.3%
14	Tennessee	17,106,000,000	2.2%
15	Missouri	16,212,000,000	2.1%
16	Virginia	15,515,000,000	2.0%
17	Maryland	14,331,000,000	1.9%
18	Kansas	13,775,000,000	1.8%
19	Wisconsin	13,772,000,000	1.8%
20	Washington	13,108,000,000	1.7%
21	Louisiana	12,616,000,000	1.7%
22	Minnesota	12,443,000,000	1.6%
23	Arizona	12,138,000,000	1.6%
24	Alabama	12,119,000,000	1.6%
25	Kentucky	10,655,000,000	1.4%
26	South Carolina	10,177,000,000	1.3%
27	Connecticut	9,226,000,000	1.2%
28	Hawaii	9,155,000,000	1.2%
29	Iowa	8,899,000,000	1.2%
30	Oklahoma	8,869,000,000	1.2%
31	Colorado	8,644,000,000	1.1%
32	Oregon	8,382,000,000	1.1%
33	Mississippi	7,456,000,000	1.0%
34	Arkansas	7,065,000,000	0.9%
35	Nebraska	4,917,000,000	0.6%
36	West Virginia	4,676,000,000	0.6%
37	Nevada	4,293,000,000	0.6%
38	New Mexico	3,806,000,000	0.5%
39	Utah	3,478,000,000	0.5%
40	Montana	3,135,000,000	0.4%
41	Rhode Island	3,079,000,000	0.4%
42	North Dakota	3,065,000,000	0.4%
43	South Dakota	3,051,000,000	0.4%
44	Maine	2,883,000,000	0.4%
45	Idaho	2,848,000,000	0.4%
46	New Hampshire	2,315,000,000	0.3%
47	Delaware	1,795,000,000	0.2%
48	Vermont	1,346,000,000	0.2%
49	Wyoming	1,165,000,000	0.2%
50	Alaska	875,000,000	0.1%
	District of Columbia	4,980,000,000	0.7%

Source: U.S. Bureau of the Census

"Consolidated Federal Funds Report: 2009" (CFFR/09, August 2010, http://www.census.gov/govs/cffr/)

*Total includes $4,723,000,000 in U.S. territories ($4,412,000,000 in Puerto Rico) and $263,000,000 in expenditures not distributed by state. "Other Direct Payments" include direct payments for programs other than retirement and disability. These include Medicare, excess earned income tax credits, unemployment compensation, food stamps, housing assistance, and agricultural assistance.

Per Capita Expenditures for Federal Government
"Other" Direct Payments in 2009
National Per Capita = $2,469*

ALPHA ORDER

RANK	STATE	PER CAPITA
21	Alabama	$2,574
49	Alaska	1,253
45	Arizona	1,840
27	Arkansas	2,445
34	California	2,186
47	Colorado	1,720
19	Connecticut	2,622
37	Delaware	2,028
14	Florida	2,733
43	Georgia	1,851
1	Hawaii	7,069
44	Idaho	1,842
23	Illinois	2,554
17	Indiana	2,702
8	Iowa	2,959
2	Kansas	4,887
26	Kentucky	2,470
11	Louisiana	2,809
33	Maine	2,187
25	Maryland	2,514
7	Massachusetts	3,120
18	Michigan	2,632
30	Minnesota	2,363
24	Mississippi	2,526
16	Missouri	2,708
5	Montana	3,215
13	Nebraska	2,737
48	Nevada	1,624
46	New Hampshire	1,748
20	New Jersey	2,612
42	New Mexico	1,894
12	New York	2,762
40	North Carolina	1,967
3	North Dakota	4,738
10	Ohio	2,871
29	Oklahoma	2,405
32	Oregon	2,191
6	Pennsylvania	3,174
9	Rhode Island	2,923
31	South Carolina	2,231
4	South Dakota	3,756
15	Tennessee	2,717
38	Texas	1,995
50	Utah	1,249
35	Vermont	2,165
39	Virginia	1,968
40	Washington	1,967
22	West Virginia	2,570
28	Wisconsin	2,435
36	Wyoming	2,140

RANK ORDER

RANK	STATE	PER CAPITA
1	Hawaii	$7,069
2	Kansas	4,887
3	North Dakota	4,738
4	South Dakota	3,756
5	Montana	3,215
6	Pennsylvania	3,174
7	Massachusetts	3,120
8	Iowa	2,959
9	Rhode Island	2,923
10	Ohio	2,871
11	Louisiana	2,809
12	New York	2,762
13	Nebraska	2,737
14	Florida	2,733
15	Tennessee	2,717
16	Missouri	2,708
17	Indiana	2,702
18	Michigan	2,632
19	Connecticut	2,622
20	New Jersey	2,612
21	Alabama	2,574
22	West Virginia	2,570
23	Illinois	2,554
24	Mississippi	2,526
25	Maryland	2,514
26	Kentucky	2,470
27	Arkansas	2,445
28	Wisconsin	2,435
29	Oklahoma	2,405
30	Minnesota	2,363
31	South Carolina	2,231
32	Oregon	2,191
33	Maine	2,187
34	California	2,186
35	Vermont	2,165
36	Wyoming	2,140
37	Delaware	2,028
38	Texas	1,995
39	Virginia	1,968
40	North Carolina	1,967
40	Washington	1,967
42	New Mexico	1,894
43	Georgia	1,851
44	Idaho	1,842
45	Arizona	1,840
46	New Hampshire	1,748
47	Colorado	1,720
48	Nevada	1,624
49	Alaska	1,253
50	Utah	1,249

District of Columbia — 8,305

Source: CQ Press using data from U.S. Bureau of the Census
"Consolidated Federal Funds Report: 2009" (CFFR/09, August 2010, http://www.census.gov/govs/cffr/)
*National per capita excludes expenditures and population for territories and undistributed amounts. "Other Direct Payments" include direct payments for programs other than retirement and disability. These include Medicare, excess earned income tax credits, unemployment compensation, food stamps, housing assistance, and agricultural assistance.

Federal Government Expenditures for Salaries and Wages in 2009

National Total = $299,413,000,000*

ALPHA ORDER

RANK	STATE	SALARIES	% of USA
19	Alabama	$4,704,000,000	1.6%
28	Alaska	3,128,000,000	1.0%
20	Arizona	4,618,000,000	1.5%
35	Arkansas	2,240,000,000	0.7%
2	California	23,462,000,000	7.8%
12	Colorado	6,845,000,000	2.3%
38	Connecticut	1,766,000,000	0.6%
49	Delaware	655,000,000	0.2%
7	Florida	12,215,000,000	4.1%
4	Georgia	13,631,000,000	4.6%
16	Hawaii	6,156,000,000	2.1%
41	Idaho	1,151,000,000	0.4%
11	Illinois	7,529,000,000	2.5%
26	Indiana	3,709,000,000	1.2%
39	Iowa	1,663,000,000	0.6%
22	Kansas	4,339,000,000	1.4%
13	Kentucky	6,692,000,000	2.2%
25	Louisiana	3,842,000,000	1.3%
43	Maine	1,073,000,000	0.4%
5	Maryland	13,231,000,000	4.4%
23	Massachusetts	4,266,000,000	1.4%
21	Michigan	4,478,000,000	1.5%
29	Minnesota	3,074,000,000	1.0%
32	Mississippi	2,633,000,000	0.9%
15	Missouri	6,179,000,000	2.1%
42	Montana	1,099,000,000	0.4%
40	Nebraska	1,597,000,000	0.5%
37	Nevada	1,812,000,000	0.6%
47	New Hampshire	847,000,000	0.3%
17	New Jersey	5,193,000,000	1.7%
33	New Mexico	2,523,000,000	0.8%
6	New York	12,422,000,000	4.1%
8	North Carolina	11,640,000,000	3.9%
45	North Dakota	959,000,000	0.3%
14	Ohio	6,637,000,000	2.2%
18	Oklahoma	4,710,000,000	1.6%
34	Oregon	2,409,000,000	0.8%
10	Pennsylvania	8,324,000,000	2.8%
46	Rhode Island	911,000,000	0.3%
24	South Carolina	3,865,000,000	1.3%
44	South Dakota	968,000,000	0.3%
27	Tennessee	3,562,000,000	1.2%
1	Texas	24,373,000,000	8.1%
30	Utah	2,848,000,000	1.0%
50	Vermont	578,000,000	0.2%
3	Virginia	18,253,000,000	6.1%
9	Washington	9,229,000,000	3.1%
36	West Virginia	1,870,000,000	0.6%
31	Wisconsin	2,662,000,000	0.9%
48	Wyoming	669,000,000	0.2%

RANK ORDER

RANK	STATE	SALARIES	% of USA
1	Texas	$24,373,000,000	8.1%
2	California	23,462,000,000	7.8%
3	Virginia	18,253,000,000	6.1%
4	Georgia	13,631,000,000	4.6%
5	Maryland	13,231,000,000	4.4%
6	New York	12,422,000,000	4.1%
7	Florida	12,215,000,000	4.1%
8	North Carolina	11,640,000,000	3.9%
9	Washington	9,229,000,000	3.1%
10	Pennsylvania	8,324,000,000	2.8%
11	Illinois	7,529,000,000	2.5%
12	Colorado	6,845,000,000	2.3%
13	Kentucky	6,692,000,000	2.2%
14	Ohio	6,637,000,000	2.2%
15	Missouri	6,179,000,000	2.1%
16	Hawaii	6,156,000,000	2.1%
17	New Jersey	5,193,000,000	1.7%
18	Oklahoma	4,710,000,000	1.6%
19	Alabama	4,704,000,000	1.6%
20	Arizona	4,618,000,000	1.5%
21	Michigan	4,478,000,000	1.5%
22	Kansas	4,339,000,000	1.4%
23	Massachusetts	4,266,000,000	1.4%
24	South Carolina	3,865,000,000	1.3%
25	Louisiana	3,842,000,000	1.3%
26	Indiana	3,709,000,000	1.2%
27	Tennessee	3,562,000,000	1.2%
28	Alaska	3,128,000,000	1.0%
29	Minnesota	3,074,000,000	1.0%
30	Utah	2,848,000,000	1.0%
31	Wisconsin	2,662,000,000	0.9%
32	Mississippi	2,633,000,000	0.9%
33	New Mexico	2,523,000,000	0.8%
34	Oregon	2,409,000,000	0.8%
35	Arkansas	2,240,000,000	0.7%
36	West Virginia	1,870,000,000	0.6%
37	Nevada	1,812,000,000	0.6%
38	Connecticut	1,766,000,000	0.6%
39	Iowa	1,663,000,000	0.6%
40	Nebraska	1,597,000,000	0.5%
41	Idaho	1,151,000,000	0.4%
42	Montana	1,099,000,000	0.4%
43	Maine	1,073,000,000	0.4%
44	South Dakota	968,000,000	0.3%
45	North Dakota	959,000,000	0.3%
46	Rhode Island	911,000,000	0.3%
47	New Hampshire	847,000,000	0.3%
48	Wyoming	669,000,000	0.2%
49	Delaware	655,000,000	0.2%
50	Vermont	578,000,000	0.2%
	District of Columbia	22,290,000,000	7.4%

Source: U.S. Bureau of the Census

"Consolidated Federal Funds Report: 2009" (CFFR/09, August 2010, http://www.census.gov/govs/cffr/)
*Total includes $1,654,000,000 in U.S. territories ($1,189,000,000 in Puerto Rico) and $2,231,000,000 in expenditures not distributed by state.

Per Capita Expenditures for Federal Government Salaries and Wages in 2009

National Per Capita = $963*

ALPHA ORDER

RANK	STATE	PER CAPITA
20	Alabama	$999
2	Alaska	4,478
32	Arizona	700
29	Arkansas	775
39	California	635
10	Colorado	1,362
48	Connecticut	502
31	Delaware	740
35	Florida	659
8	Georgia	1,387
1	Hawaii	4,753
30	Idaho	745
43	Illinois	583
44	Indiana	577
47	Iowa	553
6	Kansas	1,539
5	Kentucky	1,551
26	Louisiana	855
28	Maine	814
3	Maryland	2,321
36	Massachusetts	647
50	Michigan	449
42	Minnesota	584
23	Mississippi	892
17	Missouri	1,032
16	Montana	1,127
24	Nebraska	889
33	Nevada	686
37	New Hampshire	639
41	New Jersey	596
12	New Mexico	1,255
38	New York	636
13	North Carolina	1,241
7	North Dakota	1,483
45	Ohio	575
11	Oklahoma	1,277
40	Oregon	630
34	Pennsylvania	660
25	Rhode Island	865
27	South Carolina	847
15	South Dakota	1,192
46	Tennessee	566
21	Texas	983
19	Utah	1,023
22	Vermont	930
4	Virginia	2,316
9	Washington	1,385
18	West Virginia	1,028
49	Wisconsin	471
14	Wyoming	1,229

RANK ORDER

RANK	STATE	PER CAPITA
1	Hawaii	$4,753
2	Alaska	4,478
3	Maryland	2,321
4	Virginia	2,316
5	Kentucky	1,551
6	Kansas	1,539
7	North Dakota	1,483
8	Georgia	1,387
9	Washington	1,385
10	Colorado	1,362
11	Oklahoma	1,277
12	New Mexico	1,255
13	North Carolina	1,241
14	Wyoming	1,229
15	South Dakota	1,192
16	Montana	1,127
17	Missouri	1,032
18	West Virginia	1,028
19	Utah	1,023
20	Alabama	999
21	Texas	983
22	Vermont	930
23	Mississippi	892
24	Nebraska	889
25	Rhode Island	865
26	Louisiana	855
27	South Carolina	847
28	Maine	814
29	Arkansas	775
30	Idaho	745
31	Delaware	740
32	Arizona	700
33	Nevada	686
34	Pennsylvania	660
35	Florida	659
36	Massachusetts	647
37	New Hampshire	639
38	New York	636
39	California	635
40	Oregon	630
41	New Jersey	596
42	Minnesota	584
43	Illinois	583
44	Indiana	577
45	Ohio	575
46	Tennessee	566
47	Iowa	553
48	Connecticut	502
49	Wisconsin	471
50	Michigan	449

| | District of Columbia | 37,171 |

Source: CQ Press using data from U.S. Bureau of the Census
"Consolidated Federal Funds Report: 2009" (CFFR/09, August 2010, http://www.census.gov/govs/cffr/)
*National per capita excludes expenditures and population for territories and undistributed amounts.

Federal Civilian Employees in 2008

National Total = 1,860,000 Full-Time Employees*

ALPHA ORDER

RANK	STATE	EMPLOYEES	% of USA
13	Alabama	38,000	2.0%
36	Alaska	12,000	0.6%
13	Arizona	38,000	2.0%
34	Arkansas	14,000	0.8%
1	California	157,000	8.4%
15	Colorado	37,000	2.0%
43	Connecticut	8,000	0.4%
50	Delaware	3,000	0.2%
5	Florida	84,000	4.5%
6	Georgia	74,000	4.0%
24	Hawaii	23,000	1.2%
41	Idaho	9,000	0.5%
10	Illinois	49,000	2.6%
25	Indiana	22,000	1.2%
41	Iowa	9,000	0.5%
33	Kansas	16,000	0.9%
25	Kentucky	22,000	1.2%
27	Louisiana	21,000	1.1%
38	Maine	10,000	0.5%
4	Maryland	117,000	6.3%
20	Massachusetts	27,000	1.5%
19	Michigan	28,000	1.5%
32	Minnesota	17,000	0.9%
30	Mississippi	19,000	1.0%
16	Missouri	36,000	1.9%
38	Montana	10,000	0.5%
38	Nebraska	10,000	0.5%
37	Nevada	11,000	0.6%
48	New Hampshire	4,000	0.2%
18	New Jersey	30,000	1.6%
23	New Mexico	24,000	1.3%
7	New York	69,000	3.7%
12	North Carolina	39,000	2.1%
46	North Dakota	6,000	0.3%
10	Ohio	49,000	2.6%
17	Oklahoma	34,000	1.8%
28	Oregon	20,000	1.1%
8	Pennsylvania	67,000	3.6%
45	Rhode Island	7,000	0.4%
28	South Carolina	20,000	1.1%
43	South Dakota	8,000	0.4%
22	Tennessee	26,000	1.4%
3	Texas	130,000	7.0%
20	Utah	27,000	1.5%
48	Vermont	4,000	0.2%
2	Virginia	138,000	7.4%
9	Washington	51,000	2.7%
31	West Virginia	18,000	1.0%
34	Wisconsin	14,000	0.8%
47	Wyoming	5,000	0.3%

RANK ORDER

RANK	STATE	EMPLOYEES	% of USA
1	California	157,000	8.4%
2	Virginia	138,000	7.4%
3	Texas	130,000	7.0%
4	Maryland	117,000	6.3%
5	Florida	84,000	4.5%
6	Georgia	74,000	4.0%
7	New York	69,000	3.7%
8	Pennsylvania	67,000	3.6%
9	Washington	51,000	2.7%
10	Illinois	49,000	2.6%
10	Ohio	49,000	2.6%
12	North Carolina	39,000	2.1%
13	Alabama	38,000	2.0%
13	Arizona	38,000	2.0%
15	Colorado	37,000	2.0%
16	Missouri	36,000	1.9%
17	Oklahoma	34,000	1.8%
18	New Jersey	30,000	1.6%
19	Michigan	28,000	1.5%
20	Massachusetts	27,000	1.5%
20	Utah	27,000	1.5%
22	Tennessee	26,000	1.4%
23	New Mexico	24,000	1.3%
24	Hawaii	23,000	1.2%
25	Indiana	22,000	1.2%
25	Kentucky	22,000	1.2%
27	Louisiana	21,000	1.1%
28	Oregon	20,000	1.1%
28	South Carolina	20,000	1.1%
30	Mississippi	19,000	1.0%
31	West Virginia	18,000	1.0%
32	Minnesota	17,000	0.9%
33	Kansas	16,000	0.9%
34	Arkansas	14,000	0.8%
34	Wisconsin	14,000	0.8%
36	Alaska	12,000	0.6%
37	Nevada	11,000	0.6%
38	Maine	10,000	0.5%
38	Montana	10,000	0.5%
38	Nebraska	10,000	0.5%
41	Idaho	9,000	0.5%
41	Iowa	9,000	0.5%
43	Connecticut	8,000	0.4%
43	South Dakota	8,000	0.4%
45	Rhode Island	7,000	0.4%
46	North Dakota	6,000	0.3%
47	Wyoming	5,000	0.3%
48	New Hampshire	4,000	0.2%
48	Vermont	4,000	0.2%
50	Delaware	3,000	0.2%
	District of Columbia	149,000	8.0%

Source: U.S. Office of Personnel Management
Unpublished data (http://www.opm.gov/feddata/)
*Full-time employees. Excludes Central Intelligence Agency, Defense Intelligence Agency, and National Security Agency.

Rate of Federal Civilian Employees in 2008

National Rate = 61 Full-Time Employees per 10,000 Population*

ALPHA ORDER

RANK	STATE	RATE
13	Alabama	81
4	Alaska	174
23	Arizona	58
30	Arkansas	49
34	California	43
17	Colorado	75
50	Connecticut	23
43	Delaware	34
32	Florida	46
15	Georgia	76
2	Hawaii	179
22	Idaho	59
40	Illinois	38
43	Indiana	34
46	Iowa	30
24	Kansas	57
29	Kentucky	51
31	Louisiana	47
15	Maine	76
1	Maryland	207
39	Massachusetts	41
48	Michigan	28
45	Minnesota	33
19	Mississippi	65
21	Missouri	60
6	Montana	103
25	Nebraska	56
36	Nevada	42
46	New Hampshire	30
41	New Jersey	35
5	New Mexico	121
41	New York	35
36	North Carolina	42
10	North Dakota	94
34	Ohio	43
12	Oklahoma	93
26	Oregon	53
26	Pennsylvania	53
18	Rhode Island	66
33	South Carolina	44
7	South Dakota	99
36	Tennessee	42
26	Texas	53
7	Utah	99
20	Vermont	64
3	Virginia	177
14	Washington	78
7	West Virginia	99
49	Wisconsin	25
10	Wyoming	94

RANK ORDER

RANK	STATE	RATE
1	Maryland	207
2	Hawaii	179
3	Virginia	177
4	Alaska	174
5	New Mexico	121
6	Montana	103
7	South Dakota	99
7	Utah	99
7	West Virginia	99
10	North Dakota	94
10	Wyoming	94
12	Oklahoma	93
13	Alabama	81
14	Washington	78
15	Georgia	76
15	Maine	76
17	Colorado	75
18	Rhode Island	66
19	Mississippi	65
20	Vermont	64
21	Missouri	60
22	Idaho	59
23	Arizona	58
24	Kansas	57
25	Nebraska	56
26	Oregon	53
26	Pennsylvania	53
26	Texas	53
29	Kentucky	51
30	Arkansas	49
31	Louisiana	47
32	Florida	46
33	South Carolina	44
34	California	43
34	Ohio	43
36	Nevada	42
36	North Carolina	42
36	Tennessee	42
39	Massachusetts	41
40	Illinois	38
41	New Jersey	35
41	New York	35
43	Delaware	34
43	Indiana	34
45	Minnesota	33
46	Iowa	30
46	New Hampshire	30
48	Michigan	28
49	Wisconsin	25
50	Connecticut	23

District of Columbia	2,525

Source: CQ Press using data from U.S. Office of Personnel Management
Unpublished data (http://www.opm.gov/feddata/)

*Full-time employees. Excludes Central Intelligence Agency, Defense Intelligence Agency, and National Security Agency.

X. Government Finances: State and Local

State and Local Government Total Revenue in 2008

National Total = $2,660,474,770,000*

ALPHA ORDER

RANK	STATE	REVENUE	% of USA
26	Alabama	$31,834,272,000	1.2%
36	Alaska	18,793,269,000	0.7%
16	Arizona	47,674,582,000	1.8%
35	Arkansas	19,633,471,000	0.7%
1	California	354,000,382,000	13.3%
17	Colorado	47,107,619,000	1.8%
25	Connecticut	33,283,844,000	1.3%
47	Delaware	8,406,881,000	0.3%
4	Florida	147,940,364,000	5.6%
11	Georgia	73,064,147,000	2.7%
40	Hawaii	11,932,711,000	0.4%
42	Idaho	10,546,803,000	0.4%
6	Illinois	104,194,499,000	3.9%
18	Indiana	46,431,221,000	1.7%
30	Iowa	24,979,654,000	0.9%
33	Kansas	22,671,662,000	0.9%
27	Kentucky	29,467,046,000	1.1%
21	Louisiana	44,210,528,000	1.7%
41	Maine	10,755,753,000	0.4%
20	Maryland	45,445,324,000	1.7%
10	Massachusetts	73,472,096,000	2.8%
12	Michigan	68,603,467,000	2.6%
19	Minnesota	45,665,585,000	1.7%
31	Mississippi	23,637,133,000	0.9%
22	Missouri	42,180,267,000	1.6%
46	Montana	8,520,431,000	0.3%
37	Nebraska	17,757,268,000	0.7%
34	Nevada	19,960,966,000	0.8%
43	New Hampshire	9,631,950,000	0.4%
8	New Jersey	85,934,907,000	3.2%
38	New Mexico	16,910,955,000	0.6%
2	New York	243,901,439,000	9.2%
9	North Carolina	77,177,610,000	2.9%
48	North Dakota	6,677,535,000	0.3%
7	Ohio	100,926,025,000	3.8%
29	Oklahoma	26,780,963,000	1.0%
28	Oregon	28,987,665,000	1.1%
5	Pennsylvania	109,732,032,000	4.1%
44	Rhode Island	9,437,308,000	0.4%
24	South Carolina	35,413,679,000	1.3%
50	South Dakota	5,190,199,000	0.2%
15	Tennessee	48,025,793,000	1.8%
3	Texas	196,508,083,000	7.4%
32	Utah	22,973,040,000	0.9%
49	Vermont	6,085,215,000	0.2%
14	Virginia	58,222,696,000	2.2%
13	Washington	63,206,716,000	2.4%
39	West Virginia	13,710,441,000	0.5%
23	Wisconsin	41,701,393,000	1.6%
45	Wyoming	9,377,986,000	0.4%

RANK ORDER

RANK	STATE	REVENUE	% of USA
1	California	$354,000,382,000	13.3%
2	New York	243,901,439,000	9.2%
3	Texas	196,508,083,000	7.4%
4	Florida	147,940,364,000	5.6%
5	Pennsylvania	109,732,032,000	4.1%
6	Illinois	104,194,499,000	3.9%
7	Ohio	100,926,025,000	3.8%
8	New Jersey	85,934,907,000	3.2%
9	North Carolina	77,177,610,000	2.9%
10	Massachusetts	73,472,096,000	2.8%
11	Georgia	73,064,147,000	2.7%
12	Michigan	68,603,467,000	2.6%
13	Washington	63,206,716,000	2.4%
14	Virginia	58,222,696,000	2.2%
15	Tennessee	48,025,793,000	1.8%
16	Arizona	47,674,582,000	1.8%
17	Colorado	47,107,619,000	1.8%
18	Indiana	46,431,221,000	1.7%
19	Minnesota	45,665,585,000	1.7%
20	Maryland	45,445,324,000	1.7%
21	Louisiana	44,210,528,000	1.7%
22	Missouri	42,180,267,000	1.6%
23	Wisconsin	41,701,393,000	1.6%
24	South Carolina	35,413,679,000	1.3%
25	Connecticut	33,283,844,000	1.3%
26	Alabama	31,834,272,000	1.2%
27	Kentucky	29,467,046,000	1.1%
28	Oregon	28,987,665,000	1.1%
29	Oklahoma	26,780,963,000	1.0%
30	Iowa	24,979,654,000	0.9%
31	Mississippi	23,637,133,000	0.9%
32	Utah	22,973,040,000	0.9%
33	Kansas	22,671,662,000	0.9%
34	Nevada	19,960,966,000	0.8%
35	Arkansas	19,633,471,000	0.7%
36	Alaska	18,793,269,000	0.7%
37	Nebraska	17,757,268,000	0.7%
38	New Mexico	16,910,955,000	0.6%
39	West Virginia	13,710,441,000	0.5%
40	Hawaii	11,932,711,000	0.4%
41	Maine	10,755,753,000	0.4%
42	Idaho	10,546,803,000	0.4%
43	New Hampshire	9,631,950,000	0.4%
44	Rhode Island	9,437,308,000	0.4%
45	Wyoming	9,377,986,000	0.4%
46	Montana	8,520,431,000	0.3%
47	Delaware	8,406,881,000	0.3%
48	North Dakota	6,677,535,000	0.3%
49	Vermont	6,085,215,000	0.2%
50	South Dakota	5,190,199,000	0.2%
	District of Columbia	11,789,895,000	0.4%

Source: U.S. Bureau of the Census, Governments Division
    "2008 State and Local Government Finances" (http://www.census.gov/govs/estimate/index.html)
*Total revenue includes all money received from external sources. This includes taxes, intergovernmental transfers and insurance trust revenue, and revenue from government owned utilities and other commercial or auxiliary enterprise.

Per Capita State and Local Government Revenue in 2008

National Per Capita = $8,741*

ALPHA ORDER				RANK ORDER		
RANK	STATE	PER CAPITA		RANK	STATE	PER CAPITA
49	Alabama	$6,806		1	Alaska	$27,311
1	Alaska	27,311		2	Wyoming	17,595
41	Arizona	7,335		3	New York	12,528
48	Arkansas	6,846		4	Massachusetts	11,228
10	California	9,677		5	North Dakota	10,411
13	Colorado	9,545		6	Nebraska	9,965
14	Connecticut	9,502		7	Louisiana	9,932
12	Delaware	9,595		8	New Jersey	9,919
31	Florida	8,030		9	Vermont	9,798
37	Georgia	7,534		10	California	9,677
15	Hawaii	9,268		11	Washington	9,626
45	Idaho	6,905		12	Delaware	9,595
26	Illinois	8,113		13	Colorado	9,545
43	Indiana	7,268		14	Connecticut	9,502
24	Iowa	8,343		15	Hawaii	9,268
27	Kansas	8,105		16	Rhode Island	8,958
46	Kentucky	6,872		17	Montana	8,802
7	Louisiana	9,932		18	Ohio	8,755
25	Maine	8,150		19	Pennsylvania	8,732
30	Maryland	8,031		20	Minnesota	8,731
4	Massachusetts	11,228		21	New Mexico	8,512
47	Michigan	6,859		22	Utah	8,423
20	Minnesota	8,731		23	North Carolina	8,346
29	Mississippi	8,039		24	Iowa	8,343
44	Missouri	7,082		25	Maine	8,150
17	Montana	8,802		26	Illinois	8,113
6	Nebraska	9,965		27	Kansas	8,105
35	Nevada	7,631		28	Texas	8,085
42	New Hampshire	7,287		29	Mississippi	8,039
8	New Jersey	9,919		30	Maryland	8,031
21	New Mexico	8,512		31	Florida	8,030
3	New York	12,528		32	South Carolina	7,864
23	North Carolina	8,346		33	Tennessee	7,696
5	North Dakota	10,411		34	Oregon	7,663
18	Ohio	8,755		35	Nevada	7,631
40	Oklahoma	7,349		36	West Virginia	7,554
34	Oregon	7,663		37	Georgia	7,534
19	Pennsylvania	8,732		38	Virginia	7,469
16	Rhode Island	8,958		39	Wisconsin	7,410
32	South Carolina	7,864		40	Oklahoma	7,349
50	South Dakota	6,451		41	Arizona	7,335
33	Tennessee	7,696		42	New Hampshire	7,287
28	Texas	8,085		43	Indiana	7,268
22	Utah	8,423		44	Missouri	7,082
9	Vermont	9,798		45	Idaho	6,905
38	Virginia	7,469		46	Kentucky	6,872
11	Washington	9,626		47	Michigan	6,859
36	West Virginia	7,554		48	Arkansas	6,846
39	Wisconsin	7,410		49	Alabama	6,806
2	Wyoming	17,595		50	South Dakota	6,451

District of Columbia 19,980

Source: CQ Press using data from U.S. Bureau of the Census, Governments Division
"2008 State and Local Government Finances" (http://www.census.gov/govs/estimate/index.html)
*Total revenue includes all money received from external sources. This includes taxes, intergovernmental transfers and insurance trust revenue, and revenue from government owned utilities and other commercial or auxiliary enterprise.

State and Local Government Revenue from the Federal Government in 2008

National Total = $481,380,023,000

ALPHA ORDER

RANK	STATE	REVENUE	% of USA
21	Alabama	$8,059,950,000	1.7%
39	Alaska	2,443,774,000	0.5%
14	Arizona	9,689,177,000	2.0%
31	Arkansas	4,771,826,000	1.0%
1	California	57,719,733,000	12.0%
29	Colorado	5,632,605,000	1.2%
32	Connecticut	4,734,785,000	1.0%
50	Delaware	1,342,511,000	0.3%
4	Florida	23,272,332,000	4.8%
11	Georgia	14,043,929,000	2.9%
40	Hawaii	2,291,019,000	0.5%
42	Idaho	2,120,413,000	0.4%
7	Illinois	17,369,416,000	3.6%
18	Indiana	8,564,919,000	1.8%
30	Iowa	4,816,391,000	1.0%
35	Kansas	3,682,749,000	0.8%
25	Kentucky	7,022,395,000	1.5%
9	Louisiana	15,144,821,000	3.1%
38	Maine	2,554,771,000	0.5%
19	Maryland	8,229,265,000	1.7%
13	Massachusetts	11,239,013,000	2.3%
10	Michigan	14,877,190,000	3.1%
23	Minnesota	7,854,041,000	1.6%
20	Mississippi	8,188,853,000	1.7%
16	Missouri	9,130,107,000	1.9%
43	Montana	2,101,201,000	0.4%
37	Nebraska	2,773,637,000	0.6%
41	Nevada	2,260,701,000	0.5%
46	New Hampshire	1,747,799,000	0.4%
12	New Jersey	11,502,644,000	2.4%
33	New Mexico	4,527,301,000	0.9%
2	New York	44,739,182,000	9.3%
8	North Carolina	15,181,438,000	3.2%
49	North Dakota	1,359,889,000	0.3%
6	Ohio	18,654,263,000	3.9%
27	Oklahoma	5,940,226,000	1.2%
28	Oregon	5,859,012,000	1.2%
5	Pennsylvania	19,083,303,000	4.0%
45	Rhode Island	2,071,758,000	0.4%
26	South Carolina	7,006,265,000	1.5%
48	South Dakota	1,431,133,000	0.3%
17	Tennessee	8,849,984,000	1.8%
3	Texas	33,062,188,000	6.9%
34	Utah	3,810,777,000	0.8%
47	Vermont	1,475,927,000	0.3%
22	Virginia	7,968,765,000	1.7%
15	Washington	9,320,738,000	1.9%
36	West Virginia	3,382,351,000	0.7%
24	Wisconsin	7,372,888,000	1.5%
44	Wyoming	2,089,680,000	0.4%

RANK ORDER

RANK	STATE	REVENUE	% of USA
1	California	$57,719,733,000	12.0%
2	New York	44,739,182,000	9.3%
3	Texas	33,062,188,000	6.9%
4	Florida	23,272,332,000	4.8%
5	Pennsylvania	19,083,303,000	4.0%
6	Ohio	18,654,263,000	3.9%
7	Illinois	17,369,416,000	3.6%
8	North Carolina	15,181,438,000	3.2%
9	Louisiana	15,144,821,000	3.1%
10	Michigan	14,877,190,000	3.1%
11	Georgia	14,043,929,000	2.9%
12	New Jersey	11,502,644,000	2.4%
13	Massachusetts	11,239,013,000	2.3%
14	Arizona	9,689,177,000	2.0%
15	Washington	9,320,738,000	1.9%
16	Missouri	9,130,107,000	1.9%
17	Tennessee	8,849,984,000	1.8%
18	Indiana	8,564,919,000	1.8%
19	Maryland	8,229,265,000	1.7%
20	Mississippi	8,188,853,000	1.7%
21	Alabama	8,059,950,000	1.7%
22	Virginia	7,968,765,000	1.7%
23	Minnesota	7,854,041,000	1.6%
24	Wisconsin	7,372,888,000	1.5%
25	Kentucky	7,022,395,000	1.5%
26	South Carolina	7,006,265,000	1.5%
27	Oklahoma	5,940,226,000	1.2%
28	Oregon	5,859,012,000	1.2%
29	Colorado	5,632,605,000	1.2%
30	Iowa	4,816,391,000	1.0%
31	Arkansas	4,771,826,000	1.0%
32	Connecticut	4,734,785,000	1.0%
33	New Mexico	4,527,301,000	0.9%
34	Utah	3,810,777,000	0.8%
35	Kansas	3,682,749,000	0.8%
36	West Virginia	3,382,351,000	0.7%
37	Nebraska	2,773,637,000	0.6%
38	Maine	2,554,771,000	0.5%
39	Alaska	2,443,774,000	0.5%
40	Hawaii	2,291,019,000	0.5%
41	Nevada	2,260,701,000	0.5%
42	Idaho	2,120,413,000	0.4%
43	Montana	2,101,201,000	0.4%
44	Wyoming	2,089,680,000	0.4%
45	Rhode Island	2,071,758,000	0.4%
46	New Hampshire	1,747,799,000	0.4%
47	Vermont	1,475,927,000	0.3%
48	South Dakota	1,431,133,000	0.3%
49	North Dakota	1,359,889,000	0.3%
50	Delaware	1,342,511,000	0.3%
	District of Columbia	3,010,988,000	0.6%

Source: U.S. Bureau of the Census, Governments Division
"2008 State and Local Government Finances" (http://www.census.gov/govs/estimate/index.html)

Per Capita State and Local Government Revenue
from the Federal Government in 2008
National Per Capita = $1,582

ALPHA ORDER

RANK	STATE	PER CAPITA
15	Alabama	$1,723
2	Alaska	3,551
31	Arizona	1,491
17	Arkansas	1,664
23	California	1,578
48	Colorado	1,141
40	Connecticut	1,352
28	Delaware	1,532
47	Florida	1,263
34	Georgia	1,448
13	Hawaii	1,779
38	Idaho	1,388
40	Illinois	1,352
42	Indiana	1,341
22	Iowa	1,609
45	Kansas	1,317
19	Kentucky	1,638
3	Louisiana	3,402
11	Maine	1,936
33	Maryland	1,454
16	Massachusetts	1,718
32	Michigan	1,487
30	Minnesota	1,502
4	Mississippi	2,785
27	Missouri	1,533
8	Montana	2,171
24	Nebraska	1,557
50	Nevada	864
44	New Hampshire	1,322
43	New Jersey	1,328
7	New Mexico	2,279
6	New York	2,298
18	North Carolina	1,642
9	North Dakota	2,120
21	Ohio	1,618
20	Oklahoma	1,630
26	Oregon	1,549
29	Pennsylvania	1,519
10	Rhode Island	1,967
25	South Carolina	1,556
13	South Dakota	1,779
36	Tennessee	1,418
39	Texas	1,360
37	Utah	1,397
5	Vermont	2,377
49	Virginia	1,022
35	Washington	1,420
12	West Virginia	1,864
46	Wisconsin	1,310
1	Wyoming	3,921

RANK ORDER

RANK	STATE	PER CAPITA
1	Wyoming	$3,921
2	Alaska	3,551
3	Louisiana	3,402
4	Mississippi	2,785
5	Vermont	2,377
6	New York	2,298
7	New Mexico	2,279
8	Montana	2,171
9	North Dakota	2,120
10	Rhode Island	1,967
11	Maine	1,936
12	West Virginia	1,864
13	Hawaii	1,779
13	South Dakota	1,779
15	Alabama	1,723
16	Massachusetts	1,718
17	Arkansas	1,664
18	North Carolina	1,642
19	Kentucky	1,638
20	Oklahoma	1,630
21	Ohio	1,618
22	Iowa	1,609
23	California	1,578
24	Nebraska	1,557
25	South Carolina	1,556
26	Oregon	1,549
27	Missouri	1,533
28	Delaware	1,532
29	Pennsylvania	1,519
30	Minnesota	1,502
31	Arizona	1,491
32	Michigan	1,487
33	Maryland	1,454
34	Georgia	1,448
35	Washington	1,420
36	Tennessee	1,418
37	Utah	1,397
38	Idaho	1,388
39	Texas	1,360
40	Connecticut	1,352
40	Illinois	1,352
42	Indiana	1,341
43	New Jersey	1,328
44	New Hampshire	1,322
45	Kansas	1,317
46	Wisconsin	1,310
47	Florida	1,263
48	Colorado	1,141
49	Virginia	1,022
50	Nevada	864

| | District of Columbia | 5,103 |

Source: CQ Press using data from U.S. Bureau of the Census, Governments Division
"2008 State and Local Government Finances" (http://www.census.gov/govs/estimate/index.html)

Percent of State and Local Government Revenue
from the Federal Government in 2008
National Percent = 18.1%*

ALPHA ORDER

RANK	STATE	PERCENT
5	Alabama	25.3
48	Alaska	13.0
18	Arizona	20.3
8	Arkansas	24.3
38	California	16.3
49	Colorado	12.0
45	Connecticut	14.2
40	Delaware	16.0
41	Florida	15.7
24	Georgia	19.2
24	Hawaii	19.2
20	Idaho	20.1
36	Illinois	16.7
27	Indiana	18.4
23	Iowa	19.3
39	Kansas	16.2
10	Kentucky	23.8
2	Louisiana	34.3
10	Maine	23.8
30	Maryland	18.1
43	Massachusetts	15.3
15	Michigan	21.7
34	Minnesota	17.2
1	Mississippi	34.6
16	Missouri	21.6
6	Montana	24.7
42	Nebraska	15.6
50	Nevada	11.3
30	New Hampshire	18.1
47	New Jersey	13.4
4	New Mexico	26.8
29	New York	18.3
22	North Carolina	19.7
17	North Dakota	20.4
26	Ohio	18.5
13	Oklahoma	22.2
19	Oregon	20.2
33	Pennsylvania	17.4
14	Rhode Island	22.0
21	South Carolina	19.8
3	South Dakota	27.6
27	Tennessee	18.4
35	Texas	16.8
37	Utah	16.6
8	Vermont	24.3
46	Virginia	13.7
44	Washington	14.7
6	West Virginia	24.7
32	Wisconsin	17.7
12	Wyoming	22.3

RANK ORDER

RANK	STATE	PERCENT
1	Mississippi	34.6
2	Louisiana	34.3
3	South Dakota	27.6
4	New Mexico	26.8
5	Alabama	25.3
6	Montana	24.7
6	West Virginia	24.7
8	Arkansas	24.3
8	Vermont	24.3
10	Kentucky	23.8
10	Maine	23.8
12	Wyoming	22.3
13	Oklahoma	22.2
14	Rhode Island	22.0
15	Michigan	21.7
16	Missouri	21.6
17	North Dakota	20.4
18	Arizona	20.3
19	Oregon	20.2
20	Idaho	20.1
21	South Carolina	19.8
22	North Carolina	19.7
23	Iowa	19.3
24	Georgia	19.2
24	Hawaii	19.2
26	Ohio	18.5
27	Indiana	18.4
27	Tennessee	18.4
29	New York	18.3
30	Maryland	18.1
30	New Hampshire	18.1
32	Wisconsin	17.7
33	Pennsylvania	17.4
34	Minnesota	17.2
35	Texas	16.8
36	Illinois	16.7
37	Utah	16.6
38	California	16.3
39	Kansas	16.2
40	Delaware	16.0
41	Florida	15.7
42	Nebraska	15.6
43	Massachusetts	15.3
44	Washington	14.7
45	Connecticut	14.2
46	Virginia	13.7
47	New Jersey	13.4
48	Alaska	13.0
49	Colorado	12.0
50	Nevada	11.3

| | District of Columbia | 25.5 |

Source: CQ Press using data from U.S. Bureau of the Census, Governments Division
"2008 State and Local Government Finances" (http://www.census.gov/govs/estimate/index.html)
*As a percent of total revenue.

State and Local Government Own Source Revenue in 2008

National Total = $1,944,398,462,000*

ALPHA ORDER

RANK	STATE	REVENUE	% of USA
25	Alabama	$24,395,667,000	1.3%
32	Alaska	15,908,248,000	0.8%
19	Arizona	33,207,195,000	1.7%
36	Arkansas	13,639,188,000	0.7%
1	California	270,097,354,000	13.9%
20	Colorado	31,589,183,000	1.6%
23	Connecticut	27,704,547,000	1.4%
45	Delaware	6,550,507,000	0.3%
4	Florida	112,799,967,000	5.8%
10	Georgia	49,853,144,000	2.6%
40	Hawaii	9,372,283,000	0.5%
42	Idaho	7,870,467,000	0.4%
5	Illinois	78,143,916,000	4.0%
16	Indiana	35,680,116,000	1.8%
30	Iowa	18,332,931,000	0.9%
31	Kansas	17,644,389,000	0.9%
28	Kentucky	21,217,215,000	1.1%
24	Louisiana	27,215,401,000	1.4%
41	Maine	8,074,450,000	0.4%
15	Maryland	36,943,345,000	1.9%
13	Massachusetts	47,700,177,000	2.5%
9	Michigan	58,241,481,000	3.0%
17	Minnesota	35,546,341,000	1.8%
35	Mississippi	14,896,463,000	0.8%
22	Missouri	29,916,182,000	1.5%
47	Montana	5,392,845,000	0.3%
38	Nebraska	11,333,713,000	0.6%
33	Nevada	15,754,722,000	0.8%
43	New Hampshire	7,185,224,000	0.4%
7	New Jersey	69,827,902,000	3.6%
37	New Mexico	12,704,767,000	0.7%
2	New York	184,106,296,000	9.5%
11	North Carolina	49,376,808,000	2.5%
48	North Dakota	4,816,286,000	0.2%
8	Ohio	68,534,445,000	3.5%
29	Oklahoma	18,990,993,000	1.0%
27	Oregon	21,326,109,000	1.1%
6	Pennsylvania	76,931,147,000	4.0%
44	Rhode Island	6,901,490,000	0.4%
26	South Carolina	24,264,961,000	1.2%
50	South Dakota	3,959,479,000	0.2%
21	Tennessee	30,353,770,000	1.6%
3	Texas	131,112,634,000	6.7%
34	Utah	15,121,826,000	0.8%
49	Vermont	4,086,565,000	0.2%
12	Virginia	48,595,065,000	2.5%
14	Washington	43,369,497,000	2.2%
39	West Virginia	10,136,882,000	0.5%
18	Wisconsin	34,623,422,000	1.8%
46	Wyoming	6,039,749,000	0.3%

RANK ORDER

RANK	STATE	REVENUE	% of USA
1	California	$270,097,354,000	13.9%
2	New York	184,106,296,000	9.5%
3	Texas	131,112,634,000	6.7%
4	Florida	112,799,967,000	5.8%
5	Illinois	78,143,916,000	4.0%
6	Pennsylvania	76,931,147,000	4.0%
7	New Jersey	69,827,902,000	3.6%
8	Ohio	68,534,445,000	3.5%
9	Michigan	58,241,481,000	3.0%
10	Georgia	49,853,144,000	2.6%
11	North Carolina	49,376,808,000	2.5%
12	Virginia	48,595,065,000	2.5%
13	Massachusetts	47,700,177,000	2.5%
14	Washington	43,369,497,000	2.2%
15	Maryland	36,943,345,000	1.9%
16	Indiana	35,680,116,000	1.8%
17	Minnesota	35,546,341,000	1.8%
18	Wisconsin	34,623,422,000	1.8%
19	Arizona	33,207,195,000	1.7%
20	Colorado	31,589,183,000	1.6%
21	Tennessee	30,353,770,000	1.6%
22	Missouri	29,916,182,000	1.5%
23	Connecticut	27,704,547,000	1.4%
24	Louisiana	27,215,401,000	1.4%
25	Alabama	24,395,667,000	1.3%
26	South Carolina	24,264,961,000	1.2%
27	Oregon	21,326,109,000	1.1%
28	Kentucky	21,217,215,000	1.1%
29	Oklahoma	18,990,993,000	1.0%
30	Iowa	18,332,931,000	0.9%
31	Kansas	17,644,389,000	0.9%
32	Alaska	15,908,248,000	0.8%
33	Nevada	15,754,722,000	0.8%
34	Utah	15,121,826,000	0.8%
35	Mississippi	14,896,463,000	0.8%
36	Arkansas	13,639,188,000	0.7%
37	New Mexico	12,704,767,000	0.7%
38	Nebraska	11,333,713,000	0.6%
39	West Virginia	10,136,882,000	0.5%
40	Hawaii	9,372,283,000	0.5%
41	Maine	8,074,450,000	0.4%
42	Idaho	7,870,467,000	0.4%
43	New Hampshire	7,185,224,000	0.4%
44	Rhode Island	6,901,490,000	0.4%
45	Delaware	6,550,507,000	0.3%
46	Wyoming	6,039,749,000	0.3%
47	Montana	5,392,845,000	0.3%
48	North Dakota	4,816,286,000	0.2%
49	Vermont	4,086,565,000	0.2%
50	South Dakota	3,959,479,000	0.2%
	District of Columbia	7,011,708,000	0.4%

Source: U.S. Bureau of the Census, Governments Division
   "2008 State and Local Government Finances" (http://www.census.gov/govs/estimate/index.html)
*Own source revenue includes taxes, current charges, and miscellaneous general revenue. Excluded are intergovernmental transfers, insurance trust revenue, and revenue from government owned utilities and other commercial or auxiliary enterprise.

Per Capita State and Local Government Own Source Revenue in 2008

National Per Capita = $6,388*

<table>
<thead>
<tr><th colspan="3">ALPHA ORDER</th><th colspan="3">RANK ORDER</th></tr>
<tr><th>RANK</th><th>STATE</th><th>PER CAPITA</th><th>RANK</th><th>STATE</th><th>PER CAPITA</th></tr>
</thead>
<tbody>
<tr><td>40</td><td>Alabama</td><td>$5,216</td><td>1</td><td>Alaska</td><td>$23,118</td></tr>
<tr><td>1</td><td>Alaska</td><td>23,118</td><td>2</td><td>Wyoming</td><td>11,332</td></tr>
<tr><td>44</td><td>Arizona</td><td>5,109</td><td>3</td><td>New York</td><td>9,457</td></tr>
<tr><td>50</td><td>Arkansas</td><td>4,756</td><td>4</td><td>New Jersey</td><td>8,060</td></tr>
<tr><td>8</td><td>California</td><td>7,384</td><td>5</td><td>Connecticut</td><td>7,909</td></tr>
<tr><td>16</td><td>Colorado</td><td>6,401</td><td>6</td><td>North Dakota</td><td>7,509</td></tr>
<tr><td>5</td><td>Connecticut</td><td>7,909</td><td>7</td><td>Delaware</td><td>7,476</td></tr>
<tr><td>7</td><td>Delaware</td><td>7,476</td><td>8</td><td>California</td><td>7,384</td></tr>
<tr><td>23</td><td>Florida</td><td>6,122</td><td>9</td><td>Massachusetts</td><td>7,290</td></tr>
<tr><td>43</td><td>Georgia</td><td>5,141</td><td>10</td><td>Hawaii</td><td>7,280</td></tr>
<tr><td>10</td><td>Hawaii</td><td>7,280</td><td>11</td><td>Minnesota</td><td>6,796</td></tr>
<tr><td>42</td><td>Idaho</td><td>5,152</td><td>12</td><td>Washington</td><td>6,605</td></tr>
<tr><td>27</td><td>Illinois</td><td>6,085</td><td>13</td><td>Vermont</td><td>6,580</td></tr>
<tr><td>32</td><td>Indiana</td><td>5,585</td><td>14</td><td>Rhode Island</td><td>6,551</td></tr>
<tr><td>22</td><td>Iowa</td><td>6,123</td><td>15</td><td>Maryland</td><td>6,529</td></tr>
<tr><td>19</td><td>Kansas</td><td>6,307</td><td>16</td><td>Colorado</td><td>6,401</td></tr>
<tr><td>47</td><td>Kentucky</td><td>4,948</td><td>17</td><td>New Mexico</td><td>6,395</td></tr>
<tr><td>26</td><td>Louisiana</td><td>6,114</td><td>18</td><td>Nebraska</td><td>6,360</td></tr>
<tr><td>25</td><td>Maine</td><td>6,118</td><td>19</td><td>Kansas</td><td>6,307</td></tr>
<tr><td>15</td><td>Maryland</td><td>6,529</td><td>20</td><td>Virginia</td><td>6,234</td></tr>
<tr><td>9</td><td>Massachusetts</td><td>7,290</td><td>21</td><td>Wisconsin</td><td>6,152</td></tr>
<tr><td>30</td><td>Michigan</td><td>5,823</td><td>22</td><td>Iowa</td><td>6,123</td></tr>
<tr><td>11</td><td>Minnesota</td><td>6,796</td><td>23</td><td>Florida</td><td>6,122</td></tr>
<tr><td>45</td><td>Mississippi</td><td>5,066</td><td>23</td><td>Pennsylvania</td><td>6,122</td></tr>
<tr><td>46</td><td>Missouri</td><td>5,023</td><td>25</td><td>Maine</td><td>6,118</td></tr>
<tr><td>34</td><td>Montana</td><td>5,571</td><td>26</td><td>Louisiana</td><td>6,114</td></tr>
<tr><td>18</td><td>Nebraska</td><td>6,360</td><td>27</td><td>Illinois</td><td>6,085</td></tr>
<tr><td>28</td><td>Nevada</td><td>6,023</td><td>28</td><td>Nevada</td><td>6,023</td></tr>
<tr><td>36</td><td>New Hampshire</td><td>5,436</td><td>29</td><td>Ohio</td><td>5,945</td></tr>
<tr><td>4</td><td>New Jersey</td><td>8,060</td><td>30</td><td>Michigan</td><td>5,823</td></tr>
<tr><td>17</td><td>New Mexico</td><td>6,395</td><td>31</td><td>Oregon</td><td>5,637</td></tr>
<tr><td>3</td><td>New York</td><td>9,457</td><td>32</td><td>Indiana</td><td>5,585</td></tr>
<tr><td>39</td><td>North Carolina</td><td>5,340</td><td>32</td><td>West Virginia</td><td>5,585</td></tr>
<tr><td>6</td><td>North Dakota</td><td>7,509</td><td>34</td><td>Montana</td><td>5,571</td></tr>
<tr><td>29</td><td>Ohio</td><td>5,945</td><td>35</td><td>Utah</td><td>5,545</td></tr>
<tr><td>41</td><td>Oklahoma</td><td>5,212</td><td>36</td><td>New Hampshire</td><td>5,436</td></tr>
<tr><td>31</td><td>Oregon</td><td>5,637</td><td>37</td><td>Texas</td><td>5,395</td></tr>
<tr><td>23</td><td>Pennsylvania</td><td>6,122</td><td>38</td><td>South Carolina</td><td>5,388</td></tr>
<tr><td>14</td><td>Rhode Island</td><td>6,551</td><td>39</td><td>North Carolina</td><td>5,340</td></tr>
<tr><td>38</td><td>South Carolina</td><td>5,388</td><td>40</td><td>Alabama</td><td>5,216</td></tr>
<tr><td>48</td><td>South Dakota</td><td>4,921</td><td>41</td><td>Oklahoma</td><td>5,212</td></tr>
<tr><td>49</td><td>Tennessee</td><td>4,864</td><td>42</td><td>Idaho</td><td>5,152</td></tr>
<tr><td>37</td><td>Texas</td><td>5,395</td><td>43</td><td>Georgia</td><td>5,141</td></tr>
<tr><td>35</td><td>Utah</td><td>5,545</td><td>44</td><td>Arizona</td><td>5,109</td></tr>
<tr><td>13</td><td>Vermont</td><td>6,580</td><td>45</td><td>Mississippi</td><td>5,066</td></tr>
<tr><td>20</td><td>Virginia</td><td>6,234</td><td>46</td><td>Missouri</td><td>5,023</td></tr>
<tr><td>12</td><td>Washington</td><td>6,605</td><td>47</td><td>Kentucky</td><td>4,948</td></tr>
<tr><td>32</td><td>West Virginia</td><td>5,585</td><td>48</td><td>South Dakota</td><td>4,921</td></tr>
<tr><td>21</td><td>Wisconsin</td><td>6,152</td><td>49</td><td>Tennessee</td><td>4,864</td></tr>
<tr><td>2</td><td>Wyoming</td><td>11,332</td><td>50</td><td>Arkansas</td><td>4,756</td></tr>
<tr><td></td><td></td><td></td><td></td><td>District of Columbia</td><td>11,883</td></tr>
</tbody>
</table>

Source: CQ Press using data from U.S. Bureau of the Census, Governments Division
"2008 State and Local Government Finances" (http://www.census.gov/govs/estimate/index.html)
*Own source revenue includes taxes, current charges, and miscellaneous general revenue. Excluded are intergovernmental transfers, insurance trust revenue, and revenue from government owned utilities and other commercial or auxiliary enterprise.

State and Local Government Tax Revenue in 2008

National Total = $1,330,411,772,000

ALPHA ORDER

RANK	STATE	REVENUE	% of USA
26	Alabama	$14,040,755,000	1.1%
33	Alaska	9,735,074,000	0.7%
19	Arizona	22,992,377,000	1.7%
34	Arkansas	9,405,740,000	0.7%
1	California	186,014,884,000	14.0%
22	Colorado	19,636,243,000	1.5%
18	Connecticut	23,115,325,000	1.7%
45	Delaware	3,712,421,000	0.3%
4	Florida	73,351,398,000	5.5%
11	Georgia	33,632,501,000	2.5%
39	Hawaii	6,736,782,000	0.5%
43	Idaho	4,939,722,000	0.4%
5	Illinois	57,834,014,000	4.3%
20	Indiana	22,954,400,000	1.7%
31	Iowa	11,541,176,000	0.9%
30	Kansas	11,877,315,000	0.9%
25	Kentucky	14,156,697,000	1.1%
24	Louisiana	17,950,501,000	1.3%
41	Maine	5,932,772,000	0.4%
15	Maryland	27,651,053,000	2.1%
10	Massachusetts	33,997,340,000	2.6%
9	Michigan	37,649,871,000	2.8%
16	Minnesota	24,723,888,000	1.9%
36	Mississippi	9,212,798,000	0.7%
21	Missouri	19,872,542,000	1.5%
47	Montana	3,448,016,000	0.3%
38	Nebraska	7,508,042,000	0.6%
32	Nevada	10,587,743,000	0.8%
42	New Hampshire	4,962,804,000	0.4%
7	New Jersey	53,790,897,000	4.0%
37	New Mexico	7,746,740,000	0.6%
2	New York	138,287,941,000	10.4%
12	North Carolina	33,207,939,000	2.5%
48	North Dakota	3,174,007,000	0.2%
8	Ohio	46,660,185,000	3.5%
29	Oklahoma	12,314,542,000	0.9%
28	Oregon	12,531,550,000	0.9%
6	Pennsylvania	54,109,616,000	4.1%
44	Rhode Island	4,873,788,000	0.4%
27	South Carolina	13,162,705,000	1.0%
50	South Dakota	2,499,901,000	0.2%
23	Tennessee	18,999,627,000	1.4%
3	Texas	86,382,692,000	6.5%
35	Utah	9,371,460,000	0.7%
49	Vermont	2,935,601,000	0.2%
13	Virginia	32,706,639,000	2.5%
14	Washington	28,589,571,000	2.1%
40	West Virginia	6,428,072,000	0.5%
17	Wisconsin	24,372,341,000	1.8%
46	Wyoming	3,693,784,000	0.3%

RANK ORDER

RANK	STATE	REVENUE	% of USA
1	California	$186,014,884,000	14.0%
2	New York	138,287,941,000	10.4%
3	Texas	86,382,692,000	6.5%
4	Florida	73,351,398,000	5.5%
5	Illinois	57,834,014,000	4.3%
6	Pennsylvania	54,109,616,000	4.1%
7	New Jersey	53,790,897,000	4.0%
8	Ohio	46,660,185,000	3.5%
9	Michigan	37,649,871,000	2.8%
10	Massachusetts	33,997,340,000	2.6%
11	Georgia	33,632,501,000	2.5%
12	North Carolina	33,207,939,000	2.5%
13	Virginia	32,706,639,000	2.5%
14	Washington	28,589,571,000	2.1%
15	Maryland	27,651,053,000	2.1%
16	Minnesota	24,723,888,000	1.9%
17	Wisconsin	24,372,341,000	1.8%
18	Connecticut	23,115,325,000	1.7%
19	Arizona	22,992,377,000	1.7%
20	Indiana	22,954,400,000	1.7%
21	Missouri	19,872,542,000	1.5%
22	Colorado	19,636,243,000	1.5%
23	Tennessee	18,999,627,000	1.4%
24	Louisiana	17,950,501,000	1.3%
25	Kentucky	14,156,697,000	1.1%
26	Alabama	14,040,755,000	1.1%
27	South Carolina	13,162,705,000	1.0%
28	Oregon	12,531,550,000	0.9%
29	Oklahoma	12,314,542,000	0.9%
30	Kansas	11,877,315,000	0.9%
31	Iowa	11,541,176,000	0.9%
32	Nevada	10,587,743,000	0.8%
33	Alaska	9,735,074,000	0.7%
34	Arkansas	9,405,740,000	0.7%
35	Utah	9,371,460,000	0.7%
36	Mississippi	9,212,798,000	0.7%
37	New Mexico	7,746,740,000	0.6%
38	Nebraska	7,508,042,000	0.6%
39	Hawaii	6,736,782,000	0.5%
40	West Virginia	6,428,072,000	0.5%
41	Maine	5,932,772,000	0.4%
42	New Hampshire	4,962,804,000	0.4%
43	Idaho	4,939,722,000	0.4%
44	Rhode Island	4,873,788,000	0.4%
45	Delaware	3,712,421,000	0.3%
46	Wyoming	3,693,784,000	0.3%
47	Montana	3,448,016,000	0.3%
48	North Dakota	3,174,007,000	0.2%
49	Vermont	2,935,601,000	0.2%
50	South Dakota	2,499,901,000	0.2%
	District of Columbia	5,397,980,000	0.4%

Source: U.S. Bureau of the Census, Governments Division
"2008 State and Local Government Finances" (http://www.census.gov/govs/estimate/index.html)

Per Capita State and Local Government Tax Revenue in 2008

National Per Capita = $4,371

ALPHA ORDER

RANK	STATE	PER CAPITA
49	Alabama	$3,002
1	Alaska	14,147
37	Arizona	3,538
44	Arkansas	3,280
8	California	5,085
27	Colorado	3,979
4	Connecticut	6,599
20	Delaware	4,237
26	Florida	3,981
38	Georgia	3,468
6	Hawaii	5,233
45	Idaho	3,234
14	Illinois	4,503
32	Indiana	3,593
29	Iowa	3,855
19	Kansas	4,246
43	Kentucky	3,302
25	Louisiana	4,032
15	Maine	4,496
10	Maryland	4,887
7	Massachusetts	5,196
30	Michigan	3,764
11	Minnesota	4,727
46	Mississippi	3,133
41	Missouri	3,336
34	Montana	3,562
21	Nebraska	4,213
23	Nevada	4,048
31	New Hampshire	3,754
5	New Jersey	6,209
28	New Mexico	3,899
2	New York	7,103
33	North Carolina	3,591
9	North Dakota	4,948
23	Ohio	4,048
40	Oklahoma	3,379
42	Oregon	3,313
18	Pennsylvania	4,306
13	Rhode Island	4,626
50	South Carolina	2,923
47	South Dakota	3,107
48	Tennessee	3,045
35	Texas	3,554
39	Utah	3,436
11	Vermont	4,727
22	Virginia	4,196
16	Washington	4,354
36	West Virginia	3,542
17	Wisconsin	4,331
3	Wyoming	6,930

RANK ORDER

RANK	STATE	PER CAPITA
1	Alaska	$14,147
2	New York	7,103
3	Wyoming	6,930
4	Connecticut	6,599
5	New Jersey	6,209
6	Hawaii	5,233
7	Massachusetts	5,196
8	California	5,085
9	North Dakota	4,948
10	Maryland	4,887
11	Minnesota	4,727
11	Vermont	4,727
13	Rhode Island	4,626
14	Illinois	4,503
15	Maine	4,496
16	Washington	4,354
17	Wisconsin	4,331
18	Pennsylvania	4,306
19	Kansas	4,246
20	Delaware	4,237
21	Nebraska	4,213
22	Virginia	4,196
23	Nevada	4,048
23	Ohio	4,048
25	Louisiana	4,032
26	Florida	3,981
27	Colorado	3,979
28	New Mexico	3,899
29	Iowa	3,855
30	Michigan	3,764
31	New Hampshire	3,754
32	Indiana	3,593
33	North Carolina	3,591
34	Montana	3,562
35	Texas	3,554
36	West Virginia	3,542
37	Arizona	3,538
38	Georgia	3,468
39	Utah	3,436
40	Oklahoma	3,379
41	Missouri	3,336
42	Oregon	3,313
43	Kentucky	3,302
44	Arkansas	3,280
45	Idaho	3,234
46	Mississippi	3,133
47	South Dakota	3,107
48	Tennessee	3,045
49	Alabama	3,002
50	South Carolina	2,923
	District of Columbia	9,148

Source: CQ Press using data from U.S. Bureau of the Census, Governments Division
"2008 State and Local Government Finances" (http://www.census.gov/govs/estimate/index.html)

Percent of State and Local Government Revenue from Taxes in 2008

National Percent = 50.0%

ALPHA ORDER

RANK	STATE	PERCENT
38	Alabama	44.1
15	Alaska	51.8
21	Arizona	48.2
25	Arkansas	47.9
13	California	52.5
43	Colorado	41.7
1	Connecticut	69.4
37	Delaware	44.2
18	Florida	49.6
33	Georgia	46.0
6	Hawaii	56.5
29	Idaho	46.8
8	Illinois	55.5
19	Indiana	49.4
31	Iowa	46.2
14	Kansas	52.4
24	Kentucky	48.0
45	Louisiana	40.6
9	Maine	55.2
3	Maryland	60.8
30	Massachusetts	46.3
10	Michigan	54.9
11	Minnesota	54.1
49	Mississippi	39.0
27	Missouri	47.1
46	Montana	40.5
42	Nebraska	42.3
12	Nevada	53.0
17	New Hampshire	51.5
2	New Jersey	62.6
35	New Mexico	45.8
5	New York	56.7
41	North Carolina	43.0
26	North Dakota	47.5
31	Ohio	46.2
33	Oklahoma	46.0
40	Oregon	43.2
20	Pennsylvania	49.3
16	Rhode Island	51.6
50	South Carolina	37.2
21	South Dakota	48.2
47	Tennessee	39.6
39	Texas	44.0
44	Utah	40.8
21	Vermont	48.2
7	Virginia	56.2
36	Washington	45.2
28	West Virginia	46.9
4	Wisconsin	58.4
48	Wyoming	39.4

RANK ORDER

RANK	STATE	PERCENT
1	Connecticut	69.4
2	New Jersey	62.6
3	Maryland	60.8
4	Wisconsin	58.4
5	New York	56.7
6	Hawaii	56.5
7	Virginia	56.2
8	Illinois	55.5
9	Maine	55.2
10	Michigan	54.9
11	Minnesota	54.1
12	Nevada	53.0
13	California	52.5
14	Kansas	52.4
15	Alaska	51.8
16	Rhode Island	51.6
17	New Hampshire	51.5
18	Florida	49.6
19	Indiana	49.4
20	Pennsylvania	49.3
21	Arizona	48.2
21	South Dakota	48.2
21	Vermont	48.2
24	Kentucky	48.0
25	Arkansas	47.9
26	North Dakota	47.5
27	Missouri	47.1
28	West Virginia	46.9
29	Idaho	46.8
30	Massachusetts	46.3
31	Iowa	46.2
31	Ohio	46.2
33	Georgia	46.0
33	Oklahoma	46.0
35	New Mexico	45.8
36	Washington	45.2
37	Delaware	44.2
38	Alabama	44.1
39	Texas	44.0
40	Oregon	43.2
41	North Carolina	43.0
42	Nebraska	42.3
43	Colorado	41.7
44	Utah	40.8
45	Louisiana	40.6
46	Montana	40.5
47	Tennessee	39.6
48	Wyoming	39.4
49	Mississippi	39.0
50	South Carolina	37.2
	District of Columbia	45.8

Source: CQ Press using data from U.S. Bureau of the Census, Governments Division
"2008 State and Local Government Finances" (http://www.census.gov/govs/estimate/index.html)

State and Local Government Tax Revenue
as a Percent of Personal Income in 2008
National Percent = 10.7% of Personal Income*

ALPHA ORDER

RANK	STATE	PERCENT
45	Alabama	8.9
1	Alaska	31.9
25	Arizona	10.3
35	Arkansas	10.0
10	California	11.5
42	Colorado	9.1
10	Connecticut	11.5
23	Delaware	10.4
37	Florida	9.9
38	Georgia	9.8
4	Hawaii	12.3
38	Idaho	9.8
23	Illinois	10.4
25	Indiana	10.3
30	Iowa	10.1
19	Kansas	10.6
27	Kentucky	10.2
19	Louisiana	10.6
4	Maine	12.3
30	Maryland	10.1
27	Massachusetts	10.2
17	Michigan	10.7
16	Minnesota	10.9
27	Mississippi	10.2
42	Missouri	9.1
30	Montana	10.1
21	Nebraska	10.5
30	Nevada	10.1
49	New Hampshire	8.6
6	New Jersey	12.0
9	New Mexico	11.6
2	New York	14.8
30	North Carolina	10.1
8	North Dakota	11.9
13	Ohio	11.2
41	Oklahoma	9.2
44	Oregon	9.0
17	Pennsylvania	10.7
15	Rhode Island	11.1
45	South Carolina	8.9
50	South Dakota	7.9
48	Tennessee	8.7
45	Texas	8.9
21	Utah	10.5
6	Vermont	12.0
40	Virginia	9.4
35	Washington	10.0
13	West Virginia	11.2
12	Wisconsin	11.4
3	Wyoming	13.7

RANK ORDER

RANK	STATE	PERCENT
1	Alaska	31.9
2	New York	14.8
3	Wyoming	13.7
4	Hawaii	12.3
4	Maine	12.3
6	New Jersey	12.0
6	Vermont	12.0
8	North Dakota	11.9
9	New Mexico	11.6
10	California	11.5
10	Connecticut	11.5
12	Wisconsin	11.4
13	Ohio	11.2
13	West Virginia	11.2
15	Rhode Island	11.1
16	Minnesota	10.9
17	Michigan	10.7
17	Pennsylvania	10.7
19	Kansas	10.6
19	Louisiana	10.6
21	Nebraska	10.5
21	Utah	10.5
23	Delaware	10.4
23	Illinois	10.4
25	Arizona	10.3
25	Indiana	10.3
27	Kentucky	10.2
27	Massachusetts	10.2
27	Mississippi	10.2
30	Iowa	10.1
30	Maryland	10.1
30	Montana	10.1
30	Nevada	10.1
30	North Carolina	10.1
35	Arkansas	10.0
35	Washington	10.0
37	Florida	9.9
38	Georgia	9.8
38	Idaho	9.8
40	Virginia	9.4
41	Oklahoma	9.2
42	Colorado	9.1
42	Missouri	9.1
44	Oregon	9.0
45	Alabama	8.9
45	South Carolina	8.9
45	Texas	8.9
48	Tennessee	8.7
49	New Hampshire	8.6
50	South Dakota	7.9

	District of Columbia	13.4

Source: CQ Press using data from Bureau of Economic Analysis and U.S. Census Bureau
    "Annual State Personal Income" (http://www.bea.gov/regional/spi/) and
      "2008 State and Local Government Finances" (http://www.census.gov/govs/estimate/index.html)
*The personal income total used for this table is the sum of state estimates. This total differs from the national income and product accounts (NIPA) estimate of personal income because it omits the earnings of federal civilian and military personnel stationed abroad and of U.S. residents employed abroad temporarily by private U.S. firms.

State and Local Government General Sales Tax Revenue in 2008

National Total = $304,434,833,000*

ALPHA ORDER

RANK	STATE	REVENUE	% of USA
22	Alabama	$4,148,232,000	1.4%
46	Alaska	214,647,000	0.1%
10	Arizona	9,108,974,000	3.0%
25	Arkansas	3,715,891,000	1.2%
1	California	41,089,543,000	13.5%
17	Colorado	5,259,552,000	1.7%
27	Connecticut	3,545,734,000	1.2%
47	Delaware	0	0.0%
4	Florida	22,852,595,000	7.5%
6	Georgia	9,770,932,000	3.2%
34	Hawaii	2,619,595,000	0.9%
38	Idaho	1,347,452,000	0.4%
8	Illinois	9,309,321,000	3.1%
16	Indiana	5,738,829,000	1.9%
36	Iowa	2,431,216,000	0.8%
31	Kansas	3,059,541,000	1.0%
32	Kentucky	2,875,836,000	0.9%
15	Louisiana	7,107,737,000	2.3%
41	Maine	1,060,557,000	0.3%
24	Maryland	3,748,933,000	1.2%
23	Massachusetts	4,098,089,000	1.3%
13	Michigan	8,225,599,000	2.7%
20	Minnesota	4,668,525,000	1.5%
30	Mississippi	3,135,390,000	1.0%
18	Missouri	5,055,423,000	1.7%
47	Montana	0	0.0%
37	Nebraska	1,875,530,000	0.6%
28	Nevada	3,373,043,000	1.1%
47	New Hampshire	0	0.0%
11	New Jersey	8,915,515,000	2.9%
33	New Mexico	2,765,950,000	0.9%
3	New York	23,032,617,000	7.6%
14	North Carolina	7,225,971,000	2.4%
44	North Dakota	622,166,000	0.2%
7	Ohio	9,523,835,000	3.1%
26	Oklahoma	3,611,865,000	1.2%
47	Oregon	0	0.0%
9	Pennsylvania	9,190,350,000	3.0%
43	Rhode Island	846,870,000	0.3%
29	South Carolina	3,174,420,000	1.0%
42	South Dakota	1,003,308,000	0.3%
12	Tennessee	8,793,990,000	2.9%
2	Texas	27,076,344,000	8.9%
35	Utah	2,612,849,000	0.9%
45	Vermont	344,402,000	0.1%
19	Virginia	4,736,329,000	1.6%
5	Washington	13,732,876,000	4.5%
40	West Virginia	1,109,822,000	0.4%
21	Wisconsin	4,567,730,000	1.5%
39	Wyoming	1,216,295,000	0.4%

RANK ORDER

RANK	STATE	REVENUE	% of USA
1	California	$41,089,543,000	13.5%
2	Texas	27,076,344,000	8.9%
3	New York	23,032,617,000	7.6%
4	Florida	22,852,595,000	7.5%
5	Washington	13,732,876,000	4.5%
6	Georgia	9,770,932,000	3.2%
7	Ohio	9,523,835,000	3.1%
8	Illinois	9,309,321,000	3.1%
9	Pennsylvania	9,190,350,000	3.0%
10	Arizona	9,108,974,000	3.0%
11	New Jersey	8,915,515,000	2.9%
12	Tennessee	8,793,990,000	2.9%
13	Michigan	8,225,599,000	2.7%
14	North Carolina	7,225,971,000	2.4%
15	Louisiana	7,107,737,000	2.3%
16	Indiana	5,738,829,000	1.9%
17	Colorado	5,259,552,000	1.7%
18	Missouri	5,055,423,000	1.7%
19	Virginia	4,736,329,000	1.6%
20	Minnesota	4,668,525,000	1.5%
21	Wisconsin	4,567,730,000	1.5%
22	Alabama	4,148,232,000	1.4%
23	Massachusetts	4,098,089,000	1.3%
24	Maryland	3,748,933,000	1.2%
25	Arkansas	3,715,891,000	1.2%
26	Oklahoma	3,611,865,000	1.2%
27	Connecticut	3,545,734,000	1.2%
28	Nevada	3,373,043,000	1.1%
29	South Carolina	3,174,420,000	1.0%
30	Mississippi	3,135,390,000	1.0%
31	Kansas	3,059,541,000	1.0%
32	Kentucky	2,875,836,000	0.9%
33	New Mexico	2,765,950,000	0.9%
34	Hawaii	2,619,595,000	0.9%
35	Utah	2,612,849,000	0.9%
36	Iowa	2,431,216,000	0.8%
37	Nebraska	1,875,530,000	0.6%
38	Idaho	1,347,452,000	0.4%
39	Wyoming	1,216,295,000	0.4%
40	West Virginia	1,109,822,000	0.4%
41	Maine	1,060,557,000	0.3%
42	South Dakota	1,003,308,000	0.3%
43	Rhode Island	846,870,000	0.3%
44	North Dakota	622,166,000	0.2%
45	Vermont	344,402,000	0.1%
46	Alaska	214,647,000	0.1%
47	Delaware	0	0.0%
47	Montana	0	0.0%
47	New Hampshire	0	0.0%
47	Oregon	0	0.0%
	District of Columbia	894,613,000	0.3%

Source: U.S. Bureau of the Census, Governments Division
"2008 State and Local Government Finances" (http://www.census.gov/govs/estimate/index.html)
*Does not include special sales taxes such as those on sale of alcohol, gasoline, or tobacco.

Per Capita State and Local Government General Sales Tax Revenue in 2008

National Per Capita = $1,000*

ALPHA ORDER

RANK	STATE	PER CAPITA
27	Alabama	$887
46	Alaska	312
6	Arizona	1,402
8	Arkansas	1,296
13	California	1,123
16	Colorado	1,066
20	Connecticut	1,012
47	Delaware	0
11	Florida	1,240
21	Georgia	1,008
3	Hawaii	2,035
28	Idaho	882
38	Illinois	725
25	Indiana	898
32	Iowa	812
15	Kansas	1,094
40	Kentucky	671
4	Louisiana	1,597
34	Maine	804
41	Maryland	663
42	Massachusetts	626
31	Michigan	822
26	Minnesota	893
16	Mississippi	1,066
29	Missouri	849
47	Montana	0
18	Nebraska	1,053
9	Nevada	1,290
47	New Hampshire	0
19	New Jersey	1,029
7	New Mexico	1,392
12	New York	1,183
36	North Carolina	781
23	North Dakota	970
30	Ohio	826
22	Oklahoma	991
47	Oregon	0
37	Pennsylvania	731
34	Rhode Island	804
39	South Carolina	705
10	South Dakota	1,247
5	Tennessee	1,409
14	Texas	1,114
24	Utah	958
45	Vermont	555
44	Virginia	608
2	Washington	2,091
43	West Virginia	612
32	Wisconsin	812
1	Wyoming	2,282

RANK ORDER

RANK	STATE	PER CAPITA
1	Wyoming	$2,282
2	Washington	2,091
3	Hawaii	2,035
4	Louisiana	1,597
5	Tennessee	1,409
6	Arizona	1,402
7	New Mexico	1,392
8	Arkansas	1,296
9	Nevada	1,290
10	South Dakota	1,247
11	Florida	1,240
12	New York	1,183
13	California	1,123
14	Texas	1,114
15	Kansas	1,094
16	Colorado	1,066
16	Mississippi	1,066
18	Nebraska	1,053
19	New Jersey	1,029
20	Connecticut	1,012
21	Georgia	1,008
22	Oklahoma	991
23	North Dakota	970
24	Utah	958
25	Indiana	898
26	Minnesota	893
27	Alabama	887
28	Idaho	882
29	Missouri	849
30	Ohio	826
31	Michigan	822
32	Iowa	812
32	Wisconsin	812
34	Maine	804
34	Rhode Island	804
36	North Carolina	781
37	Pennsylvania	731
38	Illinois	725
39	South Carolina	705
40	Kentucky	671
41	Maryland	663
42	Massachusetts	626
43	West Virginia	612
44	Virginia	608
45	Vermont	555
46	Alaska	312
47	Delaware	0
47	Montana	0
47	New Hampshire	0
47	Oregon	0
	District of Columbia	1,516

Source: CQ Press using data from U.S. Bureau of the Census, Governments Division
   "2008 State and Local Government Finances" (http://www.census.gov/govs/estimate/index.html)
*Does not include special sales taxes such as those on sale of alcohol, gasoline, or tobacco.

State and Local Government Property Tax Revenue in 2008

National Total = $409,685,567,000

ALPHA ORDER

RANK	STATE	REVENUE	% of USA
33	Alabama	$2,305,795,000	0.6%
47	Alaska	1,068,390,000	0.3%
18	Arizona	6,704,621,000	1.6%
39	Arkansas	1,462,089,000	0.4%
1	California	52,758,875,000	12.9%
21	Colorado	6,130,312,000	1.5%
14	Connecticut	8,324,933,000	2.0%
50	Delaware	605,062,000	0.1%
4	Florida	30,260,538,000	7.4%
12	Georgia	10,219,678,000	2.5%
41	Hawaii	1,253,263,000	0.3%
43	Idaho	1,180,555,000	0.3%
6	Illinois	21,294,904,000	5.2%
17	Indiana	6,934,939,000	1.7%
26	Iowa	3,719,350,000	0.9%
27	Kansas	3,687,330,000	0.9%
31	Kentucky	2,779,552,000	0.7%
30	Louisiana	2,837,882,000	0.7%
36	Maine	2,157,216,000	0.5%
20	Maryland	6,611,158,000	1.6%
10	Massachusetts	11,664,990,000	2.8%
8	Michigan	14,126,726,000	3.4%
19	Minnesota	6,634,723,000	1.6%
34	Mississippi	2,299,453,000	0.6%
22	Missouri	5,480,147,000	1.3%
45	Montana	1,175,033,000	0.3%
32	Nebraska	2,485,283,000	0.6%
28	Nevada	3,215,685,000	0.8%
29	New Hampshire	3,057,145,000	0.7%
5	New Jersey	22,707,703,000	5.5%
46	New Mexico	1,124,094,000	0.3%
2	New York	39,068,724,000	9.5%
15	North Carolina	7,870,474,000	1.9%
49	North Dakota	740,022,000	0.2%
9	Ohio	13,572,615,000	3.3%
37	Oklahoma	2,112,601,000	0.5%
25	Oregon	4,257,253,000	1.0%
7	Pennsylvania	15,536,582,000	3.8%
38	Rhode Island	2,063,660,000	0.5%
24	South Carolina	4,299,365,000	1.0%
48	South Dakota	858,704,000	0.2%
23	Tennessee	4,669,642,000	1.1%
3	Texas	33,539,916,000	8.2%
35	Utah	2,218,041,000	0.5%
44	Vermont	1,177,064,000	0.3%
11	Virginia	10,569,062,000	2.6%
16	Washington	7,809,112,000	1.9%
42	West Virginia	1,237,603,000	0.3%
13	Wisconsin	8,829,539,000	2.2%
40	Wyoming	1,259,936,000	0.3%

RANK ORDER

RANK	STATE	REVENUE	% of USA
1	California	$52,758,875,000	12.9%
2	New York	39,068,724,000	9.5%
3	Texas	33,539,916,000	8.2%
4	Florida	30,260,538,000	7.4%
5	New Jersey	22,707,703,000	5.5%
6	Illinois	21,294,904,000	5.2%
7	Pennsylvania	15,536,582,000	3.8%
8	Michigan	14,126,726,000	3.4%
9	Ohio	13,572,615,000	3.3%
10	Massachusetts	11,664,990,000	2.8%
11	Virginia	10,569,062,000	2.6%
12	Georgia	10,219,678,000	2.5%
13	Wisconsin	8,829,539,000	2.2%
14	Connecticut	8,324,933,000	2.0%
15	North Carolina	7,870,474,000	1.9%
16	Washington	7,809,112,000	1.9%
17	Indiana	6,934,939,000	1.7%
18	Arizona	6,704,621,000	1.6%
19	Minnesota	6,634,723,000	1.6%
20	Maryland	6,611,158,000	1.6%
21	Colorado	6,130,312,000	1.5%
22	Missouri	5,480,147,000	1.3%
23	Tennessee	4,669,642,000	1.1%
24	South Carolina	4,299,365,000	1.0%
25	Oregon	4,257,253,000	1.0%
26	Iowa	3,719,350,000	0.9%
27	Kansas	3,687,330,000	0.9%
28	Nevada	3,215,685,000	0.8%
29	New Hampshire	3,057,145,000	0.7%
30	Louisiana	2,837,882,000	0.7%
31	Kentucky	2,779,552,000	0.7%
32	Nebraska	2,485,283,000	0.6%
33	Alabama	2,305,795,000	0.6%
34	Mississippi	2,299,453,000	0.6%
35	Utah	2,218,041,000	0.5%
36	Maine	2,157,216,000	0.5%
37	Oklahoma	2,112,601,000	0.5%
38	Rhode Island	2,063,660,000	0.5%
39	Arkansas	1,462,089,000	0.4%
40	Wyoming	1,259,936,000	0.3%
41	Hawaii	1,253,263,000	0.3%
42	West Virginia	1,237,603,000	0.3%
43	Idaho	1,180,555,000	0.3%
44	Vermont	1,177,064,000	0.3%
45	Montana	1,175,033,000	0.3%
46	New Mexico	1,124,094,000	0.3%
47	Alaska	1,068,390,000	0.3%
48	South Dakota	858,704,000	0.2%
49	North Dakota	740,022,000	0.2%
50	Delaware	605,062,000	0.1%
	District of Columbia	1,728,228,000	0.4%

Source: U.S. Bureau of the Census, Governments Division
 "2008 State and Local Government Finances" (http://www.census.gov/govs/estimate/index.html)

Per Capita State and Local Government Property Tax Revenue in 2008

National Per Capita = $1,346

ALPHA ORDER

RANK	STATE	PER CAPITA
50	Alabama	$493
13	Alaska	1,553
34	Arizona	1,032
49	Arkansas	510
14	California	1,442
21	Colorado	1,242
2	Connecticut	2,377
43	Delaware	691
10	Florida	1,642
33	Georgia	1,054
35	Hawaii	973
41	Idaho	773
9	Illinois	1,658
31	Indiana	1,086
21	Iowa	1,242
19	Kansas	1,318
45	Kentucky	648
46	Louisiana	638
11	Maine	1,635
28	Maryland	1,168
8	Massachusetts	1,783
15	Michigan	1,412
20	Minnesota	1,268
40	Mississippi	782
37	Missouri	920
25	Montana	1,214
16	Nebraska	1,395
24	Nevada	1,229
4	New Hampshire	2,313
1	New Jersey	2,621
48	New Mexico	566
5	New York	2,007
38	North Carolina	851
29	North Dakota	1,154
27	Ohio	1,177
47	Oklahoma	580
30	Oregon	1,125
23	Pennsylvania	1,236
6	Rhode Island	1,959
36	South Carolina	955
32	South Dakota	1,067
42	Tennessee	748
17	Texas	1,380
39	Utah	813
7	Vermont	1,895
18	Virginia	1,356
26	Washington	1,189
44	West Virginia	682
12	Wisconsin	1,569
3	Wyoming	2,364

RANK ORDER

RANK	STATE	PER CAPITA
1	New Jersey	$2,621
2	Connecticut	2,377
3	Wyoming	2,364
4	New Hampshire	2,313
5	New York	2,007
6	Rhode Island	1,959
7	Vermont	1,895
8	Massachusetts	1,783
9	Illinois	1,658
10	Florida	1,642
11	Maine	1,635
12	Wisconsin	1,569
13	Alaska	1,553
14	California	1,442
15	Michigan	1,412
16	Nebraska	1,395
17	Texas	1,380
18	Virginia	1,356
19	Kansas	1,318
20	Minnesota	1,268
21	Colorado	1,242
21	Iowa	1,242
23	Pennsylvania	1,236
24	Nevada	1,229
25	Montana	1,214
26	Washington	1,189
27	Ohio	1,177
28	Maryland	1,168
29	North Dakota	1,154
30	Oregon	1,125
31	Indiana	1,086
32	South Dakota	1,067
33	Georgia	1,054
34	Arizona	1,032
35	Hawaii	973
36	South Carolina	955
37	Missouri	920
38	North Carolina	851
39	Utah	813
40	Mississippi	782
41	Idaho	773
42	Tennessee	748
43	Delaware	691
44	West Virginia	682
45	Kentucky	648
46	Louisiana	638
47	Oklahoma	580
48	New Mexico	566
49	Arkansas	510
50	Alabama	493

District of Columbia   2,929

Source: CQ Press using data from U.S. Bureau of the Census, Governments Division
"2008 State and Local Government Finances" (http://www.census.gov/govs/estimate/index.html)

State and Local Government Property Tax as a Percent of State and Local Government Total Revenue in 2008
National Percent = 15.4%

ALPHA ORDER

RANK	STATE	PERCENT
46	Alabama	7.2
50	Alaska	5.7
25	Arizona	14.1
45	Arkansas	7.4
18	California	14.9
31	Colorado	13.0
3	Connecticut	25.0
46	Delaware	7.2
7	Florida	20.5
26	Georgia	14.0
37	Hawaii	10.5
35	Idaho	11.2
8	Illinois	20.4
18	Indiana	14.9
18	Iowa	14.9
14	Kansas	16.3
42	Kentucky	9.4
49	Louisiana	6.4
9	Maine	20.1
22	Maryland	14.5
17	Massachusetts	15.9
6	Michigan	20.6
22	Minnesota	14.5
39	Mississippi	9.7
31	Missouri	13.0
28	Montana	13.8
26	Nebraska	14.0
15	Nevada	16.1
1	New Hampshire	31.7
2	New Jersey	26.4
48	New Mexico	6.6
16	New York	16.0
38	North Carolina	10.2
36	North Dakota	11.1
29	Ohio	13.4
44	Oklahoma	7.9
21	Oregon	14.7
24	Pennsylvania	14.2
4	Rhode Island	21.9
34	South Carolina	12.1
13	South Dakota	16.5
39	Tennessee	9.7
12	Texas	17.1
39	Utah	9.7
10	Vermont	19.3
11	Virginia	18.2
33	Washington	12.4
43	West Virginia	9.0
5	Wisconsin	21.2
29	Wyoming	13.4

RANK ORDER

RANK	STATE	PERCENT
1	New Hampshire	31.7
2	New Jersey	26.4
3	Connecticut	25.0
4	Rhode Island	21.9
5	Wisconsin	21.2
6	Michigan	20.6
7	Florida	20.5
8	Illinois	20.4
9	Maine	20.1
10	Vermont	19.3
11	Virginia	18.2
12	Texas	17.1
13	South Dakota	16.5
14	Kansas	16.3
15	Nevada	16.1
16	New York	16.0
17	Massachusetts	15.9
18	California	14.9
18	Indiana	14.9
18	Iowa	14.9
21	Oregon	14.7
22	Maryland	14.5
22	Minnesota	14.5
24	Pennsylvania	14.2
25	Arizona	14.1
26	Georgia	14.0
26	Nebraska	14.0
28	Montana	13.8
29	Ohio	13.4
29	Wyoming	13.4
31	Colorado	13.0
31	Missouri	13.0
33	Washington	12.4
34	South Carolina	12.1
35	Idaho	11.2
36	North Dakota	11.1
37	Hawaii	10.5
38	North Carolina	10.2
39	Mississippi	9.7
39	Tennessee	9.7
39	Utah	9.7
42	Kentucky	9.4
43	West Virginia	9.0
44	Oklahoma	7.9
45	Arkansas	7.4
46	Alabama	7.2
46	Delaware	7.2
48	New Mexico	6.6
49	Louisiana	6.4
50	Alaska	5.7

District of Columbia — 14.7

Source: CQ Press using data from U.S. Bureau of the Census, Governments Division
"2008 State and Local Government Finances" (http://www.census.gov/govs/estimate/index.html)

State and Local Government Property Tax Revenue as a Percent of State and Local Government Own Source Revenue in 2008
National Percent = 21.1%*

ALPHA ORDER

RANK	STATE	PERCENT
47	Alabama	9.5
50	Alaska	6.7
23	Arizona	20.2
45	Arkansas	10.7
27	California	19.5
28	Colorado	19.4
3	Connecticut	30.0
48	Delaware	9.2
7	Florida	26.8
20	Georgia	20.5
41	Hawaii	13.4
39	Idaho	15.0
6	Illinois	27.3
28	Indiana	19.4
22	Iowa	20.3
18	Kansas	20.9
42	Kentucky	13.1
46	Louisiana	10.4
8	Maine	26.7
33	Maryland	17.9
11	Massachusetts	24.5
12	Michigan	24.3
30	Minnesota	18.7
36	Mississippi	15.4
31	Missouri	18.3
14	Montana	21.8
13	Nebraska	21.9
21	Nevada	20.4
1	New Hampshire	42.5
2	New Jersey	32.5
49	New Mexico	8.8
17	New York	21.2
35	North Carolina	15.9
36	North Dakota	15.4
26	Ohio	19.8
44	Oklahoma	11.1
25	Oregon	20.0
23	Pennsylvania	20.2
4	Rhode Island	29.9
34	South Carolina	17.7
15	South Dakota	21.7
36	Tennessee	15.4
9	Texas	25.6
40	Utah	14.7
5	Vermont	28.8
15	Virginia	21.7
32	Washington	18.0
43	West Virginia	12.2
10	Wisconsin	25.5
18	Wyoming	20.9

RANK ORDER

RANK	STATE	PERCENT
1	New Hampshire	42.5
2	New Jersey	32.5
3	Connecticut	30.0
4	Rhode Island	29.9
5	Vermont	28.8
6	Illinois	27.3
7	Florida	26.8
8	Maine	26.7
9	Texas	25.6
10	Wisconsin	25.5
11	Massachusetts	24.5
12	Michigan	24.3
13	Nebraska	21.9
14	Montana	21.8
15	South Dakota	21.7
15	Virginia	21.7
17	New York	21.2
18	Kansas	20.9
18	Wyoming	20.9
20	Georgia	20.5
21	Nevada	20.4
22	Iowa	20.3
23	Arizona	20.2
23	Pennsylvania	20.2
25	Oregon	20.0
26	Ohio	19.8
27	California	19.5
28	Colorado	19.4
28	Indiana	19.4
30	Minnesota	18.7
31	Missouri	18.3
32	Washington	18.0
33	Maryland	17.9
34	South Carolina	17.7
35	North Carolina	15.9
36	Mississippi	15.4
36	North Dakota	15.4
36	Tennessee	15.4
39	Idaho	15.0
40	Utah	14.7
41	Hawaii	13.4
42	Kentucky	13.1
43	West Virginia	12.2
44	Oklahoma	11.1
45	Arkansas	10.7
46	Louisiana	10.4
47	Alabama	9.5
48	Delaware	9.2
49	New Mexico	8.8
50	Alaska	6.7

District of Columbia   24.6

Source: CQ Press using data from U.S. Bureau of the Census, Governments Division
"2008 State and Local Government Finances" (http://www.census.gov/govs/estimate/index.html)
*Own source revenue includes taxes, current charges, and miscellaneous general revenue. Excluded are intergovernmental transfers, insurance trust revenue, and revenue from government owned utilities and other commercial or auxiliary enterprise.

State and Local Tax Burden as a Percent of Income in 2008

National Percent = 9.7% of Income*

ALPHA ORDER				RANK ORDER		
RANK	STATE	PERCENT		RANK	STATE	PERCENT
38	Alabama	8.6		1	New Jersey	11.8
50	Alaska	6.4		2	New York	11.7
41	Arizona	8.5		3	Connecticut	11.1
14	Arkansas	10.0		4	Maryland	10.8
6	California	10.5		5	Hawaii	10.6
34	Colorado	9.0		6	California	10.5
3	Connecticut	11.1		7	Ohio	10.4
23	Delaware	9.5		8	Vermont	10.3
47	Florida	7.4		9	Minnesota	10.2
16	Georgia	9.9		9	Pennsylvania	10.2
5	Hawaii	10.6		9	Rhode Island	10.2
13	Idaho	10.1		9	Wisconsin	10.2
29	Illinois	9.3		13	Idaho	10.1
25	Indiana	9.4		14	Arkansas	10.0
29	Iowa	9.3		14	Maine	10.0
21	Kansas	9.6		16	Georgia	9.9
25	Kentucky	9.4		17	Nebraska	9.8
42	Louisiana	8.4		17	North Carolina	9.8
14	Maine	10.0		17	Oklahoma	9.8
4	Maryland	10.8		17	Virginia	9.8
23	Massachusetts	9.5		21	Kansas	9.6
25	Michigan	9.4		21	Utah	9.6
9	Minnesota	10.2		23	Delaware	9.5
35	Mississippi	8.9		23	Massachusetts	9.5
32	Missouri	9.2		25	Indiana	9.4
38	Montana	8.6		25	Kentucky	9.4
17	Nebraska	9.8		25	Michigan	9.4
49	Nevada	6.6		25	Oregon	9.4
46	New Hampshire	7.6		29	Illinois	9.3
1	New Jersey	11.8		29	Iowa	9.3
38	New Mexico	8.6		29	West Virginia	9.3
2	New York	11.7		32	Missouri	9.2
17	North Carolina	9.8		32	North Dakota	9.2
32	North Dakota	9.2		34	Colorado	9.0
7	Ohio	10.4		35	Mississippi	8.9
17	Oklahoma	9.8		35	Washington	8.9
25	Oregon	9.4		37	South Carolina	8.8
9	Pennsylvania	10.2		38	Alabama	8.6
9	Rhode Island	10.2		38	Montana	8.6
37	South Carolina	8.8		38	New Mexico	8.6
45	South Dakota	7.9		41	Arizona	8.5
44	Tennessee	8.3		42	Louisiana	8.4
42	Texas	8.4		42	Texas	8.4
21	Utah	9.6		44	Tennessee	8.3
8	Vermont	10.3		45	South Dakota	7.9
17	Virginia	9.8		46	New Hampshire	7.6
35	Washington	8.9		47	Florida	7.4
29	West Virginia	9.3		48	Wyoming	7.0
9	Wisconsin	10.2		49	Nevada	6.6
48	Wyoming	7.0		50	Alaska	6.4
					District of Columbia	10.3

Source: The Tax Foundation
   "State and Local Tax Burdens: All States, One Year, 1977-2008" (www.taxfoundation.org/research/show/336.html)
*All state and local taxes.

State and Local Government Total Expenditures in 2008

National Total = $2,838,835,748,000*

ALPHA ORDER

RANK	STATE	EXPENDITURES	% of USA
25	Alabama	$38,201,262,000	1.3%
40	Alaska	12,902,612,000	0.5%
15	Arizona	52,533,341,000	1.9%
35	Arkansas	20,171,693,000	0.7%
1	California	415,436,973,000	14.6%
23	Colorado	42,536,683,000	1.5%
26	Connecticut	35,080,819,000	1.2%
45	Delaware	9,071,609,000	0.3%
4	Florida	158,174,504,000	5.6%
10	Georgia	77,708,516,000	2.7%
39	Hawaii	13,214,951,000	0.5%
42	Idaho	10,781,357,000	0.4%
5	Illinois	115,626,761,000	4.1%
19	Indiana	49,265,601,000	1.7%
30	Iowa	25,785,440,000	0.9%
32	Kansas	23,473,117,000	0.8%
28	Kentucky	34,358,625,000	1.2%
21	Louisiana	45,938,065,000	1.6%
41	Maine	11,175,171,000	0.4%
16	Maryland	51,224,896,000	1.8%
12	Massachusetts	67,895,215,000	2.4%
9	Michigan	83,962,165,000	3.0%
17	Minnesota	50,844,301,000	1.8%
31	Mississippi	25,171,039,000	0.9%
22	Missouri	45,101,940,000	1.6%
46	Montana	8,116,199,000	0.3%
37	Nebraska	18,351,450,000	0.6%
34	Nevada	21,462,154,000	0.8%
44	New Hampshire	9,967,742,000	0.4%
8	New Jersey	91,728,638,000	3.2%
36	New Mexico	19,264,191,000	0.7%
2	New York	263,436,826,000	9.3%
11	North Carolina	72,873,169,000	2.6%
50	North Dakota	5,615,939,000	0.2%
7	Ohio	102,919,573,000	3.6%
29	Oklahoma	27,429,577,000	1.0%
27	Oregon	34,560,605,000	1.2%
6	Pennsylvania	111,863,060,000	3.9%
43	Rhode Island	10,576,149,000	0.4%
24	South Carolina	39,740,999,000	1.4%
49	South Dakota	5,833,025,000	0.2%
20	Tennessee	49,128,077,000	1.7%
3	Texas	188,686,230,000	6.6%
33	Utah	22,203,709,000	0.8%
48	Vermont	6,039,076,000	0.2%
14	Virginia	63,272,066,000	2.2%
13	Washington	66,692,198,000	2.3%
38	West Virginia	13,686,366,000	0.5%
18	Wisconsin	49,283,373,000	1.7%
47	Wyoming	7,520,051,000	0.3%

RANK ORDER

RANK	STATE	EXPENDITURES	% of USA
1	California	$415,436,973,000	14.6%
2	New York	263,436,826,000	9.3%
3	Texas	188,686,230,000	6.6%
4	Florida	158,174,504,000	5.6%
5	Illinois	115,626,761,000	4.1%
6	Pennsylvania	111,863,060,000	3.9%
7	Ohio	102,919,573,000	3.6%
8	New Jersey	91,728,638,000	3.2%
9	Michigan	83,962,165,000	3.0%
10	Georgia	77,708,516,000	2.7%
11	North Carolina	72,873,169,000	2.6%
12	Massachusetts	67,895,215,000	2.4%
13	Washington	66,692,198,000	2.3%
14	Virginia	63,272,066,000	2.2%
15	Arizona	52,533,341,000	1.9%
16	Maryland	51,224,896,000	1.8%
17	Minnesota	50,844,301,000	1.8%
18	Wisconsin	49,283,373,000	1.7%
19	Indiana	49,265,601,000	1.7%
20	Tennessee	49,128,077,000	1.7%
21	Louisiana	45,938,065,000	1.6%
22	Missouri	45,101,940,000	1.6%
23	Colorado	42,536,683,000	1.5%
24	South Carolina	39,740,999,000	1.4%
25	Alabama	38,201,262,000	1.3%
26	Connecticut	35,080,819,000	1.2%
27	Oregon	34,560,605,000	1.2%
28	Kentucky	34,358,625,000	1.2%
29	Oklahoma	27,429,577,000	1.0%
30	Iowa	25,785,440,000	0.9%
31	Mississippi	25,171,039,000	0.9%
32	Kansas	23,473,117,000	0.8%
33	Utah	22,203,709,000	0.8%
34	Nevada	21,462,154,000	0.8%
35	Arkansas	20,171,693,000	0.7%
36	New Mexico	19,264,191,000	0.7%
37	Nebraska	18,351,450,000	0.6%
38	West Virginia	13,686,366,000	0.5%
39	Hawaii	13,214,951,000	0.5%
40	Alaska	12,902,612,000	0.5%
41	Maine	11,175,171,000	0.4%
42	Idaho	10,781,357,000	0.4%
43	Rhode Island	10,576,149,000	0.4%
44	New Hampshire	9,967,742,000	0.4%
45	Delaware	9,071,609,000	0.3%
46	Montana	8,116,199,000	0.3%
47	Wyoming	7,520,051,000	0.3%
48	Vermont	6,039,076,000	0.2%
49	South Dakota	5,833,025,000	0.2%
50	North Dakota	5,615,939,000	0.2%
	District of Columbia	12,948,650,000	0.5%

Source: U.S. Bureau of the Census, Governments Division
"2008 State and Local Government Finances" (http://www.census.gov/govs/estimate/index.html)
*Total expenditures includes all money paid other than for retirement of debt and extension of loans. Includes payments from all sources of funds including current revenues and proceeds from borrowing and prior year fund balances. Includes intergovernmental transfers and expenditures for government owned utilities and other commercial or auxiliary enterprise, and insurance trust expenditures.

Per Capita State and Local Government Total Expenditures in 2008

National Per Capita = $9,327*

ALPHA ORDER

RANK	STATE	PER CAPITA
34	Alabama	$8,167
1	Alaska	18,750
37	Arizona	8,083
50	Arkansas	7,034
4	California	11,357
25	Colorado	8,619
13	Connecticut	10,015
7	Delaware	10,353
27	Florida	8,585
38	Georgia	8,013
10	Hawaii	10,264
49	Idaho	7,058
19	Illinois	9,003
43	Indiana	7,712
26	Iowa	8,612
31	Kansas	8,391
38	Kentucky	8,013
8	Louisiana	10,320
29	Maine	8,468
18	Maryland	9,052
6	Massachusetts	10,376
30	Michigan	8,394
15	Minnesota	9,721
28	Mississippi	8,561
44	Missouri	7,572
32	Montana	8,384
9	Nebraska	10,299
33	Nevada	8,205
45	New Hampshire	7,541
5	New Jersey	10,588
16	New Mexico	9,696
3	New York	13,532
40	North Carolina	7,881
24	North Dakota	8,755
20	Ohio	8,928
47	Oklahoma	7,527
17	Oregon	9,136
21	Pennsylvania	8,902
12	Rhode Island	10,039
22	South Carolina	8,825
48	South Dakota	7,250
41	Tennessee	7,873
42	Texas	7,763
35	Utah	8,141
14	Vermont	9,724
36	Virginia	8,117
11	Washington	10,157
45	West Virginia	7,541
23	Wisconsin	8,757
2	Wyoming	14,109

RANK ORDER

RANK	STATE	PER CAPITA
1	Alaska	$18,750
2	Wyoming	14,109
3	New York	13,532
4	California	11,357
5	New Jersey	10,588
6	Massachusetts	10,376
7	Delaware	10,353
8	Louisiana	10,320
9	Nebraska	10,299
10	Hawaii	10,264
11	Washington	10,157
12	Rhode Island	10,039
13	Connecticut	10,015
14	Vermont	9,724
15	Minnesota	9,721
16	New Mexico	9,696
17	Oregon	9,136
18	Maryland	9,052
19	Illinois	9,003
20	Ohio	8,928
21	Pennsylvania	8,902
22	South Carolina	8,825
23	Wisconsin	8,757
24	North Dakota	8,755
25	Colorado	8,619
26	Iowa	8,612
27	Florida	8,585
28	Mississippi	8,561
29	Maine	8,468
30	Michigan	8,394
31	Kansas	8,391
32	Montana	8,384
33	Nevada	8,205
34	Alabama	8,167
35	Utah	8,141
36	Virginia	8,117
37	Arizona	8,083
38	Georgia	8,013
38	Kentucky	8,013
40	North Carolina	7,881
41	Tennessee	7,873
42	Texas	7,763
43	Indiana	7,712
44	Missouri	7,572
45	New Hampshire	7,541
45	West Virginia	7,541
47	Oklahoma	7,527
48	South Dakota	7,250
49	Idaho	7,058
50	Arkansas	7,034

District of Columbia   21,944

Source: CQ Press using data from U.S. Bureau of the Census, Governments Division
"2008 State and Local Government Finances" (http://www.census.gov/govs/estimate/index.html)
*Total expenditures includes all money paid other than for retirement of debt and extension of loans. Includes payments from all sources of funds including current revenues and proceeds from borrowing and prior year fund balances. Includes intergovernmental transfers and expenditures for government owned utilities and other commercial or auxiliary enterprise, and insurance trust expenditures.

State and Local Government Direct General Expenditures in 2008

National Total = $2,400,204,391,000*

ALPHA ORDER

RANK	STATE	EXPENDITURES	% of USA
25	Alabama	$32,626,999,000	1.4%
40	Alaska	11,523,049,000	0.5%
18	Arizona	43,224,342,000	1.8%
35	Arkansas	17,889,789,000	0.7%
1	California	335,283,145,000	14.0%
23	Colorado	35,590,778,000	1.5%
26	Connecticut	30,414,805,000	1.3%
45	Delaware	8,075,212,000	0.3%
4	Florida	138,485,305,000	5.8%
10	Georgia	65,289,945,000	2.7%
39	Hawaii	11,704,272,000	0.5%
42	Idaho	9,696,865,000	0.4%
5	Illinois	96,218,534,000	4.0%
16	Indiana	44,442,422,000	1.9%
30	Iowa	23,030,762,000	1.0%
32	Kansas	20,892,716,000	0.9%
27	Kentucky	29,470,620,000	1.2%
20	Louisiana	41,361,852,000	1.7%
41	Maine	10,308,612,000	0.4%
15	Maryland	45,739,567,000	1.9%
13	Massachusetts	56,605,696,000	2.4%
9	Michigan	72,284,062,000	3.0%
17	Minnesota	44,063,910,000	1.8%
31	Mississippi	22,453,830,000	0.9%
21	Missouri	39,260,434,000	1.6%
46	Montana	7,257,684,000	0.3%
37	Nebraska	13,715,413,000	0.6%
34	Nevada	18,232,369,000	0.8%
44	New Hampshire	8,927,324,000	0.4%
8	New Jersey	78,874,990,000	3.3%
36	New Mexico	17,273,326,000	0.7%
2	New York	212,375,369,000	8.8%
11	North Carolina	63,365,371,000	2.6%
50	North Dakota	5,119,057,000	0.2%
7	Ohio	86,440,267,000	3.6%
29	Oklahoma	24,005,390,000	1.0%
28	Oregon	28,141,787,000	1.2%
6	Pennsylvania	94,696,611,000	3.9%
43	Rhode Island	8,965,035,000	0.4%
24	South Carolina	33,653,008,000	1.4%
49	South Dakota	5,222,910,000	0.2%
22	Tennessee	37,817,306,000	1.6%
3	Texas	163,012,027,000	6.8%
33	Utah	18,716,344,000	0.8%
48	Vermont	5,435,948,000	0.2%
12	Virginia	57,090,540,000	2.4%
14	Washington	53,590,184,000	2.2%
38	West Virginia	12,420,246,000	0.5%
19	Wisconsin	42,439,720,000	1.8%
47	Wyoming	6,801,662,000	0.3%

RANK ORDER

RANK	STATE	EXPENDITURES	% of USA
1	California	$335,283,145,000	14.0%
2	New York	212,375,369,000	8.8%
3	Texas	163,012,027,000	6.8%
4	Florida	138,485,305,000	5.8%
5	Illinois	96,218,534,000	4.0%
6	Pennsylvania	94,696,611,000	3.9%
7	Ohio	86,440,267,000	3.6%
8	New Jersey	78,874,990,000	3.3%
9	Michigan	72,284,062,000	3.0%
10	Georgia	65,289,945,000	2.7%
11	North Carolina	63,365,371,000	2.6%
12	Virginia	57,090,540,000	2.4%
13	Massachusetts	56,605,696,000	2.4%
14	Washington	53,590,184,000	2.2%
15	Maryland	45,739,567,000	1.9%
16	Indiana	44,442,422,000	1.9%
17	Minnesota	44,063,910,000	1.8%
18	Arizona	43,224,342,000	1.8%
19	Wisconsin	42,439,720,000	1.8%
20	Louisiana	41,361,852,000	1.7%
21	Missouri	39,260,434,000	1.6%
22	Tennessee	37,817,306,000	1.6%
23	Colorado	35,590,778,000	1.5%
24	South Carolina	33,653,008,000	1.4%
25	Alabama	32,626,999,000	1.4%
26	Connecticut	30,414,805,000	1.3%
27	Kentucky	29,470,620,000	1.2%
28	Oregon	28,141,787,000	1.2%
29	Oklahoma	24,005,390,000	1.0%
30	Iowa	23,030,762,000	1.0%
31	Mississippi	22,453,830,000	0.9%
32	Kansas	20,892,716,000	0.9%
33	Utah	18,716,344,000	0.8%
34	Nevada	18,232,369,000	0.8%
35	Arkansas	17,889,789,000	0.7%
36	New Mexico	17,273,326,000	0.7%
37	Nebraska	13,715,413,000	0.6%
38	West Virginia	12,420,246,000	0.5%
39	Hawaii	11,704,272,000	0.5%
40	Alaska	11,523,049,000	0.5%
41	Maine	10,308,612,000	0.4%
42	Idaho	9,696,865,000	0.4%
43	Rhode Island	8,965,035,000	0.4%
44	New Hampshire	8,927,324,000	0.4%
45	Delaware	8,075,212,000	0.3%
46	Montana	7,257,684,000	0.3%
47	Wyoming	6,801,662,000	0.3%
48	Vermont	5,435,948,000	0.2%
49	South Dakota	5,222,910,000	0.2%
50	North Dakota	5,119,057,000	0.2%
	District of Columbia	10,676,980,000	0.4%

Source: U.S. Bureau of the Census, Governments Division
"2008 State and Local Government Finances" (http://www.census.gov/govs/estimate/index.html)
*Direct general expenditures include expenditures for current operations, assistance and subsidies, interest on debt, and capital outlay. Excludes intergovernmental transfers, expenditures for government owned utilities and other commercial or auxiliary enterprise, and insurance trust expenditures.

Per Capita State and Local Government Direct General Expenditures in 2008

National Per Capita = $7,886*

ALPHA ORDER

RANK	STATE	PER CAPITA
34	Alabama	$6,975
1	Alaska	16,746
44	Arizona	6,651
49	Arkansas	6,238
6	California	9,166
33	Colorado	7,212
11	Connecticut	8,683
5	Delaware	9,216
24	Florida	7,517
42	Georgia	6,732
8	Hawaii	9,091
48	Idaho	6,348
27	Illinois	7,492
36	Indiana	6,957
20	Iowa	7,692
29	Kansas	7,469
37	Kentucky	6,873
4	Louisiana	9,292
18	Maine	7,811
16	Maryland	8,083
12	Massachusetts	8,651
32	Michigan	7,227
14	Minnesota	8,424
21	Mississippi	7,637
45	Missouri	6,591
26	Montana	7,497
19	Nebraska	7,697
35	Nevada	6,970
41	New Hampshire	6,754
7	New Jersey	9,104
10	New Mexico	8,694
3	New York	10,909
39	North Carolina	6,852
17	North Dakota	7,981
25	Ohio	7,498
46	Oklahoma	6,588
30	Oregon	7,439
23	Pennsylvania	7,536
13	Rhode Island	8,510
28	South Carolina	7,473
47	South Dakota	6,492
50	Tennessee	6,060
43	Texas	6,707
38	Utah	6,862
9	Vermont	8,753
31	Virginia	7,324
15	Washington	8,162
40	West Virginia	6,844
22	Wisconsin	7,541
2	Wyoming	12,762

RANK ORDER

RANK	STATE	PER CAPITA
1	Alaska	$16,746
2	Wyoming	12,762
3	New York	10,909
4	Louisiana	9,292
5	Delaware	9,216
6	California	9,166
7	New Jersey	9,104
8	Hawaii	9,091
9	Vermont	8,753
10	New Mexico	8,694
11	Connecticut	8,683
12	Massachusetts	8,651
13	Rhode Island	8,510
14	Minnesota	8,424
15	Washington	8,162
16	Maryland	8,083
17	North Dakota	7,981
18	Maine	7,811
19	Nebraska	7,697
20	Iowa	7,692
21	Mississippi	7,637
22	Wisconsin	7,541
23	Pennsylvania	7,536
24	Florida	7,517
25	Ohio	7,498
26	Montana	7,497
27	Illinois	7,492
28	South Carolina	7,473
29	Kansas	7,469
30	Oregon	7,439
31	Virginia	7,324
32	Michigan	7,227
33	Colorado	7,212
34	Alabama	6,975
35	Nevada	6,970
36	Indiana	6,957
37	Kentucky	6,873
38	Utah	6,862
39	North Carolina	6,852
40	West Virginia	6,844
41	New Hampshire	6,754
42	Georgia	6,732
43	Texas	6,707
44	Arizona	6,651
45	Missouri	6,591
46	Oklahoma	6,588
47	South Dakota	6,492
48	Idaho	6,348
49	Arkansas	6,238
50	Tennessee	6,060
	District of Columbia	18,094

Source: CQ Press using data from U.S. Bureau of the Census, Governments Division
   "2008 State and Local Government Finances" (http://www.census.gov/govs/estimate/index.html)
*Direct general expenditures include expenditures for current operations, assistance and subsidies, interest on debt, and capital outlay. Excludes intergovernmental transfers, expenditures for government owned utilities and other commercial or auxiliary enterprise, and insurance trust expenditures.

State and Local Government Debt Outstanding in 2008

National Total = $2,550,934,283,000*

ALPHA ORDER

RANK	STATE	DEBT	% of USA
28	Alabama	$28,007,987,000	1.1%
41	Alaska	9,960,329,000	0.4%
17	Arizona	43,583,270,000	1.7%
37	Arkansas	12,938,901,000	0.5%
1	California	341,094,015,000	13.4%
15	Colorado	49,970,881,000	2.0%
23	Connecticut	36,789,007,000	1.4%
43	Delaware	7,942,626,000	0.3%
4	Florida	142,128,526,000	5.6%
14	Georgia	50,561,739,000	2.0%
40	Hawaii	10,444,929,000	0.4%
46	Idaho	5,729,839,000	0.2%
5	Illinois	124,162,818,000	4.9%
16	Indiana	46,548,499,000	1.8%
33	Iowa	15,456,614,000	0.6%
30	Kansas	20,972,593,000	0.8%
21	Kentucky	38,394,606,000	1.5%
26	Louisiana	31,886,906,000	1.3%
44	Maine	7,796,070,000	0.3%
22	Maryland	37,964,537,000	1.5%
7	Massachusetts	92,828,024,000	3.6%
9	Michigan	75,247,072,000	2.9%
19	Minnesota	41,651,295,000	1.6%
35	Mississippi	13,333,799,000	0.5%
20	Missouri	41,124,143,000	1.6%
45	Montana	6,472,038,000	0.3%
34	Nebraska	14,013,754,000	0.5%
29	Nevada	24,897,602,000	1.0%
39	New Hampshire	10,525,889,000	0.4%
8	New Jersey	87,971,714,000	3.4%
36	New Mexico	13,252,708,000	0.5%
2	New York	269,741,763,000	10.6%
13	North Carolina	51,202,200,000	2.0%
49	North Dakota	3,655,746,000	0.1%
10	Ohio	68,658,927,000	2.7%
31	Oklahoma	16,943,456,000	0.7%
27	Oregon	29,416,336,000	1.2%
6	Pennsylvania	118,611,401,000	4.6%
38	Rhode Island	11,395,427,000	0.4%
24	South Carolina	36,553,542,000	1.4%
47	South Dakota	5,247,237,000	0.2%
25	Tennessee	35,774,886,000	1.4%
3	Texas	215,877,683,000	8.5%
32	Utah	16,729,359,000	0.7%
48	Vermont	4,342,328,000	0.2%
12	Virginia	54,699,888,000	2.1%
11	Washington	64,547,668,000	2.5%
42	West Virginia	9,837,479,000	0.4%
18	Wisconsin	42,119,562,000	1.7%
50	Wyoming	2,345,954,000	0.1%

RANK ORDER

RANK	STATE	DEBT	% of USA
1	California	$341,094,015,000	13.4%
2	New York	269,741,763,000	10.6%
3	Texas	215,877,683,000	8.5%
4	Florida	142,128,526,000	5.6%
5	Illinois	124,162,818,000	4.9%
6	Pennsylvania	118,611,401,000	4.6%
7	Massachusetts	92,828,024,000	3.6%
8	New Jersey	87,971,714,000	3.4%
9	Michigan	75,247,072,000	2.9%
10	Ohio	68,658,927,000	2.7%
11	Washington	64,547,668,000	2.5%
12	Virginia	54,699,888,000	2.1%
13	North Carolina	51,202,200,000	2.0%
14	Georgia	50,561,739,000	2.0%
15	Colorado	49,970,881,000	2.0%
16	Indiana	46,548,499,000	1.8%
17	Arizona	43,583,270,000	1.7%
18	Wisconsin	42,119,562,000	1.7%
19	Minnesota	41,651,295,000	1.6%
20	Missouri	41,124,143,000	1.6%
21	Kentucky	38,394,606,000	1.5%
22	Maryland	37,964,537,000	1.5%
23	Connecticut	36,789,007,000	1.4%
24	South Carolina	36,553,542,000	1.4%
25	Tennessee	35,774,886,000	1.4%
26	Louisiana	31,886,906,000	1.3%
27	Oregon	29,416,336,000	1.2%
28	Alabama	28,007,987,000	1.1%
29	Nevada	24,897,602,000	1.0%
30	Kansas	20,972,593,000	0.8%
31	Oklahoma	16,943,456,000	0.7%
32	Utah	16,729,359,000	0.7%
33	Iowa	15,456,614,000	0.6%
34	Nebraska	14,013,754,000	0.5%
35	Mississippi	13,333,799,000	0.5%
36	New Mexico	13,252,708,000	0.5%
37	Arkansas	12,938,901,000	0.5%
38	Rhode Island	11,395,427,000	0.4%
39	New Hampshire	10,525,889,000	0.4%
40	Hawaii	10,444,929,000	0.4%
41	Alaska	9,960,329,000	0.4%
42	West Virginia	9,837,479,000	0.4%
43	Delaware	7,942,626,000	0.3%
44	Maine	7,796,070,000	0.3%
45	Montana	6,472,038,000	0.3%
46	Idaho	5,729,839,000	0.2%
47	South Dakota	5,247,237,000	0.2%
48	Vermont	4,342,328,000	0.2%
49	North Dakota	3,655,746,000	0.1%
50	Wyoming	2,345,954,000	0.1%
	District of Columbia	9,580,711,000	0.4%

Source: U.S. Bureau of the Census, Governments Division
   "2008 State and Local Government Finances" (http://www.census.gov/govs/estimate/index.html)
*Includes short-term, long-term, full faith and credit, nonguaranteed, and public debt for private purposes.

Per Capita State and Local Government Debt Outstanding in 2008

National Per Capita = $8,381*

ALPHA ORDER

RANK	STATE	PER CAPITA
37	Alabama	$5,988
1	Alaska	14,475
32	Arizona	6,706
48	Arkansas	4,512
12	California	9,325
7	Colorado	10,125
5	Connecticut	10,502
13	Delaware	9,065
22	Florida	7,714
44	Georgia	5,214
17	Hawaii	8,113
50	Idaho	3,751
9	Illinois	9,668
26	Indiana	7,287
45	Iowa	5,163
24	Kansas	7,497
14	Kentucky	8,954
27	Louisiana	7,163
39	Maine	5,907
31	Maryland	6,709
2	Massachusetts	14,186
23	Michigan	7,523
18	Minnesota	7,963
47	Mississippi	4,535
30	Missouri	6,904
33	Montana	6,686
20	Nebraska	7,864
10	Nevada	9,518
18	New Hampshire	7,963
6	New Jersey	10,154
34	New Mexico	6,671
3	New York	13,856
42	North Carolina	5,537
41	North Dakota	5,699
38	Ohio	5,956
46	Oklahoma	4,650
21	Oregon	7,776
11	Pennsylvania	9,439
4	Rhode Island	10,817
16	South Carolina	8,117
35	South Dakota	6,522
40	Tennessee	5,733
15	Texas	8,882
36	Utah	6,134
29	Vermont	6,992
28	Virginia	7,017
8	Washington	9,830
43	West Virginia	5,420
25	Wisconsin	7,484
49	Wyoming	4,402

RANK ORDER

RANK	STATE	PER CAPITA
1	Alaska	$14,475
2	Massachusetts	14,186
3	New York	13,856
4	Rhode Island	10,817
5	Connecticut	10,502
6	New Jersey	10,154
7	Colorado	10,125
8	Washington	9,830
9	Illinois	9,668
10	Nevada	9,518
11	Pennsylvania	9,439
12	California	9,325
13	Delaware	9,065
14	Kentucky	8,954
15	Texas	8,882
16	South Carolina	8,117
17	Hawaii	8,113
18	Minnesota	7,963
18	New Hampshire	7,963
20	Nebraska	7,864
21	Oregon	7,776
22	Florida	7,714
23	Michigan	7,523
24	Kansas	7,497
25	Wisconsin	7,484
26	Indiana	7,287
27	Louisiana	7,163
28	Virginia	7,017
29	Vermont	6,992
30	Missouri	6,904
31	Maryland	6,709
32	Arizona	6,706
33	Montana	6,686
34	New Mexico	6,671
35	South Dakota	6,522
36	Utah	6,134
37	Alabama	5,988
38	Ohio	5,956
39	Maine	5,907
40	Tennessee	5,733
41	North Dakota	5,699
42	North Carolina	5,537
43	West Virginia	5,420
44	Georgia	5,214
45	Iowa	5,163
46	Oklahoma	4,650
47	Mississippi	4,535
48	Arkansas	4,512
49	Wyoming	4,402
50	Idaho	3,751

District of Columbia — 16,236

Source: CQ Press using data from U.S. Bureau of the Census, Governments Division
"2008 State and Local Government Finances" (http://www.census.gov/govs/estimate/index.html)
*Includes short-term, long-term, full faith and credit, nonguaranteed, and public debt for private purposes.

State and Local Government Full-Time Equivalent Employees in 2009

National Total = 16,627,330 FTE Employees*

ALPHA ORDER

RANK	STATE	EMPLOYEES	% of USA
21	Alabama	286,050	1.7%
44	Alaska	53,449	0.3%
18	Arizona	305,611	1.8%
33	Arkansas	162,844	1.0%
1	California	1,835,410	11.0%
24	Colorado	275,876	1.7%
31	Connecticut	186,860	1.1%
47	Delaware	48,547	0.3%
4	Florida	882,597	5.3%
9	Georgia	529,528	3.2%
40	Hawaii	75,444	0.5%
39	Idaho	78,817	0.5%
5	Illinois	642,662	3.9%
14	Indiana	345,475	2.1%
32	Iowa	179,507	1.1%
28	Kansas	202,223	1.2%
26	Kentucky	242,167	1.5%
23	Louisiana	276,902	1.7%
41	Maine	71,991	0.4%
19	Maryland	301,113	1.8%
16	Massachusetts	325,354	2.0%
11	Michigan	473,876	2.8%
22	Minnesota	281,760	1.7%
30	Mississippi	193,626	1.2%
17	Missouri	324,736	2.0%
43	Montana	56,631	0.3%
36	Nebraska	117,971	0.7%
37	Nevada	115,363	0.7%
42	New Hampshire	71,663	0.4%
10	New Jersey	503,915	3.0%
35	New Mexico	129,755	0.8%
3	New York	1,252,259	7.5%
8	North Carolina	556,894	3.3%
49	North Dakota	41,658	0.3%
6	Ohio	616,305	3.7%
27	Oklahoma	217,737	1.3%
29	Oregon	198,698	1.2%
7	Pennsylvania	595,810	3.6%
45	Rhode Island	52,348	0.3%
25	South Carolina	254,476	1.5%
48	South Dakota	47,908	0.3%
15	Tennessee	325,447	2.0%
2	Texas	1,413,681	8.5%
34	Utah	140,058	0.8%
50	Vermont	38,447	0.2%
12	Virginia	444,667	2.7%
13	Washington	362,997	2.2%
38	West Virginia	101,354	0.6%
20	Wisconsin	292,671	1.8%
46	Wyoming	51,645	0.3%

RANK ORDER

RANK	STATE	EMPLOYEES	% of USA
1	California	1,835,410	11.0%
2	Texas	1,413,681	8.5%
3	New York	1,252,259	7.5%
4	Florida	882,597	5.3%
5	Illinois	642,662	3.9%
6	Ohio	616,305	3.7%
7	Pennsylvania	595,810	3.6%
8	North Carolina	556,894	3.3%
9	Georgia	529,528	3.2%
10	New Jersey	503,915	3.0%
11	Michigan	473,876	2.8%
12	Virginia	444,667	2.7%
13	Washington	362,997	2.2%
14	Indiana	345,475	2.1%
15	Tennessee	325,447	2.0%
16	Massachusetts	325,354	2.0%
17	Missouri	324,736	2.0%
18	Arizona	305,611	1.8%
19	Maryland	301,113	1.8%
20	Wisconsin	292,671	1.8%
21	Alabama	286,050	1.7%
22	Minnesota	281,760	1.7%
23	Louisiana	276,902	1.7%
24	Colorado	275,876	1.7%
25	South Carolina	254,476	1.5%
26	Kentucky	242,167	1.5%
27	Oklahoma	217,737	1.3%
28	Kansas	202,223	1.2%
29	Oregon	198,698	1.2%
30	Mississippi	193,626	1.2%
31	Connecticut	186,860	1.1%
32	Iowa	179,507	1.1%
33	Arkansas	162,844	1.0%
34	Utah	140,058	0.8%
35	New Mexico	129,755	0.8%
36	Nebraska	117,971	0.7%
37	Nevada	115,363	0.7%
38	West Virginia	101,354	0.6%
39	Idaho	78,817	0.5%
40	Hawaii	75,444	0.5%
41	Maine	71,991	0.4%
42	New Hampshire	71,663	0.4%
43	Montana	56,631	0.3%
44	Alaska	53,449	0.3%
45	Rhode Island	52,348	0.3%
46	Wyoming	51,645	0.3%
47	Delaware	48,547	0.3%
48	South Dakota	47,908	0.3%
49	North Dakota	41,658	0.3%
50	Vermont	38,447	0.2%
	District of Columbia	44,547	0.3%

Source: U.S. Bureau of the Census, Governments Division
"Government Employment and Payroll" (http://www.census.gov/govs/apes/index.html)
*As of March 2009.

Rate of State and Local Government Full-Time Equivalent Employees in 2009

National Rate = 542 State/Local Government Employees per 10,000 Population*

ALPHA ORDER

RANK	STATE	RATE
11	Alabama	607
2	Alaska	765
49	Arizona	463
20	Arkansas	564
43	California	497
25	Colorado	549
35	Connecticut	531
26	Delaware	548
46	Florida	476
31	Georgia	539
16	Hawaii	582
40	Idaho	510
42	Illinois	498
32	Indiana	538
12	Iowa	597
3	Kansas	717
22	Kentucky	561
10	Louisiana	616
27	Maine	546
36	Maryland	528
45	Massachusetts	493
47	Michigan	475
33	Minnesota	535
5	Mississippi	656
29	Missouri	542
17	Montana	581
4	Nebraska	657
50	Nevada	436
30	New Hampshire	541
18	New Jersey	579
6	New Mexico	646
8	New York	641
13	North Carolina	594
7	North Dakota	644
34	Ohio	534
14	Oklahoma	591
37	Oregon	519
48	Pennsylvania	473
43	Rhode Island	497
23	South Carolina	558
15	South Dakota	590
39	Tennessee	517
19	Texas	570
41	Utah	503
9	Vermont	618
20	Virginia	564
28	Washington	545
24	West Virginia	557
38	Wisconsin	518
1	Wyoming	949

RANK ORDER

RANK	STATE	RATE
1	Wyoming	949
2	Alaska	765
3	Kansas	717
4	Nebraska	657
5	Mississippi	656
6	New Mexico	646
7	North Dakota	644
8	New York	641
9	Vermont	618
10	Louisiana	616
11	Alabama	607
12	Iowa	597
13	North Carolina	594
14	Oklahoma	591
15	South Dakota	590
16	Hawaii	582
17	Montana	581
18	New Jersey	579
19	Texas	570
20	Arkansas	564
20	Virginia	564
22	Kentucky	561
23	South Carolina	558
24	West Virginia	557
25	Colorado	549
26	Delaware	548
27	Maine	546
28	Washington	545
29	Missouri	542
30	New Hampshire	541
31	Georgia	539
32	Indiana	538
33	Minnesota	535
34	Ohio	534
35	Connecticut	531
36	Maryland	528
37	Oregon	519
38	Wisconsin	518
39	Tennessee	517
40	Idaho	510
41	Utah	503
42	Illinois	498
43	California	497
43	Rhode Island	497
45	Massachusetts	493
46	Florida	476
47	Michigan	475
48	Pennsylvania	473
49	Arizona	463
50	Nevada	436

District of Columbia 743

Source: CQ Press using data from U.S. Bureau of the Census, Governments Division
    "Government Employment and Payroll" (http://www.census.gov/govs/apes/index.html)
*As of March 2009.

Average Annual Earnings of Full-Time State and Local Government Employees in 2009
National Average = $51,914*

ALPHA ORDER				RANK ORDER		
RANK	STATE	SALARY		RANK	STATE	SALARY
43	Alabama	$41,612		1	California	$69,292
5	Alaska	61,312		2	New Jersey	64,264
22	Arizona	49,870		3	Washington	61,935
46	Arkansas	40,073		4	Connecticut	61,758
1	California	69,292		5	Alaska	61,312
18	Colorado	51,660		6	New York	61,115
4	Connecticut	61,758		7	Nevada	60,084
17	Delaware	51,750		8	Maryland	59,671
23	Florida	48,724		9	Massachusetts	58,359
38	Georgia	42,836		10	Rhode Island	58,034
15	Hawaii	52,640		11	Michigan	56,146
39	Idaho	42,686		12	Illinois	55,558
12	Illinois	55,558		13	Minnesota	55,146
33	Indiana	44,107		14	Wisconsin	52,662
19	Iowa	50,622		15	Hawaii	52,640
40	Kansas	42,202		16	Oregon	51,767
48	Kentucky	39,798		17	Delaware	51,750
36	Louisiana	43,253		18	Colorado	51,660
35	Maine	43,333		19	Iowa	50,622
8	Maryland	59,671		20	Ohio	50,322
9	Massachusetts	58,359		21	Pennsylvania	49,921
11	Michigan	56,146		22	Arizona	49,870
13	Minnesota	55,146		23	Florida	48,724
50	Mississippi	37,513		24	Wyoming	48,646
44	Missouri	41,274		25	Utah	47,816
34	Montana	43,977		26	Virginia	47,575
29	Nebraska	45,668		27	Vermont	47,091
7	Nevada	60,084		28	New Hampshire	47,088
28	New Hampshire	47,088		29	Nebraska	45,668
2	New Jersey	64,264		30	North Carolina	44,520
37	New Mexico	43,067		31	North Dakota	44,289
6	New York	61,115		32	Texas	44,110
30	North Carolina	44,520		33	Indiana	44,107
31	North Dakota	44,289		34	Montana	43,977
20	Ohio	50,322		35	Maine	43,333
45	Oklahoma	40,140		36	Louisiana	43,253
16	Oregon	51,767		37	New Mexico	43,067
21	Pennsylvania	49,921		38	Georgia	42,836
10	Rhode Island	58,034		39	Idaho	42,686
41	South Carolina	42,190		40	Kansas	42,202
47	South Dakota	39,905		41	South Carolina	42,190
42	Tennessee	41,672		42	Tennessee	41,672
32	Texas	44,110		43	Alabama	41,612
25	Utah	47,816		44	Missouri	41,274
27	Vermont	47,091		45	Oklahoma	40,140
26	Virginia	47,575		46	Arkansas	40,073
3	Washington	61,935		47	South Dakota	39,905
49	West Virginia	39,130		48	Kentucky	39,798
14	Wisconsin	52,662		49	West Virginia	39,130
24	Wyoming	48,646		50	Mississippi	37,513

	District of Columbia	60,101

Source: CQ Press using data from U.S. Bureau of the Census, Governments Division
    "Government Employment and Payroll" (http://www.census.gov/govs/apes/index.html)
*March 2009 full-time payroll (multiplied by 12) divided by full-time employees.

State Government Total Revenue in 2008

National Total = $1,619,127,732,000*

ALPHA ORDER

RANK	STATE	REVENUE	% of USA
28	Alabama	$18,353,578,000	1.1%
31	Alaska	16,027,757,000	1.0%
19	Arizona	27,697,541,000	1.7%
34	Arkansas	15,106,880,000	0.9%
1	California	201,069,818,000	12.4%
20	Colorado	26,503,025,000	1.6%
25	Connecticut	22,160,095,000	1.4%
45	Delaware	6,658,241,000	0.4%
5	Florida	68,621,353,000	4.2%
12	Georgia	41,153,807,000	2.5%
39	Hawaii	9,298,617,000	0.6%
42	Idaho	7,107,284,000	0.4%
7	Illinois	58,523,576,000	3.6%
17	Indiana	29,314,749,000	1.8%
32	Iowa	15,939,920,000	1.0%
35	Kansas	13,541,510,000	0.8%
26	Kentucky	20,581,938,000	1.3%
15	Louisiana	30,307,726,000	1.9%
41	Maine	7,656,061,000	0.5%
18	Maryland	28,422,851,000	1.8%
9	Massachusetts	51,759,773,000	3.2%
11	Michigan	42,259,206,000	2.6%
16	Minnesota	29,707,313,000	1.8%
30	Mississippi	16,278,166,000	1.0%
23	Missouri	25,243,465,000	1.6%
46	Montana	6,402,859,000	0.4%
40	Nebraska	8,387,599,000	0.5%
38	Nevada	10,438,721,000	0.6%
47	New Hampshire	6,284,782,000	0.4%
8	New Jersey	55,046,270,000	3.4%
36	New Mexico	12,892,523,000	0.8%
2	New York	147,340,334,000	9.1%
10	North Carolina	51,421,057,000	3.2%
49	North Dakota	5,018,609,000	0.3%
6	Ohio	65,614,628,000	4.1%
27	Oklahoma	18,656,746,000	1.2%
29	Oregon	17,138,167,000	1.1%
4	Pennsylvania	71,142,087,000	4.4%
44	Rhode Island	6,691,311,000	0.4%
24	South Carolina	23,119,297,000	1.4%
50	South Dakota	2,910,381,000	0.2%
21	Tennessee	25,699,084,000	1.6%
3	Texas	119,094,697,000	7.4%
33	Utah	15,407,801,000	1.0%
48	Vermont	5,148,584,000	0.3%
14	Virginia	36,232,142,000	2.2%
13	Washington	36,659,905,000	2.3%
37	West Virginia	10,724,135,000	0.7%
22	Wisconsin	25,643,528,000	1.6%
43	Wyoming	6,718,235,000	0.4%

RANK ORDER

RANK	STATE	REVENUE	% of USA
1	California	$201,069,818,000	12.4%
2	New York	147,340,334,000	9.1%
3	Texas	119,094,697,000	7.4%
4	Pennsylvania	71,142,087,000	4.4%
5	Florida	68,621,353,000	4.2%
6	Ohio	65,614,628,000	4.1%
7	Illinois	58,523,576,000	3.6%
8	New Jersey	55,046,270,000	3.4%
9	Massachusetts	51,759,773,000	3.2%
10	North Carolina	51,421,057,000	3.2%
11	Michigan	42,259,206,000	2.6%
12	Georgia	41,153,807,000	2.5%
13	Washington	36,659,905,000	2.3%
14	Virginia	36,232,142,000	2.2%
15	Louisiana	30,307,726,000	1.9%
16	Minnesota	29,707,313,000	1.8%
17	Indiana	29,314,749,000	1.8%
18	Maryland	28,422,851,000	1.8%
19	Arizona	27,697,541,000	1.7%
20	Colorado	26,503,025,000	1.6%
21	Tennessee	25,699,084,000	1.6%
22	Wisconsin	25,643,528,000	1.6%
23	Missouri	25,243,465,000	1.6%
24	South Carolina	23,119,297,000	1.4%
25	Connecticut	22,160,095,000	1.4%
26	Kentucky	20,581,938,000	1.3%
27	Oklahoma	18,656,746,000	1.2%
28	Alabama	18,353,578,000	1.1%
29	Oregon	17,138,167,000	1.1%
30	Mississippi	16,278,166,000	1.0%
31	Alaska	16,027,757,000	1.0%
32	Iowa	15,939,920,000	1.0%
33	Utah	15,407,801,000	1.0%
34	Arkansas	15,106,880,000	0.9%
35	Kansas	13,541,510,000	0.8%
36	New Mexico	12,892,523,000	0.8%
37	West Virginia	10,724,135,000	0.7%
38	Nevada	10,438,721,000	0.6%
39	Hawaii	9,298,617,000	0.6%
40	Nebraska	8,387,599,000	0.5%
41	Maine	7,656,061,000	0.5%
42	Idaho	7,107,284,000	0.4%
43	Wyoming	6,718,235,000	0.4%
44	Rhode Island	6,691,311,000	0.4%
45	Delaware	6,658,241,000	0.4%
46	Montana	6,402,859,000	0.4%
47	New Hampshire	6,284,782,000	0.4%
48	Vermont	5,148,584,000	0.3%
49	North Dakota	5,018,609,000	0.3%
50	South Dakota	2,910,381,000	0.2%
	District of Columbia**	NA	NA

Source: U.S. Bureau of the Census, Governments Division
  "2008 State and Local Government Finances" (http://www.census.gov/govs/estimate/index.html)
*Total revenue includes all money received from external sources. This includes taxes, intergovernmental transfers and
insurance trust revenue, and revenue from government owned utilities and other commercial or auxiliary enterprise.
**Not applicable.

Per Capita State Government Total Revenue in 2008

National Per Capita = $5,330*

ALPHA ORDER				RANK ORDER		
RANK	STATE	PER CAPITA		RANK	STATE	PER CAPITA
48	Alabama	$3,924		1	Alaska	$23,292
1	Alaska	23,292		2	Wyoming	12,605
42	Arizona	4,262		3	Vermont	8,290
27	Arkansas	5,268		4	Massachusetts	7,910
24	California	5,497		5	North Dakota	7,824
25	Colorado	5,370		6	Delaware	7,599
14	Connecticut	6,326		7	New York	7,568
6	Delaware	7,599		8	Hawaii	7,222
49	Florida	3,725		9	Louisiana	6,808
43	Georgia	4,244		10	Montana	6,614
8	Hawaii	7,222		11	New Mexico	6,489
36	Idaho	4,653		12	New Jersey	6,354
39	Illinois	4,557		13	Rhode Island	6,351
38	Indiana	4,589		14	Connecticut	6,326
26	Iowa	5,324		15	West Virginia	5,909
32	Kansas	4,841		16	Maine	5,801
33	Kentucky	4,800		17	Ohio	5,692
9	Louisiana	6,808		18	Minnesota	5,680
16	Maine	5,801		19	Pennsylvania	5,661
30	Maryland	5,023		20	Utah	5,649
4	Massachusetts	7,910		21	Washington	5,583
45	Michigan	4,225		22	North Carolina	5,561
18	Minnesota	5,680		23	Mississippi	5,536
23	Mississippi	5,536		24	California	5,497
44	Missouri	4,238		25	Colorado	5,370
10	Montana	6,614		26	Iowa	5,324
35	Nebraska	4,707		27	Arkansas	5,268
47	Nevada	3,991		28	South Carolina	5,134
34	New Hampshire	4,754		29	Oklahoma	5,120
12	New Jersey	6,354		30	Maryland	5,023
11	New Mexico	6,489		31	Texas	4,900
7	New York	7,568		32	Kansas	4,841
22	North Carolina	5,561		33	Kentucky	4,800
5	North Dakota	7,824		34	New Hampshire	4,754
17	Ohio	5,692		35	Nebraska	4,707
29	Oklahoma	5,120		36	Idaho	4,653
41	Oregon	4,530		37	Virginia	4,648
19	Pennsylvania	5,661		38	Indiana	4,589
13	Rhode Island	6,351		39	Illinois	4,557
28	South Carolina	5,134		39	Wisconsin	4,557
50	South Dakota	3,617		41	Oregon	4,530
46	Tennessee	4,118		42	Arizona	4,262
31	Texas	4,900		43	Georgia	4,244
20	Utah	5,649		44	Missouri	4,238
3	Vermont	8,290		45	Michigan	4,225
37	Virginia	4,648		46	Tennessee	4,118
21	Washington	5,583		47	Nevada	3,991
15	West Virginia	5,909		48	Alabama	3,924
39	Wisconsin	4,557		49	Florida	3,725
2	Wyoming	12,605		50	South Dakota	3,617

District of Columbia**   NA

Source: CQ Press using data from U.S. Bureau of the Census, Governments Division
    "2008 State and Local Government Finances" (http://www.census.gov/govs/estimate/index.html)
*Total revenue includes all money received from external sources. This includes taxes, intergovernmental transfers and insurance trust revenue, and revenue from government owned utilities and other commercial or auxiliary enterprise.
**Not applicable.

State Government Intergovernmental Revenue in 2008

National Total = $446,109,032,000*

ALPHA ORDER

RANK	STATE	REVENUE	% of USA
20	Alabama	$7,712,748,000	1.7%
39	Alaska	2,190,854,000	0.5%
14	Arizona	8,887,402,000	2.0%
31	Arkansas	4,533,851,000	1.0%
1	California	51,914,572,000	11.6%
28	Colorado	4,945,496,000	1.1%
32	Connecticut	4,344,898,000	1.0%
48	Delaware	1,335,675,000	0.3%
4	Florida	19,876,444,000	4.5%
11	Georgia	13,090,193,000	2.9%
41	Hawaii	2,092,852,000	0.5%
43	Idaho	2,005,348,000	0.4%
7	Illinois	14,739,992,000	3.3%
16	Indiana	8,349,018,000	1.9%
30	Iowa	4,630,352,000	1.0%
34	Kansas	3,495,517,000	0.8%
26	Kentucky	6,630,599,000	1.5%
8	Louisiana	14,180,841,000	3.2%
38	Maine	2,427,894,000	0.5%
21	Maryland	7,525,060,000	1.7%
13	Massachusetts	10,047,618,000	2.3%
10	Michigan	13,359,341,000	3.0%
23	Minnesota	7,255,639,000	1.6%
19	Mississippi	7,718,794,000	1.7%
15	Missouri	8,500,589,000	1.9%
44	Montana	1,919,126,000	0.4%
37	Nebraska	2,560,819,000	0.6%
45	Nevada	1,857,810,000	0.4%
46	New Hampshire	1,830,369,000	0.4%
12	New Jersey	11,217,573,000	2.5%
33	New Mexico	4,322,241,000	1.0%
2	New York	46,623,511,000	10.5%
9	North Carolina	13,650,362,000	3.1%
50	North Dakota	1,233,474,000	0.3%
5	Ohio	17,093,617,000	3.8%
27	Oklahoma	5,705,546,000	1.3%
29	Oregon	4,835,171,000	1.1%
6	Pennsylvania	16,170,286,000	3.6%
42	Rhode Island	2,088,153,000	0.5%
24	South Carolina	7,018,905,000	1.6%
49	South Dakota	1,256,446,000	0.3%
17	Tennessee	8,308,154,000	1.9%
3	Texas	33,603,488,000	7.5%
35	Utah	3,441,961,000	0.8%
47	Vermont	1,420,594,000	0.3%
22	Virginia	7,403,481,000	1.7%
18	Washington	8,303,676,000	1.9%
36	West Virginia	3,274,439,000	0.7%
25	Wisconsin	7,013,591,000	1.6%
40	Wyoming	2,164,652,000	0.5%

RANK ORDER

RANK	STATE	REVENUE	% of USA
1	California	$51,914,572,000	11.6%
2	New York	46,623,511,000	10.5%
3	Texas	33,603,488,000	7.5%
4	Florida	19,876,444,000	4.5%
5	Ohio	17,093,617,000	3.8%
6	Pennsylvania	16,170,286,000	3.6%
7	Illinois	14,739,992,000	3.3%
8	Louisiana	14,180,841,000	3.2%
9	North Carolina	13,650,362,000	3.1%
10	Michigan	13,359,341,000	3.0%
11	Georgia	13,090,193,000	2.9%
12	New Jersey	11,217,573,000	2.5%
13	Massachusetts	10,047,618,000	2.3%
14	Arizona	8,887,402,000	2.0%
15	Missouri	8,500,589,000	1.9%
16	Indiana	8,349,018,000	1.9%
17	Tennessee	8,308,154,000	1.9%
18	Washington	8,303,676,000	1.9%
19	Mississippi	7,718,794,000	1.7%
20	Alabama	7,712,748,000	1.7%
21	Maryland	7,525,060,000	1.7%
22	Virginia	7,403,481,000	1.7%
23	Minnesota	7,255,639,000	1.6%
24	South Carolina	7,018,905,000	1.6%
25	Wisconsin	7,013,591,000	1.6%
26	Kentucky	6,630,599,000	1.5%
27	Oklahoma	5,705,546,000	1.3%
28	Colorado	4,945,496,000	1.1%
29	Oregon	4,835,171,000	1.1%
30	Iowa	4,630,352,000	1.0%
31	Arkansas	4,533,851,000	1.0%
32	Connecticut	4,344,898,000	1.0%
33	New Mexico	4,322,241,000	1.0%
34	Kansas	3,495,517,000	0.8%
35	Utah	3,441,961,000	0.8%
36	West Virginia	3,274,439,000	0.7%
37	Nebraska	2,560,819,000	0.6%
38	Maine	2,427,894,000	0.5%
39	Alaska	2,190,854,000	0.5%
40	Wyoming	2,164,652,000	0.5%
41	Hawaii	2,092,852,000	0.5%
42	Rhode Island	2,088,153,000	0.5%
43	Idaho	2,005,348,000	0.4%
44	Montana	1,919,126,000	0.4%
45	Nevada	1,857,810,000	0.4%
46	New Hampshire	1,830,369,000	0.4%
47	Vermont	1,420,594,000	0.3%
48	Delaware	1,335,675,000	0.3%
49	South Dakota	1,256,446,000	0.3%
50	North Dakota	1,233,474,000	0.3%
	District of Columbia**	NA	NA

Source: U.S. Bureau of the Census, Governments Division

"2008 State and Local Government Finances" (http://www.census.gov/govs/estimate/index.html)

*Includes revenue from federal and local government sources.

**Not applicable.

Per Capita State Government Intergovernmental Revenue in 2008

National Per Capita = $1,469*

ALPHA ORDER

ALPHA ORDER

RANK	STATE	PER CAPITA
13	Alabama	$1,649
3	Alaska	3,184
31	Arizona	1,367
15	Arkansas	1,581
27	California	1,419
48	Colorado	1,002
45	Connecticut	1,240
22	Delaware	1,524
47	Florida	1,079
32	Georgia	1,350
14	Hawaii	1,626
36	Idaho	1,313
46	Illinois	1,148
37	Indiana	1,307
19	Iowa	1,547
43	Kansas	1,250
20	Kentucky	1,546
2	Louisiana	3,186
11	Maine	1,840
35	Maryland	1,330
21	Massachusetts	1,535
33	Michigan	1,336
28	Minnesota	1,387
4	Mississippi	2,625
26	Missouri	1,427
8	Montana	1,982
25	Nebraska	1,437
50	Nevada	710
29	New Hampshire	1,385
38	New Jersey	1,295
7	New Mexico	2,176
5	New York	2,395
24	North Carolina	1,476
10	North Dakota	1,923
23	Ohio	1,483
16	Oklahoma	1,566
40	Oregon	1,278
39	Pennsylvania	1,287
8	Rhode Island	1,982
18	South Carolina	1,559
17	South Dakota	1,562
34	Tennessee	1,331
30	Texas	1,383
42	Utah	1,262
6	Vermont	2,287
49	Virginia	950
41	Washington	1,265
12	West Virginia	1,804
44	Wisconsin	1,246
1	Wyoming	4,061

RANK ORDER

RANK	STATE	PER CAPITA
1	Wyoming	$4,061
2	Louisiana	3,186
3	Alaska	3,184
4	Mississippi	2,625
5	New York	2,395
6	Vermont	2,287
7	New Mexico	2,176
8	Montana	1,982
8	Rhode Island	1,982
10	North Dakota	1,923
11	Maine	1,840
12	West Virginia	1,804
13	Alabama	1,649
14	Hawaii	1,626
15	Arkansas	1,581
16	Oklahoma	1,566
17	South Dakota	1,562
18	South Carolina	1,559
19	Iowa	1,547
20	Kentucky	1,546
21	Massachusetts	1,535
22	Delaware	1,524
23	Ohio	1,483
24	North Carolina	1,476
25	Nebraska	1,437
26	Missouri	1,427
27	California	1,419
28	Minnesota	1,387
29	New Hampshire	1,385
30	Texas	1,383
31	Arizona	1,367
32	Georgia	1,350
33	Michigan	1,336
34	Tennessee	1,331
35	Maryland	1,330
36	Idaho	1,313
37	Indiana	1,307
38	New Jersey	1,295
39	Pennsylvania	1,287
40	Oregon	1,278
41	Washington	1,265
42	Utah	1,262
43	Kansas	1,250
44	Wisconsin	1,246
45	Connecticut	1,240
46	Illinois	1,148
47	Florida	1,079
48	Colorado	1,002
49	Virginia	950
50	Nevada	710
	District of Columbia**	NA

Source: CQ Press using data from U.S. Bureau of the Census, Governments Division
   "2008 State and Local Government Finances" (http://www.census.gov/govs/estimate/index.html)
*Includes revenue from federal and local government sources.
**Not applicable.

State Government Own Source Revenue in 2008

National Total = $1,067,794,913,000*

ALPHA ORDER

RANK	STATE	REVENUE	% of USA
25	Alabama	$14,261,387,000	1.3%
27	Alaska	13,684,079,000	1.3%
19	Arizona	18,200,136,000	1.7%
32	Arkansas	10,227,364,000	1.0%
1	California	142,381,414,000	13.3%
24	Colorado	14,653,905,000	1.4%
20	Connecticut	17,723,007,000	1.7%
41	Delaware	5,229,417,000	0.5%
4	Florida	47,841,034,000	4.5%
14	Georgia	23,581,356,000	2.2%
39	Hawaii	7,209,131,000	0.7%
43	Idaho	4,758,847,000	0.4%
6	Illinois	40,516,164,000	3.8%
18	Indiana	20,894,584,000	2.0%
31	Iowa	10,383,161,000	1.0%
33	Kansas	10,009,264,000	0.9%
26	Kentucky	14,219,911,000	1.3%
23	Louisiana	15,688,281,000	1.5%
42	Maine	5,228,231,000	0.5%
16	Maryland	21,290,385,000	2.0%
10	Massachusetts	31,559,803,000	3.0%
9	Michigan	35,791,807,000	3.4%
15	Minnesota	22,426,447,000	2.1%
36	Mississippi	8,811,304,000	0.8%
22	Missouri	15,711,301,000	1.5%
46	Montana	3,571,495,000	0.3%
40	Nebraska	5,796,920,000	0.5%
37	Nevada	7,540,647,000	0.7%
45	New Hampshire	3,876,855,000	0.4%
7	New Jersey	40,178,127,000	3.8%
35	New Mexico	9,390,964,000	0.9%
2	New York	86,386,295,000	8.1%
11	North Carolina	29,446,981,000	2.8%
49	North Dakota	3,421,614,000	0.3%
8	Ohio	37,342,750,000	3.5%
29	Oklahoma	12,120,666,000	1.1%
30	Oregon	11,812,834,000	1.1%
5	Pennsylvania	44,629,889,000	4.2%
44	Rhode Island	4,299,256,000	0.4%
28	South Carolina	13,500,454,000	1.3%
50	South Dakota	2,169,713,000	0.2%
21	Tennessee	16,870,016,000	1.6%
3	Texas	65,371,486,000	6.1%
34	Utah	9,740,937,000	0.9%
48	Vermont	3,436,373,000	0.3%
12	Virginia	28,737,821,000	2.7%
13	Washington	23,969,151,000	2.2%
38	West Virginia	7,479,873,000	0.7%
17	Wisconsin	20,962,378,000	2.0%
47	Wyoming	3,459,698,000	0.3%

RANK ORDER

RANK	STATE	REVENUE	% of USA
1	California	$142,381,414,000	13.3%
2	New York	86,386,295,000	8.1%
3	Texas	65,371,486,000	6.1%
4	Florida	47,841,034,000	4.5%
5	Pennsylvania	44,629,889,000	4.2%
6	Illinois	40,516,164,000	3.8%
7	New Jersey	40,178,127,000	3.8%
8	Ohio	37,342,750,000	3.5%
9	Michigan	35,791,807,000	3.4%
10	Massachusetts	31,559,803,000	3.0%
11	North Carolina	29,446,981,000	2.8%
12	Virginia	28,737,821,000	2.7%
13	Washington	23,969,151,000	2.2%
14	Georgia	23,581,356,000	2.2%
15	Minnesota	22,426,447,000	2.1%
16	Maryland	21,290,385,000	2.0%
17	Wisconsin	20,962,378,000	2.0%
18	Indiana	20,894,584,000	2.0%
19	Arizona	18,200,136,000	1.7%
20	Connecticut	17,723,007,000	1.7%
21	Tennessee	16,870,016,000	1.6%
22	Missouri	15,711,301,000	1.5%
23	Louisiana	15,688,281,000	1.5%
24	Colorado	14,653,905,000	1.4%
25	Alabama	14,261,387,000	1.3%
26	Kentucky	14,219,911,000	1.3%
27	Alaska	13,684,079,000	1.3%
28	South Carolina	13,500,454,000	1.3%
29	Oklahoma	12,120,666,000	1.1%
30	Oregon	11,812,834,000	1.1%
31	Iowa	10,383,161,000	1.0%
32	Arkansas	10,227,364,000	1.0%
33	Kansas	10,009,264,000	0.9%
34	Utah	9,740,937,000	0.9%
35	New Mexico	9,390,964,000	0.9%
36	Mississippi	8,811,304,000	0.8%
37	Nevada	7,540,647,000	0.7%
38	West Virginia	7,479,873,000	0.7%
39	Hawaii	7,209,131,000	0.7%
40	Nebraska	5,796,920,000	0.5%
41	Delaware	5,229,417,000	0.5%
42	Maine	5,228,231,000	0.5%
43	Idaho	4,758,847,000	0.4%
44	Rhode Island	4,299,256,000	0.4%
45	New Hampshire	3,876,855,000	0.4%
46	Montana	3,571,495,000	0.3%
47	Wyoming	3,459,698,000	0.3%
48	Vermont	3,436,373,000	0.3%
49	North Dakota	3,421,614,000	0.3%
50	South Dakota	2,169,713,000	0.2%

District of Columbia**   NA   NA

Source: U.S. Bureau of the Census, Governments Division
"2008 State and Local Government Finances" (http://www.census.gov/govs/estimate/index.html)
*Own source revenue includes taxes, current charges, and miscellaneous general revenue. Excluded are intergovernmental transfers, insurance trust revenue, and revenue from government owned utilities and other commercial or auxiliary enterprise.
**Not applicable.

Per Capita State Government Own Source Revenue in 2008

National Per Capita = $3,515*

ALPHA ORDER			RANK ORDER		
RANK	STATE	PER CAPITA	RANK	STATE	PER CAPITA
38	Alabama	$3,049	1	Alaska	$19,886
1	Alaska	19,886	2	Wyoming	6,491
44	Arizona	2,800	3	Delaware	5,968
25	Arkansas	3,566	4	Hawaii	5,599
16	California	3,892	5	Vermont	5,533
41	Colorado	2,969	6	North Dakota	5,334
7	Connecticut	5,059	7	Connecticut	5,059
3	Delaware	5,968	8	Massachusetts	4,823
49	Florida	2,597	9	New Mexico	4,727
50	Georgia	2,432	10	New Jersey	4,638
4	Hawaii	5,599	11	New York	4,437
37	Idaho	3,115	12	Minnesota	4,288
35	Illinois	3,155	13	West Virginia	4,121
31	Indiana	3,271	14	Rhode Island	4,081
28	Iowa	3,468	15	Maine	3,962
22	Kansas	3,578	16	California	3,892
30	Kentucky	3,316	17	Maryland	3,762
27	Louisiana	3,524	18	Wisconsin	3,725
15	Maine	3,962	19	Montana	3,689
17	Maryland	3,762	20	Virginia	3,686
8	Massachusetts	4,823	21	Washington	3,650
22	Michigan	3,578	22	Kansas	3,578
12	Minnesota	4,288	22	Michigan	3,578
40	Mississippi	2,997	24	Utah	3,572
48	Missouri	2,638	25	Arkansas	3,566
19	Montana	3,689	26	Pennsylvania	3,552
32	Nebraska	3,253	27	Louisiana	3,524
43	Nevada	2,883	28	Iowa	3,468
42	New Hampshire	2,933	29	Oklahoma	3,326
10	New Jersey	4,638	30	Kentucky	3,316
9	New Mexico	4,727	31	Indiana	3,271
11	New York	4,437	32	Nebraska	3,253
34	North Carolina	3,184	33	Ohio	3,239
6	North Dakota	5,334	34	North Carolina	3,184
33	Ohio	3,239	35	Illinois	3,155
29	Oklahoma	3,326	36	Oregon	3,123
36	Oregon	3,123	37	Idaho	3,115
26	Pennsylvania	3,552	38	Alabama	3,049
14	Rhode Island	4,081	39	South Carolina	2,998
39	South Carolina	2,998	40	Mississippi	2,997
46	South Dakota	2,697	41	Colorado	2,969
45	Tennessee	2,703	42	New Hampshire	2,933
47	Texas	2,690	43	Nevada	2,883
24	Utah	3,572	44	Arizona	2,800
5	Vermont	5,533	45	Tennessee	2,703
20	Virginia	3,686	46	South Dakota	2,697
21	Washington	3,650	47	Texas	2,690
13	West Virginia	4,121	48	Missouri	2,638
18	Wisconsin	3,725	49	Florida	2,597
2	Wyoming	6,491	50	Georgia	2,432

District of Columbia** NA

Source: CQ Press using data from U.S. Bureau of the Census, Governments Division
   "2008 State and Local Government Finances" (http://www.census.gov/govs/estimate/index.html)
*Own source revenue includes taxes, current charges, and miscellaneous general revenue. Excluded are intergovernmental transfers, insurance trust revenue, and revenue from government owned utilities and other commercial or auxiliary enterprise.
**Not applicable.

Profits of State Lotteries in 2010

National Total = $17,877,070,000*

ALPHA ORDER

RANK	STATE	PROFITS	% of USA
NA	Alabama**	NA	NA
NA	Alaska**	NA	NA
26	Arizona	141,900,000	0.8%
32	Arkansas	82,700,000	0.5%
4	California	1,055,180,000	5.9%
31	Colorado	112,900,000	0.6%
19	Connecticut	285,500,000	1.6%
20	Delaware	275,500,000	1.5%
2	Florida	1,247,000,000	7.0%
8	Georgia	883,900,000	4.9%
NA	Hawaii**	NA	NA
39	Idaho	36,500,000	0.2%
11	Illinois	657,880,000	3.7%
24	Indiana	188,800,000	1.1%
36	Iowa	57,910,000	0.3%
34	Kansas	69,030,000	0.4%
23	Kentucky	214,300,000	1.2%
27	Louisiana	134,080,000	0.8%
37	Maine	52,200,000	0.3%
14	Maryland	510,610,000	2.9%
7	Massachusetts	903,500,000	5.1%
10	Michigan	704,200,000	3.9%
28	Minnesota	122,250,000	0.7%
NA	Mississippi**	NA	NA
22	Missouri	256,040,000	1.4%
42	Montana	10,610,000	0.1%
40	Nebraska	32,350,000	0.2%
NA	Nevada**	NA	NA
35	New Hampshire	66,080,000	0.4%
5	New Jersey	924,160,000	5.2%
38	New Mexico	43,600,000	0.2%
1	New York	2,666,380,000	14.9%
15	North Carolina	430,790,000	2.4%
43	North Dakota	6,330,000	0.0%
9	Ohio	728,600,000	4.1%
33	Oklahoma	69,970,000	0.4%
13	Oregon	516,700,000	2.9%
6	Pennsylvania	915,740,000	5.1%
17	Rhode Island	344,650,000	1.9%
21	South Carolina	272,430,000	1.5%
30	South Dakota	116,910,000	0.7%
18	Tennessee	288,900,000	1.6%
3	Texas	1,100,000,000	6.2%
NA	Utah**	NA	NA
41	Vermont	21,640,000	0.1%
16	Virginia	430,000,000	2.4%
29	Washington	121,350,000	0.7%
12	West Virginia	568,900,000	3.2%
25	Wisconsin	143,100,000	0.8%
NA	Wyoming**	NA	NA

RANK ORDER

RANK	STATE	PROFITS	% of USA
1	New York	$2,666,380,000	14.9%
2	Florida	1,247,000,000	7.0%
3	Texas	1,100,000,000	6.2%
4	California	1,055,180,000	5.9%
5	New Jersey	924,160,000	5.2%
6	Pennsylvania	915,740,000	5.1%
7	Massachusetts	903,500,000	5.1%
8	Georgia	883,900,000	4.9%
9	Ohio	728,600,000	4.1%
10	Michigan	704,200,000	3.9%
11	Illinois	657,880,000	3.7%
12	West Virginia	568,900,000	3.2%
13	Oregon	516,700,000	2.9%
14	Maryland	510,610,000	2.9%
15	North Carolina	430,790,000	2.4%
16	Virginia	430,000,000	2.4%
17	Rhode Island	344,650,000	1.9%
18	Tennessee	288,900,000	1.6%
19	Connecticut	285,500,000	1.6%
20	Delaware	275,500,000	1.5%
21	South Carolina	272,430,000	1.5%
22	Missouri	256,040,000	1.4%
23	Kentucky	214,300,000	1.2%
24	Indiana	188,800,000	1.1%
25	Wisconsin	143,100,000	0.8%
26	Arizona	141,900,000	0.8%
27	Louisiana	134,080,000	0.8%
28	Minnesota	122,250,000	0.7%
29	Washington	121,350,000	0.7%
30	South Dakota	116,910,000	0.7%
31	Colorado	112,900,000	0.6%
32	Arkansas	82,700,000	0.5%
33	Oklahoma	69,970,000	0.4%
34	Kansas	69,030,000	0.4%
35	New Hampshire	66,080,000	0.4%
36	Iowa	57,910,000	0.3%
37	Maine	52,200,000	0.3%
38	New Mexico	43,600,000	0.2%
39	Idaho	36,500,000	0.2%
40	Nebraska	32,350,000	0.2%
41	Vermont	21,640,000	0.1%
42	Montana	10,610,000	0.1%
43	North Dakota	6,330,000	0.0%
NA	Alabama**	NA	NA
NA	Alaska**	NA	NA
NA	Hawaii**	NA	NA
NA	Mississippi**	NA	NA
NA	Nevada**	NA	NA
NA	Utah**	NA	NA
NA	Wyoming**	NA	NA
	District of Columbia	66,000,000	0.4%

Source: North American Association of State and Provincial Lotteries, Willoughby Hills, OH
"Lottery Sales and Profits" (http://www.naspl.org/index.cfm?fuseaction=content&PageID=3&PageCategory=3)
*Reported profits for fiscal year 2010 on sales of $58,816,600,000. National total does not include profits for Puerto Rico.
**No lottery as of fiscal year 2010.

Per Capita Profits of State Lotteries in 2010

National Per Capita = $61.35*

ALPHA ORDER			RANK ORDER		
RANK	STATE	PER CAPITA	RANK	STATE	PER CAPITA
NA	Alabama**	NA	1	Rhode Island	$327.24
NA	Alaska**	NA	2	West Virginia	312.62
37	Arizona	21.51	3	Delaware	311.26
29	Arkansas	28.62	4	South Dakota	143.91
30	California	28.55	5	Massachusetts	137.03
35	Colorado	22.47	6	New York	136.45
11	Connecticut	81.15	7	Oregon	135.06
3	Delaware	311.26	8	New Jersey	106.13
14	Florida	67.27	9	Georgia	89.93
9	Georgia	89.93	10	Maryland	89.59
NA	Hawaii**	NA	11	Connecticut	81.15
33	Idaho	23.61	12	Pennsylvania	72.65
18	Illinois	50.96	13	Michigan	70.63
28	Indiana	29.39	14	Florida	67.27
38	Iowa	19.25	15	Ohio	63.12
32	Kansas	24.49	16	South Carolina	59.73
20	Kentucky	49.67	17	Virginia	54.55
27	Louisiana	29.85	18	Illinois	50.96
25	Maine	39.60	19	New Hampshire	49.89
10	Maryland	89.59	20	Kentucky	49.67
5	Massachusetts	137.03	21	North Carolina	45.92
13	Michigan	70.63	22	Tennessee	45.88
34	Minnesota	23.21	23	Texas	44.39
NA	Mississippi**	NA	24	Missouri	42.76
24	Missouri	42.76	25	Maine	39.60
42	Montana	10.88	26	Vermont	34.80
41	Nebraska	18.01	27	Louisiana	29.85
NA	Nevada**	NA	28	Indiana	29.39
19	New Hampshire	49.89	29	Arkansas	28.62
8	New Jersey	106.13	30	California	28.55
36	New Mexico	21.70	31	Wisconsin	25.31
6	New York	136.45	32	Kansas	24.49
21	North Carolina	45.92	33	Idaho	23.61
43	North Dakota	9.79	34	Minnesota	23.21
15	Ohio	63.12	35	Colorado	22.47
39	Oklahoma	18.98	36	New Mexico	21.70
7	Oregon	135.06	37	Arizona	21.51
12	Pennsylvania	72.65	38	Iowa	19.25
1	Rhode Island	327.24	39	Oklahoma	18.98
16	South Carolina	59.73	40	Washington	18.21
4	South Dakota	143.91	41	Nebraska	18.01
22	Tennessee	45.88	42	Montana	10.88
23	Texas	44.39	43	North Dakota	9.79
NA	Utah**	NA	NA	Alabama**	NA
26	Vermont	34.80	NA	Alaska**	NA
17	Virginia	54.55	NA	Hawaii**	NA
40	Washington	18.21	NA	Mississippi**	NA
2	West Virginia	312.62	NA	Nevada**	NA
31	Wisconsin	25.31	NA	Utah**	NA
NA	Wyoming**	NA	NA	Wyoming**	NA

District of Columbia   110.06

Source: CQ Press using data from North American Association of State and Provincial Lotteries, Willoughby Hills, OH
"Lottery Sales and Profits" (http://www.naspl.org/index.cfm?fuseaction=content&PageID=3&PageCategory=3)
*For fiscal year 2010. National rate is based on population of states with a lottery.
**No lottery as of fiscal year 2010.

Projected vs. Actual State Tax Collections in 2010

National Percent = 95.8% of Projected Taxes*

ALPHA ORDER

RANK	STATE	PERCENT
35	Alabama	93.7
47	Alaska	85.7
9	Arizona	100.0
21	Arkansas	96.9
32	California	94.6
34	Colorado	94.0
11	Connecticut	99.4
30	Delaware	95.7
2	Florida	102.3
43	Georgia	89.2
1	Hawaii	105.7
39	Idaho	91.9
22	Illinois	96.7
38	Indiana	92.5
20	Iowa	97.3
17	Kansas	97.7
45	Kentucky	85.9
45	Louisiana	85.9
4	Maine	102.1
24	Maryland	96.5
7	Massachusetts	100.5
13	Michigan	98.3
14	Minnesota	98.0
40	Mississippi	91.8
44	Missouri	87.3
49	Montana	80.4
25	Nebraska	96.4
41	Nevada	91.2
3	New Hampshire	102.2
31	New Jersey	95.3
50	New Mexico	79.9
33	New York	94.1
14	North Carolina	98.0
27	North Dakota	96.2
6	Ohio	100.7
48	Oklahoma	82.7
28	Oregon	95.9
26	Pennsylvania	96.3
18	Rhode Island	97.6
36	South Carolina	93.4
18	South Dakota	97.6
14	Tennessee	98.0
9	Texas	100.0
22	Utah	96.7
5	Vermont	100.9
7	Virginia	100.5
37	Washington	93.1
28	West Virginia	95.9
12	Wisconsin	98.5
42	Wyoming	89.3

RANK ORDER

RANK	STATE	PERCENT
1	Hawaii	105.7
2	Florida	102.3
3	New Hampshire	102.2
4	Maine	102.1
5	Vermont	100.9
6	Ohio	100.7
7	Massachusetts	100.5
7	Virginia	100.5
9	Arizona	100.0
9	Texas	100.0
11	Connecticut	99.4
12	Wisconsin	98.5
13	Michigan	98.3
14	Minnesota	98.0
14	North Carolina	98.0
14	Tennessee	98.0
17	Kansas	97.7
18	Rhode Island	97.6
18	South Dakota	97.6
20	Iowa	97.3
21	Arkansas	96.9
22	Illinois	96.7
22	Utah	96.7
24	Maryland	96.5
25	Nebraska	96.4
26	Pennsylvania	96.3
27	North Dakota	96.2
28	Oregon	95.9
28	West Virginia	95.9
30	Delaware	95.7
31	New Jersey	95.3
32	California	94.6
33	New York	94.1
34	Colorado	94.0
35	Alabama	93.7
36	South Carolina	93.4
37	Washington	93.1
38	Indiana	92.5
39	Idaho	91.9
40	Mississippi	91.8
41	Nevada	91.2
42	Wyoming	89.3
43	Georgia	89.2
44	Missouri	87.3
45	Kentucky	85.9
45	Louisiana	85.9
47	Alaska	85.7
48	Oklahoma	82.7
49	Montana	80.4
50	New Mexico	79.9

District of Columbia**   NA

Source: CQ Press using data from National Association of State Budget Officers
     "The Fiscal Survey of States" (Fall 2010, http://www.nasbo.org/)
*For fiscal year 2010. This table compares sales, personal, and corporate income tax collections projected in adopting budgets
with the amount collected.
**Not available.

State Government Tax Revenue in 2009

National Total = $715,086,270,000

ALPHA ORDER

RANK	STATE	REVENUE	% of USA
26	Alabama	$8,306,446,000	1.2%
36	Alaska	4,953,342,000	0.7%
20	Arizona	11,864,046,000	1.7%
28	Arkansas	7,467,679,000	1.0%
1	California	101,007,459,000	14.1%
25	Colorado	8,682,822,000	1.2%
19	Connecticut	12,927,619,000	1.8%
43	Delaware	2,806,031,000	0.4%
4	Florida	31,956,841,000	4.5%
15	Georgia	16,077,948,000	2.2%
39	Hawaii	4,712,651,000	0.7%
42	Idaho	3,171,863,000	0.4%
6	Illinois	29,268,349,000	4.1%
17	Indiana	14,900,123,000	2.1%
31	Iowa	6,984,279,000	1.0%
32	Kansas	6,694,630,000	0.9%
24	Kentucky	9,755,544,000	1.4%
23	Louisiana	10,014,637,000	1.4%
41	Maine	3,489,105,000	0.5%
16	Maryland	15,126,893,000	2.1%
11	Massachusetts	19,699,494,000	2.8%
9	Michigan	22,757,818,000	3.2%
12	Minnesota	17,161,299,000	2.4%
33	Mississippi	6,470,593,000	0.9%
22	Missouri	10,345,250,000	1.4%
48	Montana	2,407,400,000	0.3%
40	Nebraska	4,000,939,000	0.6%
34	Nevada	5,564,170,000	0.8%
49	New Hampshire	2,125,722,000	0.3%
7	New Jersey	27,074,472,000	3.8%
37	New Mexico	4,851,689,000	0.7%
2	New York	65,029,871,000	9.1%
10	North Carolina	20,496,106,000	2.9%
47	North Dakota	2,414,010,000	0.3%
8	Ohio	23,952,422,000	3.3%
27	Oklahoma	8,160,670,000	1.1%
29	Oregon	7,419,494,000	1.0%
5	Pennsylvania	30,071,179,000	4.2%
45	Rhode Island	2,586,184,000	0.4%
30	South Carolina	7,146,034,000	1.0%
50	South Dakota	1,333,835,000	0.2%
21	Tennessee	10,442,552,000	1.5%
3	Texas	40,786,857,000	5.7%
35	Utah	5,422,858,000	0.8%
46	Vermont	2,505,665,000	0.4%
14	Virginia	16,331,388,000	2.3%
13	Washington	16,408,838,000	2.3%
38	West Virginia	4,788,157,000	0.7%
18	Wisconsin	14,402,506,000	2.0%
44	Wyoming	2,760,491,000	0.4%

RANK ORDER

RANK	STATE	REVENUE	% of USA
1	California	$101,007,459,000	14.1%
2	New York	65,029,871,000	9.1%
3	Texas	40,786,857,000	5.7%
4	Florida	31,956,841,000	4.5%
5	Pennsylvania	30,071,179,000	4.2%
6	Illinois	29,268,349,000	4.1%
7	New Jersey	27,074,472,000	3.8%
8	Ohio	23,952,422,000	3.3%
9	Michigan	22,757,818,000	3.2%
10	North Carolina	20,496,106,000	2.9%
11	Massachusetts	19,699,494,000	2.8%
12	Minnesota	17,161,299,000	2.4%
13	Washington	16,408,838,000	2.3%
14	Virginia	16,331,388,000	2.3%
15	Georgia	16,077,948,000	2.2%
16	Maryland	15,126,893,000	2.1%
17	Indiana	14,900,123,000	2.1%
18	Wisconsin	14,402,506,000	2.0%
19	Connecticut	12,927,619,000	1.8%
20	Arizona	11,864,046,000	1.7%
21	Tennessee	10,442,552,000	1.5%
22	Missouri	10,345,250,000	1.4%
23	Louisiana	10,014,637,000	1.4%
24	Kentucky	9,755,544,000	1.4%
25	Colorado	8,682,822,000	1.2%
26	Alabama	8,306,446,000	1.2%
27	Oklahoma	8,160,670,000	1.1%
28	Arkansas	7,467,679,000	1.0%
29	Oregon	7,419,494,000	1.0%
30	South Carolina	7,146,034,000	1.0%
31	Iowa	6,984,279,000	1.0%
32	Kansas	6,694,630,000	0.9%
33	Mississippi	6,470,593,000	0.9%
34	Nevada	5,564,170,000	0.8%
35	Utah	5,422,858,000	0.8%
36	Alaska	4,953,342,000	0.7%
37	New Mexico	4,851,689,000	0.7%
38	West Virginia	4,788,157,000	0.7%
39	Hawaii	4,712,651,000	0.7%
40	Nebraska	4,000,939,000	0.6%
41	Maine	3,489,105,000	0.5%
42	Idaho	3,171,863,000	0.4%
43	Delaware	2,806,031,000	0.4%
44	Wyoming	2,760,491,000	0.4%
45	Rhode Island	2,586,184,000	0.4%
46	Vermont	2,505,665,000	0.4%
47	North Dakota	2,414,010,000	0.3%
48	Montana	2,407,400,000	0.3%
49	New Hampshire	2,125,722,000	0.3%
50	South Dakota	1,333,835,000	0.2%
	District of Columbia*	NA	NA

Source: U.S. Bureau of the Census, Governments Division
    "2009 State Government Tax Collections" (http://www.census.gov/govs/statetax/)
*Not applicable.

Per Capita State Government Tax Revenue in 2009

National Per Capita = $2,334

ALPHA ORDER

RANK	STATE	PER CAPITA
41	Alabama	$1,764
1	Alaska	7,092
40	Arizona	1,799
16	Arkansas	2,584
12	California	2,733
42	Colorado	1,728
5	Connecticut	3,674
9	Delaware	3,170
44	Florida	1,724
48	Georgia	1,636
6	Hawaii	3,639
37	Idaho	2,052
27	Illinois	2,267
25	Indiana	2,320
24	Iowa	2,322
23	Kansas	2,375
28	Kentucky	2,261
29	Louisiana	2,229
14	Maine	2,647
13	Maryland	2,654
11	Massachusetts	2,988
26	Michigan	2,283
8	Minnesota	3,259
32	Mississippi	2,192
42	Missouri	1,728
18	Montana	2,469
30	Nebraska	2,227
34	Nevada	2,105
49	New Hampshire	1,605
10	New Jersey	3,109
21	New Mexico	2,414
7	New York	3,328
33	North Carolina	2,185
4	North Dakota	3,732
35	Ohio	2,075
31	Oklahoma	2,213
39	Oregon	1,939
22	Pennsylvania	2,386
20	Rhode Island	2,456
50	South Carolina	1,567
47	South Dakota	1,642
45	Tennessee	1,659
46	Texas	1,646
38	Utah	1,947
3	Vermont	4,030
36	Virginia	2,072
19	Washington	2,462
15	West Virginia	2,631
17	Wisconsin	2,547
2	Wyoming	5,072

RANK ORDER

RANK	STATE	PER CAPITA
1	Alaska	$7,092
2	Wyoming	5,072
3	Vermont	4,030
4	North Dakota	3,732
5	Connecticut	3,674
6	Hawaii	3,639
7	New York	3,328
8	Minnesota	3,259
9	Delaware	3,170
10	New Jersey	3,109
11	Massachusetts	2,988
12	California	2,733
13	Maryland	2,654
14	Maine	2,647
15	West Virginia	2,631
16	Arkansas	2,584
17	Wisconsin	2,547
18	Montana	2,469
19	Washington	2,462
20	Rhode Island	2,456
21	New Mexico	2,414
22	Pennsylvania	2,386
23	Kansas	2,375
24	Iowa	2,322
25	Indiana	2,320
26	Michigan	2,283
27	Illinois	2,267
28	Kentucky	2,261
29	Louisiana	2,229
30	Nebraska	2,227
31	Oklahoma	2,213
32	Mississippi	2,192
33	North Carolina	2,185
34	Nevada	2,105
35	Ohio	2,075
36	Virginia	2,072
37	Idaho	2,052
38	Utah	1,947
39	Oregon	1,939
40	Arizona	1,799
41	Alabama	1,764
42	Colorado	1,728
42	Missouri	1,728
44	Florida	1,724
45	Tennessee	1,659
46	Texas	1,646
47	South Dakota	1,642
48	Georgia	1,636
49	New Hampshire	1,605
50	South Carolina	1,567
	District of Columbia*	NA

Source: CQ Press using data from U.S. Bureau of the Census, Governments Division
"2009 State Government Tax Collections" (http://www.census.gov/govs/statetax/)
*Not applicable.

State Government Tax Revenue as a Percent of Personal Income in 2009

National Percent = 5.9% of Personal Income*

ALPHA ORDER

RANK	STATE	PERCENT
40	Alabama	5.3
1	Alaska	16.4
37	Arizona	5.4
7	Arkansas	8.0
21	California	6.4
49	Colorado	4.1
18	Connecticut	6.7
8	Delaware	7.9
46	Florida	4.4
41	Georgia	4.8
5	Hawaii	8.6
20	Idaho	6.5
37	Illinois	5.4
16	Indiana	6.8
23	Iowa	6.2
27	Kansas	6.0
15	Kentucky	7.0
29	Louisiana	5.9
10	Maine	7.3
36	Maryland	5.5
27	Massachusetts	6.0
19	Michigan	6.6
9	Minnesota	7.8
12	Mississippi	7.2
41	Missouri	4.8
14	Montana	7.1
33	Nebraska	5.7
35	Nevada	5.6
50	New Hampshire	3.8
23	New Jersey	6.2
10	New Mexico	7.3
12	New York	7.2
22	North Carolina	6.3
4	North Dakota	9.2
32	Ohio	5.8
23	Oklahoma	6.2
37	Oregon	5.4
29	Pennsylvania	5.9
29	Rhode Island	5.9
41	South Carolina	4.8
47	South Dakota	4.3
41	Tennessee	4.8
47	Texas	4.3
23	Utah	6.2
3	Vermont	10.3
45	Virginia	4.7
33	Washington	5.7
6	West Virginia	8.2
16	Wisconsin	6.8
2	Wyoming	10.5

RANK ORDER

RANK	STATE	PERCENT
1	Alaska	16.4
2	Wyoming	10.5
3	Vermont	10.3
4	North Dakota	9.2
5	Hawaii	8.6
6	West Virginia	8.2
7	Arkansas	8.0
8	Delaware	7.9
9	Minnesota	7.8
10	Maine	7.3
10	New Mexico	7.3
12	Mississippi	7.2
12	New York	7.2
14	Montana	7.1
15	Kentucky	7.0
16	Indiana	6.8
16	Wisconsin	6.8
18	Connecticut	6.7
19	Michigan	6.6
20	Idaho	6.5
21	California	6.4
22	North Carolina	6.3
23	Iowa	6.2
23	New Jersey	6.2
23	Oklahoma	6.2
23	Utah	6.2
27	Kansas	6.0
27	Massachusetts	6.0
29	Louisiana	5.9
29	Pennsylvania	5.9
29	Rhode Island	5.9
32	Ohio	5.8
33	Nebraska	5.7
33	Washington	5.7
35	Nevada	5.6
36	Maryland	5.5
37	Arizona	5.4
37	Illinois	5.4
37	Oregon	5.4
40	Alabama	5.3
41	Georgia	4.8
41	Missouri	4.8
41	South Carolina	4.8
41	Tennessee	4.8
45	Virginia	4.7
46	Florida	4.4
47	South Dakota	4.3
47	Texas	4.3
49	Colorado	4.1
50	New Hampshire	3.8

District of Columbia**	NA

Source: CQ Press using data from U.S. Bureau of the Census, Governments Division
"2009 State Government Tax Collections" (http://www.census.gov/govs/statetax/)
U.S. Department of Commerce, Bureau of Economic Analysis
"Annual State Personal Income" (http://www.bea.doc.gov/bea/regional/spi/)
*National figure does not include personal income or taxes from the District of Columbia.
**Not applicable.

State Government Individual Income Tax Revenue in 2009

National Total = $245,930,476,000

ALPHA ORDER

RANK	STATE	REVENUE	% of USA
24	Alabama	$2,662,759,000	1.1%
44	Alaska	0	0.0%
25	Arizona	2,575,753,000	1.0%
29	Arkansas	2,238,958,000	0.9%
1	California	44,355,959,000	18.0%
18	Colorado	4,403,446,000	1.8%
13	Connecticut	6,376,921,000	2.6%
38	Delaware	910,693,000	0.4%
44	Florida	0	0.0%
10	Georgia	7,801,185,000	3.2%
34	Hawaii	1,338,702,000	0.5%
35	Idaho	1,175,604,000	0.5%
7	Illinois	9,183,002,000	3.7%
19	Indiana	4,313,759,000	1.8%
23	Iowa	2,703,190,000	1.1%
22	Kansas	2,731,559,000	1.1%
20	Kentucky	3,315,368,000	1.3%
21	Louisiana	2,940,633,000	1.2%
33	Maine	1,370,710,000	0.6%
12	Maryland	6,478,236,000	2.6%
3	Massachusetts	10,599,085,000	4.3%
15	Michigan	5,856,751,000	2.4%
11	Minnesota	6,948,119,000	2.8%
32	Mississippi	1,485,592,000	0.6%
17	Missouri	4,771,576,000	1.9%
39	Montana	827,196,000	0.3%
30	Nebraska	1,602,091,000	0.7%
44	Nevada	0	0.0%
43	New Hampshire	98,191,000	0.0%
4	New Jersey	10,476,267,000	4.3%
37	New Mexico	932,442,000	0.4%
2	New York	36,840,019,000	15.0%
5	North Carolina	9,560,353,000	3.9%
41	North Dakota	370,165,000	0.2%
9	Ohio	8,323,352,000	3.4%
26	Oklahoma	2,544,576,000	1.0%
16	Oregon	5,434,777,000	2.2%
6	Pennsylvania	9,550,238,000	3.9%
36	Rhode Island	960,885,000	0.4%
27	South Carolina	2,351,324,000	1.0%
44	South Dakota	0	0.0%
42	Tennessee	221,685,000	0.1%
44	Texas	0	0.0%
28	Utah	2,319,632,000	0.9%
40	Vermont	532,911,000	0.2%
8	Virginia	8,918,232,000	3.6%
44	Washington	0	0.0%
31	West Virginia	1,557,403,000	0.6%
14	Wisconsin	5,971,177,000	2.4%
44	Wyoming	0	0.0%

RANK ORDER

RANK	STATE	REVENUE	% of USA
1	California	$44,355,959,000	18.0%
2	New York	36,840,019,000	15.0%
3	Massachusetts	10,599,085,000	4.3%
4	New Jersey	10,476,267,000	4.3%
5	North Carolina	9,560,353,000	3.9%
6	Pennsylvania	9,550,238,000	3.9%
7	Illinois	9,183,002,000	3.7%
8	Virginia	8,918,232,000	3.6%
9	Ohio	8,323,352,000	3.4%
10	Georgia	7,801,185,000	3.2%
11	Minnesota	6,948,119,000	2.8%
12	Maryland	6,478,236,000	2.6%
13	Connecticut	6,376,921,000	2.6%
14	Wisconsin	5,971,177,000	2.4%
15	Michigan	5,856,751,000	2.4%
16	Oregon	5,434,777,000	2.2%
17	Missouri	4,771,576,000	1.9%
18	Colorado	4,403,446,000	1.8%
19	Indiana	4,313,759,000	1.8%
20	Kentucky	3,315,368,000	1.3%
21	Louisiana	2,940,633,000	1.2%
22	Kansas	2,731,559,000	1.1%
23	Iowa	2,703,190,000	1.1%
24	Alabama	2,662,759,000	1.1%
25	Arizona	2,575,753,000	1.0%
26	Oklahoma	2,544,576,000	1.0%
27	South Carolina	2,351,324,000	1.0%
28	Utah	2,319,632,000	0.9%
29	Arkansas	2,238,958,000	0.9%
30	Nebraska	1,602,091,000	0.7%
31	West Virginia	1,557,403,000	0.6%
32	Mississippi	1,485,592,000	0.6%
33	Maine	1,370,710,000	0.6%
34	Hawaii	1,338,702,000	0.5%
35	Idaho	1,175,604,000	0.5%
36	Rhode Island	960,885,000	0.4%
37	New Mexico	932,442,000	0.4%
38	Delaware	910,693,000	0.4%
39	Montana	827,196,000	0.3%
40	Vermont	532,911,000	0.2%
41	North Dakota	370,165,000	0.2%
42	Tennessee	221,685,000	0.1%
43	New Hampshire	98,191,000	0.0%
44	Alaska	0	0.0%
44	Florida	0	0.0%
44	Nevada	0	0.0%
44	South Dakota	0	0.0%
44	Texas	0	0.0%
44	Washington	0	0.0%
44	Wyoming	0	0.0%

District of Columbia*   NA   NA

Source: U.S. Bureau of the Census, Governments Division
"2009 State Government Tax Collections" (http://www.census.gov/govs/statetax/)
*Not applicable.

Per Capita State Government Individual Income Tax Revenue in 2009

National Per Capita = $803

ALPHA ORDER

RANK	STATE	PER CAPITA
37	Alabama	$565
44	Alaska	0
41	Arizona	391
26	Arkansas	775
7	California	1,200
19	Colorado	876
2	Connecticut	1,813
13	Delaware	1,029
44	Florida	0
25	Georgia	794
12	Hawaii	1,034
28	Idaho	761
31	Illinois	711
33	Indiana	672
17	Iowa	899
15	Kansas	969
27	Kentucky	768
34	Louisiana	655
11	Maine	1,040
8	Maryland	1,137
3	Massachusetts	1,607
35	Michigan	587
5	Minnesota	1,319
39	Mississippi	503
24	Missouri	797
22	Montana	848
18	Nebraska	892
44	Nevada	0
42	New Hampshire	74
6	New Jersey	1,203
40	New Mexico	464
1	New York	1,885
14	North Carolina	1,019
36	North Dakota	572
30	Ohio	721
32	Oklahoma	690
4	Oregon	1,421
29	Pennsylvania	758
16	Rhode Island	912
38	South Carolina	516
44	South Dakota	0
43	Tennessee	35
44	Texas	0
23	Utah	833
20	Vermont	857
9	Virginia	1,131
44	Washington	0
21	West Virginia	856
10	Wisconsin	1,056
44	Wyoming	0

RANK ORDER

RANK	STATE	PER CAPITA
1	New York	$1,885
2	Connecticut	1,813
3	Massachusetts	1,607
4	Oregon	1,421
5	Minnesota	1,319
6	New Jersey	1,203
7	California	1,200
8	Maryland	1,137
9	Virginia	1,131
10	Wisconsin	1,056
11	Maine	1,040
12	Hawaii	1,034
13	Delaware	1,029
14	North Carolina	1,019
15	Kansas	969
16	Rhode Island	912
17	Iowa	899
18	Nebraska	892
19	Colorado	876
20	Vermont	857
21	West Virginia	856
22	Montana	848
23	Utah	833
24	Missouri	797
25	Georgia	794
26	Arkansas	775
27	Kentucky	768
28	Idaho	761
29	Pennsylvania	758
30	Ohio	721
31	Illinois	711
32	Oklahoma	690
33	Indiana	672
34	Louisiana	655
35	Michigan	587
36	North Dakota	572
37	Alabama	565
38	South Carolina	516
39	Mississippi	503
40	New Mexico	464
41	Arizona	391
42	New Hampshire	74
43	Tennessee	35
44	Alaska	0
44	Florida	0
44	Nevada	0
44	South Dakota	0
44	Texas	0
44	Washington	0
44	Wyoming	0
	District of Columbia*	NA

Source: CQ Press using data from U.S. Bureau of the Census, Governments Division
"2009 State Government Tax Collections" (http://www.census.gov/govs/statetax/)
*Not applicable.

State Government Corporation Net Income Tax Revenue in 2009

National Total = $40,477,747,000

ALPHA ORDER

RANK	STATE	REVENUE	% of USA
21	Alabama	$493,972,000	1.2%
17	Alaska	632,123,000	1.6%
19	Arizona	592,187,000	1.5%
27	Arkansas	346,215,000	0.9%
1	California	9,535,679,000	23.6%
29	Colorado	329,545,000	0.8%
23	Connecticut	444,061,000	1.1%
36	Delaware	208,677,000	0.5%
5	Florida	1,836,800,000	4.5%
14	Georgia	694,717,000	1.7%
45	Hawaii	78,597,000	0.2%
41	Idaho	142,240,000	0.4%
3	Illinois	2,752,353,000	6.8%
9	Indiana	838,974,000	2.1%
32	Iowa	264,365,000	0.7%
26	Kansas	370,889,000	0.9%
25	Kentucky	389,634,000	1.0%
18	Louisiana	612,545,000	1.5%
40	Maine	143,086,000	0.4%
12	Maryland	749,001,000	1.9%
6	Massachusetts	1,789,553,000	4.4%
13	Michigan	703,250,000	1.7%
11	Minnesota	779,055,000	1.9%
30	Mississippi	324,301,000	0.8%
31	Missouri	278,661,000	0.7%
39	Montana	164,255,000	0.4%
38	Nebraska	198,442,000	0.5%
47	Nevada	0	0.0%
22	New Hampshire	493,431,000	1.2%
4	New Jersey	2,528,913,000	6.2%
37	New Mexico	203,584,000	0.5%
2	New York	4,427,675,000	10.9%
8	North Carolina	901,445,000	2.2%
42	North Dakota	129,542,000	0.3%
20	Ohio	521,363,000	1.3%
28	Oklahoma	342,762,000	0.8%
33	Oregon	258,778,000	0.6%
7	Pennsylvania	1,740,532,000	4.3%
43	Rhode Island	108,497,000	0.3%
35	South Carolina	219,484,000	0.5%
46	South Dakota	48,772,000	0.1%
10	Tennessee	816,261,000	2.0%
47	Texas	0	0.0%
34	Utah	245,880,000	0.6%
44	Vermont	86,759,000	0.2%
16	Virginia	633,490,000	1.6%
47	Washington	0	0.0%
24	West Virginia	420,530,000	1.0%
15	Wisconsin	656,872,000	1.6%
47	Wyoming	0	0.0%

RANK ORDER

RANK	STATE	REVENUE	% of USA
1	California	$9,535,679,000	23.6%
2	New York	4,427,675,000	10.9%
3	Illinois	2,752,353,000	6.8%
4	New Jersey	2,528,913,000	6.2%
5	Florida	1,836,800,000	4.5%
6	Massachusetts	1,789,553,000	4.4%
7	Pennsylvania	1,740,532,000	4.3%
8	North Carolina	901,445,000	2.2%
9	Indiana	838,974,000	2.1%
10	Tennessee	816,261,000	2.0%
11	Minnesota	779,055,000	1.9%
12	Maryland	749,001,000	1.9%
13	Michigan	703,250,000	1.7%
14	Georgia	694,717,000	1.7%
15	Wisconsin	656,872,000	1.6%
16	Virginia	633,490,000	1.6%
17	Alaska	632,123,000	1.6%
18	Louisiana	612,545,000	1.5%
19	Arizona	592,187,000	1.5%
20	Ohio	521,363,000	1.3%
21	Alabama	493,972,000	1.2%
22	New Hampshire	493,431,000	1.2%
23	Connecticut	444,061,000	1.1%
24	West Virginia	420,530,000	1.0%
25	Kentucky	389,634,000	1.0%
26	Kansas	370,889,000	0.9%
27	Arkansas	346,215,000	0.9%
28	Oklahoma	342,762,000	0.8%
29	Colorado	329,545,000	0.8%
30	Mississippi	324,301,000	0.8%
31	Missouri	278,661,000	0.7%
32	Iowa	264,365,000	0.7%
33	Oregon	258,778,000	0.6%
34	Utah	245,880,000	0.6%
35	South Carolina	219,484,000	0.5%
36	Delaware	208,677,000	0.5%
37	New Mexico	203,584,000	0.5%
38	Nebraska	198,442,000	0.5%
39	Montana	164,255,000	0.4%
40	Maine	143,086,000	0.4%
41	Idaho	142,240,000	0.4%
42	North Dakota	129,542,000	0.3%
43	Rhode Island	108,497,000	0.3%
44	Vermont	86,759,000	0.2%
45	Hawaii	78,597,000	0.2%
46	South Dakota	48,772,000	0.1%
47	Nevada	0	0.0%
47	Texas	0	0.0%
47	Washington	0	0.0%
47	Wyoming	0	0.0%
	District of Columbia*	NA	NA

Source: U.S. Bureau of the Census, Governments Division
"2009 State Government Tax Collections" (http://www.census.gov/govs/statetax/)
*Not applicable.

Per Capita State Government Corporation Net Income Tax Revenue in 2009

National Per Capita = $132

RANK	STATE	PER CAPITA
26	Alabama	$105
1	Alaska	905
33	Arizona	90
21	Arkansas	120
5	California	258
41	Colorado	66
20	Connecticut	126
6	Delaware	236
29	Florida	99
38	Georgia	71
42	Hawaii	61
32	Idaho	92
9	Illinois	213
17	Indiana	131
35	Iowa	88
16	Kansas	132
33	Kentucky	90
15	Louisiana	136
25	Maine	109
17	Maryland	131
4	Massachusetts	271
38	Michigan	71
12	Minnesota	148
23	Mississippi	110
45	Missouri	47
11	Montana	168
23	Nebraska	110
47	Nevada	0
2	New Hampshire	373
3	New Jersey	290
28	New Mexico	101
8	New York	227
30	North Carolina	96
10	North Dakota	200
46	Ohio	45
31	Oklahoma	93
40	Oregon	68
14	Pennsylvania	138
27	Rhode Island	103
44	South Carolina	48
43	South Dakota	60
19	Tennessee	130
47	Texas	0
35	Utah	88
13	Vermont	140
37	Virginia	80
47	Washington	0
7	West Virginia	231
22	Wisconsin	116
47	Wyoming	0

RANK	STATE	PER CAPITA
1	Alaska	$905
2	New Hampshire	373
3	New Jersey	290
4	Massachusetts	271
5	California	258
6	Delaware	236
7	West Virginia	231
8	New York	227
9	Illinois	213
10	North Dakota	200
11	Montana	168
12	Minnesota	148
13	Vermont	140
14	Pennsylvania	138
15	Louisiana	136
16	Kansas	132
17	Indiana	131
17	Maryland	131
19	Tennessee	130
20	Connecticut	126
21	Arkansas	120
22	Wisconsin	116
23	Mississippi	110
23	Nebraska	110
25	Maine	109
26	Alabama	105
27	Rhode Island	103
28	New Mexico	101
29	Florida	99
30	North Carolina	96
31	Oklahoma	93
32	Idaho	92
33	Arizona	90
33	Kentucky	90
35	Iowa	88
35	Utah	88
37	Virginia	80
38	Georgia	71
38	Michigan	71
40	Oregon	68
41	Colorado	66
42	Hawaii	61
43	South Dakota	60
44	South Carolina	48
45	Missouri	47
46	Ohio	45
47	Nevada	0
47	Texas	0
47	Washington	0
47	Wyoming	0

District of Columbia*   NA

Source: CQ Press using data from U.S. Bureau of the Census, Governments Division
    "2009 State Government Tax Collections" (http://www.census.gov/govs/statetax/)
*Not applicable.

State Government General Sales Tax Revenue in 2009

National Total = $227,702,510,000*

ALPHA ORDER

RANK	STATE	REVENUE	% of USA
34	Alabama	$2,069,535,000	0.9%
46	Alaska	0	0.0%
13	Arizona	5,675,531,000	2.5%
27	Arkansas	2,765,996,000	1.2%
1	California	28,972,302,000	12.7%
33	Colorado	2,123,671,000	0.9%
21	Connecticut	3,290,050,000	1.4%
46	Delaware	0	0.0%
3	Florida	19,228,000,000	8.4%
14	Georgia	5,306,491,000	2.3%
29	Hawaii	2,461,618,000	1.1%
38	Idaho	1,206,137,000	0.5%
9	Illinois	7,470,532,000	3.3%
12	Indiana	6,205,638,000	2.7%
31	Iowa	2,201,396,000	1.0%
30	Kansas	2,227,183,000	1.0%
26	Kentucky	2,857,665,000	1.3%
24	Louisiana	2,963,758,000	1.3%
40	Maine	1,012,357,000	0.4%
19	Maryland	3,851,341,000	1.7%
18	Massachusetts	3,880,087,000	1.7%
6	Michigan	8,998,942,000	4.0%
16	Minnesota	4,375,200,000	1.9%
23	Mississippi	3,026,497,000	1.3%
22	Missouri	3,030,477,000	1.3%
46	Montana	0	0.0%
37	Nebraska	1,504,174,000	0.7%
28	Nevada	2,684,029,000	1.2%
46	New Hampshire	0	0.0%
8	New Jersey	8,264,162,000	3.6%
35	New Mexico	1,887,343,000	0.8%
4	New York	11,073,898,000	4.9%
15	North Carolina	4,963,434,000	2.2%
44	North Dakota	607,171,000	0.3%
10	Ohio	7,328,388,000	3.2%
32	Oklahoma	2,162,693,000	0.9%
46	Oregon	0	0.0%
7	Pennsylvania	8,496,182,000	3.7%
42	Rhode Island	814,511,000	0.4%
25	South Carolina	2,910,183,000	1.3%
43	South Dakota	756,598,000	0.3%
11	Tennessee	6,356,962,000	2.8%
2	Texas	21,034,946,000	9.2%
36	Utah	1,744,035,000	0.8%
45	Vermont	321,162,000	0.1%
20	Virginia	3,372,974,000	1.5%
5	Washington	10,035,359,000	4.4%
39	West Virginia	1,110,017,000	0.5%
17	Wisconsin	4,084,147,000	1.8%
41	Wyoming	989,738,000	0.4%

RANK ORDER

RANK	STATE	REVENUE	% of USA
1	California	$28,972,302,000	12.7%
2	Texas	21,034,946,000	9.2%
3	Florida	19,228,000,000	8.4%
4	New York	11,073,898,000	4.9%
5	Washington	10,035,359,000	4.4%
6	Michigan	8,998,942,000	4.0%
7	Pennsylvania	8,496,182,000	3.7%
8	New Jersey	8,264,162,000	3.6%
9	Illinois	7,470,532,000	3.3%
10	Ohio	7,328,388,000	3.2%
11	Tennessee	6,356,962,000	2.8%
12	Indiana	6,205,638,000	2.7%
13	Arizona	5,675,531,000	2.5%
14	Georgia	5,306,491,000	2.3%
15	North Carolina	4,963,434,000	2.2%
16	Minnesota	4,375,200,000	1.9%
17	Wisconsin	4,084,147,000	1.8%
18	Massachusetts	3,880,087,000	1.7%
19	Maryland	3,851,341,000	1.7%
20	Virginia	3,372,974,000	1.5%
21	Connecticut	3,290,050,000	1.4%
22	Missouri	3,030,477,000	1.3%
23	Mississippi	3,026,497,000	1.3%
24	Louisiana	2,963,758,000	1.3%
25	South Carolina	2,910,183,000	1.3%
26	Kentucky	2,857,665,000	1.3%
27	Arkansas	2,765,996,000	1.2%
28	Nevada	2,684,029,000	1.2%
29	Hawaii	2,461,618,000	1.1%
30	Kansas	2,227,183,000	1.0%
31	Iowa	2,201,396,000	1.0%
32	Oklahoma	2,162,693,000	0.9%
33	Colorado	2,123,671,000	0.9%
34	Alabama	2,069,535,000	0.9%
35	New Mexico	1,887,343,000	0.8%
36	Utah	1,744,035,000	0.8%
37	Nebraska	1,504,174,000	0.7%
38	Idaho	1,206,137,000	0.5%
39	West Virginia	1,110,017,000	0.5%
40	Maine	1,012,357,000	0.4%
41	Wyoming	989,738,000	0.4%
42	Rhode Island	814,511,000	0.4%
43	South Dakota	756,598,000	0.3%
44	North Dakota	607,171,000	0.3%
45	Vermont	321,162,000	0.1%
46	Alaska	0	0.0%
46	Delaware	0	0.0%
46	Montana	0	0.0%
46	New Hampshire	0	0.0%
46	Oregon	0	0.0%
	District of Columbia**	NA	NA

Source: U.S. Bureau of the Census, Governments Division
"2009 State Government Tax Collections" (http://www.census.gov/govs/statetax/)
*Does not include special sales taxes such as those on sale of alcohol, gasoline, or tobacco.
**Not applicable.

Per Capita State Government General Sales Tax Revenue in 2009

National Per Capita = $743*

ALPHA ORDER

RANK	STATE	PER CAPITA
43	Alabama	$440
46	Alaska	0
16	Arizona	860
9	Arkansas	957
21	California	784
45	Colorado	423
13	Connecticut	935
46	Delaware	0
4	Florida	1,037
39	Georgia	540
1	Hawaii	1,901
22	Idaho	780
37	Illinois	579
8	Indiana	966
25	Iowa	732
20	Kansas	790
29	Kentucky	662
30	Louisiana	660
24	Maine	768
27	Maryland	676
35	Massachusetts	588
15	Michigan	903
19	Minnesota	831
5	Mississippi	1,025
42	Missouri	506
46	Montana	0
18	Nebraska	837
6	Nevada	1,015
46	New Hampshire	0
10	New Jersey	949
11	New Mexico	939
38	New York	567
40	North Carolina	529
11	North Dakota	939
32	Ohio	635
36	Oklahoma	587
46	Oregon	0
28	Pennsylvania	674
23	Rhode Island	773
31	South Carolina	638
14	South Dakota	931
7	Tennessee	1,010
17	Texas	849
33	Utah	626
41	Vermont	517
44	Virginia	428
3	Washington	1,506
34	West Virginia	610
26	Wisconsin	722
2	Wyoming	1,818

RANK ORDER

RANK	STATE	PER CAPITA
1	Hawaii	$1,901
2	Wyoming	1,818
3	Washington	1,506
4	Florida	1,037
5	Mississippi	1,025
6	Nevada	1,015
7	Tennessee	1,010
8	Indiana	966
9	Arkansas	957
10	New Jersey	949
11	New Mexico	939
11	North Dakota	939
13	Connecticut	935
14	South Dakota	931
15	Michigan	903
16	Arizona	860
17	Texas	849
18	Nebraska	837
19	Minnesota	831
20	Kansas	790
21	California	784
22	Idaho	780
23	Rhode Island	773
24	Maine	768
25	Iowa	732
26	Wisconsin	722
27	Maryland	676
28	Pennsylvania	674
29	Kentucky	662
30	Louisiana	660
31	South Carolina	638
32	Ohio	635
33	Utah	626
34	West Virginia	610
35	Massachusetts	588
36	Oklahoma	587
37	Illinois	579
38	New York	567
39	Georgia	540
40	North Carolina	529
41	Vermont	517
42	Missouri	506
43	Alabama	440
44	Virginia	428
45	Colorado	423
46	Alaska	0
46	Delaware	0
46	Montana	0
46	New Hampshire	0
46	Oregon	0
	District of Columbia**	NA

Source: CQ Press using data from U.S. Bureau of the Census, Governments Division
   "2009 State Government Tax Collections" (http://www.census.gov/govs/statetax/)
*Does not include special sales taxes such as those on sale of alcohol, gasoline, or tobacco.
**Not applicable.

State Government Motor Fuels Sales Tax Revenue in 2009

National Total = $35,368,850,000

ALPHA ORDER

RANK	STATE	REVENUE	% of USA
23	Alabama	$546,467,000	1.5%
50	Alaska	10,064,000	0.0%
14	Arizona	813,794,000	2.3%
28	Arkansas	462,221,000	1.3%
1	California	3,180,128,000	9.0%
21	Colorado	616,589,000	1.7%
27	Connecticut	490,804,000	1.4%
46	Delaware	114,579,000	0.3%
3	Florida	2,229,827,000	6.3%
12	Georgia	861,153,000	2.4%
47	Hawaii	91,712,000	0.3%
39	Idaho	218,180,000	0.6%
7	Illinois	1,467,402,000	4.1%
15	Indiana	798,739,000	2.3%
29	Iowa	434,243,000	1.2%
31	Kansas	422,865,000	1.2%
20	Kentucky	632,655,000	1.8%
22	Louisiana	600,786,000	1.7%
38	Maine	220,772,000	0.6%
17	Maryland	734,836,000	2.1%
19	Massachusetts	654,022,000	1.8%
10	Michigan	969,959,000	2.7%
16	Minnesota	750,308,000	2.1%
30	Mississippi	425,020,000	1.2%
18	Missouri	707,331,000	2.0%
40	Montana	191,188,000	0.5%
37	Nebraska	292,857,000	0.8%
36	Nevada	298,135,000	0.8%
43	New Hampshire	132,122,000	0.4%
24	New Jersey	538,166,000	1.5%
41	New Mexico	188,943,000	0.5%
26	New York	506,741,000	1.4%
6	North Carolina	1,515,944,000	4.3%
42	North Dakota	143,796,000	0.4%
5	Ohio	1,726,742,000	4.9%
32	Oklahoma	420,109,000	1.2%
33	Oregon	397,609,000	1.1%
4	Pennsylvania	2,025,778,000	5.7%
44	Rhode Island	122,833,000	0.3%
25	South Carolina	514,667,000	1.5%
45	South Dakota	117,489,000	0.3%
13	Tennessee	815,611,000	2.3%
2	Texas	3,036,068,000	8.6%
35	Utah	350,469,000	1.0%
48	Vermont	84,044,000	0.2%
11	Virginia	891,401,000	2.5%
8	Washington	1,181,837,000	3.3%
34	West Virginia	384,538,000	1.1%
9	Wisconsin	970,173,000	2.7%
49	Wyoming	67,134,000	0.2%

RANK ORDER

RANK	STATE	REVENUE	% of USA
1	California	$3,180,128,000	9.0%
2	Texas	3,036,068,000	8.6%
3	Florida	2,229,827,000	6.3%
4	Pennsylvania	2,025,778,000	5.7%
5	Ohio	1,726,742,000	4.9%
6	North Carolina	1,515,944,000	4.3%
7	Illinois	1,467,402,000	4.1%
8	Washington	1,181,837,000	3.3%
9	Wisconsin	970,173,000	2.7%
10	Michigan	969,959,000	2.7%
11	Virginia	891,401,000	2.5%
12	Georgia	861,153,000	2.4%
13	Tennessee	815,611,000	2.3%
14	Arizona	813,794,000	2.3%
15	Indiana	798,739,000	2.3%
16	Minnesota	750,308,000	2.1%
17	Maryland	734,836,000	2.1%
18	Missouri	707,331,000	2.0%
19	Massachusetts	654,022,000	1.8%
20	Kentucky	632,655,000	1.8%
21	Colorado	616,589,000	1.7%
22	Louisiana	600,786,000	1.7%
23	Alabama	546,467,000	1.5%
24	New Jersey	538,166,000	1.5%
25	South Carolina	514,667,000	1.5%
26	New York	506,741,000	1.4%
27	Connecticut	490,804,000	1.4%
28	Arkansas	462,221,000	1.3%
29	Iowa	434,243,000	1.2%
30	Mississippi	425,020,000	1.2%
31	Kansas	422,865,000	1.2%
32	Oklahoma	420,109,000	1.2%
33	Oregon	397,609,000	1.1%
34	West Virginia	384,538,000	1.1%
35	Utah	350,469,000	1.0%
36	Nevada	298,135,000	0.8%
37	Nebraska	292,857,000	0.8%
38	Maine	220,772,000	0.6%
39	Idaho	218,180,000	0.6%
40	Montana	191,188,000	0.5%
41	New Mexico	188,943,000	0.5%
42	North Dakota	143,796,000	0.4%
43	New Hampshire	132,122,000	0.4%
44	Rhode Island	122,833,000	0.3%
45	South Dakota	117,489,000	0.3%
46	Delaware	114,579,000	0.3%
47	Hawaii	91,712,000	0.3%
48	Vermont	84,044,000	0.2%
49	Wyoming	67,134,000	0.2%
50	Alaska	10,064,000	0.0%
	District of Columbia*	NA	NA

Source: U.S. Bureau of the Census, Governments Division
"2009 State Government Tax Collections" (http://www.census.gov/govs/statetax/)
*Not applicable.

Per Capita State Government Motor Fuel Sales Tax Revenue in 2009

National Per Capita = $115

ALPHA ORDER				RANK ORDER		
RANK	STATE	PER CAPITA		RANK	STATE	PER CAPITA
34	Alabama	$116		1	North Dakota	$222
50	Alaska	14		2	West Virginia	211
27	Arizona	123		3	Montana	196
10	Arkansas	160		4	Washington	177
46	California	86		5	Wisconsin	172
27	Colorado	123		6	Maine	167
19	Connecticut	140		7	Nebraska	163
23	Delaware	129		8	North Carolina	162
31	Florida	120		9	Pennsylvania	161
45	Georgia	88		10	Arkansas	160
47	Hawaii	71		11	Kansas	150
18	Idaho	141		11	Ohio	150
35	Illinois	114		13	Kentucky	147
26	Indiana	124		14	South Dakota	145
15	Iowa	144		15	Iowa	144
11	Kansas	150		15	Mississippi	144
13	Kentucky	147		17	Minnesota	142
21	Louisiana	134		18	Idaho	141
6	Maine	167		19	Connecticut	140
23	Maryland	129		20	Vermont	135
42	Massachusetts	99		21	Louisiana	134
43	Michigan	97		22	Tennessee	130
17	Minnesota	142		23	Delaware	129
15	Mississippi	144		23	Maryland	129
32	Missouri	118		25	Utah	126
3	Montana	196		26	Indiana	124
7	Nebraska	163		27	Arizona	123
37	Nevada	113		27	Colorado	123
41	New Hampshire	100		27	Texas	123
48	New Jersey	62		27	Wyoming	123
44	New Mexico	94		31	Florida	120
49	New York	26		32	Missouri	118
8	North Carolina	162		33	Rhode Island	117
1	North Dakota	222		34	Alabama	116
11	Ohio	150		35	Illinois	114
35	Oklahoma	114		35	Oklahoma	114
40	Oregon	104		37	Nevada	113
9	Pennsylvania	161		37	South Carolina	113
33	Rhode Island	117		37	Virginia	113
37	South Carolina	113		40	Oregon	104
14	South Dakota	145		41	New Hampshire	100
22	Tennessee	130		42	Massachusetts	99
27	Texas	123		43	Michigan	97
25	Utah	126		44	New Mexico	94
20	Vermont	135		45	Georgia	88
37	Virginia	113		46	California	86
4	Washington	177		47	Hawaii	71
2	West Virginia	211		48	New Jersey	62
5	Wisconsin	172		49	New York	26
27	Wyoming	123		50	Alaska	14
				District of Columbia*		NA

Source: CQ Press using data from U.S. Bureau of the Census, Governments Division
"2009 State Government Tax Collections" (http://www.census.gov/govs/statetax/)
*Not applicable.

State Tax Rates on Gasoline in 2010

National Median = 21.50 Cents per Gallon*

ALPHA ORDER

RANK	STATE	CENTS PER GALLON
37	Alabama	18.00
50	Alaska	8.00
37	Arizona	18.00
26	Arkansas	21.50
37	California	18.00
24	Colorado	22.00
13	Connecticut	25.00
22	Delaware	23.00
46	Florida	16.00
45	Georgia	16.80
43	Hawaii	17.00
12	Idaho	26.00
30	Illinois	20.10
37	Indiana	18.00
28	Iowa	21.00
19	Kansas	24.00
17	Kentucky	24.10
31	Louisiana	20.00
7	Maine	29.50
21	Maryland	23.50
28	Massachusetts	21.00
34	Michigan	19.00
10	Minnesota	27.10
36	Mississippi	18.40
41	Missouri	17.55
11	Montana	27.00
9	Nebraska	27.70
18	Nevada	24.06
33	New Hampshire	19.63
48	New Jersey	14.50
35	New Mexico	18.88
16	New York	24.40
6	North Carolina	30.55
22	North Dakota	23.00
8	Ohio	28.00
43	Oklahoma	17.00
19	Oregon	24.00
4	Pennsylvania	31.20
5	Rhode Island	31.00
46	South Carolina	16.00
24	South Dakota	22.00
27	Tennessee	21.40
31	Texas	20.00
14	Utah	24.50
14	Vermont	24.50
42	Virginia	17.50
1	Washington	37.50
3	West Virginia	32.20
2	Wisconsin	32.90
49	Wyoming	14.00

RANK ORDER

RANK	STATE	CENTS PER GALLON
1	Washington	37.50
2	Wisconsin	32.90
3	West Virginia	32.20
4	Pennsylvania	31.20
5	Rhode Island	31.00
6	North Carolina	30.55
7	Maine	29.50
8	Ohio	28.00
9	Nebraska	27.70
10	Minnesota	27.10
11	Montana	27.00
12	Idaho	26.00
13	Connecticut	25.00
14	Utah	24.50
14	Vermont	24.50
16	New York	24.40
17	Kentucky	24.10
18	Nevada	24.06
19	Kansas	24.00
19	Oregon	24.00
21	Maryland	23.50
22	Delaware	23.00
22	North Dakota	23.00
24	Colorado	22.00
24	South Dakota	22.00
26	Arkansas	21.50
27	Tennessee	21.40
28	Iowa	21.00
28	Massachusetts	21.00
30	Illinois	20.10
31	Louisiana	20.00
31	Texas	20.00
33	New Hampshire	19.63
34	Michigan	19.00
35	New Mexico	18.88
36	Mississippi	18.40
37	Alabama	18.00
37	Arizona	18.00
37	California	18.00
37	Indiana	18.00
41	Missouri	17.55
42	Virginia	17.50
43	Hawaii	17.00
43	Oklahoma	17.00
45	Georgia	16.80
46	Florida	16.00
46	South Carolina	16.00
48	New Jersey	14.50
49	Wyoming	14.00
50	Alaska	8.00
	District of Columbia	20.00

Source: Federation of Tax Administrators
    "Motor Fuel Excise Tax Rates" (http://www.taxadmin.org/fta/rate/tax_stru.html)
*As of January 1, 2010. Federal gasoline tax rate is an additional 18.4 cents per gallon. Many states also allow additional local option taxes on gasoline.

State Government Motor Vehicle and Operators' License Tax Revenue in 2009

National Total = $22,170,081,000

ALPHA ORDER

RANK	STATE	REVENUE	% of USA
29	Alabama	$211,084,000	1.0%
47	Alaska	55,267,000	0.2%
28	Arizona	220,583,000	1.0%
33	Arkansas	158,306,000	0.7%
1	California	3,237,473,000	14.6%
26	Colorado	225,490,000	1.0%
25	Connecticut	234,175,000	1.1%
49	Delaware	52,598,000	0.2%
4	Florida	1,300,541,000	5.9%
21	Georgia	347,568,000	1.6%
40	Hawaii	100,704,000	0.5%
37	Idaho	130,004,000	0.6%
3	Illinois	1,545,018,000	7.0%
18	Indiana	411,609,000	1.9%
17	Iowa	444,666,000	2.0%
31	Kansas	187,125,000	0.8%
27	Kentucky	222,882,000	1.0%
42	Louisiana	89,139,000	0.4%
39	Maine	101,871,000	0.5%
15	Maryland	468,800,000	2.1%
20	Massachusetts	387,316,000	1.7%
6	Michigan	933,428,000	4.2%
11	Minnesota	574,009,000	2.6%
34	Mississippi	158,007,000	0.7%
23	Missouri	285,713,000	1.3%
36	Montana	146,440,000	0.7%
43	Nebraska	84,543,000	0.4%
32	Nevada	179,671,000	0.8%
38	New Hampshire	111,831,000	0.5%
12	New Jersey	548,451,000	2.5%
35	New Mexico	149,836,000	0.7%
5	New York	1,090,094,000	4.9%
9	North Carolina	703,345,000	3.2%
45	North Dakota	82,715,000	0.4%
8	Ohio	886,510,000	4.0%
10	Oklahoma	597,940,000	2.7%
16	Oregon	466,877,000	2.1%
7	Pennsylvania	886,539,000	4.0%
48	Rhode Island	52,975,000	0.2%
30	South Carolina	199,276,000	0.9%
50	South Dakota	50,717,000	0.2%
22	Tennessee	292,515,000	1.3%
2	Texas	1,603,504,000	7.2%
24	Utah	271,164,000	1.2%
46	Vermont	68,879,000	0.3%
19	Virginia	408,831,000	1.8%
13	Washington	519,231,000	2.3%
41	West Virginia	93,809,000	0.4%
14	Wisconsin	507,729,000	2.3%
44	Wyoming	83,283,000	0.4%

RANK ORDER

RANK	STATE	REVENUE	% of USA
1	California	$3,237,473,000	14.6%
2	Texas	1,603,504,000	7.2%
3	Illinois	1,545,018,000	7.0%
4	Florida	1,300,541,000	5.9%
5	New York	1,090,094,000	4.9%
6	Michigan	933,428,000	4.2%
7	Pennsylvania	886,539,000	4.0%
8	Ohio	886,510,000	4.0%
9	North Carolina	703,345,000	3.2%
10	Oklahoma	597,940,000	2.7%
11	Minnesota	574,009,000	2.6%
12	New Jersey	548,451,000	2.5%
13	Washington	519,231,000	2.3%
14	Wisconsin	507,729,000	2.3%
15	Maryland	468,800,000	2.1%
16	Oregon	466,877,000	2.1%
17	Iowa	444,666,000	2.0%
18	Indiana	411,609,000	1.9%
19	Virginia	408,831,000	1.8%
20	Massachusetts	387,316,000	1.7%
21	Georgia	347,568,000	1.6%
22	Tennessee	292,515,000	1.3%
23	Missouri	285,713,000	1.3%
24	Utah	271,164,000	1.2%
25	Connecticut	234,175,000	1.1%
26	Colorado	225,490,000	1.0%
27	Kentucky	222,882,000	1.0%
28	Arizona	220,583,000	1.0%
29	Alabama	211,084,000	1.0%
30	South Carolina	199,276,000	0.9%
31	Kansas	187,125,000	0.8%
32	Nevada	179,671,000	0.8%
33	Arkansas	158,306,000	0.7%
34	Mississippi	158,007,000	0.7%
35	New Mexico	149,836,000	0.7%
36	Montana	146,440,000	0.7%
37	Idaho	130,004,000	0.6%
38	New Hampshire	111,831,000	0.5%
39	Maine	101,871,000	0.5%
40	Hawaii	100,704,000	0.5%
41	West Virginia	93,809,000	0.4%
42	Louisiana	89,139,000	0.4%
43	Nebraska	84,543,000	0.4%
44	Wyoming	83,283,000	0.4%
45	North Dakota	82,715,000	0.4%
46	Vermont	68,879,000	0.3%
47	Alaska	55,267,000	0.2%
48	Rhode Island	52,975,000	0.2%
49	Delaware	52,598,000	0.2%
50	South Dakota	50,717,000	0.2%

District of Columbia*   NA   NA

Source: U.S. Bureau of the Census, Governments Division
"2009 State Government Tax Collections" (http://www.census.gov/govs/statetax/)
*Not applicable.

Per Capita State Government Motor Vehicle and Operators' License Tax Revenue in 2009
National Per Capita = $72.36

ALPHA ORDER

RANK	STATE	PER CAPITA
46	Alabama	$44.83
17	Alaska	79.13
49	Arizona	33.44
36	Arkansas	54.79
13	California	87.59
45	Colorado	44.88
27	Connecticut	66.56
33	Delaware	59.42
25	Florida	70.16
48	Georgia	35.36
19	Hawaii	77.75
15	Idaho	84.10
7	Illinois	119.67
30	Indiana	64.08
4	Iowa	147.83
28	Kansas	66.39
39	Kentucky	51.66
50	Louisiana	19.84
20	Maine	77.27
16	Maryland	82.25
34	Massachusetts	58.74
11	Michigan	93.63
9	Minnesota	109.00
37	Mississippi	53.53
42	Missouri	47.72
3	Montana	150.20
43	Nebraska	47.06
26	Nevada	67.98
14	New Hampshire	84.43
31	New Jersey	62.98
23	New Mexico	74.56
35	New York	55.78
22	North Carolina	74.98
5	North Dakota	127.87
21	Ohio	76.80
1	Oklahoma	162.17
6	Oregon	122.04
24	Pennsylvania	70.33
41	Rhode Island	50.30
47	South Carolina	43.69
32	South Dakota	62.43
44	Tennessee	46.46
29	Texas	64.70
10	Utah	97.38
8	Vermont	110.78
38	Virginia	51.87
18	Washington	77.91
40	West Virginia	51.55
12	Wisconsin	89.79
2	Wyoming	153.02

RANK ORDER

RANK	STATE	PER CAPITA
1	Oklahoma	$162.17
2	Wyoming	153.02
3	Montana	150.20
4	Iowa	147.83
5	North Dakota	127.87
6	Oregon	122.04
7	Illinois	119.67
8	Vermont	110.78
9	Minnesota	109.00
10	Utah	97.38
11	Michigan	93.63
12	Wisconsin	89.79
13	California	87.59
14	New Hampshire	84.43
15	Idaho	84.10
16	Maryland	82.25
17	Alaska	79.13
18	Washington	77.91
19	Hawaii	77.75
20	Maine	77.27
21	Ohio	76.80
22	North Carolina	74.98
23	New Mexico	74.56
24	Pennsylvania	70.33
25	Florida	70.16
26	Nevada	67.98
27	Connecticut	66.56
28	Kansas	66.39
29	Texas	64.70
30	Indiana	64.08
31	New Jersey	62.98
32	South Dakota	62.43
33	Delaware	59.42
34	Massachusetts	58.74
35	New York	55.78
36	Arkansas	54.79
37	Mississippi	53.53
38	Virginia	51.87
39	Kentucky	51.66
40	West Virginia	51.55
41	Rhode Island	50.30
42	Missouri	47.72
43	Nebraska	47.06
44	Tennessee	46.46
45	Colorado	44.88
46	Alabama	44.83
47	South Carolina	43.69
48	Georgia	35.36
49	Arizona	33.44
50	Louisiana	19.84

District of Columbia*   NA

Source: CQ Press using data from U.S. Bureau of the Census, Governments Division
    "2009 State Government Tax Collections" (http://www.census.gov/govs/statetax/)
*Not applicable.

State Government Tobacco Product Sales Tax Revenue in 2009

National Total = $16,677,835,000

ALPHA ORDER

RANK	STATE	REVENUE	% of USA
31	Alabama	$141,176,000	0.8%
41	Alaska	73,079,000	0.4%
16	Arizona	373,882,000	2.2%
27	Arkansas	171,038,000	1.0%
4	California	1,000,456,000	6.0%
24	Colorado	217,165,000	1.3%
17	Connecticut	316,246,000	1.9%
33	Delaware	125,505,000	0.8%
12	Florida	447,061,000	2.7%
23	Georgia	229,673,000	1.4%
39	Hawaii	88,145,000	0.5%
46	Idaho	52,918,000	0.3%
10	Illinois	582,323,000	3.5%
11	Indiana	510,585,000	3.1%
22	Iowa	238,153,000	1.4%
36	Kansas	112,943,000	0.7%
25	Kentucky	214,597,000	1.3%
29	Louisiana	145,578,000	0.9%
30	Maine	144,425,000	0.9%
15	Maryland	405,558,000	2.4%
9	Massachusetts	587,331,000	3.5%
3	Michigan	1,043,532,000	6.3%
14	Minnesota	422,780,000	2.5%
40	Mississippi	83,589,000	0.5%
37	Missouri	107,864,000	0.6%
38	Montana	89,776,000	0.5%
42	Nebraska	70,438,000	0.4%
34	Nevada	119,566,000	0.7%
26	New Hampshire	195,034,000	1.2%
7	New Jersey	747,777,000	4.5%
47	New Mexico	48,270,000	0.3%
2	New York	1,337,665,000	8.0%
21	North Carolina	243,370,000	1.5%
50	North Dakota	24,114,000	0.1%
6	Ohio	924,764,000	5.5%
19	Oklahoma	257,812,000	1.5%
20	Oregon	248,205,000	1.5%
5	Pennsylvania	989,716,000	5.9%
32	Rhode Island	130,503,000	0.8%
48	South Carolina	30,573,000	0.2%
43	South Dakota	68,323,000	0.4%
18	Tennessee	301,219,000	1.8%
1	Texas	1,556,795,000	9.3%
45	Utah	59,821,000	0.4%
44	Vermont	63,796,000	0.4%
28	Virginia	167,579,000	1.0%
13	Washington	431,998,000	2.6%
35	West Virginia	115,095,000	0.7%
8	Wisconsin	593,575,000	3.6%
49	Wyoming	26,449,000	0.2%

RANK ORDER

RANK	STATE	REVENUE	% of USA
1	Texas	$1,556,795,000	9.3%
2	New York	1,337,665,000	8.0%
3	Michigan	1,043,532,000	6.3%
4	California	1,000,456,000	6.0%
5	Pennsylvania	989,716,000	5.9%
6	Ohio	924,764,000	5.5%
7	New Jersey	747,777,000	4.5%
8	Wisconsin	593,575,000	3.6%
9	Massachusetts	587,331,000	3.5%
10	Illinois	582,323,000	3.5%
11	Indiana	510,585,000	3.1%
12	Florida	447,061,000	2.7%
13	Washington	431,998,000	2.6%
14	Minnesota	422,780,000	2.5%
15	Maryland	405,558,000	2.4%
16	Arizona	373,882,000	2.2%
17	Connecticut	316,246,000	1.9%
18	Tennessee	301,219,000	1.8%
19	Oklahoma	257,812,000	1.5%
20	Oregon	248,205,000	1.5%
21	North Carolina	243,370,000	1.5%
22	Iowa	238,153,000	1.4%
23	Georgia	229,673,000	1.4%
24	Colorado	217,165,000	1.3%
25	Kentucky	214,597,000	1.3%
26	New Hampshire	195,034,000	1.2%
27	Arkansas	171,038,000	1.0%
28	Virginia	167,579,000	1.0%
29	Louisiana	145,578,000	0.9%
30	Maine	144,425,000	0.9%
31	Alabama	141,176,000	0.8%
32	Rhode Island	130,503,000	0.8%
33	Delaware	125,505,000	0.8%
34	Nevada	119,566,000	0.7%
35	West Virginia	115,095,000	0.7%
36	Kansas	112,943,000	0.7%
37	Missouri	107,864,000	0.6%
38	Montana	89,776,000	0.5%
39	Hawaii	88,145,000	0.5%
40	Mississippi	83,589,000	0.5%
41	Alaska	73,079,000	0.4%
42	Nebraska	70,438,000	0.4%
43	South Dakota	68,323,000	0.4%
44	Vermont	63,796,000	0.4%
45	Utah	59,821,000	0.4%
46	Idaho	52,918,000	0.3%
47	New Mexico	48,270,000	0.3%
48	South Carolina	30,573,000	0.2%
49	Wyoming	26,449,000	0.2%
50	North Dakota	24,114,000	0.1%
	District of Columbia*	NA	NA

Source: U.S. Bureau of the Census, Governments Division
   "2009 State Government Tax Collections" (http://www.census.gov/govs/statetax/)
*Not applicable.

Per Capita State Government Tobacco Sales Tax Revenue in 2009

National Per Capita = $54.43

ALPHA ORDER

RANK	STATE	PER CAPITA
40	Alabama	$29.98
7	Alaska	104.63
28	Arizona	56.69
27	Arkansas	59.19
42	California	27.07
34	Colorado	43.22
10	Connecticut	89.89
2	Delaware	141.79
44	Florida	24.12
46	Georgia	23.37
22	Hawaii	68.06
38	Idaho	34.23
33	Illinois	45.10
16	Indiana	79.49
17	Iowa	79.18
35	Kansas	40.07
29	Kentucky	49.74
39	Louisiana	32.41
4	Maine	109.55
19	Maryland	71.16
11	Massachusetts	89.08
6	Michigan	104.67
14	Minnesota	80.28
41	Mississippi	28.32
49	Missouri	18.01
9	Montana	92.08
36	Nebraska	39.21
32	Nevada	45.24
1	New Hampshire	147.24
12	New Jersey	85.87
45	New Mexico	24.02
21	New York	68.45
43	North Carolina	25.94
37	North Dakota	37.28
15	Ohio	80.12
20	Oklahoma	69.92
23	Oregon	64.88
18	Pennsylvania	78.52
3	Rhode Island	123.91
50	South Carolina	6.70
13	South Dakota	84.10
31	Tennessee	47.84
26	Texas	62.82
47	Utah	21.48
8	Vermont	102.61
48	Virginia	21.26
24	Washington	64.82
25	West Virginia	63.25
5	Wisconsin	104.97
30	Wyoming	48.60

RANK ORDER

RANK	STATE	PER CAPITA
1	New Hampshire	$147.24
2	Delaware	141.79
3	Rhode Island	123.91
4	Maine	109.55
5	Wisconsin	104.97
6	Michigan	104.67
7	Alaska	104.63
8	Vermont	102.61
9	Montana	92.08
10	Connecticut	89.89
11	Massachusetts	89.08
12	New Jersey	85.87
13	South Dakota	84.10
14	Minnesota	80.28
15	Ohio	80.12
16	Indiana	79.49
17	Iowa	79.18
18	Pennsylvania	78.52
19	Maryland	71.16
20	Oklahoma	69.92
21	New York	68.45
22	Hawaii	68.06
23	Oregon	64.88
24	Washington	64.82
25	West Virginia	63.25
26	Texas	62.82
27	Arkansas	59.19
28	Arizona	56.69
29	Kentucky	49.74
30	Wyoming	48.60
31	Tennessee	47.84
32	Nevada	45.24
33	Illinois	45.10
34	Colorado	43.22
35	Kansas	40.07
36	Nebraska	39.21
37	North Dakota	37.28
38	Idaho	34.23
39	Louisiana	32.41
40	Alabama	29.98
41	Mississippi	28.32
42	California	27.07
43	North Carolina	25.94
44	Florida	24.12
45	New Mexico	24.02
46	Georgia	23.37
47	Utah	21.48
48	Virginia	21.26
49	Missouri	18.01
50	South Carolina	6.70

District of Columbia*   NA

Source: CQ Press using data from U.S. Bureau of the Census, Governments Division
   "2009 State Government Tax Collections" (http://www.census.gov/govs/statetax/)
*Not applicable.

State Tax on a Pack of Cigarettes in 2010

National Median = $1.34 per Pack*

ALPHA ORDER

RANK	STATE	TAX PER PACK
46	Alabama	$0.43
10	Alaska	2.00
10	Arizona	2.00
28	Arkansas	1.15
32	California	0.87
33	Colorado	0.84
4	Connecticut	3.00
19	Delaware	1.60
25	Florida	1.34
47	Georgia	0.37
4	Hawaii	3.00
41	Idaho	0.57
31	Illinois	0.98
30	Indiana	1.00
24	Iowa	1.36
35	Kansas	0.79
39	Kentucky	0.60
48	Louisiana	0.36
10	Maine	2.00
10	Maryland	2.00
8	Massachusetts	2.51
10	Michigan	2.00
21	Minnesota	1.56
36	Mississippi	0.68
50	Missouri	0.17
16	Montana	1.70
37	Nebraska	0.64
34	Nevada	0.80
15	New Hampshire	1.78
6	New Jersey	2.70
18	New Mexico	1.66
1	New York	4.35
44	North Carolina	0.45
45	North Dakota	0.44
26	Ohio	1.25
29	Oklahoma	1.03
27	Oregon	1.18
19	Pennsylvania	1.60
2	Rhode Island	3.46
41	South Carolina	0.57
22	South Dakota	1.53
38	Tennessee	0.62
23	Texas	1.41
16	Utah	1.70
9	Vermont	2.24
49	Virginia	0.30
3	Washington	3.03
43	West Virginia	0.55
7	Wisconsin	2.52
39	Wyoming	0.60

RANK ORDER

RANK	STATE	TAX PER PACK
1	New York	$4.35
2	Rhode Island	3.46
3	Washington	3.03
4	Connecticut	3.00
4	Hawaii	3.00
6	New Jersey	2.70
7	Wisconsin	2.52
8	Massachusetts	2.51
9	Vermont	2.24
10	Alaska	2.00
10	Arizona	2.00
10	Maine	2.00
10	Maryland	2.00
10	Michigan	2.00
15	New Hampshire	1.78
16	Montana	1.70
16	Utah	1.70
18	New Mexico	1.66
19	Delaware	1.60
19	Pennsylvania	1.60
21	Minnesota	1.56
22	South Dakota	1.53
23	Texas	1.41
24	Iowa	1.36
25	Florida	1.34
26	Ohio	1.25
27	Oregon	1.18
28	Arkansas	1.15
29	Oklahoma	1.03
30	Indiana	1.00
31	Illinois	0.98
32	California	0.87
33	Colorado	0.84
34	Nevada	0.80
35	Kansas	0.79
36	Mississippi	0.68
37	Nebraska	0.64
38	Tennessee	0.62
39	Kentucky	0.60
39	Wyoming	0.60
41	Idaho	0.57
41	South Carolina	0.57
43	West Virginia	0.55
44	North Carolina	0.45
45	North Dakota	0.44
46	Alabama	0.43
47	Georgia	0.37
48	Louisiana	0.36
49	Virginia	0.30
50	Missouri	0.17

	District of Columbia	2.50

Source: National Conference of State Legislatures (Denver, CO)
    "State Cigarette Excise Taxes: 2010" (http://www.ncsl.org/default.aspx?tabid=14349)
*As of July 1, 2010. Many states also allow additional local option taxes on cigarettes.

State Government Alcoholic Beverage Sales Tax Revenue in 2009

National Total = $5,348,822,000

ALPHA ORDER

RANK	STATE	REVENUE	% of USA
9	Alabama	$167,830,000	3.1%
31	Alaska	39,626,000	0.7%
22	Arizona	62,799,000	1.2%
27	Arkansas	45,623,000	0.9%
3	California	323,934,000	6.1%
34	Colorado	35,972,000	0.7%
26	Connecticut	47,064,000	0.9%
42	Delaware	15,519,000	0.3%
2	Florida	590,400,000	11.0%
10	Georgia	166,618,000	3.1%
25	Hawaii	47,242,000	0.9%
48	Idaho	8,122,000	0.2%
11	Illinois	157,622,000	2.9%
28	Indiana	43,498,000	0.8%
43	Iowa	14,704,000	0.3%
16	Kansas	111,589,000	2.1%
15	Kentucky	111,596,000	2.1%
23	Louisiana	56,881,000	1.1%
40	Maine	17,438,000	0.3%
36	Maryland	29,168,000	0.5%
21	Massachusetts	72,598,000	1.4%
13	Michigan	140,488,000	2.6%
20	Minnesota	75,225,000	1.4%
29	Mississippi	42,464,000	0.8%
35	Missouri	31,990,000	0.6%
37	Montana	28,095,000	0.5%
38	Nebraska	26,925,000	0.5%
33	Nevada	37,867,000	0.7%
45	New Hampshire	12,451,000	0.2%
17	New Jersey	105,488,000	2.0%
32	New Mexico	39,251,000	0.7%
7	New York	206,453,000	3.9%
6	North Carolina	264,067,000	4.9%
49	North Dakota	7,161,000	0.1%
18	Ohio	93,782,000	1.8%
19	Oklahoma	90,064,000	1.7%
41	Oregon	15,852,000	0.3%
4	Pennsylvania	294,334,000	5.5%
46	Rhode Island	10,819,000	0.2%
12	South Carolina	150,146,000	2.8%
44	South Dakota	14,232,000	0.3%
14	Tennessee	116,056,000	2.2%
1	Texas	796,949,000	14.9%
30	Utah	40,762,000	0.8%
39	Vermont	20,682,000	0.4%
8	Virginia	180,096,000	3.4%
5	Washington	276,082,000	5.2%
47	West Virginia	9,479,000	0.2%
24	Wisconsin	54,047,000	1.0%
50	Wyoming	1,672,000	0.0%

RANK ORDER

RANK	STATE	REVENUE	% of USA
1	Texas	$796,949,000	14.9%
2	Florida	590,400,000	11.0%
3	California	323,934,000	6.1%
4	Pennsylvania	294,334,000	5.5%
5	Washington	276,082,000	5.2%
6	North Carolina	264,067,000	4.9%
7	New York	206,453,000	3.9%
8	Virginia	180,096,000	3.4%
9	Alabama	167,830,000	3.1%
10	Georgia	166,618,000	3.1%
11	Illinois	157,622,000	2.9%
12	South Carolina	150,146,000	2.8%
13	Michigan	140,488,000	2.6%
14	Tennessee	116,056,000	2.2%
15	Kentucky	111,596,000	2.1%
16	Kansas	111,589,000	2.1%
17	New Jersey	105,488,000	2.0%
18	Ohio	93,782,000	1.8%
19	Oklahoma	90,064,000	1.7%
20	Minnesota	75,225,000	1.4%
21	Massachusetts	72,598,000	1.4%
22	Arizona	62,799,000	1.2%
23	Louisiana	56,881,000	1.1%
24	Wisconsin	54,047,000	1.0%
25	Hawaii	47,242,000	0.9%
26	Connecticut	47,064,000	0.9%
27	Arkansas	45,623,000	0.9%
28	Indiana	43,498,000	0.8%
29	Mississippi	42,464,000	0.8%
30	Utah	40,762,000	0.8%
31	Alaska	39,626,000	0.7%
32	New Mexico	39,251,000	0.7%
33	Nevada	37,867,000	0.7%
34	Colorado	35,972,000	0.7%
35	Missouri	31,990,000	0.6%
36	Maryland	29,168,000	0.5%
37	Montana	28,095,000	0.5%
38	Nebraska	26,925,000	0.5%
39	Vermont	20,682,000	0.4%
40	Maine	17,438,000	0.3%
41	Oregon	15,852,000	0.3%
42	Delaware	15,519,000	0.3%
43	Iowa	14,704,000	0.3%
44	South Dakota	14,232,000	0.3%
45	New Hampshire	12,451,000	0.2%
46	Rhode Island	10,819,000	0.2%
47	West Virginia	9,479,000	0.2%
48	Idaho	8,122,000	0.2%
49	North Dakota	7,161,000	0.1%
50	Wyoming	1,672,000	0.0%
	District of Columbia*	NA	NA

Source: U.S. Bureau of the Census, Governments Division
"2009 State Government Tax Collections" (http://www.census.gov/govs/statetax/)
*Not applicable.

Per Capita State Government Alcoholic Beverage Sales Tax Revenue in 2009

National Per Capita = $17.46

ALPHA ORDER

RANK	STATE	PER CAPITA
5	Alabama	$35.64
1	Alaska	56.73
38	Arizona	9.52
21	Arkansas	15.79
40	California	8.76
42	Colorado	7.16
28	Connecticut	13.38
18	Delaware	17.53
9	Florida	31.85
20	Georgia	16.95
4	Hawaii	36.48
45	Idaho	5.25
31	Illinois	12.21
43	Indiana	6.77
48	Iowa	4.89
3	Kansas	39.59
12	Kentucky	25.87
30	Louisiana	12.66
29	Maine	13.23
47	Maryland	5.12
34	Massachusetts	11.01
27	Michigan	14.09
26	Minnesota	14.28
24	Mississippi	14.38
44	Missouri	5.34
10	Montana	28.82
22	Nebraska	14.99
25	Nevada	14.33
39	New Hampshire	9.40
32	New Jersey	12.11
16	New Mexico	19.53
35	New York	10.56
11	North Carolina	28.15
33	North Dakota	11.07
41	Ohio	8.12
13	Oklahoma	24.43
49	Oregon	4.14
14	Pennsylvania	23.35
36	Rhode Island	10.27
7	South Carolina	32.92
19	South Dakota	17.52
17	Tennessee	18.43
8	Texas	32.16
23	Utah	14.64
6	Vermont	33.26
15	Virginia	22.85
2	Washington	41.43
46	West Virginia	5.21
37	Wisconsin	9.56
50	Wyoming	3.07

RANK ORDER

RANK	STATE	PER CAPITA
1	Alaska	$56.73
2	Washington	41.43
3	Kansas	39.59
4	Hawaii	36.48
5	Alabama	35.64
6	Vermont	33.26
7	South Carolina	32.92
8	Texas	32.16
9	Florida	31.85
10	Montana	28.82
11	North Carolina	28.15
12	Kentucky	25.87
13	Oklahoma	24.43
14	Pennsylvania	23.35
15	Virginia	22.85
16	New Mexico	19.53
17	Tennessee	18.43
18	Delaware	17.53
19	South Dakota	17.52
20	Georgia	16.95
21	Arkansas	15.79
22	Nebraska	14.99
23	Utah	14.64
24	Mississippi	14.38
25	Nevada	14.33
26	Minnesota	14.28
27	Michigan	14.09
28	Connecticut	13.38
29	Maine	13.23
30	Louisiana	12.66
31	Illinois	12.21
32	New Jersey	12.11
33	North Dakota	11.07
34	Massachusetts	11.01
35	New York	10.56
36	Rhode Island	10.27
37	Wisconsin	9.56
38	Arizona	9.52
39	New Hampshire	9.40
40	California	8.76
41	Ohio	8.12
42	Colorado	7.16
43	Indiana	6.77
44	Missouri	5.34
45	Idaho	5.25
46	West Virginia	5.21
47	Maryland	5.12
48	Iowa	4.89
49	Oregon	4.14
50	Wyoming	3.07

District of Columbia*   NA

Source: CQ Press using data from U.S. Bureau of the Census, Governments Division
"2009 State Government Tax Collections" (http://www.census.gov/govs/statetax/)
*Not applicable.

State Government Total Expenditures in 2008

National Total = $1,733,861,802,000*

ALPHA ORDER

RANK	STATE	EXPENDITURES	% of USA
25	Alabama	$24,892,739,000	1.4%
39	Alaska	10,115,914,000	0.6%
20	Arizona	30,778,930,000	1.8%
33	Arkansas	15,655,753,000	0.9%
1	California	246,683,951,000	14.2%
27	Colorado	22,806,051,000	1.3%
26	Connecticut	23,528,530,000	1.4%
44	Delaware	7,151,941,000	0.4%
4	Florida	77,195,462,000	4.5%
12	Georgia	41,165,128,000	2.4%
38	Hawaii	10,533,869,000	0.6%
42	Idaho	7,675,083,000	0.4%
7	Illinois	63,368,160,000	3.7%
19	Indiana	30,783,257,000	1.8%
31	Iowa	16,522,737,000	1.0%
34	Kansas	14,968,811,000	0.9%
24	Kentucky	25,421,531,000	1.5%
17	Louisiana	33,003,929,000	1.9%
41	Maine	8,151,041,000	0.5%
16	Maryland	34,029,818,000	2.0%
11	Massachusetts	45,634,948,000	2.6%
9	Michigan	56,869,012,000	3.3%
15	Minnesota	34,283,510,000	2.0%
30	Mississippi	18,642,916,000	1.1%
22	Missouri	26,788,804,000	1.5%
46	Montana	6,137,669,000	0.4%
40	Nebraska	8,443,129,000	0.5%
36	Nevada	10,845,375,000	0.6%
45	New Hampshire	6,601,654,000	0.4%
8	New Jersey	58,539,173,000	3.4%
32	New Mexico	15,793,049,000	0.9%
2	New York	157,397,509,000	9.1%
10	North Carolina	46,707,349,000	2.7%
49	North Dakota	4,125,920,000	0.2%
6	Ohio	67,788,590,000	3.9%
29	Oklahoma	19,517,639,000	1.1%
28	Oregon	22,386,883,000	1.3%
5	Pennsylvania	71,635,287,000	4.1%
43	Rhode Island	7,495,870,000	0.4%
21	South Carolina	27,593,614,000	1.6%
50	South Dakota	3,698,335,000	0.2%
23	Tennessee	26,253,469,000	1.5%
3	Texas	99,126,766,000	5.7%
35	Utah	14,293,669,000	0.8%
48	Vermont	5,070,156,000	0.3%
13	Virginia	39,765,229,000	2.3%
14	Washington	39,689,815,000	2.3%
37	West Virginia	10,596,812,000	0.6%
18	Wisconsin	32,625,430,000	1.9%
47	Wyoming	5,081,586,000	0.3%

RANK ORDER

RANK	STATE	EXPENDITURES	% of USA
1	California	$246,683,951,000	14.2%
2	New York	157,397,509,000	9.1%
3	Texas	99,126,766,000	5.7%
4	Florida	77,195,462,000	4.5%
5	Pennsylvania	71,635,287,000	4.1%
6	Ohio	67,788,590,000	3.9%
7	Illinois	63,368,160,000	3.7%
8	New Jersey	58,539,173,000	3.4%
9	Michigan	56,869,012,000	3.3%
10	North Carolina	46,707,349,000	2.7%
11	Massachusetts	45,634,948,000	2.6%
12	Georgia	41,165,128,000	2.4%
13	Virginia	39,765,229,000	2.3%
14	Washington	39,689,815,000	2.3%
15	Minnesota	34,283,510,000	2.0%
16	Maryland	34,029,818,000	2.0%
17	Louisiana	33,003,929,000	1.9%
18	Wisconsin	32,625,430,000	1.9%
19	Indiana	30,783,257,000	1.8%
20	Arizona	30,778,930,000	1.8%
21	South Carolina	27,593,614,000	1.6%
22	Missouri	26,788,804,000	1.5%
23	Tennessee	26,253,469,000	1.5%
24	Kentucky	25,421,531,000	1.5%
25	Alabama	24,892,739,000	1.4%
26	Connecticut	23,528,530,000	1.4%
27	Colorado	22,806,051,000	1.3%
28	Oregon	22,386,883,000	1.3%
29	Oklahoma	19,517,639,000	1.1%
30	Mississippi	18,642,916,000	1.1%
31	Iowa	16,522,737,000	1.0%
32	New Mexico	15,793,049,000	0.9%
33	Arkansas	15,655,753,000	0.9%
34	Kansas	14,968,811,000	0.9%
35	Utah	14,293,669,000	0.8%
36	Nevada	10,845,375,000	0.6%
37	West Virginia	10,596,812,000	0.6%
38	Hawaii	10,533,869,000	0.6%
39	Alaska	10,115,914,000	0.6%
40	Nebraska	8,443,129,000	0.5%
41	Maine	8,151,041,000	0.5%
42	Idaho	7,675,083,000	0.4%
43	Rhode Island	7,495,870,000	0.4%
44	Delaware	7,151,941,000	0.4%
45	New Hampshire	6,601,654,000	0.4%
46	Montana	6,137,669,000	0.4%
47	Wyoming	5,081,586,000	0.3%
48	Vermont	5,070,156,000	0.3%
49	North Dakota	4,125,920,000	0.2%
50	South Dakota	3,698,335,000	0.2%
	District of Columbia**	NA	NA

Source: U.S. Bureau of the Census, Governments Division
"2008 State and Local Government Finances" (http://www.census.gov/govs/estimate/index.html)
*Total expenditures includes all money paid other than for retirement of debt and extension of loans. Includes payments from all sources of funds including current revenues and proceeds from borrowing and prior year fund balances. Includes intergovernmental transfers and expenditures for government owned utilities and other commercial or auxiliary enterprise, and insurance trust expenditures. **Not applicable.

Per Capita State Government Total Expenditures in 2008

National Per Capita = $5,708*

ALPHA ORDER

RANK	STATE	PER CAPITA
33	Alabama	$5,322
1	Alaska	14,701
42	Arizona	4,736
30	Arkansas	5,459
12	California	6,744
43	Colorado	4,621
13	Connecticut	6,717
5	Delaware	8,162
48	Florida	4,190
46	Georgia	4,245
3	Hawaii	8,182
37	Idaho	5,025
39	Illinois	4,934
40	Indiana	4,819
29	Iowa	5,519
32	Kansas	5,351
22	Kentucky	5,929
8	Louisiana	7,414
18	Maine	6,176
21	Maryland	6,014
10	Massachusetts	6,974
28	Michigan	5,685
14	Minnesota	6,554
16	Mississippi	6,341
45	Missouri	4,498
17	Montana	6,340
41	Nebraska	4,738
49	Nevada	4,146
38	New Hampshire	4,994
11	New Jersey	6,757
7	New Mexico	7,949
6	New York	8,085
36	North Carolina	5,051
15	North Dakota	6,432
24	Ohio	5,880
31	Oklahoma	5,356
23	Oregon	5,918
27	Pennsylvania	5,701
9	Rhode Island	7,115
19	South Carolina	6,127
44	South Dakota	4,597
47	Tennessee	4,207
50	Texas	4,079
34	Utah	5,241
4	Vermont	8,164
35	Virginia	5,101
20	Washington	6,045
25	West Virginia	5,839
26	Wisconsin	5,797
2	Wyoming	9,534

RANK ORDER

RANK	STATE	PER CAPITA
1	Alaska	$14,701
2	Wyoming	9,534
3	Hawaii	8,182
4	Vermont	8,164
5	Delaware	8,162
6	New York	8,085
7	New Mexico	7,949
8	Louisiana	7,414
9	Rhode Island	7,115
10	Massachusetts	6,974
11	New Jersey	6,757
12	California	6,744
13	Connecticut	6,717
14	Minnesota	6,554
15	North Dakota	6,432
16	Mississippi	6,341
17	Montana	6,340
18	Maine	6,176
19	South Carolina	6,127
20	Washington	6,045
21	Maryland	6,014
22	Kentucky	5,929
23	Oregon	5,918
24	Ohio	5,880
25	West Virginia	5,839
26	Wisconsin	5,797
27	Pennsylvania	5,701
28	Michigan	5,685
29	Iowa	5,519
30	Arkansas	5,459
31	Oklahoma	5,356
32	Kansas	5,351
33	Alabama	5,322
34	Utah	5,241
35	Virginia	5,101
36	North Carolina	5,051
37	Idaho	5,025
38	New Hampshire	4,994
39	Illinois	4,934
40	Indiana	4,819
41	Nebraska	4,738
42	Arizona	4,736
43	Colorado	4,621
44	South Dakota	4,597
45	Missouri	4,498
46	Georgia	4,245
47	Tennessee	4,207
48	Florida	4,190
49	Nevada	4,146
50	Texas	4,079

District of Columbia**   NA

Source: CQ Press using data from U.S. Bureau of the Census, Governments Division
   "2008 State and Local Government Finances" (http://www.census.gov/govs/estimate/index.html)
*Total expenditures includes all money paid other than for retirement of debt and extension of loans. Includes payments from all sources of funds including current revenues and proceeds from borrowing and prior year fund balances. Includes intergovernmental transfers and expenditures for government owned utilities and other commercial or auxiliary enterprise, and insurance trust expenditures. **Not applicable.

State Government Direct General Expenditures in 2008

National Total = $1,024,665,561,000*

ALPHA ORDER

RANK	STATE	EXPENDITURES	% of USA
26	Alabama	$15,449,791,000	1.5%
37	Alaska	7,660,896,000	0.7%
23	Arizona	17,327,014,000	1.7%
33	Arkansas	9,962,544,000	1.0%
1	California	115,138,857,000	11.2%
27	Colorado	13,063,274,000	1.3%
25	Connecticut	15,826,426,000	1.5%
42	Delaware	5,389,391,000	0.5%
4	Florida	49,452,759,000	4.8%
12	Georgia	25,749,530,000	2.5%
36	Hawaii	9,429,236,000	0.9%
44	Idaho	4,769,082,000	0.5%
6	Illinois	39,560,213,000	3.9%
17	Indiana	20,448,300,000	2.0%
31	Iowa	10,687,341,000	1.0%
35	Kansas	9,431,027,000	0.9%
22	Kentucky	17,662,081,000	1.7%
15	Louisiana	23,960,421,000	2.3%
39	Maine	6,089,598,000	0.6%
16	Maryland	21,819,005,000	2.1%
9	Massachusetts	31,146,311,000	3.0%
10	Michigan	30,312,437,000	3.0%
18	Minnesota	19,066,463,000	1.9%
30	Mississippi	11,665,118,000	1.1%
19	Missouri	17,982,716,000	1.8%
46	Montana	4,104,857,000	0.4%
40	Nebraska	6,042,455,000	0.6%
41	Nevada	5,459,729,000	0.5%
45	New Hampshire	4,220,470,000	0.4%
8	New Jersey	35,882,870,000	3.5%
32	New Mexico	10,064,457,000	1.0%
2	New York	75,400,805,000	7.4%
11	North Carolina	28,624,243,000	2.8%
48	North Dakota	2,984,497,000	0.3%
7	Ohio	36,475,341,000	3.6%
28	Oklahoma	12,817,199,000	1.3%
29	Oregon	12,435,083,000	1.2%
5	Pennsylvania	42,685,050,000	4.2%
43	Rhode Island	5,174,660,000	0.5%
24	South Carolina	17,269,097,000	1.7%
50	South Dakota	2,720,277,000	0.3%
21	Tennessee	17,905,741,000	1.7%
3	Texas	63,607,080,000	6.2%
34	Utah	9,916,600,000	1.0%
47	Vermont	3,366,430,000	0.3%
13	Virginia	25,268,743,000	2.5%
14	Washington	24,948,203,000	2.4%
38	West Virginia	7,538,880,000	0.7%
20	Wisconsin	17,907,687,000	1.7%
49	Wyoming	2,795,276,000	0.3%

RANK ORDER

RANK	STATE	EXPENDITURES	% of USA
1	California	$115,138,857,000	11.2%
2	New York	75,400,805,000	7.4%
3	Texas	63,607,080,000	6.2%
4	Florida	49,452,759,000	4.8%
5	Pennsylvania	42,685,050,000	4.2%
6	Illinois	39,560,213,000	3.9%
7	Ohio	36,475,341,000	3.6%
8	New Jersey	35,882,870,000	3.5%
9	Massachusetts	31,146,311,000	3.0%
10	Michigan	30,312,437,000	3.0%
11	North Carolina	28,624,243,000	2.8%
12	Georgia	25,749,530,000	2.5%
13	Virginia	25,268,743,000	2.5%
14	Washington	24,948,203,000	2.4%
15	Louisiana	23,960,421,000	2.3%
16	Maryland	21,819,005,000	2.1%
17	Indiana	20,448,300,000	2.0%
18	Minnesota	19,066,463,000	1.9%
19	Missouri	17,982,716,000	1.8%
20	Wisconsin	17,907,687,000	1.7%
21	Tennessee	17,905,741,000	1.7%
22	Kentucky	17,662,081,000	1.7%
23	Arizona	17,327,014,000	1.7%
24	South Carolina	17,269,097,000	1.7%
25	Connecticut	15,826,426,000	1.5%
26	Alabama	15,449,791,000	1.5%
27	Colorado	13,063,274,000	1.3%
28	Oklahoma	12,817,199,000	1.3%
29	Oregon	12,435,083,000	1.2%
30	Mississippi	11,665,118,000	1.1%
31	Iowa	10,687,341,000	1.0%
32	New Mexico	10,064,457,000	1.0%
33	Arkansas	9,962,544,000	1.0%
34	Utah	9,916,600,000	1.0%
35	Kansas	9,431,027,000	0.9%
36	Hawaii	9,429,236,000	0.9%
37	Alaska	7,660,896,000	0.7%
38	West Virginia	7,538,880,000	0.7%
39	Maine	6,089,598,000	0.6%
40	Nebraska	6,042,455,000	0.6%
41	Nevada	5,459,729,000	0.5%
42	Delaware	5,389,391,000	0.5%
43	Rhode Island	5,174,660,000	0.5%
44	Idaho	4,769,082,000	0.5%
45	New Hampshire	4,220,470,000	0.4%
46	Montana	4,104,857,000	0.4%
47	Vermont	3,366,430,000	0.3%
48	North Dakota	2,984,497,000	0.3%
49	Wyoming	2,795,276,000	0.3%
50	South Dakota	2,720,277,000	0.3%

District of Columbia** NA NA

Source: U.S. Bureau of the Census, Governments Division
     "2008 State and Local Government Finances" (http://www.census.gov/govs/estimate/index.html)
*Direct general expenditures include expenditures for current operations, assistance and subsidies, interest on debt, and capital outlay. Excludes intergovernmental transfers, expenditures for government owned utilities and other commercial or auxiliary enterprise, and insurance trust expenditures.
**Not applicable.

Per Capita State Government Direct General Expenditures in 2008

National Per Capita = $3,373*

ALPHA ORDER

RANK	STATE	PER CAPITA
31	Alabama	$3,303
1	Alaska	11,133
46	Arizona	2,666
26	Arkansas	3,474
38	California	3,148
48	Colorado	2,647
12	Connecticut	4,518
3	Delaware	6,151
45	Florida	2,684
47	Georgia	2,655
2	Hawaii	7,324
39	Idaho	3,122
41	Illinois	3,080
34	Indiana	3,201
24	Iowa	3,570
30	Kansas	3,371
16	Kentucky	4,119
5	Louisiana	5,383
11	Maine	4,614
19	Maryland	3,856
9	Massachusetts	4,760
42	Michigan	3,030
22	Minnesota	3,645
17	Mississippi	3,967
43	Missouri	3,019
13	Montana	4,240
28	Nebraska	3,391
50	Nevada	2,087
35	New Hampshire	3,193
15	New Jersey	4,142
7	New Mexico	5,066
18	New York	3,873
40	North Carolina	3,095
10	North Dakota	4,653
37	Ohio	3,164
25	Oklahoma·	3,517
32	Oregon	3,287
27	Pennsylvania	3,397
8	Rhode Island	4,912
20	South Carolina	3,835
29	South Dakota	3,381
44	Tennessee	2,869
49	Texas	2,617
23	Utah	3,636
4	Vermont	5,421
33	Virginia	3,241
21	Washington	3,800
14	West Virginia	4,154
36	Wisconsin	3,182
6	Wyoming	5,245

RANK ORDER

RANK	STATE	PER CAPITA
1	Alaska	$11,133
2	Hawaii	7,324
3	Delaware	6,151
4	Vermont	5,421
5	Louisiana	5,383
6	Wyoming	5,245
7	New Mexico	5,066
8	Rhode Island	4,912
9	Massachusetts	4,760
10	North Dakota	4,653
11	Maine	4,614
12	Connecticut	4,518
13	Montana	4,240
14	West Virginia	4,154
15	New Jersey	4,142
16	Kentucky	4,119
17	Mississippi	3,967
18	New York	3,873
19	Maryland	3,856
20	South Carolina	3,835
21	Washington	3,800
22	Minnesota	3,645
23	Utah	3,636
24	Iowa	3,570
25	Oklahoma	3,517
26	Arkansas	3,474
27	Pennsylvania	3,397
28	Nebraska	3,391
29	South Dakota	3,381
30	Kansas	3,371
31	Alabama	3,303
32	Oregon	3,287
33	Virginia	3,241
34	Indiana	3,201
35	New Hampshire	3,193
36	Wisconsin	3,182
37	Ohio	3,164
38	California	3,148
39	Idaho	3,122
40	North Carolina	3,095
41	Illinois	3,080
42	Michigan	3,030
43	Missouri	3,019
44	Tennessee	2,869
45	Florida	2,684
46	Arizona	2,666
47	Georgia	2,655
48	Colorado	2,647
49	Texas	2,617
50	Nevada	2,087

District of Columbia**　　　　NA

Source: CQ Press using data from U.S. Bureau of the Census, Governments Division
   "2008 State and Local Government Finances" (http://www.census.gov/govs/estimate/index.html)
*Direct general expenditures include expenditures for current operations, assistance and subsidies, interest on debt, and capital outlay. Excludes intergovernmental transfers, expenditures for government owned utilities and other commercial or auxiliary enterprise, and insurance trust expenditures.
**Not applicable.

State Government Debt Outstanding in 2008

National Total = $1,004,180,935,000*

ALPHA ORDER

RANK	STATE	DEBT	% of USA
29	Alabama	$8,472,097,000	0.8%
33	Alaska	6,491,713,000	0.6%
25	Arizona	10,519,389,000	1.0%
43	Arkansas	4,283,024,000	0.4%
1	California	121,929,578,000	12.1%
20	Colorado	15,879,387,000	1.6%
10	Connecticut	27,554,245,000	2.7%
39	Delaware	5,722,757,000	0.6%
6	Florida	42,320,929,000	4.2%
22	Georgia	13,072,416,000	1.3%
36	Hawaii	6,028,067,000	0.6%
46	Idaho	3,379,159,000	0.3%
4	Illinois	58,436,829,000	5.8%
16	Indiana	19,916,264,000	2.0%
32	Iowa	7,235,998,000	0.7%
38	Kansas	5,836,651,000	0.6%
23	Kentucky	12,209,861,000	1.2%
19	Louisiana	16,387,658,000	1.6%
40	Maine	5,296,282,000	0.5%
13	Maryland	23,070,309,000	2.3%
3	Massachusetts	71,892,262,000	7.2%
9	Michigan	29,065,260,000	2.9%
26	Minnesota	9,538,669,000	0.9%
35	Mississippi	6,331,031,000	0.6%
17	Missouri	19,708,834,000	2.0%
41	Montana	4,924,359,000	0.5%
48	Nebraska	2,719,139,000	0.3%
44	Nevada	4,248,696,000	0.4%
30	New Hampshire	7,908,632,000	0.8%
5	New Jersey	52,785,000,000	5.3%
31	New Mexico	7,763,822,000	0.8%
2	New York	114,240,227,000	11.4%
18	North Carolina	19,605,315,000	2.0%
49	North Dakota	1,951,959,000	0.2%
11	Ohio	26,885,476,000	2.7%
27	Oklahoma	9,129,789,000	0.9%
24	Oregon	11,647,145,000	1.2%
7	Pennsylvania	40,100,004,000	4.0%
28	Rhode Island	8,911,977,000	0.9%
21	South Carolina	15,212,910,000	1.5%
45	South Dakota	3,408,138,000	0.3%
42	Tennessee	4,366,410,000	0.4%
8	Texas	33,299,313,000	3.3%
37	Utah	5,907,105,000	0.6%
47	Vermont	3,371,915,000	0.3%
15	Virginia	21,875,483,000	2.2%
12	Washington	23,524,009,000	2.3%
34	West Virginia	6,365,585,000	0.6%
14	Wisconsin	22,107,148,000	2.2%
50	Wyoming	1,342,710,000	0.1%

RANK ORDER

RANK	STATE	DEBT	% of USA
1	California	$121,929,578,000	12.1%
2	New York	114,240,227,000	11.4%
3	Massachusetts	71,892,262,000	7.2%
4	Illinois	58,436,829,000	5.8%
5	New Jersey	52,785,000,000	5.3%
6	Florida	42,320,929,000	4.2%
7	Pennsylvania	40,100,004,000	4.0%
8	Texas	33,299,313,000	3.3%
9	Michigan	29,065,260,000	2.9%
10	Connecticut	27,554,245,000	2.7%
11	Ohio	26,885,476,000	2.7%
12	Washington	23,524,009,000	2.3%
13	Maryland	23,070,309,000	2.3%
14	Wisconsin	22,107,148,000	2.2%
15	Virginia	21,875,483,000	2.2%
16	Indiana	19,916,264,000	2.0%
17	Missouri	19,708,834,000	2.0%
18	North Carolina	19,605,315,000	2.0%
19	Louisiana	16,387,658,000	1.6%
20	Colorado	15,879,387,000	1.6%
21	South Carolina	15,212,910,000	1.5%
22	Georgia	13,072,416,000	1.3%
23	Kentucky	12,209,861,000	1.2%
24	Oregon	11,647,145,000	1.2%
25	Arizona	10,519,389,000	1.0%
26	Minnesota	9,538,669,000	0.9%
27	Oklahoma	9,129,789,000	0.9%
28	Rhode Island	8,911,977,000	0.9%
29	Alabama	8,472,097,000	0.8%
30	New Hampshire	7,908,632,000	0.8%
31	New Mexico	7,763,822,000	0.8%
32	Iowa	7,235,998,000	0.7%
33	Alaska	6,491,713,000	0.6%
34	West Virginia	6,365,585,000	0.6%
35	Mississippi	6,331,031,000	0.6%
36	Hawaii	6,028,067,000	0.6%
37	Utah	5,907,105,000	0.6%
38	Kansas	5,836,651,000	0.6%
39	Delaware	5,722,757,000	0.6%
40	Maine	5,296,282,000	0.5%
41	Montana	4,924,359,000	0.5%
42	Tennessee	4,366,410,000	0.4%
43	Arkansas	4,283,024,000	0.4%
44	Nevada	4,248,696,000	0.4%
45	South Dakota	3,408,138,000	0.3%
46	Idaho	3,379,159,000	0.3%
47	Vermont	3,371,915,000	0.3%
48	Nebraska	2,719,139,000	0.3%
49	North Dakota	1,951,959,000	0.2%
50	Wyoming	1,342,710,000	0.1%
	District of Columbia**	NA	NA

Source: U.S. Bureau of the Census, Governments Division
    "2008 State and Local Government Finances" (http://www.census.gov/govs/estimate/index.html)
*Includes short-term, long-term, full faith and credit, nonguaranteed, and public debt for private purposes.
**Not applicable.

Per Capita State Government Debt Outstanding in 2008

National Per Capita = $3,306*

ALPHA ORDER

RANK	STATE	PER CAPITA
43	Alabama	$1,811
2	Alaska	9,434
45	Arizona	1,619
47	Arkansas	1,494
22	California	3,333
24	Colorado	3,218
4	Connecticut	7,866
5	Delaware	6,531
36	Florida	2,297
49	Georgia	1,348
11	Hawaii	4,682
37	Idaho	2,212
12	Illinois	4,550
26	Indiana	3,118
34	Iowa	2,417
41	Kansas	2,086
30	Kentucky	2,847
18	Louisiana	3,681
15	Maine	4,013
14	Maryland	4,077
1	Massachusetts	10,987
29	Michigan	2,906
42	Minnesota	1,824
39	Mississippi	2,153
23	Missouri	3,309
10	Montana	5,087
46	Nebraska	1,526
44	Nevada	1,624
7	New Hampshire	5,983
6	New Jersey	6,093
17	New Mexico	3,908
8	New York	5,868
40	North Carolina	2,120
28	North Dakota	3,043
35	Ohio	2,332
33	Oklahoma	2,505
27	Oregon	3,079
25	Pennsylvania	3,191
3	Rhode Island	8,459
21	South Carolina	3,378
13	South Dakota	4,236
50	Tennessee	700
48	Texas	1,370
38	Utah	2,166
9	Vermont	5,429
31	Virginia	2,806
19	Washington	3,583
20	West Virginia	3,507
16	Wisconsin	3,928
32	Wyoming	2,519

RANK ORDER

RANK	STATE	PER CAPITA
1	Massachusetts	$10,987
2	Alaska	9,434
3	Rhode Island	8,459
4	Connecticut	7,866
5	Delaware	6,531
6	New Jersey	6,093
7	New Hampshire	5,983
8	New York	5,868
9	Vermont	5,429
10	Montana	5,087
11	Hawaii	4,682
12	Illinois	4,550
13	South Dakota	4,236
14	Maryland	4,077
15	Maine	4,013
16	Wisconsin	3,928
17	New Mexico	3,908
18	Louisiana	3,681
19	Washington	3,583
20	West Virginia	3,507
21	South Carolina	3,378
22	California	3,333
23	Missouri	3,309
24	Colorado	3,218
25	Pennsylvania	3,191
26	Indiana	3,118
27	Oregon	3,079
28	North Dakota	3,043
29	Michigan	2,906
30	Kentucky	2,847
31	Virginia	2,806
32	Wyoming	2,519
33	Oklahoma	2,505
34	Iowa	2,417
35	Ohio	2,332
36	Florida	2,297
37	Idaho	2,212
38	Utah	2,166
39	Mississippi	2,153
40	North Carolina	2,120
41	Kansas	2,086
42	Minnesota	1,824
43	Alabama	1,811
44	Nevada	1,624
45	Arizona	1,619
46	Nebraska	1,526
47	Arkansas	1,494
48	Texas	1,370
49	Georgia	1,348
50	Tennessee	700

District of Columbia**   NA

Source: CQ Press using data from U.S. Bureau of the Census, Governments Division
"2008 State and Local Government Finances" (http://www.census.gov/govs/estimate/index.html)
*Includes short-term, long-term, full faith and credit, nonguaranteed, and public debt for private purposes.
**Not applicable.

State Government Full-Time Equivalent Employees in 2009

National Total = 4,399,190 FTE Employees*

ALPHA ORDER

RANK	STATE	EMPLOYEES	% of USA
19	Alabama	89,467	2.0%
41	Alaska	26,183	0.6%
27	Arizona	68,972	1.6%
30	Arkansas	61,337	1.4%
1	California	411,142	9.3%
24	Colorado	72,778	1.7%
28	Connecticut	66,498	1.5%
40	Delaware	26,510	0.6%
4	Florida	185,630	4.2%
13	Georgia	122,582	2.8%
31	Hawaii	60,041	1.4%
42	Idaho	23,179	0.5%
10	Illinois	136,542	3.1%
15	Indiana	92,484	2.1%
33	Iowa	52,288	1.2%
36	Kansas	45,163	1.0%
21	Kentucky	81,117	1.8%
16	Louisiana	91,809	2.1%
43	Maine	21,497	0.5%
18	Maryland	89,511	2.0%
14	Massachusetts	96,865	2.2%
9	Michigan	142,924	3.2%
22	Minnesota	80,536	1.8%
32	Mississippi	57,773	1.3%
17	Missouri	90,092	2.0%
44	Montana	20,590	0.5%
38	Nebraska	32,333	0.7%
39	Nevada	29,517	0.7%
46	New Hampshire	19,591	0.4%
6	New Jersey	154,106	3.5%
35	New Mexico	48,680	1.1%
3	New York	257,490	5.9%
7	North Carolina	147,895	3.4%
47	North Dakota	17,667	0.4%
8	Ohio	142,945	3.2%
25	Oklahoma	72,198	1.6%
29	Oregon	63,086	1.4%
5	Pennsylvania	163,903	3.7%
45	Rhode Island	19,669	0.4%
23	South Carolina	77,261	1.8%
49	South Dakota	14,053	0.3%
20	Tennessee	84,387	1.9%
2	Texas	300,112	6.8%
34	Utah	51,606	1.2%
48	Vermont	14,598	0.3%
11	Virginia	125,570	2.9%
12	Washington	125,423	2.9%
37	West Virginia	39,505	0.9%
26	Wisconsin	70,457	1.6%
50	Wyoming	13,628	0.3%

RANK ORDER

RANK	STATE	EMPLOYEES	% of USA
1	California	411,142	9.3%
2	Texas	300,112	6.8%
3	New York	257,490	5.9%
4	Florida	185,630	4.2%
5	Pennsylvania	163,903	3.7%
6	New Jersey	154,106	3.5%
7	North Carolina	147,895	3.4%
8	Ohio	142,945	3.2%
9	Michigan	142,924	3.2%
10	Illinois	136,542	3.1%
11	Virginia	125,570	2.9%
12	Washington	125,423	2.9%
13	Georgia	122,582	2.8%
14	Massachusetts	96,865	2.2%
15	Indiana	92,484	2.1%
16	Louisiana	91,809	2.1%
17	Missouri	90,092	2.0%
18	Maryland	89,511	2.0%
19	Alabama	89,467	2.0%
20	Tennessee	84,387	1.9%
21	Kentucky	81,117	1.8%
22	Minnesota	80,536	1.8%
23	South Carolina	77,261	1.8%
24	Colorado	72,778	1.7%
25	Oklahoma	72,198	1.6%
26	Wisconsin	70,457	1.6%
27	Arizona	68,972	1.6%
28	Connecticut	66,498	1.5%
29	Oregon	63,086	1.4%
30	Arkansas	61,337	1.4%
31	Hawaii	60,041	1.4%
32	Mississippi	57,773	1.3%
33	Iowa	52,288	1.2%
34	Utah	51,606	1.2%
35	New Mexico	48,680	1.1%
36	Kansas	45,163	1.0%
37	West Virginia	39,505	0.9%
38	Nebraska	32,333	0.7%
39	Nevada	29,517	0.7%
40	Delaware	26,510	0.6%
41	Alaska	26,183	0.6%
42	Idaho	23,179	0.5%
43	Maine	21,497	0.5%
44	Montana	20,590	0.5%
45	Rhode Island	19,669	0.4%
46	New Hampshire	19,591	0.4%
47	North Dakota	17,667	0.4%
48	Vermont	14,598	0.3%
49	South Dakota	14,053	0.3%
50	Wyoming	13,628	0.3%
	District of Columbia**	NA	NA

Source: U.S. Bureau of the Census, Governments Division
   "Government Employment and Payroll" (http://www.census.gov/govs/apes/index.html)
*As of March 2009.
**Not applicable.

Rate of State Government Full-Time Equivalent Employees in 2009

National Rate = 144 State Government Employees per 10,000 Population*

ALPHA ORDER				RANK ORDER		
RANK	STATE	RATE		RANK	STATE	RATE
14	Alabama	190		1	Hawaii	464
2	Alaska	375		2	Alaska	375
49	Arizona	105		3	Delaware	300
9	Arkansas	212		4	North Dakota	273
47	California	111		5	Wyoming	250
36	Colorado	145		6	New Mexico	242
15	Connecticut	189		7	Vermont	235
3	Delaware	300		8	West Virginia	217
50	Florida	100		9	Arkansas	212
42	Georgia	125		10	Montana	211
1	Hawaii	464		11	Louisiana	204
32	Idaho	150		12	Mississippi	196
48	Illinois	106		12	Oklahoma	196
37	Indiana	144		14	Alabama	190
22	Iowa	174		15	Connecticut	189
27	Kansas	160		16	Kentucky	188
16	Kentucky	188		16	Washington	188
11	Louisiana	204		18	Rhode Island	187
26	Maine	163		19	Utah	185
30	Maryland	157		20	Nebraska	180
35	Massachusetts	147		21	New Jersey	177
38	Michigan	143		22	Iowa	174
31	Minnesota	153		23	South Dakota	173
12	Mississippi	196		24	South Carolina	169
32	Missouri	150		25	Oregon	165
10	Montana	211		26	Maine	163
20	Nebraska	180		27	Kansas	160
46	Nevada	112		28	Virginia	159
34	New Hampshire	148		29	North Carolina	158
21	New Jersey	177		30	Maryland	157
6	New Mexico	242		31	Minnesota	153
40	New York	132		32	Idaho	150
29	North Carolina	158		32	Missouri	150
4	North Dakota	273		34	New Hampshire	148
44	Ohio	124		35	Massachusetts	147
12	Oklahoma	196		36	Colorado	145
25	Oregon	165		37	Indiana	144
41	Pennsylvania	130		38	Michigan	143
18	Rhode Island	187		39	Tennessee	134
24	South Carolina	169		40	New York	132
23	South Dakota	173		41	Pennsylvania	130
39	Tennessee	134		42	Georgia	125
45	Texas	121		42	Wisconsin	125
19	Utah	185		44	Ohio	124
7	Vermont	235		45	Texas	121
28	Virginia	159		46	Nevada	112
16	Washington	188		47	California	111
8	West Virginia	217		48	Illinois	106
42	Wisconsin	125		49	Arizona	105
5	Wyoming	250		50	Florida	100

District of Columbia**   NA

Source: CQ Press using data from U.S. Bureau of the Census, Governments Division
"Government Employment and Payroll" (http://www.census.gov/govs/apes/index.html)
*Full-time equivalent as of March 2009.
**Not applicable.

Average Annual Earnings of Full-Time State Government Employees in 2009

National Average = $54,788*

ALPHA ORDER				RANK ORDER		
RANK	STATE	SALARY		RANK	STATE	SALARY
33	Alabama	$48,806		1	Connecticut	$69,900
8	Alaska	60,940		2	California	68,566
26	Arizona	50,582		3	New Jersey	68,232
46	Arkansas	43,956		4	Iowa	64,509
2	California	68,566		5	Minnesota	63,383
10	Colorado	60,395		5	New York	63,383
1	Connecticut	69,900		7	Rhode Island	62,209
25	Delaware	50,727		8	Alaska	60,940
41	Florida	46,521		9	Illinois	60,920
40	Georgia	46,983		10	Colorado	60,395
23	Hawaii	50,984		11	Michigan	60,273
28	Idaho	50,421		12	Nevada	60,197
9	Illinois	60,920		13	Massachusetts	59,088
29	Indiana	50,096		14	Ohio	58,830
4	Iowa	64,509		15	Wisconsin	58,535
32	Kansas	49,349		16	Washington	57,270
37	Kentucky	47,352		17	Maryland	55,272
31	Louisiana	49,572		18	Oregon	54,292
30	Maine	49,690		19	New Hampshire	53,435
17	Maryland	55,272		20	Vermont	52,674
13	Massachusetts	59,088		21	Pennsylvania	52,061
11	Michigan	60,273		22	Utah	51,516
5	Minnesota	63,383		23	Hawaii	50,984
49	Mississippi	41,403		24	Virginia	50,952
50	Missouri	40,771		25	Delaware	50,727
36	Montana	47,387		26	Arizona	50,582
42	Nebraska	46,417		27	Texas	50,498
12	Nevada	60,197		28	Idaho	50,421
19	New Hampshire	53,435		29	Indiana	50,096
3	New Jersey	68,232		30	Maine	49,690
38	New Mexico	47,253		31	Louisiana	49,572
5	New York	63,383		32	Kansas	49,349
34	North Carolina	48,386		33	Alabama	48,806
35	North Dakota	47,428		34	North Carolina	48,386
14	Ohio	58,830		35	North Dakota	47,428
44	Oklahoma	45,294		36	Montana	47,387
18	Oregon	54,292		37	Kentucky	47,352
21	Pennsylvania	52,061		38	New Mexico	47,253
7	Rhode Island	62,209		39	Wyoming	47,063
47	South Carolina	42,946		40	Georgia	46,983
45	South Dakota	44,982		41	Florida	46,521
43	Tennessee	45,525		42	Nebraska	46,417
27	Texas	50,498		43	Tennessee	45,525
22	Utah	51,516		44	Oklahoma	45,294
20	Vermont	52,674		45	South Dakota	44,982
24	Virginia	50,952		46	Arkansas	43,956
16	Washington	57,270		47	South Carolina	42,946
48	West Virginia	41,754		48	West Virginia	41,754
15	Wisconsin	58,535		49	Mississippi	41,403
39	Wyoming	47,063		50	Missouri	40,771
				District of Columbia**		NA

Source: CQ Press using data from U.S. Bureau of the Census, Governments Division
     "Government Employment and Payroll" (http://www.census.gov/govs/apes/index.html)
*March 2009 full-time payroll (multiplied by 12) divided by full-time employees.
**Not applicable.

Local Government Total Revenue in 2008

National Total = $1,530,813,774,000*

ALPHA ORDER

RANK	STATE	REVENUE	% of USA
23	Alabama	$20,312,761,000	1.3%
44	Alaska	4,059,565,000	0.3%
15	Arizona	29,767,420,000	1.9%
36	Arkansas	8,756,151,000	0.6%
1	California	246,098,635,000	16.1%
19	Colorado	25,974,080,000	1.7%
27	Connecticut	15,432,235,000	1.0%
46	Delaware	3,033,147,000	0.2%
4	Florida	101,399,365,000	6.6%
10	Georgia	43,029,511,000	2.8%
48	Hawaii	2,890,512,000	0.2%
38	Idaho	5,510,113,000	0.4%
5	Illinois	62,476,164,000	4.1%
20	Indiana	25,251,848,000	1.6%
30	Iowa	13,366,375,000	0.9%
31	Kansas	13,009,070,000	0.8%
29	Kentucky	13,397,467,000	0.9%
24	Louisiana	19,755,154,000	1.3%
41	Maine	4,498,530,000	0.3%
21	Maryland	24,459,473,000	1.6%
14	Massachusetts	31,489,291,000	2.1%
8	Michigan	44,640,717,000	2.9%
17	Minnesota	26,405,897,000	1.7%
33	Mississippi	11,881,378,000	0.8%
22	Missouri	22,657,331,000	1.5%
45	Montana	3,283,489,000	0.2%
34	Nebraska	11,348,018,000	0.7%
28	Nevada	14,370,662,000	0.9%
40	New Hampshire	4,975,862,000	0.3%
9	New Jersey	43,229,720,000	2.8%
37	New Mexico	8,052,530,000	0.5%
2	New York	151,229,364,000	9.9%
11	North Carolina	38,506,713,000	2.5%
49	North Dakota	2,404,633,000	0.2%
7	Ohio	54,536,480,000	3.6%
32	Oklahoma	12,370,172,000	0.8%
26	Oregon	17,224,842,000	1.1%
6	Pennsylvania	58,523,696,000	3.8%
43	Rhode Island	4,088,950,000	0.3%
25	South Carolina	17,786,165,000	1.2%
47	South Dakota	2,937,753,000	0.2%
16	Tennessee	28,422,527,000	1.9%
3	Texas	108,195,903,000	7.1%
35	Utah	10,681,691,000	0.7%
50	Vermont	2,358,706,000	0.2%
13	Virginia	32,817,722,000	2.1%
12	Washington	36,468,173,000	2.4%
39	West Virginia	5,030,231,000	0.3%
18	Wisconsin	26,141,938,000	1.7%
42	Wyoming	4,485,749,000	0.3%

RANK ORDER

RANK	STATE	REVENUE	% of USA
1	California	$246,098,635,000	16.1%
2	New York	151,229,364,000	9.9%
3	Texas	108,195,903,000	7.1%
4	Florida	101,399,365,000	6.6%
5	Illinois	62,476,164,000	4.1%
6	Pennsylvania	58,523,696,000	3.8%
7	Ohio	54,536,480,000	3.6%
8	Michigan	44,640,717,000	2.9%
9	New Jersey	43,229,720,000	2.8%
10	Georgia	43,029,511,000	2.8%
11	North Carolina	38,506,713,000	2.5%
12	Washington	36,468,173,000	2.4%
13	Virginia	32,817,722,000	2.1%
14	Massachusetts	31,489,291,000	2.1%
15	Arizona	29,767,420,000	1.9%
16	Tennessee	28,422,527,000	1.9%
17	Minnesota	26,405,897,000	1.7%
18	Wisconsin	26,141,938,000	1.7%
19	Colorado	25,974,080,000	1.7%
20	Indiana	25,251,848,000	1.6%
21	Maryland	24,459,473,000	1.6%
22	Missouri	22,657,331,000	1.5%
23	Alabama	20,312,761,000	1.3%
24	Louisiana	19,755,154,000	1.3%
25	South Carolina	17,786,165,000	1.2%
26	Oregon	17,224,842,000	1.1%
27	Connecticut	15,432,235,000	1.0%
28	Nevada	14,370,662,000	0.9%
29	Kentucky	13,397,467,000	0.9%
30	Iowa	13,366,375,000	0.9%
31	Kansas	13,009,070,000	0.8%
32	Oklahoma	12,370,172,000	0.8%
33	Mississippi	11,881,378,000	0.8%
34	Nebraska	11,348,018,000	0.7%
35	Utah	10,681,691,000	0.7%
36	Arkansas	8,756,151,000	0.6%
37	New Mexico	8,052,530,000	0.5%
38	Idaho	5,510,113,000	0.4%
39	West Virginia	5,030,231,000	0.3%
40	New Hampshire	4,975,862,000	0.3%
41	Maine	4,498,530,000	0.3%
42	Wyoming	4,485,749,000	0.3%
43	Rhode Island	4,088,950,000	0.3%
44	Alaska	4,059,565,000	0.3%
45	Montana	3,283,489,000	0.2%
46	Delaware	3,033,147,000	0.2%
47	South Dakota	2,937,753,000	0.2%
48	Hawaii	2,890,512,000	0.2%
49	North Dakota	2,404,633,000	0.2%
50	Vermont	2,358,706,000	0.2%
	District of Columbia	11,789,895,000	0.8%

Source: U.S. Bureau of the Census, Governments Division
"2008 State and Local Government Finances" (http://www.census.gov/govs/estimate/index.html)
*Total revenue includes all money received from external sources. This includes taxes, intergovernmental transfers and insurance trust revenue, and revenue from government owned utilities and other commercial or auxiliary enterprise.

Per Capita Local Government Total Revenue in 2008

National Per Capita = $5,029*

ALPHA ORDER

RANK	STATE	PER CAPITA
27	Alabama	$4,343
5	Alaska	5,899
18	Arizona	4,580
48	Arkansas	3,053
3	California	6,728
9	Colorado	5,263
26	Connecticut	4,406
43	Delaware	3,462
7	Florida	5,504
25	Georgia	4,437
50	Hawaii	2,245
42	Idaho	3,607
12	Illinois	4,865
33	Indiana	3,953
21	Iowa	4,464
16	Kansas	4,650
47	Kentucky	3,124
24	Louisiana	4,438
44	Maine	3,409
28	Maryland	4,322
13	Massachusetts	4,812
22	Michigan	4,463
10	Minnesota	5,048
32	Mississippi	4,041
37	Missouri	3,804
46	Montana	3,392
4	Nebraska	6,368
8	Nevada	5,494
39	New Hampshire	3,764
11	New Jersey	4,990
31	New Mexico	4,053
2	New York	7,768
30	North Carolina	4,164
40	North Dakota	3,749
14	Ohio	4,731
45	Oklahoma	3,395
20	Oregon	4,553
15	Pennsylvania	4,657
36	Rhode Island	3,881
34	South Carolina	3,950
41	South Dakota	3,652
19	Tennessee	4,555
23	Texas	4,452
35	Utah	3,917
38	Vermont	3,798
29	Virginia	4,210
6	Washington	5,554
49	West Virginia	2,772
17	Wisconsin	4,645
1	Wyoming	8,416

RANK ORDER

RANK	STATE	PER CAPITA
1	Wyoming	$8,416
2	New York	7,768
3	California	6,728
4	Nebraska	6,368
5	Alaska	5,899
6	Washington	5,554
7	Florida	5,504
8	Nevada	5,494
9	Colorado	5,263
10	Minnesota	5,048
11	New Jersey	4,990
12	Illinois	4,865
13	Massachusetts	4,812
14	Ohio	4,731
15	Pennsylvania	4,657
16	Kansas	4,650
17	Wisconsin	4,645
18	Arizona	4,580
19	Tennessee	4,555
20	Oregon	4,553
21	Iowa	4,464
22	Michigan	4,463
23	Texas	4,452
24	Louisiana	4,438
25	Georgia	4,437
26	Connecticut	4,406
27	Alabama	4,343
28	Maryland	4,322
29	Virginia	4,210
30	North Carolina	4,164
31	New Mexico	4,053
32	Mississippi	4,041
33	Indiana	3,953
34	South Carolina	3,950
35	Utah	3,917
36	Rhode Island	3,881
37	Missouri	3,804
38	Vermont	3,798
39	New Hampshire	3,764
40	North Dakota	3,749
41	South Dakota	3,652
42	Idaho	3,607
43	Delaware	3,462
44	Maine	3,409
45	Oklahoma	3,395
46	Montana	3,392
47	Kentucky	3,124
48	Arkansas	3,053
49	West Virginia	2,772
50	Hawaii	2,245

District of Columbia   19,980

Source: CQ Press using data from U.S. Bureau of the Census, Governments Division
   "2008 State and Local Government Finances" (http://www.census.gov/govs/estimate/index.html)
*Total revenue includes all money received from external sources. This includes taxes, intergovernmental transfers and insurance trust revenue, and revenue from government owned utilities and other commercial or auxiliary enterprise.

Local Government Revenue from the Federal Government in 2008

National Total = $58,229,585,000

ALPHA ORDER

RANK	STATE	REVENUE	% of USA
18	Alabama	$913,909,000	1.6%
37	Alaska	258,139,000	0.4%
17	Arizona	1,021,834,000	1.8%
36	Arkansas	260,463,000	0.4%
1	California	8,353,374,000	14.3%
21	Colorado	779,695,000	1.3%
32	Connecticut	401,858,000	0.7%
49	Delaware	58,849,000	0.1%
3	Florida	3,885,134,000	6.7%
12	Georgia	1,172,713,000	2.0%
39	Hawaii	202,266,000	0.3%
47	Idaho	134,637,000	0.2%
6	Illinois	3,091,700,000	5.3%
31	Indiana	402,085,000	0.7%
28	Iowa	420,602,000	0.7%
38	Kansas	222,488,000	0.4%
29	Kentucky	413,088,000	0.7%
16	Louisiana	1,033,560,000	1.8%
45	Maine	139,071,000	0.2%
14	Maryland	1,062,276,000	1.8%
10	Massachusetts	1,644,960,000	2.8%
9	Michigan	1,734,454,000	3.0%
22	Minnesota	739,625,000	1.3%
24	Mississippi	565,660,000	1.0%
20	Missouri	827,460,000	1.4%
40	Montana	192,241,000	0.3%
35	Nebraska	276,985,000	0.5%
25	Nevada	541,770,000	0.9%
44	New Hampshire	144,977,000	0.2%
19	New Jersey	877,965,000	1.5%
34	New Mexico	324,967,000	0.6%
2	New York	5,397,340,000	9.3%
7	North Carolina	2,215,856,000	3.8%
43	North Dakota	164,861,000	0.3%
8	Ohio	2,103,340,000	3.6%
33	Oklahoma	359,154,000	0.6%
15	Oregon	1,038,578,000	1.8%
5	Pennsylvania	3,114,913,000	5.3%
46	Rhode Island	138,648,000	0.2%
30	South Carolina	402,423,000	0.7%
41	South Dakota	191,269,000	0.3%
23	Tennessee	662,646,000	1.1%
4	Texas	3,574,966,000	6.1%
27	Utah	450,584,000	0.8%
50	Vermont	57,779,000	0.1%
13	Virginia	1,109,325,000	1.9%
11	Washington	1,322,805,000	2.3%
42	West Virginia	188,124,000	0.3%
26	Wisconsin	534,955,000	0.9%
48	Wyoming	92,226,000	0.2%

RANK ORDER

RANK	STATE	REVENUE	% of USA
1	California	$8,353,374,000	14.3%
2	New York	5,397,340,000	9.3%
3	Florida	3,885,134,000	6.7%
4	Texas	3,574,966,000	6.1%
5	Pennsylvania	3,114,913,000	5.3%
6	Illinois	3,091,700,000	5.3%
7	North Carolina	2,215,856,000	3.8%
8	Ohio	2,103,340,000	3.6%
9	Michigan	1,734,454,000	3.0%
10	Massachusetts	1,644,960,000	2.8%
11	Washington	1,322,805,000	2.3%
12	Georgia	1,172,713,000	2.0%
13	Virginia	1,109,325,000	1.9%
14	Maryland	1,062,276,000	1.8%
15	Oregon	1,038,578,000	1.8%
16	Louisiana	1,033,560,000	1.8%
17	Arizona	1,021,834,000	1.8%
18	Alabama	913,909,000	1.6%
19	New Jersey	877,965,000	1.5%
20	Missouri	827,460,000	1.4%
21	Colorado	779,695,000	1.3%
22	Minnesota	739,625,000	1.3%
23	Tennessee	662,646,000	1.1%
24	Mississippi	565,660,000	1.0%
25	Nevada	541,770,000	0.9%
26	Wisconsin	534,955,000	0.9%
27	Utah	450,584,000	0.8%
28	Iowa	420,602,000	0.7%
29	Kentucky	413,088,000	0.7%
30	South Carolina	402,423,000	0.7%
31	Indiana	402,085,000	0.7%
32	Connecticut	401,858,000	0.7%
33	Oklahoma	359,154,000	0.6%
34	New Mexico	324,967,000	0.6%
35	Nebraska	276,985,000	0.5%
36	Arkansas	260,463,000	0.4%
37	Alaska	258,139,000	0.4%
38	Kansas	222,488,000	0.4%
39	Hawaii	202,266,000	0.3%
40	Montana	192,241,000	0.3%
41	South Dakota	191,269,000	0.3%
42	West Virginia	188,124,000	0.3%
43	North Dakota	164,861,000	0.3%
44	New Hampshire	144,977,000	0.2%
45	Maine	139,071,000	0.2%
46	Rhode Island	138,648,000	0.2%
47	Idaho	134,637,000	0.2%
48	Wyoming	92,226,000	0.2%
49	Delaware	58,849,000	0.1%
50	Vermont	57,779,000	0.1%
	District of Columbia	3,010,988,000	5.2%

Source: U.S. Bureau of the Census, Governments Division
"2008 State and Local Government Finances" (http://www.census.gov/govs/estimate/index.html)

Per Capita Local Government Revenue from the Federal Government in 2008

National Per Capita = $191

ALPHA ORDER

RANK	STATE	PER CAPITA
16	Alabama	$195
1	Alaska	375
25	Arizona	157
45	Arkansas	91
11	California	228
24	Colorado	158
35	Connecticut	115
49	Delaware	67
12	Florida	211
34	Georgia	121
25	Hawaii	157
47	Idaho	88
7	Illinois	241
50	Indiana	63
31	Iowa	140
48	Kansas	80
42	Kentucky	96
10	Louisiana	232
38	Maine	105
18	Maryland	188
5	Massachusetts	251
20	Michigan	173
30	Minnesota	141
17	Mississippi	192
32	Missouri	139
15	Montana	199
27	Nebraska	155
13	Nevada	207
36	New Hampshire	110
40	New Jersey	101
23	New Mexico	164
2	New York	277
8	North Carolina	240
4	North Dakota	257
19	Ohio	182
41	Oklahoma	99
3	Oregon	275
6	Pennsylvania	248
33	Rhode Island	132
46	South Carolina	89
9	South Dakota	238
37	Tennessee	106
28	Texas	147
22	Utah	165
44	Vermont	93
29	Virginia	142
14	Washington	201
39	West Virginia	104
43	Wisconsin	95
20	Wyoming	173

RANK ORDER

RANK	STATE	PER CAPITA
1	Alaska	$375
2	New York	277
3	Oregon	275
4	North Dakota	257
5	Massachusetts	251
6	Pennsylvania	248
7	Illinois	241
8	North Carolina	240
9	South Dakota	238
10	Louisiana	232
11	California	228
12	Florida	211
13	Nevada	207
14	Washington	201
15	Montana	199
16	Alabama	195
17	Mississippi	192
18	Maryland	188
19	Ohio	182
20	Michigan	173
20	Wyoming	173
22	Utah	165
23	New Mexico	164
24	Colorado	158
25	Arizona	157
25	Hawaii	157
27	Nebraska	155
28	Texas	147
29	Virginia	142
30	Minnesota	141
31	Iowa	140
32	Missouri	139
33	Rhode Island	132
34	Georgia	121
35	Connecticut	115
36	New Hampshire	110
37	Tennessee	106
38	Maine	105
39	West Virginia	104
40	New Jersey	101
41	Oklahoma	99
42	Kentucky	96
43	Wisconsin	95
44	Vermont	93
45	Arkansas	91
46	South Carolina	89
47	Idaho	88
48	Kansas	80
49	Delaware	67
50	Indiana	63

District of Columbia	5,103

Source: CQ Press using data from U.S. Bureau of the Census, Governments Division
"2008 State and Local Government Finances" (http://www.census.gov/govs/estimate/index.html)

Local Government Own Source Revenue in 2008

National Total = $876,603,549,000*

ALPHA ORDER

RANK	STATE	REVENUE	% of USA
25	Alabama	$10,134,280,000	1.2%
44	Alaska	2,224,169,000	0.3%
17	Arizona	15,007,059,000	1.7%
36	Arkansas	3,411,824,000	0.4%
1	California	127,715,940,000	14.6%
14	Colorado	16,935,278,000	1.9%
26	Connecticut	9,981,540,000	1.1%
49	Delaware	1,321,090,000	0.2%
4	Florida	64,958,933,000	7.4%
9	Georgia	26,271,788,000	3.0%
45	Hawaii	2,163,152,000	0.2%
39	Idaho	3,111,620,000	0.4%
5	Illinois	37,627,752,000	4.3%
18	Indiana	14,785,532,000	1.7%
29	Iowa	7,949,770,000	0.9%
30	Kansas	7,635,125,000	0.9%
31	Kentucky	6,997,304,000	0.8%
23	Louisiana	11,527,120,000	1.3%
40	Maine	2,846,219,000	0.3%
16	Maryland	15,652,960,000	1.8%
15	Massachusetts	16,140,374,000	1.8%
10	Michigan	22,449,674,000	2.6%
22	Minnesota	13,119,894,000	1.5%
33	Mississippi	6,085,159,000	0.7%
19	Missouri	14,204,881,000	1.6%
46	Montana	1,821,350,000	0.2%
34	Nebraska	5,536,793,000	0.6%
28	Nevada	8,214,075,000	0.9%
38	New Hampshire	3,308,369,000	0.4%
8	New Jersey	29,649,775,000	3.4%
37	New Mexico	3,313,803,000	0.4%
2	New York	97,720,001,000	11.1%
11	North Carolina	19,929,827,000	2.3%
48	North Dakota	1,394,672,000	0.2%
7	Ohio	31,191,695,000	3.6%
32	Oklahoma	6,870,327,000	0.8%
27	Oregon	9,513,275,000	1.1%
6	Pennsylvania	32,301,258,000	3.7%
42	Rhode Island	2,602,234,000	0.3%
24	South Carolina	10,764,507,000	1.2%
47	South Dakota	1,789,766,000	0.2%
21	Tennessee	13,483,754,000	1.5%
3	Texas	65,741,148,000	7.5%
35	Utah	5,380,889,000	0.6%
50	Vermont	650,192,000	0.1%
12	Virginia	19,857,244,000	2.3%
13	Washington	19,400,346,000	2.2%
41	West Virginia	2,657,009,000	0.3%
20	Wisconsin	13,661,044,000	1.6%
43	Wyoming	2,580,051,000	0.3%

RANK ORDER

RANK	STATE	REVENUE	% of USA
1	California	$127,715,940,000	14.6%
2	New York	97,720,001,000	11.1%
3	Texas	65,741,148,000	7.5%
4	Florida	64,958,933,000	7.4%
5	Illinois	37,627,752,000	4.3%
6	Pennsylvania	32,301,258,000	3.7%
7	Ohio	31,191,695,000	3.6%
8	New Jersey	29,649,775,000	3.4%
9	Georgia	26,271,788,000	3.0%
10	Michigan	22,449,674,000	2.6%
11	North Carolina	19,929,827,000	2.3%
12	Virginia	19,857,244,000	2.3%
13	Washington	19,400,346,000	2.2%
14	Colorado	16,935,278,000	1.9%
15	Massachusetts	16,140,374,000	1.8%
16	Maryland	15,652,960,000	1.8%
17	Arizona	15,007,059,000	1.7%
18	Indiana	14,785,532,000	1.7%
19	Missouri	14,204,881,000	1.6%
20	Wisconsin	13,661,044,000	1.6%
21	Tennessee	13,483,754,000	1.5%
22	Minnesota	13,119,894,000	1.5%
23	Louisiana	11,527,120,000	1.3%
24	South Carolina	10,764,507,000	1.2%
25	Alabama	10,134,280,000	1.2%
26	Connecticut	9,981,540,000	1.1%
27	Oregon	9,513,275,000	1.1%
28	Nevada	8,214,075,000	0.9%
29	Iowa	7,949,770,000	0.9%
30	Kansas	7,635,125,000	0.9%
31	Kentucky	6,997,304,000	0.8%
32	Oklahoma	6,870,327,000	0.8%
33	Mississippi	6,085,159,000	0.7%
34	Nebraska	5,536,793,000	0.6%
35	Utah	5,380,889,000	0.6%
36	Arkansas	3,411,824,000	0.4%
37	New Mexico	3,313,803,000	0.4%
38	New Hampshire	3,308,369,000	0.4%
39	Idaho	3,111,620,000	0.4%
40	Maine	2,846,219,000	0.3%
41	West Virginia	2,657,009,000	0.3%
42	Rhode Island	2,602,234,000	0.3%
43	Wyoming	2,580,051,000	0.3%
44	Alaska	2,224,169,000	0.3%
45	Hawaii	2,163,152,000	0.2%
46	Montana	1,821,350,000	0.2%
47	South Dakota	1,789,766,000	0.2%
48	North Dakota	1,394,672,000	0.2%
49	Delaware	1,321,090,000	0.2%
50	Vermont	650,192,000	0.1%
	District of Columbia	7,011,708,000	0.8%

Source: U.S. Bureau of the Census, Governments Division
   "2008 State and Local Government Finances" (http://www.census.gov/govs/estimate/index.html)
*Own source revenue includes taxes, current charges, and miscellaneous general revenue. Excluded are intergovernmental transfers, insurance trust revenue, and revenue from government owned utilities and other commercial or auxiliary enterprise.

Per Capita Local Government Own Source Revenue in 2008

National Per Capita = $2,880*

ALPHA ORDER

RANK	STATE	PER CAPITA
35	Alabama	$2,167
7	Alaska	3,232
31	Arizona	2,309
49	Arkansas	1,190
4	California	3,491
5	Colorado	3,432
12	Connecticut	2,849
47	Delaware	1,508
3	Florida	3,526
15	Georgia	2,709
44	Hawaii	1,680
40	Idaho	2,037
11	Illinois	2,930
30	Indiana	2,314
18	Iowa	2,655
14	Kansas	2,729
46	Kentucky	1,632
19	Louisiana	2,589
37	Maine	2,157
13	Maryland	2,766
26	Massachusetts	2,467
32	Michigan	2,244
23	Minnesota	2,508
39	Mississippi	2,070
29	Missouri	2,385
43	Montana	1,881
9	Nebraska	3,107
8	Nevada	3,140
24	New Hampshire	2,503
6	New Jersey	3,422
45	New Mexico	1,668
1	New York	5,020
38	North Carolina	2,155
34	North Dakota	2,174
16	Ohio	2,706
42	Oklahoma	1,885
22	Oregon	2,515
20	Pennsylvania	2,570
25	Rhode Island	2,470
28	South Carolina	2,390
33	South Dakota	2,225
36	Tennessee	2,161
17	Texas	2,705
41	Utah	1,973
50	Vermont	1,047
21	Virginia	2,547
10	Washington	2,955
48	West Virginia	1,464
27	Wisconsin	2,428
2	Wyoming	4,841

RANK ORDER

RANK	STATE	PER CAPITA
1	New York	$5,020
2	Wyoming	4,841
3	Florida	3,526
4	California	3,491
5	Colorado	3,432
6	New Jersey	3,422
7	Alaska	3,232
8	Nevada	3,140
9	Nebraska	3,107
10	Washington	2,955
11	Illinois	2,930
12	Connecticut	2,849
13	Maryland	2,766
14	Kansas	2,729
15	Georgia	2,709
16	Ohio	2,706
17	Texas	2,705
18	Iowa	2,655
19	Louisiana	2,589
20	Pennsylvania	2,570
21	Virginia	2,547
22	Oregon	2,515
23	Minnesota	2,508
24	New Hampshire	2,503
25	Rhode Island	2,470
26	Massachusetts	2,467
27	Wisconsin	2,428
28	South Carolina	2,390
29	Missouri	2,385
30	Indiana	2,314
31	Arizona	2,309
32	Michigan	2,244
33	South Dakota	2,225
34	North Dakota	2,174
35	Alabama	2,167
36	Tennessee	2,161
37	Maine	2,157
38	North Carolina	2,155
39	Mississippi	2,070
40	Idaho	2,037
41	Utah	1,973
42	Oklahoma	1,885
43	Montana	1,881
44	Hawaii	1,680
45	New Mexico	1,668
46	Kentucky	1,632
47	Delaware	1,508
48	West Virginia	1,464
49	Arkansas	1,190
50	Vermont	1,047
	District of Columbia	11,883

Source: CQ Press using data from U.S. Bureau of the Census, Governments Division
"2008 State and Local Government Finances" (http://www.census.gov/govs/estimate/index.html)
*Own source revenue includes taxes, current charges, and miscellaneous general revenue. Excluded are intergovernmental transfers, insurance trust revenue, and revenue from government owned utilities and other commercial or auxiliary enterprise.

Local Government Tax Revenue in 2008

National Total = $548,764,528,000

ALPHA ORDER

RANK	STATE	REVENUE	% of USA
27	Alabama	$4,970,225,000	0.9%
43	Alaska	1,310,360,000	0.2%
17	Arizona	9,286,476,000	1.7%
40	Arkansas	1,875,236,000	0.3%
2	California	68,652,908,000	12.5%
16	Colorado	10,011,607,000	1.8%
20	Connecticut	8,517,355,000	1.6%
49	Delaware	781,466,000	0.1%
4	Florida	37,501,400,000	6.8%
9	Georgia	15,562,469,000	2.8%
41	Hawaii	1,589,213,000	0.3%
45	Idaho	1,287,805,000	0.2%
5	Illinois	25,943,090,000	4.7%
21	Indiana	7,838,192,000	1.4%
29	Iowa	4,649,150,000	0.8%
28	Kansas	4,717,567,000	0.9%
31	Kentucky	4,100,404,000	0.7%
23	Louisiana	6,946,631,000	1.3%
37	Maine	2,147,053,000	0.4%
13	Maryland	11,937,066,000	2.2%
12	Massachusetts	12,088,741,000	2.2%
11	Michigan	12,868,245,000	2.3%
24	Minnesota	6,402,997,000	1.2%
36	Mississippi	2,441,918,000	0.4%
19	Missouri	8,907,371,000	1.6%
47	Montana	990,087,000	0.2%
33	Nebraska	3,279,242,000	0.6%
30	Nevada	4,472,158,000	0.8%
35	New Hampshire	2,711,625,000	0.5%
6	New Jersey	23,174,387,000	4.2%
39	New Mexico	2,101,091,000	0.4%
1	New York	72,917,287,000	13.3%
15	North Carolina	10,426,737,000	1.9%
48	North Dakota	861,951,000	0.2%
8	Ohio	20,531,808,000	3.7%
32	Oklahoma	3,983,756,000	0.7%
25	Oregon	5,252,832,000	1.0%
7	Pennsylvania	21,985,876,000	4.0%
38	Rhode Island	2,112,432,000	0.4%
26	South Carolina	5,183,338,000	0.9%
46	South Dakota	1,178,533,000	0.2%
22	Tennessee	7,461,197,000	1.4%
3	Texas	41,706,739,000	7.6%
34	Utah	3,262,204,000	0.6%
50	Vermont	391,438,000	0.1%
10	Virginia	14,298,363,000	2.6%
14	Washington	10,629,738,000	1.9%
42	West Virginia	1,546,164,000	0.3%
18	Wisconsin	9,283,679,000	1.7%
44	Wyoming	1,288,941,000	0.2%

RANK ORDER

RANK	STATE	REVENUE	% of USA
1	New York	$72,917,287,000	13.3%
2	California	68,652,908,000	12.5%
3	Texas	41,706,739,000	7.6%
4	Florida	37,501,400,000	6.8%
5	Illinois	25,943,090,000	4.7%
6	New Jersey	23,174,387,000	4.2%
7	Pennsylvania	21,985,876,000	4.0%
8	Ohio	20,531,808,000	3.7%
9	Georgia	15,562,469,000	2.8%
10	Virginia	14,298,363,000	2.6%
11	Michigan	12,868,245,000	2.3%
12	Massachusetts	12,088,741,000	2.2%
13	Maryland	11,937,066,000	2.2%
14	Washington	10,629,738,000	1.9%
15	North Carolina	10,426,737,000	1.9%
16	Colorado	10,011,607,000	1.8%
17	Arizona	9,286,476,000	1.7%
18	Wisconsin	9,283,679,000	1.7%
19	Missouri	8,907,371,000	1.6%
20	Connecticut	8,517,355,000	1.6%
21	Indiana	7,838,192,000	1.4%
22	Tennessee	7,461,197,000	1.4%
23	Louisiana	6,946,631,000	1.3%
24	Minnesota	6,402,997,000	1.2%
25	Oregon	5,252,832,000	1.0%
26	South Carolina	5,183,338,000	0.9%
27	Alabama	4,970,225,000	0.9%
28	Kansas	4,717,567,000	0.9%
29	Iowa	4,649,150,000	0.8%
30	Nevada	4,472,158,000	0.8%
31	Kentucky	4,100,404,000	0.7%
32	Oklahoma	3,983,756,000	0.7%
33	Nebraska	3,279,242,000	0.6%
34	Utah	3,262,204,000	0.6%
35	New Hampshire	2,711,625,000	0.5%
36	Mississippi	2,441,918,000	0.4%
37	Maine	2,147,053,000	0.4%
38	Rhode Island	2,112,432,000	0.4%
39	New Mexico	2,101,091,000	0.4%
40	Arkansas	1,875,236,000	0.3%
41	Hawaii	1,589,213,000	0.3%
42	West Virginia	1,546,164,000	0.3%
43	Alaska	1,310,360,000	0.2%
44	Wyoming	1,288,941,000	0.2%
45	Idaho	1,287,805,000	0.2%
46	South Dakota	1,178,533,000	0.2%
47	Montana	990,087,000	0.2%
48	North Dakota	861,951,000	0.2%
49	Delaware	781,466,000	0.1%
50	Vermont	391,438,000	0.1%
	District of Columbia	5,397,980,000	1.0%

Source: U.S. Bureau of the Census, Governments Division
"2008 State and Local Government Finances" (http://www.census.gov/govs/estimate/index.html)

Per Capita Local Government Tax Revenue in 2008

National Per Capita = $1,803

ALPHA ORDER

RANK	STATE	PER CAPITA
41	Alabama	$1,063
11	Alaska	1,904
29	Arizona	1,429
49	Arkansas	654
12	California	1,877
8	Colorado	2,029
3	Connecticut	2,431
45	Delaware	892
7	Florida	2,035
24	Georgia	1,605
33	Hawaii	1,234
47	Idaho	843
9	Illinois	2,020
34	Indiana	1,227
26	Iowa	1,553
20	Kansas	1,686
44	Kentucky	956
25	Louisiana	1,561
22	Maine	1,627
5	Maryland	2,110
13	Massachusetts	1,847
32	Michigan	1,287
35	Minnesota	1,224
48	Mississippi	831
27	Missouri	1,495
43	Montana	1,023
14	Nebraska	1,840
19	Nevada	1,710
6	New Hampshire	2,051
2	New Jersey	2,675
42	New Mexico	1,058
1	New York	3,746
39	North Carolina	1,128
31	North Dakota	1,344
16	Ohio	1,781
40	Oklahoma	1,093
30	Oregon	1,389
17	Pennsylvania	1,750
10	Rhode Island	2,005
38	South Carolina	1,151
28	South Dakota	1,465
36	Tennessee	1,196
18	Texas	1,716
36	Utah	1,196
50	Vermont	630
15	Virginia	1,834
23	Washington	1,619
46	West Virginia	852
21	Wisconsin	1,650
4	Wyoming	2,418

RANK ORDER

RANK	STATE	PER CAPITA
1	New York	$3,746
2	New Jersey	2,675
3	Connecticut	2,431
4	Wyoming	2,418
5	Maryland	2,110
6	New Hampshire	2,051
7	Florida	2,035
8	Colorado	2,029
9	Illinois	2,020
10	Rhode Island	2,005
11	Alaska	1,904
12	California	1,877
13	Massachusetts	1,847
14	Nebraska	1,840
15	Virginia	1,834
16	Ohio	1,781
17	Pennsylvania	1,750
18	Texas	1,716
19	Nevada	1,710
20	Kansas	1,686
21	Wisconsin	1,650
22	Maine	1,627
23	Washington	1,619
24	Georgia	1,605
25	Louisiana	1,561
26	Iowa	1,553
27	Missouri	1,495
28	South Dakota	1,465
29	Arizona	1,429
30	Oregon	1,389
31	North Dakota	1,344
32	Michigan	1,287
33	Hawaii	1,234
34	Indiana	1,227
35	Minnesota	1,224
36	Tennessee	1,196
36	Utah	1,196
38	South Carolina	1,151
39	North Carolina	1,128
40	Oklahoma	1,093
41	Alabama	1,063
42	New Mexico	1,058
43	Montana	1,023
44	Kentucky	956
45	Delaware	892
46	West Virginia	852
47	Idaho	843
48	Mississippi	831
49	Arkansas	654
50	Vermont	630
	District of Columbia	9,148

Source: CQ Press using data from U.S. Bureau of the Census, Governments Division
"2008 State and Local Government Finances" (http://www.census.gov/govs/estimate/index.html)

Local Government Total Expenditures in 2008

National Total = $1,593,087,951,000*

ALPHA ORDER

RANK	STATE	EXPENDITURES	% of USA
23	Alabama	$20,046,415,000	1.3%
42	Alaska	4,274,918,000	0.3%
14	Arizona	32,217,566,000	2.0%
36	Arkansas	8,916,141,000	0.6%
1	California	259,358,520,000	16.3%
20	Colorado	25,992,139,000	1.6%
27	Connecticut	15,786,801,000	1.0%
46	Delaware	3,096,828,000	0.2%
4	Florida	100,978,232,000	6.3%
8	Georgia	46,997,303,000	3.0%
47	Hawaii	2,818,529,000	0.2%
39	Idaho	5,147,386,000	0.3%
5	Illinois	67,016,218,000	4.2%
19	Indiana	26,557,098,000	1.7%
30	Iowa	13,498,191,000	0.8%
31	Kansas	12,727,067,000	0.8%
29	Kentucky	13,644,526,000	0.9%
24	Louisiana	18,970,576,000	1.2%
41	Maine	4,351,378,000	0.3%
21	Maryland	25,913,713,000	1.6%
15	Massachusetts	32,174,568,000	2.0%
9	Michigan	46,855,617,000	2.9%
17	Minnesota	27,866,770,000	1.7%
34	Mississippi	11,642,274,000	0.7%
22	Missouri	23,954,808,000	1.5%
45	Montana	3,297,926,000	0.2%
33	Nebraska	11,860,019,000	0.7%
28	Nevada	14,488,427,000	0.9%
40	New Hampshire	4,900,815,000	0.3%
10	New Jersey	44,513,070,000	2.8%
37	New Mexico	7,850,201,000	0.5%
2	New York	167,708,951,000	10.5%
11	North Carolina	40,094,934,000	2.5%
50	North Dakota	2,310,156,000	0.1%
7	Ohio	53,633,696,000	3.4%
32	Oklahoma	12,261,416,000	0.8%
26	Oregon	17,829,561,000	1.1%
6	Pennsylvania	58,221,450,000	3.7%
44	Rhode Island	4,106,126,000	0.3%
25	South Carolina	17,894,354,000	1.1%
48	South Dakota	2,814,993,000	0.2%
16	Tennessee	29,386,570,000	1.8%
3	Texas	115,902,729,000	7.3%
35	Utah	10,974,628,000	0.7%
49	Vermont	2,310,207,000	0.1%
13	Virginia	34,560,899,000	2.2%
12	Washington	36,190,764,000	2.3%
38	West Virginia	5,224,359,000	0.3%
18	Wisconsin	26,791,030,000	1.7%
43	Wyoming	4,208,438,000	0.3%

RANK ORDER

RANK	STATE	EXPENDITURES	% of USA
1	California	$259,358,520,000	16.3%
2	New York	167,708,951,000	10.5%
3	Texas	115,902,729,000	7.3%
4	Florida	100,978,232,000	6.3%
5	Illinois	67,016,218,000	4.2%
6	Pennsylvania	58,221,450,000	3.7%
7	Ohio	53,633,696,000	3.4%
8	Georgia	46,997,303,000	3.0%
9	Michigan	46,855,617,000	2.9%
10	New Jersey	44,513,070,000	2.8%
11	North Carolina	40,094,934,000	2.5%
12	Washington	36,190,764,000	2.3%
13	Virginia	34,560,899,000	2.2%
14	Arizona	32,217,566,000	2.0%
15	Massachusetts	32,174,568,000	2.0%
16	Tennessee	29,386,570,000	1.8%
17	Minnesota	27,866,770,000	1.7%
18	Wisconsin	26,791,030,000	1.7%
19	Indiana	26,557,098,000	1.7%
20	Colorado	25,992,139,000	1.6%
21	Maryland	25,913,713,000	1.6%
22	Missouri	23,954,808,000	1.5%
23	Alabama	20,046,415,000	1.3%
24	Louisiana	18,970,576,000	1.2%
25	South Carolina	17,894,354,000	1.1%
26	Oregon	17,829,561,000	1.1%
27	Connecticut	15,786,801,000	1.0%
28	Nevada	14,488,427,000	0.9%
29	Kentucky	13,644,526,000	0.9%
30	Iowa	13,498,191,000	0.8%
31	Kansas	12,727,067,000	0.8%
32	Oklahoma	12,261,416,000	0.8%
33	Nebraska	11,860,019,000	0.7%
34	Mississippi	11,642,274,000	0.7%
35	Utah	10,974,628,000	0.7%
36	Arkansas	8,916,141,000	0.6%
37	New Mexico	7,850,201,000	0.5%
38	West Virginia	5,224,359,000	0.3%
39	Idaho	5,147,386,000	0.3%
40	New Hampshire	4,900,815,000	0.3%
41	Maine	4,351,378,000	0.3%
42	Alaska	4,274,918,000	0.3%
43	Wyoming	4,208,438,000	0.3%
44	Rhode Island	4,106,126,000	0.3%
45	Montana	3,297,926,000	0.2%
46	Delaware	3,096,828,000	0.2%
47	Hawaii	2,818,529,000	0.2%
48	South Dakota	2,814,993,000	0.2%
49	Vermont	2,310,207,000	0.1%
50	North Dakota	2,310,156,000	0.1%
	District of Columbia	12,948,650,000	0.8%

Source: U.S. Bureau of the Census, Governments Division
   "2008 State and Local Government Finances" (http://www.census.gov/govs/estimate/index.html)
*Total expenditures includes all money paid other than for retirement of debt and extension of loans. Includes payments from all sources of funds including current revenues and proceeds from borrowing and prior year fund balances. Includes intergovernmental transfers and expenditures for government owned utilities and other commercial or auxiliary enterprise and insurance trust expenditures.

Per Capita Local Government Total Expenditures in 2008

National Per Capita = $5,234*

ALPHA ORDER				RANK ORDER		
RANK	STATE	PER CAPITA		RANK	STATE	PER CAPITA
29	Alabama	$4,286		1	New York	$8,615
5	Alaska	6,212		2	Wyoming	7,896
13	Arizona	4,957		3	California	7,090
48	Arkansas	3,109		4	Nebraska	6,656
3	California	7,090		5	Alaska	6,212
10	Colorado	5,267		6	Nevada	5,539
26	Connecticut	4,507		7	Washington	5,512
41	Delaware	3,534		8	Florida	5,481
8	Florida	5,481		9	Minnesota	5,328
15	Georgia	4,846		10	Colorado	5,267
50	Hawaii	2,189		11	Illinois	5,218
44	Idaho	3,370		12	New Jersey	5,138
11	Illinois	5,218		13	Arizona	4,957
31	Indiana	4,157		14	Massachusetts	4,917
25	Iowa	4,508		15	Georgia	4,846
24	Kansas	4,550		16	Texas	4,769
47	Kentucky	3,182		17	Wisconsin	4,761
30	Louisiana	4,262		18	Oregon	4,713
46	Maine	3,297		19	Tennessee	4,709
23	Maryland	4,579		20	Michigan	4,684
14	Massachusetts	4,917		21	Ohio	4,652
20	Michigan	4,684		22	Pennsylvania	4,633
9	Minnesota	5,328		23	Maryland	4,579
35	Mississippi	3,960		24	Kansas	4,550
33	Missouri	4,022		25	Iowa	4,508
43	Montana	3,407		26	Connecticut	4,507
4	Nebraska	6,656		27	Virginia	4,433
6	Nevada	5,539		28	North Carolina	4,336
39	New Hampshire	3,707		29	Alabama	4,286
12	New Jersey	5,138		30	Louisiana	4,262
36	New Mexico	3,951		31	Indiana	4,157
1	New York	8,615		32	Utah	4,024
28	North Carolina	4,336		33	Missouri	4,022
40	North Dakota	3,602		34	South Carolina	3,974
21	Ohio	4,652		35	Mississippi	3,960
45	Oklahoma	3,365		36	New Mexico	3,951
18	Oregon	4,713		37	Rhode Island	3,898
22	Pennsylvania	4,633		38	Vermont	3,720
37	Rhode Island	3,898		39	New Hampshire	3,707
34	South Carolina	3,974		40	North Dakota	3,602
42	South Dakota	3,499		41	Delaware	3,534
19	Tennessee	4,709		42	South Dakota	3,499
16	Texas	4,769		43	Montana	3,407
32	Utah	4,024		44	Idaho	3,370
38	Vermont	3,720		45	Oklahoma	3,365
27	Virginia	4,433		46	Maine	3,297
7	Washington	5,512		47	Kentucky	3,182
49	West Virginia	2,879		48	Arkansas	3,109
17	Wisconsin	4,761		49	West Virginia	2,879
2	Wyoming	7,896		50	Hawaii	2,189

District of Columbia   21,944

Source: CQ Press using data from U.S. Bureau of the Census, Governments Division
   "2008 State and Local Government Finances" (http://www.census.gov/govs/estimate/index.html)
*Total expenditures includes all money paid other than for retirement of debt and extension of loans. Includes payments from all sources of funds including current revenues and proceeds from borrowing and prior year fund balances. Includes intergovernmental transfers and expenditures for government owned utilities and other commercial or auxiliary enterprise and insurance trust expenditures.

Local Government Direct General Expenditures in 2008

National Total = $1,375,538,830,000*

ALPHA ORDER

RANK	STATE	EXPENDITURES	% of USA
24	Alabama	$17,177,208,000	1.2%
43	Alaska	3,862,153,000	0.3%
14	Arizona	25,897,328,000	1.9%
35	Arkansas	7,927,245,000	0.6%
1	California	220,144,288,000	16.0%
20	Colorado	22,527,504,000	1.6%
27	Connecticut	14,588,379,000	1.1%
46	Delaware	2,685,821,000	0.2%
4	Florida	89,032,546,000	6.5%
10	Georgia	39,540,415,000	2.9%
48	Hawaii	2,275,036,000	0.2%
38	Idaho	4,927,783,000	0.4%
5	Illinois	56,658,321,000	4.1%
18	Indiana	23,994,122,000	1.7%
29	Iowa	12,343,421,000	0.9%
31	Kansas	11,461,689,000	0.8%
30	Kentucky	11,808,539,000	0.9%
23	Louisiana	17,401,431,000	1.3%
41	Maine	4,219,014,000	0.3%
19	Maryland	23,920,562,000	1.7%
15	Massachusetts	25,459,385,000	1.9%
9	Michigan	41,971,625,000	3.1%
16	Minnesota	24,997,447,000	1.8%
33	Mississippi	10,788,712,000	0.8%
21	Missouri	21,277,718,000	1.5%
45	Montana	3,152,827,000	0.2%
36	Nebraska	7,672,958,000	0.6%
28	Nevada	12,772,640,000	0.9%
40	New Hampshire	4,706,854,000	0.3%
8	New Jersey	42,992,120,000	3.1%
37	New Mexico	7,208,869,000	0.5%
2	New York	136,974,564,000	10.0%
11	North Carolina	34,741,128,000	2.5%
49	North Dakota	2,134,560,000	0.2%
7	Ohio	49,964,926,000	3.6%
32	Oklahoma	11,188,191,000	0.8%
26	Oregon	15,706,704,000	1.1%
6	Pennsylvania	52,011,561,000	3.8%
44	Rhode Island	3,790,375,000	0.3%
25	South Carolina	16,383,911,000	1.2%
47	South Dakota	2,502,633,000	0.2%
22	Tennessee	19,911,565,000	1.4%
3	Texas	99,404,947,000	7.2%
34	Utah	8,799,744,000	0.6%
50	Vermont	2,069,518,000	0.2%
12	Virginia	31,821,797,000	2.3%
13	Washington	28,641,981,000	2.1%
39	West Virginia	4,881,366,000	0.4%
17	Wisconsin	24,532,033,000	1.8%
42	Wyoming	4,006,386,000	0.3%

RANK ORDER

RANK	STATE	EXPENDITURES	% of USA
1	California	$220,144,288,000	16.0%
2	New York	136,974,564,000	10.0%
3	Texas	99,404,947,000	7.2%
4	Florida	89,032,546,000	6.5%
5	Illinois	56,658,321,000	4.1%
6	Pennsylvania	52,011,561,000	3.8%
7	Ohio	49,964,926,000	3.6%
8	New Jersey	42,992,120,000	3.1%
9	Michigan	41,971,625,000	3.1%
10	Georgia	39,540,415,000	2.9%
11	North Carolina	34,741,128,000	2.5%
12	Virginia	31,821,797,000	2.3%
13	Washington	28,641,981,000	2.1%
14	Arizona	25,897,328,000	1.9%
15	Massachusetts	25,459,385,000	1.9%
16	Minnesota	24,997,447,000	1.8%
17	Wisconsin	24,532,033,000	1.8%
18	Indiana	23,994,122,000	1.7%
19	Maryland	23,920,562,000	1.7%
20	Colorado	22,527,504,000	1.6%
21	Missouri	21,277,718,000	1.5%
22	Tennessee	19,911,565,000	1.4%
23	Louisiana	17,401,431,000	1.3%
24	Alabama	17,177,208,000	1.2%
25	South Carolina	16,383,911,000	1.2%
26	Oregon	15,706,704,000	1.1%
27	Connecticut	14,588,379,000	1.1%
28	Nevada	12,772,640,000	0.9%
29	Iowa	12,343,421,000	0.9%
30	Kentucky	11,808,539,000	0.9%
31	Kansas	11,461,689,000	0.8%
32	Oklahoma	11,188,191,000	0.8%
33	Mississippi	10,788,712,000	0.8%
34	Utah	8,799,744,000	0.6%
35	Arkansas	7,927,245,000	0.6%
36	Nebraska	7,672,958,000	0.6%
37	New Mexico	7,208,869,000	0.5%
38	Idaho	4,927,783,000	0.4%
39	West Virginia	4,881,366,000	0.4%
40	New Hampshire	4,706,854,000	0.3%
41	Maine	4,219,014,000	0.3%
42	Wyoming	4,006,386,000	0.3%
43	Alaska	3,862,153,000	0.3%
44	Rhode Island	3,790,375,000	0.3%
45	Montana	3,152,827,000	0.2%
46	Delaware	2,685,821,000	0.2%
47	South Dakota	2,502,633,000	0.2%
48	Hawaii	2,275,036,000	0.2%
49	North Dakota	2,134,560,000	0.2%
50	Vermont	2,069,518,000	0.2%
	District of Columbia	10,676,980,000	0.8%

Source: U.S. Bureau of the Census, Governments Division
"2008 State and Local Government Finances" (http://www.census.gov/govs/estimate/index.html)
*Direct general expenditures include expenditures for current operations, assistance and subsidies, interest on debt, and capital outlay. Excludes intergovernmental transfers, expenditures for government owned utilities and other commercial or auxiliary enterprise, and insurance trust expenditures.

Per Capita Local Government Direct General Expenditures in 2008

National Per Capita = $4,519*

ALPHA ORDER

RANK	STATE	PER CAPITA
30	Alabama	$3,672
4	Alaska	5,613
25	Arizona	3,985
47	Arkansas	2,764
3	California	6,018
9	Colorado	4,565
17	Connecticut	4,165
46	Delaware	3,065
7	Florida	4,832
24	Georgia	4,077
50	Hawaii	1,767
40	Idaho	3,226
10	Illinois	4,412
29	Indiana	3,756
20	Iowa	4,123
21	Kansas	4,097
48	Kentucky	2,754
26	Louisiana	3,909
42	Maine	3,197
15	Maryland	4,227
27	Massachusetts	3,891
16	Michigan	4,196
8	Minnesota	4,779
31	Mississippi	3,669
35	Missouri	3,572
39	Montana	3,257
14	Nebraska	4,306
6	Nevada	4,883
36	New Hampshire	3,561
5	New Jersey	4,963
33	New Mexico	3,628
2	New York	7,036
28	North Carolina	3,757
38	North Dakota	3,328
13	Ohio	4,334
45	Oklahoma	3,070
18	Oregon	4,152
19	Pennsylvania	4,139
34	Rhode Island	3,598
32	South Carolina	3,638
44	South Dakota	3,111
43	Tennessee	3,191
22	Texas	4,090
40	Utah	3,226
37	Vermont	3,332
23	Virginia	4,082
11	Washington	4,362
49	West Virginia	2,690
12	Wisconsin	4,359
1	Wyoming	7,517

RANK ORDER

RANK	STATE	PER CAPITA
1	Wyoming	$7,517
2	New York	7,036
3	California	6,018
4	Alaska	5,613
5	New Jersey	4,963
6	Nevada	4,883
7	Florida	4,832
8	Minnesota	4,779
9	Colorado	4,565
10	Illinois	4,412
11	Washington	4,362
12	Wisconsin	4,359
13	Ohio	4,334
14	Nebraska	4,306
15	Maryland	4,227
16	Michigan	4,196
17	Connecticut	4,165
18	Oregon	4,152
19	Pennsylvania	4,139
20	Iowa	4,123
21	Kansas	4,097
22	Texas	4,090
23	Virginia	4,082
24	Georgia	4,077
25	Arizona	3,985
26	Louisiana	3,909
27	Massachusetts	3,891
28	North Carolina	3,757
29	Indiana	3,756
30	Alabama	3,672
31	Mississippi	3,669
32	South Carolina	3,638
33	New Mexico	3,628
34	Rhode Island	3,598
35	Missouri	3,572
36	New Hampshire	3,561
37	Vermont	3,332
38	North Dakota	3,328
39	Montana	3,257
40	Idaho	3,226
40	Utah	3,226
42	Maine	3,197
43	Tennessee	3,191
44	South Dakota	3,111
45	Oklahoma	3,070
46	Delaware	3,065
47	Arkansas	2,764
48	Kentucky	2,754
49	West Virginia	2,690
50	Hawaii	1,767
	District of Columbia	18,094

Source: CQ Press using data from U.S. Bureau of the Census, Governments Division
"2008 State and Local Government Finances" (http://www.census.gov/govs/estimate/index.html)
*Direct general expenditures include expenditures for current operations, assistance and subsidies, interest on debt, and capital outlay. Excludes intergovernmental transfers, expenditures for government owned utilities and other commercial or auxiliary enterprise, and insurance trust expenditures.

Local Government Debt Outstanding in 2008

National Total = $1,546,753,348,000*

ALPHA ORDER

RANK	STATE	DEBT	% of USA
25	Alabama	$19,535,890,000	1.3%
40	Alaska	3,468,616,000	0.2%
13	Arizona	33,063,881,000	2.1%
33	Arkansas	8,655,877,000	0.6%
1	California	219,164,437,000	14.2%
12	Colorado	34,091,494,000	2.2%
32	Connecticut	9,234,762,000	0.6%
45	Delaware	2,219,869,000	0.1%
4	Florida	99,807,597,000	6.5%
10	Georgia	37,489,323,000	2.4%
38	Hawaii	4,416,862,000	0.3%
44	Idaho	2,350,680,000	0.2%
6	Illinois	65,725,989,000	4.2%
18	Indiana	26,632,235,000	1.7%
34	Iowa	8,220,616,000	0.5%
28	Kansas	15,135,942,000	1.0%
19	Kentucky	26,184,745,000	1.7%
27	Louisiana	15,499,248,000	1.0%
42	Maine	2,499,788,000	0.2%
29	Maryland	14,894,228,000	1.0%
22	Massachusetts	20,935,762,000	1.4%
7	Michigan	46,181,812,000	3.0%
15	Minnesota	32,112,626,000	2.1%
36	Mississippi	7,002,768,000	0.5%
20	Missouri	21,415,309,000	1.4%
48	Montana	1,547,679,000	0.1%
30	Nebraska	11,294,615,000	0.7%
23	Nevada	20,648,906,000	1.3%
41	New Hampshire	2,617,257,000	0.2%
11	New Jersey	35,186,714,000	2.3%
37	New Mexico	5,488,886,000	0.4%
3	New York	155,501,536,000	10.1%
16	North Carolina	31,596,885,000	2.0%
47	North Dakota	1,703,787,000	0.1%
8	Ohio	41,773,451,000	2.7%
35	Oklahoma	7,813,667,000	0.5%
26	Oregon	17,769,191,000	1.1%
5	Pennsylvania	78,511,397,000	5.1%
43	Rhode Island	2,483,450,000	0.2%
21	South Carolina	21,340,632,000	1.4%
46	South Dakota	1,839,099,000	0.1%
17	Tennessee	31,408,476,000	2.0%
2	Texas	182,578,370,000	11.8%
31	Utah	10,822,254,000	0.7%
50	Vermont	970,413,000	0.1%
14	Virginia	32,824,405,000	2.1%
9	Washington	41,023,659,000	2.7%
39	West Virginia	3,471,894,000	0.2%
24	Wisconsin	20,012,414,000	1.3%
49	Wyoming	1,003,244,000	0.1%

RANK ORDER

RANK	STATE	DEBT	% of USA
1	California	$219,164,437,000	14.2%
2	Texas	182,578,370,000	11.8%
3	New York	155,501,536,000	10.1%
4	Florida	99,807,597,000	6.5%
5	Pennsylvania	78,511,397,000	5.1%
6	Illinois	65,725,989,000	4.2%
7	Michigan	46,181,812,000	3.0%
8	Ohio	41,773,451,000	2.7%
9	Washington	41,023,659,000	2.7%
10	Georgia	37,489,323,000	2.4%
11	New Jersey	35,186,714,000	2.3%
12	Colorado	34,091,494,000	2.2%
13	Arizona	33,063,881,000	2.1%
14	Virginia	32,824,405,000	2.1%
15	Minnesota	32,112,626,000	2.1%
16	North Carolina	31,596,885,000	2.0%
17	Tennessee	31,408,476,000	2.0%
18	Indiana	26,632,235,000	1.7%
19	Kentucky	26,184,745,000	1.7%
20	Missouri	21,415,309,000	1.4%
21	South Carolina	21,340,632,000	1.4%
22	Massachusetts	20,935,762,000	1.4%
23	Nevada	20,648,906,000	1.3%
24	Wisconsin	20,012,414,000	1.3%
25	Alabama	19,535,890,000	1.3%
26	Oregon	17,769,191,000	1.1%
27	Louisiana	15,499,248,000	1.0%
28	Kansas	15,135,942,000	1.0%
29	Maryland	14,894,228,000	1.0%
30	Nebraska	11,294,615,000	0.7%
31	Utah	10,822,254,000	0.7%
32	Connecticut	9,234,762,000	0.6%
33	Arkansas	8,655,877,000	0.6%
34	Iowa	8,220,616,000	0.5%
35	Oklahoma	7,813,667,000	0.5%
36	Mississippi	7,002,768,000	0.5%
37	New Mexico	5,488,886,000	0.4%
38	Hawaii	4,416,862,000	0.3%
39	West Virginia	3,471,894,000	0.2%
40	Alaska	3,468,616,000	0.2%
41	New Hampshire	2,617,257,000	0.2%
42	Maine	2,499,788,000	0.2%
43	Rhode Island	2,483,450,000	0.2%
44	Idaho	2,350,680,000	0.2%
45	Delaware	2,219,869,000	0.1%
46	South Dakota	1,839,099,000	0.1%
47	North Dakota	1,703,787,000	0.1%
48	Montana	1,547,679,000	0.1%
49	Wyoming	1,003,244,000	0.1%
50	Vermont	970,413,000	0.1%
	District of Columbia	9,580,711,000	0.6%

Source: U.S. Bureau of the Census, Governments Division
"2008 State and Local Government Finances" (http://www.census.gov/govs/estimate/index.html)
*Includes short-term, long-term, full faith and credit, nonguaranteed, and public debt for private purposes.

Per Capita Local Government Debt Outstanding in 2008

National Per Capita = $5,082*

ALPHA ORDER

RANK	STATE	PER CAPITA
21	Alabama	$4,177
15	Alaska	5,041
14	Arizona	5,087
33	Arkansas	3,018
10	California	5,991
4	Colorado	6,908
37	Connecticut	2,636
39	Delaware	2,533
11	Florida	5,417
25	Georgia	3,866
30	Hawaii	3,431
50	Idaho	1,539
13	Illinois	5,118
22	Indiana	4,169
35	Iowa	2,746
12	Kansas	5,411
9	Kentucky	6,107
29	Louisiana	3,482
46	Maine	1,894
38	Maryland	2,632
32	Massachusetts	3,199
19	Michigan	4,617
8	Minnesota	6,139
40	Mississippi	2,382
27	Missouri	3,595
48	Montana	1,599
5	Nebraska	6,338
2	Nevada	7,894
44	New Hampshire	1,980
23	New Jersey	4,062
34	New Mexico	2,763
1	New York	7,988
31	North Carolina	3,417
36	North Dakota	2,656
26	Ohio	3,624
43	Oklahoma	2,144
18	Oregon	4,697
6	Pennsylvania	6,248
41	Rhode Island	2,357
17	South Carolina	4,739
42	South Dakota	2,286
16	Tennessee	5,033
3	Texas	7,512
24	Utah	3,968
49	Vermont	1,563
20	Virginia	4,211
6	Washington	6,248
45	West Virginia	1,913
28	Wisconsin	3,556
47	Wyoming	1,882

RANK ORDER

RANK	STATE	PER CAPITA
1	New York	$7,988
2	Nevada	7,894
3	Texas	7,512
4	Colorado	6,908
5	Nebraska	6,338
6	Pennsylvania	6,248
6	Washington	6,248
8	Minnesota	6,139
9	Kentucky	6,107
10	California	5,991
11	Florida	5,417
12	Kansas	5,411
13	Illinois	5,118
14	Arizona	5,087
15	Alaska	5,041
16	Tennessee	5,033
17	South Carolina	4,739
18	Oregon	4,697
19	Michigan	4,617
20	Virginia	4,211
21	Alabama	4,177
22	Indiana	4,169
23	New Jersey	4,062
24	Utah	3,968
25	Georgia	3,866
26	Ohio	3,624
27	Missouri	3,595
28	Wisconsin	3,556
29	Louisiana	3,482
30	Hawaii	3,431
31	North Carolina	3,417
32	Massachusetts	3,199
33	Arkansas	3,018
34	New Mexico	2,763
35	Iowa	2,746
36	North Dakota	2,656
37	Connecticut	2,636
38	Maryland	2,632
39	Delaware	2,533
40	Mississippi	2,382
41	Rhode Island	2,357
42	South Dakota	2,286
43	Oklahoma	2,144
44	New Hampshire	1,980
45	West Virginia	1,913
46	Maine	1,894
47	Wyoming	1,882
48	Montana	1,599
49	Vermont	1,563
50	Idaho	1,539

District of Columbia   16,236

Source: CQ Press using data from U.S. Bureau of the Census, Governments Division
"2008 State and Local Government Finances" (http://www.census.gov/govs/estimate/index.html)
*Includes short-term, long-term, full faith and credit, nonguaranteed, and public debt for private purposes.

Local Government Full-Time Equivalent Employees in 2009

National Total = 12,228,140 FTE Employees*

ALPHA ORDER

RANK	STATE	EMPLOYEES	% of USA
23	Alabama	196,583	1.6%
46	Alaska	27,266	0.2%
16	Arizona	236,639	1.9%
33	Arkansas	101,507	0.8%
1	California	1,424,268	11.6%
21	Colorado	203,098	1.7%
32	Connecticut	120,362	1.0%
49	Delaware	22,037	0.2%
4	Florida	696,967	5.7%
9	Georgia	406,946	3.3%
50	Hawaii	15,403	0.1%
39	Idaho	55,638	0.5%
5	Illinois	506,120	4.1%
13	Indiana	252,991	2.1%
31	Iowa	127,219	1.0%
27	Kansas	157,060	1.3%
26	Kentucky	161,050	1.3%
24	Louisiana	185,093	1.5%
41	Maine	50,494	0.4%
20	Maryland	211,602	1.7%
18	Massachusetts	228,489	1.9%
11	Michigan	330,952	2.7%
22	Minnesota	201,224	1.6%
29	Mississippi	135,853	1.1%
17	Missouri	234,644	1.9%
43	Montana	36,041	0.3%
36	Nebraska	85,638	0.7%
35	Nevada	85,846	0.7%
40	New Hampshire	52,072	0.4%
10	New Jersey	349,809	2.9%
37	New Mexico	81,075	0.7%
3	New York	994,769	8.1%
8	North Carolina	408,999	3.3%
47	North Dakota	23,991	0.2%
6	Ohio	473,360	3.9%
28	Oklahoma	145,539	1.2%
30	Oregon	135,612	1.1%
7	Pennsylvania	431,907	3.5%
45	Rhode Island	32,679	0.3%
25	South Carolina	177,215	1.4%
44	South Dakota	33,855	0.3%
14	Tennessee	241,060	2.0%
2	Texas	1,113,569	9.1%
34	Utah	88,452	0.7%
48	Vermont	23,849	0.2%
12	Virginia	319,097	2.6%
15	Washington	237,574	1.9%
38	West Virginia	61,849	0.5%
19	Wisconsin	222,214	1.8%
42	Wyoming	38,017	0.3%

RANK ORDER

RANK	STATE	EMPLOYEES	% of USA
1	California	1,424,268	11.6%
2	Texas	1,113,569	9.1%
3	New York	994,769	8.1%
4	Florida	696,967	5.7%
5	Illinois	506,120	4.1%
6	Ohio	473,360	3.9%
7	Pennsylvania	431,907	3.5%
8	North Carolina	408,999	3.3%
9	Georgia	406,946	3.3%
10	New Jersey	349,809	2.9%
11	Michigan	330,952	2.7%
12	Virginia	319,097	2.6%
13	Indiana	252,991	2.1%
14	Tennessee	241,060	2.0%
15	Washington	237,574	1.9%
16	Arizona	236,639	1.9%
17	Missouri	234,644	1.9%
18	Massachusetts	228,489	1.9%
19	Wisconsin	222,214	1.8%
20	Maryland	211,602	1.7%
21	Colorado	203,098	1.7%
22	Minnesota	201,224	1.6%
23	Alabama	196,583	1.6%
24	Louisiana	185,093	1.5%
25	South Carolina	177,215	1.4%
26	Kentucky	161,050	1.3%
27	Kansas	157,060	1.3%
28	Oklahoma	145,539	1.2%
29	Mississippi	135,853	1.1%
30	Oregon	135,612	1.1%
31	Iowa	127,219	1.0%
32	Connecticut	120,362	1.0%
33	Arkansas	101,507	0.8%
34	Utah	88,452	0.7%
35	Nevada	85,846	0.7%
36	Nebraska	85,638	0.7%
37	New Mexico	81,075	0.7%
38	West Virginia	61,849	0.5%
39	Idaho	55,638	0.5%
40	New Hampshire	52,072	0.4%
41	Maine	50,494	0.4%
42	Wyoming	38,017	0.3%
43	Montana	36,041	0.3%
44	South Dakota	33,855	0.3%
45	Rhode Island	32,679	0.3%
46	Alaska	27,266	0.2%
47	North Dakota	23,991	0.2%
48	Vermont	23,849	0.2%
49	Delaware	22,037	0.2%
50	Hawaii	15,403	0.1%
	District of Columbia	44,547	0.4%

Source: U.S. Bureau of the Census, Governments Division
    "Government Employment and Payroll" (http://www.census.gov/govs/apes/index.html)
*As of March 2009.

Rate of Local Government Full-Time Equivalent Employees in 2009

National Rate = 398 Local Government Employees per 10,000 Population*

ALPHA ORDER

RANK	STATE	RATE
9	Alabama	417
24	Alaska	390
37	Arizona	359
40	Arkansas	351
26	California	385
15	Colorado	404
43	Connecticut	342
49	Delaware	249
31	Florida	376
11	Georgia	414
50	Hawaii	119
36	Idaho	360
22	Illinois	392
19	Indiana	394
8	Iowa	423
2	Kansas	557
32	Kentucky	373
12	Louisiana	412
28	Maine	383
33	Maryland	371
41	Massachusetts	347
45	Michigan	332
30	Minnesota	382
5	Mississippi	460
22	Missouri	392
35	Montana	370
4	Nebraska	477
46	Nevada	325
20	New Hampshire	393
17	New Jersey	402
16	New Mexico	403
3	New York	509
7	North Carolina	436
33	North Dakota	371
13	Ohio	410
18	Oklahoma	395
39	Oregon	354
42	Pennsylvania	343
48	Rhode Island	310
25	South Carolina	389
9	South Dakota	417
28	Tennessee	383
6	Texas	449
47	Utah	318
27	Vermont	384
14	Virginia	405
38	Washington	356
44	West Virginia	340
20	Wisconsin	393
1	Wyoming	698

RANK ORDER

RANK	STATE	RATE
1	Wyoming	698
2	Kansas	557
3	New York	509
4	Nebraska	477
5	Mississippi	460
6	Texas	449
7	North Carolina	436
8	Iowa	423
9	Alabama	417
9	South Dakota	417
11	Georgia	414
12	Louisiana	412
13	Ohio	410
14	Virginia	405
15	Colorado	404
16	New Mexico	403
17	New Jersey	402
18	Oklahoma	395
19	Indiana	394
20	New Hampshire	393
20	Wisconsin	393
22	Illinois	392
22	Missouri	392
24	Alaska	390
25	South Carolina	389
26	California	385
27	Vermont	384
28	Maine	383
28	Tennessee	383
30	Minnesota	382
31	Florida	376
32	Kentucky	373
33	Maryland	371
33	North Dakota	371
35	Montana	370
36	Idaho	360
37	Arizona	359
38	Washington	356
39	Oregon	354
40	Arkansas	351
41	Massachusetts	347
42	Pennsylvania	343
43	Connecticut	342
44	West Virginia	340
45	Michigan	332
46	Nevada	325
47	Utah	318
48	Rhode Island	310
49	Delaware	249
50	Hawaii	119

District of Columbia — 743

Source: CQ Press using data from U.S. Bureau of the Census, Governments Division
"Government Employment and Payroll" (http://www.census.gov/govs/apes/index.html)
*Full-time equivalent as of March 2009.

Average Annual Earnings of Full-Time Local Government Employees in 2009

National Average = $50,910*

ALPHA ORDER

RANK	STATE	SALARY
44	Alabama	$38,509
4	Alaska	61,684
18	Arizona	49,668
45	Arkansas	37,775
1	California	69,503
22	Colorado	49,088
10	Connecticut	57,490
14	Delaware	53,005
19	Florida	49,307
36	Georgia	41,664
8	Hawaii	58,697
43	Idaho	39,664
13	Illinois	54,263
32	Indiana	42,075
27	Iowa	45,029
42	Kansas	40,130
49	Kentucky	36,266
41	Louisiana	40,144
38	Maine	40,704
5	Maryland	61,585
9	Massachusetts	58,057
12	Michigan	54,410
15	Minnesota	51,916
50	Mississippi	35,914
37	Missouri	41,463
33	Montana	42,074
26	Nebraska	45,403
7	Nevada	60,046
28	New Hampshire	44,846
3	New Jersey	62,534
39	New Mexico	40,673
6	New York	60,515
30	North Carolina	43,173
34	North Dakota	41,894
23	Ohio	47,950
46	Oklahoma	37,732
17	Oregon	50,530
21	Pennsylvania	49,135
11	Rhode Island	55,612
35	South Carolina	41,865
47	South Dakota	37,728
40	Tennessee	40,372
31	Texas	42,491
25	Utah	45,564
29	Vermont	43,428
24	Virginia	46,327
2	Washington	64,414
48	West Virginia	37,508
16	Wisconsin	50,792
20	Wyoming	49,259

RANK ORDER

RANK	STATE	SALARY
1	California	$69,503
2	Washington	64,414
3	New Jersey	62,534
4	Alaska	61,684
5	Maryland	61,585
6	New York	60,515
7	Nevada	60,046
8	Hawaii	58,697
9	Massachusetts	58,057
10	Connecticut	57,490
11	Rhode Island	55,612
12	Michigan	54,410
13	Illinois	54,263
14	Delaware	53,005
15	Minnesota	51,916
16	Wisconsin	50,792
17	Oregon	50,530
18	Arizona	49,668
19	Florida	49,307
20	Wyoming	49,259
21	Pennsylvania	49,135
22	Colorado	49,088
23	Ohio	47,950
24	Virginia	46,327
25	Utah	45,564
26	Nebraska	45,403
27	Iowa	45,029
28	New Hampshire	44,846
29	Vermont	43,428
30	North Carolina	43,173
31	Texas	42,491
32	Indiana	42,075
33	Montana	42,074
34	North Dakota	41,894
35	South Carolina	41,865
36	Georgia	41,664
37	Missouri	41,463
38	Maine	40,704
39	New Mexico	40,673
40	Tennessee	40,372
41	Louisiana	40,144
42	Kansas	40,130
43	Idaho	39,664
44	Alabama	38,509
45	Arkansas	37,775
46	Oklahoma	37,732
47	South Dakota	37,728
48	West Virginia	37,508
49	Kentucky	36,266
50	Mississippi	35,914

District of Columbia   60,101

Source: CQ Press using data from U.S. Bureau of the Census, Governments Division
"Government Employment and Payroll" (http://www.census.gov/govs/apes/index.html)
*March 2009 full-time payroll (multiplied by 12) divided by full-time employees.

XI. Health

Average Medical Malpractice Payment in 2006

National Average = $311,965*

ALPHA ORDER

RANK	STATE	AVERAGE PAYMENT
7	Alabama	$453,665
39	Alaska	240,511
30	Arizona	286,898
37	Arkansas	246,959
41	California	223,039
24	Colorado	312,138
4	Connecticut	500,289
3	Delaware	521,177
40	Florida**	240,363
29	Georgia	292,902
14	Hawaii	342,316
31	Idaho	281,751
1	Illinois	619,205
20	Indiana**	322,822
34	Iowa	274,281
48	Kansas**	155,285
32	Kentucky	280,599
43	Louisiana**	207,878
21	Maine	322,325
13	Maryland	347,477
6	Massachusetts	465,236
49	Michigan	138,433
5	Minnesota	480,822
35	Mississippi	258,806
18	Missouri	330,115
22	Montana	320,849
42	Nebraska**	213,081
15	Nevada	340,211
16	New Hampshire	336,032
11	New Jersey	401,144
45	New Mexico**	199,917
10	New York	405,558
12	North Carolina	366,966
27	North Dakota	301,422
25	Ohio	310,573
38	Oklahoma	245,127
26	Oregon	305,725
17	Pennsylvania**	332,376
19	Rhode Island	326,542
47	South Carolina**	174,454
8	South Dakota	422,033
23	Tennessee	317,305
46	Texas	175,644
36	Utah	247,349
50	Vermont	125,795
28	Virginia	295,840
33	Washington	277,493
44	West Virginia	204,794
2	Wisconsin**	524,041
9	Wyoming	413,553

RANK ORDER

RANK	STATE	AVERAGE PAYMENT
1	Illinois	$619,205
2	Wisconsin**	524,041
3	Delaware	521,177
4	Connecticut	500,289
5	Minnesota	480,822
6	Massachusetts	465,236
7	Alabama	453,665
8	South Dakota	422,033
9	Wyoming	413,553
10	New York	405,558
11	New Jersey	401,144
12	North Carolina	366,966
13	Maryland	347,477
14	Hawaii	342,316
15	Nevada	340,211
16	New Hampshire	336,032
17	Pennsylvania**	332,376
18	Missouri	330,115
19	Rhode Island	326,542
20	Indiana**	322,822
21	Maine	322,325
22	Montana	320,849
23	Tennessee	317,305
24	Colorado	312,138
25	Ohio	310,573
26	Oregon	305,725
27	North Dakota	301,422
28	Virginia	295,840
29	Georgia	292,902
30	Arizona	286,898
31	Idaho	281,751
32	Kentucky	280,599
33	Washington	277,493
34	Iowa	274,281
35	Mississippi	258,806
36	Utah	247,349
37	Arkansas	246,959
38	Oklahoma	245,127
39	Alaska	240,511
40	Florida**	240,363
41	California	223,039
42	Nebraska**	213,081
43	Louisiana**	207,878
44	West Virginia	204,794
45	New Mexico**	199,917
46	Texas	175,644
47	South Carolina**	174,454
48	Kansas**	155,285
49	Michigan	138,433
50	Vermont	125,795
	District of Columbia	331,628

Source: U.S. Department of Health and Human Services, Bureau of Health Professions
   "National Practitioner Data Bank, 2006 Annual Report" (http://www.npdb-hipdb.com/annualrpt.html)
*National figure includes U.S. territories and U.S. Armed Forces locations overseas.
**The figures for these states have not been adjusted for payments by state compensation funds and other similar funds.
Average payments for these states understate the actual average amounts received by claimants.

Average Annual Single Coverage Health Insurance Premium per Enrolled Employee in 2009
National Average = $4,669*

ALPHA ORDER

RANK	STATE	PREMIUM
24	Alabama	$4,647
1	Alaska	6,047
39	Arizona	4,358
50	Arkansas	3,717
25	California	4,631
29	Colorado	4,570
12	Connecticut	4,909
9	Delaware	4,955
35	Florida	4,488
21	Georgia	4,692
49	Hawaii	4,116
45	Idaho	4,248
18	Illinois	4,725
16	Indiana	4,849
37	Iowa	4,453
47	Kansas	4,236
40	Kentucky	4,336
15	Louisiana	4,861
6	Maine	5,119
14	Maryland	4,870
2	Massachusetts	5,268
11	Michigan	4,916
27	Minnesota	4,600
36	Mississippi	4,469
38	Missouri	4,393
31	Montana	4,546
41	Nebraska	4,315
26	Nevada	4,627
3	New Hampshire	5,227
13	New Jersey	4,901
32	New Mexico	4,535
5	New York	5,121
23	North Carolina	4,676
48	North Dakota	4,127
43	Ohio	4,261
46	Oklahoma	4,243
22	Oregon	4,680
17	Pennsylvania	4,749
7	Rhode Island	5,059
33	South Carolina	4,503
42	South Dakota	4,262
30	Tennessee	4,549
34	Texas	4,499
44	Utah	4,257
8	Vermont	5,001
28	Virginia	4,590
10	Washington	4,923
20	West Virginia	4,700
4	Wisconsin	5,132
19	Wyoming	4,703

RANK ORDER

RANK	STATE	PREMIUM
1	Alaska	$6,047
2	Massachusetts	5,268
3	New Hampshire	5,227
4	Wisconsin	5,132
5	New York	5,121
6	Maine	5,119
7	Rhode Island	5,059
8	Vermont	5,001
9	Delaware	4,955
10	Washington	4,923
11	Michigan	4,916
12	Connecticut	4,909
13	New Jersey	4,901
14	Maryland	4,870
15	Louisiana	4,861
16	Indiana	4,849
17	Pennsylvania	4,749
18	Illinois	4,725
19	Wyoming	4,703
20	West Virginia	4,700
21	Georgia	4,692
22	Oregon	4,680
23	North Carolina	4,676
24	Alabama	4,647
25	California	4,631
26	Nevada	4,627
27	Minnesota	4,600
28	Virginia	4,590
29	Colorado	4,570
30	Tennessee	4,549
31	Montana	4,546
32	New Mexico	4,535
33	South Carolina	4,503
34	Texas	4,499
35	Florida	4,488
36	Mississippi	4,469
37	Iowa	4,453
38	Missouri	4,393
39	Arizona	4,358
40	Kentucky	4,336
41	Nebraska	4,315
42	South Dakota	4,262
43	Ohio	4,261
44	Utah	4,257
45	Idaho	4,248
46	Oklahoma	4,243
47	Kansas	4,236
48	North Dakota	4,127
49	Hawaii	4,116
50	Arkansas	3,717
	District of Columbia	5,082

Source: U.S. Department of Health and Human Services, Agency for Healthcare Research and Quality
"Private-Sector Data by Firm Size and State" (Table II Series, Medical Expenditures Panel Survey)
(http://www.meps.ahrq.gov/mepsweb/survey_comp/Insurance.jsp)
*Enrolled employees at private-sector establishments that offer health insurance coverage.

Average Annual Family Coverage Health Insurance Premium per Enrolled Employee in 2009
National Average = $13,027*

ALPHA ORDER				RANK ORDER		
RANK	STATE	PREMIUM		RANK	STATE	PREMIUM
40	Alabama	$11,978		1	Massachusetts	$14,723
5	Alaska	14,182		2	Wisconsin	14,656
24	Arizona	12,813		3	Vermont	14,558
50	Arkansas	10,969		4	Wyoming	14,319
30	California	12,631		5	Alaska	14,182
15	Colorado	13,360		6	Connecticut	14,064
6	Connecticut	14,064		7	Louisiana	13,846
29	Delaware	12,682		8	Maryland	13,833
21	Florida	12,912		9	New Hampshire	13,822
25	Georgia	12,792		10	New York	13,757
45	Hawaii	11,826		11	New Jersey	13,750
41	Idaho	11,887		12	Illinois	13,708
12	Illinois	13,708		13	Rhode Island	13,608
22	Indiana	12,872		14	Maine	13,522
39	Iowa	12,036		15	Colorado	13,360
44	Kansas	11,829		16	Pennsylvania	13,229
34	Kentucky	12,407		17	Texas	13,221
7	Louisiana	13,846		18	Minnesota	13,202
14	Maine	13,522		19	Michigan	13,160
8	Maryland	13,833		20	North Carolina	13,087
1	Massachusetts	14,723		21	Florida	12,912
19	Michigan	13,160		22	Indiana	12,872
18	Minnesota	13,202		23	New Mexico	12,848
32	Mississippi	12,590		24	Arizona	12,813
35	Missouri	12,353		25	Georgia	12,792
49	Montana	11,365		26	Oregon	12,783
37	Nebraska	12,227		27	Washington	12,758
28	Nevada	12,700		28	Nevada	12,700
9	New Hampshire	13,822		29	Delaware	12,682
11	New Jersey	13,750		30	California	12,631
23	New Mexico	12,848		31	Virginia	12,622
10	New York	13,757		32	Mississippi	12,590
20	North Carolina	13,087		33	West Virginia	12,554
47	North Dakota	11,590		34	Kentucky	12,407
42	Ohio	11,870		35	Missouri	12,353
48	Oklahoma	11,417		36	South Carolina	12,343
26	Oregon	12,783		37	Nebraska	12,227
16	Pennsylvania	13,229		38	Tennessee	12,134
13	Rhode Island	13,608		39	Iowa	12,036
36	South Carolina	12,343		40	Alabama	11,978
46	South Dakota	11,596		41	Idaho	11,887
38	Tennessee	12,134		42	Ohio	11,870
17	Texas	13,221		43	Utah	11,869
43	Utah	11,869		44	Kansas	11,829
3	Vermont	14,558		45	Hawaii	11,826
31	Virginia	12,622		46	South Dakota	11,596
27	Washington	12,758		47	North Dakota	11,590
33	West Virginia	12,554		48	Oklahoma	11,417
2	Wisconsin	14,656		49	Montana	11,365
4	Wyoming	14,319		50	Arkansas	10,969
					District of Columbia	14,222

Source: U.S. Department of Health and Human Services, Agency for Healthcare Research and Quality
"Private-Sector Data by Firm Size and State" (Table II Series, Medical Expenditures Panel Survey)
(http://www.meps.ahrq.gov/mepsweb/survey_comp/Insurance.jsp)
*Enrolled employees at private-sector establishments that offer health insurance coverage.

Percent of Private-Sector Establishments That Offer Health Insurance: 2009

National Percent = 55.0%

ALPHA ORDER

RANK	STATE	PERCENT
12	Alabama	58.9
48	Alaska	40.5
30	Arizona	52.1
44	Arkansas	47.1
16	California	56.0
20	Colorado	55.2
3	Connecticut	63.9
9	Delaware	60.0
37	Florida	49.5
27	Georgia	52.8
1	Hawaii	85.4
47	Idaho	45.0
27	Illinois	52.8
39	Indiana	49.1
35	Iowa	50.7
17	Kansas	55.9
14	Kentucky	56.6
42	Louisiana	48.1
24	Maine	53.8
7	Maryland	61.0
6	Massachusetts	61.6
23	Michigan	54.0
19	Minnesota	55.4
41	Mississippi	48.7
13	Missouri	57.1
50	Montana	39.5
46	Nebraska	45.4
21	Nevada	55.0
10	New Hampshire	59.7
2	New Jersey	65.2
33	New Mexico	51.0
11	New York	59.1
31	North Carolina	51.6
38	North Dakota	49.2
3	Ohio	63.9
43	Oklahoma	47.4
27	Oregon	52.8
5	Pennsylvania	63.0
8	Rhode Island	60.2
26	South Carolina	53.3
40	South Dakota	48.8
18	Tennessee	55.5
34	Texas	50.9
45	Utah	46.4
15	Vermont	56.4
22	Virginia	54.1
25	Washington	53.6
36	West Virginia	50.3
32	Wisconsin	51.4
48	Wyoming	40.5

RANK ORDER

RANK	STATE	PERCENT
1	Hawaii	85.4
2	New Jersey	65.2
3	Connecticut	63.9
3	Ohio	63.9
5	Pennsylvania	63.0
6	Massachusetts	61.6
7	Maryland	61.0
8	Rhode Island	60.2
9	Delaware	60.0
10	New Hampshire	59.7
11	New York	59.1
12	Alabama	58.9
13	Missouri	57.1
14	Kentucky	56.6
15	Vermont	56.4
16	California	56.0
17	Kansas	55.9
18	Tennessee	55.5
19	Minnesota	55.4
20	Colorado	55.2
21	Nevada	55.0
22	Virginia	54.1
23	Michigan	54.0
24	Maine	53.8
25	Washington	53.6
26	South Carolina	53.3
27	Georgia	52.8
27	Illinois	52.8
27	Oregon	52.8
30	Arizona	52.1
31	North Carolina	51.6
32	Wisconsin	51.4
33	New Mexico	51.0
34	Texas	50.9
35	Iowa	50.7
36	West Virginia	50.3
37	Florida	49.5
38	North Dakota	49.2
39	Indiana	49.1
40	South Dakota	48.8
41	Mississippi	48.7
42	Louisiana	48.1
43	Oklahoma	47.4
44	Arkansas	47.1
45	Utah	46.4
46	Nebraska	45.4
47	Idaho	45.0
48	Alaska	40.5
48	Wyoming	40.5
50	Montana	39.5

District of Columbia	74.1

Source: U.S. Department of Health and Human Services, Agency for Healthcare Research and Quality
"Private-Sector Data by Firm Size and State" (Table II Series, Medical Expenditures Panel Survey)
(http://www.meps.ahrq.gov/mepsweb/survey_comp/Insurance.jsp)

Persons Not Covered by Health Insurance in 2009

National Total = 50,674,000 Uninsured

ALPHA ORDER

RANK	STATE	UNINSURED	% of USA
19	Alabama	789,000	1.6%
44	Alaska	122,000	0.2%
12	Arizona	1,273,000	2.5%
26	Arkansas	548,000	1.1%
1	California	7,345,000	14.5%
21	Colorado	762,000	1.5%
32	Connecticut	418,000	0.8%
45	Delaware	118,000	0.2%
3	Florida	4,118,000	8.1%
5	Georgia	1,985,000	3.9%
47	Hawaii	102,000	0.2%
38	Idaho	232,000	0.5%
6	Illinois	1,891,000	3.7%
16	Indiana	902,000	1.8%
35	Iowa	342,000	0.7%
34	Kansas	365,000	0.7%
23	Kentucky	694,000	1.4%
22	Louisiana	711,000	1.4%
42	Maine	133,000	0.3%
18	Maryland	793,000	1.6%
36	Massachusetts	295,000	0.6%
11	Michigan	1,350,000	2.7%
30	Minnesota	456,000	0.9%
29	Mississippi	502,000	1.0%
15	Missouri	914,000	1.8%
40	Montana	149,000	0.3%
39	Nebraska	205,000	0.4%
27	Nevada	546,000	1.1%
41	New Hampshire	138,000	0.3%
10	New Jersey	1,371,000	2.7%
31	New Mexico	430,000	0.8%
4	New York	2,837,000	5.6%
7	North Carolina	1,685,000	3.3%
49	North Dakota	67,000	0.1%
8	Ohio	1,643,000	3.2%
25	Oklahoma	659,000	1.3%
24	Oregon	678,000	1.3%
9	Pennsylvania	1,409,000	2.8%
43	Rhode Island	127,000	0.3%
20	South Carolina	766,000	1.5%
46	South Dakota	108,000	0.2%
14	Tennessee	963,000	1.9%
2	Texas	6,433,000	12.7%
33	Utah	415,000	0.8%
50	Vermont	61,000	0.1%
13	Virginia	1,014,000	2.0%
17	Washington	869,000	1.7%
37	West Virginia	253,000	0.5%
28	Wisconsin	527,000	1.0%
48	Wyoming	86,000	0.2%

RANK ORDER

RANK	STATE	UNINSURED	% of USA
1	California	7,345,000	14.5%
2	Texas	6,433,000	12.7%
3	Florida	4,118,000	8.1%
4	New York	2,837,000	5.6%
5	Georgia	1,985,000	3.9%
6	Illinois	1,891,000	3.7%
7	North Carolina	1,685,000	3.3%
8	Ohio	1,643,000	3.2%
9	Pennsylvania	1,409,000	2.8%
10	New Jersey	1,371,000	2.7%
11	Michigan	1,350,000	2.7%
12	Arizona	1,273,000	2.5%
13	Virginia	1,014,000	2.0%
14	Tennessee	963,000	1.9%
15	Missouri	914,000	1.8%
16	Indiana	902,000	1.8%
17	Washington	869,000	1.7%
18	Maryland	793,000	1.6%
19	Alabama	789,000	1.6%
20	South Carolina	766,000	1.5%
21	Colorado	762,000	1.5%
22	Louisiana	711,000	1.4%
23	Kentucky	694,000	1.4%
24	Oregon	678,000	1.3%
25	Oklahoma	659,000	1.3%
26	Arkansas	548,000	1.1%
27	Nevada	546,000	1.1%
28	Wisconsin	527,000	1.0%
29	Mississippi	502,000	1.0%
30	Minnesota	456,000	0.9%
31	New Mexico	430,000	0.8%
32	Connecticut	418,000	0.8%
33	Utah	415,000	0.8%
34	Kansas	365,000	0.7%
35	Iowa	342,000	0.7%
36	Massachusetts	295,000	0.6%
37	West Virginia	253,000	0.5%
38	Idaho	232,000	0.5%
39	Nebraska	205,000	0.4%
40	Montana	149,000	0.3%
41	New Hampshire	138,000	0.3%
42	Maine	133,000	0.3%
43	Rhode Island	127,000	0.3%
44	Alaska	122,000	0.2%
45	Delaware	118,000	0.2%
46	South Dakota	108,000	0.2%
47	Hawaii	102,000	0.2%
48	Wyoming	86,000	0.2%
49	North Dakota	67,000	0.1%
50	Vermont	61,000	0.1%
	District of Columbia	74,000	0.1%

Source: U.S. Bureau of the Census
"Income, Poverty, and Health Insurance Coverage: 2009"
(http://www.census.gov/hhes/www/hlthins/data/incpovhlth/index.html)

Percent of Population Not Covered by Health Insurance in 2009

National Percent = 15.8% of Population*

ALPHA ORDER

RANK	STATE	PERCENT
26	Alabama	13.6
7	Alaska	18.6
4	Arizona	19.1
11	Arkansas	17.7
5	California	18.9
16	Colorado	15.9
41	Connecticut	10.5
38	Delaware	11.8
3	Florida	20.9
7	Georgia	18.6
49	Hawaii	7.8
20	Idaho	14.9
25	Illinois	13.7
32	Indiana	12.6
45	Iowa	10.0
31	Kansas	12.7
18	Kentucky	15.3
9	Louisiana	18.2
46	Maine	9.8
30	Maryland	13.2
50	Massachusetts	5.1
34	Michigan	12.4
48	Minnesota	8.6
10	Mississippi	18.1
28	Missouri	13.5
17	Montana	15.7
35	Nebraska	12.2
5	Nevada	18.9
42	New Hampshire	10.4
19	New Jersey	15.2
2	New Mexico	22.6
24	New York	14.0
13	North Carolina	16.6
40	North Dakota	10.8
33	Ohio	12.5
13	Oklahoma	16.6
12	Oregon	16.9
43	Pennsylvania	10.3
39	Rhode Island	11.6
15	South Carolina	16.4
37	South Dakota	12.0
20	Tennessee	14.9
1	Texas	25.5
26	Utah	13.6
44	Vermont	10.1
29	Virginia	13.4
35	Washington	12.2
22	West Virginia	14.4
47	Wisconsin	9.1
23	Wyoming	14.3

RANK ORDER

RANK	STATE	PERCENT
1	Texas	25.5
2	New Mexico	22.6
3	Florida	20.9
4	Arizona	19.1
5	California	18.9
5	Nevada	18.9
7	Alaska	18.6
7	Georgia	18.6
9	Louisiana	18.2
10	Mississippi	18.1
11	Arkansas	17.7
12	Oregon	16.9
13	North Carolina	16.6
13	Oklahoma	16.6
15	South Carolina	16.4
16	Colorado	15.9
17	Montana	15.7
18	Kentucky	15.3
19	New Jersey	15.2
20	Idaho	14.9
20	Tennessee	14.9
22	West Virginia	14.4
23	Wyoming	14.3
24	New York	14.0
25	Illinois	13.7
26	Alabama	13.6
26	Utah	13.6
28	Missouri	13.5
29	Virginia	13.4
30	Maryland	13.2
31	Kansas	12.7
32	Indiana	12.6
33	Ohio	12.5
34	Michigan	12.4
35	Nebraska	12.2
35	Washington	12.2
37	South Dakota	12.0
38	Delaware	11.8
39	Rhode Island	11.6
40	North Dakota	10.8
41	Connecticut	10.5
42	New Hampshire	10.4
43	Pennsylvania	10.3
44	Vermont	10.1
45	Iowa	10.0
46	Maine	9.8
47	Wisconsin	9.1
48	Minnesota	8.6
49	Hawaii	7.8
50	Massachusetts	5.1

District of Columbia	10.6

Source: U.S. Bureau of the Census
   "Income, Poverty, and Health Insurance Coverage: 2009"
      (http://www.census.gov/hhes/www/hlthins/data/incpovhlth/index.html)
*Three-year average for 2007 through 2009.

Percent of Population Lacking Access to Primary Care in 2011

National Percent = 11.8% of Population*

ALPHA ORDER

RANK	STATE	PERCENT
10	Alabama	18.7
11	Alaska	17.6
14	Arizona	16.3
28	Arkansas	10.8
32	California	10.2
24	Colorado	11.6
33	Connecticut	9.0
17	Delaware	13.9
15	Florida	15.0
16	Georgia	14.0
49	Hawaii	2.8
13	Idaho	16.8
12	Illinois	17.3
39	Indiana	6.7
23	Iowa	11.9
20	Kansas	12.7
26	Kentucky	11.2
2	Louisiana	32.2
45	Maine	5.1
35	Maryland	8.3
38	Massachusetts	6.9
28	Michigan	10.8
44	Minnesota	5.4
1	Mississippi	32.4
6	Missouri	23.2
6	Montana	23.2
46	Nebraska	4.8
21	Nevada	12.5
47	New Hampshire	4.1
50	New Jersey	1.7
3	New Mexico	30.6
22	New York	12.1
40	North Carolina	6.5
8	North Dakota	22.0
41	Ohio	6.4
9	Oklahoma	21.6
25	Oregon	11.4
43	Pennsylvania	5.9
42	Rhode Island	6.3
19	South Carolina	12.9
4	South Dakota	26.7
31	Tennessee	10.3
18	Texas	13.0
33	Utah	9.0
48	Vermont	2.9
35	Virginia	8.3
27	Washington	10.9
35	West Virginia	8.3
30	Wisconsin	10.6
5	Wyoming	23.6

RANK ORDER

RANK	STATE	PERCENT
1	Mississippi	32.4
2	Louisiana	32.2
3	New Mexico	30.6
4	South Dakota	26.7
5	Wyoming	23.6
6	Missouri	23.2
6	Montana	23.2
8	North Dakota	22.0
9	Oklahoma	21.6
10	Alabama	18.7
11	Alaska	17.6
12	Illinois	17.3
13	Idaho	16.8
14	Arizona	16.3
15	Florida	15.0
16	Georgia	14.0
17	Delaware	13.9
18	Texas	13.0
19	South Carolina	12.9
20	Kansas	12.7
21	Nevada	12.5
22	New York	12.1
23	Iowa	11.9
24	Colorado	11.6
25	Oregon	11.4
26	Kentucky	11.2
27	Washington	10.9
28	Arkansas	10.8
28	Michigan	10.8
30	Wisconsin	10.6
31	Tennessee	10.3
32	California	10.2
33	Connecticut	9.0
33	Utah	9.0
35	Maryland	8.3
35	Virginia	8.3
35	West Virginia	8.3
38	Massachusetts	6.9
39	Indiana	6.7
40	North Carolina	6.5
41	Ohio	6.4
42	Rhode Island	6.3
43	Pennsylvania	5.9
44	Minnesota	5.4
45	Maine	5.1
46	Nebraska	4.8
47	New Hampshire	4.1
48	Vermont	2.9
49	Hawaii	2.8
50	New Jersey	1.7

District of Columbia   25.3

Source: CQ Press using data from U.S. Department of Health and Human Services, Division of Shortage Designation
"State Population and HPSA Designation Population Statistics" (as of January 20, 2011)
(http://datawarehouse.hrsa.gov/hpsadetail.aspx)

*Percent of population considered under-served by primary medical practitioners (Family and General Practice doctors, Internists, Ob/Gyns, and Pediatricians). An under-served population does not have primary medical care within reasonable economic and geographic bounds.

Physicians in 2009

National Total = 958,335 Physicians*

ALPHA ORDER

RANK	STATE	PHYSICIANS	% of USA
27	Alabama	11,507	1.2%
49	Alaska	1,769	0.2%
19	Arizona	16,608	1.7%
31	Arkansas	6,749	0.7%
1	California	116,489	12.2%
22	Colorado	15,222	1.6%
23	Connecticut	15,170	1.6%
46	Delaware	2,488	0.3%
4	Florida	57,066	6.0%
14	Georgia	24,092	2.5%
39	Hawaii	4,800	0.5%
43	Idaho	3,159	0.3%
6	Illinois	40,963	4.3%
21	Indiana	15,790	1.6%
33	Iowa	6,591	0.7%
30	Kansas	7,474	0.8%
28	Kentucky	11,325	1.2%
24	Louisiana	13,323	1.4%
42	Maine	4,380	0.5%
12	Maryland	27,153	2.8%
8	Massachusetts	34,612	3.6%
10	Michigan	29,133	3.0%
17	Minnesota	17,767	1.9%
34	Mississippi	6,078	0.6%
20	Missouri	16,445	1.7%
45	Montana	2,641	0.3%
37	Nebraska	5,143	0.5%
35	Nevada	5,829	0.6%
41	New Hampshire	4,515	0.5%
9	New Jersey	31,081	3.2%
36	New Mexico	5,688	0.6%
2	New York	86,506	9.0%
11	North Carolina	27,407	2.9%
48	North Dakota	1,831	0.2%
7	Ohio	35,465	3.7%
29	Oklahoma	7,476	0.8%
25	Oregon	12,777	1.3%
5	Pennsylvania	44,336	4.6%
40	Rhode Island	4,530	0.5%
26	South Carolina	11,928	1.2%
47	South Dakota	2,104	0.2%
16	Tennessee	18,839	2.0%
3	Texas	59,482	6.2%
32	Utah	6,701	0.7%
44	Vermont	2,750	0.3%
13	Virginia	25,291	2.6%
15	Washington	21,337	2.2%
38	West Virginia	4,894	0.5%
18	Wisconsin	17,024	1.8%
50	Wyoming	1,235	0.1%

RANK ORDER

RANK	STATE	PHYSICIANS	% of USA
1	California	116,489	12.2%
2	New York	86,506	9.0%
3	Texas	59,482	6.2%
4	Florida	57,066	6.0%
5	Pennsylvania	44,336	4.6%
6	Illinois	40,963	4.3%
7	Ohio	35,465	3.7%
8	Massachusetts	34,612	3.6%
9	New Jersey	31,081	3.2%
10	Michigan	29,133	3.0%
11	North Carolina	27,407	2.9%
12	Maryland	27,153	2.8%
13	Virginia	25,291	2.6%
14	Georgia	24,092	2.5%
15	Washington	21,337	2.2%
16	Tennessee	18,839	2.0%
17	Minnesota	17,767	1.9%
18	Wisconsin	17,024	1.8%
19	Arizona	16,608	1.7%
20	Missouri	16,445	1.7%
21	Indiana	15,790	1.6%
22	Colorado	15,222	1.6%
23	Connecticut	15,170	1.6%
24	Louisiana	13,323	1.4%
25	Oregon	12,777	1.3%
26	South Carolina	11,928	1.2%
27	Alabama	11,507	1.2%
28	Kentucky	11,325	1.2%
29	Oklahoma	7,476	0.8%
30	Kansas	7,474	0.8%
31	Arkansas	6,749	0.7%
32	Utah	6,701	0.7%
33	Iowa	6,591	0.7%
34	Mississippi	6,078	0.6%
35	Nevada	5,829	0.6%
36	New Mexico	5,688	0.6%
37	Nebraska	5,143	0.5%
38	West Virginia	4,894	0.5%
39	Hawaii	4,800	0.5%
40	Rhode Island	4,530	0.5%
41	New Hampshire	4,515	0.5%
42	Maine	4,380	0.5%
43	Idaho	3,159	0.3%
44	Vermont	2,750	0.3%
45	Montana	2,641	0.3%
46	Delaware	2,488	0.3%
47	South Dakota	2,104	0.2%
48	North Dakota	1,831	0.2%
49	Alaska	1,769	0.2%
50	Wyoming	1,235	0.1%
	District of Columbia	5,372	0.6%

Source: American Medical Association (Chicago, Illinois)
    "Physician Characteristics and Distribution in the U.S." (2011 Edition)
*As of December 31, 2009. Total does not include 14,041 physicians in the U.S. territories and possessions, at APOs and FPOs, or whose addresses are unknown.

Rate of Physicians in 2009

National Rate = 312 Physicians per 100,000 Population*

ALPHA ORDER

RANK	STATE	RATE
41	Alabama	244
37	Alaska	253
38	Arizona	252
44	Arkansas	234
17	California	315
20	Colorado	303
5	Connecticut	431
29	Delaware	281
18	Florida	308
40	Georgia	245
7	Hawaii	371
49	Idaho	204
16	Illinois	317
39	Indiana	246
47	Iowa	219
33	Kansas	265
34	Kentucky	263
23	Louisiana	297
13	Maine	332
2	Maryland	476
1	Massachusetts	525
24	Michigan	292
11	Minnesota	337
48	Mississippi	206
30	Missouri	275
31	Montana	271
26	Nebraska	286
46	Nevada	221
10	New Hampshire	341
8	New Jersey	357
27	New Mexico	283
3	New York	443
24	North Carolina	292
27	North Dakota	283
19	Ohio	307
50	Oklahoma	203
12	Oregon	334
9	Pennsylvania	352
6	Rhode Island	430
35	South Carolina	262
36	South Dakota	259
22	Tennessee	299
43	Texas	240
42	Utah	241
4	Vermont	442
14	Virginia	321
15	Washington	320
32	West Virginia	269
21	Wisconsin	301
45	Wyoming	227

RANK ORDER

RANK	STATE	RATE
1	Massachusetts	525
2	Maryland	476
3	New York	443
4	Vermont	442
5	Connecticut	431
6	Rhode Island	430
7	Hawaii	371
8	New Jersey	357
9	Pennsylvania	352
10	New Hampshire	341
11	Minnesota	337
12	Oregon	334
13	Maine	332
14	Virginia	321
15	Washington	320
16	Illinois	317
17	California	315
18	Florida	308
19	Ohio	307
20	Colorado	303
21	Wisconsin	301
22	Tennessee	299
23	Louisiana	297
24	Michigan	292
24	North Carolina	292
26	Nebraska	286
27	New Mexico	283
27	North Dakota	283
29	Delaware	281
30	Missouri	275
31	Montana	271
32	West Virginia	269
33	Kansas	265
34	Kentucky	263
35	South Carolina	262
36	South Dakota	259
37	Alaska	253
38	Arizona	252
39	Indiana	246
40	Georgia	245
41	Alabama	244
42	Utah	241
43	Texas	240
44	Arkansas	234
45	Wyoming	227
46	Nevada	221
47	Iowa	219
48	Mississippi	206
49	Idaho	204
50	Oklahoma	203

District of Columbia — 896

Source: CQ Press using data from American Medical Association (Chicago, Illinois)
"Physician Characteristics and Distribution in the U.S." (2011 Edition)
*As of December 31, 2009. National rate does not include physicians in the U.S. territories and possessions, at APOs and FPOs, or whose addresses are unknown.

Rate of Registered Nurses in 2009

National Rate = 842 Nurses per 100,000 Population*

ALPHA ORDER

RANK	STATE	RATE
23	Alabama	911
41	Alaska	717
50	Arizona	585
38	Arkansas	798
47	California	630
34	Colorado	831
12	Connecticut	1,017
3	Delaware	1,155
35	Florida	814
45	Georgia	665
42	Hawaii	689
43	Idaho	682
25	Illinois	901
25	Indiana	901
10	Iowa	1,022
21	Kansas	934
14	Kentucky	1,003
27	Louisiana	881
5	Maine	1,093
24	Maryland	906
2	Massachusetts	1,260
31	Michigan	849
5	Minnesota	1,093
18	Mississippi	950
8	Missouri	1,038
30	Montana	855
7	Nebraska	1,054
49	Nevada	609
13	New Hampshire	1,006
29	New Jersey	858
48	New Mexico	614
32	New York	848
20	North Carolina	940
16	North Dakota	968
11	Ohio	1,021
40	Oklahoma	742
37	Oregon	803
9	Pennsylvania	1,030
4	Rhode Island	1,104
33	South Carolina	834
1	South Dakota	1,296
15	Tennessee	984
44	Texas	678
46	Utah	635
22	Vermont	914
39	Virginia	764
35	Washington	814
17	West Virginia	953
19	Wisconsin	946
28	Wyoming	864

RANK ORDER

RANK	STATE	RATE
1	South Dakota	1,296
2	Massachusetts	1,260
3	Delaware	1,155
4	Rhode Island	1,104
5	Maine	1,093
5	Minnesota	1,093
7	Nebraska	1,054
8	Missouri	1,038
9	Pennsylvania	1,030
10	Iowa	1,022
11	Ohio	1,021
12	Connecticut	1,017
13	New Hampshire	1,006
14	Kentucky	1,003
15	Tennessee	984
16	North Dakota	968
17	West Virginia	953
18	Mississippi	950
19	Wisconsin	946
20	North Carolina	940
21	Kansas	934
22	Vermont	914
23	Alabama	911
24	Maryland	906
25	Illinois	901
25	Indiana	901
27	Louisiana	881
28	Wyoming	864
29	New Jersey	858
30	Montana	855
31	Michigan	849
32	New York	848
33	South Carolina	834
34	Colorado	831
35	Florida	814
35	Washington	814
37	Oregon	803
38	Arkansas	798
39	Virginia	764
40	Oklahoma	742
41	Alaska	717
42	Hawaii	689
43	Idaho	682
44	Texas	678
45	Georgia	665
46	Utah	635
47	California	630
48	New Mexico	614
49	Nevada	609
50	Arizona	585

District of Columbia	1,483

Source: CQ Press using data from U.S. Department of Labor, Bureau of Labor Statistics
 "Occupational Employment and Wages, 2009" (http://www.bls.gov/oes/)
*Does not include self-employed.

Rate of Dentists in 2008

National Rate = 60 Dentists per 100,000 Population*

ALPHA ORDER

RANK	STATE	RATE
48	Alabama	43
7	Alaska	73
29	Arizona	51
49	Arkansas	39
5	California	76
11	Colorado	65
6	Connecticut	75
41	Delaware	46
26	Florida	53
47	Georgia	44
2	Hawaii	81
20	Idaho	58
12	Illinois	64
38	Indiana	47
26	Iowa	53
29	Kansas	51
24	Kentucky	56
41	Louisiana	46
33	Maine	50
7	Maryland	73
1	Massachusetts	83
17	Michigan	61
17	Minnesota	61
49	Mississippi	39
38	Missouri	47
22	Montana	57
14	Nebraska	62
29	Nevada	51
14	New Hampshire	62
3	New Jersey	80
41	New Mexico	46
4	New York	77
45	North Carolina	45
29	North Dakota	51
28	Ohio	52
33	Oklahoma	50
10	Oregon	68
14	Pennsylvania	62
25	Rhode Island	54
41	South Carolina	46
33	South Dakota	50
37	Tennessee	48
45	Texas	45
12	Utah	64
20	Vermont	58
19	Virginia	60
9	Washington	70
38	West Virginia	47
22	Wisconsin	57
33	Wyoming	50

RANK ORDER

RANK	STATE	RATE
1	Massachusetts	83
2	Hawaii	81
3	New Jersey	80
4	New York	77
5	California	76
6	Connecticut	75
7	Alaska	73
7	Maryland	73
9	Washington	70
10	Oregon	68
11	Colorado	65
12	Illinois	64
12	Utah	64
14	Nebraska	62
14	New Hampshire	62
14	Pennsylvania	62
17	Michigan	61
17	Minnesota	61
19	Virginia	60
20	Idaho	58
20	Vermont	58
22	Montana	57
22	Wisconsin	57
24	Kentucky	56
25	Rhode Island	54
26	Florida	53
26	Iowa	53
28	Ohio	52
29	Arizona	51
29	Kansas	51
29	Nevada	51
29	North Dakota	51
33	Maine	50
33	Oklahoma	50
33	South Dakota	50
33	Wyoming	50
37	Tennessee	48
38	Indiana	47
38	Missouri	47
38	West Virginia	47
41	Delaware	46
41	Louisiana	46
41	New Mexico	46
41	South Carolina	46
45	North Carolina	45
45	Texas	45
47	Georgia	44
48	Alabama	43
49	Arkansas	39
49	Mississippi	39
	District of Columbia	107

Source: CQ Press using data from American Dental Association
"Distribution of Dentists, by Region and State, 2008"

*Professionally active dentists. National figure includes 65 dentists for whom state is not known.

Community Hospitals in 2009

National Total = 5,008 Hospitals*

ALPHA ORDER

RANK	STATE	HOSPITALS	% of USA
20	Alabama	108	2.2%
47	Alaska	22	0.4%
30	Arizona	72	1.4%
26	Arkansas	86	1.7%
2	California	343	6.8%
27	Colorado	81	1.6%
42	Connecticut	35	0.7%
50	Delaware	7	0.1%
3	Florida	210	4.2%
9	Georgia	152	3.0%
45	Hawaii	25	0.5%
38	Idaho	41	0.8%
5	Illinois	189	3.8%
16	Indiana	123	2.5%
17	Iowa	118	2.4%
11	Kansas	133	2.7%
21	Kentucky	104	2.1%
13	Louisiana	128	2.6%
40	Maine	37	0.7%
35	Maryland	49	1.0%
28	Massachusetts	78	1.6%
8	Michigan	158	3.2%
12	Minnesota	132	2.6%
22	Mississippi	97	1.9%
15	Missouri	125	2.5%
36	Montana	48	1.0%
24	Nebraska	87	1.7%
42	Nevada	35	0.7%
44	New Hampshire	28	0.6%
29	New Jersey	74	1.5%
40	New Mexico	37	0.7%
5	New York	189	3.8%
19	North Carolina	115	2.3%
38	North Dakota	41	0.8%
7	Ohio	183	3.7%
18	Oklahoma	116	2.3%
32	Oregon	58	1.2%
4	Pennsylvania	194	3.9%
49	Rhode Island	11	0.2%
31	South Carolina	70	1.4%
34	South Dakota	53	1.1%
10	Tennessee	137	2.7%
1	Texas	428	8.5%
37	Utah	44	0.9%
48	Vermont	14	0.3%
23	Virginia	90	1.8%
24	Washington	87	1.7%
33	West Virginia	56	1.1%
14	Wisconsin	126	2.5%
46	Wyoming	24	0.5%

RANK ORDER

RANK	STATE	HOSPITALS	% of USA
1	Texas	428	8.5%
2	California	343	6.8%
3	Florida	210	4.2%
4	Pennsylvania	194	3.9%
5	Illinois	189	3.8%
5	New York	189	3.8%
7	Ohio	183	3.7%
8	Michigan	158	3.2%
9	Georgia	152	3.0%
10	Tennessee	137	2.7%
11	Kansas	133	2.7%
12	Minnesota	132	2.6%
13	Louisiana	128	2.6%
14	Wisconsin	126	2.5%
15	Missouri	125	2.5%
16	Indiana	123	2.5%
17	Iowa	118	2.4%
18	Oklahoma	116	2.3%
19	North Carolina	115	2.3%
20	Alabama	108	2.2%
21	Kentucky	104	2.1%
22	Mississippi	97	1.9%
23	Virginia	90	1.8%
24	Nebraska	87	1.7%
24	Washington	87	1.7%
26	Arkansas	86	1.7%
27	Colorado	81	1.6%
28	Massachusetts	78	1.6%
29	New Jersey	74	1.5%
30	Arizona	72	1.4%
31	South Carolina	70	1.4%
32	Oregon	58	1.2%
33	West Virginia	56	1.1%
34	South Dakota	53	1.1%
35	Maryland	49	1.0%
36	Montana	48	1.0%
37	Utah	44	0.9%
38	Idaho	41	0.8%
38	North Dakota	41	0.8%
40	Maine	37	0.7%
40	New Mexico	37	0.7%
42	Connecticut	35	0.7%
42	Nevada	35	0.7%
44	New Hampshire	28	0.6%
45	Hawaii	25	0.5%
46	Wyoming	24	0.5%
47	Alaska	22	0.4%
48	Vermont	14	0.3%
49	Rhode Island	11	0.2%
50	Delaware	7	0.1%
	District of Columbia	10	0.2%

Source: American Hospital Association (Chicago, IL)
    "Hospital Statistics" (2011 edition)
*Community hospitals are all nonfederal, short-term general, and special hospitals whose facilities and services are available to the public.

Rate of Community Hospitals in 2009

National Rate = 1.6 Community Hospitals per 100,000 Population*

ALPHA ORDER

RANK	STATE	RATE
18	Alabama	2.3
9	Alaska	3.1
41	Arizona	1.1
12	Arkansas	3.0
47	California	0.9
28	Colorado	1.6
44	Connecticut	1.0
49	Delaware	0.8
41	Florida	1.1
32	Georgia	1.5
24	Hawaii	1.9
15	Idaho	2.7
32	Illinois	1.5
24	Indiana	1.9
7	Iowa	3.9
5	Kansas	4.7
17	Kentucky	2.4
13	Louisiana	2.8
13	Maine	2.8
47	Maryland	0.9
39	Massachusetts	1.2
28	Michigan	1.6
16	Minnesota	2.5
8	Mississippi	3.3
22	Missouri	2.1
3	Montana	4.9
4	Nebraska	4.8
37	Nevada	1.3
22	New Hampshire	2.1
49	New Jersey	0.8
26	New Mexico	1.8
44	New York	1.0
39	North Carolina	1.2
2	North Dakota	6.3
28	Ohio	1.6
9	Oklahoma	3.1
32	Oregon	1.5
32	Pennsylvania	1.5
44	Rhode Island	1.0
32	South Carolina	1.5
1	South Dakota	6.5
20	Tennessee	2.2
27	Texas	1.7
28	Utah	1.6
18	Vermont	2.3
41	Virginia	1.1
37	Washington	1.3
9	West Virginia	3.1
20	Wisconsin	2.2
6	Wyoming	4.4

RANK ORDER

RANK	STATE	RATE
1	South Dakota	6.5
2	North Dakota	6.3
3	Montana	4.9
4	Nebraska	4.8
5	Kansas	4.7
6	Wyoming	4.4
7	Iowa	3.9
8	Mississippi	3.3
9	Alaska	3.1
9	Oklahoma	3.1
9	West Virginia	3.1
12	Arkansas	3.0
13	Louisiana	2.8
13	Maine	2.8
15	Idaho	2.7
16	Minnesota	2.5
17	Kentucky	2.4
18	Alabama	2.3
18	Vermont	2.3
20	Tennessee	2.2
20	Wisconsin	2.2
22	Missouri	2.1
22	New Hampshire	2.1
24	Hawaii	1.9
24	Indiana	1.9
26	New Mexico	1.8
27	Texas	1.7
28	Colorado	1.6
28	Michigan	1.6
28	Ohio	1.6
28	Utah	1.6
32	Georgia	1.5
32	Illinois	1.5
32	Oregon	1.5
32	Pennsylvania	1.5
32	South Carolina	1.5
37	Nevada	1.3
37	Washington	1.3
39	Massachusetts	1.2
39	North Carolina	1.2
41	Arizona	1.1
41	Florida	1.1
41	Virginia	1.1
44	Connecticut	1.0
44	New York	1.0
44	Rhode Island	1.0
47	California	0.9
47	Maryland	0.9
49	Delaware	0.8
49	New Jersey	0.8
	District of Columbia	1.7

Source: CQ Press using data from American Hospital Association (Chicago, IL)
"Hospital Statistics" (2011 edition)
*Community hospitals are all nonfederal, short-term general, and special hospitals whose facilities and services are available to the public.

Births in 2008

National Total = 4,247,694 Live Births*

ALPHA ORDER

RANK	STATE	BIRTHS	% of USA
24	Alabama	64,546	1.5%
47	Alaska	11,442	0.3%
13	Arizona	99,442	2.3%
32	Arkansas	40,669	1.0%
1	California	551,779	13.0%
22	Colorado	70,031	1.6%
33	Connecticut	40,399	1.0%
44	Delaware	12,090	0.3%
4	Florida	231,445	5.4%
8	Georgia	146,603	3.5%
40	Hawaii	19,484	0.5%
38	Idaho	25,149	0.6%
5	Illinois	176,795	4.2%
15	Indiana	88,742	2.1%
34	Iowa	40,224	0.9%
31	Kansas	41,833	1.0%
26	Kentucky	58,375	1.4%
23	Louisiana	65,268	1.5%
42	Maine	13,609	0.3%
18	Maryland	77,289	1.8%
19	Massachusetts	77,022	1.8%
10	Michigan	121,127	2.9%
20	Minnesota	72,421	1.7%
30	Mississippi	44,947	1.1%
17	Missouri	80,963	1.9%
43	Montana	12,594	0.3%
37	Nebraska	26,989	0.6%
35	Nevada	39,506	0.9%
41	New Hampshire	13,683	0.3%
11	New Jersey	112,710	2.7%
36	New Mexico	30,173	0.7%
3	New York	250,383	5.9%
9	North Carolina	130,839	3.1%
48	North Dakota	8,938	0.2%
7	Ohio	148,821	3.5%
28	Oklahoma	54,781	1.3%
29	Oregon	49,096	1.2%
6	Pennsylvania	149,273	3.5%
46	Rhode Island	12,048	0.3%
25	South Carolina	63,071	1.5%
45	South Dakota	12,071	0.3%
16	Tennessee	85,560	2.0%
2	Texas	405,554	9.5%
27	Utah	55,634	1.3%
50	Vermont	6,339	0.1%
12	Virginia	106,686	2.5%
14	Washington	90,321	2.1%
39	West Virginia	21,501	0.5%
21	Wisconsin	72,261	1.7%
49	Wyoming	8,038	0.2%

RANK ORDER

RANK	STATE	BIRTHS	% of USA
1	California	551,779	13.0%
2	Texas	405,554	9.5%
3	New York	250,383	5.9%
4	Florida	231,445	5.4%
5	Illinois	176,795	4.2%
6	Pennsylvania	149,273	3.5%
7	Ohio	148,821	3.5%
8	Georgia	146,603	3.5%
9	North Carolina	130,839	3.1%
10	Michigan	121,127	2.9%
11	New Jersey	112,710	2.7%
12	Virginia	106,686	2.5%
13	Arizona	99,442	2.3%
14	Washington	90,321	2.1%
15	Indiana	88,742	2.1%
16	Tennessee	85,560	2.0%
17	Missouri	80,963	1.9%
18	Maryland	77,289	1.8%
19	Massachusetts	77,022	1.8%
20	Minnesota	72,421	1.7%
21	Wisconsin	72,261	1.7%
22	Colorado	70,031	1.6%
23	Louisiana	65,268	1.5%
24	Alabama	64,546	1.5%
25	South Carolina	63,071	1.5%
26	Kentucky	58,375	1.4%
27	Utah	55,634	1.3%
28	Oklahoma	54,781	1.3%
29	Oregon	49,096	1.2%
30	Mississippi	44,947	1.1%
31	Kansas	41,833	1.0%
32	Arkansas	40,669	1.0%
33	Connecticut	40,399	1.0%
34	Iowa	40,224	0.9%
35	Nevada	39,506	0.9%
36	New Mexico	30,173	0.7%
37	Nebraska	26,989	0.6%
38	Idaho	25,149	0.6%
39	West Virginia	21,501	0.5%
40	Hawaii	19,484	0.5%
41	New Hampshire	13,683	0.3%
42	Maine	13,609	0.3%
43	Montana	12,594	0.3%
44	Delaware	12,090	0.3%
45	South Dakota	12,071	0.3%
46	Rhode Island	12,048	0.3%
47	Alaska	11,442	0.3%
48	North Dakota	8,938	0.2%
49	Wyoming	8,038	0.2%
50	Vermont	6,339	0.1%
	District of Columbia	9,130	0.2%

Source: U.S. Department of Health and Human Services, National Center for Health Statistics
  "National Vital Statistics Reports" (Vol. 59, No. 1, December 2010, http://www.cdc.gov/nchs/births.htm)
*Final data by state of residence.

Birth Rate in 2008

National Rate = 14.0 Live Births per 1,000 Population*

ALPHA ORDER

RANK	STATE	RATE
25	Alabama	13.8
2	Alaska	16.7
5	Arizona	15.3
18	Arkansas	14.2
13	California	15.0
18	Colorado	14.2
46	Connecticut	11.5
25	Delaware	13.8
41	Florida	12.6
9	Georgia	15.1
9	Hawaii	15.1
4	Idaho	16.5
29	Illinois	13.7
22	Indiana	13.9
34	Iowa	13.4
16	Kansas	14.9
29	Kentucky	13.7
17	Louisiana	14.8
49	Maine	10.3
29	Maryland	13.7
44	Massachusetts	11.9
42	Michigan	12.1
22	Minnesota	13.9
5	Mississippi	15.3
29	Missouri	13.7
35	Montana	13.0
9	Nebraska	15.1
7	Nevada	15.2
48	New Hampshire	10.4
35	New Jersey	13.0
7	New Mexico	15.2
39	New York	12.8
18	North Carolina	14.2
22	North Dakota	13.9
35	Ohio	13.0
13	Oklahoma	15.0
35	Oregon	13.0
43	Pennsylvania	12.0
46	Rhode Island	11.5
21	South Carolina	14.1
13	South Dakota	15.0
25	Tennessee	13.8
2	Texas	16.7
1	Utah	20.3
50	Vermont	10.2
29	Virginia	13.7
25	Washington	13.8
45	West Virginia	11.8
39	Wisconsin	12.8
9	Wyoming	15.1

RANK ORDER

RANK	STATE	RATE
1	Utah	20.3
2	Alaska	16.7
2	Texas	16.7
4	Idaho	16.5
5	Arizona	15.3
5	Mississippi	15.3
7	Nevada	15.2
7	New Mexico	15.2
9	Georgia	15.1
9	Hawaii	15.1
9	Nebraska	15.1
9	Wyoming	15.1
13	California	15.0
13	Oklahoma	15.0
13	South Dakota	15.0
16	Kansas	14.9
17	Louisiana	14.8
18	Arkansas	14.2
18	Colorado	14.2
18	North Carolina	14.2
21	South Carolina	14.1
22	Indiana	13.9
22	Minnesota	13.9
22	North Dakota	13.9
25	Alabama	13.8
25	Delaware	13.8
25	Tennessee	13.8
25	Washington	13.8
29	Illinois	13.7
29	Kentucky	13.7
29	Maryland	13.7
29	Missouri	13.7
29	Virginia	13.7
34	Iowa	13.4
35	Montana	13.0
35	New Jersey	13.0
35	Ohio	13.0
35	Oregon	13.0
39	New York	12.8
39	Wisconsin	12.8
41	Florida	12.6
42	Michigan	12.1
43	Pennsylvania	12.0
44	Massachusetts	11.9
45	West Virginia	11.8
46	Connecticut	11.5
46	Rhode Island	11.5
48	New Hampshire	10.4
49	Maine	10.3
50	Vermont	10.2

District of Columbia   15.4

Source: U.S. Department of Health and Human Services, National Center for Health Statistics
"National Vital Statistics Reports" (Vol. 59, No. 1, December 2010, http://www.cdc.gov/nchs/births.htm)
*Final data by state of residence.

Births of Low Birthweight as a Percent of All Births in 2008

National Percent = 8.2% of Live Births*

ALPHA ORDER

RANK	STATE	PERCENT
3	Alabama	10.6
50	Alaska	6.0
35	Arizona	7.1
7	Arkansas	9.2
39	California	6.8
12	Colorado	8.9
29	Connecticut	8.0
16	Delaware	8.5
13	Florida	8.8
5	Georgia	9.6
27	Hawaii	8.1
44	Idaho	6.5
18	Illinois	8.4
21	Indiana	8.3
43	Iowa	6.6
34	Kansas	7.2
7	Kentucky	9.2
2	Louisiana	10.8
42	Maine	6.7
7	Maryland	9.2
32	Massachusetts	7.8
14	Michigan	8.6
47	Minnesota	6.4
1	Mississippi	11.8
27	Missouri	8.1
33	Montana	7.4
36	Nebraska	7.0
29	Nevada	8.0
44	New Hampshire	6.5
18	New Jersey	8.4
16	New Mexico	8.5
26	New York	8.2
11	North Carolina	9.1
39	North Dakota	6.8
14	Ohio	8.6
21	Oklahoma	8.3
49	Oregon	6.1
21	Pennsylvania	8.3
31	Rhode Island	7.9
4	South Carolina	9.9
44	South Dakota	6.5
7	Tennessee	9.2
18	Texas	8.4
39	Utah	6.8
36	Vermont	7.0
21	Virginia	8.3
48	Washington	6.3
6	West Virginia	9.5
36	Wisconsin	7.0
21	Wyoming	8.3

RANK ORDER

RANK	STATE	PERCENT
1	Mississippi	11.8
2	Louisiana	10.8
3	Alabama	10.6
4	South Carolina	9.9
5	Georgia	9.6
6	West Virginia	9.5
7	Arkansas	9.2
7	Kentucky	9.2
7	Maryland	9.2
7	Tennessee	9.2
11	North Carolina	9.1
12	Colorado	8.9
13	Florida	8.8
14	Michigan	8.6
14	Ohio	8.6
16	Delaware	8.5
16	New Mexico	8.5
18	Illinois	8.4
18	New Jersey	8.4
18	Texas	8.4
21	Indiana	8.3
21	Oklahoma	8.3
21	Pennsylvania	8.3
21	Virginia	8.3
21	Wyoming	8.3
26	New York	8.2
27	Hawaii	8.1
27	Missouri	8.1
29	Connecticut	8.0
29	Nevada	8.0
31	Rhode Island	7.9
32	Massachusetts	7.8
33	Montana	7.4
34	Kansas	7.2
35	Arizona	7.1
36	Nebraska	7.0
36	Vermont	7.0
36	Wisconsin	7.0
39	California	6.8
39	North Dakota	6.8
39	Utah	6.8
42	Maine	6.7
43	Iowa	6.6
44	Idaho	6.5
44	New Hampshire	6.5
44	South Dakota	6.5
47	Minnesota	6.4
48	Washington	6.3
49	Oregon	6.1
50	Alaska	6.0

District of Columbia	10.5

Source: U.S. Department of Health and Human Services, National Center for Health Statistics
"National Vital Statistics Reports" (Vol. 59, No. 1, December 2010, http://www.cdc.gov/nchs/births.htm)
*Final data by state of residence. Births of less than 2,500 grams (5 pounds 8 ounces).

Births to Teenage Mothers as a Percent of All Births in 2008

National Percent = 10.2% of Live Births*

ALPHA ORDER

RANK	STATE	PERCENT
7	Alabama	13.3
24	Alaska	9.9
12	Arizona	12.1
3	Arkansas	14.6
28	California	9.4
27	Colorado	9.5
44	Connecticut	6.9
23	Delaware	10.2
21	Florida	10.4
13	Georgia	11.8
38	Hawaii	8.3
33	Idaho	9.0
26	Illinois	9.8
18	Indiana	10.8
34	Iowa	8.9
20	Kansas	10.5
9	Kentucky	13.1
5	Louisiana	13.5
39	Maine	8.2
35	Maryland	8.5
50	Massachusetts	6.0
24	Michigan	9.9
46	Minnesota	6.7
1	Mississippi	16.0
15	Missouri	11.3
21	Montana	10.4
35	Nebraska	8.5
18	Nevada	10.8
48	New Hampshire	6.6
49	New Jersey	6.2
2	New Mexico	15.0
44	New York	6.9
14	North Carolina	11.6
42	North Dakota	7.5
16	Ohio	10.9
4	Oklahoma	13.7
32	Oregon	9.1
31	Pennsylvania	9.2
29	Rhode Island	9.3
8	South Carolina	13.2
29	South Dakota	9.3
10	Tennessee	13.0
6	Texas	13.4
46	Utah	6.7
43	Vermont	7.4
39	Virginia	8.2
39	Washington	8.2
11	West Virginia	12.9
37	Wisconsin	8.4
16	Wyoming	10.9

RANK ORDER

RANK	STATE	PERCENT
1	Mississippi	16.0
2	New Mexico	15.0
3	Arkansas	14.6
4	Oklahoma	13.7
5	Louisiana	13.5
6	Texas	13.4
7	Alabama	13.3
8	South Carolina	13.2
9	Kentucky	13.1
10	Tennessee	13.0
11	West Virginia	12.9
12	Arizona	12.1
13	Georgia	11.8
14	North Carolina	11.6
15	Missouri	11.3
16	Ohio	10.9
16	Wyoming	10.9
18	Indiana	10.8
18	Nevada	10.8
20	Kansas	10.5
21	Florida	10.4
21	Montana	10.4
23	Delaware	10.2
24	Alaska	9.9
24	Michigan	9.9
26	Illinois	9.8
27	Colorado	9.5
28	California	9.4
29	Rhode Island	9.3
29	South Dakota	9.3
31	Pennsylvania	9.2
32	Oregon	9.1
33	Idaho	9.0
34	Iowa	8.9
35	Maryland	8.5
35	Nebraska	8.5
37	Wisconsin	8.4
38	Hawaii	8.3
39	Maine	8.2
39	Virginia	8.2
39	Washington	8.2
42	North Dakota	7.5
43	Vermont	7.4
44	Connecticut	6.9
44	New York	6.9
46	Minnesota	6.7
46	Utah	6.7
48	New Hampshire	6.6
49	New Jersey	6.2
50	Massachusetts	6.0

| | District of Columbia | 11.9 |

Source: CQ Press using data from U.S. Department of Health and Human Services, National Center for Health Statistics
"National Vital Statistics Reports" (Vol. 59, No. 1, December 2010, http://www.cdc.gov/nchs/births.htm)
"Vital Stats" (http://www.cdc.gov/nchs/VitalStats.htm)
*Final data. Live births to women 15 to 19 years old by state of residence.

Births to Unmarried Women as a Percent of All Births in 2008

National Percent = 40.6% of Live Births*

ALPHA ORDER

RANK	STATE	PERCENT
27	Alabama	39.9
33	Alaska	37.6
8	Arizona	45.3
9	Arkansas	44.6
25	California	40.2
49	Colorado	24.9
35	Connecticut	36.4
4	Delaware	48.0
6	Florida	46.9
7	Georgia	45.4
31	Hawaii	37.9
48	Idaho	25.3
23	Illinois	40.7
13	Indiana	43.3
39	Iowa	35.2
32	Kansas	37.8
23	Kentucky	40.7
2	Louisiana	53.0
28	Maine	39.7
15	Maryland	42.4
42	Massachusetts	34.0
25	Michigan	40.2
46	Minnesota	33.3
1	Mississippi	54.5
21	Missouri	40.9
34	Montana	36.7
44	Nebraska	33.9
14	Nevada	42.5
47	New Hampshire	32.9
40	New Jersey	35.0
3	New Mexico	52.9
20	New York	41.4
17	North Carolina	42.0
45	North Dakota	33.6
12	Ohio	43.4
16	Oklahoma	42.3
37	Oregon	36.1
22	Pennsylvania	40.8
11	Rhode Island	43.9
5	South Carolina	47.8
30	South Dakota	38.4
10	Tennessee	44.1
19	Texas	41.7
50	Utah	20.4
29	Vermont	38.8
38	Virginia	35.8
42	Washington	34.0
17	West Virginia	42.0
36	Wisconsin	36.3
41	Wyoming	34.6

RANK ORDER

RANK	STATE	PERCENT
1	Mississippi	54.5
2	Louisiana	53.0
3	New Mexico	52.9
4	Delaware	48.0
5	South Carolina	47.8
6	Florida	46.9
7	Georgia	45.4
8	Arizona	45.3
9	Arkansas	44.6
10	Tennessee	44.1
11	Rhode Island	43.9
12	Ohio	43.4
13	Indiana	43.3
14	Nevada	42.5
15	Maryland	42.4
16	Oklahoma	42.3
17	North Carolina	42.0
17	West Virginia	42.0
19	Texas	41.7
20	New York	41.4
21	Missouri	40.9
22	Pennsylvania	40.8
23	Illinois	40.7
23	Kentucky	40.7
25	California	40.2
25	Michigan	40.2
27	Alabama	39.9
28	Maine	39.7
29	Vermont	38.8
30	South Dakota	38.4
31	Hawaii	37.9
32	Kansas	37.8
33	Alaska	37.6
34	Montana	36.7
35	Connecticut	36.4
36	Wisconsin	36.3
37	Oregon	36.1
38	Virginia	35.8
39	Iowa	35.2
40	New Jersey	35.0
41	Wyoming	34.6
42	Massachusetts	34.0
42	Washington	34.0
44	Nebraska	33.9
45	North Dakota	33.6
46	Minnesota	33.3
47	New Hampshire	32.9
48	Idaho	25.3
49	Colorado	24.9
50	Utah	20.4
	District of Columbia	57.8

Source: U.S. Department of Health and Human Services, National Center for Health Statistics
"National Vital Statistics Reports" (Vol. 59, No. 1, December 2010, http://www.cdc.gov/nchs/births.htm)
*Final data by state of residence.

Percent of Women Receiving Late or No Prenatal Care in 2008

National Percent = 7.0% of Women*

<table>
<tr><td colspan="3">ALPHA ORDER</td><td colspan="3">RANK ORDER</td></tr>
<tr><td>RANK</td><td>STATE</td><td>PERCENT</td><td>RANK</td><td>STATE</td><td>PERCENT</td></tr>
<tr><td>NA</td><td>Alabama**</td><td>NA</td><td>1</td><td>Texas</td><td>12.4</td></tr>
<tr><td>NA</td><td>Alaska**</td><td>NA</td><td>2</td><td>New Mexico</td><td>10.8</td></tr>
<tr><td>NA</td><td>Arizona**</td><td>NA</td><td>3</td><td>Delaware</td><td>9.5</td></tr>
<tr><td>NA</td><td>Arkansas**</td><td>NA</td><td>4</td><td>Tennessee</td><td>8.7</td></tr>
<tr><td>25</td><td>California</td><td>3.6</td><td>5</td><td>Colorado</td><td>7.9</td></tr>
<tr><td>5</td><td>Colorado</td><td>7.9</td><td>6</td><td>South Carolina</td><td>7.8</td></tr>
<tr><td>NA</td><td>Connecticut**</td><td>NA</td><td>7</td><td>Georgia</td><td>7.7</td></tr>
<tr><td>3</td><td>Delaware</td><td>9.5</td><td>8</td><td>Wyoming</td><td>7.6</td></tr>
<tr><td>9</td><td>Florida</td><td>7.3</td><td>9</td><td>Florida</td><td>7.3</td></tr>
<tr><td>7</td><td>Georgia</td><td>7.7</td><td>10</td><td>Ohio</td><td>7.2</td></tr>
<tr><td>NA</td><td>Hawaii**</td><td>NA</td><td>10</td><td>Washington</td><td>7.2</td></tr>
<tr><td>17</td><td>Idaho</td><td>6.0</td><td>12</td><td>Indiana</td><td>7.1</td></tr>
<tr><td>NA</td><td>Illinois**</td><td>NA</td><td>13</td><td>Pennsylvania</td><td>7.0</td></tr>
<tr><td>12</td><td>Indiana</td><td>7.1</td><td>14</td><td>North Dakota</td><td>6.6</td></tr>
<tr><td>23</td><td>Iowa</td><td>4.5</td><td>15</td><td>New York</td><td>6.3</td></tr>
<tr><td>20</td><td>Kansas</td><td>5.3</td><td>16</td><td>South Dakota</td><td>6.2</td></tr>
<tr><td>17</td><td>Kentucky</td><td>6.0</td><td>17</td><td>Idaho</td><td>6.0</td></tr>
<tr><td>NA</td><td>Louisiana**</td><td>NA</td><td>17</td><td>Kentucky</td><td>6.0</td></tr>
<tr><td>NA</td><td>Maine**</td><td>NA</td><td>19</td><td>Oregon</td><td>5.5</td></tr>
<tr><td>NA</td><td>Maryland**</td><td>NA</td><td>20</td><td>Kansas</td><td>5.3</td></tr>
<tr><td>NA</td><td>Massachusetts**</td><td>NA</td><td>20</td><td>Montana</td><td>5.3</td></tr>
<tr><td>22</td><td>Michigan</td><td>4.6</td><td>22</td><td>Michigan</td><td>4.6</td></tr>
<tr><td>NA</td><td>Minnesota**</td><td>NA</td><td>23</td><td>Iowa</td><td>4.5</td></tr>
<tr><td>NA</td><td>Mississippi**</td><td>NA</td><td>24</td><td>Nebraska</td><td>4.4</td></tr>
<tr><td>NA</td><td>Missouri**</td><td>NA</td><td>25</td><td>California</td><td>3.6</td></tr>
<tr><td>20</td><td>Montana</td><td>5.3</td><td>25</td><td>New Hampshire</td><td>3.6</td></tr>
<tr><td>24</td><td>Nebraska</td><td>4.4</td><td>27</td><td>Vermont</td><td>2.8</td></tr>
<tr><td>NA</td><td>Nevada**</td><td>NA</td><td>NA</td><td>Alabama**</td><td>NA</td></tr>
<tr><td>25</td><td>New Hampshire</td><td>3.6</td><td>NA</td><td>Alaska**</td><td>NA</td></tr>
<tr><td>NA</td><td>New Jersey**</td><td>NA</td><td>NA</td><td>Arizona**</td><td>NA</td></tr>
<tr><td>2</td><td>New Mexico</td><td>10.8</td><td>NA</td><td>Arkansas**</td><td>NA</td></tr>
<tr><td>15</td><td>New York</td><td>6.3</td><td>NA</td><td>Connecticut**</td><td>NA</td></tr>
<tr><td>NA</td><td>North Carolina**</td><td>NA</td><td>NA</td><td>Hawaii**</td><td>NA</td></tr>
<tr><td>14</td><td>North Dakota</td><td>6.6</td><td>NA</td><td>Illinois**</td><td>NA</td></tr>
<tr><td>10</td><td>Ohio</td><td>7.2</td><td>NA</td><td>Louisiana**</td><td>NA</td></tr>
<tr><td>NA</td><td>Oklahoma**</td><td>NA</td><td>NA</td><td>Maine**</td><td>NA</td></tr>
<tr><td>19</td><td>Oregon</td><td>5.5</td><td>NA</td><td>Maryland**</td><td>NA</td></tr>
<tr><td>13</td><td>Pennsylvania</td><td>7.0</td><td>NA</td><td>Massachusetts**</td><td>NA</td></tr>
<tr><td>NA</td><td>Rhode Island**</td><td>NA</td><td>NA</td><td>Minnesota**</td><td>NA</td></tr>
<tr><td>6</td><td>South Carolina</td><td>7.8</td><td>NA</td><td>Mississippi**</td><td>NA</td></tr>
<tr><td>16</td><td>South Dakota</td><td>6.2</td><td>NA</td><td>Missouri**</td><td>NA</td></tr>
<tr><td>4</td><td>Tennessee</td><td>8.7</td><td>NA</td><td>Nevada**</td><td>NA</td></tr>
<tr><td>1</td><td>Texas</td><td>12.4</td><td>NA</td><td>New Jersey**</td><td>NA</td></tr>
<tr><td>NA</td><td>Utah**</td><td>NA</td><td>NA</td><td>North Carolina**</td><td>NA</td></tr>
<tr><td>27</td><td>Vermont</td><td>2.8</td><td>NA</td><td>Oklahoma**</td><td>NA</td></tr>
<tr><td>NA</td><td>Virginia**</td><td>NA</td><td>NA</td><td>Rhode Island**</td><td>NA</td></tr>
<tr><td>10</td><td>Washington</td><td>7.2</td><td>NA</td><td>Utah**</td><td>NA</td></tr>
<tr><td>NA</td><td>West Virginia**</td><td>NA</td><td>NA</td><td>Virginia**</td><td>NA</td></tr>
<tr><td>NA</td><td>Wisconsin**</td><td>NA</td><td>NA</td><td>West Virginia**</td><td>NA</td></tr>
<tr><td>8</td><td>Wyoming</td><td>7.6</td><td>NA</td><td>Wisconsin**</td><td>NA</td></tr>
<tr><td></td><td></td><td></td><td>NA</td><td>District of Columbia**</td><td>NA</td></tr>
</table>

Source: CQ Press using data from U.S. Department of Health and Human Services, National Center for Health Statistics
    "Vital Stats" (http://www.cdc.gov/nchs/VitalStats.htm)
*Final data by state of residence. "Late" means care begun in third trimester. National figure is for reporting states only.
**Not available.

Reported Legal Abortions in 2006

Reporting States' Total = 846,181 Abortions*

ALPHA ORDER

RANK	STATE	ABORTIONS	% of USA
18	Alabama	11,654	1.4%
42	Alaska	1,923	0.2%
22	Arizona	10,836	1.3%
31	Arkansas	4,988	0.6%
NA	California**	NA	NA
21	Colorado	11,048	1.3%
15	Connecticut	14,112	1.7%
33	Delaware	4,804	0.6%
2	Florida	95,586	11.3%
9	Georgia	30,550	3.6%
34	Hawaii	3,990	0.5%
45	Idaho	1,249	0.1%
4	Illinois	46,467	5.5%
23	Indiana	10,614	1.3%
29	Iowa	6,722	0.8%
20	Kansas	11,173	1.3%
35	Kentucky	3,912	0.5%
NA	Louisiana**	NA	NA
39	Maine	2,670	0.3%
25	Maryland	9,530	1.1%
13	Massachusetts	24,246	2.9%
11	Michigan	25,636	3.0%
16	Minnesota	14,065	1.7%
37	Mississippi	2,949	0.3%
26	Missouri	7,556	0.9%
40	Montana	2,119	0.3%
38	Nebraska	2,927	0.3%
19	Nevada	11,471	1.4%
NA	New Hampshire**	NA	NA
8	New Jersey	30,986	3.7%
30	New Mexico	6,087	0.7%
1	New York	127,437	15.1%
6	North Carolina	35,088	4.1%
44	North Dakota	1,298	0.2%
7	Ohio	32,936	3.9%
27	Oklahoma	7,088	0.8%
17	Oregon	11,732	1.4%
5	Pennsylvania	36,731	4.3%
32	Rhode Island	4,828	0.6%
28	South Carolina	7,005	0.8%
46	South Dakota	748	0.1%
14	Tennessee	17,883	2.1%
3	Texas	81,883	9.7%
36	Utah	3,753	0.4%
43	Vermont	1,610	0.2%
10	Virginia	27,349	3.2%
12	Washington	24,627	2.9%
41	West Virginia	2,036	0.2%
24	Wisconsin	9,580	1.1%
47	Wyoming	7	0.0%

RANK ORDER

RANK	STATE	ABORTIONS	% of USA
1	New York	127,437	15.1%
2	Florida	95,586	11.3%
3	Texas	81,883	9.7%
4	Illinois	46,467	5.5%
5	Pennsylvania	36,731	4.3%
6	North Carolina	35,088	4.1%
7	Ohio	32,936	3.9%
8	New Jersey	30,986	3.7%
9	Georgia	30,550	3.6%
10	Virginia	27,349	3.2%
11	Michigan	25,636	3.0%
12	Washington	24,627	2.9%
13	Massachusetts	24,246	2.9%
14	Tennessee	17,883	2.1%
15	Connecticut	14,112	1.7%
16	Minnesota	14,065	1.7%
17	Oregon	11,732	1.4%
18	Alabama	11,654	1.4%
19	Nevada	11,471	1.4%
20	Kansas	11,173	1.3%
21	Colorado	11,048	1.3%
22	Arizona	10,836	1.3%
23	Indiana	10,614	1.3%
24	Wisconsin	9,580	1.1%
25	Maryland	9,530	1.1%
26	Missouri	7,556	0.9%
27	Oklahoma	7,088	0.8%
28	South Carolina	7,005	0.8%
29	Iowa	6,722	0.8%
30	New Mexico	6,087	0.7%
31	Arkansas	4,988	0.6%
32	Rhode Island	4,828	0.6%
33	Delaware	4,804	0.6%
34	Hawaii	3,990	0.5%
35	Kentucky	3,912	0.5%
36	Utah	3,753	0.4%
37	Mississippi	2,949	0.3%
38	Nebraska	2,927	0.3%
39	Maine	2,670	0.3%
40	Montana	2,119	0.3%
41	West Virginia	2,036	0.2%
42	Alaska	1,923	0.2%
43	Vermont	1,610	0.2%
44	North Dakota	1,298	0.2%
45	Idaho	1,249	0.1%
46	South Dakota	748	0.1%
47	Wyoming	7	0.0%
NA	California**	NA	NA
NA	Louisiana**	NA	NA
NA	New Hampshire**	NA	NA
	District of Columbia	2,692	0.3%

Source: U.S. Department of Health and Human Services, Centers for Disease Control and Prevention
   "Abortion Surveillance-United States, 2006" (MMWR, Vol. 58, No. SS-8, 11/27/09, http://www.cdc.gov/mmwr/mmwr_ss.html)
*By state of occurrence. Total is for reporting states only.
**Not reported.

Reported Legal Abortions per 1,000 Live Births in 2006

Reporting States' Ratio = 233 Abortions per 1,000 Live Births*

ALPHA ORDER

RANK	STATE	RATIO
26	Alabama	184
27	Alaska	175
39	Arizona	106
35	Arkansas	122
NA	California**	NA
30	Colorado	156
5	Connecticut	337
3	Delaware	401
2	Florida	404
20	Georgia	206
19	Hawaii	210
46	Idaho	52
12	Illinois	257
36	Indiana	120
29	Iowa	166
10	Kansas	273
43	Kentucky	67
NA	Louisiana**	NA
25	Maine	189
34	Maryland	123
6	Massachusetts	312
23	Michigan	201
24	Minnesota	191
44	Mississippi	64
41	Missouri	93
28	Montana	169
38	Nebraska	110
7	Nevada	287
NA	New Hampshire**	NA
11	New Jersey	269
22	New Mexico	203
1	New York	510
9	North Carolina	274
31	North Dakota	151
17	Ohio	219
33	Oklahoma	131
16	Oregon	241
15	Pennsylvania	246
4	Rhode Island	390
37	South Carolina	113
45	South Dakota	63
18	Tennessee	212
21	Texas	205
42	Utah	70
14	Vermont	247
13	Virginia	254
8	Washington	283
40	West Virginia	97
32	Wisconsin	132
47	Wyoming	1

RANK ORDER

RANK	STATE	RATIO
1	New York	510
2	Florida	404
3	Delaware	401
4	Rhode Island	390
5	Connecticut	337
6	Massachusetts	312
7	Nevada	287
8	Washington	283
9	North Carolina	274
10	Kansas	273
11	New Jersey	269
12	Illinois	257
13	Virginia	254
14	Vermont	247
15	Pennsylvania	246
16	Oregon	241
17	Ohio	219
18	Tennessee	212
19	Hawaii	210
20	Georgia	206
21	Texas	205
22	New Mexico	203
23	Michigan	201
24	Minnesota	191
25	Maine	189
26	Alabama	184
27	Alaska	175
28	Montana	169
29	Iowa	166
30	Colorado	156
31	North Dakota	151
32	Wisconsin	132
33	Oklahoma	131
34	Maryland	123
35	Arkansas	122
36	Indiana	120
37	South Carolina	113
38	Nebraska	110
39	Arizona	106
40	West Virginia	97
41	Missouri	93
42	Utah	70
43	Kentucky	67
44	Mississippi	64
45	South Dakota	63
46	Idaho	52
47	Wyoming	1
NA	California**	NA
NA	Louisiana**	NA
NA	New Hampshire**	NA
	District of Columbia	316

Source: U.S. Department of Health and Human Services, Centers for Disease Control and Prevention
    "Abortion Surveillance-United States, 2006" (MMWR, Vol. 58, No. SS-8, 11/27/09, http://www.cdc.gov/mmwr/mmwr_ss.html)
*By state of occurrence. National figure is for reporting states only.
**Not reported.

Infant Deaths in 2007

National Total = 29,138 Infant Deaths*

ALPHA ORDER					RANK ORDER			
RANK	STATE		DEATHS	% of USA	RANK	STATE	DEATHS	% of USA
15	Alabama		641	2.2%	1	California	2,944	10.1%
47	Alaska		72	0.2%	2	Texas	2,564	8.8%
13	Arizona		711	2.4%	3	Florida	1,685	5.8%
30	Arkansas		317	1.1%	4	New York	1,412	4.8%
1	California		2,944	10.1%	5	Illinois	1,217	4.2%
24	Colorado		433	1.5%	6	Georgia	1,206	4.1%
33	Connecticut		276	0.9%	7	Ohio	1,160	4.0%
41	Delaware		91	0.3%	8	Pennsylvania	1,139	3.9%
3	Florida		1,685	5.8%	9	North Carolina	1,112	3.8%
6	Georgia		1,206	4.1%	10	Michigan	995	3.4%
40	Hawaii		124	0.4%	11	Virginia	848	2.9%
38	Idaho		169	0.6%	12	Tennessee	721	2.5%
5	Illinois		1,217	4.2%	13	Arizona	711	2.4%
14	Indiana		681	2.3%	14	Indiana	681	2.3%
35	Iowa		225	0.8%	15	Alabama	641	2.2%
29	Kansas		333	1.1%	16	Maryland	625	2.1%
27	Kentucky		397	1.4%	17	Missouri	613	2.1%
18	Louisiana		608	2.1%	18	Louisiana	608	2.1%
43	Maine		89	0.3%	19	New Jersey	601	2.1%
16	Maryland		625	2.1%	20	South Carolina	539	1.8%
28	Massachusetts		384	1.3%	21	Wisconsin	470	1.6%
10	Michigan		995	3.4%	22	Oklahoma	469	1.6%
26	Minnesota		409	1.4%	23	Mississippi	467	1.6%
23	Mississippi		467	1.6%	24	Colorado	433	1.5%
17	Missouri		613	2.1%	25	Washington	429	1.5%
44	Montana		79	0.3%	26	Minnesota	409	1.4%
37	Nebraska		182	0.6%	27	Kentucky	397	1.4%
34	Nevada		262	0.9%	28	Massachusetts	384	1.3%
46	New Hampshire		76	0.3%	29	Kansas	333	1.1%
19	New Jersey		601	2.1%	30	Arkansas	317	1.1%
36	New Mexico		192	0.7%	31	Oregon	284	1.0%
4	New York		1,412	4.8%	32	Utah	280	1.0%
9	North Carolina		1,112	3.8%	33	Connecticut	276	0.9%
48	North Dakota		66	0.2%	34	Nevada	262	0.9%
7	Ohio		1,160	4.0%	35	Iowa	225	0.8%
22	Oklahoma		469	1.6%	36	New Mexico	192	0.7%
31	Oregon		284	1.0%	37	Nebraska	182	0.6%
8	Pennsylvania		1,139	3.9%	38	Idaho	169	0.6%
41	Rhode Island		91	0.3%	39	West Virginia	164	0.6%
20	South Carolina		539	1.8%	40	Hawaii	124	0.4%
44	South Dakota		79	0.3%	41	Delaware	91	0.3%
12	Tennessee		721	2.5%	41	Rhode Island	91	0.3%
2	Texas		2,564	8.8%	43	Maine	89	0.3%
32	Utah		280	1.0%	44	Montana	79	0.3%
50	Vermont		33	0.1%	44	South Dakota	79	0.3%
11	Virginia		848	2.9%	46	New Hampshire	76	0.3%
25	Washington		429	1.5%	47	Alaska	72	0.2%
39	West Virginia		164	0.6%	48	North Dakota	66	0.2%
21	Wisconsin		470	1.6%	49	Wyoming	58	0.2%
49	Wyoming		58	0.2%	50	Vermont	33	0.1%
						District of Columbia	116	0.4%

Source: U.S. Department of Health and Human Services, National Center for Health Statistics
    "National Vital Statistics Reports" (Vol. 58, No. 19, May 20, 2010, http://www.cdc.gov/nchs/deaths.htm)
*Final data. Deaths of infants under 1 year old by state of residence.

Infant Mortality Rate in 2007

National Rate = 6.8 Infant Deaths per 1,000 Live Births*

ALPHA ORDER

RANK	STATE	RATE
2	Alabama	9.9
30	Alaska	6.5
24	Arizona	6.9
13	Arkansas	7.7
45	California	5.2
39	Colorado	6.1
29	Connecticut	6.6
17	Delaware	7.5
23	Florida	7.1
8	Georgia	8.0
30	Hawaii	6.5
25	Idaho	6.8
27	Illinois	6.7
15	Indiana	7.6
43	Iowa	5.5
10	Kansas	7.9
27	Kentucky	6.7
3	Louisiana	9.2
36	Maine	6.3
8	Maryland	8.0
49	Massachusetts	4.9
10	Michigan	7.9
41	Minnesota	5.6
1	Mississippi	10.0
17	Missouri	7.5
33	Montana	6.4
25	Nebraska	6.8
33	Nevada	6.4
44	New Hampshire	5.4
45	New Jersey	5.2
36	New Mexico	6.3
41	New York	5.6
5	North Carolina	8.5
17	North Dakota	7.5
13	Ohio	7.7
5	Oklahoma	8.5
40	Oregon	5.8
15	Pennsylvania	7.6
21	Rhode Island	7.4
4	South Carolina	8.6
33	South Dakota	6.4
7	Tennessee	8.3
36	Texas	6.3
47	Utah	5.1
47	Vermont	5.1
12	Virginia	7.8
50	Washington	4.8
17	West Virginia	7.5
30	Wisconsin	6.5
21	Wyoming	7.4

RANK ORDER

RANK	STATE	RATE
1	Mississippi	10.0
2	Alabama	9.9
3	Louisiana	9.2
4	South Carolina	8.6
5	North Carolina	8.5
5	Oklahoma	8.5
7	Tennessee	8.3
8	Georgia	8.0
8	Maryland	8.0
10	Kansas	7.9
10	Michigan	7.9
12	Virginia	7.8
13	Arkansas	7.7
13	Ohio	7.7
15	Indiana	7.6
15	Pennsylvania	7.6
17	Delaware	7.5
17	Missouri	7.5
17	North Dakota	7.5
17	West Virginia	7.5
21	Rhode Island	7.4
21	Wyoming	7.4
23	Florida	7.1
24	Arizona	6.9
25	Idaho	6.8
25	Nebraska	6.8
27	Illinois	6.7
27	Kentucky	6.7
29	Connecticut	6.6
30	Alaska	6.5
30	Hawaii	6.5
30	Wisconsin	6.5
33	Montana	6.4
33	Nevada	6.4
33	South Dakota	6.4
36	Maine	6.3
36	New Mexico	6.3
36	Texas	6.3
39	Colorado	6.1
40	Oregon	5.8
41	Minnesota	5.6
41	New York	5.6
43	Iowa	5.5
44	New Hampshire	5.4
45	California	5.2
45	New Jersey	5.2
47	Utah	5.1
47	Vermont	5.1
49	Massachusetts	4.9
50	Washington	4.8

| | District of Columbia | 13.1 |

Source: U.S. Department of Health and Human Services, National Center for Health Statistics
"National Vital Statistics Reports" (Vol. 58, No. 19, May 20, 2010, http://www.cdc.gov/nchs/deaths.htm)
*Final data. Deaths of infants under 1 year old by state of residence.

Deaths in 2008

National Total = 2,473,018 Deaths*

ALPHA ORDER

RANK	STATE	DEATHS	% of USA
18	Alabama	47,712	1.9%
50	Alaska	3,483	0.1%
20	Arizona	45,610	1.8%
29	Arkansas	29,310	1.2%
1	California	234,229	9.5%
28	Colorado	31,256	1.3%
31	Connecticut	28,797	1.2%
45	Delaware	7,623	0.3%
2	Florida	170,668	6.9%
11	Georgia	69,942	2.8%
43	Hawaii	9,475	0.4%
40	Idaho	10,942	0.4%
7	Illinois	103,615	4.2%
14	Indiana	56,743	2.3%
32	Iowa	28,533	1.2%
33	Kansas	24,969	1.0%
22	Kentucky	41,280	1.7%
23	Louisiana	41,217	1.7%
39	Maine	12,531	0.5%
21	Maryland	43,885	1.8%
16	Massachusetts	53,521	2.2%
8	Michigan	88,418	3.6%
25	Minnesota	38,487	1.6%
30	Mississippi	28,980	1.2%
15	Missouri	56,566	2.3%
44	Montana	8,903	0.4%
37	Nebraska	15,455	0.6%
35	Nevada	20,790	0.8%
41	New Hampshire	10,268	0.4%
10	New Jersey	69,993	2.8%
36	New Mexico	15,996	0.6%
4	New York	148,660	6.0%
9	North Carolina	77,277	3.1%
47	North Dakota	5,870	0.2%
6	Ohio	109,749	4.4%
26	Oklahoma	37,061	1.5%
27	Oregon	31,939	1.3%
5	Pennsylvania	127,450	5.2%
42	Rhode Island	9,740	0.4%
24	South Carolina	40,305	1.6%
46	South Dakota	7,080	0.3%
13	Tennessee	58,882	2.4%
3	Texas	165,197	6.7%
38	Utah	13,991	0.6%
48	Vermont	5,213	0.2%
12	Virginia	59,093	2.4%
17	Washington	48,603	2.0%
34	West Virginia	21,549	0.9%
19	Wisconsin	46,799	1.9%
49	Wyoming	4,222	0.2%

RANK ORDER

RANK	STATE	DEATHS	% of USA
1	California	234,229	9.5%
2	Florida	170,668	6.9%
3	Texas	165,197	6.7%
4	New York	148,660	6.0%
5	Pennsylvania	127,450	5.2%
6	Ohio	109,749	4.4%
7	Illinois	103,615	4.2%
8	Michigan	88,418	3.6%
9	North Carolina	77,277	3.1%
10	New Jersey	69,993	2.8%
11	Georgia	69,942	2.8%
12	Virginia	59,093	2.4%
13	Tennessee	58,882	2.4%
14	Indiana	56,743	2.3%
15	Missouri	56,566	2.3%
16	Massachusetts	53,521	2.2%
17	Washington	48,603	2.0%
18	Alabama	47,712	1.9%
19	Wisconsin	46,799	1.9%
20	Arizona	45,610	1.8%
21	Maryland	43,885	1.8%
22	Kentucky	41,280	1.7%
23	Louisiana	41,217	1.7%
24	South Carolina	40,305	1.6%
25	Minnesota	38,487	1.6%
26	Oklahoma	37,061	1.5%
27	Oregon	31,939	1.3%
28	Colorado	31,256	1.3%
29	Arkansas	29,310	1.2%
30	Mississippi	28,980	1.2%
31	Connecticut	28,797	1.2%
32	Iowa	28,533	1.2%
33	Kansas	24,969	1.0%
34	West Virginia	21,549	0.9%
35	Nevada	20,790	0.8%
36	New Mexico	15,996	0.6%
37	Nebraska	15,455	0.6%
38	Utah	13,991	0.6%
39	Maine	12,531	0.5%
40	Idaho	10,942	0.4%
41	New Hampshire	10,268	0.4%
42	Rhode Island	9,740	0.4%
43	Hawaii	9,475	0.4%
44	Montana	8,903	0.4%
45	Delaware	7,623	0.3%
46	South Dakota	7,080	0.3%
47	North Dakota	5,870	0.2%
48	Vermont	5,213	0.2%
49	Wyoming	4,222	0.2%
50	Alaska	3,483	0.1%
	District of Columbia	5,139	0.2%

Source: U.S. Department of Health and Human Services, National Center for Health Statistics
"National Vital Statistics Reports" (Vol. 59, No. 2, December 9, 2010, http://www.cdc.gov/nchs/deaths.htm)
*Preliminary data by state of residence.

Age-Adjusted Death Rate in 2008

National Rate = 758.7 Deaths per 100,000 Population*

ALPHA ORDER

RANK	STATE	RATE
4	Alabama	930.3
32	Alaska	739.6
49	Arizona	650.6
7	Arkansas	899.2
47	California	658.8
40	Colorado	708.6
43	Connecticut	691.4
20	Delaware	780.8
44	Florida	679.0
13	Georgia	835.4
50	Hawaii	589.0
36	Idaho	721.7
23	Illinois	772.0
14	Indiana	835.1
30	Iowa	744.0
19	Kansas	784.7
6	Kentucky	901.2
5	Louisiana	922.0
25	Maine	764.1
24	Maryland	771.6
42	Massachusetts	705.9
16	Michigan	811.7
46	Minnesota	675.2
2	Mississippi	950.0
10	Missouri	847.0
18	Montana	785.9
31	Nebraska	741.1
9	Nevada	868.2
39	New Hampshire	712.5
37	New Jersey	716.8
27	New Mexico	758.2
45	New York	675.8
15	North Carolina	825.6
38	North Dakota	713.0
11	Ohio	844.0
3	Oklahoma	932.2
29	Oregon	747.9
17	Pennsylvania	796.5
28	Rhode Island	749.6
12	South Carolina	839.7
41	South Dakota	708.4
8	Tennessee	889.7
21	Texas	777.3
48	Utah	656.9
35	Vermont	722.2
26	Virginia	762.6
34	Washington	723.3
1	West Virginia	958.1
33	Wisconsin	729.7
22	Wyoming	772.5

RANK ORDER

RANK	STATE	RATE
1	West Virginia	958.1
2	Mississippi	950.0
3	Oklahoma	932.2
4	Alabama	930.3
5	Louisiana	922.0
6	Kentucky	901.2
7	Arkansas	899.2
8	Tennessee	889.7
9	Nevada	868.2
10	Missouri	847.0
11	Ohio	844.0
12	South Carolina	839.7
13	Georgia	835.4
14	Indiana	835.1
15	North Carolina	825.6
16	Michigan	811.7
17	Pennsylvania	796.5
18	Montana	785.9
19	Kansas	784.7
20	Delaware	780.8
21	Texas	777.3
22	Wyoming	772.5
23	Illinois	772.0
24	Maryland	771.6
25	Maine	764.1
26	Virginia	762.6
27	New Mexico	758.2
28	Rhode Island	749.6
29	Oregon	747.9
30	Iowa	744.0
31	Nebraska	741.1
32	Alaska	739.6
33	Wisconsin	729.7
34	Washington	723.3
35	Vermont	722.2
36	Idaho	721.7
37	New Jersey	716.8
38	North Dakota	713.0
39	New Hampshire	712.5
40	Colorado	708.6
41	South Dakota	708.4
42	Massachusetts	705.9
43	Connecticut	691.4
44	Florida	679.0
45	New York	675.8
46	Minnesota	675.2
47	California	658.8
48	Utah	656.9
49	Arizona	650.6
50	Hawaii	589.0
	District of Columbia	849.9

Source: U.S. Department of Health and Human Services, National Center for Health Statistics
"National Vital Statistics Reports" (Vol. 59, No. 2, December 9, 2010, http://www.cdc.gov/nchs/deaths.htm)
*Preliminary data by state of residence. Age-adjusted rates eliminate the distorting effects of the aging of the population. Rates based on the year 2000 standard population.

Estimated Deaths by Cancer in 2010

National Estimated Total = 569,490 Deaths

ALPHA ORDER

RANK	STATE	DEATHS	% of USA
21	Alabama	10,150	1.8%
50	Alaska	880	0.2%
19	Arizona	10,630	1.9%
30	Arkansas	6,460	1.1%
1	California	55,710	9.8%
28	Colorado	6,880	1.2%
29	Connecticut	6,850	1.2%
45	Delaware	1,900	0.3%
2	Florida	40,880	7.2%
11	Georgia	15,570	2.7%
42	Hawaii	2,330	0.4%
41	Idaho	2,530	0.4%
7	Illinois	23,360	4.1%
15	Indiana	12,900	2.3%
31	Iowa	6,370	1.1%
33	Kansas	5,370	0.9%
22	Kentucky	9,670	1.7%
25	Louisiana	8,480	1.5%
38	Maine	3,170	0.6%
20	Maryland	10,250	1.8%
14	Massachusetts	12,990	2.3%
8	Michigan	20,740	3.6%
23	Minnesota	9,200	1.6%
32	Mississippi	6,060	1.1%
16	Missouri	12,620	2.2%
44	Montana	1,980	0.3%
36	Nebraska	3,500	0.6%
35	Nevada	4,640	0.8%
40	New Hampshire	2,660	0.5%
10	New Jersey	16,520	2.9%
37	New Mexico	3,400	0.6%
4	New York	34,540	6.1%
9	North Carolina	19,100	3.4%
47	North Dakota	1,280	0.2%
6	Ohio	24,980	4.4%
26	Oklahoma	7,660	1.3%
27	Oregon	7,510	1.3%
5	Pennsylvania	28,690	5.0%
43	Rhode Island	2,170	0.4%
24	South Carolina	9,180	1.6%
46	South Dakota	1,670	0.3%
13	Tennessee	13,600	2.4%
3	Texas	36,540	6.4%
39	Utah	2,820	0.5%
47	Vermont	1,280	0.2%
12	Virginia	14,230	2.5%
17	Washington	11,640	2.0%
34	West Virginia	4,670	0.8%
18	Wisconsin	11,310	2.0%
49	Wyoming	1,000	0.2%

RANK ORDER

RANK	STATE	DEATHS	% of USA
1	California	55,710	9.8%
2	Florida	40,880	7.2%
3	Texas	36,540	6.4%
4	New York	34,540	6.1%
5	Pennsylvania	28,690	5.0%
6	Ohio	24,980	4.4%
7	Illinois	23,360	4.1%
8	Michigan	20,740	3.6%
9	North Carolina	19,100	3.4%
10	New Jersey	16,520	2.9%
11	Georgia	15,570	2.7%
12	Virginia	14,230	2.5%
13	Tennessee	13,600	2.4%
14	Massachusetts	12,990	2.3%
15	Indiana	12,900	2.3%
16	Missouri	12,620	2.2%
17	Washington	11,640	2.0%
18	Wisconsin	11,310	2.0%
19	Arizona	10,630	1.9%
20	Maryland	10,250	1.8%
21	Alabama	10,150	1.8%
22	Kentucky	9,670	1.7%
23	Minnesota	9,200	1.6%
24	South Carolina	9,180	1.6%
25	Louisiana	8,480	1.5%
26	Oklahoma	7,660	1.3%
27	Oregon	7,510	1.3%
28	Colorado	6,880	1.2%
29	Connecticut	6,850	1.2%
30	Arkansas	6,460	1.1%
31	Iowa	6,370	1.1%
32	Mississippi	6,060	1.1%
33	Kansas	5,370	0.9%
34	West Virginia	4,670	0.8%
35	Nevada	4,640	0.8%
36	Nebraska	3,500	0.6%
37	New Mexico	3,400	0.6%
38	Maine	3,170	0.6%
39	Utah	2,820	0.5%
40	New Hampshire	2,660	0.5%
41	Idaho	2,530	0.4%
42	Hawaii	2,330	0.4%
43	Rhode Island	2,170	0.4%
44	Montana	1,980	0.3%
45	Delaware	1,900	0.3%
46	South Dakota	1,670	0.3%
47	North Dakota	1,280	0.2%
47	Vermont	1,280	0.2%
49	Wyoming	1,000	0.2%
50	Alaska	880	0.2%
	District of Columbia	960	0.2%

Source: American Cancer Society

"Cancer Facts & Figures 2010" (Copyright 2010, American Cancer Society, http://www.cancer.org/docroot/stt/stt_0.asp)

Estimated Death Rate by Cancer in 2010

National Estimated Rate = 185.5 Deaths per 100,000 Population*

ALPHA ORDER

RANK	STATE	RATE
9	Alabama	215.6
49	Alaska	126.0
44	Arizona	161.2
5	Arkansas	223.6
46	California	150.7
48	Colorado	136.9
29	Connecticut	194.7
10	Delaware	214.7
6	Florida	220.5
45	Georgia	158.4
36	Hawaii	179.9
43	Idaho	163.7
34	Illinois	180.9
22	Indiana	200.8
11	Iowa	211.8
30	Kansas	190.5
4	Kentucky	224.1
32	Louisiana	188.8
2	Maine	240.5
37	Maryland	179.8
26	Massachusetts	197.0
13	Michigan	208.0
40	Minnesota	174.7
18	Mississippi	205.3
12	Missouri	210.8
20	Montana	203.1
28	Nebraska	194.8
39	Nevada	175.6
22	New Hampshire	200.8
31	New Jersey	189.7
42	New Mexico	169.2
38	New York	176.8
19	North Carolina	203.6
25	North Dakota	197.9
7	Ohio	216.4
14	Oklahoma	207.8
27	Oregon	196.3
3	Pennsylvania	227.6
15	Rhode Island	206.0
21	South Carolina	201.3
17	South Dakota	205.6
8	Tennessee	216.0
47	Texas	147.4
50	Utah	101.3
16	Vermont	205.9
35	Virginia	180.5
40	Washington	174.7
1	West Virginia	256.6
24	Wisconsin	200.0
33	Wyoming	183.7

RANK ORDER

RANK	STATE	RATE
1	West Virginia	256.6
2	Maine	240.5
3	Pennsylvania	227.6
4	Kentucky	224.1
5	Arkansas	223.6
6	Florida	220.5
7	Ohio	216.4
8	Tennessee	216.0
9	Alabama	215.6
10	Delaware	214.7
11	Iowa	211.8
12	Missouri	210.8
13	Michigan	208.0
14	Oklahoma	207.8
15	Rhode Island	206.0
16	Vermont	205.9
17	South Dakota	205.6
18	Mississippi	205.3
19	North Carolina	203.6
20	Montana	203.1
21	South Carolina	201.3
22	Indiana	200.8
22	New Hampshire	200.8
24	Wisconsin	200.0
25	North Dakota	197.9
26	Massachusetts	197.0
27	Oregon	196.3
28	Nebraska	194.8
29	Connecticut	194.7
30	Kansas	190.5
31	New Jersey	189.7
32	Louisiana	188.8
33	Wyoming	183.7
34	Illinois	180.9
35	Virginia	180.5
36	Hawaii	179.9
37	Maryland	179.8
38	New York	176.8
39	Nevada	175.6
40	Minnesota	174.7
40	Washington	174.7
42	New Mexico	169.2
43	Idaho	163.7
44	Arizona	161.2
45	Georgia	158.4
46	California	150.7
47	Texas	147.4
48	Colorado	136.9
49	Alaska	126.0
50	Utah	101.3

District of Columbia	160.1

Source: CQ Press using data from American Cancer Society
"Cancer Facts & Figures 2010" (Copyright 2010, American Cancer Society, http://www.cancer.org/docroot/stt/stt_0.asp)
*Rates calculated using 2009 Census resident population estimates. Not age-adjusted.

Estimated New Cancer Cases in 2010

National Estimated Total = 1,529,560 New Cases*

ALPHA ORDER

RANK ORDER

RANK	STATE	CASES	% of USA
23	Alabama	23,640	1.5%
49	Alaska	2,860	0.2%
18	Arizona	29,780	1.9%
31	Arkansas	15,320	1.0%
1	California	157,320	10.3%
25	Colorado	21,340	1.4%
27	Connecticut	20,750	1.4%
45	Delaware	4,890	0.3%
2	Florida	107,000	7.0%
11	Georgia	40,480	2.6%
42	Hawaii	6,670	0.4%
41	Idaho	7,220	0.5%
7	Illinois	63,890	4.2%
16	Indiana	33,020	2.2%
30	Iowa	17,260	1.1%
33	Kansas	13,550	0.9%
22	Kentucky	24,240	1.6%
26	Louisiana	20,950	1.4%
39	Maine	8,650	0.6%
20	Maryland	27,700	1.8%
13	Massachusetts	36,040	2.4%
8	Michigan	55,660	3.6%
21	Minnesota	25,080	1.6%
32	Mississippi	14,330	0.9%
17	Missouri	31,160	2.0%
44	Montana	5,570	0.4%
37	Nebraska	9,230	0.6%
34	Nevada	12,230	0.8%
40	New Hampshire	7,810	0.5%
9	New Jersey	48,100	3.1%
38	New Mexico	9,210	0.6%
3	New York	103,340	6.8%
10	North Carolina	45,120	2.9%
48	North Dakota	3,300	0.2%
6	Ohio	64,450	4.2%
29	Oklahoma	18,670	1.2%
27	Oregon	20,750	1.4%
5	Pennsylvania	75,260	4.9%
43	Rhode Island	5,970	0.4%
24	South Carolina	23,240	1.5%
46	South Dakota	4,220	0.3%
15	Tennessee	33,070	2.2%
4	Texas	101,120	6.6%
36	Utah	9,970	0.7%
47	Vermont	3,720	0.2%
12	Virginia	36,410	2.4%
14	Washington	34,500	2.3%
35	West Virginia	10,610	0.7%
19	Wisconsin	29,610	1.9%
50	Wyoming	2,540	0.2%

RANK	STATE	CASES	% of USA
1	California	157,320	10.3%
2	Florida	107,000	7.0%
3	New York	103,340	6.8%
4	Texas	101,120	6.6%
5	Pennsylvania	75,260	4.9%
6	Ohio	64,450	4.2%
7	Illinois	63,890	4.2%
8	Michigan	55,660	3.6%
9	New Jersey	48,100	3.1%
10	North Carolina	45,120	2.9%
11	Georgia	40,480	2.6%
12	Virginia	36,410	2.4%
13	Massachusetts	36,040	2.4%
14	Washington	34,500	2.3%
15	Tennessee	33,070	2.2%
16	Indiana	33,020	2.2%
17	Missouri	31,160	2.0%
18	Arizona	29,780	1.9%
19	Wisconsin	29,610	1.9%
20	Maryland	27,700	1.8%
21	Minnesota	25,080	1.6%
22	Kentucky	24,240	1.6%
23	Alabama	23,640	1.5%
24	South Carolina	23,240	1.5%
25	Colorado	21,340	1.4%
26	Louisiana	20,950	1.4%
27	Connecticut	20,750	1.4%
27	Oregon	20,750	1.4%
29	Oklahoma	18,670	1.2%
30	Iowa	17,260	1.1%
31	Arkansas	15,320	1.0%
32	Mississippi	14,330	0.9%
33	Kansas	13,550	0.9%
34	Nevada	12,230	0.8%
35	West Virginia	10,610	0.7%
36	Utah	9,970	0.7%
37	Nebraska	9,230	0.6%
38	New Mexico	9,210	0.6%
39	Maine	8,650	0.6%
40	New Hampshire	7,810	0.5%
41	Idaho	7,220	0.5%
42	Hawaii	6,670	0.4%
43	Rhode Island	5,970	0.4%
44	Montana	5,570	0.4%
45	Delaware	4,890	0.3%
46	South Dakota	4,220	0.3%
47	Vermont	3,720	0.2%
48	North Dakota	3,300	0.2%
49	Alaska	2,860	0.2%
50	Wyoming	2,540	0.2%
	District of Columbia	2,760	0.2%

Source: American Cancer Society

"Cancer Facts & Figures 2010" (Copyright 2010, American Cancer Society, http://www.cancer.org/docroot/stt/stt_0.asp)
*These estimates are offered as a rough guide and should not be regarded as definitive. They are calculated by the American Cancer Society using a model based on 1995-2006 incidence rates. Totals do not include basal and squamous cell skin cancers or in situ carcinomas except urinary bladder.

Estimated Rate of New Cancer Cases in 2010

National Estimated Rate = 498.2 New Cases per 100,000 Population*

ALPHA ORDER			RANK ORDER		
RANK	STATE	RATE	RANK	STATE	RATE
31	Alabama	502.0	1	Maine	656.1
48	Alaska	409.5	2	Vermont	598.3
44	Arizona	451.5	3	Pennsylvania	597.1
18	Arkansas	530.2	4	Connecticut	589.8
45	California	425.6	5	New Hampshire	589.6
46	Colorado	424.7	6	West Virginia	583.0
4	Connecticut	589.8	7	Florida	577.2
14	Delaware	552.5	8	Iowa	573.8
7	Florida	577.2	9	Montana	571.3
47	Georgia	411.8	10	Rhode Island	566.8
25	Hawaii	515.0	11	Kentucky	561.9
38	Idaho	467.1	12	Ohio	558.4
32	Illinois	494.9	13	Michigan	558.3
26	Indiana	514.1	14	Delaware	552.5
8	Iowa	573.8	15	New Jersey	552.4
36	Kansas	480.7	16	Massachusetts	546.6
11	Kentucky	561.9	17	Oregon	542.4
40	Louisiana	466.4	18	Arkansas	530.2
1	Maine	656.1	19	New York	528.8
33	Maryland	486.0	20	Tennessee	525.2
16	Massachusetts	546.6	21	Wisconsin	523.6
13	Michigan	558.3	22	Missouri	520.4
37	Minnesota	476.2	23	South Dakota	519.5
34	Mississippi	485.4	24	Washington	517.7
22	Missouri	520.4	25	Hawaii	515.0
9	Montana	571.3	26	Indiana	514.1
27	Nebraska	513.7	27	Nebraska	513.7
41	Nevada	462.7	28	North Dakota	510.2
5	New Hampshire	589.6	29	South Carolina	509.5
15	New Jersey	552.4	30	Oklahoma	506.4
43	New Mexico	458.3	31	Alabama	502.0
19	New York	528.8	32	Illinois	494.9
35	North Carolina	481.0	33	Maryland	486.0
28	North Dakota	510.2	34	Mississippi	485.4
12	Ohio	558.4	35	North Carolina	481.0
30	Oklahoma	506.4	36	Kansas	480.7
17	Oregon	542.4	37	Minnesota	476.2
3	Pennsylvania	597.1	38	Idaho	467.1
10	Rhode Island	566.8	39	Wyoming	466.7
29	South Carolina	509.5	40	Louisiana	466.4
23	South Dakota	519.5	41	Nevada	462.7
20	Tennessee	525.2	42	Virginia	461.9
49	Texas	408.0	43	New Mexico	458.3
50	Utah	358.0	44	Arizona	451.5
2	Vermont	598.3	45	California	425.6
42	Virginia	461.9	46	Colorado	424.7
24	Washington	517.7	47	Georgia	411.8
6	West Virginia	583.0	48	Alaska	409.5
21	Wisconsin	523.6	49	Texas	408.0
39	Wyoming	466.7	50	Utah	358.0
				District of Columbia	460.3

Source: CQ Press using data from American Cancer Society
   "Cancer Facts & Figures 2009" (Copyright 2009, American Cancer Society, http://www.cancer.org/docroot/stt/stt_0.asp)
*These estimates are offered as a rough guide and should not be regarded as definitive. They are calculated by the American Cancer Society using a model based on 1995-2006 incidence rates. Totals do not include basal and squamous cell skin cancers or in situ carcinomas except urinary bladder. Rates calculated using 2009 Census resident population estimates.

Deaths by Accidents in 2007

National Total = 123,706 Deaths*

ALPHA ORDER

RANK	STATE	DEATHS	% of USA
17	Alabama	2,542	2.1%
46	Alaska	354	0.3%
12	Arizona	3,161	2.6%
30	Arkansas	1,391	1.1%
1	California	11,614	9.4%
26	Colorado	2,056	1.7%
31	Connecticut	1,343	1.1%
47	Delaware	309	0.2%
3	Florida	9,113	7.4%
9	Georgia	4,012	3.2%
43	Hawaii	470	0.4%
39	Idaho	641	0.5%
8	Illinois	4,367	3.5%
18	Indiana	2,499	2.0%
33	Iowa	1,252	1.0%
36	Kansas	1,205	1.0%
21	Kentucky	2,372	1.9%
19	Louisiana	2,466	2.0%
41	Maine	584	0.5%
29	Maryland	1,480	1.2%
24	Massachusetts	2,139	1.7%
10	Michigan	3,764	3.0%
25	Minnesota	2,066	1.7%
27	Mississippi	1,808	1.5%
13	Missouri	2,975	2.4%
40	Montana	614	0.5%
38	Nebraska	674	0.5%
35	Nevada	1,212	1.0%
42	New Hampshire	527	0.4%
20	New Jersey	2,425	2.0%
32	New Mexico	1,329	1.1%
5	New York	5,160	4.2%
7	North Carolina	4,389	3.5%
50	North Dakota	279	0.2%
6	Ohio	4,922	4.0%
23	Oklahoma	2,149	1.7%
28	Oregon	1,646	1.3%
4	Pennsylvania	5,568	4.5%
44	Rhode Island	416	0.3%
22	South Carolina	2,364	1.9%
45	South Dakota	366	0.3%
11	Tennessee	3,257	2.6%
2	Texas	9,392	7.6%
37	Utah	811	0.7%
48	Vermont	303	0.2%
14	Virginia	2,931	2.4%
15	Washington	2,637	2.1%
34	West Virginia	1,241	1.0%
16	Wisconsin	2,619	2.1%
49	Wyoming	299	0.2%

RANK ORDER

RANK	STATE	DEATHS	% of USA
1	California	11,614	9.4%
2	Texas	9,392	7.6%
3	Florida	9,113	7.4%
4	Pennsylvania	5,568	4.5%
5	New York	5,160	4.2%
6	Ohio	4,922	4.0%
7	North Carolina	4,389	3.5%
8	Illinois	4,367	3.5%
9	Georgia	4,012	3.2%
10	Michigan	3,764	3.0%
11	Tennessee	3,257	2.6%
12	Arizona	3,161	2.6%
13	Missouri	2,975	2.4%
14	Virginia	2,931	2.4%
15	Washington	2,637	2.1%
16	Wisconsin	2,619	2.1%
17	Alabama	2,542	2.1%
18	Indiana	2,499	2.0%
19	Louisiana	2,466	2.0%
20	New Jersey	2,425	2.0%
21	Kentucky	2,372	1.9%
22	South Carolina	2,364	1.9%
23	Oklahoma	2,149	1.7%
24	Massachusetts	2,139	1.7%
25	Minnesota	2,066	1.7%
26	Colorado	2,056	1.7%
27	Mississippi	1,808	1.5%
28	Oregon	1,646	1.3%
29	Maryland	1,480	1.2%
30	Arkansas	1,391	1.1%
31	Connecticut	1,343	1.1%
32	New Mexico	1,329	1.1%
33	Iowa	1,252	1.0%
34	West Virginia	1,241	1.0%
35	Nevada	1,212	1.0%
36	Kansas	1,205	1.0%
37	Utah	811	0.7%
38	Nebraska	674	0.5%
39	Idaho	641	0.5%
40	Montana	614	0.5%
41	Maine	584	0.5%
42	New Hampshire	527	0.4%
43	Hawaii	470	0.4%
44	Rhode Island	416	0.3%
45	South Dakota	366	0.3%
46	Alaska	354	0.3%
47	Delaware	309	0.2%
48	Vermont	303	0.2%
49	Wyoming	299	0.2%
50	North Dakota	279	0.2%
	District of Columbia	193	0.2%

Source: U.S. Department of Health and Human Services, National Center for Health Statistics
"National Vital Statistics Reports" (Vol. 58, No. 19, May 20, 2010, http://www.cdc.gov/nchs/deaths.htm)
*Final data by state of residence. Includes motor vehicle deaths, poisoning, falls, drowning, and other accidents.

Age-Adjusted Death Rate by Accidents in 2007

National Rate = 40.0 Deaths per 100,000 Population*

ALPHA ORDER

RANK	STATE	RATE
10	Alabama	53.9
8	Alaska	55.3
13	Arizona	49.4
17	Arkansas	47.6
46	California	31.9
20	Colorado	44.2
39	Connecticut	35.8
41	Delaware	34.8
18	Florida	46.5
20	Georgia	44.2
45	Hawaii	33.3
23	Idaho	43.1
44	Illinois	33.4
33	Indiana	38.7
37	Iowa	37.3
28	Kansas	41.2
9	Kentucky	55.1
6	Louisiana	57.6
25	Maine	41.5
49	Maryland	26.2
47	Massachusetts	30.8
38	Michigan	36.1
36	Minnesota	37.4
3	Mississippi	61.9
14	Missouri	48.4
4	Montana	60.2
40	Nebraska	35.7
14	Nevada	48.4
34	New Hampshire	38.5
48	New Jersey	26.8
1	New Mexico	66.7
50	New York	25.3
16	North Carolina	48.3
32	North Dakota	39.3
29	Ohio	41.1
5	Oklahoma	58.4
25	Oregon	41.5
30	Pennsylvania	40.9
42	Rhode Island	34.6
11	South Carolina	53.0
24	South Dakota	41.8
12	Tennessee	52.1
27	Texas	41.4
43	Utah	34.4
19	Vermont	44.7
35	Virginia	38.1
31	Washington	39.8
2	West Virginia	65.9
22	Wisconsin	43.8
7	Wyoming	57.0

RANK ORDER

RANK	STATE	RATE
1	New Mexico	66.7
2	West Virginia	65.9
3	Mississippi	61.9
4	Montana	60.2
5	Oklahoma	58.4
6	Louisiana	57.6
7	Wyoming	57.0
8	Alaska	55.3
9	Kentucky	55.1
10	Alabama	53.9
11	South Carolina	53.0
12	Tennessee	52.1
13	Arizona	49.4
14	Missouri	48.4
14	Nevada	48.4
16	North Carolina	48.3
17	Arkansas	47.6
18	Florida	46.5
19	Vermont	44.7
20	Colorado	44.2
20	Georgia	44.2
22	Wisconsin	43.8
23	Idaho	43.1
24	South Dakota	41.8
25	Maine	41.5
25	Oregon	41.5
27	Texas	41.4
28	Kansas	41.2
29	Ohio	41.1
30	Pennsylvania	40.9
31	Washington	39.8
32	North Dakota	39.3
33	Indiana	38.7
34	New Hampshire	38.5
35	Virginia	38.1
36	Minnesota	37.4
37	Iowa	37.3
38	Michigan	36.1
39	Connecticut	35.8
40	Nebraska	35.7
41	Delaware	34.8
42	Rhode Island	34.6
43	Utah	34.4
44	Illinois	33.4
45	Hawaii	33.3
46	California	31.9
47	Massachusetts	30.8
48	New Jersey	26.8
49	Maryland	26.2
50	New York	25.3

District of Columbia	32.4

Source: U.S. Department of Health and Human Services, National Center for Health Statistics
"National Vital Statistics Reports" (Vol. 58, No. 19, May 20, 2010, http://www.cdc.gov/nchs/deaths.htm)
*Final data by state of residence. Includes motor vehicle deaths, poisoning, falls, drowning, and other accidents. Age-adjusted rates based on the year 2000 standard population.

Deaths by Cerebrovascular Diseases in 2007

National Total = 135,952 Deaths*

ALPHA ORDER

RANK	STATE	DEATHS	% of USA
17	Alabama	2,747	2.0%
50	Alaska	157	0.1%
22	Arizona	2,207	1.6%
27	Arkansas	1,873	1.4%
1	California	14,557	10.7%
30	Colorado	1,600	1.2%
33	Connecticut	1,463	1.1%
46	Delaware	374	0.3%
3	Florida	8,781	6.5%
10	Georgia	3,894	2.9%
40	Hawaii	643	0.5%
41	Idaho	640	0.5%
7	Illinois	5,864	4.3%
15	Indiana	3,083	2.3%
29	Iowa	1,686	1.2%
32	Kansas	1,498	1.1%
25	Kentucky	2,144	1.6%
24	Louisiana	2,147	1.6%
39	Maine	664	0.5%
21	Maryland	2,364	1.7%
16	Massachusetts	2,832	2.1%
8	Michigan	4,798	3.5%
23	Minnesota	2,193	1.6%
31	Mississippi	1,589	1.2%
14	Missouri	3,229	2.4%
44	Montana	443	0.3%
35	Nebraska	921	0.7%
36	Nevada	850	0.6%
42	New Hampshire	489	0.4%
11	New Jersey	3,492	2.6%
37	New Mexico	804	0.6%
5	New York	6,160	4.5%
9	North Carolina	4,530	3.3%
47	North Dakota	330	0.2%
6	Ohio	5,905	4.3%
26	Oklahoma	2,126	1.6%
28	Oregon	1,835	1.3%
4	Pennsylvania	7,152	5.3%
43	Rhode Island	457	0.3%
20	South Carolina	2,466	1.8%
45	South Dakota	410	0.3%
12	Tennessee	3,450	2.5%
2	Texas	9,796	7.2%
38	Utah	755	0.6%
48	Vermont	269	0.2%
13	Virginia	3,313	2.4%
19	Washington	2,692	2.0%
34	West Virginia	1,113	0.8%
18	Wisconsin	2,738	2.0%
49	Wyoming	209	0.2%

RANK ORDER

RANK	STATE	DEATHS	% of USA
1	California	14,557	10.7%
2	Texas	9,796	7.2%
3	Florida	8,781	6.5%
4	Pennsylvania	7,152	5.3%
5	New York	6,160	4.5%
6	Ohio	5,905	4.3%
7	Illinois	5,864	4.3%
8	Michigan	4,798	3.5%
9	North Carolina	4,530	3.3%
10	Georgia	3,894	2.9%
11	New Jersey	3,492	2.6%
12	Tennessee	3,450	2.5%
13	Virginia	3,313	2.4%
14	Missouri	3,229	2.4%
15	Indiana	3,083	2.3%
16	Massachusetts	2,832	2.1%
17	Alabama	2,747	2.0%
18	Wisconsin	2,738	2.0%
19	Washington	2,692	2.0%
20	South Carolina	2,466	1.8%
21	Maryland	2,364	1.7%
22	Arizona	2,207	1.6%
23	Minnesota	2,193	1.6%
24	Louisiana	2,147	1.6%
25	Kentucky	2,144	1.6%
26	Oklahoma	2,126	1.6%
27	Arkansas	1,873	1.4%
28	Oregon	1,835	1.3%
29	Iowa	1,686	1.2%
30	Colorado	1,600	1.2%
31	Mississippi	1,589	1.2%
32	Kansas	1,498	1.1%
33	Connecticut	1,463	1.1%
34	West Virginia	1,113	0.8%
35	Nebraska	921	0.7%
36	Nevada	850	0.6%
37	New Mexico	804	0.6%
38	Utah	755	0.6%
39	Maine	664	0.5%
40	Hawaii	643	0.5%
41	Idaho	640	0.5%
42	New Hampshire	489	0.4%
43	Rhode Island	457	0.3%
44	Montana	443	0.3%
45	South Dakota	410	0.3%
46	Delaware	374	0.3%
47	North Dakota	330	0.2%
48	Vermont	269	0.2%
49	Wyoming	209	0.2%
50	Alaska	157	0.1%
	District of Columbia	220	0.2%

Source: U.S. Department of Health and Human Services, National Center for Health Statistics
    "National Vital Statistics Reports" (Vol. 58, No. 19, May 20, 2010, http://www.cdc.gov/nchs/deaths.htm)
*Final data by state of residence. Cerebrovascular diseases include stroke and other disorders of the blood vessels of the brain.

Age-Adjusted Death Rate by Cerebrovascular Diseases in 2007

National Rate = 42.2 Deaths per 100,000 Population*

ALPHA ORDER

RANK ORDER

RANK	STATE	RATE		RANK	STATE	RATE
2	Alabama	54.5		1	Arkansas	57.4
18	Alaska	44.3		2	Alabama	54.5
49	Arizona	32.7		3	Tennessee	53.9
1	Arkansas	57.4		4	Oklahoma	53.8
27	California	42.2		5	South Carolina	53.4
35	Colorado	39.0		6	Mississippi	53.0
46	Connecticut	34.2		7	North Carolina	50.3
33	Delaware	39.4		8	Louisiana	50.1
47	Florida	33.6		9	Georgia	49.7
9	Georgia	49.7		10	Texas	49.0
31	Hawaii	39.6		11	West Virginia	48.9
22	Idaho	43.2		12	Missouri	48.2
20	Illinois	43.9		13	Kentucky	48.1
15	Indiana	45.7		14	Kansas	46.0
28	Iowa	42.1		15	Indiana	45.7
14	Kansas	46.0		16	Ohio	45.3
13	Kentucky	48.1		17	Virginia	44.5
8	Louisiana	50.1		18	Alaska	44.3
30	Maine	40.3		18	Michigan	44.3
25	Maryland	42.7		20	Illinois	43.9
43	Massachusetts	36.5		21	Oregon	43.6
18	Michigan	44.3		22	Idaho	43.2
40	Minnesota	38.1		23	Nebraska	43.1
6	Mississippi	53.0		24	Pennsylvania	42.9
12	Missouri	48.2		25	Maryland	42.7
38	Montana	38.5		26	Wisconsin	42.3
23	Nebraska	43.1		27	California	42.2
39	Nevada	38.3		28	Iowa	42.1
45	New Hampshire	34.3		29	Washington	41.4
44	New Jersey	35.8		30	Maine	40.3
34	New Mexico	39.2		31	Hawaii	39.6
50	New York	28.2		32	Wyoming	39.5
7	North Carolina	50.3		33	Delaware	39.4
42	North Dakota	37.3		34	New Mexico	39.2
16	Ohio	45.3		35	Colorado	39.0
4	Oklahoma	53.8		36	Utah	38.9
21	Oregon	43.6		37	South Dakota	38.7
24	Pennsylvania	42.9		38	Montana	38.5
48	Rhode Island	33.5		39	Nevada	38.3
5	South Carolina	53.4		40	Minnesota	38.1
37	South Dakota	38.7		41	Vermont	37.6
3	Tennessee	53.9		42	North Dakota	37.3
10	Texas	49.0		43	Massachusetts	36.5
36	Utah	38.9		44	New Jersey	35.8
41	Vermont	37.6		45	New Hampshire	34.3
17	Virginia	44.5		46	Connecticut	34.2
29	Washington	41.4		47	Florida	33.6
11	West Virginia	48.9		48	Rhode Island	33.5
26	Wisconsin	42.3		49	Arizona	32.7
32	Wyoming	39.5		50	New York	28.2
					District of Columbia	36.9

Source: U.S. Department of Health and Human Services, National Center for Health Statistics
     "National Vital Statistics Reports" (Vol. 58, No. 19, May 20, 2010, http://www.cdc.gov/nchs/deaths.htm)
*Final data by state of residence. Cerebrovascular diseases include stroke and other disorders of the blood vessels of the brain.
Age-adjusted rates based on the year 2000 standard population.

Deaths by Diseases of the Heart in 2007

National Total = 616,067 Deaths*

ALPHA ORDER

RANK	STATE	DEATHS	% of USA
17	Alabama	11,926	1.9%
50	Alaska	613	0.1%
21	Arizona	10,302	1.7%
29	Arkansas	7,214	1.2%
1	California	61,690	10.0%
32	Colorado	6,106	1.0%
28	Connecticut	7,289	1.2%
44	Delaware	1,914	0.3%
3	Florida	42,254	6.9%
11	Georgia	16,184	2.6%
43	Hawaii	2,227	0.4%
42	Idaho	2,433	0.4%
7	Illinois	25,813	4.2%
15	Indiana	13,682	2.2%
30	Iowa	6,880	1.1%
33	Kansas	5,749	0.9%
23	Kentucky	9,916	1.6%
22	Louisiana	9,947	1.6%
39	Maine	2,852	0.5%
18	Maryland	11,314	1.8%
16	Massachusetts	12,710	2.1%
8	Michigan	24,149	3.9%
27	Minnesota	7,477	1.2%
26	Mississippi	8,037	1.3%
12	Missouri	14,338	2.3%
45	Montana	1,870	0.3%
36	Nebraska	3,520	0.6%
35	Nevada	4,591	0.7%
41	New Hampshire	2,511	0.4%
9	New Jersey	18,831	3.1%
37	New Mexico	3,305	0.5%
2	New York	49,528	8.0%
10	North Carolina	17,395	2.8%
47	North Dakota	1,414	0.2%
6	Ohio	26,757	4.3%
24	Oklahoma	9,602	1.6%
31	Oregon	6,655	1.1%
5	Pennsylvania	32,862	5.3%
40	Rhode Island	2,751	0.4%
25	South Carolina	8,992	1.5%
46	South Dakota	1,633	0.3%
13	Tennessee	14,280	2.3%
4	Texas	38,912	6.3%
38	Utah	2,980	0.5%
48	Vermont	1,166	0.2%
14	Virginia	13,750	2.2%
20	Washington	11,037	1.8%
34	West Virginia	5,208	0.8%
19	Wisconsin	11,110	1.8%
49	Wyoming	957	0.2%

RANK ORDER

RANK	STATE	DEATHS	% of USA
1	California	61,690	10.0%
2	New York	49,528	8.0%
3	Florida	42,254	6.9%
4	Texas	38,912	6.3%
5	Pennsylvania	32,862	5.3%
6	Ohio	26,757	4.3%
7	Illinois	25,813	4.2%
8	Michigan	24,149	3.9%
9	New Jersey	18,831	3.1%
10	North Carolina	17,395	2.8%
11	Georgia	16,184	2.6%
12	Missouri	14,338	2.3%
13	Tennessee	14,280	2.3%
14	Virginia	13,750	2.2%
15	Indiana	13,682	2.2%
16	Massachusetts	12,710	2.1%
17	Alabama	11,926	1.9%
18	Maryland	11,314	1.8%
19	Wisconsin	11,110	1.8%
20	Washington	11,037	1.8%
21	Arizona	10,302	1.7%
22	Louisiana	9,947	1.6%
23	Kentucky	9,916	1.6%
24	Oklahoma	9,602	1.6%
25	South Carolina	8,992	1.5%
26	Mississippi	8,037	1.3%
27	Minnesota	7,477	1.2%
28	Connecticut	7,289	1.2%
29	Arkansas	7,214	1.2%
30	Iowa	6,880	1.1%
31	Oregon	6,655	1.1%
32	Colorado	6,106	1.0%
33	Kansas	5,749	0.9%
34	West Virginia	5,208	0.8%
35	Nevada	4,591	0.7%
36	Nebraska	3,520	0.6%
37	New Mexico	3,305	0.5%
38	Utah	2,980	0.5%
39	Maine	2,852	0.5%
40	Rhode Island	2,751	0.4%
41	New Hampshire	2,511	0.4%
42	Idaho	2,433	0.4%
43	Hawaii	2,227	0.4%
44	Delaware	1,914	0.3%
45	Montana	1,870	0.3%
46	South Dakota	1,633	0.3%
47	North Dakota	1,414	0.2%
48	Vermont	1,166	0.2%
49	Wyoming	957	0.2%
50	Alaska	613	0.1%
	District of Columbia	1,434	0.2%

Source: U.S. Department of Health and Human Services, National Center for Health Statistics
   "National Vital Statistics Reports" (Vol. 58, No. 19, May 20, 2010, http://www.cdc.gov/nchs/deaths.htm)
*Final data by state of residence.

Age-Adjusted Death Rate by Diseases of the Heart in 2007

National Rate = 190.9 Deaths per 100,000 Population*

ALPHA ORDER

RANK	STATE	RATE
3	Alabama	235.5
47	Alaska	147.9
45	Arizona	152.5
7	Arkansas	221.8
28	California	177.9
48	Colorado	145.3
33	Connecticut	171.0
17	Delaware	200.2
40	Florida	162.4
14	Georgia	203.0
49	Hawaii	140.2
37	Idaho	164.1
21	Illinois	192.8
14	Indiana	203.0
30	Iowa	174.8
26	Kansas	178.7
9	Kentucky	220.9
4	Louisiana	230.0
31	Maine	172.9
16	Maryland	202.4
35	Massachusetts	165.5
8	Michigan	221.5
50	Minnesota	129.8
1	Mississippi	266.5
11	Missouri	214.4
39	Montana	163.1
36	Nebraska	165.3
18	Nevada	200.0
29	New Hampshire	174.9
22	New Jersey	191.9
42	New Mexico	159.2
6	New York	225.1
24	North Carolina	191.0
37	North Dakota	164.1
12	Ohio	204.8
2	Oklahoma	241.6
44	Oregon	156.9
19	Pennsylvania	199.4
13	Rhode Island	203.6
20	South Carolina	192.9
43	South Dakota	159.1
10	Tennessee	220.6
22	Texas	191.9
46	Utah	152.1
41	Vermont	161.2
25	Virginia	182.7
34	Washington	167.2
5	West Virginia	229.4
32	Wisconsin	171.9
27	Wyoming	178.3

RANK ORDER

RANK	STATE	RATE
1	Mississippi	266.5
2	Oklahoma	241.6
3	Alabama	235.5
4	Louisiana	230.0
5	West Virginia	229.4
6	New York	225.1
7	Arkansas	221.8
8	Michigan	221.5
9	Kentucky	220.9
10	Tennessee	220.6
11	Missouri	214.4
12	Ohio	204.8
13	Rhode Island	203.6
14	Georgia	203.0
14	Indiana	203.0
16	Maryland	202.4
17	Delaware	200.2
18	Nevada	200.0
19	Pennsylvania	199.4
20	South Carolina	192.9
21	Illinois	192.8
22	New Jersey	191.9
22	Texas	191.9
24	North Carolina	191.0
25	Virginia	182.7
26	Kansas	178.7
27	Wyoming	178.3
28	California	177.9
29	New Hampshire	174.9
30	Iowa	174.8
31	Maine	172.9
32	Wisconsin	171.9
33	Connecticut	171.0
34	Washington	167.2
35	Massachusetts	165.5
36	Nebraska	165.3
37	Idaho	164.1
37	North Dakota	164.1
39	Montana	163.1
40	Florida	162.4
41	Vermont	161.2
42	New Mexico	159.2
43	South Dakota	159.1
44	Oregon	156.9
45	Arizona	152.5
46	Utah	152.1
47	Alaska	147.9
48	Colorado	145.3
49	Hawaii	140.2
50	Minnesota	129.8
	District of Columbia	239.4

Source: U.S. Department of Health and Human Services, National Center for Health Statistics
"National Vital Statistics Reports" (Vol. 58, No. 19, May 20, 2010, http://www.cdc.gov/nchs/deaths.htm)
*Final data by state of residence. Age-adjusted rates based on the year 2000 standard population.

Deaths by Suicide in 2007

National Total = 34,598 Suicides*

RANK	STATE	DEATHS	% of USA		RANK	STATE	DEATHS	% of USA
22	Alabama	592	1.7%		1	California	3,602	10.4%
43	Alaska	149	0.4%		2	Florida	2,587	7.5%
10	Arizona	1,016	2.9%		3	Texas	2,433	7.0%
30	Arkansas	402	1.2%		4	Pennsylvania	1,441	4.2%
1	California	3,602	10.4%		5	New York	1,396	4.0%
15	Colorado	811	2.3%		6	Ohio	1,295	3.7%
37	Connecticut	271	0.8%		7	Michigan	1,131	3.3%
48	Delaware	95	0.3%		8	Illinois	1,108	3.2%
2	Florida	2,587	7.5%		9	North Carolina	1,077	3.1%
11	Georgia	997	2.9%		10	Arizona	1,016	2.9%
44	Hawaii	133	0.4%		11	Georgia	997	2.9%
38	Idaho	223	0.6%		12	Virginia	880	2.5%
8	Illinois	1,108	3.2%		13	Washington	865	2.5%
17	Indiana	790	2.3%		14	Tennessee	844	2.4%
35	Iowa	322	0.9%		15	Colorado	811	2.3%
33	Kansas	382	1.1%		16	Missouri	808	2.3%
19	Kentucky	649	1.9%		17	Indiana	790	2.3%
26	Louisiana	522	1.5%		18	Wisconsin	729	2.1%
40	Maine	191	0.6%		19	Kentucky	649	1.9%
27	Maryland	518	1.5%		20	New Jersey	596	1.7%
28	Massachusetts	516	1.5%		21	Oregon	594	1.7%
7	Michigan	1,131	3.3%		22	Alabama	592	1.7%
23	Minnesota	572	1.7%		23	Minnesota	572	1.7%
32	Mississippi	396	1.1%		24	Oklahoma	531	1.5%
16	Missouri	808	2.3%		25	South Carolina	530	1.5%
39	Montana	196	0.6%		26	Louisiana	522	1.5%
41	Nebraska	181	0.5%		27	Maryland	518	1.5%
29	Nevada	471	1.4%		28	Massachusetts	516	1.5%
42	New Hampshire	158	0.5%		29	Nevada	471	1.4%
20	New Jersey	596	1.7%		30	Arkansas	402	1.2%
31	New Mexico	401	1.2%		31	New Mexico	401	1.2%
5	New York	1,396	4.0%		32	Mississippi	396	1.1%
9	North Carolina	1,077	3.1%		33	Kansas	382	1.1%
48	North Dakota	95	0.3%		34	Utah	378	1.1%
6	Ohio	1,295	3.7%		35	Iowa	322	0.9%
24	Oklahoma	531	1.5%		36	West Virginia	300	0.9%
21	Oregon	594	1.7%		37	Connecticut	271	0.8%
4	Pennsylvania	1,441	4.2%		38	Idaho	223	0.6%
47	Rhode Island	96	0.3%		39	Montana	196	0.6%
25	South Carolina	530	1.5%		40	Maine	191	0.6%
45	South Dakota	102	0.3%		41	Nebraska	181	0.5%
14	Tennessee	844	2.4%		42	New Hampshire	158	0.5%
3	Texas	2,433	7.0%		43	Alaska	149	0.4%
34	Utah	378	1.1%		44	Hawaii	133	0.4%
50	Vermont	89	0.3%		45	South Dakota	102	0.3%
12	Virginia	880	2.5%		46	Wyoming	101	0.3%
13	Washington	865	2.5%		47	Rhode Island	96	0.3%
36	West Virginia	300	0.9%		48	Delaware	95	0.3%
18	Wisconsin	729	2.1%		48	North Dakota	95	0.3%
46	Wyoming	101	0.3%		50	Vermont	89	0.3%
						District of Columbia	36	0.1%

Source: U.S. Department of Health and Human Services, National Center for Health Statistics
"National Vital Statistics Reports" (Vol. 58, No. 19, May 20, 2010, http://www.cdc.gov/nchs/deaths.htm)
*Final data by state of residence.

Age-Adjusted Death Rate by Suicide in 2007

National Rate = 11.3 Deaths per 100,000 Population*

ALPHA ORDER

RANK ORDER

RANK	STATE	RATE		RANK	STATE	RATE
25	Alabama	12.5		1	Alaska	22.1
1	Alaska	22.1		2	New Mexico	20.4
7	Arizona	16.1		3	Wyoming	19.7
15	Arkansas	14.3		4	Montana	19.4
42	California	9.8		5	Nevada	18.3
6	Colorado	16.4		6	Colorado	16.4
48	Connecticut	7.4		7	Arizona	16.1
37	Delaware	10.7		8	West Virginia	15.9
21	Florida	13.3		9	Utah	15.4
37	Georgia	10.7		10	Oregon	15.2
43	Hawaii	9.7		11	Idaho	15.1
11	Idaho	15.1		11	Kentucky	15.1
46	Illinois	8.5		13	Oklahoma	14.7
27	Indiana	12.4		14	North Dakota	14.4
39	Iowa	10.6		15	Arkansas	14.3
18	Kansas	13.7		16	Mississippi	13.8
11	Kentucky	15.1		16	Vermont	13.8
28	Louisiana	12.2		18	Kansas	13.7
18	Maine	13.7		18	Maine	13.7
44	Maryland	9.0		20	Missouri	13.5
47	Massachusetts	7.6		21	Florida	13.3
34	Michigan	11.0		21	Tennessee	13.3
36	Minnesota	10.8		23	Washington	13.0
16	Mississippi	13.8		24	Wisconsin	12.7
20	Missouri	13.5		25	Alabama	12.5
4	Montana	19.4		25	South Dakota	12.5
41	Nebraska	10.2		27	Indiana	12.4
5	Nevada	18.3		28	Louisiana	12.2
33	New Hampshire	11.1		29	North Carolina	11.7
50	New Jersey	6.7		29	South Carolina	11.7
2	New Mexico	20.4		31	Pennsylvania	11.2
49	New York	7.0		31	Virginia	11.2
29	North Carolina	11.7		33	New Hampshire	11.1
14	North Dakota	14.4		34	Michigan	11.0
34	Ohio	11.0		34	Ohio	11.0
13	Oklahoma	14.7		36	Minnesota	10.8
10	Oregon	15.2		37	Delaware	10.7
31	Pennsylvania	11.2		37	Georgia	10.7
45	Rhode Island	8.7		39	Iowa	10.6
29	South Carolina	11.7		40	Texas	10.4
25	South Dakota	12.5		41	Nebraska	10.2
21	Tennessee	13.3		42	California	9.8
40	Texas	10.4		43	Hawaii	9.7
9	Utah	15.4		44	Maryland	9.0
16	Vermont	13.8		45	Rhode Island	8.7
31	Virginia	11.2		46	Illinois	8.5
23	Washington	13.0		47	Massachusetts	7.6
8	West Virginia	15.9		48	Connecticut	7.4
24	Wisconsin	12.7		49	New York	7.0
3	Wyoming	19.7		50	New Jersey	6.7
					District of Columbia	5.8

Source: U.S. Department of Health and Human Services, National Center for Health Statistics
"National Vital Statistics Reports" (Vol. 58, No. 19, May 20, 2010, http://www.cdc.gov/nchs/deaths.htm)
*Final data by state of residence. Age-adjusted rates based on the year 2000 standard population.

Deaths by AIDS in 2007

National Total = 11,295 Deaths*

ALPHA ORDER

RANK	STATE	DEATHS	% of USA
17	Alabama	183	1.6%
44	Alaska	7	0.1%
22	Arizona	109	1.0%
25	Arkansas	91	0.8%
3	California	1,101	9.7%
27	Colorado	82	0.7%
20	Connecticut	140	1.2%
29	Delaware	55	0.5%
1	Florida	1,530	13.5%
5	Georgia	689	6.1%
40	Hawaii	21	0.2%
45	Idaho	6	0.1%
12	Illinois	303	2.7%
24	Indiana	97	0.9%
41	Iowa	18	0.2%
38	Kansas	22	0.2%
29	Kentucky	55	0.5%
10	Louisiana	344	3.0%
42	Maine	13	0.1%
7	Maryland	436	3.9%
19	Massachusetts	143	1.3%
16	Michigan	187	1.7%
32	Minnesota	49	0.4%
18	Mississippi	163	1.4%
21	Missouri	128	1.1%
46	Montana	5	0.0%
35	Nebraska	28	0.2%
28	Nevada	80	0.7%
43	New Hampshire	10	0.1%
6	New Jersey	495	4.4%
34	New Mexico	35	0.3%
2	New York	1,342	11.9%
8	North Carolina	384	3.4%
48	North Dakota	3	0.0%
15	Ohio	207	1.8%
25	Oklahoma	91	0.8%
31	Oregon	54	0.5%
9	Pennsylvania	378	3.3%
36	Rhode Island	24	0.2%
11	South Carolina	315	2.8%
46	South Dakota	5	0.0%
13	Tennessee	252	2.2%
4	Texas	988	8.7%
37	Utah	23	0.2%
49	Vermont	2	0.0%
14	Virginia	230	2.0%
23	Washington	107	0.9%
38	West Virginia	22	0.2%
32	Wisconsin	49	0.4%
50	Wyoming	0	0.0%

RANK ORDER

RANK	STATE	DEATHS	% of USA
1	Florida	1,530	13.5%
2	New York	1,342	11.9%
3	California	1,101	9.7%
4	Texas	988	8.7%
5	Georgia	689	6.1%
6	New Jersey	495	4.4%
7	Maryland	436	3.9%
8	North Carolina	384	3.4%
9	Pennsylvania	378	3.3%
10	Louisiana	344	3.0%
11	South Carolina	315	2.8%
12	Illinois	303	2.7%
13	Tennessee	252	2.2%
14	Virginia	230	2.0%
15	Ohio	207	1.8%
16	Michigan	187	1.7%
17	Alabama	183	1.6%
18	Mississippi	163	1.4%
19	Massachusetts	143	1.3%
20	Connecticut	140	1.2%
21	Missouri	128	1.1%
22	Arizona	109	1.0%
23	Washington	107	0.9%
24	Indiana	97	0.9%
25	Arkansas	91	0.8%
25	Oklahoma	91	0.8%
27	Colorado	82	0.7%
28	Nevada	80	0.7%
29	Delaware	55	0.5%
29	Kentucky	55	0.5%
31	Oregon	54	0.5%
32	Minnesota	49	0.4%
32	Wisconsin	49	0.4%
34	New Mexico	35	0.3%
35	Nebraska	28	0.2%
36	Rhode Island	24	0.2%
37	Utah	23	0.2%
38	Kansas	22	0.2%
38	West Virginia	22	0.2%
40	Hawaii	21	0.2%
41	Iowa	18	0.2%
42	Maine	13	0.1%
43	New Hampshire	10	0.1%
44	Alaska	7	0.1%
45	Idaho	6	0.1%
46	Montana	5	0.0%
46	South Dakota	5	0.0%
48	North Dakota	3	0.0%
49	Vermont	2	0.0%
50	Wyoming	0	0.0%
	District of Columbia	194	1.7%

Source: U.S. Department of Health and Human Services, National Center for Health Statistics
   "National Vital Statistics Reports" (Vol. 58, No. 19, May 20, 2010, http://www.cdc.gov/nchs/deaths.htm)
*Final data by state of residence. AIDS is Acquired Immunodeficiency Syndrome. It is a specific group of diseases or
conditions which are indicative of severe immunosuppression related to infection with the Human Immunodeficiency Virus (HIV).

Age-Adjusted Death Rate by AIDS in 2007

National Rate = 3.7 Deaths per 100,000 Population*

ALPHA ORDER

RANK	STATE	RATE
13	Alabama	4.0
NA	Alaska**	NA
26	Arizona	1.8
15	Arkansas	3.2
17	California	3.0
30	Colorado	1.6
14	Connecticut	3.6
7	Delaware	6.2
1	Florida	8.3
4	Georgia	7.1
30	Hawaii	1.6
NA	Idaho**	NA
21	Illinois	2.3
33	Indiana	1.5
NA	Iowa**	NA
40	Kansas	0.8
35	Kentucky	1.3
1	Louisiana	8.3
NA	Maine**	NA
3	Maryland	7.4
24	Massachusetts	2.0
26	Michigan	1.8
38	Minnesota	0.9
8	Mississippi	5.9
22	Missouri	2.2
NA	Montana**	NA
29	Nebraska	1.7
16	Nevada	3.1
NA	New Hampshire**	NA
9	New Jersey	5.3
25	New Mexico	1.9
6	New York	6.6
11	North Carolina	4.1
NA	North Dakota**	NA
26	Ohio	1.8
20	Oklahoma	2.7
34	Oregon	1.4
18	Pennsylvania	2.9
22	Rhode Island	2.2
4	South Carolina	7.1
NA	South Dakota**	NA
11	Tennessee	4.1
10	Texas	4.3
37	Utah	1.0
NA	Vermont**	NA
19	Virginia	2.8
30	Washington	1.6
36	West Virginia	1.2
38	Wisconsin	0.9
NA	Wyoming**	NA

RANK ORDER

RANK	STATE	RATE
1	Florida	8.3
1	Louisiana	8.3
3	Maryland	7.4
4	Georgia	7.1
4	South Carolina	7.1
6	New York	6.6
7	Delaware	6.2
8	Mississippi	5.9
9	New Jersey	5.3
10	Texas	4.3
11	North Carolina	4.1
11	Tennessee	4.1
13	Alabama	4.0
14	Connecticut	3.6
15	Arkansas	3.2
16	Nevada	3.1
17	California	3.0
18	Pennsylvania	2.9
19	Virginia	2.8
20	Oklahoma	2.7
21	Illinois	2.3
22	Missouri	2.2
22	Rhode Island	2.2
24	Massachusetts	2.0
25	New Mexico	1.9
26	Arizona	1.8
26	Michigan	1.8
26	Ohio	1.8
29	Nebraska	1.7
30	Colorado	1.6
30	Hawaii	1.6
30	Washington	1.6
33	Indiana	1.5
34	Oregon	1.4
35	Kentucky	1.3
36	West Virginia	1.2
37	Utah	1.0
38	Minnesota	0.9
38	Wisconsin	0.9
40	Kansas	0.8
NA	Alaska**	NA
NA	Idaho**	NA
NA	Iowa**	NA
NA	Maine**	NA
NA	Montana**	NA
NA	New Hampshire**	NA
NA	North Dakota**	NA
NA	South Dakota**	NA
NA	Vermont**	NA
NA	Wyoming**	NA

District of Columbia	32.8

Source: U.S. Department of Health and Human Services, National Center for Health Statistics
"National Vital Statistics Reports" (Vol. 58, No. 19, May 20, 2010, http://www.cdc.gov/nchs/deaths.htm)
*Final data by state of residence. AIDS is Acquired Immunodeficiency Syndrome. It is a specific group of diseases or conditions which are indicative of severe immunosuppression related to infection with the Human Immunodeficiency Virus (HIV). Age-adjusted rates based on the year 2000 standard population.
**Insufficient data to determine a reliable rate.

Adult Per Capita Alcohol Consumption in 2007

National Per Capita = 2.6 Gallons Consumed per Adult 21 Years and Older*

ALPHA ORDER

RANK	STATE	PER CAPITA
40	Alabama	2.3
5	Alaska	3.3
18	Arizona	2.8
46	Arkansas	2.1
24	California	2.7
9	Colorado	3.1
24	Connecticut	2.7
3	Delaware	3.7
10	Florida	3.0
37	Georgia	2.4
15	Hawaii	2.9
10	Idaho	3.0
24	Illinois	2.7
37	Indiana	2.4
30	Iowa	2.6
44	Kansas	2.2
46	Kentucky	2.1
10	Louisiana	3.0
18	Maine	2.8
34	Maryland	2.5
18	Massachusetts	2.8
34	Michigan	2.5
18	Minnesota	2.8
30	Mississippi	2.6
24	Missouri	2.7
7	Montana	3.2
24	Nebraska	2.7
2	Nevada	4.1
1	New Hampshire	4.8
30	New Jersey	2.6
18	New Mexico	2.8
40	New York	2.3
40	North Carolina	2.3
5	North Dakota	3.3
40	Ohio	2.3
44	Oklahoma	2.2
15	Oregon	2.9
34	Pennsylvania	2.5
15	Rhode Island	2.9
18	South Carolina	2.8
10	South Dakota	3.0
46	Tennessee	2.1
30	Texas	2.6
50	Utah	1.6
10	Vermont	3.0
37	Virginia	2.4
24	Washington	2.7
49	West Virginia	2.0
4	Wisconsin	3.4
7	Wyoming	3.2

RANK ORDER

RANK	STATE	PER CAPITA
1	New Hampshire	4.8
2	Nevada	4.1
3	Delaware	3.7
4	Wisconsin	3.4
5	Alaska	3.3
5	North Dakota	3.3
7	Montana	3.2
7	Wyoming	3.2
9	Colorado	3.1
10	Florida	3.0
10	Idaho	3.0
10	Louisiana	3.0
10	South Dakota	3.0
10	Vermont	3.0
15	Hawaii	2.9
15	Oregon	2.9
15	Rhode Island	2.9
18	Arizona	2.8
18	Maine	2.8
18	Massachusetts	2.8
18	Minnesota	2.8
18	New Mexico	2.8
18	South Carolina	2.8
24	California	2.7
24	Connecticut	2.7
24	Illinois	2.7
24	Missouri	2.7
24	Nebraska	2.7
24	Washington	2.7
30	Iowa	2.6
30	Mississippi	2.6
30	New Jersey	2.6
30	Texas	2.6
34	Maryland	2.5
34	Michigan	2.5
34	Pennsylvania	2.5
37	Georgia	2.4
37	Indiana	2.4
37	Virginia	2.4
40	Alabama	2.3
40	New York	2.3
40	North Carolina	2.3
40	Ohio	2.3
44	Kansas	2.2
44	Oklahoma	2.2
46	Arkansas	2.1
46	Kentucky	2.1
46	Tennessee	2.1
49	West Virginia	2.0
50	Utah	1.6

District of Columbia   4.5

Source: CQ Press using data from U.S. Dept of Health and Human Services, National Institute on Alcohol Abuse and Alcoholism "Volume Beverage and Ethanol Consumption for States" (http://www.niaaa.nih.gov/Resources/)

*This is apparent consumption of actual alcohol, not entire volume of an alcoholic beverage (for example, wine is roughly 11% absolute alcohol content). Apparent consumption is based on several sources which together approximate sales but do not actually measure consumption. Accordingly, figures for some states may be skewed by purchases by nonresidents.

Percent of Adults Who Smoke: 2009

National Median = 17.9% of Adults*

ALPHA ORDER

RANK	STATE	PERCENT
7	Alabama	22.5
12	Alaska	20.6
40	Arizona	16.1
11	Arkansas	21.5
49	California	12.9
33	Colorado	17.1
43	Connecticut	15.4
23	Delaware	18.3
33	Florida	17.1
29	Georgia	17.7
43	Hawaii	15.4
39	Idaho	16.3
21	Illinois	18.6
5	Indiana	23.1
32	Iowa	17.2
28	Kansas	17.8
1	Kentucky	25.6
8	Louisiana	22.1
31	Maine	17.3
45	Maryland	15.2
47	Massachusetts	15.0
18	Michigan	19.6
36	Minnesota	16.8
4	Mississippi	23.3
5	Missouri	23.1
36	Montana	16.8
38	Nebraska	16.7
9	Nevada	22.0
41	New Hampshire	15.8
41	New Jersey	15.8
25	New Mexico	17.9
24	New York	18.0
14	North Carolina	20.3
21	North Dakota	18.6
14	Ohio	20.3
3	Oklahoma	25.5
25	Oregon	17.9
16	Pennsylvania	20.2
46	Rhode Island	15.1
13	South Carolina	20.4
30	South Dakota	17.5
9	Tennessee	22.0
25	Texas	17.9
50	Utah	9.8
33	Vermont	17.1
19	Virginia	19.0
48	Washington	14.9
1	West Virginia	25.6
20	Wisconsin	18.8
17	Wyoming	19.9

RANK ORDER

RANK	STATE	PERCENT
1	Kentucky	25.6
1	West Virginia	25.6
3	Oklahoma	25.5
4	Mississippi	23.3
5	Indiana	23.1
5	Missouri	23.1
7	Alabama	22.5
8	Louisiana	22.1
9	Nevada	22.0
9	Tennessee	22.0
11	Arkansas	21.5
12	Alaska	20.6
13	South Carolina	20.4
14	North Carolina	20.3
14	Ohio	20.3
16	Pennsylvania	20.2
17	Wyoming	19.9
18	Michigan	19.6
19	Virginia	19.0
20	Wisconsin	18.8
21	Illinois	18.6
21	North Dakota	18.6
23	Delaware	18.3
24	New York	18.0
25	New Mexico	17.9
25	Oregon	17.9
25	Texas	17.9
28	Kansas	17.8
29	Georgia	17.7
30	South Dakota	17.5
31	Maine	17.3
32	Iowa	17.2
33	Colorado	17.1
33	Florida	17.1
33	Vermont	17.1
36	Minnesota	16.8
36	Montana	16.8
38	Nebraska	16.7
39	Idaho	16.3
40	Arizona	16.1
41	New Hampshire	15.8
41	New Jersey	15.8
43	Connecticut	15.4
43	Hawaii	15.4
45	Maryland	15.2
46	Rhode Island	15.1
47	Massachusetts	15.0
48	Washington	14.9
49	California	12.9
50	Utah	9.8

District of Columbia   15.3

Source: U.S. Department of Health and Human Services, Centers for Disease Control and Prevention
    "2009 Behavioral Risk Factor Surveillance Summary Prevalence Data" (http://apps.nccd.cdc.gov/brfss/)
*Persons 18 and older who have smoked more than 100 cigarettes during their lifetime and who currently smoke every day or some days.

Percent of Adults Overweight or Obese: 2009

National Median = 63.1% of Adults*

ALPHA ORDER

RANK	STATE	PERCENT
3	Alabama	68.2
29	Alaska	63.3
24	Arizona	64.2
12	Arkansas	66.6
40	California	61.3
50	Colorado	55.7
45	Connecticut	59.0
27	Delaware	63.7
28	Florida	63.4
19	Georgia	65.3
48	Hawaii	57.8
40	Idaho	61.3
23	Illinois	64.5
20	Indiana	65.2
7	Iowa	67.2
22	Kansas	64.6
9	Kentucky	67.1
4	Louisiana	67.6
24	Maine	64.2
32	Maryland	62.9
49	Massachusetts	57.5
15	Michigan	65.6
29	Minnesota	63.3
1	Mississippi	70.3
15	Missouri	65.6
36	Montana	62.1
21	Nebraska	64.9
31	Nevada	63.0
33	New Hampshire	62.8
37	New Jersey	61.9
38	New Mexico	61.8
44	New York	60.2
18	North Carolina	65.4
13	North Dakota	66.2
10	Ohio	66.8
6	Oklahoma	67.4
42	Oregon	60.6
26	Pennsylvania	64.1
39	Rhode Island	61.6
14	South Carolina	65.9
7	South Dakota	67.2
2	Tennessee	69.0
10	Texas	66.8
47	Utah	58.0
46	Vermont	58.2
42	Virginia	60.6
34	Washington	62.4
5	West Virginia	67.5
15	Wisconsin	65.6
35	Wyoming	62.2

RANK ORDER

RANK	STATE	PERCENT
1	Mississippi	70.3
2	Tennessee	69.0
3	Alabama	68.2
4	Louisiana	67.6
5	West Virginia	67.5
6	Oklahoma	67.4
7	Iowa	67.2
7	South Dakota	67.2
9	Kentucky	67.1
10	Ohio	66.8
10	Texas	66.8
12	Arkansas	66.6
13	North Dakota	66.2
14	South Carolina	65.9
15	Michigan	65.6
15	Missouri	65.6
15	Wisconsin	65.6
18	North Carolina	65.4
19	Georgia	65.3
20	Indiana	65.2
21	Nebraska	64.9
22	Kansas	64.6
23	Illinois	64.5
24	Arizona	64.2
24	Maine	64.2
26	Pennsylvania	64.1
27	Delaware	63.7
28	Florida	63.4
29	Alaska	63.3
29	Minnesota	63.3
31	Nevada	63.0
32	Maryland	62.9
33	New Hampshire	62.8
34	Washington	62.4
35	Wyoming	62.2
36	Montana	62.1
37	New Jersey	61.9
38	New Mexico	61.8
39	Rhode Island	61.6
40	California	61.3
40	Idaho	61.3
42	Oregon	60.6
42	Virginia	60.6
44	New York	60.2
45	Connecticut	59.0
46	Vermont	58.2
47	Utah	58.0
48	Hawaii	57.8
49	Massachusetts	57.5
50	Colorado	55.7
	District of Columbia	51.7

Source: CQ Press using data from U.S. Department of Health and Human Services, Centers for Disease Control and Prevention
"2009 Behavioral Risk Factor Surveillance Summary Prevalence Data" (http://apps.nccd.cdc.gov/brfss/)

*Persons 18 and older. Overweight is defined as a Body Mass Index (BMI) of 25.0 to 29.9 regardless of sex. Obese is a BMI of 30.0 or greater. BMI is a ratio of height to weight. As an example, a person 5' 8" and weighing 165 pounds has a BMI of 25. The same height at 197 pounds has a BMI of 30. See http://www.cdc.gov/healthyweight/assessing/bmi/index.html.

Percent of Children Aged 19 to 35 Months Fully Immunized in 2009

National Percent = 70.5%*

ALPHA ORDER

RANK	STATE	PERCENT
43	Alabama	63.9
49	Alaska	56.6
38	Arizona	66.4
46	Arkansas	61.5
17	California	72.2
40	Colorado	66.1
6	Connecticut	76.0
31	Delaware	69.2
32	Florida	68.7
12	Georgia	73.1
21	Hawaii	71.0
23	Idaho	70.5
13	Illinois	72.8
35	Indiana	67.3
1	Iowa	78.1
18	Kansas	71.7
34	Kentucky	67.5
10	Louisiana	74.9
16	Maine	72.3
2	Maryland	77.9
6	Massachusetts	76.0
5	Michigan	76.5
19	Minnesota	71.6
9	Mississippi	75.2
50	Missouri	56.2
45	Montana	61.7
41	Nebraska	65.4
44	Nevada	62.6
11	New Hampshire	73.3
36	New Jersey	67.2
24	New Mexico	70.2
36	New York	67.2
4	North Carolina	76.7
3	North Dakota	77.0
15	Ohio	72.4
39	Oklahoma	66.3
25	Oregon	69.9
29	Pennsylvania	69.4
26	Rhode Island	69.7
22	South Carolina	70.9
27	South Dakota	69.6
14	Tennessee	72.5
20	Texas	71.3
30	Utah	69.3
48	Vermont	59.9
33	Virginia	68.6
42	Washington	64.9
47	West Virginia	60.9
8	Wisconsin	75.9
27	Wyoming	69.6

RANK ORDER

RANK	STATE	PERCENT
1	Iowa	78.1
2	Maryland	77.9
3	North Dakota	77.0
4	North Carolina	76.7
5	Michigan	76.5
6	Connecticut	76.0
6	Massachusetts	76.0
8	Wisconsin	75.9
9	Mississippi	75.2
10	Louisiana	74.9
11	New Hampshire	73.3
12	Georgia	73.1
13	Illinois	72.8
14	Tennessee	72.5
15	Ohio	72.4
16	Maine	72.3
17	California	72.2
18	Kansas	71.7
19	Minnesota	71.6
20	Texas	71.3
21	Hawaii	71.0
22	South Carolina	70.9
23	Idaho	70.5
24	New Mexico	70.2
25	Oregon	69.9
26	Rhode Island	69.7
27	South Dakota	69.6
27	Wyoming	69.6
29	Pennsylvania	69.4
30	Utah	69.3
31	Delaware	69.2
32	Florida	68.7
33	Virginia	68.6
34	Kentucky	67.5
35	Indiana	67.3
36	New Jersey	67.2
36	New York	67.2
38	Arizona	66.4
39	Oklahoma	66.3
40	Colorado	66.1
41	Nebraska	65.4
42	Washington	64.9
43	Alabama	63.9
44	Nevada	62.6
45	Montana	61.7
46	Arkansas	61.5
47	West Virginia	60.9
48	Vermont	59.9
49	Alaska	56.6
50	Missouri	56.2

	District of Columbia	63.8

Source: U.S. Department of Health and Human Services, Centers for Disease Control and Prevention
   "State Vaccination Coverage Levels" (MMWR, Vol. 59, No. 36, September 17, 2010, http://www.cdc.gov/mmwr/)
*Fully immunized (4:3:1:3:3:1:4 series) children received four doses of DTP/DT/DTaP (Diphtheria, Tetanus, Pertussis [Whooping Cough], Acellular Pertussis), three doses of OPV (Oral Poliovirus Vaccine), one dose of MCV (Measles-Containing Vaccine), three doses of Hib (Haemophilus influenzae type b), three doses of Hepatitis B vaccine, one dose of Varicella (chickenpox) vaccine, and four doses of PCV (pneumococcal conjugate vaccine). This differs from previous "fully" immunized tables.

XII. Households and Housing

Households in 2009

National Total = 113,616,229 Households*

ALPHA ORDER

RANK	STATE	HOUSEHOLDS	% of USA
23	Alabama	1,848,051	1.6%
49	Alaska	236,597	0.2%
18	Arizona	2,276,865	2.0%
31	Arkansas	1,124,947	1.0%
1	California	12,214,891	10.8%
22	Colorado	1,910,146	1.7%
29	Connecticut	1,326,329	1.2%
45	Delaware	327,252	0.3%
4	Florida	6,987,647	6.2%
10	Georgia	3,469,250	3.1%
42	Hawaii	446,136	0.4%
39	Idaho	558,466	0.5%
6	Illinois	4,757,452	4.2%
14	Indiana	2,477,548	2.2%
30	Iowa	1,226,804	1.1%
32	Kansas	1,104,976	1.0%
25	Kentucky	1,694,197	1.5%
26	Louisiana	1,688,027	1.5%
40	Maine	544,855	0.5%
20	Maryland	2,095,122	1.8%
15	Massachusetts	2,475,492	2.2%
8	Michigan	3,819,736	3.4%
21	Minnesota	2,085,767	1.8%
33	Mississippi	1,095,026	1.0%
17	Missouri	2,339,684	2.1%
44	Montana	375,287	0.3%
38	Nebraska	711,223	0.6%
34	Nevada	965,715	0.8%
41	New Hampshire	506,342	0.4%
11	New Jersey	3,154,926	2.8%
37	New Mexico	742,104	0.7%
3	New York	7,187,555	6.3%
9	North Carolina	3,646,095	3.2%
47	North Dakota	279,014	0.2%
7	Ohio	4,526,404	4.0%
28	Oklahoma	1,430,019	1.3%
27	Oregon	1,485,919	1.3%
5	Pennsylvania	4,916,869	4.3%
43	Rhode Island	406,343	0.4%
24	South Carolina	1,730,232	1.5%
46	South Dakota	316,638	0.3%
16	Tennessee	2,447,066	2.2%
2	Texas	8,527,938	7.5%
35	Utah	863,122	0.8%
48	Vermont	251,736	0.2%
12	Virginia	2,971,489	2.6%
13	Washington	2,559,288	2.3%
36	West Virginia	748,517	0.7%
19	Wisconsin	2,272,274	2.0%
50	Wyoming	213,571	0.2%

RANK ORDER

RANK	STATE	HOUSEHOLDS	% of USA
1	California	12,214,891	10.8%
2	Texas	8,527,938	7.5%
3	New York	7,187,555	6.3%
4	Florida	6,987,647	6.2%
5	Pennsylvania	4,916,869	4.3%
6	Illinois	4,757,452	4.2%
7	Ohio	4,526,404	4.0%
8	Michigan	3,819,736	3.4%
9	North Carolina	3,646,095	3.2%
10	Georgia	3,469,250	3.1%
11	New Jersey	3,154,926	2.8%
12	Virginia	2,971,489	2.6%
13	Washington	2,559,288	2.3%
14	Indiana	2,477,548	2.2%
15	Massachusetts	2,475,492	2.2%
16	Tennessee	2,447,066	2.2%
17	Missouri	2,339,684	2.1%
18	Arizona	2,276,865	2.0%
19	Wisconsin	2,272,274	2.0%
20	Maryland	2,095,122	1.8%
21	Minnesota	2,085,767	1.8%
22	Colorado	1,910,146	1.7%
23	Alabama	1,848,051	1.6%
24	South Carolina	1,730,232	1.5%
25	Kentucky	1,694,197	1.5%
26	Louisiana	1,688,027	1.5%
27	Oregon	1,485,919	1.3%
28	Oklahoma	1,430,019	1.3%
29	Connecticut	1,326,329	1.2%
30	Iowa	1,226,804	1.1%
31	Arkansas	1,124,947	1.0%
32	Kansas	1,104,976	1.0%
33	Mississippi	1,095,026	1.0%
34	Nevada	965,715	0.8%
35	Utah	863,122	0.8%
36	West Virginia	748,517	0.7%
37	New Mexico	742,104	0.7%
38	Nebraska	711,223	0.6%
39	Idaho	558,466	0.5%
40	Maine	544,855	0.5%
41	New Hampshire	506,342	0.4%
42	Hawaii	446,136	0.4%
43	Rhode Island	406,343	0.4%
44	Montana	375,287	0.3%
45	Delaware	327,252	0.3%
46	South Dakota	316,638	0.3%
47	North Dakota	279,014	0.2%
48	Vermont	251,736	0.2%
49	Alaska	236,597	0.2%
50	Wyoming	213,571	0.2%
	District of Columbia	249,280	0.2%

Source: U.S. Bureau of the Census
    "2009 American Community Survey" (http://www.census.gov/acs/www/)
*A household includes all persons who occupy a housing unit. A household consists of a single family, one person living alone,
two or more families living together, or any other group of related or unrelated persons who share living arrangements.

Persons per Household in 2009

National Rate = 2.63 Persons per Household*

ALPHA ORDER

RANK	STATE	PERSONS
36	Alabama	2.48
3	Alaska	2.86
4	Arizona	2.84
33	Arkansas	2.49
2	California	2.96
19	Colorado	2.57
19	Connecticut	2.57
14	Delaware	2.63
17	Florida	2.59
7	Georgia	2.75
6	Hawaii	2.82
8	Idaho	2.71
13	Illinois	2.64
28	Indiana	2.52
47	Iowa	2.37
36	Kansas	2.48
40	Kentucky	2.47
17	Louisiana	2.59
49	Maine	2.35
11	Maryland	2.65
22	Massachusetts	2.56
25	Michigan	2.54
43	Minnesota	2.46
16	Mississippi	2.60
33	Missouri	2.49
27	Montana	2.53
44	Nebraska	2.45
9	Nevada	2.70
25	New Hampshire	2.54
9	New Jersey	2.70
11	New Mexico	2.65
14	New York	2.63
33	North Carolina	2.49
50	North Dakota	2.22
36	Ohio	2.48
31	Oklahoma	2.50
28	Oregon	2.52
40	Pennsylvania	2.47
31	Rhode Island	2.50
23	South Carolina	2.55
40	South Dakota	2.47
30	Tennessee	2.51
4	Texas	2.84
1	Utah	3.17
46	Vermont	2.38
19	Virginia	2.57
23	Washington	2.55
47	West Virginia	2.37
45	Wisconsin	2.42
36	Wyoming	2.48

RANK ORDER

RANK	STATE	PERSONS
1	Utah	3.17
2	California	2.96
3	Alaska	2.86
4	Arizona	2.84
4	Texas	2.84
6	Hawaii	2.82
7	Georgia	2.75
8	Idaho	2.71
9	Nevada	2.70
9	New Jersey	2.70
11	Maryland	2.65
11	New Mexico	2.65
13	Illinois	2.64
14	Delaware	2.63
14	New York	2.63
16	Mississippi	2.60
17	Florida	2.59
17	Louisiana	2.59
19	Colorado	2.57
19	Connecticut	2.57
19	Virginia	2.57
22	Massachusetts	2.56
23	South Carolina	2.55
23	Washington	2.55
25	Michigan	2.54
25	New Hampshire	2.54
27	Montana	2.53
28	Indiana	2.52
28	Oregon	2.52
30	Tennessee	2.51
31	Oklahoma	2.50
31	Rhode Island	2.50
33	Arkansas	2.49
33	Missouri	2.49
33	North Carolina	2.49
36	Alabama	2.48
36	Kansas	2.48
36	Ohio	2.48
36	Wyoming	2.48
40	Kentucky	2.47
40	Pennsylvania	2.47
40	South Dakota	2.47
43	Minnesota	2.46
44	Nebraska	2.45
45	Wisconsin	2.42
46	Vermont	2.38
47	Iowa	2.37
47	West Virginia	2.37
49	Maine	2.35
50	North Dakota	2.22
	District of Columbia	2.26

Source: U.S. Bureau of the Census
   "2009 American Community Survey" (http://www.census.gov/acs/www/)
*A household includes all persons who occupy a housing unit. A household consists of a single family, one person living alone,
two or more families living together, or any other group of related or unrelated persons who share living arrangements.

Percent of Households with One Person in 2009

National Percent = 27.5% of Households*

ALPHA ORDER

RANK	STATE	PERCENT
14	Alabama	28.4
45	Alaska	25.3
36	Arizona	27.0
34	Arkansas	27.4
47	California	24.4
24	Colorado	27.9
36	Connecticut	27.0
41	Delaware	26.5
18	Florida	28.3
40	Georgia	26.6
48	Hawaii	23.5
49	Idaho	22.9
12	Illinois	28.8
31	Indiana	27.6
18	Iowa	28.3
13	Kansas	28.5
24	Kentucky	27.9
22	Louisiana	28.0
10	Maine	29.3
31	Maryland	27.6
4	Massachusetts	30.0
14	Michigan	28.4
14	Minnesota	28.4
36	Mississippi	27.0
18	Missouri	28.3
3	Montana	30.7
11	Nebraska	29.1
42	Nevada	26.2
44	New Hampshire	26.0
42	New Jersey	26.2
21	New Mexico	28.1
6	New York	29.7
28	North Carolina	27.7
1	North Dakota	31.2
8	Ohio	29.4
14	Oklahoma	28.4
34	Oregon	27.4
8	Pennsylvania	29.4
2	Rhode Island	30.9
28	South Carolina	27.7
5	South Dakota	29.8
22	Tennessee	28.0
46	Texas	24.9
50	Utah	19.0
24	Vermont	27.9
36	Virginia	27.0
27	Washington	27.8
7	West Virginia	29.5
28	Wisconsin	27.7
31	Wyoming	27.6

RANK ORDER

RANK	STATE	PERCENT
1	North Dakota	31.2
2	Rhode Island	30.9
3	Montana	30.7
4	Massachusetts	30.0
5	South Dakota	29.8
6	New York	29.7
7	West Virginia	29.5
8	Ohio	29.4
8	Pennsylvania	29.4
10	Maine	29.3
11	Nebraska	29.1
12	Illinois	28.8
13	Kansas	28.5
14	Alabama	28.4
14	Michigan	28.4
14	Minnesota	28.4
14	Oklahoma	28.4
18	Florida	28.3
18	Iowa	28.3
18	Missouri	28.3
21	New Mexico	28.1
22	Louisiana	28.0
22	Tennessee	28.0
24	Colorado	27.9
24	Kentucky	27.9
24	Vermont	27.9
27	Washington	27.8
28	North Carolina	27.7
28	South Carolina	27.7
28	Wisconsin	27.7
31	Indiana	27.6
31	Maryland	27.6
31	Wyoming	27.6
34	Arkansas	27.4
34	Oregon	27.4
36	Arizona	27.0
36	Connecticut	27.0
36	Mississippi	27.0
36	Virginia	27.0
40	Georgia	26.6
41	Delaware	26.5
42	Nevada	26.2
42	New Jersey	26.2
44	New Hampshire	26.0
45	Alaska	25.3
46	Texas	24.9
47	California	24.4
48	Hawaii	23.5
49	Idaho	22.9
50	Utah	19.0
	District of Columbia	46.6

Source: CQ Press using data from U.S. Bureau of the Census
"2009 American Community Survey" (http://www.census.gov/acs/www/)
*A household includes all persons who occupy a housing unit. A household consists of a single family, one person living alone, two or more families living together, or any other group of related or unrelated persons who share living arrangements.

Percent of Households Headed by Married Couples in 2009

National Percent = 49.1% of Households*

ALPHA ORDER

RANK	STATE	PERCENT
42	Alabama	47.9
20	Alaska	50.4
29	Arizona	49.4
22	Arkansas	50.3
28	California	49.5
11	Colorado	50.8
20	Connecticut	50.4
36	Delaware	48.8
43	Florida	47.7
38	Georgia	48.3
7	Hawaii	51.3
2	Idaho	57.6
37	Illinois	48.6
14	Indiana	50.5
5	Iowa	51.9
14	Kansas	50.5
14	Kentucky	50.5
49	Louisiana	45.9
26	Maine	49.8
38	Maryland	48.3
44	Massachusetts	47.2
32	Michigan	49.2
6	Minnesota	51.6
47	Mississippi	46.3
30	Missouri	49.3
24	Montana	50.1
10	Nebraska	51.0
45	Nevada	46.8
4	New Hampshire	53.5
9	New Jersey	51.1
45	New Mexico	46.8
50	New York	44.7
34	North Carolina	49.1
14	North Dakota	50.5
41	Ohio	48.0
32	Oklahoma	49.2
26	Oregon	49.8
34	Pennsylvania	49.1
48	Rhode Island	46.1
40	South Carolina	48.2
8	South Dakota	51.2
30	Tennessee	49.3
13	Texas	50.6
1	Utah	61.7
25	Vermont	49.9
11	Virginia	50.8
23	Washington	50.2
14	West Virginia	50.5
14	Wisconsin	50.5
3	Wyoming	54.5

RANK ORDER

RANK	STATE	PERCENT
1	Utah	61.7
2	Idaho	57.6
3	Wyoming	54.5
4	New Hampshire	53.5
5	Iowa	51.9
6	Minnesota	51.6
7	Hawaii	51.3
8	South Dakota	51.2
9	New Jersey	51.1
10	Nebraska	51.0
11	Colorado	50.8
11	Virginia	50.8
13	Texas	50.6
14	Indiana	50.5
14	Kansas	50.5
14	Kentucky	50.5
14	North Dakota	50.5
14	West Virginia	50.5
14	Wisconsin	50.5
20	Alaska	50.4
20	Connecticut	50.4
22	Arkansas	50.3
23	Washington	50.2
24	Montana	50.1
25	Vermont	49.9
26	Maine	49.8
26	Oregon	49.8
28	California	49.5
29	Arizona	49.4
30	Missouri	49.3
30	Tennessee	49.3
32	Michigan	49.2
32	Oklahoma	49.2
34	North Carolina	49.1
34	Pennsylvania	49.1
36	Delaware	48.8
37	Illinois	48.6
38	Georgia	48.3
38	Maryland	48.3
40	South Carolina	48.2
41	Ohio	48.0
42	Alabama	47.9
43	Florida	47.7
44	Massachusetts	47.2
45	Nevada	46.8
45	New Mexico	46.8
47	Mississippi	46.3
48	Rhode Island	46.1
49	Louisiana	45.9
50	New York	44.7
	District of Columbia	22.7

Source: CQ Press using data from U.S. Bureau of the Census
  "2009 American Community Survey" (http://www.census.gov/acs/www/)
*A household includes all persons who occupy a housing unit. A household consists of a single family, one person living alone,
two or more families living together, or any other group of related or unrelated persons who share living arrangements.

Percent of Households Headed by Single Mothers in 2009

National Percent = 7.4% of Households*

ALPHA ORDER

RANK	STATE	PERCENT
4	Alabama	8.6
17	Alaska	7.5
24	Arizona	7.1
4	Arkansas	8.6
24	California	7.1
42	Colorado	6.1
20	Connecticut	7.4
8	Delaware	8.1
24	Florida	7.1
3	Georgia	9.1
46	Hawaii	5.7
40	Idaho	6.2
24	Illinois	7.1
22	Indiana	7.3
38	Iowa	6.3
30	Kansas	6.7
9	Kentucky	8.0
2	Louisiana	9.2
31	Maine	6.6
11	Maryland	7.9
38	Massachusetts	6.3
20	Michigan	7.4
43	Minnesota	6.0
1	Mississippi	10.2
13	Missouri	7.8
47	Montana	5.6
34	Nebraska	6.5
22	Nevada	7.3
44	New Hampshire	5.8
28	New Jersey	7.0
9	New Mexico	8.0
13	New York	7.8
11	North Carolina	7.9
49	North Dakota	5.0
13	Ohio	7.8
17	Oklahoma	7.5
37	Oregon	6.4
34	Pennsylvania	6.5
16	Rhode Island	7.6
7	South Carolina	8.4
31	South Dakota	6.6
17	Tennessee	7.5
4	Texas	8.6
48	Utah	5.4
34	Vermont	6.5
29	Virginia	6.8
40	Washington	6.2
44	West Virginia	5.8
31	Wisconsin	6.6
49	Wyoming	5.0

RANK ORDER

RANK	STATE	PERCENT
1	Mississippi	10.2
2	Louisiana	9.2
3	Georgia	9.1
4	Alabama	8.6
4	Arkansas	8.6
4	Texas	8.6
7	South Carolina	8.4
8	Delaware	8.1
9	Kentucky	8.0
9	New Mexico	8.0
11	Maryland	7.9
11	North Carolina	7.9
13	Missouri	7.8
13	New York	7.8
13	Ohio	7.8
16	Rhode Island	7.6
17	Alaska	7.5
17	Oklahoma	7.5
17	Tennessee	7.5
20	Connecticut	7.4
20	Michigan	7.4
22	Indiana	7.3
22	Nevada	7.3
24	Arizona	7.1
24	California	7.1
24	Florida	7.1
24	Illinois	7.1
28	New Jersey	7.0
29	Virginia	6.8
30	Kansas	6.7
31	Maine	6.6
31	South Dakota	6.6
31	Wisconsin	6.6
34	Nebraska	6.5
34	Pennsylvania	6.5
34	Vermont	6.5
37	Oregon	6.4
38	Iowa	6.3
38	Massachusetts	6.3
40	Idaho	6.2
40	Washington	6.2
42	Colorado	6.1
43	Minnesota	6.0
44	New Hampshire	5.8
44	West Virginia	5.8
46	Hawaii	5.7
47	Montana	5.6
48	Utah	5.4
49	North Dakota	5.0
49	Wyoming	5.0

District of Columbia 8.7

Source: CQ Press using data from U.S. Bureau of the Census
   "2009 American Community Survey" (http://www.census.gov/acs/www/)
*No spouse present in household with children under 18 years old. A household includes all persons who occupy a housing unit.
A household consists of a single family, one person living alone, two or more families living together, or any other group of
related or unrelated persons who share living arrangements.

Percent of Households Headed by Single Fathers in 2009

National Percent = 2.3% of Households*

ALPHA ORDER

RANK	STATE	PERCENT
45	Alabama	1.9
2	Alaska	3.0
4	Arizona	2.8
37	Arkansas	2.0
4	California	2.8
37	Colorado	2.0
48	Connecticut	1.8
22	Delaware	2.2
32	Florida	2.1
22	Georgia	2.2
8	Hawaii	2.7
9	Idaho	2.6
22	Illinois	2.2
12	Indiana	2.4
17	Iowa	2.3
9	Kansas	2.6
37	Kentucky	2.0
17	Louisiana	2.3
22	Maine	2.2
37	Maryland	2.0
50	Massachusetts	1.7
22	Michigan	2.2
32	Minnesota	2.1
9	Mississippi	2.6
17	Missouri	2.3
22	Montana	2.2
45	Nebraska	1.9
2	Nevada	3.0
32	New Hampshire	2.1
37	New Jersey	2.0
1	New Mexico	3.3
37	New York	2.0
17	North Carolina	2.3
45	North Dakota	1.9
22	Ohio	2.2
4	Oklahoma	2.8
22	Oregon	2.2
37	Pennsylvania	2.0
22	Rhode Island	2.2
22	South Carolina	2.2
48	South Dakota	1.8
17	Tennessee	2.3
12	Texas	2.4
32	Utah	2.1
12	Vermont	2.4
32	Virginia	2.1
12	Washington	2.4
37	West Virginia	2.0
12	Wisconsin	2.4
4	Wyoming	2.8

RANK ORDER

RANK	STATE	PERCENT
1	New Mexico	3.3
2	Alaska	3.0
2	Nevada	3.0
4	Arizona	2.8
4	California	2.8
4	Oklahoma	2.8
4	Wyoming	2.8
8	Hawaii	2.7
9	Idaho	2.6
9	Kansas	2.6
9	Mississippi	2.6
12	Indiana	2.4
12	Texas	2.4
12	Vermont	2.4
12	Washington	2.4
12	Wisconsin	2.4
17	Iowa	2.3
17	Louisiana	2.3
17	Missouri	2.3
17	North Carolina	2.3
17	Tennessee	2.3
22	Delaware	2.2
22	Georgia	2.2
22	Illinois	2.2
22	Maine	2.2
22	Michigan	2.2
22	Montana	2.2
22	Ohio	2.2
22	Oregon	2.2
22	Rhode Island	2.2
22	South Carolina	2.2
32	Florida	2.1
32	Minnesota	2.1
32	New Hampshire	2.1
32	Utah	2.1
32	Virginia	2.1
37	Arkansas	2.0
37	Colorado	2.0
37	Kentucky	2.0
37	Maryland	2.0
37	New Jersey	2.0
37	New York	2.0
37	Pennsylvania	2.0
37	West Virginia	2.0
45	Alabama	1.9
45	Nebraska	1.9
45	North Dakota	1.9
48	Connecticut	1.8
48	South Dakota	1.8
50	Massachusetts	1.7

District of Columbia 1.6

Source: CQ Press using data from U.S. Bureau of the Census
   "2009 American Community Survey" (http://www.census.gov/acs/www/)
*No spouse present in household with children under 18 years old. A household includes all persons who occupy a housing unit.
A household consists of a single family, one person living alone, two or more families living together, or any other group of
related or unrelated persons who share living arrangements.

Housing Units in 2009

National Total = 129,969,653 Housing Units*

ALPHA ORDER

RANK	STATE	HOUSING UNITS	% of USA
22	Alabama	2,182,343	1.7%
49	Alaska	283,878	0.2%
16	Arizona	2,752,991	2.1%
31	Arkansas	1,310,624	1.0%
1	California	13,433,718	10.3%
23	Colorado	2,167,850	1.7%
29	Connecticut	1,445,825	1.1%
45	Delaware	396,222	0.3%
3	Florida	8,852,754	6.8%
10	Georgia	4,063,548	3.1%
42	Hawaii	515,625	0.4%
40	Idaho	647,502	0.5%
6	Illinois	5,292,016	4.1%
14	Indiana	2,809,559	2.2%
30	Iowa	1,344,080	1.0%
33	Kansas	1,234,057	0.9%
26	Kentucky	1,934,973	1.5%
25	Louisiana	1,963,354	1.5%
39	Maine	704,578	0.5%
20	Maryland	2,341,194	1.8%
17	Massachusetts	2,748,321	2.1%
8	Michigan	4,541,680	3.5%
21	Minnesota	2,332,916	1.8%
32	Mississippi	1,282,090	1.0%
18	Missouri	2,682,066	2.1%
44	Montana	441,279	0.3%
38	Nebraska	791,863	0.6%
34	Nevada	1,137,997	0.9%
41	New Hampshire	600,090	0.5%
11	New Jersey	3,526,453	2.7%
37	New Mexico	878,043	0.7%
4	New York	8,017,881	6.2%
9	North Carolina	4,258,625	3.3%
47	North Dakota	316,435	0.2%
7	Ohio	5,094,126	3.9%
27	Oklahoma	1,650,387	1.3%
28	Oregon	1,639,498	1.3%
5	Pennsylvania	5,518,558	4.2%
43	Rhode Island	452,191	0.3%
24	South Carolina	2,084,231	1.6%
46	South Dakota	365,563	0.3%
15	Tennessee	2,780,857	2.1%
2	Texas	9,724,220	7.5%
35	Utah	952,999	0.7%
48	Vermont	314,246	0.2%
12	Virginia	3,330,465	2.6%
13	Washington	2,814,238	2.2%
36	West Virginia	893,771	0.7%
19	Wisconsin	2,587,350	2.0%
50	Wyoming	249,388	0.2%

RANK ORDER

RANK	STATE	HOUSING UNITS	% of USA
1	California	13,433,718	10.3%
2	Texas	9,724,220	7.5%
3	Florida	8,852,754	6.8%
4	New York	8,017,881	6.2%
5	Pennsylvania	5,518,558	4.2%
6	Illinois	5,292,016	4.1%
7	Ohio	5,094,126	3.9%
8	Michigan	4,541,680	3.5%
9	North Carolina	4,258,625	3.3%
10	Georgia	4,063,548	3.1%
11	New Jersey	3,526,453	2.7%
12	Virginia	3,330,465	2.6%
13	Washington	2,814,238	2.2%
14	Indiana	2,809,559	2.2%
15	Tennessee	2,780,857	2.1%
16	Arizona	2,752,991	2.1%
17	Massachusetts	2,748,321	2.1%
18	Missouri	2,682,066	2.1%
19	Wisconsin	2,587,350	2.0%
20	Maryland	2,341,194	1.8%
21	Minnesota	2,332,916	1.8%
22	Alabama	2,182,343	1.7%
23	Colorado	2,167,850	1.7%
24	South Carolina	2,084,231	1.6%
25	Louisiana	1,963,354	1.5%
26	Kentucky	1,934,973	1.5%
27	Oklahoma	1,650,387	1.3%
28	Oregon	1,639,498	1.3%
29	Connecticut	1,445,825	1.1%
30	Iowa	1,344,080	1.0%
31	Arkansas	1,310,624	1.0%
32	Mississippi	1,282,090	1.0%
33	Kansas	1,234,057	0.9%
34	Nevada	1,137,997	0.9%
35	Utah	952,999	0.7%
36	West Virginia	893,771	0.7%
37	New Mexico	878,043	0.7%
38	Nebraska	791,863	0.6%
39	Maine	704,578	0.5%
40	Idaho	647,502	0.5%
41	New Hampshire	600,090	0.5%
42	Hawaii	515,625	0.4%
43	Rhode Island	452,191	0.3%
44	Montana	441,279	0.3%
45	Delaware	396,222	0.3%
46	South Dakota	365,563	0.3%
47	North Dakota	316,435	0.2%
48	Vermont	314,246	0.2%
49	Alaska	283,878	0.2%
50	Wyoming	249,388	0.2%
	District of Columbia	285,135	0.2%

Source: U.S. Bureau of the Census
    "Housing Unit Estimates" (http://www.census.gov/popest/housing/HU-EST2009.html)
*A housing unit is a house, an apartment, a mobile home, a group of rooms, or a single room that is occupied (or if vacant, is intended for occupancy) as separate living quarters. Separate living quarters are those in which the occupants live and eat separately from any other persons in the building and which have direct access from the outside of the building or through a common hall.

Housing Units per Square Mile in 2009

National Average = 36.8 Housing Units*

ALPHA ORDER

RANK	STATE	HOUSING UNITS
25	Alabama	43.1
50	Alaska	0.5
34	Arizona	24.2
33	Arkansas	25.2
13	California	86.2
38	Colorado	20.9
4	Connecticut	298.7
6	Delaware	203.3
8	Florida	165.2
18	Georgia	70.7
16	Hawaii	80.2
44	Idaho	7.8
11	Illinois	95.3
17	Indiana	78.4
35	Iowa	24.1
40	Kansas	15.1
22	Kentucky	49.0
24	Louisiana	45.4
37	Maine	22.8
5	Maryland	241.2
3	Massachusetts	352.3
15	Michigan	80.3
31	Minnesota	29.3
32	Mississippi	27.3
27	Missouri	39.0
48	Montana	3.0
43	Nebraska	10.3
42	Nevada	10.4
21	New Hampshire	67.0
1	New Jersey	479.5
45	New Mexico	7.2
7	New York	170.1
12	North Carolina	87.6
47	North Dakota	4.6
9	Ohio	124.7
35	Oklahoma	24.1
39	Oregon	17.1
10	Pennsylvania	123.4
2	Rhode Island	437.3
19	South Carolina	69.3
46	South Dakota	4.8
20	Tennessee	67.4
28	Texas	37.2
41	Utah	11.6
30	Vermont	34.1
14	Virginia	84.3
26	Washington	42.4
28	West Virginia	37.2
23	Wisconsin	47.8
49	Wyoming	2.6

RANK ORDER

RANK	STATE	HOUSING UNITS
1	New Jersey	479.5
2	Rhode Island	437.3
3	Massachusetts	352.3
4	Connecticut	298.7
5	Maryland	241.2
6	Delaware	203.3
7	New York	170.1
8	Florida	165.2
9	Ohio	124.7
10	Pennsylvania	123.4
11	Illinois	95.3
12	North Carolina	87.6
13	California	86.2
14	Virginia	84.3
15	Michigan	80.3
16	Hawaii	80.2
17	Indiana	78.4
18	Georgia	70.7
19	South Carolina	69.3
20	Tennessee	67.4
21	New Hampshire	67.0
22	Kentucky	49.0
23	Wisconsin	47.8
24	Louisiana	45.4
25	Alabama	43.1
26	Washington	42.4
27	Missouri	39.0
28	Texas	37.2
28	West Virginia	37.2
30	Vermont	34.1
31	Minnesota	29.3
32	Mississippi	27.3
33	Arkansas	25.2
34	Arizona	24.2
35	Iowa	24.1
35	Oklahoma	24.1
37	Maine	22.8
38	Colorado	20.9
39	Oregon	17.1
40	Kansas	15.1
41	Utah	11.6
42	Nevada	10.4
43	Nebraska	10.3
44	Idaho	7.8
45	New Mexico	7.2
46	South Dakota	4.8
47	North Dakota	4.6
48	Montana	3.0
49	Wyoming	2.6
50	Alaska	0.5

District of Columbia   4,674.3

Source: CQ Press using data from U.S. Bureau of the Census
    "Housing Unit Estimates" (http://www.census.gov/popest/housing/HU-EST2009.html)
*Based on land area. A housing unit is a house, an apartment, a mobile home, a group of rooms, or a single room that is occupied (or if vacant, is intended for occupancy) as separate living quarters. Separate living quarters are those in which the occupants live and eat separately from any other persons in the building and which have direct access from the outside of the building or through a common hall.

Percent of Housing Units That Are Owner-Occupied: 2009

National Percent = 65.9% of Housing Units*

ALPHA ORDER

RANK	STATE	PERCENT
15	Alabama	69.6
41	Alaska	65.2
35	Arizona	67.1
39	Arkansas	66.0
49	California	56.6
36	Colorado	67.0
22	Connecticut	68.8
2	Delaware	73.6
25	Florida	68.5
36	Georgia	67.0
48	Hawaii	56.7
8	Idaho	71.5
27	Illinois	68.0
13	Indiana	70.4
7	Iowa	72.1
31	Kansas	67.8
23	Kentucky	68.6
29	Louisiana	67.9
5	Maine	72.7
23	Maryland	68.6
43	Massachusetts	64.2
4	Michigan	73.2
1	Minnesota	73.7
16	Mississippi	69.5
20	Missouri	69.1
18	Montana	69.2
32	Nebraska	67.2
47	Nevada	59.3
6	New Hampshire	72.5
38	New Jersey	66.1
17	New Mexico	69.3
50	New York	55.0
32	North Carolina	67.2
39	North Dakota	66.0
27	Ohio	68.0
32	Oklahoma	67.2
46	Oregon	63.1
12	Pennsylvania	70.5
45	Rhode Island	63.4
14	South Carolina	70.1
29	South Dakota	67.9
18	Tennessee	69.2
44	Texas	63.7
8	Utah	71.5
10	Vermont	71.3
26	Virginia	68.1
42	Washington	64.3
2	West Virginia	73.6
21	Wisconsin	69.0
11	Wyoming	70.9

RANK ORDER

RANK	STATE	PERCENT
1	Minnesota	73.7
2	Delaware	73.6
2	West Virginia	73.6
4	Michigan	73.2
5	Maine	72.7
6	New Hampshire	72.5
7	Iowa	72.1
8	Idaho	71.5
8	Utah	71.5
10	Vermont	71.3
11	Wyoming	70.9
12	Pennsylvania	70.5
13	Indiana	70.4
14	South Carolina	70.1
15	Alabama	69.6
16	Mississippi	69.5
17	New Mexico	69.3
18	Montana	69.2
18	Tennessee	69.2
20	Missouri	69.1
21	Wisconsin	69.0
22	Connecticut	68.8
23	Kentucky	68.6
23	Maryland	68.6
25	Florida	68.5
26	Virginia	68.1
27	Illinois	68.0
27	Ohio	68.0
29	Louisiana	67.9
29	South Dakota	67.9
31	Kansas	67.8
32	Nebraska	67.2
32	North Carolina	67.2
32	Oklahoma	67.2
35	Arizona	67.1
36	Colorado	67.0
36	Georgia	67.0
38	New Jersey	66.1
39	Arkansas	66.0
39	North Dakota	66.0
41	Alaska	65.2
42	Washington	64.3
43	Massachusetts	64.2
44	Texas	63.7
45	Rhode Island	63.4
46	Oregon	63.1
47	Nevada	59.3
48	Hawaii	56.7
49	California	56.6
50	New York	55.0
	District of Columbia	44.8

Source: U.S. Bureau of the Census
   "2009 American Community Survey" (http://www.census.gov/acs/www/)
*For occupied housing units.

New Housing Units Authorized in 2010

National Total = 598,033 Units*

ALPHA ORDER

RANK	STATE	UNITS	% of USA
21	Alabama	10,233	1.7%
50	Alaska	904	0.2%
15	Arizona	12,235	2.0%
30	Arkansas	6,905	1.2%
2	California	43,128	7.2%
18	Colorado	11,779	2.0%
38	Connecticut	3,765	0.6%
41	Delaware	3,076	0.5%
3	Florida	39,524	6.6%
9	Georgia	17,731	3.0%
40	Hawaii	3,430	0.6%
35	Idaho	4,584	0.8%
19	Illinois	11,596	1.9%
14	Indiana	12,988	2.2%
28	Iowa	7,312	1.2%
36	Kansas	4,523	0.8%
31	Kentucky	6,844	1.1%
20	Louisiana	11,515	1.9%
42	Maine	2,962	0.5%
16	Maryland	12,183	2.0%
25	Massachusetts	8,648	1.4%
24	Michigan	9,256	1.5%
22	Minnesota	9,656	1.6%
34	Mississippi	4,794	0.8%
27	Missouri	8,260	1.4%
45	Montana	2,196	0.4%
33	Nebraska	5,013	0.8%
32	Nevada	6,402	1.1%
44	New Hampshire	2,737	0.5%
13	New Jersey	13,318	2.2%
37	New Mexico	4,511	0.8%
8	New York	20,205	3.4%
4	North Carolina	33,728	5.6%
39	North Dakota	3,558	0.6%
12	Ohio	13,509	2.3%
26	Oklahoma	8,267	1.4%
29	Oregon	7,302	1.2%
5	Pennsylvania	21,339	3.6%
49	Rhode Island	949	0.2%
11	South Carolina	14,452	2.4%
43	South Dakota	2,913	0.5%
10	Tennessee	16,325	2.7%
1	Texas	84,753	14.2%
23	Utah	9,441	1.6%
48	Vermont	1,530	0.3%
6	Virginia	21,215	3.5%
7	Washington	20,235	3.4%
47	West Virginia	1,673	0.3%
17	Wisconsin	11,834	2.0%
46	Wyoming	2,126	0.4%

RANK ORDER

RANK	STATE	UNITS	% of USA
1	Texas	84,753	14.2%
2	California	43,128	7.2%
3	Florida	39,524	6.6%
4	North Carolina	33,728	5.6%
5	Pennsylvania	21,339	3.6%
6	Virginia	21,215	3.5%
7	Washington	20,235	3.4%
8	New York	20,205	3.4%
9	Georgia	17,731	3.0%
10	Tennessee	16,325	2.7%
11	South Carolina	14,452	2.4%
12	Ohio	13,509	2.3%
13	New Jersey	13,318	2.2%
14	Indiana	12,988	2.2%
15	Arizona	12,235	2.0%
16	Maryland	12,183	2.0%
17	Wisconsin	11,834	2.0%
18	Colorado	11,779	2.0%
19	Illinois	11,596	1.9%
20	Louisiana	11,515	1.9%
21	Alabama	10,233	1.7%
22	Minnesota	9,656	1.6%
23	Utah	9,441	1.6%
24	Michigan	9,256	1.5%
25	Massachusetts	8,648	1.4%
26	Oklahoma	8,267	1.4%
27	Missouri	8,260	1.4%
28	Iowa	7,312	1.2%
29	Oregon	7,302	1.2%
30	Arkansas	6,905	1.2%
31	Kentucky	6,844	1.1%
32	Nevada	6,402	1.1%
33	Nebraska	5,013	0.8%
34	Mississippi	4,794	0.8%
35	Idaho	4,584	0.8%
36	Kansas	4,523	0.8%
37	New Mexico	4,511	0.8%
38	Connecticut	3,765	0.6%
39	North Dakota	3,558	0.6%
40	Hawaii	3,430	0.6%
41	Delaware	3,076	0.5%
42	Maine	2,962	0.5%
43	South Dakota	2,913	0.5%
44	New Hampshire	2,737	0.5%
45	Montana	2,196	0.4%
46	Wyoming	2,126	0.4%
47	West Virginia	1,673	0.3%
48	Vermont	1,530	0.3%
49	Rhode Island	949	0.2%
50	Alaska	904	0.2%
	District of Columbia	671	0.1%

Source: U.S. Bureau of the Census
"New Privately Owned Housing Units Authorized" (http://www.census.gov/const/www/C40/table2.html)
*Preliminary and unadjusted year to date as of December 2010. Includes single and multifamily privately owned units. Based on approximately 19,000 places in the U.S. having building permit systems.

Value of New Housing Units Authorized in 2010

National Total = $101,007,616,000*

ALPHA ORDER

RANK	STATE	VALUE	% of USA
26	Alabama	$1,452,819,000	1.4%
49	Alaska	205,182,000	0.2%
12	Arizona	2,405,269,000	2.4%
31	Arkansas	853,976,000	0.8%
2	California	8,968,342,000	8.9%
10	Colorado	2,664,197,000	2.6%
33	Connecticut	804,309,000	0.8%
45	Delaware	364,785,000	0.4%
3	Florida	7,842,807,000	7.8%
9	Georgia	2,703,206,000	2.7%
37	Hawaii	769,341,000	0.8%
36	Idaho	773,690,000	0.8%
13	Illinois	2,359,509,000	2.3%
17	Indiana	1,988,469,000	2.0%
29	Iowa	1,190,531,000	1.2%
38	Kansas	745,742,000	0.7%
30	Kentucky	988,821,000	1.0%
20	Louisiana	1,808,046,000	1.8%
41	Maine	479,975,000	0.5%
18	Maryland	1,943,062,000	1.9%
23	Massachusetts	1,683,107,000	1.7%
24	Michigan	1,529,056,000	1.5%
21	Minnesota	1,752,087,000	1.7%
39	Mississippi	646,253,000	0.6%
27	Missouri	1,275,422,000	1.3%
46	Montana	328,961,000	0.3%
35	Nebraska	776,403,000	0.8%
32	Nevada	827,187,000	0.8%
40	New Hampshire	488,812,000	0.5%
16	New Jersey	2,016,723,000	2.0%
34	New Mexico	777,343,000	0.8%
8	New York	3,190,873,000	3.2%
4	North Carolina	5,017,250,000	5.0%
42	North Dakota	450,459,000	0.4%
14	Ohio	2,299,019,000	2.3%
28	Oklahoma	1,214,189,000	1.2%
25	Oregon	1,472,770,000	1.5%
6	Pennsylvania	3,465,368,000	3.4%
50	Rhode Island	156,811,000	0.2%
11	South Carolina	2,524,555,000	2.5%
43	South Dakota	431,293,000	0.4%
15	Tennessee	2,173,979,000	2.2%
1	Texas	13,331,790,000	13.2%
22	Utah	1,719,933,000	1.7%
48	Vermont	247,751,000	0.2%
7	Virginia	3,248,894,000	3.2%
5	Washington	4,011,038,000	4.0%
47	West Virginia	269,407,000	0.3%
19	Wisconsin	1,858,306,000	1.8%
44	Wyoming	414,065,000	0.4%

RANK ORDER

RANK	STATE	VALUE	% of USA
1	Texas	$13,331,790,000	13.2%
2	California	8,968,342,000	8.9%
3	Florida	7,842,807,000	7.8%
4	North Carolina	5,017,250,000	5.0%
5	Washington	4,011,038,000	4.0%
6	Pennsylvania	3,465,368,000	3.4%
7	Virginia	3,248,894,000	3.2%
8	New York	3,190,873,000	3.2%
9	Georgia	2,703,206,000	2.7%
10	Colorado	2,664,197,000	2.6%
11	South Carolina	2,524,555,000	2.5%
12	Arizona	2,405,269,000	2.4%
13	Illinois	2,359,509,000	2.3%
14	Ohio	2,299,019,000	2.3%
15	Tennessee	2,173,979,000	2.2%
16	New Jersey	2,016,723,000	2.0%
17	Indiana	1,988,469,000	2.0%
18	Maryland	1,943,062,000	1.9%
19	Wisconsin	1,858,306,000	1.8%
20	Louisiana	1,808,046,000	1.8%
21	Minnesota	1,752,087,000	1.7%
22	Utah	1,719,933,000	1.7%
23	Massachusetts	1,683,107,000	1.7%
24	Michigan	1,529,056,000	1.5%
25	Oregon	1,472,770,000	1.5%
26	Alabama	1,452,819,000	1.4%
27	Missouri	1,275,422,000	1.3%
28	Oklahoma	1,214,189,000	1.2%
29	Iowa	1,190,531,000	1.2%
30	Kentucky	988,821,000	1.0%
31	Arkansas	853,976,000	0.8%
32	Nevada	827,187,000	0.8%
33	Connecticut	804,309,000	0.8%
34	New Mexico	777,343,000	0.8%
35	Nebraska	776,403,000	0.8%
36	Idaho	773,690,000	0.8%
37	Hawaii	769,341,000	0.8%
38	Kansas	745,742,000	0.7%
39	Mississippi	646,253,000	0.6%
40	New Hampshire	488,812,000	0.5%
41	Maine	479,975,000	0.5%
42	North Dakota	450,459,000	0.4%
43	South Dakota	431,293,000	0.4%
44	Wyoming	414,065,000	0.4%
45	Delaware	364,785,000	0.4%
46	Montana	328,961,000	0.3%
47	West Virginia	269,407,000	0.3%
48	Vermont	247,751,000	0.2%
49	Alaska	205,182,000	0.2%
50	Rhode Island	156,811,000	0.2%
	District of Columbia	96,433,000	0.1%

Source: U.S. Bureau of the Census
    "New Privately Owned Housing Units Authorized" (http://www.census.gov/const/www/C40/table2.html)
*Preliminary and unadjusted year to date as of December 2010. Includes single and multifamily privately owned units. Based on approximately 19,000 places in the U.S. having building permit systems.

Average Value of New Housing Units in 2010

National Average = $168,900 per Unit*

ALPHA ORDER			RANK ORDER		
RANK	STATE	VALUE	RANK	STATE	VALUE
44	Alabama	$141,974	1	Alaska	$226,971
1	Alaska	226,971	2	Colorado	226,182
10	Arizona	196,589	3	Hawaii	224,298
49	Arkansas	123,675	4	Connecticut	213,628
5	California	207,947	5	California	207,947
2	Colorado	226,182	6	Illinois	203,476
4	Connecticut	213,628	7	Oregon	201,694
50	Delaware	118,591	8	Florida	198,432
8	Florida	198,432	9	Washington	198,223
37	Georgia	152,456	10	Arizona	196,589
3	Hawaii	224,298	11	Wyoming	194,762
19	Idaho	168,781	12	Massachusetts	194,624
6	Illinois	203,476	13	Utah	182,177
36	Indiana	153,100	14	Minnesota	181,451
23	Iowa	162,819	15	New Hampshire	178,594
22	Kansas	164,878	16	South Carolina	174,686
43	Kentucky	144,480	17	New Mexico	172,322
32	Louisiana	157,017	18	Ohio	170,184
25	Maine	162,044	19	Idaho	168,781
28	Maryland	159,490	20	Rhode Island	165,238
12	Massachusetts	194,624	21	Michigan	165,196
21	Michigan	165,196	22	Kansas	164,878
14	Minnesota	181,451	23	Iowa	162,819
45	Mississippi	134,805	24	Pennsylvania	162,396
34	Missouri	154,409	25	Maine	162,044
39	Montana	149,800	26	Vermont	161,929
33	Nebraska	154,878	27	West Virginia	161,032
47	Nevada	129,208	28	Maryland	159,490
15	New Hampshire	178,594	29	New York	157,925
38	New Jersey	151,428	30	Texas	157,302
17	New Mexico	172,322	31	Wisconsin	157,031
29	New York	157,925	32	Louisiana	157,017
40	North Carolina	148,756	33	Nebraska	154,878
48	North Dakota	126,605	34	Missouri	154,409
18	Ohio	170,184	35	Virginia	153,141
42	Oklahoma	146,872	36	Indiana	153,100
7	Oregon	201,694	37	Georgia	152,456
24	Pennsylvania	162,396	38	New Jersey	151,428
20	Rhode Island	165,238	39	Montana	149,800
16	South Carolina	174,686	40	North Carolina	148,756
41	South Dakota	148,058	41	South Dakota	148,058
46	Tennessee	133,169	42	Oklahoma	146,872
30	Texas	157,302	43	Kentucky	144,480
13	Utah	182,177	44	Alabama	141,974
26	Vermont	161,929	45	Mississippi	134,805
35	Virginia	153,141	46	Tennessee	133,169
9	Washington	198,223	47	Nevada	129,208
27	West Virginia	161,032	48	North Dakota	126,605
31	Wisconsin	157,031	49	Arkansas	123,675
11	Wyoming	194,762	50	Delaware	118,591
				District of Columbia	143,715

Source: CQ Press using data from U.S. Bureau of the Census
    "New Privately Owned Housing Units Authorized" (http://www.census.gov/const/www/C40/table2.html)
*Preliminary and unadjusted year to date as of December 2010. Includes single and multifamily privately owned units. Based
on approximately 19,000 places in the U.S. having building permit systems.

Median Value of Owner-Occupied Housing in 2009

National Median = $185,200*

ALPHA ORDER

RANK ORDER

RANK	STATE	MEDIAN		RANK	STATE	MEDIAN
44	Alabama	$119,600		1	Hawaii	$517,600
15	Alaska	232,900		2	California	384,200
21	Arizona	187,700		3	New Jersey	348,300
48	Arkansas	102,900		4	Massachusetts	338,500
2	California	384,200		5	Maryland	318,600
14	Colorado	237,800		6	New York	306,000
7	Connecticut	291,200		7	Connecticut	291,200
13	Delaware	249,400		8	Washington	287,200
23	Florida	182,400		9	Rhode Island	267,100
29	Georgia	162,800		10	Oregon	257,400
1	Hawaii	517,600		11	Virginia	252,600
26	Idaho	171,700		12	New Hampshire	249,700
19	Illinois	202,200		13	Delaware	249,400
42	Indiana	123,100		14	Colorado	237,800
43	Iowa	122,000		15	Alaska	232,900
40	Kansas	125,500		16	Utah	224,700
45	Kentucky	117,800		17	Vermont	216,300
35	Louisiana	135,400		18	Nevada	207,600
24	Maine	177,500		19	Illinois	202,200
5	Maryland	318,600		20	Minnesota	200,400
4	Massachusetts	338,500		21	Arizona	187,700
37	Michigan	132,200		22	Wyoming	184,000
20	Minnesota	200,400		23	Florida	182,400
49	Mississippi	98,000		24	Maine	177,500
32	Missouri	139,700		25	Montana	176,300
25	Montana	176,300		26	Idaho	171,700
41	Nebraska	123,300		27	Wisconsin	170,800
18	Nevada	207,600		28	Pennsylvania	164,700
12	New Hampshire	249,700		29	Georgia	162,800
3	New Jersey	348,300		30	New Mexico	160,900
30	New Mexico	160,900		31	North Carolina	155,500
6	New York	306,000		32	Missouri	139,700
31	North Carolina	155,500		33	South Carolina	137,500
46	North Dakota	116,800		34	Tennessee	137,300
36	Ohio	134,600		35	Louisiana	135,400
47	Oklahoma	107,700		36	Ohio	134,600
10	Oregon	257,400		37	Michigan	132,200
28	Pennsylvania	164,700		38	South Dakota	126,200
9	Rhode Island	267,100		39	Texas	125,800
33	South Carolina	137,500		40	Kansas	125,500
38	South Dakota	126,200		41	Nebraska	123,300
34	Tennessee	137,300		42	Indiana	123,100
39	Texas	125,800		43	Iowa	122,000
16	Utah	224,700		44	Alabama	119,600
17	Vermont	216,300		45	Kentucky	117,800
11	Virginia	252,600		46	North Dakota	116,800
8	Washington	287,200		47	Oklahoma	107,700
50	West Virginia	94,500		48	Arkansas	102,900
27	Wisconsin	170,800		49	Mississippi	98,000
22	Wyoming	184,000		50	West Virginia	94,500
					District of Columbia	443,700

Source: U.S. Bureau of the Census
   "2009 American Community Survey" (http://www.census.gov/acs/www/)
*Housing units with a mortgage.

Percent Change in House Prices: 2009 to 2010

National Percent Change = 3.2% Decrease*

ALPHA ORDER

RANK	STATE	PERCENT CHANGE
32	Alabama	(3.6)
2	Alaska	4.2
48	Arizona	(9.3)
37	Arkansas	(4.4)
18	California	(1.5)
27	Colorado	(2.9)
25	Connecticut	(2.6)
42	Delaware	(6.0)
44	Florida	(6.5)
49	Georgia	(9.5)
43	Hawaii	(6.1)
50	Idaho	(9.8)
33	Illinois	(3.7)
10	Indiana	0.1
23	Iowa	(2.2)
20	Kansas	(1.7)
9	Kentucky	0.2
4	Louisiana	1.7
5	Maine	1.2
39	Maryland	(5.4)
7	Massachusetts	0.6
31	Michigan	(3.5)
22	Minnesota	(1.9)
30	Mississippi	(3.2)
15	Missouri	(1.1)
28	Montana	(3.0)
17	Nebraska	(1.3)
45	Nevada	(6.7)
12	New Hampshire	(0.6)
16	New Jersey	(1.2)
34	New Mexico	(3.9)
14	New York	(0.7)
39	North Carolina	(5.4)
3	North Dakota	3.9
28	Ohio	(3.0)
12	Oklahoma	(0.6)
47	Oregon	(8.1)
19	Pennsylvania	(1.6)
20	Rhode Island	(1.7)
46	South Carolina	(7.7)
8	South Dakota	0.3
26	Tennessee	(2.7)
6	Texas	1.1
41	Utah	(5.7)
36	Vermont	(4.1)
11	Virginia	(0.5)
35	Washington	(4.0)
1	West Virginia	4.4
24	Wisconsin	(2.3)
37	Wyoming	(4.4)

RANK ORDER

RANK	STATE	PERCENT CHANGE
1	West Virginia	4.4
2	Alaska	4.2
3	North Dakota	3.9
4	Louisiana	1.7
5	Maine	1.2
6	Texas	1.1
7	Massachusetts	0.6
8	South Dakota	0.3
9	Kentucky	0.2
10	Indiana	0.1
11	Virginia	(0.5)
12	New Hampshire	(0.6)
12	Oklahoma	(0.6)
14	New York	(0.7)
15	Missouri	(1.1)
16	New Jersey	(1.2)
17	Nebraska	(1.3)
18	California	(1.5)
19	Pennsylvania	(1.6)
20	Kansas	(1.7)
20	Rhode Island	(1.7)
22	Minnesota	(1.9)
23	Iowa	(2.2)
24	Wisconsin	(2.3)
25	Connecticut	(2.6)
26	Tennessee	(2.7)
27	Colorado	(2.9)
28	Montana	(3.0)
28	Ohio	(3.0)
30	Mississippi	(3.2)
31	Michigan	(3.5)
32	Alabama	(3.6)
33	Illinois	(3.7)
34	New Mexico	(3.9)
35	Washington	(4.0)
36	Vermont	(4.1)
37	Arkansas	(4.4)
37	Wyoming	(4.4)
39	Maryland	(5.4)
39	North Carolina	(5.4)
41	Utah	(5.7)
42	Delaware	(6.0)
43	Hawaii	(6.1)
44	Florida	(6.5)
45	Nevada	(6.7)
46	South Carolina	(7.7)
47	Oregon	(8.1)
48	Arizona	(9.3)
49	Georgia	(9.5)
50	Idaho	(9.8)

District of Columbia 5.3

Source: Federal Housing Finance Agency
  "House Price Index" (http://www.fhfa.gov/Default.aspx?Page=14)
*Single-family house prices. As of September 30, 2010.

Percent Change in House Prices: 2006 to 2010

National Percent Change = 8.4% Decrease*

<table>
<tr><td colspan="3">ALPHA ORDER</td><td colspan="3">RANK ORDER</td></tr>
<tr><td>RANK</td><td>STATE</td><td>PERCENT CHANGE</td><td>RANK</td><td>STATE</td><td>PERCENT CHANGE</td></tr>
<tr><td>13</td><td>Alabama</td><td>4.2</td><td>1</td><td>North Dakota</td><td>19.5</td></tr>
<tr><td>8</td><td>Alaska</td><td>10.5</td><td>2</td><td>Louisiana</td><td>16.2</td></tr>
<tr><td>47</td><td>Arizona</td><td>(35.7)</td><td>3</td><td>Texas</td><td>13.7</td></tr>
<tr><td>27</td><td>Arkansas</td><td>(1.6)</td><td>4</td><td>Oklahoma</td><td>11.9</td></tr>
<tr><td>49</td><td>California</td><td>(39.7)</td><td>5</td><td>Wyoming</td><td>11.8</td></tr>
<tr><td>24</td><td>Colorado</td><td>(0.7)</td><td>6</td><td>Montana</td><td>10.9</td></tr>
<tr><td>37</td><td>Connecticut</td><td>(9.3)</td><td>7</td><td>South Dakota</td><td>10.8</td></tr>
<tr><td>34</td><td>Delaware</td><td>(7.5)</td><td>8</td><td>Alaska</td><td>10.5</td></tr>
<tr><td>48</td><td>Florida</td><td>(36.6)</td><td>9</td><td>West Virginia</td><td>9.3</td></tr>
<tr><td>41</td><td>Georgia</td><td>(13.4)</td><td>10</td><td>New Mexico</td><td>5.1</td></tr>
<tr><td>39</td><td>Hawaii</td><td>(11.0)</td><td>11</td><td>North Carolina</td><td>4.5</td></tr>
<tr><td>32</td><td>Idaho</td><td>(4.4)</td><td>12</td><td>Kansas</td><td>4.4</td></tr>
<tr><td>35</td><td>Illinois</td><td>(7.9)</td><td>13</td><td>Alabama</td><td>4.2</td></tr>
<tr><td>26</td><td>Indiana</td><td>(1.5)</td><td>13</td><td>Kentucky</td><td>4.2</td></tr>
<tr><td>18</td><td>Iowa</td><td>2.9</td><td>15</td><td>Utah</td><td>3.7</td></tr>
<tr><td>12</td><td>Kansas</td><td>4.4</td><td>16</td><td>Tennessee</td><td>3.3</td></tr>
<tr><td>13</td><td>Kentucky</td><td>4.2</td><td>17</td><td>Mississippi</td><td>3.0</td></tr>
<tr><td>2</td><td>Louisiana</td><td>16.2</td><td>18</td><td>Iowa</td><td>2.9</td></tr>
<tr><td>29</td><td>Maine</td><td>(3.1)</td><td>19</td><td>Pennsylvania</td><td>2.4</td></tr>
<tr><td>44</td><td>Maryland</td><td>(14.8)</td><td>20</td><td>Vermont</td><td>1.4</td></tr>
<tr><td>40</td><td>Massachusetts</td><td>(11.9)</td><td>21</td><td>Nebraska</td><td>0.8</td></tr>
<tr><td>46</td><td>Michigan</td><td>(26.8)</td><td>22</td><td>South Carolina</td><td>0.7</td></tr>
<tr><td>42</td><td>Minnesota</td><td>(13.5)</td><td>23</td><td>Washington</td><td>(0.2)</td></tr>
<tr><td>17</td><td>Mississippi</td><td>3.0</td><td>24</td><td>Colorado</td><td>(0.7)</td></tr>
<tr><td>27</td><td>Missouri</td><td>(1.6)</td><td>24</td><td>New York</td><td>(0.7)</td></tr>
<tr><td>6</td><td>Montana</td><td>10.9</td><td>26</td><td>Indiana</td><td>(1.5)</td></tr>
<tr><td>21</td><td>Nebraska</td><td>0.8</td><td>27</td><td>Arkansas</td><td>(1.6)</td></tr>
<tr><td>50</td><td>Nevada</td><td>(50.0)</td><td>27</td><td>Missouri</td><td>(1.6)</td></tr>
<tr><td>43</td><td>New Hampshire</td><td>(14.6)</td><td>29</td><td>Maine</td><td>(3.1)</td></tr>
<tr><td>36</td><td>New Jersey</td><td>(8.9)</td><td>30</td><td>Virginia</td><td>(4.1)</td></tr>
<tr><td>10</td><td>New Mexico</td><td>5.1</td><td>31</td><td>Wisconsin</td><td>(4.3)</td></tr>
<tr><td>24</td><td>New York</td><td>(0.7)</td><td>32</td><td>Idaho</td><td>(4.4)</td></tr>
<tr><td>11</td><td>North Carolina</td><td>4.5</td><td>33</td><td>Oregon</td><td>(6.1)</td></tr>
<tr><td>1</td><td>North Dakota</td><td>19.5</td><td>34</td><td>Delaware</td><td>(7.5)</td></tr>
<tr><td>38</td><td>Ohio</td><td>(9.6)</td><td>35</td><td>Illinois</td><td>(7.9)</td></tr>
<tr><td>4</td><td>Oklahoma</td><td>11.9</td><td>36</td><td>New Jersey</td><td>(8.9)</td></tr>
<tr><td>33</td><td>Oregon</td><td>(6.1)</td><td>37</td><td>Connecticut</td><td>(9.3)</td></tr>
<tr><td>19</td><td>Pennsylvania</td><td>2.4</td><td>38</td><td>Ohio</td><td>(9.6)</td></tr>
<tr><td>45</td><td>Rhode Island</td><td>(18.4)</td><td>39</td><td>Hawaii</td><td>(11.0)</td></tr>
<tr><td>22</td><td>South Carolina</td><td>0.7</td><td>40</td><td>Massachusetts</td><td>(11.9)</td></tr>
<tr><td>7</td><td>South Dakota</td><td>10.8</td><td>41</td><td>Georgia</td><td>(13.4)</td></tr>
<tr><td>16</td><td>Tennessee</td><td>3.3</td><td>42</td><td>Minnesota</td><td>(13.5)</td></tr>
<tr><td>3</td><td>Texas</td><td>13.7</td><td>43</td><td>New Hampshire</td><td>(14.6)</td></tr>
<tr><td>15</td><td>Utah</td><td>3.7</td><td>44</td><td>Maryland</td><td>(14.8)</td></tr>
<tr><td>20</td><td>Vermont</td><td>1.4</td><td>45</td><td>Rhode Island</td><td>(18.4)</td></tr>
<tr><td>30</td><td>Virginia</td><td>(4.1)</td><td>46</td><td>Michigan</td><td>(26.8)</td></tr>
<tr><td>23</td><td>Washington</td><td>(0.2)</td><td>47</td><td>Arizona</td><td>(35.7)</td></tr>
<tr><td>9</td><td>West Virginia</td><td>9.3</td><td>48</td><td>Florida</td><td>(36.6)</td></tr>
<tr><td>31</td><td>Wisconsin</td><td>(4.3)</td><td>49</td><td>California</td><td>(39.7)</td></tr>
<tr><td>5</td><td>Wyoming</td><td>11.8</td><td>50</td><td>Nevada</td><td>(50.0)</td></tr>
<tr><td></td><td></td><td></td><td></td><td>District of Columbia</td><td>3.2</td></tr>
</table>

Source: Federal Housing Finance Agency
   "House Price Index" (http://www.fhfa.gov/Default.aspx?Page=14)
*Single-family house prices. As of September 30, 2010.

Existing Home Sales in 2010

National Total = 4,163,000 Homes*

ALPHA ORDER

RANK	STATE	HOMES	% of USA
22	Alabama	63,600	1.5%
43	Alaska	16,800	0.4%
9	Arizona	131,200	3.2%
28	Arkansas	53,200	1.3%
1	California	439,600	10.6%
18	Colorado	76,400	1.8%
34	Connecticut	37,200	0.9%
48	Delaware	8,800	0.2%
3	Florida	350,000	8.4%
6	Georgia	148,800	3.6%
41	Hawaii	18,400	0.4%
35	Idaho	26,000	0.6%
7	Illinois	142,400	3.4%
14	Indiana	88,000	2.1%
32	Iowa	41,200	1.0%
31	Kansas	41,600	1.0%
27	Kentucky	58,000	1.4%
29	Louisiana	46,400	1.1%
40	Maine	19,200	0.5%
21	Maryland	65,200	1.6%
14	Massachusetts	88,000	2.1%
10	Michigan	119,600	2.9%
24	Minnesota	60,800	1.5%
33	Mississippi	37,600	0.9%
19	Missouri	74,400	1.8%
42	Montana	17,600	0.4%
37	Nebraska	24,400	0.6%
16	Nevada	87,200	2.1%
44	New Hampshire	16,400	0.4%
13	New Jersey	101,000	2.4%
36	New Mexico	24,800	0.6%
4	New York	195,600	4.7%
11	North Carolina	112,800	2.7%
47	North Dakota	9,200	0.2%
5	Ohio	188,400	4.5%
25	Oklahoma	58,800	1.4%
30	Oregon	44,400	1.1%
8	Pennsylvania	135,200	3.2%
45	Rhode Island	12,000	0.3%
25	South Carolina	58,800	1.4%
45	South Dakota	12,000	0.3%
17	Tennessee	83,200	2.0%
2	Texas	358,400	8.6%
39	Utah	22,000	0.5%
49	Vermont	8,000	0.2%
12	Virginia	103,200	2.5%
20	Washington	68,400	1.6%
37	West Virginia	24,400	0.6%
23	Wisconsin	61,600	1.5%
50	Wyoming	7,200	0.2%

RANK ORDER

RANK	STATE	HOMES	% of USA
1	California	439,600	10.6%
2	Texas	358,400	8.6%
3	Florida	350,000	8.4%
4	New York	195,600	4.7%
5	Ohio	188,400	4.5%
6	Georgia	148,800	3.6%
7	Illinois	142,400	3.4%
8	Pennsylvania	135,200	3.2%
9	Arizona	131,200	3.2%
10	Michigan	119,600	2.9%
11	North Carolina	112,800	2.7%
12	Virginia	103,200	2.5%
13	New Jersey	101,000	2.4%
14	Indiana	88,000	2.1%
14	Massachusetts	88,000	2.1%
16	Nevada	87,200	2.1%
17	Tennessee	83,200	2.0%
18	Colorado	76,400	1.8%
19	Missouri	74,400	1.8%
20	Washington	68,400	1.6%
21	Maryland	65,200	1.6%
22	Alabama	63,600	1.5%
23	Wisconsin	61,600	1.5%
24	Minnesota	60,800	1.5%
25	Oklahoma	58,800	1.4%
25	South Carolina	58,800	1.4%
27	Kentucky	58,000	1.4%
28	Arkansas	53,200	1.3%
29	Louisiana	46,400	1.1%
30	Oregon	44,400	1.1%
31	Kansas	41,600	1.0%
32	Iowa	41,200	1.0%
33	Mississippi	37,600	0.9%
34	Connecticut	37,200	0.9%
35	Idaho	26,000	0.6%
36	New Mexico	24,800	0.6%
37	Nebraska	24,400	0.6%
37	West Virginia	24,400	0.6%
39	Utah	22,000	0.5%
40	Maine	19,200	0.5%
41	Hawaii	18,400	0.4%
42	Montana	17,600	0.4%
43	Alaska	16,800	0.4%
44	New Hampshire	16,400	0.4%
45	Rhode Island	12,000	0.3%
45	South Dakota	12,000	0.3%
47	North Dakota	9,200	0.2%
48	Delaware	8,800	0.2%
49	Vermont	8,000	0.2%
50	Wyoming	7,200	0.2%
	District of Columbia	8,000	0.2%

Source: National Association of Realtors®, Economics and Research Division
   "Existing Home Sales" (http://www.realtor.org/research/research/metroprice)
*Seasonally adjusted preliminary data as of September 2010. Includes existing houses, apartment condos, and co-ops. Excludes new construction.

Percent Change in Existing Home Sales: 2009 to 2010

National Percent Change = 21.2% Decrease*

ALPHA ORDER

RANK	STATE	PERCENT CHANGE
14	Alabama	(16.3)
34	Alaska	(26.3)
7	Arizona	(13.7)
10	Arkansas	(15.3)
5	California	(13.0)
23	Colorado	(21.1)
17	Connecticut	(18.4)
44	Delaware	(31.3)
1	Florida	(1.0)
13	Georgia	(15.8)
2	Hawaii	(4.2)
3	Idaho	(8.5)
31	Illinois	(24.6)
12	Indiana	(15.4)
40	Iowa	(29.5)
38	Kansas	(28.3)
29	Kentucky	(24.1)
19	Louisiana	(18.9)
8	Maine	(14.3)
6	Maryland	(13.3)
20	Massachusetts	(19.7)
42	Michigan	(30.1)
50	Minnesota	(37.4)
4	Mississippi	(11.3)
46	Missouri	(32.4)
26	Montana	(21.4)
48	Nebraska	(33.0)
16	Nevada	(17.4)
9	New Hampshire	(14.6)
27	New Jersey	(22.2)
30	New Mexico	(24.4)
37	New York	(27.1)
24	North Carolina	(21.2)
49	North Dakota	(34.3)
36	Ohio	(27.0)
43	Oklahoma	(30.7)
25	Oregon	(21.3)
35	Pennsylvania	(26.7)
32	Rhode Island	(25.0)
20	South Carolina	(19.7)
45	South Dakota	(31.8)
28	Tennessee	(23.2)
22	Texas	(20.8)
40	Utah	(29.5)
39	Vermont	(28.6)
15	Virginia	(17.0)
18	Washington	(18.6)
10	West Virginia	(15.3)
47	Wisconsin	(32.5)
32	Wyoming	(25.0)

RANK ORDER

RANK	STATE	PERCENT CHANGE
1	Florida	(1.0)
2	Hawaii	(4.2)
3	Idaho	(8.5)
4	Mississippi	(11.3)
5	California	(13.0)
6	Maryland	(13.3)
7	Arizona	(13.7)
8	Maine	(14.3)
9	New Hampshire	(14.6)
10	Arkansas	(15.3)
10	West Virginia	(15.3)
12	Indiana	(15.4)
13	Georgia	(15.8)
14	Alabama	(16.3)
15	Virginia	(17.0)
16	Nevada	(17.4)
17	Connecticut	(18.4)
18	Washington	(18.6)
19	Louisiana	(18.9)
20	Massachusetts	(19.7)
20	South Carolina	(19.7)
22	Texas	(20.8)
23	Colorado	(21.1)
24	North Carolina	(21.2)
25	Oregon	(21.3)
26	Montana	(21.4)
27	New Jersey	(22.2)
28	Tennessee	(23.2)
29	Kentucky	(24.1)
30	New Mexico	(24.4)
31	Illinois	(24.6)
32	Rhode Island	(25.0)
32	Wyoming	(25.0)
34	Alaska	(26.3)
35	Pennsylvania	(26.7)
36	Ohio	(27.0)
37	New York	(27.1)
38	Kansas	(28.3)
39	Vermont	(28.6)
40	Iowa	(29.5)
40	Utah	(29.5)
42	Michigan	(30.1)
43	Oklahoma	(30.7)
44	Delaware	(31.3)
45	South Dakota	(31.8)
46	Missouri	(32.4)
47	Wisconsin	(32.5)
48	Nebraska	(33.0)
49	North Dakota	(34.3)
50	Minnesota	(37.4)

District of Columbia   (9.1)

Source: National Association of Realtors®, Economics and Research Division
    "Existing Home Sales" (http://www.realtor.org/research/research/metroprice)
*Seasonally adjusted preliminary data as of September 2010. Includes existing houses, apartment condos, and co-ops. Excludes new construction.

Median Monthly Mortgage Payment in 2009

National Median = $1,505*

Source: U.S. Bureau of the Census
"2009 American Community Survey" (http://www.census.gov/acs/www/)
*Monthly housing costs for owner-occupied housing.

Percent of Home Owners Spending 30% or More of Household Income on Housing Costs: 2009
National Percent = 37.5% of Home Owners*

ALPHA ORDER

RANK	STATE	PERCENT
37	Alabama	29.5
31	Alaska	32.8
9	Arizona	40.9
42	Arkansas	27.1
1	California	52.2
23	Colorado	35.7
12	Connecticut	40.5
20	Delaware	36.0
2	Florida	49.2
22	Georgia	35.9
2	Hawaii	49.2
17	Idaho	36.6
15	Illinois	38.2
41	Indiana	27.4
49	Iowa	23.3
47	Kansas	25.2
40	Kentucky	27.9
39	Louisiana	28.6
19	Maine	36.3
14	Maryland	38.5
13	Massachusetts	40.0
17	Michigan	36.6
28	Minnesota	33.6
29	Mississippi	33.1
38	Missouri	29.1
25	Montana	34.7
46	Nebraska	25.4
4	Nevada	47.1
8	New Hampshire	41.1
5	New Jersey	46.8
27	New Mexico	34.2
9	New York	40.9
33	North Carolina	32.3
50	North Dakota	21.3
36	Ohio	31.1
44	Oklahoma	25.8
7	Oregon	41.5
32	Pennsylvania	32.6
6	Rhode Island	43.3
34	South Carolina	32.1
45	South Dakota	25.6
30	Tennessee	32.9
35	Texas	31.2
24	Utah	35.4
16	Vermont	38.1
20	Virginia	36.0
9	Washington	40.9
48	West Virginia	24.2
26	Wisconsin	34.5
43	Wyoming	26.7

RANK ORDER

RANK	STATE	PERCENT
1	California	52.2
2	Florida	49.2
2	Hawaii	49.2
4	Nevada	47.1
5	New Jersey	46.8
6	Rhode Island	43.3
7	Oregon	41.5
8	New Hampshire	41.1
9	Arizona	40.9
9	New York	40.9
9	Washington	40.9
12	Connecticut	40.5
13	Massachusetts	40.0
14	Maryland	38.5
15	Illinois	38.2
16	Vermont	38.1
17	Idaho	36.6
17	Michigan	36.6
19	Maine	36.3
20	Delaware	36.0
20	Virginia	36.0
22	Georgia	35.9
23	Colorado	35.7
24	Utah	35.4
25	Montana	34.7
26	Wisconsin	34.5
27	New Mexico	34.2
28	Minnesota	33.6
29	Mississippi	33.1
30	Tennessee	32.9
31	Alaska	32.8
32	Pennsylvania	32.6
33	North Carolina	32.3
34	South Carolina	32.1
35	Texas	31.2
36	Ohio	31.1
37	Alabama	29.5
38	Missouri	29.1
39	Louisiana	28.6
40	Kentucky	27.9
41	Indiana	27.4
42	Arkansas	27.1
43	Wyoming	26.7
44	Oklahoma	25.8
45	South Dakota	25.6
46	Nebraska	25.4
47	Kansas	25.2
48	West Virginia	24.2
49	Iowa	23.3
50	North Dakota	21.3
	District of Columbia	38.9

Source: U.S. Bureau of the Census
   "2009 American Community Survey" (http://www.census.gov/acs/www/)
*For owner-occupied housing units with a mortgage.

Homeownership Rate in 2009

National Rate = 67.4%*

ALPHA ORDER

RANK	STATE	RATE
9	Alabama	74.1
40	Alaska	66.8
34	Arizona	68.9
35	Arkansas	68.5
49	California	57.0
36	Colorado	68.4
23	Connecticut	70.5
2	Delaware	76.5
21	Florida	70.9
38	Georgia	67.4
48	Hawaii	59.5
4	Idaho	75.5
32	Illinois	69.1
16	Indiana	72.0
14	Iowa	72.4
38	Kansas	67.4
19	Kentucky	71.2
18	Louisiana	71.9
11	Maine	74.0
29	Maryland	69.6
45	Massachusetts	65.1
6	Michigan	74.5
13	Minnesota	72.9
4	Mississippi	75.5
16	Missouri	72.0
22	Montana	70.7
25	Nebraska	70.2
47	Nevada	62.4
3	New Hampshire	76.0
41	New Jersey	65.9
32	New Mexico	69.1
50	New York	54.4
26	North Carolina	70.1
42	North Dakota	65.7
27	Ohio	69.7
29	Oklahoma	69.6
37	Oregon	68.2
15	Pennsylvania	72.2
46	Rhode Island	62.9
7	South Carolina	74.4
29	South Dakota	69.6
20	Tennessee	71.1
44	Texas	65.4
9	Utah	74.1
8	Vermont	74.3
27	Virginia	69.7
43	Washington	65.5
1	West Virginia	78.7
24	Wisconsin	70.4
12	Wyoming	73.8

RANK ORDER

RANK	STATE	RATE
1	West Virginia	78.7
2	Delaware	76.5
3	New Hampshire	76.0
4	Idaho	75.5
4	Mississippi	75.5
6	Michigan	74.5
7	South Carolina	74.4
8	Vermont	74.3
9	Alabama	74.1
9	Utah	74.1
11	Maine	74.0
12	Wyoming	73.8
13	Minnesota	72.9
14	Iowa	72.4
15	Pennsylvania	72.2
16	Indiana	72.0
16	Missouri	72.0
18	Louisiana	71.9
19	Kentucky	71.2
20	Tennessee	71.1
21	Florida	70.9
22	Montana	70.7
23	Connecticut	70.5
24	Wisconsin	70.4
25	Nebraska	70.2
26	North Carolina	70.1
27	Ohio	69.7
27	Virginia	69.7
29	Maryland	69.6
29	Oklahoma	69.6
29	South Dakota	69.6
32	Illinois	69.1
32	New Mexico	69.1
34	Arizona	68.9
35	Arkansas	68.5
36	Colorado	68.4
37	Oregon	68.2
38	Georgia	67.4
38	Kansas	67.4
40	Alaska	66.8
41	New Jersey	65.9
42	North Dakota	65.7
43	Washington	65.5
44	Texas	65.4
45	Massachusetts	65.1
46	Rhode Island	62.9
47	Nevada	62.4
48	Hawaii	59.5
49	California	57.0
50	New York	54.4
	District of Columbia	44.9

Source: U.S. Bureau of the Census
"Housing Vacancies and Homeownership, Annual Statistics: 2009"
(http://www.census.gov/hhes/www/housing/hvs/annual09/ann09ind.html)
*Percent of households occupied by the owner.

Properties with Foreclosure Filings in 2010

National Total = 2,871,891 Properties*

ALPHA ORDER

RANK	STATE	PROPERTIES	% of USA
28	Alabama	20,869	0.7%
45	Alaska	2,654	0.1%
3	Arizona	155,878	5.4%
29	Arkansas	19,757	0.7%
1	California	546,669	19.0%
11	Colorado	54,041	1.9%
27	Connecticut	21,705	0.8%
41	Delaware	4,727	0.2%
2	Florida	485,286	16.9%
6	Georgia	130,966	4.6%
34	Hawaii	12,425	0.4%
30	Idaho	19,088	0.7%
4	Illinois	151,304	5.3%
14	Indiana	44,172	1.5%
37	Iowa	8,663	0.3%
35	Kansas	11,415	0.4%
33	Kentucky	12,656	0.4%
32	Louisiana	15,753	0.5%
42	Maine	3,502	0.1%
17	Maryland	42,446	1.5%
22	Massachusetts	36,092	1.3%
5	Michigan	135,874	4.7%
26	Minnesota	31,315	1.1%
39	Mississippi	5,280	0.2%
23	Missouri	33,944	1.2%
44	Montana	3,307	0.1%
43	Nebraska	3,377	0.1%
9	Nevada	106,160	3.7%
38	New Hampshire	7,703	0.3%
10	New Jersey	64,808	2.3%
36	New Mexico	11,133	0.4%
15	New York	43,913	1.5%
18	North Carolina	40,151	1.4%
49	North Dakota	488	0.0%
8	Ohio	108,160	3.8%
31	Oklahoma	17,718	0.6%
21	Oregon	36,958	1.3%
13	Pennsylvania	51,278	1.8%
40	Rhode Island	5,246	0.2%
24	South Carolina	33,063	1.2%
47	South Dakota	1,244	0.0%
20	Tennessee	39,206	1.4%
7	Texas	118,923	4.1%
25	Utah	32,520	1.1%
50	Vermont	393	0.0%
12	Virginia	51,588	1.8%
16	Washington	43,856	1.5%
46	West Virginia	1,329	0.0%
19	Wisconsin	39,920	1.4%
48	Wyoming	815	0.0%

RANK ORDER

RANK	STATE	PROPERTIES	% of USA
1	California	546,669	19.0%
2	Florida	485,286	16.9%
3	Arizona	155,878	5.4%
4	Illinois	151,304	5.3%
5	Michigan	135,874	4.7%
6	Georgia	130,966	4.6%
7	Texas	118,923	4.1%
8	Ohio	108,160	3.8%
9	Nevada	106,160	3.7%
10	New Jersey	64,808	2.3%
11	Colorado	54,041	1.9%
12	Virginia	51,588	1.8%
13	Pennsylvania	51,278	1.8%
14	Indiana	44,172	1.5%
15	New York	43,913	1.5%
16	Washington	43,856	1.5%
17	Maryland	42,446	1.5%
18	North Carolina	40,151	1.4%
19	Wisconsin	39,920	1.4%
20	Tennessee	39,206	1.4%
21	Oregon	36,958	1.3%
22	Massachusetts	36,092	1.3%
23	Missouri	33,944	1.2%
24	South Carolina	33,063	1.2%
25	Utah	32,520	1.1%
26	Minnesota	31,315	1.1%
27	Connecticut	21,705	0.8%
28	Alabama	20,869	0.7%
29	Arkansas	19,757	0.7%
30	Idaho	19,088	0.7%
31	Oklahoma	17,718	0.6%
32	Louisiana	15,753	0.5%
33	Kentucky	12,656	0.4%
34	Hawaii	12,425	0.4%
35	Kansas	11,415	0.4%
36	New Mexico	11,133	0.4%
37	Iowa	8,663	0.3%
38	New Hampshire	7,703	0.3%
39	Mississippi	5,280	0.2%
40	Rhode Island	5,246	0.2%
41	Delaware	4,727	0.2%
42	Maine	3,502	0.1%
43	Nebraska	3,377	0.1%
44	Montana	3,307	0.1%
45	Alaska	2,654	0.1%
46	West Virginia	1,329	0.0%
47	South Dakota	1,244	0.0%
48	Wyoming	815	0.0%
49	North Dakota	488	0.0%
50	Vermont	393	0.0%
	District of Columbia	2,153	0.1%

Source: RealtyTrac

"Record 2.9 Million U.S. Properties Receive Foreclosure Filings in 2010" (Press Release, January 13, 2011, www.realtytrac.com)
*Foreclosure filings include foreclosure-related documents filed in all phases of foreclosure.

Percent of Housing Units Receiving Foreclosure Filings in 2010

National Rate = 2.2% of Housing Units*

ALPHA ORDER				RANK ORDER		
RANK	STATE	PERCENT		RANK	STATE	PERCENT
33	Alabama	1.0		1	Nevada	9.4
35	Alaska	0.9		2	Arizona	5.7
2	Arizona	5.7		3	Florida	5.5
21	Arkansas	1.5		4	California	4.1
4	California	4.1		5	Utah	3.4
10	Colorado	2.5		6	Georgia	3.3
21	Connecticut	1.5		7	Idaho	3.0
29	Delaware	1.2		7	Michigan	3.0
3	Florida	5.5		9	Illinois	2.9
6	Georgia	3.3		10	Colorado	2.5
11	Hawaii	2.4		11	Hawaii	2.4
7	Idaho	3.0		12	Oregon	2.3
9	Illinois	2.9		13	Ohio	2.1
16	Indiana	1.6		14	Maryland	1.8
40	Iowa	0.7		14	New Jersey	1.8
35	Kansas	0.9		16	Indiana	1.6
40	Kentucky	0.7		16	South Carolina	1.6
38	Louisiana	0.8		16	Virginia	1.6
43	Maine	0.5		16	Washington	1.6
14	Maryland	1.8		16	Wisconsin	1.6
24	Massachusetts	1.3		21	Arkansas	1.5
7	Michigan	3.0		21	Connecticut	1.5
24	Minnesota	1.3		23	Tennessee	1.4
44	Mississippi	0.4		24	Massachusetts	1.3
24	Missouri	1.3		24	Minnesota	1.3
38	Montana	0.8		24	Missouri	1.3
44	Nebraska	0.4		24	New Hampshire	1.3
1	Nevada	9.4		24	New Mexico	1.3
24	New Hampshire	1.3		29	Delaware	1.2
14	New Jersey	1.8		29	Rhode Island	1.2
24	New Mexico	1.3		29	Texas	1.2
42	New York	0.6		32	Oklahoma	1.1
33	North Carolina	1.0		33	Alabama	1.0
48	North Dakota	0.2		33	North Carolina	1.0
13	Ohio	2.1		35	Alaska	0.9
32	Oklahoma	1.1		35	Kansas	0.9
12	Oregon	2.3		35	Pennsylvania	0.9
35	Pennsylvania	0.9		38	Louisiana	0.8
29	Rhode Island	1.2		38	Montana	0.8
16	South Carolina	1.6		40	Iowa	0.7
46	South Dakota	0.3		40	Kentucky	0.7
23	Tennessee	1.4		42	New York	0.6
29	Texas	1.2		43	Maine	0.5
5	Utah	3.4		44	Mississippi	0.4
50	Vermont	0.1		44	Nebraska	0.4
16	Virginia	1.6		46	South Dakota	0.3
16	Washington	1.6		46	Wyoming	0.3
48	West Virginia	0.2		48	North Dakota	0.2
16	Wisconsin	1.6		48	West Virginia	0.2
46	Wyoming	0.3		50	Vermont	0.1
					District of Columbia	0.8

Source: RealtyTrac
"Record 2.9 Million U.S. Properties Receive Foreclosure Filings in 2010" (Press Release, January 13, 2011, www.realtytrac.com)
*Foreclosure filings include foreclosure-related documents filed in all phases of foreclosure.

Percent Change in Properties Receiving Foreclosure Filings: 2009 to 2010

National Percent Change = 1.7% Increase*

ALPHA ORDER			RANK ORDER		
RANK	STATE	PERCENT CHANGE	RANK	STATE	PERCENT CHANGE
36	Alabama	4.9	1	Vermont**	174.8
30	Alaska	8.7	2	Montana**	140.9
45	Arizona	(4.5)	3	Nebraska**	83.0
19	Arkansas	19.4	4	South Dakota**	62.6
50	California	(13.6)	5	Delaware**	55.8
32	Colorado	7.0	6	New Mexico**	54.4
28	Connecticut	10.3	7	Iowa**	52.5
5	Delaware**	55.8	8	North Carolina	41.5
47	Florida	(6.1)	9	Hawaii	38.0
17	Georgia	23.4	10	Oklahoma**	37.0
9	Hawaii	38.0	11	Louisiana**	34.1
27	Idaho	11.2	12	South Carolina	31.4
22	Illinois	15.4	13	Kentucky**	30.7
34	Indiana	6.7	14	Kansas**	26.1
7	Iowa**	52.5	15	North Dakota**	25.1
14	Kansas**	26.1	16	Washington	24.4
13	Kentucky**	30.7	17	Georgia	23.4
11	Louisiana**	34.1	18	Utah	19.8
29	Maine	10.2	19	Arkansas	19.4
42	Maryland	(1.9)	20	Missouri	19.0
39	Massachusetts	(0.1)	21	Texas	18.9
23	Michigan	14.9	22	Illinois	15.4
41	Minnesota	(1.2)	23	Michigan	14.9
43	Mississippi	(2.3)	24	Pennsylvania	14.6
20	Missouri	19.0	25	Wyoming	13.7
2	Montana**	140.9	26	Wisconsin	13.2
3	Nebraska**	83.0	27	Idaho	11.2
46	Nevada	(5.3)	28	Connecticut	10.3
33	New Hampshire	6.8	29	Maine	10.2
38	New Jersey	2.5	30	Alaska	8.7
6	New Mexico**	54.4	31	Oregon	8.3
49	New York	(12.8)	32	Colorado	7.0
8	North Carolina	41.5	33	New Hampshire	6.8
15	North Dakota**	25.1	34	Indiana	6.7
35	Ohio	6.4	35	Ohio	6.4
10	Oklahoma**	37.0	36	Alabama	4.9
31	Oregon	8.3	37	Rhode Island	3.6
24	Pennsylvania	14.6	38	New Jersey	2.5
37	Rhode Island	3.6	39	Massachusetts	(0.1)
12	South Carolina	31.4	40	Virginia	(1.0)
4	South Dakota**	62.6	41	Minnesota	(1.2)
44	Tennessee	(3.8)	42	Maryland	(1.9)
21	Texas	18.9	43	Mississippi	(2.3)
18	Utah	19.8	44	Tennessee	(3.8)
1	Vermont**	174.8	45	Arizona	(4.5)
40	Virginia	(1.0)	46	Nevada	(5.3)
16	Washington	24.4	47	Florida	(6.1)
48	West Virginia	(10.1)	48	West Virginia	(10.1)
26	Wisconsin	13.2	49	New York	(12.8)
25	Wyoming	13.7	50	California	(13.6)
				District of Columbia	(33.5)

Source: RealtyTrac

"Record 2.9 Million U.S. Properties Receive Foreclosure Filings in 2010" (Press Release, January 13, 2011, www.realtytrac.com)

*Foreclosure filings include foreclosure-related documents filed in all phases of foreclosure.

**Actual increase may not be as high due to data collection changes or improvements.

Median Monthly Rental Payment in 2009

National Median = $842*

ALPHA ORDER

RANK	STATE	MEDIAN
40	Alabama	$657
5	Alaska	1,007
16	Arizona	859
47	Arkansas	606
2	California	1,155
17	Colorado	851
6	Connecticut	1,006
12	Delaware	949
11	Florida	952
21	Georgia	800
1	Hawaii	1,293
33	Idaho	694
19	Illinois	828
34	Indiana	687
46	Iowa	611
37	Kansas	671
45	Kentucky	613
29	Louisiana	715
26	Maine	722
3	Maryland	1,108
9	Massachusetts	988
28	Michigan	716
24	Minnesota	757
41	Mississippi	644
39	Missouri	668
44	Montana	627
41	Nebraska	644
7	Nevada	993
13	New Hampshire	918
3	New Jersey	1,108
36	New Mexico	680
10	New York	984
27	North Carolina	720
48	North Dakota	564
38	Ohio	670
43	Oklahoma	636
20	Oregon	819
25	Pennsylvania	738
15	Rhode Island	890
31	South Carolina	706
49	South Dakota	562
35	Tennessee	682
23	Texas	788
22	Utah	793
18	Vermont	829
8	Virginia	989
14	Washington	911
50	West Virginia	552
30	Wisconsin	708
32	Wyoming	700

RANK ORDER

RANK	STATE	MEDIAN
1	Hawaii	$1,293
2	California	1,155
3	Maryland	1,108
3	New Jersey	1,108
5	Alaska	1,007
6	Connecticut	1,006
7	Nevada	993
8	Virginia	989
9	Massachusetts	988
10	New York	984
11	Florida	952
12	Delaware	949
13	New Hampshire	918
14	Washington	911
15	Rhode Island	890
16	Arizona	859
17	Colorado	851
18	Vermont	829
19	Illinois	828
20	Oregon	819
21	Georgia	800
22	Utah	793
23	Texas	788
24	Minnesota	757
25	Pennsylvania	738
26	Maine	722
27	North Carolina	720
28	Michigan	716
29	Louisiana	715
30	Wisconsin	708
31	South Carolina	706
32	Wyoming	700
33	Idaho	694
34	Indiana	687
35	Tennessee	682
36	New Mexico	680
37	Kansas	671
38	Ohio	670
39	Missouri	668
40	Alabama	657
41	Mississippi	644
41	Nebraska	644
43	Oklahoma	636
44	Montana	627
45	Kentucky	613
46	Iowa	611
47	Arkansas	606
48	North Dakota	564
49	South Dakota	562
50	West Virginia	552
	District of Columbia	1,059

Source: U.S. Bureau of the Census
    "2009 American Community Survey" (http://www.census.gov/acs/www/)
*Monthly housing costs for renter-occupied housing.

Percent of Renters Spending 30% or More of Household Income on Rent and Utilities: 2009
National Percent = 47.7% of Renters

ALPHA ORDER

RANK	STATE	PERCENT
33	Alabama	44.2
48	Alaska	36.6
13	Arizona	48.0
38	Arkansas	42.8
2	California	52.8
9	Colorado	49.3
8	Connecticut	49.4
5	Delaware	49.9
1	Florida	55.9
14	Georgia	47.6
3	Hawaii	52.3
36	Idaho	44.0
15	Illinois	47.4
29	Indiana	45.3
44	Iowa	40.2
40	Kansas	41.9
41	Kentucky	41.7
32	Louisiana	44.3
20	Maine	46.5
10	Maryland	49.2
21	Massachusetts	46.3
4	Michigan	51.6
19	Minnesota	46.8
35	Mississippi	44.1
37	Missouri	43.1
46	Montana	38.2
45	Nebraska	39.1
5	Nevada	49.9
23	New Hampshire	45.8
5	New Jersey	49.9
39	New Mexico	42.2
11	New York	48.8
25	North Carolina	45.6
47	North Dakota	36.7
22	Ohio	46.0
42	Oklahoma	41.4
12	Oregon	48.5
33	Pennsylvania	44.2
18	Rhode Island	46.9
31	South Carolina	44.9
49	South Dakota	36.2
27	Tennessee	45.5
27	Texas	45.5
23	Utah	45.8
17	Vermont	47.2
25	Virginia	45.6
16	Washington	47.3
43	West Virginia	40.5
29	Wisconsin	45.3
50	Wyoming	32.8

RANK ORDER

RANK	STATE	PERCENT
1	Florida	55.9
2	California	52.8
3	Hawaii	52.3
4	Michigan	51.6
5	Delaware	49.9
5	Nevada	49.9
5	New Jersey	49.9
8	Connecticut	49.4
9	Colorado	49.3
10	Maryland	49.2
11	New York	48.8
12	Oregon	48.5
13	Arizona	48.0
14	Georgia	47.6
15	Illinois	47.4
16	Washington	47.3
17	Vermont	47.2
18	Rhode Island	46.9
19	Minnesota	46.8
20	Maine	46.5
21	Massachusetts	46.3
22	Ohio	46.0
23	New Hampshire	45.8
23	Utah	45.8
25	North Carolina	45.6
25	Virginia	45.6
27	Tennessee	45.5
27	Texas	45.5
29	Indiana	45.3
29	Wisconsin	45.3
31	South Carolina	44.9
32	Louisiana	44.3
33	Alabama	44.2
33	Pennsylvania	44.2
35	Mississippi	44.1
36	Idaho	44.0
37	Missouri	43.1
38	Arkansas	42.8
39	New Mexico	42.2
40	Kansas	41.9
41	Kentucky	41.7
42	Oklahoma	41.4
43	West Virginia	40.5
44	Iowa	40.2
45	Nebraska	39.1
46	Montana	38.2
47	North Dakota	36.7
48	Alaska	36.6
49	South Dakota	36.2
50	Wyoming	32.8
	District of Columbia	46.7

Source: U.S. Bureau of the Census
"2009 American Community Survey" (http://www.census.gov/acs/www/)

State and Local Government Expenditures
for Housing and Community Development in 2008
National Total = $50,974,243,000*

ALPHA ORDER

RANK	STATE	EXPENDITURES	% of USA
26	Alabama	$415,104,000	0.8%
30	Alaska	270,906,000	0.5%
23	Arizona	537,257,000	1.1%
40	Arkansas	173,205,000	0.3%
1	California	10,285,043,000	20.2%
18	Colorado	707,724,000	1.4%
19	Connecticut	666,396,000	1.3%
45	Delaware	117,561,000	0.2%
4	Florida	2,436,064,000	4.8%
10	Georgia	1,239,499,000	2.4%
37	Hawaii	199,058,000	0.4%
49	Idaho	53,462,000	0.1%
6	Illinois	2,011,562,000	3.9%
20	Indiana	660,103,000	1.3%
41	Iowa	163,917,000	0.3%
39	Kansas	188,734,000	0.4%
27	Kentucky	294,579,000	0.6%
2	Louisiana	5,423,117,000	10.6%
31	Maine	244,926,000	0.5%
13	Maryland	1,041,725,000	2.0%
9	Massachusetts	1,763,337,000	3.5%
15	Michigan	1,010,258,000	2.0%
17	Minnesota	846,219,000	1.7%
33	Mississippi	231,699,000	0.5%
22	Missouri	618,657,000	1.2%
46	Montana	111,316,000	0.2%
35	Nebraska	203,846,000	0.4%
32	Nevada	234,927,000	0.5%
38	New Hampshire	190,169,000	0.4%
11	New Jersey	1,188,406,000	2.3%
42	New Mexico	159,374,000	0.3%
3	New York	4,661,341,000	9.1%
16	North Carolina	868,768,000	1.7%
48	North Dakota	77,357,000	0.2%
5	Ohio	2,138,080,000	4.2%
34	Oklahoma	215,434,000	0.4%
24	Oregon	485,865,000	1.0%
8	Pennsylvania	1,916,906,000	3.8%
36	Rhode Island	202,209,000	0.4%
25	South Carolina	446,486,000	0.9%
47	South Dakota	92,630,000	0.2%
21	Tennessee	650,174,000	1.3%
7	Texas	1,919,668,000	3.8%
29	Utah	273,073,000	0.5%
44	Vermont	122,852,000	0.2%
14	Virginia	1,035,636,000	2.0%
12	Washington	1,146,807,000	2.2%
43	West Virginia	157,442,000	0.3%
28	Wisconsin	284,262,000	0.6%
50	Wyoming	20,580,000	0.0%

RANK ORDER

RANK	STATE	EXPENDITURES	% of USA
1	California	$10,285,043,000	20.2%
2	Louisiana	5,423,117,000	10.6%
3	New York	4,661,341,000	9.1%
4	Florida	2,436,064,000	4.8%
5	Ohio	2,138,080,000	4.2%
6	Illinois	2,011,562,000	3.9%
7	Texas	1,919,668,000	3.8%
8	Pennsylvania	1,916,906,000	3.8%
9	Massachusetts	1,763,337,000	3.5%
10	Georgia	1,239,499,000	2.4%
11	New Jersey	1,188,406,000	2.3%
12	Washington	1,146,807,000	2.2%
13	Maryland	1,041,725,000	2.0%
14	Virginia	1,035,636,000	2.0%
15	Michigan	1,010,258,000	2.0%
16	North Carolina	868,768,000	1.7%
17	Minnesota	846,219,000	1.7%
18	Colorado	707,724,000	1.4%
19	Connecticut	666,396,000	1.3%
20	Indiana	660,103,000	1.3%
21	Tennessee	650,174,000	1.3%
22	Missouri	618,657,000	1.2%
23	Arizona	537,257,000	1.1%
24	Oregon	485,865,000	1.0%
25	South Carolina	446,486,000	0.9%
26	Alabama	415,104,000	0.8%
27	Kentucky	294,579,000	0.6%
28	Wisconsin	284,262,000	0.6%
29	Utah	273,073,000	0.5%
30	Alaska	270,906,000	0.5%
31	Maine	244,926,000	0.5%
32	Nevada	234,927,000	0.5%
33	Mississippi	231,699,000	0.5%
34	Oklahoma	215,434,000	0.4%
35	Nebraska	203,846,000	0.4%
36	Rhode Island	202,209,000	0.4%
37	Hawaii	199,058,000	0.4%
38	New Hampshire	190,169,000	0.4%
39	Kansas	188,734,000	0.4%
40	Arkansas	173,205,000	0.3%
41	Iowa	163,917,000	0.3%
42	New Mexico	159,374,000	0.3%
43	West Virginia	157,442,000	0.3%
44	Vermont	122,852,000	0.2%
45	Delaware	117,561,000	0.2%
46	Montana	111,316,000	0.2%
47	South Dakota	92,630,000	0.2%
48	North Dakota	77,357,000	0.2%
49	Idaho	53,462,000	0.1%
50	Wyoming	20,580,000	0.0%
	District of Columbia	570,523,000	1.1%

Source: U.S. Bureau of the Census, Governments Division
   "2008 State and Local Government Finances" (http://www.census.gov/govs/estimate/index.html)
*Direct general expenditures.

Per Capita State and Local Government Expenditures
for Housing and Community Development in 2008
National Per Capita = $167*

ALPHA ORDER

RANK	STATE	PER CAPITA
37	Alabama	$89
2	Alaska	394
39	Arizona	83
45	Arkansas	60
3	California	281
18	Colorado	143
8	Connecticut	190
20	Delaware	134
22	Florida	132
23	Georgia	128
15	Hawaii	155
50	Idaho	35
14	Illinois	157
31	Indiana	103
47	Iowa	55
44	Kansas	67
43	Kentucky	69
1	Louisiana	1,218
9	Maine	186
11	Maryland	184
4	Massachusetts	269
32	Michigan	101
13	Minnesota	162
41	Mississippi	79
29	Missouri	104
26	Montana	115
28	Nebraska	114
36	Nevada	90
17	New Hampshire	144
19	New Jersey	137
40	New Mexico	80
5	New York	239
35	North Carolina	94
25	North Dakota	121
10	Ohio	185
46	Oklahoma	59
23	Oregon	128
16	Pennsylvania	153
7	Rhode Island	192
34	South Carolina	99
26	South Dakota	115
29	Tennessee	104
41	Texas	79
33	Utah	100
6	Vermont	198
21	Virginia	133
12	Washington	175
38	West Virginia	87
48	Wisconsin	51
49	Wyoming	39

RANK ORDER

RANK	STATE	PER CAPITA
1	Louisiana	$1,218
2	Alaska	394
3	California	281
4	Massachusetts	269
5	New York	239
6	Vermont	198
7	Rhode Island	192
8	Connecticut	190
9	Maine	186
10	Ohio	185
11	Maryland	184
12	Washington	175
13	Minnesota	162
14	Illinois	157
15	Hawaii	155
16	Pennsylvania	153
17	New Hampshire	144
18	Colorado	143
19	New Jersey	137
20	Delaware	134
21	Virginia	133
22	Florida	132
23	Georgia	128
23	Oregon	128
25	North Dakota	121
26	Montana	115
26	South Dakota	115
28	Nebraska	114
29	Missouri	104
29	Tennessee	104
31	Indiana	103
32	Michigan	101
33	Utah	100
34	South Carolina	99
35	North Carolina	94
36	Nevada	90
37	Alabama	89
38	West Virginia	87
39	Arizona	83
40	New Mexico	80
41	Mississippi	79
41	Texas	79
43	Kentucky	69
44	Kansas	67
45	Arkansas	60
46	Oklahoma	59
47	Iowa	55
48	Wisconsin	51
49	Wyoming	39
50	Idaho	35
	District of Columbia	967

Source: CQ Press using data from U.S. Bureau of the Census, Governments Division
   "2008 State and Local Government Finances" (http://www.census.gov/govs/estimate/index.html)
*Direct general expenditures.

XIII. Population

Apportionment Population in 2010

National Total = 309,183,463*

ALPHA ORDER

RANK	STATE	POPULATION	% of USA
23	Alabama	4,802,982	1.6%
47	Alaska	721,523	0.2%
16	Arizona	6,412,700	2.1%
32	Arkansas	2,926,229	0.9%
1	California	37,341,989	12.1%
22	Colorado	5,044,930	1.6%
29	Connecticut	3,581,628	1.2%
45	Delaware	900,877	0.3%
4	Florida	18,900,773	6.1%
9	Georgia	9,727,566	3.1%
40	Hawaii	1,366,862	0.4%
39	Idaho	1,573,499	0.5%
5	Illinois	12,864,380	4.2%
15	Indiana	6,501,582	2.1%
30	Iowa	3,053,787	1.0%
33	Kansas	2,863,813	0.9%
26	Kentucky	4,350,606	1.4%
25	Louisiana	4,553,962	1.5%
41	Maine	1,333,074	0.4%
19	Maryland	5,789,929	1.9%
14	Massachusetts	6,559,644	2.1%
8	Michigan	9,911,626	3.2%
21	Minnesota	5,314,879	1.7%
31	Mississippi	2,978,240	1.0%
18	Missouri	6,011,478	1.9%
44	Montana	994,416	0.3%
38	Nebraska	1,831,825	0.6%
35	Nevada	2,709,432	0.9%
42	New Hampshire	1,321,445	0.4%
11	New Jersey	8,807,501	2.8%
36	New Mexico	2,067,273	0.7%
3	New York	19,421,055	6.3%
10	North Carolina	9,565,781	3.1%
48	North Dakota	675,905	0.2%
7	Ohio	11,568,495	3.7%
28	Oklahoma	3,764,882	1.2%
27	Oregon	3,848,606	1.2%
6	Pennsylvania	12,734,905	4.1%
43	Rhode Island	1,055,247	0.3%
24	South Carolina	4,645,975	1.5%
46	South Dakota	819,761	0.3%
17	Tennessee	6,375,431	2.1%
2	Texas	25,268,418	8.2%
34	Utah	2,770,765	0.9%
49	Vermont	630,337	0.2%
12	Virginia	8,037,736	2.6%
13	Washington	6,753,369	2.2%
37	West Virginia	1,859,815	0.6%
20	Wisconsin	5,698,230	1.8%
50	Wyoming	568,300	0.2%

RANK ORDER

RANK	STATE	POPULATION	% of USA
1	California	37,341,989	12.1%
2	Texas	25,268,418	8.2%
3	New York	19,421,055	6.3%
4	Florida	18,900,773	6.1%
5	Illinois	12,864,380	4.2%
6	Pennsylvania	12,734,905	4.1%
7	Ohio	11,568,495	3.7%
8	Michigan	9,911,626	3.2%
9	Georgia	9,727,566	3.1%
10	North Carolina	9,565,781	3.1%
11	New Jersey	8,807,501	2.8%
12	Virginia	8,037,736	2.6%
13	Washington	6,753,369	2.2%
14	Massachusetts	6,559,644	2.1%
15	Indiana	6,501,582	2.1%
16	Arizona	6,412,700	2.1%
17	Tennessee	6,375,431	2.1%
18	Missouri	6,011,478	1.9%
19	Maryland	5,789,929	1.9%
20	Wisconsin	5,698,230	1.8%
21	Minnesota	5,314,879	1.7%
22	Colorado	5,044,930	1.6%
23	Alabama	4,802,982	1.6%
24	South Carolina	4,645,975	1.5%
25	Louisiana	4,553,962	1.5%
26	Kentucky	4,350,606	1.4%
27	Oregon	3,848,606	1.2%
28	Oklahoma	3,764,882	1.2%
29	Connecticut	3,581,628	1.2%
30	Iowa	3,053,787	1.0%
31	Mississippi	2,978,240	1.0%
32	Arkansas	2,926,229	0.9%
33	Kansas	2,863,813	0.9%
34	Utah	2,770,765	0.9%
35	Nevada	2,709,432	0.9%
36	New Mexico	2,067,273	0.7%
37	West Virginia	1,859,815	0.6%
38	Nebraska	1,831,825	0.6%
39	Idaho	1,573,499	0.5%
40	Hawaii	1,366,862	0.4%
41	Maine	1,333,074	0.4%
42	New Hampshire	1,321,445	0.4%
43	Rhode Island	1,055,247	0.3%
44	Montana	994,416	0.3%
45	Delaware	900,877	0.3%
46	South Dakota	819,761	0.3%
47	Alaska	721,523	0.2%
48	North Dakota	675,905	0.2%
49	Vermont	630,337	0.2%
50	Wyoming	568,300	0.2%
	District of Columbia**	NA	NA

Source: U.S. Bureau of the Census
   "Congressional Apportionment" (http://www.census.gov/population/apportionment/
*Apportionment population includes the resident population for the 50 states, as ascertained by the Twenty-Third Decennial Census under Title 13, United States Code, and counts of overseas U.S. military and federal civilian employees (and their dependents living with them) allocated to their home state, as reported by the employing federal agencies. The apportionment population excludes the population of the District of Columbia. **Not applicable.

Population in 2010

National Total = 309,050,816*

ALPHA ORDER

RANK	STATE	POPULATION	% of USA
23	Alabama	4,729,656	1.5%
47	Alaska	708,862	0.2%
14	Arizona	6,676,627	2.2%
32	Arkansas	2,910,236	0.9%
1	California	37,266,600	12.1%
22	Colorado	5,095,309	1.6%
29	Connecticut	3,526,937	1.1%
45	Delaware	891,464	0.3%
4	Florida	18,678,049	6.0%
9	Georgia	9,908,357	3.2%
42	Hawaii	1,300,086	0.4%
39	Idaho	1,559,796	0.5%
5	Illinois	12,944,410	4.2%
16	Indiana	6,445,295	2.1%
30	Iowa	3,023,081	1.0%
33	Kansas	2,841,121	0.9%
26	Kentucky	4,339,435	1.4%
25	Louisiana	4,529,426	1.5%
41	Maine	1,312,939	0.4%
19	Maryland	5,737,274	1.9%
15	Massachusetts	6,631,280	2.1%
8	Michigan	9,931,235	3.2%
21	Minnesota	5,290,447	1.7%
31	Mississippi	2,960,467	1.0%
18	Missouri	6,011,741	1.9%
44	Montana	980,152	0.3%
38	Nebraska	1,811,072	0.6%
35	Nevada	2,654,751	0.9%
40	New Hampshire	1,323,531	0.4%
11	New Jersey	8,732,811	2.8%
36	New Mexico	2,033,875	0.7%
3	New York	19,577,730	6.3%
10	North Carolina	9,458,888	3.1%
48	North Dakota	653,778	0.2%
7	Ohio	11,532,111	3.7%
28	Oklahoma	3,724,447	1.2%
27	Oregon	3,855,536	1.2%
6	Pennsylvania	12,632,780	4.1%
43	Rhode Island	1,056,870	0.3%
24	South Carolina	4,596,958	1.5%
46	South Dakota	820,077	0.3%
17	Tennessee	6,338,112	2.1%
2	Texas	25,213,445	8.2%
34	Utah	2,830,753	0.9%
49	Vermont	622,433	0.2%
12	Virginia	7,952,119	2.6%
13	Washington	6,746,199	2.2%
37	West Virginia	1,825,513	0.6%
20	Wisconsin	5,668,519	1.8%
50	Wyoming	547,637	0.2%

RANK ORDER

RANK	STATE	POPULATION	% of USA
1	California	37,266,600	12.1%
2	Texas	25,213,445	8.2%
3	New York	19,577,730	6.3%
4	Florida	18,678,049	6.0%
5	Illinois	12,944,410	4.2%
6	Pennsylvania	12,632,780	4.1%
7	Ohio	11,532,111	3.7%
8	Michigan	9,931,235	3.2%
9	Georgia	9,908,357	3.2%
10	North Carolina	9,458,888	3.1%
11	New Jersey	8,732,811	2.8%
12	Virginia	7,952,119	2.6%
13	Washington	6,746,199	2.2%
14	Arizona	6,676,627	2.2%
15	Massachusetts	6,631,280	2.1%
16	Indiana	6,445,295	2.1%
17	Tennessee	6,338,112	2.1%
18	Missouri	6,011,741	1.9%
19	Maryland	5,737,274	1.9%
20	Wisconsin	5,668,519	1.8%
21	Minnesota	5,290,447	1.7%
22	Colorado	5,095,309	1.6%
23	Alabama	4,729,656	1.5%
24	South Carolina	4,596,958	1.5%
25	Louisiana	4,529,426	1.5%
26	Kentucky	4,339,435	1.4%
27	Oregon	3,855,536	1.2%
28	Oklahoma	3,724,447	1.2%
29	Connecticut	3,526,937	1.1%
30	Iowa	3,023,081	1.0%
31	Mississippi	2,960,467	1.0%
32	Arkansas	2,910,236	0.9%
33	Kansas	2,841,121	0.9%
34	Utah	2,830,753	0.9%
35	Nevada	2,654,751	0.9%
36	New Mexico	2,033,875	0.7%
37	West Virginia	1,825,513	0.6%
38	Nebraska	1,811,072	0.6%
39	Idaho	1,559,796	0.5%
40	New Hampshire	1,323,531	0.4%
41	Maine	1,312,939	0.4%
42	Hawaii	1,300,086	0.4%
43	Rhode Island	1,056,870	0.3%
44	Montana	980,152	0.3%
45	Delaware	891,464	0.3%
46	South Dakota	820,077	0.3%
47	Alaska	708,862	0.2%
48	North Dakota	653,778	0.2%
49	Vermont	622,433	0.2%
50	Wyoming	547,637	0.2%
	District of Columbia	610,589	0.2%

Source: U.S. Bureau of the Census
"Population Estimates" (February 2011, http://www.census.gov/popest/estimates.php)
*Resident population estimate as of July 1, 2010.

Population in 2009

National Total = 306,656,290*

ALPHA ORDER

RANK	STATE	POPULATION	% of USA
23	Alabama	4,707,496	1.5%
47	Alaska	694,690	0.2%
15	Arizona	6,587,653	2.1%
32	Arkansas	2,887,331	0.9%
1	California	36,887,615	12.0%
22	Colorado	5,015,155	1.6%
29	Connecticut	3,514,826	1.1%
45	Delaware	884,124	0.3%
4	Florida	18,509,936	6.0%
9	Georgia	9,813,588	3.2%
42	Hawaii	1,288,285	0.4%
39	Idaho	1,544,465	0.5%
5	Illinois	12,893,278	4.2%
16	Indiana	6,417,276	2.1%
30	Iowa	3,008,331	1.0%
33	Kansas	2,817,430	0.9%
26	Kentucky	4,312,268	1.4%
25	Louisiana	4,489,490	1.5%
41	Maine	1,315,889	0.4%
19	Maryland	5,688,399	1.9%
14	Massachusetts	6,592,205	2.1%
8	Michigan	9,955,260	3.2%
21	Minnesota	5,262,824	1.7%
31	Mississippi	2,949,943	1.0%
18	Missouri	5,982,234	2.0%
44	Montana	974,163	0.3%
38	Nebraska	1,794,852	0.6%
35	Nevada	2,638,588	0.9%
40	New Hampshire	1,322,181	0.4%
11	New Jersey	8,693,723	2.8%
36	New Mexico	2,007,315	0.7%
3	New York	19,522,612	6.4%
10	North Carolina	9,357,107	3.1%
48	North Dakota	645,903	0.2%
7	Ohio	11,531,860	3.8%
28	Oklahoma	3,685,640	1.2%
27	Oregon	3,823,058	1.2%
6	Pennsylvania	12,602,112	4.1%
43	Rhode Island	1,057,451	0.3%
24	South Carolina	4,554,258	1.5%
46	South Dakota	810,814	0.3%
17	Tennessee	6,291,220	2.1%
2	Texas	24,770,651	8.1%
34	Utah	2,780,871	0.9%
49	Vermont	621,436	0.2%
12	Virginia	7,862,480	2.6%
13	Washington	6,671,597	2.2%
37	West Virginia	1,821,290	0.6%
20	Wisconsin	5,650,751	1.8%
50	Wyoming	544,391	0.2%

RANK ORDER

RANK	STATE	POPULATION	% of USA
1	California	36,887,615	12.0%
2	Texas	24,770,651	8.1%
3	New York	19,522,612	6.4%
4	Florida	18,509,936	6.0%
5	Illinois	12,893,278	4.2%
6	Pennsylvania	12,602,112	4.1%
7	Ohio	11,531,860	3.8%
8	Michigan	9,955,260	3.2%
9	Georgia	9,813,588	3.2%
10	North Carolina	9,357,107	3.1%
11	New Jersey	8,693,723	2.8%
12	Virginia	7,862,480	2.6%
13	Washington	6,671,597	2.2%
14	Massachusetts	6,592,205	2.1%
15	Arizona	6,587,653	2.1%
16	Indiana	6,417,276	2.1%
17	Tennessee	6,291,220	2.1%
18	Missouri	5,982,234	2.0%
19	Maryland	5,688,399	1.9%
20	Wisconsin	5,650,751	1.8%
21	Minnesota	5,262,824	1.7%
22	Colorado	5,015,155	1.6%
23	Alabama	4,707,496	1.5%
24	South Carolina	4,554,258	1.5%
25	Louisiana	4,489,490	1.5%
26	Kentucky	4,312,268	1.4%
27	Oregon	3,823,058	1.2%
28	Oklahoma	3,685,640	1.2%
29	Connecticut	3,514,826	1.1%
30	Iowa	3,008,331	1.0%
31	Mississippi	2,949,943	1.0%
32	Arkansas	2,887,331	0.9%
33	Kansas	2,817,430	0.9%
34	Utah	2,780,871	0.9%
35	Nevada	2,638,588	0.9%
36	New Mexico	2,007,315	0.7%
37	West Virginia	1,821,290	0.6%
38	Nebraska	1,794,852	0.6%
39	Idaho	1,544,465	0.5%
40	New Hampshire	1,322,181	0.4%
41	Maine	1,315,889	0.4%
42	Hawaii	1,288,285	0.4%
43	Rhode Island	1,057,451	0.3%
44	Montana	974,163	0.3%
45	Delaware	884,124	0.3%
46	South Dakota	810,814	0.3%
47	Alaska	694,690	0.2%
48	North Dakota	645,903	0.2%
49	Vermont	621,436	0.2%
50	Wyoming	544,391	0.2%
	District of Columbia	599,975	0.2%

Source: U.S. Bureau of the Census
    "Population Estimates" (February 2011, http://www.census.gov/popest/estimates.php)
*Resident population. Revised estimates of July 1, 2010.

Numerical Population Change: 2009 to 2010

National Total = 2,394,526 Increase*

ALPHA ORDER

RANK	STATE	GAIN/LOSS	% of USA
29	Alabama	22,160	0.9%
35	Alaska	14,172	0.6%
7	Arizona	88,974	3.7%
28	Arkansas	22,905	1.0%
2	California	378,985	15.8%
8	Colorado	80,154	3.3%
36	Connecticut	12,111	0.5%
41	Delaware	7,340	0.3%
3	Florida	168,113	7.0%
5	Georgia	94,769	4.0%
37	Hawaii	11,801	0.5%
33	Idaho	15,331	0.6%
11	Illinois	51,132	2.1%
23	Indiana	28,019	1.2%
34	Iowa	14,750	0.6%
27	Kansas	23,691	1.0%
25	Kentucky	27,167	1.1%
16	Louisiana	39,936	1.7%
49	Maine	(2,950)	
13	Maryland	48,875	2.0%
18	Massachusetts	39,075	1.6%
50	Michigan	(24,025)	
24	Minnesota	27,623	1.2%
38	Mississippi	10,524	0.4%
22	Missouri	29,507	1.2%
42	Montana	5,989	0.3%
31	Nebraska	16,220	0.7%
32	Nevada	16,163	0.7%
45	New Hampshire	1,350	0.1%
17	New Jersey	39,088	1.6%
26	New Mexico	26,560	1.1%
10	New York	55,118	2.3%
4	North Carolina	101,781	4.3%
40	North Dakota	7,875	0.3%
47	Ohio	251	0.0%
19	Oklahoma	38,807	1.6%
20	Oregon	32,478	1.4%
21	Pennsylvania	30,668	1.3%
48	Rhode Island	(581)	0.0%
15	South Carolina	42,700	1.8%
39	South Dakota	9,263	0.4%
14	Tennessee	46,892	2.0%
1	Texas	442,794	18.5%
12	Utah	49,882	2.1%
46	Vermont	997	0.0%
6	Virginia	89,639	3.7%
9	Washington	74,602	3.1%
43	West Virginia	4,223	0.2%
30	Wisconsin	17,768	0.7%
44	Wyoming	3,246	0.1%

RANK ORDER

RANK	STATE	GAIN/LOSS	% of USA
1	Texas	442,794	18.5%
2	California	378,985	15.8%
3	Florida	168,113	7.0%
4	North Carolina	101,781	4.3%
5	Georgia	94,769	4.0%
6	Virginia	89,639	3.7%
7	Arizona	88,974	3.7%
8	Colorado	80,154	3.3%
9	Washington	74,602	3.1%
10	New York	55,118	2.3%
11	Illinois	51,132	2.1%
12	Utah	49,882	2.1%
13	Maryland	48,875	2.0%
14	Tennessee	46,892	2.0%
15	South Carolina	42,700	1.8%
16	Louisiana	39,936	1.7%
17	New Jersey	39,088	1.6%
18	Massachusetts	39,075	1.6%
19	Oklahoma	38,807	1.6%
20	Oregon	32,478	1.4%
21	Pennsylvania	30,668	1.3%
22	Missouri	29,507	1.2%
23	Indiana	28,019	1.2%
24	Minnesota	27,623	1.2%
25	Kentucky	27,167	1.1%
26	New Mexico	26,560	1.1%
27	Kansas	23,691	1.0%
28	Arkansas	22,905	1.0%
29	Alabama	22,160	0.9%
30	Wisconsin	17,768	0.7%
31	Nebraska	16,220	0.7%
32	Nevada	16,163	0.7%
33	Idaho	15,331	0.6%
34	Iowa	14,750	0.6%
35	Alaska	14,172	0.6%
36	Connecticut	12,111	0.5%
37	Hawaii	11,801	0.5%
38	Mississippi	10,524	0.4%
39	South Dakota	9,263	0.4%
40	North Dakota	7,875	0.3%
41	Delaware	7,340	0.3%
42	Montana	5,989	0.3%
43	West Virginia	4,223	0.2%
44	Wyoming	3,246	0.1%
45	New Hampshire	1,350	0.1%
46	Vermont	997	0.0%
47	Ohio	251	0.0%
48	Rhode Island	(581)	0.0%
49	Maine	(2,950)	
50	Michigan	(24,025)	
	District of Columbia	10,614	0.4%

Source: CQ Press using data from U.S. Bureau of the Census
  "Population Estimates" (February 2011, http://www.census.gov/popest/estimates.php)
*Resident population from July 1, 2009 to July 1, 2010.

Percent Change in Population: 2009 to 2010

National Percent Change = 0.8% Increase*

ALPHA ORDER

RANK	STATE	PERCENT CHANGE
32	Alabama	0.5
1	Alaska	2.0
5	Arizona	1.4
22	Arkansas	0.8
13	California	1.0
4	Colorado	1.6
40	Connecticut	0.3
22	Delaware	0.8
16	Florida	0.9
13	Georgia	1.0
16	Hawaii	0.9
13	Idaho	1.0
36	Illinois	0.4
36	Indiana	0.4
32	Iowa	0.5
22	Kansas	0.8
27	Kentucky	0.6
16	Louisiana	0.9
49	Maine	(0.2)
16	Maryland	0.9
27	Massachusetts	0.6
49	Michigan	(0.2)
32	Minnesota	0.5
36	Mississippi	0.4
32	Missouri	0.5
27	Montana	0.6
16	Nebraska	0.9
27	Nevada	0.6
46	New Hampshire	0.1
36	New Jersey	0.4
6	New Mexico	1.3
40	New York	0.3
8	North Carolina	1.1
7	North Dakota	1.2
47	Ohio	0.0
8	Oklahoma	1.1
22	Oregon	0.8
43	Pennsylvania	0.2
48	Rhode Island	(0.1)
16	South Carolina	0.9
8	South Dakota	1.1
26	Tennessee	0.7
2	Texas	1.8
2	Utah	1.8
43	Vermont	0.2
8	Virginia	1.1
8	Washington	1.1
43	West Virginia	0.2
40	Wisconsin	0.3
27	Wyoming	0.6

RANK ORDER

RANK	STATE	PERCENT CHANGE
1	Alaska	2.0
2	Texas	1.8
2	Utah	1.8
4	Colorado	1.6
5	Arizona	1.4
6	New Mexico	1.3
7	North Dakota	1.2
8	North Carolina	1.1
8	Oklahoma	1.1
8	South Dakota	1.1
8	Virginia	1.1
8	Washington	1.1
13	California	1.0
13	Georgia	1.0
13	Idaho	1.0
16	Florida	0.9
16	Hawaii	0.9
16	Louisiana	0.9
16	Maryland	0.9
16	Nebraska	0.9
16	South Carolina	0.9
22	Arkansas	0.8
22	Delaware	0.8
22	Kansas	0.8
22	Oregon	0.8
26	Tennessee	0.7
27	Kentucky	0.6
27	Massachusetts	0.6
27	Montana	0.6
27	Nevada	0.6
27	Wyoming	0.6
32	Alabama	0.5
32	Iowa	0.5
32	Minnesota	0.5
32	Missouri	0.5
36	Illinois	0.4
36	Indiana	0.4
36	Mississippi	0.4
36	New Jersey	0.4
40	Connecticut	0.3
40	New York	0.3
40	Wisconsin	0.3
43	Pennsylvania	0.2
43	Vermont	0.2
43	West Virginia	0.2
46	New Hampshire	0.1
47	Ohio	0.0
48	Rhode Island	(0.1)
49	Maine	(0.2)
49	Michigan	(0.2)
	District of Columbia	1.8

Source: CQ Press using data from U.S. Bureau of the Census
"Population Estimates" (February 2011, http://www.census.gov/popest/estimates.php)
*Resident population from July 1, 2009 to July 1, 2010.

Population in 2000 Census

National Total = 281,421,906*

ALPHA ORDER

RANK	STATE	POPULATION	% of USA
23	Alabama	4,447,100	1.6%
48	Alaska	626,932	0.2%
20	Arizona	5,130,632	1.8%
33	Arkansas	2,673,400	0.9%
1	California	33,871,648	12.0%
24	Colorado	4,301,261	1.5%
29	Connecticut	3,405,565	1.2%
45	Delaware	783,600	0.3%
4	Florida	15,982,378	5.7%
10	Georgia	8,186,453	2.9%
42	Hawaii	1,211,537	0.4%
39	Idaho	1,293,953	0.5%
5	Illinois	12,419,293	4.4%
14	Indiana	6,080,485	2.2%
30	Iowa	2,926,324	1.0%
32	Kansas	2,688,418	1.0%
25	Kentucky	4,041,769	1.4%
22	Louisiana	4,468,976	1.6%
40	Maine	1,274,923	0.5%
19	Maryland	5,296,486	1.9%
13	Massachusetts	6,349,097	2.3%
8	Michigan	9,938,444	3.5%
21	Minnesota	4,919,479	1.7%
31	Mississippi	2,844,658	1.0%
17	Missouri	5,595,211	2.0%
44	Montana	902,195	0.3%
38	Nebraska	1,711,263	0.6%
35	Nevada	1,998,257	0.7%
41	New Hampshire	1,235,786	0.4%
9	New Jersey	8,414,350	3.0%
36	New Mexico	1,819,046	0.6%
3	New York	18,976,457	6.7%
11	North Carolina	8,049,313	2.9%
47	North Dakota	642,200	0.2%
7	Ohio	11,353,140	4.0%
27	Oklahoma	3,450,654	1.2%
28	Oregon	3,421,399	1.2%
6	Pennsylvania	12,281,054	4.4%
43	Rhode Island	1,048,319	0.4%
26	South Carolina	4,012,012	1.4%
46	South Dakota	754,844	0.3%
16	Tennessee	5,689,283	2.0%
2	Texas	20,851,820	7.4%
34	Utah	2,233,169	0.8%
49	Vermont	608,827	0.2%
12	Virginia	7,078,515	2.5%
15	Washington	5,894,121	2.1%
37	West Virginia	1,808,344	0.6%
18	Wisconsin	5,363,675	1.9%
50	Wyoming	493,782	0.2%

RANK ORDER

RANK	STATE	POPULATION	% of USA
1	California	33,871,648	12.0%
2	Texas	20,851,820	7.4%
3	New York	18,976,457	6.7%
4	Florida	15,982,378	5.7%
5	Illinois	12,419,293	4.4%
6	Pennsylvania	12,281,054	4.4%
7	Ohio	11,353,140	4.0%
8	Michigan	9,938,444	3.5%
9	New Jersey	8,414,350	3.0%
10	Georgia	8,186,453	2.9%
11	North Carolina	8,049,313	2.9%
12	Virginia	7,078,515	2.5%
13	Massachusetts	6,349,097	2.3%
14	Indiana	6,080,485	2.2%
15	Washington	5,894,121	2.1%
16	Tennessee	5,689,283	2.0%
17	Missouri	5,595,211	2.0%
18	Wisconsin	5,363,675	1.9%
19	Maryland	5,296,486	1.9%
20	Arizona	5,130,632	1.8%
21	Minnesota	4,919,479	1.7%
22	Louisiana	4,468,976	1.6%
23	Alabama	4,447,100	1.6%
24	Colorado	4,301,261	1.5%
25	Kentucky	4,041,769	1.4%
26	South Carolina	4,012,012	1.4%
27	Oklahoma	3,450,654	1.2%
28	Oregon	3,421,399	1.2%
29	Connecticut	3,405,565	1.2%
30	Iowa	2,926,324	1.0%
31	Mississippi	2,844,658	1.0%
32	Kansas	2,688,418	1.0%
33	Arkansas	2,673,400	0.9%
34	Utah	2,233,169	0.8%
35	Nevada	1,998,257	0.7%
36	New Mexico	1,819,046	0.6%
37	West Virginia	1,808,344	0.6%
38	Nebraska	1,711,263	0.6%
39	Idaho	1,293,953	0.5%
40	Maine	1,274,923	0.5%
41	New Hampshire	1,235,786	0.4%
42	Hawaii	1,211,537	0.4%
43	Rhode Island	1,048,319	0.4%
44	Montana	902,195	0.3%
45	Delaware	783,600	0.3%
46	South Dakota	754,844	0.3%
47	North Dakota	642,200	0.2%
48	Alaska	626,932	0.2%
49	Vermont	608,827	0.2%
50	Wyoming	493,782	0.2%
	District of Columbia	572,059	0.2%

Source: U.S. Bureau of the Census
"First Census 2000 Results" (December 28, 2000, http://www.census.gov/main/www/cen2000.html)
*Resident population as of April 2000 Census.

Projected State Population in 2030

National Total = 363,584,435*

ALPHA ORDER

RANK	STATE	POPULATION	% of USA
24	Alabama	4,874,243	1.3%
46	Alaska	867,674	0.2%
10	Arizona	10,712,397	2.9%
32	Arkansas	3,240,208	0.9%
1	California	46,444,861	12.8%
22	Colorado	5,792,357	1.6%
30	Connecticut	3,688,630	1.0%
45	Delaware	1,012,658	0.3%
3	Florida	28,685,769	7.9%
8	Georgia	12,017,838	3.3%
41	Hawaii	1,466,046	0.4%
37	Idaho	1,969,624	0.5%
5	Illinois	13,432,892	3.7%
18	Indiana	6,810,108	1.9%
34	Iowa	2,955,172	0.8%
35	Kansas	2,940,084	0.8%
27	Kentucky	4,554,998	1.3%
26	Louisiana	4,802,633	1.3%
42	Maine	1,411,097	0.4%
16	Maryland	7,022,251	1.9%
17	Massachusetts	7,012,009	1.9%
11	Michigan	10,694,172	2.9%
20	Minnesota	6,306,130	1.7%
33	Mississippi	3,092,410	0.9%
19	Missouri	6,430,173	1.8%
44	Montana	1,044,898	0.3%
38	Nebraska	1,820,247	0.5%
28	Nevada	4,282,102	1.2%
40	New Hampshire	1,646,471	0.5%
13	New Jersey	9,802,440	2.7%
36	New Mexico	2,099,708	0.6%
4	New York	19,477,429	5.4%
7	North Carolina	12,227,739	3.4%
49	North Dakota	606,566	0.2%
9	Ohio	11,550,528	3.2%
29	Oklahoma	3,913,251	1.1%
25	Oregon	4,833,918	1.3%
6	Pennsylvania	12,768,184	3.5%
43	Rhode Island	1,152,941	0.3%
23	South Carolina	5,148,569	1.4%
47	South Dakota	800,462	0.2%
15	Tennessee	7,380,634	2.0%
2	Texas	33,317,744	9.2%
31	Utah	3,485,367	1.0%
48	Vermont	711,867	0.2%
12	Virginia	9,825,019	2.7%
14	Washington	8,624,801	2.4%
39	West Virginia	1,719,959	0.5%
21	Wisconsin	6,150,764	1.7%
50	Wyoming	522,979	0.1%

RANK ORDER

RANK	STATE	POPULATION	% of USA
1	California	46,444,861	12.8%
2	Texas	33,317,744	9.2%
3	Florida	28,685,769	7.9%
4	New York	19,477,429	5.4%
5	Illinois	13,432,892	3.7%
6	Pennsylvania	12,768,184	3.5%
7	North Carolina	12,227,739	3.4%
8	Georgia	12,017,838	3.3%
9	Ohio	11,550,528	3.2%
10	Arizona	10,712,397	2.9%
11	Michigan	10,694,172	2.9%
12	Virginia	9,825,019	2.7%
13	New Jersey	9,802,440	2.7%
14	Washington	8,624,801	2.4%
15	Tennessee	7,380,634	2.0%
16	Maryland	7,022,251	1.9%
17	Massachusetts	7,012,009	1.9%
18	Indiana	6,810,108	1.9%
19	Missouri	6,430,173	1.8%
20	Minnesota	6,306,130	1.7%
21	Wisconsin	6,150,764	1.7%
22	Colorado	5,792,357	1.6%
23	South Carolina	5,148,569	1.4%
24	Alabama	4,874,243	1.3%
25	Oregon	4,833,918	1.3%
26	Louisiana	4,802,633	1.3%
27	Kentucky	4,554,998	1.3%
28	Nevada	4,282,102	1.2%
29	Oklahoma	3,913,251	1.1%
30	Connecticut	3,688,630	1.0%
31	Utah	3,485,367	1.0%
32	Arkansas	3,240,208	0.9%
33	Mississippi	3,092,410	0.9%
34	Iowa	2,955,172	0.8%
35	Kansas	2,940,084	0.8%
36	New Mexico	2,099,708	0.6%
37	Idaho	1,969,624	0.5%
38	Nebraska	1,820,247	0.5%
39	West Virginia	1,719,959	0.5%
40	New Hampshire	1,646,471	0.5%
41	Hawaii	1,466,046	0.4%
42	Maine	1,411,097	0.4%
43	Rhode Island	1,152,941	0.3%
44	Montana	1,044,898	0.3%
45	Delaware	1,012,658	0.3%
46	Alaska	867,674	0.2%
47	South Dakota	800,462	0.2%
48	Vermont	711,867	0.2%
49	North Dakota	606,566	0.2%
50	Wyoming	522,979	0.1%
	District of Columbia	433,414	0.1%

Source: U.S. Bureau of the Census
"State Interim Population Projections: 2004-2030 "
(http://www.census.gov/population/www/projections/projectionsagesex.html)
*Based on 2000 Census.

Population per Square Mile in 2010

National Rate = 87.5 Persons per Square Mile*

ALPHA ORDER

RANK	STATE	RATE
27	Alabama	93.4
50	Alaska	1.2
33	Arizona	58.8
34	Arkansas	55.9
11	California	239.2
37	Colorado	49.2
4	Connecticut	728.7
6	Delaware	457.4
8	Florida	348.5
18	Georgia	172.3
13	Hawaii	202.3
44	Idaho	18.9
12	Illinois	233.2
16	Indiana	179.9
36	Iowa	54.1
40	Kansas	34.7
22	Kentucky	109.9
23	Louisiana	104.9
38	Maine	42.6
5	Maryland	591.2
3	Massachusetts	850.1
17	Michigan	175.7
31	Minnesota	66.5
32	Mississippi	63.1
28	Missouri	87.5
48	Montana	6.7
43	Nebraska	23.6
42	Nevada	24.2
21	New Hampshire	147.8
1	New Jersey	1,187.5
45	New Mexico	16.8
7	New York	415.4
15	North Carolina	194.6
47	North Dakota	9.5
10	Ohio	282.2
35	Oklahoma	54.3
39	Oregon	40.2
9	Pennsylvania	282.4
2	Rhode Island	1,022.1
20	South Carolina	152.9
46	South Dakota	10.8
19	Tennessee	153.7
26	Texas	96.5
41	Utah	34.4
30	Vermont	67.5
14	Virginia	201.4
25	Washington	101.5
29	West Virginia	75.9
24	Wisconsin	104.7
49	Wyoming	5.6

RANK ORDER

RANK	STATE	RATE
1	New Jersey	1,187.5
2	Rhode Island	1,022.1
3	Massachusetts	850.1
4	Connecticut	728.7
5	Maryland	591.2
6	Delaware	457.4
7	New York	415.4
8	Florida	348.5
9	Pennsylvania	282.4
10	Ohio	282.2
11	California	239.2
12	Illinois	233.2
13	Hawaii	202.3
14	Virginia	201.4
15	North Carolina	194.6
16	Indiana	179.9
17	Michigan	175.7
18	Georgia	172.3
19	Tennessee	153.7
20	South Carolina	152.9
21	New Hampshire	147.8
22	Kentucky	109.9
23	Louisiana	104.9
24	Wisconsin	104.7
25	Washington	101.5
26	Texas	96.5
27	Alabama	93.4
28	Missouri	87.5
29	West Virginia	75.9
30	Vermont	67.5
31	Minnesota	66.5
32	Mississippi	63.1
33	Arizona	58.8
34	Arkansas	55.9
35	Oklahoma	54.3
36	Iowa	54.1
37	Colorado	49.2
38	Maine	42.6
39	Oregon	40.2
40	Kansas	34.7
41	Utah	34.4
42	Nevada	24.2
43	Nebraska	23.6
44	Idaho	18.9
45	New Mexico	16.8
46	South Dakota	10.8
47	North Dakota	9.5
48	Montana	6.7
49	Wyoming	5.6
50	Alaska	1.2
	District of Columbia	10,009.7

Source: CQ Press using data from U.S. Bureau of the Census
"Population Estimates" (February 2011, http://www.census.gov/popest/estimates.php)
*Resident population. Based on land area of states.

Male Population in 2009

National Total = 151,449,490 Males

ALPHA ORDER

RANK	STATE	MALES	% of USA
23	Alabama	2,281,612	1.5%
47	Alaska	362,225	0.2%
14	Arizona	3,306,841	2.2%
32	Arkansas	1,415,500	0.9%
1	California	18,505,202	12.2%
22	Colorado	2,531,085	1.7%
29	Connecticut	1,717,636	1.1%
45	Delaware	429,662	0.3%
4	Florida	9,123,926	6.0%
9	Georgia	4,835,262	3.2%
40	Hawaii	654,421	0.4%
39	Idaho	775,918	0.5%
5	Illinois	6,359,626	4.2%
16	Indiana	3,164,688	2.1%
30	Iowa	1,485,609	1.0%
34	Kansas	1,399,823	0.9%
26	Kentucky	2,117,406	1.4%
25	Louisiana	2,185,135	1.4%
42	Maine	643,580	0.4%
20	Maryland	2,763,806	1.8%
15	Massachusetts	3,204,983	2.1%
8	Michigan	4,902,854	3.2%
21	Minnesota	2,620,570	1.7%
31	Mississippi	1,431,040	0.9%
18	Missouri	2,926,002	1.9%
44	Montana	487,981	0.3%
38	Nebraska	891,652	0.6%
35	Nevada	1,346,046	0.9%
41	New Hampshire	652,948	0.4%
11	New Jersey	4,268,344	2.8%
36	New Mexico	994,635	0.7%
3	New York	9,499,163	6.3%
10	North Carolina	4,590,185	3.0%
48	North Dakota	325,000	0.2%
7	Ohio	5,633,403	3.7%
28	Oklahoma	1,821,974	1.2%
27	Oregon	1,897,054	1.3%
6	Pennsylvania	6,138,709	4.1%
43	Rhode Island	511,490	0.3%
24	South Carolina	2,221,134	1.5%
46	South Dakota	405,920	0.3%
17	Tennessee	3,069,243	2.0%
2	Texas	12,378,092	8.2%
33	Utah	1,400,974	0.9%
49	Vermont	306,024	0.2%
12	Virginia	3,874,865	2.6%
13	Washington	3,328,953	2.2%
37	West Virginia	892,120	0.6%
19	Wisconsin	2,809,066	1.9%
50	Wyoming	277,040	0.2%

RANK ORDER

RANK	STATE	MALES	% of USA
1	California	18,505,202	12.2%
2	Texas	12,378,092	8.2%
3	New York	9,499,163	6.3%
4	Florida	9,123,926	6.0%
5	Illinois	6,359,626	4.2%
6	Pennsylvania	6,138,709	4.1%
7	Ohio	5,633,403	3.7%
8	Michigan	4,902,854	3.2%
9	Georgia	4,835,262	3.2%
10	North Carolina	4,590,185	3.0%
11	New Jersey	4,268,344	2.8%
12	Virginia	3,874,865	2.6%
13	Washington	3,328,953	2.2%
14	Arizona	3,306,841	2.2%
15	Massachusetts	3,204,983	2.1%
16	Indiana	3,164,688	2.1%
17	Tennessee	3,069,243	2.0%
18	Missouri	2,926,002	1.9%
19	Wisconsin	2,809,066	1.9%
20	Maryland	2,763,806	1.8%
21	Minnesota	2,620,570	1.7%
22	Colorado	2,531,085	1.7%
23	Alabama	2,281,612	1.5%
24	South Carolina	2,221,134	1.5%
25	Louisiana	2,185,135	1.4%
26	Kentucky	2,117,406	1.4%
27	Oregon	1,897,054	1.3%
28	Oklahoma	1,821,974	1.2%
29	Connecticut	1,717,636	1.1%
30	Iowa	1,485,609	1.0%
31	Mississippi	1,431,040	0.9%
32	Arkansas	1,415,500	0.9%
33	Utah	1,400,974	0.9%
34	Kansas	1,399,823	0.9%
35	Nevada	1,346,046	0.9%
36	New Mexico	994,635	0.7%
37	West Virginia	892,120	0.6%
38	Nebraska	891,652	0.6%
39	Idaho	775,918	0.5%
40	Hawaii	654,421	0.4%
41	New Hampshire	652,948	0.4%
42	Maine	643,580	0.4%
43	Rhode Island	511,490	0.3%
44	Montana	487,981	0.3%
45	Delaware	429,662	0.3%
46	South Dakota	405,920	0.3%
47	Alaska	362,225	0.2%
48	North Dakota	325,000	0.2%
49	Vermont	306,024	0.2%
50	Wyoming	277,040	0.2%
	District of Columbia	283,063	0.2%

Source: CQ Press using data from U.S. Bureau of the Census
   "SC-EST2009-AGESEX_RES - State Characteristic Estimates" (http://www.census.gov/popest/datasets.html)

Female Population in 2009

National Total = 155,557,060 Females

ALPHA ORDER

RANK	STATE	FEMALES	% of USA
23	Alabama	2,427,096	1.6%
47	Alaska	336,248	0.2%
15	Arizona	3,288,937	2.1%
32	Arkansas	1,473,950	0.9%
1	California	18,456,462	11.9%
22	Colorado	2,493,663	1.6%
29	Connecticut	1,800,652	1.2%
45	Delaware	455,460	0.3%
4	Florida	9,414,043	6.1%
9	Georgia	4,993,949	3.2%
42	Hawaii	640,757	0.4%
39	Idaho	769,883	0.5%
5	Illinois	6,550,783	4.2%
16	Indiana	3,258,425	2.1%
30	Iowa	1,522,247	1.0%
33	Kansas	1,418,924	0.9%
26	Kentucky	2,196,707	1.4%
25	Louisiana	2,306,941	1.5%
40	Maine	674,721	0.4%
19	Maryland	2,935,672	1.9%
13	Massachusetts	3,388,604	2.2%
8	Michigan	5,066,873	3.3%
21	Minnesota	2,645,644	1.7%
31	Mississippi	1,520,956	1.0%
18	Missouri	3,061,578	2.0%
44	Montana	487,008	0.3%
38	Nebraska	904,967	0.6%
35	Nevada	1,297,039	0.8%
41	New Hampshire	671,627	0.4%
11	New Jersey	4,439,395	2.9%
36	New Mexico	1,015,036	0.7%
3	New York	10,042,290	6.5%
10	North Carolina	4,790,699	3.1%
48	North Dakota	321,844	0.2%
7	Ohio	5,909,242	3.8%
28	Oklahoma	1,865,076	1.2%
27	Oregon	1,928,603	1.2%
6	Pennsylvania	6,466,058	4.2%
43	Rhode Island	541,719	0.3%
24	South Carolina	2,340,108	1.5%
46	South Dakota	406,463	0.3%
17	Tennessee	3,227,011	2.1%
2	Texas	12,404,210	8.0%
34	Utah	1,383,598	0.9%
49	Vermont	315,736	0.2%
12	Virginia	4,007,725	2.6%
14	Washington	3,335,242	2.1%
37	West Virginia	927,657	0.6%
20	Wisconsin	2,845,708	1.8%
50	Wyoming	267,230	0.2%

RANK ORDER

RANK	STATE	FEMALES	% of USA
1	California	18,456,462	11.9%
2	Texas	12,404,210	8.0%
3	New York	10,042,290	6.5%
4	Florida	9,414,043	6.1%
5	Illinois	6,550,783	4.2%
6	Pennsylvania	6,466,058	4.2%
7	Ohio	5,909,242	3.8%
8	Michigan	5,066,873	3.3%
9	Georgia	4,993,949	3.2%
10	North Carolina	4,790,699	3.1%
11	New Jersey	4,439,395	2.9%
12	Virginia	4,007,725	2.6%
13	Massachusetts	3,388,604	2.2%
14	Washington	3,335,242	2.1%
15	Arizona	3,288,937	2.1%
16	Indiana	3,258,425	2.1%
17	Tennessee	3,227,011	2.1%
18	Missouri	3,061,578	2.0%
19	Maryland	2,935,672	1.9%
20	Wisconsin	2,845,708	1.8%
21	Minnesota	2,645,644	1.7%
22	Colorado	2,493,663	1.6%
23	Alabama	2,427,096	1.6%
24	South Carolina	2,340,108	1.5%
25	Louisiana	2,306,941	1.5%
26	Kentucky	2,196,707	1.4%
27	Oregon	1,928,603	1.2%
28	Oklahoma	1,865,076	1.2%
29	Connecticut	1,800,652	1.2%
30	Iowa	1,522,247	1.0%
31	Mississippi	1,520,956	1.0%
32	Arkansas	1,473,950	0.9%
33	Kansas	1,418,924	0.9%
34	Utah	1,383,598	0.9%
35	Nevada	1,297,039	0.8%
36	New Mexico	1,015,036	0.7%
37	West Virginia	927,657	0.6%
38	Nebraska	904,967	0.6%
39	Idaho	769,883	0.5%
40	Maine	674,721	0.4%
41	New Hampshire	671,627	0.4%
42	Hawaii	640,757	0.4%
43	Rhode Island	541,719	0.3%
44	Montana	487,008	0.3%
45	Delaware	455,460	0.3%
46	South Dakota	406,463	0.3%
47	Alaska	336,248	0.2%
48	North Dakota	321,844	0.2%
49	Vermont	315,736	0.2%
50	Wyoming	267,230	0.2%
	District of Columbia	316,594	0.2%

Source: CQ Press using data from U.S. Bureau of the Census
"SC-EST2009-AGESEX_RES - State Characteristic Estimates" (http://www.census.gov/popest/datasets.html)

Male to Female Ratio in 2009

National Ratio = 97.4 Males per 100 Females

ALPHA ORDER

RANK	STATE	RATIO
50	Alabama	94.0
1	Alaska	107.7
9	Arizona	100.5
34	Arkansas	96.0
10	California	100.3
5	Colorado	101.5
37	Connecticut	95.4
47	Delaware	94.3
26	Florida	96.9
28	Georgia	96.8
4	Hawaii	102.1
8	Idaho	100.8
24	Illinois	97.1
24	Indiana	97.1
22	Iowa	97.6
16	Kansas	98.7
31	Kentucky	96.4
43	Louisiana	94.7
37	Maine	95.4
48	Maryland	94.1
44	Massachusetts	94.6
28	Michigan	96.8
15	Minnesota	99.1
48	Mississippi	94.1
36	Missouri	95.6
11	Montana	100.2
18	Nebraska	98.5
2	Nevada	103.8
23	New Hampshire	97.2
33	New Jersey	96.1
20	New Mexico	98.0
44	New York	94.6
35	North Carolina	95.8
7	North Dakota	101.0
39	Ohio	95.3
21	Oklahoma	97.7
19	Oregon	98.4
41	Pennsylvania	94.9
46	Rhode Island	94.4
41	South Carolina	94.9
12	South Dakota	99.9
40	Tennessee	95.1
13	Texas	99.8
6	Utah	101.3
26	Vermont	96.9
30	Virginia	96.7
13	Washington	99.8
32	West Virginia	96.2
16	Wisconsin	98.7
3	Wyoming	103.7

RANK ORDER

RANK	STATE	RATIO
1	Alaska	107.7
2	Nevada	103.8
3	Wyoming	103.7
4	Hawaii	102.1
5	Colorado	101.5
6	Utah	101.3
7	North Dakota	101.0
8	Idaho	100.8
9	Arizona	100.5
10	California	100.3
11	Montana	100.2
12	South Dakota	99.9
13	Texas	99.8
13	Washington	99.8
15	Minnesota	99.1
16	Kansas	98.7
16	Wisconsin	98.7
18	Nebraska	98.5
19	Oregon	98.4
20	New Mexico	98.0
21	Oklahoma	97.7
22	Iowa	97.6
23	New Hampshire	97.2
24	Illinois	97.1
24	Indiana	97.1
26	Florida	96.9
26	Vermont	96.9
28	Georgia	96.8
28	Michigan	96.8
30	Virginia	96.7
31	Kentucky	96.4
32	West Virginia	96.2
33	New Jersey	96.1
34	Arkansas	96.0
35	North Carolina	95.8
36	Missouri	95.6
37	Connecticut	95.4
37	Maine	95.4
39	Ohio	95.3
40	Tennessee	95.1
41	Pennsylvania	94.9
41	South Carolina	94.9
43	Louisiana	94.7
44	Massachusetts	94.6
44	New York	94.6
46	Rhode Island	94.4
47	Delaware	94.3
48	Maryland	94.1
48	Mississippi	94.1
50	Alabama	94.0
	District of Columbia	89.4

Source: CQ Press using data from U.S. Bureau of the Census
"SC-EST2009-AGESEX_RES - State Characteristic Estimates" (http://www.census.gov/popest/datasets.html)

White Population in 2009

National Total = 244,298,393 White Persons*

ALPHA ORDER

RANK	STATE	WHITES	% of USA
25	Alabama	3,340,085	1.4%
49	Alaska	490,858	0.2%
13	Arizona	5,677,252	2.3%
33	Arkansas	2,328,347	1.0%
1	California	28,244,628	11.6%
21	Colorado	4,495,567	1.8%
27	Connecticut	2,956,387	1.2%
45	Delaware	654,500	0.3%
3	Florida	14,725,600	6.0%
11	Georgia	6,391,950	2.6%
50	Hawaii	391,377	0.2%
39	Idaho	1,459,145	0.6%
6	Illinois	10,195,829	4.2%
15	Indiana	5,637,786	2.3%
30	Iowa	2,824,723	1.2%
32	Kansas	2,495,350	1.0%
22	Kentucky	3,865,858	1.6%
28	Louisiana	2,902,958	1.2%
40	Maine	1,267,444	0.5%
23	Maryland	3,588,912	1.5%
14	Massachusetts	5,664,723	2.3%
8	Michigan	8,091,776	3.3%
20	Minnesota	4,664,703	1.9%
35	Mississippi	1,784,587	0.7%
17	Missouri	5,084,023	2.1%
43	Montana	880,107	0.4%
38	Nebraska	1,637,009	0.7%
34	Nevada	2,122,890	0.9%
41	New Hampshire	1,261,735	0.5%
10	New Jersey	6,599,311	2.7%
37	New Mexico	1,680,251	0.7%
4	New York	14,350,944	5.9%
9	North Carolina	6,917,452	2.8%
47	North Dakota	589,112	0.2%
7	Ohio	9,771,805	4.0%
29	Oklahoma	2,876,092	1.2%
24	Oregon	3,435,729	1.4%
5	Pennsylvania	10,741,619	4.4%
42	Rhode Island	930,287	0.4%
26	South Carolina	3,140,443	1.3%
44	South Dakota	713,702	0.3%
19	Tennessee	5,048,678	2.1%
2	Texas	20,351,522	8.3%
31	Utah	2,580,338	1.1%
46	Vermont	598,423	0.2%
12	Virginia	5,735,104	2.3%
16	Washington	5,584,302	2.3%
36	West Virginia	1,718,074	0.7%
18	Wisconsin	5,056,461	2.1%
48	Wyoming	509,018	0.2%

RANK ORDER

RANK	STATE	WHITES	% of USA
1	California	28,244,628	11.6%
2	Texas	20,351,522	8.3%
3	Florida	14,725,600	6.0%
4	New York	14,350,944	5.9%
5	Pennsylvania	10,741,619	4.4%
6	Illinois	10,195,829	4.2%
7	Ohio	9,771,805	4.0%
8	Michigan	8,091,776	3.3%
9	North Carolina	6,917,452	2.8%
10	New Jersey	6,599,311	2.7%
11	Georgia	6,391,950	2.6%
12	Virginia	5,735,104	2.3%
13	Arizona	5,677,252	2.3%
14	Massachusetts	5,664,723	2.3%
15	Indiana	5,637,786	2.3%
16	Washington	5,584,302	2.3%
17	Missouri	5,084,023	2.1%
18	Wisconsin	5,056,461	2.1%
19	Tennessee	5,048,678	2.1%
20	Minnesota	4,664,703	1.9%
21	Colorado	4,495,567	1.8%
22	Kentucky	3,865,858	1.6%
23	Maryland	3,588,912	1.5%
24	Oregon	3,435,729	1.4%
25	Alabama	3,340,085	1.4%
26	South Carolina	3,140,443	1.3%
27	Connecticut	2,956,387	1.2%
28	Louisiana	2,902,958	1.2%
29	Oklahoma	2,876,092	1.2%
30	Iowa	2,824,723	1.2%
31	Utah	2,580,338	1.1%
32	Kansas	2,495,350	1.0%
33	Arkansas	2,328,347	1.0%
34	Nevada	2,122,890	0.9%
35	Mississippi	1,784,587	0.7%
36	West Virginia	1,718,074	0.7%
37	New Mexico	1,680,251	0.7%
38	Nebraska	1,637,009	0.7%
39	Idaho	1,459,145	0.6%
40	Maine	1,267,444	0.5%
41	New Hampshire	1,261,735	0.5%
42	Rhode Island	930,287	0.4%
43	Montana	880,107	0.4%
44	South Dakota	713,702	0.3%
45	Delaware	654,500	0.3%
46	Vermont	598,423	0.2%
47	North Dakota	589,112	0.2%
48	Wyoming	509,018	0.2%
49	Alaska	490,858	0.2%
50	Hawaii	391,377	0.2%
	District of Columbia	243,617	0.1%

Source: U.S. Bureau of the Census

"State Population Estimates - Characteristics" (http://www.census.gov/popest/states/asrh/)

*"White" is defined by Census as a person having origins in any of the original peoples of Europe, North Africa, or the Middle East. There are 199,851,240 non-Hispanic whites. Census states "Race is a self-identification data item in which respondents choose the race or races with which they most closely identify."

Percent of Population White in 2009

National Percent = 79.6% White*

ALPHA ORDER

RANK	STATE	PERCENT
43	Alabama	70.9
44	Alaska	70.3
21	Arizona	86.1
31	Arkansas	80.6
37	California	76.4
14	Colorado	89.5
26	Connecticut	84.0
39	Delaware	73.9
34	Florida	79.4
46	Georgia	65.0
50	Hawaii	30.2
4	Idaho	94.4
35	Illinois	79.0
20	Indiana	87.8
6	Iowa	93.9
17	Kansas	88.5
13	Kentucky	89.6
47	Louisiana	64.6
2	Maine	96.1
48	Maryland	63.0
22	Massachusetts	85.9
30	Michigan	81.2
16	Minnesota	88.6
49	Mississippi	60.5
24	Missouri	84.9
11	Montana	90.3
9	Nebraska	91.1
32	Nevada	80.3
3	New Hampshire	95.3
38	New Jersey	75.8
28	New Mexico	83.6
41	New York	73.4
40	North Carolina	73.7
9	North Dakota	91.1
25	Ohio	84.7
36	Oklahoma	78.0
12	Oregon	89.8
23	Pennsylvania	85.2
18	Rhode Island	88.3
45	South Carolina	68.9
19	South Dakota	87.9
33	Tennessee	80.2
29	Texas	82.1
8	Utah	92.7
1	Vermont	96.2
42	Virginia	72.8
27	Washington	83.8
4	West Virginia	94.4
15	Wisconsin	89.4
7	Wyoming	93.5

RANK ORDER

RANK	STATE	PERCENT
1	Vermont	96.2
2	Maine	96.1
3	New Hampshire	95.3
4	Idaho	94.4
4	West Virginia	94.4
6	Iowa	93.9
7	Wyoming	93.5
8	Utah	92.7
9	Nebraska	91.1
9	North Dakota	91.1
11	Montana	90.3
12	Oregon	89.8
13	Kentucky	89.6
14	Colorado	89.5
15	Wisconsin	89.4
16	Minnesota	88.6
17	Kansas	88.5
18	Rhode Island	88.3
19	South Dakota	87.9
20	Indiana	87.8
21	Arizona	86.1
22	Massachusetts	85.9
23	Pennsylvania	85.2
24	Missouri	84.9
25	Ohio	84.7
26	Connecticut	84.0
27	Washington	83.8
28	New Mexico	83.6
29	Texas	82.1
30	Michigan	81.2
31	Arkansas	80.6
32	Nevada	80.3
33	Tennessee	80.2
34	Florida	79.4
35	Illinois	79.0
36	Oklahoma	78.0
37	California	76.4
38	New Jersey	75.8
39	Delaware	73.9
40	North Carolina	73.7
41	New York	73.4
42	Virginia	72.8
43	Alabama	70.9
44	Alaska	70.3
45	South Carolina	68.9
46	Georgia	65.0
47	Louisiana	64.6
48	Maryland	63.0
49	Mississippi	60.5
50	Hawaii	30.2
	District of Columbia	40.6

Source: CQ Press using data from U.S. Bureau of the Census

"State Population Estimates - Characteristics" (http://www.census.gov/popest/states/asrh/)

*"White" is defined by Census as a person having origins in any of the original peoples of Europe, North Africa, or the Middle East. Non-Hispanic whites comprise 65.1% of the total population. Census states "Race is a self-identification data item in which respondents choose the race or races with which they most closely identify."

Black Population in 2009

National Total = 39,641,060 Black Persons*

ALPHA ORDER

RANK	STATE	BLACKS	% of USA
16	Alabama	1,240,739	3.1%
42	Alaska	29,396	0.1%
27	Arizona	290,422	0.7%
22	Arkansas	455,447	1.1%
5	California	2,453,695	6.2%
30	Colorado	221,919	0.6%
23	Connecticut	366,375	0.9%
32	Delaware	187,198	0.5%
2	Florida	2,983,327	7.5%
4	Georgia	2,970,607	7.5%
40	Hawaii	41,553	0.1%
44	Idaho	15,827	0.0%
7	Illinois	1,926,551	4.9%
20	Indiana	588,163	1.5%
34	Iowa	84,054	0.2%
33	Kansas	174,689	0.4%
25	Kentucky	339,435	0.9%
10	Louisiana	1,443,141	3.6%
45	Maine	15,327	0.0%
8	Maryland	1,691,143	4.3%
21	Massachusetts	468,838	1.2%
11	Michigan	1,413,582	3.6%
29	Minnesota	249,909	0.6%
17	Mississippi	1,097,462	2.8%
19	Missouri	688,360	1.7%
49	Montana	7,282	0.0%
35	Nebraska	83,400	0.2%
31	Nevada	218,469	0.6%
43	New Hampshire	18,114	0.0%
15	New Jersey	1,259,682	3.2%
39	New Mexico	62,773	0.2%
1	New York	3,352,100	8.5%
6	North Carolina	2,027,898	5.1%
47	North Dakota	7,813	0.0%
12	Ohio	1,395,368	3.5%
26	Oklahoma	296,880	0.7%
36	Oregon	78,348	0.2%
13	Pennsylvania	1,370,987	3.5%
37	Rhode Island	67,617	0.2%
14	South Carolina	1,287,368	3.2%
46	South Dakota	10,000	0.0%
18	Tennessee	1,060,260	2.7%
3	Texas	2,977,306	7.5%
41	Utah	38,164	0.1%
50	Vermont	5,917	0.0%
9	Virginia	1,573,645	4.0%
28	Washington	258,711	0.7%
38	West Virginia	66,433	0.2%
24	Wisconsin	347,797	0.9%
48	Wyoming	7,638	0.0%

RANK ORDER

RANK	STATE	BLACKS	% of USA
1	New York	3,352,100	8.5%
2	Florida	2,983,327	7.5%
3	Texas	2,977,306	7.5%
4	Georgia	2,970,607	7.5%
5	California	2,453,695	6.2%
6	North Carolina	2,027,898	5.1%
7	Illinois	1,926,551	4.9%
8	Maryland	1,691,143	4.3%
9	Virginia	1,573,645	4.0%
10	Louisiana	1,443,141	3.6%
11	Michigan	1,413,582	3.6%
12	Ohio	1,395,368	3.5%
13	Pennsylvania	1,370,987	3.5%
14	South Carolina	1,287,368	3.2%
15	New Jersey	1,259,682	3.2%
16	Alabama	1,240,739	3.1%
17	Mississippi	1,097,462	2.8%
18	Tennessee	1,060,260	2.7%
19	Missouri	688,360	1.7%
20	Indiana	588,163	1.5%
21	Massachusetts	468,838	1.2%
22	Arkansas	455,447	1.1%
23	Connecticut	366,375	0.9%
24	Wisconsin	347,797	0.9%
25	Kentucky	339,435	0.9%
26	Oklahoma	296,880	0.7%
27	Arizona	290,422	0.7%
28	Washington	258,711	0.7%
29	Minnesota	249,909	0.6%
30	Colorado	221,919	0.6%
31	Nevada	218,469	0.6%
32	Delaware	187,198	0.5%
33	Kansas	174,689	0.4%
34	Iowa	84,054	0.2%
35	Nebraska	83,400	0.2%
36	Oregon	78,348	0.2%
37	Rhode Island	67,617	0.2%
38	West Virginia	66,433	0.2%
39	New Mexico	62,773	0.2%
40	Hawaii	41,553	0.1%
41	Utah	38,164	0.1%
42	Alaska	29,396	0.1%
43	New Hampshire	18,114	0.0%
44	Idaho	15,827	0.0%
45	Maine	15,327	0.0%
46	South Dakota	10,000	0.0%
47	North Dakota	7,813	0.0%
48	Wyoming	7,638	0.0%
49	Montana	7,282	0.0%
50	Vermont	5,917	0.0%
	District of Columbia	323,931	0.8%

Source: U.S. Bureau of the Census
    "State Population Estimates - Characteristics" (http://www.census.gov/popest/states/asrh/)
*"Black" is defined by Census as a person having origins in any of the Black racial groups of Africa. Census states "Race is a self-identification data item in which respondents choose the race or races with which they most closely identify."

Percent of Population Black in 2009

National Percent = 12.9% Black*

ALPHA ORDER

RANK	STATE	PERCENT
6	Alabama	26.3
35	Alaska	4.2
33	Arizona	4.4
13	Arkansas	15.8
27	California	6.6
33	Colorado	4.4
21	Connecticut	10.4
8	Delaware	21.1
12	Florida	16.1
3	Georgia	30.2
38	Hawaii	3.2
48	Idaho	1.0
14	Illinois	14.9
22	Indiana	9.2
40	Iowa	2.8
29	Kansas	6.2
25	Kentucky	7.9
2	Louisiana	32.1
45	Maine	1.2
4	Maryland	29.7
26	Massachusetts	7.1
16	Michigan	14.2
31	Minnesota	4.7
1	Mississippi	37.2
19	Missouri	11.5
50	Montana	0.7
32	Nebraska	4.6
23	Nevada	8.3
42	New Hampshire	1.4
15	New Jersey	14.5
39	New Mexico	3.1
10	New York	17.2
7	North Carolina	21.6
45	North Dakota	1.2
17	Ohio	12.1
24	Oklahoma	8.1
41	Oregon	2.0
20	Pennsylvania	10.9
28	Rhode Island	6.4
5	South Carolina	28.2
45	South Dakota	1.2
11	Tennessee	16.8
18	Texas	12.0
42	Utah	1.4
48	Vermont	1.0
9	Virginia	20.0
36	Washington	3.9
37	West Virginia	3.7
29	Wisconsin	6.2
42	Wyoming	1.4

RANK ORDER

RANK	STATE	PERCENT
1	Mississippi	37.2
2	Louisiana	32.1
3	Georgia	30.2
4	Maryland	29.7
5	South Carolina	28.2
6	Alabama	26.3
7	North Carolina	21.6
8	Delaware	21.1
9	Virginia	20.0
10	New York	17.2
11	Tennessee	16.8
12	Florida	16.1
13	Arkansas	15.8
14	Illinois	14.9
15	New Jersey	14.5
16	Michigan	14.2
17	Ohio	12.1
18	Texas	12.0
19	Missouri	11.5
20	Pennsylvania	10.9
21	Connecticut	10.4
22	Indiana	9.2
23	Nevada	8.3
24	Oklahoma	8.1
25	Kentucky	7.9
26	Massachusetts	7.1
27	California	6.6
28	Rhode Island	6.4
29	Kansas	6.2
29	Wisconsin	6.2
31	Minnesota	4.7
32	Nebraska	4.6
33	Arizona	4.4
33	Colorado	4.4
35	Alaska	4.2
36	Washington	3.9
37	West Virginia	3.7
38	Hawaii	3.2
39	New Mexico	3.1
40	Iowa	2.8
41	Oregon	2.0
42	New Hampshire	1.4
42	Utah	1.4
42	Wyoming	1.4
45	Maine	1.2
45	North Dakota	1.2
45	South Dakota	1.2
48	Idaho	1.0
48	Vermont	1.0
50	Montana	0.7

District of Columbia 54.0

Source: CQ Press using data from U.S. Bureau of the Census
"State Population Estimates - Characteristics" (http://www.census.gov/popest/states/asrh/)
*"Black" is defined by Census as a person having origins in any of the Black racial groups of Africa. Census states "Race is a self-identification data item in which respondents choose the race or races with which they most closely identify."

Hispanic Population in 2009

National Total = 48,419,324 Hispanics*

ALPHA ORDER

RANK	STATE	HISPANICS	% of USA
34	Alabama	152,516	0.3%
42	Alaska	44,480	0.1%
5	Arizona	2,031,650	4.2%
31	Arkansas	172,991	0.4%
1	California	13,681,375	28.3%
8	Colorado	1,018,204	2.1%
17	Connecticut	434,471	0.9%
41	Delaware	63,892	0.1%
3	Florida	3,992,297	8.2%
10	Georgia	819,887	1.7%
38	Hawaii	115,967	0.2%
32	Idaho	165,285	0.3%
6	Illinois	1,968,599	4.1%
21	Indiana	350,676	0.7%
36	Iowa	134,402	0.3%
26	Kansas	263,307	0.5%
39	Kentucky	115,416	0.2%
33	Louisiana	162,981	0.3%
48	Maine	18,265	0.0%
20	Maryland	411,133	0.8%
15	Massachusetts	582,881	1.2%
19	Michigan	421,106	0.9%
28	Minnesota	226,384	0.5%
40	Mississippi	74,447	0.2%
30	Missouri	203,907	0.4%
45	Montana	30,265	0.1%
35	Nebraska	150,470	0.3%
12	Nevada	700,294	1.4%
44	New Hampshire	36,867	0.1%
7	New Jersey	1,452,824	3.0%
9	New Mexico	915,738	1.9%
4	New York	3,274,385	6.8%
11	North Carolina	717,662	1.5%
49	North Dakota	14,718	0.0%
23	Ohio	326,413	0.7%
24	Oklahoma	301,840	0.6%
18	Oregon	428,469	0.9%
14	Pennsylvania	646,524	1.3%
37	Rhode Island	127,849	0.3%
29	South Carolina	206,760	0.4%
46	South Dakota	23,455	0.0%
27	Tennessee	261,793	0.5%
2	Texas	9,148,056	18.9%
22	Utah	343,164	0.7%
50	Vermont	9,184	0.0%
16	Virginia	569,921	1.2%
13	Washington	687,367	1.4%
47	West Virginia	22,662	0.0%
25	Wisconsin	299,123	0.6%
43	Wyoming	43,977	0.1%

RANK ORDER

RANK	STATE	HISPANICS	% of USA
1	California	13,681,375	28.3%
2	Texas	9,148,056	18.9%
3	Florida	3,992,297	8.2%
4	New York	3,274,385	6.8%
5	Arizona	2,031,650	4.2%
6	Illinois	1,968,599	4.1%
7	New Jersey	1,452,824	3.0%
8	Colorado	1,018,204	2.1%
9	New Mexico	915,738	1.9%
10	Georgia	819,887	1.7%
11	North Carolina	717,662	1.5%
12	Nevada	700,294	1.4%
13	Washington	687,367	1.4%
14	Pennsylvania	646,524	1.3%
15	Massachusetts	582,881	1.2%
16	Virginia	569,921	1.2%
17	Connecticut	434,471	0.9%
18	Oregon	428,469	0.9%
19	Michigan	421,106	0.9%
20	Maryland	411,133	0.8%
21	Indiana	350,676	0.7%
22	Utah	343,164	0.7%
23	Ohio	326,413	0.7%
24	Oklahoma	301,840	0.6%
25	Wisconsin	299,123	0.6%
26	Kansas	263,307	0.5%
27	Tennessee	261,793	0.5%
28	Minnesota	226,384	0.5%
29	South Carolina	206,760	0.4%
30	Missouri	203,907	0.4%
31	Arkansas	172,991	0.4%
32	Idaho	165,285	0.3%
33	Louisiana	162,981	0.3%
34	Alabama	152,516	0.3%
35	Nebraska	150,470	0.3%
36	Iowa	134,402	0.3%
37	Rhode Island	127,849	0.3%
38	Hawaii	115,967	0.2%
39	Kentucky	115,416	0.2%
40	Mississippi	74,447	0.2%
41	Delaware	63,892	0.1%
42	Alaska	44,480	0.1%
43	Wyoming	43,977	0.1%
44	New Hampshire	36,867	0.1%
45	Montana	30,265	0.1%
46	South Dakota	23,455	0.0%
47	West Virginia	22,662	0.0%
48	Maine	18,265	0.0%
49	North Dakota	14,718	0.0%
50	Vermont	9,184	0.0%
	District of Columbia	53,025	0.1%

Source: U.S. Bureau of the Census
    "State Population Estimates - Characteristics" (http://www.census.gov/popest/states/asrh/)
*Persons of Hispanic origin may be of any race. Census states "Race is a self-identification data item in which respondents choose the race or races with which they most closely identify."

Percent of Population Hispanic in 2009

National Percent = 15.8% Hispanic*

ALPHA ORDER

RANK	STATE	PERCENT
40	Alabama	3.2
28	Alaska	6.4
4	Arizona	30.8
29	Arkansas	6.0
2	California	37.0
7	Colorado	20.3
11	Connecticut	12.3
25	Delaware	7.2
6	Florida	21.5
21	Georgia	8.3
18	Hawaii	9.0
15	Idaho	10.7
10	Illinois	15.2
30	Indiana	5.5
33	Iowa	4.5
17	Kansas	9.3
45	Kentucky	2.7
38	Louisiana	3.6
49	Maine	1.4
25	Maryland	7.2
19	Massachusetts	8.8
36	Michigan	4.2
35	Minnesota	4.3
46	Mississippi	2.5
39	Missouri	3.4
41	Montana	3.1
20	Nebraska	8.4
5	Nevada	26.5
43	New Hampshire	2.8
9	New Jersey	16.7
1	New Mexico	45.6
8	New York	16.8
24	North Carolina	7.7
47	North Dakota	2.3
43	Ohio	2.8
22	Oklahoma	8.2
14	Oregon	11.2
32	Pennsylvania	5.1
13	Rhode Island	12.1
33	South Carolina	4.5
42	South Dakota	2.9
36	Tennessee	4.2
3	Texas	36.9
11	Utah	12.3
48	Vermont	1.5
25	Virginia	7.2
16	Washington	10.3
50	West Virginia	1.2
31	Wisconsin	5.3
23	Wyoming	8.1

RANK ORDER

RANK	STATE	PERCENT
1	New Mexico	45.6
2	California	37.0
3	Texas	36.9
4	Arizona	30.8
5	Nevada	26.5
6	Florida	21.5
7	Colorado	20.3
8	New York	16.8
9	New Jersey	16.7
10	Illinois	15.2
11	Connecticut	12.3
11	Utah	12.3
13	Rhode Island	12.1
14	Oregon	11.2
15	Idaho	10.7
16	Washington	10.3
17	Kansas	9.3
18	Hawaii	9.0
19	Massachusetts	8.8
20	Nebraska	8.4
21	Georgia	8.3
22	Oklahoma	8.2
23	Wyoming	8.1
24	North Carolina	7.7
25	Delaware	7.2
25	Maryland	7.2
25	Virginia	7.2
28	Alaska	6.4
29	Arkansas	6.0
30	Indiana	5.5
31	Wisconsin	5.3
32	Pennsylvania	5.1
33	Iowa	4.5
33	South Carolina	4.5
35	Minnesota	4.3
36	Michigan	4.2
36	Tennessee	4.2
38	Louisiana	3.6
39	Missouri	3.4
40	Alabama	3.2
41	Montana	3.1
42	South Dakota	2.9
43	New Hampshire	2.8
43	Ohio	2.8
45	Kentucky	2.7
46	Mississippi	2.5
47	North Dakota	2.3
48	Vermont	1.5
49	Maine	1.4
50	West Virginia	1.2

District of Columbia 8.8

Source: CQ Press using data from U.S. Bureau of the Census
"State Population Estimates - Characteristics" (http://www.census.gov/popest/states/asrh/)
*Persons of Hispanic origin may be of any race. Census states "Race is a self-identification data item in which respondents choose the race or races with which they most closely identify."

Asian Population in 2009

National Total = 14,013,954 Asians*

ALPHA ORDER

RANK	STATE	ASIANS	% of USA
33	Alabama	49,031	0.3%
35	Alaska	34,590	0.2%
19	Arizona	173,314	1.2%
36	Arkansas	33,713	0.2%
1	California	4,689,992	33.5%
21	Colorado	136,984	1.0%
22	Connecticut	126,996	0.9%
40	Delaware	26,512	0.2%
8	Florida	445,494	3.2%
13	Georgia	290,045	2.1%
6	Hawaii	502,372	3.6%
43	Idaho	18,301	0.1%
5	Illinois	567,673	4.1%
24	Indiana	93,813	0.7%
32	Iowa	49,975	0.4%
28	Kansas	64,863	0.5%
34	Kentucky	46,111	0.3%
27	Louisiana	65,928	0.5%
44	Maine	12,757	0.1%
12	Maryland	297,997	2.1%
10	Massachusetts	334,709	2.4%
14	Michigan	241,597	1.7%
15	Minnesota	198,574	1.4%
42	Mississippi	25,726	0.2%
25	Missouri	91,035	0.6%
48	Montana	6,810	0.0%
37	Nebraska	30,509	0.2%
18	Nevada	173,909	1.2%
41	New Hampshire	25,931	0.2%
4	New Jersey	683,454	4.9%
38	New Mexico	30,160	0.2%
2	New York	1,387,848	9.9%
16	North Carolina	192,121	1.4%
49	North Dakota	5,328	0.0%
17	Ohio	184,606	1.3%
29	Oklahoma	62,699	0.4%
20	Oregon	142,728	1.0%
11	Pennsylvania	317,580	2.3%
39	Rhode Island	29,366	0.2%
30	South Carolina	60,212	0.4%
47	South Dakota	7,219	0.1%
26	Tennessee	87,769	0.6%
3	Texas	883,806	6.3%
31	Utah	57,120	0.4%
46	Vermont	7,298	0.1%
9	Virginia	397,476	2.8%
7	Washington	463,995	3.3%
45	West Virginia	12,201	0.1%
23	Wisconsin	121,716	0.9%
50	Wyoming	4,554	0.0%

RANK ORDER

RANK	STATE	ASIANS	% of USA
1	California	4,689,992	33.5%
2	New York	1,387,848	9.9%
3	Texas	883,806	6.3%
4	New Jersey	683,454	4.9%
5	Illinois	567,673	4.1%
6	Hawaii	502,372	3.6%
7	Washington	463,995	3.3%
8	Florida	445,494	3.2%
9	Virginia	397,476	2.8%
10	Massachusetts	334,709	2.4%
11	Pennsylvania	317,580	2.3%
12	Maryland	297,997	2.1%
13	Georgia	290,045	2.1%
14	Michigan	241,597	1.7%
15	Minnesota	198,574	1.4%
16	North Carolina	192,121	1.4%
17	Ohio	184,606	1.3%
18	Nevada	173,909	1.2%
19	Arizona	173,314	1.2%
20	Oregon	142,728	1.0%
21	Colorado	136,984	1.0%
22	Connecticut	126,996	0.9%
23	Wisconsin	121,716	0.9%
24	Indiana	93,813	0.7%
25	Missouri	91,035	0.6%
26	Tennessee	87,769	0.6%
27	Louisiana	65,928	0.5%
28	Kansas	64,863	0.5%
29	Oklahoma	62,699	0.4%
30	South Carolina	60,212	0.4%
31	Utah	57,120	0.4%
32	Iowa	49,975	0.4%
33	Alabama	49,031	0.3%
34	Kentucky	46,111	0.3%
35	Alaska	34,590	0.2%
36	Arkansas	33,713	0.2%
37	Nebraska	30,509	0.2%
38	New Mexico	30,160	0.2%
39	Rhode Island	29,366	0.2%
40	Delaware	26,512	0.2%
41	New Hampshire	25,931	0.2%
42	Mississippi	25,726	0.2%
43	Idaho	18,301	0.1%
44	Maine	12,757	0.1%
45	West Virginia	12,201	0.1%
46	Vermont	7,298	0.1%
47	South Dakota	7,219	0.1%
48	Montana	6,810	0.0%
49	North Dakota	5,328	0.0%
50	Wyoming	4,554	0.0%
	District of Columbia	19,437	0.1%

Source: U.S. Bureau of the Census
    "State Population Estimates - Characteristics" (http://www.census.gov/popest/states/asrh/)
*Census states "Race is a self-identification data item in which respondents choose the race or races with which they most closely identify."

Percent of Population Asian in 2009

National Percent = 4.6% Asian*

ALPHA ORDER

RANK	STATE	PERCENT
43	Alabama	1.0
9	Alaska	5.0
20	Arizona	2.6
39	Arkansas	1.2
2	California	12.7
19	Colorado	2.7
14	Connecticut	3.6
16	Delaware	3.0
22	Florida	2.4
16	Georgia	3.0
1	Hawaii	38.8
39	Idaho	1.2
11	Illinois	4.4
33	Indiana	1.5
29	Iowa	1.7
24	Kansas	2.3
42	Kentucky	1.1
33	Louisiana	1.5
43	Maine	1.0
7	Maryland	5.2
8	Massachusetts	5.1
22	Michigan	2.4
12	Minnesota	3.8
45	Mississippi	0.9
33	Missouri	1.5
49	Montana	0.7
29	Nebraska	1.7
6	Nevada	6.6
27	New Hampshire	2.0
3	New Jersey	7.8
33	New Mexico	1.5
4	New York	7.1
27	North Carolina	2.0
47	North Dakota	0.8
32	Ohio	1.6
29	Oklahoma	1.7
13	Oregon	3.7
21	Pennsylvania	2.5
18	Rhode Island	2.8
38	South Carolina	1.3
45	South Dakota	0.9
37	Tennessee	1.4
14	Texas	3.6
26	Utah	2.1
39	Vermont	1.2
9	Virginia	5.0
5	Washington	7.0
49	West Virginia	0.7
25	Wisconsin	2.2
47	Wyoming	0.8

RANK ORDER

RANK	STATE	PERCENT
1	Hawaii	38.8
2	California	12.7
3	New Jersey	7.8
4	New York	7.1
5	Washington	7.0
6	Nevada	6.6
7	Maryland	5.2
8	Massachusetts	5.1
9	Alaska	5.0
9	Virginia	5.0
11	Illinois	4.4
12	Minnesota	3.8
13	Oregon	3.7
14	Connecticut	3.6
14	Texas	3.6
16	Delaware	3.0
16	Georgia	3.0
18	Rhode Island	2.8
19	Colorado	2.7
20	Arizona	2.6
21	Pennsylvania	2.5
22	Florida	2.4
22	Michigan	2.4
24	Kansas	2.3
25	Wisconsin	2.2
26	Utah	2.1
27	New Hampshire	2.0
27	North Carolina	2.0
29	Iowa	1.7
29	Nebraska	1.7
29	Oklahoma	1.7
32	Ohio	1.6
33	Indiana	1.5
33	Louisiana	1.5
33	Missouri	1.5
33	New Mexico	1.5
37	Tennessee	1.4
38	South Carolina	1.3
39	Arkansas	1.2
39	Idaho	1.2
39	Vermont	1.2
42	Kentucky	1.1
43	Alabama	1.0
43	Maine	1.0
45	Mississippi	0.9
45	South Dakota	0.9
47	North Dakota	0.8
47	Wyoming	0.8
49	Montana	0.7
49	West Virginia	0.7

District of Columbia	3.2

Source: CQ Press using data from U.S. Bureau of the Census
"State Population Estimates - Characteristics" (http://www.census.gov/popest/states/asrh/)
*Census states "Race is a self-identification data item in which respondents choose the race or races with which they most closely identify."

American Indian Population in 2009

National Total = 3,151,284 American Indians*

ALPHA ORDER

RANK	STATE	INDIANS	% of USA
31	Alabama	24,851	0.8%
9	Alaska	106,398	3.4%
2	Arizona	320,587	10.2%
30	Arkansas	25,195	0.8%
1	California	447,424	14.2%
15	Colorado	62,231	2.0%
41	Connecticut	13,586	0.4%
49	Delaware	3,474	0.1%
10	Florida	93,723	3.0%
21	Georgia	37,427	1.2%
44	Hawaii	8,136	0.3%
32	Idaho	23,986	0.8%
18	Illinois	45,873	1.5%
36	Indiana	20,698	0.7%
42	Iowa	13,248	0.4%
27	Kansas	29,355	0.9%
43	Kentucky	11,593	0.4%
28	Louisiana	29,025	0.9%
45	Maine	8,067	0.3%
34	Maryland	21,134	0.7%
35	Massachusetts	20,812	0.7%
14	Michigan	62,485	2.0%
12	Minnesota	66,640	2.1%
39	Mississippi	15,500	0.5%
24	Missouri	31,135	1.0%
13	Montana	62,873	2.0%
37	Nebraska	19,999	0.6%
19	Nevada	39,588	1.3%
48	New Hampshire	3,848	0.1%
23	New Jersey	31,574	1.0%
4	New Mexico	195,403	6.2%
8	New York	110,304	3.5%
6	North Carolina	117,497	3.7%
22	North Dakota	36,258	1.2%
25	Ohio	30,008	1.0%
3	Oklahoma	296,182	9.4%
16	Oregon	59,665	1.9%
29	Pennsylvania	28,593	0.9%
46	Rhode Island	6,801	0.2%
38	South Carolina	19,614	0.6%
11	South Dakota	68,976	2.2%
33	Tennessee	21,737	0.7%
5	Texas	193,482	6.1%
20	Utah	39,289	1.2%
50	Vermont	2,452	0.1%
26	Virginia	29,587	0.9%
7	Washington	117,121	3.7%
47	West Virginia	4,320	0.1%
17	Wisconsin	57,060	1.8%
40	Wyoming	14,118	0.4%

RANK ORDER

RANK	STATE	INDIANS	% of USA
1	California	447,424	14.2%
2	Arizona	320,587	10.2%
3	Oklahoma	296,182	9.4%
4	New Mexico	195,403	6.2%
5	Texas	193,482	6.1%
6	North Carolina	117,497	3.7%
7	Washington	117,121	3.7%
8	New York	110,304	3.5%
9	Alaska	106,398	3.4%
10	Florida	93,723	3.0%
11	South Dakota	68,976	2.2%
12	Minnesota	66,640	2.1%
13	Montana	62,873	2.0%
14	Michigan	62,485	2.0%
15	Colorado	62,231	2.0%
16	Oregon	59,665	1.9%
17	Wisconsin	57,060	1.8%
18	Illinois	45,873	1.5%
19	Nevada	39,588	1.3%
20	Utah	39,289	1.2%
21	Georgia	37,427	1.2%
22	North Dakota	36,258	1.2%
23	New Jersey	31,574	1.0%
24	Missouri	31,135	1.0%
25	Ohio	30,008	1.0%
26	Virginia	29,587	0.9%
27	Kansas	29,355	0.9%
28	Louisiana	29,025	0.9%
29	Pennsylvania	28,593	0.9%
30	Arkansas	25,195	0.8%
31	Alabama	24,851	0.8%
32	Idaho	23,986	0.8%
33	Tennessee	21,737	0.7%
34	Maryland	21,134	0.7%
35	Massachusetts	20,812	0.7%
36	Indiana	20,698	0.7%
37	Nebraska	19,999	0.6%
38	South Carolina	19,614	0.6%
39	Mississippi	15,500	0.5%
40	Wyoming	14,118	0.4%
41	Connecticut	13,586	0.4%
42	Iowa	13,248	0.4%
43	Kentucky	11,593	0.4%
44	Hawaii	8,136	0.3%
45	Maine	8,067	0.3%
46	Rhode Island	6,801	0.2%
47	West Virginia	4,320	0.1%
48	New Hampshire	3,848	0.1%
49	Delaware	3,474	0.1%
50	Vermont	2,452	0.1%
	District of Columbia	2,352	0.1%

Source: U.S. Bureau of the Census
   "State Population Estimates - Characteristics" (http://www.census.gov/popest/states/asrh/)
*Includes Alaska Native populations. Census states "Race is a self-identification data item in which respondents choose the race or races with which they most closely identify."

Percent of Population American Indian in 2009

National Percent = 1.0% American Indian*

ALPHA ORDER

RANK	STATE	PERCENT
29	Alabama	0.5
1	Alaska	15.2
7	Arizona	4.9
21	Arkansas	0.9
16	California	1.2
16	Colorado	1.2
33	Connecticut	0.4
33	Delaware	0.4
29	Florida	0.5
33	Georgia	0.4
23	Hawaii	0.6
10	Idaho	1.6
33	Illinois	0.4
43	Indiana	0.3
33	Iowa	0.4
19	Kansas	1.0
43	Kentucky	0.3
23	Louisiana	0.6
23	Maine	0.6
33	Maryland	0.4
43	Massachusetts	0.3
23	Michigan	0.6
14	Minnesota	1.3
29	Mississippi	0.5
29	Missouri	0.5
5	Montana	6.4
18	Nebraska	1.1
12	Nevada	1.5
43	New Hampshire	0.3
33	New Jersey	0.4
2	New Mexico	9.7
23	New York	0.6
14	North Carolina	1.3
6	North Dakota	5.6
43	Ohio	0.3
4	Oklahoma	8.0
10	Oregon	1.6
49	Pennsylvania	0.2
23	Rhode Island	0.6
33	South Carolina	0.4
3	South Dakota	8.5
43	Tennessee	0.3
22	Texas	0.8
13	Utah	1.4
33	Vermont	0.4
33	Virginia	0.4
9	Washington	1.8
49	West Virginia	0.2
19	Wisconsin	1.0
8	Wyoming	2.6

RANK ORDER

RANK	STATE	PERCENT
1	Alaska	15.2
2	New Mexico	9.7
3	South Dakota	8.5
4	Oklahoma	8.0
5	Montana	6.4
6	North Dakota	5.6
7	Arizona	4.9
8	Wyoming	2.6
9	Washington	1.8
10	Idaho	1.6
10	Oregon	1.6
12	Nevada	1.5
13	Utah	1.4
14	Minnesota	1.3
14	North Carolina	1.3
16	California	1.2
16	Colorado	1.2
18	Nebraska	1.1
19	Kansas	1.0
19	Wisconsin	1.0
21	Arkansas	0.9
22	Texas	0.8
23	Hawaii	0.6
23	Louisiana	0.6
23	Maine	0.6
23	Michigan	0.6
23	New York	0.6
23	Rhode Island	0.6
29	Alabama	0.5
29	Florida	0.5
29	Mississippi	0.5
29	Missouri	0.5
33	Connecticut	0.4
33	Delaware	0.4
33	Georgia	0.4
33	Illinois	0.4
33	Iowa	0.4
33	Maryland	0.4
33	New Jersey	0.4
33	South Carolina	0.4
33	Vermont	0.4
33	Virginia	0.4
43	Indiana	0.3
43	Kentucky	0.3
43	Massachusetts	0.3
43	New Hampshire	0.3
43	Ohio	0.3
43	Tennessee	0.3
49	Pennsylvania	0.2
49	West Virginia	0.2
	District of Columbia	0.4

Source: CQ Press using data from U.S. Bureau of the Census
"State Population Estimates - Characteristics" (http://www.census.gov/popest/states/asrh/)
*Includes Alaska Native populations. Census states "Race is a self-identification data item in which respondents choose the race or races with which they most closely identify."

Mixed Race Population in 2009

National Total = 5,323,506 Mixed Race*

ALPHA ORDER

RANK	STATE	MIXED RACE	% of USA
29	Alabama	51,776	1.0%
37	Alaska	32,507	0.6%
15	Arizona	120,561	2.3%
34	Arkansas	43,268	0.8%
1	California	966,467	18.2%
17	Colorado	100,344	1.9%
28	Connecticut	52,072	1.0%
46	Delaware	12,908	0.2%
4	Florida	271,190	5.1%
13	Georgia	130,390	2.4%
5	Hawaii	233,029	4.4%
39	Idaho	26,356	0.5%
7	Illinois	165,158	3.1%
23	Indiana	79,377	1.5%
36	Iowa	34,247	0.6%
27	Kansas	52,253	1.0%
32	Kentucky	48,677	0.9%
31	Louisiana	49,080	0.9%
45	Maine	14,222	0.3%
20	Maryland	95,514	1.8%
18	Massachusetts	98,852	1.9%
9	Michigan	155,850	2.9%
22	Minnesota	82,819	1.6%
38	Mississippi	27,597	0.5%
21	Missouri	88,147	1.7%
43	Montana	17,210	0.3%
40	Nebraska	24,023	0.5%
25	Nevada	73,753	1.4%
44	New Hampshire	14,409	0.3%
14	New Jersey	125,777	2.4%
35	New Mexico	38,008	0.7%
3	New York	319,689	6.0%
16	North Carolina	118,754	2.2%
49	North Dakota	8,015	0.2%
8	Ohio	156,307	2.9%
10	Oklahoma	151,250	2.8%
19	Oregon	97,817	1.8%
11	Pennsylvania	139,802	2.6%
42	Rhode Island	17,646	0.3%
30	South Carolina	50,697	1.0%
47	South Dakota	12,013	0.2%
24	Tennessee	73,945	1.4%
2	Texas	344,423	6.5%
33	Utah	48,032	0.9%
50	Vermont	7,448	0.1%
12	Virginia	139,618	2.6%
6	Washington	206,681	3.9%
41	West Virginia	18,247	0.3%
26	Wisconsin	69,124	1.3%
48	Wyoming	8,427	0.2%

RANK ORDER

RANK	STATE	MIXED RACE	% of USA
1	California	966,467	18.2%
2	Texas	344,423	6.5%
3	New York	319,689	6.0%
4	Florida	271,190	5.1%
5	Hawaii	233,029	4.4%
6	Washington	206,681	3.9%
7	Illinois	165,158	3.1%
8	Ohio	156,307	2.9%
9	Michigan	155,850	2.9%
10	Oklahoma	151,250	2.8%
11	Pennsylvania	139,802	2.6%
12	Virginia	139,618	2.6%
13	Georgia	130,390	2.4%
14	New Jersey	125,777	2.4%
15	Arizona	120,561	2.3%
16	North Carolina	118,754	2.2%
17	Colorado	100,344	1.9%
18	Massachusetts	98,852	1.9%
19	Oregon	97,817	1.8%
20	Maryland	95,514	1.8%
21	Missouri	88,147	1.7%
22	Minnesota	82,819	1.6%
23	Indiana	79,377	1.5%
24	Tennessee	73,945	1.4%
25	Nevada	73,753	1.4%
26	Wisconsin	69,124	1.3%
27	Kansas	52,253	1.0%
28	Connecticut	52,072	1.0%
29	Alabama	51,776	1.0%
30	South Carolina	50,697	1.0%
31	Louisiana	49,080	0.9%
32	Kentucky	48,677	0.9%
33	Utah	48,032	0.9%
34	Arkansas	43,268	0.8%
35	New Mexico	38,008	0.7%
36	Iowa	34,247	0.6%
37	Alaska	32,507	0.6%
38	Mississippi	27,597	0.5%
39	Idaho	26,356	0.5%
40	Nebraska	24,023	0.5%
41	West Virginia	18,247	0.3%
42	Rhode Island	17,646	0.3%
43	Montana	17,210	0.3%
44	New Hampshire	14,409	0.3%
45	Maine	14,222	0.3%
46	Delaware	12,908	0.2%
47	South Dakota	12,013	0.2%
48	Wyoming	8,427	0.2%
49	North Dakota	8,015	0.2%
50	Vermont	7,448	0.1%
	District of Columbia	9,730	0.2%

Source: U.S. Bureau of the Census
   "State Population Estimates - Characteristics" (http://www.census.gov/popest/states/asrh/)
*Census states "Race is a self-identification data item in which respondents choose the race or races with which they most closely identify." The 2000 Census was the first to allow respondents to identify themselves as one or more races.

Percent of Population of Mixed Race in 2009

National Percent = 1.7% Mixed Race*

ALPHA ORDER

RANK	STATE	PERCENT
41	Alabama	1.1
2	Alaska	4.7
11	Arizona	1.8
21	Arkansas	1.5
6	California	2.6
8	Colorado	2.0
21	Connecticut	1.5
21	Delaware	1.5
21	Florida	1.5
32	Georgia	1.3
1	Hawaii	18.0
14	Idaho	1.7
32	Illinois	1.3
36	Indiana	1.2
41	Iowa	1.1
9	Kansas	1.9
41	Kentucky	1.1
41	Louisiana	1.1
41	Maine	1.1
14	Maryland	1.7
21	Massachusetts	1.5
18	Michigan	1.6
18	Minnesota	1.6
50	Mississippi	0.9
21	Missouri	1.5
11	Montana	1.8
32	Nebraska	1.3
5	Nevada	2.8
41	New Hampshire	1.1
29	New Jersey	1.4
9	New Mexico	1.9
18	New York	1.6
32	North Carolina	1.3
36	North Dakota	1.2
29	Ohio	1.4
3	Oklahoma	4.1
6	Oregon	2.6
41	Pennsylvania	1.1
14	Rhode Island	1.7
41	South Carolina	1.1
21	South Dakota	1.5
36	Tennessee	1.2
29	Texas	1.4
14	Utah	1.7
36	Vermont	1.2
11	Virginia	1.8
4	Washington	3.1
49	West Virginia	1.0
36	Wisconsin	1.2
21	Wyoming	1.5

RANK ORDER

RANK	STATE	PERCENT
1	Hawaii	18.0
2	Alaska	4.7
3	Oklahoma	4.1
4	Washington	3.1
5	Nevada	2.8
6	California	2.6
6	Oregon	2.6
8	Colorado	2.0
9	Kansas	1.9
9	New Mexico	1.9
11	Arizona	1.8
11	Montana	1.8
11	Virginia	1.8
14	Idaho	1.7
14	Maryland	1.7
14	Rhode Island	1.7
14	Utah	1.7
18	Michigan	1.6
18	Minnesota	1.6
18	New York	1.6
21	Arkansas	1.5
21	Connecticut	1.5
21	Delaware	1.5
21	Florida	1.5
21	Massachusetts	1.5
21	Missouri	1.5
21	South Dakota	1.5
21	Wyoming	1.5
29	New Jersey	1.4
29	Ohio	1.4
29	Texas	1.4
32	Georgia	1.3
32	Illinois	1.3
32	Nebraska	1.3
32	North Carolina	1.3
36	Indiana	1.2
36	North Dakota	1.2
36	Tennessee	1.2
36	Vermont	1.2
36	Wisconsin	1.2
41	Alabama	1.1
41	Iowa	1.1
41	Kentucky	1.1
41	Louisiana	1.1
41	Maine	1.1
41	New Hampshire	1.1
41	Pennsylvania	1.1
41	South Carolina	1.1
49	West Virginia	1.0
50	Mississippi	0.9

| | District of Columbia | 1.6 |

Source: CQ Press using data from U.S. Bureau of the Census
"State Population Estimates - Characteristics" (http://www.census.gov/popest/states/asrh/)
*Census states "Race is a self-identification data item in which respondents choose the race or races with which they most closely identify." The 2000 Census was the first to allow respondents to identify themselves as one or more races.

Median Age in 2009

National Median = 36.8 Years Old

ALPHA ORDER

RANK	STATE	MEDIAN AGE
25	Alabama	37.4
49	Alaska	32.8
43	Arizona	35.0
27	Arkansas	37.0
45	California	34.8
39	Colorado	35.7
7	Connecticut	39.5
14	Delaware	38.4
5	Florida	40.0
46	Georgia	34.7
24	Hawaii	37.5
47	Idaho	34.1
34	Illinois	36.2
32	Indiana	36.8
18	Iowa	38.0
35	Kansas	35.9
19	Kentucky	37.7
42	Louisiana	35.4
1	Maine	42.2
19	Maryland	37.7
9	Massachusetts	39.0
12	Michigan	38.5
26	Minnesota	37.3
43	Mississippi	35.0
22	Missouri	37.6
9	Montana	39.0
37	Nebraska	35.8
41	Nevada	35.5
4	New Hampshire	40.4
11	New Jersey	38.8
40	New Mexico	35.6
16	New York	38.1
29	North Carolina	36.9
33	North Dakota	36.3
12	Ohio	38.5
37	Oklahoma	35.8
16	Oregon	38.1
6	Pennsylvania	39.9
8	Rhode Island	39.2
22	South Carolina	37.6
29	South Dakota	36.9
19	Tennessee	37.7
48	Texas	33.0
50	Utah	28.8
2	Vermont	41.2
29	Virginia	36.9
27	Washington	37.0
3	West Virginia	40.5
15	Wisconsin	38.2
35	Wyoming	35.9

RANK ORDER

RANK	STATE	MEDIAN AGE
1	Maine	42.2
2	Vermont	41.2
3	West Virginia	40.5
4	New Hampshire	40.4
5	Florida	40.0
6	Pennsylvania	39.9
7	Connecticut	39.5
8	Rhode Island	39.2
9	Massachusetts	39.0
9	Montana	39.0
11	New Jersey	38.8
12	Michigan	38.5
12	Ohio	38.5
14	Delaware	38.4
15	Wisconsin	38.2
16	New York	38.1
16	Oregon	38.1
18	Iowa	38.0
19	Kentucky	37.7
19	Maryland	37.7
19	Tennessee	37.7
22	Missouri	37.6
22	South Carolina	37.6
24	Hawaii	37.5
25	Alabama	37.4
26	Minnesota	37.3
27	Arkansas	37.0
27	Washington	37.0
29	North Carolina	36.9
29	South Dakota	36.9
29	Virginia	36.9
32	Indiana	36.8
33	North Dakota	36.3
34	Illinois	36.2
35	Kansas	35.9
35	Wyoming	35.9
37	Nebraska	35.8
37	Oklahoma	35.8
39	Colorado	35.7
40	New Mexico	35.6
41	Nevada	35.5
42	Louisiana	35.4
43	Arizona	35.0
43	Mississippi	35.0
45	California	34.8
46	Georgia	34.7
47	Idaho	34.1
48	Texas	33.0
49	Alaska	32.8
50	Utah	28.8
	District of Columbia	35.1

Source: U.S. Bureau of the Census
"State Population Estimates - Characteristics" (http://www.census.gov/popest/states/asrh/)

Population under 5 Years Old in 2009

National Total = 21,299,656

ALPHA ORDER

RANK	STATE	POPULATION	% of USA
24	Alabama	315,210	1.5%
47	Alaska	54,463	0.3%
13	Arizona	518,431	2.4%
33	Arkansas	204,785	1.0%
1	California	2,753,801	12.9%
20	Colorado	364,481	1.7%
31	Connecticut	210,470	1.0%
45	Delaware	59,726	0.3%
4	Florida	1,166,005	5.5%
6	Georgia	751,215	3.5%
40	Hawaii	88,987	0.4%
38	Idaho	124,936	0.6%
5	Illinois	893,952	4.2%
15	Indiana	445,604	2.1%
34	Iowa	203,997	1.0%
32	Kansas	205,385	1.0%
26	Kentucky	288,022	1.4%
23	Louisiana	319,438	1.5%
42	Maine	70,762	0.3%
19	Maryland	380,606	1.8%
18	Massachusetts	385,851	1.8%
10	Michigan	616,055	2.9%
22	Minnesota	363,975	1.7%
30	Mississippi	222,503	1.0%
17	Missouri	403,529	1.9%
43	Montana	62,438	0.3%
37	Nebraska	134,717	0.6%
35	Nevada	203,570	1.0%
41	New Hampshire	74,689	0.4%
11	New Jersey	555,282	2.6%
36	New Mexico	151,988	0.7%
3	New York	1,223,080	5.7%
9	North Carolina	664,837	3.1%
48	North Dakota	43,401	0.2%
8	Ohio	739,526	3.5%
28	Oklahoma	271,861	1.3%
29	Oregon	247,909	1.2%
7	Pennsylvania	746,813	3.5%
44	Rhode Island	60,139	0.3%
25	South Carolina	311,013	1.5%
46	South Dakota	59,640	0.3%
16	Tennessee	425,565	2.0%
2	Texas	2,073,513	9.7%
27	Utah	273,723	1.3%
50	Vermont	32,474	0.2%
12	Virginia	533,143	2.5%
14	Washington	450,617	2.1%
39	West Virginia	105,976	0.5%
21	Wisconsin	364,068	1.7%
49	Wyoming	40,341	0.2%

RANK ORDER

RANK	STATE	POPULATION	% of USA
1	California	2,753,801	12.9%
2	Texas	2,073,513	9.7%
3	New York	1,223,080	5.7%
4	Florida	1,166,005	5.5%
5	Illinois	893,952	4.2%
6	Georgia	751,215	3.5%
7	Pennsylvania	746,813	3.5%
8	Ohio	739,526	3.5%
9	North Carolina	664,837	3.1%
10	Michigan	616,055	2.9%
11	New Jersey	555,282	2.6%
12	Virginia	533,143	2.5%
13	Arizona	518,431	2.4%
14	Washington	450,617	2.1%
15	Indiana	445,604	2.1%
16	Tennessee	425,565	2.0%
17	Missouri	403,529	1.9%
18	Massachusetts	385,851	1.8%
19	Maryland	380,606	1.8%
20	Colorado	364,481	1.7%
21	Wisconsin	364,068	1.7%
22	Minnesota	363,975	1.7%
23	Louisiana	319,438	1.5%
24	Alabama	315,210	1.5%
25	South Carolina	311,013	1.5%
26	Kentucky	288,022	1.4%
27	Utah	273,723	1.3%
28	Oklahoma	271,861	1.3%
29	Oregon	247,909	1.2%
30	Mississippi	222,503	1.0%
31	Connecticut	210,470	1.0%
32	Kansas	205,385	1.0%
33	Arkansas	204,785	1.0%
34	Iowa	203,997	1.0%
35	Nevada	203,570	1.0%
36	New Mexico	151,988	0.7%
37	Nebraska	134,717	0.6%
38	Idaho	124,936	0.6%
39	West Virginia	105,976	0.5%
40	Hawaii	88,987	0.4%
41	New Hampshire	74,689	0.4%
42	Maine	70,762	0.3%
43	Montana	62,438	0.3%
44	Rhode Island	60,139	0.3%
45	Delaware	59,726	0.3%
46	South Dakota	59,640	0.3%
47	Alaska	54,463	0.3%
48	North Dakota	43,401	0.2%
49	Wyoming	40,341	0.2%
50	Vermont	32,474	0.2%
	District of Columbia	37,144	0.2%

Source: U.S. Bureau of the Census
"State Population Estimates - Characteristics" (http://www.census.gov/popest/states/asrh/)

Percent of Population under 5 Years Old in 2009

National Percent = 6.9% of Population

ALPHA ORDER

RANK	STATE	PERCENT
29	Alabama	6.7
5	Alaska	7.8
4	Arizona	7.9
17	Arkansas	7.1
9	California	7.5
14	Colorado	7.3
43	Connecticut	6.0
29	Delaware	6.7
40	Florida	6.3
7	Georgia	7.6
20	Hawaii	6.9
3	Idaho	8.1
20	Illinois	6.9
20	Indiana	6.9
24	Iowa	6.8
14	Kansas	7.3
29	Kentucky	6.7
17	Louisiana	7.1
49	Maine	5.4
29	Maryland	6.7
44	Massachusetts	5.9
42	Michigan	6.2
20	Minnesota	6.9
9	Mississippi	7.5
29	Missouri	6.7
36	Montana	6.4
36	New Jersey	6.4
7	New Mexico	7.6
40	New York	6.3
17	North Carolina	7.1
29	North Dakota	6.7
36	Ohio	6.4
12	Oklahoma	7.4
35	Oregon	6.5
44	Pennsylvania	5.9
47	Rhode Island	5.7
24	South Carolina	6.8
14	South Dakota	7.3
24	Tennessee	6.8
2	Texas	8.4
1	Utah	9.8
50	Vermont	5.2
24	Virginia	6.8
24	Washington	6.8
46	West Virginia	5.8
36	Wisconsin	6.4
12	Wyoming	7.4

RANK ORDER

RANK	STATE	PERCENT
1	Utah	9.8
2	Texas	8.4
3	Idaho	8.1
4	Arizona	7.9
5	Alaska	7.8
6	Nevada	7.7
7	Georgia	7.6
7	New Mexico	7.6
9	California	7.5
9	Mississippi	7.5
9	Nebraska	7.5
12	Oklahoma	7.4
12	Wyoming	7.4
14	Colorado	7.3
14	Kansas	7.3
14	South Dakota	7.3
17	Arkansas	7.1
17	Louisiana	7.1
17	North Carolina	7.1
20	Hawaii	6.9
20	Illinois	6.9
20	Indiana	6.9
20	Minnesota	6.9
24	Iowa	6.8
24	South Carolina	6.8
24	Tennessee	6.8
24	Virginia	6.8
24	Washington	6.8
29	Alabama	6.7
29	Delaware	6.7
29	Kentucky	6.7
29	Maryland	6.7
29	Missouri	6.7
29	North Dakota	6.7
35	Oregon	6.5
36	Montana	6.4
36	New Jersey	6.4
36	Ohio	6.4
36	Wisconsin	6.4
40	Florida	6.3
40	New York	6.3
42	Michigan	6.2
43	Connecticut	6.0
44	Massachusetts	5.9
44	Pennsylvania	5.9
46	West Virginia	5.8
47	Rhode Island	5.7
48	New Hampshire	5.6
49	Maine	5.4
50	Vermont	5.2
	District of Columbia	6.2

Source: CQ Press using data from U.S. Bureau of the Census
"State Population Estimates - Characteristics" (http://www.census.gov/popest/states/asrh/)

Population 5 to 17 Years Old in 2009

National Total = 53,248,559

ALPHA ORDER				
RANK	STATE	POPULATION	% of USA	
23	Alabama	813,654	1.5%	
47	Alaska	129,083	0.2%	
13	Arizona	1,213,588	2.3%	
33	Arkansas	505,183	0.9%	
1	California	6,681,881	12.5%	
22	Colorado	863,282	1.6%	
29	Connecticut	597,515	1.1%	
45	Delaware	147,267	0.3%	
4	Florida	2,891,768	5.4%	
8	Georgia	1,832,577	3.4%	
41	Hawaii	201,374	0.4%	
38	Idaho	294,254	0.6%	
5	Illinois	2,283,425	4.3%	
14	Indiana	1,143,761	2.1%	
32	Iowa	509,158	1.0%	
34	Kansas	499,566	0.9%	
26	Kentucky	726,301	1.4%	
24	Louisiana	803,948	1.5%	
42	Maine	200,414	0.4%	
19	Maryland	971,329	1.8%	
17	Massachusetts	1,047,151	2.0%	
9	Michigan	1,733,837	3.3%	
21	Minnesota	896,822	1.7%	
31	Mississippi	545,239	1.0%	
18	Missouri	1,027,809	1.9%	
44	Montana	157,390	0.3%	
37	Nebraska	316,924	0.6%	
35	Nevada	477,463	0.9%	
40	New Hampshire	214,382	0.4%	
11	New Jersey	1,490,566	2.8%	
36	New Mexico	358,250	0.7%	
3	New York	3,201,003	6.0%	
10	North Carolina	1,613,130	3.0%	
48	North Dakota	100,570	0.2%	
7	Ohio	1,974,815	3.7%	
27	Oklahoma	646,988	1.2%	
28	Oregon	624,902	1.2%	
6	Pennsylvania	2,028,319	3.8%	
43	Rhode Island	166,686	0.3%	
25	South Carolina	769,719	1.4%	
46	South Dakota	139,976	0.3%	
16	Tennessee	1,067,687	2.0%	
2	Texas	4,822,456	9.1%	
30	Utah	595,101	1.1%	
49	Vermont	93,801	0.2%	
12	Virginia	1,314,039	2.5%	
15	Washington	1,118,975	2.1%	
39	West Virginia	280,473	0.5%	
20	Wisconsin	946,182	1.8%	
50	Wyoming	91,684	0.2%	

RANK ORDER				
RANK	STATE	POPULATION	% of USA	
1	California	6,681,881	12.5%	
2	Texas	4,822,456	9.1%	
3	New York	3,201,003	6.0%	
4	Florida	2,891,768	5.4%	
5	Illinois	2,283,425	4.3%	
6	Pennsylvania	2,028,319	3.8%	
7	Ohio	1,974,815	3.7%	
8	Georgia	1,832,577	3.4%	
9	Michigan	1,733,837	3.3%	
10	North Carolina	1,613,130	3.0%	
11	New Jersey	1,490,566	2.8%	
12	Virginia	1,314,039	2.5%	
13	Arizona	1,213,588	2.3%	
14	Indiana	1,143,761	2.1%	
15	Washington	1,118,975	2.1%	
16	Tennessee	1,067,687	2.0%	
17	Massachusetts	1,047,151	2.0%	
18	Missouri	1,027,809	1.9%	
19	Maryland	971,329	1.8%	
20	Wisconsin	946,182	1.8%	
21	Minnesota	896,822	1.7%	
22	Colorado	863,282	1.6%	
23	Alabama	813,654	1.5%	
24	Louisiana	803,948	1.5%	
25	South Carolina	769,719	1.4%	
26	Kentucky	726,301	1.4%	
27	Oklahoma	646,988	1.2%	
28	Oregon	624,902	1.2%	
29	Connecticut	597,515	1.1%	
30	Utah	595,101	1.1%	
31	Mississippi	545,239	1.0%	
32	Iowa	509,158	1.0%	
33	Arkansas	505,183	0.9%	
34	Kansas	499,566	0.9%	
35	Nevada	477,463	0.9%	
36	New Mexico	358,250	0.7%	
37	Nebraska	316,924	0.6%	
38	Idaho	294,254	0.6%	
39	West Virginia	280,473	0.5%	
40	New Hampshire	214,382	0.4%	
41	Hawaii	201,374	0.4%	
42	Maine	200,414	0.4%	
43	Rhode Island	166,686	0.3%	
44	Montana	157,390	0.3%	
45	Delaware	147,267	0.3%	
46	South Dakota	139,976	0.3%	
47	Alaska	129,083	0.2%	
48	North Dakota	100,570	0.2%	
49	Vermont	93,801	0.2%	
50	Wyoming	91,684	0.2%	
	District of Columbia	76,892	0.1%	

Source: U.S. Bureau of the Census
"State Population Estimates - Characteristics" (http://www.census.gov/popest/states/asrh/)

Percent of Population 5 to 17 Years Old in 2009

National Percent = 17.3% of Population

ALPHA ORDER

RANK	STATE	PERCENT
19	Alabama	17.3
5	Alaska	18.5
7	Arizona	18.4
16	Arkansas	17.5
8	California	18.1
20	Colorado	17.2
26	Connecticut	17.0
37	Delaware	16.6
45	Florida	15.6
4	Georgia	18.6
46	Hawaii	15.5
3	Idaho	19.0
13	Illinois	17.7
11	Indiana	17.8
30	Iowa	16.9
13	Kansas	17.7
32	Kentucky	16.8
10	Louisiana	17.9
49	Maine	15.2
26	Maryland	17.0
43	Massachusetts	15.9
18	Michigan	17.4
26	Minnesota	17.0
5	Mississippi	18.5
20	Missouri	17.2
41	Montana	16.1
15	Nebraska	17.6
8	Nevada	18.1
40	New Hampshire	16.2
24	New Jersey	17.1
11	New Mexico	17.8
38	New York	16.4
20	North Carolina	17.2
46	North Dakota	15.5
24	Ohio	17.1
16	Oklahoma	17.5
39	Oregon	16.3
41	Pennsylvania	16.1
44	Rhode Island	15.8
30	South Carolina	16.9
20	South Dakota	17.2
26	Tennessee	17.0
2	Texas	19.5
1	Utah	21.4
50	Vermont	15.1
35	Virginia	16.7
32	Washington	16.8
48	West Virginia	15.4
35	Wisconsin	16.7
32	Wyoming	16.8

RANK ORDER

RANK	STATE	PERCENT
1	Utah	21.4
2	Texas	19.5
3	Idaho	19.0
4	Georgia	18.6
5	Alaska	18.5
5	Mississippi	18.5
7	Arizona	18.4
8	California	18.1
8	Nevada	18.1
10	Louisiana	17.9
11	Indiana	17.8
11	New Mexico	17.8
13	Illinois	17.7
13	Kansas	17.7
15	Nebraska	17.6
16	Arkansas	17.5
16	Oklahoma	17.5
18	Michigan	17.4
19	Alabama	17.3
20	Colorado	17.2
20	Missouri	17.2
20	North Carolina	17.2
20	South Dakota	17.2
24	New Jersey	17.1
24	Ohio	17.1
26	Connecticut	17.0
26	Maryland	17.0
26	Minnesota	17.0
26	Tennessee	17.0
30	Iowa	16.9
30	South Carolina	16.9
32	Kentucky	16.8
32	Washington	16.8
32	Wyoming	16.8
35	Virginia	16.7
35	Wisconsin	16.7
37	Delaware	16.6
38	New York	16.4
39	Oregon	16.3
40	New Hampshire	16.2
41	Montana	16.1
41	Pennsylvania	16.1
43	Massachusetts	15.9
44	Rhode Island	15.8
45	Florida	15.6
46	Hawaii	15.5
46	North Dakota	15.5
48	West Virginia	15.4
49	Maine	15.2
50	Vermont	15.1

| District of Columbia | | 12.8 |

Source: CQ Press using data from U.S. Bureau of the Census
"State Population Estimates - Characteristics" (http://www.census.gov/popest/states/asrh/)

Population 18 Years Old and Older in 2009

National Total = 232,458,335

ALPHA ORDER

ALPHA ORDER

RANK	STATE	POPULATION	% of USA
23	Alabama	3,579,844	1.5%
47	Alaska	514,927	0.2%
15	Arizona	4,863,759	2.1%
32	Arkansas	2,179,482	0.9%
1	California	27,525,982	11.8%
22	Colorado	3,796,985	1.6%
29	Connecticut	2,710,303	1.2%
45	Delaware	678,129	0.3%
4	Florida	14,480,196	6.2%
9	Georgia	7,245,419	3.1%
42	Hawaii	1,004,817	0.4%
39	Idaho	1,126,611	0.5%
6	Illinois	9,733,032	4.2%
16	Indiana	4,833,748	2.1%
30	Iowa	2,294,701	1.0%
33	Kansas	2,113,796	0.9%
26	Kentucky	3,299,790	1.4%
25	Louisiana	3,368,690	1.4%
40	Maine	1,047,125	0.5%
19	Maryland	4,347,543	1.9%
13	Massachusetts	5,160,585	2.2%
8	Michigan	7,619,835	3.3%
21	Minnesota	4,005,417	1.7%
31	Mississippi	2,184,254	0.9%
18	Missouri	4,556,242	2.0%
44	Montana	755,161	0.3%
38	Nebraska	1,344,978	0.6%
34	Nevada	1,962,052	0.8%
41	New Hampshire	1,035,504	0.4%
11	New Jersey	6,661,891	2.9%
36	New Mexico	1,499,433	0.6%
3	New York	15,117,370	6.5%
10	North Carolina	7,102,917	3.1%
48	North Dakota	502,873	0.2%
7	Ohio	8,828,304	3.8%
28	Oklahoma	2,768,201	1.2%
27	Oregon	2,952,846	1.3%
5	Pennsylvania	9,829,635	4.2%
43	Rhode Island	826,384	0.4%
24	South Carolina	3,480,510	1.5%
46	South Dakota	612,767	0.3%
17	Tennessee	4,803,002	2.1%
2	Texas	17,886,333	7.7%
35	Utah	1,915,748	0.8%
49	Vermont	495,485	0.2%
12	Virginia	6,035,408	2.6%
14	Washington	5,094,603	2.2%
37	West Virginia	1,433,328	0.6%
20	Wisconsin	4,344,524	1.9%
50	Wyoming	412,245	0.2%

RANK ORDER

RANK	STATE	POPULATION	% of USA
1	California	27,525,982	11.8%
2	Texas	17,886,333	7.7%
3	New York	15,117,370	6.5%
4	Florida	14,480,196	6.2%
5	Pennsylvania	9,829,635	4.2%
6	Illinois	9,733,032	4.2%
7	Ohio	8,828,304	3.8%
8	Michigan	7,619,835	3.3%
9	Georgia	7,245,419	3.1%
10	North Carolina	7,102,917	3.1%
11	New Jersey	6,661,891	2.9%
12	Virginia	6,035,408	2.6%
13	Massachusetts	5,160,585	2.2%
14	Washington	5,094,603	2.2%
15	Arizona	4,863,759	2.1%
16	Indiana	4,833,748	2.1%
17	Tennessee	4,803,002	2.1%
18	Missouri	4,556,242	2.0%
19	Maryland	4,347,543	1.9%
20	Wisconsin	4,344,524	1.9%
21	Minnesota	4,005,417	1.7%
22	Colorado	3,796,985	1.6%
23	Alabama	3,579,844	1.5%
24	South Carolina	3,480,510	1.5%
25	Louisiana	3,368,690	1.4%
26	Kentucky	3,299,790	1.4%
27	Oregon	2,952,846	1.3%
28	Oklahoma	2,768,201	1.2%
29	Connecticut	2,710,303	1.2%
30	Iowa	2,294,701	1.0%
31	Mississippi	2,184,254	0.9%
32	Arkansas	2,179,482	0.9%
33	Kansas	2,113,796	0.9%
34	Nevada	1,962,052	0.8%
35	Utah	1,915,748	0.8%
36	New Mexico	1,499,433	0.6%
37	West Virginia	1,433,328	0.6%
38	Nebraska	1,344,978	0.6%
39	Idaho	1,126,611	0.5%
40	Maine	1,047,125	0.5%
41	New Hampshire	1,035,504	0.4%
42	Hawaii	1,004,817	0.4%
43	Rhode Island	826,384	0.4%
44	Montana	755,161	0.3%
45	Delaware	678,129	0.3%
46	South Dakota	612,767	0.3%
47	Alaska	514,927	0.2%
48	North Dakota	502,873	0.2%
49	Vermont	495,485	0.2%
50	Wyoming	412,245	0.2%
	District of Columbia	485,621	0.2%

Source: U.S. Bureau of the Census
"State Population Estimates - Characteristics" (http://www.census.gov/popest/states/asrh/)

Percent of Population 18 Years Old and Older in 2009

National Percent = 75.7% of Population

ALPHA ORDER

RANK	STATE	PERCENT
29	Alabama	76.0
45	Alaska	73.7
45	Arizona	73.7
33	Arkansas	75.4
42	California	74.5
32	Colorado	75.6
14	Connecticut	77.0
16	Delaware	76.6
7	Florida	78.1
45	Georgia	73.7
10	Hawaii	77.6
48	Idaho	72.9
33	Illinois	75.4
36	Indiana	75.3
23	Iowa	76.3
38	Kansas	75.0
18	Kentucky	76.5
38	Louisiana	75.0
2	Maine	79.4
23	Maryland	76.3
5	Massachusetts	78.3
21	Michigan	76.4
27	Minnesota	76.1
44	Mississippi	74.0
27	Missouri	76.1
11	Montana	77.5
40	Nebraska	74.9
43	Nevada	74.2
6	New Hampshire	78.2
18	New Jersey	76.5
41	New Mexico	74.6
12	New York	77.4
30	North Carolina	75.7
9	North Dakota	77.7
18	Ohio	76.5
37	Oklahoma	75.1
13	Oregon	77.2
8	Pennsylvania	78.0
4	Rhode Island	78.5
23	South Carolina	76.3
33	South Dakota	75.4
23	Tennessee	76.3
49	Texas	72.2
50	Utah	68.8
1	Vermont	79.7
16	Virginia	76.6
21	Washington	76.4
3	West Virginia	78.8
15	Wisconsin	76.8
30	Wyoming	75.7

RANK ORDER

RANK	STATE	PERCENT
1	Vermont	79.7
2	Maine	79.4
3	West Virginia	78.8
4	Rhode Island	78.5
5	Massachusetts	78.3
6	New Hampshire	78.2
7	Florida	78.1
8	Pennsylvania	78.0
9	North Dakota	77.7
10	Hawaii	77.6
11	Montana	77.5
12	New York	77.4
13	Oregon	77.2
14	Connecticut	77.0
15	Wisconsin	76.8
16	Delaware	76.6
16	Virginia	76.6
18	Kentucky	76.5
18	New Jersey	76.5
18	Ohio	76.5
21	Michigan	76.4
21	Washington	76.4
23	Iowa	76.3
23	Maryland	76.3
23	South Carolina	76.3
23	Tennessee	76.3
27	Minnesota	76.1
27	Missouri	76.1
29	Alabama	76.0
30	North Carolina	75.7
30	Wyoming	75.7
32	Colorado	75.6
33	Arkansas	75.4
33	Illinois	75.4
33	South Dakota	75.4
36	Indiana	75.3
37	Oklahoma	75.1
38	Kansas	75.0
38	Louisiana	75.0
40	Nebraska	74.9
41	New Mexico	74.6
42	California	74.5
43	Nevada	74.2
44	Mississippi	74.0
45	Alaska	73.7
45	Arizona	73.7
45	Georgia	73.7
48	Idaho	72.9
49	Texas	72.2
50	Utah	68.8

	District of Columbia	81.0

Source: CQ Press using data from U.S. Bureau of the Census
"State Population Estimates - Characteristics" (http://www.census.gov/popest/states/asrh/)

Population 18 to 24 Years Old in 2009

National Total = 30,412,035

ALPHA ORDER

RANK	STATE	POPULATION	% of USA
24	Alabama	465,249	1.5%
48	Alaska	79,696	0.3%
16	Arizona	610,920	2.0%
34	Arkansas	273,263	0.9%
1	California	3,746,026	12.3%
22	Colorado	500,695	1.6%
30	Connecticut	340,550	1.1%
47	Delaware	83,522	0.3%
4	Florida	1,667,090	5.5%
9	Georgia	979,688	3.2%
41	Hawaii	124,841	0.4%
39	Idaho	161,387	0.5%
5	Illinois	1,298,744	4.3%
15	Indiana	643,920	2.1%
31	Iowa	321,355	1.1%
33	Kansas	307,284	1.0%
26	Kentucky	416,470	1.4%
23	Louisiana	477,506	1.6%
42	Maine	118,353	0.4%
20	Maryland	547,538	1.8%
13	Massachusetts	668,112	2.2%
8	Michigan	995,230	3.3%
21	Minnesota	526,091	1.7%
32	Mississippi	313,729	1.0%
17	Missouri	592,454	1.9%
44	Montana	104,243	0.3%
37	Nebraska	196,793	0.6%
35	Nevada	228,809	0.8%
40	New Hampshire	130,242	0.4%
12	New Jersey	756,033	2.5%
36	New Mexico	202,276	0.7%
3	New York	1,923,887	6.3%
10	North Carolina	942,328	3.1%
45	North Dakota	88,808	0.3%
7	Ohio	1,084,493	3.6%
27	Oklahoma	386,532	1.3%
28	Oregon	364,365	1.2%
6	Pennsylvania	1,219,844	4.0%
43	Rhode Island	112,088	0.4%
25	South Carolina	452,903	1.5%
46	South Dakota	87,586	0.3%
19	Tennessee	585,173	1.9%
2	Texas	2,523,258	8.3%
29	Utah	341,926	1.1%
49	Vermont	68,869	0.2%
11	Virginia	814,917	2.7%
14	Washington	644,616	2.1%
38	West Virginia	169,767	0.6%
18	Wisconsin	590,593	1.9%
50	Wyoming	59,634	0.2%

RANK ORDER

RANK	STATE	POPULATION	% of USA
1	California	3,746,026	12.3%
2	Texas	2,523,258	8.3%
3	New York	1,923,887	6.3%
4	Florida	1,667,090	5.5%
5	Illinois	1,298,744	4.3%
6	Pennsylvania	1,219,844	4.0%
7	Ohio	1,084,493	3.6%
8	Michigan	995,230	3.3%
9	Georgia	979,688	3.2%
10	North Carolina	942,328	3.1%
11	Virginia	814,917	2.7%
12	New Jersey	756,033	2.5%
13	Massachusetts	668,112	2.2%
14	Washington	644,616	2.1%
15	Indiana	643,920	2.1%
16	Arizona	610,920	2.0%
17	Missouri	592,454	1.9%
18	Wisconsin	590,593	1.9%
19	Tennessee	585,173	1.9%
20	Maryland	547,538	1.8%
21	Minnesota	526,091	1.7%
22	Colorado	500,695	1.6%
23	Louisiana	477,506	1.6%
24	Alabama	465,249	1.5%
25	South Carolina	452,903	1.5%
26	Kentucky	416,470	1.4%
27	Oklahoma	386,532	1.3%
28	Oregon	364,365	1.2%
29	Utah	341,926	1.1%
30	Connecticut	340,550	1.1%
31	Iowa	321,355	1.1%
32	Mississippi	313,729	1.0%
33	Kansas	307,284	1.0%
34	Arkansas	273,263	0.9%
35	Nevada	228,809	0.8%
36	New Mexico	202,276	0.7%
37	Nebraska	196,793	0.6%
38	West Virginia	169,767	0.6%
39	Idaho	161,387	0.5%
40	New Hampshire	130,242	0.4%
41	Hawaii	124,841	0.4%
42	Maine	118,353	0.4%
43	Rhode Island	112,088	0.4%
44	Montana	104,243	0.3%
45	North Dakota	88,808	0.3%
46	South Dakota	87,586	0.3%
47	Delaware	83,522	0.3%
48	Alaska	79,696	0.3%
49	Vermont	68,869	0.2%
50	Wyoming	59,634	0.2%
	District of Columbia	72,339	0.2%

Source: U.S. Bureau of the Census
"State Population Estimates - Characteristics" (http://www.census.gov/popest/states/asrh/)

Percent of Population 18 to 24 Years Old in 2009

National Percent = 9.9% of Population

ALPHA ORDER

RANK	STATE	PERCENT
29	Alabama	9.9
3	Alaska	11.4
44	Arizona	9.3
40	Arkansas	9.5
19	California	10.1
23	Colorado	10.0
34	Connecticut	9.7
42	Delaware	9.4
47	Florida	9.0
23	Georgia	10.0
38	Hawaii	9.6
15	Idaho	10.4
19	Illinois	10.1
23	Indiana	10.0
9	Iowa	10.7
7	Kansas	10.9
34	Kentucky	9.7
11	Louisiana	10.6
47	Maine	9.0
38	Maryland	9.6
19	Massachusetts	10.1
23	Michigan	10.0
23	Minnesota	10.0
11	Mississippi	10.6
29	Missouri	9.9
9	Montana	10.7
5	Nebraska	11.0
49	Nevada	8.7
32	New Hampshire	9.8
49	New Jersey	8.7
19	New Mexico	10.1
32	New York	9.8
23	North Carolina	10.0
1	North Dakota	13.7
42	Ohio	9.4
14	Oklahoma	10.5
40	Oregon	9.5
34	Pennsylvania	9.7
11	Rhode Island	10.6
29	South Carolina	9.9
8	South Dakota	10.8
44	Tennessee	9.3
18	Texas	10.2
2	Utah	12.3
4	Vermont	11.1
17	Virginia	10.3
34	Washington	9.7
44	West Virginia	9.3
15	Wisconsin	10.4
5	Wyoming	11.0

RANK ORDER

RANK	STATE	PERCENT
1	North Dakota	13.7
2	Utah	12.3
3	Alaska	11.4
4	Vermont	11.1
5	Nebraska	11.0
5	Wyoming	11.0
7	Kansas	10.9
8	South Dakota	10.8
9	Iowa	10.7
9	Montana	10.7
11	Louisiana	10.6
11	Mississippi	10.6
11	Rhode Island	10.6
14	Oklahoma	10.5
15	Idaho	10.4
15	Wisconsin	10.4
17	Virginia	10.3
18	Texas	10.2
19	California	10.1
19	Illinois	10.1
19	Massachusetts	10.1
19	New Mexico	10.1
23	Colorado	10.0
23	Georgia	10.0
23	Indiana	10.0
23	Michigan	10.0
23	Minnesota	10.0
23	North Carolina	10.0
29	Alabama	9.9
29	Missouri	9.9
29	South Carolina	9.9
32	New Hampshire	9.8
32	New York	9.8
34	Connecticut	9.7
34	Kentucky	9.7
34	Pennsylvania	9.7
34	Washington	9.7
38	Hawaii	9.6
38	Maryland	9.6
40	Arkansas	9.5
40	Oregon	9.5
42	Delaware	9.4
42	Ohio	9.4
44	Arizona	9.3
44	Tennessee	9.3
44	West Virginia	9.3
47	Florida	9.0
47	Maine	9.0
49	Nevada	8.7
49	New Jersey	8.7
	District of Columbia	12.1

Source: CQ Press using data from U.S. Bureau of the Census
"State Population Estimates - Characteristics" (http://www.census.gov/popest/states/asrh/)

Population 25 to 44 Years Old in 2009

National Total = 83,096,278

ALPHA ORDER

RANK ORDER

RANK	STATE	POPULATION	% of USA
23	Alabama	1,235,509	1.5%
46	Alaska	197,248	0.2%
14	Arizona	1,826,751	2.2%
33	Arkansas	755,915	0.9%
1	California	10,604,180	12.8%
21	Colorado	1,445,400	1.7%
29	Connecticut	899,649	1.1%
44	Delaware	232,837	0.3%
4	Florida	4,789,059	5.8%
8	Georgia	2,830,740	3.4%
40	Hawaii	360,037	0.4%
39	Idaho	400,329	0.5%
5	Illinois	3,544,995	4.3%
17	Indiana	1,689,050	2.0%
34	Iowa	734,622	0.9%
35	Kansas	717,645	0.9%
26	Kentucky	1,162,402	1.4%
25	Louisiana	1,186,325	1.4%
42	Maine	322,409	0.4%
18	Maryland	1,557,085	1.9%
15	Massachusetts	1,787,350	2.2%
10	Michigan	2,536,880	3.1%
22	Minnesota	1,394,305	1.7%
32	Mississippi	761,785	0.9%
19	Missouri	1,554,391	1.9%
45	Montana	231,769	0.3%
38	Nebraska	451,666	0.5%
31	Nevada	769,608	0.9%
41	New Hampshire	333,694	0.4%
11	New Jersey	2,363,679	2.8%
36	New Mexico	523,059	0.6%
3	New York	5,351,598	6.4%
9	North Carolina	2,553,673	3.1%
48	North Dakota	153,582	0.2%
7	Ohio	2,998,151	3.6%
28	Oklahoma	957,235	1.2%
27	Oregon	1,028,645	1.2%
6	Pennsylvania	3,187,617	3.8%
43	Rhode Island	274,622	0.3%
24	South Carolina	1,200,366	1.4%
47	South Dakota	196,143	0.2%
16	Tennessee	1,710,134	2.1%
2	Texas	7,064,651	8.5%
30	Utah	775,481	0.9%
49	Vermont	148,584	0.2%
12	Virginia	2,194,699	2.6%
13	Washington	1,855,094	2.2%
37	West Virginia	459,606	0.6%
20	Wisconsin	1,449,006	1.7%
50	Wyoming	139,035	0.2%

RANK	STATE	POPULATION	% of USA
1	California	10,604,180	12.8%
2	Texas	7,064,651	8.5%
3	New York	5,351,598	6.4%
4	Florida	4,789,059	5.8%
5	Illinois	3,544,995	4.3%
6	Pennsylvania	3,187,617	3.8%
7	Ohio	2,998,151	3.6%
8	Georgia	2,830,740	3.4%
9	North Carolina	2,553,673	3.1%
10	Michigan	2,536,880	3.1%
11	New Jersey	2,363,679	2.8%
12	Virginia	2,194,699	2.6%
13	Washington	1,855,094	2.2%
14	Arizona	1,826,751	2.2%
15	Massachusetts	1,787,350	2.2%
16	Tennessee	1,710,134	2.1%
17	Indiana	1,689,050	2.0%
18	Maryland	1,557,085	1.9%
19	Missouri	1,554,391	1.9%
20	Wisconsin	1,449,006	1.7%
21	Colorado	1,445,400	1.7%
22	Minnesota	1,394,305	1.7%
23	Alabama	1,235,509	1.5%
24	South Carolina	1,200,366	1.4%
25	Louisiana	1,186,325	1.4%
26	Kentucky	1,162,402	1.4%
27	Oregon	1,028,645	1.2%
28	Oklahoma	957,235	1.2%
29	Connecticut	899,649	1.1%
30	Utah	775,481	0.9%
31	Nevada	769,608	0.9%
32	Mississippi	761,785	0.9%
33	Arkansas	755,915	0.9%
34	Iowa	734,622	0.9%
35	Kansas	717,645	0.9%
36	New Mexico	523,059	0.6%
37	West Virginia	459,606	0.6%
38	Nebraska	451,666	0.5%
39	Idaho	400,329	0.5%
40	Hawaii	360,037	0.4%
41	New Hampshire	333,694	0.4%
42	Maine	322,409	0.4%
43	Rhode Island	274,622	0.3%
44	Delaware	232,837	0.3%
45	Montana	231,769	0.3%
46	Alaska	197,248	0.2%
47	South Dakota	196,143	0.2%
48	North Dakota	153,582	0.2%
49	Vermont	148,584	0.2%
50	Wyoming	139,035	0.2%
	District of Columbia	197,983	0.2%

Source: CQ Press using data from U.S. Bureau of the Census
"SC-EST2009-AGESEX_RES - State Characteristic Estimates" (http://www.census.gov/popest/datasets.html)

Percent of Population 25 to 44 Years Old in 2009

National Percent = 27.1% of Population

ALPHA ORDER

RANK	STATE	PERCENT
26	Alabama	26.2
6	Alaska	28.2
11	Arizona	27.7
26	Arkansas	26.2
4	California	28.7
2	Colorado	28.8
36	Connecticut	25.6
23	Delaware	26.3
34	Florida	25.8
2	Georgia	28.8
7	Hawaii	27.8
33	Idaho	25.9
12	Illinois	27.5
23	Indiana	26.3
46	Iowa	24.4
38	Kansas	25.5
19	Kentucky	26.9
22	Louisiana	26.4
45	Maine	24.5
14	Maryland	27.3
17	Massachusetts	27.1
40	Michigan	25.4
21	Minnesota	26.5
34	Mississippi	25.8
29	Missouri	26.0
49	Montana	23.8
44	Nebraska	25.1
1	Nevada	29.1
43	New Hampshire	25.2
17	New Jersey	27.1
29	New Mexico	26.0
13	New York	27.4
15	North Carolina	27.2
50	North Dakota	23.7
29	Ohio	26.0
29	Oklahoma	26.0
19	Oregon	26.9
41	Pennsylvania	25.3
28	Rhode Island	26.1
23	South Carolina	26.3
47	South Dakota	24.1
15	Tennessee	27.2
5	Texas	28.5
7	Utah	27.8
48	Vermont	23.9
7	Virginia	27.8
7	Washington	27.8
41	West Virginia	25.3
36	Wisconsin	25.6
38	Wyoming	25.5

RANK ORDER

RANK	STATE	PERCENT
1	Nevada	29.1
2	Colorado	28.8
2	Georgia	28.8
4	California	28.7
5	Texas	28.5
6	Alaska	28.2
7	Hawaii	27.8
7	Utah	27.8
7	Virginia	27.8
7	Washington	27.8
11	Arizona	27.7
12	Illinois	27.5
13	New York	27.4
14	Maryland	27.3
15	North Carolina	27.2
15	Tennessee	27.2
17	Massachusetts	27.1
17	New Jersey	27.1
19	Kentucky	26.9
19	Oregon	26.9
21	Minnesota	26.5
22	Louisiana	26.4
23	Delaware	26.3
23	Indiana	26.3
23	South Carolina	26.3
26	Alabama	26.2
26	Arkansas	26.2
28	Rhode Island	26.1
29	Missouri	26.0
29	New Mexico	26.0
29	Ohio	26.0
29	Oklahoma	26.0
33	Idaho	25.9
34	Florida	25.8
34	Mississippi	25.8
36	Connecticut	25.6
36	Wisconsin	25.6
38	Kansas	25.5
38	Wyoming	25.5
40	Michigan	25.4
41	Pennsylvania	25.3
41	West Virginia	25.3
43	New Hampshire	25.2
44	Nebraska	25.1
45	Maine	24.5
46	Iowa	24.4
47	South Dakota	24.1
48	Vermont	23.9
49	Montana	23.8
50	North Dakota	23.7
	District of Columbia	33.0

Source: CQ Press using data from U.S. Bureau of the Census
"SC-EST2009-AGESEX_RES - State Characteristic Estimates" (http://www.census.gov/popest/datasets.html)

Population 45 to 64 Years Old in 2009

National Total = 79,379,432

<table>
<tr><td colspan="4">ALPHA ORDER</td><td colspan="4">RANK ORDER</td></tr>
<tr><td>RANK</td><td>STATE</td><td>POPULATION</td><td>% of USA</td><td>RANK</td><td>STATE</td><td>POPULATION</td><td>% of USA</td></tr>
<tr><td>23</td><td>Alabama</td><td>1,228,037</td><td>1.5%</td><td>1</td><td>California</td><td>9,027,721</td><td>11.4%</td></tr>
<tr><td>48</td><td>Alaska</td><td>185,134</td><td>0.2%</td><td>2</td><td>Texas</td><td>5,759,209</td><td>7.3%</td></tr>
<tr><td>18</td><td>Arizona</td><td>1,559,354</td><td>2.0%</td><td>3</td><td>New York</td><td>5,222,130</td><td>6.6%</td></tr>
<tr><td>31</td><td>Arkansas</td><td>736,623</td><td>0.9%</td><td>4</td><td>Florida</td><td>4,828,206</td><td>6.1%</td></tr>
<tr><td>1</td><td>California</td><td>9,027,721</td><td>11.4%</td><td>5</td><td>Pennsylvania</td><td>3,475,908</td><td>4.4%</td></tr>
<tr><td>22</td><td>Colorado</td><td>1,317,310</td><td>1.7%</td><td>6</td><td>Illinois</td><td>3,294,820</td><td>4.2%</td></tr>
<tr><td>28</td><td>Connecticut</td><td>982,049</td><td>1.2%</td><td>7</td><td>Ohio</td><td>3,140,344</td><td>4.0%</td></tr>
<tr><td>45</td><td>Delaware</td><td>235,077</td><td>0.3%</td><td>8</td><td>Michigan</td><td>2,747,953</td><td>3.5%</td></tr>
<tr><td>4</td><td>Florida</td><td>4,828,206</td><td>6.1%</td><td>9</td><td>Georgia</td><td>2,420,177</td><td>3.0%</td></tr>
<tr><td>9</td><td>Georgia</td><td>2,420,177</td><td>3.0%</td><td>10</td><td>North Carolina</td><td>2,414,891</td><td>3.0%</td></tr>
<tr><td>42</td><td>Hawaii</td><td>331,759</td><td>0.4%</td><td>11</td><td>New Jersey</td><td>2,369,155</td><td>3.0%</td></tr>
<tr><td>41</td><td>Idaho</td><td>377,477</td><td>0.5%</td><td>12</td><td>Virginia</td><td>2,065,702</td><td>2.6%</td></tr>
<tr><td>6</td><td>Illinois</td><td>3,294,820</td><td>4.2%</td><td>13</td><td>Massachusetts</td><td>1,810,609</td><td>2.3%</td></tr>
<tr><td>15</td><td>Indiana</td><td>1,672,187</td><td>2.1%</td><td>14</td><td>Washington</td><td>1,788,691</td><td>2.3%</td></tr>
<tr><td>30</td><td>Iowa</td><td>794,430</td><td>1.0%</td><td>15</td><td>Indiana</td><td>1,672,187</td><td>2.1%</td></tr>
<tr><td>33</td><td>Kansas</td><td>721,321</td><td>0.9%</td><td>16</td><td>Tennessee</td><td>1,666,742</td><td>2.1%</td></tr>
<tr><td>25</td><td>Kentucky</td><td>1,150,582</td><td>1.4%</td><td>17</td><td>Missouri</td><td>1,586,972</td><td>2.0%</td></tr>
<tr><td>26</td><td>Louisiana</td><td>1,150,563</td><td>1.4%</td><td>18</td><td>Arizona</td><td>1,559,354</td><td>2.0%</td></tr>
<tr><td>39</td><td>Maine</td><td>400,746</td><td>0.5%</td><td>19</td><td>Maryland</td><td>1,548,124</td><td>2.0%</td></tr>
<tr><td>19</td><td>Maryland</td><td>1,548,124</td><td>2.0%</td><td>20</td><td>Wisconsin</td><td>1,543,646</td><td>1.9%</td></tr>
<tr><td>13</td><td>Massachusetts</td><td>1,810,609</td><td>2.3%</td><td>21</td><td>Minnesota</td><td>1,413,966</td><td>1.8%</td></tr>
<tr><td>8</td><td>Michigan</td><td>2,747,953</td><td>3.5%</td><td>22</td><td>Colorado</td><td>1,317,310</td><td>1.7%</td></tr>
<tr><td>21</td><td>Minnesota</td><td>1,413,966</td><td>1.8%</td><td>23</td><td>Alabama</td><td>1,228,037</td><td>1.5%</td></tr>
<tr><td>32</td><td>Mississippi</td><td>731,827</td><td>0.9%</td><td>24</td><td>South Carolina</td><td>1,204,018</td><td>1.5%</td></tr>
<tr><td>17</td><td>Missouri</td><td>1,586,972</td><td>2.0%</td><td>25</td><td>Kentucky</td><td>1,150,582</td><td>1.4%</td></tr>
<tr><td>44</td><td>Montana</td><td>277,246</td><td>0.3%</td><td>26</td><td>Louisiana</td><td>1,150,563</td><td>1.4%</td></tr>
<tr><td>38</td><td>Nebraska</td><td>455,889</td><td>0.6%</td><td>27</td><td>Oregon</td><td>1,042,974</td><td>1.3%</td></tr>
<tr><td>34</td><td>Nevada</td><td>656,792</td><td>0.8%</td><td>28</td><td>Connecticut</td><td>982,049</td><td>1.2%</td></tr>
<tr><td>40</td><td>New Hampshire</td><td>392,321</td><td>0.5%</td><td>29</td><td>Oklahoma</td><td>928,472</td><td>1.2%</td></tr>
<tr><td>11</td><td>New Jersey</td><td>2,369,155</td><td>3.0%</td><td>30</td><td>Iowa</td><td>794,430</td><td>1.0%</td></tr>
<tr><td>37</td><td>New Mexico</td><td>512,756</td><td>0.6%</td><td>31</td><td>Arkansas</td><td>736,623</td><td>0.9%</td></tr>
<tr><td>3</td><td>New York</td><td>5,222,130</td><td>6.6%</td><td>32</td><td>Mississippi</td><td>731,827</td><td>0.9%</td></tr>
<tr><td>10</td><td>North Carolina</td><td>2,414,891</td><td>3.0%</td><td>33</td><td>Kansas</td><td>721,321</td><td>0.9%</td></tr>
<tr><td>49</td><td>North Dakota</td><td>165,613</td><td>0.2%</td><td>34</td><td>Nevada</td><td>656,792</td><td>0.8%</td></tr>
<tr><td>7</td><td>Ohio</td><td>3,140,344</td><td>4.0%</td><td>35</td><td>Utah</td><td>547,182</td><td>0.7%</td></tr>
<tr><td>29</td><td>Oklahoma</td><td>928,472</td><td>1.2%</td><td>36</td><td>West Virginia</td><td>516,398</td><td>0.7%</td></tr>
<tr><td>27</td><td>Oregon</td><td>1,042,974</td><td>1.3%</td><td>37</td><td>New Mexico</td><td>512,756</td><td>0.6%</td></tr>
<tr><td>5</td><td>Pennsylvania</td><td>3,475,908</td><td>4.4%</td><td>38</td><td>Nebraska</td><td>455,889</td><td>0.6%</td></tr>
<tr><td>43</td><td>Rhode Island</td><td>289,078</td><td>0.4%</td><td>39</td><td>Maine</td><td>400,746</td><td>0.5%</td></tr>
<tr><td>24</td><td>South Carolina</td><td>1,204,018</td><td>1.5%</td><td>40</td><td>New Hampshire</td><td>392,321</td><td>0.5%</td></tr>
<tr><td>46</td><td>South Dakota</td><td>211,306</td><td>0.3%</td><td>41</td><td>Idaho</td><td>377,477</td><td>0.5%</td></tr>
<tr><td>16</td><td>Tennessee</td><td>1,666,742</td><td>2.1%</td><td>42</td><td>Hawaii</td><td>331,759</td><td>0.4%</td></tr>
<tr><td>2</td><td>Texas</td><td>5,759,209</td><td>7.3%</td><td>43</td><td>Rhode Island</td><td>289,078</td><td>0.4%</td></tr>
<tr><td>35</td><td>Utah</td><td>547,182</td><td>0.7%</td><td>44</td><td>Montana</td><td>277,246</td><td>0.3%</td></tr>
<tr><td>47</td><td>Vermont</td><td>188,121</td><td>0.2%</td><td>45</td><td>Delaware</td><td>235,077</td><td>0.3%</td></tr>
<tr><td>12</td><td>Virginia</td><td>2,065,702</td><td>2.6%</td><td>46</td><td>South Dakota</td><td>211,306</td><td>0.3%</td></tr>
<tr><td>14</td><td>Washington</td><td>1,788,691</td><td>2.3%</td><td>47</td><td>Vermont</td><td>188,121</td><td>0.2%</td></tr>
<tr><td>36</td><td>West Virginia</td><td>516,398</td><td>0.7%</td><td>48</td><td>Alaska</td><td>185,134</td><td>0.2%</td></tr>
<tr><td>20</td><td>Wisconsin</td><td>1,543,646</td><td>1.9%</td><td>49</td><td>North Dakota</td><td>165,613</td><td>0.2%</td></tr>
<tr><td>50</td><td>Wyoming</td><td>146,709</td><td>0.2%</td><td>50</td><td>Wyoming</td><td>146,709</td><td>0.2%</td></tr>
<tr><td></td><td></td><td></td><td></td><td></td><td>District of Columbia</td><td>145,115</td><td>0.2%</td></tr>
</table>

Source: U.S. Bureau of the Census
    "State Population Estimates - Characteristics" (http://www.census.gov/popest/states/asrh/)

Percent of Population 45 to 64 Years Old in 2009

National Percent = 25.9% of Population

ALPHA ORDER

RANK	STATE	PERCENT
29	Alabama	26.1
22	Alaska	26.5
48	Arizona	23.6
38	Arkansas	25.5
46	California	24.4
27	Colorado	26.2
6	Connecticut	27.9
21	Delaware	26.6
30	Florida	26.0
45	Georgia	24.6
34	Hawaii	25.6
46	Idaho	24.4
38	Illinois	25.5
30	Indiana	26.0
25	Iowa	26.4
34	Kansas	25.6
19	Kentucky	26.7
34	Louisiana	25.6
1	Maine	30.4
13	Maryland	27.2
9	Massachusetts	27.5
7	Michigan	27.6
17	Minnesota	26.8
43	Mississippi	24.8
22	Missouri	26.5
4	Montana	28.4
41	Nebraska	25.4
43	Nevada	24.8
3	New Hampshire	29.6
13	New Jersey	27.2
38	New Mexico	25.5
19	New York	26.7
33	North Carolina	25.7
34	North Dakota	25.6
13	Ohio	27.2
42	Oklahoma	25.2
11	Oregon	27.3
7	Pennsylvania	27.6
10	Rhode Island	27.4
25	South Carolina	26.4
30	South Dakota	26.0
22	Tennessee	26.5
49	Texas	23.2
50	Utah	19.7
2	Vermont	30.3
27	Virginia	26.2
17	Washington	26.8
4	West Virginia	28.4
11	Wisconsin	27.3
16	Wyoming	27.0

RANK ORDER

RANK	STATE	PERCENT
1	Maine	30.4
2	Vermont	30.3
3	New Hampshire	29.6
4	Montana	28.4
4	West Virginia	28.4
6	Connecticut	27.9
7	Michigan	27.6
7	Pennsylvania	27.6
9	Massachusetts	27.5
10	Rhode Island	27.4
11	Oregon	27.3
11	Wisconsin	27.3
13	Maryland	27.2
13	New Jersey	27.2
13	Ohio	27.2
16	Wyoming	27.0
17	Minnesota	26.8
17	Washington	26.8
19	Kentucky	26.7
19	New York	26.7
21	Delaware	26.6
22	Alaska	26.5
22	Missouri	26.5
22	Tennessee	26.5
25	Iowa	26.4
25	South Carolina	26.4
27	Colorado	26.2
27	Virginia	26.2
29	Alabama	26.1
30	Florida	26.0
30	Indiana	26.0
30	South Dakota	26.0
33	North Carolina	25.7
34	Hawaii	25.6
34	Kansas	25.6
34	Louisiana	25.6
34	North Dakota	25.6
38	Arkansas	25.5
38	Illinois	25.5
38	New Mexico	25.5
41	Nebraska	25.4
42	Oklahoma	25.2
43	Mississippi	24.8
43	Nevada	24.8
45	Georgia	24.6
46	California	24.4
46	Idaho	24.4
48	Arizona	23.6
49	Texas	23.2
50	Utah	19.7
	District of Columbia	24.2

Source: CQ Press using data from U.S. Bureau of the Census
   "State Population Estimates - Characteristics" (http://www.census.gov/popest/states/asrh/)

Population 65 Years Old and Older in 2009

National Total = 39,570,590

ALPHA ORDER

RANK	STATE	POPULATION	% of USA
22	Alabama	651,049	1.6%
50	Alaska	52,849	0.1%
14	Arizona	866,734	2.2%
31	Arkansas	413,681	1.0%
1	California	4,148,055	10.5%
26	Colorado	533,580	1.3%
29	Connecticut	488,055	1.2%
45	Delaware	126,693	0.3%
2	Florida	3,195,841	8.1%
11	Georgia	1,014,814	2.6%
40	Hawaii	188,180	0.5%
41	Idaho	187,418	0.5%
7	Illinois	1,594,473	4.0%
16	Indiana	828,591	2.1%
30	Iowa	444,294	1.1%
33	Kansas	367,546	0.9%
24	Kentucky	570,336	1.4%
25	Louisiana	554,296	1.4%
39	Maine	205,617	0.5%
20	Maryland	694,796	1.8%
13	Massachusetts	894,514	2.3%
8	Michigan	1,339,772	3.4%
21	Minnesota	671,055	1.7%
32	Mississippi	376,913	1.0%
17	Missouri	822,425	2.1%
44	Montana	141,903	0.4%
38	Nebraska	240,630	0.6%
34	Nevada	306,843	0.8%
42	New Hampshire	179,247	0.5%
10	New Jersey	1,173,024	3.0%
36	New Mexico	261,342	0.7%
3	New York	2,619,755	6.6%
9	North Carolina	1,192,025	3.0%
47	North Dakota	94,870	0.2%
6	Ohio	1,605,316	4.1%
28	Oklahoma	495,962	1.3%
27	Oregon	516,862	1.3%
5	Pennsylvania	1,946,266	4.9%
43	Rhode Island	150,596	0.4%
23	South Carolina	623,223	1.6%
46	South Dakota	117,732	0.3%
15	Tennessee	840,953	2.1%
4	Texas	2,539,215	6.4%
37	Utah	251,159	0.6%
48	Vermont	89,911	0.2%
12	Virginia	960,090	2.4%
18	Washington	806,202	2.0%
35	West Virginia	287,557	0.7%
19	Wisconsin	761,279	1.9%
49	Wyoming	66,867	0.2%

RANK ORDER

RANK	STATE	POPULATION	% of USA
1	California	4,148,055	10.5%
2	Florida	3,195,841	8.1%
3	New York	2,619,755	6.6%
4	Texas	2,539,215	6.4%
5	Pennsylvania	1,946,266	4.9%
6	Ohio	1,605,316	4.1%
7	Illinois	1,594,473	4.0%
8	Michigan	1,339,772	3.4%
9	North Carolina	1,192,025	3.0%
10	New Jersey	1,173,024	3.0%
11	Georgia	1,014,814	2.6%
12	Virginia	960,090	2.4%
13	Massachusetts	894,514	2.3%
14	Arizona	866,734	2.2%
15	Tennessee	840,953	2.1%
16	Indiana	828,591	2.1%
17	Missouri	822,425	2.1%
18	Washington	806,202	2.0%
19	Wisconsin	761,279	1.9%
20	Maryland	694,796	1.8%
21	Minnesota	671,055	1.7%
22	Alabama	651,049	1.6%
23	South Carolina	623,223	1.6%
24	Kentucky	570,336	1.4%
25	Louisiana	554,296	1.4%
26	Colorado	533,580	1.3%
27	Oregon	516,862	1.3%
28	Oklahoma	495,962	1.3%
29	Connecticut	488,055	1.2%
30	Iowa	444,294	1.1%
31	Arkansas	413,681	1.0%
32	Mississippi	376,913	1.0%
33	Kansas	367,546	0.9%
34	Nevada	306,843	0.8%
35	West Virginia	287,557	0.7%
36	New Mexico	261,342	0.7%
37	Utah	251,159	0.6%
38	Nebraska	240,630	0.6%
39	Maine	205,617	0.5%
40	Hawaii	188,180	0.5%
41	Idaho	187,418	0.5%
42	New Hampshire	179,247	0.5%
43	Rhode Island	150,596	0.4%
44	Montana	141,903	0.4%
45	Delaware	126,693	0.3%
46	South Dakota	117,732	0.3%
47	North Dakota	94,870	0.2%
48	Vermont	89,911	0.2%
49	Wyoming	66,867	0.2%
50	Alaska	52,849	0.1%
	District of Columbia	70,184	0.2%

Source: U.S. Bureau of the Census
"State Population Estimates - Characteristics" (http://www.census.gov/popest/states/asrh/)

Percent of Population 65 Years Old and Older in 2009

National Percent = 12.9% of Population

ALPHA ORDER

RANK	STATE	PERCENT
16	Alabama	13.8
50	Alaska	7.6
30	Arizona	13.1
11	Arkansas	14.3
45	California	11.2
46	Colorado	10.6
14	Connecticut	13.9
11	Delaware	14.3
1	Florida	17.2
47	Georgia	10.3
8	Hawaii	14.5
42	Idaho	12.1
37	Illinois	12.4
33	Indiana	12.9
5	Iowa	14.8
31	Kansas	13.0
29	Kentucky	13.2
38	Louisiana	12.3
3	Maine	15.6
40	Maryland	12.2
19	Massachusetts	13.6
25	Michigan	13.4
35	Minnesota	12.7
34	Mississippi	12.8
17	Missouri	13.7
7	Montana	14.6
25	Nebraska	13.4
44	Nevada	11.6
20	New Hampshire	13.5
20	New Jersey	13.5
31	New Mexico	13.0
25	New York	13.4
35	North Carolina	12.7
6	North Dakota	14.7
14	Ohio	13.9
20	Oklahoma	13.5
20	Oregon	13.5
4	Pennsylvania	15.4
11	Rhode Island	14.3
17	South Carolina	13.7
8	South Dakota	14.5
25	Tennessee	13.4
48	Texas	10.2
49	Utah	9.0
8	Vermont	14.5
40	Virginia	12.2
42	Washington	12.1
2	West Virginia	15.8
20	Wisconsin	13.5
38	Wyoming	12.3

RANK ORDER

RANK	STATE	PERCENT
1	Florida	17.2
2	West Virginia	15.8
3	Maine	15.6
4	Pennsylvania	15.4
5	Iowa	14.8
6	North Dakota	14.7
7	Montana	14.6
8	Hawaii	14.5
8	South Dakota	14.5
8	Vermont	14.5
11	Arkansas	14.3
11	Delaware	14.3
11	Rhode Island	14.3
14	Connecticut	13.9
14	Ohio	13.9
16	Alabama	13.8
17	Missouri	13.7
17	South Carolina	13.7
19	Massachusetts	13.6
20	New Hampshire	13.5
20	New Jersey	13.5
20	Oklahoma	13.5
20	Oregon	13.5
20	Wisconsin	13.5
25	Michigan	13.4
25	Nebraska	13.4
25	New York	13.4
25	Tennessee	13.4
29	Kentucky	13.2
30	Arizona	13.1
31	Kansas	13.0
31	New Mexico	13.0
33	Indiana	12.9
34	Mississippi	12.8
35	Minnesota	12.7
35	North Carolina	12.7
37	Illinois	12.4
38	Louisiana	12.3
38	Wyoming	12.3
40	Maryland	12.2
40	Virginia	12.2
42	Idaho	12.1
42	Washington	12.1
44	Nevada	11.6
45	California	11.2
46	Colorado	10.6
47	Georgia	10.3
48	Texas	10.2
49	Utah	9.0
50	Alaska	7.6

District of Columbia	11.7

Source: CQ Press using data from U.S. Bureau of the Census
"State Population Estimates - Characteristics" (http://www.census.gov/popest/states/asrh/)

Population 85 Years Old and Older in 2009

National Total = 5,630,661

ALPHA ORDER

RANK	STATE	POPULATION	% of USA
22	Alabama	82,058	1.5%
50	Alaska	4,747	0.1%
12	Arizona	119,767	2.1%
32	Arkansas	57,085	1.0%
1	California	602,502	10.7%
30	Colorado	67,431	1.2%
23	Connecticut	77,064	1.4%
47	Delaware	16,196	0.3%
2	Florida	515,070	9.1%
13	Georgia	119,679	2.1%
39	Hawaii	31,751	0.6%
42	Idaho	25,262	0.4%
6	Illinois	233,635	4.1%
16	Indiana	117,559	2.1%
25	Iowa	76,148	1.4%
31	Kansas	60,498	1.1%
27	Kentucky	73,077	1.3%
28	Louisiana	70,291	1.2%
40	Maine	28,388	0.5%
21	Maryland	89,272	1.6%
11	Massachusetts	141,722	2.5%
8	Michigan	183,004	3.3%
19	Minnesota	106,196	1.9%
33	Mississippi	50,019	0.9%
14	Missouri	119,499	2.1%
45	Montana	20,174	0.4%
34	Nebraska	39,544	0.7%
37	Nevada	32,346	0.6%
43	New Hampshire	24,713	0.4%
9	New Jersey	171,833	3.1%
36	New Mexico	34,890	0.6%
3	New York	386,876	6.9%
10	North Carolina	148,967	2.6%
46	North Dakota	17,360	0.3%
7	Ohio	227,420	4.0%
29	Oklahoma	68,633	1.2%
26	Oregon	74,458	1.3%
5	Pennsylvania	309,253	5.5%
41	Rhode Island	25,493	0.5%
24	South Carolina	76,644	1.4%
44	South Dakota	20,205	0.4%
20	Tennessee	104,945	1.9%
4	Texas	330,660	5.9%
38	Utah	32,168	0.6%
48	Vermont	12,443	0.2%
15	Virginia	119,255	2.1%
18	Washington	112,816	2.0%
35	West Virginia	38,205	0.7%
17	Wisconsin	114,942	2.0%
49	Wyoming	8,807	0.2%

RANK ORDER

RANK	STATE	POPULATION	% of USA
1	California	602,502	10.7%
2	Florida	515,070	9.1%
3	New York	386,876	6.9%
4	Texas	330,660	5.9%
5	Pennsylvania	309,253	5.5%
6	Illinois	233,635	4.1%
7	Ohio	227,420	4.0%
8	Michigan	183,004	3.3%
9	New Jersey	171,833	3.1%
10	North Carolina	148,967	2.6%
11	Massachusetts	141,722	2.5%
12	Arizona	119,767	2.1%
13	Georgia	119,679	2.1%
14	Missouri	119,499	2.1%
15	Virginia	119,255	2.1%
16	Indiana	117,559	2.1%
17	Wisconsin	114,942	2.0%
18	Washington	112,816	2.0%
19	Minnesota	106,196	1.9%
20	Tennessee	104,945	1.9%
21	Maryland	89,272	1.6%
22	Alabama	82,058	1.5%
23	Connecticut	77,064	1.4%
24	South Carolina	76,644	1.4%
25	Iowa	76,148	1.4%
26	Oregon	74,458	1.3%
27	Kentucky	73,077	1.3%
28	Louisiana	70,291	1.2%
29	Oklahoma	68,633	1.2%
30	Colorado	67,431	1.2%
31	Kansas	60,498	1.1%
32	Arkansas	57,085	1.0%
33	Mississippi	50,019	0.9%
34	Nebraska	39,544	0.7%
35	West Virginia	38,205	0.7%
36	New Mexico	34,890	0.6%
37	Nevada	32,346	0.6%
38	Utah	32,168	0.6%
39	Hawaii	31,751	0.6%
40	Maine	28,388	0.5%
41	Rhode Island	25,493	0.5%
42	Idaho	25,262	0.4%
43	New Hampshire	24,713	0.4%
44	South Dakota	20,205	0.4%
45	Montana	20,174	0.4%
46	North Dakota	17,360	0.3%
47	Delaware	16,196	0.3%
48	Vermont	12,443	0.2%
49	Wyoming	8,807	0.2%
50	Alaska	4,747	0.1%
	District of Columbia	9,691	0.2%

Source: U.S. Bureau of the Census
"State Population Estimates - Characteristics" (http://www.census.gov/popest/states/asrh/)

Percent of Population 85 Years Old and Older in 2009

National Percent = 1.8% of Population

ALPHA ORDER

RANK	STATE	PERCENT
31	Alabama	1.7
50	Alaska	0.7
26	Arizona	1.8
15	Arkansas	2.0
38	California	1.6
45	Colorado	1.3
8	Connecticut	2.2
26	Delaware	1.8
1	Florida	2.8
47	Georgia	1.2
3	Hawaii	2.5
38	Idaho	1.6
26	Illinois	1.8
26	Indiana	1.8
3	Iowa	2.5
11	Kansas	2.1
31	Kentucky	1.7
38	Louisiana	1.6
8	Maine	2.2
38	Maryland	1.6
11	Massachusetts	2.1
26	Michigan	1.8
15	Minnesota	2.0
31	Mississippi	1.7
15	Missouri	2.0
11	Montana	2.1
8	Nebraska	2.2
47	Nevada	1.2
23	New Hampshire	1.9
15	New Jersey	2.0
31	New Mexico	1.7
15	New York	2.0
38	North Carolina	1.6
2	North Dakota	2.7
15	Ohio	2.0
23	Oklahoma	1.9
23	Oregon	1.9
3	Pennsylvania	2.5
7	Rhode Island	2.4
31	South Carolina	1.7
3	South Dakota	2.5
31	Tennessee	1.7
45	Texas	1.3
47	Utah	1.2
15	Vermont	2.0
44	Virginia	1.5
31	Washington	1.7
11	West Virginia	2.1
15	Wisconsin	2.0
38	Wyoming	1.6

RANK ORDER

RANK	STATE	PERCENT
1	Florida	2.8
2	North Dakota	2.7
3	Hawaii	2.5
3	Iowa	2.5
3	Pennsylvania	2.5
3	South Dakota	2.5
7	Rhode Island	2.4
8	Connecticut	2.2
8	Maine	2.2
8	Nebraska	2.2
11	Kansas	2.1
11	Massachusetts	2.1
11	Montana	2.1
11	West Virginia	2.1
15	Arkansas	2.0
15	Minnesota	2.0
15	Missouri	2.0
15	New Jersey	2.0
15	New York	2.0
15	Ohio	2.0
15	Vermont	2.0
15	Wisconsin	2.0
23	New Hampshire	1.9
23	Oklahoma	1.9
23	Oregon	1.9
26	Arizona	1.8
26	Delaware	1.8
26	Illinois	1.8
26	Indiana	1.8
26	Michigan	1.8
31	Alabama	1.7
31	Kentucky	1.7
31	Mississippi	1.7
31	New Mexico	1.7
31	South Carolina	1.7
31	Tennessee	1.7
31	Washington	1.7
38	California	1.6
38	Idaho	1.6
38	Louisiana	1.6
38	Maryland	1.6
38	North Carolina	1.6
38	Wyoming	1.6
44	Virginia	1.5
45	Colorado	1.3
45	Texas	1.3
47	Georgia	1.2
47	Nevada	1.2
47	Utah	1.2
50	Alaska	0.7
	District of Columbia	1.6

Source: CQ Press using data from U.S. Bureau of the Census
"State Population Estimates - Characteristics" (http://www.census.gov/popest/states/asrh/)

Percent of Native Population Born in Their State of Residence: 2009

National Percent = 67.5%

<table>
<tr><td colspan="3">ALPHA ORDER</td><td colspan="3">RANK ORDER</td></tr>
<tr><td>RANK</td><td>STATE</td><td>PERCENT</td><td>RANK</td><td>STATE</td><td>PERCENT</td></tr>
<tr><td>13</td><td>Alabama</td><td>72.4</td><td>1</td><td>New York</td><td>81.9</td></tr>
<tr><td>48</td><td>Alaska</td><td>43.3</td><td>2</td><td>Michigan</td><td>81.4</td></tr>
<tr><td>46</td><td>Arizona</td><td>43.8</td><td>3</td><td>Louisiana</td><td>81.3</td></tr>
<tr><td>30</td><td>Arkansas</td><td>63.8</td><td>4</td><td>Pennsylvania</td><td>78.9</td></tr>
<tr><td>11</td><td>California</td><td>73.5</td><td>5</td><td>Ohio</td><td>78.2</td></tr>
<tr><td>44</td><td>Colorado</td><td>46.9</td><td>6</td><td>Illinois</td><td>77.4</td></tr>
<tr><td>27</td><td>Connecticut</td><td>64.5</td><td>7</td><td>Iowa</td><td>75.5</td></tr>
<tr><td>42</td><td>Delaware</td><td>50.1</td><td>8</td><td>Wisconsin</td><td>75.3</td></tr>
<tr><td>47</td><td>Florida</td><td>43.5</td><td>9</td><td>Massachusetts</td><td>74.4</td></tr>
<tr><td>34</td><td>Georgia</td><td>61.4</td><td>10</td><td>Minnesota</td><td>74.1</td></tr>
<tr><td>26</td><td>Hawaii</td><td>64.8</td><td>11</td><td>California</td><td>73.5</td></tr>
<tr><td>43</td><td>Idaho</td><td>48.7</td><td>12</td><td>Mississippi</td><td>73.1</td></tr>
<tr><td>6</td><td>Illinois</td><td>77.4</td><td>13</td><td>Alabama</td><td>72.4</td></tr>
<tr><td>17</td><td>Indiana</td><td>71.6</td><td>13</td><td>West Virginia</td><td>72.4</td></tr>
<tr><td>7</td><td>Iowa</td><td>75.5</td><td>15</td><td>Kentucky</td><td>72.3</td></tr>
<tr><td>32</td><td>Kansas</td><td>62.4</td><td>15</td><td>Texas</td><td>72.3</td></tr>
<tr><td>15</td><td>Kentucky</td><td>72.3</td><td>17</td><td>Indiana</td><td>71.6</td></tr>
<tr><td>3</td><td>Louisiana</td><td>81.3</td><td>17</td><td>North Dakota</td><td>71.6</td></tr>
<tr><td>24</td><td>Maine</td><td>66.9</td><td>19</td><td>Nebraska</td><td>70.2</td></tr>
<tr><td>38</td><td>Maryland</td><td>55.0</td><td>20</td><td>Missouri</td><td>68.9</td></tr>
<tr><td>9</td><td>Massachusetts</td><td>74.4</td><td>21</td><td>Rhode Island</td><td>68.4</td></tr>
<tr><td>2</td><td>Michigan</td><td>81.4</td><td>22</td><td>Utah</td><td>67.9</td></tr>
<tr><td>10</td><td>Minnesota</td><td>74.1</td><td>23</td><td>South Dakota</td><td>67.7</td></tr>
<tr><td>12</td><td>Mississippi</td><td>73.1</td><td>24</td><td>Maine</td><td>66.9</td></tr>
<tr><td>20</td><td>Missouri</td><td>68.9</td><td>25</td><td>New Jersey</td><td>66.0</td></tr>
<tr><td>36</td><td>Montana</td><td>56.3</td><td>26</td><td>Hawaii</td><td>64.8</td></tr>
<tr><td>19</td><td>Nebraska</td><td>70.2</td><td>27</td><td>Connecticut</td><td>64.5</td></tr>
<tr><td>50</td><td>Nevada</td><td>29.7</td><td>27</td><td>Tennessee</td><td>64.5</td></tr>
<tr><td>45</td><td>New Hampshire</td><td>44.7</td><td>29</td><td>Oklahoma</td><td>63.9</td></tr>
<tr><td>25</td><td>New Jersey</td><td>66.0</td><td>30</td><td>Arkansas</td><td>63.8</td></tr>
<tr><td>35</td><td>New Mexico</td><td>57.0</td><td>31</td><td>North Carolina</td><td>62.6</td></tr>
<tr><td>1</td><td>New York</td><td>81.9</td><td>32</td><td>Kansas</td><td>62.4</td></tr>
<tr><td>31</td><td>North Carolina</td><td>62.6</td><td>33</td><td>South Carolina</td><td>62.0</td></tr>
<tr><td>17</td><td>North Dakota</td><td>71.6</td><td>34</td><td>Georgia</td><td>61.4</td></tr>
<tr><td>5</td><td>Ohio</td><td>78.2</td><td>35</td><td>New Mexico</td><td>57.0</td></tr>
<tr><td>29</td><td>Oklahoma</td><td>63.9</td><td>36</td><td>Montana</td><td>56.3</td></tr>
<tr><td>41</td><td>Oregon</td><td>50.6</td><td>36</td><td>Virginia</td><td>56.3</td></tr>
<tr><td>4</td><td>Pennsylvania</td><td>78.9</td><td>38</td><td>Maryland</td><td>55.0</td></tr>
<tr><td>21</td><td>Rhode Island</td><td>68.4</td><td>39</td><td>Vermont</td><td>54.7</td></tr>
<tr><td>33</td><td>South Carolina</td><td>62.0</td><td>40</td><td>Washington</td><td>54.0</td></tr>
<tr><td>23</td><td>South Dakota</td><td>67.7</td><td>41</td><td>Oregon</td><td>50.6</td></tr>
<tr><td>27</td><td>Tennessee</td><td>64.5</td><td>42</td><td>Delaware</td><td>50.1</td></tr>
<tr><td>15</td><td>Texas</td><td>72.3</td><td>43</td><td>Idaho</td><td>48.7</td></tr>
<tr><td>22</td><td>Utah</td><td>67.9</td><td>44</td><td>Colorado</td><td>46.9</td></tr>
<tr><td>39</td><td>Vermont</td><td>54.7</td><td>45</td><td>New Hampshire</td><td>44.7</td></tr>
<tr><td>36</td><td>Virginia</td><td>56.3</td><td>46</td><td>Arizona</td><td>43.8</td></tr>
<tr><td>40</td><td>Washington</td><td>54.0</td><td>47</td><td>Florida</td><td>43.5</td></tr>
<tr><td>13</td><td>West Virginia</td><td>72.4</td><td>48</td><td>Alaska</td><td>43.3</td></tr>
<tr><td>8</td><td>Wisconsin</td><td>75.3</td><td>49</td><td>Wyoming</td><td>42.4</td></tr>
<tr><td>49</td><td>Wyoming</td><td>42.4</td><td>50</td><td>Nevada</td><td>29.7</td></tr>
<tr><td></td><td></td><td></td><td></td><td>District of Columbia</td><td>46.2</td></tr>
</table>

Source: U.S. Bureau of the Census
   "2009 American Community Survey" (http://www.census.gov/acs/www/index.html)

Domestic Migration of Population: 2008 to 2009

National Net Migration = 0 People*

ALPHA ORDER

RANK	STATE	NET MIGRATION
13	Alabama	11,044
27	Alaska	979
11	Arizona	15,111
17	Arkansas	5,298
50	California	(98,798)
4	Colorado	35,591
41	Connecticut	(7,824)
21	Delaware	2,580
44	Florida	(31,179)
6	Georgia	26,604
36	Hawaii	(5,298)
24	Idaho	1,555
47	Illinois	(48,249)
40	Indiana	(6,805)
32	Iowa	(2,135)
31	Kansas	(1,242)
16	Kentucky	6,268
12	Louisiana	14,647
34	Maine	(2,937)
43	Maryland	(11,163)
19	Massachusetts	3,614
48	Michigan	(87,339)
42	Minnesota	(8,813)
37	Mississippi	(5,529)
28	Missouri	(124)
22	Montana	2,410
29	Nebraska	(956)
35	Nevada	(3,801)
33	New Hampshire	(2,602)
45	New Jersey	(31,690)
20	New Mexico	3,366
49	New York	(98,178)
2	North Carolina	59,108
25	North Dakota	1,375
46	Ohio	(36,278)
8	Oklahoma	18,345
10	Oregon	16,173
26	Pennsylvania	1,346
39	Rhode Island	(6,172)
5	South Carolina	31,480
23	South Dakota	1,619
7	Tennessee	20,605
1	Texas	143,423
14	Utah	8,623
30	Vermont	(975)
9	Virginia	18,238
3	Washington	38,201
18	West Virginia	4,510
38	Wisconsin	(5,672)
15	Wyoming	7,192

RANK ORDER

RANK	STATE	NET MIGRATION
1	Texas	143,423
2	North Carolina	59,108
3	Washington	38,201
4	Colorado	35,591
5	South Carolina	31,480
6	Georgia	26,604
7	Tennessee	20,605
8	Oklahoma	18,345
9	Virginia	18,238
10	Oregon	16,173
11	Arizona	15,111
12	Louisiana	14,647
13	Alabama	11,044
14	Utah	8,623
15	Wyoming	7,192
16	Kentucky	6,268
17	Arkansas	5,298
18	West Virginia	4,510
19	Massachusetts	3,614
20	New Mexico	3,366
21	Delaware	2,580
22	Montana	2,410
23	South Dakota	1,619
24	Idaho	1,555
25	North Dakota	1,375
26	Pennsylvania	1,346
27	Alaska	979
28	Missouri	(124)
29	Nebraska	(956)
30	Vermont	(975)
31	Kansas	(1,242)
32	Iowa	(2,135)
33	New Hampshire	(2,602)
34	Maine	(2,937)
35	Nevada	(3,801)
36	Hawaii	(5,298)
37	Mississippi	(5,529)
38	Wisconsin	(5,672)
39	Rhode Island	(6,172)
40	Indiana	(6,805)
41	Connecticut	(7,824)
42	Minnesota	(8,813)
43	Maryland	(11,163)
44	Florida	(31,179)
45	New Jersey	(31,690)
46	Ohio	(36,278)
47	Illinois	(48,249)
48	Michigan	(87,339)
49	New York	(98,178)
50	California	(98,798)

| | District of Columbia | 4,454 |

Source: U.S. Bureau of the Census
   "Components of Population Change" (http://www.census.gov/popest/datasets.html)
*From July 1, 2008 to July 1, 2009. Includes armed forces residing in each state. Net Domestic Migration is the difference between domestic inmigration to an area and domestic outmigration from it during the period. Domestic inmigration and outmigration consist of moves where both the origins and destinations are within the United States (excluding Puerto Rico).

Net International Migration: 2008 to 2009

National Net = 854,905 Immigrants*

ALPHA ORDER

RANK	STATE	IMMIGRANTS	% of USA
29	Alabama	5,319	0.6%
43	Alaska	1,022	0.1%
8	Arizona	26,997	3.2%
34	Arkansas	3,662	0.4%
1	California	165,600	19.4%
16	Colorado	13,078	1.5%
18	Connecticut	11,322	1.3%
40	Delaware	2,016	0.2%
3	Florida	87,381	10.2%
7	Georgia	27,346	3.2%
33	Hawaii	4,033	0.5%
39	Idaho	2,179	0.3%
6	Illinois	35,839	4.2%
22	Indiana	9,194	1.1%
36	Iowa	3,189	0.4%
30	Kansas	5,003	0.6%
32	Kentucky	4,598	0.5%
35	Louisiana	3,476	0.4%
44	Maine	828	0.1%
13	Maryland	19,565	2.3%
9	Massachusetts	24,518	2.9%
15	Michigan	15,446	1.8%
20	Minnesota	10,066	1.2%
41	Mississippi	1,939	0.2%
26	Missouri	6,133	0.7%
50	Montana	344	0.0%
38	Nebraska	3,069	0.4%
19	Nevada	10,969	1.3%
42	New Hampshire	1,787	0.2%
5	New Jersey	37,360	4.4%
31	New Mexico	4,828	0.6%
4	New York	75,099	8.8%
10	North Carolina	21,211	2.5%
47	North Dakota	521	0.1%
17	Ohio	11,835	1.4%
28	Oklahoma	5,340	0.6%
23	Oregon	8,599	1.0%
14	Pennsylvania	18,480	2.2%
37	Rhode Island	3,096	0.4%
24	South Carolina	7,265	0.8%
45	South Dakota	688	0.1%
21	Tennessee	9,474	1.1%
2	Texas	88,116	10.3%
27	Utah	5,957	0.7%
48	Vermont	421	0.0%
11	Virginia	20,928	2.4%
12	Washington	19,956	2.3%
46	West Virginia	558	0.1%
25	Wisconsin	6,798	0.8%
49	Wyoming	361	0.0%

RANK ORDER

RANK	STATE	IMMIGRANTS	% of USA
1	California	165,600	19.4%
2	Texas	88,116	10.3%
3	Florida	87,381	10.2%
4	New York	75,099	8.8%
5	New Jersey	37,360	4.4%
6	Illinois	35,839	4.2%
7	Georgia	27,346	3.2%
8	Arizona	26,997	3.2%
9	Massachusetts	24,518	2.9%
10	North Carolina	21,211	2.5%
11	Virginia	20,928	2.4%
12	Washington	19,956	2.3%
13	Maryland	19,565	2.3%
14	Pennsylvania	18,480	2.2%
15	Michigan	15,446	1.8%
16	Colorado	13,078	1.5%
17	Ohio	11,835	1.4%
18	Connecticut	11,322	1.3%
19	Nevada	10,969	1.3%
20	Minnesota	10,066	1.2%
21	Tennessee	9,474	1.1%
22	Indiana	9,194	1.1%
23	Oregon	8,599	1.0%
24	South Carolina	7,265	0.8%
25	Wisconsin	6,798	0.8%
26	Missouri	6,133	0.7%
27	Utah	5,957	0.7%
28	Oklahoma	5,340	0.6%
29	Alabama	5,319	0.6%
30	Kansas	5,003	0.6%
31	New Mexico	4,828	0.6%
32	Kentucky	4,598	0.5%
33	Hawaii	4,033	0.5%
34	Arkansas	3,662	0.4%
35	Louisiana	3,476	0.4%
36	Iowa	3,189	0.4%
37	Rhode Island	3,096	0.4%
38	Nebraska	3,069	0.4%
39	Idaho	2,179	0.3%
40	Delaware	2,016	0.2%
41	Mississippi	1,939	0.2%
42	New Hampshire	1,787	0.2%
43	Alaska	1,022	0.1%
44	Maine	828	0.1%
45	South Dakota	688	0.1%
46	West Virginia	558	0.1%
47	North Dakota	521	0.1%
48	Vermont	421	0.0%
49	Wyoming	361	0.0%
50	Montana	344	0.0%
	District of Columbia	2,096	0.2%

Source: U.S. Bureau of the Census
  "Components of Population Change" (http://www.census.gov/popest/datasets.html)
*From July 1, 2008 to July 1, 2009. Net International Migration is the difference between migration to an area from outside the United States (immigration) and migration from the area to outside the United States (emigration) during the period. Includes legal immigration and estimates of undocumented immigration.

Percent of Population Foreign Born: 2009

National Percent = 12.5% of Population*

ALPHA ORDER

RANK	STATE	PERCENT
43	Alabama	3.1
23	Alaska	7.0
9	Arizona	14.0
35	Arkansas	4.2
1	California	26.9
17	Colorado	9.7
11	Connecticut	13.1
20	Delaware	8.4
5	Florida	18.8
19	Georgia	9.4
6	Hawaii	17.3
25	Idaho	6.3
10	Illinois	13.5
34	Indiana	4.4
37	Iowa	3.9
27	Kansas	6.1
45	Kentucky	3.0
40	Louisiana	3.4
41	Maine	3.3
12	Maryland	12.8
8	Massachusetts	14.3
26	Michigan	6.2
24	Minnesota	6.8
48	Mississippi	2.0
39	Missouri	3.6
48	Montana	2.0
28	Nebraska	5.9
4	Nevada	19.2
30	New Hampshire	5.2
3	New Jersey	20.2
16	New Mexico	9.8
2	New York	21.4
22	North Carolina	7.1
47	North Dakota	2.4
38	Ohio	3.8
31	Oklahoma	5.1
18	Oregon	9.6
29	Pennsylvania	5.5
13	Rhode Island	12.7
32	South Carolina	4.5
46	South Dakota	2.7
35	Tennessee	4.2
7	Texas	16.1
21	Utah	7.8
41	Vermont	3.3
15	Virginia	10.2
14	Washington	12.2
50	West Virginia	1.3
32	Wisconsin	4.5
43	Wyoming	3.1

RANK ORDER

RANK	STATE	PERCENT
1	California	26.9
2	New York	21.4
3	New Jersey	20.2
4	Nevada	19.2
5	Florida	18.8
6	Hawaii	17.3
7	Texas	16.1
8	Massachusetts	14.3
9	Arizona	14.0
10	Illinois	13.5
11	Connecticut	13.1
12	Maryland	12.8
13	Rhode Island	12.7
14	Washington	12.2
15	Virginia	10.2
16	New Mexico	9.8
17	Colorado	9.7
18	Oregon	9.6
19	Georgia	9.4
20	Delaware	8.4
21	Utah	7.8
22	North Carolina	7.1
23	Alaska	7.0
24	Minnesota	6.8
25	Idaho	6.3
26	Michigan	6.2
27	Kansas	6.1
28	Nebraska	5.9
29	Pennsylvania	5.5
30	New Hampshire	5.2
31	Oklahoma	5.1
32	South Carolina	4.5
32	Wisconsin	4.5
34	Indiana	4.4
35	Arkansas	4.2
35	Tennessee	4.2
37	Iowa	3.9
38	Ohio	3.8
39	Missouri	3.6
40	Louisiana	3.4
41	Maine	3.3
41	Vermont	3.3
43	Alabama	3.1
43	Wyoming	3.1
45	Kentucky	3.0
46	South Dakota	2.7
47	North Dakota	2.4
48	Mississippi	2.0
48	Montana	2.0
50	West Virginia	1.3

District of Columbia — 12.0

Source: U.S. Bureau of the Census

"2009 American Community Survey" (http://www.census.gov/acs/www/index.html)

*"Foreign born" are persons not born in the United States, Puerto Rico, a U.S. Island Area, or abroad of American parent or parents.

Percent of Population Speaking a Language Other than English at Home in 2009
National Percent = 20.0%*

ALPHA ORDER

RANK	STATE	PERCENT
46	Alabama	4.6
16	Alaska	16.4
7	Arizona	27.7
36	Arkansas	6.8
1	California	43.1
15	Colorado	16.7
13	Connecticut	20.4
22	Delaware	11.4
8	Florida	26.3
21	Georgia	12.5
9	Hawaii	24.9
25	Idaho	9.9
10	Illinois	21.7
34	Indiana	7.6
38	Iowa	6.5
23	Kansas	10.1
47	Kentucky	4.5
32	Louisiana	8.2
35	Maine	7.3
17	Maryland	15.3
12	Massachusetts	20.6
29	Michigan	9.2
26	Minnesota	9.8
49	Mississippi	3.7
43	Missouri	5.8
45	Montana	4.8
27	Nebraska	9.6
5	Nevada	28.5
33	New Hampshire	8.0
5	New Jersey	28.5
2	New Mexico	35.8
4	New York	29.0
23	North Carolina	10.1
44	North Dakota	5.0
39	Ohio	6.3
30	Oklahoma	8.6
18	Oregon	14.6
27	Pennsylvania	9.6
11	Rhode Island	21.1
39	South Carolina	6.3
39	South Dakota	6.3
42	Tennessee	6.0
3	Texas	34.2
19	Utah	13.8
48	Vermont	4.4
20	Virginia	13.5
14	Washington	17.0
50	West Virginia	2.3
31	Wisconsin	8.3
36	Wyoming	6.8

RANK ORDER

RANK	STATE	PERCENT
1	California	43.1
2	New Mexico	35.8
3	Texas	34.2
4	New York	29.0
5	Nevada	28.5
5	New Jersey	28.5
7	Arizona	27.7
8	Florida	26.3
9	Hawaii	24.9
10	Illinois	21.7
11	Rhode Island	21.1
12	Massachusetts	20.6
13	Connecticut	20.4
14	Washington	17.0
15	Colorado	16.7
16	Alaska	16.4
17	Maryland	15.3
18	Oregon	14.6
19	Utah	13.8
20	Virginia	13.5
21	Georgia	12.5
22	Delaware	11.4
23	Kansas	10.1
23	North Carolina	10.1
25	Idaho	9.9
26	Minnesota	9.8
27	Nebraska	9.6
27	Pennsylvania	9.6
29	Michigan	9.2
30	Oklahoma	8.6
31	Wisconsin	8.3
32	Louisiana	8.2
33	New Hampshire	8.0
34	Indiana	7.6
35	Maine	7.3
36	Arkansas	6.8
36	Wyoming	6.8
38	Iowa	6.5
39	Ohio	6.3
39	South Carolina	6.3
39	South Dakota	6.3
42	Tennessee	6.0
43	Missouri	5.8
44	North Dakota	5.0
45	Montana	4.8
46	Alabama	4.6
47	Kentucky	4.5
48	Vermont	4.4
49	Mississippi	3.7
50	West Virginia	2.3
	District of Columbia	12.6

Source: U.S. Bureau of the Census

"2009 American Community Survey" (http://www.census.gov/acs/www/index.html)

*Population five years old and older.

Percent of Population Speaking Spanish at Home in 2009

National Percent = 12.4%*

ALPHA ORDER

RANK	STATE	PERCENT
38	Alabama	2.8
29	Alaska	4.2
4	Arizona	21.5
26	Arkansas	5.1
2	California	28.7
10	Colorado	11.9
12	Connecticut	10.3
25	Delaware	5.6
6	Florida	19.3
17	Georgia	7.2
44	Hawaii	2.0
16	Idaho	7.3
9	Illinois	12.6
29	Indiana	4.2
33	Iowa	3.7
19	Kansas	6.7
40	Kentucky	2.3
36	Louisiana	3.0
48	Maine	1.0
22	Maryland	6.0
17	Massachusetts	7.2
36	Michigan	3.0
34	Minnesota	3.5
42	Mississippi	2.2
39	Missouri	2.6
46	Montana	1.5
21	Nebraska	6.4
5	Nevada	20.0
40	New Hampshire	2.3
7	New Jersey	14.4
3	New Mexico	28.4
8	New York	14.1
20	North Carolina	6.6
47	North Dakota	1.4
43	Ohio	2.1
24	Oklahoma	5.9
14	Oregon	8.7
31	Pennsylvania	3.9
11	Rhode Island	10.6
31	South Carolina	3.9
45	South Dakota	1.8
35	Tennessee	3.4
1	Texas	29.2
13	Utah	9.2
50	Vermont	0.8
22	Virginia	6.0
15	Washington	7.4
49	West Virginia	0.9
28	Wisconsin	4.3
27	Wyoming	4.5

RANK ORDER

RANK	STATE	PERCENT
1	Texas	29.2
2	California	28.7
3	New Mexico	28.4
4	Arizona	21.5
5	Nevada	20.0
6	Florida	19.3
7	New Jersey	14.4
8	New York	14.1
9	Illinois	12.6
10	Colorado	11.9
11	Rhode Island	10.6
12	Connecticut	10.3
13	Utah	9.2
14	Oregon	8.7
15	Washington	7.4
16	Idaho	7.3
17	Georgia	7.2
17	Massachusetts	7.2
19	Kansas	6.7
20	North Carolina	6.6
21	Nebraska	6.4
22	Maryland	6.0
22	Virginia	6.0
24	Oklahoma	5.9
25	Delaware	5.6
26	Arkansas	5.1
27	Wyoming	4.5
28	Wisconsin	4.3
29	Alaska	4.2
29	Indiana	4.2
31	Pennsylvania	3.9
31	South Carolina	3.9
33	Iowa	3.7
34	Minnesota	3.5
35	Tennessee	3.4
36	Louisiana	3.0
36	Michigan	3.0
38	Alabama	2.8
39	Missouri	2.6
40	Kentucky	2.3
40	New Hampshire	2.3
42	Mississippi	2.2
43	Ohio	2.1
44	Hawaii	2.0
45	South Dakota	1.8
46	Montana	1.5
47	North Dakota	1.4
48	Maine	1.0
49	West Virginia	0.9
50	Vermont	0.8

District of Columbia	6.3

Source: U.S. Bureau of the Census
   "2009 American Community Survey" (http://www.census.gov/acs/www/index.html)
*Population five years old and older.

Marriages in 2009

National Total = 2,077,000 Marriages*

ALPHA ORDER					RANK ORDER			
RANK	STATE	MARRIAGES	% of USA		RANK	STATE	MARRIAGES	% of USA
19	Alabama	37,284	1.8%		1	California	213,922	10.3%
46	Alaska	5,525	0.3%		2	Texas	179,776	8.7%
21	Arizona	35,338	1.7%		3	Florida	141,175	6.8%
24	Arkansas	31,622	1.5%		4	New York	120,137	5.8%
1	California	213,922	10.3%		5	Nevada	108,150	5.2%
18	Colorado	37,439	1.8%		6	Illinois	72,741	3.5%
34	Connecticut	19,800	1.0%		7	North Carolina	65,817	3.2%
47	Delaware	5,138	0.2%		8	Ohio	64,766	3.1%
3	Florida	141,175	6.8%		9	Pennsylvania	64,218	3.1%
10	Georgia	63,640	3.1%		10	Georgia	63,640	3.1%
32	Hawaii	22,215	1.1%		11	Tennessee	55,239	2.7%
37	Idaho	13,873	0.7%		12	Virginia	54,108	2.6%
6	Illinois	72,741	3.5%		13	Michigan	53,143	2.6%
14	Indiana	52,900	2.5%		14	Indiana	52,900	2.5%
33	Iowa	21,172	1.0%		15	New Jersey	46,291	2.2%
35	Kansas	18,475	0.9%		16	Washington	40,357	1.9%
22	Kentucky	33,422	1.6%		17	Missouri	39,767	1.9%
27	Louisiana	28,716	1.4%		18	Colorado	37,439	1.8%
41	Maine	9,446	0.5%		19	Alabama	37,284	1.8%
23	Maryland	32,403	1.6%		20	Massachusetts	36,701	1.8%
20	Massachusetts	36,701	1.8%		21	Arizona	35,338	1.7%
13	Michigan	53,143	2.6%		22	Kentucky	33,422	1.6%
28	Minnesota	28,382	1.4%		23	Maryland	32,403	1.6%
36	Mississippi	14,480	0.7%		24	Arkansas	31,622	1.5%
17	Missouri	39,767	1.9%		25	Wisconsin	30,271	1.5%
43	Montana	7,132	0.3%		26	South Carolina	29,164	1.4%
38	Nebraska	12,468	0.6%		27	Louisiana	28,716	1.4%
5	Nevada	108,150	5.2%		28	Minnesota	28,382	1.4%
42	New Hampshire	8,509	0.4%		29	Utah	23,888	1.2%
15	New Jersey	46,291	2.2%		30	Oklahoma	23,539	1.1%
40	New Mexico	10,208	0.5%		31	Oregon	23,530	1.1%
4	New York	120,137	5.8%		32	Hawaii	22,215	1.1%
7	North Carolina	65,817	3.2%		33	Iowa	21,172	1.0%
50	North Dakota	4,305	0.2%		34	Connecticut	19,800	1.0%
8	Ohio	64,766	3.1%		35	Kansas	18,475	0.9%
30	Oklahoma	23,539	1.1%		36	Mississippi	14,480	0.7%
31	Oregon	23,530	1.1%		37	Idaho	13,873	0.7%
9	Pennsylvania	64,218	3.1%		38	Nebraska	12,468	0.6%
44	Rhode Island	6,540	0.3%		39	West Virginia	12,422	0.6%
26	South Carolina	29,164	1.4%		40	New Mexico	10,208	0.5%
45	South Dakota	5,874	0.3%		41	Maine	9,446	0.5%
11	Tennessee	55,239	2.7%		42	New Hampshire	8,509	0.4%
2	Texas	179,776	8.7%		43	Montana	7,132	0.3%
29	Utah	23,888	1.2%		44	Rhode Island	6,540	0.3%
49	Vermont	4,701	0.2%		45	South Dakota	5,874	0.3%
12	Virginia	54,108	2.6%		46	Alaska	5,525	0.3%
16	Washington	40,357	1.9%		47	Delaware	5,138	0.2%
39	West Virginia	12,422	0.6%		48	Wyoming	4,718	0.2%
25	Wisconsin	30,271	1.5%		49	Vermont	4,701	0.2%
48	Wyoming	4,718	0.2%		50	North Dakota	4,305	0.2%
						District of Columbia	1,892	0.1%

Source: U.S. Department of Health and Human Services, National Center for Health Statistics
"National Vital Statistics Reports" (Vol. 58, No. 25, August 27, 2010, http://www.cdc.gov/nchs/data/nvsr/nvsr58/nvsr58_25.pdf)
*Provisional data by state of occurrence.

Marriage Rate in 2009

National Rate = 6.8 Marriages per 1,000 Population*

ALPHA ORDER

RANK	STATE	RATE
9	Alabama	7.9
9	Alaska	7.9
43	Arizona	5.4
3	Arkansas	10.9
36	California	5.8
14	Colorado	7.5
39	Connecticut	5.6
36	Delaware	5.8
12	Florida	7.6
27	Georgia	6.5
2	Hawaii	17.2
4	Idaho	9.0
39	Illinois	5.6
8	Indiana	8.2
19	Iowa	7.0
25	Kansas	6.6
11	Kentucky	7.7
28	Louisiana	6.4
17	Maine	7.2
38	Maryland	5.7
39	Massachusetts	5.6
46	Michigan	5.3
43	Minnesota	5.4
50	Mississippi	4.9
25	Missouri	6.6
15	Montana	7.3
21	Nebraska	6.9
1	Nevada	40.9
28	New Hampshire	6.4
46	New Jersey	5.3
48	New Mexico	5.1
34	New York	6.1
19	North Carolina	7.0
24	North Dakota	6.7
39	Ohio	5.6
28	Oklahoma	6.4
32	Oregon	6.2
48	Pennsylvania	5.1
32	Rhode Island	6.2
28	South Carolina	6.4
17	South Dakota	7.2
5	Tennessee	8.8
15	Texas	7.3
7	Utah	8.6
12	Vermont	7.6
21	Virginia	6.9
34	Washington	6.1
23	West Virginia	6.8
43	Wisconsin	5.4
6	Wyoming	8.7

RANK ORDER

RANK	STATE	RATE
1	Nevada	40.9
2	Hawaii	17.2
3	Arkansas	10.9
4	Idaho	9.0
5	Tennessee	8.8
6	Wyoming	8.7
7	Utah	8.6
8	Indiana	8.2
9	Alabama	7.9
9	Alaska	7.9
11	Kentucky	7.7
12	Florida	7.6
12	Vermont	7.6
14	Colorado	7.5
15	Montana	7.3
15	Texas	7.3
17	Maine	7.2
17	South Dakota	7.2
19	Iowa	7.0
19	North Carolina	7.0
21	Nebraska	6.9
21	Virginia	6.9
23	West Virginia	6.8
24	North Dakota	6.7
25	Kansas	6.6
25	Missouri	6.6
27	Georgia	6.5
28	Louisiana	6.4
28	New Hampshire	6.4
28	Oklahoma	6.4
28	South Carolina	6.4
32	Oregon	6.2
32	Rhode Island	6.2
34	New York	6.1
34	Washington	6.1
36	California	5.8
36	Delaware	5.8
38	Maryland	5.7
39	Connecticut	5.6
39	Illinois	5.6
39	Massachusetts	5.6
39	Ohio	5.6
43	Arizona	5.4
43	Minnesota	5.4
43	Wisconsin	5.4
46	Michigan	5.3
46	New Jersey	5.3
48	New Mexico	5.1
48	Pennsylvania	5.1
50	Mississippi	4.9

District of Columbia	3.2

Source: CQ Press using data from U.S. Department of Health and Human Services, National Center for Health Statistics
"National Vital Statistics Reports" (Vol. 58, No. 25, August 27, 2010, http://www.cdc.gov/nchs/data/nvsr/nvsr58/nvsr58_25.pdf)
*Provisional data by state of occurrence.

Estimated Median Age of Men at First Marriage: 2009

National Median = 28.4 Years*

ALPHA ORDER

RANK	STATE	AGE
40	Alabama	26.9
34	Alaska	27.3
20	Arizona	28.4
46	Arkansas	26.2
8	California	29.3
28	Colorado	27.8
5	Connecticut	29.7
12	Delaware	29.1
14	Florida	28.9
23	Georgia	28.0
18	Hawaii	28.5
49	Idaho	25.7
8	Illinois	29.3
37	Indiana	27.1
40	Iowa	26.9
31	Kansas	27.7
40	Kentucky	26.9
33	Louisiana	27.5
28	Maine	27.8
8	Maryland	29.3
2	Massachusetts	30.3
18	Michigan	28.5
15	Minnesota	28.6
43	Mississippi	26.8
28	Missouri	27.8
13	Montana	29.0
34	Nebraska	27.3
25	Nevada	27.9
4	New Hampshire	29.8
3	New Jersey	30.2
31	New Mexico	27.7
1	New York	30.4
25	North Carolina	27.9
38	North Dakota	27.0
15	Ohio	28.6
48	Oklahoma	26.0
15	Oregon	28.6
8	Pennsylvania	29.3
6	Rhode Island	29.6
22	South Carolina	28.1
47	South Dakota	26.1
38	Tennessee	27.0
34	Texas	27.3
49	Utah	25.7
7	Vermont	29.4
25	Virginia	27.9
23	Washington	28.0
44	West Virginia	26.6
21	Wisconsin	28.3
45	Wyoming	26.3

RANK ORDER

RANK	STATE	AGE
1	New York	30.4
2	Massachusetts	30.3
3	New Jersey	30.2
4	New Hampshire	29.8
5	Connecticut	29.7
6	Rhode Island	29.6
7	Vermont	29.4
8	California	29.3
8	Illinois	29.3
8	Maryland	29.3
8	Pennsylvania	29.3
12	Delaware	29.1
13	Montana	29.0
14	Florida	28.9
15	Minnesota	28.6
15	Ohio	28.6
15	Oregon	28.6
18	Hawaii	28.5
18	Michigan	28.5
20	Arizona	28.4
21	Wisconsin	28.3
22	South Carolina	28.1
23	Georgia	28.0
23	Washington	28.0
25	Nevada	27.9
25	North Carolina	27.9
25	Virginia	27.9
28	Colorado	27.8
28	Maine	27.8
28	Missouri	27.8
31	Kansas	27.7
31	New Mexico	27.7
33	Louisiana	27.5
34	Alaska	27.3
34	Nebraska	27.3
34	Texas	27.3
37	Indiana	27.1
38	North Dakota	27.0
38	Tennessee	27.0
40	Alabama	26.9
40	Iowa	26.9
40	Kentucky	26.9
43	Mississippi	26.8
44	West Virginia	26.6
45	Wyoming	26.3
46	Arkansas	26.2
47	South Dakota	26.1
48	Oklahoma	26.0
49	Idaho	25.7
49	Utah	25.7
	District of Columbia	31.5

Source: U.S. Bureau of the Census
"2009 American Community Survey" (http://www.census.gov/acs/www/index.html)
*The median age at first marriage is calculated indirectly by estimating the proportion of young people who will marry during their lifetime, calculating one-half of this proportion, and determining the age (at the time of the survey) of people at this half-way mark. It does not represent the actual median age of the population who married during the calendar year.

Estimated Median Age of Women at First Marriage: 2009

National Median = 26.5 Years*

ALPHA ORDER

RANK	STATE	AGE
36	Alabama	25.7
41	Alaska	25.4
24	Arizona	26.1
46	Arkansas	24.9
11	California	27.3
28	Colorado	26.0
5	Connecticut	27.7
17	Delaware	26.6
13	Florida	27.0
24	Georgia	26.1
7	Hawaii	27.5
50	Idaho	23.1
9	Illinois	27.4
24	Indiana	26.1
33	Iowa	25.8
29	Kansas	25.9
43	Kentucky	25.2
24	Louisiana	26.1
13	Maine	27.0
9	Maryland	27.4
2	Massachusetts	28.9
17	Michigan	26.6
19	Minnesota	26.5
36	Mississippi	25.7
33	Missouri	25.8
33	Montana	25.8
36	Nebraska	25.7
22	Nevada	26.3
6	New Hampshire	27.6
4	New Jersey	28.0
29	New Mexico	25.9
3	New York	28.6
29	North Carolina	25.9
43	North Dakota	25.2
15	Ohio	26.9
47	Oklahoma	24.5
23	Oregon	26.2
7	Pennsylvania	27.5
1	Rhode Island	29.0
21	South Carolina	26.4
40	South Dakota	25.5
39	Tennessee	25.6
41	Texas	25.4
48	Utah	24.1
12	Vermont	27.2
16	Virginia	26.7
29	Washington	25.9
45	West Virginia	25.0
19	Wisconsin	26.5
49	Wyoming	23.7

RANK ORDER

RANK	STATE	AGE
1	Rhode Island	29.0
2	Massachusetts	28.9
3	New York	28.6
4	New Jersey	28.0
5	Connecticut	27.7
6	New Hampshire	27.6
7	Hawaii	27.5
7	Pennsylvania	27.5
9	Illinois	27.4
9	Maryland	27.4
11	California	27.3
12	Vermont	27.2
13	Florida	27.0
13	Maine	27.0
15	Ohio	26.9
16	Virginia	26.7
17	Delaware	26.6
17	Michigan	26.6
19	Minnesota	26.5
19	Wisconsin	26.5
21	South Carolina	26.4
22	Nevada	26.3
23	Oregon	26.2
24	Arizona	26.1
24	Georgia	26.1
24	Indiana	26.1
24	Louisiana	26.1
28	Colorado	26.0
29	Kansas	25.9
29	New Mexico	25.9
29	North Carolina	25.9
29	Washington	25.9
33	Iowa	25.8
33	Missouri	25.8
33	Montana	25.8
36	Alabama	25.7
36	Mississippi	25.7
36	Nebraska	25.7
39	Tennessee	25.6
40	South Dakota	25.5
41	Alaska	25.4
41	Texas	25.4
43	Kentucky	25.2
43	North Dakota	25.2
45	West Virginia	25.0
46	Arkansas	24.9
47	Oklahoma	24.5
48	Utah	24.1
49	Wyoming	23.7
50	Idaho	23.1
	District of Columbia	29.6

Source: U.S. Bureau of the Census
  "2009 American Community Survey" (http://www.census.gov/acs/www/index.html)
*The median age at first marriage is calculated indirectly by estimating the proportion of young people who will marry during their lifetime, calculating one-half of this proportion, and determining the age (at the time of the survey) of people at this half-way mark. It does not represent the actual median age of the population who married during the calendar year.

Ratio of Unmarried Men to Unmarried Women: 2009

National Ratio = 112.9 Unmarried Men for Every 100 Unmarried Women*

ALPHA ORDER

RANK	STATE	RATIO
40	Alabama	108.8
3	Alaska	129.0
9	Arizona	119.2
30	Arkansas	111.3
13	California	117.7
6	Colorado	121.6
43	Connecticut	107.9
50	Delaware	103.8
18	Florida	115.5
42	Georgia	108.3
2	Hawaii	130.1
4	Idaho	124.4
32	Illinois	111.2
34	Indiana	110.7
29	Iowa	111.7
18	Kansas	115.5
23	Kentucky	114.0
46	Louisiana	106.2
41	Maine	108.7
49	Maryland	105.4
45	Massachusetts	106.5
35	Michigan	110.6
24	Minnesota	113.6
47	Mississippi	106.1
30	Missouri	111.3
14	Montana	117.4
16	Nebraska	115.9
7	Nevada	119.9
36	New Hampshire	110.3
25	New Jersey	112.9
18	New Mexico	115.5
44	New York	107.2
28	North Carolina	111.8
5	North Dakota	121.8
37	Ohio	110.2
10	Oklahoma	118.6
21	Oregon	114.4
38	Pennsylvania	110.0
48	Rhode Island	105.5
39	South Carolina	109.9
12	South Dakota	118.2
33	Tennessee	111.1
15	Texas	116.3
22	Utah	114.2
16	Vermont	115.9
26	Virginia	112.4
11	Washington	118.4
8	West Virginia	119.8
27	Wisconsin	112.0
1	Wyoming	136.4

RANK ORDER

RANK	STATE	RATIO
1	Wyoming	136.4
2	Hawaii	130.1
3	Alaska	129.0
4	Idaho	124.4
5	North Dakota	121.8
6	Colorado	121.6
7	Nevada	119.9
8	West Virginia	119.8
9	Arizona	119.2
10	Oklahoma	118.6
11	Washington	118.4
12	South Dakota	118.2
13	California	117.7
14	Montana	117.4
15	Texas	116.3
16	Nebraska	115.9
16	Vermont	115.9
18	Florida	115.5
18	Kansas	115.5
18	New Mexico	115.5
21	Oregon	114.4
22	Utah	114.2
23	Kentucky	114.0
24	Minnesota	113.6
25	New Jersey	112.9
26	Virginia	112.4
27	Wisconsin	112.0
28	North Carolina	111.8
29	Iowa	111.7
30	Arkansas	111.3
30	Missouri	111.3
32	Illinois	111.2
33	Tennessee	111.1
34	Indiana	110.7
35	Michigan	110.6
36	New Hampshire	110.3
37	Ohio	110.2
38	Pennsylvania	110.0
39	South Carolina	109.9
40	Alabama	108.8
41	Maine	108.7
42	Georgia	108.3
43	Connecticut	107.9
44	New York	107.2
45	Massachusetts	106.5
46	Louisiana	106.2
47	Mississippi	106.1
48	Rhode Island	105.5
49	Maryland	105.4
50	Delaware	103.8
	District of Columbia	91.1

Source: U.S. Bureau of the Census
   "2009 American Community Survey" (http://www.census.gov/acs/www/index.html)
*Population 15 to 44 years old.

Divorces in 2009

Reporting States' Total = 820,669 Divorces*

ALPHA ORDER

ALPHA ORDER / RANK ORDER

RANK	STATE	DIVORCES	% of USA	RANK	STATE	DIVORCES	% of USA
16	Alabama	20,158	2.5%	1	Florida	79,915	9.7%
40	Alaska	3,324	0.4%	2	Texas	76,909	9.4%
14	Arizona	23,140	2.8%	3	New York	46,070	5.6%
21	Arkansas	16,262	2.0%	4	Ohio	36,861	4.5%
NA	California**	NA	NA	5	North Carolina	36,708	4.5%
15	Colorado	21,197	2.6%	6	Illinois	32,746	4.0%
27	Connecticut	10,837	1.3%	7	Michigan	32,456	4.0%
38	Delaware	3,417	0.4%	8	Pennsylvania	28,828	3.5%
1	Florida	79,915	9.7%	9	Virginia	28,527	3.5%
NA	Georgia**	NA	NA	10	Washington	26,251	3.2%
NA	Hawaii**	NA	NA	11	Tennessee	25,843	3.1%
32	Idaho	7,700	0.9%	12	New Jersey	23,978	2.9%
6	Illinois	32,746	4.0%	13	Missouri	23,299	2.8%
NA	Indiana**	NA	NA	14	Arizona	23,140	2.8%
33	Iowa	7,298	0.9%	15	Colorado	21,197	2.6%
29	Kansas	10,303	1.3%	16	Alabama	20,158	2.5%
17	Kentucky	19,931	2.4%	17	Kentucky	19,931	2.4%
NA	Louisiana**	NA	NA	18	Nevada	17,682	2.2%
35	Maine	5,323	0.6%	19	Wisconsin	17,270	2.1%
22	Maryland	15,221	1.9%	20	Oklahoma	16,858	2.1%
24	Massachusetts	12,725	1.6%	21	Arkansas	16,262	2.0%
7	Michigan	32,456	4.0%	22	Maryland	15,221	1.9%
NA	Minnesota**	NA	NA	23	Oregon	13,277	1.6%
26	Mississippi	12,210	1.5%	24	Massachusetts	12,725	1.6%
13	Missouri	23,299	2.8%	25	South Carolina	12,222	1.5%
37	Montana	3,904	0.5%	26	Mississippi	12,210	1.5%
34	Nebraska	5,379	0.7%	27	Connecticut	10,837	1.3%
18	Nevada	17,682	2.2%	28	Utah	10,739	1.3%
36	New Hampshire	4,868	0.6%	29	Kansas	10,303	1.3%
12	New Jersey	23,978	2.9%	30	West Virginia	9,237	1.1%
31	New Mexico	7,969	1.0%	31	New Mexico	7,969	1.0%
3	New York	46,070	5.6%	32	Idaho	7,700	0.9%
5	North Carolina	36,708	4.5%	33	Iowa	7,298	0.9%
44	North Dakota	1,596	0.2%	34	Nebraska	5,379	0.7%
4	Ohio	36,861	4.5%	35	Maine	5,323	0.6%
20	Oklahoma	16,858	2.1%	36	New Hampshire	4,868	0.6%
23	Oregon	13,277	1.6%	37	Montana	3,904	0.5%
8	Pennsylvania	28,828	3.5%	38	Delaware	3,417	0.4%
39	Rhode Island	3,345	0.4%	39	Rhode Island	3,345	0.4%
25	South Carolina	12,222	1.5%	40	Alaska	3,324	0.4%
42	South Dakota	2,627	0.3%	41	Wyoming	2,833	0.3%
11	Tennessee	25,843	3.1%	42	South Dakota	2,627	0.3%
2	Texas	76,909	9.4%	43	Vermont	2,102	0.3%
28	Utah	10,739	1.3%	44	North Dakota	1,596	0.2%
43	Vermont	2,102	0.3%	NA	California**	NA	NA
9	Virginia	28,527	3.5%	NA	Georgia**	NA	NA
10	Washington	26,251	3.2%	NA	Hawaii**	NA	NA
30	West Virginia	9,237	1.1%	NA	Indiana**	NA	NA
19	Wisconsin	17,270	2.1%	NA	Louisiana**	NA	NA
41	Wyoming	2,833	0.3%	NA	Minnesota**	NA	NA
					District of Columbia	1,324	0.2%

Source: U.S. Department of Health and Human Services, National Center for Health Statistics
"National Vital Statistics Reports" (Vol. 58, No. 25, August 27, 2010, http://www.cdc.gov/nchs/data/nvsr/nvsr58/nvsr58_25.pdf)
*Provisional data by state of occurrence. National total is only for reporting states.
**Not available.

Divorce Rate in 2009

Reporting States' Rate = 3.4 Divorces per 1,000 Population*

ALPHA ORDER

RANK	STATE	RATE
9	Alabama	4.3
6	Alaska	4.8
25	Arizona	3.5
2	Arkansas	5.6
NA	California**	NA
11	Colorado	4.2
32	Connecticut	3.1
17	Delaware	3.9
9	Florida	4.3
NA	Georgia**	NA
NA	Hawaii**	NA
5	Idaho	5.0
39	Illinois	2.5
NA	Indiana**	NA
41	Iowa	2.4
22	Kansas	3.7
7	Kentucky	4.6
NA	Louisiana**	NA
14	Maine	4.0
37	Maryland	2.7
44	Massachusetts	1.9
28	Michigan	3.3
NA	Minnesota**	NA
12	Mississippi	4.1
17	Missouri	3.9
14	Montana	4.0
35	Nebraska	3.0
1	Nevada	6.7
22	New Hampshire	3.7
36	New Jersey	2.8
14	New Mexico	4.0
41	New York	2.4
17	North Carolina	3.9
39	North Dakota	2.5
29	Ohio	3.2
7	Oklahoma	4.6
25	Oregon	3.5
43	Pennsylvania	2.3
29	Rhode Island	3.2
37	South Carolina	2.7
29	South Dakota	3.2
12	Tennessee	4.1
32	Texas	3.1
17	Utah	3.9
27	Vermont	3.4
24	Virginia	3.6
17	Washington	3.9
4	West Virginia	5.1
32	Wisconsin	3.1
3	Wyoming	5.2

RANK ORDER

RANK	STATE	RATE
1	Nevada	6.7
2	Arkansas	5.6
3	Wyoming	5.2
4	West Virginia	5.1
5	Idaho	5.0
6	Alaska	4.8
7	Kentucky	4.6
7	Oklahoma	4.6
9	Alabama	4.3
9	Florida	4.3
11	Colorado	4.2
12	Mississippi	4.1
12	Tennessee	4.1
14	Maine	4.0
14	Montana	4.0
14	New Mexico	4.0
17	Delaware	3.9
17	Missouri	3.9
17	North Carolina	3.9
17	Utah	3.9
17	Washington	3.9
22	Kansas	3.7
22	New Hampshire	3.7
24	Virginia	3.6
25	Arizona	3.5
25	Oregon	3.5
27	Vermont	3.4
28	Michigan	3.3
29	Ohio	3.2
29	Rhode Island	3.2
29	South Dakota	3.2
32	Connecticut	3.1
32	Texas	3.1
32	Wisconsin	3.1
35	Nebraska	3.0
36	New Jersey	2.8
37	Maryland	2.7
37	South Carolina	2.7
39	Illinois	2.5
39	North Dakota	2.5
41	Iowa	2.4
41	New York	2.4
43	Pennsylvania	2.3
44	Massachusetts	1.9
NA	California**	NA
NA	Georgia**	NA
NA	Hawaii**	NA
NA	Indiana**	NA
NA	Louisiana**	NA
NA	Minnesota**	NA

District of Columbia 2.2

Source: CQ Press using data from U.S. Department of Health and Human Services, National Center for Health Statistics
"National Vital Statistics Reports" (Vol. 58, No. 25, August 27, 2010, http://www.cdc.gov/nchs/data/nvsr/nvsr58/nvsr58_25.pdf)
*Provisional data by state of occurrence. National rate is only for reporting states.
**Not available.

Average Family Size in 2009

National Average = 3.23 Persons per Family

RANK	STATE	PERSONS	RANK	STATE	PERSONS
35	Alabama	3.06	1	Utah	3.65
4	Alaska	3.43	2	California	3.56
3	Arizona	3.49	3	Arizona	3.49
39	Arkansas	3.04	4	Alaska	3.43
2	California	3.56	4	Texas	3.43
18	Colorado	3.17	6	Georgia	3.35
22	Connecticut	3.15	6	Hawaii	3.35
18	Delaware	3.17	8	New York	3.31
15	Florida	3.20	9	Illinois	3.30
6	Georgia	3.35	9	Nevada	3.30
6	Hawaii	3.35	11	New Mexico	3.29
17	Idaho	3.19	12	New Jersey	3.28
9	Illinois	3.30	13	Maryland	3.26
28	Indiana	3.08	14	Massachusetts	3.22
48	Iowa	2.90	15	Florida	3.20
39	Kansas	3.04	15	Louisiana	3.20
44	Kentucky	3.01	17	Idaho	3.19
15	Louisiana	3.20	18	Colorado	3.17
49	Maine	2.88	18	Delaware	3.17
13	Maryland	3.26	18	Mississippi	3.17
14	Massachusetts	3.22	21	Rhode Island	3.16
23	Michigan	3.14	22	Connecticut	3.15
39	Minnesota	3.04	23	Michigan	3.14
18	Mississippi	3.17	23	Montana	3.14
35	Missouri	3.06	25	South Carolina	3.13
23	Montana	3.14	25	Virginia	3.13
42	Nebraska	3.03	27	Washington	3.12
9	Nevada	3.30	28	Indiana	3.08
29	New Hampshire	3.07	29	New Hampshire	3.07
12	New Jersey	3.28	29	Ohio	3.07
11	New Mexico	3.29	29	Oklahoma	3.07
8	New York	3.31	29	Oregon	3.07
35	North Carolina	3.06	29	Pennsylvania	3.07
50	North Dakota	2.80	29	Tennessee	3.07
29	Ohio	3.07	35	Alabama	3.06
29	Oklahoma	3.07	35	Missouri	3.06
29	Oregon	3.07	35	North Carolina	3.06
29	Pennsylvania	3.07	35	South Dakota	3.06
21	Rhode Island	3.16	39	Arkansas	3.04
25	South Carolina	3.13	39	Kansas	3.04
35	South Dakota	3.06	39	Minnesota	3.04
29	Tennessee	3.07	42	Nebraska	3.03
4	Texas	3.43	43	Wyoming	3.02
1	Utah	3.65	44	Kentucky	3.01
46	Vermont	2.92	45	Wisconsin	2.96
25	Virginia	3.13	46	Vermont	2.92
27	Washington	3.12	47	West Virginia	2.91
47	West Virginia	2.91	48	Iowa	2.90
45	Wisconsin	2.96	49	Maine	2.88
43	Wyoming	3.02	50	North Dakota	2.80
				District of Columbia	3.38

Source: U.S. Bureau of the Census
  "2009 American Community Survey" (http://www.census.gov/acs/www/)

Seats in the U.S. House of Representatives in 2012

National Total = 435 Seats*

ALPHA ORDER

RANK	STATE	SEATS	% of USA
22	Alabama	7	1.6%
44	Alaska	1	0.2%
14	Arizona	9	2.1%
30	Arkansas	4	0.9%
1	California	53	12.2%
22	Colorado	7	1.6%
27	Connecticut	5	1.1%
44	Delaware	1	0.2%
3	Florida	27	6.2%
8	Georgia	14	3.2%
39	Hawaii	2	0.5%
39	Idaho	2	0.5%
5	Illinois	18	4.1%
14	Indiana	9	2.1%
30	Iowa	4	0.9%
30	Kansas	4	0.9%
25	Kentucky	6	1.4%
25	Louisiana	6	1.4%
39	Maine	2	0.5%
18	Maryland	8	1.8%
14	Massachusetts	9	2.1%
8	Michigan	14	3.2%
18	Minnesota	8	1.8%
30	Mississippi	4	0.9%
18	Missouri	8	1.8%
44	Montana	1	0.2%
36	Nebraska	3	0.7%
30	Nevada	4	0.9%
39	New Hampshire	2	0.5%
11	New Jersey	12	2.8%
36	New Mexico	3	0.7%
3	New York	27	6.2%
10	North Carolina	13	3.0%
44	North Dakota	1	0.2%
7	Ohio	16	3.7%
27	Oklahoma	5	1.1%
27	Oregon	5	1.1%
5	Pennsylvania	18	4.1%
39	Rhode Island	2	0.5%
22	South Carolina	7	1.6%
44	South Dakota	1	0.2%
14	Tennessee	9	2.1%
2	Texas	36	8.3%
30	Utah	4	0.9%
44	Vermont	1	0.2%
12	Virginia	11	2.5%
13	Washington	10	2.3%
36	West Virginia	3	0.7%
18	Wisconsin	8	1.8%
44	Wyoming	1	0.2%

RANK ORDER

RANK	STATE	SEATS	% of USA
1	California	53	12.2%
2	Texas	36	8.3%
3	Florida	27	6.2%
3	New York	27	6.2%
5	Illinois	18	4.1%
5	Pennsylvania	18	4.1%
7	Ohio	16	3.7%
8	Georgia	14	3.2%
8	Michigan	14	3.2%
10	North Carolina	13	3.0%
11	New Jersey	12	2.8%
12	Virginia	11	2.5%
13	Washington	10	2.3%
14	Arizona	9	2.1%
14	Indiana	9	2.1%
14	Massachusetts	9	2.1%
14	Tennessee	9	2.1%
18	Maryland	8	1.8%
18	Minnesota	8	1.8%
18	Missouri	8	1.8%
18	Wisconsin	8	1.8%
22	Alabama	7	1.6%
22	Colorado	7	1.6%
22	South Carolina	7	1.6%
25	Kentucky	6	1.4%
25	Louisiana	6	1.4%
27	Connecticut	5	1.1%
27	Oklahoma	5	1.1%
27	Oregon	5	1.1%
30	Arkansas	4	0.9%
30	Iowa	4	0.9%
30	Kansas	4	0.9%
30	Mississippi	4	0.9%
30	Nevada	4	0.9%
30	Utah	4	0.9%
36	Nebraska	3	0.7%
36	New Mexico	3	0.7%
36	West Virginia	3	0.7%
39	Hawaii	2	0.5%
39	Idaho	2	0.5%
39	Maine	2	0.5%
39	New Hampshire	2	0.5%
39	Rhode Island	2	0.5%
44	Alaska	1	0.2%
44	Delaware	1	0.2%
44	Montana	1	0.2%
44	North Dakota	1	0.2%
44	South Dakota	1	0.2%
44	Vermont	1	0.2%
44	Wyoming	1	0.2%
	District of Columbia	0	0.0%

Source: U.S. Bureau of the Census
    "Congressional Apportionment" (http://www.census.gov/population/apportionment/
*This table shows the number of seats after reapportionment of the 2010 Census. This apportionment becomes effective with the Congress elected in November 2012 and that will take office in January 2013.
**The District of Columbia has one non-voting delegate. Each state has two members in the U.S. Senate.

Estimated Population per U.S. House Seat in 2012

National Rate = 710,767 Persons per House Member*

ALPHA ORDER				RANK ORDER		
RANK	STATE	RATE		RANK	STATE	RATE
37	Alabama	686,140		1	Montana	994,416
20	Alaska	721,523		2	Delaware	900,877
26	Arizona	712,522		3	South Dakota	819,761
13	Arkansas	731,557		4	Idaho	786,750
31	California	704,566		5	Oregon	769,721
21	Colorado	720,704		6	Iowa	763,447
23	Connecticut	716,326		7	Louisiana	758,994
2	Delaware	900,877		8	Oklahoma	752,976
33	Florida	700,029		9	Missouri	751,435
34	Georgia	694,826		10	Mississippi	744,560
38	Hawaii	683,431		11	North Carolina	735,829
4	Idaho	786,750		12	New Jersey	733,958
25	Illinois	714,688		13	Arkansas	731,557
19	Indiana	722,398		14	Virginia	730,703
6	Iowa	763,447		15	Massachusetts	728,849
24	Kansas	715,953		16	Kentucky	725,101
16	Kentucky	725,101		17	Maryland	723,741
7	Louisiana	758,994		18	Ohio	723,031
42	Maine	666,537		19	Indiana	722,398
17	Maryland	723,741		20	Alaska	721,523
15	Massachusetts	728,849		21	Colorado	720,704
29	Michigan	707,973		22	New York	719,298
43	Minnesota	664,360		23	Connecticut	716,326
10	Mississippi	744,560		24	Kansas	715,953
9	Missouri	751,435		25	Illinois	714,688
1	Montana	994,416		26	Arizona	712,522
48	Nebraska	610,608		27	Wisconsin	712,279
39	Nevada	677,358		28	Tennessee	708,381
45	New Hampshire	660,723		29	Michigan	707,973
12	New Jersey	733,958		30	Pennsylvania	707,495
36	New Mexico	689,091		31	California	704,566
22	New York	719,298		32	Texas	701,901
11	North Carolina	735,829		33	Florida	700,029
40	North Dakota	675,905		34	Georgia	694,826
18	Ohio	723,031		35	Utah	692,691
8	Oklahoma	752,976		36	New Mexico	689,091
5	Oregon	769,721		37	Alabama	686,140
30	Pennsylvania	707,495		38	Hawaii	683,431
50	Rhode Island	527,624		39	Nevada	677,358
44	South Carolina	663,711		40	North Dakota	675,905
3	South Dakota	819,761		41	Washington	675,337
28	Tennessee	708,381		42	Maine	666,537
32	Texas	701,901		43	Minnesota	664,360
35	Utah	692,691		44	South Carolina	663,711
46	Vermont	630,337		45	New Hampshire	660,723
14	Virginia	730,703		46	Vermont	630,337
41	Washington	675,337		47	West Virginia	619,938
47	West Virginia	619,938		48	Nebraska	610,608
27	Wisconsin	712,279		49	Wyoming	568,300
49	Wyoming	568,300		50	Rhode Island	527,624

District of Columbia**   NA

Source: CQ Press using data from U.S. Bureau of the Census
"Congressional Apportionment" (http://www.census.gov/population/apportionment/
*National rate based on the Census apportionment population and does not include population of the District of Columbia. The District has one non-voting delegate. Each state has two members in the U.S. Senate. This table is based only on U.S. Representatives and not U.S. Senate members. This table reflects reapportionment resulting from the 2010 census but not taking effect until the 2012 election. **Not applicable.

State Legislators in 2011

National Total = 7,382 Legislators*

ALPHA ORDER

RANK	STATE	LEGISLATORS	% of USA
27	Alabama	140	1.9%
49	Alaska	60	0.8%
43	Arizona	90	1.2%
30	Arkansas	135	1.8%
35	California	120	1.6%
42	Colorado	100	1.4%
9	Connecticut	187	2.5%
48	Delaware	62	0.8%
18	Florida	160	2.2%
3	Georgia	236	3.2%
46	Hawaii	76	1.0%
39	Idaho	105	1.4%
13	Illinois	177	2.4%
19	Indiana	150	2.0%
19	Iowa	150	2.0%
17	Kansas	165	2.2%
29	Kentucky	138	1.9%
25	Louisiana	144	2.0%
10	Maine	186	2.5%
8	Maryland	188	2.5%
6	Massachusetts	200	2.7%
23	Michigan	148	2.0%
5	Minnesota	201	2.7%
14	Mississippi	174	2.4%
7	Missouri	197	2.7%
19	Montana	150	2.0%
50	Nebraska	49	0.7%
47	Nevada	63	0.9%
1	New Hampshire	424	5.7%
35	New Jersey	120	1.6%
38	New Mexico	112	1.5%
4	New York	212	2.9%
15	North Carolina	170	2.3%
26	North Dakota	141	1.9%
32	Ohio	132	1.8%
22	Oklahoma	149	2.0%
43	Oregon	90	1.2%
2	Pennsylvania	253	3.4%
37	Rhode Island	113	1.5%
15	South Carolina	170	2.3%
39	South Dakota	105	1.4%
32	Tennessee	132	1.8%
11	Texas	181	2.5%
41	Utah	104	1.4%
12	Vermont	180	2.4%
27	Virginia	140	1.9%
24	Washington	147	2.0%
31	West Virginia	134	1.8%
32	Wisconsin	132	1.8%
43	Wyoming	90	1.2%

RANK ORDER

RANK	STATE	LEGISLATORS	% of USA
1	New Hampshire	424	5.7%
2	Pennsylvania	253	3.4%
3	Georgia	236	3.2%
4	New York	212	2.9%
5	Minnesota	201	2.7%
6	Massachusetts	200	2.7%
7	Missouri	197	2.7%
8	Maryland	188	2.5%
9	Connecticut	187	2.5%
10	Maine	186	2.5%
11	Texas	181	2.5%
12	Vermont	180	2.4%
13	Illinois	177	2.4%
14	Mississippi	174	2.4%
15	North Carolina	170	2.3%
15	South Carolina	170	2.3%
17	Kansas	165	2.2%
18	Florida	160	2.2%
19	Indiana	150	2.0%
19	Iowa	150	2.0%
19	Montana	150	2.0%
22	Oklahoma	149	2.0%
23	Michigan	148	2.0%
24	Washington	147	2.0%
25	Louisiana	144	2.0%
26	North Dakota	141	1.9%
27	Alabama	140	1.9%
27	Virginia	140	1.9%
29	Kentucky	138	1.9%
30	Arkansas	135	1.8%
31	West Virginia	134	1.8%
32	Ohio	132	1.8%
32	Tennessee	132	1.8%
32	Wisconsin	132	1.8%
35	California	120	1.6%
35	New Jersey	120	1.6%
37	Rhode Island	113	1.5%
38	New Mexico	112	1.5%
39	Idaho	105	1.4%
39	South Dakota	105	1.4%
41	Utah	104	1.4%
42	Colorado	100	1.4%
43	Arizona	90	1.2%
43	Oregon	90	1.2%
43	Wyoming	90	1.2%
46	Hawaii	76	1.0%
47	Nevada	63	0.9%
48	Delaware	62	0.8%
49	Alaska	60	0.8%
50	Nebraska	49	0.7%
	District of Columbia**	NA	NA

Source: National Conference of State Legislatures (Denver, CO)
 "2010 Post-Election Partisan Composition of State Legislatures" (http://www.ncsl.org/?tabid=21352)
*There are 1,971 state senators (including Nebraska's 49 unicameral seats) and 5,411 state house members.
**Not applicable.

Population per State Legislator in 2011

National Rate = 41,783 Population per Legislator*

ALPHA ORDER

RANK	STATE	RATE
22	Alabama	33,783
42	Alaska	11,814
6	Arizona	74,185
32	Arkansas	21,557
1	California	310,555
12	Colorado	50,953
34	Connecticut	18,861
40	Delaware	14,378
3	Florida	116,738
20	Georgia	41,985
37	Hawaii	17,106
39	Idaho	14,855
7	Illinois	73,132
16	Indiana	42,969
33	Iowa	20,154
36	Kansas	17,219
25	Kentucky	31,445
24	Louisiana	31,454
45	Maine	7,059
26	Maryland	30,517
23	Massachusetts	33,156
9	Michigan	67,103
30	Minnesota	26,321
38	Mississippi	17,014
27	Missouri	30,516
46	Montana	6,534
21	Nebraska	36,961
19	Nevada	42,139
50	New Hampshire	3,122
8	New Jersey	72,773
35	New Mexico	18,160
4	New York	92,348
11	North Carolina	55,641
48	North Dakota	4,637
5	Ohio	87,364
31	Oklahoma	24,996
18	Oregon	42,839
13	Pennsylvania	49,932
43	Rhode Island	9,353
29	South Carolina	27,041
44	South Dakota	7,810
14	Tennessee	48,016
2	Texas	139,301
28	Utah	27,219
49	Vermont	3,458
10	Virginia	56,801
15	Washington	45,893
41	West Virginia	13,623
17	Wisconsin	42,943
47	Wyoming	6,085

RANK ORDER

RANK	STATE	RATE
1	California	310,555
2	Texas	139,301
3	Florida	116,738
4	New York	92,348
5	Ohio	87,364
6	Arizona	74,185
7	Illinois	73,132
8	New Jersey	72,773
9	Michigan	67,103
10	Virginia	56,801
11	North Carolina	55,641
12	Colorado	50,953
13	Pennsylvania	49,932
14	Tennessee	48,016
15	Washington	45,893
16	Indiana	42,969
17	Wisconsin	42,943
18	Oregon	42,839
19	Nevada	42,139
20	Georgia	41,985
21	Nebraska	36,961
22	Alabama	33,783
23	Massachusetts	33,156
24	Louisiana	31,454
25	Kentucky	31,445
26	Maryland	30,517
27	Missouri	30,516
28	Utah	27,219
29	South Carolina	27,041
30	Minnesota	26,321
31	Oklahoma	24,996
32	Arkansas	21,557
33	Iowa	20,154
34	Connecticut	18,861
35	New Mexico	18,160
36	Kansas	17,219
37	Hawaii	17,106
38	Mississippi	17,014
39	Idaho	14,855
40	Delaware	14,378
41	West Virginia	13,623
42	Alaska	11,814
43	Rhode Island	9,353
44	South Dakota	7,810
45	Maine	7,059
46	Montana	6,534
47	Wyoming	6,085
48	North Dakota	4,637
49	Vermont	3,458
50	New Hampshire	3,122
	District of Columbia**	NA

Source: CQ Press using data from National Conference of State Legislatures (Denver, CO)
 "2010 Post-Election Partisan Composition of State Legislatures" (http://www.ncsl.org/?tabid=21352)
*There are 1,971 state senators (including Nebraska's 49 unicameral seats) and 5,411 state house members. National rate does not include population for the District of Columbia. Calculated using 2010 population estimates.
**Not applicable.

Registered Voters in 2008

National Total = 146,311,000

ALPHA ORDER

RANK	STATE	REGISTERED	% of USA
22	Alabama	2,438,000	1.7%
48	Alaska	345,000	0.2%
20	Arizona	2,874,000	2.0%
33	Arkansas	1,317,000	0.9%
1	California	14,885,000	10.2%
23	Colorado	2,437,000	1.7%
29	Connecticut	1,761,000	1.2%
45	Delaware	447,000	0.3%
3	Florida	8,774,000	6.0%
10	Georgia	4,624,000	3.2%
43	Hawaii	522,000	0.4%
41	Idaho	723,000	0.5%
6	Illinois	6,151,000	4.2%
16	Indiana	3,105,000	2.1%
30	Iowa	1,630,000	1.1%
32	Kansas	1,343,000	0.9%
26	Kentucky	2,259,000	1.5%
24	Louisiana	2,393,000	1.6%
39	Maine	801,000	0.5%
21	Maryland	2,828,000	1.9%
14	Massachusetts	3,293,000	2.3%
8	Michigan	5,531,000	3.8%
18	Minnesota	2,931,000	2.0%
31	Mississippi	1,589,000	1.1%
15	Missouri	3,224,000	2.2%
44	Montana	516,000	0.4%
36	Nebraska	939,000	0.6%
34	Nevada	1,147,000	0.8%
40	New Hampshire	756,000	0.5%
11	New Jersey	4,022,000	2.7%
37	New Mexico	937,000	0.6%
4	New York	8,458,000	5.8%
9	North Carolina	4,902,000	3.4%
47	North Dakota	399,000	0.3%
7	Ohio	6,108,000	4.2%
28	Oklahoma	1,798,000	1.2%
27	Oregon	1,961,000	1.3%
5	Pennsylvania	6,451,000	4.4%
42	Rhode Island	568,000	0.4%
25	South Carolina	2,385,000	1.6%
46	South Dakota	442,000	0.3%
19	Tennessee	2,921,000	2.0%
2	Texas	10,123,000	6.9%
35	Utah	1,056,000	0.7%
48	Vermont	345,000	0.2%
12	Virginia	3,950,000	2.7%
13	Washington	3,299,000	2.3%
38	West Virginia	917,000	0.6%
17	Wisconsin	3,095,000	2.1%
50	Wyoming	270,000	0.2%

RANK ORDER

RANK	STATE	REGISTERED	% of USA
1	California	14,885,000	10.2%
2	Texas	10,123,000	6.9%
3	Florida	8,774,000	6.0%
4	New York	8,458,000	5.8%
5	Pennsylvania	6,451,000	4.4%
6	Illinois	6,151,000	4.2%
7	Ohio	6,108,000	4.2%
8	Michigan	5,531,000	3.8%
9	North Carolina	4,902,000	3.4%
10	Georgia	4,624,000	3.2%
11	New Jersey	4,022,000	2.7%
12	Virginia	3,950,000	2.7%
13	Washington	3,299,000	2.3%
14	Massachusetts	3,293,000	2.3%
15	Missouri	3,224,000	2.2%
16	Indiana	3,105,000	2.1%
17	Wisconsin	3,095,000	2.1%
18	Minnesota	2,931,000	2.0%
19	Tennessee	2,921,000	2.0%
20	Arizona	2,874,000	2.0%
21	Maryland	2,828,000	1.9%
22	Alabama	2,438,000	1.7%
23	Colorado	2,437,000	1.7%
24	Louisiana	2,393,000	1.6%
25	South Carolina	2,385,000	1.6%
26	Kentucky	2,259,000	1.5%
27	Oregon	1,961,000	1.3%
28	Oklahoma	1,798,000	1.2%
29	Connecticut	1,761,000	1.2%
30	Iowa	1,630,000	1.1%
31	Mississippi	1,589,000	1.1%
32	Kansas	1,343,000	0.9%
33	Arkansas	1,317,000	0.9%
34	Nevada	1,147,000	0.8%
35	Utah	1,056,000	0.7%
36	Nebraska	939,000	0.6%
37	New Mexico	937,000	0.6%
38	West Virginia	917,000	0.6%
39	Maine	801,000	0.5%
40	New Hampshire	756,000	0.5%
41	Idaho	723,000	0.5%
42	Rhode Island	568,000	0.4%
43	Hawaii	522,000	0.4%
44	Montana	516,000	0.4%
45	Delaware	447,000	0.3%
46	South Dakota	442,000	0.3%
47	North Dakota	399,000	0.3%
48	Alaska	345,000	0.2%
48	Vermont	345,000	0.2%
50	Wyoming	270,000	0.2%
	District of Columbia	324,000	0.2%

Source: U.S. Bureau of the Census
"Voting and Registration" (Table 4a, http://www.census.gov/hhes/www/socdemo/voting/index.html)

Percent of Eligible Voters Reported Registered in 2008

National Percent = 71.0%*

ALPHA ORDER

RANK	STATE	PERCENT
28	Alabama	71.6
19	Alaska	73.7
39	Arizona	68.9
47	Arkansas	64.9
41	California	68.2
26	Colorado	72.2
20	Connecticut	73.5
18	Delaware	73.8
33	Florida	70.4
30	Georgia	71.0
50	Hawaii	59.1
39	Idaho	68.9
31	Illinois	70.9
42	Indiana	68.1
9	Iowa	76.3
36	Kansas	69.7
21	Kentucky	73.0
4	Louisiana	78.3
2	Maine	79.7
17	Maryland	73.9
24	Massachusetts	72.6
5	Michigan	77.1
2	Minnesota	79.7
6	Mississippi	77.0
14	Missouri	74.5
29	Montana	71.3
13	Nebraska	74.9
44	Nevada	66.9
10	New Hampshire	76.0
31	New Jersey	70.9
37	New Mexico	69.3
46	New York	65.8
11	North Carolina	75.7
1	North Dakota	83.7
21	Ohio	73.0
34	Oklahoma	70.1
21	Oregon	73.0
34	Pennsylvania	70.1
12	Rhode Island	75.5
14	South Carolina	74.5
7	South Dakota	76.9
48	Tennessee	64.5
43	Texas	67.3
49	Utah	59.7
25	Vermont	72.5
16	Virginia	74.3
27	Washington	71.7
45	West Virginia	66.1
8	Wisconsin	76.4
37	Wyoming	69.3

RANK ORDER

RANK	STATE	PERCENT
1	North Dakota	83.7
2	Maine	79.7
2	Minnesota	79.7
4	Louisiana	78.3
5	Michigan	77.1
6	Mississippi	77.0
7	South Dakota	76.9
8	Wisconsin	76.4
9	Iowa	76.3
10	New Hampshire	76.0
11	North Carolina	75.7
12	Rhode Island	75.5
13	Nebraska	74.9
14	Missouri	74.5
14	South Carolina	74.5
16	Virginia	74.3
17	Maryland	73.9
18	Delaware	73.8
19	Alaska	73.7
20	Connecticut	73.5
21	Kentucky	73.0
21	Ohio	73.0
21	Oregon	73.0
24	Massachusetts	72.6
25	Vermont	72.5
26	Colorado	72.2
27	Washington	71.7
28	Alabama	71.6
29	Montana	71.3
30	Georgia	71.0
31	Illinois	70.9
31	New Jersey	70.9
33	Florida	70.4
34	Oklahoma	70.1
34	Pennsylvania	70.1
36	Kansas	69.7
37	New Mexico	69.3
37	Wyoming	69.3
39	Arizona	68.9
39	Idaho	68.9
41	California	68.2
42	Indiana	68.1
43	Texas	67.3
44	Nevada	66.9
45	West Virginia	66.1
46	New York	65.8
47	Arkansas	64.9
48	Tennessee	64.5
49	Utah	59.7
50	Hawaii	59.1
	District of Columbia	78.3

Source: U.S. Bureau of the Census
"Voting and Registration" (Table 4a, http://www.census.gov/hhes/www/socdemo/voting/index.html)
*As a percent of citizen population 18 and older.

Persons Voting in 2008

National Total = 131,144,000

ALPHA ORDER

RANK	STATE	VOTERS	% of USA
24	Alabama	2,126,000	1.6%
49	Alaska	304,000	0.2%
21	Arizona	2,497,000	1.9%
33	Arkansas	1,092,000	0.8%
1	California	13,828,000	10.5%
22	Colorado	2,308,000	1.8%
28	Connecticut	1,610,000	1.2%
45	Delaware	408,000	0.3%
3	Florida	7,951,000	6.1%
10	Georgia	4,183,000	3.2%
44	Hawaii	457,000	0.3%
41	Idaho	644,000	0.5%
7	Illinois	5,436,000	4.1%
18	Indiana	2,758,000	2.1%
30	Iowa	1,501,000	1.1%
32	Kansas	1,219,000	0.9%
26	Kentucky	1,952,000	1.5%
23	Louisiana	2,149,000	1.6%
39	Maine	716,000	0.5%
19	Maryland	2,611,000	2.0%
14	Massachusetts	3,044,000	2.3%
8	Michigan	4,865,000	3.7%
17	Minnesota	2,759,000	2.1%
31	Mississippi	1,439,000	1.1%
16	Missouri	2,846,000	2.2%
43	Montana	473,000	0.4%
37	Nebraska	844,000	0.6%
34	Nevada	1,027,000	0.8%
40	New Hampshire	708,000	0.5%
12	New Jersey	3,637,000	2.8%
36	New Mexico	846,000	0.6%
4	New York	7,559,000	5.8%
9	North Carolina	4,370,000	3.3%
47	North Dakota	321,000	0.2%
6	Ohio	5,483,000	4.2%
29	Oklahoma	1,507,000	1.1%
27	Oregon	1,818,000	1.4%
5	Pennsylvania	5,747,000	4.4%
42	Rhode Island	507,000	0.4%
25	South Carolina	2,100,000	1.6%
46	South Dakota	390,000	0.3%
20	Tennessee	2,516,000	1.9%
2	Texas	8,435,000	6.4%
35	Utah	939,000	0.7%
48	Vermont	308,000	0.2%
11	Virginia	3,650,000	2.8%
13	Washington	3,073,000	2.3%
38	West Virginia	741,000	0.6%
15	Wisconsin	2,887,000	2.2%
50	Wyoming	250,000	0.2%

RANK ORDER

RANK	STATE	VOTERS	% of USA
1	California	13,828,000	10.5%
2	Texas	8,435,000	6.4%
3	Florida	7,951,000	6.1%
4	New York	7,559,000	5.8%
5	Pennsylvania	5,747,000	4.4%
6	Ohio	5,483,000	4.2%
7	Illinois	5,436,000	4.1%
8	Michigan	4,865,000	3.7%
9	North Carolina	4,370,000	3.3%
10	Georgia	4,183,000	3.2%
11	Virginia	3,650,000	2.8%
12	New Jersey	3,637,000	2.8%
13	Washington	3,073,000	2.3%
14	Massachusetts	3,044,000	2.3%
15	Wisconsin	2,887,000	2.2%
16	Missouri	2,846,000	2.2%
17	Minnesota	2,759,000	2.1%
18	Indiana	2,758,000	2.1%
19	Maryland	2,611,000	2.0%
20	Tennessee	2,516,000	1.9%
21	Arizona	2,497,000	1.9%
22	Colorado	2,308,000	1.8%
23	Louisiana	2,149,000	1.6%
24	Alabama	2,126,000	1.6%
25	South Carolina	2,100,000	1.6%
26	Kentucky	1,952,000	1.5%
27	Oregon	1,818,000	1.4%
28	Connecticut	1,610,000	1.2%
29	Oklahoma	1,507,000	1.1%
30	Iowa	1,501,000	1.1%
31	Mississippi	1,439,000	1.1%
32	Kansas	1,219,000	0.9%
33	Arkansas	1,092,000	0.8%
34	Nevada	1,027,000	0.8%
35	Utah	939,000	0.7%
36	New Mexico	846,000	0.6%
37	Nebraska	844,000	0.6%
38	West Virginia	741,000	0.6%
39	Maine	716,000	0.5%
40	New Hampshire	708,000	0.5%
41	Idaho	644,000	0.5%
42	Rhode Island	507,000	0.4%
43	Montana	473,000	0.4%
44	Hawaii	457,000	0.3%
45	Delaware	408,000	0.3%
46	South Dakota	390,000	0.3%
47	North Dakota	321,000	0.2%
48	Vermont	308,000	0.2%
49	Alaska	304,000	0.2%
50	Wyoming	250,000	0.2%
	District of Columbia	306,000	0.2%

Source: U.S. Bureau of the Census
"Voting and Registration" (Table 4a, http://www.census.gov/hhes/www/socdemo/voting/index.html)

Percent of Eligible Population Reported Voting in 2008

National Percent = 63.6%*

ALPHA ORDER

RANK	STATE	PERCENT
37	Alabama	62.4
26	Alaska	65.0
41	Arizona	59.9
47	Arkansas	53.8
32	California	63.4
9	Colorado	68.4
19	Connecticut	67.2
17	Delaware	67.3
31	Florida	63.8
29	Georgia	64.2
50	Hawaii	51.8
39	Idaho	61.4
35	Illinois	62.6
40	Indiana	60.5
6	Iowa	70.2
33	Kansas	63.3
34	Kentucky	63.1
5	Louisiana	70.3
2	Maine	71.2
10	Maryland	68.3
20	Massachusetts	67.1
11	Michigan	67.8
1	Minnesota	75.0
7	Mississippi	69.7
22	Missouri	65.8
25	Montana	65.4
17	Nebraska	67.3
41	Nevada	59.9
2	New Hampshire	71.2
30	New Jersey	64.1
35	New Mexico	62.6
43	New York	58.8
14	North Carolina	67.5
14	North Dakota	67.5
24	Ohio	65.5
44	Oklahoma	58.7
13	Oregon	67.6
37	Pennsylvania	62.4
16	Rhode Island	67.4
23	South Carolina	65.6
11	South Dakota	67.8
46	Tennessee	55.5
45	Texas	56.1
49	Utah	53.1
27	Vermont	64.7
8	Virginia	68.7
21	Washington	66.8
48	West Virginia	53.4
2	Wisconsin	71.2
28	Wyoming	64.3

RANK ORDER

RANK	STATE	PERCENT
1	Minnesota	75.0
2	Maine	71.2
2	New Hampshire	71.2
2	Wisconsin	71.2
5	Louisiana	70.3
6	Iowa	70.2
7	Mississippi	69.7
8	Virginia	68.7
9	Colorado	68.4
10	Maryland	68.3
11	Michigan	67.8
11	South Dakota	67.8
13	Oregon	67.6
14	North Carolina	67.5
14	North Dakota	67.5
16	Rhode Island	67.4
17	Delaware	67.3
17	Nebraska	67.3
19	Connecticut	67.2
20	Massachusetts	67.1
21	Washington	66.8
22	Missouri	65.8
23	South Carolina	65.6
24	Ohio	65.5
25	Montana	65.4
26	Alaska	65.0
27	Vermont	64.7
28	Wyoming	64.3
29	Georgia	64.2
30	New Jersey	64.1
31	Florida	63.8
32	California	63.4
33	Kansas	63.3
34	Kentucky	63.1
35	Illinois	62.6
35	New Mexico	62.6
37	Alabama	62.4
37	Pennsylvania	62.4
39	Idaho	61.4
40	Indiana	60.5
41	Arizona	59.9
41	Nevada	59.9
43	New York	58.8
44	Oklahoma	58.7
45	Texas	56.1
46	Tennessee	55.5
47	Arkansas	53.8
48	West Virginia	53.4
49	Utah	53.1
50	Hawaii	51.8
	District of Columbia	74.1

Source: U.S. Bureau of the Census
   "Voting and Registration" (Table 4a, http://www.census.gov/hhes/www/socdemo/voting/index.html)
*As a percent of citizen population 18 and older.

Percent of Registered Population Reported Voting in 2008

National Percent = 89.6%*

ALPHA ORDER

RANK	STATE	PERCENT
42	Alabama	87.2
38	Alaska	88.1
43	Arizona	86.9
48	Arkansas	82.9
6	California	92.9
1	Colorado	94.7
14	Connecticut	91.4
15	Delaware	91.3
17	Florida	90.6
19	Georgia	90.5
41	Hawaii	87.5
30	Idaho	89.1
35	Illinois	88.4
34	Indiana	88.8
12	Iowa	92.1
16	Kansas	90.8
44	Kentucky	86.4
23	Louisiana	89.8
26	Maine	89.4
11	Maryland	92.3
9	Massachusetts	92.4
40	Michigan	88.0
2	Minnesota	94.1
17	Mississippi	90.6
36	Missouri	88.3
13	Montana	91.7
22	Nebraska	89.9
25	Nevada	89.5
3	New Hampshire	93.7
20	New Jersey	90.4
21	New Mexico	90.3
26	New York	89.4
30	North Carolina	89.1
50	North Dakota	80.5
23	Ohio	89.8
46	Oklahoma	83.8
7	Oregon	92.7
30	Pennsylvania	89.1
28	Rhode Island	89.3
38	South Carolina	88.1
37	South Dakota	88.2
45	Tennessee	86.1
47	Texas	83.3
33	Utah	88.9
28	Vermont	89.3
9	Virginia	92.4
5	Washington	93.1
49	West Virginia	80.8
4	Wisconsin	93.3
8	Wyoming	92.6

RANK ORDER

RANK	STATE	PERCENT
1	Colorado	94.7
2	Minnesota	94.1
3	New Hampshire	93.7
4	Wisconsin	93.3
5	Washington	93.1
6	California	92.9
7	Oregon	92.7
8	Wyoming	92.6
9	Massachusetts	92.4
9	Virginia	92.4
11	Maryland	92.3
12	Iowa	92.1
13	Montana	91.7
14	Connecticut	91.4
15	Delaware	91.3
16	Kansas	90.8
17	Florida	90.6
17	Mississippi	90.6
19	Georgia	90.5
20	New Jersey	90.4
21	New Mexico	90.3
22	Nebraska	89.9
23	Louisiana	89.8
23	Ohio	89.8
25	Nevada	89.5
26	Maine	89.4
26	New York	89.4
28	Rhode Island	89.3
28	Vermont	89.3
30	Idaho	89.1
30	North Carolina	89.1
30	Pennsylvania	89.1
33	Utah	88.9
34	Indiana	88.8
35	Illinois	88.4
36	Missouri	88.3
37	South Dakota	88.2
38	Alaska	88.1
38	South Carolina	88.1
40	Michigan	88.0
41	Hawaii	87.5
42	Alabama	87.2
43	Arizona	86.9
44	Kentucky	86.4
45	Tennessee	86.1
46	Oklahoma	83.8
47	Texas	83.3
48	Arkansas	82.9
49	West Virginia	80.8
50	North Dakota	80.5

District of Columbia 94.4

Source: CQ Press using data from U.S. Bureau of the Census
    "Voting and Registration" (Table 4a, http://www.census.gov/hhes/www/socdemo/voting/index.html)
*As a percent of citizen population 18 and older who are registered to vote.

XIV. Social Welfare

Poverty Rate in 2009

National Rate = 13.6% of Population in Poverty*

ALPHA ORDER

RANK	STATE	PERCENT
7	Alabama	16.7
48	Alaska	8.7
13	Arizona	15.2
2	Arkansas	18.1
24	California	13.3
28	Colorado	12.2
46	Connecticut	9.0
39	Delaware	10.7
21	Florida	13.6
12	Georgia	15.3
45	Hawaii	9.3
24	Idaho	13.3
26	Illinois	12.6
22	Indiana	13.4
36	Iowa	11.5
30	Kansas	12.1
3	Kentucky	18.0
4	Louisiana	17.9
27	Maine	12.4
49	Maryland	8.4
43	Massachusetts	10.1
15	Michigan	15.1
42	Minnesota	10.2
1	Mississippi	21.4
19	Missouri	13.8
16	Montana	14.9
34	Nebraska	11.7
35	Nevada	11.6
50	New Hampshire	7.8
46	New Jersey	9.0
5	New Mexico	17.8
18	New York	13.9
13	North Carolina	15.2
28	North Dakota	12.2
17	Ohio	14.0
10	Oklahoma	16.1
20	Oregon	13.7
30	Pennsylvania	12.1
32	Rhode Island	11.9
11	South Carolina	16.0
22	South Dakota	13.4
9	Tennessee	16.4
8	Texas	16.6
40	Utah	10.3
38	Vermont	10.9
40	Virginia	10.3
33	Washington	11.8
6	West Virginia	17.4
37	Wisconsin	11.4
44	Wyoming	9.7

RANK ORDER

RANK	STATE	PERCENT
1	Mississippi	21.4
2	Arkansas	18.1
3	Kentucky	18.0
4	Louisiana	17.9
5	New Mexico	17.8
6	West Virginia	17.4
7	Alabama	16.7
8	Texas	16.6
9	Tennessee	16.4
10	Oklahoma	16.1
11	South Carolina	16.0
12	Georgia	15.3
13	Arizona	15.2
13	North Carolina	15.2
15	Michigan	15.1
16	Montana	14.9
17	Ohio	14.0
18	New York	13.9
19	Missouri	13.8
20	Oregon	13.7
21	Florida	13.6
22	Indiana	13.4
22	South Dakota	13.4
24	California	13.3
24	Idaho	13.3
26	Illinois	12.6
27	Maine	12.4
28	Colorado	12.2
28	North Dakota	12.2
30	Kansas	12.1
30	Pennsylvania	12.1
32	Rhode Island	11.9
33	Washington	11.8
34	Nebraska	11.7
35	Nevada	11.6
36	Iowa	11.5
37	Wisconsin	11.4
38	Vermont	10.9
39	Delaware	10.7
40	Utah	10.3
40	Virginia	10.3
42	Minnesota	10.2
43	Massachusetts	10.1
44	Wyoming	9.7
45	Hawaii	9.3
46	Connecticut	9.0
46	New Jersey	9.0
48	Alaska	8.7
49	Maryland	8.4
50	New Hampshire	7.8
	District of Columbia	17.4

Source: U.S. Bureau of the Census
 "2009 American Community Survey" (http://www.census.gov/acs/www/)
*Three-year average: 2007-2009. The poverty threshold for a family of four (two children) in 2009 was $22,050.

Percent of Senior Citizens Living in Poverty in 2009

National Percent = 9.5%*

ALPHA ORDER

RANK	STATE	PERCENT
9	Alabama	11.3
50	Alaska	3.2
29	Arizona	8.4
5	Arkansas	12.0
22	California	8.7
25	Colorado	8.6
48	Connecticut	6.4
47	Delaware	6.5
15	Florida	10.2
6	Georgia	11.9
44	Hawaii	7.3
32	Idaho	8.3
22	Illinois	8.7
34	Indiana	7.9
44	Iowa	7.3
37	Kansas	7.8
2	Kentucky	12.7
3	Louisiana	12.4
19	Maine	8.8
34	Maryland	7.9
19	Massachusetts	8.8
28	Michigan	8.5
25	Minnesota	8.6
1	Mississippi	15.0
25	Missouri	8.6
22	Montana	8.7
37	Nebraska	7.8
42	Nevada	7.5
46	New Hampshire	6.7
34	New Jersey	7.9
4	New Mexico	12.2
9	New York	11.3
16	North Carolina	10.0
8	North Dakota	11.5
29	Ohio	8.4
17	Oklahoma	9.5
29	Oregon	8.4
19	Pennsylvania	8.8
18	Rhode Island	9.1
11	South Carolina	11.2
13	South Dakota	10.6
12	Tennessee	11.1
7	Texas	11.8
43	Utah	7.4
37	Vermont	7.8
33	Virginia	8.2
40	Washington	7.7
14	West Virginia	10.3
40	Wisconsin	7.7
48	Wyoming	6.4

RANK ORDER

RANK	STATE	PERCENT
1	Mississippi	15.0
2	Kentucky	12.7
3	Louisiana	12.4
4	New Mexico	12.2
5	Arkansas	12.0
6	Georgia	11.9
7	Texas	11.8
8	North Dakota	11.5
9	Alabama	11.3
9	New York	11.3
11	South Carolina	11.2
12	Tennessee	11.1
13	South Dakota	10.6
14	West Virginia	10.3
15	Florida	10.2
16	North Carolina	10.0
17	Oklahoma	9.5
18	Rhode Island	9.1
19	Maine	8.8
19	Massachusetts	8.8
19	Pennsylvania	8.8
22	California	8.7
22	Illinois	8.7
22	Montana	8.7
25	Colorado	8.6
25	Minnesota	8.6
25	Missouri	8.6
28	Michigan	8.5
29	Arizona	8.4
29	Ohio	8.4
29	Oregon	8.4
32	Idaho	8.3
33	Virginia	8.2
34	Indiana	7.9
34	Maryland	7.9
34	New Jersey	7.9
37	Kansas	7.8
37	Nebraska	7.8
37	Vermont	7.8
40	Washington	7.7
40	Wisconsin	7.7
42	Nevada	7.5
43	Utah	7.4
44	Hawaii	7.3
44	Iowa	7.3
46	New Hampshire	6.7
47	Delaware	6.5
48	Connecticut	6.4
48	Wyoming	6.4
50	Alaska	3.2

District of Columbia	14.6

Source: U.S. Bureau of the Census
   "2009 American Community Survey" (http://www.census.gov/acs/www/)
*People 65 years and older living with incomes below the poverty level.

Percent of Children Living in Poverty in 2009

National Percent = 20.0%*

ALPHA ORDER

RANK	STATE	PERCENT
5	Alabama	24.7
45	Alaska	12.8
11	Arizona	23.4
2	Arkansas	27.2
22	California	19.9
29	Colorado	17.4
48	Connecticut	12.1
34	Delaware	16.5
18	Florida	21.3
14	Georgia	22.3
40	Hawaii	13.8
26	Idaho	18.1
24	Illinois	18.9
20	Indiana	20.0
36	Iowa	15.7
27	Kansas	17.6
3	Kentucky	25.6
8	Louisiana	24.2
30	Maine	17.1
49	Maryland	11.6
43	Massachusetts	13.1
12	Michigan	22.5
38	Minnesota	14.1
1	Mississippi	31.0
19	Missouri	20.7
17	Montana	21.4
37	Nebraska	15.2
27	Nevada	17.6
50	New Hampshire	10.8
41	New Jersey	13.5
4	New Mexico	25.3
20	New York	20.0
12	North Carolina	22.5
44	North Dakota	13.0
16	Ohio	21.9
15	Oklahoma	22.2
23	Oregon	19.2
30	Pennsylvania	17.1
32	Rhode Island	16.9
6	South Carolina	24.4
25	South Dakota	18.5
9	Tennessee	23.9
6	Texas	24.4
47	Utah	12.2
42	Vermont	13.3
39	Virginia	13.9
35	Washington	16.2
10	West Virginia	23.6
33	Wisconsin	16.7
46	Wyoming	12.6

RANK ORDER

RANK	STATE	PERCENT
1	Mississippi	31.0
2	Arkansas	27.2
3	Kentucky	25.6
4	New Mexico	25.3
5	Alabama	24.7
6	South Carolina	24.4
6	Texas	24.4
8	Louisiana	24.2
9	Tennessee	23.9
10	West Virginia	23.6
11	Arizona	23.4
12	Michigan	22.5
12	North Carolina	22.5
14	Georgia	22.3
15	Oklahoma	22.2
16	Ohio	21.9
17	Montana	21.4
18	Florida	21.3
19	Missouri	20.7
20	Indiana	20.0
20	New York	20.0
22	California	19.9
23	Oregon	19.2
24	Illinois	18.9
25	South Dakota	18.5
26	Idaho	18.1
27	Kansas	17.6
27	Nevada	17.6
29	Colorado	17.4
30	Maine	17.1
30	Pennsylvania	17.1
32	Rhode Island	16.9
33	Wisconsin	16.7
34	Delaware	16.5
35	Washington	16.2
36	Iowa	15.7
37	Nebraska	15.2
38	Minnesota	14.1
39	Virginia	13.9
40	Hawaii	13.8
41	New Jersey	13.5
42	Vermont	13.3
43	Massachusetts	13.1
44	North Dakota	13.0
45	Alaska	12.8
46	Wyoming	12.6
47	Utah	12.2
48	Connecticut	12.1
49	Maryland	11.6
50	New Hampshire	10.8

District of Columbia	29.4

Source: U.S. Bureau of the Census
"2009 American Community Survey" (http://www.census.gov/acs/www/)
*Children 17 and under living in families with incomes below the poverty level.

Percent of Families Living in Poverty in 2009

National Percent = 10.5%*

ALPHA ORDER				RANK ORDER		
RANK	STATE	PERCENT		RANK	STATE	PERCENT
6	Alabama	13.4		1	Mississippi	17.3
48	Alaska	6.2		2	Arkansas	14.8
14	Arizona	11.6		3	Kentucky	14.4
2	Arkansas	14.8		4	West Virginia	13.9
21	California	10.6		5	New Mexico	13.6
29	Colorado	8.9		6	Alabama	13.4
45	Connecticut	6.7		6	Texas	13.4
41	Delaware	7.1		8	Louisiana	13.3
19	Florida	10.7		9	Tennessee	13.1
11	Georgia	12.7		10	South Carolina	12.9
38	Hawaii	7.5		11	Georgia	12.7
22	Idaho	9.9		12	Oklahoma	12.1
22	Illinois	9.9		13	North Carolina	11.9
19	Indiana	10.7		14	Arizona	11.6
37	Iowa	7.7		14	Michigan	11.6
26	Kansas	9.0		16	Ohio	11.1
3	Kentucky	14.4		17	Missouri	10.9
8	Louisiana	13.3		18	New York	10.8
33	Maine	8.3		19	Florida	10.7
49	Maryland	6.1		19	Indiana	10.7
42	Massachusetts	7.0		21	California	10.6
14	Michigan	11.6		22	Idaho	9.9
42	Minnesota	7.0		22	Illinois	9.9
1	Mississippi	17.3		22	Montana	9.9
17	Missouri	10.9		25	Oregon	9.8
22	Montana	9.9		26	Kansas	9.0
32	Nebraska	8.4		26	Nevada	9.0
26	Nevada	9.0		26	South Dakota	9.0
50	New Hampshire	5.5		29	Colorado	8.9
42	New Jersey	7.0		30	Pennsylvania	8.6
5	New Mexico	13.6		30	Rhode Island	8.6
18	New York	10.8		32	Nebraska	8.4
13	North Carolina	11.9		33	Maine	8.3
46	North Dakota	6.6		34	Wisconsin	8.2
16	Ohio	11.1		35	Washington	8.1
12	Oklahoma	12.1		36	Utah	7.8
25	Oregon	9.8		37	Iowa	7.7
30	Pennsylvania	8.6		38	Hawaii	7.5
30	Rhode Island	8.6		38	Virginia	7.5
10	South Carolina	12.9		40	Vermont	7.3
26	South Dakota	9.0		41	Delaware	7.1
9	Tennessee	13.1		42	Massachusetts	7.0
6	Texas	13.4		42	Minnesota	7.0
36	Utah	7.8		42	New Jersey	7.0
40	Vermont	7.3		45	Connecticut	6.7
38	Virginia	7.5		46	North Dakota	6.6
35	Washington	8.1		47	Wyoming	6.3
4	West Virginia	13.9		48	Alaska	6.2
34	Wisconsin	8.2		49	Maryland	6.1
47	Wyoming	6.3		50	New Hampshire	5.5

District of Columbia   14.6

Source: CQ Press using data from U.S. Bureau of the Census
   "2009 American Community Survey" (http://www.census.gov/acs/www/)
*Families living with incomes below the poverty level.

Percent of Female-Headed Families with Children Living in Poverty in 2009

National Percent = 38.2%*

ALPHA ORDER

RANK	STATE	PERCENT
5	Alabama	46.0
48	Alaska	28.8
35	Arizona	34.6
3	Arkansas	49.5
37	California	33.5
32	Colorado	34.9
42	Connecticut	31.0
48	Delaware	28.8
30	Florida	35.5
22	Georgia	38.3
43	Hawaii	30.6
26	Idaho	36.9
20	Illinois	38.6
13	Indiana	42.6
21	Iowa	38.4
19	Kansas	38.7
4	Kentucky	49.2
7	Louisiana	45.3
34	Maine	34.8
50	Maryland	24.8
39	Massachusetts	31.9
12	Michigan	42.7
38	Minnesota	33.2
1	Mississippi	51.5
14	Missouri	42.2
11	Montana	42.9
24	Nebraska	37.5
44	Nevada	30.5
45	New Hampshire	30.3
46	New Jersey	30.0
17	New Mexico	40.6
29	New York	36.1
15	North Carolina	41.6
27	North Dakota	36.5
9	Ohio	43.6
6	Oklahoma	45.5
23	Oregon	38.2
24	Pennsylvania	37.5
28	Rhode Island	36.4
10	South Carolina	43.1
32	South Dakota	34.9
8	Tennessee	44.2
16	Texas	40.9
47	Utah	29.6
31	Vermont	35.2
40	Virginia	31.7
36	Washington	34.1
2	West Virginia	51.0
18	Wisconsin	39.1
41	Wyoming	31.6

RANK ORDER

RANK	STATE	PERCENT
1	Mississippi	51.5
2	West Virginia	51.0
3	Arkansas	49.5
4	Kentucky	49.2
5	Alabama	46.0
6	Oklahoma	45.5
7	Louisiana	45.3
8	Tennessee	44.2
9	Ohio	43.6
10	South Carolina	43.1
11	Montana	42.9
12	Michigan	42.7
13	Indiana	42.6
14	Missouri	42.2
15	North Carolina	41.6
16	Texas	40.9
17	New Mexico	40.6
18	Wisconsin	39.1
19	Kansas	38.7
20	Illinois	38.6
21	Iowa	38.4
22	Georgia	38.3
23	Oregon	38.2
24	Nebraska	37.5
24	Pennsylvania	37.5
26	Idaho	36.9
27	North Dakota	36.5
28	Rhode Island	36.4
29	New York	36.1
30	Florida	35.5
31	Vermont	35.2
32	Colorado	34.9
32	South Dakota	34.9
34	Maine	34.8
35	Arizona	34.6
36	Washington	34.1
37	California	33.5
38	Minnesota	33.2
39	Massachusetts	31.9
40	Virginia	31.7
41	Wyoming	31.6
42	Connecticut	31.0
43	Hawaii	30.6
44	Nevada	30.5
45	New Hampshire	30.3
46	New Jersey	30.0
47	Utah	29.6
48	Alaska	28.8
48	Delaware	28.8
50	Maryland	24.8

| District of Columbia | 41.0 |

Source: CQ Press using data from U.S. Bureau of the Census
  "2009 American Community Survey" (http://www.census.gov/acs/www/)
*Households headed by females with own children under 18 years living with them with incomes below the poverty level as a percent of all such female-headed households.

State and Local Government Expenditures for Public Welfare Programs in 2008

National Total = $404,623,719,000*

ALPHA ORDER					RANK ORDER			
RANK	STATE	EXPENDITURES	% of USA		RANK	STATE	EXPENDITURES	% of USA
27	Alabama	$4,568,526,000	1.1%		1	California	$50,989,250,000	12.6%
45	Alaska	1,415,111,000	0.3%		2	New York	43,947,540,000	10.9%
20	Arizona	7,231,148,000	1.8%		3	Texas	22,710,876,000	5.6%
32	Arkansas	3,785,357,000	0.9%		4	Pennsylvania	20,255,477,000	5.0%
1	California	50,989,250,000	12.6%		5	Florida	19,519,621,000	4.8%
29	Colorado	4,198,320,000	1.0%		6	Ohio	16,650,814,000	4.1%
25	Connecticut	5,184,673,000	1.3%		7	Illinois	16,234,989,000	4.0%
44	Delaware	1,442,513,000	0.4%		8	New Jersey	12,619,691,000	3.1%
5	Florida	19,519,621,000	4.8%		9	Massachusetts	12,381,876,000	3.1%
13	Georgia	9,354,361,000	2.3%		10	Michigan	11,649,252,000	2.9%
43	Hawaii	1,627,702,000	0.4%		11	North Carolina	10,475,705,000	2.6%
41	Idaho	1,642,494,000	0.4%		12	Minnesota	10,016,722,000	2.5%
7	Illinois	16,234,989,000	4.0%		13	Georgia	9,354,361,000	2.3%
14	Indiana	8,347,985,000	2.1%		14	Indiana	8,347,985,000	2.1%
31	Iowa	3,890,942,000	1.0%		15	Tennessee	8,189,423,000	2.0%
34	Kansas	3,204,499,000	0.8%		16	Virginia	8,069,375,000	2.0%
22	Kentucky	6,126,955,000	1.5%		17	Washington	7,741,518,000	1.9%
23	Louisiana	5,758,344,000	1.4%		18	Wisconsin	7,479,999,000	1.8%
36	Maine	2,505,673,000	0.6%		19	Maryland	7,331,315,000	1.8%
19	Maryland	7,331,315,000	1.8%		20	Arizona	7,231,148,000	1.8%
9	Massachusetts	12,381,876,000	3.1%		21	Missouri	6,355,091,000	1.6%
10	Michigan	11,649,252,000	2.9%		22	Kentucky	6,126,955,000	1.5%
12	Minnesota	10,016,722,000	2.5%		23	Louisiana	5,758,344,000	1.4%
28	Mississippi	4,245,159,000	1.0%		24	South Carolina	5,451,353,000	1.3%
21	Missouri	6,355,091,000	1.6%		25	Connecticut	5,184,673,000	1.3%
47	Montana	904,079,000	0.2%		26	Oklahoma	4,812,498,000	1.2%
39	Nebraska	2,142,817,000	0.5%		27	Alabama	4,568,526,000	1.1%
40	Nevada	1,826,677,000	0.5%		28	Mississippi	4,245,159,000	1.0%
42	New Hampshire	1,637,239,000	0.4%		29	Colorado	4,198,320,000	1.0%
8	New Jersey	12,619,691,000	3.1%		30	Oregon	4,102,675,000	1.0%
33	New Mexico	3,673,476,000	0.9%		31	Iowa	3,890,942,000	1.0%
2	New York	43,947,540,000	10.9%		32	Arkansas	3,785,357,000	0.9%
11	North Carolina	10,475,705,000	2.6%		33	New Mexico	3,673,476,000	0.9%
49	North Dakota	809,950,000	0.2%		34	Kansas	3,204,499,000	0.8%
6	Ohio	16,650,814,000	4.1%		35	West Virginia	2,543,813,000	0.6%
26	Oklahoma	4,812,498,000	1.2%		36	Maine	2,505,673,000	0.6%
30	Oregon	4,102,675,000	1.0%		37	Utah	2,267,922,000	0.6%
4	Pennsylvania	20,255,477,000	5.0%		38	Rhode Island	2,153,558,000	0.5%
38	Rhode Island	2,153,558,000	0.5%		39	Nebraska	2,142,817,000	0.5%
24	South Carolina	5,451,353,000	1.3%		40	Nevada	1,826,677,000	0.5%
48	South Dakota	818,950,000	0.2%		41	Idaho	1,642,494,000	0.4%
15	Tennessee	8,189,423,000	2.0%		42	New Hampshire	1,637,239,000	0.4%
3	Texas	22,710,876,000	5.6%		43	Hawaii	1,627,702,000	0.4%
37	Utah	2,267,922,000	0.6%		44	Delaware	1,442,513,000	0.4%
46	Vermont	1,254,399,000	0.3%		45	Alaska	1,415,111,000	0.3%
16	Virginia	8,069,375,000	2.0%		46	Vermont	1,254,399,000	0.3%
17	Washington	7,741,518,000	1.9%		47	Montana	904,079,000	0.2%
35	West Virginia	2,543,813,000	0.6%		48	South Dakota	818,950,000	0.2%
18	Wisconsin	7,479,999,000	1.8%		49	North Dakota	809,950,000	0.2%
50	Wyoming	671,019,000	0.2%		50	Wyoming	671,019,000	0.2%
						District of Columbia	2,404,998,000	0.6%

Source: U.S. Bureau of the Census, Governments Division
"2008 State and Local Government Finances" (http://www.census.gov/govs/estimate/index.html)
*Direct general expenditures. Includes funds for cash assistance programs, medical and other vendor payments, welfare institutions, and other public welfare programs.

Per Capita State and Local Government Expenditures
for Public Welfare Programs in 2008
National Per Capita = $1,329*

ALPHA ORDER

RANK	STATE	PER CAPITA
44	Alabama	$977
2	Alaska	2,056
37	Arizona	1,113
20	Arkansas	1,320
17	California	1,394
48	Colorado	851
11	Connecticut	1,480
9	Delaware	1,646
41	Florida	1,059
45	Georgia	965
26	Hawaii	1,264
39	Idaho	1,075
26	Illinois	1,264
22	Indiana	1,307
23	Iowa	1,300
35	Kansas	1,146
15	Kentucky	1,429
25	Louisiana	1,294
6	Maine	1,899
24	Maryland	1,296
7	Massachusetts	1,892
34	Michigan	1,165
5	Minnesota	1,915
13	Mississippi	1,444
40	Missouri	1,067
46	Montana	934
32	Nebraska	1,203
50	Nevada	698
30	New Hampshire	1,239
12	New Jersey	1,457
8	New Mexico	1,849
1	New York	2,257
36	North Carolina	1,133
28	North Dakota	1,263
13	Ohio	1,444
19	Oklahoma	1,321
38	Oregon	1,085
10	Pennsylvania	1,612
3	Rhode Island	2,044
31	South Carolina	1,211
43	South Dakota	1,018
21	Tennessee	1,312
46	Texas	934
49	Utah	832
4	Vermont	2,020
42	Virginia	1,035
33	Washington	1,179
16	West Virginia	1,402
18	Wisconsin	1,329
29	Wyoming	1,259

RANK ORDER

RANK	STATE	PER CAPITA
1	New York	$2,257
2	Alaska	2,056
3	Rhode Island	2,044
4	Vermont	2,020
5	Minnesota	1,915
6	Maine	1,899
7	Massachusetts	1,892
8	New Mexico	1,849
9	Delaware	1,646
10	Pennsylvania	1,612
11	Connecticut	1,480
12	New Jersey	1,457
13	Mississippi	1,444
13	Ohio	1,444
15	Kentucky	1,429
16	West Virginia	1,402
17	California	1,394
18	Wisconsin	1,329
19	Oklahoma	1,321
20	Arkansas	1,320
21	Tennessee	1,312
22	Indiana	1,307
23	Iowa	1,300
24	Maryland	1,296
25	Louisiana	1,294
26	Hawaii	1,264
26	Illinois	1,264
28	North Dakota	1,263
29	Wyoming	1,259
30	New Hampshire	1,239
31	South Carolina	1,211
32	Nebraska	1,203
33	Washington	1,179
34	Michigan	1,165
35	Kansas	1,146
36	North Carolina	1,133
37	Arizona	1,113
38	Oregon	1,085
39	Idaho	1,075
40	Missouri	1,067
41	Florida	1,059
42	Virginia	1,035
43	South Dakota	1,018
44	Alabama	977
45	Georgia	965
46	Montana	934
46	Texas	934
48	Colorado	851
49	Utah	832
50	Nevada	698
	District of Columbia	4,076

Source: CQ Press using data from U.S. Bureau of the Census, Governments Division
"2008 State and Local Government Finances" (http://www.census.gov/govs/estimate/index.html)
*Direct general expenditures. Includes funds for cash assistance programs, medical and other vendor payments, welfare institutions, and other public welfare programs.

State and Local Government Spending for Public Welfare Programs as a Percent of All State and Local Government Expenditures in 2008
National Percent = 16.9%*

ALPHA ORDER

RANK	STATE	PERCENT
41	Alabama	14.0
46	Alaska	12.3
24	Arizona	16.7
9	Arkansas	21.2
35	California	15.2
48	Colorado	11.8
20	Connecticut	17.0
18	Delaware	17.9
39	Florida	14.1
38	Georgia	14.3
42	Hawaii	13.9
21	Idaho	16.9
21	Illinois	16.9
16	Indiana	18.8
21	Iowa	16.9
34	Kansas	15.3
10	Kentucky	20.8
42	Louisiana	13.9
1	Maine	24.3
29	Maryland	16.0
5	Massachusetts	21.9
28	Michigan	16.1
4	Minnesota	22.7
15	Mississippi	18.9
26	Missouri	16.2
45	Montana	12.5
33	Nebraska	15.6
49	Nevada	10.0
17	New Hampshire	18.3
29	New Jersey	16.0
8	New Mexico	21.3
11	New York	20.7
25	North Carolina	16.5
31	North Dakota	15.8
14	Ohio	19.3
13	Oklahoma	20.0
36	Oregon	14.6
7	Pennsylvania	21.4
2	Rhode Island	24.0
26	South Carolina	16.2
32	South Dakota	15.7
6	Tennessee	21.7
42	Texas	13.9
47	Utah	12.1
3	Vermont	23.1
39	Virginia	14.1
37	Washington	14.4
12	West Virginia	20.5
19	Wisconsin	17.6
50	Wyoming	9.9

RANK ORDER

RANK	STATE	PERCENT
1	Maine	24.3
2	Rhode Island	24.0
3	Vermont	23.1
4	Minnesota	22.7
5	Massachusetts	21.9
6	Tennessee	21.7
7	Pennsylvania	21.4
8	New Mexico	21.3
9	Arkansas	21.2
10	Kentucky	20.8
11	New York	20.7
12	West Virginia	20.5
13	Oklahoma	20.0
14	Ohio	19.3
15	Mississippi	18.9
16	Indiana	18.8
17	New Hampshire	18.3
18	Delaware	17.9
19	Wisconsin	17.6
20	Connecticut	17.0
21	Idaho	16.9
21	Illinois	16.9
21	Iowa	16.9
24	Arizona	16.7
25	North Carolina	16.5
26	Missouri	16.2
26	South Carolina	16.2
28	Michigan	16.1
29	Maryland	16.0
29	New Jersey	16.0
31	North Dakota	15.8
32	South Dakota	15.7
33	Nebraska	15.6
34	Kansas	15.3
35	California	15.2
36	Oregon	14.6
37	Washington	14.4
38	Georgia	14.3
39	Florida	14.1
39	Virginia	14.1
41	Alabama	14.0
42	Hawaii	13.9
42	Louisiana	13.9
42	Texas	13.9
45	Montana	12.5
46	Alaska	12.3
47	Utah	12.1
48	Colorado	11.8
49	Nevada	10.0
50	Wyoming	9.9

District of Columbia — 22.5

Source: CQ Press using data from U.S. Bureau of the Census, Governments Division
"2008 State and Local Government Finances" (http://www.census.gov/govs/estimate/index.html)
*As a percent of direct general expenditures. Includes funds for cash assistance programs, medical and other vendor payments, welfare institutions, and other public welfare programs.

Social Security (OASDI) Payments in 2008

National Total = $615,152,000,000*

ALPHA ORDER

RANK	STATE	PAYMENTS	% of USA
20	Alabama	$11,089,000,000	1.8%
50	Alaska	818,000,000	0.1%
19	Arizona	12,162,000,000	2.0%
31	Arkansas	6,807,000,000	1.1%
1	California	56,447,000,000	9.2%
29	Colorado	7,640,000,000	1.2%
27	Connecticut	7,961,000,000	1.3%
45	Delaware	2,081,000,000	0.3%
2	Florida	42,985,000,000	7.0%
11	Georgia	15,908,000,000	2.6%
42	Hawaii	2,557,000,000	0.4%
41	Idaho	2,926,000,000	0.5%
7	Illinois	24,565,000,000	4.0%
13	Indiana	14,202,000,000	2.3%
30	Iowa	6,864,000,000	1.1%
33	Kansas	5,765,000,000	0.9%
24	Kentucky	9,687,000,000	1.6%
25	Louisiana	8,495,000,000	1.4%
39	Maine	3,220,000,000	0.5%
23	Maryland	10,010,000,000	1.6%
15	Massachusetts	13,405,000,000	2.2%
8	Michigan	23,903,000,000	3.9%
21	Minnesota	10,228,000,000	1.7%
32	Mississippi	6,325,000,000	1.0%
16	Missouri	13,230,000,000	2.2%
44	Montana	2,102,000,000	0.3%
38	Nebraska	3,578,000,000	0.6%
35	Nevada	4,614,000,000	0.8%
40	New Hampshire	3,006,000,000	0.5%
10	New Jersey	18,895,000,000	3.1%
36	New Mexico	3,774,000,000	0.6%
3	New York	39,929,000,000	6.5%
9	North Carolina	19,473,000,000	3.2%
48	North Dakota	1,346,000,000	0.2%
6	Ohio	24,797,000,000	4.0%
28	Oklahoma	7,836,000,000	1.3%
26	Oregon	8,114,000,000	1.3%
5	Pennsylvania	31,162,000,000	5.1%
43	Rhode Island	2,387,000,000	0.4%
22	South Carolina	10,155,000,000	1.7%
46	South Dakota	1,663,000,000	0.3%
14	Tennessee	13,778,000,000	2.2%
4	Texas	37,403,000,000	6.1%
37	Utah	3,608,000,000	0.6%
47	Vermont	1,437,000,000	0.2%
12	Virginia	14,588,000,000	2.4%
17	Washington	12,699,000,000	2.1%
34	West Virginia	5,167,000,000	0.8%
18	Wisconsin	12,482,000,000	2.0%
49	Wyoming	1,046,000,000	0.2%

RANK ORDER

RANK	STATE	PAYMENTS	% of USA
1	California	$56,447,000,000	9.2%
2	Florida	42,985,000,000	7.0%
3	New York	39,929,000,000	6.5%
4	Texas	37,403,000,000	6.1%
5	Pennsylvania	31,162,000,000	5.1%
6	Ohio	24,797,000,000	4.0%
7	Illinois	24,565,000,000	4.0%
8	Michigan	23,903,000,000	3.9%
9	North Carolina	19,473,000,000	3.2%
10	New Jersey	18,895,000,000	3.1%
11	Georgia	15,908,000,000	2.6%
12	Virginia	14,588,000,000	2.4%
13	Indiana	14,202,000,000	2.3%
14	Tennessee	13,778,000,000	2.2%
15	Massachusetts	13,405,000,000	2.2%
16	Missouri	13,230,000,000	2.2%
17	Washington	12,699,000,000	2.1%
18	Wisconsin	12,482,000,000	2.0%
19	Arizona	12,162,000,000	2.0%
20	Alabama	11,089,000,000	1.8%
21	Minnesota	10,228,000,000	1.7%
22	South Carolina	10,155,000,000	1.7%
23	Maryland	10,010,000,000	1.6%
24	Kentucky	9,687,000,000	1.6%
25	Louisiana	8,495,000,000	1.4%
26	Oregon	8,114,000,000	1.3%
27	Connecticut	7,961,000,000	1.3%
28	Oklahoma	7,836,000,000	1.3%
29	Colorado	7,640,000,000	1.2%
30	Iowa	6,864,000,000	1.1%
31	Arkansas	6,807,000,000	1.1%
32	Mississippi	6,325,000,000	1.0%
33	Kansas	5,765,000,000	0.9%
34	West Virginia	5,167,000,000	0.8%
35	Nevada	4,614,000,000	0.8%
36	New Mexico	3,774,000,000	0.6%
37	Utah	3,608,000,000	0.6%
38	Nebraska	3,578,000,000	0.6%
39	Maine	3,220,000,000	0.5%
40	New Hampshire	3,006,000,000	0.5%
41	Idaho	2,926,000,000	0.5%
42	Hawaii	2,557,000,000	0.4%
43	Rhode Island	2,387,000,000	0.4%
44	Montana	2,102,000,000	0.3%
45	Delaware	2,081,000,000	0.3%
46	South Dakota	1,663,000,000	0.3%
47	Vermont	1,437,000,000	0.2%
48	North Dakota	1,346,000,000	0.2%
49	Wyoming	1,046,000,000	0.2%
50	Alaska	818,000,000	0.1%
	District of Columbia	775,000,000	0.1%

Source: Social Security Administration
"Social Security Bulletin, Annual Statistical Supplement 2009" (http://www.ssa.gov/policy/docs/statcomps/supplement/2009/)
*"OASDI" is Old Age, Survivors and Disability Insurance. National total includes $10,058,000,000 in payments to recipients in U.S. territories and foreign countries.

Per Capita Social Security (OASDI) Payments in 2008

National Per Capita = $1,988*

<table>
<tr><th colspan="3">ALPHA ORDER</th><th colspan="3">RANK ORDER</th></tr>
<tr><th>RANK</th><th>STATE</th><th>PER CAPITA</th><th>RANK</th><th>STATE</th><th>PER CAPITA</th></tr>
<tr><td>7</td><td>Alabama</td><td>$2,371</td><td>1</td><td>West Virginia</td><td>$2,847</td></tr>
<tr><td>50</td><td>Alaska</td><td>1,189</td><td>2</td><td>Pennsylvania</td><td>2,480</td></tr>
<tr><td>41</td><td>Arizona</td><td>1,871</td><td>3</td><td>Maine</td><td>2,440</td></tr>
<tr><td>6</td><td>Arkansas</td><td>2,374</td><td>4</td><td>Michigan</td><td>2,390</td></tr>
<tr><td>47</td><td>California</td><td>1,543</td><td>5</td><td>Delaware</td><td>2,375</td></tr>
<tr><td>46</td><td>Colorado</td><td>1,548</td><td>6</td><td>Arkansas</td><td>2,374</td></tr>
<tr><td>12</td><td>Connecticut</td><td>2,273</td><td>7</td><td>Alabama</td><td>2,371</td></tr>
<tr><td>5</td><td>Delaware</td><td>2,375</td><td>8</td><td>Florida</td><td>2,333</td></tr>
<tr><td>8</td><td>Florida</td><td>2,333</td><td>9</td><td>Vermont</td><td>2,314</td></tr>
<tr><td>45</td><td>Georgia</td><td>1,640</td><td>10</td><td>Iowa</td><td>2,293</td></tr>
<tr><td>33</td><td>Hawaii</td><td>1,986</td><td>11</td><td>New Hampshire</td><td>2,274</td></tr>
<tr><td>37</td><td>Idaho</td><td>1,916</td><td>12</td><td>Connecticut</td><td>2,273</td></tr>
<tr><td>38</td><td>Illinois</td><td>1,913</td><td>13</td><td>Rhode Island</td><td>2,266</td></tr>
<tr><td>16</td><td>Indiana</td><td>2,223</td><td>14</td><td>Kentucky</td><td>2,259</td></tr>
<tr><td>10</td><td>Iowa</td><td>2,293</td><td>15</td><td>South Carolina</td><td>2,255</td></tr>
<tr><td>29</td><td>Kansas</td><td>2,061</td><td>16</td><td>Indiana</td><td>2,223</td></tr>
<tr><td>14</td><td>Kentucky</td><td>2,259</td><td>17</td><td>Missouri</td><td>2,221</td></tr>
<tr><td>39</td><td>Louisiana</td><td>1,908</td><td>18</td><td>Wisconsin</td><td>2,218</td></tr>
<tr><td>3</td><td>Maine</td><td>2,440</td><td>19</td><td>Tennessee</td><td>2,208</td></tr>
<tr><td>43</td><td>Maryland</td><td>1,769</td><td>20</td><td>New Jersey</td><td>2,181</td></tr>
<tr><td>31</td><td>Massachusetts</td><td>2,049</td><td>21</td><td>Montana</td><td>2,171</td></tr>
<tr><td>4</td><td>Michigan</td><td>2,390</td><td>22</td><td>Mississippi</td><td>2,151</td></tr>
<tr><td>35</td><td>Minnesota</td><td>1,955</td><td>22</td><td>Ohio</td><td>2,151</td></tr>
<tr><td>22</td><td>Mississippi</td><td>2,151</td><td>24</td><td>Oklahoma</td><td>2,150</td></tr>
<tr><td>17</td><td>Missouri</td><td>2,221</td><td>25</td><td>Oregon</td><td>2,145</td></tr>
<tr><td>21</td><td>Montana</td><td>2,171</td><td>26</td><td>North Carolina</td><td>2,106</td></tr>
<tr><td>32</td><td>Nebraska</td><td>2,008</td><td>27</td><td>North Dakota</td><td>2,098</td></tr>
<tr><td>44</td><td>Nevada</td><td>1,764</td><td>28</td><td>South Dakota</td><td>2,067</td></tr>
<tr><td>11</td><td>New Hampshire</td><td>2,274</td><td>29</td><td>Kansas</td><td>2,061</td></tr>
<tr><td>20</td><td>New Jersey</td><td>2,181</td><td>30</td><td>New York</td><td>2,051</td></tr>
<tr><td>40</td><td>New Mexico</td><td>1,900</td><td>31</td><td>Massachusetts</td><td>2,049</td></tr>
<tr><td>30</td><td>New York</td><td>2,051</td><td>32</td><td>Nebraska</td><td>2,008</td></tr>
<tr><td>26</td><td>North Carolina</td><td>2,106</td><td>33</td><td>Hawaii</td><td>1,986</td></tr>
<tr><td>27</td><td>North Dakota</td><td>2,098</td><td>34</td><td>Wyoming</td><td>1,963</td></tr>
<tr><td>22</td><td>Ohio</td><td>2,151</td><td>35</td><td>Minnesota</td><td>1,955</td></tr>
<tr><td>24</td><td>Oklahoma</td><td>2,150</td><td>36</td><td>Washington</td><td>1,934</td></tr>
<tr><td>25</td><td>Oregon</td><td>2,145</td><td>37</td><td>Idaho</td><td>1,916</td></tr>
<tr><td>2</td><td>Pennsylvania</td><td>2,480</td><td>38</td><td>Illinois</td><td>1,913</td></tr>
<tr><td>13</td><td>Rhode Island</td><td>2,266</td><td>39</td><td>Louisiana</td><td>1,908</td></tr>
<tr><td>15</td><td>South Carolina</td><td>2,255</td><td>40</td><td>New Mexico</td><td>1,900</td></tr>
<tr><td>28</td><td>South Dakota</td><td>2,067</td><td>41</td><td>Arizona</td><td>1,871</td></tr>
<tr><td>19</td><td>Tennessee</td><td>2,208</td><td>41</td><td>Virginia</td><td>1,871</td></tr>
<tr><td>48</td><td>Texas</td><td>1,539</td><td>43</td><td>Maryland</td><td>1,769</td></tr>
<tr><td>49</td><td>Utah</td><td>1,323</td><td>44</td><td>Nevada</td><td>1,764</td></tr>
<tr><td>9</td><td>Vermont</td><td>2,314</td><td>45</td><td>Georgia</td><td>1,640</td></tr>
<tr><td>41</td><td>Virginia</td><td>1,871</td><td>46</td><td>Colorado</td><td>1,548</td></tr>
<tr><td>36</td><td>Washington</td><td>1,934</td><td>47</td><td>California</td><td>1,543</td></tr>
<tr><td>1</td><td>West Virginia</td><td>2,847</td><td>48</td><td>Texas</td><td>1,539</td></tr>
<tr><td>18</td><td>Wisconsin</td><td>2,218</td><td>49</td><td>Utah</td><td>1,323</td></tr>
<tr><td>34</td><td>Wyoming</td><td>1,963</td><td>50</td><td>Alaska</td><td>1,189</td></tr>
</table>

District of Columbia   1,313

Source: CQ Press using data from Social Security Administration
"Social Security Bulletin, Annual Statistical Supplement 2009" (http://www.ssa.gov/policy/docs/statcomps/supplement/2009/)
*"OASDI" is Old Age, Survivors and Disability Insurance. National per capita does not include payments or population in U.S. territories and foreign countries.

Social Security (OASDI) Monthly Payments in 2008

National Total = $53,666,109,000*

ALPHA ORDER

RANK	STATE	PAYMENTS	% of USA
20	Alabama	$951,795,000	1.8%
50	Alaska	71,226,000	0.1%
19	Arizona	1,072,700,000	2.0%
31	Arkansas	587,570,000	1.1%
1	California	4,947,266,000	9.2%
29	Colorado	671,777,000	1.3%
27	Connecticut	701,732,000	1.3%
45	Delaware	182,835,000	0.3%
2	Florida	3,791,084,000	7.1%
11	Georgia	1,389,721,000	2.6%
42	Hawaii	227,489,000	0.4%
41	Idaho	256,999,000	0.5%
7	Illinois	2,139,985,000	4.0%
13	Indiana	1,238,360,000	2.3%
30	Iowa	599,606,000	1.1%
33	Kansas	504,138,000	0.9%
24	Kentucky	827,189,000	1.5%
25	Louisiana	717,667,000	1.3%
39	Maine	279,889,000	0.5%
23	Maryland	876,540,000	1.6%
15	Massachusetts	1,170,915,000	2.2%
8	Michigan	2,083,982,000	3.9%
21	Minnesota	900,039,000	1.7%
32	Mississippi	541,975,000	1.0%
16	Missouri	1,150,109,000	2.1%
44	Montana	183,908,000	0.3%
38	Nebraska	312,526,000	0.6%
35	Nevada	407,088,000	0.8%
40	New Hampshire	260,778,000	0.5%
10	New Jersey	1,663,434,000	3.1%
36	New Mexico	328,701,000	0.6%
3	New York	3,496,208,000	6.5%
9	North Carolina	1,705,531,000	3.2%
48	North Dakota	116,143,000	0.2%
6	Ohio	2,144,294,000	4.0%
28	Oklahoma	678,765,000	1.3%
26	Oregon	714,690,000	1.3%
5	Pennsylvania	2,710,656,000	5.1%
43	Rhode Island	209,452,000	0.4%
22	South Carolina	888,484,000	1.7%
46	South Dakota	145,585,000	0.3%
14	Tennessee	1,196,982,000	2.2%
4	Texas	3,237,555,000	6.0%
37	Utah	317,103,000	0.6%
47	Vermont	126,027,000	0.2%
12	Virginia	1,273,789,000	2.4%
17	Washington	1,117,592,000	2.1%
34	West Virginia	437,536,000	0.8%
18	Wisconsin	1,096,491,000	2.0%
49	Wyoming	91,622,000	0.2%

RANK ORDER

RANK	STATE	PAYMENTS	% of USA
1	California	$4,947,266,000	9.2%
2	Florida	3,791,084,000	7.1%
3	New York	3,496,208,000	6.5%
4	Texas	3,237,555,000	6.0%
5	Pennsylvania	2,710,656,000	5.1%
6	Ohio	2,144,294,000	4.0%
7	Illinois	2,139,985,000	4.0%
8	Michigan	2,083,982,000	3.9%
9	North Carolina	1,705,531,000	3.2%
10	New Jersey	1,663,434,000	3.1%
11	Georgia	1,389,721,000	2.6%
12	Virginia	1,273,789,000	2.4%
13	Indiana	1,238,360,000	2.3%
14	Tennessee	1,196,982,000	2.2%
15	Massachusetts	1,170,915,000	2.2%
16	Missouri	1,150,109,000	2.1%
17	Washington	1,117,592,000	2.1%
18	Wisconsin	1,096,491,000	2.0%
19	Arizona	1,072,700,000	2.0%
20	Alabama	951,795,000	1.8%
21	Minnesota	900,039,000	1.7%
22	South Carolina	888,484,000	1.7%
23	Maryland	876,540,000	1.6%
24	Kentucky	827,189,000	1.5%
25	Louisiana	717,667,000	1.3%
26	Oregon	714,690,000	1.3%
27	Connecticut	701,732,000	1.3%
28	Oklahoma	678,765,000	1.3%
29	Colorado	671,777,000	1.3%
30	Iowa	599,606,000	1.1%
31	Arkansas	587,570,000	1.1%
32	Mississippi	541,975,000	1.0%
33	Kansas	504,138,000	0.9%
34	West Virginia	437,536,000	0.8%
35	Nevada	407,088,000	0.8%
36	New Mexico	328,701,000	0.6%
37	Utah	317,103,000	0.6%
38	Nebraska	312,526,000	0.6%
39	Maine	279,889,000	0.5%
40	New Hampshire	260,778,000	0.5%
41	Idaho	256,999,000	0.5%
42	Hawaii	227,489,000	0.4%
43	Rhode Island	209,452,000	0.4%
44	Montana	183,908,000	0.3%
45	Delaware	182,835,000	0.3%
46	South Dakota	145,585,000	0.3%
47	Vermont	126,027,000	0.2%
48	North Dakota	116,143,000	0.2%
49	Wyoming	91,622,000	0.2%
50	Alaska	71,226,000	0.1%
	District of Columbia	67,272,000	0.1%

Source: Social Security Administration
"Social Security Bulletin, Annual Statistical Supplement 2009" (http://www.ssa.gov/policy/docs/statcomps/supplement/2009/)
*For December 2008. "OASDI" is Old Age, Survivors and Disability Insurance. National total includes $855,309,000 in payments to recipients in U.S. territories and foreign countries.

Social Security (OASDI) Beneficiaries in 2008

National Total = 50,898,244*

ALPHA ORDER

RANK	STATE	BENEFICIARIES	% of USA
20	Alabama	952,511	1.9%
50	Alaska	71,145	0.1%
19	Arizona	986,539	1.9%
29	Arkansas	602,017	1.2%
1	California	4,678,517	9.2%
28	Colorado	635,816	1.2%
30	Connecticut	599,533	1.2%
45	Delaware	161,314	0.3%
2	Florida	3,547,492	7.0%
11	Georgia	1,347,932	2.6%
42	Hawaii	212,890	0.4%
40	Idaho	247,847	0.5%
7	Illinois	1,948,578	3.8%
14	Indiana	1,121,662	2.2%
32	Iowa	563,610	1.1%
33	Kansas	464,699	0.9%
22	Kentucky	844,573	1.7%
25	Louisiana	748,171	1.5%
39	Maine	286,123	0.6%
24	Maryland	802,066	1.6%
16	Massachusetts	1,094,012	2.1%
8	Michigan	1,840,547	3.6%
23	Minnesota	831,763	1.6%
31	Mississippi	567,786	1.1%
15	Missouri	1,106,923	2.2%
44	Montana	180,802	0.4%
38	Nebraska	297,811	0.6%
35	Nevada	374,289	0.7%
41	New Hampshire	237,498	0.5%
10	New Jersey	1,407,621	2.8%
36	New Mexico	335,471	0.7%
4	New York	3,143,642	6.2%
9	North Carolina	1,631,266	3.2%
48	North Dakota	117,130	0.2%
6	Ohio	2,021,874	4.0%
26	Oklahoma	669,673	1.3%
27	Oregon	659,719	1.3%
5	Pennsylvania	2,481,695	4.9%
43	Rhode Island	196,161	0.4%
21	South Carolina	850,368	1.7%
46	South Dakota	146,991	0.3%
13	Tennessee	1,168,699	2.3%
3	Texas	3,192,227	6.3%
37	Utah	299,088	0.6%
47	Vermont	120,249	0.2%
12	Virginia	1,207,101	2.4%
17	Washington	1,008,804	2.0%
34	West Virginia	429,613	0.8%
18	Wisconsin	1,000,788	2.0%
49	Wyoming	85,755	0.2%

RANK ORDER

RANK	STATE	BENEFICIARIES	% of USA
1	California	4,678,517	9.2%
2	Florida	3,547,492	7.0%
3	Texas	3,192,227	6.3%
4	New York	3,143,642	6.2%
5	Pennsylvania	2,481,695	4.9%
6	Ohio	2,021,874	4.0%
7	Illinois	1,948,578	3.8%
8	Michigan	1,840,547	3.6%
9	North Carolina	1,631,266	3.2%
10	New Jersey	1,407,621	2.8%
11	Georgia	1,347,932	2.6%
12	Virginia	1,207,101	2.4%
13	Tennessee	1,168,699	2.3%
14	Indiana	1,121,662	2.2%
15	Missouri	1,106,923	2.2%
16	Massachusetts	1,094,012	2.1%
17	Washington	1,008,804	2.0%
18	Wisconsin	1,000,788	2.0%
19	Arizona	986,539	1.9%
20	Alabama	952,511	1.9%
21	South Carolina	850,368	1.7%
22	Kentucky	844,573	1.7%
23	Minnesota	831,763	1.6%
24	Maryland	802,066	1.6%
25	Louisiana	748,171	1.5%
26	Oklahoma	669,673	1.3%
27	Oregon	659,719	1.3%
28	Colorado	635,816	1.2%
29	Arkansas	602,017	1.2%
30	Connecticut	599,533	1.2%
31	Mississippi	567,786	1.1%
32	Iowa	563,610	1.1%
33	Kansas	464,699	0.9%
34	West Virginia	429,613	0.8%
35	Nevada	374,289	0.7%
36	New Mexico	335,471	0.7%
37	Utah	299,088	0.6%
38	Nebraska	297,811	0.6%
39	Maine	286,123	0.6%
40	Idaho	247,847	0.5%
41	New Hampshire	237,498	0.5%
42	Hawaii	212,890	0.4%
43	Rhode Island	196,161	0.4%
44	Montana	180,802	0.4%
45	Delaware	161,314	0.3%
46	South Dakota	146,991	0.3%
47	Vermont	120,249	0.2%
48	North Dakota	117,130	0.2%
49	Wyoming	85,755	0.2%
50	Alaska	71,145	0.1%
	District of Columbia	71,468	0.1%

Source: Social Security Administration
  "Social Security Bulletin, Annual Statistical Supplement 2009" (http://www.ssa.gov/policy/docs/statcomps/supplement/2009/)
*For December 2008. "OASDI" is Old Age, Survivors and Disability Insurance. National total includes 1,298,375 beneficiaries in U.S. territories and foreign countries.

Average Monthly Social Security (OASDI) Payment in 2008

National Average = $1,065 Each Month per Beneficiary*

ALPHA ORDER

RANK	STATE	AVERAGE BENEFIT
42	Alabama	$999
41	Alaska	1,001
14	Arizona	1,087
48	Arkansas	976
26	California	1,057
26	Colorado	1,057
2	Connecticut	1,170
3	Delaware	1,133
19	Florida	1,069
35	Georgia	1,031
19	Hawaii	1,069
34	Idaho	1,037
8	Illinois	1,098
7	Indiana	1,104
23	Iowa	1,064
15	Kansas	1,085
46	Kentucky	979
49	Louisiana	959
47	Maine	978
11	Maryland	1,093
18	Massachusetts	1,070
4	Michigan	1,132
17	Minnesota	1,082
50	Mississippi	955
33	Missouri	1,039
38	Montana	1,017
29	Nebraska	1,049
13	Nevada	1,088
8	New Hampshire	1,098
1	New Jersey	1,182
45	New Mexico	980
5	New York	1,112
31	North Carolina	1,046
43	North Dakota	992
24	Ohio	1,061
39	Oklahoma	1,014
16	Oregon	1,083
12	Pennsylvania	1,092
21	Rhode Island	1,068
32	South Carolina	1,045
44	South Dakota	990
36	Tennessee	1,024
39	Texas	1,014
25	Utah	1,060
30	Vermont	1,048
28	Virginia	1,055
6	Washington	1,108
37	West Virginia	1,018
10	Wisconsin	1,096
21	Wyoming	1,068

RANK ORDER

RANK	STATE	AVERAGE BENEFIT
1	New Jersey	$1,182
2	Connecticut	1,170
3	Delaware	1,133
4	Michigan	1,132
5	New York	1,112
6	Washington	1,108
7	Indiana	1,104
8	Illinois	1,098
8	New Hampshire	1,098
10	Wisconsin	1,096
11	Maryland	1,093
12	Pennsylvania	1,092
13	Nevada	1,088
14	Arizona	1,087
15	Kansas	1,085
16	Oregon	1,083
17	Minnesota	1,082
18	Massachusetts	1,070
19	Florida	1,069
19	Hawaii	1,069
21	Rhode Island	1,068
21	Wyoming	1,068
23	Iowa	1,064
24	Ohio	1,061
25	Utah	1,060
26	California	1,057
26	Colorado	1,057
28	Virginia	1,055
29	Nebraska	1,049
30	Vermont	1,048
31	North Carolina	1,046
32	South Carolina	1,045
33	Missouri	1,039
34	Idaho	1,037
35	Georgia	1,031
36	Tennessee	1,024
37	West Virginia	1,018
38	Montana	1,017
39	Oklahoma	1,014
39	Texas	1,014
41	Alaska	1,001
42	Alabama	999
43	North Dakota	992
44	South Dakota	990
45	New Mexico	980
46	Kentucky	979
47	Maine	978
48	Arkansas	976
49	Louisiana	959
50	Mississippi	955
	District of Columbia	941

Source: CQ Press using data from Social Security Administration
"Social Security Bulletin, Annual Statistical Supplement 2009" (http://www.ssa.gov/policy/docs/statcomps/supplement/2009/)
*As of December 2008. "OASDI" is Old Age, Survivors and Disability Insurance. National average does not include beneficiaries or payments in U.S. territories or foreign countries.

Social Security Supplemental Security Income Beneficiaries in 2008

National Total = 7,520,501 Beneficiaries*

ALPHA ORDER

RANK	STATE	BENEFICIARIES	% of USA
13	Alabama	166,743	2.2%
48	Alaska	11,614	0.2%
23	Arizona	103,065	1.4%
25	Arkansas	99,072	1.3%
1	California	1,271,916	16.9%
31	Colorado	59,891	0.8%
33	Connecticut	55,376	0.7%
45	Delaware	14,797	0.2%
4	Florida	444,840	5.9%
9	Georgia	212,803	2.8%
42	Hawaii	23,610	0.3%
40	Idaho	24,655	0.3%
6	Illinois	265,628	3.5%
21	Indiana	108,094	1.4%
34	Iowa	45,434	0.6%
35	Kansas	41,903	0.6%
11	Kentucky	186,809	2.5%
14	Louisiana	165,454	2.2%
37	Maine	33,915	0.5%
24	Maryland	100,726	1.3%
12	Massachusetts	182,455	2.4%
8	Michigan	232,581	3.1%
28	Minnesota	80,673	1.1%
20	Mississippi	122,455	1.6%
19	Missouri	124,449	1.7%
43	Montana	16,033	0.2%
41	Nebraska	23,727	0.3%
36	Nevada	36,679	0.5%
44	New Hampshire	15,811	0.2%
16	New Jersey	159,751	2.1%
32	New Mexico	57,605	0.8%
2	New York	658,265	8.8%
10	North Carolina	208,409	2.8%
49	North Dakota	8,032	0.1%
7	Ohio	265,273	3.5%
27	Oklahoma	87,829	1.2%
30	Oregon	66,354	0.9%
5	Pennsylvania	339,697	4.5%
38	Rhode Island	31,548	0.4%
22	South Carolina	107,142	1.4%
47	South Dakota	13,083	0.2%
15	Tennessee	165,151	2.2%
3	Texas	566,281	7.5%
39	Utah	25,443	0.3%
46	Vermont	14,353	0.2%
17	Virginia	141,822	1.9%
18	Washington	124,974	1.7%
29	West Virginia	79,688	1.1%
26	Wisconsin	99,014	1.3%
50	Wyoming	5,903	0.1%

RANK ORDER

RANK	STATE	BENEFICIARIES	% of USA
1	California	1,271,916	16.9%
2	New York	658,265	8.8%
3	Texas	566,281	7.5%
4	Florida	444,840	5.9%
5	Pennsylvania	339,697	4.5%
6	Illinois	265,628	3.5%
7	Ohio	265,273	3.5%
8	Michigan	232,581	3.1%
9	Georgia	212,803	2.8%
10	North Carolina	208,409	2.8%
11	Kentucky	186,809	2.5%
12	Massachusetts	182,455	2.4%
13	Alabama	166,743	2.2%
14	Louisiana	165,454	2.2%
15	Tennessee	165,151	2.2%
16	New Jersey	159,751	2.1%
17	Virginia	141,822	1.9%
18	Washington	124,974	1.7%
19	Missouri	124,449	1.7%
20	Mississippi	122,455	1.6%
21	Indiana	108,094	1.4%
22	South Carolina	107,142	1.4%
23	Arizona	103,065	1.4%
24	Maryland	100,726	1.3%
25	Arkansas	99,072	1.3%
26	Wisconsin	99,014	1.3%
27	Oklahoma	87,829	1.2%
28	Minnesota	80,673	1.1%
29	West Virginia	79,688	1.1%
30	Oregon	66,354	0.9%
31	Colorado	59,891	0.8%
32	New Mexico	57,605	0.8%
33	Connecticut	55,376	0.7%
34	Iowa	45,434	0.6%
35	Kansas	41,903	0.6%
36	Nevada	36,679	0.5%
37	Maine	33,915	0.5%
38	Rhode Island	31,548	0.4%
39	Utah	25,443	0.3%
40	Idaho	24,655	0.3%
41	Nebraska	23,727	0.3%
42	Hawaii	23,610	0.3%
43	Montana	16,033	0.2%
44	New Hampshire	15,811	0.2%
45	Delaware	14,797	0.2%
46	Vermont	14,353	0.2%
47	South Dakota	13,083	0.2%
48	Alaska	11,614	0.2%
49	North Dakota	8,032	0.1%
50	Wyoming	5,903	0.1%
	District of Columbia	22,827	0.3%

Source: Social Security Administration
"Social Security Bulletin, Annual Statistical Supplement 2009" (http://www.ssa.gov/policy/docs/statcomps/supplement/2009/)
*For December 2008. National total includes 849 beneficiaries in U.S. territories or otherwise not distributed by state. The SSI program provides income support to persons age 65 and older and blind or disabled adults and children.

Average Monthly Social Security
Supplemental Security Income Payment in 2008
National Average = $447.00 Each Month per Beneficiary*

ALPHA ORDER

RANK	STATE	AVERAGE BENEFIT
36	Alabama	$429.56
29	Alaska	435.14
9	Arizona	457.56
38	Arkansas	426.78
14	California	452.23
31	Colorado	433.20
11	Connecticut	453.76
18	Delaware	447.49
23	Florida	443.83
37	Georgia	429.01
8	Hawaii	457.66
27	Idaho	436.95
1	Illinois	475.18
13	Indiana	452.91
43	Iowa	419.17
28	Kansas	436.36
19	Kentucky	446.04
22	Louisiana	444.86
45	Maine	418.29
7	Maryland	463.03
16	Massachusetts	449.53
3	Michigan	473.34
10	Minnesota	456.77
40	Mississippi	423.79
26	Missouri	437.73
39	Montana	424.22
44	Nebraska	418.68
20	Nevada	445.19
35	New Hampshire	429.64
30	New Jersey	435.06
32	New Mexico	431.79
6	New York	464.08
47	North Carolina	417.16
50	North Dakota	388.44
5	Ohio	468.95
24	Oklahoma	439.98
17	Oregon	448.74
4	Pennsylvania	472.56
15	Rhode Island	449.77
41	South Carolina	421.79
49	South Dakota	404.58
34	Tennessee	429.97
42	Texas	420.74
25	Utah	438.20
48	Vermont	415.63
33	Virginia	431.43
2	Washington	474.60
12	West Virginia	453.22
20	Wisconsin	445.19
46	Wyoming	417.42

RANK ORDER

RANK	STATE	AVERAGE BENEFIT
1	Illinois	$475.18
2	Washington	474.60
3	Michigan	473.34
4	Pennsylvania	472.56
5	Ohio	468.95
6	New York	464.08
7	Maryland	463.03
8	Hawaii	457.66
9	Arizona	457.56
10	Minnesota	456.77
11	Connecticut	453.76
12	West Virginia	453.22
13	Indiana	452.91
14	California	452.23
15	Rhode Island	449.77
16	Massachusetts	449.53
17	Oregon	448.74
18	Delaware	447.49
19	Kentucky	446.04
20	Nevada	445.19
20	Wisconsin	445.19
22	Louisiana	444.86
23	Florida	443.83
24	Oklahoma	439.98
25	Utah	438.20
26	Missouri	437.73
27	Idaho	436.95
28	Kansas	436.36
29	Alaska	435.14
30	New Jersey	435.06
31	Colorado	433.20
32	New Mexico	431.79
33	Virginia	431.43
34	Tennessee	429.97
35	New Hampshire	429.64
36	Alabama	429.56
37	Georgia	429.01
38	Arkansas	426.78
39	Montana	424.22
40	Mississippi	423.79
41	South Carolina	421.79
42	Texas	420.74
43	Iowa	419.17
44	Nebraska	418.68
45	Maine	418.29
46	Wyoming	417.42
47	North Carolina	417.16
48	Vermont	415.63
49	South Dakota	404.58
50	North Dakota	388.44

District of Columbia — 480.10

Source: Social Security Administration
"Social Security Bulletin, Annual Statistical Supplement 2009" (http://www.ssa.gov/policy/docs/statcomps/supplement/2009/)
*As of December 2008. National average includes payments to beneficiaries in U.S. territories and foreign countries. The SSI program provides income support to persons age 65 and older and blind or disabled adults and children.

Medicare Enrollees in 2009

National Total = 46,520,716 Enrollees*

ALPHA ORDER					RANK ORDER			
RANK	STATE	ENROLLEES	% of USA		RANK	STATE	ENROLLEES	% of USA
20	Alabama	827,594	1.8%		1	California	4,619,642	9.9%
50	Alaska	62,707	0.1%		2	Florida	3,289,117	7.1%
18	Arizona	899,487	1.9%		3	New York	2,937,045	6.3%
30	Arkansas	520,377	1.1%		4	Texas	2,899,787	6.2%
1	California	4,619,642	9.9%		5	Pennsylvania	2,252,011	4.8%
27	Colorado	601,992	1.3%		6	Ohio	1,870,284	4.0%
29	Connecticut	558,107	1.2%		7	Illinois	1,806,475	3.9%
45	Delaware	145,065	0.3%		8	Michigan	1,614,512	3.5%
2	Florida	3,289,117	7.1%		9	North Carolina	1,447,965	3.1%
11	Georgia	1,193,887	2.6%		10	New Jersey	1,304,311	2.8%
42	Hawaii	200,305	0.4%		11	Georgia	1,193,887	2.6%
40	Idaho	221,962	0.5%		12	Virginia	1,109,909	2.4%
7	Illinois	1,806,475	3.9%		13	Massachusetts	1,039,299	2.2%
16	Indiana	985,107	2.1%		14	Tennessee	1,031,204	2.2%
31	Iowa	511,615	1.1%		15	Missouri	985,325	2.1%
33	Kansas	425,444	0.9%		16	Indiana	985,107	2.1%
24	Kentucky	743,418	1.6%		17	Washington	938,166	2.0%
25	Louisiana	671,294	1.4%		18	Arizona	899,487	1.9%
39	Maine	259,090	0.6%		19	Wisconsin	891,742	1.9%
22	Maryland	764,123	1.6%		20	Alabama	827,594	1.8%
13	Massachusetts	1,039,299	2.2%		21	Minnesota	766,806	1.6%
8	Michigan	1,614,512	3.5%		22	Maryland	764,123	1.6%
21	Minnesota	766,806	1.6%		23	South Carolina	748,651	1.6%
32	Mississippi	487,978	1.0%		24	Kentucky	743,418	1.6%
15	Missouri	985,325	2.1%		25	Louisiana	671,294	1.4%
44	Montana	164,635	0.4%		26	Oregon	602,246	1.3%
37	Nebraska	275,617	0.6%		27	Colorado	601,992	1.3%
35	Nevada	343,026	0.7%		28	Oklahoma	591,793	1.3%
41	New Hampshire	217,378	0.5%		29	Connecticut	558,107	1.2%
10	New Jersey	1,304,311	2.8%		30	Arkansas	520,377	1.1%
36	New Mexico	303,827	0.7%		31	Iowa	511,615	1.1%
3	New York	2,937,045	6.3%		32	Mississippi	487,978	1.0%
9	North Carolina	1,447,965	3.1%		33	Kansas	425,444	0.9%
47	North Dakota	107,998	0.2%		34	West Virginia	377,244	0.8%
6	Ohio	1,870,284	4.0%		35	Nevada	343,026	0.7%
28	Oklahoma	591,793	1.3%		36	New Mexico	303,827	0.7%
26	Oregon	602,246	1.3%		37	Nebraska	275,617	0.6%
5	Pennsylvania	2,252,011	4.8%		38	Utah	273,860	0.6%
43	Rhode Island	180,233	0.4%		39	Maine	259,090	0.6%
23	South Carolina	748,651	1.6%		40	Idaho	221,962	0.5%
46	South Dakota	134,470	0.3%		41	New Hampshire	217,378	0.5%
14	Tennessee	1,031,204	2.2%		42	Hawaii	200,305	0.4%
4	Texas	2,899,787	6.2%		43	Rhode Island	180,233	0.4%
38	Utah	273,860	0.6%		44	Montana	164,635	0.4%
48	Vermont	107,950	0.2%		45	Delaware	145,065	0.3%
12	Virginia	1,109,909	2.4%		46	South Dakota	134,470	0.3%
17	Washington	938,166	2.0%		47	North Dakota	107,998	0.2%
34	West Virginia	377,244	0.8%		48	Vermont	107,950	0.2%
19	Wisconsin	891,742	1.9%		49	Wyoming	78,223	0.2%
49	Wyoming	78,223	0.2%		50	Alaska	62,707	0.1%
						District of Columbia	76,694	0.2%

Source: U.S. Department of Health and Human Services, Centers for Medicare and Medicaid Services
"2010 Data Compendium" (http://www.cms.hhs.gov/DataCompendium/)
*Includes aged and disabled enrollees. Total includes 653,166 enrollees in Puerto Rico and other outlying areas, foreign countries, or whose address is unknown.

Percent of Population Enrolled in Medicare in 2009

National Percent = 14.8% of Population*

ALPHA ORDER

RANK STATE PERCENT

RANK	STATE	PERCENT
6	Alabama	17.6
50	Alaska	9.0
42	Arizona	13.6
3	Arkansas	18.0
45	California	12.5
47	Colorado	12.0
23	Connecticut	15.9
18	Delaware	16.4
5	Florida	17.7
46	Georgia	12.1
27	Hawaii	15.5
38	Idaho	14.4
41	Illinois	14.0
30	Indiana	15.3
10	Iowa	17.0
32	Kansas	15.1
8	Kentucky	17.2
35	Louisiana	14.9
2	Maine	19.7
43	Maryland	13.4
25	Massachusetts	15.8
21	Michigan	16.2
36	Minnesota	14.6
14	Mississippi	16.5
15	Missouri	16.5
11	Montana	16.9
29	Nebraska	15.3
44	Nevada	13.0
17	New Hampshire	16.4
34	New Jersey	15.0
31	New Mexico	15.1
33	New York	15.0
28	North Carolina	15.4
12	North Dakota	16.7
20	Ohio	16.2
22	Oklahoma	16.1
26	Oregon	15.7
4	Pennsylvania	17.9
9	Rhode Island	17.1
16	South Carolina	16.4
13	South Dakota	16.6
19	Tennessee	16.4
48	Texas	11.7
49	Utah	9.8
7	Vermont	17.4
39	Virginia	14.1
40	Washington	14.1
1	West Virginia	20.7
24	Wisconsin	15.8
37	Wyoming	14.4

RANK ORDER

RANK STATE PERCENT

RANK	STATE	PERCENT
1	West Virginia	20.7
2	Maine	19.7
3	Arkansas	18.0
4	Pennsylvania	17.9
5	Florida	17.7
6	Alabama	17.6
7	Vermont	17.4
8	Kentucky	17.2
9	Rhode Island	17.1
10	Iowa	17.0
11	Montana	16.9
12	North Dakota	16.7
13	South Dakota	16.6
14	Mississippi	16.5
15	Missouri	16.5
16	South Carolina	16.4
17	New Hampshire	16.4
18	Delaware	16.4
19	Tennessee	16.4
20	Ohio	16.2
21	Michigan	16.2
22	Oklahoma	16.1
23	Connecticut	15.9
24	Wisconsin	15.8
25	Massachusetts	15.8
26	Oregon	15.7
27	Hawaii	15.5
28	North Carolina	15.4
29	Nebraska	15.3
30	Indiana	15.3
31	New Mexico	15.1
32	Kansas	15.1
33	New York	15.0
34	New Jersey	15.0
35	Louisiana	14.9
36	Minnesota	14.6
37	Wyoming	14.4
38	Idaho	14.4
39	Virginia	14.1
40	Washington	14.1
41	Illinois	14.0
42	Arizona	13.6
43	Maryland	13.4
44	Nevada	13.0
45	California	12.5
46	Georgia	12.1
47	Colorado	12.0
48	Texas	11.7
49	Utah	9.8
50	Alaska	9.0
	District of Columbia	12.8

Source: U.S. Department of Health and Human Services, Centers for Medicare and Medicaid Services
"2010 Data Compendium" (http://www.cms.hhs.gov/DataCompendium/)
*Includes aged and disabled enrollees. National rate includes only residents of the 50 states and the District of Columbia.

Medicare Program Payments in 2009

National Total = $316,915,000,000*

ALPHA ORDER

RANK	STATE	PAYMENTS	% of USA
18	Alabama	$5,471,000,000	1.7%
50	Alaska	477,000,000	0.2%
24	Arizona	4,751,000,000	1.5%
29	Arkansas	3,435,000,000	1.1%
1	California	28,389,000,000	9.0%
31	Colorado	3,214,000,000	1.0%
25	Connecticut	4,635,000,000	1.5%
41	Delaware	1,272,000,000	0.4%
2	Florida	25,292,000,000	8.0%
11	Georgia	8,484,000,000	2.7%
47	Hawaii	702,000,000	0.2%
42	Idaho	1,104,000,000	0.3%
5	Illinois	15,334,000,000	4.8%
15	Indiana	7,183,000,000	2.3%
30	Iowa	3,224,000,000	1.0%
32	Kansas	3,038,000,000	1.0%
19	Kentucky	5,380,000,000	1.7%
20	Louisiana	5,342,000,000	1.7%
37	Maine	1,689,000,000	0.5%
14	Maryland	7,336,000,000	2.3%
12	Massachusetts	8,441,000,000	2.7%
8	Michigan	12,180,000,000	3.8%
27	Minnesota	4,153,000,000	1.3%
28	Mississippi	4,150,000,000	1.3%
17	Missouri	6,743,000,000	2.1%
44	Montana	907,000,000	0.3%
36	Nebraska	1,954,000,000	0.6%
35	Nevada	2,083,000,000	0.7%
38	New Hampshire	1,586,000,000	0.5%
9	New Jersey	11,895,000,000	3.8%
39	New Mexico	1,543,000,000	0.5%
4	New York	20,896,000,000	6.6%
10	North Carolina	10,006,000,000	3.2%
48	North Dakota	652,000,000	0.2%
6	Ohio	12,651,000,000	4.0%
26	Oklahoma	4,446,000,000	1.4%
34	Oregon	2,315,000,000	0.7%
7	Pennsylvania	12,567,000,000	4.0%
43	Rhode Island	988,000,000	0.3%
21	South Carolina	5,330,000,000	1.7%
45	South Dakota	859,000,000	0.3%
16	Tennessee	6,892,000,000	2.2%
3	Texas	24,514,000,000	7.7%
40	Utah	1,370,000,000	0.4%
46	Vermont	772,000,000	0.2%
13	Virginia	7,414,000,000	2.3%
22	Washington	5,217,000,000	1.6%
33	West Virginia	2,382,000,000	0.8%
23	Wisconsin	5,002,000,000	1.6%
49	Wyoming	507,000,000	0.2%

RANK ORDER

RANK	STATE	PAYMENTS	% of USA
1	California	$28,389,000,000	9.0%
2	Florida	25,292,000,000	8.0%
3	Texas	24,514,000,000	7.7%
4	New York	20,896,000,000	6.6%
5	Illinois	15,334,000,000	4.8%
6	Ohio	12,651,000,000	4.0%
7	Pennsylvania	12,567,000,000	4.0%
8	Michigan	12,180,000,000	3.8%
9	New Jersey	11,895,000,000	3.8%
10	North Carolina	10,006,000,000	3.2%
11	Georgia	8,484,000,000	2.7%
12	Massachusetts	8,441,000,000	2.7%
13	Virginia	7,414,000,000	2.3%
14	Maryland	7,336,000,000	2.3%
15	Indiana	7,183,000,000	2.3%
16	Tennessee	6,892,000,000	2.2%
17	Missouri	6,743,000,000	2.1%
18	Alabama	5,471,000,000	1.7%
19	Kentucky	5,380,000,000	1.7%
20	Louisiana	5,342,000,000	1.7%
21	South Carolina	5,330,000,000	1.7%
22	Washington	5,217,000,000	1.6%
23	Wisconsin	5,002,000,000	1.6%
24	Arizona	4,751,000,000	1.5%
25	Connecticut	4,635,000,000	1.5%
26	Oklahoma	4,446,000,000	1.4%
27	Minnesota	4,153,000,000	1.3%
28	Mississippi	4,150,000,000	1.3%
29	Arkansas	3,435,000,000	1.1%
30	Iowa	3,224,000,000	1.0%
31	Colorado	3,214,000,000	1.0%
32	Kansas	3,038,000,000	1.0%
33	West Virginia	2,382,000,000	0.8%
34	Oregon	2,315,000,000	0.7%
35	Nevada	2,083,000,000	0.7%
36	Nebraska	1,954,000,000	0.6%
37	Maine	1,689,000,000	0.5%
38	New Hampshire	1,586,000,000	0.5%
39	New Mexico	1,543,000,000	0.5%
40	Utah	1,370,000,000	0.4%
41	Delaware	1,272,000,000	0.4%
42	Idaho	1,104,000,000	0.3%
43	Rhode Island	988,000,000	0.3%
44	Montana	907,000,000	0.3%
45	South Dakota	859,000,000	0.3%
46	Vermont	772,000,000	0.2%
47	Hawaii	702,000,000	0.2%
48	North Dakota	652,000,000	0.2%
49	Wyoming	507,000,000	0.2%
50	Alaska	477,000,000	0.2%
	District of Columbia	747,000,000	0.2%

Source: U.S. Department of Health and Human Services, Centers for Medicare and Medicaid Services
   "Health Care Financing Review, 2010 Statistical Supplement" (http://cms.hhs.gov/MedicareMedicaidStatSupp)
*Figures for calendar year 2009. Includes payments to aged and disabled enrollees. Total does not include payments to beneficiaries in Puerto Rico and other outlying areas.

Medicare Program Payments per Enrollee in 2009

National Rate = $9,121*

ALPHA ORDER

RANK	STATE	PER ENROLLEE
24	Alabama	$8,496
36	Alaska	7,744
27	Arizona	8,405
34	Arkansas	7,847
11	California	9,411
31	Colorado	7,998
9	Connecticut	9,968
14	Delaware	9,139
1	Florida	10,894
28	Georgia	8,320
50	Hawaii	5,802
43	Idaho	6,929
12	Illinois	9,367
17	Indiana	8,650
42	Iowa	7,257
30	Kansas	8,071
23	Kentucky	8,517
3	Louisiana	10,338
41	Maine	7,264
5	Maryland	10,322
8	Massachusetts	9,988
6	Michigan	10,085
19	Minnesota	8,647
10	Mississippi	9,479
22	Missouri	8,528
47	Montana	6,576
33	Nebraska	7,906
21	Nevada	8,619
32	New Hampshire	7,951
4	New Jersey	10,327
45	New Mexico	6,782
7	New York	10,014
26	North Carolina	8,433
49	North Dakota	6,453
13	Ohio	9,202
16	Oklahoma	8,826
48	Oregon	6,561
15	Pennsylvania	9,036
17	Rhode Island	8,650
25	South Carolina	8,453
44	South Dakota	6,927
20	Tennessee	8,642
2	Texas	10,413
39	Utah	7,352
40	Vermont	7,338
36	Virginia	7,744
38	Washington	7,376
29	West Virginia	8,200
35	Wisconsin	7,815
46	Wyoming	6,774

RANK ORDER

RANK	STATE	PER ENROLLEE
1	Florida	$10,894
2	Texas	10,413
3	Louisiana	10,338
4	New Jersey	10,327
5	Maryland	10,322
6	Michigan	10,085
7	New York	10,014
8	Massachusetts	9,988
9	Connecticut	9,968
10	Mississippi	9,479
11	California	9,411
12	Illinois	9,367
13	Ohio	9,202
14	Delaware	9,139
15	Pennsylvania	9,036
16	Oklahoma	8,826
17	Indiana	8,650
17	Rhode Island	8,650
19	Minnesota	8,647
20	Tennessee	8,642
21	Nevada	8,619
22	Missouri	8,528
23	Kentucky	8,517
24	Alabama	8,496
25	South Carolina	8,453
26	North Carolina	8,433
27	Arizona	8,405
28	Georgia	8,320
29	West Virginia	8,200
30	Kansas	8,071
31	Colorado	7,998
32	New Hampshire	7,951
33	Nebraska	7,906
34	Arkansas	7,847
35	Wisconsin	7,815
36	Alaska	7,744
36	Virginia	7,744
38	Washington	7,376
39	Utah	7,352
40	Vermont	7,338
41	Maine	7,264
42	Iowa	7,257
43	Idaho	6,929
44	South Dakota	6,927
45	New Mexico	6,782
46	Wyoming	6,774
47	Montana	6,576
48	Oregon	6,561
49	North Dakota	6,453
50	Hawaii	5,802

	District of Columbia	10,910

Source: U.S. Department of Health and Human Services, Centers for Medicare and Medicaid Services
"Health Care Financing Review, 2010 Statistical Supplement" (http://cms.hhs.gov/MedicareMedicaidStatSupp)
*Figures for calendar year 2009. Includes payments to aged and disabled enrollees. National figure does not include enrollees in managed care plans in the denominator used to calculate average payments. National rate also does not include payments or enrollees in Puerto Rico and other outlying areas.

Medicaid Enrollment in 2009

National Total = 52,355,471 Enrollees*

ALPHA ORDER

RANK	STATE	ENROLLEES	% of USA
22	Alabama	825,655	1.6%
47	Alaska	107,440	0.2%
11	Arizona	1,312,189	2.5%
28	Arkansas	655,766	1.3%
1	California	7,131,538	13.6%
31	Colorado	494,699	0.9%
32	Connecticut	474,288	0.9%
43	Delaware	173,846	0.3%
4	Florida	2,589,982	4.9%
10	Georgia	1,443,271	2.8%
37	Hawaii	248,984	0.5%
41	Idaho	206,846	0.4%
5	Illinois	2,344,100	4.5%
17	Indiana	1,041,295	2.0%
33	Iowa	414,201	0.8%
35	Kansas	291,720	0.6%
23	Kentucky	789,371	1.5%
14	Louisiana	1,147,955	2.2%
36	Maine	279,439	0.5%
21	Maryland	830,172	1.6%
12	Massachusetts	1,227,224	2.3%
8	Michigan	1,732,487	3.3%
26	Minnesota	682,193	1.3%
25	Mississippi	692,296	1.3%
19	Missouri	900,302	1.7%
48	Montana	90,392	0.2%
40	Nebraska	225,523	0.4%
39	Nevada	230,067	0.4%
45	New Hampshire	128,858	0.2%
18	New Jersey	1,006,067	1.9%
30	New Mexico	497,782	1.0%
2	New York	4,557,053	8.7%
9	North Carolina	1,537,651	2.9%
50	North Dakota	63,752	0.1%
6	Ohio	2,028,863	3.9%
27	Oklahoma	656,221	1.3%
29	Oregon	513,079	1.0%
7	Pennsylvania	1,976,439	3.8%
42	Rhode Island	181,572	0.3%
24	South Carolina	776,610	1.5%
46	South Dakota	115,597	0.2%
13	Tennessee	1,184,092	2.3%
3	Texas	3,513,243	6.7%
38	Utah	247,040	0.5%
44	Vermont	155,283	0.3%
20	Virginia	854,858	1.6%
16	Washington	1,074,361	2.1%
34	West Virginia	330,565	0.6%
15	Wisconsin	1,102,516	2.1%
49	Wyoming	67,366	0.1%

RANK ORDER

RANK	STATE	ENROLLEES	% of USA
1	California	7,131,538	13.6%
2	New York	4,557,053	8.7%
3	Texas	3,513,243	6.7%
4	Florida	2,589,982	4.9%
5	Illinois	2,344,100	4.5%
6	Ohio	2,028,863	3.9%
7	Pennsylvania	1,976,439	3.8%
8	Michigan	1,732,487	3.3%
9	North Carolina	1,537,651	2.9%
10	Georgia	1,443,271	2.8%
11	Arizona	1,312,189	2.5%
12	Massachusetts	1,227,224	2.3%
13	Tennessee	1,184,092	2.3%
14	Louisiana	1,147,955	2.2%
15	Wisconsin	1,102,516	2.1%
16	Washington	1,074,361	2.1%
17	Indiana	1,041,295	2.0%
18	New Jersey	1,006,067	1.9%
19	Missouri	900,302	1.7%
20	Virginia	854,858	1.6%
21	Maryland	830,172	1.6%
22	Alabama	825,655	1.6%
23	Kentucky	789,371	1.5%
24	South Carolina	776,610	1.5%
25	Mississippi	692,296	1.3%
26	Minnesota	682,193	1.3%
27	Oklahoma	656,221	1.3%
28	Arkansas	655,766	1.3%
29	Oregon	513,079	1.0%
30	New Mexico	497,782	1.0%
31	Colorado	494,699	0.9%
32	Connecticut	474,288	0.9%
33	Iowa	414,201	0.8%
34	West Virginia	330,565	0.6%
35	Kansas	291,720	0.6%
36	Maine	279,439	0.5%
37	Hawaii	248,984	0.5%
38	Utah	247,040	0.5%
39	Nevada	230,067	0.4%
40	Nebraska	225,523	0.4%
41	Idaho	206,846	0.4%
42	Rhode Island	181,572	0.3%
43	Delaware	173,846	0.3%
44	Vermont	155,283	0.3%
45	New Hampshire	128,858	0.2%
46	South Dakota	115,597	0.2%
47	Alaska	107,440	0.2%
48	Montana	90,392	0.2%
49	Wyoming	67,366	0.1%
50	North Dakota	63,752	0.1%
	District of Columbia	161,041	0.3%

Source: U.S. Department of Health and Human Services, Centers for Medicare and Medicaid Services
    "2009 Medicaid Managed Care Enrollment Report" (http://www.cms.hhs.gov/MedicaidDataSourcesGenInfo/)
*Unduplicated enrollment as of December 31, 2009. National total includes 1,042,150 Medicaid enrollees in Puerto Rico and the
Virgin Islands.

Percent of Population Enrolled in Medicaid in 2009

National Percent = 16.7% of Population*

ALPHA ORDER

RANK ORDER

RANK	STATE	PERCENT	RANK	STATE	PERCENT
20	Alabama	17.5	1	Louisiana	25.6
28	Alaska	15.4	2	Vermont	25.0
8	Arizona	19.9	3	New Mexico	24.8
6	Arkansas	22.7	4	Mississippi	23.5
11	California	19.3	5	New York	23.3
46	Colorado	9.8	6	Arkansas	22.7
36	Connecticut	13.5	7	Maine	21.2
9	Delaware	19.6	8	Arizona	19.9
34	Florida	14.0	9	Delaware	19.6
30	Georgia	14.7	10	Wisconsin	19.5
12	Hawaii	19.2	11	California	19.3
37	Idaho	13.4	12	Hawaii	19.2
16	Illinois	18.2	13	Tennessee	18.8
25	Indiana	16.2	14	Massachusetts	18.6
35	Iowa	13.8	15	Kentucky	18.3
44	Kansas	10.3	16	Illinois	18.2
15	Kentucky	18.3	16	West Virginia	18.2
1	Louisiana	25.6	18	Oklahoma	17.8
7	Maine	21.2	19	Ohio	17.6
31	Maryland	14.6	20	Alabama	17.5
14	Massachusetts	18.6	21	Michigan	17.4
21	Michigan	17.4	22	Rhode Island	17.2
39	Minnesota	13.0	23	South Carolina	17.0
4	Mississippi	23.5	24	North Carolina	16.4
29	Missouri	15.0	25	Indiana	16.2
48	Montana	9.3	26	Washington	16.1
40	Nebraska	12.6	27	Pennsylvania	15.7
50	Nevada	8.7	28	Alaska	15.4
47	New Hampshire	9.7	29	Missouri	15.0
42	New Jersey	11.6	30	Georgia	14.7
3	New Mexico	24.8	31	Maryland	14.6
5	New York	23.3	32	South Dakota	14.2
24	North Carolina	16.4	32	Texas	14.2
45	North Dakota	9.9	34	Florida	14.0
19	Ohio	17.6	35	Iowa	13.8
18	Oklahoma	17.8	36	Connecticut	13.5
37	Oregon	13.4	37	Idaho	13.4
27	Pennsylvania	15.7	37	Oregon	13.4
22	Rhode Island	17.2	39	Minnesota	13.0
23	South Carolina	17.0	40	Nebraska	12.6
32	South Dakota	14.2	41	Wyoming	12.4
13	Tennessee	18.8	42	New Jersey	11.6
32	Texas	14.2	43	Virginia	10.8
49	Utah	8.9	44	Kansas	10.3
2	Vermont	25.0	45	North Dakota	9.9
43	Virginia	10.8	46	Colorado	9.8
26	Washington	16.1	47	New Hampshire	9.7
16	West Virginia	18.2	48	Montana	9.3
10	Wisconsin	19.5	49	Utah	8.9
41	Wyoming	12.4	50	Nevada	8.7

District of Columbia 26.9

Source: CQ Press using data from U.S. Department of Health and Human Services, Centers for Medicare and Medicaid Services
"2009 Medicaid Managed Care Enrollment Report" (http://www.cms.hhs.gov/MedicaidDataSourcesGenInfo/)
*Unduplicated enrollment as of December 31, 2009. National percent does not include recipients or population in U.S. territories.

Estimated Medicaid Expenditures in 2010

National Total = $353,837,000,000*

ALPHA ORDER

RANK	STATE	EXPENDITURES	% of USA
26	Alabama	$4,857,000,000	1.4%
46	Alaska	1,120,000,000	0.3%
14	Arizona	7,663,000,000	2.2%
30	Arkansas	4,161,000,000	1.2%
1	California	48,326,000,000	13.7%
27	Colorado	4,770,000,000	1.3%
25	Connecticut	4,980,000,000	1.4%
44	Delaware	1,258,000,000	0.4%
4	Florida	18,810,000,000	5.3%
13	Georgia	7,674,000,000	2.2%
41	Hawaii	1,456,000,000	0.4%
40	Idaho	1,506,000,000	0.4%
5	Illinois	15,551,000,000	4.4%
22	Indiana	6,172,000,000	1.7%
32	Iowa	3,370,000,000	1.0%
35	Kansas	2,509,000,000	0.7%
23	Kentucky	5,693,000,000	1.6%
19	Louisiana	6,626,000,000	1.9%
36	Maine	2,395,000,000	0.7%
18	Maryland	6,661,000,000	1.9%
10	Massachusetts	9,465,000,000	2.7%
8	Michigan	11,529,000,000	3.3%
17	Minnesota	6,774,000,000	1.9%
28	Mississippi	4,255,000,000	1.2%
11	Missouri	8,071,000,000	2.3%
47	Montana	930,000,000	0.3%
39	Nebraska	1,649,000,000	0.5%
43	Nevada	1,364,000,000	0.4%
42	New Hampshire	1,374,000,000	0.4%
9	New Jersey	10,254,000,000	2.9%
33	New Mexico	3,363,000,000	1.0%
2	New York	37,025,000,000	10.5%
7	North Carolina	11,796,000,000	3.3%
49	North Dakota	665,000,000	0.2%
6	Ohio	12,654,000,000	3.6%
29	Oklahoma	4,203,000,000	1.2%
31	Oregon	3,948,000,000	1.1%
3	Pennsylvania	19,427,000,000	5.5%
37	Rhode Island	1,958,000,000	0.6%
24	South Carolina	5,005,000,000	1.4%
48	South Dakota	850,000,000	0.2%
12	Tennessee	7,684,000,000	2.2%
16	Texas	7,322,000,000	2.1%
38	Utah	1,811,000,000	0.5%
45	Vermont	1,213,000,000	0.3%
21	Virginia	6,554,000,000	1.9%
15	Washington	7,440,000,000	2.1%
34	West Virginia	2,551,000,000	0.7%
20	Wisconsin	6,586,000,000	1.9%
50	Wyoming	559,000,000	0.2%

RANK ORDER

RANK	STATE	EXPENDITURES	% of USA
1	California	$48,326,000,000	13.7%
2	New York	37,025,000,000	10.5%
3	Pennsylvania	19,427,000,000	5.5%
4	Florida	18,810,000,000	5.3%
5	Illinois	15,551,000,000	4.4%
6	Ohio	12,654,000,000	3.6%
7	North Carolina	11,796,000,000	3.3%
8	Michigan	11,529,000,000	3.3%
9	New Jersey	10,254,000,000	2.9%
10	Massachusetts	9,465,000,000	2.7%
11	Missouri	8,071,000,000	2.3%
12	Tennessee	7,684,000,000	2.2%
13	Georgia	7,674,000,000	2.2%
14	Arizona	7,663,000,000	2.2%
15	Washington	7,440,000,000	2.1%
16	Texas	7,322,000,000	2.1%
17	Minnesota	6,774,000,000	1.9%
18	Maryland	6,661,000,000	1.9%
19	Louisiana	6,626,000,000	1.9%
20	Wisconsin	6,586,000,000	1.9%
21	Virginia	6,554,000,000	1.9%
22	Indiana	6,172,000,000	1.7%
23	Kentucky	5,693,000,000	1.6%
24	South Carolina	5,005,000,000	1.4%
25	Connecticut	4,980,000,000	1.4%
26	Alabama	4,857,000,000	1.4%
27	Colorado	4,770,000,000	1.3%
28	Mississippi	4,255,000,000	1.2%
29	Oklahoma	4,203,000,000	1.2%
30	Arkansas	4,161,000,000	1.2%
31	Oregon	3,948,000,000	1.1%
32	Iowa	3,370,000,000	1.0%
33	New Mexico	3,363,000,000	1.0%
34	West Virginia	2,551,000,000	0.7%
35	Kansas	2,509,000,000	0.7%
36	Maine	2,395,000,000	0.7%
37	Rhode Island	1,958,000,000	0.6%
38	Utah	1,811,000,000	0.5%
39	Nebraska	1,649,000,000	0.5%
40	Idaho	1,506,000,000	0.4%
41	Hawaii	1,456,000,000	0.4%
42	New Hampshire	1,374,000,000	0.4%
43	Nevada	1,364,000,000	0.4%
44	Delaware	1,258,000,000	0.4%
45	Vermont	1,213,000,000	0.3%
46	Alaska	1,120,000,000	0.3%
47	Montana	930,000,000	0.3%
48	South Dakota	850,000,000	0.2%
49	North Dakota	665,000,000	0.2%
50	Wyoming	559,000,000	0.2%
	District of Columbia**	NA	NA

Source: National Association of State Budget Officers
"2009 State Expenditure Report" (http://www.nasbo.org)
*Estimates for fiscal year 2010.
**Not available.

Percent Change in Medicaid Expenditures: 2009 to 2010

National Percent Change = 8.2% Increase*

ALPHA ORDER

RANK	STATE	PERCENT CHANGE
47	Alabama	(3.8)
14	Alaska	10.0
48	Arizona	(3.9)
6	Arkansas	16.3
1	California	20.1
4	Colorado	17.7
49	Connecticut	(7.5)
5	Delaware	16.8
3	Florida	18.4
43	Georgia	1.1
16	Hawaii	9.4
32	Idaho	4.5
20	Illinois	8.4
12	Indiana	10.3
23	Iowa	7.6
36	Kansas	3.5
37	Kentucky	3.3
24	Louisiana	7.4
45	Maine	(0.9)
25	Maryland	7.2
18	Massachusetts	9.1
16	Michigan	9.4
42	Minnesota	2.2
46	Mississippi	(1.2)
21	Missouri	7.9
11	Montana	10.6
40	Nebraska	2.5
41	Nevada	2.3
33	New Hampshire	4.2
27	New Jersey	5.9
29	New Mexico	5.6
7	New York	14.2
14	North Carolina	10.0
2	North Dakota	20.0
50	Ohio	(9.9)
27	Oklahoma	5.9
8	Oregon	12.6
44	Pennsylvania	0.8
26	Rhode Island	6.9
38	South Carolina	3.2
10	South Dakota	10.7
35	Tennessee	4.0
18	Texas	9.1
30	Utah	5.1
13	Vermont	10.2
22	Virginia	7.8
39	Washington	3.0
31	West Virginia	4.8
9	Wisconsin	11.1
34	Wyoming	4.1

RANK ORDER

RANK	STATE	PERCENT CHANGE
1	California	20.1
2	North Dakota	20.0
3	Florida	18.4
4	Colorado	17.7
5	Delaware	16.8
6	Arkansas	16.3
7	New York	14.2
8	Oregon	12.6
9	Wisconsin	11.1
10	South Dakota	10.7
11	Montana	10.6
12	Indiana	10.3
13	Vermont	10.2
14	Alaska	10.0
14	North Carolina	10.0
16	Hawaii	9.4
16	Michigan	9.4
18	Massachusetts	9.1
18	Texas	9.1
20	Illinois	8.4
21	Missouri	7.9
22	Virginia	7.8
23	Iowa	7.6
24	Louisiana	7.4
25	Maryland	7.2
26	Rhode Island	6.9
27	New Jersey	5.9
27	Oklahoma	5.9
29	New Mexico	5.6
30	Utah	5.1
31	West Virginia	4.8
32	Idaho	4.5
33	New Hampshire	4.2
34	Wyoming	4.1
35	Tennessee	4.0
36	Kansas	3.5
37	Kentucky	3.3
38	South Carolina	3.2
39	Washington	3.0
40	Nebraska	2.5
41	Nevada	2.3
42	Minnesota	2.2
43	Georgia	1.1
44	Pennsylvania	0.8
45	Maine	(0.9)
46	Mississippi	(1.2)
47	Alabama	(3.8)
48	Arizona	(3.9)
49	Connecticut	(7.5)
50	Ohio	(9.9)

District of Columbia**   NA

Source: National Association of State Budget Officers
"2009 State Expenditure Report" (http://www.nasbo.org)
*Estimates for fiscal year 2010.
**Not available.

Percent of Population Receiving Public Aid in 2008

National Percent = 3.8% of Population*

ALPHA ORDER

RANK	STATE	PERCENT
9	Alabama	4.5
28	Alaska	2.8
24	Arizona	2.9
13	Arkansas	4.1
1	California	7.0
48	Colorado	1.6
38	Connecticut	2.5
21	Delaware	3.2
24	Florida	2.9
35	Georgia	2.6
24	Hawaii	2.9
47	Idaho	1.8
38	Illinois	2.5
19	Indiana	3.4
28	Iowa	2.8
35	Kansas	2.6
2	Kentucky	5.8
11	Louisiana	4.2
10	Maine	4.4
33	Maryland	2.7
11	Massachusetts	4.2
15	Michigan	3.9
40	Minnesota	2.4
4	Mississippi	5.0
18	Missouri	3.5
35	Montana	2.6
43	Nebraska	2.3
44	Nevada	2.2
46	New Hampshire	2.1
28	New Jersey	2.8
6	New Mexico	4.9
7	New York	4.7
28	North Carolina	2.8
44	North Dakota	2.2
14	Ohio	4.0
24	Oklahoma	2.9
23	Oregon	3.0
17	Pennsylvania	3.6
7	Rhode Island	4.7
21	South Carolina	3.2
40	South Dakota	2.4
4	Tennessee	5.0
28	Texas	2.8
49	Utah	1.4
20	Vermont	3.3
33	Virginia	2.7
15	Washington	3.9
3	West Virginia	5.5
40	Wisconsin	2.4
50	Wyoming	1.2

RANK ORDER

RANK	STATE	PERCENT
1	California	7.0
2	Kentucky	5.8
3	West Virginia	5.5
4	Mississippi	5.0
4	Tennessee	5.0
6	New Mexico	4.9
7	New York	4.7
7	Rhode Island	4.7
9	Alabama	4.5
10	Maine	4.4
11	Louisiana	4.2
11	Massachusetts	4.2
13	Arkansas	4.1
14	Ohio	4.0
15	Michigan	3.9
15	Washington	3.9
17	Pennsylvania	3.6
18	Missouri	3.5
19	Indiana	3.4
20	Vermont	3.3
21	Delaware	3.2
21	South Carolina	3.2
23	Oregon	3.0
24	Arizona	2.9
24	Florida	2.9
24	Hawaii	2.9
24	Oklahoma	2.9
28	Alaska	2.8
28	Iowa	2.8
28	New Jersey	2.8
28	North Carolina	2.8
28	Texas	2.8
33	Maryland	2.7
33	Virginia	2.7
35	Georgia	2.6
35	Kansas	2.6
35	Montana	2.6
38	Connecticut	2.5
38	Illinois	2.5
40	Minnesota	2.4
40	South Dakota	2.4
40	Wisconsin	2.4
43	Nebraska	2.3
44	Nevada	2.2
44	North Dakota	2.2
46	New Hampshire	2.1
47	Idaho	1.8
48	Colorado	1.6
49	Utah	1.4
50	Wyoming	1.2

| | District of Columbia | 6.0 |

Source: CQ Press using data from U.S. Social Security Administration and
U.S. Department of Health and Human Services

*As of December 2008. Includes recipients of Temporary Assistance to Needy Families (TANF) and/or Supplemental Security Income payments.

Recipients of Temporary Assistance to
Needy Families (TANF) Payments in 2010
National Total = 4,334,354 Monthly Recipients*

ALPHA ORDER

RANK	STATE	RECIPIENTS	% of USA
22	Alabama	51,555	1.2%
NA	Alaska**	NA	NA
16	Arizona	67,908	1.6%
39	Arkansas	18,760	0.4%
1	California	1,424,405	32.9%
30	Colorado	29,887	0.7%
29	Connecticut	33,742	0.8%
42	Delaware	15,212	0.4%
9	Florida	102,735	2.4%
27	Georgia	37,095	0.9%
33	Hawaii	25,241	0.6%
48	Idaho	2,644	0.1%
17	Illinois	61,574	1.4%
11	Indiana	86,943	2.0%
24	Iowa	44,975	1.0%
28	Kansas	36,279	0.8%
18	Kentucky	60,904	1.4%
35	Louisiana	22,783	0.5%
32	Maine	25,354	0.6%
19	Maryland	58,239	1.3%
10	Massachusetts	96,363	2.2%
4	Michigan	173,215	4.0%
23	Minnesota	49,222	1.1%
34	Mississippi	25,216	0.6%
12	Missouri	84,515	1.9%
44	Montana	9,245	0.2%
38	Nebraska	18,778	0.4%
31	Nevada	26,925	0.6%
43	New Hampshire	11,072	0.3%
13	New Jersey	79,656	1.8%
21	New Mexico	51,909	1.2%
2	New York	268,887	6.2%
25	North Carolina	44,368	1.0%
47	North Dakota	4,835	0.1%
3	Ohio	237,168	5.5%
37	Oklahoma	20,215	0.5%
15	Oregon	71,212	1.6%
7	Pennsylvania	125,367	2.9%
40	Rhode Island	17,203	0.4%
26	South Carolina	41,669	1.0%
45	South Dakota	6,791	0.2%
6	Tennessee	156,164	3.6%
8	Texas	113,772	2.6%
41	Utah	16,846	0.4%
46	Vermont	6,155	0.1%
14	Virginia	79,373	1.8%
5	Washington	160,374	3.7%
36	West Virginia	21,554	0.5%
20	Wisconsin	53,639	1.2%
49	Wyoming	695	0.0%

RANK ORDER

RANK	STATE	RECIPIENTS	% of USA
1	California	1,424,405	32.9%
2	New York	268,887	6.2%
3	Ohio	237,168	5.5%
4	Michigan	173,215	4.0%
5	Washington	160,374	3.7%
6	Tennessee	156,164	3.6%
7	Pennsylvania	125,367	2.9%
8	Texas	113,772	2.6%
9	Florida	102,735	2.4%
10	Massachusetts	96,363	2.2%
11	Indiana	86,943	2.0%
12	Missouri	84,515	1.9%
13	New Jersey	79,656	1.8%
14	Virginia	79,373	1.8%
15	Oregon	71,212	1.6%
16	Arizona	67,908	1.6%
17	Illinois	61,574	1.4%
18	Kentucky	60,904	1.4%
19	Maryland	58,239	1.3%
20	Wisconsin	53,639	1.2%
21	New Mexico	51,909	1.2%
22	Alabama	51,555	1.2%
23	Minnesota	49,222	1.1%
24	Iowa	44,975	1.0%
25	North Carolina	44,368	1.0%
26	South Carolina	41,669	1.0%
27	Georgia	37,095	0.9%
28	Kansas	36,279	0.8%
29	Connecticut	33,742	0.8%
30	Colorado	29,887	0.7%
31	Nevada	26,925	0.6%
32	Maine	25,354	0.6%
33	Hawaii	25,241	0.6%
34	Mississippi	25,216	0.6%
35	Louisiana	22,783	0.5%
36	West Virginia	21,554	0.5%
37	Oklahoma	20,215	0.5%
38	Nebraska	18,778	0.4%
39	Arkansas	18,760	0.4%
40	Rhode Island	17,203	0.4%
41	Utah	16,846	0.4%
42	Delaware	15,212	0.4%
43	New Hampshire	11,072	0.3%
44	Montana	9,245	0.2%
45	South Dakota	6,791	0.2%
46	Vermont	6,155	0.1%
47	North Dakota	4,835	0.1%
48	Idaho	2,644	0.1%
49	Wyoming	695	0.0%
NA	Alaska**	NA	NA
	District of Columbia	15,022	0.3%

Source: U.S. Department of Health and Human Services, Administration for Children and Families
"TANF Caseload Data" (http://www.acf.hhs.gov/programs/ofa/data-reports/index.htm)
*As of June 2010. Welfare reform replaced the Aid to Families with Dependent Children program (AFDC) with Temporary Assistance to Needy Families (TANF) as of July 1, 1997. National total includes 40,694 recipients in U.S. territories (36,175 in Puerto Rico).
**Not available.

Percent Change in TANF Recipients: 2009 to 2010

National Percent Change = 6.1% Increase*

ALPHA ORDER

RANK	STATE	PERCENT CHANGE
5	Alabama	18.5
NA	Alaska**	NA
49	Arizona	(16.2)
43	Arkansas	(2.2)
24	California	6.1
3	Colorado	24.1
32	Connecticut	3.6
6	Delaware	18.0
37	Florida	2.7
42	Georgia	(1.3)
8	Hawaii	16.0
13	Idaho	9.9
7	Illinois	16.3
48	Indiana	(14.2)
15	Iowa	9.4
30	Kansas	4.4
39	Kentucky	2.1
35	Louisiana	3.1
34	Maine	3.3
21	Maryland	6.8
32	Massachusetts	3.6
20	Michigan	7.4
40	Minnesota	1.6
12	Mississippi	10.4
41	Missouri	0.6
27	Montana	5.3
17	Nebraska	9.2
4	Nevada	20.9
46	New Hampshire	(12.4)
28	New Jersey	4.8
9	New Mexico	15.7
36	New York	2.8
47	North Carolina	(13.3)
45	North Dakota	(10.2)
10	Ohio	12.1
31	Oklahoma	4.1
1	Oregon	37.2
23	Pennsylvania	6.4
28	Rhode Island	4.8
11	South Carolina	11.1
16	South Dakota	9.3
38	Tennessee	2.5
14	Texas	9.7
22	Utah	6.6
44	Vermont	(3.7)
26	Virginia	5.7
19	Washington	8.7
25	West Virginia	5.8
2	Wisconsin	31.4
18	Wyoming	8.9

RANK ORDER

RANK	STATE	PERCENT CHANGE
1	Oregon	37.2
2	Wisconsin	31.4
3	Colorado	24.1
4	Nevada	20.9
5	Alabama	18.5
6	Delaware	18.0
7	Illinois	16.3
8	Hawaii	16.0
9	New Mexico	15.7
10	Ohio	12.1
11	South Carolina	11.1
12	Mississippi	10.4
13	Idaho	9.9
14	Texas	9.7
15	Iowa	9.4
16	South Dakota	9.3
17	Nebraska	9.2
18	Wyoming	8.9
19	Washington	8.7
20	Michigan	7.4
21	Maryland	6.8
22	Utah	6.6
23	Pennsylvania	6.4
24	California	6.1
25	West Virginia	5.8
26	Virginia	5.7
27	Montana	5.3
28	New Jersey	4.8
28	Rhode Island	4.8
30	Kansas	4.4
31	Oklahoma	4.1
32	Connecticut	3.6
32	Massachusetts	3.6
34	Maine	3.3
35	Louisiana	3.1
36	New York	2.8
37	Florida	2.7
38	Tennessee	2.5
39	Kentucky	2.1
40	Minnesota	1.6
41	Missouri	0.6
42	Georgia	(1.3)
43	Arkansas	(2.2)
44	Vermont	(3.7)
45	North Dakota	(10.2)
46	New Hampshire	(12.4)
47	North Carolina	(13.3)
48	Indiana	(14.2)
49	Arizona	(16.2)
NA	Alaska**	NA
	District of Columbia**	NA

Source: CQ Press using data from U.S. Department of Health and Human Services, Administration for Children and Families
"TANF Caseload Data" (http://www.acf.hhs.gov/programs/ofa/data-reports/index.htm)
*June 2009 to June 2010. Welfare reform replaced the Aid to Families with Dependent Children program (AFDC) with Temporary
Assistance to Needy Families (TANF) as of July 1, 1997. National percent includes recipients in U.S. territories.
**Not available.

TANF Work Participation Rates in 2008

National Rate = 29.4%*

ALPHA ORDER

RANK	STATE	PERCENT
25	Alabama	37.4
14	Alaska	42.8
36	Arizona	27.8
20	Arkansas	38.8
39	California	25.1
31	Colorado	32.3
37	Connecticut	25.3
9	Delaware	48.8
16	Florida	42.4
4	Georgia	59.0
29	Hawaii	34.4
3	Idaho	59.5
15	Illinois	42.6
33	Indiana	29.4
18	Iowa	41.1
44	Kansas	19.6
22	Kentucky	38.0
19	Louisiana	40.0
50	Maine	11.4
28	Maryland	36.9
12	Massachusetts	44.7
30	Michigan	33.6
32	Minnesota	29.9
1	Mississippi	63.2
49	Missouri	14.2
13	Montana	44.2
6	Nebraska	51.2
17	Nevada	42.1
10	New Hampshire	47.4
45	New Jersey	18.9
24	New Mexico	37.5
26	New York	37.3
40	North Carolina	24.5
8	North Dakota	50.2
40	Ohio	24.5
35	Oklahoma	29.2
42	Oregon	24.1
21	Pennsylvania	38.6
48	Rhode Island	17.5
5	South Carolina	51.7
2	South Dakota	62.2
38	Tennessee	25.2
34	Texas	29.3
23	Utah	37.6
43	Vermont	23.2
11	Virginia	45.4
46	Washington	18.3
47	West Virginia	17.6
27	Wisconsin	37.1
7	Wyoming	50.5

RANK ORDER

RANK	STATE	PERCENT
1	Mississippi	63.2
2	South Dakota	62.2
3	Idaho	59.5
4	Georgia	59.0
5	South Carolina	51.7
6	Nebraska	51.2
7	Wyoming	50.5
8	North Dakota	50.2
9	Delaware	48.8
10	New Hampshire	47.4
11	Virginia	45.4
12	Massachusetts	44.7
13	Montana	44.2
14	Alaska	42.8
15	Illinois	42.6
16	Florida	42.4
17	Nevada	42.1
18	Iowa	41.1
19	Louisiana	40.0
20	Arkansas	38.8
21	Pennsylvania	38.6
22	Kentucky	38.0
23	Utah	37.6
24	New Mexico	37.5
25	Alabama	37.4
26	New York	37.3
27	Wisconsin	37.1
28	Maryland	36.9
29	Hawaii	34.4
30	Michigan	33.6
31	Colorado	32.3
32	Minnesota	29.9
33	Indiana	29.4
34	Texas	29.3
35	Oklahoma	29.2
36	Arizona	27.8
37	Connecticut	25.3
38	Tennessee	25.2
39	California	25.1
40	North Carolina	24.5
40	Ohio	24.5
42	Oregon	24.1
43	Vermont	23.2
44	Kansas	19.6
45	New Jersey	18.9
46	Washington	18.3
47	West Virginia	17.6
48	Rhode Island	17.5
49	Missouri	14.2
50	Maine	11.4
	District of Columbia	49.6

Source: U.S. Department of Health and Human Services, Administration for Children and Families
"Table 1A: TANF Work Participation Rates" (http://www.acf.hhs.gov/programs/ofa/particip/2008/tab1a.htm)
*For fiscal year 2008. Percent of parents in TANF families who work for at least 30 hours per week, or 20 hours per week if they have children under age six. Welfare reform replaced the Aid to Families with Dependent Children program (AFDC) with Temporary Assistance to Needy Families (TANF) as of July 1, 1997. National average includes recipients in U.S. territories.

Average Monthly TANF Assistance per Family in 2008

National Average = $382.95*

ALPHA ORDER				RANK ORDER		
RANK	STATE	PER FAMILY		RANK	STATE	PER FAMILY
44	Alabama	$171.64		1	Alaska	$512.52
1	Alaska	512.52		2	New York	488.85
31	Arizona	234.06		3	Hawaii	476.84
50	Arkansas	123.11		4	Massachusetts	441.86
6	California	436.20		5	New Hampshire	440.92
38	Colorado	200.67		6	California	436.20
8	Connecticut	393.42		7	Vermont	428.23
36	Delaware	207.40		8	Connecticut	393.42
32	Florida	223.32		9	Washington	375.14
46	Georgia	161.52		10	Utah	372.10
3	Hawaii	476.84		11	Rhode Island	352.77
16	Idaho	302.40		12	Oregon	344.28
49	Illinois	127.63		13	Maryland	329.95
43	Indiana	175.40		14	South Dakota	320.45
26	Iowa	256.56		15	Montana	312.16
28	Kansas	242.24		16	Idaho	302.40
35	Kentucky	208.01		17	Nevada	300.27
39	Louisiana	197.52		18	Wisconsin	297.97
19	Maine	289.82		19	Maine	289.82
13	Maryland	329.95		20	Minnesota	286.39
4	Massachusetts	441.86		21	Ohio	274.17
24	Michigan	259.94		22	New Mexico	273.68
20	Minnesota	286.39		23	North Dakota	265.16
41	Mississippi	187.69		24	Michigan	259.94
34	Missouri	215.46		25	West Virginia	259.12
15	Montana	312.16		26	Iowa	256.56
37	Nebraska	207.32		27	New Jersey	252.66
17	Nevada	300.27		28	Kansas	242.24
5	New Hampshire	440.92		29	Pennsylvania	238.58
27	New Jersey	252.66		30	Texas	234.38
22	New Mexico	273.68		31	Arizona	234.06
2	New York	488.85		32	Florida	223.32
40	North Carolina	189.25		33	Virginia	218.40
23	North Dakota	265.16		34	Missouri	215.46
21	Ohio	274.17		35	Kentucky	208.01
48	Oklahoma	130.65		36	Delaware	207.40
12	Oregon	344.28		37	Nebraska	207.32
29	Pennsylvania	238.58		38	Colorado	200.67
11	Rhode Island	352.77		39	Louisiana	197.52
45	South Carolina	162.45		40	North Carolina	189.25
14	South Dakota	320.45		41	Mississippi	187.69
47	Tennessee	136.86		42	Wyoming	185.43
30	Texas	234.38		43	Indiana	175.40
10	Utah	372.10		44	Alabama	171.64
7	Vermont	428.23		45	South Carolina	162.45
33	Virginia	218.40		46	Georgia	161.52
9	Washington	375.14		47	Tennessee	136.86
25	West Virginia	259.12		48	Oklahoma	130.65
18	Wisconsin	297.97		49	Illinois	127.63
42	Wyoming	185.43		50	Arkansas	123.11
					District of Columbia	280.95

Source: U.S. Department of Health and Human Services, Administration for Children and Families
    "Average Monthly Amount of Assistance" (http://www.acf.hhs.gov/programs/ofa/character/FY2008/tab41.htm)
*For fiscal year 2008.   Welfare reform replaced the Aid to Families with Dependent Children program (AFDC) with Temporary
Assistance to Needy Families (TANF) as of July 1, 1997. National average includes families in U.S. territories.

Percent of Households with Food Insecurity in 2009

National Percent = 13.5% of Households*

ALPHA ORDER

RANK	STATE	PERCENT
7	Alabama	15.0
25	Alaska	12.9
13	Arizona	14.5
1	Arkansas	17.7
16	California	14.1
30	Colorado	12.2
38	Connecticut	11.4
47	Delaware	9.5
14	Florida	14.2
4	Georgia	15.6
38	Hawaii	11.4
35	Idaho	11.6
30	Illinois	12.2
29	Indiana	12.3
36	Iowa	11.5
14	Kansas	14.2
22	Kentucky	13.4
44	Louisiana	10.0
9	Maine	14.8
42	Maryland	11.1
44	Massachusetts	10.0
22	Michigan	13.4
43	Minnesota	10.5
3	Mississippi	17.1
7	Missouri	15.0
27	Montana	12.4
30	Nebraska	12.2
26	Nevada	12.8
49	New Hampshire	8.9
36	New Jersey	11.5
12	New Mexico	14.7
27	New York	12.4
9	North Carolina	14.8
50	North Dakota	6.7
9	Ohio	14.8
5	Oklahoma	15.2
18	Oregon	13.9
33	Pennsylvania	11.8
19	Rhode Island	13.7
21	South Carolina	13.5
41	South Dakota	11.2
6	Tennessee	15.1
2	Texas	17.4
33	Utah	11.8
20	Vermont	13.6
48	Virginia	9.2
17	Washington	14.0
22	West Virginia	13.4
38	Wisconsin	11.4
46	Wyoming	9.8

RANK ORDER

RANK	STATE	PERCENT
1	Arkansas	17.7
2	Texas	17.4
3	Mississippi	17.1
4	Georgia	15.6
5	Oklahoma	15.2
6	Tennessee	15.1
7	Alabama	15.0
7	Missouri	15.0
9	Maine	14.8
9	North Carolina	14.8
9	Ohio	14.8
12	New Mexico	14.7
13	Arizona	14.5
14	Florida	14.2
14	Kansas	14.2
16	California	14.1
17	Washington	14.0
18	Oregon	13.9
19	Rhode Island	13.7
20	Vermont	13.6
21	South Carolina	13.5
22	Kentucky	13.4
22	Michigan	13.4
22	West Virginia	13.4
25	Alaska	12.9
26	Nevada	12.8
27	Montana	12.4
27	New York	12.4
29	Indiana	12.3
30	Colorado	12.2
30	Illinois	12.2
30	Nebraska	12.2
33	Pennsylvania	11.8
33	Utah	11.8
35	Idaho	11.6
36	Iowa	11.5
36	New Jersey	11.5
38	Connecticut	11.4
38	Hawaii	11.4
38	Wisconsin	11.4
41	South Dakota	11.2
42	Maryland	11.1
43	Minnesota	10.5
44	Louisiana	10.0
44	Massachusetts	10.0
46	Wyoming	9.8
47	Delaware	9.5
48	Virginia	9.2
49	New Hampshire	8.9
50	North Dakota	6.7

District of Columbia   12.9

Source: U.S. Department of Agriculture, Economic Research Service
"Household Food Security in the United States, 2009" (http://www.ers.usda.gov/Publications/ERR108/)
*Three-year average for 2007-2009. Refers to households for which access to enough food is limited by a lack of money and other resources. About one-third of food-insecure households have very low food security, meaning that at times the food intake of some household members is reduced and their normal eating patterns are disrupted.

Supplemental Nutrition Assistance Program Benefits in 2010

National Total = $64,704,631,665*

ALPHA ORDER

RANK	STATE	BENEFITS	% of USA
18	Alabama	$1,226,018,708	1.9%
45	Alaska	159,413,978	0.2%
12	Arizona	1,587,702,249	2.5%
29	Arkansas	686,400,617	1.1%
1	California	5,694,135,988	8.8%
28	Colorado	687,709,379	1.1%
31	Connecticut	569,684,382	0.9%
44	Delaware	171,155,272	0.3%
4	Florida	4,416,942,533	6.8%
8	Georgia	2,565,169,527	4.0%
38	Hawaii	358,144,853	0.6%
40	Idaho	299,552,014	0.5%
6	Illinois	2,784,473,892	4.3%
15	Indiana	1,291,225,153	2.0%
33	Iowa	526,119,310	0.8%
36	Kansas	402,630,483	0.6%
20	Kentucky	1,186,291,238	1.8%
16	Louisiana	1,285,916,247	2.0%
39	Maine	356,097,335	0.6%
26	Maryland	877,975,713	1.4%
21	Massachusetts	1,165,907,744	1.8%
5	Michigan	2,808,763,231	4.3%
30	Minnesota	625,094,300	1.0%
27	Mississippi	846,542,922	1.3%
14	Missouri	1,361,300,993	2.1%
43	Montana	176,546,027	0.3%
42	Nebraska	237,577,180	0.4%
35	Nevada	414,596,369	0.6%
47	New Hampshire	151,813,784	0.2%
23	New Jersey	1,030,292,837	1.6%
32	New Mexico	541,806,403	0.8%
3	New York	4,984,900,302	7.7%
10	North Carolina	2,072,127,398	3.2%
49	North Dakota	95,014,675	0.1%
7	Ohio	2,733,689,660	4.2%
25	Oklahoma	899,655,548	1.4%
22	Oregon	1,067,273,327	1.6%
9	Pennsylvania	2,332,575,204	3.6%
41	Rhode Island	237,618,372	0.4%
17	South Carolina	1,256,298,352	1.9%
46	South Dakota	153,075,454	0.2%
11	Tennessee	1,966,107,581	3.0%
2	Texas	5,447,397,414	8.4%
37	Utah	366,903,456	0.6%
48	Vermont	124,311,833	0.2%
19	Virginia	1,213,496,417	1.9%
13	Washington	1,386,585,984	2.1%
34	West Virginia	486,939,521	0.8%
24	Wisconsin	1,000,416,198	1.5%
50	Wyoming	51,674,879	0.1%

RANK ORDER

RANK	STATE	BENEFITS	% of USA
1	California	$5,694,135,988	8.8%
2	Texas	5,447,397,414	8.4%
3	New York	4,984,900,302	7.7%
4	Florida	4,416,942,533	6.8%
5	Michigan	2,808,763,231	4.3%
6	Illinois	2,784,473,892	4.3%
7	Ohio	2,733,689,660	4.2%
8	Georgia	2,565,169,527	4.0%
9	Pennsylvania	2,332,575,204	3.6%
10	North Carolina	2,072,127,398	3.2%
11	Tennessee	1,966,107,581	3.0%
12	Arizona	1,587,702,249	2.5%
13	Washington	1,386,585,984	2.1%
14	Missouri	1,361,300,993	2.1%
15	Indiana	1,291,225,153	2.0%
16	Louisiana	1,285,916,247	2.0%
17	South Carolina	1,256,298,352	1.9%
18	Alabama	1,226,018,708	1.9%
19	Virginia	1,213,496,417	1.9%
20	Kentucky	1,186,291,238	1.8%
21	Massachusetts	1,165,907,744	1.8%
22	Oregon	1,067,273,327	1.6%
23	New Jersey	1,030,292,837	1.6%
24	Wisconsin	1,000,416,198	1.5%
25	Oklahoma	899,655,548	1.4%
26	Maryland	877,975,713	1.4%
27	Mississippi	846,542,922	1.3%
28	Colorado	687,709,379	1.1%
29	Arkansas	686,400,617	1.1%
30	Minnesota	625,094,300	1.0%
31	Connecticut	569,684,382	0.9%
32	New Mexico	541,806,403	0.8%
33	Iowa	526,119,310	0.8%
34	West Virginia	486,939,521	0.8%
35	Nevada	414,596,369	0.6%
36	Kansas	402,630,483	0.6%
37	Utah	366,903,456	0.6%
38	Hawaii	358,144,853	0.6%
39	Maine	356,097,335	0.6%
40	Idaho	299,552,014	0.5%
41	Rhode Island	237,618,372	0.4%
42	Nebraska	237,577,180	0.4%
43	Montana	176,546,027	0.3%
44	Delaware	171,155,272	0.3%
45	Alaska	159,413,978	0.2%
46	South Dakota	153,075,454	0.2%
47	New Hampshire	151,813,784	0.2%
48	Vermont	124,311,833	0.2%
49	North Dakota	95,014,675	0.1%
50	Wyoming	51,674,879	0.1%
	District of Columbia	195,893,308	0.3%

Source: U.S. Department of Agriculture, Food, Nutrition and Consumer Services
   "Supplemental Nutrition Assistance Program" (http://www.fns.usda.gov/pd/snapmain.htm)
*Preliminary data for fiscal year 2010. National total includes $139,676,121 to U.S. territories. Costs are for benefits only and exclude administrative expenditures. Program formerly called the Food Stamp Program.

Monthly Supplemental Nutrition Assistance Program Recipients in 2010

National Total = 40,301,666 Recipients*

ALPHA ORDER

RANK	STATE	RECIPIENTS	% of USA
17	Alabama	805,095	2.0%
48	Alaska	76,445	0.2%
12	Arizona	1,018,171	2.5%
28	Arkansas	466,598	1.2%
2	California	3,238,548	8.0%
30	Colorado	404,679	1.0%
34	Connecticut	336,064	0.8%
44	Delaware	112,513	0.3%
4	Florida	2,603,185	6.5%
8	Georgia	1,591,078	3.9%
42	Hawaii	138,166	0.3%
39	Idaho	194,033	0.5%
6	Illinois	1,645,722	4.1%
16	Indiana	813,403	2.0%
33	Iowa	340,304	0.8%
36	Kansas	269,710	0.7%
20	Kentucky	778,114	1.9%
15	Louisiana	825,918	2.0%
38	Maine	229,731	0.6%
27	Maryland	560,848	1.4%
21	Massachusetts	749,121	1.9%
5	Michigan	1,776,368	4.4%
29	Minnesota	430,346	1.1%
26	Mississippi	575,674	1.4%
14	Missouri	901,349	2.2%
43	Montana	113,570	0.3%
40	Nebraska	162,817	0.4%
35	Nevada	278,105	0.7%
45	New Hampshire	104,375	0.3%
24	New Jersey	622,022	1.5%
31	New Mexico	356,822	0.9%
3	New York	2,757,836	6.8%
10	North Carolina	1,346,495	3.3%
49	North Dakota	59,888	0.1%
7	Ohio	1,607,422	4.0%
25	Oklahoma	582,492	1.4%
23	Oregon	704,822	1.7%
9	Pennsylvania	1,574,783	3.9%
41	Rhode Island	138,966	0.3%
18	South Carolina	797,110	2.0%
46	South Dakota	95,336	0.2%
11	Tennessee	1,224,023	3.0%
1	Texas	3,551,581	8.8%
37	Utah	247,405	0.6%
47	Vermont	85,538	0.2%
19	Virginia	786,157	2.0%
13	Washington	956,004	2.4%
32	West Virginia	341,156	0.8%
22	Wisconsin	715,213	1.8%
50	Wyoming	34,799	0.1%

RANK ORDER

RANK	STATE	RECIPIENTS	% of USA
1	Texas	3,551,581	8.8%
2	California	3,238,548	8.0%
3	New York	2,757,836	6.8%
4	Florida	2,603,185	6.5%
5	Michigan	1,776,368	4.4%
6	Illinois	1,645,722	4.1%
7	Ohio	1,607,422	4.0%
8	Georgia	1,591,078	3.9%
9	Pennsylvania	1,574,783	3.9%
10	North Carolina	1,346,495	3.3%
11	Tennessee	1,224,023	3.0%
12	Arizona	1,018,171	2.5%
13	Washington	956,004	2.4%
14	Missouri	901,349	2.2%
15	Louisiana	825,918	2.0%
16	Indiana	813,403	2.0%
17	Alabama	805,095	2.0%
18	South Carolina	797,110	2.0%
19	Virginia	786,157	2.0%
20	Kentucky	778,114	1.9%
21	Massachusetts	749,121	1.9%
22	Wisconsin	715,213	1.8%
23	Oregon	704,822	1.7%
24	New Jersey	622,022	1.5%
25	Oklahoma	582,492	1.4%
26	Mississippi	575,674	1.4%
27	Maryland	560,848	1.4%
28	Arkansas	466,598	1.2%
29	Minnesota	430,346	1.1%
30	Colorado	404,679	1.0%
31	New Mexico	356,822	0.9%
32	West Virginia	341,156	0.8%
33	Iowa	340,304	0.8%
34	Connecticut	336,064	0.8%
35	Nevada	278,105	0.7%
36	Kansas	269,710	0.7%
37	Utah	247,405	0.6%
38	Maine	229,731	0.6%
39	Idaho	194,033	0.5%
40	Nebraska	162,817	0.4%
41	Rhode Island	138,966	0.3%
42	Hawaii	138,166	0.3%
43	Montana	113,570	0.3%
44	Delaware	112,513	0.3%
45	New Hampshire	104,375	0.3%
46	South Dakota	95,336	0.2%
47	Vermont	85,538	0.2%
48	Alaska	76,445	0.2%
49	North Dakota	59,888	0.1%
50	Wyoming	34,799	0.1%
	District of Columbia	118,493	0.3%

Source: U.S. Department of Agriculture, Food, Nutrition and Consumer Services
    "Supplemental Nutrition Assistance Program" (http://www.fns.usda.gov/pd/snapmain.htm)
*Preliminary for fiscal year 2010. National total includes 57,254 recipients in U.S. territories. Program was formerly called the Food Stamp Program.

Average Monthly Supplemental Nutrition Assistance Program
Benefit per Recipient in 2010
National Average = $133.79 per Recipient*

ALPHA ORDER

RANK	STATE	PER RECIPIENT
32	Alabama	$126.90
2	Alaska	173.78
20	Arizona	129.95
42	Arkansas	122.59
4	California	146.52
7	Colorado	141.62
9	Connecticut	141.26
33	Delaware	126.77
8	Florida	141.40
12	Georgia	134.35
1	Hawaii	216.01
27	Idaho	128.65
10	Illinois	141.00
15	Indiana	132.29
25	Iowa	128.84
37	Kansas	124.40
31	Kentucky	127.05
21	Louisiana	129.75
24	Maine	129.17
19	Maryland	130.45
22	Massachusetts	129.70
17	Michigan	131.77
47	Minnesota	121.05
43	Mississippi	122.54
36	Missouri	125.86
23	Montana	129.54
44	Nebraska	121.60
38	Nevada	124.23
45	New Hampshire	121.21
11	New Jersey	138.03
34	New Mexico	126.54
3	New York	150.63
29	North Carolina	128.24
16	North Dakota	132.21
6	Ohio	141.72
26	Oklahoma	128.71
35	Oregon	126.19
41	Pennsylvania	123.43
5	Rhode Island	142.49
18	South Carolina	131.34
14	South Dakota	133.80
13	Tennessee	133.86
30	Texas	127.82
40	Utah	123.58
46	Vermont	121.11
28	Virginia	128.63
48	Washington	120.87
49	West Virginia	118.94
50	Wisconsin	116.56
39	Wyoming	123.75

RANK ORDER

RANK	STATE	PER RECIPIENT
1	Hawaii	$216.01
2	Alaska	173.78
3	New York	150.63
4	California	146.52
5	Rhode Island	142.49
6	Ohio	141.72
7	Colorado	141.62
8	Florida	141.40
9	Connecticut	141.26
10	Illinois	141.00
11	New Jersey	138.03
12	Georgia	134.35
13	Tennessee	133.86
14	South Dakota	133.80
15	Indiana	132.29
16	North Dakota	132.21
17	Michigan	131.77
18	South Carolina	131.34
19	Maryland	130.45
20	Arizona	129.95
21	Louisiana	129.75
22	Massachusetts	129.70
23	Montana	129.54
24	Maine	129.17
25	Iowa	128.84
26	Oklahoma	128.71
27	Idaho	128.65
28	Virginia	128.63
29	North Carolina	128.24
30	Texas	127.82
31	Kentucky	127.05
32	Alabama	126.90
33	Delaware	126.77
34	New Mexico	126.54
35	Oregon	126.19
36	Missouri	125.86
37	Kansas	124.40
38	Nevada	124.23
39	Wyoming	123.75
40	Utah	123.58
41	Pennsylvania	123.43
42	Arkansas	122.59
43	Mississippi	122.54
44	Nebraska	121.60
45	New Hampshire	121.21
46	Vermont	121.11
47	Minnesota	121.05
48	Washington	120.87
49	West Virginia	118.94
50	Wisconsin	116.56
	District of Columbia	137.77

Source: U.S. Department of Agriculture, Food, Nutrition and Consumer Services
"Supplemental Nutrition Assistance Program" (http://www.fns.usda.gov/pd/snapmain.htm)
*Preliminary for fiscal year 2010. National average includes recipients in U.S. territories. Program formerly called the Food Stamp Program.

Percent of Population Receiving
Supplemental Nutrition Assistance Program Benefits in 2010
National Percent = 13.1%*

ALPHA ORDER

RANK	STATE	PERCENT
11	Alabama	17.1
35	Alaska	10.9
15	Arizona	15.4
13	Arkansas	16.1
45	California	8.8
47	Colorado	8.1
40	Connecticut	9.6
25	Delaware	12.7
21	Florida	14.0
12	Georgia	16.2
36	Hawaii	10.7
28	Idaho	12.6
25	Illinois	12.7
25	Indiana	12.7
34	Iowa	11.3
40	Kansas	9.6
6	Kentucky	18.0
4	Louisiana	18.4
10	Maine	17.4
39	Maryland	9.8
33	Massachusetts	11.4
7	Michigan	17.8
46	Minnesota	8.2
1	Mississippi	19.5
16	Missouri	15.1
32	Montana	11.6
43	Nebraska	9.1
37	Nevada	10.5
48	New Hampshire	7.9
49	New Jersey	7.1
7	New Mexico	17.8
20	New York	14.1
17	North Carolina	14.4
42	North Dakota	9.3
22	Ohio	13.9
14	Oklahoma	15.8
4	Oregon	18.4
30	Pennsylvania	12.5
24	Rhode Island	13.2
9	South Carolina	17.5
31	South Dakota	11.7
2	Tennessee	19.4
18	Texas	14.3
44	Utah	8.9
23	Vermont	13.8
38	Virginia	10.0
18	Washington	14.3
3	West Virginia	18.7
28	Wisconsin	12.6
50	Wyoming	6.4

RANK ORDER

RANK	STATE	PERCENT
1	Mississippi	19.5
2	Tennessee	19.4
3	West Virginia	18.7
4	Louisiana	18.4
4	Oregon	18.4
6	Kentucky	18.0
7	Michigan	17.8
7	New Mexico	17.8
9	South Carolina	17.5
10	Maine	17.4
11	Alabama	17.1
12	Georgia	16.2
13	Arkansas	16.1
14	Oklahoma	15.8
15	Arizona	15.4
16	Missouri	15.1
17	North Carolina	14.4
18	Texas	14.3
18	Washington	14.3
20	New York	14.1
21	Florida	14.0
22	Ohio	13.9
23	Vermont	13.8
24	Rhode Island	13.2
25	Delaware	12.7
25	Illinois	12.7
25	Indiana	12.7
28	Idaho	12.6
28	Wisconsin	12.6
30	Pennsylvania	12.5
31	South Dakota	11.7
32	Montana	11.6
33	Massachusetts	11.4
34	Iowa	11.3
35	Alaska	10.9
36	Hawaii	10.7
37	Nevada	10.5
38	Virginia	10.0
39	Maryland	9.8
40	Connecticut	9.6
40	Kansas	9.6
42	North Dakota	9.3
43	Nebraska	9.1
44	Utah	8.9
45	California	8.8
46	Minnesota	8.2
47	Colorado	8.1
48	New Hampshire	7.9
49	New Jersey	7.1
50	Wyoming	6.4

District of Columbia   19.8

Source: CQ Press using data from U.S. Department of Agriculture, Food, Nutrition and Consumer Services
"Supplemental Nutrition Assistance Program" (http://www.fns.usda.gov/pd/snapmain.htm)
*Preliminary data for fiscal year 2010. National rate does not include recipients in U.S. territories. Program formerly called the Food Stamp Program. Rate calculated using 2009 estimated population.

Percent of Households Receiving
Supplemental Nutrition Assistance Program Benefits in 2010
National Percent = 16.4% of Households*

ALPHA ORDER

RANK	STATE	PERCENT
15	Alabama	18.7
36	Alaska	12.9
14	Arizona	19.3
18	Arkansas	17.6
41	California	11.4
49	Colorado	9.2
33	Connecticut	13.6
28	Delaware	15.4
13	Florida	19.6
12	Georgia	19.7
27	Hawaii	15.6
30	Idaho	14.0
26	Illinois	16.3
30	Indiana	14.0
37	Iowa	12.8
43	Kansas	11.1
7	Kentucky	20.8
6	Louisiana	20.9
5	Maine	21.0
38	Maryland	12.7
24	Massachusetts	16.5
3	Michigan	22.7
44	Minnesota	10.1
4	Mississippi	22.6
20	Missouri	17.5
33	Montana	13.6
45	Nebraska	9.9
35	Nevada	13.4
46	New Hampshire	9.8
48	New Jersey	9.6
11	New Mexico	20.3
10	New York	20.4
22	North Carolina	16.8
46	North Dakota	9.8
23	Ohio	16.6
18	Oklahoma	17.6
1	Oregon	25.2
29	Pennsylvania	15.1
17	Rhode Island	17.9
7	South Carolina	20.8
39	South Dakota	12.6
2	Tennessee	23.4
24	Texas	16.5
41	Utah	11.4
21	Vermont	16.9
40	Virginia	12.3
16	Washington	18.5
9	West Virginia	20.7
30	Wisconsin	14.0
50	Wyoming	6.8

RANK ORDER

RANK	STATE	PERCENT
1	Oregon	25.2
2	Tennessee	23.4
3	Michigan	22.7
4	Mississippi	22.6
5	Maine	21.0
6	Louisiana	20.9
7	Kentucky	20.8
7	South Carolina	20.8
9	West Virginia	20.7
10	New York	20.4
11	New Mexico	20.3
12	Georgia	19.7
13	Florida	19.6
14	Arizona	19.3
15	Alabama	18.7
16	Washington	18.5
17	Rhode Island	17.9
18	Arkansas	17.6
18	Oklahoma	17.6
20	Missouri	17.5
21	Vermont	16.9
22	North Carolina	16.8
23	Ohio	16.6
24	Massachusetts	16.5
24	Texas	16.5
26	Illinois	16.3
27	Hawaii	15.6
28	Delaware	15.4
29	Pennsylvania	15.1
30	Idaho	14.0
30	Indiana	14.0
30	Wisconsin	14.0
33	Connecticut	13.6
33	Montana	13.6
35	Nevada	13.4
36	Alaska	12.9
37	Iowa	12.8
38	Maryland	12.7
39	South Dakota	12.6
40	Virginia	12.3
41	California	11.4
41	Utah	11.4
43	Kansas	11.1
44	Minnesota	10.1
45	Nebraska	9.9
46	New Hampshire	9.8
46	North Dakota	9.8
48	New Jersey	9.6
49	Colorado	9.2
50	Wyoming	6.8
	District of Columbia	26.5

Source: CQ Press using data from U.S. Department of Agriculture, Food, Nutrition and Consumer Services
"Supplemental Nutrition Assistance Program" (http://www.fns.usda.gov/pd/snapmain.htm)
*Preliminary data for fiscal year 2010. Percent calculated using 2009 estimated total households. National percent excludes
households in U.S. territories. Program formerly called the Food Stamp Program.

Average Monthly Participants in Women, Infants, and Children (WIC) Special Nutrition Program in 2010
National Total = 9,175,199 Participants*

ALPHA ORDER

RANK	STATE	PARTICIPANTS	% of USA
20	Alabama	145,001	1.6%
42	Alaska	27,020	0.3%
11	Arizona	206,741	2.3%
30	Arkansas	98,963	1.1%
1	California	1,459,406	15.9%
28	Colorado	109,643	1.2%
36	Connecticut	58,111	0.6%
44	Delaware	23,617	0.3%
4	Florida	509,733	5.6%
5	Georgia	311,995	3.4%
40	Hawaii	37,029	0.4%
38	Idaho	47,046	0.5%
6	Illinois	307,201	3.3%
13	Indiana	174,118	1.9%
33	Iowa	74,685	0.8%
31	Kansas	77,363	0.8%
21	Kentucky	139,087	1.5%
17	Louisiana	155,619	1.7%
41	Maine	27,118	0.3%
19	Maryland	147,848	1.6%
26	Massachusetts	125,647	1.4%
10	Michigan	256,229	2.8%
22	Minnesota	138,508	1.5%
29	Mississippi	102,224	1.1%
18	Missouri	151,224	1.6%
46	Montana	20,741	0.2%
39	Nebraska	45,267	0.5%
34	Nevada	74,344	0.8%
47	New Hampshire	17,897	0.2%
14	New Jersey	171,060	1.9%
35	New Mexico	65,472	0.7%
3	New York	512,547	5.6%
8	North Carolina	272,447	3.0%
49	North Dakota	14,621	0.2%
7	Ohio	297,672	3.2%
24	Oklahoma	133,002	1.4%
27	Oregon	114,140	1.2%
9	Pennsylvania	262,270	2.9%
43	Rhode Island	25,525	0.3%
23	South Carolina	134,001	1.5%
45	South Dakota	22,778	0.2%
15	Tennessee	170,588	1.9%
2	Texas	1,036,220	11.3%
32	Utah	75,389	0.8%
48	Vermont	16,804	0.2%
16	Virginia	160,400	1.7%
12	Washington	194,572	2.1%
37	West Virginia	51,798	0.6%
25	Wisconsin	126,535	1.4%
50	Wyoming	13,650	0.1%

RANK ORDER

RANK	STATE	PARTICIPANTS	% of USA
1	California	1,459,406	15.9%
2	Texas	1,036,220	11.3%
3	New York	512,547	5.6%
4	Florida	509,733	5.6%
5	Georgia	311,995	3.4%
6	Illinois	307,201	3.3%
7	Ohio	297,672	3.2%
8	North Carolina	272,447	3.0%
9	Pennsylvania	262,270	2.9%
10	Michigan	256,229	2.8%
11	Arizona	206,741	2.3%
12	Washington	194,572	2.1%
13	Indiana	174,118	1.9%
14	New Jersey	171,060	1.9%
15	Tennessee	170,588	1.9%
16	Virginia	160,400	1.7%
17	Louisiana	155,619	1.7%
18	Missouri	151,224	1.6%
19	Maryland	147,848	1.6%
20	Alabama	145,001	1.6%
21	Kentucky	139,087	1.5%
22	Minnesota	138,508	1.5%
23	South Carolina	134,001	1.5%
24	Oklahoma	133,002	1.4%
25	Wisconsin	126,535	1.4%
26	Massachusetts	125,647	1.4%
27	Oregon	114,140	1.2%
28	Colorado	109,643	1.2%
29	Mississippi	102,224	1.1%
30	Arkansas	98,963	1.1%
31	Kansas	77,363	0.8%
32	Utah	75,389	0.8%
33	Iowa	74,685	0.8%
34	Nevada	74,344	0.8%
35	New Mexico	65,472	0.7%
36	Connecticut	58,111	0.6%
37	West Virginia	51,798	0.6%
38	Idaho	47,046	0.5%
39	Nebraska	45,267	0.5%
40	Hawaii	37,029	0.4%
41	Maine	27,118	0.3%
42	Alaska	27,020	0.3%
43	Rhode Island	25,525	0.3%
44	Delaware	23,617	0.3%
45	South Dakota	22,778	0.2%
46	Montana	20,741	0.2%
47	New Hampshire	17,897	0.2%
48	Vermont	16,804	0.2%
49	North Dakota	14,621	0.2%
50	Wyoming	13,650	0.1%
	District of Columbia	16,946	0.2%

Source: U.S. Department of Agriculture, Food, Nutrition and Consumer Services
"WIC Program (http://www.fns.usda.gov/pd/wicmain.htm)
*Preliminary data for fiscal year 2010. National total includes 217,342 participants in outlying areas not shown separately (Puerto Rico has 192,084 participants).

Average Monthly Benefit per Participant in Women, Infants, and Children (WIC) Special Nutrition Program in 2010
National Average = $41.52*

<table>
<tr><td colspan="3">ALPHA ORDER</td><td colspan="3">RANK ORDER</td></tr>
<tr><td>RANK</td><td>STATE</td><td>AVERAGE BENEFIT</td><td>RANK</td><td>STATE</td><td>AVERAGE BENEFIT</td></tr>
<tr><td>9</td><td>Alabama</td><td>$45.91</td><td>1</td><td>Mississippi</td><td>$52.23</td></tr>
<tr><td>6</td><td>Alaska</td><td>47.94</td><td>2</td><td>Georgia</td><td>51.65</td></tr>
<tr><td>34</td><td>Arizona</td><td>37.74</td><td>3</td><td>New York</td><td>51.42</td></tr>
<tr><td>19</td><td>Arkansas</td><td>41.08</td><td>4</td><td>Hawaii</td><td>50.09</td></tr>
<tr><td>8</td><td>California</td><td>47.22</td><td>5</td><td>Louisiana</td><td>48.14</td></tr>
<tr><td>38</td><td>Colorado</td><td>35.81</td><td>6</td><td>Alaska</td><td>47.94</td></tr>
<tr><td>13</td><td>Connecticut</td><td>44.09</td><td>7</td><td>New Jersey</td><td>47.80</td></tr>
<tr><td>31</td><td>Delaware</td><td>38.46</td><td>8</td><td>California</td><td>47.22</td></tr>
<tr><td>22</td><td>Florida</td><td>40.43</td><td>9</td><td>Alabama</td><td>45.91</td></tr>
<tr><td>2</td><td>Georgia</td><td>51.65</td><td>10</td><td>Rhode Island</td><td>44.97</td></tr>
<tr><td>4</td><td>Hawaii</td><td>50.09</td><td>11</td><td>Illinois</td><td>44.62</td></tr>
<tr><td>41</td><td>Idaho</td><td>34.61</td><td>12</td><td>Vermont</td><td>44.26</td></tr>
<tr><td>11</td><td>Illinois</td><td>44.62</td><td>13</td><td>Connecticut</td><td>44.09</td></tr>
<tr><td>33</td><td>Indiana</td><td>38.23</td><td>14</td><td>Kentucky</td><td>43.65</td></tr>
<tr><td>40</td><td>Iowa</td><td>35.16</td><td>15</td><td>North Dakota</td><td>43.58</td></tr>
<tr><td>39</td><td>Kansas</td><td>35.48</td><td>16</td><td>Pennsylvania</td><td>42.85</td></tr>
<tr><td>14</td><td>Kentucky</td><td>43.65</td><td>17</td><td>South Dakota</td><td>42.56</td></tr>
<tr><td>5</td><td>Louisiana</td><td>48.14</td><td>18</td><td>South Carolina</td><td>42.37</td></tr>
<tr><td>27</td><td>Maine</td><td>39.04</td><td>19</td><td>Arkansas</td><td>41.08</td></tr>
<tr><td>24</td><td>Maryland</td><td>39.52</td><td>20</td><td>Minnesota</td><td>40.88</td></tr>
<tr><td>25</td><td>Massachusetts</td><td>39.15</td><td>21</td><td>West Virginia</td><td>40.59</td></tr>
<tr><td>30</td><td>Michigan</td><td>38.73</td><td>22</td><td>Florida</td><td>40.43</td></tr>
<tr><td>20</td><td>Minnesota</td><td>40.88</td><td>23</td><td>North Carolina</td><td>39.68</td></tr>
<tr><td>1</td><td>Mississippi</td><td>52.23</td><td>24</td><td>Maryland</td><td>39.52</td></tr>
<tr><td>45</td><td>Missouri</td><td>33.50</td><td>25</td><td>Massachusetts</td><td>39.15</td></tr>
<tr><td>36</td><td>Montana</td><td>36.29</td><td>26</td><td>Wisconsin</td><td>39.14</td></tr>
<tr><td>28</td><td>Nebraska</td><td>38.92</td><td>27</td><td>Maine</td><td>39.04</td></tr>
<tr><td>47</td><td>Nevada</td><td>33.28</td><td>28</td><td>Nebraska</td><td>38.92</td></tr>
<tr><td>46</td><td>New Hampshire</td><td>33.46</td><td>29</td><td>Washington</td><td>38.86</td></tr>
<tr><td>7</td><td>New Jersey</td><td>47.80</td><td>30</td><td>Michigan</td><td>38.73</td></tr>
<tr><td>42</td><td>New Mexico</td><td>33.79</td><td>31</td><td>Delaware</td><td>38.46</td></tr>
<tr><td>3</td><td>New York</td><td>51.42</td><td>32</td><td>Tennessee</td><td>38.27</td></tr>
<tr><td>23</td><td>North Carolina</td><td>39.68</td><td>33</td><td>Indiana</td><td>38.23</td></tr>
<tr><td>15</td><td>North Dakota</td><td>43.58</td><td>34</td><td>Arizona</td><td>37.74</td></tr>
<tr><td>44</td><td>Ohio</td><td>33.52</td><td>35</td><td>Oklahoma</td><td>37.44</td></tr>
<tr><td>35</td><td>Oklahoma</td><td>37.44</td><td>36</td><td>Montana</td><td>36.29</td></tr>
<tr><td>37</td><td>Oregon</td><td>36.25</td><td>37</td><td>Oregon</td><td>36.25</td></tr>
<tr><td>16</td><td>Pennsylvania</td><td>42.85</td><td>38</td><td>Colorado</td><td>35.81</td></tr>
<tr><td>10</td><td>Rhode Island</td><td>44.97</td><td>39</td><td>Kansas</td><td>35.48</td></tr>
<tr><td>18</td><td>South Carolina</td><td>42.37</td><td>40</td><td>Iowa</td><td>35.16</td></tr>
<tr><td>17</td><td>South Dakota</td><td>42.56</td><td>41</td><td>Idaho</td><td>34.61</td></tr>
<tr><td>32</td><td>Tennessee</td><td>38.27</td><td>42</td><td>New Mexico</td><td>33.79</td></tr>
<tr><td>50</td><td>Texas</td><td>26.86</td><td>43</td><td>Utah</td><td>33.65</td></tr>
<tr><td>43</td><td>Utah</td><td>33.65</td><td>44</td><td>Ohio</td><td>33.52</td></tr>
<tr><td>12</td><td>Vermont</td><td>44.26</td><td>45</td><td>Missouri</td><td>33.50</td></tr>
<tr><td>48</td><td>Virginia</td><td>32.43</td><td>46</td><td>New Hampshire</td><td>33.46</td></tr>
<tr><td>29</td><td>Washington</td><td>38.86</td><td>47</td><td>Nevada</td><td>33.28</td></tr>
<tr><td>21</td><td>West Virginia</td><td>40.59</td><td>48</td><td>Virginia</td><td>32.43</td></tr>
<tr><td>26</td><td>Wisconsin</td><td>39.14</td><td>49</td><td>Wyoming</td><td>28.57</td></tr>
<tr><td>49</td><td>Wyoming</td><td>28.57</td><td>50</td><td>Texas</td><td>26.86</td></tr>
<tr><td></td><td></td><td></td><td></td><td>District of Columbia</td><td>37.47</td></tr>
</table>

Source: U.S. Department of Agriculture, Food, Nutrition and Consumer Services
"WIC Program (http://www.fns.usda.gov/pd/wicmain.htm)
*Preliminary data for fiscal year 2010. National average includes outlying areas and Indian reservations not shown separately.

Percent of Public Elementary and Secondary School Students Eligible for Free or Reduced-Price Meals in 2009
National Percent = 43.8%*

ALPHA ORDER

RANK	STATE	PERCENT
8	Alabama	52.4
37	Alaska	34.1
15	Arizona	47.5
4	Arkansas	57.1
8	California	52.4
33	Colorado	35.4
47	Connecticut	30.2
24	Delaware	39.5
13	Florida	49.6
6	Georgia	53.0
21	Hawaii	41.7
23	Idaho	39.7
25	Illinois	39.3
19	Indiana	41.8
36	Iowa	34.4
18	Kansas	42.9
10	Kentucky	51.6
2	Louisiana	64.9
30	Maine	38.1
34	Maryland	34.7
46	Massachusetts	30.7
19	Michigan	41.8
42	Minnesota	32.7
1	Mississippi	68.3
27	Missouri	38.7
31	Montana	36.7
28	Nebraska	38.4
26	Nevada	39.0
50	New Hampshire	20.5
49	New Jersey	30.0
3	New Mexico	61.7
17	New York	44.7
38	North Carolina	33.9
43	North Dakota	31.6
32	Ohio	36.4
5	Oklahoma	56.1
16	Oregon	46.0
40	Pennsylvania	33.4
22	Rhode Island	39.8
7	South Carolina	52.5
34	South Dakota	34.7
11	Tennessee	50.0
14	Texas	48.8
44	Utah	31.2
48	Vermont	30.1
41	Virginia	33.1
29	Washington	38.2
11	West Virginia	50.0
39	Wisconsin	33.5
45	Wyoming	31.0

RANK ORDER

RANK	STATE	PERCENT
1	Mississippi	68.3
2	Louisiana	64.9
3	New Mexico	61.7
4	Arkansas	57.1
5	Oklahoma	56.1
6	Georgia	53.0
7	South Carolina	52.5
8	Alabama	52.4
8	California	52.4
10	Kentucky	51.6
11	Tennessee	50.0
11	West Virginia	50.0
13	Florida	49.6
14	Texas	48.8
15	Arizona	47.5
16	Oregon	46.0
17	New York	44.7
18	Kansas	42.9
19	Indiana	41.8
19	Michigan	41.8
21	Hawaii	41.7
22	Rhode Island	39.8
23	Idaho	39.7
24	Delaware	39.5
25	Illinois	39.3
26	Nevada	39.0
27	Missouri	38.7
28	Nebraska	38.4
29	Washington	38.2
30	Maine	38.1
31	Montana	36.7
32	Ohio	36.4
33	Colorado	35.4
34	Maryland	34.7
34	South Dakota	34.7
36	Iowa	34.4
37	Alaska	34.1
38	North Carolina	33.9
39	Wisconsin	33.5
40	Pennsylvania	33.4
41	Virginia	33.1
42	Minnesota	32.7
43	North Dakota	31.6
44	Utah	31.2
45	Wyoming	31.0
46	Massachusetts	30.7
47	Connecticut	30.2
48	Vermont	30.1
49	New Jersey	30.0
50	New Hampshire	20.5

| | District of Columbia | 67.1 |

Source: CQ Press using data from U.S. Department of Education, National Center for Education Statistics
"Common Core of Data (CCD) Database" (http://nces.ed.gov/ccd/)
*Preliminary data for school year 2008-2009.

Child Support Collections in 2009

National Total = $26,038,654,947*

ALPHA ORDER

RANK	STATE	COLLECTIONS	% of USA
28	Alabama	$265,980,685	1.0%
41	Alaska	96,515,095	0.4%
25	Arizona	314,771,703	1.2%
32	Arkansas	202,024,048	0.8%
2	California	2,145,379,995	8.2%
26	Colorado	281,289,812	1.1%
30	Connecticut	253,250,384	1.0%
45	Delaware	73,584,549	0.3%
7	Florida	1,289,345,860	5.0%
15	Georgia	588,950,868	2.3%
40	Hawaii	98,558,516	0.4%
38	Idaho	141,005,005	0.5%
9	Illinois	796,917,883	3.1%
13	Indiana	604,252,006	2.3%
24	Iowa	328,521,904	1.3%
35	Kansas	181,226,810	0.7%
21	Kentucky	393,627,221	1.5%
22	Louisiana	339,495,471	1.3%
39	Maine	103,670,074	0.4%
20	Maryland	489,617,761	1.9%
18	Massachusetts	547,003,552	2.1%
6	Michigan	1,391,917,746	5.3%
14	Minnesota	598,101,027	2.3%
29	Mississippi	253,796,409	1.0%
17	Missouri	554,441,257	2.1%
49	Montana	54,389,670	0.2%
33	Nebraska	188,771,393	0.7%
37	Nevada	153,947,716	0.6%
43	New Hampshire	82,354,776	0.3%
8	New Jersey	1,075,169,861	4.1%
42	New Mexico	92,221,126	0.4%
4	New York	1,622,629,967	6.2%
10	North Carolina	655,187,240	2.5%
44	North Dakota	79,058,817	0.3%
3	Ohio	1,721,706,006	6.6%
27	Oklahoma	270,574,118	1.0%
23	Oregon	339,026,784	1.3%
5	Pennsylvania	1,424,996,960	5.5%
47	Rhode Island	60,942,159	0.2%
31	South Carolina	244,465,949	0.9%
46	South Dakota	72,996,116	0.3%
19	Tennessee	530,651,486	2.0%
1	Texas	2,676,095,948	10.3%
36	Utah	169,161,896	0.6%
50	Vermont	47,392,646	0.2%
16	Virginia	588,056,330	2.3%
11	Washington	643,732,608	2.5%
34	West Virginia	187,540,473	0.7%
12	Wisconsin	611,255,026	2.3%
48	Wyoming	60,419,481	0.2%

RANK ORDER

RANK	STATE	COLLECTIONS	% of USA
1	Texas	$2,676,095,948	10.3%
2	California	2,145,379,995	8.2%
3	Ohio	1,721,706,006	6.6%
4	New York	1,622,629,967	6.2%
5	Pennsylvania	1,424,996,960	5.5%
6	Michigan	1,391,917,746	5.3%
7	Florida	1,289,345,860	5.0%
8	New Jersey	1,075,169,861	4.1%
9	Illinois	796,917,883	3.1%
10	North Carolina	655,187,240	2.5%
11	Washington	643,732,608	2.5%
12	Wisconsin	611,255,026	2.3%
13	Indiana	604,252,006	2.3%
14	Minnesota	598,101,027	2.3%
15	Georgia	588,950,868	2.3%
16	Virginia	588,056,330	2.3%
17	Missouri	554,441,257	2.1%
18	Massachusetts	547,003,552	2.1%
19	Tennessee	530,651,486	2.0%
20	Maryland	489,617,761	1.9%
21	Kentucky	393,627,221	1.5%
22	Louisiana	339,495,471	1.3%
23	Oregon	339,026,784	1.3%
24	Iowa	328,521,904	1.3%
25	Arizona	314,771,703	1.2%
26	Colorado	281,289,812	1.1%
27	Oklahoma	270,574,118	1.0%
28	Alabama	265,980,685	1.0%
29	Mississippi	253,796,409	1.0%
30	Connecticut	253,250,384	1.0%
31	South Carolina	244,465,949	0.9%
32	Arkansas	202,024,048	0.8%
33	Nebraska	188,771,393	0.7%
34	West Virginia	187,540,473	0.7%
35	Kansas	181,226,810	0.7%
36	Utah	169,161,896	0.6%
37	Nevada	153,947,716	0.6%
38	Idaho	141,005,005	0.5%
39	Maine	103,670,074	0.4%
40	Hawaii	98,558,516	0.4%
41	Alaska	96,515,095	0.4%
42	New Mexico	92,221,126	0.4%
43	New Hampshire	82,354,776	0.3%
44	North Dakota	79,058,817	0.3%
45	Delaware	73,584,549	0.3%
46	South Dakota	72,996,116	0.3%
47	Rhode Island	60,942,159	0.2%
48	Wyoming	60,419,481	0.2%
49	Montana	54,389,670	0.2%
50	Vermont	47,392,646	0.2%
	District of Columbia	52,664,754	0.2%

Source: U.S. Department of Health and Human Services, Office of Child Support Enforcement
"Child Support Enforcement Preliminary Data Report" (http://www.acf.hhs.gov/programs/cse/pubs/)
*Fiscal year 2009. Total does not include $346,937,880 collected in U.S. territories.

XV. Transportation

Federal Highway Funding in 2010

National Total = $38,363,650,000*

ALPHA ORDER

RANK	STATE	FUNDS	% of USA
16	Alabama	$759,490,000	2.0%
33	Alaska	429,490,000	1.1%
17	Arizona	749,060,000	2.0%
28	Arkansas	503,673,000	1.3%
1	California	3,601,446,000	9.4%
27	Colorado	527,375,000	1.4%
29	Connecticut	498,352,000	1.3%
50	Delaware	162,355,000	0.4%
3	Florida	1,919,342,000	5.0%
8	Georgia	1,303,829,000	3.4%
49	Hawaii	163,445,000	0.4%
41	Idaho	284,624,000	0.7%
6	Illinois	1,369,022,000	3.6%
13	Indiana	965,912,000	2.5%
32	Iowa	465,991,000	1.2%
36	Kansas	375,633,000	1.0%
20	Kentucky	659,819,000	1.7%
19	Louisiana	684,458,000	1.8%
47	Maine	175,412,000	0.5%
26	Maryland	596,354,000	1.6%
25	Massachusetts	606,268,000	1.6%
9	Michigan	1,056,502,000	2.8%
22	Minnesota	633,005,000	1.7%
31	Mississippi	472,328,000	1.2%
14	Missouri	922,396,000	2.4%
35	Montana	382,744,000	1.0%
40	Nebraska	285,045,000	0.7%
38	Nevada	336,248,000	0.9%
48	New Hampshire	165,951,000	0.4%
12	New Jersey	991,301,000	2.6%
37	New Mexico	366,271,000	1.0%
4	New York	1,669,277,000	4.4%
10	North Carolina	1,053,573,000	2.7%
44	North Dakota	243,629,000	0.6%
7	Ohio	1,341,675,000	3.5%
24	Oklahoma	612,191,000	1.6%
30	Oregon	474,219,000	1.2%
5	Pennsylvania	1,644,105,000	4.3%
45	Rhode Island	206,791,000	0.5%
23	South Carolina	629,722,000	1.6%
42	South Dakota	271,497,000	0.7%
15	Tennessee	838,455,000	2.2%
2	Texas	3,217,725,000	8.4%
39	Utah	312,512,000	0.8%
46	Vermont	184,096,000	0.5%
11	Virginia	1,013,690,000	2.6%
21	Washington	657,331,000	1.7%
34	West Virginia	426,625,000	1.1%
18	Wisconsin	742,717,000	1.9%
43	Wyoming	257,319,000	0.7%

RANK ORDER

RANK	STATE	FUNDS	% of USA
1	California	$3,601,446,000	9.4%
2	Texas	3,217,725,000	8.4%
3	Florida	1,919,342,000	5.0%
4	New York	1,669,277,000	4.4%
5	Pennsylvania	1,644,105,000	4.3%
6	Illinois	1,369,022,000	3.6%
7	Ohio	1,341,675,000	3.5%
8	Georgia	1,303,829,000	3.4%
9	Michigan	1,056,502,000	2.8%
10	North Carolina	1,053,573,000	2.7%
11	Virginia	1,013,690,000	2.6%
12	New Jersey	991,301,000	2.6%
13	Indiana	965,912,000	2.5%
14	Missouri	922,396,000	2.4%
15	Tennessee	838,455,000	2.2%
16	Alabama	759,490,000	2.0%
17	Arizona	749,060,000	2.0%
18	Wisconsin	742,717,000	1.9%
19	Louisiana	684,458,000	1.8%
20	Kentucky	659,819,000	1.7%
21	Washington	657,331,000	1.7%
22	Minnesota	633,005,000	1.7%
23	South Carolina	629,722,000	1.6%
24	Oklahoma	612,191,000	1.6%
25	Massachusetts	606,268,000	1.6%
26	Maryland	596,354,000	1.6%
27	Colorado	527,375,000	1.4%
28	Arkansas	503,673,000	1.3%
29	Connecticut	498,352,000	1.3%
30	Oregon	474,219,000	1.2%
31	Mississippi	472,328,000	1.2%
32	Iowa	465,991,000	1.2%
33	Alaska	429,490,000	1.1%
34	West Virginia	426,625,000	1.1%
35	Montana	382,744,000	1.0%
36	Kansas	375,633,000	1.0%
37	New Mexico	366,271,000	1.0%
38	Nevada	336,248,000	0.9%
39	Utah	312,512,000	0.8%
40	Nebraska	285,045,000	0.7%
41	Idaho	284,624,000	0.7%
42	South Dakota	271,497,000	0.7%
43	Wyoming	257,319,000	0.7%
44	North Dakota	243,629,000	0.6%
45	Rhode Island	206,791,000	0.5%
46	Vermont	184,096,000	0.5%
47	Maine	175,412,000	0.5%
48	New Hampshire	165,951,000	0.4%
49	Hawaii	163,445,000	0.4%
50	Delaware	162,355,000	0.4%
	District of Columbia	153,363,000	0.4%

Source: U.S. Department of Transportation, Federal Highway Administration
"Federal-aid Highway Fund Apportionments" (http://www.fhwa.dot.gov/policyinformation/statistics/2009/)
*Fiscal Year 2010.

Per Capita Federal Highway Funding in 2010

National Per Capita = $124*

ALPHA ORDER

RANK	STATE	PER CAPITA
14	Alabama	$161
1	Alaska	606
39	Arizona	112
12	Arkansas	173
47	California	97
44	Colorado	104
22	Connecticut	141
9	Delaware	182
46	Florida	103
25	Georgia	132
33	Hawaii	126
9	Idaho	182
42	Illinois	106
21	Indiana	150
17	Iowa	154
25	Kansas	132
19	Kentucky	152
20	Louisiana	151
24	Maine	134
44	Maryland	104
49	Massachusetts	91
42	Michigan	106
36	Minnesota	120
15	Mississippi	160
18	Missouri	153
3	Montana	390
16	Nebraska	157
31	Nevada	127
34	New Hampshire	125
38	New Jersey	114
11	New Mexico	180
50	New York	85
40	North Carolina	111
4	North Dakota	373
37	Ohio	116
13	Oklahoma	164
35	Oregon	123
29	Pennsylvania	130
8	Rhode Island	196
23	South Carolina	137
5	South Dakota	331
25	Tennessee	132
30	Texas	128
41	Utah	110
6	Vermont	296
31	Virginia	127
47	Washington	97
7	West Virginia	234
28	Wisconsin	131
2	Wyoming	470

RANK ORDER

RANK	STATE	PER CAPITA
1	Alaska	$606
2	Wyoming	470
3	Montana	390
4	North Dakota	373
5	South Dakota	331
6	Vermont	296
7	West Virginia	234
8	Rhode Island	196
9	Delaware	182
9	Idaho	182
11	New Mexico	180
12	Arkansas	173
13	Oklahoma	164
14	Alabama	161
15	Mississippi	160
16	Nebraska	157
17	Iowa	154
18	Missouri	153
19	Kentucky	152
20	Louisiana	151
21	Indiana	150
22	Connecticut	141
23	South Carolina	137
24	Maine	134
25	Georgia	132
25	Kansas	132
25	Tennessee	132
28	Wisconsin	131
29	Pennsylvania	130
30	Texas	128
31	Nevada	127
31	Virginia	127
33	Hawaii	126
34	New Hampshire	125
35	Oregon	123
36	Minnesota	120
37	Ohio	116
38	New Jersey	114
39	Arizona	112
40	North Carolina	111
41	Utah	110
42	Illinois	106
42	Michigan	106
44	Colorado	104
44	Maryland	104
46	Florida	103
47	California	97
47	Washington	97
49	Massachusetts	91
50	New York	85
	District of Columbia	251

Source: CQ Press using data from U.S. Department of Transportation, Federal Highway Administration
"Federal-aid Highway Fund Apportionments" (http://www.fhwa.dot.gov/policyinformation/statistics/2009/)
*Fiscal Year 2010 apportionments. Calculated with 2010 population estimates.

Public Road and Street Mileage in 2008

National Total = 4,042,768 Miles*

ALPHA ORDER

RANK	STATE	MILES	% of USA
18	Alabama	97,325	2.4%
46	Alaska	15,328	0.4%
33	Arizona	60,439	1.5%
17	Arkansas	99,812	2.5%
2	California	172,512	4.3%
22	Colorado	88,266	2.2%
44	Connecticut	21,365	0.5%
49	Delaware	6,281	0.2%
11	Florida	121,386	3.0%
8	Georgia	121,875	3.0%
50	Hawaii	4,362	0.1%
35	Idaho	47,788	1.2%
4	Illinois	139,492	3.5%
19	Indiana	95,613	2.4%
14	Iowa	114,226	2.8%
3	Kansas	140,609	3.5%
26	Kentucky	78,749	1.9%
32	Louisiana	61,093	1.5%
43	Maine	22,829	0.6%
41	Maryland	31,385	0.8%
39	Massachusetts	36,104	0.9%
10	Michigan	121,666	3.0%
5	Minnesota	138,239	3.4%
27	Mississippi	74,886	1.9%
6	Missouri	129,717	3.2%
28	Montana	74,171	1.8%
20	Nebraska	93,615	2.3%
40	Nevada	33,907	0.8%
45	New Hampshire	16,006	0.4%
37	New Jersey	38,753	1.0%
30	New Mexico	68,384	1.7%
13	New York	114,473	2.8%
16	North Carolina	105,103	2.6%
23	North Dakota	86,842	2.1%
7	Ohio	122,973	3.0%
15	Oklahoma	113,325	2.8%
34	Oregon	59,250	1.5%
9	Pennsylvania	121,772	3.0%
48	Rhode Island	6,404	0.2%
31	South Carolina	66,254	1.6%
25	South Dakota	82,149	2.0%
21	Tennessee	92,173	2.3%
1	Texas	306,404	7.6%
36	Utah	44,705	1.1%
47	Vermont	14,423	0.4%
29	Virginia	73,903	1.8%
24	Washington	83,527	2.1%
38	West Virginia	38,452	1.0%
12	Wisconsin	114,843	2.8%
42	Wyoming	28,105	0.7%

RANK ORDER

RANK	STATE	MILES	% of USA
1	Texas	306,404	7.6%
2	California	172,512	4.3%
3	Kansas	140,609	3.5%
4	Illinois	139,492	3.5%
5	Minnesota	138,239	3.4%
6	Missouri	129,717	3.2%
7	Ohio	122,973	3.0%
8	Georgia	121,875	3.0%
9	Pennsylvania	121,772	3.0%
10	Michigan	121,666	3.0%
11	Florida	121,386	3.0%
12	Wisconsin	114,843	2.8%
13	New York	114,473	2.8%
14	Iowa	114,226	2.8%
15	Oklahoma	113,325	2.8%
16	North Carolina	105,103	2.6%
17	Arkansas	99,812	2.5%
18	Alabama	97,325	2.4%
19	Indiana	95,613	2.4%
20	Nebraska	93,615	2.3%
21	Tennessee	92,173	2.3%
22	Colorado	88,266	2.2%
23	North Dakota	86,842	2.1%
24	Washington	83,527	2.1%
25	South Dakota	82,149	2.0%
26	Kentucky	78,749	1.9%
27	Mississippi	74,886	1.9%
28	Montana	74,171	1.8%
29	Virginia	73,903	1.8%
30	New Mexico	68,384	1.7%
31	South Carolina	66,254	1.6%
32	Louisiana	61,093	1.5%
33	Arizona	60,439	1.5%
34	Oregon	59,250	1.5%
35	Idaho	47,788	1.2%
36	Utah	44,705	1.1%
37	New Jersey	38,753	1.0%
38	West Virginia	38,452	1.0%
39	Massachusetts	36,104	0.9%
40	Nevada	33,907	0.8%
41	Maryland	31,385	0.8%
42	Wyoming	28,105	0.7%
43	Maine	22,829	0.6%
44	Connecticut	21,365	0.5%
45	New Hampshire	16,006	0.4%
46	Alaska	15,328	0.4%
47	Vermont	14,423	0.4%
48	Rhode Island	6,404	0.2%
49	Delaware	6,281	0.2%
50	Hawaii	4,362	0.1%
	District of Columbia	1,505	0.0%

Source: U.S. Department of Transportation, Federal Highway Administration
"Highway Statistics 2008" (Table HM-10, http://www.fhwa.dot.gov/policyinformation/statistics/2008/index.cfm)
*Does not include 16,572 miles of roads and streets in Puerto Rico.

Percent of Public Road and Street Mileage Federally Funded in 2008

National Percent = 24.5% of Public Road and Street Mileage*

ALPHA ORDER

RANK	STATE	PERCENT
23	Alabama	24.7
10	Alaska	28.6
39	Arizona	21.5
38	Arkansas	21.8
2	California	32.0
44	Colorado	19.8
8	Connecticut	28.8
25	Delaware	24.4
40	Florida	21.4
19	Georgia	25.3
1	Hawaii	35.9
32	Idaho	23.5
20	Illinois	25.2
29	Indiana	23.6
35	Iowa	22.7
22	Kansas	24.8
49	Kentucky	17.6
37	Louisiana	21.9
13	Maine	27.7
21	Maryland	25.0
4	Massachusetts	30.8
6	Michigan	29.9
28	Minnesota	23.8
9	Mississippi	28.7
29	Missouri	23.6
45	Montana	19.7
36	Nebraska	22.0
48	Nevada	19.0
41	New Hampshire	21.3
18	New Jersey	26.6
50	New Mexico	16.8
27	New York	24.0
43	North Carolina	20.9
42	North Dakota	21.1
29	Ohio	23.6
12	Oklahoma	27.9
5	Oregon	30.5
34	Pennsylvania	23.1
14	Rhode Island	27.4
3	South Carolina	31.7
26	South Dakota	24.1
47	Tennessee	19.2
15	Texas	27.2
46	Utah	19.5
17	Vermont	26.8
7	Virginia	28.9
33	Washington	23.3
16	West Virginia	27.1
24	Wisconsin	24.6
11	Wyoming	28.1

RANK ORDER

RANK	STATE	PERCENT
1	Hawaii	35.9
2	California	32.0
3	South Carolina	31.7
4	Massachusetts	30.8
5	Oregon	30.5
6	Michigan	29.9
7	Virginia	28.9
8	Connecticut	28.8
9	Mississippi	28.7
10	Alaska	28.6
11	Wyoming	28.1
12	Oklahoma	27.9
13	Maine	27.7
14	Rhode Island	27.4
15	Texas	27.2
16	West Virginia	27.1
17	Vermont	26.8
18	New Jersey	26.6
19	Georgia	25.3
20	Illinois	25.2
21	Maryland	25.0
22	Kansas	24.8
23	Alabama	24.7
24	Wisconsin	24.6
25	Delaware	24.4
26	South Dakota	24.1
27	New York	24.0
28	Minnesota	23.8
29	Indiana	23.6
29	Missouri	23.6
29	Ohio	23.6
32	Idaho	23.5
33	Washington	23.3
34	Pennsylvania	23.1
35	Iowa	22.7
36	Nebraska	22.0
37	Louisiana	21.9
38	Arkansas	21.8
39	Arizona	21.5
40	Florida	21.4
41	New Hampshire	21.3
42	North Dakota	21.1
43	North Carolina	20.9
44	Colorado	19.8
45	Montana	19.7
46	Utah	19.5
47	Tennessee	19.2
48	Nevada	19.0
49	Kentucky	17.6
50	New Mexico	16.8

District of Columbia	30.2

Source: CQ Press using data from U.S. Department of Transportation, Federal Highway Administration
"Highway Statistics 2008" (Table HM-10, http://www.fhwa.dot.gov/policyinformation/statistics/2008/index.cfm)
*National percent does not include federally-funded highway miles in Puerto Rico.

Interstate Highway Mileage in 2008

National Total = 46,750 Miles*

ALPHA ORDER					RANK ORDER			
RANK	STATE	MILES	% of USA		RANK	STATE	MILES	% of USA
25	Alabama	905	1.9%		1	Texas	3,234	6.9%
17	Alaska	1,082	2.3%		2	California	2,460	5.3%
13	Arizona	1,168	2.5%		3	Illinois	2,182	4.7%
35	Arkansas	656	1.4%		4	Pennsylvania	1,792	3.8%
2	California	2,460	5.3%		5	New York	1,705	3.6%
19	Colorado	953	2.0%		6	Ohio	1,574	3.4%
45	Connecticut	346	0.7%		7	Florida	1,471	3.1%
50	Delaware	41	0.1%		8	Michigan	1,243	2.7%
7	Florida	1,471	3.1%		9	Georgia	1,242	2.7%
9	Georgia	1,242	2.7%		10	Montana	1,192	2.5%
49	Hawaii	55	0.1%		11	Missouri	1,181	2.5%
36	Idaho	612	1.3%		12	Indiana	1,171	2.5%
3	Illinois	2,182	4.7%		13	Arizona	1,168	2.5%
12	Indiana	1,171	2.5%		14	North Carolina	1,125	2.4%
28	Iowa	781	1.7%		15	Virginia	1,119	2.4%
26	Kansas	874	1.9%		16	Tennessee	1,105	2.4%
30	Kentucky	762	1.6%		17	Alaska	1,082	2.3%
24	Louisiana	906	1.9%		18	New Mexico	1,000	2.1%
44	Maine	366	0.8%		19	Colorado	953	2.0%
41	Maryland	481	1.0%		20	Utah	936	2.0%
37	Massachusetts	573	1.2%		21	Oklahoma	933	2.0%
8	Michigan	1,243	2.7%		22	Minnesota	918	2.0%
22	Minnesota	918	2.0%		23	Wyoming	913	2.0%
33	Mississippi	698	1.5%		24	Louisiana	906	1.9%
11	Missouri	1,181	2.5%		25	Alabama	905	1.9%
10	Montana	1,192	2.5%		26	Kansas	874	1.9%
41	Nebraska	481	1.0%		27	South Carolina	843	1.8%
39	Nevada	570	1.2%		28	Iowa	781	1.7%
47	New Hampshire	225	0.5%		29	Washington	764	1.6%
43	New Jersey	431	0.9%		30	Kentucky	762	1.6%
18	New Mexico	1,000	2.1%		31	Wisconsin	743	1.6%
5	New York	1,705	3.6%		32	Oregon	729	1.6%
14	North Carolina	1,125	2.4%		33	Mississippi	698	1.5%
38	North Dakota	571	1.2%		34	South Dakota	679	1.5%
6	Ohio	1,574	3.4%		35	Arkansas	656	1.4%
21	Oklahoma	933	2.0%		36	Idaho	612	1.3%
32	Oregon	729	1.6%		37	Massachusetts	573	1.2%
4	Pennsylvania	1,792	3.8%		38	North Dakota	571	1.2%
48	Rhode Island	72	0.2%		39	Nevada	570	1.2%
27	South Carolina	843	1.8%		40	West Virginia	554	1.2%
34	South Dakota	679	1.5%		41	Maryland	481	1.0%
16	Tennessee	1,105	2.4%		41	Nebraska	481	1.0%
1	Texas	3,234	6.9%		43	New Jersey	431	0.9%
20	Utah	936	2.0%		44	Maine	366	0.8%
46	Vermont	320	0.7%		45	Connecticut	346	0.7%
15	Virginia	1,119	2.4%		46	Vermont	320	0.7%
29	Washington	764	1.6%		47	New Hampshire	225	0.5%
40	West Virginia	554	1.2%		48	Rhode Island	72	0.2%
31	Wisconsin	743	1.6%		49	Hawaii	55	0.1%
23	Wyoming	913	2.0%		50	Delaware	41	0.1%
						District of Columbia	13	0.0%

Source: U.S. Department of Transportation, Federal Highway Administration
 "Highway Statistics 2008" (Table HM-15, http://www.fhwa.dot.gov/policyinformation/statistics/2008/index.cfm)
*Does not include 265 miles of highway in Puerto Rico that are part of the interstate system.

Toll Road Mileage in 2008

National Total = 4,919.6 Miles

ALPHA ORDER

RANK ORDER

RANK	STATE	MILES	% of USA
27	Alabama	0.7	0.0%
28	Alaska	0.0	0.0%
28	Arizona	0.0	0.0%
28	Arkansas	0.0	0.0%
14	California	95.8	1.9%
17	Colorado	84.0	1.7%
28	Connecticut	0.0	0.0%
18	Delaware	56.7	1.2%
1	Florida	685.8	13.9%
24	Georgia	6.2	0.1%
28	Hawaii	0.0	0.0%
28	Idaho	0.0	0.0%
7	Illinois	284.1	5.8%
10	Indiana	156.8	3.2%
28	Iowa	0.0	0.0%
9	Kansas	236.0	4.8%
15	Kentucky	93.6	1.9%
25	Louisiana	1.5	0.0%
13	Maine	106.2	2.2%
20	Maryland	27.6	0.6%
12	Massachusetts	138.2	2.8%
28	Michigan	0.0	0.0%
28	Minnesota	0.0	0.0%
28	Mississippi	0.0	0.0%
28	Missouri	0.0	0.0%
28	Montana	0.0	0.0%
28	Nebraska	0.0	0.0%
23	Nevada	6.4	0.1%
11	New Hampshire	155.4	3.2%
5	New Jersey	359.9	7.3%
28	New Mexico	0.0	0.0%
3	New York	567.6	11.5%
28	North Carolina	0.0	0.0%
28	North Dakota	0.0	0.0%
8	Ohio	241.2	4.9%
2	Oklahoma	595.5	12.1%
28	Oregon	0.0	0.0%
4	Pennsylvania	533.0	10.8%
28	Rhode Island	0.0	0.0%
21	South Carolina	23.5	0.5%
28	South Dakota	0.0	0.0%
28	Tennessee	0.0	0.0%
6	Texas	308.0	6.3%
26	Utah	1.0	0.0%
22	Vermont	11.9	0.2%
19	Virginia	56.2	1.1%
28	Washington	0.0	0.0%
16	West Virginia	86.8	1.8%
28	Wisconsin	0.0	0.0%
28	Wyoming	0.0	0.0%

RANK	STATE	MILES	% of USA
1	Florida	685.8	13.9%
2	Oklahoma	595.5	12.1%
3	New York	567.6	11.5%
4	Pennsylvania	533.0	10.8%
5	New Jersey	359.9	7.3%
6	Texas	308.0	6.3%
7	Illinois	284.1	5.8%
8	Ohio	241.2	4.9%
9	Kansas	236.0	4.8%
10	Indiana	156.8	3.2%
11	New Hampshire	155.4	3.2%
12	Massachusetts	138.2	2.8%
13	Maine	106.2	2.2%
14	California	95.8	1.9%
15	Kentucky	93.6	1.9%
16	West Virginia	86.8	1.8%
17	Colorado	84.0	1.7%
18	Delaware	56.7	1.2%
19	Virginia	56.2	1.1%
20	Maryland	27.6	0.6%
21	South Carolina	23.5	0.5%
22	Vermont	11.9	0.2%
23	Nevada	6.4	0.1%
24	Georgia	6.2	0.1%
25	Louisiana	1.5	0.0%
26	Utah	1.0	0.0%
27	Alabama	0.7	0.0%
28	Alaska	0.0	0.0%
28	Arizona	0.0	0.0%
28	Arkansas	0.0	0.0%
28	Connecticut	0.0	0.0%
28	Hawaii	0.0	0.0%
28	Idaho	0.0	0.0%
28	Iowa	0.0	0.0%
28	Michigan	0.0	0.0%
28	Minnesota	0.0	0.0%
28	Mississippi	0.0	0.0%
28	Missouri	0.0	0.0%
28	Montana	0.0	0.0%
28	Nebraska	0.0	0.0%
28	New Mexico	0.0	0.0%
28	North Carolina	0.0	0.0%
28	North Dakota	0.0	0.0%
28	Oregon	0.0	0.0%
28	Rhode Island	0.0	0.0%
28	South Dakota	0.0	0.0%
28	Tennessee	0.0	0.0%
28	Washington	0.0	0.0%
28	Wisconsin	0.0	0.0%
28	Wyoming	0.0	0.0%
	District of Columbia	0.0	0.0%

Source: U.S. Department of Transportation, Bureau of Transportation Statistics
"State Transportation Statistics 2009" (http://www.bts.gov/publications/state_transportation_statistics/)

Rural Road and Street Mileage in 2008

National Total = 2,977,228 Rural Miles*

ALPHA ORDER

RANK	STATE	MILES	% of USA
18	Alabama	75,390	2.5%
42	Alaska	12,987	0.4%
35	Arizona	37,522	1.3%
9	Arkansas	87,627	2.9%
13	California	83,483	2.8%
23	Colorado	68,921	2.3%
47	Connecticut	6,228	0.2%
48	Delaware	3,302	0.1%
34	Florida	40,366	1.4%
14	Georgia	83,261	2.8%
49	Hawaii	2,052	0.1%
33	Idaho	42,128	1.4%
6	Illinois	98,202	3.3%
20	Indiana	71,299	2.4%
5	Iowa	102,919	3.5%
2	Kansas	127,859	4.3%
24	Kentucky	66,213	2.2%
32	Louisiana	44,758	1.5%
40	Maine	19,837	0.7%
41	Maryland	14,051	0.5%
45	Massachusetts	7,978	0.3%
11	Michigan	85,853	2.9%
3	Minnesota	117,613	4.0%
26	Mississippi	63,929	2.1%
4	Missouri	106,765	3.6%
21	Montana	71,115	2.4%
10	Nebraska	87,297	2.9%
38	Nevada	26,741	0.9%
44	New Hampshire	11,098	0.4%
46	New Jersey	7,298	0.2%
28	New Mexico	60,386	2.0%
25	New York	66,071	2.2%
19	North Carolina	71,674	2.4%
12	North Dakota	84,945	2.9%
16	Ohio	78,260	2.6%
7	Oklahoma	97,268	3.3%
31	Oregon	46,260	1.6%
17	Pennsylvania	76,484	2.6%
50	Rhode Island	1,214	0.0%
30	South Carolina	49,833	1.7%
15	South Dakota	79,217	2.7%
22	Tennessee	69,719	2.3%
1	Texas	212,999	7.2%
36	Utah	33,632	1.1%
43	Vermont	12,965	0.4%
29	Virginia	50,334	1.7%
27	Washington	60,784	2.0%
37	West Virginia	33,092	1.1%
8	Wisconsin	92,572	3.1%
39	Wyoming	25,427	0.9%

RANK ORDER

RANK	STATE	MILES	% of USA
1	Texas	212,999	7.2%
2	Kansas	127,859	4.3%
3	Minnesota	117,613	4.0%
4	Missouri	106,765	3.6%
5	Iowa	102,919	3.5%
6	Illinois	98,202	3.3%
7	Oklahoma	97,268	3.3%
8	Wisconsin	92,572	3.1%
9	Arkansas	87,627	2.9%
10	Nebraska	87,297	2.9%
11	Michigan	85,853	2.9%
12	North Dakota	84,945	2.9%
13	California	83,483	2.8%
14	Georgia	83,261	2.8%
15	South Dakota	79,217	2.7%
16	Ohio	78,260	2.6%
17	Pennsylvania	76,484	2.6%
18	Alabama	75,390	2.5%
19	North Carolina	71,674	2.4%
20	Indiana	71,299	2.4%
21	Montana	71,115	2.4%
22	Tennessee	69,719	2.3%
23	Colorado	68,921	2.3%
24	Kentucky	66,213	2.2%
25	New York	66,071	2.2%
26	Mississippi	63,929	2.1%
27	Washington	60,784	2.0%
28	New Mexico	60,386	2.0%
29	Virginia	50,334	1.7%
30	South Carolina	49,833	1.7%
31	Oregon	46,260	1.6%
32	Louisiana	44,758	1.5%
33	Idaho	42,128	1.4%
34	Florida	40,366	1.4%
35	Arizona	37,522	1.3%
36	Utah	33,632	1.1%
37	West Virginia	33,092	1.1%
38	Nevada	26,741	0.9%
39	Wyoming	25,427	0.9%
40	Maine	19,837	0.7%
41	Maryland	14,051	0.5%
42	Alaska	12,987	0.4%
43	Vermont	12,965	0.4%
44	New Hampshire	11,098	0.4%
45	Massachusetts	7,978	0.3%
46	New Jersey	7,298	0.2%
47	Connecticut	6,228	0.2%
48	Delaware	3,302	0.1%
49	Hawaii	2,052	0.1%
50	Rhode Island	1,214	0.0%
	District of Columbia	0	0.0%

Source: U.S. Department of Transportation, Federal Highway Administration
    "Highway Statistics 2008" (Table HM-10, http://www.fhwa.dot.gov/policyinformation/statistics/2008/index.cfm)
*Does not include 3,105 miles of rural roads and streets in Puerto Rico.

Urban Road and Street Mileage in 2008

National Total = 1,065,540 Urban Miles*

ALPHA ORDER

RANK	STATE	MILES	% of USA
20	Alabama	21,935	2.1%
47	Alaska	2,341	0.2%
16	Arizona	22,917	2.2%
31	Arkansas	12,185	1.1%
2	California	89,029	8.4%
22	Colorado	19,345	1.8%
27	Connecticut	15,137	1.4%
44	Delaware	2,979	0.3%
3	Florida	81,020	7.6%
8	Georgia	38,614	3.6%
48	Hawaii	2,310	0.2%
38	Idaho	5,660	0.5%
7	Illinois	41,290	3.9%
13	Indiana	24,314	2.3%
32	Iowa	11,307	1.1%
29	Kansas	12,750	1.2%
30	Kentucky	12,536	1.2%
25	Louisiana	16,335	1.5%
43	Maine	2,992	0.3%
23	Maryland	17,334	1.6%
12	Massachusetts	28,126	2.6%
9	Michigan	35,813	3.4%
21	Minnesota	20,626	1.9%
34	Mississippi	10,957	1.0%
15	Missouri	22,952	2.2%
42	Montana	3,056	0.3%
37	Nebraska	6,318	0.6%
36	Nevada	7,166	0.7%
41	New Hampshire	4,908	0.5%
11	New Jersey	31,455	3.0%
35	New Mexico	7,998	0.8%
4	New York	48,402	4.5%
10	North Carolina	33,429	3.1%
49	North Dakota	1,897	0.2%
6	Ohio	44,713	4.2%
26	Oklahoma	16,057	1.5%
28	Oregon	12,990	1.2%
5	Pennsylvania	45,288	4.3%
40	Rhode Island	5,190	0.5%
24	South Carolina	16,421	1.5%
45	South Dakota	2,932	0.3%
18	Tennessee	22,454	2.1%
1	Texas	93,405	8.8%
33	Utah	11,073	1.0%
50	Vermont	1,458	0.1%
14	Virginia	23,569	2.2%
17	Washington	22,743	2.1%
39	West Virginia	5,360	0.5%
19	Wisconsin	22,271	2.1%
46	Wyoming	2,678	0.3%

RANK ORDER

RANK	STATE	MILES	% of USA
1	Texas	93,405	8.8%
2	California	89,029	8.4%
3	Florida	81,020	7.6%
4	New York	48,402	4.5%
5	Pennsylvania	45,288	4.3%
6	Ohio	44,713	4.2%
7	Illinois	41,290	3.9%
8	Georgia	38,614	3.6%
9	Michigan	35,813	3.4%
10	North Carolina	33,429	3.1%
11	New Jersey	31,455	3.0%
12	Massachusetts	28,126	2.6%
13	Indiana	24,314	2.3%
14	Virginia	23,569	2.2%
15	Missouri	22,952	2.2%
16	Arizona	22,917	2.2%
17	Washington	22,743	2.1%
18	Tennessee	22,454	2.1%
19	Wisconsin	22,271	2.1%
20	Alabama	21,935	2.1%
21	Minnesota	20,626	1.9%
22	Colorado	19,345	1.8%
23	Maryland	17,334	1.6%
24	South Carolina	16,421	1.5%
25	Louisiana	16,335	1.5%
26	Oklahoma	16,057	1.5%
27	Connecticut	15,137	1.4%
28	Oregon	12,990	1.2%
29	Kansas	12,750	1.2%
30	Kentucky	12,536	1.2%
31	Arkansas	12,185	1.1%
32	Iowa	11,307	1.1%
33	Utah	11,073	1.0%
34	Mississippi	10,957	1.0%
35	New Mexico	7,998	0.8%
36	Nevada	7,166	0.7%
37	Nebraska	6,318	0.6%
38	Idaho	5,660	0.5%
39	West Virginia	5,360	0.5%
40	Rhode Island	5,190	0.5%
41	New Hampshire	4,908	0.5%
42	Montana	3,056	0.3%
43	Maine	2,992	0.3%
44	Delaware	2,979	0.3%
45	South Dakota	2,932	0.3%
46	Wyoming	2,678	0.3%
47	Alaska	2,341	0.2%
48	Hawaii	2,310	0.2%
49	North Dakota	1,897	0.2%
50	Vermont	1,458	0.1%
	District of Columbia	1,505	0.1%

Source: U.S. Department of Transportation, Federal Highway Administration
   "Highway Statistics 2008" (Table HM-10, http://www.fhwa.dot.gov/policyinformation/statistics/2008/index.cfm)
*Does not include 13,467 miles of urban roads and streets in Puerto Rico.

Percent of Roadways in Mediocre or Poor Condition: 2008

National Percent = 17.9%*

ALPHA ORDER

RANK	STATE	PERCENT
37	Alabama	9.5
8	Alaska	32.4
34	Arizona	10.3
17	Arkansas	24.4
3	California	40.5
32	Colorado	11.9
27	Connecticut	14.2
26	Delaware	15.4
49	Florida	4.5
44	Georgia	7.9
2	Hawaii	46.1
5	Idaho	35.2
24	Illinois	16.8
33	Indiana	11.1
25	Iowa	16.2
7	Kansas	32.6
50	Kentucky	3.4
13	Louisiana	26.8
19	Maine	20.9
6	Maryland	34.6
28	Massachusetts	13.8
18	Michigan	21.7
46	Minnesota	7.8
21	Mississippi	18.1
14	Missouri	26.6
47	Montana	6.6
35	Nebraska	10.2
36	Nevada	9.6
20	New Hampshire	20.8
1	New Jersey	49.5
10	New Mexico	29.4
16	New York	25.6
39	North Carolina	8.6
38	North Dakota	9.1
48	Ohio	6.3
9	Oklahoma	32.3
40	Oregon	8.5
15	Pennsylvania	26.1
12	Rhode Island	28.9
29	South Carolina	13.0
22	South Dakota	17.9
44	Tennessee	7.9
31	Texas	12.2
43	Utah	8.0
4	Vermont	36.3
42	Virginia	8.2
30	Washington	12.8
10	West Virginia	29.4
23	Wisconsin	17.7
40	Wyoming	8.5

RANK ORDER

RANK	STATE	PERCENT
1	New Jersey	49.5
2	Hawaii	46.1
3	California	40.5
4	Vermont	36.3
5	Idaho	35.2
6	Maryland	34.6
7	Kansas	32.6
8	Alaska	32.4
9	Oklahoma	32.3
10	New Mexico	29.4
10	West Virginia	29.4
12	Rhode Island	28.9
13	Louisiana	26.8
14	Missouri	26.6
15	Pennsylvania	26.1
16	New York	25.6
17	Arkansas	24.4
18	Michigan	21.7
19	Maine	20.9
20	New Hampshire	20.8
21	Mississippi	18.1
22	South Dakota	17.9
23	Wisconsin	17.7
24	Illinois	16.8
25	Iowa	16.2
26	Delaware	15.4
27	Connecticut	14.2
28	Massachusetts	13.8
29	South Carolina	13.0
30	Washington	12.8
31	Texas	12.2
32	Colorado	11.9
33	Indiana	11.1
34	Arizona	10.3
35	Nebraska	10.2
36	Nevada	9.6
37	Alabama	9.5
38	North Dakota	9.1
39	North Carolina	8.6
40	Oregon	8.5
40	Wyoming	8.5
42	Virginia	8.2
43	Utah	8.0
44	Georgia	7.9
44	Tennessee	7.9
46	Minnesota	7.8
47	Montana	6.6
48	Ohio	6.3
49	Florida	4.5
50	Kentucky	3.4

District of Columbia	96.0

Source: CQ Press using data from U.S. Department of Transportation, Bureau of Transportation Statistics
"State Transportation Statistics 2009" (http://www.bts.gov/publications/state_transportation_statistics/)
*Does not include 3,632 miles for which the condition is not reported. Road condition ratings are derived from the International Roughness Index (IRI) and the Present Serviceability Rating (PSR). States are required to report to the Federal Highway Administration (FHWA) IRI data for the Interstate system, other principal arterials, rural minor arterials, and the National Highway System regardless of functional system.

Bridges in 2010

National Total = 602,273 Bridges*

ALPHA ORDER

RANK	STATE	BRIDGES	% of USA
15	Alabama	16,018	2.7%
48	Alaska	1,134	0.2%
29	Arizona	7,578	1.3%
23	Arkansas	12,587	2.1%
6	California	24,557	4.1%
27	Colorado	8,506	1.4%
38	Connecticut	4,191	0.7%
49	Delaware	861	0.1%
24	Florida	11,912	2.0%
17	Georgia	14,670	2.4%
47	Hawaii	1,137	0.2%
39	Idaho	4,132	0.7%
3	Illinois	26,337	4.4%
11	Indiana	18,548	3.1%
5	Iowa	24,731	4.1%
4	Kansas	25,329	4.2%
19	Kentucky	13,849	2.3%
21	Louisiana	13,361	2.2%
45	Maine	2,393	0.4%
34	Maryland	5,195	0.9%
36	Massachusetts	5,113	0.8%
25	Michigan	10,928	1.8%
22	Minnesota	13,108	2.2%
14	Mississippi	17,065	2.8%
7	Missouri	24,245	4.0%
35	Montana	5,119	0.8%
16	Nebraska	15,376	2.6%
46	Nevada	1,753	0.3%
44	New Hampshire	2,409	0.4%
32	New Jersey	6,520	1.1%
40	New Mexico	3,903	0.6%
13	New York	17,365	2.9%
12	North Carolina	18,099	3.0%
37	North Dakota	4,418	0.7%
2	Ohio	28,033	4.7%
8	Oklahoma	23,692	3.9%
30	Oregon	7,255	1.2%
9	Pennsylvania	22,359	3.7%
50	Rhode Island	757	0.1%
26	South Carolina	9,252	1.5%
33	South Dakota	5,891	1.0%
10	Tennessee	19,892	3.3%
1	Texas	51,440	8.5%
42	Utah	2,911	0.5%
43	Vermont	2,712	0.5%
20	Virginia	13,522	2.2%
28	Washington	7,755	1.3%
31	West Virginia	7,069	1.2%
18	Wisconsin	13,982	2.3%
41	Wyoming	3,060	0.5%

RANK ORDER

RANK	STATE	BRIDGES	% of USA
1	Texas	51,440	8.5%
2	Ohio	28,033	4.7%
3	Illinois	26,337	4.4%
4	Kansas	25,329	4.2%
5	Iowa	24,731	4.1%
6	California	24,557	4.1%
7	Missouri	24,245	4.0%
8	Oklahoma	23,692	3.9%
9	Pennsylvania	22,359	3.7%
10	Tennessee	19,892	3.3%
11	Indiana	18,548	3.1%
12	North Carolina	18,099	3.0%
13	New York	17,365	2.9%
14	Mississippi	17,065	2.8%
15	Alabama	16,018	2.7%
16	Nebraska	15,376	2.6%
17	Georgia	14,670	2.4%
18	Wisconsin	13,982	2.3%
19	Kentucky	13,849	2.3%
20	Virginia	13,522	2.2%
21	Louisiana	13,361	2.2%
22	Minnesota	13,108	2.2%
23	Arkansas	12,587	2.1%
24	Florida	11,912	2.0%
25	Michigan	10,928	1.8%
26	South Carolina	9,252	1.5%
27	Colorado	8,506	1.4%
28	Washington	7,755	1.3%
29	Arizona	7,578	1.3%
30	Oregon	7,255	1.2%
31	West Virginia	7,069	1.2%
32	New Jersey	6,520	1.1%
33	South Dakota	5,891	1.0%
34	Maryland	5,195	0.9%
35	Montana	5,119	0.8%
36	Massachusetts	5,113	0.8%
37	North Dakota	4,418	0.7%
38	Connecticut	4,191	0.7%
39	Idaho	4,132	0.7%
40	New Mexico	3,903	0.6%
41	Wyoming	3,060	0.5%
42	Utah	2,911	0.5%
43	Vermont	2,712	0.5%
44	New Hampshire	2,409	0.4%
45	Maine	2,393	0.4%
46	Nevada	1,753	0.3%
47	Hawaii	1,137	0.2%
48	Alaska	1,134	0.2%
49	Delaware	861	0.1%
50	Rhode Island	757	0.1%
	District of Columbia	244	0.0%

Source: U.S. Department of Transportation, Federal Highway Administration
"Deficient Bridges by State and Highway System, 2010" (http://www.fhwa.dot.gov/bridge/deficient.htm)
*As of December 2010. Includes federal-aid and nonfederal-aid system bridges. National total does not include 2,201 bridges in Puerto Rico.

Deficient Bridges in 2010

National Total = 145,538 Deficient Bridges*

ALPHA ORDER

RANK	STATE	BRIDGES	% of USA
18	Alabama	3,676	2.5%
48	Alaska	280	0.2%
37	Arizona	903	0.6%
20	Arkansas	2,814	1.9%
3	California	7,091	4.9%
34	Colorado	1,399	1.0%
33	Connecticut	1,411	1.0%
50	Delaware	161	0.1%
28	Florida	1,883	1.3%
21	Georgia	2,729	1.9%
45	Hawaii	507	0.3%
40	Idaho	787	0.5%
14	Illinois	4,002	2.7%
13	Indiana	4,003	2.8%
6	Iowa	6,599	4.5%
10	Kansas	4,899	3.4%
11	Kentucky	4,311	3.0%
16	Louisiana	3,829	2.6%
41	Maine	771	0.5%
35	Maryland	1,322	0.9%
23	Massachusetts	2,548	1.8%
22	Michigan	2,726	1.9%
31	Minnesota	1,537	1.1%
12	Mississippi	4,019	2.8%
4	Missouri	7,021	4.8%
38	Montana	877	0.6%
17	Nebraska	3,794	2.6%
49	Nevada	208	0.1%
42	New Hampshire	747	0.5%
25	New Jersey	2,280	1.6%
44	New Mexico	642	0.4%
8	New York	6,467	4.4%
9	North Carolina	4,976	3.4%
36	North Dakota	943	0.6%
7	Ohio	6,598	4.5%
5	Oklahoma	6,811	4.7%
30	Oregon	1,650	1.1%
1	Pennsylvania	9,608	6.6%
47	Rhode Island	396	0.3%
26	South Carolina	1,995	1.4%
32	South Dakota	1,425	1.0%
15	Tennessee	3,856	2.6%
2	Texas	9,133	6.3%
46	Utah	420	0.3%
39	Vermont	861	0.6%
19	Virginia	3,429	2.4%
27	Washington	1,971	1.4%
24	West Virginia	2,543	1.7%
29	Wisconsin	1,861	1.3%
43	Wyoming	661	0.5%

RANK ORDER

RANK	STATE	BRIDGES	% of USA
1	Pennsylvania	9,608	6.6%
2	Texas	9,133	6.3%
3	California	7,091	4.9%
4	Missouri	7,021	4.8%
5	Oklahoma	6,811	4.7%
6	Iowa	6,599	4.5%
7	Ohio	6,598	4.5%
8	New York	6,467	4.4%
9	North Carolina	4,976	3.4%
10	Kansas	4,899	3.4%
11	Kentucky	4,311	3.0%
12	Mississippi	4,019	2.8%
13	Indiana	4,003	2.8%
14	Illinois	4,002	2.7%
15	Tennessee	3,856	2.6%
16	Louisiana	3,829	2.6%
17	Nebraska	3,794	2.6%
18	Alabama	3,676	2.5%
19	Virginia	3,429	2.4%
20	Arkansas	2,814	1.9%
21	Georgia	2,729	1.9%
22	Michigan	2,726	1.9%
23	Massachusetts	2,548	1.8%
24	West Virginia	2,543	1.7%
25	New Jersey	2,280	1.6%
26	South Carolina	1,995	1.4%
27	Washington	1,971	1.4%
28	Florida	1,883	1.3%
29	Wisconsin	1,861	1.3%
30	Oregon	1,650	1.1%
31	Minnesota	1,537	1.1%
32	South Dakota	1,425	1.0%
33	Connecticut	1,411	1.0%
34	Colorado	1,399	1.0%
35	Maryland	1,322	0.9%
36	North Dakota	943	0.6%
37	Arizona	903	0.6%
38	Montana	877	0.6%
39	Vermont	861	0.6%
40	Idaho	787	0.5%
41	Maine	771	0.5%
42	New Hampshire	747	0.5%
43	Wyoming	661	0.5%
44	New Mexico	642	0.4%
45	Hawaii	507	0.3%
46	Utah	420	0.3%
47	Rhode Island	396	0.3%
48	Alaska	280	0.2%
49	Nevada	208	0.1%
50	Delaware	161	0.1%
	District of Columbia	158	0.1%

Source: U.S. Department of Transportation, Federal Highway Administration
"Deficient Bridges by State and Highway System, 2010" (http://www.fhwa.dot.gov/bridge/deficient.htm)
*As of December 2010. Includes federal-aid and nonfederal-aid system bridges. National total does not include 1,095 deficient bridges in Puerto Rico. Bridges classified as deficient are either functionally obsolete or structurally deficient and are not necessarily unsafe.

Deficient Bridges as a Percent of Total Bridges in 2010

National Percent = 24.2% of Bridges are Deficient*

ALPHA ORDER

RANK	STATE	PERCENT
28	Alabama	22.9
23	Alaska	24.7
48	Arizona	11.9
30	Arkansas	22.4
14	California	28.9
42	Colorado	16.4
8	Connecticut	33.7
38	Delaware	18.7
44	Florida	15.8
39	Georgia	18.6
3	Hawaii	44.6
37	Idaho	19.0
45	Illinois	15.2
31	Indiana	21.6
18	Iowa	26.7
36	Kansas	19.3
11	Kentucky	31.1
15	Louisiana	28.7
9	Maine	32.2
19	Maryland	25.4
2	Massachusetts	49.8
22	Michigan	24.9
50	Minnesota	11.7
26	Mississippi	23.6
13	Missouri	29.0
41	Montana	17.1
23	Nebraska	24.7
48	Nevada	11.9
12	New Hampshire	31.0
7	New Jersey	35.0
42	New Mexico	16.4
5	New York	37.2
17	North Carolina	27.5
34	North Dakota	21.3
27	Ohio	23.5
15	Oklahoma	28.7
29	Oregon	22.7
4	Pennsylvania	43.0
1	Rhode Island	52.3
31	South Carolina	21.6
25	South Dakota	24.2
35	Tennessee	19.4
40	Texas	17.8
46	Utah	14.4
10	Vermont	31.7
19	Virginia	25.4
19	Washington	25.4
6	West Virginia	36.0
47	Wisconsin	13.3
31	Wyoming	21.6

RANK ORDER

RANK	STATE	PERCENT
1	Rhode Island	52.3
2	Massachusetts	49.8
3	Hawaii	44.6
4	Pennsylvania	43.0
5	New York	37.2
6	West Virginia	36.0
7	New Jersey	35.0
8	Connecticut	33.7
9	Maine	32.2
10	Vermont	31.7
11	Kentucky	31.1
12	New Hampshire	31.0
13	Missouri	29.0
14	California	28.9
15	Louisiana	28.7
15	Oklahoma	28.7
17	North Carolina	27.5
18	Iowa	26.7
19	Maryland	25.4
19	Virginia	25.4
19	Washington	25.4
22	Michigan	24.9
23	Alaska	24.7
23	Nebraska	24.7
25	South Dakota	24.2
26	Mississippi	23.6
27	Ohio	23.5
28	Alabama	22.9
29	Oregon	22.7
30	Arkansas	22.4
31	Indiana	21.6
31	South Carolina	21.6
31	Wyoming	21.6
34	North Dakota	21.3
35	Tennessee	19.4
36	Kansas	19.3
37	Idaho	19.0
38	Delaware	18.7
39	Georgia	18.6
40	Texas	17.8
41	Montana	17.1
42	Colorado	16.4
42	New Mexico	16.4
44	Florida	15.8
45	Illinois	15.2
46	Utah	14.4
47	Wisconsin	13.3
48	Arizona	11.9
48	Nevada	11.9
50	Minnesota	11.7

District of Columbia — 64.8

Source: CQ Press using data from U.S. Department of Transportation, Federal Highway Administration
"Deficient Bridges by State and Highway System, 2010" (http://www.fhwa.dot.gov/bridge/deficient.htm)
*As of December 2010. Includes federal-aid and nonfederal-aid system bridges. National percent does not include bridges in Puerto Rico. Bridges classified as deficient are either functionally obsolete or structurally deficient and are not necessarily unsafe.

Vehicle-Miles of Travel in 2008

National Total = 2,973,509,000,000 Miles

<table>
<tr><td colspan="4">ALPHA ORDER</td><td colspan="4">RANK ORDER</td></tr>
<tr><th>RANK</th><th>STATE</th><th>MILES</th><th>% of USA</th><th>RANK</th><th>STATE</th><th>MILES</th><th>% of USA</th></tr>
<tr><td>17</td><td>Alabama</td><td>59,303,000,000</td><td>2.0%</td><td>1</td><td>California</td><td>327,286,000,000</td><td>11.0%</td></tr>
<tr><td>50</td><td>Alaska</td><td>4,865,000,000</td><td>0.2%</td><td>2</td><td>Texas</td><td>235,382,000,000</td><td>7.9%</td></tr>
<tr><td>16</td><td>Arizona</td><td>61,628,000,000</td><td>2.1%</td><td>3</td><td>Florida</td><td>198,616,000,000</td><td>6.7%</td></tr>
<tr><td>30</td><td>Arkansas</td><td>33,163,000,000</td><td>1.1%</td><td>4</td><td>New York</td><td>134,085,000,000</td><td>4.5%</td></tr>
<tr><td>1</td><td>California</td><td>327,286,000,000</td><td>11.0%</td><td>5</td><td>Georgia</td><td>109,057,000,000</td><td>3.7%</td></tr>
<tr><td>25</td><td>Colorado</td><td>47,860,000,000</td><td>1.6%</td><td>6</td><td>Ohio</td><td>108,302,000,000</td><td>3.6%</td></tr>
<tr><td>31</td><td>Connecticut</td><td>31,737,000,000</td><td>1.1%</td><td>7</td><td>Pennsylvania</td><td>107,848,000,000</td><td>3.6%</td></tr>
<tr><td>46</td><td>Delaware</td><td>8,976,000,000</td><td>0.3%</td><td>8</td><td>Illinois</td><td>106,079,000,000</td><td>3.6%</td></tr>
<tr><td>3</td><td>Florida</td><td>198,616,000,000</td><td>6.7%</td><td>9</td><td>Michigan</td><td>101,825,000,000</td><td>3.4%</td></tr>
<tr><td>5</td><td>Georgia</td><td>109,057,000,000</td><td>3.7%</td><td>10</td><td>North Carolina</td><td>101,712,000,000</td><td>3.4%</td></tr>
<tr><td>43</td><td>Hawaii</td><td>10,278,000,000</td><td>0.3%</td><td>11</td><td>Virginia</td><td>82,278,000,000</td><td>2.8%</td></tr>
<tr><td>39</td><td>Idaho</td><td>15,251,000,000</td><td>0.5%</td><td>12</td><td>New Jersey</td><td>73,629,000,000</td><td>2.5%</td></tr>
<tr><td>8</td><td>Illinois</td><td>106,079,000,000</td><td>3.6%</td><td>13</td><td>Indiana</td><td>70,973,000,000</td><td>2.4%</td></tr>
<tr><td>13</td><td>Indiana</td><td>70,973,000,000</td><td>2.4%</td><td>14</td><td>Tennessee</td><td>69,469,000,000</td><td>2.3%</td></tr>
<tr><td>32</td><td>Iowa</td><td>30,713,000,000</td><td>1.0%</td><td>15</td><td>Missouri</td><td>68,273,000,000</td><td>2.3%</td></tr>
<tr><td>33</td><td>Kansas</td><td>29,727,000,000</td><td>1.0%</td><td>16</td><td>Arizona</td><td>61,628,000,000</td><td>2.1%</td></tr>
<tr><td>26</td><td>Kentucky</td><td>47,534,000,000</td><td>1.6%</td><td>17</td><td>Alabama</td><td>59,303,000,000</td><td>2.0%</td></tr>
<tr><td>27</td><td>Louisiana</td><td>45,091,000,000</td><td>1.5%</td><td>18</td><td>Minnesota</td><td>57,995,000,000</td><td>2.0%</td></tr>
<tr><td>40</td><td>Maine</td><td>14,559,000,000</td><td>0.5%</td><td>19</td><td>Wisconsin</td><td>57,462,000,000</td><td>1.9%</td></tr>
<tr><td>21</td><td>Maryland</td><td>55,023,000,000</td><td>1.9%</td><td>20</td><td>Washington</td><td>55,558,000,000</td><td>1.9%</td></tr>
<tr><td>22</td><td>Massachusetts</td><td>54,505,000,000</td><td>1.8%</td><td>21</td><td>Maryland</td><td>55,023,000,000</td><td>1.9%</td></tr>
<tr><td>9</td><td>Michigan</td><td>101,825,000,000</td><td>3.4%</td><td>22</td><td>Massachusetts</td><td>54,505,000,000</td><td>1.8%</td></tr>
<tr><td>18</td><td>Minnesota</td><td>57,995,000,000</td><td>2.0%</td><td>23</td><td>South Carolina</td><td>49,597,000,000</td><td>1.7%</td></tr>
<tr><td>28</td><td>Mississippi</td><td>43,711,000,000</td><td>1.5%</td><td>24</td><td>Oklahoma</td><td>48,499,000,000</td><td>1.6%</td></tr>
<tr><td>15</td><td>Missouri</td><td>68,273,000,000</td><td>2.3%</td><td>25</td><td>Colorado</td><td>47,860,000,000</td><td>1.6%</td></tr>
<tr><td>42</td><td>Montana</td><td>10,812,000,000</td><td>0.4%</td><td>26</td><td>Kentucky</td><td>47,534,000,000</td><td>1.6%</td></tr>
<tr><td>38</td><td>Nebraska</td><td>19,170,000,000</td><td>0.6%</td><td>27</td><td>Louisiana</td><td>45,091,000,000</td><td>1.5%</td></tr>
<tr><td>36</td><td>Nevada</td><td>20,780,000,000</td><td>0.7%</td><td>28</td><td>Mississippi</td><td>43,711,000,000</td><td>1.5%</td></tr>
<tr><td>41</td><td>New Hampshire</td><td>13,040,000,000</td><td>0.4%</td><td>29</td><td>Oregon</td><td>33,468,000,000</td><td>1.1%</td></tr>
<tr><td>12</td><td>New Jersey</td><td>73,629,000,000</td><td>2.5%</td><td>30</td><td>Arkansas</td><td>33,163,000,000</td><td>1.1%</td></tr>
<tr><td>34</td><td>New Mexico</td><td>26,279,000,000</td><td>0.9%</td><td>31</td><td>Connecticut</td><td>31,737,000,000</td><td>1.1%</td></tr>
<tr><td>4</td><td>New York</td><td>134,085,000,000</td><td>4.5%</td><td>32</td><td>Iowa</td><td>30,713,000,000</td><td>1.0%</td></tr>
<tr><td>10</td><td>North Carolina</td><td>101,712,000,000</td><td>3.4%</td><td>33</td><td>Kansas</td><td>29,727,000,000</td><td>1.0%</td></tr>
<tr><td>48</td><td>North Dakota</td><td>7,820,000,000</td><td>0.3%</td><td>34</td><td>New Mexico</td><td>26,279,000,000</td><td>0.9%</td></tr>
<tr><td>6</td><td>Ohio</td><td>108,302,000,000</td><td>3.6%</td><td>35</td><td>Utah</td><td>25,974,000,000</td><td>0.9%</td></tr>
<tr><td>24</td><td>Oklahoma</td><td>48,499,000,000</td><td>1.6%</td><td>36</td><td>Nevada</td><td>20,780,000,000</td><td>0.7%</td></tr>
<tr><td>29</td><td>Oregon</td><td>33,468,000,000</td><td>1.1%</td><td>37</td><td>West Virginia</td><td>20,774,000,000</td><td>0.7%</td></tr>
<tr><td>7</td><td>Pennsylvania</td><td>107,848,000,000</td><td>3.6%</td><td>38</td><td>Nebraska</td><td>19,170,000,000</td><td>0.6%</td></tr>
<tr><td>47</td><td>Rhode Island</td><td>8,187,000,000</td><td>0.3%</td><td>39</td><td>Idaho</td><td>15,251,000,000</td><td>0.5%</td></tr>
<tr><td>23</td><td>South Carolina</td><td>49,597,000,000</td><td>1.7%</td><td>40</td><td>Maine</td><td>14,559,000,000</td><td>0.5%</td></tr>
<tr><td>45</td><td>South Dakota</td><td>8,986,000,000</td><td>0.3%</td><td>41</td><td>New Hampshire</td><td>13,040,000,000</td><td>0.4%</td></tr>
<tr><td>14</td><td>Tennessee</td><td>69,469,000,000</td><td>2.3%</td><td>42</td><td>Montana</td><td>10,812,000,000</td><td>0.4%</td></tr>
<tr><td>2</td><td>Texas</td><td>235,382,000,000</td><td>7.9%</td><td>43</td><td>Hawaii</td><td>10,278,000,000</td><td>0.3%</td></tr>
<tr><td>35</td><td>Utah</td><td>25,974,000,000</td><td>0.9%</td><td>44</td><td>Wyoming</td><td>9,447,000,000</td><td>0.3%</td></tr>
<tr><td>49</td><td>Vermont</td><td>7,312,000,000</td><td>0.2%</td><td>45</td><td>South Dakota</td><td>8,986,000,000</td><td>0.3%</td></tr>
<tr><td>11</td><td>Virginia</td><td>82,278,000,000</td><td>2.8%</td><td>46</td><td>Delaware</td><td>8,976,000,000</td><td>0.3%</td></tr>
<tr><td>20</td><td>Washington</td><td>55,558,000,000</td><td>1.9%</td><td>47</td><td>Rhode Island</td><td>8,187,000,000</td><td>0.3%</td></tr>
<tr><td>37</td><td>West Virginia</td><td>20,774,000,000</td><td>0.7%</td><td>48</td><td>North Dakota</td><td>7,820,000,000</td><td>0.3%</td></tr>
<tr><td>19</td><td>Wisconsin</td><td>57,462,000,000</td><td>1.9%</td><td>49</td><td>Vermont</td><td>7,312,000,000</td><td>0.2%</td></tr>
<tr><td>44</td><td>Wyoming</td><td>9,447,000,000</td><td>0.3%</td><td>50</td><td>Alaska</td><td>4,865,000,000</td><td>0.2%</td></tr>
<tr><td></td><td></td><td></td><td></td><td></td><td>District of Columbia</td><td>3,611,000,000</td><td>0.1%</td></tr>
</table>

Source: U.S. Department of Transportation, Federal Highway Administration
"Highway Statistics 2008" (Table VM-2, http://www.fhwa.dot.gov/policyinformation/statistics/2008/index.cfm)

Highway Fatalities in 2009

National Total = 33,808 Fatalities

ALPHA ORDER

RANK	STATE	FATALITIES	% of USA
14	Alabama	848	2.5%
50	Alaska	64	0.2%
16	Arizona	807	2.4%
22	Arkansas	585	1.7%
1	California	3,081	9.1%
27	Colorado	465	1.4%
38	Connecticut	223	0.7%
45	Delaware	116	0.3%
3	Florida	2,558	7.6%
5	Georgia	1,284	3.8%
47	Hawaii	109	0.3%
37	Idaho	226	0.7%
10	Illinois	911	2.7%
21	Indiana	693	2.0%
31	Iowa	372	1.1%
29	Kansas	386	1.1%
17	Kentucky	791	2.3%
15	Louisiana	821	2.4%
41	Maine	159	0.5%
25	Maryland	547	1.6%
34	Massachusetts	334	1.0%
13	Michigan	871	2.6%
28	Minnesota	421	1.2%
20	Mississippi	700	2.1%
12	Missouri	878	2.6%
40	Montana	221	0.7%
38	Nebraska	223	0.7%
36	Nevada	243	0.7%
46	New Hampshire	110	0.3%
23	New Jersey	583	1.7%
32	New Mexico	361	1.1%
7	New York	1,156	3.4%
4	North Carolina	1,314	3.9%
42	North Dakota	140	0.4%
8	Ohio	1,021	3.0%
19	Oklahoma	738	2.2%
30	Oregon	377	1.1%
6	Pennsylvania	1,256	3.7%
48	Rhode Island	83	0.2%
11	South Carolina	894	2.6%
44	South Dakota	131	0.4%
9	Tennessee	989	2.9%
2	Texas	3,071	9.1%
35	Utah	244	0.7%
49	Vermont	74	0.2%
18	Virginia	757	2.2%
26	Washington	492	1.5%
33	West Virginia	356	1.1%
24	Wisconsin	561	1.7%
43	Wyoming	134	0.4%

RANK ORDER

RANK	STATE	FATALITIES	% of USA
1	California	3,081	9.1%
2	Texas	3,071	9.1%
3	Florida	2,558	7.6%
4	North Carolina	1,314	3.9%
5	Georgia	1,284	3.8%
6	Pennsylvania	1,256	3.7%
7	New York	1,156	3.4%
8	Ohio	1,021	3.0%
9	Tennessee	989	2.9%
10	Illinois	911	2.7%
11	South Carolina	894	2.6%
12	Missouri	878	2.6%
13	Michigan	871	2.6%
14	Alabama	848	2.5%
15	Louisiana	821	2.4%
16	Arizona	807	2.4%
17	Kentucky	791	2.3%
18	Virginia	757	2.2%
19	Oklahoma	738	2.2%
20	Mississippi	700	2.1%
21	Indiana	693	2.0%
22	Arkansas	585	1.7%
23	New Jersey	583	1.7%
24	Wisconsin	561	1.7%
25	Maryland	547	1.6%
26	Washington	492	1.5%
27	Colorado	465	1.4%
28	Minnesota	421	1.2%
29	Kansas	386	1.1%
30	Oregon	377	1.1%
31	Iowa	372	1.1%
32	New Mexico	361	1.1%
33	West Virginia	356	1.1%
34	Massachusetts	334	1.0%
35	Utah	244	0.7%
36	Nevada	243	0.7%
37	Idaho	226	0.7%
38	Connecticut	223	0.7%
38	Nebraska	223	0.7%
40	Montana	221	0.7%
41	Maine	159	0.5%
42	North Dakota	140	0.4%
43	Wyoming	134	0.4%
44	South Dakota	131	0.4%
45	Delaware	116	0.3%
46	New Hampshire	110	0.3%
47	Hawaii	109	0.3%
48	Rhode Island	83	0.2%
49	Vermont	74	0.2%
50	Alaska	64	0.2%
	District of Columbia	29	0.1%

Source: U.S. Department of Transportation, National Highway Traffic Safety Administration
"Traffic Safety Facts 2009, Early Edition" (http://www.nhtsa.dot.gov/)

Highway Fatalities in 2008

National Total = 37,261 Fatalities

RANK	STATE	FATALITIES	% of USA
12	Alabama	966	2.6%
50	Alaska	62	0.2%
14	Arizona	937	2.5%
23	Arkansas	600	1.6%
1	California	3,434	9.2%
26	Colorado	548	1.5%
37	Connecticut	264	0.7%
44	Delaware	121	0.3%
3	Florida	2,978	8.0%
4	Georgia	1,493	4.0%
46	Hawaii	107	0.3%
38	Idaho	232	0.6%
9	Illinois	1,043	2.8%
19	Indiana	814	2.2%
30	Iowa	412	1.1%
31	Kansas	385	1.0%
17	Kentucky	826	2.2%
16	Louisiana	912	2.4%
42	Maine	155	0.4%
24	Maryland	591	1.6%
34	Massachusetts	363	1.0%
11	Michigan	980	2.6%
28	Minnesota	456	1.2%
20	Mississippi	783	2.1%
13	Missouri	960	2.6%
39	Montana	229	0.6%
40	Nebraska	208	0.6%
35	Nevada	324	0.9%
43	New Hampshire	139	0.4%
25	New Jersey	590	1.6%
33	New Mexico	366	1.0%
7	New York	1,231	3.3%
6	North Carolina	1,433	3.8%
47	North Dakota	104	0.3%
8	Ohio	1,190	3.2%
21	Oklahoma	749	2.0%
29	Oregon	416	1.1%
5	Pennsylvania	1,468	3.9%
49	Rhode Island	65	0.2%
15	South Carolina	920	2.5%
45	South Dakota	119	0.3%
10	Tennessee	1,035	2.8%
2	Texas	3,382	9.1%
36	Utah	275	0.7%
48	Vermont	73	0.2%
18	Virginia	824	2.2%
27	Washington	521	1.4%
32	West Virginia	380	1.0%
22	Wisconsin	605	1.6%
41	Wyoming	159	0.4%

RANK	STATE	FATALITIES	% of USA
1	California	3,434	9.2%
2	Texas	3,382	9.1%
3	Florida	2,978	8.0%
4	Georgia	1,493	4.0%
5	Pennsylvania	1,468	3.9%
6	North Carolina	1,433	3.8%
7	New York	1,231	3.3%
8	Ohio	1,190	3.2%
9	Illinois	1,043	2.8%
10	Tennessee	1,035	2.8%
11	Michigan	980	2.6%
12	Alabama	966	2.6%
13	Missouri	960	2.6%
14	Arizona	937	2.5%
15	South Carolina	920	2.5%
16	Louisiana	912	2.4%
17	Kentucky	826	2.2%
18	Virginia	824	2.2%
19	Indiana	814	2.2%
20	Mississippi	783	2.1%
21	Oklahoma	749	2.0%
22	Wisconsin	605	1.6%
23	Arkansas	600	1.6%
24	Maryland	591	1.6%
25	New Jersey	590	1.6%
26	Colorado	548	1.5%
27	Washington	521	1.4%
28	Minnesota	456	1.2%
29	Oregon	416	1.1%
30	Iowa	412	1.1%
31	Kansas	385	1.0%
32	West Virginia	380	1.0%
33	New Mexico	366	1.0%
34	Massachusetts	363	1.0%
35	Nevada	324	0.9%
36	Utah	275	0.7%
37	Connecticut	264	0.7%
38	Idaho	232	0.6%
39	Montana	229	0.6%
40	Nebraska	208	0.6%
41	Wyoming	159	0.4%
42	Maine	155	0.4%
43	New Hampshire	139	0.4%
44	Delaware	121	0.3%
45	South Dakota	119	0.3%
46	Hawaii	107	0.3%
47	North Dakota	104	0.3%
48	Vermont	73	0.2%
49	Rhode Island	65	0.2%
50	Alaska	62	0.2%
	District of Columbia	34	0.1%

Source: U.S. Department of Transportation, National Highway Traffic Safety Administration
"Traffic Safety Facts-Speeding" (http://www.nhtsa.dot.gov/portal/site/nhtsa/)

Highway Fatality Rate in 2008

National Rate = 1.25 Fatalities per 100 Million Vehicle-Miles of Travel

ALPHA ORDER

RANK	STATE	RATE
9	Alabama	1.63
27	Alaska	1.27
12	Arizona	1.52
5	Arkansas	1.81
37	California	1.05
29	Colorado	1.15
46	Connecticut	0.83
22	Delaware	1.35
14	Florida	1.50
20	Georgia	1.37
39	Hawaii	1.04
12	Idaho	1.52
42	Illinois	0.98
29	Indiana	1.15
23	Iowa	1.34
26	Kansas	1.30
7	Kentucky	1.74
2	Louisiana	2.02
35	Maine	1.06
33	Maryland	1.07
50	Massachusetts	0.67
43	Michigan	0.96
48	Minnesota	0.79
6	Mississippi	1.79
17	Missouri	1.41
1	Montana	2.12
32	Nebraska	1.09
10	Nevada	1.56
33	New Hampshire	1.07
47	New Jersey	0.80
19	New Mexico	1.39
45	New York	0.92
17	North Carolina	1.41
24	North Dakota	1.33
31	Ohio	1.10
11	Oklahoma	1.54
28	Oregon	1.24
21	Pennsylvania	1.36
48	Rhode Island	0.79
3	South Carolina	1.85
25	South Dakota	1.32
15	Tennessee	1.49
16	Texas	1.44
35	Utah	1.06
40	Vermont	1.00
40	Virginia	1.00
44	Washington	0.94
4	West Virginia	1.83
37	Wisconsin	1.05
8	Wyoming	1.68

RANK ORDER

RANK	STATE	RATE
1	Montana	2.12
2	Louisiana	2.02
3	South Carolina	1.85
4	West Virginia	1.83
5	Arkansas	1.81
6	Mississippi	1.79
7	Kentucky	1.74
8	Wyoming	1.68
9	Alabama	1.63
10	Nevada	1.56
11	Oklahoma	1.54
12	Arizona	1.52
12	Idaho	1.52
14	Florida	1.50
15	Tennessee	1.49
16	Texas	1.44
17	Missouri	1.41
17	North Carolina	1.41
19	New Mexico	1.39
20	Georgia	1.37
21	Pennsylvania	1.36
22	Delaware	1.35
23	Iowa	1.34
24	North Dakota	1.33
25	South Dakota	1.32
26	Kansas	1.30
27	Alaska	1.27
28	Oregon	1.24
29	Colorado	1.15
29	Indiana	1.15
31	Ohio	1.10
32	Nebraska	1.09
33	Maryland	1.07
33	New Hampshire	1.07
35	Maine	1.06
35	Utah	1.06
37	California	1.05
37	Wisconsin	1.05
39	Hawaii	1.04
40	Vermont	1.00
40	Virginia	1.00
42	Illinois	0.98
43	Michigan	0.96
44	Washington	0.94
45	New York	0.92
46	Connecticut	0.83
47	New Jersey	0.80
48	Minnesota	0.79
48	Rhode Island	0.79
50	Massachusetts	0.67
	District of Columbia	0.94

Source: CQ Press using data from U.S. Department of Transportation, National Highway Traffic Safety Administration
"Traffic Safety Facts-Speeding" (http://www.nhtsa.dot.gov/portal/site/nhtsa/)
"Highway Statistics 2008" (Table VM-2, http://www.fhwa.dot.gov/policyinformation/statistics/2008/index.cfm)

Percent of Traffic Fatalities That Were Speeding-Related: 2009

National Percent = 31.3%*

ALPHA ORDER

RANK	STATE	PERCENT
12	Alabama	38.6
8	Alaska	40.6
23	Arizona	35.1
46	Arkansas	17.9
22	California	35.3
17	Colorado	36.8
3	Connecticut	46.2
14	Delaware	37.9
41	Florida	20.9
45	Georgia	18.5
1	Hawaii	54.1
19	Idaho	35.8
20	Illinois	35.7
35	Indiana	25.1
47	Iowa	16.7
34	Kansas	26.7
42	Kentucky	19.5
23	Louisiana	35.1
13	Maine	38.4
27	Maryland	33.6
38	Massachusetts	22.8
36	Michigan	23.5
39	Minnesota	22.6
49	Mississippi	15.1
4	Missouri	43.2
11	Montana	38.9
50	Nebraska	13.5
16	Nevada	37.4
21	New Hampshire	35.5
48	New Jersey	16.3
44	New Mexico	19.1
29	New York	31.8
10	North Carolina	39.3
37	North Dakota	22.9
33	Ohio	28.1
30	Oklahoma	31.7
28	Oregon	33.2
2	Pennsylvania	50.5
25	Rhode Island	33.7
15	South Carolina	37.7
31	South Dakota	31.3
40	Tennessee	21.1
9	Texas	40.0
5	Utah	42.6
32	Vermont	29.7
43	Virginia	19.4
6	Washington	42.3
25	West Virginia	33.7
18	Wisconsin	36.2
7	Wyoming	41.8

RANK ORDER

RANK	STATE	PERCENT
1	Hawaii	54.1
2	Pennsylvania	50.5
3	Connecticut	46.2
4	Missouri	43.2
5	Utah	42.6
6	Washington	42.3
7	Wyoming	41.8
8	Alaska	40.6
9	Texas	40.0
10	North Carolina	39.3
11	Montana	38.9
12	Alabama	38.6
13	Maine	38.4
14	Delaware	37.9
15	South Carolina	37.7
16	Nevada	37.4
17	Colorado	36.8
18	Wisconsin	36.2
19	Idaho	35.8
20	Illinois	35.7
21	New Hampshire	35.5
22	California	35.3
23	Arizona	35.1
23	Louisiana	35.1
25	Rhode Island	33.7
25	West Virginia	33.7
27	Maryland	33.6
28	Oregon	33.2
29	New York	31.8
30	Oklahoma	31.7
31	South Dakota	31.3
32	Vermont	29.7
33	Ohio	28.1
34	Kansas	26.7
35	Indiana	25.1
36	Michigan	23.5
37	North Dakota	22.9
38	Massachusetts	22.8
39	Minnesota	22.6
40	Tennessee	21.1
41	Florida	20.9
42	Kentucky	19.5
43	Virginia	19.4
44	New Mexico	19.1
45	Georgia	18.5
46	Arkansas	17.9
47	Iowa	16.7
48	New Jersey	16.3
49	Mississippi	15.1
50	Nebraska	13.5

District of Columbia   34.5

Source: CQ Press using data from U.S. Department of Transportation, National Highway Traffic Safety Administration
"Traffic Safety Facts 2009, Early Edition" (http://www.nhtsa.dot.gov/)
*A speeding-related crash is if the driver was charged with a speeding-related offense or if an officer indicated that racing, driving too fast for conditions, or exceeding the posted speed limit was a contributing factor in the crash.

Percent of Vehicles Involved in Fatal Crashes That Were Large Trucks: 2008

National Percent = 8.1%*

ALPHA ORDER				RANK ORDER		
RANK	STATE	PERCENT		RANK	STATE	PERCENT
12	Alabama	9.6		1	North Dakota	15.3
45	Alaska	5.5		2	Wyoming	15.0
27	Arizona	7.9		3	Nebraska	14.4
10	Arkansas	9.8		4	Iowa	12.1
38	California	6.4		5	Indiana	11.4
25	Colorado	8.1		5	Kansas	11.4
32	Connecticut	7.2		7	Oklahoma	10.7
47	Delaware	4.6		8	Idaho	10.5
38	Florida	6.4		9	Maine	10.3
24	Georgia	8.6		10	Arkansas	9.8
49	Hawaii	4.3		11	Minnesota	9.7
8	Idaho	10.5		12	Alabama	9.6
16	Illinois	9.5		12	New Mexico	9.6
5	Indiana	11.4		12	Pennsylvania	9.6
4	Iowa	12.1		12	West Virginia	9.6
5	Kansas	11.4		16	Illinois	9.5
21	Kentucky	8.9		17	Montana	9.4
21	Louisiana	8.9		18	Missouri	9.3
9	Maine	10.3		19	Texas	9.1
42	Maryland	6.1		19	Utah	9.1
48	Massachusetts	4.5		21	Kentucky	8.9
38	Michigan	6.4		21	Louisiana	8.9
11	Minnesota	9.7		23	South Dakota	8.8
33	Mississippi	7.1		24	Georgia	8.6
18	Missouri	9.3		25	Colorado	8.1
17	Montana	9.4		25	Ohio	8.1
3	Nebraska	14.4		27	Arizona	7.9
46	Nevada	4.7		28	Wisconsin	7.8
41	New Hampshire	6.2		29	North Carolina	7.6
43	New Jersey	5.9		29	Washington	7.6
12	New Mexico	9.6		31	Oregon	7.5
36	New York	6.6		32	Connecticut	7.2
29	North Carolina	7.6		33	Mississippi	7.1
1	North Dakota	15.3		34	South Carolina	7.0
25	Ohio	8.1		35	Tennessee	6.7
7	Oklahoma	10.7		36	New York	6.6
31	Oregon	7.5		37	Virginia	6.5
12	Pennsylvania	9.6		38	California	6.4
50	Rhode Island	2.5		38	Florida	6.4
34	South Carolina	7.0		38	Michigan	6.4
23	South Dakota	8.8		41	New Hampshire	6.2
35	Tennessee	6.7		42	Maryland	6.1
19	Texas	9.1		43	New Jersey	5.9
19	Utah	9.1		43	Vermont	5.9
43	Vermont	5.9		45	Alaska	5.5
37	Virginia	6.5		46	Nevada	4.7
29	Washington	7.6		47	Delaware	4.6
12	West Virginia	9.6		48	Massachusetts	4.5
28	Wisconsin	7.8		49	Hawaii	4.3
2	Wyoming	15.0		50	Rhode Island	2.5
					District of Columbia	4.5

Source: U.S. Department of Transportation, National Highway Traffic Safety Administration
    "Traffic Safety Facts-Large Trucks" (http://www.nhtsa.dot.gov/portal/site/nhtsa/)
*Large trucks are those with gross vehicle weight greater than 10,000 pounds. In 2008, 4,006 large trucks were involved in fatal crashes.

Lives Saved by Child Restraints, Seat Belts, Air Bags, and Motorcycle Helmets in 2009
National Total = 16,886 Lives

ALPHA ORDER

RANK	STATE	LIVES	% of USA
12	Alabama	426	2.5%
47	Alaska	38	0.2%
21	Arizona	304	1.8%
24	Arkansas	279	1.7%
1	California	1,771	10.5%
29	Colorado	210	1.2%
38	Connecticut	104	0.6%
44	Delaware	52	0.3%
3	Florida	1,026	6.1%
5	Georgia	657	3.9%
49	Hawaii	31	0.2%
37	Idaho	116	0.7%
10	Illinois	456	2.7%
16	Indiana	378	2.2%
31	Iowa	196	1.2%
32	Kansas	187	1.1%
13	Kentucky	409	2.4%
18	Louisiana	364	2.2%
41	Maine	87	0.5%
20	Maryland	310	1.8%
34	Massachusetts	134	0.8%
8	Michigan	516	3.1%
28	Minnesota	220	1.3%
22	Mississippi	298	1.8%
15	Missouri	381	2.3%
40	Montana	95	0.6%
39	Nebraska	101	0.6%
36	Nevada	127	0.8%
46	New Hampshire	51	0.3%
26	New Jersey	260	1.5%
30	New Mexico	202	1.2%
6	New York	612	3.6%
4	North Carolina	778	4.6%
42	North Dakota	69	0.4%
11	Ohio	437	2.6%
19	Oklahoma	349	2.1%
27	Oregon	246	1.5%
7	Pennsylvania	562	3.3%
50	Rhode Island	20	0.1%
14	South Carolina	403	2.4%
44	South Dakota	52	0.3%
9	Tennessee	489	2.9%
2	Texas	1,756	10.4%
35	Utah	133	0.8%
48	Vermont	37	0.2%
17	Virginia	374	2.2%
23	Washington	281	1.7%
33	West Virginia	173	1.0%
25	Wisconsin	261	1.5%
43	Wyoming	58	0.3%

RANK ORDER

RANK	STATE	LIVES	% of USA
1	California	1,771	10.5%
2	Texas	1,756	10.4%
3	Florida	1,026	6.1%
4	North Carolina	778	4.6%
5	Georgia	657	3.9%
6	New York	612	3.6%
7	Pennsylvania	562	3.3%
8	Michigan	516	3.1%
9	Tennessee	489	2.9%
10	Illinois	456	2.7%
11	Ohio	437	2.6%
12	Alabama	426	2.5%
13	Kentucky	409	2.4%
14	South Carolina	403	2.4%
15	Missouri	381	2.3%
16	Indiana	378	2.2%
17	Virginia	374	2.2%
18	Louisiana	364	2.2%
19	Oklahoma	349	2.1%
20	Maryland	310	1.8%
21	Arizona	304	1.8%
22	Mississippi	298	1.8%
23	Washington	281	1.7%
24	Arkansas	279	1.7%
25	Wisconsin	261	1.5%
26	New Jersey	260	1.5%
27	Oregon	246	1.5%
28	Minnesota	220	1.3%
29	Colorado	210	1.2%
30	New Mexico	202	1.2%
31	Iowa	196	1.2%
32	Kansas	187	1.1%
33	West Virginia	173	1.0%
34	Massachusetts	134	0.8%
35	Utah	133	0.8%
36	Nevada	127	0.8%
37	Idaho	116	0.7%
38	Connecticut	104	0.6%
39	Nebraska	101	0.6%
40	Montana	95	0.6%
41	Maine	87	0.5%
42	North Dakota	69	0.4%
43	Wyoming	58	0.3%
44	Delaware	52	0.3%
44	South Dakota	52	0.3%
46	New Hampshire	51	0.3%
47	Alaska	38	0.2%
48	Vermont	37	0.2%
49	Hawaii	31	0.2%
50	Rhode Island	20	0.1%
	District of Columbia	6	0.0%

Source: CQ Press using data from U.S. Department of Transportation, National Highway Traffic Safety Administration "Traffic Safety Facts-Lives Saved" (http://www.nhtsa.gov/)

Safety Belt Usage Rate in 2009

National Rate = 84.0% Use Safety Belts

ALPHA ORDER				RANK ORDER		
RANK	STATE	PERCENT		RANK	STATE	PERCENT
15	Alabama	90.0		1	Michigan	98.0
22	Alaska	86.1		2	Hawaii	97.9
35	Arizona	80.8		3	Oregon	96.6
45	Arkansas	74.4		4	Washington	96.4
5	California	95.3		5	California	95.3
34	Colorado	81.1		6	Maryland	94.0
24	Connecticut	85.9		7	Iowa	93.1
18	Delaware	88.4		8	Texas	92.9
26	Florida	85.2		9	New Jersey	92.7
17	Georgia	88.9		10	Indiana	92.6
2	Hawaii	97.9		11	Illinois	91.7
38	Idaho	79.2		12	Nevada	91.0
11	Illinois	91.7		13	Minnesota	90.2
10	Indiana	92.6		14	New Mexico	90.1
7	Iowa	93.1		15	Alabama	90.0
41	Kansas	77.0		16	North Carolina	89.5
37	Kentucky	79.7		17	Georgia	88.9
44	Louisiana	74.5		18	Delaware	88.4
30	Maine	82.6		19	New York	88.0
6	Maryland	94.0		20	Pennsylvania	87.9
47	Massachusetts	73.6		21	West Virginia	87.0
1	Michigan	98.0		22	Alaska	86.1
13	Minnesota	90.2		22	Utah	86.1
42	Mississippi	76.0		24	Connecticut	85.9
40	Missouri	77.2		25	Vermont	85.3
38	Montana	79.2		26	Florida	85.2
27	Nebraska	84.8		27	Nebraska	84.8
12	Nevada	91.0		28	Oklahoma	84.2
49	New Hampshire	68.9		29	Ohio	83.6
9	New Jersey	92.7		30	Maine	82.6
14	New Mexico	90.1		31	Virginia	82.3
19	New York	88.0		32	North Dakota	81.5
16	North Carolina	89.5		32	South Carolina	81.5
32	North Dakota	81.5		34	Colorado	81.1
29	Ohio	83.6		35	Arizona	80.8
28	Oklahoma	84.2		36	Tennessee	80.6
3	Oregon	96.6		37	Kentucky	79.7
20	Pennsylvania	87.9		38	Idaho	79.2
43	Rhode Island	74.7		38	Montana	79.2
32	South Carolina	81.5		40	Missouri	77.2
48	South Dakota	72.1		41	Kansas	77.0
36	Tennessee	80.6		42	Mississippi	76.0
8	Texas	92.9		43	Rhode Island	74.7
22	Utah	86.1		44	Louisiana	74.5
25	Vermont	85.3		45	Arkansas	74.4
31	Virginia	82.3		46	Wisconsin	73.8
4	Washington	96.4		47	Massachusetts	73.6
21	West Virginia	87.0		48	South Dakota	72.1
46	Wisconsin	73.8		49	New Hampshire	68.9
50	Wyoming	67.6		50	Wyoming	67.6
					District of Columbia	93.0

Source: U.S. Department of Transportation, National Highway Traffic Safety Administration
"Seat Belt Use in 2009" (http://www-nrd.nhtsa.dot.gov/Pubs/811324.pdf)

Percent of Passenger Car Occupant Fatalities
Where Victim Used a Seat Belt in 2008
National Percent = 42% of Passenger Car Occupant Fatalities*

ALPHA ORDER

RANK	STATE	PERCENT
30	Alabama	36
20	Alaska	44
34	Arizona	34
40	Arkansas	32
1	California	58
10	Colorado	49
22	Connecticut	42
6	Delaware	51
25	Florida	40
28	Georgia	37
20	Hawaii	44
28	Idaho	37
18	Illinois	45
18	Indiana	45
23	Iowa	41
40	Kansas	32
30	Kentucky	36
40	Louisiana	32
17	Maine	47
4	Maryland	55
43	Massachusetts	30
6	Michigan	51
13	Minnesota	48
34	Mississippi	34
45	Missouri	29
46	Montana	28
26	Nebraska	39
10	Nevada	49
48	New Hampshire	26
13	New Jersey	48
13	New Mexico	48
6	New York	51
13	North Carolina	48
50	North Dakota	23
23	Ohio	41
33	Oklahoma	35
1	Oregon	58
37	Pennsylvania	33
49	Rhode Island	25
37	South Carolina	33
43	South Dakota	30
34	Tennessee	34
9	Texas	50
5	Utah	54
10	Vermont	49
30	Virginia	36
3	Washington	56
37	West Virginia	33
27	Wisconsin	38
46	Wyoming	28

RANK ORDER

RANK	STATE	PERCENT
1	California	58
1	Oregon	58
3	Washington	56
4	Maryland	55
5	Utah	54
6	Delaware	51
6	Michigan	51
6	New York	51
9	Texas	50
10	Colorado	49
10	Nevada	49
10	Vermont	49
13	Minnesota	48
13	New Jersey	48
13	New Mexico	48
13	North Carolina	48
17	Maine	47
18	Illinois	45
18	Indiana	45
20	Alaska	44
20	Hawaii	44
22	Connecticut	42
23	Iowa	41
23	Ohio	41
25	Florida	40
26	Nebraska	39
27	Wisconsin	38
28	Georgia	37
28	Idaho	37
30	Alabama	36
30	Kentucky	36
30	Virginia	36
33	Oklahoma	35
34	Arizona	34
34	Mississippi	34
34	Tennessee	34
37	Pennsylvania	33
37	South Carolina	33
37	West Virginia	33
40	Arkansas	32
40	Kansas	32
40	Louisiana	32
43	Massachusetts	30
43	South Dakota	30
45	Missouri	29
46	Montana	28
46	Wyoming	28
48	New Hampshire	26
49	Rhode Island	25
50	North Dakota	23

District of Columbia   36

Source: U.S. Department of Transportation, National Highway Safety Administration
"Traffic Safety Facts-Occupant Protection" (http://www.nhtsa.dot.gov/portal/site/nhtsa/)
*Only those fatalities where seat belts are known to have been used are counted.

Fatalities in Alcohol-Related Crashes in 2009

National Total = 12,744 Fatalities*

ALPHA ORDER

ALPHA ORDER

RANK ORDER

RANK	STATE	FATALITIES	% of USA
14	Alabama	325	2.6%
50	Alaska	22	0.2%
19	Arizona	260	2.0%
24	Arkansas	211	1.7%
2	California	1,118	8.8%
27	Colorado	178	1.4%
35	Connecticut	114	0.9%
46	Delaware	48	0.4%
3	Florida	904	7.1%
7	Georgia	394	3.1%
40	Hawaii	59	0.5%
39	Idaho	65	0.5%
9	Illinois	381	3.0%
21	Indiana	249	2.0%
34	Iowa	118	0.9%
28	Kansas	177	1.4%
22	Kentucky	239	1.9%
11	Louisiana	366	2.9%
45	Maine	53	0.4%
25	Maryland	194	1.5%
32	Massachusetts	130	1.0%
15	Michigan	291	2.3%
31	Minnesota	131	1.0%
18	Mississippi	264	2.1%
12	Missouri	358	2.8%
36	Montana	92	0.7%
38	Nebraska	88	0.7%
37	Nevada	90	0.7%
48	New Hampshire	36	0.3%
26	New Jersey	185	1.5%
33	New Mexico	129	1.0%
8	New York	388	3.0%
5	North Carolina	430	3.4%
40	North Dakota	59	0.5%
10	Ohio	378	3.0%
17	Oklahoma	265	2.1%
29	Oregon	141	1.1%
4	Pennsylvania	470	3.7%
47	Rhode Island	40	0.3%
6	South Carolina	423	3.3%
40	South Dakota	59	0.5%
13	Tennessee	345	2.7%
1	Texas	1,437	11.3%
43	Utah	54	0.4%
49	Vermont	28	0.2%
16	Virginia	278	2.2%
23	Washington	232	1.8%
30	West Virginia	134	1.1%
20	Wisconsin	251	2.0%
43	Wyoming	54	0.4%

RANK	STATE	FATALITIES	% of USA
1	Texas	1,437	11.3%
2	California	1,118	8.8%
3	Florida	904	7.1%
4	Pennsylvania	470	3.7%
5	North Carolina	430	3.4%
6	South Carolina	423	3.3%
7	Georgia	394	3.1%
8	New York	388	3.0%
9	Illinois	381	3.0%
10	Ohio	378	3.0%
11	Louisiana	366	2.9%
12	Missouri	358	2.8%
13	Tennessee	345	2.7%
14	Alabama	325	2.6%
15	Michigan	291	2.3%
16	Virginia	278	2.2%
17	Oklahoma	265	2.1%
18	Mississippi	264	2.1%
19	Arizona	260	2.0%
20	Wisconsin	251	2.0%
21	Indiana	249	2.0%
22	Kentucky	239	1.9%
23	Washington	232	1.8%
24	Arkansas	211	1.7%
25	Maryland	194	1.5%
26	New Jersey	185	1.5%
27	Colorado	178	1.4%
28	Kansas	177	1.4%
29	Oregon	141	1.1%
30	West Virginia	134	1.1%
31	Minnesota	131	1.0%
32	Massachusetts	130	1.0%
33	New Mexico	129	1.0%
34	Iowa	118	0.9%
35	Connecticut	114	0.9%
36	Montana	92	0.7%
37	Nevada	90	0.7%
38	Nebraska	88	0.7%
39	Idaho	65	0.5%
40	Hawaii	59	0.5%
40	North Dakota	59	0.5%
40	South Dakota	59	0.5%
43	Utah	54	0.4%
43	Wyoming	54	0.4%
45	Maine	53	0.4%
46	Delaware	48	0.4%
47	Rhode Island	40	0.3%
48	New Hampshire	36	0.3%
49	Vermont	28	0.2%
50	Alaska	22	0.2%
	District of Columbia	12	0.1%

Source: U.S. Department of Transportation, National Highway Traffic Safety Administration
"Traffic Safety Facts: Alcohol-Impaired Driving" (http://www.nhtsa.gov/staticfiles/ncsa/pdf/2010/811385.pdf)
*Drivers with Blood Alcohol Content (BAC) of .01 or more. "Legally Drunk" BAC differs from state to state but is often .08 or higher.

Fatalities in Alcohol-Related Crashes
as a Percent of All Highway Fatalities in 2009
National Percent = 38% of Highway Fatalities*

ALPHA ORDER

RANK	STATE	PERCENT
19	Alabama	38
34	Alaska	35
43	Arizona	32
29	Arkansas	36
29	California	36
19	Colorado	38
2	Connecticut	51
11	Delaware	42
34	Florida	35
46	Georgia	31
1	Hawaii	54
49	Idaho	29
11	Illinois	42
29	Indiana	36
43	Iowa	32
7	Kansas	46
48	Kentucky	30
8	Louisiana	45
39	Maine	33
34	Maryland	35
17	Massachusetts	39
39	Michigan	33
46	Minnesota	31
19	Mississippi	38
15	Missouri	41
11	Montana	42
17	Nebraska	39
23	Nevada	37
39	New Hampshire	33
43	New Jersey	32
29	New Mexico	36
38	New York	34
39	North Carolina	33
11	North Dakota	42
23	Ohio	37
29	Oklahoma	36
23	Oregon	37
23	Pennsylvania	37
3	Rhode Island	48
4	South Carolina	47
8	South Dakota	45
34	Tennessee	35
4	Texas	47
50	Utah	22
23	Vermont	37
23	Virginia	37
4	Washington	47
19	West Virginia	38
8	Wisconsin	45
16	Wyoming	40

RANK ORDER

RANK	STATE	PERCENT
1	Hawaii	54
2	Connecticut	51
3	Rhode Island	48
4	South Carolina	47
4	Texas	47
4	Washington	47
7	Kansas	46
8	Louisiana	45
8	South Dakota	45
8	Wisconsin	45
11	Delaware	42
11	Illinois	42
11	Montana	42
11	North Dakota	42
15	Missouri	41
16	Wyoming	40
17	Massachusetts	39
17	Nebraska	39
19	Alabama	38
19	Colorado	38
19	Mississippi	38
19	West Virginia	38
23	Nevada	37
23	Ohio	37
23	Oregon	37
23	Pennsylvania	37
23	Vermont	37
23	Virginia	37
29	Arkansas	36
29	California	36
29	Indiana	36
29	New Mexico	36
29	Oklahoma	36
34	Alaska	35
34	Florida	35
34	Maryland	35
34	Tennessee	35
38	New York	34
39	Maine	33
39	Michigan	33
39	New Hampshire	33
39	North Carolina	33
43	Arizona	32
43	Iowa	32
43	New Jersey	32
46	Georgia	31
46	Minnesota	31
48	Kentucky	30
49	Idaho	29
50	Utah	22

District of Columbia	41

Source: U.S. Department of Transportation, National Highway Traffic Safety Administration
"Traffic Safety Facts: Alcohol-Impaired Driving" (http://www.nhtsa.gov/staticfiles/ncsa/pdf/2010/811385.pdf)
*Drivers with Blood Alcohol Content (BAC) of .01 or more. "Legally Drunk" BAC differs from state to state but is often .08 or higher.

Percent of Fatal Traffic Accidents Involving Older Drivers in 2008

National Percent = 11.1%*

ALPHA ORDER

RANK	STATE	PERCENT
48	Alabama	8.6
47	Alaska	8.8
27	Arizona	11.2
24	Arkansas	11.4
45	California	9.0
27	Colorado	11.2
26	Connecticut	11.3
33	Delaware	10.5
27	Florida	11.2
31	Georgia	11.0
37	Hawaii	10.1
42	Idaho	9.3
24	Illinois	11.4
39	Indiana	9.6
4	Iowa	14.7
11	Kansas	13.3
32	Kentucky	10.6
50	Louisiana	7.9
4	Maine	14.7
34	Maryland	10.4
20	Massachusetts	12.0
7	Michigan	14.3
8	Minnesota	14.2
34	Mississippi	10.4
21	Missouri	11.9
36	Montana	10.2
3	Nebraska	16.0
43	Nevada	9.2
22	New Hampshire	11.8
12	New Jersey	13.0
45	New Mexico	9.0
10	New York	13.7
30	North Carolina	11.1
41	North Dakota	9.5
16	Ohio	12.6
15	Oklahoma	12.8
18	Oregon	12.5
16	Pennsylvania	12.6
2	Rhode Island	18.5
38	South Carolina	10.0
6	South Dakota	14.5
12	Tennessee	13.0
49	Texas	8.5
44	Utah	9.1
1	Vermont	18.6
23	Virginia	11.6
19	Washington	12.1
9	West Virginia	13.8
12	Wisconsin	13.0
39	Wyoming	9.6

RANK ORDER

RANK	STATE	PERCENT
1	Vermont	18.6
2	Rhode Island	18.5
3	Nebraska	16.0
4	Iowa	14.7
4	Maine	14.7
6	South Dakota	14.5
7	Michigan	14.3
8	Minnesota	14.2
9	West Virginia	13.8
10	New York	13.7
11	Kansas	13.3
12	New Jersey	13.0
12	Tennessee	13.0
12	Wisconsin	13.0
15	Oklahoma	12.8
16	Ohio	12.6
16	Pennsylvania	12.6
18	Oregon	12.5
19	Washington	12.1
20	Massachusetts	12.0
21	Missouri	11.9
22	New Hampshire	11.8
23	Virginia	11.6
24	Arkansas	11.4
24	Illinois	11.4
26	Connecticut	11.3
27	Arizona	11.2
27	Colorado	11.2
27	Florida	11.2
30	North Carolina	11.1
31	Georgia	11.0
32	Kentucky	10.6
33	Delaware	10.5
34	Maryland	10.4
34	Mississippi	10.4
36	Montana	10.2
37	Hawaii	10.1
38	South Carolina	10.0
39	Indiana	9.6
39	Wyoming	9.6
41	North Dakota	9.5
42	Idaho	9.3
43	Nevada	9.2
44	Utah	9.1
45	California	9.0
45	New Mexico	9.0
47	Alaska	8.8
48	Alabama	8.6
49	Texas	8.5
50	Louisiana	7.9

District of Columbia 13.6

Source: CQ Press using data from U.S. Department of Transportation, National Highway Traffic Safety Administration
"Traffic Safety Facts-Older Population" (http://www.nhtsa.dot.gov/portal/site/nhtsa/)
*Drivers 65 years old and older. People 65 or older make up 13 percent of the total U.S. population.

Percent of Highway Fatalities Who Were Young Drivers: 2008

National Percent = 7.4% of Fatalities*

ALPHA ORDER

RANK	STATE	PERCENT
6	Alabama	9.6
17	Alaska	8.1
46	Arizona	5.1
10	Arkansas	8.8
43	California	6.3
25	Colorado	7.5
42	Connecticut	6.4
47	Delaware	5.0
38	Florida	6.5
38	Georgia	6.5
38	Hawaii	6.5
4	Idaho	9.9
19	Illinois	7.7
6	Indiana	9.6
29	Iowa	7.0
10	Kansas	8.8
32	Kentucky	6.9
34	Louisiana	6.8
14	Maine	8.4
27	Maryland	7.1
13	Massachusetts	8.5
29	Michigan	7.0
29	Minnesota	7.0
25	Mississippi	7.5
8	Missouri	9.2
15	Montana	8.3
1	Nebraska	12.0
50	Nevada	4.6
12	New Hampshire	8.6
44	New Jersey	6.1
36	New Mexico	6.6
47	New York	5.0
36	North Carolina	6.6
19	North Dakota	7.7
35	Ohio	6.7
3	Oklahoma	10.1
47	Oregon	5.0
23	Pennsylvania	7.6
19	Rhode Island	7.7
19	South Carolina	7.7
23	South Dakota	7.6
9	Tennessee	9.1
16	Texas	8.2
45	Utah	5.5
2	Vermont	11.0
5	Virginia	9.7
38	Washington	6.5
27	West Virginia	7.1
17	Wisconsin	8.1
32	Wyoming	6.9

RANK ORDER

RANK	STATE	PERCENT
1	Nebraska	12.0
2	Vermont	11.0
3	Oklahoma	10.1
4	Idaho	9.9
5	Virginia	9.7
6	Alabama	9.6
6	Indiana	9.6
8	Missouri	9.2
9	Tennessee	9.1
10	Arkansas	8.8
10	Kansas	8.8
12	New Hampshire	8.6
13	Massachusetts	8.5
14	Maine	8.4
15	Montana	8.3
16	Texas	8.2
17	Alaska	8.1
17	Wisconsin	8.1
19	Illinois	7.7
19	North Dakota	7.7
19	Rhode Island	7.7
19	South Carolina	7.7
23	Pennsylvania	7.6
23	South Dakota	7.6
25	Colorado	7.5
25	Mississippi	7.5
27	Maryland	7.1
27	West Virginia	7.1
29	Iowa	7.0
29	Michigan	7.0
29	Minnesota	7.0
32	Kentucky	6.9
32	Wyoming	6.9
34	Louisiana	6.8
35	Ohio	6.7
36	New Mexico	6.6
36	North Carolina	6.6
38	Florida	6.5
38	Georgia	6.5
38	Hawaii	6.5
38	Washington	6.5
42	Connecticut	6.4
43	California	6.3
44	New Jersey	6.1
45	Utah	5.5
46	Arizona	5.1
47	Delaware	5.0
47	New York	5.0
47	Oregon	5.0
50	Nevada	4.6

District of Columbia**   NA

Source: CQ Press using data from U.S. Department of Transportation, National Highway Traffic Safety Administration
"Traffic Safety Facts-Young Drivers" (http://www.nhtsa.dot.gov/portal/site/nhtsa/)
*Drivers 15 to 20 years old. Based on 2,739 fatalities of young drivers. An additional 3,689 passengers and nonoccupants were killed in crashes involving young drivers. Young drivers accounted for 6.4 percent of all drivers.
**Not available.

Licensed Drivers in 2008

National Total = 208,320,601 Licensed Drivers

ALPHA ORDER

RANK	STATE	DRIVERS	% of USA
21	Alabama	3,753,550	1.8%
48	Alaska	503,162	0.2%
17	Arizona	4,315,579	2.1%
30	Arkansas	2,055,189	1.0%
1	California	23,697,667	11.4%
22	Colorado	3,605,682	1.7%
27	Connecticut	2,883,324	1.4%
45	Delaware	651,877	0.3%
3	Florida	14,033,844	6.7%
10	Georgia	6,257,484	3.0%
42	Hawaii	884,767	0.4%
39	Idaho	1,038,314	0.5%
6	Illinois	8,260,940	4.0%
12	Indiana	5,550,469	2.7%
32	Iowa	1,989,663	1.0%
31	Kansas	2,021,905	1.0%
26	Kentucky	2,932,659	1.4%
25	Louisiana	2,998,162	1.4%
41	Maine	1,006,057	0.5%
20	Maryland	3,786,650	1.8%
15	Massachusetts	4,674,058	2.2%
8	Michigan	7,118,378	3.4%
23	Minnesota	3,190,183	1.5%
33	Mississippi	1,935,764	0.9%
18	Missouri	4,196,682	2.0%
44	Montana	738,982	0.4%
38	Nebraska	1,346,406	0.6%
35	Nevada	1,678,550	0.8%
40	New Hampshire	1,031,158	0.5%
11	New Jersey	5,782,155	2.8%
36	New Mexico	1,365,249	0.7%
4	New York	11,284,545	5.4%
9	North Carolina	6,457,000	3.1%
49	North Dakota	473,019	0.2%
7	Ohio	7,962,266	3.8%
29	Oklahoma	2,301,848	1.1%
28	Oregon	2,856,085	1.4%
5	Pennsylvania	8,646,273	4.2%
43	Rhode Island	748,351	0.4%
24	South Carolina	3,185,408	1.5%
46	South Dakota	597,326	0.3%
16	Tennessee	4,450,644	2.1%
2	Texas	15,374,063	7.4%
34	Utah	1,687,306	0.8%
47	Vermont	541,990	0.3%
13	Virginia	5,301,182	2.5%
14	Washington	4,953,872	2.4%
37	West Virginia	1,360,926	0.7%
19	Wisconsin	4,075,764	2.0%
50	Wyoming	404,489	0.2%

RANK ORDER

RANK	STATE	DRIVERS	% of USA
1	California	23,697,667	11.4%
2	Texas	15,374,063	7.4%
3	Florida	14,033,844	6.7%
4	New York	11,284,545	5.4%
5	Pennsylvania	8,646,273	4.2%
6	Illinois	8,260,940	4.0%
7	Ohio	7,962,266	3.8%
8	Michigan	7,118,378	3.4%
9	North Carolina	6,457,000	3.1%
10	Georgia	6,257,484	3.0%
11	New Jersey	5,782,155	2.8%
12	Indiana	5,550,469	2.7%
13	Virginia	5,301,182	2.5%
14	Washington	4,953,872	2.4%
15	Massachusetts	4,674,058	2.2%
16	Tennessee	4,450,644	2.1%
17	Arizona	4,315,579	2.1%
18	Missouri	4,196,682	2.0%
19	Wisconsin	4,075,764	2.0%
20	Maryland	3,786,650	1.8%
21	Alabama	3,753,550	1.8%
22	Colorado	3,605,682	1.7%
23	Minnesota	3,190,183	1.5%
24	South Carolina	3,185,408	1.5%
25	Louisiana	2,998,162	1.4%
26	Kentucky	2,932,659	1.4%
27	Connecticut	2,883,324	1.4%
28	Oregon	2,856,085	1.4%
29	Oklahoma	2,301,848	1.1%
30	Arkansas	2,055,189	1.0%
31	Kansas	2,021,905	1.0%
32	Iowa	1,989,663	1.0%
33	Mississippi	1,935,764	0.9%
34	Utah	1,687,306	0.8%
35	Nevada	1,678,550	0.8%
36	New Mexico	1,365,249	0.7%
37	West Virginia	1,360,926	0.7%
38	Nebraska	1,346,406	0.6%
39	Idaho	1,038,314	0.5%
40	New Hampshire	1,031,158	0.5%
41	Maine	1,006,057	0.5%
42	Hawaii	884,767	0.4%
43	Rhode Island	748,351	0.4%
44	Montana	738,982	0.4%
45	Delaware	651,877	0.3%
46	South Dakota	597,326	0.3%
47	Vermont	541,990	0.3%
48	Alaska	503,162	0.2%
49	North Dakota	473,019	0.2%
50	Wyoming	404,489	0.2%
	District of Columbia	373,735	0.2%

Source: U.S. Department of Transportation, Federal Highway Administration
"Highway Statistics 2008" (Table DL-22, http://www.fhwa.dot.gov/policyinformation/statistics/2008/index.cfm)

Licensed Drivers per 1,000 Driving Age Population in 2008

National Ratio = 871 Licensed Drivers

ALPHA ORDER

RANK	STATE	RATIO
4	Alabama	1,022
10	Alaska	952
34	Arizona	867
19	Arkansas	920
46	California	832
15	Colorado	933
3	Connecticut	1,034
14	Delaware	943
12	Florida	948
41	Georgia	844
39	Hawaii	854
26	Idaho	898
47	Illinois	819
1	Indiana	1,116
44	Iowa	838
17	Kansas	927
33	Kentucky	868
32	Louisiana	873
15	Maine	933
40	Maryland	850
28	Massachusetts	891
24	Michigan	900
49	Minnesota	776
37	Mississippi	857
23	Missouri	901
8	Montana	954
6	Nebraska	970
44	Nevada	838
5	New Hampshire	973
42	New Jersey	841
29	New Mexico	887
50	New York	722
27	North Carolina	893
20	North Dakota	917
31	Ohio	876
48	Oklahoma	811
13	Oregon	944
35	Pennsylvania	862
30	Rhode Island	879
24	South Carolina	900
11	South Dakota	950
22	Tennessee	907
43	Texas	839
38	Utah	856
2	Vermont	1,063
36	Virginia	861
8	Washington	954
18	West Virginia	923
21	Wisconsin	911
7	Wyoming	965

RANK ORDER

RANK	STATE	RATIO
1	Indiana	1,116
2	Vermont	1,063
3	Connecticut	1,034
4	Alabama	1,022
5	New Hampshire	973
6	Nebraska	970
7	Wyoming	965
8	Montana	954
8	Washington	954
10	Alaska	952
11	South Dakota	950
12	Florida	948
13	Oregon	944
14	Delaware	943
15	Colorado	933
15	Maine	933
17	Kansas	927
18	West Virginia	923
19	Arkansas	920
20	North Dakota	917
21	Wisconsin	911
22	Tennessee	907
23	Missouri	901
24	Michigan	900
24	South Carolina	900
26	Idaho	898
27	North Carolina	893
28	Massachusetts	891
29	New Mexico	887
30	Rhode Island	879
31	Ohio	876
32	Louisiana	873
33	Kentucky	868
34	Arizona	867
35	Pennsylvania	862
36	Virginia	861
37	Mississippi	857
38	Utah	856
39	Hawaii	854
40	Maryland	850
41	Georgia	844
42	New Jersey	841
43	Texas	839
44	Iowa	838
44	Nevada	838
46	California	832
47	Illinois	819
48	Oklahoma	811
49	Minnesota	776
50	New York	722
	District of Columbia	758

Source: CQ Press using data from U.S. Department of Transportation, Federal Highway Administration "Highway Statistics 2008" (Table DL-22, http://www.fhwa.dot.gov/policyinformation/statistics/2008/index.cfm)

Motor Vehicle Registrations in 2008

National Total = 248,164,738 Motor Vehicles*

ALPHA ORDER

RANK	STATE	VEHICLES	% of USA
20	Alabama	4,729,791	1.9%
48	Alaska	690,756	0.3%
22	Arizona	4,373,232	1.8%
32	Arkansas	2,040,988	0.8%
1	California	33,483,061	13.5%
35	Colorado	1,618,219	0.7%
29	Connecticut	3,093,744	1.2%
45	Delaware	867,744	0.3%
3	Florida	16,461,925	6.6%
8	Georgia	8,569,625	3.5%
42	Hawaii	945,491	0.4%
39	Idaho	1,318,233	0.5%
7	Illinois	9,793,821	3.9%
14	Indiana	5,847,546	2.4%
26	Iowa	3,430,867	1.4%
30	Kansas	2,448,768	1.0%
24	Kentucky	3,604,048	1.5%
23	Louisiana	3,979,188	1.6%
41	Maine	1,074,465	0.4%
21	Maryland	4,525,233	1.8%
15	Massachusetts	5,328,349	2.1%
9	Michigan	7,945,471	3.2%
19	Minnesota	4,783,491	1.9%
33	Mississippi	2,034,907	0.8%
18	Missouri	4,865,776	2.0%
43	Montana	926,975	0.4%
34	Nebraska	1,756,628	0.7%
37	Nevada	1,417,214	0.6%
40	New Hampshire	1,213,955	0.5%
12	New Jersey	6,246,882	2.5%
36	New Mexico	1,569,771	0.6%
4	New York	11,088,903	4.5%
11	North Carolina	6,248,829	2.5%
47	North Dakota	717,221	0.3%
5	Ohio	10,933,169	4.4%
27	Oklahoma	3,291,970	1.3%
28	Oregon	3,105,673	1.3%
6	Pennsylvania	10,366,408	4.2%
46	Rhode Island	794,380	0.3%
25	South Carolina	3,603,960	1.5%
44	South Dakota	907,384	0.4%
16	Tennessee	5,098,147	2.1%
2	Texas	18,207,948	7.3%
31	Utah	2,438,685	1.0%
50	Vermont	581,466	0.2%
10	Virginia	6,525,948	2.6%
13	Washington	5,979,710	2.4%
38	West Virginia	1,402,030	0.6%
17	Wisconsin	4,998,903	2.0%
49	Wyoming	664,041	0.3%

RANK ORDER

RANK	STATE	VEHICLES	% of USA
1	California	33,483,061	13.5%
2	Texas	18,207,948	7.3%
3	Florida	16,461,925	6.6%
4	New York	11,088,903	4.5%
5	Ohio	10,933,169	4.4%
6	Pennsylvania	10,366,408	4.2%
7	Illinois	9,793,821	3.9%
8	Georgia	8,569,625	3.5%
9	Michigan	7,945,471	3.2%
10	Virginia	6,525,948	2.6%
11	North Carolina	6,248,829	2.5%
12	New Jersey	6,246,882	2.5%
13	Washington	5,979,710	2.4%
14	Indiana	5,847,546	2.4%
15	Massachusetts	5,328,349	2.1%
16	Tennessee	5,098,147	2.1%
17	Wisconsin	4,998,903	2.0%
18	Missouri	4,865,776	2.0%
19	Minnesota	4,783,491	1.9%
20	Alabama	4,729,791	1.9%
21	Maryland	4,525,233	1.8%
22	Arizona	4,373,232	1.8%
23	Louisiana	3,979,188	1.6%
24	Kentucky	3,604,048	1.5%
25	South Carolina	3,603,960	1.5%
26	Iowa	3,430,867	1.4%
27	Oklahoma	3,291,970	1.3%
28	Oregon	3,105,673	1.3%
29	Connecticut	3,093,744	1.2%
30	Kansas	2,448,768	1.0%
31	Utah	2,438,685	1.0%
32	Arkansas	2,040,988	0.8%
33	Mississippi	2,034,907	0.8%
34	Nebraska	1,756,628	0.7%
35	Colorado	1,618,219	0.7%
36	New Mexico	1,569,771	0.6%
37	Nevada	1,417,214	0.6%
38	West Virginia	1,402,030	0.6%
39	Idaho	1,318,233	0.5%
40	New Hampshire	1,213,955	0.5%
41	Maine	1,074,465	0.4%
42	Hawaii	945,491	0.4%
43	Montana	926,975	0.4%
44	South Dakota	907,384	0.4%
45	Delaware	867,744	0.3%
46	Rhode Island	794,380	0.3%
47	North Dakota	717,221	0.3%
48	Alaska	690,756	0.3%
49	Wyoming	664,041	0.3%
50	Vermont	581,466	0.2%
	District of Columbia	223,799	0.1%

Source: U.S. Department of Transportation, Federal Highway Administration
   "Highway Statistics 2008" (Table MV-1, http://www.fhwa.dot.gov/policyinformation/statistics/2008/index.cfm)
*Includes automobiles, trucks and buses. Does not include motorcycles.

Motor Vehicles per Driving Age Population in 2008

National Rate = 1.04 Motor Vehicles*

ALPHA ORDER

RANK	STATE	RATE
6	Alabama	1.29
5	Alaska	1.31
46	Arizona	0.88
42	Arkansas	0.91
12	California	1.18
50	Colorado	0.42
24	Connecticut	1.11
8	Delaware	1.26
24	Florida	1.11
14	Georgia	1.16
42	Hawaii	0.91
19	Idaho	1.14
39	Illinois	0.97
12	Indiana	1.18
2	Iowa	1.44
22	Kansas	1.12
26	Kentucky	1.07
14	Louisiana	1.16
36	Maine	1.00
32	Maryland	1.02
32	Massachusetts	1.02
36	Michigan	1.00
14	Minnesota	1.16
45	Mississippi	0.90
28	Missouri	1.04
10	Montana	1.20
7	Nebraska	1.27
48	Nevada	0.71
19	New Hampshire	1.14
42	New Jersey	0.91
32	New Mexico	1.02
48	New York	0.71
47	North Carolina	0.86
4	North Dakota	1.39
10	Ohio	1.20
14	Oklahoma	1.16
30	Oregon	1.03
30	Pennsylvania	1.03
41	Rhode Island	0.93
32	South Carolina	1.02
2	South Dakota	1.44
28	Tennessee	1.04
38	Texas	0.99
9	Utah	1.24
19	Vermont	1.14
27	Virginia	1.06
18	Washington	1.15
40	West Virginia	0.95
22	Wisconsin	1.12
1	Wyoming	1.58

RANK ORDER

RANK	STATE	RATE
1	Wyoming	1.58
2	Iowa	1.44
2	South Dakota	1.44
4	North Dakota	1.39
5	Alaska	1.31
6	Alabama	1.29
7	Nebraska	1.27
8	Delaware	1.26
9	Utah	1.24
10	Montana	1.20
10	Ohio	1.20
12	California	1.18
12	Indiana	1.18
14	Georgia	1.16
14	Louisiana	1.16
14	Minnesota	1.16
14	Oklahoma	1.16
18	Washington	1.15
19	Idaho	1.14
19	New Hampshire	1.14
19	Vermont	1.14
22	Kansas	1.12
22	Wisconsin	1.12
24	Connecticut	1.11
24	Florida	1.11
26	Kentucky	1.07
27	Virginia	1.06
28	Missouri	1.04
28	Tennessee	1.04
30	Oregon	1.03
30	Pennsylvania	1.03
32	Maryland	1.02
32	Massachusetts	1.02
32	New Mexico	1.02
32	South Carolina	1.02
36	Maine	1.00
36	Michigan	1.00
38	Texas	0.99
39	Illinois	0.97
40	West Virginia	0.95
41	Rhode Island	0.93
42	Arkansas	0.91
42	Hawaii	0.91
42	New Jersey	0.91
45	Mississippi	0.90
46	Arizona	0.88
47	North Carolina	0.86
48	Nevada	0.71
48	New York	0.71
50	Colorado	0.42

	District of Columbia	0.45

Source: CQ Press using data from U.S. Department of Transportation, Federal Highway Administration
"Highway Statistics 2008" (Table MV-1, http://www.fhwa.dot.gov/policyinformation/statistics/2008/index.cfm)
*Persons age 16 and older. Motor Vehicles include automobiles, trucks and buses. Motorcycles are not included.

Average Travel Time to Work in 2009

National Average = 25.1 Minutes*

RANK	STATE	MINUTES
22	Alabama	23.6
47	Alaska	17.7
18	Arizona	24.3
39	Arkansas	21.1
8	California	26.6
17	Colorado	24.5
18	Connecticut	24.3
22	Delaware	23.6
11	Florida	25.4
7	Georgia	26.9
10	Hawaii	25.5
42	Idaho	19.8
4	Illinois	28.0
30	Indiana	22.9
43	Iowa	18.5
43	Kansas	18.5
33	Kentucky	22.6
15	Louisiana	24.7
30	Maine	22.9
2	Maryland	31.3
5	Massachusetts	27.3
21	Michigan	23.7
34	Minnesota	22.5
22	Mississippi	23.6
25	Missouri	23.2
48	Montana	16.8
46	Nebraska	17.9
29	Nevada	23.1
9	New Hampshire	25.7
3	New Jersey	29.8
37	New Mexico	21.6
1	New York	31.4
25	North Carolina	23.2
50	North Dakota	16.6
32	Ohio	22.8
41	Oklahoma	20.5
35	Oregon	22.1
11	Pennsylvania	25.4
25	Rhode Island	23.2
25	South Carolina	23.2
49	South Dakota	16.7
20	Tennessee	24.0
16	Texas	24.6
40	Utah	21.0
36	Vermont	21.9
6	Virginia	27.2
11	Washington	25.4
14	West Virginia	25.1
38	Wisconsin	21.2
45	Wyoming	18.0

RANK	STATE	MINUTES
1	New York	31.4
2	Maryland	31.3
3	New Jersey	29.8
4	Illinois	28.0
5	Massachusetts	27.3
6	Virginia	27.2
7	Georgia	26.9
8	California	26.6
9	New Hampshire	25.7
10	Hawaii	25.5
11	Florida	25.4
11	Pennsylvania	25.4
11	Washington	25.4
14	West Virginia	25.1
15	Louisiana	24.7
16	Texas	24.6
17	Colorado	24.5
18	Arizona	24.3
18	Connecticut	24.3
20	Tennessee	24.0
21	Michigan	23.7
22	Alabama	23.6
22	Delaware	23.6
22	Mississippi	23.6
25	Missouri	23.2
25	North Carolina	23.2
25	Rhode Island	23.2
25	South Carolina	23.2
29	Nevada	23.1
30	Indiana	22.9
30	Maine	22.9
32	Ohio	22.8
33	Kentucky	22.6
34	Minnesota	22.5
35	Oregon	22.1
36	Vermont	21.9
37	New Mexico	21.6
38	Wisconsin	21.2
39	Arkansas	21.1
40	Utah	21.0
41	Oklahoma	20.5
42	Idaho	19.8
43	Iowa	18.5
43	Kansas	18.5
45	Wyoming	18.0
46	Nebraska	17.9
47	Alaska	17.7
48	Montana	16.8
49	South Dakota	16.7
50	North Dakota	16.6
	District of Columbia	29.2

Source: U.S. Bureau of the Census
"2009 American Community Survey" (http://www.census.gov/acs/www/)
*Workers 16 and older not working at home.

Percent of Commuters Who Drive to Work Alone: 2009

National Percent = 76.1%*

RANK	STATE	PERCENT
1	Alabama	84.4
48	Alaska	68.2
37	Arizona	75.9
14	Arkansas	81.1
43	California	73.0
40	Colorado	74.3
24	Connecticut	78.9
17	Delaware	80.5
22	Florida	79.3
27	Georgia	78.4
49	Hawaii	67.7
31	Idaho	77.5
41	Illinois	73.5
4	Indiana	83.0
24	Iowa	78.9
13	Kansas	81.2
12	Kentucky	81.5
10	Louisiana	81.8
28	Maine	78.3
42	Maryland	73.4
46	Massachusetts	71.9
6	Michigan	82.6
29	Minnesota	78.0
2	Mississippi	83.5
15	Missouri	81.0
38	Montana	75.3
18	Nebraska	80.4
23	Nevada	79.2
7	New Hampshire	82.2
47	New Jersey	71.4
30	New Mexico	77.9
50	New York	54.0
16	North Carolina	80.8
26	North Dakota	78.5
4	Ohio	83.0
8	Oklahoma	82.0
45	Oregon	72.0
35	Pennsylvania	76.8
19	Rhode Island	80.3
8	South Carolina	82.0
33	South Dakota	77.3
3	Tennessee	83.4
21	Texas	79.6
36	Utah	76.1
39	Vermont	74.8
31	Virginia	77.5
44	Washington	72.1
11	West Virginia	81.7
20	Wisconsin	79.8
34	Wyoming	77.2

RANK	STATE	PERCENT
1	Alabama	84.4
2	Mississippi	83.5
3	Tennessee	83.4
4	Indiana	83.0
4	Ohio	83.0
6	Michigan	82.6
7	New Hampshire	82.2
8	Oklahoma	82.0
8	South Carolina	82.0
10	Louisiana	81.8
11	West Virginia	81.7
12	Kentucky	81.5
13	Kansas	81.2
14	Arkansas	81.1
15	Missouri	81.0
16	North Carolina	80.8
17	Delaware	80.5
18	Nebraska	80.4
19	Rhode Island	80.3
20	Wisconsin	79.8
21	Texas	79.6
22	Florida	79.3
23	Nevada	79.2
24	Connecticut	78.9
24	Iowa	78.9
26	North Dakota	78.5
27	Georgia	78.4
28	Maine	78.3
29	Minnesota	78.0
30	New Mexico	77.9
31	Idaho	77.5
31	Virginia	77.5
33	South Dakota	77.3
34	Wyoming	77.2
35	Pennsylvania	76.8
36	Utah	76.1
37	Arizona	75.9
38	Montana	75.3
39	Vermont	74.8
40	Colorado	74.3
41	Illinois	73.5
42	Maryland	73.4
43	California	73.0
44	Washington	72.1
45	Oregon	72.0
46	Massachusetts	71.9
47	New Jersey	71.4
48	Alaska	68.2
49	Hawaii	67.7
50	New York	54.0
	District of Columbia	36.5

Source: U.S. Bureau of the Census
    "2009 American Community Survey" (http://www.census.gov/acs/www/)
*Workers 16 and older who traveled to work by car, truck or van.

Percent of Commuters Who Drive to Work in Carpools: 2009

National Percent = 10.0%*

ALPHA ORDER

RANK	STATE	PERCENT
22	Alabama	10.3
2	Alaska	13.3
3	Arizona	11.8
5	Arkansas	11.6
5	California	11.6
27	Colorado	10.1
46	Connecticut	8.4
44	Delaware	8.9
19	Florida	10.4
10	Georgia	11.0
1	Hawaii	14.0
10	Idaho	11.0
40	Illinois	9.0
37	Indiana	9.2
33	Iowa	9.8
36	Kansas	9.5
16	Kentucky	10.6
16	Louisiana	10.6
27	Maine	10.1
29	Maryland	10.0
48	Massachusetts	8.2
40	Michigan	9.0
37	Minnesota	9.2
14	Mississippi	10.7
29	Missouri	10.0
33	Montana	9.8
25	Nebraska	10.2
22	Nevada	10.3
49	New Hampshire	8.0
45	New Jersey	8.7
7	New Mexico	11.5
50	New York	7.4
14	North Carolina	10.7
16	North Dakota	10.6
46	Ohio	8.4
10	Oklahoma	11.0
19	Oregon	10.4
40	Pennsylvania	9.0
40	Rhode Island	9.0
29	South Carolina	10.0
25	South Dakota	10.2
33	Tennessee	9.8
8	Texas	11.4
4	Utah	11.7
29	Vermont	10.0
19	Virginia	10.4
9	Washington	11.3
22	West Virginia	10.3
37	Wisconsin	9.2
13	Wyoming	10.9

RANK ORDER

RANK	STATE	PERCENT
1	Hawaii	14.0
2	Alaska	13.3
3	Arizona	11.8
4	Utah	11.7
5	Arkansas	11.6
5	California	11.6
7	New Mexico	11.5
8	Texas	11.4
9	Washington	11.3
10	Georgia	11.0
10	Idaho	11.0
10	Oklahoma	11.0
13	Wyoming	10.9
14	Mississippi	10.7
14	North Carolina	10.7
16	Kentucky	10.6
16	Louisiana	10.6
16	North Dakota	10.6
19	Florida	10.4
19	Oregon	10.4
19	Virginia	10.4
22	Alabama	10.3
22	Nevada	10.3
22	West Virginia	10.3
25	Nebraska	10.2
25	South Dakota	10.2
27	Colorado	10.1
27	Maine	10.1
29	Maryland	10.0
29	Missouri	10.0
29	South Carolina	10.0
29	Vermont	10.0
33	Iowa	9.8
33	Montana	9.8
33	Tennessee	9.8
36	Kansas	9.5
37	Indiana	9.2
37	Minnesota	9.2
37	Wisconsin	9.2
40	Illinois	9.0
40	Michigan	9.0
40	Pennsylvania	9.0
40	Rhode Island	9.0
44	Delaware	8.9
45	New Jersey	8.7
46	Connecticut	8.4
46	Ohio	8.4
48	Massachusetts	8.2
49	New Hampshire	8.0
50	New York	7.4
	District of Columbia	6.7

Source: U.S. Bureau of the Census
   "2009 American Community Survey" (http://www.census.gov/acs/www/)
*Workers 16 and older who traveled to work by car, truck or van.

Percent of Commuters Who Travel to Work by Public Transportation: 2009

National Percent = 5.0%*

ALPHA ORDER

RANK	STATE	PERCENT
45	Alabama	0.4
26	Alaska	1.4
20	Arizona	2.1
45	Arkansas	0.4
9	California	5.2
15	Colorado	3.3
10	Connecticut	4.5
13	Delaware	3.8
21	Florida	1.9
18	Georgia	2.5
6	Hawaii	6.0
34	Idaho	1.0
4	Illinois	8.8
32	Indiana	1.1
30	Iowa	1.2
45	Kansas	0.4
30	Kentucky	1.2
28	Louisiana	1.3
40	Maine	0.7
4	Maryland	8.8
3	Massachusetts	9.4
28	Michigan	1.3
14	Minnesota	3.4
45	Mississippi	0.4
25	Missouri	1.5
38	Montana	0.8
41	Nebraska	0.6
16	Nevada	3.1
41	New Hampshire	0.6
2	New Jersey	10.6
32	New Mexico	1.1
1	New York	26.6
34	North Carolina	1.0
50	North Dakota	0.3
23	Ohio	1.8
45	Oklahoma	0.4
12	Oregon	4.1
8	Pennsylvania	5.3
17	Rhode Island	2.8
41	South Carolina	0.6
44	South Dakota	0.5
38	Tennessee	0.8
24	Texas	1.6
19	Utah	2.4
36	Vermont	0.9
11	Virginia	4.4
7	Washington	5.9
36	West Virginia	0.9
21	Wisconsin	1.9
26	Wyoming	1.4

RANK ORDER

RANK	STATE	PERCENT
1	New York	26.6
2	New Jersey	10.6
3	Massachusetts	9.4
4	Illinois	8.8
4	Maryland	8.8
6	Hawaii	6.0
7	Washington	5.9
8	Pennsylvania	5.3
9	California	5.2
10	Connecticut	4.5
11	Virginia	4.4
12	Oregon	4.1
13	Delaware	3.8
14	Minnesota	3.4
15	Colorado	3.3
16	Nevada	3.1
17	Rhode Island	2.8
18	Georgia	2.5
19	Utah	2.4
20	Arizona	2.1
21	Florida	1.9
21	Wisconsin	1.9
23	Ohio	1.8
24	Texas	1.6
25	Missouri	1.5
26	Alaska	1.4
26	Wyoming	1.4
28	Louisiana	1.3
28	Michigan	1.3
30	Iowa	1.2
30	Kentucky	1.2
32	Indiana	1.1
32	New Mexico	1.1
34	Idaho	1.0
34	North Carolina	1.0
36	Vermont	0.9
36	West Virginia	0.9
38	Montana	0.8
38	Tennessee	0.8
40	Maine	0.7
41	Nebraska	0.6
41	New Hampshire	0.6
41	South Carolina	0.6
44	South Dakota	0.5
45	Alabama	0.4
45	Arkansas	0.4
45	Kansas	0.4
45	Mississippi	0.4
45	Oklahoma	0.4
50	North Dakota	0.3
	District of Columbia	37.1

Source: U.S. Bureau of the Census
   "2009 American Community Survey" (http://www.census.gov/acs/www/)
*Workers 16 and older.

Annual Miles per Vehicle in 2008

National Annual Average = 11,982 Miles*

ALPHA ORDER

RANK	STATE	MILES
21	Alabama	12,538
50	Alaska	7,043
10	Arizona	14,092
5	Arkansas	16,249
47	California	9,775
1	Colorado	29,576
43	Connecticut	10,258
41	Delaware	10,344
27	Florida	12,065
18	Georgia	12,726
35	Hawaii	10,871
30	Idaho	11,569
36	Illinois	10,831
24	Indiana	12,137
49	Iowa	8,952
23	Kansas	12,140
15	Kentucky	13,189
32	Louisiana	11,332
14	Maine	13,550
22	Maryland	12,159
44	Massachusetts	10,229
17	Michigan	12,815
25	Minnesota	12,124
2	Mississippi	21,481
11	Missouri	14,031
29	Montana	11,664
33	Nebraska	10,913
8	Nevada	14,663
38	New Hampshire	10,742
28	New Jersey	11,787
3	New Mexico	16,741
26	New York	12,092
4	North Carolina	16,277
34	North Dakota	10,903
45	Ohio	9,906
7	Oklahoma	14,733
37	Oregon	10,776
40	Pennsylvania	10,404
42	Rhode Island	10,306
12	South Carolina	13,762
46	South Dakota	9,903
13	Tennessee	13,626
16	Texas	12,927
39	Utah	10,651
20	Vermont	12,575
19	Virginia	12,608
48	Washington	9,291
6	West Virginia	14,817
31	Wisconsin	11,495
9	Wyoming	14,227

RANK ORDER

RANK	STATE	MILES
1	Colorado	29,576
2	Mississippi	21,481
3	New Mexico	16,741
4	North Carolina	16,277
5	Arkansas	16,249
6	West Virginia	14,817
7	Oklahoma	14,733
8	Nevada	14,663
9	Wyoming	14,227
10	Arizona	14,092
11	Missouri	14,031
12	South Carolina	13,762
13	Tennessee	13,626
14	Maine	13,550
15	Kentucky	13,189
16	Texas	12,927
17	Michigan	12,815
18	Georgia	12,726
19	Virginia	12,608
20	Vermont	12,575
21	Alabama	12,538
22	Maryland	12,159
23	Kansas	12,140
24	Indiana	12,137
25	Minnesota	12,124
26	New York	12,092
27	Florida	12,065
28	New Jersey	11,787
29	Montana	11,664
30	Idaho	11,569
31	Wisconsin	11,495
32	Louisiana	11,332
33	Nebraska	10,913
34	North Dakota	10,903
35	Hawaii	10,871
36	Illinois	10,831
37	Oregon	10,776
38	New Hampshire	10,742
39	Utah	10,651
40	Pennsylvania	10,404
41	Delaware	10,344
42	Rhode Island	10,306
43	Connecticut	10,258
44	Massachusetts	10,229
45	Ohio	9,906
46	South Dakota	9,903
47	California	9,775
48	Washington	9,291
49	Iowa	8,952
50	Alaska	7,043

District of Columbia   16,135

Source: CQ Press using data from U.S. Department of Transportation, Federal Highway Administration
"Highway Statistics 2008" (Tables MV-1 and VM-2, http://www.fhwa.dot.gov/policyinformation/statistics/2008/index.cfm)
*Includes automobiles, trucks, buses and motorcycles.

Average Miles per Gallon in 2008

National Average = 17.4 Miles per Gallon*

ALPHA ORDER

RANK	STATE	MILES PER GALLON
17	Alabama	18.1
50	Alaska	9.6
20	Arizona	17.8
33	Arkansas	16.7
10	California	18.4
12	Colorado	18.2
19	Connecticut	18.0
9	Delaware	18.5
1	Florida	21.1
12	Georgia	18.2
1	Hawaii	21.1
20	Idaho	17.8
31	Illinois	16.8
33	Indiana	16.7
48	Iowa	14.3
27	Kansas	17.2
37	Kentucky	16.3
37	Louisiana	16.3
23	Maine	17.6
25	Maryland	17.4
25	Massachusetts	17.4
7	Michigan	19.2
10	Minnesota	18.4
4	Mississippi	19.7
33	Missouri	16.7
42	Montana	15.2
40	Nebraska	15.8
46	Nevada	14.5
37	New Hampshire	16.3
47	New Jersey	14.4
6	New Mexico	19.3
5	New York	19.4
12	North Carolina	18.2
45	North Dakota	14.6
30	Ohio	16.9
12	Oklahoma	18.2
33	Oregon	16.7
29	Pennsylvania	17.0
17	Rhode Island	18.1
41	South Carolina	15.6
43	South Dakota	14.9
23	Tennessee	17.6
44	Texas	14.8
20	Utah	17.8
8	Vermont	19.1
31	Virginia	16.8
27	Washington	17.2
3	West Virginia	20.0
12	Wisconsin	18.2
49	Wyoming	13.5

RANK ORDER

RANK	STATE	MILES PER GALLON
1	Florida	21.1
1	Hawaii	21.1
3	West Virginia	20.0
4	Mississippi	19.7
5	New York	19.4
6	New Mexico	19.3
7	Michigan	19.2
8	Vermont	19.1
9	Delaware	18.5
10	California	18.4
10	Minnesota	18.4
12	Colorado	18.2
12	Georgia	18.2
12	North Carolina	18.2
12	Oklahoma	18.2
12	Wisconsin	18.2
17	Alabama	18.1
17	Rhode Island	18.1
19	Connecticut	18.0
20	Arizona	17.8
20	Idaho	17.8
20	Utah	17.8
23	Maine	17.6
23	Tennessee	17.6
25	Maryland	17.4
25	Massachusetts	17.4
27	Kansas	17.2
27	Washington	17.2
29	Pennsylvania	17.0
30	Ohio	16.9
31	Illinois	16.8
31	Virginia	16.8
33	Arkansas	16.7
33	Indiana	16.7
33	Missouri	16.7
33	Oregon	16.7
37	Kentucky	16.3
37	Louisiana	16.3
37	New Hampshire	16.3
40	Nebraska	15.8
41	South Carolina	15.6
42	Montana	15.2
43	South Dakota	14.9
44	Texas	14.8
45	North Dakota	14.6
46	Nevada	14.5
47	New Jersey	14.4
48	Iowa	14.3
49	Wyoming	13.5
50	Alaska	9.6

District of Columbia   28.3

Source: CQ Press using data from U.S. Department of Transportation, Federal Highway Administration
 "Highway Statistics 2008" (Table VM-2, http://www.fhwa.dot.gov/policyinformation/statistics/2008/index.cfm)
*Total vehicle-miles for 2008 divided by total highway motor-fuel use. Includes gasoline, gasohol, diesel, and other "special fuels."

Airports in 2008

National Total = 13,362 Airports*

ALPHA ORDER			
RANK	STATE	AIRPORTS	% of USA
32	Alabama	185	1.4%
3	Alaska	532	4.0%
31	Arizona	190	1.4%
25	Arkansas	218	1.6%
4	California	514	3.8%
22	Colorado	254	1.9%
46	Connecticut	55	0.4%
48	Delaware	31	0.2%
6	Florida	491	3.7%
17	Georgia	337	2.5%
49	Hawaii	30	0.2%
26	Idaho	217	1.6%
2	Illinois	536	4.0%
7	Indiana	476	3.6%
28	Iowa	204	1.5%
14	Kansas	352	2.6%
34	Kentucky	157	1.2%
24	Louisiana	222	1.7%
38	Maine	107	0.8%
35	Maryland	149	1.1%
43	Massachusetts	77	0.6%
12	Michigan	378	2.8%
14	Minnesota	352	2.6%
30	Mississippi	193	1.4%
11	Missouri	383	2.9%
23	Montana	223	1.7%
27	Nebraska	216	1.6%
41	Nevada	92	0.7%
47	New Hampshire	53	0.4%
39	New Jersey	99	0.7%
36	New Mexico	145	1.1%
10	New York	400	3.0%
18	North Carolina	317	2.4%
21	North Dakota	269	2.0%
5	Ohio	502	3.8%
19	Oklahoma	296	2.2%
16	Oregon	343	2.6%
8	Pennsylvania	442	3.3%
50	Rhode Island	10	0.1%
33	South Carolina	160	1.2%
36	South Dakota	145	1.1%
29	Tennessee	194	1.5%
1	Texas	1,417	10.6%
40	Utah	93	0.7%
45	Vermont	59	0.4%
20	Virginia	281	2.1%
13	Washington	359	2.7%
44	West Virginia	72	0.5%
8	Wisconsin	442	3.3%
42	Wyoming	91	0.7%

RANK ORDER			
RANK	STATE	AIRPORTS	% of USA
1	Texas	1,417	10.6%
2	Illinois	536	4.0%
3	Alaska	532	4.0%
4	California	514	3.8%
5	Ohio	502	3.8%
6	Florida	491	3.7%
7	Indiana	476	3.6%
8	Pennsylvania	442	3.3%
8	Wisconsin	442	3.3%
10	New York	400	3.0%
11	Missouri	383	2.9%
12	Michigan	378	2.8%
13	Washington	359	2.7%
14	Kansas	352	2.6%
14	Minnesota	352	2.6%
16	Oregon	343	2.6%
17	Georgia	337	2.5%
18	North Carolina	317	2.4%
19	Oklahoma	296	2.2%
20	Virginia	281	2.1%
21	North Dakota	269	2.0%
22	Colorado	254	1.9%
23	Montana	223	1.7%
24	Louisiana	222	1.7%
25	Arkansas	218	1.6%
26	Idaho	217	1.6%
27	Nebraska	216	1.6%
28	Iowa	204	1.5%
29	Tennessee	194	1.5%
30	Mississippi	193	1.4%
31	Arizona	190	1.4%
32	Alabama	185	1.4%
33	South Carolina	160	1.2%
34	Kentucky	157	1.2%
35	Maryland	149	1.1%
36	New Mexico	145	1.1%
36	South Dakota	145	1.1%
38	Maine	107	0.8%
39	New Jersey	99	0.7%
40	Utah	93	0.7%
41	Nevada	92	0.7%
42	Wyoming	91	0.7%
43	Massachusetts	77	0.6%
44	West Virginia	72	0.5%
45	Vermont	59	0.4%
46	Connecticut	55	0.4%
47	New Hampshire	53	0.4%
48	Delaware	31	0.2%
49	Hawaii	30	0.2%
50	Rhode Island	10	0.1%
	District of Columbia	2	0.0%

Source: U.S. Department of Transportation, Bureau of Transportation Statistics
"State Transportation Statistics 2009" (http://www.bts.gov/publications/state_transportation_statistics/)
*This table comprises all U.S. public use and private use airports.   Public use facilities are open to the public with no prior authorization or permission required. Private use facilities are not open to the general public and include medical, law enforcement, corporate, and other such facilities.

Inland Waterway Mileage in 2008

National Total = 29,620 Miles*

ALPHA ORDER

RANK	STATE	MILES	% of USA
6	Alabama	1,270	4.3%
1	Alaska	5,500	18.6%
40	Arizona	0	0.0%
3	Arkansas	1,860	6.3%
26	California	290	1.0%
40	Colorado	0	0.0%
31	Connecticut	120	0.4%
34	Delaware	100	0.3%
5	Florida	1,540	5.2%
14	Georgia	720	2.4%
40	Hawaii	0	0.0%
33	Idaho	110	0.4%
8	Illinois	1,100	3.7%
24	Indiana	350	1.2%
19	Iowa	490	1.7%
31	Kansas	120	0.4%
4	Kentucky	1,590	5.4%
2	Louisiana	2,820	9.5%
37	Maine	70	0.2%
18	Maryland	530	1.8%
35	Massachusetts	90	0.3%
40	Michigan	0	0.0%
27	Minnesota	260	0.9%
12	Mississippi	870	2.9%
10	Missouri	1,030	3.5%
40	Montana	0	0.0%
25	Nebraska	320	1.1%
40	Nevada	0	0.0%
39	New Hampshire	10	0.0%
23	New Jersey	360	1.2%
40	New Mexico	0	0.0%
22	New York	390	1.3%
7	North Carolina	1,150	3.9%
40	North Dakota	0	0.0%
21	Ohio	440	1.5%
30	Oklahoma	150	0.5%
15	Oregon	680	2.3%
27	Pennsylvania	260	0.9%
38	Rhode Island	40	0.1%
20	South Carolina	480	1.6%
36	South Dakota	80	0.3%
11	Tennessee	950	3.2%
13	Texas	830	2.8%
40	Utah	0	0.0%
40	Vermont	0	0.0%
17	Virginia	670	2.3%
9	Washington	1,060	3.6%
15	West Virginia	680	2.3%
29	Wisconsin	230	0.8%
40	Wyoming	0	0.0%

RANK ORDER

RANK	STATE	MILES	% of USA
1	Alaska	5,500	18.6%
2	Louisiana	2,820	9.5%
3	Arkansas	1,860	6.3%
4	Kentucky	1,590	5.4%
5	Florida	1,540	5.2%
6	Alabama	1,270	4.3%
7	North Carolina	1,150	3.9%
8	Illinois	1,100	3.7%
9	Washington	1,060	3.6%
10	Missouri	1,030	3.5%
11	Tennessee	950	3.2%
12	Mississippi	870	2.9%
13	Texas	830	2.8%
14	Georgia	720	2.4%
15	Oregon	680	2.3%
15	West Virginia	680	2.3%
17	Virginia	670	2.3%
18	Maryland	530	1.8%
19	Iowa	490	1.7%
20	South Carolina	480	1.6%
21	Ohio	440	1.5%
22	New York	390	1.3%
23	New Jersey	360	1.2%
24	Indiana	350	1.2%
25	Nebraska	320	1.1%
26	California	290	1.0%
27	Minnesota	260	0.9%
27	Pennsylvania	260	0.9%
29	Wisconsin	230	0.8%
30	Oklahoma	150	0.5%
31	Connecticut	120	0.4%
31	Kansas	120	0.4%
33	Idaho	110	0.4%
34	Delaware	100	0.3%
35	Massachusetts	90	0.3%
36	South Dakota	80	0.3%
37	Maine	70	0.2%
38	Rhode Island	40	0.1%
39	New Hampshire	10	0.0%
40	Arizona	0	0.0%
40	Colorado	0	0.0%
40	Hawaii	0	0.0%
40	Michigan	0	0.0%
40	Montana	0	0.0%
40	Nevada	0	0.0%
40	New Mexico	0	0.0%
40	North Dakota	0	0.0%
40	Utah	0	0.0%
40	Vermont	0	0.0%
40	Wyoming	0	0.0%
	District of Columbia	10	0.0%

Source: U.S. Department of Transportation, Bureau of Transportation Statistics
    "State Transportation Statistics 2009" (http://www.bts.gov/publications/state_transportation_statistics/)
*Waterway mileage was determined by including the length of channels 1) with a controlling draft of nine feet or greater, 2) with commercial cargo traffic reported for 1998 and 1999, but 3) were not offshore. Channels within major bays are included (e.g., Chesapeake Bay, San Francisco Bay, Puget Sound, Long Island Sound, and major sounds and straits in southeastern Alaska). Channels in the Great Lakes are not included. Approximately 4,300 miles are counted twice as several are state boundaries.

Percent of Recreational Boating Accidents Involving Alcohol: 2009

National Percent = 8.4% of Accidents*

ALPHA ORDER

RANK	STATE	PERCENT
14	Alabama	13.3
4	Alaska	21.1
35	Arizona	6.0
17	Arkansas	11.5
44	California	4.6
10	Colorado	15.0
8	Connecticut	16.1
48	Delaware	0.0
38	Florida	5.4
30	Georgia	8.3
48	Hawaii	0.0
16	Idaho	12.2
17	Illinois	11.5
43	Indiana	4.8
13	Iowa	13.5
48	Kansas	0.0
8	Kentucky	16.1
6	Louisiana	19.2
19	Maine	11.4
31	Maryland	7.5
24	Massachusetts	9.8
26	Michigan	9.2
12	Minnesota	14.6
40	Mississippi	5.1
34	Missouri	7.3
10	Montana	15.0
5	Nebraska	19.4
27	Nevada	9.0
42	New Hampshire	5.0
46	New Jersey	3.2
36	New Mexico	5.9
33	New York	7.4
27	North Carolina	9.0
1	North Dakota	28.6
29	Ohio	8.6
37	Oklahoma	5.5
31	Oregon	7.5
21	Pennsylvania	10.3
45	Rhode Island	4.0
39	South Carolina	5.3
3	South Dakota	23.8
15	Tennessee	12.8
22	Texas	10.1
47	Utah	1.1
2	Vermont	25.0
40	Virginia	5.1
23	Washington	9.9
25	West Virginia	9.4
7	Wisconsin	17.6
20	Wyoming	11.1

RANK ORDER

RANK	STATE	PERCENT
1	North Dakota	28.6
2	Vermont	25.0
3	South Dakota	23.8
4	Alaska	21.1
5	Nebraska	19.4
6	Louisiana	19.2
7	Wisconsin	17.6
8	Connecticut	16.1
8	Kentucky	16.1
10	Colorado	15.0
10	Montana	15.0
12	Minnesota	14.6
13	Iowa	13.5
14	Alabama	13.3
15	Tennessee	12.8
16	Idaho	12.2
17	Arkansas	11.5
17	Illinois	11.5
19	Maine	11.4
20	Wyoming	11.1
21	Pennsylvania	10.3
22	Texas	10.1
23	Washington	9.9
24	Massachusetts	9.8
25	West Virginia	9.4
26	Michigan	9.2
27	Nevada	9.0
27	North Carolina	9.0
29	Ohio	8.6
30	Georgia	8.3
31	Maryland	7.5
31	Oregon	7.5
33	New York	7.4
34	Missouri	7.3
35	Arizona	6.0
36	New Mexico	5.9
37	Oklahoma	5.5
38	Florida	5.4
39	South Carolina	5.3
40	Mississippi	5.1
40	Virginia	5.1
42	New Hampshire	5.0
43	Indiana	4.8
44	California	4.6
45	Rhode Island	4.0
46	New Jersey	3.2
47	Utah	1.1
48	Delaware	0.0
48	Hawaii	0.0
48	Kansas	0.0
	District of Columbia	0.0

Source: CQ Press using data from United States Coast Guard
"Boating Statistics 2009" (http://www.uscgboating.org/statistics/accident_statistics.aspx)
*Alcohol involvement in a boating accident includes any accident in which alcoholic beverages are consumed in the boat and the investigating official has determined that the operator was impaired or affected while operating the boat.

Railroad Accidents and Incidents in 2009

National Total = 11,120*

ALPHA ORDER

RANK	STATE	ACCIDENTS	% of USA
16	Alabama	205	1.8%
34	Alaska	117	1.1%
30	Arizona	126	1.1%
22	Arkansas	183	1.6%
5	California	721	6.5%
23	Colorado	174	1.6%
31	Connecticut	125	1.1%
43	Delaware	46	0.4%
15	Florida	222	2.0%
7	Georgia	292	2.6%
50	Hawaii	0	0.0%
42	Idaho	61	0.5%
2	Illinois	1,024	9.2%
8	Indiana	278	2.5%
21	Iowa	187	1.7%
17	Kansas	204	1.8%
26	Kentucky	154	1.4%
14	Louisiana	224	2.0%
47	Maine	19	0.2%
32	Maryland	123	1.1%
11	Massachusetts	249	2.2%
25	Michigan	166	1.5%
18	Minnesota	202	1.8%
35	Mississippi	110	1.0%
13	Missouri	236	2.1%
28	Montana	147	1.3%
12	Nebraska	243	2.2%
45	Nevada	27	0.2%
49	New Hampshire	6	0.1%
6	New Jersey	459	4.1%
40	New Mexico	86	0.8%
1	New York	1,071	9.6%
24	North Carolina	167	1.5%
39	North Dakota	87	0.8%
9	Ohio	269	2.4%
29	Oklahoma	137	1.2%
36	Oregon	108	1.0%
4	Pennsylvania	747	6.7%
48	Rhode Island	12	0.1%
37	South Carolina	104	0.9%
44	South Dakota	40	0.4%
19	Tennessee	198	1.8%
3	Texas	768	6.9%
41	Utah	73	0.7%
45	Vermont	27	0.2%
20	Virginia	193	1.7%
10	Washington	251	2.3%
33	West Virginia	122	1.1%
27	Wisconsin	150	1.3%
38	Wyoming	94	0.8%

RANK ORDER

RANK	STATE	ACCIDENTS	% of USA
1	New York	1,071	9.6%
2	Illinois	1,024	9.2%
3	Texas	768	6.9%
4	Pennsylvania	747	6.7%
5	California	721	6.5%
6	New Jersey	459	4.1%
7	Georgia	292	2.6%
8	Indiana	278	2.5%
9	Ohio	269	2.4%
10	Washington	251	2.3%
11	Massachusetts	249	2.2%
12	Nebraska	243	2.2%
13	Missouri	236	2.1%
14	Louisiana	224	2.0%
15	Florida	222	2.0%
16	Alabama	205	1.8%
17	Kansas	204	1.8%
18	Minnesota	202	1.8%
19	Tennessee	198	1.8%
20	Virginia	193	1.7%
21	Iowa	187	1.7%
22	Arkansas	183	1.6%
23	Colorado	174	1.6%
24	North Carolina	167	1.5%
25	Michigan	166	1.5%
26	Kentucky	154	1.4%
27	Wisconsin	150	1.3%
28	Montana	147	1.3%
29	Oklahoma	137	1.2%
30	Arizona	126	1.1%
31	Connecticut	125	1.1%
32	Maryland	123	1.1%
33	West Virginia	122	1.1%
34	Alaska	117	1.1%
35	Mississippi	110	1.0%
36	Oregon	108	1.0%
37	South Carolina	104	0.9%
38	Wyoming	94	0.8%
39	North Dakota	87	0.8%
40	New Mexico	86	0.8%
41	Utah	73	0.7%
42	Idaho	61	0.5%
43	Delaware	46	0.4%
44	South Dakota	40	0.4%
45	Nevada	27	0.2%
45	Vermont	27	0.2%
47	Maine	19	0.2%
48	Rhode Island	12	0.1%
49	New Hampshire	6	0.1%
50	Hawaii	0	0.0%
	District of Columbia	86	0.8%

Source: U.S. Department of Transportation, Federal Railroad Administration
   "Railroad Accidents and Incidents 2009" (http://safetydata.fra.dot.gov/officeofsafety/)
*Accidents or incidents include all events reportable to the U.S. Department of Transportation. These include train accidents causing damage above an established threshold; highway-rail grade crossing incidents involving impact between railroad equipment and highway users at crossings; and all other reportable incidents that cause a fatality or injury to any person or an occupational illness to a railroad employee.

Railroad Mileage Operated in 2008

National Total = 139,887 Miles of Railroad*

ALPHA ORDER

RANK	STATE	MILES	% of USA
16	Alabama	3,271	2.3%
45	Alaska	506	0.4%
35	Arizona	1,679	1.2%
25	Arkansas	2,780	2.0%
4	California	5,200	3.7%
26	Colorado	2,663	1.9%
47	Connecticut	330	0.2%
48	Delaware	218	0.2%
23	Florida	2,874	2.1%
7	Georgia	4,720	3.4%
50	Hawaii	0	0.0%
37	Idaho	1,591	1.1%
2	Illinois	7,306	5.2%
9	Indiana	4,448	3.2%
11	Iowa	3,925	2.8%
6	Kansas	4,849	3.5%
29	Kentucky	2,558	1.8%
24	Louisiana	2,789	2.0%
40	Maine	1,151	0.8%
43	Maryland	759	0.5%
42	Massachusetts	952	0.7%
12	Michigan	3,735	2.7%
8	Minnesota	4,528	3.2%
28	Mississippi	2,618	1.9%
10	Missouri	4,078	2.9%
22	Montana	3,179	2.3%
19	Nebraska	3,215	2.3%
39	Nevada	1,192	0.9%
46	New Hampshire	415	0.3%
41	New Jersey	993	0.7%
34	New Mexico	1,835	1.3%
13	New York	3,528	2.5%
17	North Carolina	3,250	2.3%
15	North Dakota	3,478	2.5%
3	Ohio	5,318	3.8%
18	Oklahoma	3,240	2.3%
32	Oregon	2,155	1.5%
5	Pennsylvania	5,139	3.7%
49	Rhode Island	87	0.1%
30	South Carolina	2,289	1.6%
36	South Dakota	1,675	1.2%
27	Tennessee	2,641	1.9%
1	Texas	10,743	7.7%
38	Utah	1,365	1.0%
44	Vermont	590	0.4%
21	Virginia	3,205	2.3%
20	Washington	3,209	2.3%
31	West Virginia	2,232	1.6%
14	Wisconsin	3,503	2.5%
33	Wyoming	1,860	1.3%

RANK ORDER

RANK	STATE	MILES	% of USA
1	Texas	10,743	7.7%
2	Illinois	7,306	5.2%
3	Ohio	5,318	3.8%
4	California	5,200	3.7%
5	Pennsylvania	5,139	3.7%
6	Kansas	4,849	3.5%
7	Georgia	4,720	3.4%
8	Minnesota	4,528	3.2%
9	Indiana	4,448	3.2%
10	Missouri	4,078	2.9%
11	Iowa	3,925	2.8%
12	Michigan	3,735	2.7%
13	New York	3,528	2.5%
14	Wisconsin	3,503	2.5%
15	North Dakota	3,478	2.5%
16	Alabama	3,271	2.3%
17	North Carolina	3,250	2.3%
18	Oklahoma	3,240	2.3%
19	Nebraska	3,215	2.3%
20	Washington	3,209	2.3%
21	Virginia	3,205	2.3%
22	Montana	3,179	2.3%
23	Florida	2,874	2.1%
24	Louisiana	2,789	2.0%
25	Arkansas	2,780	2.0%
26	Colorado	2,663	1.9%
27	Tennessee	2,641	1.9%
28	Mississippi	2,618	1.9%
29	Kentucky	2,558	1.8%
30	South Carolina	2,289	1.6%
31	West Virginia	2,232	1.6%
32	Oregon	2,155	1.5%
33	Wyoming	1,860	1.3%
34	New Mexico	1,835	1.3%
35	Arizona	1,679	1.2%
36	South Dakota	1,675	1.2%
37	Idaho	1,591	1.1%
38	Utah	1,365	1.0%
39	Nevada	1,192	0.9%
40	Maine	1,151	0.8%
41	New Jersey	993	0.7%
42	Massachusetts	952	0.7%
43	Maryland	759	0.5%
44	Vermont	590	0.4%
45	Alaska	506	0.4%
46	New Hampshire	415	0.3%
47	Connecticut	330	0.2%
48	Delaware	218	0.2%
49	Rhode Island	87	0.1%
50	Hawaii	0	0.0%
	District of Columbia	23	0.0%

Source: Association of American Railroads
  "Railroads and States" (http://www.aar.org/KeyIssues/Railroads-States.aspx)
*Includes Class I and non-Class I miles. Excludes trackage rights. Synonymous with route-miles, so that a mile of single track
is counted the same as a mile of double track.

Sources

ACT, Inc.
500 ACT Drive, P.O. Box 168
Iowa City, IA 52243-0168
319-337-1000
www.act.org

Administration for Children and Families
U.S. Dept. of Health and Human Services
370 L'Enfant Promenade, SW
Washington, DC 20201
202-401-9215
www.acf.hhs.gov

American Cancer Society, Inc.
1599 Clifton Road, NE
Atlanta, GA 30329-4251
800-227-2345
www.cancer.org

American Dental Association
211 E. Chicago Ave.
Chicago, IL 60611-2678
312-440-2500
www.ada.org

American Hospital Association
155 N. Wacker Drive
Chicago, IL 60606
312-422-3000
www.aha.org

American Medical Association
515 North State Street
Chicago, IL 60610
800-621-8335
www.ama-assn.org

Association of American Railroads
425 Third Street, SW
Suite 1000
Washington, DC 20024
202-639-2100
www.aar.org

Bureau of the Census
4600 Silver Hill Road
Washington, DC 20233-0001
800-923-8282
www.census.gov

Bureau of Economic Analysis
U.S. Department of Commerce
1441 L Street, NW
Washington, DC 20230
202-606-9900
www.bea.gov

Bureau of Justice Statistics
U.S. Department of Justice
810 Seventh St., NW
Washington, DC 20531
202-307-0765
www.ojp.usdoj.gov/bjs/

Bureau of Labor Statistics
U.S. Department of Labor
2 Massachusetts Ave., NE
Washington, DC 20212-0001
202-691-5200
www.bls.gov

Bureau of Transportation Statistics
US Department of Transportation
1200 New Jersey Ave., SE
Washington DC 20590
800-853-1351
www.bts.gov

Centers for Disease Control and Prevention
1600 Clifton Road
Atlanta, GA 30333
800-232-4636
www.cdc.gov

Centers for Medicare and Medicaid Services
7500 Security Boulevard
Baltimore, MD 21244-1850
877-267-2323
www.cms.hhs.gov

College Board
45 Columbus Avenue
New York, NY 10023-6992
212-713-8000
www.collegeboard.com

Economic Research Service
U.S. Department of Agriculture
1800 M Street, NW
Washington, DC 20036-5831
202-694-5050
www.ers.usda.gov

Energy Information Administration
US Department of Energy
1000 Independence Avenue, SW
Washington, DC 20585
202-586-8800
www.eia.doe.gov

Environmental Protection Agency
Ariel Rios Building
1200 Pennsylvania Ave, NW
Washington, DC 20464
202-272-0167
www.epa.gov

Federal Bureau of Investigation
J Edgar Hoover Building
935 Pennsylvania Avenue, NW
Washington, DC 20535
202-324-3000
www.fbi.gov

Federal Highway Administration
US Department of Transportation
1200 New Jersey Ave., SE
Washington, DC 20590
202-366-0660
www.fhwa.dot.gov

Federation of Tax Administrators
444 North Capitol St., NW, Ste 348
Washington, DC 20001
202-624-5890
www.taxadmin.org

Food and Nutrition Service
U.S. Department of Agriculture
3101 Park Center Drive
Alexandria, VA 22302
703-305-2281
www.fns.usda.gov/fns/

General Services Administration
One Constitution Square
1275 First Street, NE
Washington, DC 20417
202-501-1231
www.gsa.gov

Health Resources and Services Administration
Division of Practitioner Data Banks
5600 Fishers Lane
Rockville MD 20857
800-767-6732
www.hrsa.gov

Institute of Museum and Library Services
1800 M Street, NW, 9th Floor
Washington DC 20036-5802
202-653-4657
www.imls.gov

Internal Revenue Service
U.S. Department of the Treasury
10th Street and Pennsylvania Avenue, NW
Washington, DC 20004
800-829-1040
www.irs.gov

Medical Expenditure Panel Survey
Agency for Healthcare Research and Quality
540 Gaither Road
Rockville MD 20850
301-427-1364
www.meps.ahrq.gov

National Agricultural Statistics Service
1400 Independence Avenue, SW
Washington, DC 20250
800-727-9540
www.nass.usda.gov

National Assembly of State Arts Agencies
1029 Vermont Ave., NW 2nd Fl
Washington, DC 20005
202-347-6352
www.nasaa-arts.org

National Association of Realtors
430 N. Michigan Ave
Chicago, IL 60611
800-874-6500
www.realtor.org

National Association of State Park Directors
8829 Woodyhill Road
Raleigh, NC 27613
919-676-8365
www.naspd.org

National Center for Education Statistics
U.S. Department of Education
1990 K Street, NW
Washington, DC 20006
202-502-7300
http://nces.ed.gov

National Center for Health Statistics
U.S. Department of Health and Human Services
3311 Toledo Road
Hyattsville, MD 20782
800-232-4636
www.cdc.gov/nchs/

National Conference of State Legislatures
770 E. First Place
Denver, CO 80230
303-346-7700
www.ncsl.org

National Education Association
1201 16th Street, NW
Washington, DC 20036-3290
202-833-4000
www.nea.org

National Highway Traffic Safety Administration
1200 New Jersey Ave., SE
Washington, DC 20590
888-327-4236
www.nhtsa.dot.gov

National Institute on Alcohol Abuse And Alcoholism
5635 Fishers Lane, MSC 9304
Bethesda, MD 20892-9304
301-443-3860
www.niaaa.nih.gov/

National Oceanic & Atmospheric Administration
U.S. Department of Commerce
1401 Constitution Ave., NW, Rm 5128
Washington, DC 20230
202-482-6090
www.noaa.gov

Social Security Administration
Windsor Park Building
6401 Security Boulevard
Baltimore, MD 21235
800-772-1213 (information)
www.ssa.gov

Storm Prediction Center
National Weather Service
120 David Boren Blvd
Norman, OK 73072
405-579-0771
www.spc.noaa.gov

Tax Foundation
529 14th Street, NW
Suite 420
Washington, DC 20036
202-464-6200
www.taxfoundation.org

U.S. Department of Defense
Directorate for Public Inquiry and Analysis
Room 2E565 The Pentagon
1400 Defense Pentagon
Washington, DC 20301-1400
703-571-3343
www.defenselink.mil

U.S. Department of Veterans Affairs
810 Vermont Avenue, NW
Washington, DC 20420
202-273-5400
www.va.gov

U.S. Geological Survey
12201 Sunrise Valley Drive
Reston, VA 20192
703-648-9051
www.usgs.gov

Index